CONTEMPORARY
Black
Biography

ISSN-1058-1316

CONTEMPORARY

Black

Biography

Profiles from the International Black Community

Volume 115

GALE
CENGAGE Learning·

Farmington Hills, Mich • San Francisco • New York • Waterville, Maine
Meriden, Conn • Mason, Ohio • Chicago

GALE
CENGAGE Learning

**Contemporary Black Biography,
Volume 115**

**Kepos Media, Inc.: Deborah A. Ring, Derek
Jacques, and Paula Kepos, editors**

Project Editor: Margaret Mazurkiewicz

Image Research and Acquisitions: Moriam
Aigoro, Ashley M. Maynard

Editorial Support Services: Nataliya
Mikheyeva

Manufacturing: Dorothy Maki, Rita
Wimberley

Composition and Prepress: Mary Beth
Trimper, Gary Leach

Imaging: John Watkins

Advisory Board

Contents

Introduction ix

Cumulative Nationality Index 167

Cumulative Occupation Index 189

Cumulative Subject Index 219

Cumulative Name Index 269

Marcia Anderson 1

   Highest-ranking African-American woman in the U.S. Army

Kofi Awoonor 4

   Ghanaian poet killed in 2013 shopping mall terrorist attack in Kenya

Zelmo Beaty..7

   All-Star center in two basketball leagues

Gael Bigirimana 10

   Up-and-coming Burundian soccer player

Blitz the Ambassador...13

   Ghanaian-American hip-hop artist

Arthur M. Brazier 16

   Pastor and community organizer on Chicago's South Side

Aja Brown 19

   Youngest-ever mayor of Compton, California

Paul Bryant 22

   Jazz organist and pianist

Cedric the Entertainer...24

   Charismatic comedian known for film and television roles

Ndugu Chancler 28

   Accomplished drummer and producer

Dave Chappelle 31

   Irreverent comedian who addresses racial issues

Ciara 35

   Grammy-winning pop singer and model

Stanley Clarke 38

   Jazz, rock, and pop bassist

Tom Colbert 41

   First African American appointed to the Oklahoma Supreme Court

Ertharin Cousin...43

   Executive director of the United Nations World Food Programme

Antonio Cromartie...46

   Defensive back for the New York Jets

Andraé Crouch...49

   Grammy-winning gospel singer and pastor

Arthur Crudup 53

   Blues musician admired by Elvis Presley

Cow Cow Davenport..55

   Influential pianist who played blues and boogie-woogie

Ben Davis 57

   First black golf pro in Michigan

Lois M. DeBerry 59

   Longtime state legislator in Tennessee

Aretha Franklin 62

   Music icon known as the "Queen of Soul"

Curtis Fuller 67

   Important jazz trombonist

Red Garland 70

   Self-taught jazz pianist who collaborated with Miles Davis

Geto Boys 73

   Controversial Houston-based rap group

L. C. Greenwood 76

   Anchor of the Pittsburgh Steelers' "Steel Curtain" defense in the 1970s

Jrue Holiday..80

   Young center for the New Orleans Pelicans

Loleatta Holloway 82

   Disco singer whose hit "Love Sensation" has been widely sampled

Big Walter Horton 85

   Chicago blues harmonica player and vocalist

Bobby Hutcherson 88
  Leading jazz vibraphonist
Mo Ibrahim 91
  *Sudanese billionaire who established foundation to
  promote African development*
Phillip Jackson 95
  *Activist who founded Black Star Project and Million
  Father March*
Wilson Kipsang 98
  Kenyan marathoner who set new world record in 2013
Julius Lester 101
  Award-winning author of books for young adults
Jamal Lewis 106
  *Baltimore Ravens running back whose off-the-field
  conduct made headlines*
Evelyn Gibson Lowery 109
  Activist who fought for civil rights alongside husband
William Lynch Jr. 112
  Democratic political strategist
Gloria Lynne 114
  Jazz and R&B vocalist who blended the genres
Master P 117
  Rapper, producer, and entrepreneur
Pumeza Matshikiza 122
  Rising South African opera star
Niecy Nash 125
  *Actress and comedian known for roles on Reno 911!
  and Clean House*
Kadir Nelson 128
  Author and illustrator of award-winning children's books
Solomon Northup 131
  *Freed slave who penned influential account of his
  experiences*

Ken Norton 135
  Boxer famous for defeating Muhammad Ali
Paul Oliver 138
  *NFL player whose suicide reignited concussion
  concerns*
Maxine Powell 141
  Style maven for Motown Records
Don Robey 144
  *Pioneering R&B producer and founder of Peacock
  Records*
Romanthony 146
  *House music producer who appeared on 2000 hit "One
  More Time"*
Ashton Springer Jr. 148
  First major African-American producer on Broadway
Sage Steele 151
  Host of ESPN's SportsCenter and NBA Countdown
Sevyn Streeter 154
  Singer and songwriter who made solo debut in 2013
A Taste of Honey 156
  *Disco group known for their 1978 hit "Boogie Oogie
  Oogie"*
Tavares 158
  *R&B group heard on the soundtrack for Saturday Night
  Fever*
Tinie Tempah 161
  *British rapper who debuted in 2010 with the album
  Disc-Overy*
Ora Mae Washington 164
  *Exceptional athlete who won championships in tennis
  and basketball*

Introduction

Contemporary Black Biography provides informative biographical profiles of the important and influential persons of African heritage who form the international black community: men and women who have changed today's world and are shaping tomorrow's. *Contemporary Black Biography* covers persons of various nationalities in a wide variety of fields, including architecture, art, business, dance, education, fashion, film, industry, journalism, law, literature, medicine, music, politics and government, publishing, religion, science and technology, social issues, sports, television, theater, and others. In addition to in-depth coverage of names found in today's headlines, *Contemporary Black Biography* provides coverage of selected individuals from earlier in this century whose influence continues to impact on contemporary life. *Contemporary Black Biography* also provides coverage of important and influential persons who are not yet household names and are therefore likely to be ignored by other biographical reference series. Each volume also includes listee updates on names previously appearing in *CBB*.

Designed for Quick Research and Interesting Reading

- **Attractive page design** incorporates textual subheads, making it easy to find the information you're looking for.

- **Easy-to-locate data sections** provide quick access to vital personal statistics, career information, major awards, and mailing addresses, when available.

- **Informative biographical essays** trace the subject's personal and professional life with the kind of in-depth analysis you need.

- **To further enhance your appreciation** of the subject, most entries include photographic portraits.

- **Sources for additional information** direct the user to selected books, magazines, and newspapers where more information on the individuals can be obtained.

Helpful Indexes Make It Easy to Find the Information You Need

Contemporary Black Biography includes cumulative Nationality, Occupation, Subject, and Name indexes that make it easy to locate entries in a variety of useful ways.

Available in Electronic Formats

Diskette/Magnetic Tape. Contemporary Black Biography is available for licensing on magnetic tape or diskette in a fielded format. Either the complete database or a custom selection of entries may be ordered. The database is available for internal data processing and nonpublishing purposes only. For more information, call (800) 877-GALE.

On-line. Contemporary Black Biography is available on-line through Mead Data Central's NEXIS Service in the NEXIS, PEOPLE and SPORTS Libraries in the GALBIO file and Gale's Biography Resource Center.

Disclaimer

Contemporary Black Biography uses and lists websites as sources and these websites may become obsolete.

We Welcome Your Suggestions

The editors welcome your comments and suggestions for enhancing and improving *Contemporary Black Biography*. If you would like to suggest persons for inclusion in the series, please submit these names to the editors. Mail comments or suggestions to:

The Editor

Contemporary Black Biography

Gale, Cengage Learning

27500 Drake Rd.

Farmington Hills, MI 48331-3535

Phone: (800) 347-4253

Marcia Anderson

1958(?)—

U.S. Army officer

In 2011 Marcia Anderson became the highest-ranking African-American woman in the U.S. Army when she was promoted to major general. Her promotion to two-star general followed more than three decades of service in the armed forces, both on active duty and in the U.S. Army Reserve. Early in her military career, Anderson distinguished herself as a trainer. Her first major command was the 6th Brigade, 95th Division at Fort Sill, Oklahoma, where she oversaw training exercises for drill sergeants and professional development courses for army officers. As she rose through the ranks, her responsibility included training for the entire First Army Division West, headquartered at Fort Hood, Texas. In 2007 Anderson became a brigadier general (a one-star general) in the U.S. Army Reserve. She moved from the training realm into human resources and in 2010 was made deputy commander of the U.S. Army Human Resources Command at Fort Knox, Kentucky. The following year she was promoted to major general and was reassigned to the Pentagon as a deputy chief of the U.S. Army Reserve. Anderson has a law degree and since 1998 has served as a law clerk for the U.S. Bankruptcy Court for the Western District of Wisconsin.

Anderson was born Marcia Mahan during the late 1950s in Beloit, Wisconsin, a small city along the state's southern border with Illinois. Her parents divorced when she was a toddler, and Anderson and her younger brother were raised by their mother. When Anderson was in the second grade, the family moved to East St. Louis, Illinois, to live with her maternal grandmother. The city underwent hard times during the

1960s, suffering from high poverty and crime rates. According to Lauren McLane of the Carlisle, Pennsylvania, *Sentinel,* Anderson later recalled, "I knew what drive-by shootings were before they knew what they were in L.A." She was a shy girl but remembered her mother and grandmother being strong role models who encouraged her to excel at whatever she did. After graduating from Rosati-Kain High School, a girls' Catholic school in St. Louis, Missouri, she attended Creighton University in Omaha, Nebraska, a private Catholic Jesuit college. There Anderson decided to sign up for the Reserve Officers' Training Corps (ROTC), a training program operated by the U.S. military through which graduates can become officers.

ROTC participants attend regular college courses and also undergo military training. In exchange they commit to serve in the armed forces for a set number of years. In 1979 Anderson graduated from Creighton University with a degree in political science. That year she was also commissioned as a second lieutenant in the U.S. Army. After completing her commitment period, she signed up as a reservist. Army reservists work in civilian careers but spend at least one weekend per month and two weeks per year in military service. During wartime they can be called to active duty. As a reservist during the 1980s, Anderson worked her way up to the rank of captain and enjoyed her role in training new recruits. She continued to reenlist in the U.S. Army Reserve even as she worked in the private sector and attended law school at Rutgers University, where she earned a law degree.

At a Glance . . .

Born Marcia Mahan in 1958(?) in Beloit, WI; daughter of Rudy Mahan (a sandblaster) and mother (a clerk); married Amos Anderson (a school administrator), 2000; children: one stepdaughter. *Military service:* U.S. Army, commissioned second lieutenant, 1979; brigadier general, 2007–11; major general, 2011—. *Education:* Creighton University, BA, political science, 1979; Rutgers University, JD, 1990s; U.S. Army War College, master's degree, strategic studies.

Career: U.S. Army officer, commissioned second lieutenant, 1979; U.S. Army Reserve officer, 1980s—, including 6th Brigade, 95th Division (Institutional Training), commander, 2005–06; 95th Division (Institutional Training), assistant division commander, operations, 2006–07; 85th Support Command (Regional Support Group West), commander, 2007–08(?); First Army West, deputy commanding general, support, 2008(?)–10; U.S. Army Human Resources Command, deputy commander, 2010–11; U.S. Army Reserve, deputy chief, 2011—; U.S. Bankruptcy Court for the Western District of Wisconsin, law clerk, 1998—.

Memberships: Wisconsin Board of Veterans Affairs; Women in Focus; Center for Veterans Issues.

Awards: Legion of Merit (with one Oak Leaf Cluster), Meritorious Service Medal (with three Oak Leaf Clusters), U.S. Army; Army Commendation Medal; Army Achievement Medal; Parachutist Badge, U.S. Army; Physical Fitness Badge, U.S. Army; Women of Distinction, Young Women's Christian Association, 2008; Benjamin L. Hooks Distinguished Service Award, National Association for the Advancement of Colored People, 2012; Distinguished Member of the Regiment, U.S. Army, 2013.

Addresses: *Office*—U.S. Bankruptcy Court for the Western District of Wisconsin, 120 North Henry St., Room 340, Madison, WI 53703. *Office*—Office of the Chief, U.S. Army Reserve, 2400 Army Pentagon, Washington, DC 20310-2400.

In 1985 Anderson began a long career in the federal judiciary. The federal court system includes 94 judicial districts that are grouped into 12 regional circuits. Anderson first worked as the operations manager in the clerk's office in the Second Circuit, which is headquartered in New York City. Eventually she became a supervising staff attorney and worked with the circuit's Bankruptcy Appellate Panel, a panel of judges that heard appeals of decisions made by bankruptcy judges. In 1998 Anderson became a law clerk—a prestigious position—at the U.S. Bankruptcy Court for the Western District of Wisconsin, which is headquartered in Madison.

Anderson balanced her demanding civilian law career with her ever-increasing responsibilities in the U.S. Army Reserve. In 2005 she was given command of the 6th Brigade, 95th Division (Institutional Training), headquartered at Fort Sill. There she oversaw the Drill Sergeant School and was responsible for professional development education, including intermediate level education and combined arms exercise courses, for officers throughout an eight-state area. The following year she was appointed assistant division commander-operations for the 6th Brigade, 95th Division. By this time Anderson had risen to the rank of colonel. In 2007 she was promoted to brigadier general (a one-star general), becoming only the second African-American woman in U.S. Army history to achieve that rank, after Hazel W. Johnson-Brown. Anderson assumed command of the reserve's 85th Support Command (Regional Support Group West) in Arlington Heights, Illinois. In this role she oversaw the programs of the First Army, which specialized in mobilization, training, and deployment of reserve forces. Later she became deputy commanding general-support of First Army West, headquartered at Fort Hood.

In 2010 Anderson took a one-year leave of absence from her civilian job to go into active military service. She was named deputy commander of the U.S. Army Human Resources Command (HRC) at Fort Knox. Previously the army had operated separate HRC offices at multiple locations across the country. Anderson was charged with consolidating these operations at Fort Knox to provide one portal through which army soldiers, veterans, and retirees as well as army families could obtain human resources services. Her work in this capacity earned her a promotion recommendation from her superiors. On September 29, 2011, she was promoted to major general, becoming the first African-American woman ever to attain that rank in the U.S. Army. Along with the promotion to two-star general came a new assignment to the Pentagon in Washington, DC. Anderson was named deputy chief, Army Reserve (Individual Mobilization Augmentation), making her a senior adviser in the area of soldier deployment, mobilization, and demobilization.

Sources

Periodicals

Capital Times, March 6, 2008, p. D1.
Jet, June 2, 2008, p. 14.

Sentinel (Carlisle, PA), February 24, 2012.
Wisconsin State Journal, May 30, 2008, p. B3; September 29, 2011; July 10, 2012.

Online

"Bankruptcy Clerk Becomes Army Reserve's Highest Ranking African-American Woman," U.S. Courts, November 2011, http://www.uscourts.gov/news/TheThirdBranch/11-11-01/Bankruptcy_Clerk_Becomes_Army_Reserve_s_Highest_Ranking_African-American_Woman.aspx (accessed November 19, 2013).

"Deputy Reserve Chief Receives NAACP Award," U.S. Army, July 13, 2012, http://www.army.mil/article/83609/ (accessed November 19, 2013).

"Gwen Moore to Host Major General Marcia M. Anderson at State of the Union," Office of Congresswoman Gwen Moore, January 23, 2012, http://gwenmoore.house.gov/press-releases/gwen-moore-to-host-major-general-marcia-m-anderson-at-state-of-the-union/ (accessed November 19, 2013).

"HRC History," U.S. Army, 2013, https://www.hrc.army.mil/STAFF/HRC%20History (accessed November 19, 2013).

Lamb, Brian, "Maj. Gen. Marcia Anderson," C-SPAN, December 11, 2011, http://www.q-and-a.org/Transcript/?ProgramID=1369 (accessed November 19, 2013).

"Maj. Gen. Marcia M. Anderson," U.S. Army, 2013, http://www.army.mil/africanamericans/profiles/anderson.html (accessed November 19, 2013).

"Major General Marcia M. Anderson," U.S. Army, 2013, http://www.usar.army.mil/ourstory/leadership/Pages/Major-General-Marcia-M–Anderson.aspx (accessed November 19, 2013).

Quebec, Joel, "Deputy Chief, Army Reserve Is Honored as Adjutant General Distinguished Member of the Regiment," U.S. Army, June 3, 2013, http://www.army.mil/article/104640/Deputy_Chief__Army_Reserve_is_honored_as_Adjutant_General_Distinguished_Member_of_the_Regiment/ (accessed November 19, 2013).

Wales, Andrea, "HRC Deputy Becomes Army's First Female African-American Major General," U.S. Army, September 29, 2011, http://www.army.mil/article/66413/ (accessed November 19, 2013).

—Kim Masters Evans

Kofi Awoonor

1935–2013

Poet, writer, diplomat

One of West Africa's best-known writers, Ghanaian poet Kofi Awoonor integrated traditional African forms of expression with the techniques of modern poetry. The resulting body of work formed a unique poetic chronicle of West African life in the late 20th century, encompassing both the effects of European colonialism and the influence that Africa exerted on other cultures around the world. Once closely aligned with the pre-eminent leader of modern Ghana, Kwame Nkrumah, Awoonor endured imprisonment for his political beliefs but later emerged as an important political figure himself in later life.

Influenced by African Heritage

The son of a tailor and the grandson of a woman who was a traditional singer of dirges (songs of lament) in the Ewe culture, Kofi Awoonor was born in his grand-father's house in Wheta, Ghana (then known as the Gold Coast), on March 13, 1935. He was baptized in the Presbyterian faith and given the name George Awoonor-Williams, but he was raised in his mother's large extended family and was exposed more often to traditional Ewe culture than to Western religion. Most important were Ewe songs and folktales, which influenced Awoonor's early poetry. In an essay published in the *Contemporary Authors Autobiography Series,* Awoonor stated that his early work represented "very much an effort to move the oral poetry from which I learnt so much into perhaps a higher literary plane, even if it lost much in the process."

Awoonor's family was poor, but when he was nine years old, his family sent him away to attend school; he earned a place to live by working as a servant for a wealthy family. Financing his entire education in this way, Awoonor was able to attend the University of Ghana in Accra, the capital. He graduated in 1960 and continued to teach at the university and to write. His first book of poetry, *Rediscovery and Other Poems,* was published in Nigeria in 1964. Critic Derek Wright, quoted on the Poetry Foundation Ghana website, noted that Awoonor's work "both drew on a personal family heirloom and opened up a channel into a broader African heritage."

During this period Awoonor became allied with the charismatic Nkrumah, who became a symbol of the aspirations of West Africa's newly independent countries and of African cultural pride in general. That friendship led in 1964 to a job in Accra with Ghana's Ministry of Information, but after Nkrumah's government was overturned in a coup d'état in 1966, Awoonor left the country. He landed for a year at the University of London, and in 1968 he came to the United States and enrolled at the State University of New York at Stony Brook on Long Island.

Wrote Experimental Novel

Earning a master's degree and later a doctorate in comparative literature at Stony Brook, Awoonor both deepened his poetry and began to gain wider recognition for it. His first book of poetry was reissued, with added material, by Doubleday as *Night of My Blood* in

At a Glance . . .

Born George Awoonor-Williams on March 13, 1935, in Wheta, Ghana; died on September 21, 2013, in Nairobi, Kenya; son of Atsu E. (a tailor) and Kosiwo (Nyidevu) Awoonor; married; six children. *Religion:* Traditional ancestralist. *Education:* University College of Ghana, BA, 1960; University College, London, MA, 1970; State University of New York at Stony Brook, PhD, 1972.

Career: University of Ghana, Accra, lecturer and researcher, 1960–64; Ghana Ministry of Information, director of films, 1964–67; State University of New York at Stony Brook, assistant professor of English, 1968–75; University of Cape Coast, Ghana, state professor, 1976; served as Ghanaian ambassador to Brazil and other South American countries, 1983–88; Ghanaian ambassador to Cuba, 1988–90; Ghanaian ambassador to the United Nations, 1990–94; continued to serve in Ghanaian government.

Awards: Longmans Fellow, University of London, 1967–68; National Book Council (Ghana) Award for poetry, 1979.

1971. He also wrote plays and an experimental novel called *This Earth, My Brother,* published that same year. Awoonor's poetry often dealt with themes of loss and exile; it had the flavor of traditional songs of lament while making reference to Ghana's history and the uprooting effects of English colonialism. *This Earth, My Brother* mirrored Awoonor's own African upbringing and transplantation to the West, mixing realistic narrative with poetic elements.

Awoonor's 1973 volume *Ride Me, Memory* incorporated African-American culture and music into a stylistic mix that also employed traditional African oral styles of ritual insult and abuse; it earned Awoonor a reputation as one of the key writers, along with Nigerian novelist Chinua Achebe, who could interpret the African world for English-speaking Western audiences. One of his best-known poems, "The Weaver Bird," originally appeared in *Rediscovery and Other Poems* and was widely reprinted. It used a common African form—a poem about an animal—to comment on the effects of European domination of Africa; the weaver bird is a creature that destroys the tree in which it takes up residence.

The collection of poems that Awoonor had submitted as his doctoral dissertation was published as *The Breast*

of the Earth in 1975. By that time Awoonor had become professor and chair of the comparative literature program at Stony Brook. That year the poet took a one-year sabbatical to return home to Ghana, intending to teach at the country's Cape Coast University. But the trip had disastrous results—he was put in prison on charges of harboring a subversive on December 31, 1975, amid rumors of a possible coup. Despite heavy international pressure organized largely by Awoonor's U.S. colleagues, he was held for a year, during which time he had little contact with the outside world.

Wrote Poetry While in Prison

Awoonor continued to write while in Ghana's Ussher Fort prison, and his work of this period was published in 1978 as *The House By the Sea*. These poems marked a new and more political direction in Awoonor's work. Perhaps unsurprisingly, his life after his release from prison in 1976 became more and more entwined with the politics and government of his homeland. Awoonor taught at Cape Coast University from 1977 to 1982, but then he embarked on a period of service to the Ghanaian government in various capacities. He became Ghana's ambassador to Brazil in 1984 and was named ambassador to Cuba in 1988. And from 1990 to 1994, Awoonor was the Ghanaian ambassador to the United Nations in New York.

Noted for his advocacy of African causes at the United Nations, Awoonor penned a variety of nonfiction works during this period, including two full-length books on Ghanaian history and a general study, *Africa: The Marginalised Continent* (1995). He returned to poetry, however, with the *Latin American and Caribbean Notebook* (1992), a work drawn from Awoonor's residence in those regions. That work and his 1992 novel *Comes the Voyager at Last* won less critical favor than Awoonor's earlier books.

In the late 1990s, Awoonor, entering his seventh decade, plunged once again into the world of Ghanaian domestic politics. He served in the administration of Ghanaian president Jerry Rawlings as an aide and economic planner, drawing criticism at one point for an offhand remark that praised Accra's notorious traffic jams as a sign of economic resilience. In this last stage of his career, Awoonor joined a procession of modern African writers, including Senegalese president Léopold Sédar Senghor and Ivorian poet Bernard Binlin Dadié, who turned to civic affairs later in life.

Killed in Shopping Mall Terrorist Attack

In September of 2013, at the age of 78, Awoonor traveled to Nairobi, Kenya to participate in the Storymoja Hay Festival, an international celebration of writing and storytelling; Awoonor was one of the most

eminent African writers invited. On the first morning of the festival, Saturday, September 21, Awoonor and his son Afetsi went to Nairobi's Westgate shopping mall to do some shopping. The timing of their arrival, however, coincided with a terror attack led by al-Shabab, a group of Somali Islamist militants, that eventually would develop into an 80-hour siege, killing 67 people and injuring hundreds more. Inside the mall, 10 to 15 al-Shabab members killed fired automatic weapons and grenades, sometimes separating Muslims from non-Muslims and sometimes killing indiscriminately. By Sunday morning—even as the siege in the mall continued—it was confirmed that Awoonor was among the dead. Awoonor's son Afetsi was injured but survived the attack.

On September 23 festival organizers honored Awoonor with a tribute held at the National Museum. Though the attack was then still ongoing, 150 people attended, including fellow Ghanaian poet Kwame Dawes and Nigerian-American writer Teju Cole, as well as members of Awoonor's family.

Awoonor's remains were flown back to Ghana on September 25. Hailed as the nation's most important writer, Awoonor's death was met in Ghana with outpourings of poetry and grief as well as a state memorial service. The University of Nebraska Press was set to release a collection of his poems entitled *The Promise of Hope,* spanning 50 years of Awoonor's work, in 2014.

Selected writings

Rediscovery and Other Poems, Mbari Publications, 1964.
Night of My Blood, Doubleday, 1971.
This Earth, My Brother, Heinemann, 1971.
Ride Me Memory, Greenfield Review, 1973.
The Breast of the Earth: A Survey of the History, Culture, and Literature of Africa South of the Sahara, Anchor Press, 1975.
The House By the Sea, Greenfield Review, 1978.
Ghana: A Political History from Pre-European to Modern Times, Sedco Publishing and Woeli Publishing, 1990.
Comes the Voyager at Last, Africa World Press, 1992.
Latin American and Caribbean Notebook, Africa World Press, 1992.
Africa: The Marginalised Continent, Woeli Publishing, 1995.
The African Predicament: Collected Essays, Sub-Saharan Publishers, 2006.

Sources

Books

Contemporary Authors Autobiography Series, vol. 13, Gale, 1991.

Periodicals

Africa News, August 24, 1999; May 13, 2000; April 11, 2002.
Guardian (London), September 23, 2013; September 27, 2013.
New York Times, February 4, 1976, p. 8; February 22, 1976, p. 48; November 18, 1976, p. 8.
Observer (London), September 21, 2013.
Straits Times (Malaysia), September 11, 1993.

Online

Edwards, Jocelyn, "Ghana Mourns Loss of Poet Killed in Kenya," Associated Press, September 25, 2013, http://bigstory.ap.org/article/ghana-mourns-loss-poet-killed-kenya (accessed January 15, 2014).
Garland, Muthoni, "Muthoni Garland, CEO of Storymoja on the Tribute evening for Prof. Kofi Awoonor last night," Hay Festivals, September 24, 2013, http://blog.hayfestival.org/index.php/2013/09/muthoni-garland-ceo-of-storymoja-on-the-tribute-evening-for-prof-kofi-awoonor-last-night/ (accessed November 19, 2013).
"Kofi Awoonor," Poetry Foundation Ghana, http://www.poetryfoundationghana.org/index.php/en/poets-connect/poets-directory/item/496-kofi-awoonor (accessed January 15, 2014).

—Kay Eastman and James M. Manheim

Zelmo Beaty

1939–2013

Professional basketball player

In 1961 Zelmo Beaty was a star basketball player at the historically black Prairie View A&M University in Texas when he was discovered by St. Louis Hawks scout Marty Blake. At the time few teams in the National Basketball Association (NBA) scouted players at all-black colleges. But at six feet, nine inches tall, and with obvious talents on the court, Beaty could not be missed. Selected as the third overall pick in the 1962 NBA draft, he played with the Hawks from 1962 to 1969, averaging 14.25 points and 11.2 rebounds per game. Beaty established himself as center who could compete at his position with bigger stars such as Wilt Chamberlain and Julius Erving, in spite of his slightly smaller frame. He became known early in his career as an extremely physical player, muscling for baskets and rebounds and earning the nicknames "Big Z" and "The Franchise."

Beaty's fierceness on the court sometimes got him into trouble. In both the 1962–63 and 1965–66 seasons with the Hawks, he racked up the most personal fouls in the NBA, and in 1963–64, he tied for most disqualifications from games. He was both feared and respected by other players in the league. Former Utah Jazz coach and Chicago Bulls player Jerry Sloan described Beaty to the *Salt Lake Tribune* as "a terrific player … big and strong and nasty. The kind of guy you wanted on your team." According to sportswriter Dan Pattinson on the website Remember the ABA, Former Indiana Pacers coach Bobby Leonard, whose team often faced Beaty and the Hawks, said of the center, "He was a banger! He was not only physically tough, but mentally tough, too. But at the same time, he played the game with dignity and grace. His play demanded respect."

Left Hawks for Rival League

During his seven seasons with the St. Louis (later Atlanta) Hawks, Beaty established himself as a leader both on and off the court. Serving as a player representative to the NBA players' union, he grew increasingly frustrated with the NBA's salary levels, which were significantly lower than those of the rival American Basketball Association, which was formed in 1967. Beaty said that the Hawks—after signing him as a rookie for $15,000—never paid him more than $37,000 in one year. When the opportunity arose for him to take a four-year, $800,000 contract to play for the ABA's Los Angeles Stars, he took it.

As free agency status did not yet exist in the NBA, Beaty was legally required to sit out a year (1970–71) in order to be released from his contract with Hawks. During that year the Los Angeles Stars were sold to a new owner, who moved the team to Salt Lake City, Utah. Beaty was upset by the unexpected move to a city where politics and culture were dominated by the Mormon church (which historically had not welcomed African Americans) and where there was virtually no black population. Initially he refused to go to Salt Lake City, but he eventually agreed after Mormon leaders reassured team owner Larry Miller that they would do everything they could to support and accommodate the new team.

At a Glance . . .

Born Zelmo Beaty Jr. on October 25, 1939, in Hillister, TX; died on August 27, 2013, in Bellevue, WA; married Ann; children: Debra, Darryl. *Education:* Prairie View A&M University, BA, 1962.

Career: St. Louis/Atlanta Hawks, center, 1962–69; Utah Stars (American Basketball Association), center, 1970–74; Los Angeles Lakers, center, 1974–75; Virginia Squires (American Basketball Association), coach, 1975–76.

Awards: National Basketball Association (NBA) All-Rookie First Team, 1963; NBA All-Star selection 1966, 1968; American Basketball Association (ABA) Playoffs Most Valuable Player, 1971; ABA All-Star selection, 1971–73; All-ABA Second Team, 1971, 1973; ABA All-Time Team.

Those promises were kept, and the team did well in Utah, winning the ABA championship in Beaty's first year with the team. "The most memorable game of my career came in Utah when we won the ABA title in 1971," Beaty said in an interview with *Basketball Digest* in 2003. "But it wasn't so much for what happened during the game. It's always great to win a championship, but I actually think it was the reaction of the fans after we had won the championship that made it so special. Here's what happened: As soon as we had beat the Kentucky Colonels, the fans were on that floor so fast, the players could not get off. The next thing we knew, they had us hoisted on their shoulders and were carrying us off the floor." Beaty went on to play for four years with the Stars, where he averaged more than 20 points and 10 rebounds per game. Beaty played in the ABA All-Star Game in three of his four years with the Stars, and he was twice named to the All-ABA Second Team.

Led ABA Players Association

Beaty's leadership and success as a black player in Utah was critical in establishing a precedent for a successful basketball franchise in Salt Lake City, and Beaty assumed an even more important role off the court when he was elected president of the ABA Players Association. Beaty had been disappointed by his previous professional relationship with the Hawks, where he had felt betrayed by the team's management. In the ABA he lobbied for better pension packages for retired players, helping create a sense of legitimacy and fairness in the new league. As a result, both the ABA and

NBA—two leagues in competition for the same talent—were forced to improve their treatment of players.

Though Beaty never signed the kind of multimillion-dollar contracts often given to star athletes today, he is remembered as a key figure in paving the way for professional athletes—black athletes in particular—to gain more agency in their contracts. On the website Remember the ABA, sportswriter Dan Pattison wrote of Beaty, "He was a goodwill ambassador for the state and city. He commanded respect just by the way he carried himself." It was Beaty's penchant for activism and diplomacy, combined with his consistent team play and personal dignity, that earned him the nickname "The Franchise."

Toward the end of his playing career, Beaty suffered from repeated knee injuries, necessitating nine surgeries. He left the Stars in 1974 and returned to the NBA, where he played one season with the Los Angeles Lakers in 1974–75 before retiring.

Turned to Teaching after Basketball

Beaty always said that he had wanted to be a carpenter as a boy, and after retiring from basketball, he was able to fulfill that dream by building his own house in Bellevue, Washington. After his basketball career he coached the ABA's Virginia Squires for one season in 1975–76, worked for many years in the financial planning sector, and then—on a friend's suggestion—applied to be a substitute teacher in the Washington Public School district. To his surprise he was hired, and he began working for the district as a substitute.

Beaty was adamant that children needed more male role models in school, as most teachers then were female. Speaking of his role as a mentor, Beaty told *Basketball Digest,* "I like to teach physical education. I'm sort of a gym rat. I like to deal with kids on that level where they come and have fun. I also believe this country is in a lot of trouble when it comes to kids and health. There are just too many kids that go home every night to sit in front of a computer and eat ice cream. They really don't have a chance to be healthy."

Over the course of his 12-year career in the NBA and ABA, Beaty averaged 17 points and 11 rebounds per game. Many historians of the game believe that he was an under-recognized player, in light of all that he achieved in the league, both on and off the court. Although he was inducted into the Utah Sports Hall of Fame in 2004, it seems that Beaty never quite escaped from the shadows of stars such as Irving and Chamberlain. After a four-year battle with cancer, Beaty died on August 27, 2013, at the age of 73. (Some sources incorrectly give his death date as September 7.) That same weekend that the Naismith Memorial Basketball Hall of Fame announced its 12 new inductees; Beaty was not on the list.

Sources

Books

Marecek, Greg, *Full Court: The Untold Stories of the St. Louis Hawks,* Reedy Press, 2006.

Pluto, Terry, *Loose Balls: The Short, Wild Life of the American Basketball Association as told by the Players, Coaches, and Movers and Shakers Who Made it Happen,* Fireside, 1991.

Periodicals

Basketball Digest, May 2003, p. 76.
New York Times, September 11, 2013, p. B17.
Salt Lake Tribune, September 12, 2013.

Online

Fatsis, Stefan, "Remember Zelmo Beaty," Slate.com, September 9, 2013, http://www.slate.com/articles/sports/sports_nut/2013/09/remember_zelmo_beaty_an_obituary_for_slate_s_favorite_basketball_player.html (accessed January 17, 2014).

Pattison, Dan, "Zelmo Beaty Tribute," Remember the ABA, http://www.remembertheaba.com/ABAArticles/PattisonArticleBeaty.html (accessed December 19, 2013).

"Zelmo Beaty," Basketball-Reference.com, http://www.basketball-reference.com/players/b/beatyze01.html (accessed December 19, 2013).

—Ben Bloch

Gael Bigirimana

1993—

Professional soccer player

Bigirimana, Gael, photograph. Chris Brunskill/The FA/ Getty Images.

Gael Bigirimana was just 18 years old when he signed as a midfielder for Newcastle United, one of England's Premier League (top-tier) football (soccer) clubs, in July of 2012. Bigirimana's youthful success is one of European football's most inspirational stories. Bigirimana was an 11-year-old war refugee from the African nation of Burundi, newly arrived in England, when he confidently presented himself as a prospect to the coaching staff of the Coventry City Sky Blues, a second-tier (or Championship Division) football team in England. Bigirimana rose swiftly through the ranks of Coventry's youth system and turned pro in the summer of 2011, already a fan favorite. In his first season as a senior player for Coventry City, Bigirimana was named Football League Championship Apprentice of the Year. Coventry executives only reluctantly released the teenage sensation to Newcastle United. On July 7, 2012, shortly after the trade was announced, Tim Fisher, the managing director of Coventry City, told Lee Ryder of the Newcastle *Evening Chronicle,* "Gael is a great talent and we would, obviously, have liked him to stay here at Coventry. But when the Premier League comes calling it becomes increasingly difficult to stand in the player's way."

Bigirimana has been embraced by the British press as a shining example both on and off the field. "It is not just Bigi's abilities on the pitch which make him special," a staffer for the *Evening Chronicle* wrote on February 15, 2013. "His lifestyle could not be further removed from the nightclubs … and hedonistic behavior associated with many footballers. A star of Newcastle's various community projects, he volunteers to visit schools so youngsters can learn from his life story, to see you can get a chance with the right attitude and talent." During a workshop for at-risk teens held at St. James Park, Newcastle's home stadium, on April 10, 2013, Bigirimana told the *Evening Chronicle,* "With my faith, I feel that God has given me the opportunity to be where I am so I want to give back to the others of my generation.… I look back and can't believe that it's happened. It's crazy for me. I just have to be grateful and remember that my story isn't for me, it's for other people."

Impressed Coventry City Scouts

Bigirimana was born in Bujumbura, Burundi's capital, on October 22, 1993. Although his family, including

At a Glance . . .

Born Gael Bigirimana on October 22, 1993, in Bujumbura, Burundi; son of Bonnet Bigirimana (a town planner) and Esperance Bigirimana (a hairstylist). *Religion:* Christian.

Career: Coventry City Youth, 2005–11; Coventry City FC, Championship Division, 2011–12; Newcastle United FC, Premier League, 2012—.

Awards: Apprentice of the Year Award, Championship Division, The Football League (England and Wales), 2012.

Addresses: c/o Newcastle United, St. James Park, Newcastle upon Tyne, NE1 4ST, United Kingdom.

three older siblings, lived in just one room, their standard of living was comfortable by Burundian standards. Bigirimana's Burundian father, Bonnet, was a town planner, and his Rwandan mother, Esperance, braided hair. In addition, his oldest brother, Passey, worked for the local shopkeeper. Gael first learned to play football barefoot in the dusty streets of his Bujumbura neighborhood. At the time his favorite football team was the powerhouse Spanish squad Real Madrid.

The Bigirimana family was displaced by the escalating civil war in Burundi between rival ethnic groups, the Hutu and the Tutsi. When Gael was seven years old, he fled to Uganda with his father, sister, and two brothers. His mother escaped to England to live with a relative. The family was reunited near Coventry City four years later. Shortly thereafter Bigirimana's mother sent him on a fateful trip to buy a pint of milk. On the way home he spied the Coventry City training academy and decided to ask scouts there for a trial. As Bigirimana recalled the meeting in an interview with Simon Bird of the London *Mirror,* "They said when I got to school and got in the team they would come and watch me and I was happy—I was overjoyed. But when I was jogging away, they stopped me then and there and told me to come back the next day. They have explained to me since that they saw athletic speed—but I was not really running!"

Coventry scout Ray Gooding took Bigirimana under his wing, steering him through levels of play in which he was given the opportunity to compete against more experienced boys in older age groups. By the time he was 17, Bigirimana had graduated from the youth system of the Coventry Sky Blues. Bigirimana made his professional debut for the Sky Blues' first team on August 8, 2011, in a match against Leicester City. He

went on to play 25 more games that first season and also appeared in matches for two domestic trophies, the Football Association Challenge Cup and the League Cup. Having been placed on the first team at such a young age, Bigirimana attended extra class sessions with the Sky Blues' education officer so that he could catch up on his studies.

Signed with Newcastle United

Bigirimana's aggressive ball playing and tough-tackling style of play at central midfield earned him a great deal of notice. He was one of the few bright lights on a struggling Coventry team that, by the end of the season, had been downgraded from the second tier to the third tier. After Bigirimana was named the recipient of the Championship League Apprentice Award, Newcastle United manager Alan Pardew moved quickly to lure him to his team before he was approached with offers from rival Premier League clubs. Bigirimana signed with Newcastle on July 6, 2012, in a five-year deal that reportedly paid him £500,000 up front, with another £500,000 written into the agreement based on his performance.

Although it was assumed that Bigirimana would go straight into Pardew's development squad at Newcastle, he got more playing time than expected because of injuries that had sidelined star midfielder Cheick Tioté. Bigirimana made his preseason debut in a Europa League competition in Greece on August 23, 2012, and saw his first Premier League play just three weeks into the season in a match against Aston Villa during which he made a key tackle to secure a 1–1 draw. Bigirimana appeared in more than 20 matches during the 2012–13 season, including a December 5, 2012, game in which he netted the third goal in a 3–0 win over Wigan Athletic, making him the first Burundian ever to score in English Premier League competition.

The sports press was impressed with Bigirimana's transition to first-team, first-tier play. Ex-footballer and sports journalist Malcolm MacDonald wrote in the Newcastle *Evening Chronicle* for September 29, 2012, "I like the look of Bigirimana in midfield. For a kid of only 18 he has an awful lot to offer and looks comfortable in good company. He rattles a few players rather than standing on ceremony and I like that in a young man." Hamza Nkuutu, a cricket player and writer for the *New Times* of Rwanda, enthused on October 14, 2012, "Since joining Newcastle in July, a side that finished 5th in the English Premier League last season, and playing the Europa League, the youngster [Bigirimana] has not looked out of place whatsoever, instead he has been assured in his nine appearances so far. His range of passing and retrieving possession is top drawer and you can see that with more learning and settling in the new environment, it's just a matter of time before he establishes himself in Alan Pardew's side

whose major weapon is hard work and team-work ethic."

Late in the spring of 2013, Bigirimana was named to England's Under-20 World Cup squad. His selection put to rest rumors that Bigirimana would commit his international future to Rwanda. Despite his promising first season with Newcastle, Bigirimana dropped in Pardew's pecking order for the 2013–14 season. With Newcastle having plummeted in the rankings and Cheick Tioté and other veteran midfielders back in action, Bigirimana has had few opportunities. Football insiders have urged Pardew to put Bigirimana on loan to a lower-tier club, possibly Coventry City, so that he can get the regular playing time necessary to his development. Pardew has said that he is struggling to find a suitable option for Bigirimana and, as Steph Clark noted in the *Northern Echo* for October 9, 2013, "Bigirimana's situation is a little different [from other standout young players] with the midfielder having already impressed in the Premier League and the Europa League for Newcastle, but with Cheick Tioté, Yohan Cabaye, Vurnon Anita, and Moussa Sissoko all vying for central midfield roles."

Bigirimana initially balked at the idea of a transfer, vowing to fight for a promotion from Newcastle's fringe lineup. On September 5, 2013, he told Miles Starforth of the *Shields Gazette,* "People can say it's best for me to go on loan, but I'm not going anywhere. I'm going to stay here. I'm going to be patient, and I'm going to work my socks off. I showed last year that I didn't look out of place in the big games.... My target this season is to fight. You never know how the season can change." However, in a November 7, 2013, interview with Ed Harrison, a blogger for Newcastle United, Bigirimana appeared to have accepted the loan solution. He told Harrison, "I am in love with Newcastle now, every time I don't make the squad I watch the game and I see how passionate fans are, I want to be part of that. If I want to be one of the top players at this club I need to get experience, I need to go out on loan.... But it's so that when I come back, I will be an even better player for Newcastle United." In an article published in the *Coventry Telegraph* for November 18, 2013, Coventry City manager Steven Pressley denied any interest in signing Bigirimana during the midseason transfer window, January 1–31, 2014.

Sources

Periodicals

Coventry (UK) Observer, March 12, 2012.
Coventry (UK) Telegraph, November 18, 2013.
Evening Chronicle (Newcastle, UK), July 7, 2012; September 29, 2012; December 5, 2012; April 10, 2013; August 28, 2013.
Mirror (London), October 24, 2012.
New Times (Rwanda), October 14, 2012; December 5, 2012.
Northern Echo (UK), October 9, 2013.
Shields Gazette (South Shields, UK), September 5, 2013.

Online

Fletcher, Paul, "Coventry's Boy from Burundi," BBC Sport, March 12, 2012, http://www.bbc.co.uk/blogs/paulfletcher/2012/03/coventrys_boy_from_burundi.html (accessed January 13, 2014).

"Gael Bigirimana," Newcastle United, http://www.nufc.co.uk/page/Teams/PlayerProfile/0,,10278~52504,00.html (accessed January 13, 2014).

"Gael Bigirimana Tells of Journey from Burundi to Newcastle," ChronicleLive.co.uk, February 15, 2013, http://www.chroniclelive.co.uk/news/local-news/gael-bigirimana-tells-journey-burundi-1352831 (accessed January 13, 2014).

Harrison, Ed, "Newcastle Youngster—I'm in Love with the Club," *Newcastle United Blog,* November 7, 2013, http://www.nufcblog.com/2013/11/07/newcastle-youngster-im-in-love-with-the-club/ (accessed January 13, 2014).

Murphy, Chris, and Ben Monro-Davies, "Premier League Dream for Gael Bigirimana after 'Miracle Journey,'" CNN.com, October 9, 2013, http://www.cnn.com/2013/10/09/sport/football/gael-bigirimana-newcastle-burundi-football/ (accessed January 13, 2014).

Ryder, Lee, "Pardew: Bigirimana Can Become NUFC Favorite," ChronicleLive.co.uk, July 7, 2012, http://www.chroniclelive.co.uk/sport/football/football-news/pardew-bigirimana-can-become-nufc-1367418 (accessed January 13, 2014).

—Janet Mullane

Blitz the Ambassador

1982—

Hip-hop artist

Blitz the Ambassador, photograph. Jack Vartoogian/Getty Images.

Blitz the Ambassador is a Ghanaian-American hip-hop artist whose distinctive music combines the influence of old-school rappers such as Chuck D with African sounds such as Afrobeat and Ghanaian highlife. The result is neither Western nor African but rather a seamless hybrid of the two cultures in which the rapper has lived. Born in Ghana and based for nearly a decade in New York City, Blitz has produced two well-regarded albums, *Stereotype* (2009) and *Native Sun* (2011), both released on his own label. In 2013 he released the EP *The Warm-Up,* a prelude to his third studio album that included the popular singles "Dikembe!" and "African in New York." As he seeks to expand the boundaries of hip-hop, Blitz views himself as an ambassador for African music—hence his moniker. "I realized that there's a specific role that I need to be playing," he explained to Michel Martin of National Public Radio (NPR). "And that role is about bridging gaps and … expanding the culture that I've been blessed to be a part of and letting people see that, in fact, it is a global culture and people all over the world are a part of hip-hop culture."

Influenced by American Hip-Hop

Blitz the Ambassador was born Samuel Bazawule in April of 1982 in Accra, the capital of Ghana. The second of four children, he grew up in a household that valued education and art. His father was a human rights lawyer for the United Nations, and his mother was a teacher. As a boy Blitz had access to his father's large library of books and music, which included Middle Eastern music as well as albums by American jazz and Motown singers and African artists such as Hugh Masekela. "It was great, with books on one hand and vinyl on the other hand in the house. You really can't go wrong," he said in an interview with the Victoria, Canada, *Times Colonist.*

By the early 1990s, American rap and hip-hop were making their way to Africa, and the music's influence spread quickly. Blitz and his friends devoured tapes brought from overseas, listening to acts such as Public Enemy, A Tribe Called Quest, Rakim, and KRS-One. Public Enemy's seminal album *It Takes a Nation of Millions to Hold Us Back* (1988)—especially the track

At a Glance . . .

Born Samuel Bazawule in April of 1982 in Accra, Ghana. *Education:* Kent State University, BA, business administration, 2005.

Career: Founded record label, Embassy MVMT, 2000s; recording artist, 2004—.

Awards: Best New Artist, Ghana Music Awards, 2000; Vilchek Prize for Creative Promise in Contemporary Music, Vilchek Foundation, 2013.

Addresses: *Office*—Embassy MVMT, 80 Hanson Place, Suite 102, Brooklyn, NY 11217. *Web*—http://blitz.mvmt.com.

"Bring the Noise"—had a profound effect on Blitz. "That's where it began for me," he told NPR in October of 2013. "My parents hated the song and hated the title, because it was noisy. But it really, really informed me." The social consciousness of early rappers such as Public Enemy, the first hip-hop act to tour in Ghana, resonated with a generation of young Africans. The music had "an urgency that the music that we had back home did not have at the time. There was a kind of social commentary, a political commentary of life … that was very appealing to young people that also didn't have much of a voice at the time," Blitz told Martin.

Blitz began performing hip-hop as a teenager and was discovered by the Ghanaian producer Hammer of The Last Two, who first brought the young rapper into the studio. Blitz made a guest appearance with the Ghanaian artist Deeba on a track of the same name. That song was a local hit, and Blitz quickly became a sensation, earning best new artist honors at the Ghana Music Awards in 2000.

Fused Western and African Genres

Soon thereafter Blitz moved to the United States, stopping first in New York City, where he spent time with family. He then attended college for four years in Ohio, earning a bachelor's degree in business administration from Kent State University. Living in a small town in the Midwest was a culture shock for the Ghanaian: "Imagine the difference," he told Rob Boffard of the online magazine *Huck.* "Coming to New York, where there's a diverse cultural environment, you feel safe because there's something for everyone there, and then you go to Ohio and it's like, 'Wow, there are two kinds of people here!' There were white folks and

African-Americans. It's a small pool. If you were an international person in that town, you were a student…. It was very, very different." That experience helped shape Blitz's understanding of the immigrant experience and how immigrants survive in a completely different culture.

While he was a student, Blitz honed his musical skills. He performed live at local shows, opening for the rapper Rakim, and released the EPs *Soul Rebel* in 2004 and *Double Consciousness* in 2005. After finishing his undergraduate degree in 2005, he moved to New York City to pursue a career as a hip-hop artist. Finding that the major music labels were unreceptive to his unique style of hip-hop, he eventually decided to form his own label, Embassy MVMT. "I was tired of record labels telling me I had to be like somebody else," he said in an interview posted on the website of Center Stage Theater in Atlanta, Georgia.

In 2009 Blitz released another EP, *StereoLive,* as well as his first full-length album, *Stereotype.* His sophomore album, *Native Sun,* followed in 2011. Blitz's music pushes the boundaries of hip-hop in a global direction, incorporating diverse elements of both African and Western music, including Afrobeat, highlife (a Ghanaian genre), R&B, funk, and jazz. Likewise, his lyrics are a pastiche of several languages, including Akan (the language of Ghana), English, and a west African pigeon English. In contrast to much mainstream American hip-hop, which relies heavily on sampled music and electronic instrumentation, Blitz works with live musicians, backed by his 12-piece Embassy Ensemble. Many of his raps use a 6/8 time signature, which is common in Afrobeat music but not in hip-hop, creating an unusual sound.

Created Hybrid Sound

Blitz fuses all of these diverse components to create a hybrid sound that reflects both his African roots and his American experience. "[Y]ou … find points where [the different elements] intersect," Blitz said on his website. "You have to create something so that you can't tell where the hip hop begins and where the Afrobeat ends, and where highlife stops and future beats start. You have to create a world of equal parts."

Blitz's 2011 album *Native Sun,* which is accompanied by a companion short film, traces the evolution of the rapper's hip-hop consciousness. "*Native Sun* the album is a journey backwards, back through hip hop, the Caribbean soundsystem culture that preceded it, back to its African roots," while "[t]he film looks forward, to what could be," he explained on his website. "Both are about … letting go of old notions and embracing new ideas. The sound in itself speaks to that." Collaborations on the album pay tribute to Blitz's earliest influences, with an appearance by Chuck D on the track

"The Oracle," and feature a lineup of new African artists, such as the Parisian R&B duo Les Nubians (on "Dear Africa"), the Afro-German singer Corneille (on "Best I Can"), the Congolese MC Baloji (on "Wahala"), and the Canadian rapper Shad (on "Native Sun").

In 2013 Blitz released the EP *The Warm-Up* as a prelude to his third studio album, *Afropolitan Dreams,* which was expected in early 2014. The release included the singles "African in New York," which borrows from Sting's "Alien in New York" and Jay-Z's "99 Problems," and "Dikembe!," an homage to the Congoborn professional basketball player Dikembe Mutombo.

Selected discography

EPs

Soul Rebel, 2004.
Double Consciousness, 2005.
StereoLive, 2009.
The Warm-Up (includes "Dikembe!" and "African in New York"), 2013.

Studio albums

Stereotype, Embassy MVMT, 2009.
Native Sun, Embassy MVMT, 2011.

Sources

Periodicals

Guardian (London), May 20, 2011.
Times Colonist (Victoria, Canada), July 10, 2013.

Online

Blitz the Ambassador, http://blitz.mvmt.com (accessed January 6, 2014).
"Blitz the Ambassador: A New Face for Hip-Hop's Foreign Policy," Brooklyn Bodega, July 24, 2009, http://brooklynbodega.wpengine.com/blitz-the-ambassador-a-new-face-for-hip-hops-foreign-policy-2/ (accessed January 6, 2014).
"Blitz: The Ambassador of Hip-Hop and African Music," National Public Radio, October 7, 2013, http://www.npr.org/2013/10/07/230126264/blitz-the-ambassador-of-hip-hop-and-african-music (accessed January 6, 2014).
Boffard, Rob, "Blitz the Ambassador from Accra," Huck, July 25, 2012, http://www.huckmagazine.com/features/blitz-the-ambassador/ (accessed January 6, 2014).
Gallafant, Alex, "Ghanaian Rapper Blitz the Ambassador," Public Radio International, May 4, 2011, http://www.pri.org/stories/2011-05-04/ghanaian-rapper-blitz-ambassador (accessed January 6, 2014).
Kelley, Frannie, "From Ghana to Brooklyn: Learning from Hip-Hop," *Weekend Edition,* National Public Radio, July 9, 2011, http://www.npr.org/2011/07/10/137702818/from-ghana-to-brooklyn-learning-from-hip-hop (accessed January 6, 2014).
Martin, Michel, "Blitz the Ambassador: Fighting against Invisibility," *Tell Me More,* National Public Radio, September 8, 2013, http://www.npr.org/2013/11/27/247481464/blitz-the-ambassador-fighting-against-invisibility (accessed January 6, 2014).
"Rival Entertainment Presents: Blitz the Ambassador." Center Stage Theater-Atlanta, http://www.centerstage-atlanta.com/show/?id=1089&artist=BLITZ=THE=AMBASSADOR (accessed January 14, 2013).

—Deborah A. Ring

Arthur M. Brazier

1921–2010

Clergyman, community organizer

Bishop Arthur M. Brazier made many contributions to his hometown of Chicago throughout his lengthy life, which he devoted to clerical service and civic activism. Beginning in the 1960s Brazier helped devise an effective, pragmatic model of community organizing and grassroots urban neighborhood development to address structural inequities in housing and education. The Reverend Martin Luther King Jr. chose to stage a civil rights campaign in Chicago in 1966 in response to an invitation from Brazier and his colleagues. Over nearly a half century in the pulpit of the Apostolic Church of God, located in the Woodlawn neighborhood on the city's South Side, Brazier built the largest congregation in Chicago, becoming a prominent and deeply respected figure in the city.

Took over Storefront Church from Mother

Arthur Monroe Brazier was born July 22, 1921, on the South Side of Chicago, youngest of five children of Robert and Geneva Brazier. His family was deeply affected by the Great Depression, so after a year at Wendell Phillips High School in the Bronzeville neighborhood, Brazier quit school for the opportunity to contribute to the family income by taking any available work. When the United States entered World War II, Brazier was drafted into the U.S. Army and served as staff sergeant from 1942 to 1945, stationed in Burma and India.

Returning to Chicago after his discharge, Brazier grew interested in religious life, thanks to the influence of his mother, a lay pastor with the Universal Church of Christ. He was baptized in 1947, an event that he later cited as the moment when he committed his life to the Lord. He was married early in 1948 to Esther Isabelle Holmes, who would remain by his side for the rest of his life; the couple had four children. That same year Brazier found steady employment as a mailman. He kept the job for 12 years but increasingly felt called to preach. Following his mother's death in 1949, Brazier stepped in to become assistant pastor, then pastor of her storefront church on the South Side. In 1955 Brazier began attending Moody Bible Institute at night, concluding his formal studies for the ministry six years later. In 1960 he accepted an offer to become pastor of the Apostolic Church of God in Woodlawn, merging it with his Universal Church of Christ congregation; the combined flock consisted of about 100 members.

Battled University Encroachment on Black Neighborhoods

The young minister took a sincere interest in improving neighborhood conditions. At the time Woodlawn suffered from high unemployment, dilapidated ghetto housing, overcrowded and segregated schools, and rampant gang activity. Brazier's search for solutions brought him to Chicago's most experienced community organizer, Saul Alinsky, the author of *Reveille for Radicals* (1946). Working with Alinsky's Industrial Areas Foundation and its associate director, Nicholas von Hoffman, Brazier and other South Side clergy and residents came together in early 1961 to create what

At a Glance . . .

Born Arthur Monroe Brazier on July 22, 1921, in Chicago, IL; died on October 22, 2010, in Chicago, IL; son of Robert and Geneva Brazier; married Esther Isabelle Holmes, February 21, 1948; children: Lola, Byron, Janice, Rosalyn. *Military service:* U.S. Army, staff sergeant, 1942–45. *Religion:* Pentecostal. *Education:* Graduated from the Moody Bible Institute, 1961.

Career: U.S. Postal Service, letter carrier, 1948–60; Universal Church of Christ, Chicago, pastor, 1952–60; Apostolic Church of God, Chicago, pastor, 1960–2008; Center for Community Change, staff member, vice president, 1970s–86; Pentecostal Assemblies of the World, Sixth Episcopal District, appointed diocesan bishop, 1976.

Memberships: Coordinating Council of Community Organizations; Fund for Community Redevelopment and Revitalization; New Communities Program-Woodlawn; Public Building Commission, City of Chicago; Woodlawn Children's Promise Community; The Woodlawn Organization; Woodlawn Preservation and Investment Corporation.

became known as The Woodlawn Organization (TWO), the first and most successful African-American community advocacy group in any Northern city. Brazier was the group's founding president and retained that title until the end of the decade. In 1962 the TWO called a public school strike to protest the installation of portable classrooms on wheels in overcrowded local schools. The group excoriated Chicago schools superintendent Benjamin Willis by christening the mobile classrooms "Willis Wagons." The name stuck—but, unfortunately, so did the wagons.

The following year the organization strengthened its reputation as the authentic voice of the neighborhood in a dramatic confrontation with the University of Chicago. The private university, whose campus straddled Woodlawn and the adjacent South Side neighborhood of Hyde Park, sought to expand southward. University leaders, along with private developers and powerful allies in city government, presented their blueprints as an innovative exercise in urban renewal and slum clearance. However, the TWO—and its main spokesman, Brazier—argued that the city's white power structure was attempting to seize the neighborhood and displace its black population. The group made such a stink that the university eventually was

forced to shelve its plans. Years later the university and the TWO's successor organizations formed a cooperative partnership in several community development initiatives.

Brazier was instrumental in founding the Coordinating Council of Community Organizations, which was led by Chicago schoolteacher Albert Raby and active in the struggle for school integration. In 1965 the council invited the Southern Christian Leadership Conference (SCLC), King's organization, to participate in a civil rights demonstration in Chicago. Recognizing the groundwork that the TWO and other groups had laid, King and his colleagues decided to make Chicago the theater for the nonviolent freedom movement's first major campaign in the North. Early in 1966 King and his family moved into an apartment in a slum district on the west side. The civil rights groups crafted a series of actions to call attention to inequalities and racial discrimination in housing. The Reverend Jesse Jackson also initiated Operation Breadbasket, a project of the SCLC that was intended to provide economic uplift to the black community, in Chicago. The civil rights marches drew a hostile response in white neighborhoods; King was struck by a thrown rock during a march on August 5. Although the Chicago freedom movement brought about significant progress in public housing and mortgage access for African Americans, some historians regard it as a partial success, at best, for the nationwide movement.

Witnessed Community Rejuvenation

Under Brazier's leadership the TWO developed Model Cities programs that directed community members' energies toward achieving collective empowerment in health care, housing, employment, education, and welfare. Brazier narrated the growth of these innovative projects in the book *Black Self-Determination: The Story of The Woodlawn Organization,* published in 1969. Starting in the early 1970s, the TWO became involved in rehabilitating and building hundreds of residential structures in the neighborhood.

In 1976 the Pentecostal Assemblies of the World elevated Brazier from the title of elder to diocesan bishop, making responsible for supervising dozens of churches statewide within its Sixth Episcopal District. Brazier also became a part-time staff member of the Washington, DC–based Center for Community Change, training organizers and civic groups around the country in community revitalization methods, particularly with regard to housing and land use. He eventually was named a vice president of the organization, resigning in 1986 in order to concentrate on local efforts, especially his own church. The Apostolic Church of God was on its way to becoming a megachurch, with a 12-acre campus and a congregation of nearly 20,000, while its surrounding area, the formerly

blighted East 63rd Street, was beginning to enjoy a renaissance.

The bishop was increasingly recognized as a city elder, and his weekly sermons were often heard on local television. In 1986 Brazier was named to the Chicago Public Building Commission under the city's first African-American mayor, Harold Washington. With the founding of the Woodlawn Preservation and Investment Corporation in 1987, Brazier and his colleagues crossed from housing advocacy to development and management of affordable and mixed-income housing complexes. Several years later he brought community stake holders together to create a sister organization, the Fund for Community Redevelopment and Revitalization, to combat longtime disinvestment in the neighborhood. Several major grants, including one from the MacArthur Foundation, and an infusion of support from the University of Chicago helped spur construction and community renovations. In 1997 the city tore down a stretch of the El—the city's elevated train line—along East 63rd Street, largely in response to Bishop Brazier's vociferous argument that the tracks impeded development on the commercial thoroughfare.

In 2008 Brazier spearheaded the formation of the Woodlawn Children's Promise Community, a coalition to mobilize community assets on behalf of local youth and families. That year on Father's Day, Chicagoan Barack Obama, who had clinched the Democratic presidential nomination days earlier, delivered an important campaign speech from the pulpit of the Apostolic Church of God. That September the bishop installed his son, Byron Brazier, as the church's new pastor.

Even at age 87, Brazier refused to slow down: just weeks after his retirement, the pastor emeritus was named the first senior fellow of the Chicago Local Initiative Support Corporation, a major community development institution. All the while Brazier was battling prostate cancer. The disease finally took his life on October 22, 2010. His memorial service one week later was attended by the mayor of Chicago, the governor of Illinois, the state's two senators, First Lady Michelle Obama, and roughly 4,000 mourners. In 2013 Chicago mayor Rahm Emanuel announced his intention to rename a major South Side thoroughfare, Stony Island Avenue, after Bishop Brazier.

Selected writings

Black Self-Determination: The Story of the Woodlawn Organization, William B. Eerdmans, 1969.
Saved By Grace and Grace Alone, Saving Grace Ministries, 1993.
From Milk to Meat, Treasure House, 1996.

Sources

Books

Dortch, Sammie M., *When God Calls: A Biography of Bishop Arthur M. Brazier.* Chicago: William B. Eerdmans, 1996.

Periodicals

Chicago Reader, November 6, 1997.
Chicago Tribune, October 22, 2010.

Online

"Behold the Man: The Life Story of Bishop Arthur M. Brazier," Apostolic Church of God, http://www.acog-chicago.org/site/epage/88518_875.htm (accessed November 23, 2013).
"Bishop Arthur M. Brazier, Tireless Advocate for Woodlawn Community, 1921–2010," University of Chicago, October 22, 2010, http://news.uchicago.edu/article/2010/10/21/bishop-arthur-m-brazier-tireless-advocate-woodlawn-community-1921-2010 (accessed November 23, 2013).
Lane, L., "Woodlawn Mourns the Passing of Bishop Arthur M. Brazier." New Communities Project-Woodlawn, http://www.ncp-woodlawn.org/display.aspx?pointer=10355 (accessed November 23, 2013).

—Roger K. Smith

Aja Brown

1982—

Urban planner, politician

In June of 2013, 31-year-old Aja Brown was elected as the youngest-ever mayor of Compton, California, a city whose gang violence and urban decay have been immortalized in gangsta rap music since the 1980s. During campaign appearances Brown emphatically told audiences, "I know what it takes to move cities forward." Nearly 64 percent of Compton's voters agreed, and Brown handily defeated both the incumbent and a former mayor to become not just the youngest but also the first female mayor of the city in more than 40 years. Within four months she had slashed the city's budget deficit, restructured its loan debt by negotiating lower interest rates, initiated much-needed neighborhood policing and gang intervention programs, and gained the respect of at least some of her critics, who saw her as an outsider despite the family roots that had drawn her to Compton.

Brown was born in Los Angeles in 1982. She and her twin brother were raised in Altadena by their mother, Brenda Jackson, who was left a single parent after a divorce. As a child Jackson had lived in Compton until her mother, Lena Young, was brutally raped and murdered in their home in 1973. The crime was never solved. Jackson moved away from Compton soon afterward. Her daughter, Aja (pronounced "Asia"), who never knew her grandmother, grew up hearing stories about life in Compton before it was overrun by crime. Although Compton had never been her hometown, after earning degrees in urban planning and development and working in the field for nearly a decade, Brown decided to move to the city of her family's roots with her husband, Van Brown. She explained to Patrick

Range McDonald of *LA Weekly,* "We wanted to be where we could make a difference."

Brown excelled in high school as an athlete and a scholar, and from an early age she was fascinated by civic renewal and rebuilding efforts. Amy Ephron reported in *Vogue,* "When Aja was ten, she would beg her mother to take her … to Old Pasadena, which at the time was undergoing a preservation and renovation project…. She just wanted to watch the buildings go up." Brown would eventually take a leadership role in such projects, but education came first. In order to pay for college, Brown earned scholarships and grants but worked regularly as well, which required discipline and focus. In an interview with McDonald, Brown explained, "I didn't have a traditional college experience," referring to the social life of most University of Southern California students. She and her husband, whom she began dating at age 17, were married in 2003.

While working on her master's degree, Brown was hired by the City of Gardena, California, as an economic development analyst to handle brownfield coordination and remediation—that is, the reuse of industrial sites contaminated by hazardous substances that must be removed before the property can be used for another purpose. Two years later she was hired by the City of Inglewood, where she led other aspects of economic development and planning. In 2007 she joined the City of Pasadena as a planning commissioner. Finally, in 2009, Brown was tapped to focus on redevelopment efforts for the city of Compton. She worked for the city's Community Redevelopment

At a Glance . . .

Born Aja Lena Clinkscale on April 17, 1982, in Los Angeles, CA; daughter of Brenda Jackson (an executive assistant); married Van Brown (an oil industry safety manager), November 12, 2003. *Education:* University of Southern California, BS, policy, planning, and development, 2004, MS, planning and development, 2005.

Career: City of Gardena, CA, economic development analyst, brownfield coordinator, 2004–06; City of Inglewood, CA, senior administrative analyst, senior planner, 2006–09; City of Pasadena, CA, planning commissioner, 2007–09; City of Compton, CA, Community Redevelopment Agency, project manager, 2009–11; Urban Vision Community Development Corporation, cofounder, principal, 2011–13; City of Compton, mayor, 2013—.

Memberships: American Planning Association; Community Redevelopment Association; International Council of Shopping Centers; Urban Land Institute's Young Leaders Group.

Addresses: *Office*—City of Compton, 205 S. Willowbrook Ave., Compton, CA 90220. *Web*—https://www.facebook.com/ajalenabrown. *Twitter*—@AjaLBrown.

Agency to raise development resources in the form of grants, corporate investments, in-kind contributions (donated services), and a $100 million tax allocation bond. She also was instrumental in adding a Blue Line mass transit station, extending service to and from Los Angeles.

Despite her mother's concerns about their safety, Brown and her husband bought a townhouse in Compton in 2009. In addition to Brown's work with the city, the young couple were active members of Faith Inspirational Missionary Baptist Church, where they mentored youth and participated in community outreach and assistance programs. In 2011 Compton's budget crisis forced layoffs in the Community Redevelopment Agency. In August that year Aja and Van Brown founded the Urban Vision Community Development Corporation, a nonprofit foundation targeting local needs with small business loans and mentoring, education programs, and scholarships. Brown began to consider running for office as a way of contributing to the renewal of her adopted city.

With her youthful enthusiasm, experience as an urban planner, and a vision of Compton as a vibrant city attractive to young professionals such as herself, Brown was an unexpectedly controversial candidate in the mayoral race in 2013. In the *LA Weekly* McDonald noted that the city "nurtures a deep, historical distrust of 'outsiders,'" which was how many in the community perceived Brown. Retired police sergeant John Baker told McDonald, "She's only been there for four years. She doesn't know the culture of Compton." In the *Los Angeles Daily News,* Compton voter Floyd Hooper noted that some residents suspected that she was running for mayor only as "a stepping stone to get to the Assembly or Senate." Nonetheless, two-thirds of Compton's voters selected Brown as their mayor. Explaining her sense of connection to Compton, Brown told McDonald that running for mayor of the city held a personal significance for her: "Growing up there was a big void in my life and my mother's life.... [this is] part of rectifying a part of my past tragedy."

The influence of "outsiders" who supported Brown's candidacy, including the Los Angeles County Federation of Labor and county supervisor Mark Ridley-Thomas, was also resisted by the Compton "old guard" power structure. Some were supporters of the incumbent mayor, Eric Perrodin, while others wanted to return former mayor Omar Bradley to city hall. Both men had endured legal and ethical challenges while in office, and voters seemed eager to reject them as symbolic of a culture of corruption and failure. In fact, Brown was not the only new face on the political scene in Compton in 2013. Isaac Galvan, a 26-year-old Latino candidate, defeated longtime incumbent council member Lillie Dobson. In so doing, Galvan became the first Latino council member in a city that was two-thirds Latino, with no prior council representation.

Although a dark moment from Compton's past motivated Brown to strive for change, it is her vision for the present and future that others are counting on as inspiration. From establishing a weekly farmer's market to improve access to fresh produce and a healthier diet, to recruiting permanent jobs in e-commerce, Brown has a very specific model of renewal in mind. Citing the infrastructure of freeways, trains, and proximity to Los Angeles's resources such as the airport and seaports, she compared Compton to the New York borough of Brooklyn, which underwent its own rebirth. Brown told the London *Guardian,* "Just look at all the resources here. You kind of wonder why Compton hasn't progressed to the level that it should." In a November of 2013 interview with Southern California Public Radio, she also offered a nod to Pasadena, which may be more familiar to her constituents: "When I grew up [there] Colorado Blvd. was a hotspot for drugs, gangs, prostitution, pawn shops, and now it's one of the higher end retail magnets in North L.A. County." She continued, "If it can happen there, it can happen here."

Sources

Periodicals

Guardian (London), October 15, 2013.
LA Weekly, July 18, 2013.
Los Angeles Daily News, June 4, 2013.
Los Angeles Times, June 1, 2013.
Vogue, September 2013.

Online

Aja Brown, LinkedIn, http://www.linkedin.com/in/ajabrown (accessed November 22, 2013).

Brenda Jackson, Facebook, https://www.facebook.com/brenda.jackson.39904 (accessed December 1, 2013).

Garrova, Robert, "Compton Mayor Aja Brown Takes Cues from Old Town Pasadena," Southern California Public Radio, November 22, 2013, http://www.scpr.org/programs/offramp/2013/11/22/34807/compton-mayor-aja-brown-takes-cues-from-old-town-p/ (accessed November 25, 2013).

Jonathan Clinkscale, Facebook, https://www.facebook.com/profile.php?id=8619654&fref=browse_search (accessed December 1, 2013).

"A New Vision for Compton," Aja Brown for Mayor, http://visionforcompton.org/ (accessed November 30, 2013).

Siegler, Kirk, "New Mayor Asks Compton: What Can Brown Do For You?," National Public Radio, November 4, 2013, http://www.npr.org/blogs/codeswitch/2013/11/04/242956747/new-mayor-asks-compton-what-can-brown-do-for-you (accessed November 25, 2013).

—Pamela Willwerth Aue

Paul Bryant

1933–2010

Jazz organist and pianist

Although he never became quite as famous as some of his peers, the organist and pianist Paul Bryant was a major figure in the development of the cool, rhythmically complex jazz long associated with the West Coast. A fixture on the Los Angeles jazz scene for more than half a century, he was best known for blending the melodic freedom characteristic of that genre with the rhythms and textures of the blues. According to Fresh Sound Records, which reissued several classic albums Bryant completed in the early 1960s, Bryant "had a hard-hitting, two-fisted style that exploited the [organ's range] to the limit."

Paul Carlton Bryant was born on September 22, 1933, in Asbury Park, New Jersey, a small town not far from New York City. The son of Gene Odom and Maxwell Bryant, he moved with his mother to Los Angeles when he was a child. They settled in that fast-growing city's South Central district, an area that already was emerging as a center of African-American culture. Bryant's mother had a strong interest in music and performance, and on the family's arrival in California, she enrolled Bryant in the John Gray Conservatory of Music, where he began piano lessons. His talent and stage presence were soon visible, and by the age of about seven, he had appeared in a number of amateur and semiprofessional productions, many of which featured his singing, dancing, and acting as well as his piano skills. It was not long before movie producers in nearby Hollywood took notice of Bryant, and over the course of the 1940s, he had small roles in several films, among the best known of which was *I Married An*

Angel (1942), a musical starring Jeanette MacDonald and Nelson Eddy.

Like many child stars, Bryant found acting jobs more difficult to obtain as he aged, and by the time he reached his mid-teens, his focus was squarely on music. At Jefferson High School, a predominately African-American institution well-known for its music programs, he joined a jazz band that also featured the drummer Ed Thigpen and the trumpeter Art Farmer, both of whom later joined Bryant in the professional ranks. After graduation he entered the U.S. Air Force, where he served for several years as part of a touring orchestra, playing gigs for military personnel around the country. He then returned to Los Angeles and began his career in earnest, playing piano in the city's jazz clubs, many of them clustered along Central Avenue, a vibrant arts and business district and a focal point for the African-American community. A familiar figure in that area for decades, Bryant was sometimes billed as the "Central Avenue Kid." One of his favorite haunts there was Dynamite Jackson's, a club that also had a branch on West Adams Boulevard, several miles to the northwest. Both locations regularly hosted many of the city's leading musicians, among them the saxophonist Curtis Amy, who became a close collaborator.

By the late 1950s Bryant's proficiency on the piano was well-known across Southern California. It was at that moment, however, that he shifted his approach, turning his attention to the organ, an instrument well suited to the bluesy, gospel-inflected jazz that was his hallmark. In later years he recalled his embrace of the

At a Glance . . .

Born Paul Carlton Bryant on September 22, 1933, in Asbury Park, NJ; died on December 4, 2010, in West Hollywood, CA; son of Gene Odom and Maxwell Bryant; married Shirley Jean Harris, 1957; children: two. *Military service:* U.S. Air Force, 1950s.

Career: Jazz organist and pianist, 1950s–2010.

organ matter-of-factly, saying simply that it allowed him to do things the piano did not.

A major break soon followed. In 1960 Dick Bock, the founder of a small but highly regarded label called Pacific Jazz, heard Amy at Dynamite Jackson's, offered him a contract, and began to recruit other musicians for a backing band. Bryant, then working at a club called Mardi's, was asked to serve both as organist and as Amy's coleader. Joining them in the studio were the trombonist Roy Brewster, the drummer Jimmy Miller, and the bassist Clarence S. Jones. Their sessions together resulted in an album called *The Blues Message,* released in 1960 under the names of Amy and Bryant. Deeply infused with the rhythms of the blues, it was anchored by a song Bryant had written called "Searchin'," which soon inspired him to compose a follow-up, "Still Searchin'"; the latter appeared on his next album, *Burnin'* (1960), completed without the help of Amy.

The next few years were arguably the height of Bryant's career, at least in terms of his recorded output. In addition to coleading another major album with Amy, *Meetin' Here* (1961), he also backed the saxophonist Johnny Griffin on *Grab This!* (1963), described by Ronnie D. Lankford Jr. of AllMusic.com as "a fine album" that was "greatly aided by the organ of Paul Bryant." Among the tracks Lankford singled out for praise was a "wonderful" Bryant composition called "Offering Time," which Lankford characterized as "a slow blues piece with a strong groove."

The jazz world, meanwhile, was changing rapidly. Although Bryant continued to record steadily through 1964, a year in which he released two solo albums (*Something's Happening* and *Groove Time*), the public's growing enthusiasm for newer styles such as free jazz cut significantly into his record sales. He responded to that shift, as did many of his peers, by focusing once again on live gigs in neighborhood clubs. With the aid of what was, by all accounts, a warm and personable

demeanor, he attracted a strong following that allowed him to withstand the vagaries of public taste and industry economics for the next four decades.

Active professionally until his mid-70s, Bryant was eventually forced to curtail his performance schedule because of health concerns. An honored guest at music festivals in and around Los Angeles, he served for many years as an unofficial spokesman for the city's jazz community. On December 4, 2010, roughly three years after his last major performance on a public stage, he died of surgical complications at Cedars-Sinai Medical Center in West Hollywood, California. Joining his family in mourning were dozens of colleagues and friends, many of whom gathered at a nearby church to recall what Scott Gold of the *Los Angeles Times* described as his "infectious smile and precocious skills."

Selected discography

(With Curtis Amy) *The Blues Message* (includes "Searchin'"), Pacific Jazz, 1960.
Burnin' (includes "Still Searchin'"), Pacific Jazz, 1960.
(With Curtis Amy) *Meetin' Here,* Pacific Jazz, 1961.
Johnny Griffin, *Grab This!* (includes "Offering Time"), Riverside, 1963.
Something's Happening, Fantasy, 1964.
Groove Time, Fantasy, 1964.

Sources

Periodicals

Los Angeles Times, January 14, 2010.

Online

"*The Blues Message* (2 LPs on 1 CD)," Fresh Sound Records, http://www.freshsoundrecords.com/the _blues_message_2_lps_on_1_cd-cd-5467.html (accessed November 7, 2013).
Harrod, James A., and Earl Anthony, "Curtis Amy/ Paul Bryant Quintet," Jazz Scene USA, May 5, 2013, http://jazzsceneusa.blogspot.com/2013/05 /jazz-scene-u.html (accessed November 7, 2013).
Lankford, Ronnie D., Jr., "Paul Bryant: *Grab This!,*" AllMusic.com, http://www.allmusic.com/album/ grab-this%21-mw0000118753 (accessed November 9, 2013).
"Paul Bryant Discography," JazzLists.com, http:// www.jazzlists.com/SJ_Paul_Bryant.htm (accessed November 7, 2013),
Wynn, Ron, "Paul Bryant: Artist Biography," AllMusic .com, http://www.allmusic.com/artist/paul-bryant -mn0000013044 (accessed November 8, 2013).

—R. Anthony Kugler

Cedric the Entertainer

1964—

Comedian, actor, producer

A member of the phenomenally successful "Original Kings of Comedy" tour in the late 1990s, the man known as Cedric the Entertainer has built a comedic brand grounded in an Everyman quality that resonates with a wide spectrum of audiences. Although he eagerly listened to Richard Pryor and Eddie Murphy as a child, Cedric told the *Detroit News* that the late Robin Harris had the strongest influence on him. "His delivery was pretty much guy-around-the-corner.... I recognized that that's the way I would want to do comedy, as someone you felt familiar with."

Cedric the Entertainer, photograph. Vincent Sandoval/Getty Images.

Cedric the Entertainer was born Cedric Antonio Kyles in Jefferson City, Missouri, on April 14, 1964. His mother, a school reading specialist, encouraged his talents as a performer—but not, at first, as a comedian. "He was always singing and dancing in plays. I couldn't nail down the comedic part because that didn't come until later," she told *Jet*. In 2013 Cedric told The DailyBeast.com the story a little differently: "My mom raised us to go to school and get a good, dependable job when you graduate.... [she] didn't want to hear anything about me being a stand-up comedian."

Made Stand-Up Comedy Debut

At Southeast Missouri State University, Cedric majored in mass communication. After graduating in 1987 he took a job as an insurance claims representative with a State Farm agency, along with college friend Eric C. Rhone, who eventually would become Cedric's business manager. Cedric entered a stand-up comedy competition in Chicago and walked away with a $500 prize. Another first prize in the Miller Genuine Draft Comedy Search led to more tours and the realization that life as a comedian was within his reach. In a 2012 Rhone told James Baer of the Missouri Chesterfield Patch website that after several years at State Farm, "[W]e had to make a decision. We quit our jobs on the same day, we put our clothes in UPS boxes, shipped them to Los Angeles, and the rest you might say is history."

Cedric's breakthrough came in Dallas in 1989, when he was in the audience at a comedy club in which fellow African-American comedian Steve Harvey was a principal player. As the audience endured an unsuccessful act from a visiting headliner, Cedric asked the house manager if he could perform a five-minute set at no

stand-up segment on *It's Showtime at the Apollo* and later performed on HBO's *Def Comedy Jam*. The next year he became the host of BET's *Comic View*, which featured a segment of his own, "Ced's Comedy Crockpot." Cedric won the Richard Pryor Comic of the Year Award in 1994. Harvey became a mentor to Cedric, which led to a continuing role for the young comic on the hit sitcom *The Steve Harvey Show* as high school coach Cedric Jackie Robinson. The role brought Cedric four consecutive NAACP Image awards for outstanding supporting actor in a comedy series.

The "Original Kings of Comedy" tour cemented Cedric's status as a star in urban America. That tour, which became the top-grossing comedy program of all time and pointed to a pent-up demand for high-quality entertainment among black audiences, featured the comedy of Cedric alongside D. L. Hughley, Harvey, and Bernie Mac. Running from 1998 into 1999, the program first spawned a recording, which won a 1999 Grammy Award nomination for best spoken comedy album, and then Spike Lee's acclaimed film of the same name in 2000.

Cedric was now on the radar of Hollywood talent spotters. He landed parts in a string of films released in 2001, including *Kingdom Come, Serving Sara,* and *Dr. Doolittle 2,* in which he was heard as the voice of a bear in a zoo. More voice acting work would follow over the next decade, including the Disney Channel's *The Proud Family,* the *Madagascar* franchise of films starting in 2005, and the 2006 animated feature *Charlotte's Web.*

Cedric became a national celebrity after he appeared in a television commercial broadcast during the Super Bowl in January of 2001. The commercial featured Cedric bringing an attractive date home to his apartment. Offering her something to drink, he goes to the kitchen for two bottles of Bud Light beer. Once he is safely out of her sight, he erupts into an enthusiastic dance—but forgets that by so doing he is shaking the still-closed beer bottles. Thus his date is drenched when her bottle is opened.

Launched Film Career

The Bud Light commercial ranked number one out of 57 ads broadcast during the Super Bowl, according to viewer polls. "I definitely noticed a difference in how people respond to me after the Super Bowl when I was out and about," Cedric told the *Los Angeles Times.* The following year Cedric appeared in another highly ranked Bud Light commercial. The exposure boded well for Cedric's growing career. He was featured on his own variety show, *Cedric the Entertainer Presents,* on Fox in 2002. But his film career, which had started with supporting roles, soon eclipsed his television work.

Cedric's role in *Barbershop* and its sequel, *Barbershop 2: Back in Business,* garnered the most attention. As

charge. His short act brought the house down, and impressed Harvey, who brought Cedric back to Dallas to headline his own show.

As a comedian Cedric was notable for his almost total avoidance of profanity—in stark contrast to the vast majority of other touring comedians, both black and white. "If I use a curse word it's because of the character I'm portraying," he explained to *Jet.* "I use curse words like a Lawry's seasoning salt. It's hidden somewhere inside the joke. I use it as a tenderizer." Cedric explained to Baer, "I enjoy those off-color jokes as much as the next guy and profanity doesn't really bother me if it makes sense. I just feel it isn't my best way of telling my kind of jokes."

Landed First Television Gig

Cedric first appeared on television in 1992 in a

Eddie, a curmudgeonly barber, Cedric spouted off-color jokes about some of the civil rights movement's greatest heroes. "Rosa Parks didn't do nothing but sit her Black ass down," Cedric's character, Eddie, grumbles in *Barbershop*. The role drew the ire of some in the black community, and Rosa Parks herself refused to attend the NAACP Image Awards that Cedric hosted in 2003. Cedric took the negative attention in stride. "The point of the barbershop was that, while in there, people could speak their truth even if it wasn't the truth," he explained to Davina Morris of the *Voice*. His character Eddie, he continued, was "an antagonist.... He'd say things to get people fired up so they could give their own opinions ... the controversy it sparked outside the film inspired people to talk about these heroes and research their stories to find out why Eddie said the things he did." The sequel was less controversial, and in the end Cedric's congenial personality and warmth overshadowed the outcries. Cedric told Kam Williams of the *Afro-American* that he "never experienced any personal attacks. I talked with Jesse Jackson and Rosa Parks, afterwards, and the King family, and we all arrived at an understanding about it with one another. Nobody ever blamed me, personally."

To make the leap to leading roles in feature films, Cedric and his longtime manager Rhone founded their own production company, A Bird and A Bear Entertainment, in 2002. The company's first film, *The Johnson Family Vacation* (2004), grossed more than $30 million. Cedric explained to Alan Hughes of *Black Enterprise* that producing films was about control. "Often, especially as African Americans, [we're] accused of doing things on-screen that [are] considered buffoonery or something to that nature. Well, that's really determined by the writers and the powers-the people writing the check." Cedric hoped to develop projects with "a certain Cedric The Entertainer kind of energy to them," he told Hughes. He subsequently produced and appeared in several films, including *The Honeymooners* (2005), *Code Name: The Cleaner* (2007), and *Dance Fu* (2011). Cedric also continued to appear in movies produced by other studios, including *Cadillac Records* (2008), *Street Kings* (2008), *All's Faire in Love* (2009), *Caught on Tape* (2013), and *A Haunted House* (2013).

Built a Brand for Expansion

A Bird and A Bear took Cedric back into television as well, with *Cedric: Taking You Higher* (2006), *All Star Comedy Jam* (2009), and the TV Land series *The Soul Man*, costarring Niecy Nash. In 2011 Cedric was tapped to host NBC's short-lived summer game show *It's Worth What?* Two years later ABC hired him to replace Meredith Vieira as the host of the daily game show *Who Wants to Be A Millionaire?* This appeared to be a successful move both for himself and for the show; in November of 2013, two months into his first season, viewership was up 11 percent among women ages 25 to 54, a key daytime demographic. Among all viewers between 18 and 49, viewership was up 20 percent.

Cedric's business acumen led him to forge endorsement deals with McDonalds and Budweiser, building on his Super Bowl commercial audience appeal, and to invest in selected high-tech startup companies, such as Qloo Inc. (pronounced "clue"), which went public in November of 2013. In 2011 he also spun his own creative ideas into a line of high-end men's hats called Who Ced? The online niche business reflected his personal affinity for stylish headwear. In an interview with Lora Koldny of the *Wall Street Journal*, Cedric likened entrepreneurship to building an entertainment audience. In both cases, he said, "You need people who are loyal to you and willing to follow you anywhere and at all times. That's how you build and audience, and that's how you build a business with some longevity." He continued, "You have to remain true to what you introduced to the audience, and drive that through."

The Cedric the Entertainer brand includes not just career and lifestyle deals but charitable efforts as well. The Cedric the Entertainer Charitable Foundation was established to offer scholarships and outreach programs to inner-city youth and their families in his hometown of St. Louis, with plans to expand the programming nationally.

Selected works

Television

It's Showtime at the Apollo, 1992.
Comic View, BET, 1993–94.
Def Comedy Jam, HBO, 1995.
The Steve Harvey Show, The WB, 1996–2002.
(Voice) *The Proud Family,* Disney, 2001–05.
Cedric The Entertainer Presents, Fox, 2002.
Cedric: Taking You Higher (television movie), HBO, 2006.
The Law (television movie), ABC, 2009.
(Voice) *Merry Madagascar* (short), NBC, 2009.
Caribbean Comedy Classic (television movie), RISARC Productions, 2010.
It's Worth What?, NBC, 2011.
The Soul Man, TV Land, 2012–13.
Who Wants to Be a Millionaire?, ABC, 2013—.

Films

Ride, Dimension Films, 1998.
The Original Kings of Comedy, Paramount Pictures, 2000.
Big Momma's House, Twentieth Century Fox, 2000.
(Voice) *Dr. Dolittle 2,* Twentieth Century Fox, 2001.
Kingdom Come, Fox Searchlight, 2001.
Barbershop, MGM, 2002.
(Voice) *Ice Age,* Twentieth Century Fox, 2002.
Serving Sara, Paramount, 2002.
Intolerable Cruelty, Universal Pictures, 2003.

Woman Thou Art Loosed, Magnolia Pictures, 2004.
Barbershop 2: Back in Business, MGM, 2004.
Johnson Family Vacation, A Bird and a Bear Entertainment, 2004.
Lemony Snicket's A Series of Unfortunate Events, Paramount Pictures, 2004.
Man of the House, Columbia Pictures, 2005.
Be Cool, MGM, 2005.
The Honeymooners, A Bird and a Bear Entertainment, 2005.
(Voice) *Madagascar,* DreamWorks, 2005.
(Voice) *Charlotte's Web,* Paramount Pictures, 2006.
Code Name: The Cleaner, A Bird and a Bear Entertainment, 2007.
Talk to Me, Focus Features, 2007.
Welcome Home, Roscoe Jenkins, Universal Pictures, 2008.
Street Kings, Fox Searchlight, 2008.
Cadillac Records, Sony, 2008.
(Voice) *Madagascar: Escape 2 Africa,* DreamWorks, 2008.
All's Faire in Love, Patriot Pictures, 2009.
Dance Fu, A Bird and a Bear Entertainment, 2011.
Larry Crowne, Universal Pictures, 2011.
(Voice) *Madagascar 3: Europe's Most Wanted,* DreamWorks, 2012.
Caught on Tape, Lionsgate, 2013.
A Haunted House, Automatik Entertainment, 2013.
(Voice) *Planes,* Disney, 2013.

Sources

Periodicals

Afro-American, March 15–21, 2003, p. 7; October 24, 2003, p. B1.
Black Enterprise, July 2001, p. 64; December 2004, p. 130.
Chicago Sun-Times, February 5, 2001, p. 51.
Crain's New York Business, November 14, 2013.
Detroit News, November 21, 2013.
Essence, April 2001, p. 80.
Interview, August 2000, p. 57.
Jet, September 20, 1999, p. 58; March 12, 2001, p. 58.
Los Angeles Times, February 6, 2001, p. F1; June 20, 2003, p. E32.
New York Daily News, August 21, 2013.
New York Post, November 5, 2013.
New York Times, August 18, 2000, p. E12.
USA Today, January 30, 2001, p. B3.
Voice, October 19, 2003, p. 4.
Washington Informer, January 4–10, 2007, p. 29.

Online

Baer, James, "Cedric the Entertainer: His Manager Lives in Frontenac," Chesterfield.Patch.com, July 11, 2012, http://chesterfield.patch.com/groups/business-news/p/cedric-the-entertainer-his-manager-lives-in-frontenac (accessed November 30, 2013).

Caslin, Yvette, "Cedric the Entertainer Launches New Line of Hats," RollingOut.com, March 21, 2011, http://rollingout.com/entertainment/cedric-the-entertainer-launches-new-line-of-hats/ (accessed November 24, 2013).

"Cedric the Entertainer," Behind the Voice Actors, http://www.behindthevoiceactors.com/Cedric-the-Entertainer/ (accessed November 30, 2013).

"Cedric the Entertainer, Manager Officially Bring Tourists to St. Louis," Chesterfield.Patch.com, July 11, 2012, http://chesterfield.patch.com/groups/business-news/p/eric-rhone-is-an-official-missouri-tourism-ambassador20d14ee5e0 (accessed November 30, 2013).

Fleming-Dixon, Jamie, "Niecy Nash & Cedric The Entertainer Speak on Love, Family and The Soul Man," ForColoredGurls.com, June 18, 2013, http://forcoloredgurls.com/2013/06/niecy-nash-cedric-the-entertainer-speak-on-love-family-and-the-soul-man/ (accessed November 24, 2013).

Koldny, Lora, "Cedric The Entertainer: Building An Audience Is Like Building a Startup," *Venture Capital Dispatch* (*Wall Street Journal* blog), November 19, 2013, http://blogs.wsj.com/venturecapital/2013/11/19/cedric-the-entertainer-building-an-audience-is-like-building-a-startup/ (accessed November 24, 2013).

Samuels, Allison, "Cedric the Entertainer Wants to Make You a Millionaire," TheDailyBeast.com, September 2, 2013, http://www.thedailybeast.com/articles/2013/09/02/cedric-the-entertainer-wants-to-make-you-a-millionaire.html (accessed November 24, 2013).

Tschorn, Adam, "Cedric the Entertainer Throws His Hat in the Ring with Who Ced?," *All the Rage* (*Los Angeles Times* blog), August 30, 2011, http://latimesblogs.latimes.com/alltherage/2011/08/cedric-the-entertainer-launches-a-line-of-hats-.html (accessed November 24, 2013).

Who Ced, http://whoced.com/ (accessed November 24, 2013).

—Ashyia Henderson, James Manheim, Sara Pendergast, and Pamela Willwerth Aue

Ndugu Chancler

1952—

Drummer, producer, educator

The percussionist and producer Ndugu Chancler has been at the forefront of American music since the 1970s. Trained in the jazz tradition, he has worked with some of that genre's leading figures, including the trumpeter Miles Davis and the pianist Herbie Hancock. As of 2013, however, Chancler was best known for his many contributions to pop, including important collaborations with the stars Carlos Santana and Michael Jackson. A passionate advocate for music education, Chancler balanced his work onstage and in the studio with academic appointments at such institutions as the University of Southern California, where he served as an adjunct assistant professor of jazz studies and popular music.

Leon Chancler, known since the early 1970s as Ndugu Chancler, was born on July 1, 1952, in Shreveport, Louisiana. Raised in a household devoted to both gospel music and the blues, he moved with his family to Los Angeles, California, around the age of eight. His study of the drums began roughly five years later, when a band teacher in his junior high school taught him the basics of rhythm and introduced him to the art of jazz

Chancler, Ndugu, photograph. Victor Spinelli/WireImage/Getty Images.

drumming. In a 2011 interview with Bill Milkowski of *Drum!* magazine, Chancler recalled that through this teacher's efforts, he was able to attend the 1966 Pacific Jazz Festival not far from Los Angeles. There he saw several great percussionists in person for the first time. "And from that point," he told Milkowski, "I was turned on. When I saw all these great drummers, my whole life spun around and I said, 'That's what I want to do, and that's what I'm going to do.'"

Driven by that enthusiasm, Chancler made rapid strides. While he was still a student at Locke High School on the south side of Los Angeles, he had a number of professional gigs, appearing alongside such stars as fellow drummer Willie Bobo, the trumpeter Gerald Wilson, and Hancock. Hancock offered Chancler a spot in his band when he graduated. Chancler turned down that offer, choosing instead to fulfill his mother's desire to see him enrolled in college. Hancock called him again soon thereafter, however, this time for the studio sessions that resulted in the influential album *Mwandishi*, released in 1970. Chancler's rousing, uncompromising performance on that recording proved a model for much of his later work.

At a Glance . . .

Born Leon Chancler on July 1, 1952, in Shreveport, LA. *Education:* Attended California State University, Dominguez Hills, late 1960s(?)–early 1970s(?).

Career: Drummer, late 1960s—; producer, 1970s—; faculty member at the University of Southern California and other institutions, 1980s(?)—.

Addresses: *Office*—Department of Jazz Studies, University of Southern California, Thornton School of Music, Los Angeles, CA 90089-0851. *Web*—http://www.nduguchancler.com.

Mwandishi appeared at a time when jazz was changing rapidly. As listeners began to embrace fusion—the free-form, electrically amplified style pioneered by Hancock and Davis—Chancler found himself in demand for gigs across California. For a time he balanced these performances with coursework in music education at California State University, Dominguez Hills. His partners in this period included the trumpeter Freddie Hubbard, with whom he was playing one night when Davis, on the lookout for a new drummer, happened to be in the audience. That fortuitous event led to Chancler's participation in a famous tour Davis made through Europe in the fall of 1971. Although the experience was relatively brief, it proved pivotal to Chancler's development as an artist. "Miles' band took me over the edge in terms of musical concept," he told Milkowski. "It also gave me the freedom to not be afraid to be the stylistic fence-straddler that I was. As much as I love jazz, I love music and was always playing different forms of it. With Miles, he let me know that was okay and that, in fact, would be the way to go."

In keeping with that philosophy, Chancler moved steadily toward pop, R&B, and rock over the course of the 1970s. In 1974, for example, he joined Santana's eponymous group, and over the next three years he helped that influential ensemble complete several major albums, including *Borboletta* (1974), *Amigos* (1976), and *Festival* (1977). Also around this time he began collaborating with George Duke, a keyboardist who shared both Chancler's eclecticism and his growing interest in composition. One of Duke's largest hits, a funk classic from 1977 called "Reach for It," grew directly out of their partnership; the cowriting credit Chancler earned for the song was one of several he accumulated as the decade progressed.

As his songwriting prowess became known, Chancler began to take an active role in album production, and by the start of the 1980s, he had firmly established himself in that field. One of his most prominent production projects was *Straight to the Bank,* a 1978 recording by the noted percussionist Bill Summers. Chancler also earned a number of coproduction credits over the years, perhaps most notably for *The Platinum Collection* (2009), a career-spanning compilation by the R&B star Tina Turner.

Amid the demands of his production career, Chancler continued to find time for drumming, both for his own groups and for other artists. Some of his most prominent work for other artists was done with Jackson, whose landmark albums *Thriller* (1982) and *Bad* (1987) Chancler helped complete. While both albums sold tens of millions of copies around the world, *Thriller* was particularly influential; as of the fall of 2013, more than three decades after its initial release, it was still considered the most popular album in the history of recorded music. Anchoring that success was the song "Billie Jean," which hit number one on singles charts worldwide. The distinctive drumbeat behind Jackson's soaring vocals on that track was Chancler's.

Chancler's solo work, meanwhile, allowed him to explore tempos and rhythms on his own terms. Much of his earliest work in this area was done with a group he founded called the Chocolate Jam Company, which released two albums, *The Spread of the Future* (1979) and *Do I Make You Feel Better?* (1980). Both recordings encapsulated the funky, syncopated style typical of the era. Since their release Chancler has continued to issue albums at irregular intervals, many of which have returned to the jazz tempos with which he began his career. Typical of these recordings were *Old Friends New Friends* (1988), released on the MCA label, and the self-produced *Old Friends Live* (2010).

Selected discography

Herbie Hancock, *Mwandishi,* Warner, 1970.
Santana, *Borboletta,* Columbia, 1974.
Santana, *Amigos,* Columbia, 1976.
Santana, *Festival,* Columbia, 1977.
George Duke, *Reach for It* (includes "Reach for It"), Epic, 1977.
(Producer and drummer) Bill Summers, *Straight to the Bank,* Prestige, 1978.
Ndugu and the Chocolate Jam Company, *The Spread of the Future,* Epic, 1979.
Ndugu and the Chocolate Jam Company, *Do I Make You Feel Better?,* Epic, 1980.
Michael Jackson, *Thriller* (includes "Billie Jean"), Epic, 1982.
Michael Jackson, *Bad,* Epic, 1987.
Old Friends New Friends, MCA, 1988.
(Coproducer) Tina Turner, *The Platinum Collection,* Capitol, 2009.
Old Friends Live, self-produced, 2010.

Sources

Periodicals

Drum!, April 2011.

Online

"Leon 'Ndugu' Chancler," DrummerWorld.com, http://www.drummerworld.com/drummers/Ndugu_Chancler.html (accessed November 13, 2013).

"Ndugu Chancler: About," NduguChancler.com, http://www.nduguchancler.com/about.html (accessed November 13, 2013).

"Ndugu Chancler," University of Southern California, http://www.usc.edu/schools/music/private/faculty/ndugu.php (accessed November 13, 2013).

Wynn, Ron, "Leon 'Ndugu' Chancler: Artist Biography," AllMusic.com, http://www.allmusic.com/artist/leon-ndugu-chancler-mn0000378362 (accessed November 13, 2013).

—R. Anthony Kugler

Dave Chappelle

1973—

Comedian, actor

Chappelle, Dave, photograph. Larry Marano/WireImage/Getty Images.

From young age Dave Chappelle could make people laugh. Influenced by comedians such as Richard Pryor and Bill Cosby and cartoon characters such as Bugs Bunny, Chappelle realized the power of his natural talent and made serious goals for his art. As a teenager he crafted his standup comedy act out of the realties of his life growing up black in Washington, DC. Racism and racial division became his main targets, subjects that he approached with an outrageous irreverence that often shocked his audiences into shouts of laughter. Though Chappelle has worked toward recognition and success, he has continually refused to tone down his style or dilute his outspoken African-American point of view in order to make his comedy more acceptable. As a result he has gained fame and success on his own terms. Following an extended break from the entertainment world after he walked away from his successful comedy series, *Chappelle's Show,* the comedian returned to the stage in 2011.

Began Performing as a Teenager

Born David Khari Webber Chappelle on August 24, 1973, in Washington, DC, Chappelle's parents divorced when he was two years old, and he grew up in the city and the nearby suburb of Silver Springs, Maryland. His summers were often spent in Yellow Springs, Ohio, with his father, who was a professor at Antioch University. Chappelle enjoyed the peaceful rural atmosphere of Yellow Springs, and as an adult, his home on a farm there would become a family refuge from the hectic entertainment worlds of New York and Los Angeles.

From a young age the routine of school wore on Chappelle. As he told James Lipton in a 2013 interview for the Bravo series *Inside the Actors Studio,* "I never liked school. From the first day, I walked in there I said, 'I hate this place. I hate its guts.'" Chappelle decided to become a comedian after his mother bought him a copy of *Time* magazine in 1987, which highlighted the comedy career of Bill Cosby. Within the year, at age 14, Chappelle began performing standup comedy in clubs in Washington. His mother, a Unitarian minister, was supportive of her son's talent and frequently accompanied him as a chaperone when he performed in nightclubs and bars. After a few years on stage, Chappelle began to win comedy contests, and by the time he was a senior in

At a Glance . . .

Born David Khari Webber Chappelle on August 24, 1973, in Washington, DC; son of William David Chappelle III (a professor) and Yvonne Reed (a professor and Unitarian minister); married Elaine, 2001; children: Sulayman, Ibrahim, Sonal. *Religion:* Muslim.

Career: Comedian, 1987—; actor, 1992—.

Memberships: Screen Actors Guild.

Awards: NAMIC (National Association for Multi-Ethnicity in Communications) Vision Awards, Best Comedic Performance, 2004, 2005, for *Chappelle's Show.*

Addresses: *Talent agent*—The Gersh Agency, 9465 Wilshire Blvd., 6th Floor, Beverly Hills, CA 90212. *Twitter*—@DaveChappelle.

high school, he was traveling to comedy clubs across the country, excused from school by the principal so that he could pursue his career.

After graduating high school Chappelle's lack of interest in attending college went against the family grain. As he told Lipton, "I was the first person in my family not to go to college that had not been a slave." Chappelle made a bargain with his parents: instead of going to college right away, he would go to New York to work on his comedy act. If he did not succeed after one year, he would consider college. While working with other comics in the Washington area, Chappelle had learned a lot about the comedy clubs of New York, and he began to feel that he had to go there to become a real success in comedy.

Found Success on Television and Film

Chappelle's dedication and nerve were tested at amateur night at the famous Apollo Theater in Harlem. As he shared with Lipton, "I remember looking out and seeing everybody booing, everybody, even old people. I was like, 'who boos a child pursuing his dreams?' ... And that was the best thing that ever happened to me ... That night was so liberating because I failed so far beyond my wildest nightmares of failing, it was like ... this is not that bad. And after that, I was fearless." Within a few weeks Chappelle had landed gigs at several hot New York comedy clubs and gave a successful performance at the Montreal Comedy Festival. In 1992 he won critical and popular acclaim for his television appearance on HBO's *Def Comedy Jam.* As

his popularity began to rise, he was a regular guest on late-night television shows such as *Politically Incorrect, The Late Show With David Letterman, The Howard Stern Show,* and *Late Night With Conan O'Brien.*

In 1993 Chappelle landed his first film role in the Mel Brooks comedy *Robin Hood: Men in Tights.* He had small roles in several other films, but it was his role as the nasty comic Reggie Warrington in Eddie Murphy's 1996 film *The Nutty Professor* that brought him to the attention of Hollywood. Suddenly Chappelle was in demand for character roles, and he did several films in the next few years. In 1998 he cowrote his first film, *Half Baked,* a tribute to Cheech and Chong, the comedy duo who made a series of drug-related slapstick comedies in the late 1970s and 1980s. Though *Half Baked* enjoyed some success, Chappelle was disappointed with his first filmmaking experience. He felt that the studio had weakened the film by trying to make it more acceptable to conservative audiences. He did not like losing control over his work, and the experience would influence his later choices.

Chappelle worked on developing television pilots beginning in the early 1990s. After creating more than 10 of them, one pilot, called *Buddies,* was picked up by ABC. But, as Chappelle recalled in an interview with *60 Minutes,* "It was a bad show. It was bad. I mean when we were doing it, I could tell this was not gonna work." Indeed, *Buddies* aired for only 13 episodes before it was cancelled.

Walked Away from $50 Million Contract

The year 1998 marked a dark time in the comedian's life. His father suffered a stroke, and then a deal fell through with the Fox network to air *Dave Chappelle,* a situation comedy about Chappelle's struggles as a young comedian in New York. "They fly me out for a creative meeting. I'm in a room full of white people, and they proceed to tell me why we need more white people on the show, so it can have a more universal appeal," the comedian told Jenny Hontz of *Variety.* Chappelle canceled the deal and returned to Ohio to be with his father, who died shortly thereafter. In response to that loss and his disenchantment with Hollywood, Chappelle bought a farm in Yellow Springs, ready to abandon show business altogether. In 2000, however, Chappelle produced a successful one-man show for HBO called *Dave Chappelle: Killin' Them Softly,* which sold more than one million copies on DVD.

In 2003 Comedy Central offered Chappelle a chance to do television on his own terms. *Chappelle's Show,* a half-hour program repeated several times each week, featured Chappelle and a cast of regulars and guests performing satirical skits. Cable television proved to be a more comfortable location for Chappelle's outra-

geous comedy, and the show soon developed a devoted following. Though no topic was safe from Chappelle's sharp satire, racism remained a major focus of his biting humor. His first show, for example, featured Chappelle playing a blind leader of a white supremacist movement who does not realize that he is black.

Though *Chappelle's Show* was designed for hilarity, there was a serious political message in the show's attacks on racism and bigotry. Critics recognized the similarities between Chappelle's comedy and that of comedian Richard Pryor during the 1970s. Pryor's wife spoke for her ailing husband on *60 Minutes,* saying that Pryor approved of Chappelle's work and has "passed the torch" to him. Chappelle's respect for Pryor showed in his response: "That's a lot of pressure. He was the best, man. For him to say that is, you know, that's something, I don't even know if I'll attempt to live up to that."

When the first season of *Chappelle's Show* was released on DVD, it sold more than two million copies, a sales record for a television series. In 2004 Chappelle signed a two-year, $50 million contract to continue the series, but rumors behind-the-scenes problems began to circulate. The next year Chappelle walked off the set and seemed to vanish, not even telling his wife that he was leaving. Headlines speculated as to his whereabouts amid rumors of drugs and mental health problems. In an interview with Oprah Winfrey in 2006, Chappelle disclosed that he had gone to South Africa to visit friends and family and to take a break. "I felt like it was a place where I could really reflect … And here's the other thing: I was gone for two weeks! They made it sound like it was so mysterious."

Returned to Stage

Chappelle's abrupt exit from Comedy Central reflected his continuing disillusionment with show business and his refusal to perform under anyone's terms but his own. As *Chappelle's Show* gained in popularity—and profitability—the comedian began to lose creative control. More importantly, however, the show's content began to make him feel "socially irresponsible." An epiphany struck during a sketch about blackface comedy, reminiscent of 19th-century minstrel shows in which white people painted their faces black to caricaturize black people. Although Chappelle acknowledged "a good-spirited intention behind" the Comedy Central skit, the laughter of a particular white set member made him question the humor. He began to worry that some might perceive the comedy in the wrong way. "That concerned me," he told Oprah. "I don't want black people to be disappointed in me for putting that [message] out there."

Following his return from Africa, Chappelle took an extended break from comedy. In 2011 he returned his focus to his primary love, stand-up comedy. His comeback was rocky, however. On several occasions, Chappelle walked off stage in the middle of a show because of hecklers, including dates in Miami, Florida, in July of 2011; Austin, Texas, in June of 2012; and Hartford, Connecticut, in August of 2013. "I'm going through some real tough, some real times. Some nitty gritty stuff," Chappelle reflected during his *Inside the Actors Studio* interview. "When you go through things like this, it helps you put it all into perspective. I'm famous today, people like me today. They might not like me tomorrow, you never know. You can't count on it, the world can't tell you who you are. You just got to figure out who you are and be that, for better or worse."

Selected works

Films

Undercover Blues, MGM, 1993.
Robin Hood: Men in Tights, Twentieth Century Fox, 1993.
Getting In, Trimark Home Video, 1994.
The Nutty Professor, Universal Pictures, 1996.
Joe's Apartment, Fox, 1996.
The Real Blonde, Paramount Pictures, 1997.
Con Air, Buena Vista Pictures, 1997.
You've Got Mail, Warner Bros., 1998.
Woo, New Line Cinema, 1998.
Half Baked, Universal Pictures, 1998.
Blue Streak, Columbia Pictures, 1999.
200 Cigarettes, Paramount Pictures, 1999.
Screwed, Universal Pictures, 2000.
Undercover Brother, Universal Pictures, 2002.

Television

Def Comedy Jam, HBO, 1992.
Buddies, ABC, 1996.
The Dave Chappelle Project, Fox, 1998.
Dave Chappelle: Killin' Them Softly, Comedy Central, 2000.
Chappelle's Show, Comedy Central, 2003–06.
Dave Chappelle: For What It's Worth, Showtime, 2004.

Sources

Periodicals

Chicago Tribune, July 30, 1993.
Economist, August 31, 2013.
Jet, August 23, 2004, p. 37.
New York Times, August 15, 2013.
Time, May 15, 2005.
Variety, July 8, 1998.

Online

"Chappelle's Story," Oprah.com, February 3, 2006, http://www.oprah.com/oprahshow/Chappelles -Story/1, (accessed November 24, 2013).

Chapman, Reg, "One-on-One with Dave Chappelle," CBS Minnesota, November 14, 2013, http://minnesota.cbslocal.com/2013/11/14/one-on-one-with-dave-chappelle/ (accessed November 24, 2013).

"Chappelle: 'An Act of Freedom,'" *60 Minutes,* CBS, October 19, 2004, http://www.cbsnews.com/news/chappelle-an-act-of-freedom-19-10-2004/ (accessed January 20, 2014).

"Chappelle's Show," Comedy Central, http://www.comedycentral.com/shows/chappelle-s-show (accessed January 20, 2014).

Cosme, Shante, "Dave Chappelle Tells a Single Joke and Gets Booed Off Stage," Complex.com, July 25, 2011, http://www.complex.com/pop-culture/2011/07/dave-chappelle-heckled-booed-bombs (accessed November 26, 2013).

"Dave Chappelle," *Inside the Actors Studio,* April 19, 2013, http://www.youtube.com/watch?v=s0ifcBk9HXM (accessed December 1, 2013).

Harris, Aisha, "What Happened with Dave Chappelle Thursday Night?" Slate.com, August 30, 2013, http://www.slate.com/blogs/browbeat/2013/08/30/dave_chappelle_in_hartford_walks_off_stage_heckled_what_happened_video.html (accessed November 24, 2013).

Luippold, Ross, "Dave Chappelle In Austin: Hecklers Throw Off Comedy Legend's Texas Show," Huffington Post, June 20, 2012, http://www.huffingtonpost.com/2012/06/20/dave-chappelle-in-austin-heckled_n_1613748.html (accessed November 26, 2013).

Paunescu, Delia, "Hear Dave Chappelle Explain Why He Walked Off the Stage Last Week," Vulture.com, September 4, 2013, http://www.vulture.com/2013/09/dave-chappelle-explains-leaving-stage-last-week.html (accessed November 24, 2013).

—Tina Gianoulis and Candice Mancini

Ciara

1985—

Singer, songwriter, model

Ciara, photograph. Jacopo Raule/FilmMagic/Getty Images.

Young R&B vocalist Ciara (pronounced "Sierra") rose to pop stardom in the summer of 2004, when her single "Goodies" spent seven weeks at number one on both the pop and R&B charts, its subtly layered beats pounding out of stereos all over North America. A striking beauty with long hair and strong dance moves, Ciara quickly dispelled any idea that she was a one-hit wonder. Her debut album, *Goodies,* released that year, matched the success of its title track, spawning two more major hits and selling three million copies. Since then the singer has produced four more studio albums, including her most recent, 2013's *Ciara.*

Born on October 25, 1985, in Austin, Texas, Ciara Princess Harris grew up in a military family. Her father was in the U.S. Army and her mother in the U.S. Air Force. Their postings took the family to New York, California, the desert Southwest, and Germany before the family finally settled in the Atlanta, Georgia, area. Attending North Clayton High School in Atlanta's southern suburbs, she was a member of the track team, competing in relays, the long jump, and the triple jump. She then moved to Riverdale High School, where she was captain of the cheerleading squad.

By the end of high school, Ciara had already decided what she wanted to do with her life. When she was a freshman, she had seen the girl group Destiny's Child, led by Beyoncé, perform live on *Good Morning America.* While other young girls might have stared at the television and dreamed, Ciara took action. She began writing songs and soon found a manager who landed her a songwriting gig at the up-and-coming Red Zone Entertainment studio. For a short time, after winning a contest, she performed with an all-girl group called Hearsay, but she soon went her own way. She wrote songs for the R&B singer Mýa and kept aiming toward the goal of hearing her own music on the radio.

Her prediction came true when she met Atlanta producer Jazze Pha, whom she called her musical soul mate. In 2002 Ciara was signed to Jazze Pha's Sho' Nuff label. That opportunity, in turn, provided the young singer with an entrée into the corridors of Atlanta's phenomenally successful urban hit-making machine. Jazze Pha gave Ciara's demo recording to Arista Records head L. A. Reid, who then passed it on to Lil Jon, the hot producer of the moment and a key

At a Glance . . .

Born Ciara Princess Harris on October 25, 1985, in Austin, TX.

Career: Recording artist, 2004—; model, 2006—.

Awards: ASCAP (American Society of Composers, Authors and Publishers) Pop Music Awards, Most Performed Songs, 2005, for "Goodies," 2006, for "Goodies," "1, 2 Step," and "Oh," 2007, for "Like You" and "So What"; BET Awards, Best Collaboration, 2005, for "1, 2 Step"; Grammy Award, Best Short-Form Music Video, 2006, for "Lose Control" (with Missy Elliott); MTV Video Awards, Best Dance Video, Best Hip-Hop Video, 2005, for "Lose Control."

Addresses: *Web*—http://onlyciara.com/.

figure in bringing the hip-hop subgenre known as crunk to national popularity.

Yet Ciara was much more than just a pretty face slotted into a producer's vision. The beat for her single "Goodies" was Lil Jon's, but the lyrics, as with most of her songs, were her own. She was reluctant at first to work with the rhythm track that the producer had given her, and in fact she disliked crunk music in the beginning. "If you're lookin' for the goodies, keep on lookin', 'cause they stay in the jar," Ciara sang, in contrast to the sexual promiscuousness of which other female stars boasted. The song had a musically minimal feel, with repeated notes and even rhythms that complemented its chaste message.

Having crossed the first hurdle to stardom, Ciara did not lose her ambitious edge; she listened to the music of veteran artists such as Janet Jackson in search of clues to their longevity. Two more singles from the *Goodies* album, the dance-ready "1, 2 Step" (with an assist from established hip-hop star Missy Elliott, who also would collaborate on the singles "Work" and "Lose Control") and the more sensual "Oh" (featuring Ludacris), emerged as hits later in 2004. Both singles reached number two on the Billboard Hot 100, and *Goodies* topped out at number three on the Billboard 200 albums chart. The high-powered guest artists testified to industry expectations that Ciara was an emerging star.

Ciara: The Evolution came out in 2006, reaching number one on both the pop and R&B lists. The album was broken down into five sections, each marked by a brief spoken-word interlude. Hits included "Get Up," "Like a Boy," and "Promise." Rapper 50 Cent made

an appearance on the song "Can't Leave 'Em Alone" and would soon be linked romantically to Ciara, who reportedly had just gotten over a relationship with the rapper Bow Wow. In a generally positive review, a critic from *Entertainment Weekly* wrote, "Ciara's comfort with rave-inspired beats sets her apart from Cassie, Amerie, Rihanna, and other would-Beyoncés."

A beauty as well as a talent, Ciara began receiving offers to model, and in 2006 she appeared in ads for Rocawear, the clothing company owned by Jay-Z. She opened for Jay-Z in concert in 2009, as well as for Britney Spears. That same year, after several months of delay, her third album was released. *Fantasy Ride* showcased considerable growth as a vocalist as the singer parried with male partners such as Justin Timberlake, Chris Brown, and The-Dream, but sales were lackluster. A *New York Times* review singled out "High Price," produced by Tricky Stewart and The-Dream, for praise, noting that Ciara's "vocals are manipulated to sound like opera, a spooky, ethereal effect that's both innovative and surprisingly natural." For her next album, *Basic Instinct* (2010), Ciara reunited with Stewart and The-Dream for seven tracks, notably "Speechless," which many fans consider to be her best work. BBC Music critic Matthew Horton hailed the album as one of the best R&B releases of the year, calling it "vibrant, addictive and sleek," but Jive Records dropped her from the label the next year.

After five years on top of the charts, Ciara enjoyed fewer hits with her later releases and began doing more modeling after signing a deal with Wilhelmina Models in 2009, as well as occasional acting gigs. *French Vogue* and *V Magazine* featured her in fashion spreads. In 2013 Ciara announced her engagement to the rapper Future, with whom she collaborated on the track "Body Party" from her self-titled album, which had come out earlier that year on the Epic label.

Selected discography

Goodies (includes "Goodies," "1, 2 Step," and "Oh"), LaFace, 2004.
Ciara: The Evolution (includes "Get Up," "Like a Boy," "Promise," and "Can't Leave 'Em Alone"), LaFace, 2006.
Fantasy Ride (includes "High Price"), LaFace, 2009.
Basic Instinct (includes "Speechless"), LaFace/Jive, 2010.
Ciara (includes "Body Party"), Epic, 2013.

Sources

Periodicals

Atlanta Journal-Constitution, September 9, 2004, p. P9.
Ebony, June 2005, p. 28.
Entertainment Weekly, July 22, 2005; December 30, 2005; December 4, 2006.

Interview, May 2004, p. 52; July 2005, p. 74.
Los Angeles Daily News , May 13, 2005, p. U21.
New York Times, May 3, 2009.
People, October 18, 2004, p. 132.
St. Louis Post-Dispatch, August 25, 2005, p. 5.
USA Today, July 26, 2004.

Online

"Ciara," AllMusic.com, http://www.allmusic.com/artist/ciara-mn0000215513 (accessed January 20, 2014).

Halperin, Valerie, "Outkast, Ciara Headed for L.A. Reid's Epic Records," HollywoodReporter.com, September 15, 2011, http://www.hollywoodreporter.com/news/outkast-ciara-headed-la-reids-235952 (accessed January 20, 2014).

Horton, Matthew, review of *Basic Instinct,* BBC Music, 2010, http://www.bbc.co.uk/music/reviews/45fd (accessed January 20, 2014).

Muhammad, Latifah, "Ciara Talks Blossoming Modeling Career," The Boombox, October 5, 2010, http://theboombox.com/ciara-talks-blossoming-modeling-career/ (accessed January 20, 2014).

—James M. Manheim and Mark Swartz

Stanley Clarke

1951—

Jazz, rock, and pop bassist, composer, conductor, orchestrator, music executive

Clarke, Stanley, photograph. Kevin Winter/WireImage/Getty Images.

A master of the bass, Stanley Clarke has been bringing that long-neglected instrument to the attention of rock, pop, and fusion fans since the late 1960s. As of the fall of 2013, he had garnered three Grammy Awards and one Latin Grammy. He is especially well known for his long collaboration with the pianist Chick Corea, his partner in an influential fusion ensemble called Return to Forever (RTF). Adept at handling a wide range of styles and tempos, Clarke has also done extensive work in Hollywood, writing scores for films and television programs and launching his own record label.

Born on June 30, 1951, in Philadelphia, Pennsylvania, Stanley Marvin Clarke grew up there in an atmosphere filled with music. As a child he studied at least three other instruments (accordion, violin, and cello) before taking up the bass. Known even as a teenager for his eclectic music tastes, he made rapid progress, moving from band classes at Roxborough High School to advanced studies at the Philadelphia Musical Academy, a venerable institution that later became part of the University of the Arts. Clarke then settled in New York City, where he began his career in earnest.

Upon his arrival in New York in 1971, Clarke found a vibrant community of jazz musicians, many of whom were experimenting with fusion, a blend of jazz and rock that was rapidly gaining attention. Fusion's emphasis on driving rhythms meshed well with Clarke's growing efforts to bring the bass, one of the anchors of the rhythm section, out of the relative obscurity in which it had languished for many years. Although older bassists, such as Charles Mingus and Scott LaFaro, had done a great deal in that area as well, Clarke's youth and his taste for rock and roll put him in a unique position to shape the instrument's role as jazz continued to evolve.

The focus of much of Clarke's work in the early 1970s, widely regarded as one of his most creative periods, was RTF, a group that released eight albums in the space of just a few years. In 1975 one of those recordings, *No Mystery*, earned Clarke and his bandmates a Grammy Award for best jazz performance by a group. "We really didn't realize how much of an impact we were having on people at the time," Clarke later recalled, in a comment quoted on the website of the

At a Glance . . .

Born Stanley Marvin Clarke on June 30, 1951, in Philadelphia, PA; married Carolyn Reese, 1974. *Education:* Attended Philadelphia Musical Academy (later part of the University of the Arts), late 1960s–early 1970s(?).

Career: Independent musician, early 1970s—; Return to Forever (jazz group), cofounder, early 1970s; Roxboro Entertainment Group, founder, 2010—.

Awards: Grammy Award, Best Jazz Performance by a Group, 1975, for *No Mystery* (with Return to Forever), Best Contemporary Jazz Album, 2010, for *The Stanley Clarke Band,* Best Jazz Instrumental Album, 2011, for *Forever,* Latin Grammy Award, Best Instrumental Album, 2011, for *Forever.*

Addresses: *Office*—Roxboro Entertainment Group, P.O. Box 1662, Topanga, CA 90290-1662. *Web*—http://StanleyClarke.com.

Concord Music Group. "We were touring so much then, we would just make a record and then go back on the road."

Also during this period Clarke began releasing the solo albums that have arguably done more to establish his reputation than any other facet of his career. While his solo debut, *Stanley Clarke* (1974), won strong reviews, its follow-up, *School Days* (1976), was so virtuosic that its appearance came to be regarded by bassists worldwide as a pivotal moment in their own development. Anchored by its title track, which quickly became a standard, the album introduced the rock fans who had missed RTF's releases to several innovative features of Clarke's style, most notably his habit of "slapping" the strings. Designed primarily to add percussion, the technique has become a standard tool for bassists everywhere.

In addition to his solo projects, Clarke also began number of intensive collaborations. In the early 1980s, for example, he joined the keyboardist George Duke in a new group known as the Clarke/Duke Project (CDP). Offering a distinctive mix of funk and fusion, they reached a broad national audience in 1981 with a piece called "Sweet Baby." Although some fans of Clarke's earlier work objected to what they considered CDP's smooth, commercialized tone, record buyers around the country disagreed, sending "Sweet Baby" to num-

ber 19 on *Billboard* magazine's pop chart and to number six on its R&B list.

In the 1980s Clarke began to turn his attention to the film and television industries. One of his earliest credits came in 1987, when he composed music for the children's program *Pee-Wee's Playhouse.* His work there was nominated for an Emmy Award. Clarke went on to fill a variety of roles in Hollywood, serving as a composer, orchestrator, conductor, or musician on dozens of major projects. In 2000, for example, he wrote and conducted the music for *Romeo Must Die,* a crime drama starring Jet Li and Aaliyah. He also composed much of the music for *Lincoln Heights,* a well-regarded drama series on ABC.

Amid the growing demands of his Hollywood career, Clarke continued to find time to complete albums, including *If This Bass Could Only Talk* (1988), released on the Portrait label, and *Live at the Greek* (1993), on which he was backed by a stellar band that included the drummer Billy Cobham and the saxophonist Najee. Both of those recordings won enthusiastic reviews. With the release of *The Stanley Clarke Band* in 2010, Clarke captured his next Grammy, for best contemporary jazz album. *The Stanley Clarke Band* featured contributions by the pianists Ruslan Sirota and Hiromi, the saxophonist Bob Sheppard, and other top-notch musicians. It was followed the next year by *Forever,* which won both a Grammy (for best jazz instrumental album) and a Latin Grammy (for best instrumental album). A joint project with two of his old partners from RTF, Corea and the drummer Lenny White, *Forever* included several new compositions as well as updated renditions of RTF favorites, such as "500 Miles High."

A passionate advocate for music education, Clarke returned to his high school in 2012 to work with students. Many of his education initiatives were run through the Roxboro Entertainment Group, a record label he founded in 2010 and named, significantly, for his alma mater. Based in Topanga, California, not far from downtown Hollywood, Roxboro boasted a number of well-known artists on its roster in 2013, including the composer Kennard Ramsey and the guitarist Lloyd Gregory. "The thing that I love most about Roxboro," Clarke told Nate Jackson of the *Los Angeles Times* in 2011, "is that it creates an energy in the business and hopefully it will fulfill some dreams for some people."

A review of Clarke's website, StanleyClarke.com, in November of 2013 revealed upcoming gigs in Florida and California.

Selected discography

Singles

Clarke/Duke Project, "Sweet Baby," 1981.

Albums

Stanley Clarke, Epic, 1974.
(With Return to Forever) *No Mystery,* Polydor, 1975.
School Days (includes "School Days"), Epic, 1976.
If This Bass Could Only Talk, Portrait, 1988.
Live at the Greek, Epic, 1993.
The Stanley Clarke Band, Heads Up, 2010.
(With Chick Corea and Lenny White) *Forever* (includes "500 Miles High"), Concord, 2011.

Television

(Composer) *Pee-Wee's Playhouse,* CBS, 1987.
(Composer) *Lincoln Heights,* ABC, 2007.

Films

(Composer and conductor) *Romeo Must Die,* Warner Brothers, 2000.

Sources

Periodicals

Los Angeles Times, March 19, 2011.

Online

"About Stanley Clarke," Concord Music Group, http://www2.concordmusicgroup.com/artists/Stanley-Clarke/ (accessed November 20, 2013).
Dye, David, "Stanley Clarke: A Lyrical Bass Player," National Public Radio, November 26, 2007, http://www.npr.org/templates/story/story.php?storyId=15879188 (accessed November 20, 2013).
"His Story," StanleyClarke.com, http://stanleyclarke.com/his-story/ (accessed November 20, 2013).
Yanow, Scott, "Stanley Clarke: Artist Biography," All-Music.com, http://www.allmusic.com/artist/stanley-clarke-mn0000745316/biography (accessed November 20, 2013).

—R. Anthony Kugler

Tom Colbert

1949—

Judge

Tom Colbert is the sitting chief justice of the Oklahoma Supreme Court, the first African-American in Oklahoma's history to serve on the state's highest court. Appointed to the Supreme Court in 2004 by Oklahoma governor Brad Henry, Colbert was chosen by the other eight members of the court to serve as chief justice in 2012. Colbert's term will expire at the end of 2014.

Colbert was born in Oklahoma City in 1949 and grew up in a household with his single mother, three sisters, and grandfather. As a high school student in the 1960s, a guidance counselor advised him that he was not "smart enough to go to college," a statement that Colbert cited as both hurtful and motivating. The comment convinced him not only to go to college but to aim high in all that he did in life. "It wasn't that I went to college to prove my guidance counselor wrong," he told the Oklahoma City *Journal Record,* "but I went because I was inspired and encouraged by others in my life. I went because they encouraged me." One of the people who encouraged him was his high school track coach, who played a role in Colbert's decision to go to college as well as in his achievements as an All-American in track and field.

Colbert earned an associate's degree from Eastern Oklahoma State College in Wilburton and went on to earn a bachelor's degree from Kentucky State University in 1973. After graduating from college he served in the U.S. Army's criminal investigation division before he was honorably discharged in 1975. he returned to Eastern Kentucky University to earn a master's degree

in education in 1976. He worked as a teacher in the Chicago public school system until 1980, when he went back to his home state to attend law school at the University of Oklahoma, earning his law degree in just two years. "My wife and son were still in Chicago," he told the Journal Record. "I didn't want to spend any more time away from them than necessary ... I was on a mission."

After completing law school Colbert held a prestigious position as assistant dean at Marquette University Law School in Milwaukee, Wisconsin. But Colbert was not completed satisfied with academic life. He wanted to gain practical, real-world experience, so in 1984 he took a job as assistant district attorney in Oklahoma County. He served in this position for two years before partnering with another lawyer, Vicki Miles-LaGrange, to form a private practice. Five years later, in 1989, he left the firm to establish his own practice, Colbert and Associates.

In 2000 Oklahoma governor Frank Keating appointed Colbert to the Oklahoma Court of Civil Appeals, an intermediate appellate court, where he served for four years before becoming the first African American appointed to the Oklahoma Supreme Court by Democratic governor Brad Henry. Upon his swearing-in as chief justice in January of 2013, Colbert recalled that he had almost resigned from his seat on the Supreme Court to pursue other opportunities, but his mother and wife had convinced him of the significance of his role as the first and only African-American on Oklahoma's highest court. They reminded him that he had a

At a Glance . . .

Born Thomas Colbert on December 30, 1949, in Oklahoma City, OK; married Doretha Maria Guion (an educator); three children. *Education:* Eastern Oklahoma State College, AA, 1970; Kentucky State University, BS, 1973; Eastern Kentucky University, MEd, 1976; University of Oklahoma School of Law, JD, 1982.

Career: Marquette University Law School, assistant dean, 1982–84; Oklahoma County, OK, assistant district attorney, 1984–86; Miles-LaGrange and Colbert, partner, 1986–89; Oklahoma Department of Human Services, attorney, 1988–89; Colbert and Associates, attorney, 1989–2000; Oklahoma Department of Human Services, attorney, 1999–2000; Oklahoma Court of Civil Appeals, judge, 2000–2004; Oklahoma State Supreme Court, judge, 2004–13, chief justice, 2013–.

Memberships: American Bar Association; National Bar Association; Oklahoma Bar Association; Phi Delta Phi Legal Fraternity; Tulsa County Bar Association.

Addresses: *Office*—Oklahoma Judicial Center, 2100 N. Lincoln Blvd., Suite 4, Oklahoma City, OK 73105.

duty to those who had struggled for civil rights before him to remain on the court and eventually become chief justice. "They were right," Colbert said in his interview with the *Journal Record.* "Here I am on the doorstep of making it to the next level, and it would be very selfish for me to worry about my own opportunities when someone else may never get the opportunity to stand where I'm standing, being a minority." Colbert was sworn in as chief justice by retired Oklahoma County district judge Charles Owens, who become the first-ever black judge in the state of Oklahoma when he was appointed in 1968.

Since Colbert's appointment to Oklahoma's high court, tensions have arisen between the state legislature and the Supreme Court with regard to the process of judicial selection. Members of Oklahoma's generally conservative legislature have complained that the state's Supreme Court has denied too many proposed bills on the basis of their constitutionality. Some Re-

publicans in the state house have requested a legislative inquiry into the process of judicial appointments and the possibility of term limits for Supreme Court judges, sowing the seeds of a partisan-oriented struggle between the legislature and the court. Republicans in the legislature have cited their dismay that eight of the state's nine Supreme Court justices have been appointed by Democratic governors.

Colbert responded to this situation by explaining that "our responsibility is to interpret the laws and we, in interpreting law, must make sure that it's consistent with the state and federal constitutions," he said in an Associated Press report published in the *Bartlesville Examiner-Enterprise.* Colbert downplayed the significance of any rift, stating, "all of us, I think we have a good working relationship with the Legislature as well as the executive branch." He has stated that believes the state's process for appointing judges—in which a judicial nominating committee gives three names to the presiding governor for selection—is fair.

Colbert's current term on the Oklahoma Supreme Court will expire on December 31, 2014. According to state law, Colbert must file for direct election in order to retain his seat for another six-year term.

Sources

Periodicals

Bartlesville (OK) Examiner-Enterprise, September 29, 2013.
Daily Oklahoman, January 5, 2013.
Journal Record (Oklahoma City, OK), November 1, 2013.
Tulsa (OK) World, January 5, 2013, A1.

Online

"Chief Justice Tom Colbert, District No. 6," Supreme Court of the State of Oklahoma, http://www.oscn.net/oscn/schome/colbert.htm (accessed December 20, 2013).
McGuigan, Patrick B. "Tom Colbert Becomes Chief Justice of Oklahoma State Supreme Court," Capitol-BeatOK.com, January 5, 2013, http://capitolbeatok.com/reports/tom-colbert-becomes-chief-justice-of-oklahoma-state-supreme-court/ (accessed December 20, 2013).
"Tom Colbert," Judgepedia.org, http://judgepedia.org/Tom_Colbert / (accessed December 20, 2013).

—Ben Bloch

Ertharin Cousin

1957—

Administrator of nongovernmental organization

Cousin, Ertharin, photograph. Jonathan Ernst/Chicago Tribune/ MCT via Getty Images.

In 2012 Ertharin Cousin became the executive director of the United Nations World Food Programme (WFP), which is headquartered in Rome, Italy. The WFP is the world's largest humanitarian organization devoted to combatting global hunger and malnutrition. It is financed entirely through donations and works to meet urgent food needs and to develop long-term solutions to food insecurity and malnutrition. Cousin brought to the position more than two decades of experience, including corporate work in the U.S. retail food industry and a two-year stint as a top executive at America's Second Harvest (later renamed Feeding America), the largest nonprofit hunger-relief organization in the United States. The politically connected Democrat also worked in the administration of President Bill Clinton during the 1990s as the White House liaison to the U.S. State Department. In 2009 President Barack Obama appointed her as the U.S. representative to United Nations agencies concerned with food and agriculture. Ambassador Cousin served in that capacity for nearly three years before being recommended by President Obama to fill the top spot at the WFP.

Ertharin Cousin was born in 1957 in Chicago, Illinois, and grew up on Polk Street in the Lawndale neighborhood on the city's West Side. The economically depressed area was plagued by poverty and crime. Cousin took the last name of her mother, Annie Cousin, who was a social worker and city administrator. Her father, Julius Riley, was a community volunteer and was active in local politics. The city's schools were racially segregated at the time, so Cousin attended St. Louise de Marillac Catholic School in the nearby suburb of La Grange Park. From there she went to the Lane Technical College Preparatory High School on the city's North Side, graduating in 1975. Cousin majored in criminal justice at the University of Illinois at Chicago, receiving a bachelor's degree in 1979. Next she attended law school at the University of Georgia, earning a juris doctorate in 1982. Following law school Cousin returned to Chicago and over the following decade worked as a private attorney and in government relations for AT&T. She briefly served as the Illinois assistant attorney general and held positions on the Chicago Ethics Board and at the Metropolitan Water Reclamation District of Greater Chicago.

At a Glance . . .

Born Ertharin Cousin in 1957 in Chicago, IL; daughter of Julius Riley (a community activist) and Annie Cousin (a social worker); married Deryll Moore, 1990s (divorced); children: Maurice. *Politics:* Democrat. *Education:* University of Illinois at Chicago, BA, criminal justice, 1979; University of Georgia, JD, 1982.

Career: Private attorney, 1980s; State of Illinois, assistant attorney general, 1980s or early 1990s; Democratic National Committee, deputy chief of staff, 1990s; White House, liaison to U.S. State Department, 1994–96; Jewel Food Stores, vice president for government and community affairs, 1997–99; Albertsons Inc., group vice president of public affairs, 1999–2001, senior vice president of public relations and government affairs, 2001–04; America's Second Harvest (later Feeding America), chief operating officer and executive vice president, 2004–06; Polk Street Group, founder and president, 2006—; U.S. State Department, representative to the United Nations food and agriculture agencies, 2009–12; United Nations World Food Programme, executive director, 2012—.

Memberships: Chicago Ethics Board; Chicago Black Women Lawyers; Illinois Hate Crimes Commission; Executive Leadership Council; Chicago Urban League; Access Living; International Food and Agriculture Development; National Association for the Advancement of Colored People.

Awards: Meritorious Service Award, U.S. Department of State, 1996; Alumni Achievement Award, University of Illinois at Chicago, 2013.

Addresses: *Office*—United Nations World Food Programme, Via C.G. Viola 68, Parco dei Medici, 00148 Rome, Italy.

Cousin was heavily involved in politics and during the early 1990s became a deputy chief of staff for the Democratic National Committee and campaigned for Bill Clinton during the presidential election campaign in 1992. Clinton later selected Cousin to be the White House liaison to the U.S. State Department, a position she filled from 1994 to 1996. She was a senior adviser to Secretary of State Warren Christopher regarding the Olympic Games held in Atlanta, Georgia, in the summer of 1996.

The following year Cousin took a corporate job with Jewel Food Stores, Inc., a grocery store chain centered in the Midwest. In 1999 the chain was purchased by Albertsons Inc., then one of the largest retail grocers in the nation with approximately 2,500 stores. Cousin rose to senior vice president of public relations and government affairs at Albertsons before leaving in 2004 to work at America's Second Harvest (later renamed Feeding America). The nonprofit hunger-relief organization—the largest of its kind in the United States—partners with hundreds of food banks and related charities to procure, store, and distribute donated food to needy people around the country. Cousin served as chief operating officer and executive vice president of the organization for two years.

In 2006 Cousin founded a public relations firm in Chicago named after the street on which she grew up. The Polk Street Group specializes in forging public–private business partnerships, helping corporations craft socially responsible community projects, and supporting urban retail development. The politically active Cousin was acquainted with then–U.S. Senator Barack Obama, who was from Chicago. Jerry Hagstrom of the *National Journal* noted that Cousin first met Obama at a voter registration drive on the South Side of Chicago. She told Hagstrom that at the time, the Obamas "lived about a block and a half from me, and I would see [Obama] at the grocery store. So during the general election for the Senate, I tried to be helpful to them as much as I could."

When Senator Obama began his campaign for the presidency in 2007, Cousin served as one of his senior advisers. He won the election in November of 2008 and took office in January of 2009. Later that year President Obama nominated Cousin as the U.S. representative (with the rank of ambassador) to the United Nations agencies for food and agriculture—the World Food Programme, the Food and Agriculture Organization, and the International Fund for Agricultural Development. All three agencies are headquartered in Rome, Italy. Cousin's nomination was approved by the U.S. Senate in August of 2009. During her nearly three years as ambassador, Cousin helped lead the U.S. response to food crises in Haiti (the result of a devastating earthquake in January of 2010), Pakistan (following monsoon-driven flooding in the summer of 2010), and East Africa, which suffered a severe drought beginning in 2011.

In 2012, based on recommendations from President Obama and U.S. Secretary of State Hilary Clinton, Cousin was appointed by United Nations Secretary-General Ban Ki-moon to head the WFP, the largest hunger-relief organization in the world. Cousin became the agency's 12th executive director. The WFP combats hunger by providing emergency life-saving food deliveries and by fostering long-term solutions to chronic food shortages, such as in drought-stricken areas. The United States is by far the largest donor to

the WFP, accounting for nearly 40 percent of the agency's total donations during 2013. In a WFP biography for Cousin, the agency stated, "As the leader of the world's largest humanitarian organization with approximately 13,500 staff serving over 90 million beneficiaries in more than 70 countries across the world, [Cousin] is an exceptional advocate for improving the lives of hungry people worldwide, and travels extensively to raise awareness of food insecurity and chronic malnutrition." In 2013 Cousin was ranked number 49 on *Forbes* magazine's international list of "Power Women." According to *Forbes,* in her role as executive director of the WFP, Cousin oversaw an annual budget of nearly $4 billion in 2013 and helped provide food to more than 97 million people around the world.

Sources

Periodicals

Advocate, 2013.
AtLAS, Winter 2012.
Black Enterprise, June 2000, p. 96.
Chicago Tribune, April 3, 2012.
Daily Beast, July 11, 2013.
Food & Fiber Letter, July 6, 2009, p. 10.
Forbes, May 2013.
Jet, July 2, 2001, p. 6.
National Journal, December 11, 2009.
Seafood Business, April 2004, p. 42.
State Magazine, November 2009, p. 38.

Online

"2010 Speaker Biographies: Ertharin Cousin," U.S. Department of Agriculture, 2010, http://www.fsa .usda.gov/Internet/FSA_File/2010_ifadc_biogra phies.pdf (accessed November 20, 2013).
"About: Contributions to WFP 2013," World Food Programme, 2013, http://www.wfp.org/about/ funding/year/2013 (accessed November 20, 2013).
"Alumni Five Awards: A Celebration of Distinguished Alumni," University of Illinois at Chicago, 2013, http://www.uiaa.org/uic/programs/alumni_five/ (accessed November 20, 2013).
"Ertharin Cousin Named U.S. Ambassador to United Nations Agencies for Food and Agriculture," US Newswire, June 22, 2009, http://www.prnewswire .com/news-releases/ertharin-cousin-named-us-am bassador-to-united-nations-agencies-for-food-and-ag riculture-61836467.html (accessed November 19, 2013).
"Ertharin Cousin's Biography," World Food Programme, 2013, http://www.wfp.org/about/cor porate-information/executive-director/biography (accessed November 19, 2013).
"Jewel-Osco Executive to Lead Parent Company's Nationwide Public Affairs Activities," PR Newswire, February 15, 2000, http://www.thefreelibary.com/ Jewel-Osco+Executive+to+Lead+Parent+Company's+Na tionwide+Public...-a059447002 (accessed January 15, 2014).

—Kim Masters Evans

Antonio Cromartie

1984—

Professional football player

Cromartie, Antonio, photograph. Joe Robbins/Getty Images.

In 2013 Antonio Cromartie was the starting defensive cornerback for the New York Jets of the National Football League (NFL). Although Cromartie's career has been inconsistent over his seven years in the NFL, first with the San Diego Chargers and then with the Jets, he remains one of the fastest, most dynamic, and most athletic defensive players in the league. Cromartie's performance on the field, however, has sometimes been overshadowed by tabloid headlines about his large family: the defensive back has fathered at least 10 children by eight women and has often failed to keep up with his child support payments.

Chosen as First-Round Draft Pick

Antonio Tyrell Cromartie was born on April 15, 1984, in Tallahassee, Florida. The oldest of four children, he was raised by his single mother, Cassandra Gardner, growing up in a poor household. His mother was sometimes unable to pay their utility bills, and the electricity was frequently turned off in the home. His family moved often, living in 11 different places by the time he was in the sixth grade. Cromartie began

playing football in grade school and went on to become a star athlete at Lincoln High School in Tallahassee, where he was personally recruited Bobby Bowden, the head coach of the hometown Florida State University Seminoles.

At Florida State Cromartie competed in both football and track and field. A member of the Seminoles track team that won the 2004 Atlantic Coast Conference championship, he ran the 400-meter relay and excelled at the triple jump, setting a personal record of 14.05 meters. He played two years of college football, although he started only one game. Cromartie was prone to angry outbursts at his teammates and frequently got into fights that prevented him from becoming a regular starter for the team.

During a routine voluntary workout between his sophomore and junior years, Cromartie tore the anterior cruciate ligament (ACL) in his left knee. The injury kept him sidelined for his entire junior season as he underwent surgery, followed by an intense eight-month rehabilitation. During this time Cromartie's mother was diagnosed with breast cancer. She lacked health insurance or other resources to pay for her treatment, and

At a Glance . . .

Born Antonio Tyrell Cromartie on April 15, 1984, in Tallahassee, FL; son of Cassandra Gardner; married Terricka Cason, July 12, 2010; children: Alonzo Pierre, Karis Marie, Antonio Jr., Deyjah, Tyler Jae, London Jaye, Leilani, Julian, Jerzie, Jagger. *Education:* Attended Florida State University, 2003–05.

Career: San Diego Chargers, cornerback, 2006–09; New York Jets, cornerback, 2010—.

Awards: *USA Today* Defensive High School Player of the Year, 2002; All-Atlantic Coast Conference First Team, 2004; National Football League (NFL) Alumni Defensive Back of the Year, 2007; NFL All-Pro selection, 2007; NFL Pro Bowl selection 2007, 2012.

Addresses: *Office*—c/o New York Jets, 1 Jets Dr., Florham Park, NJ. *Web*—http://www.cro31.com. *Twitter*—@CRO31.

so Cromartie made the decision to enter the NFL draft early, skipping his senior season at Florida State. Many draft analysts speculated that he would have been selected higher in the draft had he played his senior season (thus proving that his knee injury was not a future liability), but his performance at the 2006 pro day—when draft prospects demonstrate their skills for pro team scouts—was so strong that he was judged one of the fastest and most versatile defensive players in that year's draft class. Cromartie was selected in the first round of the draft by the San Diego Chargers and signed a five-year, $13.5 million contract with the team.

Set NFL Records with Chargers

Throughout his four seasons in San Diego, the Chargers used Cromartie as both a cornerback and a kickoff and punt return specialist. He played in his first big game late in his rookie season when he returned a kickoff 91 yards against the Oakland Raiders. His performance that season would establish Cromartie as one of the top defensive players in the league. With 10 regular-season interceptions, he set a Chargers franchise record and led the NFL. Playing at home against the Houston Texans during the eighth week of the season, he returned an interception 70 yards for a touchdown and recovered a fumble that he ran for another touchdown.

In week nine of the 2007 season, on the road against the Minnesota Vikings, Cromartie set an NFL record

for longest play when he returned Ryan Longwell's missed 58-yard field goal attempt, going 109 yards for a touchdown. Cromartie stood at the back of the end zone and received the short kick at the longest possible distance from the opposing end zone (the field is 100 yards long and each end zone is 10 yards), running it back untouched for the record and the score. The following week, at home against the Indianapolis Colts, Cromartie had three interceptions on one of the league's best passers, quarterback Peyton Manning, becoming the first player ever to intercept Manning three times in a regular-season game.

The Chargers made it to the American Football Conference (AFC) Championship in 2007, losing to the New England Patriots. Cromartie had two postseason interceptions in addition to his 10 during the regular season. That year he was selected to the AFC Pro Bowl team, intercepting two passes in the annual game in Hawaii.

After his banner 2007 season, opposing teams took notice of Cromartie's prowess on the field. Although he claimed that he could top his personal record of 10 interceptions in a season, Cromartie's numbers dropped significantly in 2008 and 2009, as the league's offensive coordinators and quarterbacks became wary of throwing the ball in his direction. Although he started for the entire season in 2008, he was held to only two interceptions and committed a number of costly pass interference penalties. Cromartie later announced that he had played the entire season with a partial hip fracture.

In 2009 Cromartie's numbers continued to drop, and the Chargers began to question his effort when, in a loss against the New York Jets, he appeared to have an opportunity to tackle running back Shonn Greene but refrained from making contact, allowing Greene to run 53 yards for a touchdown. That game would be his last in San Diego: at the end of season, he was traded to the New York Jets for a third-round 2011 draft pick.

Signed with New York Jets

Cromartie's first seasons with the Jets were unremarkable. He arrived under some scrutiny because of the circumstances of his departure from the Chargers. Cromartie had been disciplined several times by Chargers coach Norv Turner for tweeting about team matters, including a public denouncement of the team's cafeteria food, for which the league fined him $2,500. Cromartie also earned attention in the tabloids for reportedly having seven children by six different women living in five states and failing to keep up with his child support. The Jets reportedly gave Cromartie a $500,000 advance on his salary so that he could address these paternity issues.

Cromartie played inconsistently throughout the 2010 and 2011 seasons with the Jets. Although he contin-

ued to make big plays for the team, he also gave up considerably more touchdowns to the wide receivers he was assigned to cover. The Jets made it to the playoffs in 2010, when Cromartie executed a crucial late-game kickoff return that allowed the Jets to kick a game-winning field goal and advance to the AFC Championship. The Jets lost to the Pittsburgh Steelers, 24–19.

Since 2010 Cromartie has received frequent media attention for his growing family—his 10th child was born in 2011—and for financial troubles, including a near-foreclosure on a home purchased for his mother in Tallahassee. On the sixth season of the HBO series *Hard Knocks,* Cromartie famously struggled to name all of his children, although he later suggested that producers had urged him to speak slowly to heighten the comedic value of the scene. He spoke publicly about undergoing a vasectomy in 2011 and about his greater commitment to fiscal responsibility, saying that he wants to be a responsible father and a role model to a younger generation of athletes.

Sources

Books

Nicholas Dawidoff, *Collision Low Crossers: A Year Inside the Turbulent World of NFL Football,* Little, Brown, 2013.

Periodicals

Journal of Sports Media, vol. 6, no. 1 (Spring 2011), pp. 115–120.
Newsday (New York), June 1, 2013.
New York Daily News, April 19, 2011.
New York Post, March 8, 2010; April 15, 2012; May 20, 2012; September 7, 2013.
San Diego Union-Tribune, February 17, 2010.
Sporting News, May 5, 2008, pp. 24–33.

Online

"Antonio Cromartie," Florida State University Seminoles, http://www.seminoles.com/sports/m-footbl/mtt/antonio_cromartie_86022.html (accessed November 30, 2013).
"Antonio Cromartie," New York Jets, http://www.newyorkjets.com/team/roster/antonio-cromartie/ca33331d-4119-43f8-b860-1c4e534ccb1c/ (accessed November 30, 2013).
"Antonio Cromartie," San Diego Chargers, http://www.chargers.com/team/roster/antonio-cromartie/b06c1da0-199d-414f-87e3-f24ffa54cca9/ (accessed November 30, 2013).
"Chargers Cornerback's Return Longest Play in NFL History," ESPN.com, November 4, 2007, http://sports.espn.go.com/nfl/news/story?id=3094481 (accessed November 30, 2013).
Clayton, John, "Cromartie's First Start at Corner a Smash Hit," ESPN.com, November 12, 2007, http://sports.espn.go.com/nfl/columns/story?columnist=clayton_john&id=3106487 (accessed November 30, 2013).
"Cromartie Tweets Food, Then Gets Fined," ESPN.com, August 4, 2009, http://sports.espn.go.com/nfl/trainingcamp09/news/story?id=4376876 (accessed November 30, 2013).
Florio, Mike, "Cromartie Addresses Tackling, Child Support," Pro Football Talk, March 5, 2010, http://profootballtalk.nbcsports.com/2010/03/05/cromartie-addresses-tackling-child-support/ (accessed November 30, 2013).

Other

Hard Knocks, season 6, HBO, 2010, http://www.nfl.com/videos/nfl-network-hard-knocks/0ap2000000209179/Hard-Knocks-Antonio-Cromartie-s-kids (accessed November 30, 2013).

—Ben Bloch

Andraé Crouch

1942—

Gospel singer, composer, pianist, producer, preacher

Over a 40-year career, contemporary gospel music pioneer Andraé Crouch has become one of the most influential musicians in the United States. Both the black gospel performers who draw on R&B and the white contemporary Christian artists who blur the line between sacred and secular with middle-of-the-road romantic styles owe Crouch a musical debt.

Crouch was born in Los Angeles on July 1, 1942. His twin sister Sandra and older brother Benjamin were both musicians, and he is also the

Crouch, Andraé, photograph. Frederick Breedon/Getty Images.

cousin of noted jazz critic Stanley Crouch. The three Crouch children sang in a trio at the behest of their father, who had begun to preach in order to strengthen his prayers to God that his son might be given musical talent. One Sunday when Andraé was 11 years old, his father preached at a church in Val Verde, California, and then called Andraé to the piano to accompany the choir on the hymn "What a Friend We Have in Jesus." Although Andraé, according to his own recollections, had never played the piano before, he performed successfully.

Crouch moved with his family to the San Fernando Valley suburb of Pacoima when he was in junior high

school. Music helped Crouch overcome shyness and a stammering impediment. "I started singing what I had to say," he recalled to *People* magazine in 1995. "People became music to me because everything they said was a song." Indeed, Crouch began composing songs at age 14 and never slowed down.

Formed Group with Billy Preston

In high school Crouch formed a group called the COGICS (an acronym for Church of God in Christ Singers) that also included vocalist Billy Preston, of "Will It Go Round in Circles?" fame. Crouch later attended Valley Junior College and Life Bible College in the Los Angeles area and counseled recovering drug addicts, but his heart was in music. By the mid-1960s he had put together another group, the Disciples, and the first of six Andraé Crouch and the Disciples albums, *Take the Message Everywhere,* was released in 1969 on the Light label.

Crouch's solo career began with the album *Just Andraé* in 1973, and throughout the 1970s his reputation rose steadily. Crouch and the Disciples toured world-

At a Glance . . .

Born Andraé Edward Crouch on July 1, 1942, in Los Angeles, CA; son of Benjamin Jerome (a preacher and dry-cleaning business owner) and Catherine Dorothea Crouch. *Religion:* Church of God in Christ. *Education:* Attended Valley Junior College, San Fernando, CA; Life Bible Institute, Los Angeles.

Career: Drug addiction counselor, 1960s; recording artist, 1969—; founded and toured with Andraé Crouch and the Disciples, 1969–82; New Christ Memorial Church of God in Christ, San Fernando, CA, pastor, 1994—.

Awards: Grammy Awards: Best Soul Gospel Performance, 1975, for *Take Me Back*; Best Soul Gospel Performance, Contemporary, 1978, for *Live in London*, 1979, for *I'll Be Thinking of You*, 1980, for *The Lord's Prayer*, 1981, for *Don't Give Up*; Best Soul Gospel Performance, Male, 1984, for "Always Remember"; Dove Awards, 1977, 1978, 1985, 1993, 1997, 1998; inducted into Gospel Music Hall of Fame, 1998; Best Pop/Contemporary Gospel Album, 2004, for *Mercy*; Hollywood Walk of Fame, 2004; Salute to Gospel Music Lifetime Achievement Award, National Academy of Recording Arts and Sciences, 2005; inducted into Christian Music Hall of Fame, 2007.

Addresses: *Agent*—Demetrius Stewart, PureSprings Gospel, 5214 Maryland Way, Suite 300, Brentwood, TN 37027. *Office*—New Christ Memorial Church of God in Christ, 13333 Vaughn St., San Fernando, CA 91340.

wide, and in 1975 and 1979 they performed to sellout crowds at New York's Carnegie Hall. They pushed the boundaries of gospel by introducing features of contemporary R&B, gaining new fans from far outside the usual gospel sphere. Crouch's crossover gospel encompassed several aspects of secular music, including pop-style vocal arrangements, production techniques, and, most important, Crouch's crooning vocals, which were miles removed from the intense fervor of traditional gospel.

The Disciples broke another barrier of secular culture with an appearance on NBC's *Saturday Night Live* in 1980; Crouch later was invited back to the show for a solo performance. Crouch and the Disciples took home Grammy Awards every year from 1978 through 1981, and Crouch's presence on the annual Dove

Christian music awards roster was practically guaranteed for several years. Crouch did not let stardom interfere with his songwriting activities, and several of his compositions from the 1970s, including "Through It All" and "Take Me Back," are now part of the gospel tradition's standard repertoire.

Endured Criticism from Gospel Traditionalists

Despite his success Crouch was criticized by followers of traditional gospel, some of whom felt that his use of secular styles diluted the religious content of his lyrics. These concerns flared into the open with the 1981 release of Crouch's solo album *Don't Give Up*, which made an explicit bid for sales in the secular market with its up-to-the-minute studio techniques and topical lyrics. Crouch weathered the storm, telling *Billboard* that "[e]very album I've done has been controversial … It's not anything new for me. It's just time for me to say it." The album was released on the mainstream Warner Brothers label, but Crouch also continued to record for the more gospel-oriented Light label in the early 1980s.

The singer added a Grammy Award for his 1984 album *No Time to Lose*. Then spiritual and physical exhaustion set in. In 1982 Crouch had been arrested on cocaine possession charges, but he had maintained that the substance found in his car was instant chicken soup powder. Police eventually declined to press charges, but the experience took its toll on Crouch. "I had been traveling so much, I just decided it was time I got off the road at least part of the time and devoted some time to my family and to my church," he told *American Visions*.

During the mid-1980s he produced and composed songs for other artists, including pop superstar Michael Jackson, and gained critical acclaim for the historically detailed music he composed and arranged for the 1985 film *The Color Purple*. He also composed and arranged music for the NBC comedy series *Amen* from 1986 to 1991.

Took over Father's Ministry

Crouch's life took a new direction after his mother, father, and older brother Benjamin all died within a short period between 1993 and 1994. Shortly before his death, Crouch's father had maintained that his son was destined for the ministry—an idea that Crouch had always strongly resisted. "But, he knew I was going to be [a minister] one day," Crouch recalled to *Jet*. "And before he died, he said, 'Andraé, I want you to be ready. Have three black suits ready at all times.'" Crouch took over the ministry at the Christ Memorial Church of God in Christ in Pacoima after his father's death, although he had little training as a preacher. His brother helped Crouch with the transition before he, too, died several months later.

During those days Crouch was unsure of his mission. But, he told *People* magazine, he had an otherworldly experience that convinced him to step into the pulpit: a mysterious force threw him to the floor as he sat one day listening to a sermon, and he heard a voice telling him to take over the church. "You will tell me yes," Crouch remembered hearing. "I've put too much into you for you to say no. Not 'right on,' not 'uh-huh.' 'Yes!'" The next night, Crouch remembered, he slept through the night for the first time since his mother had died.

Attendance at the church soon doubled, and the ministry consumed the lion's share of his energies. Crouch released the album *Mercy* in 1994 and continued to compose and make appearances as a performer. He received the Grammy Award for best pop/contemporary gospel album for *Mercy* that year. His pivotal place in gospel music history was illustrated by the release in 1996 of the album *Tribute: The Songs of Andraé Crouch.* Of the countless gospel artists for whom Crouch's influence was critical, the album featured a representative selection including the Winans, Take 6, and Michael W. Smith.

After two back-to-back albums in 1997 and 1998—*Pray* and *Gift of Christmas*—Crouch took a break from the music scene to focus on family and preaching. Despite the controversies that had shadowed his own progressive music in the 1970s, he was critical of certain recent trends including the incursion of rap styles into gospel music.

Celebrated 40 Years of Music

In 2004 Crouch was honored with a star on the Hollywood Walk of Fame, a recognition given to only two gospel artists before him: the Reverend James Cleveland and Mahalia Jackson both received stars posthumously. In 2006 Crouch released the album *Mighty Wind,* which celebrated the 40 years he had spent in the music business. He told Farai Chideya of National Public Radio, "You know, at first, when this record came out and they told me that they would like to celebrate 40 years, and I said, 'who would want to buy a record of a guy that's been playing music for 40 years?' And then, I know that I heard the voice of God say, 'Andrae, boy, I kept you here, man. And you could be gone, but I've never failed you and I've always given you music.' And so He's been faithful on his part. And I just wanted to, you know, keep up what He has given me. And I don't think that it will ever drain out of me. I think that … as long as I want to do music, I think that God will continually pour it into me."

That year Crouch also recalled an uncomfortable moment from the 1970s when audience members discovered for the first time, during a live concert in Fort Worth, Texas, that Andraé Crouch and the Disciples were black. In an interview published in the Los Angeles Times, he acknowledged that some people had walked out, but once the concert began, the music the audience had come to hear kept them there. He remembered the occasion as an opportunity to build a bridge over the racial divide, noting, "Some of my best friends today were people in that concert." He also laughingly described the mood at the moment the audience first saw the band: "It was like turning the stove on from burning hot, scorching hot, to low," continuing, "It would be like, from cayenne pepper to bubble gum."

In July of 2009 Crouch and his 25-voice gospel choir participated in the public memorial service for Michael Jackson, performing one of Crouch's signature pieces, "Soon and Very Soon." Crouch had arranged Jackson's 1987 hit "Man in the Mirror" and worked with him on other projects over the years as well.

Two years later Crouch released *The Journey,* another studio album that featured the vocals of Kim Burrell, Take 6, Chaka Khan, and Sheila E. "I was surprised that some of these people said yes when I asked them to be a part of this project," Crouch told TheGrio.com. "I have always loved their music, their concepts, and the gift that God has given them. I did not think they would be so willing to sing a song with me or for me." *The Journey* was nominated for a Grammy Award in 2012.

On October 13, 2013, Crouch experienced an episode of fainting while taking a shower at his home in Los Angeles and was rushed to a hospital as a precaution. Crouch is diabetic and has experienced other health concerns at times in the past. After several hours of observation, doctors released him. In a statement reported by NewsOne.com two days later, Crouch noted that he felt he had recovered fully from the event, but also acknowledged, "Diabetes is no fun."

Selected works

Albums

With the Disciples

Take the Message Everywhere, Light, 1969.
Keep on Singin', Light, 1971.
Soulfully, Light, 1972.
Live at Carnegie Hall, Compendia Music Group, 1973.
Take Me Back, Light, 1975.
This is Another Day, Light, 1976.
Live in London, Light, 1978.

Solo albums

Just Andraé, Light, 1973.
I'll Be Thinking of You, Light, 1979.
Don't Give Up, Warner Bros., 1981.
Finally, Light, 1982.

No Time to Lose, Light, 1984.
Autograph, Light, 1986.
Mercy, Qwest, 1994.
Pray, Qwest, 1997.
Gift of Christmas, Qwest, 1998.
Take the Message Everywhere, Artemis Gospel, 2005.
Mighty Wind, Verity, 2006.
The Journey, Riverphlo Entertainment, 2011.

Books

Through It All, Word, 1974.

Television

(Composer, musical director) *Amen,* NBC, 1986–91.

Films

(Music arranger, conductor) *The Color Purple,* Warner Bros., 1985.
(Choir master, choral arranger) *The Lion King,* Disney, 1994.

Sources

Books

Crouch, Andraé, *Through It All,* Word, 1974.
Hitchcock, H. Wiley, and Stanley Sadie, eds., *The New Grove Dictionary of American Music,* Macmillan, 1986.
Larkin, Colin, ed., *The Encyclopedia of Popular Music,* Muze UK, 1998.

Periodicals

American Visions, August/September 1994, p. 48.
Billboard, November 7, 1981; September 14, 1996, p. 10.
Christianity Today, March 4, 1983, p. 66.
Jet, September 13, 1982, p. 64; October 16, 1995, p. 32.
Los Angeles Times, July 7, 2006.
People, October 23, 1995, p. 103.

Online

"Andrae Crouch," AllMusic.com, http://www.allmusic.com/artist/andra%C3%A9-crouch-mn0000031263 (accessed November 29, 2013).
"Andrae Crouch and the Disciples," Gospel Music Association Hall of Fame, http://www.gmahalloffame.org/site/andrae-crouch-the-disciples/ (accessed November 29, 2013).
"Andrae Crouch's Musical 'Journey' Is Far from Over," TheGrio.com, December 21, 2011, http://www.thegrio.com/entertainment/andrae-crouch.php (accessed November 29, 2013).
Chideya, Farai, "Gospel Singer Andrae Crouch: 'Mighty Wind,'" National Public Radio, June 12, 2006, http://www.npr.org/templates/story/story.php?storyId=5478515 (accessed January 14, 2014).
Manuel-Logan, Ruth, "Gospel Icon Andrae Crouch Rushed to Hospital after Falling Ill," NewsOne.com, October 15, 2013, http://newsone.com/2740565/andrae-crouch-hospital-ill/ (accessed November 25, 2013).

—James M. Manheim and Pamela Willwerth Aue

Arthur Crudup

1905–1974

Blues vocalist, guitarist, songwriter

Crudup, Arthur, photograph. Gilles Petard/Redferns/Getty Images.

Although he has sometimes been called the "Father of Rock and Roll" for his influence on such stars as Elvis Presley, the blues vocalist, guitarist, and songwriter Arthur "Big Boy" Crudup never earned a steady living from music. Despite a string of popular singles in the 1940s and 1950s, his royalties were meager, and he often had to rely on farmwork and other odd jobs to make ends meet. His influence was nevertheless considerable, and in the last years of his life, he was increasingly regarded as an elder statesmen of the blues. "Down in Tupelo, Mississippi, I used to hear old Arthur Crudup bang his box the way I do now," Presley once said, in a comment quoted by the Blues Foundation's Jim O'Neal. "I said if I ever got to the place [where] I could feel all old Arthur felt, I'd be a music man like nobody ever saw."

Arthur Crudup was born on August 24, 1905, in Forest, a small community in central Mississippi. He spent much of his early life working in the fields around his home, and his formal education was limited. While he enjoyed singing gospel music, he did not take up the guitar until he was in his early 30s. He learned to play the instrument with the help of several mentors, including the local stars Papa Harvey Hull and George Lee. Crudup progressed rapidly, and within a few years he was playing professionally in the small bars known throughout the South as juke joints. Although he soon attracted a local following, his earnings from the bars were never enough to support him, and he had to balance his nascent music career with the kind of manual labor he had been doing since childhood. Around 1940 he left Mississippi for Chicago, Illinois, a move that proved crucial to his subsequent development as an artist.

By his own account Crudup faced some significant difficulties upon his arrival in the Midwest, and for a time he was homeless. In 1941 his luck turned when a well-known producer named Lester Melrose heard him playing on the street and invited him to perform at a house party. In attendance at that event were a number of established stars, including his fellow guitarists Tampa Red and Big Bill Broonzy, whose approval of the new arrival helped convince Melrose to offer Crudup a contract with RCA. His recording debut followed soon thereafter.

Crudup later had deals with several other companies but has always been most closely associated with RCA and its Bluebird subsidiary. Between 1941 and about 1954, he released a steady stream of singles for the label, many of which became national hits. Among the most prominent of these were a pair of songs released in 1946, "So Glad You're Mine" and "That's All Right." Both were later covered by Presley, as was "My Baby Left Me" (1950). By the time "My Baby Left Me" was released, Crudup was one of the most visible blues stars in the country. His remuneration from RCA failed to reflect that success, however, and his relationship with the company soured. He responded, at first, by recording for several other labels under a pseudonym, a common practice at the time. The situation continued to deteriorate, however, and around 1954 Crudup parted ways with RCA permanently.

The decade that followed was difficult for Crudup in a number of ways. Although he continued to perform when he could, he faced growing competition in Chicago. By the end of the 1950s, he was spending most of his time in Mississippi, playing juke joints and working in the fields. A break came in the early 1960s when he signed a contract with Fire Records, a label based in New York City. That agreement, however, resulted in relatively little new work. Instead, Fire simply revised and repackaged many of Crudup's earlier hits. More significant was a deal Crudup signed in the late 1960s with Delmark Records, a small label in Chicago that was rapidly gaining a national reputation for its blues expertise. His work for Delmark, particularly a 1969 album called *Crudup's Mood,* won strong reviews and revitalized his career. Many of his new fans in this period were college students, who embraced traditional blues artists with growing enthusiasm over the course of the 1960s. Thanks in part to their support, Crudup began to obtain gigs in venues that were larger, better equipped, and more remunerative than the average juke joint. At one point he even appeared in Europe, where he shared the stage with a number of British blues-rock enthusiasts, among them the drummer Hughie Flint and the guitarist and vocalist Dave Kelly.

Amid this success, however, Crudup's financial health remained precarious, and even in the last years of his life, he was still heavily involved in farmwork. At one point, noted the Mississippi Blues Commission, he ran a small business that transported migrant workers between his native state and rural Virginia. On March 28, 1974, Crudup died in Nassawadox, a tiny community on Virginia's Eastern Shore. Among his survivors were three sons (George, James, and Jonas), all of whom followed him into the music business, where they had some success performing as the Malibus and later as the Crudup Brothers.

Crudup's legacy extends beyond his music to encompass another aspect of his career, namely his long struggle to obtain fair payments for his contributions. Although many of his peers also faced difficulties in this area, Crudup's experiences came to be viewed as especially egregious. While racism was undoubtedly a significant factor in his troubled relationship with producers in the 1940s and 1950s, white performers of that period were also frequently subjected to treatment that was later regarded as unfair. Contracts then were typically one sided. With a few exceptions, artists did not begin to wield significant power in their dealings with labels until the 1960s. While that shift came too late to bring much benefit to Crudup himself, a measure of justice was obtained for him after his death, when his family was finally able to obtain some of the royalties he had been owed for decades.

Selected discography

Singles

"Rock Me Mamma," 1944.
"So Glad You're Mine," 1946.
"That's All Right," 1946.
"My Baby Left Me," 1950.

Albums

Crudup's Mood, Delmark, 1969.

Sources

Online

"Arthur 'Big Boy' Crudup," Discogs.com, http://www .discogs.com/artist/Arthur+%22Big+Boy%22 +Crudup (accessed October 30, 2013).
"Arthur 'Big Boy' Crudup," Mississippi Blues Commission, http://www.msbluestrail.org/blues-trail-mark ers/arthur-crudup (accessed October 30, 2013).
Dahl, Bill, "Arthur 'Big Boy' Crudup: Artist Biography," AllMusic.com, http://www.allmusic.com/ artist/arthur-big-boy-crudup-mn0000603680/bio graphy (accessed October 30, 2013).
O'Neal, Jim, "Past Hall of Fame Inductees: Arthur 'Big Boy' Crudup," Blues Foundation, https://blues.org/ #ref=halloffame_inductees (accessed October 30, 2013).

—R. Anthony Kugler

Cow Cow Davenport

1894–1955

Jazz and blues pianist

Although much of his work has faded from public memory, the pianist and vocalist Cow Cow Davenport had a significant influence on the development of both jazz and the blues. One of the founders of "boogie-woogie," a fast-paced style that mixed those genres, he worked for many years in vaudeville, where he drew particular notice for his abilities as an accompanist. In 2011 a prominent blogger and critic known only as "Record Fiend" described him as "one of the most important and influential blues pianists."

The son of a pastor and a church organist, Cow Cow Davenport was born Charles Edward Davenport on April 26, 1894 (some sources give April 23), in Anniston, Alabama, an industrial city east of Birmingham. His study of the piano began with lessons from his mother when he was still a boy. His talent was soon evident, and by the middle of his teens, he was adept at both the hymns his mother had taught him and at ragtime, a jazz style many considered disreputable at the time. Among those who disapproved of it were his parents and his teachers at a theological seminary he had entered with the goal of following his father into the ministry. Those plans went awry, however, as his penchant for secular music grew; according to one frequently recounted story, he was expelled for playing ragtime in church. His career as an entertainer started soon thereafter.

Davenport began, as did many of his peers, by joining a medicine show, a traveling ensemble that offered a mix of music and comedy to audiences across the South. Typically organized by manufacturers of patent medicines, advertisements for which were incorporated into their programs, medicine shows had much in common with vaudeville, and performers routinely moved back and forth between the two. By the 1920s Davenport was doing much of his work under the auspices of the Theater Owners Booking Association (TOBA), a powerful group that controlled a large proportion of the African-American vaudeville market in that segregated era. Among Davenport's most important partners on the TOBA circuit was the vocalist Dora Carr, with whom he performed under the name of Davenport and Company until Carr's marriage around 1928. Davenport then moved to Chicago, Illinois, where he worked as a talent scout for Brunswick and Vocalion, two of the leading producers of what were known at the time as "race records"—a broad term that encompassed all music marketed primarily to African Americans.

Meanwhile, Davenport's own recording career was developing quickly. Many of his first recordings were not records but rolls designed for use in the automatic player pianos popular at the time. By the mid-1920s, however, Davenport was also recording standard-format singles, many of which were later gathered by Document Records into a collection titled *The Accompanist (1924–1929)*. Released in 1993, the album featured a number of tracks with Carr, including "(If You Think You're Gonna Get What I Got) You Got Another Thought Coming to You" and "You Might Pizen [Poison] Me," both of which featured the humorous, slightly off-color lyrics for which vaudeville was famous.

At a Glance . . .

Born Charles Edward Davenport on April 26(?), 1894, in Anniston, AL; died on December 3, 1955, in Cleveland, OH.

Career: Independent musician, 1910s(?)–55.

Davenport was best known for a solo instrumental he wrote called "Cow Cow Blues." He recorded it several times, most prominently for Brunswick in 1928, around the time of his departure from Carr. A light-hearted number with a memorable bass line, it gave a strong boost to his career, in part because it increased his visibility on the vaudeville circuit. Over the following decade, Davenport balanced his work in Chicago with regular appearances at TOBA theaters, often sharing the stage with a fellow pianist named Sammy Price. Around 1938, however, Davenport suffered a severe blow. A stroke left his right hand essentially paralyzed. Unable to play the piano, he relied for a while on purely vocal work. Those gigs were not easy to obtain, however, and by the early 1940s he had been forced to find employment outside the music industry. Although he eventually recovered the use of his hand, he was unable to regain his momentum as a pianist. For the rest of his life, he typically played small, out-of-the-way venues, many of them near his home in Cleveland, Ohio.

The music Davenport had helped to develop exploded in popularity. Once virtually unknown outside the African-American community, boogie-woogie was picked up by white bandleaders such as Freddie Slack around the start of World War II. In 1942 Slack's orchestra released "Cow Cow Boogie," a song that strongly recalled, at least superficially, Davenport's "Cow Cow Blues" of the 1920s. Anchored by the vocals of a young singer named Ella Mae Morse, it reached number one on the national charts, selling enough copies to become the first gold record in the history of the Capitol label, then in its infancy. A wave of boogie-woogie hits followed, including several from the Andrews Sisters, then one of the most popular groups in the country.

Although the boogie-woogie craze was essentially over by the end of the 1940s, many of its essential features—particularly its emphasis on upbeat, dance-friendly rhythms—had a significant influence on later styles, including rock and roll, a genre with deep roots in Cleveland, Davenport's adopted home. Just as the first rock records were reaching the airwaves, thanks in part to the efforts of the Cleveland disc jockey Alan Freed, Davenport's health, which he had never fully recovered after his stroke, took a turn for the worse. On December 3, 1955, he died in Cleveland of circulatory problems. He was 61.

Davenport's death was not widely noticed at the time. In the years since, however, there has been a considerable effort to recognize and honor his contributions. One of the highlights of that ongoing project was the release of the Document Records compilation in 1993. The growth of the Internet has helped as well. As of November of 2013, a recording of "Cow Cow Blues" on YouTube had been accessed more than 14,000 times.

Selected discography

(With Dora Carr) "(If You Think You're Gonna Get What I Got) You Got Another Thought Coming to You," 1920s.
(With Dora Carr) "You Might Pizen [Poison] Me," 1920s.
"Cow Cow Blues," 1928.

Sources

Online

"Big Road Blues Show 4/8/12: House Rent Scuffle— Early Chicago Piano," Big Road Blues, April 8, 2012, http://sundayblues.org/archives/tag/cow -cow-davenport (accessed November 7, 2013).
"Charles Edward (Cow Cow) Davenport," TheBlues Trail.com, http://www.thebluestrail.com/artists/ mus_cd.htm (accessed November 7, 2013).
"Cow Cow Blues (Cow Cow Davenport)," YouTube, http://www.youtube.com/watch?v=-1G9eZcsS14 (accessed November 7, 2013).
Koda, Cub, "Cow Cow Davenport: Artist Biography," AllMusic.com, http://www.allmusic.com/artist/cow -cow-davenport-mn0000169258/biography (accessed November 7, 2013).
Record Fiend, "Cow Cow Davenport—*The Accompanist (1924–1929)* (Document, 1993)," Record Fiend, June 6, 2011, http://record-fiend.blogspot .com/2011/06/cow-cow-davenport-accompanist -1924-1929.html (accessed November 7, 2013).

—R. Anthony Kugler

Ben Davis

1912–2013

Golfer, golf instructor

Ben Davis was an athlete of firsts: the first African American to be admitted to the Michigan section of the Professional Golfers' Association (PGA), he also became, in 1968, the first African-American head golf pro at a municipal course in the United States. He was inducted into the Michigan Golf Hall of Fame in 1992 and the African American Golfers Hall of Fame in 2012. But for Davis it was the game that mattered most. "He really concentrated on the fact of being a good golfer," Davis's great-nephew, Shaun Thomas, told CandGNews.com contributor Jennie Miller at the celebration of Davis's 100th birthday in 2012. "I think maybe he wanted to be a good golfer first, and all that other stuff happened, but he wanted to put his skills at playing golf above that."

Davis died the following year, at age 101. A longtime native of Detroit, Davis's passing was noted in numerous periodicals and online tributes. Writing on MyFox-Detroit.com, Dennis Kraniak noted of Davis, "He was as well respected for his wisdom and demeanor as he was for his prodigious golf game." Thomas added, "He was always respected as a professional, and that's what he always wanted to be, and he was."

Born Erellon Benjamin Davis in 1912 in Pensacola, Florida, the future golf pro was the son of Ellis and Belle Davis and grew up with three brothers and one sister. Early on Davis showed skill on the golf course. However, as a contributor to the *Michigan Chronicle* noted, "Opportunities in the 1920's for African-Americans in golf were virtually non-existent and more along the line of a Bagger Vance, the great caddies that made white

golfers even greater." So it was that Davis's coach at the time, the legendary Toney Penna, a professional golfer and designer of golf clubs, advised his protégé to head to north, where there would be more opportunities for an African-American athlete.

Davis arrived in Detroit in 1925, a high school freshman, and graduated from Northern High School. In 1936 he launched his professional career, becoming a golf instructor at a driving range in the suburb of Ferndale. It would be three more decades before he became a member of the Michigan PGA, however. In 1952 he became a golf instructor at Rackham Golf Course, a municipal course in Huntington Woods. He would stay on at Rackham for more than half a century, eventually making history when he became the first African-American Class A head professional at that club.

Davis married Ruby Nell Day in 1953, and they were together until she died in 2010. Miller quoted Davis in a written statement thanking his wife for all he had achieved: "I owe it all to my wife, Ruby, because she (insisted) on breakfast every morning, some rest at night, (regularly) get your check-ups from your doctor, and keep a cool head." Davis managed to keep a cool head on the links, holding the course record at Rackham for eight years. Throughout his career he had six holes-in-one and also played on the Governor's Cup team for Michigan, winning all of the matches that he participated in. He also instructed professional basketball star Bob Lanier of the Detroit Pistons and boxing champion Joe Louis in the gentle art of golf. Davis was

At a Glance . . .

Born Erellon Benjamin Davis on February 19, 1912, in Pensacola, FL; died on April 9, 2013, in Southfield, MI; son of Ellis and Belle Davis; married Ruby Nell Day, 1953.

Career: Pine Crest Driving Range, Ferndale, MI, golf instructor, beginning 1936; Rackham Golf Course, Huntington Woods, MI, golf instructor, Class A Head Professional, 1952–2002; Palmer Park Golf Course, Detroit, MI, golf instructor.

Memberships: Professional Golfers' Association, Michigan Section.

Awards: Michigan Senior PGA Championship, winner, 1974; U.S. National Senior Tournament, winner, 1979; Golf Man of the Year, March of Dimes, 1981; inducted into Michigan Golf Hall of Fame, 1992; proclamation from the City of Detroit for contributions to the citizens and to the game of golf, 2007; inducted into African American Golfers Hall of Fame, 2012.

already 62 when he won the Michigan Senior PGA Championship, and he was 67 when he took the U.S. National Senior Tournament in Las Vegas.

Davis received many awards for his accomplishments. His fellow golfers honored him in with induction into halls of fame. The Ben Davis Youth Golf Tournament was named in his honor by the City of Detroit Recreation Department in 2000, and in 2007, he was presented with a proclamation commending his work with the city and for the game of golf. Into his and 80s and 90s, Davis was still active, speaking at public courses around Michigan and playing a rounds of golf until he was almost 100.

After his wife died Davis moved into an assisted living home in Southfield, Michigan, where he died on April 9, 2013. Though he was a trailblazer, opening up possibilities for future generations of African-American golfers such as Tiger Woods, Davis was always humble about his accomplishments, according to family members and to others who knew him. "To me what [Davis] really exemplifies is somebody who refused to be held down—he sought out a dream he had in life and he followed through with it," Michigan senator Vince Gregory told Miller.

Sources

Periodicals

Michigan Chronicle, April 18, 2013.

Online

"Dedicated Teacher Ben Davis Passes at 101," Michigan Golf Foundation, http://michigan-golf-foundation.com/text/BEN_DAVIS_OBIT.pdf (accessed November 14, 2013).

Kraniak, Dennis, "Legendary Rackham Golf Club Pro Ben Davis Dies at the Age of 101," MyFoxDetroit .com, http://www.myfoxdetroit.com/story/21991 246/legendary-rackham-golf-club-pro-ben-davis-has - died-at-the-age-of-101 (accessed November 14, 2013).

Leyden, Tom, "Legendary Golf Pro Ben Davis Dies AT 101," WXYZ.com, http://www.wxyz.com/dpp/ sports/legendary-golf-pro-ben-davis-dead-at-101 (accessed November 14, 2013).

Miller, Jennie, "Local Golf Legend, Pioneer Honored on 100th Birthday," CandGNews.com, http://www .candgnews.com/news/local-golf-legend-pioneer -honored-100th-birthday (accessed November 14, 2013).

"Obituary for Erellon Ben Davis," Book of Memories, http://jameshcolefh.frontrunnerpro.com/book-of -memories/1547005/Erellon-Ben-Davis/obituary .php (accessed November 14, 2013).

"Passages: Erellon Ben Davis, February 19, 1912– April 9, 2013," African American Golfer's Digest, http://africanamericangolfersdigest.com/articles/ Erellon_Ben_Davis_Obituary_2013.htm (accessed November 14, 2013).

—J. Sydney Jones

Lois M. DeBerry

1945–2013

Politician

A native of Memphis, Tennessee, Lois M. DeBerry became the second African-American woman to serve in that state's legislature and the first female speaker pro tempore of the Tennessee House of Representatives. During her more than 40 years in office, DeBerry committed herself to speaking for underrepresented members of society, including minorities, women, children, prisoners, senior citizens, and the poor. The second of five children, DeBerry's values for hard work and self-respect were instilled in her by her parents. In 2009 DeBerry was diagnosed with pancreatic cancer; the disease eventually took her life in 2013, six months after she was sworn into the House of Representatives to serve her 20th term.

Became Involved in Civil Rights Movement

The blues music that defined DeBerry's childhood city was born in the cotton fields of the Mississippi Delta. Although slavery had long been abolished by the time DeBerry was born on May 5, 1945, handfuls of former slaves and their descendants could be found in and around Memphis, a city that freed slaves had flocked to in search of work after the Civil War. During DeBerry's childhood the groundwork for the civil rights movement was being laid in Tennessee and throughout the South. The first Tennessee branch of the National Association for the Advancement of Colored People (NAACP) was chartered when DeBerry was three years old. When she was seven, black students were admitted to graduate programs at the University of Tennessee

for the first time. In 1954, when DeBerry was nine, Tennessee governor Frank G. Clement vowed to never integrate public schools; only two years later he enlisted the National Guard to begin school integration. By the time DeBerry was a teenager, her state was fully immersed in the fight for civil rights, and the month that she turned 19, the first Civil Rights Act was passed.

DeBerry became involved in the civil rights movement in the early 1960s, participating in picket lines, sit-ins, and attending the 1963 March on Washington. Her participation was an act of defiance against her parents, who wanted her to stay out of the conflict and focus on her studies. The situation became especially tense when DeBerry joined the 50-mile march from Selma to Montgomery, Alabama, in 1965. Although that decision earned her a punishment from her parents, it confirmed in DeBerry a desire to be a leader for marginalized members of society.

After she graduated from Memphis's LeMoyne-Owen College in 1971, DeBerry took a job as a counselor in a federally funded program, working with African-American families living in housing projects. The job entailed helping children find success in and out of school, a cause that was close to DeBerry's heart. However, the program was underfunded and, as the only African-American counselor, DeBerry found it impossible to make a significant impact. Initially she was disappointed, but she soon realized that she could make a difference if she chose a different career path.

At a Glance . . .

Born Lois Marie DeBerry on May 5, 1945, in Memphis, TN; died on July 28, 2013, in Memphis, TN; daughter of Samuel DeBerry (a truck driver) and Mary Page; married Charles Traughber, April 1, 1981 (chair of the Tennessee state parole board); children: Michael Boyer. *Politics:* Democrat. *Religion:* Baptist. *Education:* LeMoyne-Owen College (Memphis, TN), BA, elementary education, 1971.

Career: Tennessee House of Representatives, 1972–2013 (speaker pro tempore, 1986–2011).

Memberships: Delta Sigma Theta Sorority; The Links, Memphis chapter; National Association for the Advancement of Colored People; National Black Caucus of State Legislators, president emeritus; National Conference of State Legislators; National Organization of Black Law Enforcement Executives; State Legislative Leaders Foundation, board of directors; Tennessee Black Caucus; Women in Government, president and board of directors.

Awards: Labor Roundtable Appreciation Award, National Black Caucus of State Legislators; 100 Most Influential African Americans, *Kansas City (MO) Globe,* 1997; William M. Bugler Excellence in State Legislative Leadership Award, 2000; Legislator of the Year, National Black Caucus of State Legislators, 2003; Women of Excellence, *Tri-State Defender* (Memphis, TN), 2010; Legends Award, Women's Foundation of Memphis, 2010; Governor Ned Ray McWherter Legacy Award, Tennessee Democratic Party, 2011.

Elected to State House

At the age of 27, DeBerry entered the race for a seat representing Tennessee&';s 91st District in the state House of Representatives as a Democrat, the only female out of five candidates. When she won the election, DeBerry became the first black woman from Shelby County ever to serve in the Tennessee House. DeBerry's support from U.S. Representative Harold Ford Sr.—a key factor in her win—was criticized by some. In an article in the Memphis *Tri-State Defender,* fellow candidate George Dowdy proclaimed, "I respect Miss Deberry, but many people didn't know Miss Deberry. They voted on Harold's influence." Speaking of her victory, DeBerry declared her commitment to fellow African Americans, telling Debbie Dennie of the

Tri-State Defender, "The time has come for me to represent my people, not just in my community, but rather in the city and county as well. The time has also come for the State of Tennessee to reckon directly with the people who are responsible for its existence."

With a role model in Barbara Jordan—the first Southern black woman elected to the U.S. House of Representatives—DeBerry held true to her word. In her first session in the House, attesting to her dedication to African Americans and children, she passed a bill that required the history of blacks to be included in Tennessee history books. A champion of the rights of senior citizens, DeBerry soon after sponsored a bill that allowed seniors to attend state colleges and universities for free.

However, being a black woman in the legislature presented considerable challenges. During her first legislative session in 1973, DeBerry was advised by fellow legislators that women had no place in politics. Further, when she took the floor to speak on behalf of adding black history to textbooks, she was heckled by those who insisted that blacks had no history. Crushed, DeBerry rushed out of the chamber in tears. By the following session she had gained greater composure, and DeBerry confidently voiced her concern that all of the new interns that session were white. "The main gripe of Black Caucus is that they did not hire enough Blacks on the legislative staff, last year we had a few scattered here and there; this year we have none," she maintained on the floor. As she later told Susan Saulny of the New Orleans *Times-Picayune* for article about female legislators, "You can't be a little old nice lady. Be aggressive—that's the only way to demand respect."

Made Lasting Impact

DeBerry was reelected to the House in 1975, the same year that she became the first woman and the first black to be appointed to the Tennessee Law Enforcement Commission. That appointment, which gave her a voice in the way law enforcement was organized and run in the state, sparked her interest in the prison population. Visiting the Fort Pillow State Prison that year, DeBerry expressed concerns over the poor conditions for inmates. Among her complaints were the terrible food and the harassment of black inmates by white guards. DeBerry argued that such conditions increased the likelihood of prison riots, as had recently occurred at Tennessee State Prison in Nashville. The following year DeBerry was given the opportunity to make a difference in the matter when she became chair of the House Special Committee on Corrections. DeBerry's dedication to inmates was etched in history when the Lois M. DeBerry Special Needs Facility opened in 1992, providing medical and mental health care to inmates.

In 1986 DeBerry was elected speaker pro tempore, the second most powerful position in the House. Retaining

the title until 2011, she held the position longer than anyone else in Tennessee history. Controversy arose for DeBerry in 2004 amid unusual circumstances. Celebrating her 59th birthday at a casino, DeBerry accepted $200 from an undercover Federal Bureau of Investigation agent posing as a businessman for E-Cycle, a recycling company. The agent offered the money as a birthday gift, which DeBerry immediately lost in the slots. Although E-Cycle had no lobbyists, ethical questions were raised, and DeBerry resigned from a legislative committee on ethics reform. Although she maintained that she had done nothing wrong, she stepped down to save the committee distractions in its work, which she considered extremely important. The matter, never reaching the status of a scandal, diminished as quickly as it arose, and DeBerry returned her focus to the people she served.

"You can't go day by day and at the end of the day you have not made a difference in somebody's life," DeBerry told Betsy Peoples of *Emerge* in 1996. "That's the question that each one of us [should be asking], regardless of whether we are elected, appointed, or just a person in the community." In recognition of her commitment to her political career and her constituents, in May of 2011, the legislature passed House Joint Resolution 516, honoring DeBerry with the title of "speaker pro tempore emeritus."

Diagnosed with pancreatic cancer in 2009 after a colleague noticed that her eyes were jaundiced, DeBerry beat the odds and survived through 2010—80 percent of pancreatic cancer diagnoses end in death within the first year. In December of 2011 DeBerry received a clean bill of health from her doctor and proclaimed that she had "beat cancer." In March of 2012 she was presented with the Governor Ned Ray McWherter Legacy Award for her contributions to public service, an award that she had earned in 2011 but had been too ill to receive. On January 8, 2013, DeBerry was sworn in for a 20th term—the longest tenure ever served in the Tennessee House. Within months, however, her cancer returned, and on July 28, 2013, DeBerry died at the age of 68.

Sources

Books

DeCosta-Willis, Miriam, *Notable Black Memphians,* Cambria Press, 2008.

Periodicals

Commercial Appeal (Memphis, TN), July 28, 2013.
Emerge, November 1996.
New York Beacon, March 10, 1999.
New York Times, July 29, 2013.
Philadelphia Tribune, January 11, 1994.
Times-Picayune (New Orleans, LA), July 25, 1994.
Tri-State Defender (Memphis, TN), July 22, 1972; August 19, 1972; January 19, 1974; October 18, 1975; August 7, 1976; December 7, 1994.

Online

"Democrats Mourn Death of Rep. Lois DeBerry," Tennessee Democratic Party, July 28, 2013, http://tndp.org/blog/2013/07/28/democrats-mourn-death-of-rep-lois-deberry/ (accessed November 27, 2013).

Johnson, Lucas, "Lois DeBerry: Pancreatic Cancer Survivor," KnoxNews.com, December 20, 2011, http://blogs.knoxnews.com/humphrey/2011/12/lois-deberry-pancreatic-cancer.html (accessed December 2, 2013).

"Lois DeBerry Accepts McWherter Legacy Award," Tennessee Democratic Party, March 21, 2012, http://tndp.org/blog/2012/03/21/lois-deberry-accepts-mcwherter-legacy-award/ (accessed December 1, 2013).

"Rep. Lois DeBerry," Tennessee General Assembly, http://www.capitol.tn.gov/house/members/h91.html (accessed November 27, 2013).

"Timeline of Civil Rights in Tennessee," http://orig.jacksonsun.com/civilrights/sec2_tn_timeline.shtml (accessed December 2, 2013).

—Candice Mancini

Aretha Franklin

1942—

Singer, songwriter, pianist

Franklin, Aretha, photograph. Randy Brooke/Getty Images.

Known the world over as the "Queen of Soul," Aretha Franklin is an icon of modern music. Franklin exploded onto the music scene in the late 1960s with a series of recordings that defined the golden age of soul and propelled a phenomenal six-decade career that has influenced generations of singers, from Chaka Khan and Natalie Cole to Whitney Houston, Luther Vandross, Lauryn Hill, and Mary J. Blige. Sales of Franklin's more than 40 studio albums have exceeded 75 million, and the list of her awards and accolades is seemingly endless. She is the winner of 18 competitive and two honorary Grammy Awards. In 1987 she became the first woman inducted into the Rock and Roll Hall of Fame. She received Kennedy Center Honors in 1994, the National Medal of Arts in 1999, and the Presidential Medal of Freedom in 2005. Franklin sang at the inaugurations of Presidents Bill Clinton and Barack Obama and at the funeral for the Reverend Martin Luther King Jr. In 1985 her voice was declared a "natural resource" of her home state of Michigan. In 2012 she was inducted into the Gospel Music Hall of Fame. A *Rolling Stone* feature for November 27, 2008, placed Franklin atop its list of the "100 Greatest Singers of All Time." *New York Times* music critic Jon

Pareles wrote in a July 8, 1989, article, "Aretha Franklin's voice is one of the glories of American music. Lithe and sultry, assertive and caressing, knowing and luxuriant, her singing melts down any divisions between gospel, soul, jazz, and rock, bringing an improvisatory spirit even to the most cut-and-dried pop material."

Started as Gospel-Singing Child Prodigy

The fourth of five children, Franklin was born in Memphis, Tennessee, on March 25, 1942. Her father, Clarence LaVaughn Franklin, was an itinerant Baptist minister, and her mother, Barbara Siggers Franklin, was a gospel singer. When Aretha was a girl, the family relocated, first to Buffalo, New York, and then to Detroit, Michigan, where her father accepted a position as pastor of New Bethel Baptist Church on the city's west side. Reverend Franklin soon became a popular figure in Detroit, attracting thousands of new members to the church with his resounding, emotionally charged sermons. When Aretha was six years old, her parents separated; her mother returned to Buffalo with her oldest brother, Vaughn. In her 1999 autobiography, *Aretha: From*

These Roots, Franklin denied published reports that her mother had abandoned the family: "It is an absolute lie…. She never lost sight of her children or her parenting responsibilities—and her visits continued regularly." Franklin's mother died of a heart attack on March 7, 1952.

Franklin attended Alger Elementary School in Detroit and then Northern High School. Around the age of eight, she began teaching herself to play the piano. She became highly accomplished by mimicking what she heard on the radio and her favorite jazz recordings. By this time her father had become so well known that New Bethel attracted some of the most famous gospel vocalists of the day, including James Cleveland, Mahalia Jackson, and Clara Ward, who sometimes joined in on jam sessions at the Franklin house. Aretha and her two sisters, Erma and Carolyn, also piano players, naturally gravitated toward singing as well.

Franklin was part of the junior choir at New Bethel and sang her first solos in church at age 12. She showed such talent that her father took her on the road with his travelling gospel show. "I travelled from about the age of thirteen to sixteen with my dad, singing with the Roberta Martin Singers, the Clara Ward Singers Caravan—real gospel giants. It was great training," Franklin told biographer Mark Bego. In 1956 Chess Records, which had recorded some of Reverend Franklin's services, released a compilation of Aretha's gospel performances from New Bethel, *Songs of Faith,* her very first album. According to Bego, "The album itself is a true piece of recorded history…. [The] pure and untrained sound of fourteen-year-old Aretha singing hymns and spiritual songs is an amazing preview of the greatness to come."

At age 18, with the music industry changing around her, Franklin made the decision to branch out into secular fare. She was encouraged by family friend Sam Cooke, who had recently crossed over from gospel to pop and scored a huge hit in 1967 with "You Send Me." Already the mother of two sons, Clarence and Edward, Franklin put the boys in the care of her paternal grandmother, Rachel, so that she could pursue her dreams of a musical career. She moved to New York City, hired a manager, and signed with legendary talent scout John Hammond of Columbia Records.

Topped the Record Charts

Franklin's first Columbia album, *The Great Aretha Franklin,* was released in the fall of 1960. Five years and eight albums later, Franklin had achieved some modest success in the R&B market, but much of her material struggled to find an audience. The Columbia period produced only one pop hit, a version of the jazz standard "Rock-a-Bye Your Baby with a Dixie Melody" that peaked at number 37 on the charts. "I cherish the recordings we made together," Hammond is quoted in Jerry Wexler and David Ritz's *Rhythm and the Blues,* "but, finally, Columbia was a white company [that] misunderstood her genius."

In 1966 Franklin, with her new manager and husband, Ted White, moved over to Atlantic Records, working with producer Jerry Wexler. The savvy Wexler would shepherd Franklin to fame over the next decade by encouraging her to bring the passion of gospel into her R&B and soul recordings. Wexler had Franklin accompany herself on the piano and backed her with a funky

Memphis rhythm section and vocals provided either by her sisters Carolyn and Erma or by the group the Sweet Inspirations, which featured Cissy Houston, the mother of future singing star Whitney Houston. Wexler also brought in young rock lions such as guitarists Duane Allman and Eric Clapton for guest spots.

Franklin's 1967 Atlantic debut, *I Never Loved a Man (the Way I Love You),* sold more than one million copies and showcased the heartfelt title track, the rollicking "Baby I Love You," and the legendary "Respect," Franklin's blistering remake of the Otis Redding classic that has long been synonymous with her name. More top-10 hits followed the same year with Franklin's second Atlantic release, *Aretha Arrives,* most notably the pounding groove "Chain of Fools" and the tender "(You Make Me Feel Like) A Natural Woman."

In 1968 Franklin had another blockbuster year. She toured Europe and released three top-selling albums, including *Aretha Now,* containing the supercharged "Think," which she wrote with her husband, and "I Say a Little Prayer," a song originally written for Dionne Warwick by Burt Bacharach and Hal David. That same year Franklin won the first two of her many Grammy Awards for "Respect." The song came along at a crucial point for black activism, feminism, and sexual liberation and was embraced as an anthem of social protest. According to the Rock and Roll Hall of Fame, 1968 is significant as well as the year Aretha "was anointed the Queen of Soul. Legendary deejay Pervis Spann, the Blues Man, did the honors, ceremoniously placing a crown atop her head during a performance at Chicago's Regal Theater."

Dominated the Grammy Awards

A *Time* magazine cover story devoted to Franklin on June 28, 1968, described her vocal technique as "a direct, natural style of delivery that ranges over a full four octaves, and the breath control to spin out long phrases that curl sinuously around the beat and dangle tantalizingly from blue notes. But what really accounts for her impact goes beyond technique: it is her fierce, gritty conviction. She flexes her rich, cutting voice like a whip; she lashes her listeners—in her words—'to the bone, for deepness'…. She does not seem to be performing so much as bearing witness to a reality so simple and compelling that she could not possibly fake it." The *Time* story also suggested that Franklin's achingly powerful lyrics found their source in her turbulent personal life and the private demons of which she rarely spoke. There were reports that her husband beat her and that he had shot a production manager. By 1969 Franklin had divorced White and was rumored to have developed a drinking problem. That same year her father was arrested for possessing marijuana, and New Bethel was the site of a racially charged incident in which one police officer was killed and another wounded during a shootout with members of a black separatist group.

Amid all of the turmoil, the hits continued. Franklin won eight Grammy Awards between 1969 and 1975, including one for the 1972 gospel recording *Amazing Grace,* which sold more than two million copies. Among the many hit songs from this period are "Rock Steady," "Day Dreaming," and a cover of Simon and Garfunkel's "Bridge Over Troubled Water." By the end of the decade, however, Franklin's sound was being eclipsed by disco. She attempted to attract the disco audience with 1979's *La Diva,* but the album sold fewer than 50,000 copies, and Atlantic opted to let her contract lapse.

More personal turmoil accompanied the professional disappointments. Franklin's father was shot by a burglar during a home invasion on June 10, 1979. The shooting left Reverend Franklin in a coma from which he never recovered, and he died on July 27, 1984. In February of that year, Franklin divorced her second husband, actor Glynn Turman, whom she had married in 1978.

Achieved Crossover Success

Franklin's attention-grabbing cameo appearance in the 1980 movie *The Blues Brothers,* starring John Belushi and Dan Ackroyd, helped fuel mainstream interest in 1960s soul and inaugurated an upswing in her career. Moving to Clive Davis's Arista Records, Franklin profited from the label's slick production and commercial choice of material. The song "United Together," which appeared on her first Arista album, *Aretha* (1980), was a number three R&B hit, and Franklin won a Grammy Award in 1982 for her cover of Sam and Dave's "Hold On, I'm Comin'," from *Love All the Hurt Away* (1981). *Jump to It* (1982) was Franklin's first gold record in seven years. *Who's Zoomin' Who* (1985) went platinum, propelled by the hugely popular "Freeway of Love." Franklin scored another big hit with the single "I Knew You Were Waiting for Me," a duet with George Michael that reached number one on the adult contemporary charts in both England and the United States. More duets, with artists including Elton John and Whitney Houston, closed out the decade, which also featured a return to gospel with the Grammy-winning *One Lord, One Faith, One Baptism* (1987), an album recorded at New Bethel Baptist Church.

In a May 15, 1992, *Entertainment Weekly* piece, Dave DiMartino praised Franklin's single "If I Lose," her contribution to the soundtrack for the 1992 comedy *White Men Can't Jump,* as a striking reminder of her glory days at Atlantic, before she had become "conspicuously 'modernized'" by a string of producers at Arista. DiMartino was not alone in preferring the Queen of Soul to the "Queen of Duets," as he called Arista's overproduced version of Franklin, and sales of her records faltered throughout the 1990s until the appearance of *A Rose Is Still a Rose* (1998), her first gold album in more than a decade. With tracks pro-

duced by rising stars Sean "Puffy" Combs (later known as P. Diddy) and Lauryn Hill, *A Rose Is Still a Rose* showed that Franklin could keep up with current hip-hop sounds. Also contributing to Franklin's resurgence was her performance at the 1998 Grammy Awards, where she filled in at the last minute for ailing tenor Luciano Pavarotti with a stellar performance of the aria "Nessun dorma" from Giacomo Puccini's opera *Turandot.*

Franklin followed *A Rose Is Still a Rose* in 2003 with *So Damn Happy,* which featured collaborations with such contemporary stars as Mary J. Blige and Troy Taylor and veterans Earl Klugh and Burt Bacharach. Shortly after the release of *So Damn Happy,* Franklin left Arista to start her own label, Aretha Records. Her first album on the independent label, *A Woman Falling Out of Love,* did not appear until May of 2011, following a long period of health problems that resulted in surgery for an undisclosed illness in December of 2010. Franklin remained tight-lipped about her health issues, and rumors circulated that she was suffering from pancreatic cancer. However, the general consensus is that she underwent gastric bypass surgery and experienced severe complications. Since 2011 the singer has shed more than 80 pounds and adopted a regular exercise routine. Although she appears healthier than she has in years, her performance schedule has been only sporadic, and she has postponed several concert dates, citing lingering medical problems. Brian McCollum reported in *USA Today* on October 16, 2013, that Franklin was set to begin recording a new album in Detroit for RCA Records, teamed once again with her former Arista mentor, Clive Davis.

Selected discography

Albums

Songs of Faith, Chess Records, 1956.
The Great Aretha Franklin, Columbia, 1960.
The Electrifying Aretha Franklin, Columbia, 1962.
The Tender, the Moving, the Swinging Aretha Franklin, Columbia, 1962.
Laughing on the Outside, Columbia, 1963.
Runnin' Out of Fools, Columbia, 1964.
Unforgettable: A Tribute to Dinah Washington, Columbia, 1964.
Soul Sister, Columbia, 1966.
Aretha Arrives (includes "[You Make Me Feel Like] A Natural Woman" and "Chain of Fools"), Atlantic, 1967.
Aretha Franklin's Greatest Hits, Columbia, 1967.
I Never Loved a Man (the Way I Love You) (includes "I Never Loved a Man [the Way I Love You]," "Baby I Love You," and "Respect"), Atlantic, 1967.
Aretha in Paris, Atlantic, 1968.
Aretha Now (includes "Think" and "I Say a Little Prayer"), Atlantic, 1968.
Lady Soul, Atlantic, 1968.

Aretha's Gold, Atlantic, 1969.
Soul '69, Atlantic, 1969.
This Girl's in Love with You, Atlantic, 1970.
Aretha Live at Fillmore West (includes "Bridge Over Troubled Water"), Atlantic, 1971.
Amazing Grace, Atlantic, 1972.
In the Beginning/The World of Aretha Franklin 1960-1967, Columbia, 1972.
Young, Gifted and Black (includes "Rock Steady" and "Day Dreaming"), Atlantic, 1972.
Hey Now Hey (The Other Side of the Sky), Atlantic, 1973.
Let Me in Your Life, Atlantic, 1974.
With Everything I Feel in Me, Atlantic, 1975.
Sparkle (soundtrack), Atlantic, 1976.
Sweet Passion, Atlantic, 1977.
Ten Years of Gold, Atlantic, 1977.
Almighty Fire, Atlantic, 1978.
La Diva, Atlantic, 1979.
Aretha (includes "United Together"), Arista, 1980.
Love All the Hurt Away (includes "Hold On, I'm Comin'"), Arista, 1981.
Jump to It, Arista, 1982.
Get It Right, Arista, 1984.
Who's Zoomin' Who? (includes "Freeway of Love"), Arista, 1985.
Aretha, Arista, 1987.
One Lord, One Faith, One Baptism, Arista, 1987.
Through the Storm, Arista, 1989.
What You See Is What You Sweat, Arista, 1991.
Queen of Soul: The Atlantic Recordings, Atlantic, 1992.
Greatest Hits: 1980–1994, Arista, 1994.
A Rose Is Still a Rose, Arista, 1998.
So Damn Happy, Arista, 2003.
This Christmas, DMI, 2009.
A Woman Falling Out of Love, Aretha, 2011.

Recordings with other artists

"Think," *The Blues Brothers* (soundtrack), Atlantic, 1980.
"Jumpin' Jack Flash," *Jumpin' Jack Flash* (soundtrack), Mercury Records, 1986.
(With George Michael) "I Knew You Were Waiting (for Me)", Arista, 1987.
"If I Lose," *White Men Can't Jump* (soundtrack), EMI, 1992.
"The Makings of You," *All Men Are Brothers: A Tribute to Curtis Mayfield,* Warner Brothers, 1994.
Jewels in the Crown: All-Star Duets with the Queen, Arista, 2007.

Films

The Blues Brothers, Universal Pictures, 1980.
Blues Brothers 2000, Universal Pictures, 1998.

Books

(With David Ritz) *Aretha: From These Roots,* Villard, 1999.

Sources

Books

Bego, Mark, *Aretha Franklin: The Queen of Soul,* Da Capo Press, 2001.

Dobkin, Matt, *I Never Loved a Man the Way I Love You: Aretha Franklin, Respect, and the Making of a Soul Masterpiece,* St. Martin's Press, 2004.

Gourse, Leslie, *Aretha Franklin, Lady Soul,* Franklin Watts, 1995.

Rees, Dafydd, and Luke Crampton, *Rock Movers & Shakers: An A–Z of People Who Made Rock Happen,* Billboard, 1991.

Werner, Craig Hansen, *Higher Ground: Stevie Wonder, Aretha Franklin, Curtis Mayfield, and the Rise and Fall of American Soul,* Crown, 2004.

Wexler, Jerry, and David Ritz, *Rhythm and the Blues: A Life in American Music,* Alfred A. Knopf, 1993.

Periodicals

Billboard, February 9, 2008.
Buffalo News, September 28, 1999.
Entertainment Weekly, May 15, 1992.
Guardian (London), April 27, 2011.
Kansas City (MO) Star, May 5, 2012.
Newsweek, March 12, 2012.
New York Times, December 13, 1987; July 8, 1989; June 28, 1996; September 28, 2003; November 4, 2007.
People, May 2, 2011, 58.
Rolling Stone, November 27, 2008.
Sacramento Observer, March 30, 1994.
Time, June 28, 1968.
USA Today, October 16, 2013.

Online

"Aretha Franklin Biography," Rock and Roll Hall of Fame, http://rockhall.com/inductees/aretha-franklin/bio/ (accessed January 13, 2014).

"Aretha Franklin: Interviews and Profiles, News, Reviews," NPR Music, http://www.npr.org/artists/15662553/aretha-franklin (accessed January 13, 2014).

—Janet Mullane

Curtis Fuller

1934—

Jazz trombonist

The trombonist Curtis Fuller has been delighting jazz fans around the world since the 1950s. Known for his bright tone and technical brilliance, he has worked closely with dozens of the genre's biggest stars, including the saxophonist John Coltrane and the drummer Art Blakey. "Fuller is his own man," the critic Leo T. Sullivan once wrote, adding, "His melodic ideas are inventive and immaculately executed, with a fast and definitive articulation." The saxophonist Gigi Gryce echoed that sentiment, noting, in a comment later quoted by Eric B. Olsen, "Curtis has buckets and buckets and tons of soul."

Fuller, Curtis, photograph. David Redfern/Redferns/Getty Images.

Born in Detroit, Michigan, on December 15, 1934, Curtis DuBois Fuller was drawn to music at an early age. In a 2007 interview with Molly Murphy of the National Endowment for the Arts, he recalled watching with interest as a teacher gave his older sister piano lessons. Absorbing all he heard, he practiced later on his own. "My sister had no idea that I was sneaking these little exercises," he told Murphy. "I learned to play ... and I loved music from that point on."

Fuller's life changed dramatically in the early 1940s, when his mother, who had been raising the family

single-handedly, died. Sent with his sister to one of the Detroit area's largest orphanages, Fuller struggled to find his place until one of his teachers, a nun who knew of his interest in music, took him to see a swing band led by Illinois Jacquet, a saxophonist who at that time was working closely with the trombonist J. J. Johnson. Deeply impressed by Johnson's dazzling performance on what is widely considered one of the most difficult horns to master, Fuller took up the trombone himself in his mid-teens, and within a few years he was making rapid progress. Thanks in part to the strength of the music programs in Detroit's public school system, the city was home to dozens of extraordinarily gifted teenagers, many of whom went on to play with Fuller professionally. "There was a lot of love and real closeness," Fuller told Murphy, describing his relationship with such fellow Detroiters as the trumpeter Donald Byrd and the pianist Tommy Flanagan. When his recording career began, Fuller added, "I wanted to use the Detroit guys because I knew them."

After high school Fuller spent several years in the U.S. Army, where he had the good fortune to be assigned to a band that included the saxophonist Cannonball

Adderley. Following his discharge, Fuller returned to Detroit, where he worked with the guitarist Kenny Burrell and the multi-instrumentalist Yusuf Lateef before moving to New York City in the mid-1950s. Fuller's arrival there roughly coincided with the emergence of hard bop, a variety of jazz that mixed the improvisational solos characteristic of the genre with rhythms and melodies from gospel and the blues.

In the months that followed, Fuller worked with many of the new style's leading figures, including Coltrane, whom he backed on *Blue Train* (1957), widely regarded as a landmark album. Also during this period Fuller began releasing albums under his own name; among the most significant of these was *The Opener,* released on the Blue Note label in 1957. The album was completed with the help of a stellar backing group that included the bassist Paul Chambers, the drummer Art Taylor, the pianist Bobby Timmons, and the saxophonist Hank Mobley. Stephen Thomas Erlewine of AllMusic.com described *The Opener* as "a thoroughly impressive affair." Other important partners in this period included Bud Powell, a troubled but immensely gifted pianist, and Benny Golson, a saxophonist in an influential group called the Jazztet, with whom Fuller worked from 1959 to about 1961, when he left to join the Jazz Messengers.

Fuller's four-year tenure (1961–65) with the Messengers, a cutting-edge group led by Blakey, is widely regarded as one of the highlights of his career. His trombone can be heard on several of the long-lived ensemble's most significant albums, including *Buhaina's Delight* (1963), which was anchored by a piece Fuller wrote ("Bu's Delight"). Blakey was well-known for encouraging his band members to compose, and Fuller took full advantage of that supportive environment, contributing pieces in a variety of tempos and moods. Arguably the most prominent of these, next to "Bu's Delight," was "Time Off," which appeared on the Messengers' popular live album *Ugetsu* (1963).

After leaving the Messengers, Fuller toured and recorded with such leading figures as the trumpeter and bandleader Dizzy Gillespie, with whom Fuller played a series of gigs in Europe in the late 1960s. Although Fuller continued to be associated with hard bop, he explored a variety of new approaches as well, particularly the electrically amplified style that came to be known as fusion. Working closely with the bassist Stanley Clarke and other fusion aficionados, Fuller completed an album called *Crankin'* in 1973. *Crankin'* illustrated the strengths and weaknesses of the new style in a forceful and dramatic fashion. By the 1980s, however, Fuller had largely returned to the sounds with which he had begun his career, working once again with Golson, Blakey, and other hard-bop pioneers. An honored figure at jazz festivals around the world, Fuller released a number of albums in the 1990s and early 2000s, including *Together in Monaco* (1996), a joint project with the saxophonist Paul Jeffrey, and *Up Jumped Spring* (2004), completed with the help of the trumpeter Brad Goode. In 2011 Fuller released *The Story of Cathy & Me,* a touching tribute to his late wife.

As he approached his eighties, Fuller was no longer as active professionally as he had been just a few years earlier. He retained his status, however, as one of the most revered figures in jazz. A particularly clear indication of his stature came in 2007, when the National Endowment for the Arts, an independent agency of the federal government, awarded him a Jazz Masters Fellowship, widely considered the genre's most prestigious honor. In a brief tribute on its website, the agency expressed the consensus of critics around the world, praising Fuller as "a remarkably fluent trombonist" with an "impeccable sense of time."

Selected discography

John Coltrane, *Blue Train,* Blue Note, 1957.
The Opener, Blue Note, 1957.
Art Blakey and the Jazz Messengers, *Buhaina's Delight* (includes "Bu's Delight"), Blue Note, 1963.
Art Blakey and the Jazz Messengers, *Ugetsu* (includes "Time Off"), Riverside, 1963.
Crankin', Mainstream, 1973.
(With Paul Jeffrey) *Together in Monaco,* Amosaya, 1996.
(With Brad Goode) *Up Jumped Spring,* Delmark, 2004.
The Story of Cathy & Me, Challenge, 2011.

Sources

Online

"Curtis Fuller: Bio," National Endowment for the Arts, http://arts.gov/honors/jazz/curtis-fuller (accessed November 9, 2013).
Erlewine, Stephen Thomas, "Curtis Fuller: *The Opener,*" AllMusic.com, accessed November 13, 2013).

Murphy, Molly, "Curtis Fuller: Interview by Molly Murphy for the NEA," National Endowment for the Arts, January 11, 2007, http://arts.gov/honors/jazz/curtis-fuller (accessed November 9, 2013).

Olsen, Eric B., and Michael Cuscuna, "Curtis Fuller," Hard Bop Homepage, http://hardbop.tripod.com/fuller.html (accessed November 9, 2013).

Sullivan, Leo T., "Curtis Fuller—Jazz Trombonist," CurtisFuller.net, http://www.curtisfuller.net/ (accessed November 9, 2013).

Wynn, Ron, "Curtis Fuller: Artist Biography," AllMusic.com, http://www.allmusic.com/artist/curtis-fuller-mn0000139566/biography (accessed November 9, 2013).

—R. Anthony Kugler

Red Garland

1923–1984

Jazz pianist

Garland, Red, photograph. GAB Archive/Redferns/Getty Images.

Although he was never as well known to the general public as some of his band mates, the pianist Red Garland was revered by critics and jazz aficionados around the world. Largely self-taught, he was admired for his innovative use of "block chords"—so named because they are played by the left and right hands in unison. While he is probably best remembered for his collaborations with the trumpeter Miles Davis in the mid-1950s, Garland also had a flourishing solo career for many years. Many of the albums he released under his own name are considered classics. "Red Garland has the sublime virtue of swing," noted the critic Ralph J. Gleason, in a comment quoted on the website of the Concord Music Group (CMG), "and a solid, deep groove."

William M. Garland, known as "Red" from an early age, was born on May 13, 1923, in Dallas, Texas. The son of an elevator operator, he turned to music as a child, taking up the clarinet and the saxophone. Much of his work on the sax was done under the tutelage of Buster Smith, a gifted stylist whose protégés also included the jazz legend Charlie Parker. Although Garland made rapid progress, quickly developing his own sense of rhythm, his efforts were interrupted in the early 1940s, when he was conscripted into the U.S. Army for several years of wartime service. It was then that he switched decisively to the piano, having been inspired to do so by a fellow soldier at an army base in Arizona. He had a few informal teachers in this period but essentially taught himself, in part by studying the recordings of such piano pioneers as Art Tatum.

After his discharge from the military, Garland returned to the Dallas area, where he began playing the piano professionally, often backing a saxophonist named Bill Blocker. Garland's major break came soon thereafter, when he auditioned successfully for a touring trumpeter named Hot Lips Page, who took Garland to New York City. When his engagement with Page was over, Garland found steady work in New York's many bars and nightclubs, where his partners included the bandleader Billy Eckstine and the saxophonist Eddie "Lockjaw" Davis. As his reputation grew, Garland began to receive job offers from farther afield, and in 1947 he moved to Philadelphia, Pennsylvania, to become house pianist at a famous club called the Blue Note. His work

At a Glance . . .

Born William M. Garland on May 13, 1923, in Dallas, TX; died on April 23, 1984, in Dallas, TX. *Military service:* U.S. Army, 1940s.

Career: Independent musician, 1940s–84; played with Miles Davis, mid-1950s.

there brought him into contact with a number of major stars, among them Davis, who soon tried to recruit Garland for a new group. At first Garland declined the offer, focusing instead on his freelance career and on an existing engagement with the saxophonist Lester Young, also a major figure. Around 1955, however, Garland's schedule finally meshed with Davis's, and the two began working together in a new quintet that included the drummer Philly Joe Jones, the bassist Paul Chambers, and the saxophonist John Coltrane.

Remembered in part for the soaring solos of Davis and Coltrane, the group worked steadily, releasing a string of influential albums between 1955 and Garland's departure roughly three years later. His tasteful, restrained style on the piano played a significant role in the success of such recordings as *Cookin' with the Miles Davis Quintet,* released by Prestige Records in 1957. Featuring one of Garland's own compositions ("Blues by Five"), *Cookin'* included "some of these musicians' finest moments," wrote the reviewer Lindsay Planer of AllMusic.com. "The immediate yet somewhat understated ability of each musician to react with ingenuity and precision," noted Planer, "is expressed in the consistency and singularity of each solo as it is maintained from one musician to the next without the slightest deviation."

Around 1958 Garland left the quintet to focus on his nascent solo career. A few of his best-known works as a leader, notably *Red Garland's Piano* (1957), were released when he was still with Davis, but most followed his departure. Typically working with just a bassist (often Chambers) and a drummer behind him, Garland completed a string of highly regarded albums in the late 1950s and early 1960s. Among the most prominent of these were *Red Alone,* a collection of ballads released in 1960, and *When There Are Grey Skies,* completed two years later with the help of the drummer Charlie Persip and the bassist Wendell Marshall.

Garland worked steadily until the mid-1960s, when his career began to be affected by various shifts in public taste, arguably the most significant of which was a growing preference for so-called free jazz. Like many musicians of his generation, Garland disliked the new style, which eschewed the traditional structures of melody and harmony in favor of near-constant improvisation. That shift occurred as the jazz world as a whole was contracting, pressured in part by the rise of R&B and rock. As his bookings declined, Garland began to think about retirement. Around 1968 he moved back to Dallas and quietly reentered private life, where he remained for roughly eight years. In 1976 he made a tentative return by playing some local gigs. The positive response those generated led to a resumption of touring and recording. By the late 1970s there were growing signs of renewed interest in classic jazz, and for the remainder of his life, Garland enjoyed strong support from fans and critics alike.

Although his recording schedule was somewhat less hectic in this period than it had been several decades earlier, Garland remained active in the studio, releasing several major albums. Among the most prominent of these was a collection of standards called *Misty Red* (1982). Roughly two years after its release, on April 23, 1984, Garland died of a heart attack in his hometown of Dallas. News of his passing prompted tributes from fans and colleagues around the world, several of whom recalled, in particular, the joy he had expressed on his return to the jazz world in the 1970s. "It put some sense into me," he once said of his return, in a comment quoted by CMG. "I thought jazz was all finished, but now I see there are still people who love jazz…. I'll stay out here as long as the reception stays as beautiful as it's been."

Selected discography

Red Garland's Piano, Prestige, 1957.
Miles Davis, *Cookin' with the Miles Davis Quintet* (includes "Blues by Five"), Prestige, 1957.
Red Alone, Prestige, 1960.
When There Are Grey Skies, Prestige, 1962.
Misty Red, Timeless, 1982.

Sources

Online

"About Red Garland," Concord Music Group, http://www2.concordmusicgroup.com/artists/red-garland/ (accessed October 26, 2013).

Myers, Marc, "Red Garland and Charlie Parker," Jazz Wax.com, February 12, 2010, http://www.jazzwax.com/2010/02/red-garland-and-charlie-parker.html (accessed October 26, 2013).

Planer, Lindsay, *"Cookin' with the Miles Davis Quintet:* Review," AllMusic.com, http://www.allmusic.com/album/cookin-with-the-miles-davis-quintet-mw0000649470 (accessed October 30, 2013).

Simpson, Joel, "Red Garland," AllAboutJazz.com, October 24, 2013, http://musicians.allaboutjazz.com/musician.php?id=6951#.UmvXVJ3D_IV (accessed October 26, 2013).

Yanow, Scott, "Red Garland: Biography," AllMusic

.com, http://www.allmusic.com/artist/red-garland -mn0000882950/biography (accessed October 26, 2013).

—R. Anthony Kugler

Geto Boys

Rap group

The Houston-based rap group the Geto Boys earned notoriety in the early 1990s for their violent and explicit lyrics, which touched on misogyny, necrophilia, and psychotic experiences, rivaling even 2 Live Crew as the most hated rappers in America. When Geffen Records refused to release their 1990 album *The Geto Boys,* the group suddenly found themselves at the center of a national debate over graphic rap lyrics. Nevertheless, the Geto Boys were pioneers of the "Dirty South" brand of rap, and two of their tracks, "Mind of a Lunatic" and "Mind Playing Tricks on Me," are regarded today as rap classics, in spite of—or perhaps because of—their graphic and (to some) offensive lyrics.

Geto Boys, photograph. Orlando Garcia/Getty Images.

Scarface (Brad Jordan) and "Willie D" Dennis. Born in Houston in 1970, Scarface had begun his rap career as Akshun before joining the Geto Boys. Born in 1966, Willie D was a boxer as well as a rapper.

Early in 1990 the Geto Boys released *Grip It! On That Other Level* on the Rap-a-Lot label. It caught the attention of Rick Rubin, a producer and music executive known for his work in both rap (Run-D.M.C., Public Enemy, and the Beastie Boys) and heavy metal (Slayer). Rubin took 10 of the 12 tracks on that album, re-recorded some of the vocals, and put them in a different order. He made the record into a self-titled album and ditched the awkward cover photo for four black-and-white mug shots. Rubin was set to release the result on Geffen Records, but the graphic nature of the lyrics prompted the label to renege on the deal—largely as a result of pressure from Tipper Gore, the wife of soon-to-be vice president Al Gore, and her Parents Music Resource Center. In October of 1990 Giant Records distributed *The Geto Boys,* which bore this message from Rubin's label: "Def American Recordings is opposed to censorship. Our manufacturer and distributor, however, do not condone or endorse the content of this recording, which they find violent, sexist, racist, and indecent."

The Geto Boys (originally Ghetto Boys) formed in Houston, Texas, in 1986, at a time when hip-hop music was primarily coming from the two coasts. The group's original lineup, put together by James "Lil' J" Smith for his Rap-a-Lot label, comprised Prince Johnny C, the Slim Jukebox, and DJ Ready Red. Their 1988 debut *Making Trouble* fizzled, and Prince Johnny C and the Slim Jukebox soon quit the group. Smith added Bushwick Bill (born Richard Shaw in Jamaica in 1966 and raised in the Bushwick neighborhood of Brooklyn), a dwarf who had been introducing the band onstage, to the lineup. He was joined by

The final track on *Grip It!*, "Mind of a Lunatic," featured violent, unprintable lyrics, which only fueled a national debate about explicit rap music that had begun the previous year following the release of 2 Live Crew's album *As Nasty As They Wanna Be.* The controversy intensified when the lawyer of two Kansas teenagers who were on trial for murder claimed that the defendants were "temporarily hypnotized" by "Mind of a Lunatic." Pundits from all sides of the culture wars weighed in on whether the misogynistic and cruel lyrics represented a harmless fantasy, the genuine inner lives of urban African-American males, or a crass marketing gimmick meant to sell more albums.

Speaking to the *Los Angeles Times,* Bushwick Bill defended the lyrics, arguing that they reflected the group's reality. "This is the reality I've seen on the news and around me growing up: *Texas Chainsaw Massacre* and Freddie Krueger [of *Nightmare on Elm Street*]. When I turn on the TV there's always someone getting raped, someone getting killed." Writing in the *New York Times,* music critic Jon Pareles described their first major-label album: "With songs about mutilation, rape and murder, graphically described and shouted over ominous funk, it makes the 2 Live Crew's lewd scenarios sound like a society luncheon." Pareles conceded that the world sketched by the Geto Boys was terrifying, concluding, "If it weren't scary, it would be a lie."

A violent episode in the life of Bushwick Bill both fueled the band's myth and revealed the extent of the Geto Boys' real-life traumas. As chronicled in the song "Ever So Clear," Bill became suicidal after drinking too much one night in May of 1991. He asked his girlfriend to shoot him, but she refused, and a scuffle ensued. The gun went off, and he lost his eye. A photo of Bill in the hospital, flanked by his band mates, made the cover of their summer release *We Can't Be Stopped* (1991).

Critics considered the album uneven at best, but it did contain a bona fide hip-hop classic in "Mind Playing Tricks on Me." The first-person account of the life of a man who, in Scarface's verse, "sleep[s] with my finger on the trigger," is set to a catchy sample from Isaac Hayes's "Hung Up On My Baby." The single made it to number one on the rap chart and number 23 on the Billboard Hot 100. The song and its video conclude with Bushwick Bill realizing that the man that he thought he was punching in the face was just a hallucination: "My hands were all bloody from punchin' on the concrete." Scarface told an interviewer that his

grandmother had come up with the title and explicitly connected the song to drug use and paranoia. In 2012 *Rolling Stone* ranked "Mind Playing Tricks on Me" as the fifth-greatest hip-hop song of all time.

The Geto Boys toured intermittently and issued albums sporadically in the following years, most notably, 1996's *The Resurrection,* which critic Stephen Thomas Erlewine of AllMusic.com hailed as "the leanest, meanest, and funkiest thing they've ever recorded." In 2005, after another seven-year separation, the three rappers reunited for the album *The Foundation.*

By the early 1990s all three members of the Geto Boys had begun solo careers. Willie D released several solo records, including *Play Witcha Mama* (1994) and *Loved by Few, Hated by Many* (2000), and ran into legal troubles around an incident of assault. Bushwick Bill was arrested on a drug possession charge in 2010, and deportation proceedings were initiated, but he eventually was granted legal permanent resident status. Around this time he publicly gave up rapping about sex and violence, embracing instead a born-again Christian outlook in his life and music. Scarface, whom comedian Chris Rock once called "the most underrated rapper of all time," issued several successful solo albums and gradually spent more time on the business side of music, serving as coordinator and president of Def Jam South and stewarding the career of rapper Ludacris. "The first four or five lines have got to be memorable," said Scarface in a 2013 interview. "If you ain't crying when the song is done, you ain't wrote the right record."

Selected discography

Making Trouble, Rap-a-Lot, 1988.
Grip It! On That Other Level (includes "Mind of a Lunatic"), Rap-a-Lot, 1989.
The Geto Boys (includes "Mind of a Lunatic"), Rap-a-Lot, 1990.
We Can't Be Stopped (includes "Mind Playing Tricks on Me"), Rap-a-Lot, 1991.
Till Death Do Us Part, Rap-a-Lot, 1993.
The Resurrection, Rap-a-Lot, 1996.
Da Good da Bad & da Ugly, Rap-a-Lot, 1998.
The Foundation, Rap-a-Lot, 2005.

Sources

Periodicals

Los Angeles Times, July 22, 1990.
New York Times, October 7, 1990.
Rolling Stone, October 22, 2004.
XXL, October 22, 2010.

Online

"Best Of Hard Knock TV: Scarface Talks Writing Process, Rick Rubin, Geto Boys Album, Mind Playing Tricks on Me," YouTube, April 22, 2013, http://

www.youtube.com/watch?v=l4x7bhUR_H8 (accessed January 20, 2014).

Erlewine, Stephen Thomas, "Geto Boys: *The Resurrection,*" AllMusic.com, http://www.allmusic.com/album/the-resurrection-mw0000180254 (accessed January 20, 2014).

Koshkin, Brett, "How Tipper Gore Helped the Geto Boys Popularize Southern Rap," *Sound of the City* (*Village Voice* blog), June 20, 2013, http://blogs.villagevoice.com/music/2013/06/tipper_gore_vs _geto_boys.php (accessed January 20, 2014).

Mack, Bayer L., "Willie D.: Knuckle Up," HipHopDX.com, December 29, 2004, http://www.hiphopdx.com/index/interviews/id.351/title.willie-d-knuckle-up (accessed January 20, 2014).

"Top 25 Albums," ChrisRock.com, http://www.chrisrock.com/category/top-25-albums (accessed January 20, 2014).

—Mark Swartz

L. C. Greenwood

1946–2013

Professional football player

Greenwood, L. C., photograph. George Gojkovich/Getty Images.

Defensive end L. C. Greenwood is remembered as a star of the Pittsburgh Steelers' famed "Steel Curtain" in the 1970s, a fearsome defensive line that was among the best in National Football League (NFL) history. The Steel Curtain—made up of the "front four" of Greenwood, "Mean Joe" Greene, Ernie "Fats" Holmes, and Dwight "Mad Dog" White—was the mainstay of the Steelers dynasty in the 1970s, which won six division championships and four Super Bowls in a six-year span. At six feet, six inches and nearly 250 pounds, Greenwood cut a formidable figure on the defensive line. A master of the quarterback sack, he racked up 73.5 in his 13-year NFL career (1969–81), all of which he played for the Steelers. Known for his flair on and off the field, Greenwood took to wearing specially designed gold high-top cleats (the Steelers' colors are black and gold), and he continued to don gold sneakers long after his playing career was over. Despite his impressive statistics—he was twice named an All-Pro and was selected to six Pro Bowls—Greenwood has not been elected to the Pro Football Hall of Fame, to the consternation of his fans and former teammates.

Played Football for Fun

L. C. Henderson Greenwood was born on September 8, 1946, in rural Canton, Mississippi, the eldest of nine children. In his book *About Three Bricks Shy of a Load*, about the Steelers' 1973 season, Roy Blount Jr. noted that Greenwood had once told him that his initials stood for "Lover Cool," but in later interviews, the defensive end admitted that the letters did not stand for anything. Greenwood's father, Moses Greenwood, was a factory foreman who also ran a farm on the side to provide for his large family. A hardworking man, the elder Greenwood expected the same effort of his son. "My old man was working his behind off, and it was my responsibility as the oldest to contribute," Greenwood recalled in a 2011 interview with the *Pittsburgh Tribune-Review*. Greenwood picked cotton from August to December each year, earning $2.50 for 100 pounds. While in his teens he started his own company, doing odd jobs.

As a student at Rogers High School, Greenwood played football and basketball, but his father forced him to choose one sport, so as to leave time for his chores

At a Glance . . .

Born L. C. Henderson Greenwood on September 8, 1946, in Canton, MS; died on September 29, 2013, in Pittsburgh, PA; son of Moses Greenwood Sr.; children: Chelsea, Fernando. *Education:* Arkansas Agricultural, Mechanical and Normal College (now the University of Arkansas at Pine Bluff), BA, vocational education, 1969.

Career: Pittsburgh Steelers, defensive end, 1969–81.

Awards: National Football League (NFL) Pro Bowl selection, 1973–76, 1978–79; NFL All-Pro First Team, 1974–75; NFL 1970s All-Decade Team; Super Bowl Silver Anniversary Team, 1991; inducted into Mississippi Sports Hall of Fame, 1996; named to Steelers All-Time Team, 2007.

at home. Greenwood chose football. "I picked football because it was physical," Greenwood told the *Tribune-Review*. "It was a way for me to get out my aggression. My folks would leave home and I was in charge, and all my brothers and sisters would plot against me, and I couldn't fight back ... so I took it out on people on the football field." As a high school senior Greenwood received All-State honors and drew attention from colleges throughout the South. However, he looked at football as a means to an end, allowing him to attend college on a scholarship. "I was just playing football because it was fun," he told the *Tribune-Review*. "I never dreamed of being in the NFL or playing professionally."

Greenwood earned a full athletic scholarship to play football at Arkansas Agricultural, Mechanical and Normal College (now the University of Arkansas at Pine Bluff). Initially he intended to pursue a career as a vocational teacher. In Greenwood's freshman year, Arkansas's starting defensive end was injured, and Greenwood replaced him. For the next four years, Greenwood was a starter at either defensive end or defensive tackle. In his senior year, when he was named an *Ebony* magazine All-American, Greenwood was scouted by the Dallas Cowboys and performed drills for Coach Tom Landry. "He had me do a 40-yard dash, and he pulled out a stopwatch," Greenwood recalled to the *Tribune-Review*, referring to the sprint traditionally used to evaluate football players' speed. "I didn't even know what [a stopwatch] was because I'd never seen one. [Landry] said I did really well. A month later the draft started, and my coach said I'd get picked up. I was shocked."

Anchored "Steel Curtain" Defensive Line

Dallas passed on Greenwood, concerned that a knee injury would prevent him from playing, but he was chosen in the 10th round as the 238th pick by the Pittsburgh Steelers—a team that Greenwood had never even heard of. "All of a sudden I'm in the NFL, and to that point I had seen exactly one pro football game on television: The Cowboys vs. the Redskins," he told the *Tribune-Review*. Greenwood signed with the Steelers for the league-minimum salary of $13,500, teaching high school in the off-season. He joined the team the same year as his fellow defensive lineman "Mean Joe" Greene.

In 1971 Greenwood became a starter at left defensive end, making up one-quarter of the Steelers' front four, a defensive line that was nicknamed the "Steel Curtain" in a local radio contest. Greenwood quickly became known for his remarkable speed and agility. "He was like a greyhound," Greene told the *Tribune-Review* in 2011. "He would just zoom right past everyone on the field." Those qualities, combined with Greenwood's imposing size and power, made for a formidable defensive end. He specialized in the quarterback sack, making 73.5 sacks over the course of his career (although the NFL did not officially begin recording sacks until 1982). Greenwood led the Steelers in sacks for six consecutive years, and to this day he ranks second all-time in franchise history. He also recovered 14 fumbles, including five in 1971 alone, second best in the league.

The Steelers dominated the NFL in the 1970s, taking six division championships and winning four Super Bowls. Greenwood's performance was key to those victories. In Super Bowl IX in 1975, Greenwood batted down two passes by Minnesota Vikings quarterback Fran Tarkenton, helping lead the Steelers to a 16–6 win and the first championship in franchise history. In Super Bowl X the next year, the Steelers won their second straight championship, defeating the Dallas Cowboys 21–17. In that game Greenwood sacked Cowboys quarterback Roger Staubach four times (a record had the NFL been keeping track of sacks at the time). The Steelers won two more Super Bowls, besting the Dallas Cowboys again in 1979 and the Los Angeles Rams in 1980. In all Greenwood had five sacks in four Super Bowl appearances.

Off the field Greenwood was known to be a snazzy dresser. On Monday mornings after games, the Pittsburgh announcer Myron Cope often called the players downtown for a "dress-off" between Greenwood and the Steelers running back John "Frenchy" Fuqua. On one occasion Greenwood appeared in blue tights and a cape, but he was upstaged by Fuqua, who donned platform shoes with clear heels containing fish from his aquarium. Greenwood's sense of style was apparent on the field as well. In 1973, after he suffered an ankle

injury, a Steelers athletic trainer recommended that he wear high-top cleats for an upcoming game. Greenwood and equipment manager Tony Parisi decided to spray-paint the shoes gold, reasoning that the announcers would be better able to credit Greenwood's tackles. After wearing the cleats in two games, both of which the Steelers won, Greenwood chose to continue wearing them, having them specially made by Nike. The shoe company even paid Greenwood's $100 fine to the NFL for each game in which he wore the nonregulation shoes.

Left Out of Hall of Fame

Greenwood ended his NFL career in 1982, when the Steelers released him following a knee injury. In his 13 years with the Steelers—the longest tenure in franchise history to that date—he was named to the All-Pro first team twice, in 1974 and 1975, and made six trips to the Pro Bowl.

During his playing days, Greenwood was nicknamed "Hollywood Bags," a reference to his plan to take up acting after his football career was over. (He reportedly had his bags packed so that he could go to Hollywood at a moment's notice). He later joined the Screen Actors Guild and appeared in 10 television commercials, including a memorable spot for Miller Lite in which he apologized to all the quarterbacks he had sacked in the past.

In retirement Greenwood became a fixture in Pittsburgh. Well before the end of his playing career, he had prepared for life after football, founding his own company—Greenwood Enterprises, a construction and paving contractor—in 1974. "I knew enough not to count on football to support me forever," he told the *Tribune-Review.* He later partnered with Jim McDonald to form Greenwood-McDonald Supply, an electrical supply company. In 2002 Greenwood established Greenwood Manufacturing, a corrugated packing manufacturer. In his business ventures, he applied the lessons he had learned while playing football. "The skill sets are similar," he said in a 2012 interview with *Diversity Executive* magazine. "You need to work hard in both, learn how to be effective in your role, learn how to do it well and increase your capabilities by testing yourself every day. You also have to have a steel exterior. Just like losing a game, you need to be prepared for rejection in business."

Despite Greenwood's impressive statistics, he has not been inducted into the Pro Football Hall of Fame. A finalist six times (in 1991, 1995, 1996, 2002, 2005, and 2006), he never garnered enough support in his years of eligibility. Some have speculated that the committee passed over Greenwood because so many other Steelers are already enshrined in the Hall of Fame, including nine of Greenwood's teammates. (Greenwood still could be elected by a special veterans committee.) In 1996 Greenwood was inducted into the Mississippi Sports Hall of Fame, and in 2007 he was named to the Steelers All-Time Team.

Greenwood suffered kidney failure two weeks after undergoing back surgery. He died at a Pittsburgh hospital on September 29, 2013, at age 67. His funeral was attended by Greene, the last surviving member of the Steel Curtain defensive line.

Sources

Books

Blount, Roy, Jr., *About Three Bricks Shy of a Load ... And the Load Filled Up,* University of Pittsburgh Press, 2004.

Periodicals

Jackson (MS) Free Press, October 3, 2013.
New York Times, September 30, 2013.
Pittsburgh Post-Gazette, September 29, 2013.
Pittsburgh Tribune-Review, September 18, 2011.
Sports Illustrated, December 2, 2002.

Online

Brown, Scott, "L. C. Greenwood Dies at 67," ESPN.com, September 29, 2013, http://espn.go.com/nfl/story/_/id/9744968/ (accessed December 17, 2013).

Cattel, Jeffrey, "Playing Both Sides of the Ball," Diversity-Executive.com, August 15, 2012, http://diversity-executive.com/articles/view/playing-both-sides-of-the-ball (accessed December 17, 2013).

Cleveland, Rick, "RIP: L. C. Greenwood, of Canton, Sack Master," Mississippi Sports Hall of Fame, September 30, 2013, http://msfame.com/news-updates/rip-l-c-greenwood-of-canton-sack-master/ (accessed December 17, 2013).

"Hall of Famers: Yearly Finalists," Pro Football Hall of Fame, http://www.profootballhof.com/hof/YearlyFinalistsAlltimeAlphabeticalListing.aspx (accessed December 17, 2013).

Hornbuckle, Adam R., "L. C. Greenwood (1946–2013)," Encyclopedia of Arkansas History and Culture, http://www.encyclopediaofarkansas.net/encyclopedia/entry-detail.aspx?entryID=7315 (accessed December 17, 2013).

Labriola, Bob, "L. C. Greenwood, 67," Steelers.com, September 30, 2013, http://www.steelers.com/news/article-1/LC-Greenwood-67/5548d9c7-4dff-4bc5-8dff-496b7b842ede (accessed December 17, 2013).

"L. C. Greenwood," Pro-Football-Reference.com, http://www.pro-football-reference.com/players/G/GreeL.00.htm (accessed December 17, 2013).

O'Brien, Jim, "L. C. Greenwood Still Working to Please His Father Moses," Pittsburgh Sports Daily Bulletin, January 10, 2013, http://pittsburghsports

dailybulletin.wordpress.com/2013/01/10/jim -obrien-l-c-greenwood-still-working-to-please-his -father-moses/ (accessed December 17, 2013).

The Official Site for L. C. Greenwood, http://www .lcgreenwood68.com/ (accessed December 17, 2013).

Pomerantz, Gary M., "The Curtain Falls on the '70s Steelers," WSJ.com, October 2, 2013, http://on line.wsj.com/news/articles/SB10001424052702 3 04176904579111213754067206 (accessed December 17, 2013).

—Deborah A. Ring

Jrue Holiday

1990—

Professional basketball player

Holiday, Jrue, photograph. Ethan Miller/Getty Images.

In 2013 Jrue Holiday became the starting point guard for the New Orleans Pelicans of the National Basketball Association (NBA). Drafted after playing for only one year at the University of California, Los Angeles (UCLA), Holiday was one of the youngest players ever drafted, at age 18, and the first player born in the 1990s to play in the NBA. Known for his composure on the court and for his exceptional quickness, the six-foot, four-inch guard has shown marked improvement during his short career in the NBA. In 2013 he was selected to his first All-Star team as a reserve guard.

Jrue Randall Holiday (his first name is pronounced "Drew") was born on June 12, 1990, in Mission Hills, California. Both of his parents were former college basketball players. His mother, Toya Decree Holiday, played for Arizona State University, where she was named the PAC-10 Conference's player of the year in 1982. His father, Shawn, also played college ball at Arizona State before going on to California State University, Los Angeles. Jrue Holiday began dribbling a basketball as early as two years old. As a boy he played basketball for the R. C. Bulls of the Amateur Athletic Union, playing against future NBA players such as

DeMar DeRozan, Malcolm Lee, and Brandon Jennings. "He always had that athleticism and that drive," a family friend told the New Orleans *Times-Picayune* in a 2013 article. "He'd always joke around, 'I'm going to be in the NBA soon' or 'When I get older I'm going to be in the NBA.' He never gave up on his dreams."

As a senior at Campbell Hall Episcopal High School, a private school in North Hollywood, Holiday was ranked as the number-one point guard prospect in the country and the number-two overall prospect. Recruited by UCLA head coach Ben Howland, Holiday chose that school over the University of Washington. He played just one year of college hoops before entering the NBA draft at age 18 in 2009, when he was selected in the first round with the 17th overall by the Philadelphia 76ers. NBA scouts had assessed Holiday as a well-rounded player with a tremendous basketball IQ, exceptional physical abilities, and level-headed maturity. There was little doubt that he would succeed in the NBA—even as one of the youngest players in the league.

In 2009–10, his rookie season with the 76ers, Holiday started 51 of the 73 games in which he played. In the

At a Glance . . .

Born Jrue Randall Holiday on June 12, 1990, in Mission Hills, CA; son of Shawn Holiday and Toya Decree Holiday; married Lauren Cheney, July 7, 2013. *Education:* Attended University of California, Los Angles, 2007–08.

Career: Philadelphia 76ers, point guard, 2009–13; New Orleans Pelicans, point guard, 2013—.

Awards: Gatorade National Player of the Year, Boys Basketball, 2008; McDonald's All-American, 2008; National Basketball Association (NBA) All-Star selection, 2013.

Addresses: *Office*—c/o New Orleans Pelicans, 5800 Airline Dr., Metairie, LA 20003. *Twitter*—@Jrue_Holiday11.

next three seasons, he was a starter in every game in which he played. Over the course of four years with the 76ers, Holiday averaged 13.4 points per game, with 3.6 rebounds, 5.8 assists, 1.4 steals, and a .781 free throw percentage. Showing consistent improvement from year to year, in 2013 he was nominated as the NBA's most improved player of the year, in addition to being selected to his first All-Star team.

During the off-season in 2013, Holiday was surprised to learn that he had been traded to the New Orleans Pelicans. In exchange for Holiday, the 76ers had obtained the rights to their 2013 number-six draft pick, Nerlens Noel, in addition to securing a first-round draft pick for 2014. Holiday had just finished his best season with the 76ers and had just married to his college sweetheart, Lauren Cheney, who is a member of the U.S. women's soccer team. Holiday learned of the trade deal while he was on his honeymoon. As he described in press interviews, his initial shock quickly turned to excitement when he realized that he would be playing alongside such up-and-comers as Tyreke Evans (whom the Pelicans had acquired that same week from the Sacramento Kings), Ryan Anderson, Jason Smith, and Eric Gordon. Holiday described the surprise trade

as a blessing in disguise and looked forward to contributing to the team.

In his first few month as the Pelicans' point guard, Holiday performed well, raising his averages to 14.8 points per game with 8.4 assists, 4.5 rebounds, and an .810 free throw shooting percentage in the first months of the 2013–14 season.

The transition to the Pelicans, however, was not without some bumps for Holiday. In October of 2013 the point guard made headlines for an awkward verbal slip at the Pelicans' home opener against the Indiana Pacers. As the team's new star acquisition, Holiday was handed the microphone to address the crowd on opening night. "On behalf of myself and the 76ers we want to welcome you all to the first Pelican's game of the year," Holiday announced to the home crowd, seeming to have forgotten which team he played for. The media seized on the mistake and made light of the faux pas. Despite the gaffe Holiday went on to play an impressive game against the Pacers, assuring Pelicans fans that they would be in good hands for years to come.

Sources

Periodicals

Advocate (New Orleans, LA), July 22, 2013.
Sports Illustrated, February 6, 2012.
Times-Picayune (New Orleans, LA), November 28, 2013.
USA Today, June 26, 2009.

Online

"Jrue Holiday," ESPN.com, http://espn.go.com/nba/player/stats/_/id/3995/jrue-holiday (accessed November 30, 2013).
"Jrue Holiday," National Basketball Association, http://www.nba.com/playerfile/jrue_holiday/ (accessed November 30, 2013).
"Jrue Holiday," NBADraft.net, http://www.nbadraft.net/players/jrue-holiday (accessed November 30, 2013).
"Jrue Holiday," University of California, Los Angeles Bruins, http://www.uclabruins.com/ViewArticle.dbml?DB_OEM_ID=30500&ATCLID=208185086 (accessed November 30, 2013).

—Ben Bloch

Loleatta Holloway

1946–2011

Disco, R&B, and gospel singer

Holloway, Loleatta, photograph. Michael Ochs Archives/Getty Images.

As a girl Loleatta Holloway hated her voice because she thought she sounded like a woman instead of a child. As a teenager she joined her mother's 100-member gospel group and then toured with the renowned gospel group the Caravans, led by Alberta Walker. At the age of 26, Holloway embarked on a solo career; mixing disco with the ballads that she preferred, Holloway's gospel influences were apparent in her soulful undulations. Her career was stressful at times, as in the late 1980s, when she sued the Italian group Black Box for using samples of her music without her permission. Although she won the lawsuit, other artists continued to sample her songs without her consent. "You know, when sampling first came out it was OK," she said in an interview with the website Disco Disco. "What I didn't understand was they never wanted to pay me."

Holloway was born in 1946 in Chicago. To encourage her children to sing in her church, Holloway's mother assigned a song to each child in the family. But Holloway did not like the song she was assigned, preferring the song assigned to her niece, who was the same age as she, and refused to sing. One Sunday when Holloway was four years old, her niece was home

sick, and she had the opportunity to sing the song of her choice. The congregation took notice. "I just stood up and start singing that and start walking up through the whole church singing it and everybody in church just went 'wow!'" she shared in her interview with Disco Disco. "And ever since then I was like the singer of the choir."

Much to the young singer's displeasure, the church recorded her while she was singing. "I used to hate to hear it," she said in the Disco Disco interview. "To me I sounded like an old woman and I was just a little girl. And everybody would play that record and every time I found one I [broke] it up." In high school Holloway joined her mother's gospel group, the Holloway Community Singers. After her mother died in 1966, Holloway joined the Caravans, with whom she performed with Aretha Franklin in Las Vegas. When the group broke up in 1972, Holloway turned to secular music.

Under the management of songwriter and producer Floyd Smith, whom she later married, Holloway entered the disco scene. She first signed with GRC, an offshoot of Aware, but her contract collapsed after GRC's owner was arrested for making pornographic

films. In 1976 she signed with Salsoul Records' subsidiary, Gold Mind. Holloway was not crazy about her first Salsoul recording, the single "Hit and Run." "I thought it was the worst song I ever heard," she told Brewster. "I didn't wanna sing about 'I'm an old fashioned country girl' because I hadn't been born in the country, I was from Chicago, so to me it was an insult."

Her first album with Gold Mind, *Loleatta,* was released in 1977. The album included disco tunes, including "Dreamin'" and "Hit and Run," as well as ballads such as "What Now" and "Worn Out Broken Heart." Of the album, critic David Nathan proclaimed, "In the hands of Ms. Holloway, a meaningful ballad … becomes really 'something else'—she wails, she soars, she interprets and gets the song over … But her new album reflects not just Loleatta's incredible talent when it comes to ballads (which, she confesses, she prefers 'because I can really put myself into them, get into the lyrics, whether I've personally been in those situations or not') but indicates her ability to get into Philly's disco music of today."

Holloway recorded several more albums with Gold Mind and became a regular at the hottest disco clubs of the era, including two of New York's most popular gay clubs, Paradise Garage and Better Days. Although she was able to make a career out of her music, the hours were often long. Reflecting on one Christmas, Holloway told Brewster, "I did four shows that night and I got to the last club and I couldn't talk and when I got up there and it was six o'clock and they gave me a Santa Claus outfit to put on and I went up there and not a word came out. Tears started coming out my eyes." Holloway regained her voice and spirit after the crowd began singing her song for her. "It was great, they just lifted me all the way up."

She gained widespread popularity in Europe and Japan in the 1970s but remained relatively unknown in the United States. In 1980, however, she climbed to the top of the U.S. dance charts with two songs penned by songwriter Dan Hartman, "Relight My Fire" and "Love Sensation." The latter became one of the most sampled songs in music history. In 1989 Holloway became enraged when the Italian house music group Black Box used segments of "Love Sensation" for their hit "Ride On Time" without her consent. At the time

Black Box was oblivious to any wrongdoing, and member Daniele Davioli claimed that he had thought Holloway was dead at the time. Holloway and Hartman successfully sued Black Box for an undisclosed amount. However, the situation was upsetting for the singer. "I thought I was gonna lose my mind," she told Brewster. "I almost had a nervous breakdown … Someone's just taken something from you, right in front of your face … For years it destroyed me, it made me a person I don't like."

In 1984 Holloway's husband and manager, Floyd Smith, died. That same year the singer signed with Streetwise Records, and over the course of the following decade, she recorded singles for several other labels, including DJ International, Warlock, and Select. In 1991 Holloway earned notice again in the United States after singer Marky Mark (Mark Wahlberg) sampled "Love Sensation" for his 1991 pop hit "Good Vibrations." The song exceeded a million in sales, and although Holloway was compensated for the use of her vocals, she felt underappreciated. As she shared with Brewster, "the other day Marky Mark was on the TV talkin' about that record and he never even mentioned my name. I'm so used to people like this that it doesn't even phase me anymore."

Holloway's music career slowed down considerably in the 1990s, although she continued to tour occasionally. She moved to Los Angeles, and on March 21, 2011, she died of heart failure at the age of 64. "She was a very strong, powerful woman, but she was sweet at the same time," Holloway's manager, Ron Richardson, shared in an interview with BBC 6 Music. "She was also very fragile, which a lot of people didn't know."

Selected works

Albums

Loleatta, Aware, 1973.
Cry to Me, Aware, 1975.
Loleatta (includes "Dreamin'," "Hit and Run," "What Now," and "Worn Out Broken Heart"), Gold Mind Records, 1976.
Queen of the Night, Gold Mind Records/Salsoul Records, 1978.
Loleatta Holloway, Gold Mind Records, 1978.
Love Sensation (includes "Relight My Fire" and "Love Sensation"), Gold Mind Records/Salsoul Records, 1980.
Dreamin', EMI Music Distribution, 2000.

Singles

"Bring It On Up," 1971.
"Mother of Shame," 1973.
"Cry to Me," 1974.
"Rainbow '71," 1976.

"Casanova," 1975.
"I Know Where You're Coming From," 1975.
"Worn Out Broken Heart," 1976.
"Dreamin'," 1976.
"Hit and Run," 1977.
"We're Getting Stronger (The Longer We Stay Together)," 1977.
"You Light Up My Life," 1978.
"The Greatest Performance of My Life," 1979.
"That's What You Said," 1979.
"Love Sensation," 1980.
"I've Been Loving You Too Long," 1980.
"Two Became a Crowd," 1980.
"Crash Goes Love," 1984.
"So Sweet," 1987.
"Hit and Run '88 Gotta Be Number One," 1988.
"Ride on Time," 1989.
"Heartstealer," 1989.
"Set Me Free (Do That To Me)," 1991.
"Strong Enough," 1992.
"Mama Don't, Papa Won't," 1993.
"Stand Up!," 1994.
"The Queen's Anthem," 1994.
"Lifting Me Up," 1998.

Plays

Don't Bother Me, I Can't Cope, 1972.

Sources

Periodicals

Guardian (London), March 24, 2011.
Independent (London), March 25, 2011.
New York Times, March 23, 2011.

Online

Brewster, Bill, "Loleatta Holloway," DJHistory.com, January 6, 2005, http://www.djhistory.com/interviews/loleatta-holloway (accessed November 28, 2013).
"Disco Singer Loleatta Holloway Dies at 64," BBC News, March 22, 2011, http://www.bbc.co.uk/news/entertainment-arts-12822122 (accessed November 28, 2013).
Hogan, Ed, "Loleatta Holloway," AllMusic.com, http://www.allmusic.com/artist/loleatta-holloway-mn0000829125/biography (accessed November 28, 2013).
"Loleatta Holloway," Disco Disco, http://www.disco-disco.com/artists/loleatta.shtml (accessed November 28, 2013).
Nathan, David, "Loleatta Holloway April 1977 Interview," SoulMusic.com, January 1, 2011, http://www.soulmusic.com/index.asp?S=1&T=38&ART=1152 (accessed November 28, 2013).

—Candice Mancini

Big Walter Horton

1918(?)–1981

Blues harmonica player, vocalist

Horton, Big Walter, photograph. Gilles Petard/Redferns/Getty Images.

Although he typically avoided the spotlight, preferring small gigs and backup work to solo albums and publicity, the harmonica player and vocalist Big Walter Horton was a major blues figure for more than half a century. Known for his bright tone and powerful, stirring solos, he was closely associated with Chicago, Illinois, a city famous around the world for its dedication to hard-driving, electrically amplified blues—a style Horton did much to popularize. Inducted in 1982 into the Blues Foundation's Blues Hall of Fame, he was described on the foundation's website as "one of the most brilliant and creative musicians ever to play the harmonica."

Walter Horton was born on a farm in Horn Lake, a rural community in northern Mississippi, just over the state line from Memphis, Tennessee. His birth date has been the subject of considerable debate. While it is generally agreed that he was born on April 6, sources differ with regard to the year; 1917, 1918, and 1921 have all been proposed. It is clear, in any event, that he was living in Memphis by the age of about five. Diagnosed with nystagmus, a medical condition that often causes involuntary head shaking and vision problems, Horton had difficulty in school, and his formal education came to an end as early as the first grade. While his peers were in class, he did odd jobs and played a harmonica, or "harp," that his father had given him.

Horton's technique on that instrument was essentially self-taught, although he received some important tips from two older players, Will Shade and Hammie Nixon. Horton's development was rapid, and by the end of the 1920s, he was playing professionally, sometimes in the company of a well-known and influential group called the Memphis Jug Band. Most of Horton's gigs in this period, however, were impromptu appearances on the streets of Memphis. As his reputation grew, Horton began to move farther afield. Over the course of the 1930s, he traveled regularly to gigs as far away as Missouri. His partners on these trips included two guitarists, Johnny Shines and David "Honeyboy" Edwards, both of whom later joined Horton in Chicago. Also around this time he began to be recruited for backup work, both onstage and in the recording studio. He accompanied the noted

At a Glance . . .

Born Walter Horton on April 6, 1918(?), in Horn Lake, MS; died on December 8, 1981, in Chicago, IL.

Career: Independent musician, 1920s–81.

Awards: Inducted into Blues Hall of Fame, 1982.

vocalist Ma Rainey, for example, on at least one tour, while the guitarist Little Buddy Doyle recorded some tracks with him in 1939.

Significant as they were, these gigs paid relatively little, and Horton was often forced to put his harmonica aside while he looked for more remunerative work. According to Steve Huey of AllMusic.com, Horton was essentially out of the music business from around 1940 to 1948. Soon after his return, however, his career began to flourish, thanks in part to the legendary producer Sam Phillips. The founder of the Memphis-based Sun Records, Phillips brought Horton into the studio in the early 1950s. Although the singles that resulted were not released under Horton's real name and received only limited distribution, Phillips's imprimatur gave a significant boost to Horton's career. The guitarist and vocalist Eddie Taylor also aided Horton in this period, encouraging him to move to Chicago. Soon thereafter, in 1953, Horton joined a band led by another guitarist and vocalist, the legendary Muddy Waters. Horton's tenure with Waters was brief, however, and by the following year, Horton had moved on to stints with other artists, many of them connected with the Chicago-based Chess Records. He also made at least one trip back to Sun Records in Memphis, where he joined the guitarist Jimmy DeBerry for an instrumental called "Easy," which quickly became a standard.

Upon his return to Chicago, Horton balanced his time between studio work and live performance. A familiar figure in many of the city's blues clubs, he also played regularly for tips on Maxwell Street, the site of an open-air market that has attracted musicians for decades. In the studio, meanwhile, he did backup work for such stars as the vocalist Koko Taylor and recorded a number of singles that were released under his own name by Chess and other labels. Among his best-known works in this period was "Hard-Hearted Woman," a stirring piece released in the mid-1950s. It has since been covered by many other artists, including Carey Bell, one of Horton's protégés.

Horton's career changed dramatically in the years that followed, thanks in part to the explosive growth of rock and roll. When rock fans, many of them white, began to explore the genre's antecedents, they discovered blues stars such as Horton. As the enthusiasm of these new aficionados grew steadily more apparent, Argo Records offered him the chance to record a full album, *The Soul of Blues Harmonica* (1964). Several more full-length recordings followed, including *Big Walter Horton with Carey Bell* (1972) and *Fine Cuts* (1979). While all of these won praise from critics, Horton's preference for backup work remained clear. Long known for his shyness, he tended to seek out gigs that brought him together with large groups. In the 1960s and 1970s, for example, he toured widely with the Chicago Blues All Stars, an ensemble organized by producer Willie Dixon.

Amid this success Horton faced an array of challenges, many of them related to his reliance on alcohol. Years of heavy drinking did lasting damage to his finances, in part because he sometimes missed gigs while under the influence. His alcohol addiction also took a serious toll on his health, particularly toward the end of his life. Although his death in Chicago on December 8, 1981, was officially ascribed to heart failure, acute alcoholism was listed on his death certificate as a contributory factor.

News of Horton's passing quickly prompted tributes from around the world. Typical of these were the comments of the critic Michael Erlewine, who praised Horton's "big tone and spacious sense of time." Erlewine added, "Give Big Water a chance to solo and you were in for some of the most tasteful lines Chicago-style harp has ever produced."

Selected discography

Singles

(With Jimmy DeBerry) "Easy," 1950s.
"Hard-Hearted Woman," 1950s.

Albums

(With Carey Bell) *Big Walter Horton with Carey Bell*, Alligator, 1972.
Fine Cuts, Blind Pig, 1979.

Sources

Online

"Big Walter Horton," Mississippi Blues Commission, http://msbluestrail.org/blues-trail-markers/big-walter-horton (accessed November 3, 2013).

Erlewine, Michael, "Big Walter 'Shakey' Horton," BluesHarp.ca, http://www.bluesharp.ca/legends/bwalter.html (accessed November 3, 2013).

Huey, Steve, "Big Walter Horton: Artist Biography," AllMusic.com, http://www.allmusic.com/artist/big-walter-horton-mn0000064817/biography (accessed November 3, 2013).

O'Neal, Jim, "Past Hall of Fame Inductees: Big Walter Horton," Blues Foundation, https://blues.org/#ref =halloffame_inductees (accessed November 3, 2013).

—R. Anthony Kugler

Bobby Hutcherson

1941—

Jazz vibraphonist

Hutcherson, Bobby, photograph. Andrew Lepley/Redferns/Getty Images.

One of the top vibraphonists in the world, Bobby Hutcherson has been at the forefront of jazz since the late 1950s. Known for his innovative arrangements and deft handling of the mallets, he has worked closely with some of the genre's biggest names, including saxophonists Eric Dolphy and Jackie McLean. The recipient in 2010 of one of the country's highest music honors, a Jazz Masters Fellowship from the National Endowment for the Arts, Hutcherson has been praised by that organization for "adding an adventurous new voice to the free jazz and post bop eras."

The son of a brick mason, Bobby Hutcherson was born in Los Angeles, California, on January 27, 1941. He grew up in nearby Pasadena in an atmosphere filled with jazz; an older brother was a friend of the saxophonist Dexter Gordon, and an older sister was a vocalist who knew Dolphy well. Hutcherson's own study of music began with piano lessons from his aunt before he was 10 years old. By his own account, however, he was not especially enthusiastic until the age of 12, when he heard a recording by a famous ensemble that included the vibraphonist Milt Jackson.

That day, he heard a composition called "Bemsha Swing," and by his own account, the experience changed his life. Determined to emulate Jackson, Hutcherson worked on jobs with his father until he had enough money to buy his own vibraphone, an unwieldy and relatively uncommon instrument. Although he had some informal lessons with a musician named Dave Pike, Hutcherson essentially taught himself, developing his own distinctive style in the process.

Hutcherson began playing professionally when he was still in high school. The Los Angeles area was a hotbed of jazz at the time, and by his late teens he had performed with a number of distinguished musicians, including the bassist Scott LaFaro and the saxophonist Curtis Amy. Hutcherson then moved north to San Francisco, where in 1960 he joined a group led by the trombonist Al Grey and the saxophonist Billy Mitchell. That collaboration was a major break for Hutcherson. It took him to New York City's famed Birdland, one of the most prominent venues in jazz. His performances there with Grey and Mitchell in 1961 brought him to the attention of musicians across the city. In the months that followed, Hutcherson began working with a num-

At a Glance . . .

Born Bobby Hutcherson on January 27, 1941, in Los Angeles, CA.

Career: Independent musician, late 1950s—.

Awards: Jazz Masters Fellowship, National Endowment for the Arts, 2010.

Addresses: *Office*—c/o Kind of Blue Records, Recording Arts SA, CP48, CH-6836 Serfontana, Switzerland.

ber of new partners, among them McLean, whom he backed on a landmark album called *One Step Beyond.*

Released by Blue Note Records in 1963, *One Step Beyond* was filled with innovative arrangements that signaled a transition away from the blues-tinged "hard bop" that had dominated jazz since the mid-1950s. Through his work with McLean and, later, Dolphy, Hutcherson played a significant role in establishing the broad outlines of the new style, often described at the time as the "new thing" in jazz. Less melodic than hard bop, it attracted a growing audience, particularly after the release of Dolphy's 1964 album *Out to Lunch,* a recording to which Hutcherson made a number of important contributions. Soon after its release, he entered the studio to record his debut album as a leader. The result, *Dialogue* (1965), was described by Steve Huey of AllMusic.com as "a masterpiece of 'new thing' avant-garde jazz, not really free but way beyond hard bop."

A string of innovative albums followed, virtually all of them (until the late 1970s) on Blue Note, a distinguished label with which Hutcherson had a long and fruitful relationship. While many of these recordings came to be highly regarded, particularly *Components* (1965) and *Stick-Up!* (1966), their sales at the time were generally quite modest. By the end of the decade, many fans had moved on from the "new thing" to free jazz, which eschewed structured melody almost entirely, replacing it with constant or near-constant improvisation. Hutcherson, in contrast, continued to incorporate traditional structures into his work, a decision that hurt his sales amid the countercultural tumult that characterized the era. He responded to that situation with ostensible aplomb, moving back to California when opportunities for him in New York began drying up around 1967. In Los Angeles he joined forces with the saxophonist Harold Land, coleading an active and highly proficient quintet with Land until the early 1970s.

After leaving Land, Hutcherson experimented with a variety of new styles, including—briefly—fusion, which mixed jazz with the heavy rhythms and electric amplification of rock and roll. By the middle of the decade, however, Hutcherson had largely returned to the "new style" with which he had begun his career. Typical of his 1970s releases was *Cirrus* (1974), which included a piece called "Even Later," described by Scott Mortensen of MusicWeb International as "luminous [and] transcendent" and "one of Hutcherson's best."

Amid his other commitments, Hutcherson also continued to work frequently as a "sideman," helping other artists complete their albums. Over the next few decades, he made important contributions to dozens of recordings, including *Ethiopian Knights* (1972) by the trumpeter Donald Byrd, *Sama Layuca* (1974) by the pianist McCoy Tyner (on which Hutcherson played the marimba as well as the vibraphone), and a joint project with Tyner called *Manhattan Moods* (1993). Hutcherson's own groups, meanwhile, continued to move in new and sometimes unexpected directions, particularly after Blue Note ceased operations (temporarily) around 1978. Hutcherson responded to that event by moving to Columbia Records. He remained with Columbia for several years before shifting to smaller labels, such as Timeless, where he worked with the Timeless All Stars, a distinguished group that included the trombonist Curtis Fuller and the pianist Cedar Walton. Among other prominent partners in this period was the saxophonist Kenny Garrett, who helped Hutcherson finish *Skyline* (1999), his first recording for the venerable Verve label.

As he neared and then passed the 50th anniversary of his late-1950s debut, Hutcherson remained quite active. One of his biggest projects in the 21st century involved the SFJAZZ Collective, a teaching ensemble with which he played for about three years (roughly 2004–07) before returning to his own groups. In 2012, more than half a century after he arrived at Birdland with Grey and Mitchell, he released a highly regarded live album, *Somewhere in the Night.*

Selected discography

Al Grey and Billy Mitchell, *Snap Your Fingers,* Argo, 1962.
Jackie McLean, *One Step Beyond,* Blue Note, 1963.
Eric Dolphy, *Out to Lunch,* Blue Note, 1964.
Dialogue, Blue Note, 1965.
Components, Blue Note, 1965.
Stick-Up!, Blue Note, 1966.
Donald Byrd, *Ethiopian Knights,* Blue Note, 1972.
Cirrus (includes "Even Later"), Blue Note, 1974.
McCoy Tyner, *Sama Layuca,* Milestone, 1974.
Timeless All Stars, *It's Timeless,* Timeless, 1982.
(With McCoy Tyner) *Manhattan Moods,* Blue Note, 1993.
Skyline, Verve, 1999.
SFJAZZ Collective, *SFJAZZ Collective,* Nonesuch, 2004.
Somewhere in the Night, Kind of Blue, 2012.

Sources

Online

"Bobby Hutcherson: Bio," National Endowment for the Arts, http://arts.gov/honors/jazz/bobby-hutcherson (accessed November 18, 2013).

Huey, Steve, "Bobby Hutcherson: Artist Biography," AllMusic.com, http://www.allmusic.com/artist/bobby-hutcherson-mn0000081231/biography (accessed November 18, 2013).

Huey, Steve, *Dialogue:* Review," AllMusic.com, http://www.allmusic.com/album/dialogue-mw 0000217052 (accessed November 19, 2013).

Mortensen, Scott, "Bobby Hutcherson Biographical Sketch," MusicWeb International, 2006, http://www.musicweb-international.com/jazz/Hutcherson/01_BioSketch.htm (accessed November 18, 2013).

Murphy, Molly, "Bobby Hutcherson: Interview by Molly Murphy for the NEA," National Endowment for the Arts, August 13, 2009, http://arts.gov/honors/jazz/bobby-hutcherson (accessed November 18, 2013).

—R. Anthony Kugler

Mo Ibrahim

1946—

Telecommunications executive, philanthropist

Ibrahim, Mo, photograph. Carl Court/AFP/Getty Images.

Sudanese-British businessman Mohamed "Mo" Ibrahim is among the wealthiest men in the world, ranking on *Forbes* magazine's "Forbes Rich" with a net worth of $2.5 billion. Ibrahim earned his considerable fortune by building some of the first telephone networks in sub-Saharan Africa. As the founder of Celtel International, Ibrahim was a pioneer in the international mobile communications sector, and after his company was acquired for a stunning $3.4 billion in 2005, the London-based tycoon established an eponymous foundation that bestows the annual Ibrahim Prize for Achievement in African Leadership. "Africa is rich—really rich," he told journalist Michael Wines in the *New York Times*. "It's really a wonderful continent. What we need to do now is enforce good governance, and it's happening, perhaps not as quickly as I would like. All we need to do is push."

Gordon Pitts, writing in the Toronto *Globe and Mail*, called Ibrahim "one of the great success stories of today's Africa." Ibrahim is giving back to his native continent through his leadership prize and through a major effort to rebrand Africa by showing the positive aspects of the continent, not just horror stories. "All we hear about Africa in the west is Darfur, Zimbabwe, Congo, Somalia, as if that is all there is," Ibrahim told Geraldine Bedell of the London *Guardian*. "Yet there are 53 countries in Africa, and many of them are doing well." Asked by Pitts whether he is a good model for young Africans to follow, Ibrahim replied with characteristic humility: "Many African people are smarter than me—kids who could have been better. I have no claim for genius."

Became Interested in Mobile Communications

Ibrahim was born in 1946 in the town of Eshket in northern Sudan into a family of Nubian heritage, an ethnic group whose traditional homelands stretch from southern Egypt to northern Sudan. He grew up in Cairo, Egypt, where his father worked as a clerk for a cotton trade organization. The family, which numbered seven in all, lived in a small apartment that was often stifling in the heat of the warmer months. During his childhood Ibrahim dreamed of becoming a scientist like

At a Glance . . .

Born Mohamed Ibrahim in 1946 in Eshket, Sudan; married Hania Fadl (a radiologist); children: Hadeel, Hosh. *Education:* University of Alexandria, BS; University of Bradford, MS, electrical engineering; University of Birmingham, PhD, mobile communications.

Career: British Telecom, technical manager, 1983–89; Mobile Systems International (MSI), founder and president, 1989–2000; MSI-Cellular Investments/Celtel International, founder and president, 1998–2005; Mo Ibrahim Foundation, founder, 2006.

Memberships: Mo Ibrahim Foundation; London Business School, Africa Regional Advisory Board; Satya Capital, advisory board chair, 2008—.

Awards: Bishop John T. Walker Leadership Award, Africare, 2013.

Addresses: *Office*—Mo Ibrahim Foundation, 35 Portman Square, 3rd Floor North, London W1H 6LR, United Kingdom.

his role model, Albert Einstein. When he entered the University of Alexandria on a partial scholarship, he chose to study engineering.

In 1971, at the age of 25, Ibrahim began an internship with the International Telecommunications Union, a regulatory body located in Geneva, Switzerland. On his way to see a movie, he took a taxi and was enthralled by the driver's ability to communicate with the dispatcher back at the taxicab company's headquarters. That brief experience sparked his interest in mobile communications, which was then an emerging field. Mobile networks rely on radio-frequency signals—like the two-way radio in the cab—rather than actual wires, as telephone lines require.

Ibrahim earned a graduate degree in electrical engineering from the University of Bradford in Yorkshire, England, and then a doctorate in mobile communications from the University of Birmingham. He went to work for British Telecom and became a technical director at Cellnet, a joint venture between British Telecom and a private investment group that was founded in 1985 to capture the coming British mobile-phone market. He grew weary of corporate politicking, however, and quit in 1989 to become a telecommunications consultant.

Brought Telecommunications Networks to Africa

Ibrahim's company was called Mobile Systems International, or MSI, and its first office was the dining room table of the London home that he shared with his wife and two children. Over the next decade, MSI helped build mobile phone networks in other countries for major operators, becoming so successful that it was acquired by the Marconi Company, a British telecommunications company whose original corporate roots were in the General Electric Company of Britain and the pioneering Italian radio manufacturer whose name it still carried. The sale to Marconi in 2000 enriched not only Ibrahim but also many of his employees, to whom he had given shares of stock as bonuses.

Ibrahim's other company was Celtel, which began as MSI-Cellular Investments and then was spun off into a stand-alone entity in 1998. By that point Celtel was becoming the leading mobile phone service provider in sub-Saharan Africa, an area that had been written off as unfeasible by most other companies. Many larger providers had eagerly ventured into the rest of Africa but judged this part of the continent too impoverished to make investment in building a network there financially worthwhile.

Ibrahim believed otherwise, knowing that land lines were still scarce in this part of the world. Celtel moved forward with the plan, and within a few years the company was providing mobile phone service in 15 African countries, from Chad to Zambia, and had invested more than $750 million in Africa, bringing mobile communications to millions who previously had no telephone service. Ibrahim's idea proved so profitable that in 2005, a Kuwaiti company acquired Celtel for $3.4 billion.

Established Foundation to Promote African Development

Ibrahim began his second career as a philanthropist in 2006 when he established the Mo Ibrahim Foundation with his new fortune, estimated at well over $1 billion. Its main focus was to improve the lives of Africans by encouraging good governance and leadership. *New Yorker* writer Ken Auletta quoted Ibrahim as he spoke to students at the University of Ghana, outlining Africa's problem: "We are a very rich continent, the second-largest continent in the world, lush-green, plenty of resources. Everything we have. Yet we are the poorest people on earth. So, rich continent, poor people. After fifty years of independence, I don't think we can continue to blame the colonialists." Instead, as Ibrahim observed, Africa's difficulties are the result of a "catastrophic failure of leadership and governance." Ibrahim added, "There is no other explanation. We have had to a very large extent very lousy leadership in Africa: too many dictators, too many megalomaniacs,

too many thieves, who bled this continent for their personal and family interest."

Thus, Ibrahim set out to do something about the continent's poor leadership. Working with world-renowned economists and political scientists, the foundation created the Ibrahim Index of African Governance, which ranks the 48 countries of sub-Saharan Africa according to various factors, such as human rights abuses and the level of political corruption. From that, Ibrahim created a somewhat unusual prize designed to reward the best leaders in Africa. Known as the Mo Ibrahim Prize for Achievement in African Leadership, its inaugural recipient was Mozambique's Joaquim Chissano in 2007. Once a Marxist who had played a key role in his country's break with its longtime colonial master, Portugal, Chissano became Mozambique's second president in 1986 during the country's long and bloody civil war. He worked to end the conflict and bring stability and prosperity back to the country before stepping down in 2005.

The Ibrahim Prize awarded Chissano $5 million over a 10-year period, then another $200,000 annually until his death. It was the most generous prize in philanthropy—more than three times greater than the $1.5 million that comes with the Nobel Prize—and was established to encourage African leaders to leave office rather than cling to power. Ibrahim explained the impetus behind the award: unlike the heads of state of most Western countries, African leaders do not anticipate generous book deals when they leave office, nor can they expect lucrative lecture tours. In most cases they receive a woefully small pension and, in a few cases, have not even been able to live in the capital city any longer because of their reduced financial circumstances. Such a future, Ibrahim argued, encourages corruption and compels some to remain in office by any means possible, including suspending the constitution.

Promoted Political and Economic Reform

Only a handful of African leaders—about seven in all—were eligible for the initial Ibrahim Prize. According to the strict criteria associated with the prize, those under consideration were limited to leaders who had left office within the past three years and had been democratically elected. Some observers criticized the Ibrahim Prize, contending that it provided little incentive to stop corruption and abuse of office, as most leaders had access to much more than $5 million over the course of their time in office. Ibrahim termed this argument "cynical," and told Helen Coster of Forbes that such a view "assumes that all people coming to office are thieves."

Other recipients of the award have included Festus Mogae of Botswana (2008) and Pedro Pires of Cape Verde (2011). The award committee was unable to find suitable candidates in 2009, 2010, 2012, and again in 2013. Despite this, Ibrahim continues to have a positive view of the impact of his prize, as he noted to Geoffrey York in an interview with the Toronto Globe and Mail: "Because of the prize, there's a lot of noise around this. Once people start to talk, … that's what will change the game. We have to get out of the assumption that leaders are some kind of pharaohs. They are just human beings like us."

Ibrahim has also made advances on the economic front, touting Africa as an investment opportunity and acting as an unofficial international spokesman for African business. To that end he also serves as chair of the advisory board to the London-based investment fund Satya Capital, which focuses on investment opportunities in Africa. Thus far, the fund has invested in a telecommunications satellite company to supply broadband to Africa, as well as in private health, mining, food, and retail. However, as York noted, although "investors are buzzing about the rise of Africa as an emerging market these days, … Mr. Ibrahim worries that its profits are going to a tiny minority." A partial solution to this could be much closer integration between all the countries of Africa, another project Ibrahim supports.

Never Forgot His Roots

In 2008 Ibrahim made history when he appeared on the newest "Rich List" rankings of Forbes magazine. Along with a South African mining billionaire and a Nigerian who had made his fortune in sugar, Ibrahim was among the first black Africans ever to appear on the list of the world's wealthiest citizens. In an earlier issue of Forbes, he was asked what he thought about the millions of Africans whose lives were marked—and prematurely curtailed, oftentimes—by unimaginable hardships. His own good fortune, he told Coster, was "just a matter of luck. I managed to get education. I am not better than any of those unfortunate people."

In 2013 Ibrahim was the recipient of the Bishop John T. Walker Leadership Award, receiving the honor at a dinner that also honored President Barack Obama for his contributions to African development. Accepting the award—as quoted by the States News Service—Ibrahim was sanguine about the future of Africa: "Africa is moving forward—there's no question about that. It doesn't mean we are there yet. We see a great rise in the African servant society, mainly from young people and women. These two forces, I believe, are what will change Africa."

In an interview with Emily Flynn Vencat in Newsweek Ibrahim explained that because he had earned his fortune in Africa, he felt duty bound to return the favor. "I believe that us business people who have made money in Africa have a responsibility to help bring

good governance there." Asked by Auletta what he wanted his legacy to be, Ibrahim immediately responded, "I'd like to be remembered as a good African boy who didn't forget his people."

Sources

Periodicals

African Business, February 2006, p. 11; December 2006, p. 46.
Forbes, October 29, 2007, p. 52.
Globe and Mail (Toronto), May 10, 2010, p. B1; May 11, 2013, p. F4.
Guardian (London), January 31, 2009.
Newsweek, October 1, 2007, p. 74.
New Yorker, March 7, 2011, p. 45.

New York Times, October 27, 2006; October 23, 2007.
States News Service, April 23, 2013.
Telegraph (London), January 8, 2006; October 14, 2013.
Wall Street Journal, April 18, 2011; September 7, 2012.

Online

Mo Ibrahim Foundation, http://www.moibrahim foundation.org/ (accessed November 12, 2013).
"No. 462: Mohammed Ibrahim," Forbes.com, March 5, 2008, http://www.forbes.com/lists/2008/10/billionaires08_Mohammed-Ibrahim_IK9A.html (accessed March 6, 2008).

—Carol Brennan and J. Sydney Jones

Phillip Jackson

1950—

Nonprofit executive, government administrator

In 1996 Phillip Jackson founded a mentoring program in Chicago, Illinois, called the Black Star Project with the mission of helping minority students—particularly African Americans—achieve academically. At the time Jackson was an administrator with the Chicago Public Schools and was keenly aware of the lower test scores and graduation rates for black students compared to white students. The city's black youth were also exposed to numerous social ills, including street violence, gangs, and teen pregnancy. Over the years the organization gained national prominence by adding programs and services to help children and their parents develop skills for coping with these problems. In addition, Jackson encouraged black fathers (and father figures) to be strong, positive role models for the children in their lives. In 2004 he spearheaded the creation of the Million Father March, which annually encourages fathers, grandfathers, uncles, big brothers, and father figures of all types to escort children to school on the first day of school and to volunteer in the schools throughout the year.

Jackson was emphatic that parents take responsibility for the educational, social, and economic outcomes of their children. On the Black Star Project website, he stated, "Black parents are responsible for the well-being of Black children. Not the police. Not teachers. Not schools. Not preachers. Not elected officials. Not social service agencies. Black parents must hold the police, teachers, schools, preachers, elected officials, and social service agencies accountable for their actions to support the well-being of Black children. We will only solve the problems of Black youth to the degree that we create strong, empowered and engaged parents for Black children. Our actions, or inactions, will determine the future of our race."

Grew Up in Public Housing

Phillip Jackson was born in 1950 in Chicago. Little is known about his childhood other than that he was raised by his grandmother in public housing projects, including Altgeld Gardens and Robert Taylor Homes. Michael Martinez of the *Chicago Tribune* noted that Jackson grew up with five sisters in "ever-changing households." He attended seven different elementary schools and four different high schools. In 1969 he graduated from DuSable High School, a public school in the Bronzeville neighborhood on Chicago's South Side. Jackson told Martinez that he was not academically prepared for college and flunked out of the University of Illinois at Chicago after six months. However, Jackson tried again, earning credits at Olive-Harvey College and Malcolm X College, both two-year community colleges. He then studied at Roosevelt University, a private four-year school in Chicago, graduating in 1974 with honors and a degree in philosophy.

During his college years, Jackson worked as a stock clerk at a Kroch's and Brentano's bookstore. The family-owned company operated a chain of bookstores in Chicago and surrounding areas. Following graduation, Jackson worked his way up the management

ladder, eventually becoming senior vice president of operations in the early 1990s. By this time the company faced fierce competition from national book chains and began laying off employees and closing stores. According to Jackson, he left Kroch's and Brentano's in 1993 over a dispute with senior management regarding pension benefits for departing workers. The company went out of business two years later.

Jackson secured a job with the City of Chicago at the Office of Budget and Management and quickly moved up to the position of assistant budget director. In 1995 he went to work as a senior administrator for the Chicago Public Schools. There he served under school superintendent Paul Vallas, who had been tapped by Mayor Richard M. Daley to reform the city's beleaguered school system. Jackson began as Vallas's deputy chief of staff and then progressed to director of intergovernmental affairs and finally to chief of staff. During his stint with the Chicago Public Schools, Jackson became acutely aware that black students were underperforming academically compared to white students. The so-called academic gap was evidenced by large differences in test scores and graduation rates between white and minority students. Realizing that the school system was incapable of fully addressing the

problem, Jackson decided to start a private organization to help minority students perform better.

Founded Black Star Project

In 1996 Jackson founded a nonprofit organization called the Black Star Project and enlisted the aid of fellow educators and other professionals as volunteer mentors. Martinez indicated that by 1998 the program had arranged for 400 mentors to visit 85 public and private schools in the city, reaching nearly 20,000 students. Another project called The Wall was initiated to help college-bound youth perform at the collegiate level. In part from his own experience, Jackson knew that many black freshman college students struggle in their first year because of academic and cultural challenges. The Wall was a summer program that employed recent black college graduates to coach black youths and help them develop strategies for success in college. In addition, the Journey to Womanhood program arranged for professional women to mentor teenage girls and to provide them with strong, positive female role models and hopefully reduce drug use and teen pregnancy. Martinez pointed out that the Black Star Project did not receive any government funding but relied on donations and money infused into the organization by Jackson.

In 1999 Jackson left the Chicago Public Schools to become chief executive officer of the Chicago Housing Authority for a year. From there he took a position as chief of education in the office of the city's mayor. From 2001 to 2002 he served as chief executive officer and president of the Boys and Girls Clubs of Chicago, ultimately leaving that post to devote himself full time to the Black Star Project. Jackson ran unsuccessfully in the Democratic primaries for the U.S. Congress (First District) in 2006 and for the Illinois House (26th District) in 2008.

In the 21st century Jackson continued to add new programs to the Black Star Project to aid minority youths and their families. These included Destination College workshops that provided college-bound students with information about college admissions and financial aid. Parent University offered classes for the parents of Chicago Public Schools students, educating the adults about parenting skills, conflict resolution, and financial literacy. The Father's Club encouraged fathers and father figures to take the children in their lives on outings to zoos, parks, and other venues. The League of Black Parents urged black parents not only to educate their children but also to advocate on their behalf in the schools and the community at large.

In 2004 Jackson began a movement he called the Million Father March in which fathers and father figures were asked to escort their children to school on the first day of the school year. In addition, the men were encouraged to volunteer at the schools throughout the

year to provide positive male role models for the students. According to Brian DeBose of the *Washington Times*, Jackson's inspiration for the Million Father March was twofold. First, it recognized the significance of the Million Man March, the 1995 mass gathering in Washington, DC, spearheaded by Louis Farrakhan to draw attention to civil rights and social and political issues relevant to African Americans. In addition, Jackson was emulating a South American tradition in which fathers take a day off from work to travel to their children's schools and thank the teachers for their efforts. Jackson told DeBose, "We thought what would it do and what would it be like for black men to take control of the education of their children, and this is a part of that mechanism."

The Black Star Project has brought its founder national recognition. On February 26, 2013, Jackson was honored by President Barack Obama at the White House as a "Champion of Change." The program recognizes people who work to empower and inspire the members of their community. A press release from the White House noted that the Black Star Project "works to create globally competitive, globally compassionate, globally cooperative students, parents, families, and communities."

Selected writings

Opinion/editorials

"Blacks Drowning in Poverty," *Tuscaloosa News*, July 23, 2006.
"Will Another Generation of Black Males Be Lost?" *Record* (Bergen County, NJ), January 2, 2009.
"America Has Given Up on Young Black Men Like Trayvon Martin," *Wisconsin State Journal*, March 28, 2012.

Articles

"Failing Our Black Children," *Black Issues in Higher Education*, September 23, 2004.
"Occupy the Hood Calls Young People of African Descent to Improve Their World," *Public Agenda* (Accra, Ghana), November 8, 2011.

Sources

Periodicals

Atlanta Journal-Constitution, September 7, 2009, p. B5.
Chicago Tribune, June 6, 1998; March 20, 2006.
Daily Herald (Arlington Heights, IL), March 22, 2006, p. 19.
Denver Post, July 18, 2013, p. 21A.
National Journal, October 1, 2012.
The Journal: Technological Horizons in Education, October 2006, p. 14.
Washington Times, August 22, 2005, p. A01.

Online

"Champions of Change," White House, 2013, http://www.whitehouse.gov/champions (accessed November 22, 2013).
"District 26," Ballotpedia.org, 2008, http://ballotpedia.org/Illinois_House_of_Representatives_elections,_2008 (accessed November 22, 2013).
"Leadership," Black Star Project, 2013, http://blackstarproject.org/action/index.php?option=com_content&view=article&id=31&Itemid=23 (accessed November 22, 2013).
"Our Programs," Black Star Project, 2013, http://blackstarproject.org/action/index.php?option=com_content&view=section&layout=blog&id=2&Itemid=25 (accessed November 22, 2013).
"Phillip Jackson," Encore, 2011, http://www.encore.org/phillip-jackson (accessed November 22, 2013).
"Phillip Jackson," White House, 2013, http://www.whitehouse.gov/champions/educational-excellence-for-african-americans/phillip-jackson (accessed November 22, 2013).
"Toyota Partners with the Black Star Project to Launch Groundbreaking Parent University Initiative," Business Wire, October 22, 2004, http://www.businesswire.com/news/home/20041022005058/en/Toyota-Partners-Black-Star-Project-Launch-Groundbreaking (accessed January 21, 2014).

—Kim Masters Evans

Wilson Kipsang

1982—

Long-distance runner

Kenyan long-distance runner Wilson Kipsang Kiprotich set a world-record time of 2 hours, 3 minutes, and 23 seconds at the 40th Berlin Marathon on September 29, 2013. His time bested by 15 seconds the previous mark set by his compatriot, Patrick Makau, at the same race two years earlier. With his triumph in Berlin, the five-foot, 11-inch, 137-pound Kenyan, who is known in the running world by his middle name, Kipsang, brought his total number of marathon wins to seven, including back-to-back victories at Frankfurt, Germany, in 2010 and 2011 and a first-place finish in London in 2012. Kipsang began racing professionally in 2007, at age 25. He competed well in several half-marathons before making his full-marathon debut in Paris in April of 2010, where he finished third. Kipsang took the bronze medal in the men's marathon at the 2012 Olympic Games in London.

Kipsang, Wilson, photograph. Ian Walton/Getty Images.

Inspired by Countryman Paul Tergat

Kipsang was born on March 15, 1982, in Muskut Village in Keiyo District, a region of Kenya's Great Rift Valley that is famous for producing world-class runners. For many years the running community has been centered in the Rift Valley town of Iten and the surrounding area, where the high altitudes, at 8,000 feet above sea level, enhance athletes' oxygen-carrying capacity. Kipsang attended an all-boys' public high school in Tambach, just outside Iten. He graduated in 2000 and went on to become a travelling salesman of farm equipment.

Kipsang's life changed course when he learned of Kenyan Paul Tergat's record-breaking speed at the 2003 Berlin Marathon, where Tergat became the first man in history to run the 26.2 miles (42.2 kilometers) in under 2 hours and 5 minutes. Inspired by the example of Tergat, who only learned of his talent as a 20-year-old air force recruit, Kipsang began to train. He had his first success running locally for the Kenya Police, including a second-place finish in 2006 in the 10-kilometer Tegla Loroupe Peace Race, held in the Rift Valley town of Kapenguria. Kipsang worked on the police force for three years before his running career took off in 2007. That year a fellow runner arranged for Kipsang's introduction to Dutch manager Gerard van den Veen, who agreed to take Kipsang on as a substitute when

one of his regular runners had to drop out of the 10-mile Jever Fun Lauf in Schortens, Germany. Kipsang won the race, setting a world record for the distance. More international successes followed. Kipsang took second place in the Tilburg Ten Miles in the Netherlands in 2007 and 2008. He shaved more than a minute off his personal-best time to run second in the 2008 Delhi Half Marathon, clocking in at 59:16, just one second off the pace of Ethiopian winner Deriba Merga.

Kipsang improved his personal best to 58:59 at the 2009 Ras Al Khaimah Half Marathon in the United Arab Emirates, earning a second-place finish seven seconds behind Makau that put him in league with just a handful of runners who had broken the 59-minute mark. Also in 2009, Kipsang won the Egmond Half Marathon in the Netherlands and placed third in a Kenyan sweep of the Berlin Half Marathon.

Earned Spot on Olympic Team

Kipsang ran two full marathons in 2010, the typical number for elite runners, taking third place at Paris in April and first at Frankfurt in October with a time of 2:04:57. He went on to win the Frankfurt event again in November of 2011, turning in the second-fastest marathon ever with a time of 2:03:42, missing by just four seconds Makau's record time set at the Berlin Marathon a month earlier. A morning mist had made the Frankfurt track slippery, possibly impeding Kipsang's record challenge. As quoted on the website of the BMW-sponsored event, Kipsang was nonetheless pleased with his performance: "The surface was a little bit wet, so it cost us something. There was less friction, so you expend more energy. I saw we were a little slow at 35k, and I felt strong, so I decided to go for it. But I'm pretty happy. It's my personal best."

Kipsang opened 2012 with a wind-troubled third-place finish at the Ras Al Khaimah Half Marathon. He followed with a runaway win in the London Marathon on April 22, 2012. Breaking away from the field at the 12-mile mark, Kipsang turned in a time of 2:04:44, more than two minutes faster than the second-place finisher, Kenyan Martin Lel, and only four seconds off the course record. The victory earned Kipsang a spot on the three-man Kenyan Olympic team, alongside Abel Kirui and Moses Mosop. At the Summer Games in London that year, Kipsang built up an early lead but was stymied by the hot and humid conditions and winding track. By the 25-kilometer mark, his advantage was only seven seconds. Ugandan Stephen Kiprotich made a final surge to claim gold, with Kirui taking the silver medal and Kipsang the bronze.

One month after the Olympics, Kipsang prevailed at the Great North Half Marathon in England with a time of 59:06. Early in November he arrived in New York City with thousands of other runners, only to learn that the annual marathon through the five boroughs had been cancelled as a result of Hurricane Sandy. Kipsang regrouped and instead made his American debut in the Honolulu Marathon in December. In a race severely slowed by strong trade winds, Kipsang won with a time of 2:12:31.

Kipsang's next race was the New York City Half on March 17, 2013, the first major road race in the city since the devastation caused by Hurricane Sandy. In freezing temperatures and with a dusting of snow covering the track, Kipsang overcame a pack that included 21 Olympians to take the race in 1:01:02. The race was preparation for his title defense at the 2013 London Marathon, scheduled for April 21. In a March 15 interview with Chris Lotsbom of the website LetsRun.com, Kipsang explained, "Before every marathon I try to go for a half-marathon to see how the fitness is responding, to see how fast I am, to see how the endurance part is, and to also give the body a push, to get used to the competing atmosphere." The London race featured a superb group of runners, including world record holder Makau, Olympic gold medalist Stephen Kiprotich, and another Kenyan, Geoffrey Mutai, who ran the downhill Boston course (therefore exempted from official times) in an astonishing 2:03:02 in 2011. Competitors all wore black ribbons in memory of the victims of the bombings at the Boston Marathon six days earlier. Ethiopian Tsegaye Kebede, the 2010 winner, overtook Mutai at the close of the race to cross the finish line first. Kipsang finished fifth and Makau a distant 11th.

Set New Marathon World Record

The greatest highlight of Kipsang's career occurred when he smashed the world record at the Berlin Marathon on September 29, 2013. His spectacular victory at 2:03:23 beat Makau's record by 15 seconds and earned him $54,000 in prize money for finishing

first and another $68,000 for establishing a new record. "This is a dream come true," Kipsang was quoted in the Kenyan newspaper *Mwakilishi* that day. "Ten years ago, I watched Paul Tergat break the world record in Berlin, and now I have achieved the dream. I felt strong, so I attacked at 35k, because the pace had become a little too slow." Despite beefed-up security, an intruder wearing running gear and a T-shirt promoting an escort service managed to rob Kipsang of the exhilaration of breaking the tape at the finish line. The man jumped out of the crowd in front of Kipsang and was quickly taken into custody by police.

According to a report by Mike Rowbottom for the International Association of Athletics Federations, Kipsang told reporters at a November, 2013, awards banquet in Morocco that he was hard at work improving his speed. "The World record can easily be broken. There are a lot of new guys now training harder who want to go for the record. For me, I think I can do a sub-2:03. It's possible…. The main problem in the Marathon is to control your mind for two hours. You have to be aware of how you are feeling, what time you are doing your splits, what are your targets, when do you break away from the group." Kipsang added that his long-range goal was to represent Kenya at the World Championships in Beijing in 2015 and at the Summer Olympics in 2016 in Rio de Janeiro. Kipsang's first race after his history-making marathon was the 15-kilometer Pfixx Solar Montferland Run in the Netherlands on December 1, 2013. He finished a disappointing fifth, 15 seconds behind Kenyan winner Patrick Ereng's time of 43:01.

Kipsang trains in Iten, where he owns a farm and a lodging and conference center, the Keeluu Resort. He is a local favorite because he chooses up-and-comers as pacemakers. In the Kenyan tradition, he also contributes financially to the development of aspiring youngsters, many of whom are motivated to run to escape poverty. Kipsang's wife, Doreen, has been integral to his success and has begun training herself. After her husband's 2011 Frankfurt victory, she surprised fans by supplying him with traditional Kenyan fanfare brought from home, a gourd of specially treated sour milk known as *mursik*.

Sources

Books

Finn, Adharanand, *Running with the Kenyans: Discovering the Secrets of the Fastest People on Earth,* Ballantine, 2013.

Periodicals

New York Times, April 22, 2012; May 1, 2012; September 29, 2013.
Runners World, September 29, 2013.
Telegraph (London), April 22, 2012.
Washington Times, August 12, 2012.

Online

"Athlete Profile: Wilson Kipsang Kiprotich," International Association of Athletics Federations, http://www.iaaf.org/athletes/kenya/wilson-kipsang-kiprotich-237679 (accessed January 13, 2014).
"Great North Run 2012: Wilson Kipsang Wins Annual Half Marathon," BBC News, September 16, 2013, http://www.bbc.co.uk/news/uk-england-tyne-19614850 (accessed January 13, 2014).
"Kenya's Wilson Kipsang Breaks Marathon World Record in Berlin," Mwakilishi.com, September 29, 2013, http://www.mwakilishi.com/content/articles/2013/09/29/kenyas-wilson-kipsang-breaks-marathon-world-record-in-berlin.html (accessed January 13, 2014).
"Kipsang and Galimova Win Windy Honolulu Marathon," International Association of Athletics Federations, December 9, 2012, http://www.iaaf.org/news/report/kipsang-and-galimova-win-windy-honolulu-marat (accessed January 13, 2014).
"Kipsang and Kiplagat Voted AIMS Best Marathon Runners of the Year," International Association of Athletics Federations, November 9, 2013, http://www.iaaf.org/news/news/wilson-kipsang-edna-kiplagat-aims-best-marath (accessed January 13, 2014).
Lotsbom, Chris, "Wilson Kipsang Hoping to Celebrate 31st Birthday with NYC Half Win," LetsRun.com, March 15, 2013, http://www.letsrun.com/2013/03/wilson-kipsang-hoping-to-celebrate-31st-birthday-with-nyc-half-win/ (accessed January 13, 2014).
Magut, Stanley, "Kenya: Hugh Bash at Iten for World Record Holder Wilson Kipsang," AllAfrica.com, October 5, 2013, http://allafrica.com/stories/201310070365.html (accessed January 13, 2014).
"Monaco Press Points: Wilson Kipsang," International Association of Athletics Federations, November 15, 2013, http://www.iaaf.org/news/news/monaco-wilson-kipsang (accessed January 13, 2014).
Rowbottom, Mike, "Kipsang Prefers Gold over Record," International Association of Athletics Federations, November 15, 2013, http://www.iaaf.org/news/news/monaco-wilson-kipsang (accessed January 13, 2014).
"Ugandan Kiprotich Beats Kenyan Duo Kirui and Kipsang to Spring Marathon Surprise," DailyMail.co.uk, August 12, 2012, http://www.dailymail.co.uk/sport/olympics/article-2187297/London-2012-Olympics-marathon-Stephen-Kiprotich-wins.html (accessed January 13, 2014).
"Wilson Kipsang: Kenya's Man of the Moment," BMW Frankfurt Marathon, http://www.bmw-frankfurt-marathon.com/en/allgemein/news/detailview/article/1389/wilson_kipsang_kenyas_man_of_the_moment.html (accessed January 13, 2014).
"Wilson Kipsang Sets New Marathon World Record 2:02:23," YouTube, http://www.youtube.com/watch?v=lkHnEJT9hKM (accessed January 13, 2014).

—Janet Mullane

Julius Lester

1939—

Writer, professor

Julius Lester is an award-winning writer whose body of work includes more than 40 books, many of which showcase his overlapping interests in African-American history (particularly slavery), folktales, and religion. From 1971 through 2003, he also worked as a professor at the University of Massachusetts, first in the African-American Studies Department and later in the Near Eastern and Judaic Studies Department. Lester has penned both fiction and nonfiction works for readers of all ages. His portfolio includes novels for adults and picture books for children. He is a lover of folk literature and classic myths and has revisited some of their enduring characters in his own works for children. For example, his three-volume series *The Tales of Uncle Remus* (1987–90) uses colorful illustrations to retell African-American folk stories about a trickster hare named Brer Rabbit.

Lester is best known for his young adult books, which target readers in their tweens and teens. One of most acclaimed books in this category is *To Be a Slave* (1969), which includes actual firsthand accounts from slaves interspersed with Lester's commentary providing historical context. The writer values storytelling, and most of his young adult novels are fictionalized accounts that vividly bring to life the peoples and events of the past. Lester has won praise for his attention to historical detail, soul-searching characters, and lyrical prose. On his website he explains his passion for writing: "I write because there is something I want to know and the only way I can find out is to write about it. I wrote *To Be a Slave* because I wanted to know what it was like to have been a slave and I couldn't find

a book that really told me. So, I suppose I write because I have questions I need answers to, and the only way to find the answers is to write my way into them."

Embraced Civil Rights Movement

Julius Lester was born on January 27, 1939, in St. Louis, Missouri, the younger son of a Methodist minister. He grew up in Kansas City, Kansas (1941–54), and in Nashville, Tennessee (1954–61), where his father led congregations. In an interview with Powell's Books, Lester fondly remembered his seventh-grade history teacher, recalling, "So much of what I do as a writer is to try to make the past come alive. That's what Miss Caldwell did for me." He was also profoundly influenced by his father, a man who told stories in the Southern rural black tradition, and by his grandmother, who was of Eastern European Jewish descent. This connection to a Jewish ancestor helped spark a lifelong interest in spirituality that eventually led Lester to covert to Judaism as an adult.

Growing up during the 1940s and 1950s, Lester spent summers in Arkansas with his grandmother. There he was exposed to racism and segregation in the days before the civil rights movement gained strength. He was profoundly influenced by what he described in *Horn Book* as the South's atmosphere of "deathly spiritual violence." In addition to its "many restrictions on where [blacks] could live, eat, go to school, and go after dark," the South was a dangerous place where blacks faced "the constant threat of physical death if

At a Glance . . .

Born Julius Bernard Lester on January 27, 1939, in St. Louis, MO; son of W. D. Lester (a minister) and Julia (Smith) Lester (a homemaker); married Joan Steinau (a researcher), 1962 (divorced, 1970); married Alida Carolyn Fechner, March 21, 1979 (divorced); married Milan Sabatini, early 1990s; children: (first marriage) Jody, Malcolm; (second marriage) Elena (stepdaughter), David; (third marriage) Lian (adopted). *Religion:* Jewish. *Education:* Fisk University, BA, English, 1960.

Career: Writer, 1965—; Graduate Faculty of Political and Social Science (later New School for Social Research), professor of Afro-American Studies, 1968–70; producer and host of live radio shows, WBAI-FM, 1968–75; host of television program *Free Time,* WNET-TV, 1971–73; University of Massachusetts, professor of Afro-American Studies (later African-American Studies), 1971–88, acting director and associate director of Institute for Advanced Studies in Humanities, 1982–84, professor of Near Eastern and Judaic Studies, 1988–2003.

Memberships: Authors Guild.

Awards: Newbery Honor, American Library Association, 1969, for *To Be a Slave*; Lewis Carroll Shelf Award, University of Wisconsin–Madison School of Education, 1970, for *To Be a Slave,* 1972, for *The Long Journey Home: Stories from Black History,* 1973, for *The Knee-High Man and Other Tales*; Coretta Scott King Award, Author Honor, American Library Association, 1983, for *This Strange New Feeling,* 1988, for *Tales of Uncle Remus: The Adventures of Brer Rabbit,* Author Award Winner, 2006, for *Day of Tears: A Novel in Dialogue.*

Addresses: *Home*—Belchertown, MA. *Web*—http://members.authorsguild.net/juliuslester/index.htm.

you looked at a white man in what he considered the wrong way or if he didn't like your attitude."

Lester was a gifted student who could also sing and play guitar. Although his early artistic interests lay in folk music, he eventually aspired to become a writer. In 1960 Lester earned a bachelor's degree in English at Fisk University in Nashville, Tennessee. The following year he moved to New York City and became politically active in the civil rights struggle. One of his contribu-

tions was to play guitar and banjo at rallies in the South, an activity that brought friendships with like-minded musicians, such as Pete Seeger. As the 1960s progressed, the racial climate in the United States became more polarized. Lester joined the Student Nonviolent Coordinating Committee (SNCC), a group that initially embraced nonviolence but gradually took a more militant stance against whites. A talented photographer, Lester became head of the SNCC's photo department and visited North Vietnam during the Vietnam War to document the effects of U.S. bombing missions. He also traveled extensively in the South, taking pictures to help document the civil rights movement.

Some of Lester's early books were written as a response to his experiences in the civil rights struggle. Works produced in the mid- to late 1960s, such as *The Angry Children of Malcolm X* (1966), *Look Out Whitey, Black Power's Gon' Get Your Mama!* (1968), and *Revolutionary Notes* (1969), established Lester as an eloquent and impassioned defender of the new black militancy. Still, the writer brought his penetrating gaze to the movement itself, not hesitating to criticize its leaders when he detected hypocrisy.

One issue that interested Lester was the state of relations between African Americans and white American Jews. In the two decades following World War II (1941–45), the two minority groups had found common ground under the civil rights banner in their experiences with discrimination and oppression. However, by the late 1960s white Jews had become much more integrated into U.S. society than had African Americans. In addition, the black militant movement was Afrocentric and largely rejected white participation. The PBS documentary *From Swastika to Jim Crow* explained, "Through the eyes of Blacks, Jews became Whites with all the privileges their skin color won them, regardless of alliances they had in the past."

Hosted Radio Show and Began Teaching

In 1968 Lester was hired to host a radio show at WBAI-FM, a public broadcasting station in New York City. The following year he became embroiled in a disagreement between the United Federation of Teachers (UFT)—a union including many white Jewish teachers—and the largely black populace of the Ocean Hill-Brownsville section of Brooklyn. The two sides got into a bitter dispute over the power of the African-American school board to fire UFT teachers and wield greater control over the local schools. Unfortunately there were some ugly outbursts of antiblack and anti-Semitic rhetoric. Lester came under fire after he allowed a black teacher to read on the air a poem, written by a black student, that included anti-Semitic phrases.

Recalling the incident many years later in an interview with Brad Pilcher of *American Jewish Life Magazine,*

Lester defended his decision. He pointed out that his 1979 essay "The Uses of Suffering," published in the *Village Voice,* criticized black leaders who accused Jews of pressuring the White House to fire the United Nations ambassador Andrew Young (a black man) after he met secretly with leaders of the Palestine Liberation Organization (PLO). Such a meeting directly contradicted U.S. foreign policy, which favored Israeli interests over those of the PLO. Lester told Pilcher, "I have no doubt that in my obituary there will be a mention of the anti-Semitic poem incident and not what I wrote in 1979. What no one seems to grasp is that the two are the same for me in that in 1969 I thought Jews were being racist and said so. In 1979 I thought blacks were being racist and said so. In my mind these controversies were never about black-Jewish relations; they were about being true to myself and speaking out against racism." Lester kept his position at the radio station until 1973 and also spent two years (1971–73) as the host of a public television show called *Free Time.*

In 1968 Lester began teaching at the Graduate Faculty of Political and Social Science (later the New School for Social Research) in New York. He was a professor of Afro-American Studies at the university for two years. In 1971 he left for the University of Massachusetts in Amherst to serve as a professor in the new Afro-American Studies Department. Over the years, particularly in the early 1980s, Lester earned national awards for his teaching. Also during this time he converted to Judaism, a spiritual journey he describes in his autobiographical book *Lovesong: Becoming a Jew* (1988). In the book Lester accuses the black novelist James Baldwin of making anti-Semitic statements. Lester's fellow black professors in the renamed African-American Studies Department were outraged and voted to oust him from the department. Lester became a professor in the university's Near Eastern and Judaic Studies Department, a position he held until he retired in 2003.

Wrote Children's Books

Meanwhile, Lester's writing career had flourished after an editor suggested that he write for children and young adults. In 1969 Lester released two books that came to mark his future success as a writer for young people. *To Be a Slave,* a collection of first-person accounts from slaves, evolved from an oral history of slaves that Lester was compiling. The book was the runner-up for the Newbery Medal, one of the most important prizes for American children's literature. Later that year Lester published *Black Folktales,* a vividly illustrated children's book that recasts various human and animal characters from African legends and slave narratives.

During the 1970s and 1980s, Lester released a number of well-received books. *The Knee-High Man and Other Tales* assembles six black folk stories, including those of the well-known Brer Rabbit, treating them with subtle emphasis on the politics of defying racism.

Long Journey Home: Stories from Black History (1972) and *Two Love Stories* (1972) as well as *This Strange New Feeling,* published 10 years later, offer lessons in black heritage through fiction based on actual African-American experiences. For example, *Long Journey Home* explores the everyday lives of ordinary African Americans during the Reconstruction period in the decades following the Civil War.

Lester teamed with illustrator Jerry Pinkney for a children's series of Uncle Remus retellings, beginning with *The Adventures of Brer Rabbit* (1987). The cycle of titles, which came to be known as *The Tales of Uncle Remus,* continued into a fourth volume in 1994, with *The Last Tales of Uncle Remus.* In addition, Lester and Pinkney produced a children's picture book that year titled *John Henry,* about the black steel-driving man of U.S. folk legend. Also in 1994 Lester published the civil rights novel *And All Our Wounds Forgiven.* The story takes place in the 1960s and follows the rise and assassination of a fictional black civil rights leader named John Calvin Marshall, who was inspired by the Reverend Martin Luther King Jr.

Through the remainder of the 1990s and into the 21st century, Lester wrote more than 20 additional books, all but one of them for young readers. His lone adult novel of this period was *The Autobiography of God* (2004), which weaves elements of Jewish history and a murder mystery into the story of a former rabbi suffering a crisis of faith. Many of Lester's books for children produced during this time—including *What a Truly Cool World* (1998), about God's creation of the Earth, *Why Heaven Is Far Away* (2002), and *Hungry Ghosts* (2009)—have a spiritual bent. All are brightly illustrated and filled with lighthearted prose and humor. The children's book *Black Cowboy, Wild Horses: A True Story* (1998) is based on the life of Robert "Bob" Lemmon, a former slave who became a celebrated cowboy after the Civil War.

Other children's books by Lester address diverse themes, including slavery, blues singers, and race. In *Shining* (2003), Lester tells the story of a mysterious little girl born into a rural mountain village. Because she does not speak, she is shunned by the other villagers. In an interview with Harcourt Trade Publishers, Lester explained that he filled the picture book with metaphors, especially ones that equate the color black with positive images rather than negative images, for example, "black as wisdom." The author stated that "[u]sing such metaphors is a way to have readers think about and experience emotions and concepts in a fresh way." He talks at length about his approach to writing and reflects upon his life in the autobiographical *On Writing for Children & Other People* (2004).

Lester's books for tweens and teens reflect themes of importance to him. *Pharaoh's Daughter: A Novel of Ancient Egypt* (2000) imagines the life of a young Moses growing up in a royal family. *Cupid: A Tale of*

Love and Desire (2007) takes a humorous look at the god of desire from classical mythology. In *When Dad Killed Mom* (2001), Lester explores the tragic consequences of domestic violence on a family. Perhaps his most controversial book, the disturbing story includes strong language and subplots involving suicide and sexual abuse. Lester brings to life the horrors of slavery and lynching in three 21st-century works for young adults. In *Day of Tears: A Novel in Dialogue* (2005), he uses richly drawn characters to expose the cruel truths of the largest-ever U.S. slave auction, held in March of 1859 in Savannah, Georgia. *Time's Memory* (2006) relies on elements of African spiritualism to examine the slave trade from the viewpoint of Amma, the creator god. In the very graphic *Guardian* (2008), Lester details the moral atrocities of the white residents of a fictional Southern town who lynch a local black man after he is accused of raping and murdering a white woman. The book is unique because of its focus on a white viewpoint of the events, which are set in the 1940s. Most of the story is told from the perspective of a 14-year-old white boy who knows that the black man is innocent but remains silent.

In addition to his dozens of books, Lester has written more than 200 articles, essays, and book reviews for such publications as the *Boston Globe*, *Dissent*, *Forward*, *Moment*, the *New York Times*, the *New Republic*, and the *Village Voice*.

Selected works

Tracts

The Angry Children of Malcolm X, Southern Student Organizing Committee, 1966.

Books (as author)

(With Pete Seeger) *The Folksinger's Guide to the 12-String Guitar as Played by Leadbelly: An Instructional Manual*, Oak, 1965.
The Mud of Vietnam: Photographs and Poems, Folklore Press, 1967.
Look Out Whitey! Black Power's Gon' Get Your Mama!, Dial, 1968.
Black Folktales, illustrated by Tom Feelings, Baron, 1969.
Search for the New Land: History as Subjective Experience, Dial, 1969.
Revolutionary Notes, Baron, 1969.
The Long Journey Home: Stories from Black History, Dial, 1972.
The Knee-High Man and Other Tales, illustrated by Ralph Pinto, Dial, 1972.
Two Love Stories, Dial, 1972.
(With David Gahr) *Who I Am*, Dial, 1974.
All Is Well: An Autobiography, Morrow, 1976.
This Strange New Feeling, Dial, 1982.
Do Lord Remember Me, Holt, 1984.
The Tales of Uncle Remus, illustrated by Jerry Pinkney, Dial, Volume 1: *The Adventures of Brer Rabbit*, 1987; Volume 2: *The Further Adventures of Brer Rabbit*, 1988; Volume 3: *The Misadventures of Brer Rabbit, Brer Fox, Brer Wolf, the Doodang, and Other Creatures*, 1990; Volume 4: *The Last Tales of Uncle Remus*, 1994.
Lovesong: Becoming a Jew, Holt, 1988.
How Many Spots Does a Leopard Have? and Other Tales, illustrated by David Shannon, Scholastic, 1990.
Falling Pieces of the Broken Sky, Arcade, 1990.
John Henry, illustrated by Jerry Pinkney, Dial, 1994.
And All Our Wounds Forgiven, Arcade, 1994.
The Man Who Knew Too Much: A Moral Tale from the Baila of Zambia, Clarion Books, 1994.
Othello: A Novel, Scholastic, 1995.
Sam and the Tigers: A New Telling of Little Black Sambo, Puffin, 1996.
What a Truly Cool World, Scholastic, 1998.
From Slave Ship to Freedom Road, illustrated by Rod Brown, Puffin, 1998.
Black Cowboy, Wild Horses: A True Story, illustrated by Jerry Pinkney, Dial, 1998.
When the Beginning Began: Stories about God, the Creatures, and Us, illustrated by Emily Lisker, HMH, 1999.
Pharaoh's Daughter: A Novel of Ancient Egypt, Houghton Mifflin Harcourt, 2000.
Albidaro and the Mischievous Dream, illustrated by Jerry Pinkney, Dial, 2000.
Ackamarackus: Julius Lester's Sumptuously Silly Fantastically Funny Fables, illustrated by Emilie Chollat, Scholastic, 2001.
When Dad Killed Mom, HMH, 2001.
The Blues Singers: Ten Who Rocked the World, illustrated by Lisa Cohen, Jump at the Sun, 2001.
Why Heaven Is Far Away, illustrated by Joe Cepeda, Scholastic, 2002.
Shining, illustrated by John Clapp, Harcourt, 2003.
The Autobiography of God: A Novel, St. Martin's, 2004.
On Writing for Children & Other People, Dial, 2004.
Day of Tears: A Novel in Dialogue, Hyperion, 2005.
The Old African, illustrated by Jerry Pinkney, Dial, 2005.
Let's Talk about Race, illustrated by Karen Barbour, Amistad, 2005.
Time's Memory, Farrar, Straus and Giroux, 2006.
Cupid: A Tale of Love and Desire, HMH, 2007.
Guardian, Amistad, 2008.
Hungry Ghosts, illustrated by Geraldo Valerio, Dial, 2009.

Books (as editor)

(With Mary Varela) *Our Folk Tales: High John, The Conqueror, and Other Afro-American Tales*, illustrated by Jennifer Lawson, privately printed, 1967.

(With Mary Varela) Fanny Lou Hamer, *To Praise Our Bridges: An Autobiography,* KIPCO, 1967.

The Seventh Son: The Thoughts and Writings of W. E. B. Du Bois, Random House, 1971.

Stanley Couch, *Ain't No Ambulances for No Nigguhs Tonight,* Baron, 1972.

Books (as compiler)

To Be a Slave, illustrated by Tom Feelings, Dial, 1969.

(With Rae Pace Alexander) *Young and Black in America,* Random House, 1971.

Sources

Books

Carson, Claybourne, Jr., "Blacks and Jews in the Civil Rights Movement," in *Strangers & Neighbors: Relations between Blacks & Jews in the United States,* ed. Maurianne Bracey and John H. Bracey, University of Massachusetts Press, 1999, pp. 574–89.

Periodicals

American Jewish Life Magazine, January/February 2007.

Commonweal, March 25, 1988, pp. 167–69.

Horn Book, April 1984, pp. 161–69.

Jewish Week, February 15, 2011.

Los Angeles Times, July 10, 1988.

New Jersey Jewish News, February 9, 2006.

New Republic, June 27, 1988, pp. 9–10.

New York Review of Books, April 20, 1972, p. 39.

New York Times Book Review, November 3, 1968, p. 7; November 9, 1969, pp. 10, 12; February 4, 1973, p. 8; May 17, 1987.

Publishers Weekly, February 12, 1988, pp. 67–68; September 5, 1994, p. 108.

Online

"Between the Lines: Interview with Julius Lester and John Clapp," Harcourt Trade Publishers, http://www.harcourtbooks.com/authorinterviews/book-interview_Clapp.asp (accessed November 26, 2013).

"Boston Globe–Horn Book Awards: Winners and Honor Books 1967 to Present," 2013, Horn Book, Inc., http://archive.hbook.com/bghb/past/past.asp (accessed November 26, 2013).

"Coretta Scott King Book Awards—All Recipients, 1970–Present," American Library Association, 2013, http://www.ala.org/emiert/coretta-scott-king-book-awards-all-recipients-1970-present (accessed November 26, 2013).

"Faculty: Julius Lester, Professor Emeritus," University of Massachusetts, 2013, http://www.umass.edu/judaic/faculty/juliuslester.html (accessed November 26, 2013).

"From Swastika to Jim Crow," PBS, 2000, http://www.pbs.org/itvs/fromswastikatojimcrow/relations_2.html (accessed November 27, 2013).

"Julius Lester," Amazon.com, 2013, http://www.amazon.com/Julius-Lester/e/B000APHAR6/ref=ntt_athr_dp_pel_1 (accessed November 27, 2013).

"Julius Lester," Goodreads.com, 2013, http://www.goodreads.com/author/show/8161.Julius_Lester?from_search=true (accessed November 27, 2013).

"Julius Lester," Powell's Books, 2007, http://www.powells.com/kidsqa/lester.html (accessed November 27, 2013).

"Julius Lester Interview Transcript," Scholastic, http://www.scholastic.com/teachers/article/julius-lester-interview-transcript (accessed November 27, 2013).

"Julius Lester on *Guardian,*" Harper Collins, http://www.harpercollins.com/author/authorExtra.aspx?authorID=13371&isbn13=9780061558900&displayType=bookinterview (accessed November 26, 2013).

Official Website of Julius Lester, http://members.authorsguild.net/juliuslester/index.htm (accessed November 27, 2013).

—Anne Janette Johnson
and Kim Masters Evans

Jamal Lewis

1979—

Professional football player

Lewis, Jamal, photograph. Mark Cunningham/Getty Images.

Exceeding 1,000 rushing yards in seven of his 10 pro seasons and rushing for the third-highest yardage ever in a single season, Jamal Lewis is one of the best running backs ever to have played in the National Football League (NFL). Lewis's name, however, is perhaps more recognizable for his conduct off the field, including drug charges that landed him in federal prison in 2004 and a series of other legal problems in 2012. That year Lewis made headlines for a personal bankruptcy, a paternity suit, and participation in a monumental lawsuit against the NFL for withholding the effects of concussions on players. Those stories regrettably overshadowed news of Lewis's 2012 induction into the Baltimore Ravens Ring of Honor for his contributions to the team and to the game of football.

Jamal Lafitte Lewis was born in 1979 and raised in a middle-class Atlanta neighborhood. His father was a railroad conductor, and his mother was a corrections warden. As a child Lewis rode go-karts, loved sports, and idolized Walter Payton of the Chicago Bears and his older brother, John, who was six years his senior. Football was a household passion: all three Lewis men played in high school. At Frederick Douglass High School in Atlanta, Lewis was a running back and linebacker.

In his senior year at Frederick Douglass, Lewis's parents separated, his father moved out, and the couple eventually divorced. The separation created a rift between Lewis and his father, and the future football star began spending much of his time at Bowen Homes, a crime-ridden housing project located five miles from his home. When Lewis was 18, he was arrested for shoplifting a $109 polo shirt from a Macy's department store, for which he was fined $1,000 and sentenced to three years of probation. During the same time, Lewis entangled himself in Bowen's drug scene, a situation that would come to head during his career with the Ravens.

Won Super Bowl with Baltimore Ravens

During his three years at the University of Tennessee, Lewis was the school's third-best rusher, gaining 2,677 yards, even as he sat out most of his sophomore year with a knee injury. As a freshman he rushed for 1,364 yards, scored seven touchdowns, and was named the

Southeastern Conference (SEC) Freshman of the Year and second-team All-SEC. Following his junior year, in 2000, he was chosen as the fifth overall pick in the NFL draft when the Baltimore Ravens selected him in the first round. Lewis's rookie season with the Ravens lived up to the expectations of a top draft pick. Rushing for more than 1,300 yards that season, Lewis helped the Ravens clinch a win in Super Bowl XXV over the New York Giants with 102 rushing yards and a fourth-quarter touchdown.

During training camp the following season, Lewis suffered a debilitating left knee injury and had to sit out. The situation was made worse when he was caught violating the NFL's alcohol and substance abuse policy, earning a four-game suspension. In 2002 he returned to the field with renewed dedication and a surgically repaired knee. In a preseason game against the New York Jets, Lewis "was almost too pumped up," Ravens coach Brian Billick told Damon Hack of the *New York Times.* "When he had nine guys draped over him, I was like: 'Get down, son. It's over.'" Lewis's efforts were not enough for the team, however, and the 2002 season marked the first time in three years that the Ravens did not make the playoffs.

Triumph returned to both Lewis and the Ravens in the 2003 season, Baltimore made the playoffs, finishing 10–6, while Lewis scored 14 touchdowns and rushed for a spectacular 2,066 yards, an average 129.1 per game and 5.3 per carry. A highlight of the season came during a game against the Cleveland Browns in week two, when Lewis set the NFL record for the most rushing yards in a single game, with 295. Three days before that feat, on the phone with Cleveland linebacker Andra Davis, Lewis predicted that he would break the record. "It was like Babe Ruth pointing to the fence before the home run," Billick told Jamison Hensley of the *Baltimore Sun.*

Faced Legal Problems

The Ravens had a tough 2004 season, finishing 9–7 and missing the playoffs. Unfortunately for Lewis, his problems extended beyond the football field. Following a years-long Federal Bureau of Investigation probe that focused on two drug-ridden Atlanta neighborhoods— including Lewis's teen hangout, Bowen Homes—Lewis and a childhood friend were arrested for possession and intent to distribute five kilograms of cocaine. Lewis was sentenced to four months in prison, which he served at the Federal Prison Camp in Pensacola, Florida, and two months at a halfway house. At the time of his arrest, he was completing his fourth season with the Baltimore Ravens. He was suspended for two NFL games, resulting in a loss of $761,000 in wages.

Back at training camp in August of 2005, Lewis told *Los Angeles Times,* "I'm back doing what I like to do, doing what I do best ... I'm not looking back on the past and the things I just went through. My next step is really just prove people wrong." Rushing for more than 100 yards in only two games that season, 2005 was not a spectacular year for the running back. Lewis's 906 rushing yards marked the first season of his NFL career that he fell below 1,000, and his average yards per carry, 3.4, was his lowest. The Ravens ended the season 6–10, missing the playoffs for the second season in a row.

The situation improved in 2006, beginning with the Ravens' 27–0 landslide win in the season opener against the Tampa Bay Buccaneers, with Lewis snagging the team's first points. Cinching their first four games of the season, the team ended with an impressive 13–3 record but lost in the divisional playoff game against the Indianapolis Colts. Lewis—who was playing with bone spurs in his ankles—finished the 2006 season with a respectable 1,132 rushing yards and nine touchdowns.

Lewis became a free agent in 2007. Following surgery to remove his bone spurs, he took a one-year, $3.5 million contract with the Cleveland Browns, who had just finished a disappointing 4–12 season. Lewis's Cleveland debut, against the Pittsburgh Steelers, was less than dazzling. With the Ravens down 10–0, Lewis fumbled at the Browns' 40-yard line, resulting in a

40-yard touchdown pass for the Steelers. The season soon improved for the running back, however, and he rushed for 1,304 yards, an average of 4.4 per carry—his best since 2003. As Daniel Wolf of the Bleacher Report website noted, Lewis's performance "helped the Browns become the Cinderella story that season with a 10–6 record."

Called NFL a "Silent Killer"

The 2007 season would mark the pinnacle of the running back's career. In 2008 his rushing yards fell to 1,002 and 3.6 per carry. Additionally, he managed to alienate his teammates by remarking that his team's defense had given up in a game against the Denver Broncos and that the new head coach Eric Mangini pushed the team too hard at practices. Halfway through the 2009 season, suffering from the lingering effects of a concussion, Lewis announced his retirement plans. But before he could make a final decision, the Browns cut the 30-year-old running back with a year left on his contract.

Lewis's retirement did not get off to a good start. In 2012, with $25 million of debt, he filed for bankruptcy. Shortly thereafter he was arrested for child abandonment and failure to pay child support to a former girlfriend in Georgia for a child whom Lewis claimed was not his. In February of 2013 a paternity test revealed he was indeed the father of the seven-year-old boy, and Lewis was ordered to pay support. The mother's request for $5,236 per month was reduced to $663, however, because of Lewis's bankruptcy.

In 2012 Lewis joined several other former NFL players in a lawsuit against the NFL and the makers of football helmets. In a radio interview with Atlanta's WCNN, Lewis referred to the NFL as a "silent killer," arguing that players were never fully warned of the damaging effects of concussions. By the time a $765 million settlement was reached in 2013, more than 4,500 former players had joined the lawsuit. The settlement included $675 million to compensate former players for brain injuries and $75 million for baseline medical exams. In January of 2014, however, a federal judge rejected the settlement, concerned that the sum would not be enough to cover all injured players, and requested further financial documentation from the NFL.

Regardless of the controversy that has surrounded him, Lewis was celebrated as one of NFL's greatest running backs in 2012, when he was inducted into the Baltimore Ravens Ring of Honor. In addition to helping the Ravens win the Super Bowl during his rookie year, Lewis still holds team records in total rushing yards (7,801), attempts (1,822), and touchdowns (47). At the end of 2013, his 10,607 total rushing yards of placed him at number 21 on the NFL career rushing yards leaders.

Sources

Periodicals

Baltimore Sun, August 9, 2001; September 15, 2003; February 27, 2004; August 2, 2012.
Los Angeles Times, August 10, 2005.
New York Times, August 16, 2002; February 26, 2004.
Sports Illustrated, May 6, 2011.
USA Today, February 4, 2005; February 18, 2010; May 10, 2012.

Online

Clayton, John, "Lewis Stops Waiting on Ravens, Signs with Browns," ESPN.com, March 8, 2007, http://sports.espn.go.com/nfl/news/story?id=2791313 (accessed November 30, 2013).
Farrar, Doug, "Judge Anita Brody Denies Preliminary Approval for NFL Concussion Settlement," SI.com, January 14, 2014, http://nfl.si.com/2014/01/14/nfl-concussion-lawsuit-settlement-2/ (accessed January 20, 2014).
Gagnon, Brad, "Memory Loss, Headaches, Dizziness, Sensitivity to Light: Jamal Lewis Discusses the Lingering Effects of his Concussion-Filled Career," SportsRadioInterviews.com, May 9, 2012, http://sportsradiointerviews.com/2012/05/09/memory-loss-headaches-dizziness-sensitivity-to-light-jamal-lewis-discusses-the-lingering-effects-of-his-concussion-filled-career/ (accessed November 30, 2013).
"Jamal Lewis: Baltimore Roster," Inside Tennessee, http://tennessee.scout.com/a.z?s=7&p=8&c=1&nid=1805667 (accessed November 30, 2013).
Mink, Ryan, "Jamal Lewis Going into Ring of Honor," Baltimore Ravens, September 17, 2012, http://www.baltimoreravens.com/news/article-1/Jamal-Lewis-Going-Into-Ring-Of-Honor/7421fb7e-21f1-4f21-b9d8-1ebd4be75521 (accessed November 30, 2013).
Rosenthal, Gregg, "Jamal Lewis Might Not Be Able to Retire," NBC Sports, February 17, 2010, http://profootballtalk.nbcsports.com/2010/02/17/jamal-lewis-might-not-be-able-to-retire/ (accessed November 28, 2013).
Viviano, Mark, "NFL to Pay $765M to Settle Concussion Lawsuits," CBS Baltimore, August 29, 2013, http://baltimore.cbslocal.com/2013/08/29/judge-nfl-players-to-settle-concussion-lawsuits/ (accessed November 30, 2013).
Wolf, Daniel, "Farewell, Jamal Lewis: Cleveland Browns Cut Diminishing Running Back," Bleacher Report, February 17, 2010, http://bleacherreport.com/articles/347467-bye-bye-jamal-lewis-cleveland-browns-cut-diminishing-running-back (accessed November 30, 2013).

—Candice Mancini

Evelyn Gibson Lowery

1925–2013

Civil rights activist

Evelyn Gibson Lowery, the wife of the Reverend Joseph Lowery, who was known as the "dean of the civil rights movement," was an icon of the civil rights movement and a lifelong activist in her own right. The daughter of two activists, Lowery dedicated her life to fighting for the rights of the disenfranchised and played an active role in important milestones of the civil rights movement, such as the formation of the Southern Christian Leadership Conference (SCLC) and the historic Selma-to-Montgomery marches.

Followed Parents' Footsteps as Activist

Born in 1925 in Topeka, Kansas, to the Reverend Harry B. Gibson, a Methodist preacher, and his wife Evelyn, Lowery was raised in a household in which both parents were fiercely committed to fighting society's injustices. Lowery witnessed her father take leadership positions in the local chapters of the National Association for the Advancement of Colored People (NAACP) and made a decision to follow in her parents' footsteps early in life. Because her father was a preacher, the family moved often when she was a girl, although Gibson spent much of her childhood in Memphis, Tennessee. Later the family moved to Birmingham, Alabama, where Lowery enrolled at Clark College to study social work.

In 1947 Lowery's sister proposed that she go on a blind date with a young Birmingham preacher whom she knew, the Reverend Joseph Lowery. After a year of courtship, Evelyn Gibson married Reverend Lowery

on April 5, 1948. Their marriage was a close, 65-year partnership that lasted until Evelyn's death in 2013. Always by her husband's side, together the Lowerys lived a life of conviction, fighting against discrimination for more than six decades. Juanita Abernathy, the wife of civil rights activist Ralph Abernathy, told Michelle Shaw of the *Atlanta Journal-Constitution,* "She was always by Joe's side. They were always a team." As a preacher's wife Lowery found another means of fulfilling her desire to become a social worker, serving the needs of her congregation while also advocating for their rights and well-being.

Reverend Lowery graduated from the Chicago Ecumenical Institute in 1950, earning a doctorate in divinity. An ordained Methodist minister, like Evelyn's father, his calling took the family into churches across the South. From 1952 to 1963 the Lowerys lived in Mobile, Alabama, where they first began working with the Reverend Martin Luther King Jr. on a broad and organized civil rights movement. To that end, following the Montgomery Bus Boycott that took place in 1955–56, King, Reverend Lowery, and Abernathy, among others, formed the Southern Christian Leadership Conference, an organization that would become a major force in the American civil rights movement. Reverend Lowery became the organization's vice president, serving under King, the first president of the SCLC.

Fought for Civil Rights Alongside Husband

The Lowerys work with the SCLC would define the

At a Glance . . .

Born Evelyn Gibson in 1925 in Topeka, KS; died on September 26, 2013, in Atlanta, GA; daughter of Harry B. Gibson (a Methodist preacher and activist) and Evelyn Gibson (an activist); married Joseph E. Lowery (a Methodist preacher and civil rights activist), April 5, 1948; children: Yvonne Kennedy, Karen Lowery, Cheryl Lowery-Osborne. *Politics:* Democrat. *Religion:* Methodist. *Education:* Attended Clark College, Youngstown University.

Career: Civil rights activist, 1950s–2013; Evelyn G. Lowery Civil Rights Heritage Tour, founder, 1987; opened Women's Empowerment Training Center, 1988; started Bridging the Gap mentoring program, 1995.

Memberships: Southern Christian Leadership Council; Southern Christian Leadership Council/WOMEN, founder.

Awards: International Civil Rights Walk of Fame, 2004.

next three decades of their life together. In the early 1960s members of the SCLC were sued for libel for running a newspaper advertisement that criticized the Montgomery police department. When the court ruled against the SCLC, the Lowerys' assets were seized. The case was eventually overturned by the U.S. Supreme Court. In 1962 the Lowerys moved to Nashville, Tennessee, where Reverend Lowery served St. Paul's Church and the couple worked on integrating racially segregated restaurants.

By 1964 they had moved back to Birmingham, where they helped organize the historic Selma-to-Montgomery marches of 1965. A response to the murder of activist Jimmie Less Jackson by a state trooper, as well as a demonstration in support of voting rights, the marches initially were stopped in Selma when local law officials used violence to quell the marchers. After obtaining court protection for their right to march, thousands of people began the four-day walk from Selma to Montgomery. The march gathered more participants as it progressed, culminating in the arrival of a group of more than 20,000. Months later, President Lyndon B. Johnson would sign the Voting Rights Act of 1965, which outlawed voting discrimination.

Following King's death in 1968, the Lowerys moved to Atlanta, where Reverend Lowery became chair of the SCLC and, later, president. In May of 1979, while leading a protest in Decatur, Alabama, against the conviction of a mentally disabled black man accused of raping a white woman, the Lowerys became the target of violence by the Ku Klux Klan. Knowing that there had been threats, Reverend Lowery asked Evelyn to drive behind the protest in their 1977 Buick. When shots were fired at the protestors, two hit the Buick. The Lowerys kept that car thereafter as a reminder of the violence brought against them.

Helped Give Black Women a Voice

In October of 1979 Evelyn Lowery founded the Southern Christian Leadership Conference/Women's Organizational Movement for Equality Now (WOMEN) to give voice to women activists in the African-American community. Though women had long been active in the civil rights movement, they were most often seen as supporters of the primary actors, men, and were rarely invited to speak. Seeking to change that inequality, Lowery turned her focus to putting women in leadership roles. Speaking to the *Atlanta Journal-Constitution,* Lowery explained, "It was apparent women were coming into our own around the country, in leadership roles. Women have been supportive of the civil rights movement all through the years, but not in leadership roles. This was the beginning of not only being active in leadership but also vocal." Though it was initially a branch of the SCLC, WOMEN eventually became its own entity. Later, in the 1990s and 2000s, WOMEN focused its attention on AIDS awareness, health and welfare issues, and efforts to strengthen black families.

From the late 1970s on, Lowery headed a series of her own initiatives while continuing to be an active presence at marches and protests. In 1980 she founded the SCLC's Drum Major for Justice Award, which honors those who fight for social justice. She marched with the SCLC in Pickens County, Alabama, in 1982 in support of extending the Voting Rights Act of 1965, and in 1983 she took part in a march in Washington, DC, commemorating King's 1963 rally at Lincoln Memorial. The next year she was arrested while protesting against apartheid in front of the South African embassy in Washington.

In 1987 Lowery also founded the Evelyn G. Lowery Civil Rights Heritage Tour, which she ran out of her SCLC/WOMEN organization. The two-day tour throughout the state of Alabama gave participants a chance to encounter the well-known as well as the unsung heroes of the civil rights movement. Functioning as tour guide, Lowery used her extensive knowledge of the civil rights movement to bring every detail and event to light. As part of this tour, Lowery also succeeded in getting 13 monuments erected to civil rights activists in Alabama, including monuments for

Rosa Parks, Jimmie Lee Jackson, Viola Liuzzo, Mother Marie Foster, and many others. In her 60s, but far from retirement, in 1988 Lowery opened a Women's Empowerment Training Center that focused on GED and computer training, and in 1995, she started a mentoring program for girls called Bridging the Gap.

Even in her 80s, Lowery was organizing public appearances for herself and her husband and remaining active in black community. In commemoration of a lifetime of fighting injustice, she was inducted into the International Civil Rights Walk of Fame located at the Martin Luther King Jr. National Historic Site in Atlanta in 2004. Lowery died at home from complications of a stroke on September 26, 2013, at age 88. At the time of her death, her husband told CNN, "My beloved Evelyn was a special woman, whose life was committed to service, especially around the issues of empowering women." NAACP chair Roslyn M. Brock told *USA Today*, "Ms. Lowery was a drum major for justice in her own right. Her spirit lives on in the initiatives she founded and in the activists she mentored across the nation."

Sources

Periodicals

Atlanta Journal-Constitution, September 26, 2013.
USA Today, September 26, 2013.

Online

"Civil Rights Activist Evelyn Lowery Dies after Stroke," CNN.com, September 26, 2014, http://www.cnn.com/2013/09/26/us/obit-evelyn-lowery/ (accessed November 26, 2013).
"Evelyn Gibson Lowery," SCLC/Women's Organizational Movement for Equality Now, Inc., http://www.sclcwomeninc.org/founder.html (accessed November 26, 2013).
"Joseph Lowery," Biography.com, http://www.biography.com/people/joseph-lowery-11388?page=1 (accessed November 27, 2013).
SCLC/Women's Organizational Movement for Equality Now, Inc. (official website), http://www.sclcwomeninc.org/index.html (accessed November 26, 2013).

—Kay Eastman

William Lynch Jr.

1941–2013

Political strategist

William "Bill" Lynch Jr. was a longtime political strategist for the Democratic Party who led or helped manage the election campaigns of many prominent politicians, including David Dinkins (the first black mayor of New York City), President Bill Clinton, and Jesse Jackson. Lynch served as deputy mayor under Dinkins from 1990 to 1993 and was vice chair of the Democratic National Committee from 1997 to 2003. In the political arena he was savvy at forging coalitions that helped candidates get elected to office. For example, he worked on a mayoral campaign for Dinkins, who narrowly won the race in 1989 over his Republican challenger, Rudolph Giuliani. Dinkins owed his victory to votes from a majority of the city's blacks, Hispanics, and young white liberals. Over subsequent decades Lynch served on campaigns for numerous Democrats at the local, state, and national levels. His folksy, unassuming manner and shrewd political skills earned him the nickname the "rumpled genius."

Bill Lynch was born on Long Island, New York, on July 21, 1941. Little is known about his upbringing other than that his father was a potato farmer. Lynch admitted that he was better at sports than at academics during his years at Mattituck High School. After graduating he went into the U.S. Air Force and then moved to Richmond, Virginia, to attend Virginia Union University, a historically black college. However, he left before completing his degree and returned to Long Island, where he worked as a community organizer. During the late 1960s he settled in Harlem and worked in the job training center at the City University of New York in the Graduate School and University Center in New York City.

Early on Lynch developed an interest in politics and in 1975 managed the campaign of the Harlem politician Diane Lacey Winley, who won a district election. Over the following decade Lynch played a role in the national presidential campaigns of Edward "Ted" Kennedy and Jackson. Kennedy, a U.S. senator from Massachusetts, lost to President Jimmy Carter in the Democratic primary in 1980. Jackson, a black civil rights activist, ran for president four years later and finished third in the Democratic primary behind the former vice president Walter Mondale and U.S. Senator Gary Hart. During this time period Lynch also mentored two rising black stars in New York politics, David Paterson and Dinkins. Lynch ran the campaign for Paterson, who was elected to the state senate in 1985. Dinkins also won election that year as Manhattan's borough president. (Each of the city's five boroughs has a president who advocates on behalf of the residents to the New York City government.)

Dinkins made Lynch his chief of staff. In *The Power of the Mayor: David Dinkins: 1990–1993,* Chris McNickle noted, "Observers thought them something of an odd-couple—the newly elected borough president physically fit, perfectly groomed, and fastidiously attired, his new top advisor heavyset, bearded, and unkempt, projecting the demeanor and aura of a 'rumpled genius.' Yet the two men had a natural affinity for each other, and they fell easily into a relationship of mutual respect and trust." According to McNickle, it

At a Glance . . .

Born William Lynch Jr. on July 21, 1941, on Long Island, NY; died on August 9, 2013; son of William Lynch Sr. (a farmer); married Mary Lynch; children: William III, Stacy. *Military Service:* U.S. Air Force *Politics:* Democrat.

Career: Community organizer, 1960s; City University of New York, Graduate School and University Center, job trainer, 1960s–70s; private political campaign strategist, 1970s–99; Bill Lynch Associates, founder and president, 1999–2013.

Memberships: Advancement Project; Black Institute; Children's Defense Fund; Hamilton Heights-Sugar Hill Historic Commission; Museum for African Art; National Association for the Advancement of Colored People; New York Organ Donor Network; Shared Interest.

was Lynch who convinced Dinkins to run for mayor in 1989 after test opinion polls indicated strong support from black and Hispanic voters. Although the incumbent mayor—the Democrat Ed Koch—was running for a fourth term, his popularity had declined dramatically because of corruption scandals and the city's economic woes. Lynch energized minority volunteers and powerful labor union leaders to rally votes for Dinkins. In the primary election in September of 1987, Dinkins won easily with 51 percent of the vote compared to 42 percent for Koch. In the general election two months later, Dinkins bested the former U.S. attorney general Giuliani, a Republican, by a slim margin, becoming New York's first African-American mayor.

After Dinkins was inaugurated in January of 1990, he appointed Lynch deputy mayor for intergovernmental relations. Over the following four years, the political strategist served as a senior adviser to the mayor. Lynch is credited with arranging Nelson Mandela's visit to New York in June of 1990; the festivities included a ticker tape parade. Lynch later advised Mandela when he served as South Africa's president during the late 1990s. Although Dinkins had run on a platform touting racial harmony, during his term the city suffered several racially polarizing incidents that hurt him politically. The most notable was the so-called Crown Heights riot that occurred in August of 1991 in Brooklyn after a car in a motorcade for a Jewish religious leader struck and killed a black child. Already-strained relations between the neighborhood's African Americans and Hasidic Jews (an ultra-Orthodox sect) were pushed to the breaking point by the accident. Over three days, rioting by angry black protestors left one Hasidic Jew dead and more than 100 police officers injured, unsettling the city. Critics, particularly Jewish groups, accused the

Dinkins administration of failing to act quickly to quell the violence. Those assertions seriously damaged the mayor's popularity with Jewish voters. In the 1993 mayoral election—a rematch between Dinkins and Giuliani—the Republican challenger won by a slim margin.

Meanwhile Lynch had been active in the Democratic Party machine, working on the 1992 presidential campaign for Governor Bill Clinton of Arkansas, who defeated incumbent Republican president George H. W. Bush and independent candidate Ross Perot. The campaign marked the beginning of a long and close alliance between Lynch and both Bill and Hilary Clinton. In 1997 the former president was instrumental in securing Lynch the position of vice chair of the Democratic National Committee, a post he held until 2003. During this time Lynch developed kidney disease and diabetes and received a kidney transplant from his son, William Lynch III, who had become a political consultant.

In 1999 the elder Lynch founded his own firm, Bill Lynch Associates, LLC, in New York to provide consulting services to companies and labor unions. He also continued his campaign work for Democratic candidates, including Fernando Ferrer (New York City mayoral candidate in 2001 and 2005), H. Carl McCall (New York gubernatorial candidate in 2002), U.S. Senator John Kerry of Massachusetts (presidential candidate in 2004), U.S. Senator Hilary Clinton of New York (presidential candidate in 2008), and John Liu (New York City mayoral candidate in 2013). Although none of these candidacies were successful, Lynch did live to see his former protégé Paterson elected lieutenant governor of New York in 2006. When Governor Eliot Spitzer resigned two years later over a sex scandal, Paterson served out Spitzer's term, becoming the first African-American governor in the state's history. Lynch was a lifetime supporter of the National Association for the Advancement of Colored People. In early 2013 the organization's Northeast Region established the Bill Lynch Political Courage Award in his honor. Only months later, on August 9, 2013, Lynch died of complications from kidney disease. He was 72 years old.

Sources

Books

McNickle, Chris, *The Power of the Mayor: David Dinkins: 1990–1993*, Transaction, pp. 22–23.

Periodicals

Chicago Tribune, November 9, 1989.
Los Angeles Times, September 13, 1989.
New York Times, September 14, 1989; August 10, 2013; August 16, 2013.

—Kim Masters Evans

Gloria Lynne

1929(?)–2013

Jazz and R&B vocalist

A masterful vocalist known for her warm tone, magnetic stage presence, and distinctive blend of jazz and R&B, Gloria Lynne was an audience favorite for decades. Trained in the gospel tradition, she had a string of successful albums between 1958 and 2007. She is perhaps best remembered, however, for a single she released in 1964, a ballad called "I Wish You Love" that quickly became a standard. Although she went on to suffer a series of setbacks—many of them related to the public's changing tastes—she made a triumphant return to the spotlight in the late 1980s. "An excellent singer whose style falls between bop, 1950s middle-of-the-road pop, and early soul," wrote Scott Yanow of AllMusic.com, "Lynne was always capable of putting on a colorful show."

Lynne was born Gloria Mai (or Mia) Wilson in New York City on November 23, 1929 (some sources say 1931). The daughter of John Wilson, a dock worker, and his wife, Mary, Lynne grew up there near the end of the Harlem Renaissance, an especially lively and fertile period in the development of African-American culture. Within blocks of her home in Harlem, long the center of the city's black community, were dozens of cafes and nightclubs where nationally known jazz stars

Lynne, Gloria, photograph. Andrew Lepley/Redferns/Getty Images.

could be heard nightly. Initially, however, Lynne's own musical interests centered on gospel, not jazz. Trained first by her mother, herself a gifted gospel singer, Lynne was performing regularly with the choir in her church by her early teens.

Like many vocalists Lynne found the particular challenges of gospel singing, above all its characteristic emphasis on protracted notes at the upper and lower edges of the scale, to be excellent training for other styles. In her mid-teens she began to focus on secular music. A pivotal moment came when, at the age of just 15, she entered and won the famous and notoriously competitive amateur contest at the Apollo Theater, a Harlem landmark. That victory brought her to the attention of local impresarios, and it was not long before she was singing professionally in venues around the city. One of her biggest breaks came in 1958, when she released her first album, *Miss Gloria Lynne*. It won strong reviews, and in the months that followed, Lynne's primary label, Everest, released a string of follow-ups. These, too, were generally well received, and her appearance on a television special with fellow vocalist Harry Belafonte in 1961 firmly established her national reputation.

At a Glance . . .

Born Gloria Mai (or Mia) Wilson on November 23, 1929(?), in New York City, NY; died on October 15, 2013, in Newark, NJ; daughter of John Wilson (a dock worker) and Mary Wilson; married Harry Alleyne (divorced, 1968); children: one son.

Career: Independent musician, 1940s–2013.

The next few years unquestionably marked the height of Lynne's career. In addition to the praise she won for "I Wish You Love," a moving remake of an old French hit, Lynne appeared in 1966 on another Belafonte television special. Like the previous special, it brought her to the attention of the general public in a way that her albums, directed primarily at fans of vocal jazz and R&B, could not.

Although those appearances were successful, it was soon clear that public tastes were changing. As listeners turned in increasing numbers to newer, looser styles such as free jazz and disco, the tightly structured, highly melodic standards on which Lynne had built her career began to lose favor, and it became harder and harder to find gigs. While many other vocalists of her generation found themselves in similar circumstances, her situation proved especially dire because she had few royalties to sustain her between bookings. Her albums had generally sold well, but disadvantageous contracts and mismanagement kept Lynne close to poverty for much of her career. In the mid-1970s, under the onslaught of disco, her finances became so precarious that she had to leave the music industry. "The crash for me was when disco came in," she later recalled, in a comment quoted by Adam Bernstein of the *Washington Post.* "Disco seemed to have taken over the whole era in the '70s, and singers like myself were put in the background. I just wasn't able to change over."

Lynne responded to that setback with admirable aplomb, balancing a series of nine-to-five jobs with vocal exercises to keep her voice in top form. That determination helped her return to the spotlight in the late 1980s. Amid signs of a resurgence of interest in traditional jazz, Muse Records offered her a contract, her first in more than a decade. The result, an album called *A Time for Love,* reinvigorated Lynne's career and brought her a number of new fans, many of whom had not yet been born when she made her debut in the 1950s. Although *A Time for Love* and its highly regarded follow-up, *No Detour Ahead* (1992), did not end her financial troubles, they enabled her to focus on her music. By the late 1990s she was once again a favorite at nightclubs, where she continued to refine her sound, updating it slightly while respecting its roots in the classic styles of the 1940s and 1950s. The

culmination of that conservative approach, in the eyes of many critics, was *From My Heart to Yours* (2007), which Yanow of AllMusic.com described as "arguably her finest album since the 1960s." Yanow added, "Her voice remains powerful, soulful, and unwavering."

Active until the last weeks of her life, Lynne was still performing publicly as late as August of 2013, when she appeared at a New York club called 54 Below. Soon thereafter, however, her health began to decline, and on October 15, 2013, she died of heart failure at a hospital in Newark, not far from her home in East Orange, New Jersey. Among her survivors was a son from her marriage to Harry Alleyne, whom she divorced in 1968.

News of Lynne's passing quickly prompted tributes from fans, music critics, and fellow performers around the world. Many recalled, in particular, the courage and perseverance she had shown in handling the setbacks she had experienced over the course of her career. "Honest to God," she once said, in a comment quoted by Bernstein of the *Post,* "every time I would try to stray away from [music], it would come right back and grab me."

Selected discography

Singles

"I Wish You Love," 1964.

Albums

Miss Gloria Lynne, Everest, 1958.
This Little Boy of Mine, Everest, 1961.
A Time for Love, Muse, 1989.
No Detour Ahead, Muse, 1992.
From My Heart to Yours, HighNote, 2007.

Sources

Online

Bernstein, Adam, "Jazz Chanteuse Gloria Lynne Dies at 83," WashingtonPost.com, October 18, 2013, http://www.washingtonpost.com/entertainment/music/jazz-chanteuse-gloria-lynne-dies-at-83/2013/10/18/223c08c4-3808-11e3-ae46-e4248e75c8ea_story.html (accessed November 15, 2013).

Farber, Jim, "'I Wish You Love' Singer Gloria Lynne Dies at Age 83," NYDailyNews.com, October 17, 2013, http://www.nydailynews.com/entertainment/love-singer-gloria-lynne-dies-age-83-article-1.1489309 (accessed November 15, 2013).

Slotnick, Daniel E., "Gloria Lynne, Singer of 'I Wish You Love,' Dies at 83," NYTimes.com, October 18, 2013, http://www.nytimes.com/2013/10/19/arts/music/gloria-lynne-singer-of-i-wish-you-love-dies-at-83.html?_r=1&&gwh=31C25FE8E778E3C47EF5BDFE25341A85 (accessed November 15, 2013).

Yanow, Scott, "*From My Heart to Yours:* Review," AllMusic.com, http://www.allmusic.com/album/from-my-heart-to-yours-mw0000476482 (accessed November 16, 2013).

Yanow, Scott, "Gloria Lynne: Artist Biography," All Music.com, http://www.allmusic.com/artist/gloria-lynne-mn0000664883/biography (accessed November 15, 2013).

—R. Anthony Kugler

Master P

1970—

Rapper, music producer, record industry executive, entrepreneur

At the beginning of his 1995 album *99 Ways to Die,* rapper and music industry executive Master P sums up his career: "I'm not just your everyday rapper. I'm an entrepreneur." Indeed, Master P was among the earliest hip-hop moguls in the 1990s—before Sean "Diddy" Combs and Jay-Z—building a business empire centered on his music label, No Limit Records. In the span of a few years, Master P turned his small record store in California into the biggest rap label and the biggest independent label in the United States, making a fortune producing Southern-style gangsta rap. He also was the label's marquee artist, with platinum-selling albums such as *Ghetto D* (1997) and *MP Da Last Don* (1998). A savvy and streetwise businessman, Master P seized on any market opportunity he could find, expanding his business beyond music into films, clothing, footwear, sports management, real estate, and even potato chips and phone sex services. By the end of the decade, *Forbes* magazine ranked him among the highest-paid entertainment executives in the country.

By the early 2000s, as No Limit's releases began to decline in popularity, Master P had announced his

Master P, photograph. James Lemke Jr./FilmMagic/Getty Images.

retirement as a performer (even though he went on to produce several more albums) so that he could focus on his business enterprises. Devoting himself to his family, he helped launch the hip-hop career of his oldest son, Romeo (also known as Lil Romeo), and the pair formed another independent label, Guttar Music. The father and son starred on the short-lived Nickelodeon television series *Romeo!* and released an album, *Hip Hop History,* as the Miller Boyz. Master P reinvented his label, first as New No Limit in 2003 and then as No Limit Forever in 2010. He kept his enterprise centered on his family, running the business with the help of his wife and producing albums by his son and other family members.

Started Business Empire with Record Store

Master P was born Percy Miller on April 29, 1970, in New Orleans, Louisiana. The oldest of five children, he grew up in the city's rough Third Ward in the Calliope housing projects. His parents divorced when he was 11 years old, and his mother moved to California. Master

At a Glance . . .

Born Percy Miller on April 29, 1970, in New Orleans, LA; married Sonya Miller, 1991; nine children. *Education:* Attended University of Houston; Merritt College (Oakland, CA).

Career: No Limit Records, founder and chief executive officer, early 1990s, renamed New No Limit, 2003; No Limit Forever, founder, 2010; founder and chief executive officer of No Limit Films, No Limit Sports Management, No Limit Clothing, P. Miller Clothing and Footwear, No Limit Toys, P. M. Properties, Advantage Travel, Platinum Barbeque Potato Chips, and Master Piece.

Awards: Inducted into Louisiana Music Hall of Fame, 2013.

Addresses: *Twitter*—@MasterPMiller.

P and his siblings shuttled back and forth between California and New Orleans, where they were raised by their grandparents. Master P attended Booker T. Washington and Warren Easton high schools and was a standout on the basketball team at both schools. According to a 1998 *New York Times* article, he earned an athletic scholarship to play basketball for the University of Houston (the university could not confirm that detail), but after he was sidelined by an injury, he opted to return home rather than sit out the season on the bench.

When Master P was 20 years old, his family settled a medical malpractice lawsuit with a New Orleans hospital over the wrongful death of his grandfather. Master P took his share of the settlement—$10,000—and moved to California with his high school sweetheart, Sonya (whom he married in 1991). He completed two years of business courses at Merritt College in Oakland and opened a record store in Richmond, California, which later would become the headquarters of No Limit Records.

Master P quickly grasped that he could make more money producing his own music rather than just selling records made by others. He self-produced his first album, *Get Away Clean*, in 1991. He followed with *Mama's Bad Boy* in 1992 and *The Ghettos Tryin to Kill Me* in 1994, selling tapes out of the trunk of his car in Oakland and in New Orleans. The *Ghettos Tryin to Kill Me* became an underground hit, selling 200,000 copies without any radio play and turning a profit for the young company. "Start in your neighborhood and sell your records," Master P later advised an audience of young entrepreneurs at a music business workshop,

the *Chicago Tribune* reported in 1998. "Once you start making a buzz, they'll come looking for you. If you can't sell records at home, you can't sell them nowhere."

Developed Successful Marketing Strategies

Master P's instincts were spot-on. The entrepreneur took the profits from his first records and used those funds to produce several compilations of regional rap, including *West Coast Bad Boys, Vol. 1* (1994) and *Down South Hustlers: Bouncin' and Swingin'* (1995). The latter album reached the Billboard charts, rising to number 139 on the Billboard 200 and to number 13 on the Top R&B/Hip-Hop Albums list. The strategies that he employed would become the hallmark of Master P and No Limit's marketing: highlighting popular artists along with less well-known entertainers and giving customers more for their money, with longer playing time and two-for-one compilations. "What I learned in the ghetto is that everybody wants more for their money," Master P explained in a 1997 interview with the *Washington Post*. "If you sell something for $20, they wanna know how they can get $25 worth…. [T]hat's what hustling is about. You gotta be able to give your customers more for their money, 'cause that's how you're going to keep them coming back to you."

No Limit also released albums by the group Tru, a trio that included Master P and his two younger brothers, Silkk the Shocker (Vyshonn Miller) and C-Murder (Corey Miller). By the mid-1990s, the label had a roster of artists, such as Mystical and Mia X, who were not household names but were well-known among rap fans. Soon the major labels took an interest in No Limit. In 1995 Master P signed a distribution deal with Priority Records, giving that label 15 percent of the profits for distribution while No Limit retained 85 percent. The deal granted No Limit sole ownership of its master recordings, allowing the company to profit from future reissues. No Limit's first release through Priority was Master P's 1995 album *99 Ways to Die*.

That same year Master P moved No Limit Records back to Louisiana, where he assembled an in-house production team called Beats by the Pound, made up of Craig B, KLC, and Mo B. Dick. The label was prolific in its output, releasing as many as 10 albums a year. Among them was Master P's 1997 album *Ghetto D*, his best-selling release to date, topping the Billboard 200 in the fall and eventually reaching triple-platinum status. *Ghetto D* produced the hit "Make 'Em Say Uhh!," Master P's highest-ever charting single, reaching number nine on the Billboard Hot 100 and number six on the Hot Rap Singles chart.

Expanded Business beyond Music

Master P saw the necessity of diversifying his business

beyond music. "You spread out because you never know when it's going to end," he told the *New York Times* in a 1998 interview. "Business is like a seesaw going up and down. When one goes down, I have the other going up. You have to think like that if you want to survive." He first branched out into films, producing, directing, and acting in the low-budget film *I'm Bout It* in 1997. When no investor would back the project, he bankrolled it himself with profits from No Limit Records. When he could not find a distributor for the film, he added short clips to the beginning and end, labeled the film "banned in theaters across America," and released it directly to video. Once Master P had an underground hit on his hands, the video flew out of stores. Within five weeks of its release, it had sold 200,000 copies and had risen to 26th place on the video sales chart.

In 1998 Master P had no trouble finding a distributor for No Limit's second film, the comedy *I Got the Hook-Up.* Dimension Films, a division of Miramax, signed a distribution deal with No Limit, again giving the company ownership of the film. Master P wrote the screenplay, produced it, and played a starring role. Although *I Got the Hook-Up* was criticized as heralding a new era of "blaxploitation" films, it was popular at the box office, grossing $10 million. Master P went on to write, produce, and star in a string of films over the next decade and a half.

The venture into filmmaking seemed to validate No Limit's business strategy. Instead of borrowing to launch a new venture, No Limit took the profits from one venture to bankroll the next. Master P was careful to retain ownership of the product, eliminating any middle man. Each new enterprise started small and grew from there. No Limit also cross-promoted its products: the films promoted the albums, and vice versa. Most important, No Limit projects always reflected what customers wanted. "We have total control, we stay small and we constantly put records and films out," Tevester Scott, the label's business manager, told the *Baltimore Sun* in 1999. "We know what sells in our market because we are our market."

Announced Retirement as a Rapper

Master P continued to take No Limit in new directions. In 1997 he formed a sports management company, No Limit Sports Management, which represented several young professional basketball players, including Ron Mercer of the Boston Celtics and Derek Anderson of the Cleveland Cavaliers. The following year, No Limit incorporated a dozen new businesses, including a Foot Locker franchise, a gas station, a travel agency, a real estate company, and even a phone sex service. By the end of the decade, Master P was chief executive officer of such diverse ventures as No Limit Clothing, P. Miller Clothing and Footwear, No Limit Toys, P. M.

Properties, Advantage Travel, Platinum Barbeque Potato Chips, and Master Piece (a line of watches). In 1998 he ranked 10th on *Forbes* magazine's list of the top entertainers, with a net worth of $56 million.

In June of 1998, Master P released his best-selling album, *MP Da Last Don,* accompanied by a direct-to-video film of the same name. The album debuted at number one on the Billboard 200, staying there for three weeks, and eventually was certified quadruple platinum, selling more than four million copies. The album produced three charting singles: "Goodbye to My Homies," "Make 'Em Say Uhh Pt. 2," and "Hot Boys and Girls," which reached number 25, 14, and 23 on the Billboard Hot R&B/Hip-Hop Singles chart, respectively. The album was marketed as Master P's swan song, as he announced that year that he was retiring from rapping to concentrate on his business enterprises. Despite that promise, he released his eighth studio album, *Only God Can Judge Me,* the following year. In 2000 he released *Ghetto Postage.* Also in 2000 No Limit released *Goodfellas,* the debut of Master P's new group 504 Boyz. (The name refers to the area code for New Orleans.) The album rose to number one on the Top R&B/Hip-Hop Albums chart.

A lifelong basketball fan, Master P decided to pursue his childhood dream of playing professional basketball. In 1997 he tried out for the Charlotte Hornets and the Toronto Raptors before signing as a free agent with the Fort Wayne (Indiana) Fury of the Continental Basketball Association. Playing for several months as Percy Miller, he averaged just 1.9 points and 1.6 rebounds in eight games, earning $1,000 a week plus $15 per diem for expenses. Although Master P was invited to try out for the Charlotte Hornets again, he did not make the team. In 2004 he played briefly for the Las Vegas Rattlers of the American Basketball Association.

Reinvented Record Label

By the early 2000s, a number of No Limit's marquee artists had left the label, and in 2003 Master P's brother, C-Murder, was sentenced to life in prison for a nightclub shooting. That same year, No Limit Records filed for bankruptcy. Master P soon resurrected the company as New No Limit Records, and in 2004 he struck a distribution deal with Koch Records. Master P's first release on the new label was his 2004 album *Good Side, Bad Side,* followed by Tru's *The Truth* (the group's final album) in 2005.

In 2005 Master P and his oldest son, Romeo (first known as Lil Romeo), whose hip-hop career his father had helped launched, founded the independent label Guttar Music. That year Master P released his album *Living Legend: Certified D-Boy* on the new label, and in 2007 the father and son released the collaboration *Hip Hop History.* This was not the first time that Master P and his son had worked together: in 2003 the

two starred in the Nickelodeon television series *Romeo!*, which aired until 2006. By this time Master P had settled back into family life, raising his nine children with wife, Sonya. His dedication to his family undoubtedly was influenced by his childhood experience. "I look at my parents. They divorced, went their separate ways. It made me look at life. I want to make sure I keep the pieces together," he reflected in a 2002 interview with *Ebony* magazine. "I grew up without a father, so I want to make sure that my kids grow [up] knowing that I'm in their life, no matter what the situation is." In 2008 Master P launched Better Black Television, a family-friendly cable television network with programming by and for black families. The network premiered in 2010.

In late 2010 Master P reinvented his record label once again, rechristening it No Limit Forever and moving its base of operations to Los Angeles. The new label, headed by Master P's sons Romeo and Valentino Miller, had a roster of artists that included Silkk the Shocker, Atlanta rapper Alley Boy, Miss Chee, Black Don, Gangsta, and T-Bo Da Firecracker, among others. In 2013 Master P released his album *The Gift* on No Limit Forever.

Selected works

Albums

Solo albums

Get Away Clean, No Limit, 1991.
Mama's Bad Boy, No Limit, 1992.
The Ghettos Tryin to Kill Me!, No Limit, 1994.
99 Ways to Die, No Limit, 1995.
Ice Cream Man, No Limit, 1996.
Ghetto D (includes "Make 'Em Say Uhh!"), No Limit, 1997.
MP Da Last Don (includes "Goodbye to My Homies," "Make 'Em Say Uhh Pt. 2," and "Hot Boys and Girls"), No Limit, 1998.
Only God Can Judge Me, No Limit, 1999.
Ghetto Postage, No Limit, 2000.
Game Face, New No Limit, 2001.
Good Side, Bad Side, New No Limit, 2004.
Ghetto Bill, New No Limit, 2005.
Living Legend: Certified D-Boy, Guttar Music, 2005.
(With Romeo as the Miller Boyz) *Hip Hop History,* Guttar Music, 2007.
The Gift, No Limit Forever, 2013.

With Tru

Understanding the Criminal Mind, No Limit, 1992.
Who's Da Killer?, No Limit, 1993.
True, No Limit, 1995.
Tru 2 Da Game, No Limit, 1997.
Da Crime Family, No Limit, 1999.
The Truth, New No Limit, 2005.

With 504 Boyz

Goodfellas, No Limit, 2000.
Ballers, New No Limit, 2002.
Hurricane Katrina: We Gon Bounce Back, Guttar Music, 2005.

Films

I'm Bout It (video), No Limit Films, 1997.
I Got the Hook-Up, No Limit Films, 1998.
MP Da Last Don (video), No Limit Films, 1998.
Da Game of Life, No Limit Films, 1998.
The Players Club, New Line Cinema, 1998.
Foolish, No Limit Films, 1999.
No Tomorrow, No Limit Films, 1999.
911 (video), No Limit Films, 2000.
Lockdown, Evolution Entertainment, 2000.
Hot Boyz (video), No Limit Films, 2000.
Takedown, Dimension Films, 2000.
Undisputed, Miramax Films, 2002.
Dark Blue, United Artists, 2002.
Hollywood Homicide, Revolution Studios, 2003.
Bad Bizness, Epsilon Motion Pictures, 2003.
Still Bout It (video), New No Limit Films, 2004.
Decisions (video), Koch Vision, 2004.
Repos (video), Bossman/Master P, 2006.
Don't Be Scared (video), Bossman/Master P, 2006.
Paroled, Paroled Films, 2007.
Uncle P, Reveal Pictures, 2007.
Black Superman, First Look International, 2007.
Toxic, Wingman, 2008.
Soccer Mom, Bogner Entertainment, 2008.
Internet Dating, Bossman/Master P, 2008.
The Pig People, Vault Load, 2009.
The Mail Man, Bumpit Promotions, 2009.
Down and Distance, Gorilla Films, 2010.
Knock Knock Killers, Company Pictures, 2011.

Television

Crashing with Master P, MTV, 2003.
Romeo!, Nickelodeon, 2003–06.
No Excuses with Master P, VH1, 2009.

Sources

Periodicals

Baltimore Sun, January 10, 1999.
Chicago Tribune, August 6, 1998.
Ebony, June 2002.
Herald (Rock Hill, SC), January 24, 1999.
Jet, February 26, 2001; February 3, 2003; September 15, 2003.
Newsweek, June 1, 1998.
New York Times, May 13, 1998; November 9, 1998.
Wall Street Journal, June 25, 1998.
Washington Post, May 29, 1998.
Washington Times, October 27, 1999.

Online

Erlewine, Thomas, "Master P," AllMusic.com, http://www.allmusic.com/artist/master-p-mn000038 2455 (accessed January 8, 2014).

"The Rise and Fall of No Limit Records," SOHH.com, February 25, 2010, http://www.sohh.com/2010/02/special_to_sohh_the_rise_fall_of_no_limi.html (accessed January 8, 2014).

—Rory Connelly and Deborah A. Ring

Pumeza Matshikiza

1979(?)—

Opera singer

Matshikiza, Pumeza, photograph. Tony Barson/WireImage/Getty Images.

Pumeza Matshikiza has a highly unusual background for a singer rising to stardom in opera world: she comes from the black townships of South Africa. The young beauty, trained at London's Royal College of Music, has won acclaim on the European stage for her rich, joyful soprano, tackling roles from Giacomo Puccini, Wolfgang Amadeus Mozart, and other classical composers. In 2013 Matshikiza signed a recording contract with the prestigious Decca Classics label and began work on a debut album that will bridge the gap between African and European musical traditions.

Matshikiza grew up at the tail end of the apartheid era in South Africa, when legally enforced racial discrimination kept blacks disenfranchised, impoverished, and relegated to the ghetto townships on the outskirts of the nation's major cities. Her parents separated when she was an infant, and she relocated with her mother and brothers from Eastern Cape Province to Cape Town. Her mother struggled to find work and keep her children safe and nourished, sheltered in corrugated iron shacks in the crowded shanty towns of Khayelitsha, Langa, and Nyanga, among of the world's most dangerous places to live. Frequently looked after by her grandmother and other relatives, Matshikiza witnessed the extremes of crime and violence and saw people killed by "necklacing"—a gasoline-doused tire placed around the victim's neck and ignited—a common form of informal township justice. She also took part in many protests against apartheid, sometimes facing tear gas and other police crowd control. She was a teenager when the country finally ended apartheid and elected its first black president, Nelson Mandela, in 1994.

Music is deeply interwoven into the culture of South African blacks, and Matshikiza discovered her love of singing at an early age. She sang alongside her mother in their Seventh-day Adventist church choir and with her peers at Homba Public Primary School. One day early in her adolescence, while flipping the radio dial, she heard a few strains of opera and was immediately captivated by the exquisite voices and orchestration. Through the radio she immersed herself in the classical tradition and began fantasizing about a career in vocal performance.

At first Matshikiza found no encouragement from her

At a Glance . . .

Born Pumeza Matshikiza in 1979(?) in Cape Town, South Africa. *Education:* University of Cape Town, South African College of Music, performer's diploma, 2004; Royal College of Music, London, master's degree in performance, 2007.

Career: Jette Parker Young Artists Programme, Royal Opera House, London, 2007–09; Classical Opera, London, associate artist, 2010; Stuttgart State Opera, ensemble, 2011–14.

Awards: Best Performer of the Year, Friends of Cape Town Opera, 2003; First Prize, Veronica Dunne International Singing Competition, Dublin, 2010.

Addresses: *Management*—c/o Intermusica Artists' Management Ltd., 36 Graham St., Crystal Wharf, London N1 8GJ, United Kingdom.

teachers for such pursuits. A fine student with excellent grades in math and science, she began her studies at the University of Cape Town with the pragmatic goal of becoming a quantity surveyor in the construction industry. But in the heady postapartheid years, she allowed her dreams to take flight. After taking a year off from school to think over her career plans, she transferred to the South African College of Music at the university and began honing her talent under the tutelage of a first-rate voice teacher, Virginia Davids. While she was still a student, Matshikiza performed with South Africa's famous Handspring Puppet Company and toured from Western Europe to Singapore with the troupe's production of *The Confessions of Zeno* in 2002. She also sang with the Cape Town Opera and was chosen as best performer of the year by the Friends of Cape Town Opera in 2003.

Matshikiza graduated with a performer's diploma in 2004. By this time Kevin Volans, the composer of *The Confessions of Zeno,* had become a devoted admirer. Volans arranged for Matshikiza to audition for the Royal College of Music in London and paid her airfare. Her auditioners asked her not to apply anywhere else: they accepted her on the spot and offered her a full scholarship. She endured London's cold weather and homesickness as she adjusted to her new surroundings, deeply aware that she had received a rare opportunity that would require her to spend a long far from home. "Opera is a luxury in a South African context," she told

the London *Independent* newspaper in 2011, "when people have no clean water, people live without sanitation—these are basic needs. That's why South African opera singers have to leave. We have some fantastic voices, but there is not enough work for singers to make a living."

After earning her master's degree in 2007, Matshikiza received another honor: she was accepted into the Jette Parker Young Artists Program at London's Royal Opera House, a two-year paid apprenticeship with one of the world's most prestigious opera companies. She debuted on the Covent Garden stage as a flower maiden in Richard Wagner's opera *Parsifal* and sang featured roles in several other productions, including *Don Carlos, The Tales of Hoffmann, Salome, Hansel and Gretel,* and the world premiere of *The Minotaur* by Harrison Birtwistle.

Matshikiza came into her own in 2010, when she took first prize at the Veronica Dunne International Singing Competition in Dublin, Ireland, besting performers from 21 nations; a fellow South African, Sarah-Jane Brandon, finished second. That June, having joined the Classical Opera in London, she sang the title role in its production of Mozart's unfinished opera *Zaide,* receiving positive notices, although the production was widely panned. Two months later in Glasgow, Scotland, she scored a greater success as Mimi in the Opera Bohemia production of Puccini's *La Bohème.* On the Opera Britannia website, Antony Lias wrote, "Pumeza Matshikiza's Mimi was as rapt an interpretation as one could expect to hear today.... That distinctively warm and rich timbre was a joy to hear, as it cosseted Mimi's soaring climaxes with a distinctively old world charm." In 2011 the soprano signed on to a three-year contract to perform with the Stuttgart State Opera in Germany. Her roles with that company included Susanna in *The Marriage of Figaro* and Zerlina in Mozart's *Don Giovanni.*

In June of 2013 Matshikiza signed her first recording contract with Decca Classics, a label that has released the work of such star vocalists as Joan Sutherland, Marilyn Horne, and Luciano Pavarotti. Decca announced that Matshikiza's debut album, to be recorded at London's Abbey Road Studios, "will follow her musical journey from townships to the operatic stage," placing familiar arias from Mozart and Puccini alongside traditional material sung in the Xhosa language. The African Children's Choir will appear on the album on tracks such as "Wimoweh" (The Lion Sleeps Tonight) and Paul Simon's "Homeless" (from the 1986 album *Graceland*). The album, slated for release early in 2014, also will feature a new arrangement by Paul Mealor of William Ernest Henley's "Invictus," a poem that inspired Nelson Mandela during his years of imprisonment. In May of 2014 Matshikiza was scheduled to reprise her role as Mimi in the Stuttgart Opera production of *La Bohème.*

Sources

Periodicals

Independent (London), May 13, 2011.
Telegraph (London), June 10, 2010; June 21, 2013.

Online

"From Township to Opera House," Decca Classics, http://www.deccaclassics.com/us/artist/matshi kiza/ (accessed December 2, 2013).

Lias, Antony, "*La Bohème:* Opera Bohemia, Glasgow, 21st August 2010," Opera-Britannia.com, August 23, 2010, http://www.opera-britannia.com/index .php?option=com_content&view=article&id=351 :la-boheme-opera-bohemia-glasgow-21st-august-20 10&catid=8:opera-reviews&Itemid=16 (accessed December 2, 2013).

Nkozi, Bongani, "SA Songbird Wins Top Opera Prize," Media Club South Africa, February 5, 2010, http:// www.mediaclubsouthafrica.com/culture/1501-sa -songbird-wins-top-opera-prize#ixzz2lgbvcI3x (accessed November 25, 2013).

Nurse, Earl, and Soffel, Jenny, "Pumeza Matshikiza: Township Girl to Opera Diva," CNN.com, September 23, 2013, http://edition.cnn.com/2013/09/ 23/world/africa/pumeza-matshikiza-township-girl -opera/index.html (accessed November 25, 2013).

—Roger K. Smith

Niecy Nash

1970—

Film and television actress

Nash, Niecy, photograph. Jeffrey Mayer/WireImage/Getty Images.

Niecy Nash is an actress, television host, and producer who first rose to prominence in her role as Deputy Raineesha Williams on the Comedy Central series *Reno 911!* Recognizable by the flower that she always wears in her hair, Nash also was the host and producer of *Clean House,* a home-makeover series on the Style Network. Her appearance on *Clean House* won her both a daytime Emmy and a Gracie Allen Award. In 2010 she appeared in the 10th season of *Dancing with the Stars,* taking fifth place with partner Louis van Amstel. Nash has been the subject of two reality television shows on the TLC network, *Niecy Nash's Wedding Bash* (2011) and *Leave It to Niecy* (2012).

Dreamed of Television Stardom

Nash was born Carol Denise Ensley in 1970 in Palmdale, California, north of Los Angeles. She spent the first years of her life in St. Louis, Missouri. There she was cared for by her grandmother in the afternoons, when the pair watched *The Young and the Restless* and other daytime dramas. One day the soap opera was preempted by a special, and Nash was fascinated by the appearance of Lola Falana, a glamorous singer and dancer who was a frequent guest on television dramas and celebrity talk shows of the era. "I told my grandmother that's what I want to do," Nash recalled in an interview with *Boston Herald* writer Amy Amatangelo. "And she said, 'What baby?' I said, 'Be on TV and be black and fabulous.'"

Nash's family returned to the Los Angeles area when she was eight years old, and as a young woman she earned a bachelor's degree in theater arts from California State University, Dominguez Hills. In 1993 her family was devastated by the shooting death of her younger brother, Michael, in the hallway of Reseda High School in Los Angeles. During the difficult aftermath of the tragedy, Nash realized that she had a gift for making others laugh. "My mother was in a shambles, obviously, and I would come home every day and try to cheer her up," she told Amatangelo. "Eventually she came to expect it." Nash now serves as a spokesperson for the advocacy group M.A.V.I.S. (Mothers Against Violence in Schools), an organization founded by her mother.

Nash began her entertainment career as a stand-up comedian while also auditioning for roles in movies and

At a Glance . . .

Born Carol Denise Ensley on February 23, 1970, in Palmdale, CA; daughter of Margaret and Sonny Ensley; married Don Nash (a minister and real estate agent), 1991 (divorced, 2007); married Jay Tucker (an electrical engineer), 2011; children: Dominic, Donielle, Dia. *Education:* California State University, Dominguez Hills, BA, theater arts.

Career: Film and television actress, 1995—.

Awards: National Woman in the Arts Award, St. Louis Grand Center, 2007; Gracie Allen Award, Outstanding Program Host, 2007, for *Clean House*; Daytime Emmy Award, Outstanding Special Class, 2010, for *Clean House* episode "The Messiest Home in the Country"; Gracie Allen Award, Outstanding Supporting Actress in a Comedy Series, 2010, for *Reno 911!*.

Addresses: *Agent*—William Morris Endeavor Agency, 9601 Wilshire Blvd., Beverly Hills, CA 90210. *Management*—Principato Young Entertainment, 9465 Wilshire Blvd, Beverly Hills, CA 90212. *Web*—http://www.niecy-nash.com. *Twitter*—@NiecyNash.

television. She made her film debut with a bit part in the 1995 comedy *Boys on the Side* and went on to win roles on television in *City of Angels, CSI: Crime Scene Investigation,* and *The Bernie Mac Show.* In 2003 she landed a memorable role in the Comedy Central series *Reno 911!* A parody of the long-running reality series *Cops,* the show pretended to be a behind-the-scenes look at the sheriff's department in Reno, Nevada. Nash played Deputy Raineesha Williams, a character that she named after her young daughter's best friend. Among the humorous qualities that Nash brought to the character was her frequent use of mace on suspects with the slightest provocation. In addition, Nash wore a prosthetic backside to add visual humor to the role. *Reno 911!* quickly attracted a cult following for its ability to poke fun at those on both sides of the law. Adding to its exuberance and outlandishness, much of the dialogue was unscripted and improvised by the actors on set.

Hosted Hit Style Network Show

A year after *Reno 911!* premiered, Nash won a vastly different television job as the host of *Clean House,* a new show that debuted on the Style Network (now the Esquire Network). In each episode Nash followed a team of experts into homes that were in need of a clean-up crew and professional organizers, who then put the surfeit of possessions up for sale on the front lawn. The proceeds of the sale were then used to fund home renovations, with matching dollars provided by the show's producers.

Clean House also developed a loyal following, thanks in part to Nash's "no-nonsense approach, telling frat brothers whose filthy house is tackled in the season opener, 'Your mama didn't raise you like this,'" noted Gail Pennington, a television critic for the *St. Louis Post-Dispatch.* Nash left *Clean House* in 2010. She went on to be a celebrity panelist on CBS's *The Insider,* in addition to hosting her own Yahoo! web series, *Let's Talk About Love.*

Nash continues to appear in feature films, including 2005's *Guess Who,* a remake of the 1967 classic *Guess Who's Coming to Dinner;* the 2007 film version of her hit Comedy Central series, *Reno 911!: Miami;* and the 2009 drama *Not Easily Broken.* She has been a voice actor on several animated series and films, including the Cartoon Network's Adult Swim series *The Boondocks* and *Minoriteam* and the 2008 animated feature *Horton Hears a Who!*

Expanded Her Repertoire

In 2011 Nash embarked on her second marriage with electrical engineer Jay Tucker. She allowed the TLC network to chronicle the wedding in a two-hour special, *Niecy Nash's Wedding Bash.* That show was followed in 2012 with what TLC billed as "TV's First Reality Sitcom," *Leave It to Niecy.* The show follows Niecy, Jay, and their blended family—including Nash's mother Margaret, her three children, and Tucker's son—as they go about their daily lives with humor and love. Commenting on the relatively small viewership attracted in the show's first season, Nash told *Las Vegas Black Image* magazine, "I don't think 'Leave It to Niecy' was sensational enough.... when you want to love your husband and positively raise your children, I don't think some people find that interesting."

Nash has parlayed her experiences into an advice book on love and marriage, *It's Hard to Fight Naked.* Published in 2013 by Gallery Books, Nash's book offers a combination of personal anecdote and practical advice to women in search of lasting love.

Nash continues to thrive in her acting career, costarring in the hit TV Land series *The Soul Man* and the HBO comedy-drama *Getting On.* The latter has been particularly exciting for Nash, allowing her to develop her repertoire into less stereotypical realms of performance. In an interview with Essence.com, Nash reveled in the opportunity to play a character other than "the sassy Black momma, the sassy Black neighbor or the sassy Black friend." Calling her role as nurse Didi

Ortley "delicious," Nash explained, "it's so far from anything that I've had to play in such a long time. It's exciting when you're still discovering things about not only the character but yourself as a performer."

Selected works

Television

Kid Notorious, Comedy Central, 2003.
Reno 911!, Comedy Central, 2003–09.
Clean House, Style Network, 2004–10.
Minoriteam, Comedy Central, 2006.
American Dad!, Fox, 2007–12.
Do Not Disturb, Fox, 2008.
The Insider, CBS, 2009.
Dancing with the Stars, ABC, 2010.
The LeBrons, YouTube, 2011.
Niecy Nash's Wedding Bash, TLC, 2011.
Let's Talk About Love, Yahoo!, 2012.
Leave It to Niecy, TLC, 2012.
The Soul Man, TV Land, 2012—.
Getting On, HBO, 2013—.

Films

Boys on the Side, Warner Bros., 1995.
Cookie's Fortune, October Films, 1999.
The Bachelor, New Line Cinema, 1999.
Malibu's Most Wanted, Warner Bros., 2003.
Hair Show, Innovation Film Group, 2004.
Guess Who, Columbia Pictures, 2005.
Code Name: The Cleaner, New Line Cinema, 2007.
Reno 911!: Miami, Twentieth Century Fox, 2007.
(Voice) *Horton Hears a Who!,* Twentieth Century Fox, 2008.
G-Force, Walt Disney, 2009.
Not Easily Broken, Screen Gems, 2009.
The Proposal, Walt Disney, 2009.
Nurse 3D, Lionsgate, 2013.
Trust Me, Starz Digital Media, 2013.

Books

It's Hard to Fight Naked, Gallery Books, 2013.

Sources

Periodicals

Ask Deanna!, November 2009, pp. 37–39.
Boston Herald, November 20, 2005, p. 49.
Jet, July 1, 2013, p. 26.
Las Vegas Black Image, October 2012, p. 4.
New York Times, October 12, 2003; March 31, 2007, p. B13.
People, April 26, 2010, pp. 77–78.
Philadelphia Inquirer, February 22, 2007.
Star-Ledger (Newark, NJ), May 26, 2007, p. 6.
St. Louis Post-Dispatch, August 16, 2006, p. E1.
Upscale Magazine, September/October 2008, pp. 72–74.
USA Today, March 20, 2008.

Online

Niecy Nash, http://www.niecynash.com (accessed January 17, 2014).
Pendleton, Tonya, "In New Book, Nash Says It's Hard to Fight Naked," BlackAmericaWeb.com, May 14, 2013, http://blackamericaweb.com/125583/in-new-book-niecy-nash-says-its-hard-to-fight-naked/ (accessed December 20, 2013).
Sangweni, Yolanda, "Niecy Nash Happy Not Playing 'Sassy Black Friend' on HBO's 'Getting On,'" Essence.com, December 6, 2013, http://www.essence.com/2013/12/06/niecy-nash-getting-on-hbo-sassy-black-friend/ (accessed January 20, 2014).

—Carol Brennan and Ben Bloch

Kadir Nelson

1974—

Artist, illustrator, author

Nelson, Kadir, photograph. M. Phillips/WireImage/Getty Images.

Kadir Nelson is one of the most sought-after artists and illustrators working today. Best known for his oil paintings depicting African-American people and history, Nelson's work often focuses on the struggles and triumphs of ordinary African-Americans, as well as those of famous blacks such as Nelson Mandela, Jackie Robinson, and Harriet Tubman. Nelson's large, intimate, and almost photographic paintings invite viewers into the lives of legends as well as the nameless faces of countless African Americans who have played important roles in resisting slavery and racial discrimination. His work, which hangs in private collections and public galleries around the world, can also be found in numerous award-winning children's picture books, some of which Nelson has both written and illustrated.

Nelson was born in 1974 in Washington, DC, but grew up in New Jersey and in San Diego, California, where he now lives and works. A natural artist, he began drawing at the age of three, well before he could even write or spell. "Some people don't discover what their gift is for a long time but mine was apparent from a very young age and I am cognizant of that and respectful and grateful," Nelson told Sue Corbett of *Publishers*

Weekly. Nelson benefited from the attention and mentorship of an uncle who was an artist and art teacher, and he worked alongside him as he developed into a young artist. In possession of a clear talent, Nelson began entering art competitions, one of which resulted in a full scholarship to attend the Pratt Institute in Brooklyn, New York.

Nelson enrolled in the architecture program at Pratt. At the time he believed that architecture was a more practical and financially viable career than art, but he also feared that art department teachers would take away the freedom that he enjoyed as an artist, forcing him to join a school or create in a certain way. His fears alleviated by spending time with Pratt's art students, Nelson acquiesced, changing his major to art and pursuing his passion for painting. He graduated from Pratt in 1996 with honors and with the support of many of his professors who had taken notice of his hard work and progress.

His nervousness about finding employment as an artist turned out to be unfounded. Two weeks after graduating, he was hired by DreamWorks as a visual development artist to work on the 1997 film *Amistad,* about a

At a Glance . . .

Born Kadir Nelson in 1974 in Washington, DC; married Keara Nelson, 1996; children: Amel, Aya. *Politics:* Democrat. *Education:* Pratt Institute, BFA, art, 1996.

Career: Children's book illustrator, 1999—, author, 2008—.

Awards: NAACP Image Award, 2001, for *Just the Two of Us*; Coretta Scott King Award for Illustrators, American Library Association, 2005, for *Ellington Was Not a Street*; Caldecott Honor, Coretta Scott King Award for Illustrators, 2007, for *Moses: When Harriet Tubman Led Her People to Freedom*; Caldecott Honor, 2008, for *Henry's Freedom Box: A True Story from the Underground Railroad*; CASEY Award for Best Baseball Book, Robert F. Sibert Medal, Coretta Scott King Award for Authors, all 2009, for *We Are The Ship: The Story of Negro League Baseball*; Coretta Scott King Award for Authors, 2012, for *Heart and Soul: The Story of America and African-Americans.*

Addresses: *Office*—6977 Navajo Road, Ste. 124, San Diego, CA 92119. *Agent*—Steven Malk, Writers House, 21 W. 26th St., New York, New York 10010. *Web*—http://kadirnelson.com.

mutiny aboard a slave trade vessel. Around the same time, he was given the opportunity to show his work to representatives of *Sports Illustrated,* who also immediately took him on as a freelance artist. Nelson would later round out his freelance career by securing work from the Coca-Cola Company, the U.S. Postal Service, and Major League Baseball, in addition to designing album cover art for Michael Jackson and the rapper Drake.

Nelson's was introduced to illustration in 1999. While freelancing, Nelson had a painting chosen for a juried show that caught the attention of children's book author Jerdine Nolen, who asked him whether he had ever considered illustrating. Nelson was collaborating with Nolen on her book *Big Jabe* (2000) when actress Debbie Allen, one of the forces behind the making of the movie *Amistad,* asked him to illustrate her children's book *Brothers of the Knight* (1999). Nelson quickly established a reputation as an illustrator and was asked to work on a number of celebrity books, including those by Will Smith and Spike Lee. Early on Nelson's work began accumulating honors; he has

received an NAACP Image Award, several Coretta Scott King Awards, and two Caldecott Honors, among other awards.

In 2008, after nearly a decade of illustrating, Nelson published his first work of his own writing, *We Are the Ship: The Story of Negro League Baseball,* which he had been working on for seven years. Nelson conducted long and painstaking research for the book, securing as many historical images and details about baseball's Negro League as he could. In an interview with the website Reading Rockets, Nelson emphasized the amount of time that it took to do each image right: "I have to make sure that the uniforms are accurate—colors of uniforms, the ages of the players represented, color of the ballparks, and which ballparks they played in. Every last detail has to be accurate and, unfortunately, much of the records and photographs have been lost to history." The book won him a CASEY Award for best baseball book, a Robert F. Sibert Medal for best informational book for children, and the Coretta Scott King Award for Authors. Perhaps more importantly, the success of *We Are the Ship* encouraged Nelson to do more writing.

In the four years following the publication of *We Are the Ship,* Nelson illustrated a dizzying succession of books, including books on President Barack Obama, baseball pioneer Jackie Robinson, Kenyan activist Wangari Maathai, and boxer Joe Louis, before writing and illustrating another on Nelson Mandela.

His most ambitious work to date, a book titled *Heart and Soul: The Story of America and African-Americans,* was published in 2012. "I had been telling the African-American story all along," he told CNN, "but I hadn't tried to tell it all in one place." The book is a somewhat personalized tale of the history of African-Americans told through the character of an elderly woman. Nelson began his work on *Heart and Soul* by interviewing his family members. He told Sue Corbett of *Publishers Weekly,* "Someone once asked me what my work was about and I said, 'I am in hot pursuit of the truth.' History is a way to look for it. You get a general swath of it in school but that wasn't enough for me. I wanted to know the real story. And I had to begin with me. Find out more about my family, how they contributed not only to my life but to the life of our country." Nelson selected the book's opening narrative from his own family history, telling the story of a family that does not follow the black Southern tradition of eating black-eyed peas on New Year's Day because an enslaved ancestor had once been forced to eat the dish from a horse trough. *Heart and Soul* garnered widespread praise upon publication and earned Nelson another Coretta Scott King Award for Authors.

Nelson counts artists such as Normal Rockwell and N. C. Wyeth, as well as painter and muralists Charles White, Ernie Barnes, and Dean Cornwell, as major

influences on his work, telling CNN's Stephanie Siek, "I like the style, I like their technique, the emotion that comes through their work, the light and shadow, the drama, the use of color and storytelling." He added, "I think what's always most important to me is the story behind the images and in African-American history, the human drama is often very dramatic."

Nelson's paintings hang in numerous public collections, including the U.S. House of Representatives and the National Baseball Hall of Fame.

Selected works

Illustrated books

Brothers of the Knight (by Debbie Allen), Dial, 1999.
Big Jabe (by Jerdine Nolen), HarperCollins, 2000.
Salt in His Shoes: Michael Jordan in Pursuit of a Dream (by Deloris and Roslyn Jordan), Simon & Schuster, 2000.
Dancing in the Wings (by Debbie Allen), Dial, 2000.
Just the Two of Us (by Will Smith), Scholastic, 2001.
Please, Baby, Please (by Spike and Tonya Lee), Simon & Schuster, 2002.
Under the Christmas Tree (by Nikki Grimes), HarperCollins, 2002.
The Village that Vanished (by Ann Grifalconi), Dial, 2002.
Thunder Rose (by Jerdine Nolen), Harcourt, 2003.
Ellington Was Not a Street (by Ntozake Shange), Simon & Schuster, 2004.
He's Got the Whole World in His Hands, Dial, 2005.
The Real Slam Dunk (by Charisse Richardson), Dial, 2005.
Hewitt Anderson's Great Big Life (by Jerdine Nolen), Simon & Schuster, 2005.
Please, Puppy, Please (by Spike and Tonya Lee), Simon & Schuster, 2005.
Moses: When Harriet Tubman Led Her People to Freedom (by Carole Boston Weatherford), Hyperion/Jump at the Sun, 2006.
Henry's Freedom Box: A True Story from the Underground Railroad (by Ellen Levine), Scholastic, 2007.
Michael's Golden Rules (by Deloris Jordan), Simon & Schuster, 2007.
We Are the Ship: The Story of Negro League Baseball (by Kadir Nelson), Hyperion/Jump at the Sun, 2008.

Abe's Hones Words (by Doreen Rappaport), Hyperion, 2008.
Change Has Come: An Artist Celebrates Our American Spirit, Simon and Schuster, 2009.
Testing the Ice: A True Story About Jackie Robinson (by Sharon Robinson), Scholastic, 2009.
All God's Critters (by Bill Staines), Simon and Schuster, 2009.
Mama Miti: Wangari Maathai and the Trees of Kenya (by Donna Jo Napoli), Simon & Schuster/Paula Wiseman Books, 2010.
A Nation's Hope: The Story of Boxing Legend Joe Louis (by Matt de la Peña), Dial Books, 2011.
Nelson Mandela, HarperCollins, 2012.
Heart and Soul: The Story of America and African-Americans, HarperCollins, 2012.
Baby Bear, HarperCollins, 2013.

Sources

Periodicals

Publishers Weekly, July 18, 2011, p. 26.

Online

Kadir Nelson, http://www.kadirnelson.com/Artist-Biography.html (accessed November 19, 2013).
"Kadir Nelson," Scholastic, http://www.scholastic.com/teachers/contributor/kadir-nelson (accessed November 19, 2013).
Pasori, Cedar, "Interview: Artist Kadir Nelson Talks Painting Drake's 'Nothing Was The Same' Album Covers," Complex.com, http://www.complex.com/art-design/2013/08/kadir-nelson-drake-interview (accessed November 19, 2013).
Siek, Stephanie, "Q & A: 'Heart and Soul' Author Kadir Nelson on Illustrating African-American History," CNN.com, January 24, 2013, http://inamerica.blogs.cnn.com/2012/01/24/qa-heart-and-soul-author-kadir-nelson-on-illustrating-african-american-history/.
"Transcript from an Interview with Kadir Nelson," Reading Rockets, http://www.readingrockets.org/books/interviews/nelson/transcript/ (accessed November 19, 2013).

—Kay Eastman

Solomon Northup

1808–1863(?)

Solomon Northup was a free black man living in upstate New York when, in 1841, he was kidnapped and forced into slavery. Lured to Washington, DC, by a pair of unscrupulous slave catchers who promised him a lucrative job, Northup was captured and transported south to New Orleans, Louisiana, where he was sold at a slave auction. He endured brutal conditions and abuse by his master for more than a decade, until he finally managed to get word of his location to his family. With assistance from a white lawyer who enlisted the help of the governor of New York, Northup was rescued from bondage in 1853. Just months after he regained his freedom, he published *Twelve Years a Slave,* a first-hand account of his experience of slavery. Contemporary scholars consider Northup's text one of the most authentic and detailed slave narratives ever written. In 2013 Northup's story was adapted into a major motion picture.

Duped by Slave Traders

Solomon Northup was born a free black man in Minerva, New York, in 1808. His father, Mintus, had been a slave of the Northup family of Rhode Island and later New York and took his surname from his master, who emancipated his slaves in his will. For most of his life, Solomon Northup lived in Essex and Washington counties, helping his father with farm chores and working as a raftsman on the waterways of upstate New York. In 1829 he married Anne Hampton, a woman of mixed black, white, and Native American ancestry. The couple had three children.

By 1841 Northup had settled in nearby Saratoga Springs, New York, where he earned a reputation as a talented fiddle player. He worked a number of odd jobs, but in the winter of that year, he was unemployed. One day in March, Northup was approached in town by two strangers calling themselves Merrill Brown and Abram Hamilton. (Their real names were Alexander Merrill and Joseph Russell.) The men told Northup that they worked for a circus in Washington, DC, and were looking for a musical accompanist. After learning of Northup's talent on the fiddle, they asked him to join them, offering a dollar per day to follow them to New York City and three dollars for each performance Northup played. Northup accepted their offer and went home to get a change of clothes and his fiddle, leaving his wife and children.

Northup traveled with the two men first to Albany, New York, where he performed in a sort of vaudeville show, and then to New York City. Brown and Hamilton promised him high pay if he would continue on to Washington, DC. In a sign of their concern for him, they even recommended that he obtain "free papers" before he left New York State. Free papers were documents testifying that Northup was a free man, a necessary precaution for a black man traveling in a slave state (slavery was then legal in both Maryland and Washington, DC), where he might be abducted and forced into slavery. Northup did so, paying two dollars for the documents.

Upon arriving in Washington, Brown and Hamilton cemented Northup's trust by squiring him about town—they took him to the White House and Capitol grounds—and promising him a generous sum of money for his employment. Their elaborate ruse culminated the following evening, when they took him to a tavern and drugged his drink. Unconscious, Northup was transported to the Williams Slave Pen, a jail cell near the present-day National Mall, where black men

and women were held before being sold into slavery. Northup awoke in an underground cell, his hands cuffed and his legs bound in iron shackles. Finding that his money and free papers were gone, he quickly realized that he had been duped by his new "friends" and understood the horror of his situation.

Endured 12 Years of Bondage

Northup was sold for $650 to James H. Birch (spelled "Burch" in Northup's account), the commander of the auxiliary guard of the Washington, DC, police force and one of the city's most notorious slave traders. When Birch told Northup that he was to be sent to New Orleans—then the center of the slave trade, where slaves were sold as chattel at auction—Northup protested that he was a free man and demanded to be released. "You're a black liar!" Birch shouted at Northup, according to Northup's retelling. "You're a runaway from Georgia!" Northup endured a brutal beating at Birch's hands, suffering injuries so severe that he was sure he would die. "Even now," Northup wrote, "the flesh crawls upon my bones, as I recall the scene. I was all on fire. My sufferings I can compare to nothing else than the burning agonies of hell."

First Northup was transported to Richmond, Virginia, and then was sent by steamboat to New Orleans, where he was to be sold at a slave auction. En route he and two others planned a mutiny, but when one of the conspirators contracted smallpox, their plot was foiled. In New Orleans, Northup was delivered to Theophilus Freeman, a slave trader who rechristened him "Platt." Northup was sold first to William Ford, a Baptist preacher in Louisiana who treated his slaves well. In the winter of 1842, however, Ford sold Northup to John M. Tibaut (called John Tibeats in Northup's narrative), a neighboring carpenter, for $400 in repayment of a debt. Tibaut was a cruel man who violently abused his slaves. One day Tibaut attacked the slave, and in self-defense Northup responded in kind, beating his master. Such an offense was punishable by death. Tibaut threatened to lynch Northup but was dissuaded from doing so by Ford, who still retained partial

ownership of the slave. That technicality saved Northup's life.

A few days later Northup was sold to Edwin Epps, a cotton farmer who owned a plantation in Bayou Boeuf, Avoyelles Parish, Louisiana. Northrup spent his remaining years of bondage there. Epps was an alcoholic who often went on drinking binges that for lasted weeks, forcing his slaves to entertain him with song and dance. A stern taskmaster, he demanded a heavy load of cotton production each day and doled out harsh punishments to those who failed to meet their quota. Although Northup thought daily of escaping, he became convinced that doing so was impossible and feared the consequences if he were caught.

Freed in Dramatic Rescue

In June of 1852, Northup's prospects for escape improved. Epps had begun construction of a new house and had hired a Canadian carpenter named Samuel Bass, who was known to have liberal political views and to support the antislavery movement. Northup told Bass of his situation and asked for his help. The two men met in secret in a nearby field, where Bass helped Northrup write a letter to William Perry and Cephas Parker of Saratoga, New York, detailing his kidnapping. Accepting tremendous risk, Bass posted the letter in nearby Marksville, Louisiana, on August 15, 1852.

The letter arrived in Saratoga in September, and Perry and Parker forwarded the letter to Northup's wife, Anne. She, in turn, sent it to Henry B. Northup, the son of Mintus Northup's former master, who was then a lawyer in Sandy Hill, New York. Henry Northup discovered that in May of 1840, nearly a year before Solomon Northup's kidnapping, New York State had in fact passed a statute to address just such a situation. The law, which sought to protect free blacks from being abducted and forced into slavery, empowered the governor to take steps to liberate any person proven to be a free citizen of New York who was being held against his or her will in another state. The legal machinations took some time to complete. First Anne Northup submitted evidence to New York governor Washington Hunt that her husband was a free man who had been kidnapped. Then Henry Northup petitioned to have himself appointed as an official agent of the state to rescue Solomon Northup and secured federal support to do so.

Even when he had completed those arrangements, Henry Northup had to find Solomon, who had not given his location or mentioned that he was known by a different name. After many months Henry Northup finally located the slave and in January of 1853 arrived at Bayou Boeuf to reclaim Solomon Northup. The two Northups first traveled to Washington, DC, where Henry Northup signed a warrant for the arrest of Birch,

charging him with kidnapping. Birch claimed that he had believed Solomon Northup to be a slave from Georgia and had been unaware of his kidnapping. Because of his race, Northup was not allowed to testify, and Birch went free.

Published Autobiographical Account of Slavery

Solomon Northup was reunited with his wife and children on January 21, 1853. The dramatic story of his rescue quickly became a national sensation, with a full-page account published in the *New York Times* on January 20, 1853. Northup soon became a celebrity in abolitionist circles, appearing alongside the orator Frederick Douglass at an antislavery rally on February 1 in Troy, New York, where he recounted his extraordinary ordeal. Solomon and Henry Northup appeared with Douglass three days later in Albany, and soon the former slave had a full schedule of speaking engagements. Although he had performed publicly as a musician for much of his life, he was unaccustomed to such attention.

A longer and more complete version of Northup's narrative, titled *Twelve Years a Slave: Narrative of Solomon Northup, a Citizen of New-York, Kidnapped in Washington City in 1841, and Rescued in 1853, From a Cotton Plantation Near the Red River, in Louisiana,* was rushed to press in 1853 by Derby & Miller. The account was written in just three months with the aid of David Wilson, a lawyer and writer from New York who was credited as the book's editor. Scholars continue to debate whether Northup or Wilson actually wrote the text. Many historians believe that Northup likely dictated the story, providing the outline and details of the narrative, while Wilson crafted the prose. In his "Editor's Preface," Wilson states that "the only object of the editor has been to give a faithful history of Solomon Northup's life, as he received it from his lips."

Published just a year after Harriet Beecher Stowe's antislavery novel *Uncle Tom's Cabin* (1852), *Twelve Years a Slave* was dedicated to that author: "To Harriet Beecher Stowe: Whose name, throughout the world, is identified with the great reform: This narrative, affording another key to *Uncle Tom's Cabin,* is respectfully dedicated," the inscription read. Promoted by Stowe and by such abolitionist leaders as Douglass and William Lloyd Garrison, the publisher of the antislavery newspaper the *Liberator,* Northup's book was an instant hit. It sold 30,000 copies in its first three years of publication and had been reprinted in several editions by the end of the century. According to the publisher's advertisement, the *New York Tribune* extolled that "Next to *Uncle Tom's Cabin,* the extraordinary Narrative of Solomon Northup, is the most remarkable book that was ever issued from the American press," while the *Cincinnati Journal* called the book "one of the most exciting narratives, full of thrilling incidents artlessly told, with all the marks of truth."

At 330 pages, *Twelve Years a Slave* is one of the longest slave narratives ever published, and historians consider it among the most authentic firsthand accounts of the horrors of slavery. Concerned that his story be accepted as truth and not a fabrication, Northup used real names (rather than pseudonyms, as some other slave narratives did), dates, and places in his narrative in the hope that his account might aid in the eventual capture and trial of his abductors.

Died under Mysterious Circumstances

Henry and Solomon Northup eventually tracked down the two kidnappers and had them arrested. For several years, however, the case was shuffled among appeals courts in an effort to determine jurisdiction—that is, whether the crime had been committed in New York (where Northup could testify) or in Washington (where his testimony would once again be inadmissible). The case eventually was dropped, and the two men were never tried for their offenses.

What happened to Northup thereafter remains a mystery. He earned little compensation for the publication of *Twelve Years a Slave,* receiving only $3,000 for his copyright. He used the money to purchase property in Glens Falls, New York, next door to his daughter and her family. When the property was sold, however, Northup's name did not appear in the records, and his whereabouts after that time remain unknown. He is believed to have died sometime around 1863. Scholars have speculated about what happened to Northup. Some claim that foul play was involved, while others believe that he likely died of natural causes, as he would have been in poor health after so many years of bondage. Years later a team of scholars and students from Union College in Schenectady, New York, attempted to reconstruct Northup's life using photographs, family records, bills of sale, maps, and hospital records, but the researchers found no record of the date or location of his death. To this day Northup's burial location remains unknown.

In 2002 the city council of Saratoga Springs, New York, proclaimed the third Saturday in July as Solomon Northup Day, which is commemorated at an annual event called the "Celebration of Freedom." A historical marker stands on Broadway Avenue in Saratoga Springs, marking the spot where Northup first met his two kidnappers.

The scholars Sue Eakin and Joseph Logsdon edited a new annotated edition of *Twelve Years a Slave,* which was published by Louisiana State University Press in 1968. Their edition, now considered the definitive text,

retraces Northup's journey and includes additional maps and other supporting documents. In 2013 a film adaptation of Northup's account, directed by the British filmmaker Steve McQueen and starring Chiwetel Ejiofor as Northup, brought renewed attention to Northup's narrative.

Selected works

Twelve Years a Slave: Narrative of Solomon Northup, a Citizen of New-York, Kidnapped in Washington City in 1841, and Rescued in 1853, From a Cotton Plantation Near the Red River, in Louisiana, Derby & Miller, 1853.

Sources

Books

Eakin, Sue, and Joseph Logsdon, eds., *Twelve Years a Slave by Solomon Northup,* Louisiana State University Press, 1968.

Fiske, David, Clifford W. Brown, and Rachel Seligman, *Solomon Northup: The Complete Story of the Author of "Twelve Years a Slave",* ABC-CLIO, 2013.

Wilson, Carol, *Freedom at Risk: The Kidnapping of Free Blacks in America, 1780–1865,* University Press of Kentucky, 1994.

Periodicals

New York Times, January 20, 1853; September 22, 2013.

Washington Post, March 7, 1999.

Online

"Solomon Northup Day," Saratoga Springs Heritage Area Visitor Center, http://www.saratogasprings visitorcenter.com/about-the-visitors-center/solomon -northup-day (accessed January 3, 2014).

"Solomon Northup, b. 1808, Twelve Years a Slave: Narrative of Solomon Northup, a Citizen of New-York, Kidnapped in Washington City in 1841, and Rescued in 1853," Documenting the American South, http://docsouth.unc.edu/fpn/northup/men u.html (accessed January 3, 2014).

—Deborah A. Ring

Ken Norton

1943–2013

Boxer, actor

Norton, Ken, photograph. Ethan Miller/Getty Images for Keep Memory Alive.

One of the most prominent fighters in the world in the 1970s, Ken Norton reigned for several months in 1978 as the World Boxing Council's heavyweight champion. He is best remembered, however, for his stunning upset of Muhammad Ali five years earlier, when Norton famously broke the superstar's jaw in a grueling 12-round match. Known for his warm, affable demeanor outside the ring, he focused on acting after leaving the sport in the early 1980s. "For those who knew him best," the writer Lee Groves once noted, "his fortitude and positive mindset cemented what they already realized—that this was a man of uncommon character and perseverance."

Norton was born Kenneth Howard Florence on August 9, 1943, in Jacksonville, Illinois. His parents were unwed teenagers when he was born, and his father left the family soon thereafter. Raised by his mother, Ruth, and his stepfather, John Norton, in a solidly middle-class household, Norton excelled as a youth in three sports—football, basketball, and track. After high school he entered Northeast Missouri State College (later Truman State University) on an athletic scholar-

ship, remaining there until he joined the U.S. Marine Corps in 1963.

It was in the Marines that Norton first began boxing. In a 1987 interview with Rich Roberts of the *Los Angeles Times,* Norton's wife Jackie explained that he had taken up the sport in an effort "to stay out of [the war in] Vietnam"; successful participants in the Marines' amateur bouts, he knew, were sent into combat less often than their peers. Norton progressed rapidly, winning the All-Marine heavyweight title three times while compiling an amateur record of 24–2. That success convinced him to try his luck as a professional, and he began his long climb up the pro ranks soon after his discharge from the military in 1967.

Faced Ali, Foreman, and Holmes

A powerful but gracious fighter who devoted himself to physical conditioning, Norton eschewed the brash behavior and braggadocio for which many of his opponents were known. His quiet demeanor kept his profile relatively low, and he was not well-known or highly paid when he met Ali in 1973 for the first of their three

bouts. Bookmakers gave Norton virtually no chance of winning. Norton shocked the boxing world, however, with his powerful shot to Ali's jaw, his stamina through 12 hard-fought rounds, and his victory by judges' decision. "The first Ali fight gave me a chance to give my son more food, better clothes," he recalled in the 2009 documentary *Facing Ali.* "A fight with Ali gave me a chance at life, period."

In the aftermath of the upset, widely regarded as one of the best bouts of the decade, Ali and his handlers asked for a rematch, which Norton lost in a narrow decision in September of 1973. By that time, however, his reputation as a formidable contender was firmly established. Norton's next target was George Foreman, then the undisputed heavyweight champion. The two boxers squared off in front of thousands of fans in Caracas, Venezuela, in March of 1974. Foreman, then at the height of his powers, stopped Norton handily in the second round. Norton recovered quickly, however, winning bouts against several well-regarded rivals in the following months.

In September of 1976, Norton met Ali for the third and final time. Before a huge crowd at Yankee Stadium in New York City, the two traded dozens of hooks and jabs. When the match was over, the judges awarded the fight to Ali. That outcome was bitterly opposed by Norton's fans, many of whom felt that Ali's charisma had blinded the officials to his weaknesses inside the ring. The decision stood, however, and Norton ac-

cepted it with apparent aplomb. After two well-publicized comeback victories over the leading contenders Duane Bobick and Jimmy Young, Norton challenged the titleholder Leon Spinks to meet him in a championship match sanctioned by the World Boxing Council (WBC). (A boxer may hold titles from more than one group simultaneously, as Foreman did in 1974.) When Spinks declined the proposal, the WBC, following its long-standing policy in such cases, stripped him of his title and awarded it to Norton instead. Although that outcome may have been less satisfying than an actual victory, it solidified Norton's reputation as one of the best boxers in the world. That status was affirmed by the Boxing Writers Association of America, which named him fighter of the year for 1977.

Norton did not hold the title for long, however, losing by decision to Larry Holmes, a much younger man, in June of 1978. The fights that followed were anticlimactic, and Norton retired in 1981 with a professional record of 42 wins, 7 losses, and 1 draw. After his departure from the ring, he focused on his family, his business interests, and his burgeoning acting career. His first and most prominent role came in *Mandingo,* a Hollywood release that appeared in 1975, when his boxing career was at its height. As Mede, a slave forced by his master to fight without gloves, Norton shared the screen with such stars as James Mason. Although the film received mixed reviews at the time, by the end of the following decade, it had become a cult favorite. By that point Norton had also made a number of appearances on television, with cameos on several popular series, including *The A-Team* and *Knight Rider,* and a role in a made-for-television movie, *Oceans of Fire* (1986).

Suffered Serious Health Problems

Norton's life changed significantly in 1986, when he was hurt in a serious car accident in California. His injuries left him in a wheelchair for months and severely compromised his ability to communicate. With intensive physical therapy, however, Norton made major progress. As he told Roberts of the *Los Angeles Times* in 1987, with characteristic modesty and humor, "At first they thought I might die, and if I didn't die, I wouldn't be coherent. Then they thought even if I could talk, I'd be a cripple. Now I'm talkin' and walkin' and I can even chew gum at the same time."

Dramatic as his recovery was, Norton continued to face an array of serious health issues in the years that followed, including prostate cancer, two strokes, and a heart attack. He met these challenges with courage and determination, taking a proactive approach that eventually drew the notice of his peers. In 2011, for example, he volunteered for a landmark investigation into boxing's long-term effects on the human brain. "He was one of the first retired boxers to participate in the study," Dr. Charley Bernick of the Cleveland Clinic

Lou Ruvo Center for Brain Health told Steve Carp of the *Las Vegas Review-Journal,* "and his name encouraged others to get involved."

A longtime resident of the Las Vegas area, Norton died of congestive heart failure at a medical facility in Henderson, Nevada, on September 18, 2013. News of his passing quickly drew tributes from such fellow boxers as Foreman, his opponent in the famous Caracas fight of 1974. "It's a sad day," Foreman told Lance Pugmire of the *Los Angeles Times,* "but I take solace that I had the chance to be friends with him."

Norton was once asked how he wanted to be remembered. "[As] an intelligent being," he replied, in a comment later quoted by Groves. "A caring being. An individual [who], even though he was very competitive, in his heart … never wanted to injure anyone. And … a man that believed in God."

Selected works

Films

Mandingo, Paramount Pictures, 1975.
Drum, United Artists, 1976.
Delta Pi, Pegasus Films, 1985.
The Man Who Came Back, Grindstone, 2008.
Facing Ali, Lions Gate, 2009.

Television

Oceans of Fire (television movie), CBS, 1986.

Sources

Periodicals

Los Angeles Times, December 26, 1987.

Online

"Biography," KenNorton.com, http://www.kennorton.com/biography.html (accessed November 18, 2013).

Carp, Steve, "Former Heavyweight Champion Ken Norton Has Died at 70," ReviewJournal.com, September 18, 2013, http://www.reviewjournal.com/sports/boxing/former-heavyweight-champion-ken-norton-has-died-70 (accessed November 18, 2013).

Goldstein, Richard, "Ken Norton, A Championship Fighter Who Broke Ali's Jaw, Is Dead at 70," NY Times.com, September 18, 2013, http://www.nytimes.com/2013/09/19/sports/ken-norton-a-championship-fighter-who-broke-alis-jaw-is-dead-at-70.html?_r=1&&gwh=A182C6F77873E8F53D10A91D48DEC824 (accessed November 18, 2013).

Groves, Lee, "A Tribute to Ken Norton," Ring, September 20, 2013, http://ringtv.craveonline.com/blog/180941-a-tribute-to-ken-norton (accessed November 18, 2013).

"Ken Norton," International Boxing Hall of Fame, http://www.ibhof.com/pages/about/inductees/modern/norton.html (accessed November 18, 2013).

"Marine Corps Sports Hall of Fame: Ken Norton," Marine Corps Community Services, http://www.usmc-mccs.org/sports/hof/2004-norton.cfm (accessed November 18, 2013).

Pugmire, Lance, "Ken Norton Sr. Dies at 70; Former Heavyweight Boxing Champion," LATimes.com, September 18, 2013, http://www.latimes.com/obituaries/la-me-ken-norton-20130919,0,3821737.story#axzz2kzkcl8AR (accessed November 18, 2013).

Other

Facing Ali (documentary), Lionsgate, 2009.

—R. Anthony Kugler

Paul Oliver

1984–2013

Professional football player

Oliver, Paul, photograph. George Bridges/MCT/MCT via Getty Images.

Paul Oliver, a cornerback and safety for the San Diego Chargers of the National Football League (NFL) for five years, shocked his family, friends, and former teammates when he committed suicide on September 24, 2013. He was just 29 years old. "Maybe depression set in, I don't know," his uncle, David Scandrett, told Lindsay H. Jones and Ray Glier of *USA Today*. "He was playing ball, then he is like a stay-at-home mom." Oliver's pro football career had come to an abrupt end two years earlier, when the Chargers released him after five seasons. Oliver's death by self-inflicted gunshot renewed the debate over the effects of concussions on NFL players, a number of whom—including fellow Chargers player Junior Seau—have taken their lives after leaving the sport.

Born in Kennesaw, Georgia, in 1984, Oliver was a standout on the football team at Harrison High School, where he played offense as a split end and defense as a cornerback. His coach, Bruce Cobleigh, told the *Atlanta Journal-Constitution* that Oliver was "the best player who ever played here," adding, "He was very hard-working and motivated and wanted to play

football beyond college. That was his dream, and he got to do that."

Oliver's team went to three regional championships from 2000 to 2002. During his junior year, on offense, he caught 30 passes for 650 yards and eight touchdowns. On the defensive side he had 60 tackles and nine interceptions. He also returned four punts for touchdowns. As a senior Oliver focused on defense, with 65 tackles and three interceptions. That year he was named to the *Parade* magazine All-American First Team and to *USA Today*'s All-USA Second Team. The recruiting service Super Prep Elite 50 named Oliver the best player in Georgia, and other media outlets and ranking agencies tagged him as one of the best football players in the state of Georgia and in the nation.

Stood Out on Defense at Georgia

Oliver's high school performance had college recruiters knocking on his door. He had offers from a number of major university football teams, but he turned them down to attend the University of Georgia in Athens. Speaking at the time with Online Athens contributor

Chris J. Starrs, Oliver explained his choice: "It's close to home and this was the first school to offer me. I'd been here plenty of times before they offered me, and I got comfortable with the players and it was really a no-brainer. My family it less than two hours away, and they can come see me and I can go see them whenever I want."

Oliver was red-shirted his first year with the Georgia Bulldogs (that is, his playing eligibility was delayed), but in the 2004 season he played in 12 games and had nine tackles, five of them solo. He also had his first collegiate career interception and was given the Iron Man Award that year by his teammates. The next season Oliver earned the Bulldog's Most Improved Defensive Player Award, playing cornerback in all 13 season games. That same year he had 28 tackles, of which 23 were solo, and 30 yards on three interceptions. The Bulldogs were the Southern Conference champions in 2005.

Oliver had his best year at Georgia in 2006, starting 12 games as strong-side cornerback. Forty-six of his 58 season tackles were solo, and he intercepted three passes for 44 yards. When Oliver discovered that he was academically ineligible for the 2007 season, he decided to try out for the NFL supplemental draft. According to the website NFLDraftScout.com, the scouting report on Oliver described him as a "versatile cornerback with experience on the strong-side and weak-side," noting that he "might be a better fit at free safety in the National Football League." The same report termed Oliver a "hard-hitting tackler."

Drafted by San Diego Chargers

Oliver was picked up in the fourth round of the supplemental draft by the San Diego Chargers in

2007. "We had the opportunity to get a good football player today, and we took it," noted Chargers general manager A. J. Smith in an interview with *San Diego Union-Tribune* contributor Jim Trotter. "Paul Oliver is a very competitive, aggressive, confident player. He's not cautious about anything he does on the field. You know how we like depth. We'll add Paul to the mix as a Charger and time will tell." Also speaking with Trotter, Oliver expressed his feelings about making it to the NFL: "I'm feeling great, so relieved and excited—especially with being able to play for a serious contender like San Diego."

At training camp with the Chargers, Oliver was converted to the safety position on defense, as the scouting report had recommended. He sat out his first season at San Diego, but in 2008 he played in 12 games and had 13 solo tackles. In both 2009 and 2010 he played in all 16 games, with 85 solo tackles and six interceptions combined in those years. At the end of the 2010 season, however, the Chargers and Oliver could not come to an agreement over his contract, and he became a free agent.

Oliver was picked up by the Miami Dolphins, but after sustaining a concussion during training camp, he was released with an injury settlement. In September of 2011 he re-signed with the Chargers and played 13 games of that season. It would be his last in the NFL, as he was released by the team at the end of the season, having racked up 113 solo tackles during his time in San Diego. He became a free agent once again.

Faced Depression after NFL Career

After the end of his pro career, Oliver returned to his native Georgia, setting up house in Marietta with his wife, Chelsea, with whom he had two sons. But problems soon arose. As his wife later told reporters, Oliver became depressed following his retirement from football. The couple began to argue, and there was talk of a divorce. As Jones and Glier noted in their *USA Today* article, "[Oliver's] friends and family acknowledged he was having a tough time adjusting to post-football life. He was unemployed, without a college degree, and the only identity he had known as an adult was as a football player."

On September 24, 2013, Oliver and his wife were having a particularly heated argument, and she took the two young children out for a walk, hoping that her husband would calm down. When they returned Oliver brandished a gun—Glock semi-automatic pistol—and threatened to kill himself. Standing at the top of the stairs, in full view of his wife and children, he put the gun to his head and shot himself. Oliver died instantly, according to the coroner's report.

The news of Oliver's death came as a shock to his former teammates and coaches. Chargers free safety

Eric Weddle told Jones of *USA Today* that Oliver was "just a joy to be around." Weddle added, "Funny. Charismatic. Worked his tail off. Also quiet, reserved, at the same time. Just a great teammate and great friend. Great person. Never once said something bad about anyone ... Wish I would have reached out to him more and helped him in some way." Speaking with Josh Levs, Steve Almasy, and Joe Sutton of CNN, Oliver's high school coach, Cobleigh, commented, "This is surprising, shocking. He was really outgoing. He was really well-liked, a leader, hard, hard worker." Oliver's college coach, Mark Richt, told Jones, "I was crushed this morning when I heard it, quite frankly ... I haven't been able to keep it off my mind, to be honest with you. We have to find a way to reach out and help any way we can."

Oliver's death reignited a discussion about the role of concussions in chronic traumatic encephalopathy, or CTE, a degenerative brain disease that can be the result of multiple blows to the head, as often occurs in football. Brain tissue studies have shown an inordinate number of sufferers of CTE among former professional football players, a number of whom have taken their own lives.

Sources

Online

Acee, Kevin, "Oliver Returns; Mouton to IR," UTSan Diego.com, September 21, 2011, http://www.ut sandiego.com/news/2011/sep/21/oliver-returning -chargers/ (accessed November 19, 2013).

Burke, Chris, "Ex-Charger Paul Oliver Reportedly Commits Suicide," SI.com, September 25, 2013, http://nfl.si.com/2013/09/25/paul-oliver-suicide-san-diego-chargers/ (accessed November 17, 2013).

"8 Paul Oliver," GeorgiaDogs.com, http://www.geor giadogs.com/sports/m-footbl/mtt/paul_oliver_57 280.html (accessed November 19, 2013).

"Former Bulldog Paul Oliver Passes Away," Georgia Dogs.com, September 25, 2013, http://www.geor giadogs.com/sports/m-footbl/spec-rel/092513aab .html (accessed November 17, 2013).

Jones, Lindsay H., "Chargers 'Devastated' by Ex-DB Paul Oliver's Suicide," USAToday.com, September 26, 2013, http://www.usatoday.com/story/sports/ nfl/chargers/2013/09/25/paul-oliver-chargers/28 70397/ (accessed November 27, 2013).

Jones, Lindsay H., and Ray Glier, "Police: Post-Football Woes Factor in Paul Oliver's Death," USA-Today.com, October 3, 2013, http://www.usato day.com/story/sports/nfl/2013/10/03/paul-oliver -gunshot-death/2916421/ (accessed November 17, 2013).

Levs, Josh, Steve Almasy and Joe Sutton, "Paul Oliver's Suicide Is Latest in a String among Former NFL Players," CNN.com, September 26, 2013, http:// www.cnn.com/2013/09/25/us/former-nfl-player -suicide/ (accessed November 17, 2013).

"Oliver Killed Himself in Front of Family," FoxSports. com, October 4, 2013, http://msn.foxsports.com/ nfl/story/former-charger-paul-oliver-committed-sui cide-in-front-of-wife-and-kids-100213 (accessed November 17, 2013).

"Paul Oliver," NFLDraftScout.com, http://www.nfl draftscout.com/files/PaulOliver.pdf (accessed November 17, 2013).

"Paul Justin Oliver," West Cobb Funeral Home, http:// www.westcobbfuneralhome.com/sitemaker/sites/ WestCo1/obit.cgi?user=1106602Oliver (accessed November 17, 2013).

Shaw, Michelle E., "Ex-UGA Football Player Paul Oliver, 29, Dies of Apparent Suicide," AJC.com, September 25, 2013, http://www.ajc.com/news/ sports/ex-uga-football-player-paul-oliver-29-dies-of -appa/nZ7W9/ (accessed November 17, 2013).

Starrs, Chris J., "Hangin' With: Paul Oliver," Online Athens.com, September 13, 2006, http://online athens.com/stories/091306/football_200609 13021.shtml (accessed November 19, 2013).

Towers, Chip, and Todd Holcomb, "Former Georgia DB Commits Suicide," AJC.com, September 25, 2013, http://www.ajc.com/news/sports/college/ former-georgia-db-reportedly-commits-suicide/nZ7 Dw/ (accessed November 19, 2013).

Trotter, Jim, "Chargers Take a Supplement for the Secondary," UTSanDiego.com, June 13, 2007, http://www.utsandiego.com/sports/chargers/2007 0713-9999-1s13chargers.html (accessed November 19, 2013).

Weiszer, Marc, "Georgia Coach, Teammates Mourn Former Player Paul Oliver," Chronicle.Augusta.com, September 25, 2013, http://chronicle.augusta .com/latest-news/2013-09-25/georgia-coach-team mates-mourn-former-player-paul-oliver (accessed November 17, 2013).

—J. Sydney Jones

Maxine Powell

1915–2013

Fashion consultant, model, entrepreneur, educator

One of the professionals most responsible for Motown Records' international reputation for style and sophistication, Maxine Powell instilled a sense of elegance and refinement in some of the most gifted pop stars of the 1960s. A founding member of Motown's Artist Development Department, she served the label for five years (1964–69) as a finishing instructor, fashion designer, and style expert. Stressing the importance of social etiquette, posture, and stage presence, she helped launch the careers of many artists, including the Supremes' Diana Ross, who once described her, in a comment later quoted by Margalit Fox of the *New York Times,* as "the person who taught me everything I know."

Powell, Maxine, photograph. Monica Morgan/WireImage/Getty Images.

Powell was born Maxine Blair in Texarkana, Texas, on May 30, 1915. Taken to Chicago, Illinois, as an infant, she was raised there by her aunt in a middle-class household. As a child she spent many hours attending church and learning the rules of proper dress and etiquette. Under the influence of that training, she became an intent observer of human nature. As she explained in a 1994 interview with a *Contemporary Black Biography* (CBB) contributor, "When I was

young I came to realize how people were all born and conceived in the same manner; [I understood] that since all children are helpless and innocent at birth, their differences are determined by their upbringing, not color." Her belief in the importance of upbringing later encouraged Powell to instill in others the values of beauty, discipline, and positive self-image.

As a teen Powell was particularly interested in theater and dance, and as the member of a local dramatic league, she had the opportunity to study with Baron James, a prominent producer and director. Between the ages of 14 and 22, roughly, she appeared in a number of plays and dance recitals around the Midwest. She was dissatisfied with her stage voice, however, and around 1937 she decided to move from the performing arts into modeling. Her training at several charm schools in Chicago, including Madam C. J. Walker's School of Beauty Culture, provided her with the background needed for a successful modeling career. Over the course of the 1940s, she became well-known for her work in local advertisements and fashion shows. She also found time to study cosmetology, and by the end of the decade, she was working steadily as a manicurist and makeup artist.

At a Glance . . .

Born Maxine Blair on May 30, 1915, in Texarkana, TX; died on October 14, 2013, in Southfield, MI; daughter of Clarence and Gladys Blair; married James Powell (divorced). *Education:* Attended several modeling schools, 1930s–40s(?).

Career: Model, 1940s; manicurist and makeup artist, late 1940s–early 1950s; Maxine Powell Finishing and Modeling School, founder and director, 1951–64; Motown Records, finishing instructor and consultant, 1964–69; independent fashion consultant, 1969–2013; Wayne County Community College, instructor, 1971–85.

A pivotal moment in Powell's career came in 1948, when Powell traveled to Detroit, Michigan, for a stay at the Gotham Hotel, one of the finest black-owned establishments in the country. Through an acquaintance at the Gotham, she quickly found work in the city, then a booming industrial hub, and decided to remain. Soon after her arrival, she joined the Zontas Business and Professional Organization, a black civic group dedicated to the desegregation of Detroit's public venues. The connections she made within that organization proved useful to her when she opened the Maxine Powell Finishing and Modeling School in 1951. Generally regarded as Detroit's first black modeling agency, it was instrumental in breaking the color barrier that had long kept African-American models out of certain advertisements, notably those used to sell the cars that rolled off Detroit's assembly lines. Relying on her personal connections and considerable charisma, Powell gradually "convinced the auto companies to use black models," the attorney Myzell Sowell told the *Detroit News.* Sowell added, "Her contributions were tremendous."

The next stage in Powell's career began in the early 1960s, when her friend Berry Gordy, who had founded Motown several years earlier, began seeking her opinion about the young talent he was signing to his label. In his book *Where Did Our Love Go?,* Nelson George explained, "It was nothing at first; just a friend helping a friend. But as time went on she found herself caught up in the enthusiasm for Berry's record company." In 1964 Powell closed her modeling operations to join Motown as a special company consultant. After organizing the label's new finishing school, known officially as the Artist Development Department, she set out to instruct its stars (many of whom came from Detroit's housing projects) on the fine points of stage presence and public speaking. Her students included Martha Reeves, Smokey Robinson, Marvin Gaye, Stevie Wonder, the Temptations, and the Supremes, whose stage clothing she made from department-store sale items.

Powell spent two hours a day with each performer, telling the artists that they were being trained for two places: the White House and Buckingham Palace. Many of the young stars did not share her enthusiasm, however; she later described them to the *Detroit News* as "rude and crude." She explained, "They were twenty years old, and all they wanted was a hit record. I told them, 'I'm teaching you skills for life.'" In the *Detroit Free Press,* Powell recalled that Gaye, although cooperative and polite, thought himself above her methods. "I said, 'Marvin, you don't need as much training as some of them. But you sing with your eyes closed. We have to work on that.'"

Under Powell's guidance, Motown artists were groomed to play the most prominent and demanding venues in the world. "I taught positive change through body language and word power," Powell emphasized to *CBB.* "I told these young artists that they were not the best singers and dancers in the world, that our race has always had great performers. My job was to keep them from going on an ego trip—to remind them that each performance was a dress rehearsal."

Following her departure from Motown in 1969, Powell began a teaching career. In 1971 she became an instructor at Wayne County Community College, where she taught courses in personal development for 14 years. She remained active professionally for many years thereafter, serving as a freelance consultant in the fields of fashion and personal deportment. As late as 2009, for example, she was working with her former student Reeves, then serving on Detroit's city council, to bring finishing tips to schools and community groups across the city. Although her health declined sharply after she suffered a fall in the spring of 2013, her characteristic optimism and determination soon returned, and she was seen distributing business cards to hospital personnel just hours before her death in Southfield, Michigan, on October 14, 2013. At a funeral held several days later at Detroit's Hartford Memorial Baptist Church, dozens of mourners recalled her, in the words of USAToday.com's Brian McCollum, "as a woman who lived the class and elegance she taught for a living" and "as a figure who helped shape Motown's public image—and thus, the image of black America writ large."

Sources

Books

George, Nelson, *Where Did Our Love Go? The Rise and Fall of the Motown Sound,* St. Martin's Press, 1985.
Wilson, Mary, *Dream Girl: My Life as a Supreme,* St. Martin's Press, 1986.

Periodicals

Detroit Free Press Magazine, January 3, 1993, pp. 14–17.

Detroit News, May 20, 1985, pp. 1B, 10B.
Los Angeles Times, October 19, 2013.
People, October 13, 1985.

Online

Fox, Margalit, "Maxine Powell, Motown's Maven of Style, Dies at 98," NYTimes.com, http://www
.nytimes.com/2013/10/17/arts/music/maxine
-powell-motowns-maven-of-style-dies-at-98.html?_r
=2&adxnnl=1&hpw=&adxnnlx=1385055500-otHj
LHAJjZkXkOPSp5Va7w (accessed November 21,
2013).

McCollum, Brian, "Funeral Celebrates Life of Motown Figure Maxine Powell," USAToday.com, October 18, 2013, http://www.usatoday.com/story/life/ music/2013/10/18/motown-funeral-maxine-po well/3020541/ (accessed November 21, 2013).

Wang, Kevin, "Maxine Powell, Mentor to Motown Stars, Dies at 98," CNN.com, October 15, 2013, http://edition.cnn.com/2013/10/14/showbiz/mo town-mentor-powell-obit/ (accessed November 21, 2013).

Other

Additional information for the profile was obtained through Maxine Powell's personal business publications and promotional materials and through a *CBB* interview conducted on February 16, 1994, in Detroit, MI.

—John Cohassey and R. Anthony Kugler

Don Robey

1903–1975

Music executive, entrepreneur

Robey, Don, photograph. Michael Ochs Archives/Getty Images.

Although he never became a household name, the record executive Don Robey had a lasting impact on the development of popular music. As the founder and president of Peacock (later Duke-Peacock) Records, he shaped the careers of dozens of blues, gospel, and R&B stars, including the vocalist Willie Mae "Big Mama" Thornton, whose rendition of "Hound Dog" in the early 1950s was later covered by Elvis Presley in what proved one of the seminal events of the rock era. A shrewd negotiator whose hard-nosed tactics sometimes sparked controversy, Robey slowly but steadily built his organization into one of the most successful African-American businesses in the country. "Robey's name," Ed Hogan of AllMusic.com once wrote, "should be on any serious list of early pop/R&B pioneers." Writer Ronald G. Bookman echoed that sentiment, describing the Texas-born entrepreneur as nothing less than "the original king of black music."

Don Deadric Robey was born on November 1, 1903, in Houston's Fifth Ward, the center of that city's African-American community. Raised there in a middle-class household, he left school at about 16 to pursue a variety of entrepreneurial projects, including professional gambling, a taxi company, and concert promotion. His most prominent ventures before Peacock, however, involved nightclubs, such as the Harlem Grill, which he ran in Los Angeles, California, in the late 1930s and early 1940s. Robey's efforts there brought him a number of contacts in the entertainment industry, many of which proved useful to him when he returned to Houston and began to lay the groundwork for a new nightspot, the Bronze Peacock Dinner Club. Opened in 1945, it became quite successful, drawing large crowds with top-notch musicians from around the country.

Robey's interactions with the acts he booked at the Bronze Peacock soon convinced him that there were other opportunities in the music industry, and in the second half of the 1940s he opened a record store and a talent-management agency. The agency's first client, a young blues musician named Clarence "Gatemouth" Brown, played a pivotal role in the creation of Peacock Records in 1949. Unhappy with the way Brown was being treated by his label, Robey simply started his own, paying for it with the profits from his other enterprises. The fact that he was self-financed allowed

him to negotiate on his own terms, without interference from banks and business partners.

Brown was the first artist on Peacock's roster. His recordings sold well, and that success soon attracted Thornton and others. It also enabled Robey to expand aggressively. In 1952 he agreed to join forces with Duke Records, based in Memphis, Tennessee. Duke had a strong roster of R&B talent, including the vocalists Johnny Ace and Bobby "Blue" Bland. The following year, Robey gained control of the combined company, which he ran from a modest building on Houston's Erastus Street for the next two decades.

Robey's handling of Duke solidified his growing reputation as a formidable negotiator, a role he played with musicians and songwriters as well. One of his most controversial practices involved his efforts to control songwriting credits and the rights and royalties that depended on them. At the time, royalties were not well regulated, and artists all over the country were often denied fair payment for their work. Even in that climate, however, Robey's habit of listing himself as a cowriter, usually under the pseudonym "Deadric Malone," was controversial.

Nevertheless, many artists thrived at Duke-Peacock. With excellent backing musicians and a strong distribution network, Robey was able to bring regional stars, such as the vocalist O. V. Wright, to national attention. Wright was known above all for R&B, a genre in which Duke-Peacock had exceptional expertise. Under Robey's direction, the label also built one of the strongest gospel lineups in the country. Many of the singles released under its aegis by the Dixie Hummingbirds, the Mighty Clouds of Joy, and other gospel acts had a lush, rich sound that proved highly influential. Previous gospel recordings had typically been done in an austere style, with a minimum of orchestration and special effects. Robey's gospel groups, in contrast, used backing musicians to full effect, creating a sound that often resembled contemporary pop and R&B. That shift helped revive what had been a declining genre and was widely imitated by other companies.

As he built his business, Robey launched a number of subsidiary labels, many of which became well-known in their own right. Among the most prominent were the R&B-focused Back Beat, founded in 1957, and Song Bird, a gospel imprint. When Song Bird was established in 1963, the music business was changing rapidly, driven by a number of factors, including the explosive growth of rock and roll and the cultural tumult that came to characterize the era. Although many Duke-Peacock artists, among them Wright and Bland, continued to sell tens of thousands of singles, they faced growing competition, much of it from Motown Records, based in Detroit, Michigan, and Stax Records, based in Memphis. Robey managed to hang on, however, until 1973, when he sold the company to ABC Dunhill, a label based in New York City. For another two years, he remained on staff as a consultant, helping the new owners plan reissues from Duke-Peacock's extensive catalog. Robey died on June 16, 1975, leaving behind his wife, Murphy, and three children. For decades Robey had been heavily involved in a variety of community programs in Houston and across the country, including the National Association for the Advancement of Colored People and the United Negro College Fund, and he was widely mourned.

In the decades since Robey's passing, his reputation has continued to grow, fueled in part by the rapid adoption of digital media, a process that has encouraged the remastering and rerelease of many gems from the Duke-Peacock vaults. The growth of the Internet has helped as well; a recording of Thornton's "Hound Dog," for example, had been viewed well over 170,000 times on YouTube as of November of 2013.

Sources

Online

"Big Mama Thornton–Hound Dog (1952) Blues," YouTube, May 1, 2011, https://www.youtube.com/watch?v=yoHDrzw-RPg (accessed November 17, 2013).

Bookman, Ronald G., "Don D. Robey, The Original King of Black Music: 'They Call Me Mister Robey,'" EURWeb.com, June 10, 2012, http://www.eurweb.com/2012/06/don-d-robey-the-original-king-of-black-music-they-call-me-mister-robey/ (accessed November 16, 2013).

Hogan, Ed, "Don Robey: Artist Biography," AllMusic.com, http://www.allmusic.com/artist/don-robey-mn0000192354 (accessed November 16, 2013).

Rimmer, Dave, "Don Robey and Peacock Records," SoulfulKindaMusic.net, http://www.soulfulkindamusic.net/articlepeacock.htm (accessed November 16, 2013).

"Robey, Don Deadric," Texas State Historical Association, http://www.tshaonline.org/handbook/online/articles/fropc (accessed November 16, 2013).

—R. Anthony Kugler

Romanthony

1967–2013

DJ, producer, singer

Regarded as a "cult figure in the world of house music," according to the London *Guardian,* singer, DJ, and producer Romanthony is best remembered for his vocals on the 2000 track "One More Time" by the French electronic music duo Daft Punk, which became one of the biggest dance hits of its day, particularly in the United Kingdom and Europe. Romanthony first began releasing house music on his own label, Black Male Records, in the early 1990s, producing singles such as "Make This Love Right" and "Let Me Show You Love," and later issued two albums on the Glasgow Underground label, 1999's *Instinctual* and 2000's *R.Hide in Plain Site.* His career was cut short by kidney disease, which caused his death in 2013 at age 45.

Romanthony was born Anthony Wayne Moore in 1967 in Eatontown, New Jersey. Encouraged by his parents, he took guitar lessons from a young age. Later, Romanthony expressed that knowing how to play "real instruments" had helped him design electronic sounds. In a video interview conducted after "One More Time" was released in 2000, he cited the songwriting inspiration of Marvin Gaye, Jimi Hendrix, the Beatles, Chuck Berry, the Eagles, and Prince. Romanthony also was influenced by the German group Kraftwerk, which came out of Düsseldorf in 1970, and the British electronica band 808 State, which debuted in 1987. He embraced house music, a genre that arose in Chicago in the early 1980s. House music typically blends drum machines, samples, and disembodied vocals. Many house musicians are equally known for their intricate recordings and their club appearances as DJs.

His first record, an EP titled *Now You Want Me,* was released in 1992 on Romanthony's own Black Male Records label and in the United Kingdom on Azuli Records. One of his best-known tracks, "Hold On," featuring a lengthy sample of a sermon, came out in 1994. Other songs that were popular in urban clubs across the United States and Europe included "Let Me Show You Love" and "The Wanderer." Many of these tracks featured the singer Daone Remmidy, also known as Eve Angel. Romanthony's full-length debut, *Romanworld,* came out in 1997. After the DJ's death, Gerd Janson of the Red Bull Music Academy called that work "one of the few coherent house albums ever made."

As his following grew Romanthony became known for odd juxtapositions—for example, Christian gospel could be heard alongside Malcolm X, Islamic calls to prayer, and self-help advice. Many of Romanthony's recordings featured his own high-pitched voice, which bore enough resemblance to that of Prince that some people suspected that Romanthony was a pseudonym of the pop icon. *Instinctual,* an album coproduced with DJ Predator, came out in 1999. Romanthony toured internationally, deejaying at clubs and circulating his distinctive mixtapes. On a visit to Berlin, Germany, he told an interviewer in a video posted on YouTube, "My music in production is usually physical pain.... When you get a certain rhythm going at the studio, a certain sequence of melodies, sometimes, it's not funny at all, it's like the opposite of it."

The album *R.Hide in Plain Sight* was released jointly by Black Male Records and Glasgow Underground in 2000. A *New Music Express* critic wryly called it "the best Prince record since *Sign O the Times,*" contrasting it favorably with Britain's sterile house music scene.

At the Winter Music Conference in 1996, Romanthony befriended French musicians Thomas Bangalter and Guy-Manuel de Homem-Christo, who had formed a band called Daft Punk. When the act released their house-influenced debut, *Homework* (1997), it included "Teachers," which hailed the influence of the genre's leading figures, including Romanthony and producer Todd Edwards. Soon Daft Punk and Romanthony were working together.

Daft Punk released "One More Time," featuring Romanthony singing the hook, as a single in November of 2000. The French duo heavily processed Romanthony's voice, but its aching soulfulness remained apparent. The track became a number-one hit in Canada and France and reached number two on the U.K. singles chart. On the Billboard Hot 100 singles chart in the United States, "One More Time" reached number 61 and subsequently was nominated for a Grammy Award in the best dance recording category. Twelve years after its release, the website MixMag.net declared "One More Time" the greatest dance track of all time. It appeared on Daft Punk's album *Discovery*, along with another Romanthony track, "Too Long."

Speaking at the time of their hit in 2001, de Homem-Christo said, "What's odd is that Romanthony and Todd Edwards are not big in the United States at all. Their music had a big effect on us. The sound of their productions—the compression, the sound of the kick-drum and Romanthony's voice, the emotional soul—is part of how we sound today. Because they mean something to us, it was much more important for us to work with them than with other big stars."

At some point after 2001, Romanthony moved from New Jersey to Austin, Texas, keeping a lower than usual profile. He died there on May 7, 2013, of complications from kidney disease. At the time of his death, he reportedly had been working with Boys Noize (German producer and DJ Alexander Ridha) on a new collaboration.

Selected discography

Now You Want Me (EP), Black Male Records/Azuli, 1992.
Romanworld, Azuli Records, 1997.
Instinctual, Glasgow Underground, 1999.
Live in the Mix, Distance Records, 1999.
R.Hide in Plain Site, Glasgow Underground, 2000.

Sources

Periodicals

Guardian, May 20, 2013.
New Musical Express, March 21, 2000.

Online

Janson, Gerd, "Romanthony RIP," Red Bull Music Academy, May 25, 2013, http://www.redbull musicacademy.com/magazine/romanthony-rip-feature (accessed January 20, 2014).

Matthew, Terry, "Remembering Romanthony, For the First Time, Again," 5Chicago.com, May 19, 2013, http://5chicago.com/news/2013/05/19/remem bering-romanthony-for-the-first-time-again/ (accessed January 20, 2014).

"Romanthony, or the Strange Isolation of House Music," May 20, 2013, http://musicismthought .word press.com/2013/05/20/romanthony-or-the -strange-isolation-of-house-music/ (accessed January 20, 2014).

Romanthony (Slices DVD Feature), YouTube, January 3, 2013, http://www.youtube.com/watch?v=WT3 Hk7OD44U (accessed January 20, 2014).

Sherburne, Philip, "Romanthony, Daft Punk's 'One More Time' Singer, Dead at 45," Spin.com, May 19, 2013, http://www.spin.com/articles/romanthony -daft-punk-dead-obit-one-more-time/ (accessed January 20, 2014).

"What Is the Greatest Dance Track of All Time?," MixMag.net, February 15, 2013, http://www.mix mag.net/words/news/what-is-the-greatest-dance -track-of-all-time (accessed January 20, 2014).

—Mark Swartz

Ashton Springer Jr.

1930–2013

Theatrical producer, theater manager

Ashton Springer Jr. was the first black theatrical producer to become a major player on Broadway, producing a string of hit shows in the 1970s and early 1980s, including the musical revues *Bubbling Brown Sugar* (1976) and *Eubie!* (1978) and an all-black revival of *Guys and Dolls* (1976). A coin-laundry operator who stumbled into a career in the theater, Springer had his first Broadway outing in 1960 with *No Place to Be Somebody* by Charles Gordone, the first African-American playwright to win a Pulitzer Prize. Convinced that audiences would respond to theater by and about blacks, Springer mounted a series of successful productions in the late 1970s, earning two Tony Award nominations. Springer is credited with introducing the works of 20th-century black playwrights such as Gordone and Athol Fugard to mainstream audiences, as well as drawing large numbers of African Americans to the theater, helping reverse Broadway's trend of declining audience numbers. Although his stint on Broadway was brief, ending in the early 1980s amid damaging allegations of financial improprieties, Springer has come to be regarded as a trailblazer who helped open doors for other African-American producers.

Ashton Springer Jr. was born on November 1, 1930, in New York City, the son of immigrants from the West Indies. He grew up in the Bronx, where he attended Evander Childs High School. While a student there, he sang with a group called the Four Aces and promoted his first show, "Boppin' at the Bronx," which featured such big names in jazz as Charlie Parker, Miles Davis, Milt Jackson, Bud Powell, and Max Roach performing at the Bronx Winter Garden. "We made $150, and we thought that was a lot of dough at the time," Springer recalled in a 1978 interview with Paul Wilner of the *New York Times.*

Springer studied at Ohio State University, earning his degree in 1954. After college Springer returned to New York and found a job as a social worker at the Richard Lawrence Youth Center in the Bronx. On the side, he and his wife, Myra, managed a coin-operated laundry in Queens that was owned by N. Richard Nash, a playwright who was known for his 1954 drama *The Rainmaker.* Nash gave Springer a room in his office in the theater district. "A lot of famous people would come by. It was like walking around star-gazing," Springer told Wilner. Springer quickly became captivated by the theater, and he began his career on Broadway in 1960 as Nash's assistant on the musical comedy *Wildcat,* starring Lucille Ball.

A chance encounter with an old classmate would define the direction of Springer's theatrical career. In the mid-1960s he connected with Jeanne Warner, who was married to a little-known playwright named Charles Gordone. Warner gave Springer the script for Gordone's play *No Place to Be Somebody,* a gritty drama that portrayed the lives of black patrons of a New York saloon. Springer spent three years trying to raise enough money to produce the play; potential investors told him that there was little market for a play about African Americans. Finally Springer convinced Joseph Papp, a producer and director and the founder of the New York Shakespeare Festival, to stage Gordone's play at his Public Theatre. *No Place* began as a

workshop production on the Other Stage, the experimental wing of Papp's theater. After a positive response, the production moved upstairs to the larger Florence Anspacher Theater, where it was performed as part of the Public Theatre's regular programming. Thereafter the play transferred to the ANTA Playhouse on Broadway for a limited 15-show run. The following year, Gordone received the Pulitzer Prize for Drama for *No Place,* becoming the first black playwright ever to win the award. In 1971 Springer and Warner mounted a revival of the play at Broadway's Morosco Theatre, where it ran for 39 performances.

When the show went on tour beginning in 1970, Springer became convinced that there was indeed a market for African-American theater—among both black and white audiences. "White people enjoyed 'No Place' as a piece of playwriting, but black people had a tremendous identification with it—they were totally involved," he told the *New York Times.* When the play traveled to cities such as Chicago and Philadelphia, it drew large crowds of African-American theatergoers. "Black folks started coming out, and they continued to come out," Springer told Wilner.

Springer went on to produce a string of successful shows, becoming a major player on Broadway and one of only a few black producers. He initially focused his attention on works by and for African Americans. The musical review *Bubbling Brown Sugar,* set in Harlem between the 1920s and the 1940s, featured the music of great black musicians such as Cab Calloway, Louis Armstrong, Duke Ellington, and Billie Holiday. The play opened at the Church of St. Paul and St. Andrew

in February of 1975, running for 12 previews before moving to the ANTA Playhouse on Broadway, where it continued for 766 performances, earning a Tony Award nomination for best musical. Springer followed in 1976 with a revival of the musical *Guys and Dolls* featuring an all-black cast, which also received a Tony nod.

In 1978 Springer produced another musical revue, *Eubie!,* which showcased the music of ragtime and jazz pianist Eubie Blake. Playing for 439 performances, the show starred tap dancers Gregory and Maurice Hines. Even though the show was a hit, financially, *Eubie!* was a failure, barely taking in enough money to cover weekly expenses and preventing Springer from repaying investors. The New York State attorney general's office later launched an investigation into possible financial improprieties. In 1982 Springer was ordered to pay more than $120,000 in restitution to 33 investors and was temporarily barred from producing. Court documents revealed that he had previously been convicted on charges of committing forgery and petty larceny and of using counterfeit stock certificates to obtain loans, although Springer claimed that none of those offenses had been related to any theatrical production.

Following *Eubie!,* Springer produced three more Broadway shows: the musical comedy *Whoopee!, A Lesson from Aloes* by the South African playwright Fugard, and another comedy, *Inacent Black.* However, the 1982 court order virtually ended Springer's Broadway producing career. He continued to manage Broadway's Little Theatre (also known as the Helen Hayes Theatre) until 1985. In 1992 he produced a touring production of *Lotto: Experience the Dream,* and in 1999 he produced the Off-Broadway play *Rollin' on the T.B.A.* at the 27th Street Theater. Springer's final production was a 2000 Off-Broadway revival of Ntozake Shange's *for colored girls who have considered suicide/when the rainbow is enuf* at the American Place Theatre, for which Springer served as general manager.

Springer died at his home in Mamaroneck, New York, on June 15, 2013, at the age of 82. On June 24 of that year, Broadway theaters dimmed their marquees for one minute in Springer's memory.

Selected works

Plays (as a producer)

No Place to Be Somebody, New York Shakespeare Festival/Public Theatre, ANTA Playhouse, New York, 1969; revival, Morosco Theatre, New York, 1971.
Lamppost Reunion, Little Theatre, New York, 1975.
Bubbling Brown Sugar, ANTA Playhouse, New York, 1976–77.

Guys and Dolls, Broadway Theatre, New York, 1976–77.

Going Up, John Golden Theatre, New York, 1976.

Unexpected Guests, Little Theatre, New York, 1977.

Cold Storage, Lyceum Theatre, New York, 1977–78.

Eubie!, Ambassador Theatre, New York, 1978–79.

Whoopee!, ANTA Playhouse, New York, 1979.

The All Night Strut!, Theatre Four, New York, 1979.

Daddy Goodness, Forest Theatre, Philadelphia, National Theater, Washington, DC, 1979.

A Lesson from Aloes, Playhouse Theatre, New York, 1980–81.

Inacent Black, Biltmore Theatre, New York, 1981.

Lotto: Experience the Dream, touring production, 1992.

Rollin' on the T.B.A., 47th Street Theatre, New York, 1999.

(General manager) *for colored girls who have considered suicide/when the rainbow is enuf,* American Place Theatre, 2000.

Sources

Periodicals

New York Times, October 10, 1976; March 19, 1978; October 2, 1982; July 20, 2013.

Philadelphia Inquirer, November 11, 1992.

Online

Boyd, Herb, "Ashton Springer, First Major Black Producer on B'Way, Dies at 82," AmsterdamNews.com, July 29, 2013, http://amsterdamnews.com/news/2013/jul/29/ashton-springer-first-major-black-producer-bway-di/ (accessed December 13, 2013).

Simonsen, Robert, "Ashton Springer, Broadway Producer of Hit Revues, Dies at 82," Playbill.com, July 16, 2013, http://www.playbill.com/news/article/180173-Ashton-Springer-Broadway-Producer-of-Hit-Revues-Dies-at-82- (accessed December 13, 2013).

—Deborah A. Ring

Sage Steele

1972—

Journalist, sports broadcaster

Sage Steele is a sports journalist and on-air personality for ESPN. Since 2007 she has served as cohost of the network's flagship program, *SportsCenter,* while also working on segments for the National Basketball Association (NBA) Finals. In 2013 she became a coanchor of ESPN's *NBA Countdown*—a major promotion for Steele, who is one of the few women of African-American descent to make it in sports broadcasting. There are fewer still of biracial background (Steele is the daughter of a black father and a white mother). "If someone sees me on TV," Steele told Richard Deitsch in an interview for *Sports Illustrated,* "they are not thinking there is a white girl with curly hair…. They are saying there is a black girl with curly hair. But I don't look it as a pioneering role. That's not what I'm trying to do and never have been."

Born in 1972 in the Panama Canal Zone, where her father was then serving in the military, Steele grew up around the world in a household that valued athletics. Her father, Gary Steele, was the first African American to play on the varsity football squad at the U.S. Military Academy at West Point. Steele's two brothers were also enthusiastic about sports (her brother Chad is the

Steele, Sage, photograph. Neilson Barnard/Getty Images for DirecTV.

media relations director for the Baltimore Ravens), and wherever they were posted, they managed to follow American football and basketball, forging a link with life in the United States. Robin Roberts, then an ESPN commentator and one of television's first black female sports reporters, was Steele's idol.

Steele's family returned to the United States in 1989, settling in Indianapolis, Indiana, where she finished her senior year in high school at suburban Carmel High. It was her first real experience of being made to feel like a minority. With a black father and a white Catholic mother from Massachusetts, Steele had navigated the racial divide with little difficulty at various postings around the world and never had felt that she had to decide which race she belonged to. "Whenever I filled out an application," Steele told Tom Zucco of Florida's *St. Petersburg Times,* "I always checked 'both.'"

At Carmel High School, however, race was an issue. She was the only minority in a student body of almost 2,000, and she had to deal not only with racial epithets but also social rejection. Steele's parents told her that she could transfer, but she decided not to, as she

At a Glance . . .

Born on November 28, 1972, in Panama; daughter of Gary Steele (a career army officer); married Jonathan Bailey; children: three. *Education:* Indiana University, BS, sports communications, 1995.

Career: WSBT-TV, South Bend, IN, reporter, 1995–97; WISH-TV, Indianapolis, IN, reporter and weekend morning sports anchor, 1997–98; WFTS-TV, Tampa, FL, sports reporter, 1998–2001; Fox Sports Florida, sports reporter, 2000–01; Comcast SportsNet Mid-Atlantic, Bethesda, MD, anchor and sports reporter, 2001–07; ESPN, sports anchor, *SportsCenter*, 2007—, *NBA Countdown*, host, 2013—.

Addresses: *Office*—ESPN, 545 Middle St., Bristol, CT 06010. *Twitter*—@SageSteele.

explained to the *St. Petersburg Times:* "Maybe it's the military in me.… I wasn't going to let those people run me off. It was the toughest year of my life, but looking back now, I'm glad it happened." Steele credited that year with giving her the self-confidence and tenacity necessary to make it in sports journalism.

Steele chose to attend nearby Indiana University in Bloomington, where she majored in sports communications, and after graduating in 1995, she got her first job as a broadcast reporter as a trainee at WSBT-TV in South Bend. In 1997 she moved to WISH-TV, a CBS affiliate in Indianapolis, scoring a coup by reporting on the NCAA Final Four basketball tournament held that year in Indianapolis. She was "shaking like a leaf" while doing that coverage, she told the *St. Petersburg Times,* but it was one more trial by fire that she passed, bolstering her self-confidence.

In 1998 she moved to a television station in Tampa, Florida, working as the beat reporter for the Tampa Bay Buccaneers and covering the 1999 NCAA Final Four tournament. In 2000 she became one of three regional reporters for Fox SportsNet Florida, covering Super Bowl XXXV. A bigger break came for Steele when she took on the post as anchor for the fledgling Comcast SportsNet in the Baltimore and Washington, DC, region. She was the beat reporter for the Baltimore Ravens and also anchored *SportsNite,* the standard-bearer show for SportsNet.

The move to ESPN—her dream job—came in 2007, when she was hired as one of the anchors of *Sports-Center.* "I love *SportsCenter,*" Steele told *New York Post* contributor Justin Terranova. "That was my goal since I was 12 years old and I did it." She debuted on

March 14, 2007, appearing on the evening edition of *SportsCenter,* and since then has gone on to make a name for herself as a competent and knowledgeable sports journalist. In addition to *SportsCenter,* she also has appeared on other ESPN shows, including *First Take, Mike & Mike in the Morning,* and *SportsNation,* and has provided on-site coverage of the NBA Finals.

In an interview with Indiana University Sports Marketing Alliance contributor Pat Manaher, Steele commented on the pressures of her career as a sports journalist and anchor: "The pressure that goes into each highlight, each three hour show is tremendous, there is so much that goes into it.… It's indescribable, there's nothing that could fully prepare you for it." She also noted that the goal post is different for women in the industry than it is for men: "As women we have to be better.… Is that right? No, but it is how it is."

Steele's focus and work ethic were two reasons she was named to ESPN's *NBA Countdown* in 2013, cohosting the pregame show on Fridays and Sundays. "Sage is a dynamic, engaging personality and an avid follower of the NBA," noted ESPN executive vice president of production, John Wildhack, in a press release posted on ESPN MediaZone. "She has a proven track record hosting our NBA coverage, and, on Countdown, she'll help facilitate insightful discussion." In the same press release Steele remarked, "I'm thrilled to continue my career at ESPN and to embark on this exciting, new challenge." Speaking with Terranova, she further commented on this career advancement: "With this, it's the first time in my career I can concentrate on one sport.… This is truly just an awesome opportunity."

Steele's career is not the sole focus of her life. Her husband and three children are the center for her. In 2004, with young children at home, she initially turned down an offer from ESPN, feeling that she needed to focus on her family instead of on her career. She told Manaher that although she loves her work, she would "walk away today if there was a conflict between family and work." In addition to spending as much time with her family as she can, Steele also gives back to the community by volunteering for the Alzheimer's Association. "I just try to do my job, do it the right way and make my family proud," Steele told Deitsch.

Sources

Periodicals

St. Petersburg (FL) Times, June 9, 2000.

Online

Deitsch, Richard, "Sage Steele Talks NBA Countdown, Barkley Bashes Twitter, More," SI.com, October 27, 2013, http://sportsillustrated.cnn.com/more/news/20131027/sage-steele-espn-nba-countdown-media-circus/ (accessed November 24, 2013).

Manaher, Pat, "Steele Credits IU as Foundation for ESPN Success," Indiana University Sports Marketing Alliance, http://www.iusma.com/sage-steele.html (accessed November 24, 2013).

"Sage Steele," ESPN MediaZone, http://espnmediazone.com/us/bios/steele_sage/ (accessed November 24, 2013).

"Sage Steele to Host ABC's and ESPN's NBA Countdown," ESPN MediaZone, October 22, 2013, http://espnmediazone.com/us/press-releases/20 13/10/sage-steele-to-host-abcs-and-espns-nba -countdown/ (accessed November 14, 2013).

Terranova, Justin, "Sage Steele in Middle of ESPN's New-Look NBA Show," NYPost.com, November 8, 2013, http://nypost.com/2013/11/08/sage-steele -in-middle-of-espns-new-look-nba-show/ (accessed November 24, 2013).

—J. Sydney Jones

Sevyn Streeter

1986—

Singer, songwriter

Sevyn Streeter is a veteran of two short-lived girl groups, a songwriter of hits for Chris Brown, Mary J. Blige, and more, and, as of December of 2013, a solo recording artist. After stints with the groups TG4 and RichGirl, Streeter scored her first big hit with the single "It Won't Stop" in late 2013. The duet with frequent collaborator Brown left her poised for greater success in the future.

The singer was born Amber Denise Streeter in Haines City, Florida, outside of Orlando, in 1986 on the seventh

Streeter, Sevyn, photograph. John Ricard/Getty Images.

day of the seventh month—hence her stage name, Sevyn, which she adopted in 2007. The music that Streeter heard in church as a girl made a distinct impression on her. Her website lists a number of early musical influences, including Yolanda Adams, the Winans family, Michael Jackson, Celine Dion, Brandy, and Whitney Houston. She had a particular fondness for the R&B solo artists and groups of the 1990s, among them Aaliyah, 702, 112, Jagged Edge, and TLC. "They way they sang was effortless," she told Esteban Serrano of the Fuse network.

Streeter wanted to be a singer and appeared in talent shows in Tampa as a child. At the age of 10, she took

the stage at Harlem's Apollo Theater, where her rendition of the Rodgers and Hart standard "My Funny Valentine" earned her a tie for first place in the "Showtime at the Apollo" competition, a platform that had launched the career of Lauryn Hill and many others.

As a member of two different girl groups in the first decade of the 21st century, Streeter was able to explore different sides of her musical personality. In early 2001 she was invited to join TG4 (which stands for TomGurl 4 or Tom Girls Forever), the brainchild of Chris Strokes of T.U.G. Entertainment, and at age 15, she was signed to Interscope Records. The group, which was conceived as the female counterpart to the boy band B2K, scored a minor hit with the single "Virginity" in 2002, but their follow-up, "2 Minutes," failed to chart, and the group members went their separate ways. Streeter's band mate Davida Williams went on to a successful acting career.

Streeter's next project was a group called RichGirl, which was produced by Rich Harrison, best known for his work on Beyoncé and Jay-Z's smash "Crazy in Love." Harrison was impressed by a MySpace perfor-

At a Glance . . .

Born Amber Denise Streeter on July 7, 1986, in Haines City, FL.

Career: Singer with TG4, RichGirl, 2001–09; songwriter, 2011—; solo recording artist, 2013—.

Addresses: *Record company*—Atlantic Records/CBE 1290 Avenue of Americas, New York, NY 10104. *Web*— http://www.sevynstreeter.com.

mance by Streeter (who was then calling herself "Se7en"). Despite their chance in the spotlight as Beyoncé's opening act, RichGirl barely dented the charts in 2009 with "24's," a single featuring rapper Bun B, before they, too, disbanded.

Streeter told Erika Ramirez of *Billboard* that these experiences "helped mold the artist I am today." To Esteban Serrano of Fuse, she elaborated: "When you're in groups, you don't feel the need to strengthen yourself in your weaker areas. Today I feel more secure and confident as *a woman*."

RichGirl was managed by Tina Davis, who also oversaw the career of pop singer Chris Brown. That connection proved vital as Streeter earned a reputation as a songwriter, contributing "Yeah 3X," "Wet the Bed," and "Strip" to Brown's *F.A.M.E.* album (2011) and four songs to the follow-up, *Fortune* (2012). She also wrote songs for Alicia Keys, Mary J. Blige, Brandy, Trey Songz, and Kelly Rowland. In November 2013 she joined Rowland and Eve for a performance of "Gone" on BET's Black Girls Rock concert. Her two most successful songs, as of 2013, were Chris Brown's "Fine China" and Ariana Grande's "The Way."

As with most contemporary R&B songs, these songs represent the combined work of multiple collaborators. She told Kai Acevedo of the website Life and Times, "A lot of the times I'm the only female in the room when we're writing." For example, "Strip," a track on Brown's 2012 album *Fortune,* is credited to J. "Lonny" Bereal, Chris Brown, Justin Henderson, Kevin McCall, Amber Streeter, and Christopher Whitacre.

In 2013 Brown signed Streeter as a solo artist to his CBE label. Regarding this development in her career,

she told AllHipHop.com, "It took a long time for me to get to a place where I believed, 'I'm enough.'" Late in 2013 she released the EP *Call Me Crazy, But...* and her breakthrough single, "It Won't Stop," a duet with Brown that *Billboard* called "infectious." Brown himself directed the song's video. A reviewer for *The Source* wrote, "From her steamy lyrics, to her amazing vocals, to her emotion delivered through each track, Sevyn Streeter is truly a breathe of fresh air."

Streeter told *Billboard*'s Ramirez that the seven-song EP "talks abut the cycle of a relationship: the ups, the downs, the goods, the bad, the ugly, the fights, the makeups" and forecast a 2014 that would be spent working on her own debut as well as Brown's *X,* for which she cowrote the title track. She also confessed a wish to work with Beyoncé and Usher.

Selected discography

Call Me Crazy, But... (EP; includes "It Won't Stop"), Atlantic, 2013.

Sources

Periodicals

Billboard, November 26, 2013; December 12, 2013. *Source,* December 5, 2013.

Online

Acevedo, Kai, "Check the Credits: Sevyn Streeter Speaks on Writing for Alicia Keys, Chris Brown, and Mary J. Blige," LifeandTimes.com, June 4, 2013, http://lifeandtimes.com/check-the-credits-sevyn-streeter-speaks-on-writing-for-alicia-keys-chris-brown-and-mary-j-blige (accessed January 20, 2014).

"Artist of the Week: Sevyn Streeter," Ace Show Biz, http://www.aceshowbiz.com/news/view/00066491.html (accessed January 20, 2014).

Davis, Rea Melissa, "Sevyn Streeter Goes Solo and Loves It," AllHipHop.com, December 6, 2013, http://allhiphop.com/2013/12/06/sevyn-streeter-goes-solo-and-loves-it/ (accessed January 20, 2014).

Serrano, Esteban, "Fuse Favorite: Watch Sevyn Streeter on Fuse All Week," Fuse, December 9, 2013, http://www.fuse.tv/2013/12/fuse-favorites-sevyn-streeter (accessed January 20, 2014).

Sevyn Streeter, http://www.sevynstreeter.com (accessed January 20, 2014).

—Mark Swartz

A Taste of Honey

R&B group

The R&B group A Taste of Honey is best remembered for a pair of dissimilar hits, 1978's "Boogie Oogie Oogie," an iconic song of the disco era, and 1981's "Sukiyaki," a remake of a popular Japanese hit, both of which reached the pop top five. After the runaway success of their dance hit "Boogie Oogie Oogie," which topped the pop singles chart for three weeks, A Taste of Honey struggled to break out of the disco category, but they were largely unsuccessful. The group had only a handful of hits thereafter, although they remained popular in Japan. In the late 1990s Burger King resurrected "Boogie Oogie Oogie" for a television advertising campaign, introducing a new generation to the disco classic, which has been sampled by contemporary artists such as MC Lyte and Mack 10.

The group formed in Los Angeles in 1971, when bassist and guitarist Janice Marie Johnson and keyboardist Perry Kimble met at an audition for Princess Cruises and decided to start a band. They called themselves A Taste of Honey, after the Herb Alpert and the Tijuana Brass song of the same name. The group added several friends, including lead singer Greg Walker, guitarist Carlita Dorhan, and Donald Ray Johnson (no relation to Janice Johnson) on drums, and began performing at local clubs in Southern California and at nearby military bases. Walker eventually quit the group to join the band Santana, and after Dorhan departed in 1976, she was replaced by guitarist Hazel Payne. After a meeting with producers Larry and Fonce Mizell, the group signed with Capitol Records in 1978.

A Taste of Honey's first single and biggest hit is said to have been inspired by an unresponsive audience at a show at a military base. Johnson and Payne believed that the mostly male crowd was put off by the two female guitarists, and Payne is said to have yelled at the crowd, "If you're thinkin' you're too cool to boogie, boy oh boy have I got news for you! Everybody here tonight must boogie. Let me tell ya, you are no exception to the rule." That exhortation became the opening line of "Boogie Oogie Oogie," and the song's distinctive bass solo introduction was captured while Johnson was warming up before the recording session, unaware that the tape was rolling. "Boogie Oogie Oogie" was released as a 12-inch dance mix in June of 1978, debuting on the Billboard 100 singles chart at number 82. Within three months the song had risen to number one, staying there for three weeks, and eventually sold more than two million copies. The group's self-titled solo debut album reached number six on the Billboard 200 and number two on the Top R&B/Black Albums chart. At the Grammy Awards in January of 1979, A Taste of Honey was named best new artist of the year.

The platinum-selling "Boogie Oogie Oogie" was hard to top, however. By 1979 the group had been reduced to a duo consisting of Johnson and Payne. That year they released their sophomore album, *Another Taste,* and had a modest hit with "Do It Good," which reached number 13 on the R&B singles list and number 79 on the Billboard Hot 100.

After hearing Linda Ronstadt's rendition of Smokey Robinson's "Ooo Baby Baby," Johnson decided to follow suit and remake a classic song. Early in the group's career, Johnson had sung "Sukiyaki," by the Japanese singer Kyu Sakamoto, when A Taste of Honey toured Japan and performed at the Yamaha Song Festival. Johnson secured permission to redo the song and hired two translators to put the original lyrics into English. Johnson added some of her own lyrics, encouraged by producer George Duke. Executives at Capitol, however, were not enthusiastic about the song. They delayed releasing it as a single, instead

issuing "Rescue Me" and "I'm Talkin' 'Bout You" from the group's third album, *Twice as Sweet* (1980). Those two singles reached the R&B chart, rising to number 16 and number 64, respectively. Eventually the label relented, and "Sukiyaki" was released in 1981. That spring, the song rose to number one on the R&B chart and number three on the Billboard Hot 100, fueling sales of *Twice as Sweet,* which peaked at number 36 on the Billboard 200. Johnson and Payne subsequently traveled to Japan and toured with Sakamoto, donning kimonos for their performances.

A Taste of Honey had their last hit single with a cover of Smokey Robinson and the Miracles' "I'll Try Something New," which reached number nine on the R&B chart and number 41 on the Billboard Hot 100. The remake appeared on the group's fourth and final album, *Ladies of the Eighties* (1982).

After the group disbanded in the early 1980s, Johnson released a solo album on Capitol Records, *One Taste of Honey* (1984), which produced the charting single "Love Me Tonite." She followed with *Hiatus of the Heart* (2000) and *Until the Eagle Falls* (2002), both released on Tastebuds, the label that she founded. Payne subsequently toured in Japan with her own band.

Selected discography

Albums

A Taste of Honey (includes "Boogie Oogie Oogie"), Capitol Records, 1978.
Another Taste (includes "Do It Good"), Capitol Records, 1979.
Twice as Sweet (includes "Rescue Me," "I'm Talkin' 'Bout You," and "Sukiyaki"), Capitol Records, 1980.
Ladies of the Eighties (includes "I'll Try Something New"), Capitol Records, 1982.

Sources

Periodicals

Billboard, June 26, 1999, p. 27.
Jet, January 3, 1983, pp. 60–62.

Online

Hogan, Ed, "A Taste of Honey: Artist Biography," AllMusic.com, http://www.allmusic.com/artist/a-taste-of-honey-mn0000576072/biography (accessed December 16, 2013).
A Taste of Honey, http://www.janice-marie.com/honey/honeyhome.htm (accessed December 16, 2013).
"A Taste of Honey," DiscoMuseum.net, http://www.discomuseum.net/BioATasteOfHoney.html (accessed December 16, 2013).

—Deborah A. Ring

Tavares

R&B group

The R&B group Tavares is best known for their 1977 disco hit "More Than a Woman," a song written for them by the *Bee Gees* for the soundtrack to the popular film *Saturday Night Fever*. Although that song would forever associate the group with the disco era, in fact, the five Tavares brothers spent most of their musical career singing R&B graced with more subtle rhythms than disco's driving beat. Including their early years, when they called themselves Chubby and the Turnpikes, their recording career spanned the 1950s to the 1980s, during which time they released a dozen albums and placed eight singles on the Billboard top 40.

Tavares, photograph. Michael Ochs Archives/Getty Images.

The Tavares brothers were born in New Bedford, Massachusetts, in the 1940s, the sons of Feliciano "Flash" Tavares. Flash was a self-taught singer and guitarist whose chief influence was the music of the West African island nation of Cape Verde, where his parents had grown up. Flash sometimes performed with his sister, Victoria Tavares Vieira, who sang Cape Verdean songs with jazz inflections. When Aristides Pereira, the first president of Cape Verde, visited the United States, Victoria sang in his honor.

Flash's sons—Victor, Ralph, Arthur, Antone, Feliciano, and Perry Tavares—grew up in New Bedford as well as in Providence, Rhode Island, in the Fox Point and South Providence neighborhoods, which are home to a large community of Cape Verdeans. There they were immersed in the culture and music of the distant island country. The brothers' first group, Chubby and the Turnpikes, debuted in 1959, when its youngest member, Perry, nicknamed "Tiny," was nine years old. Joey Kramer, who later would join the rock group Aerosmith, played drums in their backing band. After signing with Capitol Records in 1967, the group enjoyed a few local hits, including "I Know the Inside Story" and "Nothing But Promises."

Changing their name to Tavares, the brothers made the R&B top 10 in 1973 with "Check It Out." Lead vocals were sung by the oldest brother, Victor Tavares, who dropped out of the band soon afterward. The following year Tavares, now a quintet, had a number-one R&B hit with "She's Gone," which was written by Daryl Hall and John Oates and would later become one of that duo's first hits.

With matching their suits and synchronized choreography, Tavares put on an exciting live show that won fans in concert and during frequent television appearances. In 1975 their album *In the City* was released, producing the top-10 single "It Only Takes a Minute." The group toured with the Jackson 5 and KC and the Sunshine Band. Like many of Tavares's early hits,

At a Glance . . .

Members included Ralph Tavares, born on December 10, 1941; Arthur "Pooch" Tavares, born on November 12, 1943; Antone "Chubby" Tavares, born on June 2, 1945; Feliciano "Butch" Tavares Jr., born on May 18, 1948; Perry "Tiny" Tavares, born on October 24, 1949.

Awards: Grammy Award, Album of the Year, 1978, for *Saturday Night Fever*; inducted into Cape Verdean Heritage Hall of Fame, 2006; Lifetime Achievement Award, Rhythm and Blues Music Society, 2013.

"Minute" was written and produced by Dennis Lambert and Brian Potter, who had been responsible for such hits as "One Tin Soldier" (from the *Billy Jack* soundtrack) and "Ain't No Woman (Like the One I've Got)" by the Four Tops. Nearly 20 years later, the British boy band Take That recorded a hit version of "It Only Takes a Minute."

Working with producer Freddie Perren, best known as a hit maker for the Jackson 5, Tavares made the charts frequently in the following years with songs such as "Heaven Must Be Missing an Angel," "Don't Take Away the Music," and "I Wanna See You Soon," which featured the voice of Freda Payne. The comical "Whodunit" enlisted the help of Sherlock Holmes, Ellery Queen, Charlie Chan, and other fictional detectives in search of "my baby."

By 1977 R&B was giving way to disco, with its steady dance beats. The disco craze reached its peak with the film *Saturday Night Fever*, whose soundtrack sold more than 15 million copies and won the Grammy Award for album of the year in 1978. In addition to several hits by the Bee Gees, the *Saturday Night Fever* soundtrack also featured two versions of the Bee Gees–penned song "More Than a Woman"—one by the Bee Gees and one by Tavares. In the movie, Tony Manero (played by John Travolta) and Stephanie (played by Karen Lynn Gorney) practice disco dancing alone in a studio while Tavares's version of the song plays. That version made it to number 28 on the pop chart. The Bee Gees' version, which plays while the couple dances at the disco, was never released as a single but has remained a radio favorite.

Rather than capitalize on their disco success, Tavares moved on to their next project, *Madam Butterfly*, a Philadelphia soul version of the Giacomo Puccini opera. In the words of one critic, "If, in 1979, you were hoping to hear Tavares performing a lot of disco, you were bound to find [the album] disappointing. But those who wanted Tavares to stick to pure, unadulterated Northern soul agreed that working with [producer Bobby] Martin was a very wise move." The album's single "Never Had a Love Like This Before" hit number five on the R&B chart. In 1980 the group released *Love Uprising*, their last album for Capitol Records.

New Directions and *Words and Music* came out on the RCA label in 1982 and 1983, respectively, but neither succeeded in rekindling Tavares's career. Ralph Tavares left the group in 1984 to raise his family and later became a court officer for the Fall River Superior Court in Massachusetts. In 1994 Antone "Chubby" Tavares—who continued to perform with Butch and Pooch—sang back-up vocals on a song by New Kids on the Block, and in 2012 he released a solo album titled *Jealousy*.

In September of 2013 Tavares was honored with a lifetime achievement award from the Rhythm and Blues Music Society, and all six brothers performed onstage together for the first time in 37 years. Pedro Graciano Carvalho, consul general of Cape Verde in the United States, released a statement: "The Tavares brothers' contributions to R&B and to the American culture in general are internationally recognized and a source of pride for the Cape Verdean community where they were raised and are still cherished," he said. The Tavares brothers were inducted into the Cape Verdean Heritage Hall of Fame in 2006.

Selected discography

Check It Out (includes "Check It Out"), Capitol, 1973.
Hard Core Poetry (includes "She's Gone"), Capitol, 1974.
In the City (includes "It Only Takes a Minute"), Capitol, 1975.
Sky High! (includes "Heaven Must Be Missing an Angel" and "Don't Take Away the Music"), Capitol, 1976.
Love Storm (includes "I Wanna See You Soon" and "Whodunit"), Capitol, 1977.
Future Bound, Capitol, 1978.
Saturday Night Fever (soundtrack, includes "More Than a Woman"), RSO/Polydor/Reprise, 1977.
Madam Butterfly (includes "Never Had a Love Like This Before"), Capitol, 1979.
Supercharged, Capitol, 1980.
Love Uprising, Capitol, 1980.
Loveline, Capitol, 1981.
New Directions, RCA, 1982.
Words and Music, RCA, 1983.

Sources

Periodicals

South Coast Today (New Bedford, MA), September 21, 2013.

Online

"Cape Verdean Museum Exhibit: 2006 Hall of Fame Inductees," Cape Verdean Museum, http://www .capeverdeanmuseum.org/2006halloffame.html #tavares1 (accessed January 20, 2014).

Henderson, Alex, "Tavares: *Madam Butterfly*," All Music.com, http://www.allmusic.com/album/ma dam-butterfly-mw0000477914 (accessed January 20, 2014).

"Tavares," Billboard.com, http://www.billboard.com/ artist/370877/tavares/biography (accessed January 20, 2014).

Tavares Brothers, http://www.tavaresbrothers.com/ (accessed January 20, 2014).

"Tavares/Chubby & the Turnpikes," Rhode Island Music Hall of Fame Historical Archive, http://www .ripopmusic.org/musical-artists/musicians/tavares turnpikes/ (accessed January 20, 2014).

—Mark Swartz

Tinie Tempah

1988—

Rapper

London-based British rapper Tinie Tempah emerged on the mainstream music scene in the United Kingdom and the United States in 2010 with his major-label debut album, *Disc-Overy*. The double-platinum-selling record produced four top-10 singles in the United Kingdom—including his biggest hit, "Written in the Stars," which became the anthem of the 2011 Major League Baseball postseason—and made Tinie Tempah an instant success. His 2013 follow-up, *Demonstration,* was equally successful, producing the hit singles "Chil-

Tinie Tempah, photograph. Andrew Cowie/AFP/Getty Images.

dren of the Sun" and "Trampoline." Tinie Tempah's music, while appealing to mainstream audiences, has been characterized as a groundbreaking fusion of rap and grime, a British form of electronic music that emerged in London in the early 2000s.

Became Internet Phenomenon

Tinie Tempah was born Patrick Chukwuemeka Okogwu in 1988 in London. The child of Nigerian immigrants, he grew up in a poor section of London called Aylesbury Estate in Peckham. In his teens he excelled in high school and at St. Francis Xavier Sixth

Form College, where he focused on media studies, psychology, and religious studies. He knew from the time he was 12 years old that he wanted to be a pop star, when he first began admiring British rappers such as Dizzee Rascal. It was at this age that he chose the stage name Tinie Tempah (pronounced "Tiny Tempa").

The rapper began his music career as a member of a group called the Aftershock Hooligans with Aftershock Records. Between 2005 and 2007 he recorded several songs with the group but eventually left over artistic differences. He partnered with his cousin, Dumi Oburota, an aspiring businessman and an ardent supporter of his music. Oburota took on a managerial role. With Aftershock Tinie Tempah had recorded several tracks that circulated on London's underground music scene, including an especially popular song titled "Wifey" that received considerable airplay on British music television Channel AKA.

Tinie Tempah had a strong underground presence on United Kingdom's grime music scene and cultivated a large following on the website MySpace, where he had more than a million followers. Oburota began leverag-

At a Glance . . .

Born Patrick Chukwuemeka Okogwu on November 7, 1988, in London, England; son of Patrick Okogwu (a social worker) and Rosemary Okogwu (a human resources officer). *Education:* St. Francis Xavier Sixth Form College.

Career: Recording artist, 2007—.

Awards: MOBO Awards, Best Newcomer, Best Video, for "Frisky," 2010; UGG Award, MP3 Music Awards, 2010; Urban Music Awards, Best Newcomer, Best Hip-Hop Act, Best Collaboration, for "Pass Out," 2010; BT Digital Music Award, Best Newcomer, 2010; UK Festival Award, Breakthrough Artist, 2010; Brit Awards, Best Breakthrough Act, Best Single, for "Pass Out," 2011; Ivor Novello Award, Best Contemporary Song, for "Pass Out," 2011; BET Award, Best International Act: UK, 2011; MOBO Awards, Best UK Hip Hop/Grime Act, 2011, 2013; Nigeria Entertainment Award, Best International Artist, 2012.

Addresses: *Agent*—Echo Location Talent Agency, Unit 33, Tile Yard Studios, Tile Yard Rd., London N7 9AH, United Kingdom. *Web*—http://www.tinietempah.com. *Twitter*—@tinietempah.

ing Tinie Tempah's web presence to secure live bookings in the United Kingdom while, at the same time, producing and releasing 10,000 copies of a debut record and shooting a low-budget video for "Wifey." Oburota financed these ventures through a side business buying and selling cars and by using funds that had been earmarked for student loans. Together the two cousins formed their own label called Disturbing London. "We were an independent label that tried to do major label things," Oburota said in a 2011 interview with the website HitQuarters.com. "We were making quality videos like 'Tears' and 'Hood Economics'; these videos were top at the time. We'd spent about £10,000 and because I was networking with the production company, we got a video with the production value of at least £30,000. It looked like Okogwu was signed already. The vision was always to package it well, make a product that people can buy into, and one that was as polished as possible."

Signed with Major Label Parlophone

Their strategy worked. Tinie Tempah's web popularity, combined with his self-produced debut album and

video, brought him to the tipping point of success. His big break came when one of his tracks was used on the soundtrack for a Sony PlayStation video game called *Wipeout Pure.* Soon Tinie Tempah was touring the country with his childhood idol Dizzee Rascal. In 2009, after performing at the Wireless Festival in London, he was signed to the Parlophone label. That deal led to his first major-label release, *Disc-Overy,* in 2010. The album went double platinum and produced two number-one singles, "Pass Out" and "Written in the Stars." Another single, "Frisky," reached number two on the U.K. charts, while "Miami 2 Ibiza" reached number four. The album included collaborations with a number of well-known artists, including Kelly Rowland, Ellie Goulding, Labrinth, Emeli Sandé, Eric Turner, Wiz Khalifa, Swedish House Mafia, and Range.

Tinie Tempah was catapulted into the world spotlight. That same year he appeared with American rapper Snoop Dogg at the Glastonbury Festival and with the American pop singer Rihanna at four concerts during her 2010 European tour. The rapper won the awards for best new artist and best video (for "Frisky") at the prestigious MOBO Awards, as well as best breakthrough artist and best single (for "Pass Out") at the annual Brit Awards.

Fueling his meteoric success, Tinie Tempah's number-one U.K. hit "Written in the Stars" was chosen by WWE as the official theme for its wildly popular American wrestling event, Wrestlemania XXVII. The same song also was chosen as the theme for the 2011 Major League Baseball postseason. The use of his music at two mainstream American events was a testament to Tinie Tempah's crossover appeal. As he had hoped from the start, his music transcended the niches of British rap and grime to find widespread appreciation among mainstream audiences. His success also helped bring attention to other British rappers, who have not enjoyed the level of success of their American counterparts, as well as to grime.

Tinie Tempah had equally dynamic years in 2012 and 2013. In addition to performing at major venues and festivals in Europe and the United States, he released his second album, *Demonstration,* in November of 2013. The long-awaited follow-up to his 2010 release, his sophomore effort produced two top-10 singles, "Children of the Sun" and "Trampoline." The album features collaborations with Labrinth, Big Sean, Ty Dolla $ign, Candace Pilay, Ella Eyre, Paloma Faith, Sway Clarke II, The Chemical Brothers, Emeli Sandé, John Martin, 2 Chainz, and Dizzee Rascal.

With a diversity of influences and collaborators, Tinie Tempah's music is characterized by a fusion of styles ranging from electronic to hip-hop to grime to R&B. The result is an altogether new sound—a smorgasbord of styles collapsing into each other. Tinie Tempah sees himself as having evolved from the limitations of being a rapper into the role of a complete artist. In a 2013 interview with the popular Australian website TheVine.

com, he stated, "This is the one thing that really separates British rappers from American rappers. US hip-hop is very much their thing and their culture, so they stay within that lane. But I'm from London, which is a melting pot of different music, all the genres you can think of. Whether it's indie, dance, trap, dubstep, grime, hip-hop, it's all in there, from my youth."

Selected discography

Hood Econ%mics—Room 147: The 80-Minute Course, Disturbing London, 2007.

Disc-Overy (includes "Pass Out," "Written in the Stars," "Frisky," and "Miami 2 Ibiza"), Parlophone, 2010.

Demonstration (includes "Children of the Sun" and "Trampoline"), Parlophone, 2013.

Sources

Periodicals

Daily Mirror (London), February 11, 2011, pp. 6, 7.
Evening Gazette (Middlesbrough, UK), March 19, 2010.
Guardian (London), August 18, 2012.
New York Times, February 10, 2011, p. C8.
Nottingham (UK) Post, October 24, 2013.
Sun (London), March 3, 2010.
Times (London), October 25, 2010; February 21, 2011; June 25, 2011.

Online

Blumentrath, Jay, "Interview with Dumi Oburota, Man-ager for Tinie Tempah and MD at Disturbing London," HitQuarters.com, March 7, 2011, http://www.hitquarters.com/index.php3?page=intrview/opar/intrview_DOint.html (accessed December 20, 2013).

Copsey, Robert, and Tom Mansell, "Tinie Tempah Interview: 'I've Evolved from a Rapper into an Artist,'" DigitalSpy.com, November 1, 2013, http://www.digitalspy.com/music/interviews/a528076/tinie-tempah-interview-ive-evolved-from-a-rapper-into-an-artist.html 20110418 (accessed December 20, 2013).

Meldrum, Richie, "Tinie Tempah: 'Everyone's Story Is Unique,'" TheVine.com.au, December 13, 2013, http://www.thevine.com.au/music/interviews/tine-tempah-everyones-story-is-unique-20131213-269731 (accessed December 20, 2013).

Perpetua, Matthew, "Tinie Tempah Is Optimistic about Breaking through in the U.S.," RollingStone.com, April 18, 2013, http://www.rollingstone.com/culture/blogs/rolling-stone-video-blog/video-tinie-tempeh-is-optimistic-about-breaking-through-in-the-u-s-20110418 (accessed December 20, 2013).

Savage, Mark, "Tinie Tempah: 'I Believe in the Magic of Music,'" BBC News, October 24, 2013, http://www.bbc.co.uk/news/entertainment-arts-24582845 (accessed December 20, 2013).

Tinie Tempah, http://www.tinietempah.com (accessed January 17, 2014).

"Tinie Tempah Biography Documentary," Rap Up UK, February 24, 2013, http://www.youtube.com/watch?v=Aq-HbEoHwOA (accessed January 17, 2014).

—Ben Bloch

Ora Mae Washington

1899(?)–1971

Tennis player

Ora Mae Washington was one of the finest female athletes of the 1920s and 1930s, winning championships in two sports: tennis and basketball. Competing on the American Tennis Association (ATA) circuit, Washington was the top-ranked black women's player in the United States, capturing nine singles titles between 1929 and 1937 and numerous doubles crowns. Equally talented on the basketball court, she was a standout on the Philadelphia Tribunes, one of the best black women's squads in the country in the 1930s. In spite of her accomplishments, Washington was relegated to segregated black leagues, where she faced little serious competition, and as a result she received few accolades during her lifetime. Had she been a white woman, some sports historians have speculated, she likely would have been heralded as one of the top sportswomen of her day. As her achievements have come to light in the 21st century, Washington is being recognized as a pioneer among black athletes.

Ora Mae Washington was born on January 16, 1899 (some sources give January 16 or 23, 1898, as her birth date), in Caroline County, Virginia, the fifth of nine children of John Thomas "Tommy" Washington and his wife, Laura. Washington grew up in the small rural community of File, where the family owned a farm, raising corn, wheat, vegetables, and hogs. In 1908 Washington's mother died giving birth to her ninth child. Thereafter members of the family began migrating north to Philadelphia, Pennsylvania, settling in the racially diverse Germantown neighborhood in the northern part of the city. By 1920 Washington was living there, working as a live-in servant.

Washington did not participate in organized sports until she was in her 20s. Following the death of one of Washington's sisters, an instructor at the Young Women's Christian Association (YWCA) in Germantown suggested that Washington engage in physical activity to cope with her grief. She decided to take up tennis and threw herself into the sport. Within a year she had entered her first national tournament for black players. (At the time, black and white tennis players competed on separate circuits.) She won her first championship in 1924 at the African-American National Tennis Tournament in Baltimore, Maryland, defeating Dorothy Radcliffe. Washington quickly moved into the top ranks of the black leagues in which she played—the National Tennis Organization and (beginning in 1929) the American Tennis Association—becoming the dominant women's player for more than a decade.

From 1929 to 1935 Washington went undefeated as the ATA's women's singles champion. After taking a year off, she returned to capture an eighth crown in 1937. During this time she also added 12 doubles and three mixed-doubles championships to her résumé. Washington was nearly unbeatable, dominating her competition with her powerful serve and overhead game and her agility on the court. Known for her unorthodox style of play, she held the racket above the grip and struck at the ball with short jabs, rarely completing a full stroke, and she eschewed warm-ups. Washington was also an intense competitor. According to Pamela Grundy in the book *Out of the Shadows: A Biographical History of African American Athletes* (2006), a 1931 *Chicago Defender* article noted that

At a Glance . . .

Born Ora Mae Washington on January 16(?), 1899(?), in Caroline County, VA; died on May 28, 1971, in Philadelphia, PA; daughter of John Thomas Washington (a farmer) and Laura Young Washington.

Career: Played on the National Tennis Organization and American Tennis Association circuits, 1924–47; Germantown Hornets, player and captain, 1930–31; Philadelphia Tribunes, player and coach, 1930s–40s.

Awards: Inducted into Black Athletes Hall of Fame, 1976; Temple University Sports Hall of Fame, 1980s; Women's Basketball Hall of Fame, 2009.

Washington's "superiority is so evident that her competitors are frequently beaten before the first ball crosses the net."

With few serious rivals on the black tennis circuit, Washington was eager to compete against the reigning white women's champion, Helen Wills Moody, who won eight Wimbledon singles titles and seven U.S. Open championships between 1923 and 1938. Washington was denied the opportunity, however, when Moody refused to play her because of Washington's race. Although the ATA pressed the U.S. Lawn Tennis Association (the whites-only circuit) to admit black players to its tournaments, the organization did not relent until 1948, after Washington had retired from the sport.

In the midst of her successful tennis career, Washington decided to take up basketball, excelling at that sport as well. In 1930 she joined the Germantown Hornets, an African-American women's basketball team formed at the Germantown YWCA, playing at center. Led by Washington and Lula Ballard, another tennis player, the Hornets went 22–1 in 1930–31 and declared themselves the "black national champions." In the fall of 1932, Washington left the Hornets to join the Philadelphia Tribunes, a team affiliated with the African-American newspaper of that name. The "Tribune Girls," as they were known, were the dominant team in black women's basketball, losing only six games in a nine-year span. Washington and her teammates traveled across the country, taking on all challengers, including black and white teams and high school and college squads. Washington was the Tribunes' leading scorer for a time and later served as the team's coach.

Washington played with the Philadelphia Tribunes until the early 1940s, when the team disbanded. In 1947 she won her last tennis championship; she and George Stewart defeated R. Walter Johnson and the up-and-comer Althea Gibson to take the ATA mixed-doubles title. A decade later Gibson would achieve the fame that had eluded Washington, becoming known as a pioneer among black tennis players after she won consecutive crowns at both Wimbledon and the U.S. Open in 1957 and 1958.

Retired from sports by the end of the 1940s, Washington quietly slipped out of sight, working in domestic service and later managing an apartment building that she owned. She remained active in sports, often running free tennis and basketball clinics for young players. Washington died in Philadelphia on May 28, 1971, and was buried near her hometown in Virginia. Five years later the Black Athletes Hall of Fame voted to induct her, unaware that she had died. Washington was posthumously inducted into Temple University's Sports Hall of Fame in the 1980s and the Women's Basketball Hall of Fame in 2009. In 2004 a historical marker was erected at the location of the Germantown YWCA where Washington once played.

Sources

Books

Grasso, John, *Historical Dictionary of Tennis,* Scarecrow Press, 2011.

Grundy, Pamela, "Ora Washington: The First Black Female Athletic Star," in *Out of the Shadows: A Biographical History of African American Athletes,* ed. David Kenneth Wiggins, University of Arkansas Press, 2006, pp. 79–92.

Shackleford, Susan, and Pamela Grundy, *Shattering the Glass: The Remarkable History of Women's Basketball,* New Press, 2005.

Online

"All Hail the Philadelphia Tribune Girls!," Black Fives Foundation, January 22, 2008, http://www.blackfives.org/all-hail-the-philadelpha-tribune-girls-happy-birthday-ora-mae-washington/ (accessed December 30, 2013).

"Female Black Fives Invade Philly," Black Fives Foundation, January 2, 2008, http://www.blackfives.org/female-black-fives-invade-philly/ (accessed December 30, 2013).

"Ora Washington," Women's Basketball Hall of Fame, http://www.wbhof.com/OWashington.html (accessed December 30, 2013).

"Ora Washington (1899–1971) Historical Marker," ExplorePAHistory.com, http://explorepahistory.com/hmarker.php?markerId=1-A-35A (accessed December 30, 2013).

—Deborah A. Ring

Cumulative Nationality Index

Volume numbers appear in **bold**

American

Aaliyah **30**
Aaron, Hank **5**
Aaron, Quinton **82**
Abbott, Robert Sengstacke **27**
Abdul-Jabbar, Kareem **8**
Abdullah, Kazem **97**
Abdur-Rahim, Shareef **28**
Abele, Julian **55**
Abercrumbie, P. Eric **95**
Abernathy, Ralph David **1**
Aberra, Amsale **67**
Abu-Jamal, Mumia **15**
Ace, Johnny **36**
Ackerman, Arlene **108**
Acklin, Barbara Jean **107**
Adams, Eula L. **39**
Adams, Floyd, Jr. **12**
Adams, Jenoyne **60**
Adams, Johnny **39**
Adams, Leslie **39**
Adams, Oleta **18**
Adams, Osceola Macarthy **31**
Adams, Sheila J. **25**
Adams, Yolanda **17, 67**
Adams-Campbell, Lucille L. **60**
Adams Earley, Charity **13, 34**
Adams-Ender, Clara **40**
Adderley, Julian "Cannonball" **30**
Adderley, Nat **29**
Adebimpe, Tunde **75**
Adkins, Rod **41**
Adkins, Rutherford H. **21**
Adu, Freddy **67**
Agyeman, Jaramogi Abebe **10, 63**
Ailey, Alvin **8**
Akil, Mara Brock **60, 82**
Akinmusire, Ambrose **103**
Akon **68**
Al-Amin, Jamil Abdullah **6**
Albert, Octavia V. R. **100**
Albright, Gerald **23**
Alcorn, George Edward, Jr. **59**
Aldridge, Ira **99**
Alert, Kool DJ Red **33**
Alexander, Archie Alphonso **14**
Alexander, Clifford **26**
Alexander, Elizabeth **75**
Alexander, Joseph L. **95**
Alexander, Joyce London **18**
Alexander, Khandi **43**
Alexander, Kwame **98**
Alexander, Margaret Walker **22**

Alexander, Michelle **98**
Alexander, Sadie Tanner Mossell **22**
Alexander, Shaun **58**
Ali, Hana Yasmeen **52**
Ali, Laila **27, 63**
Ali, Muhammad **2, 16, 52**
Ali, Rashied **79**
Ali, Russlynn H. **92**
Ali, Tatyana **73**
Allain, Stephanie **49**
Allen, Betty **83**
Allen, Byron **3, 24, 97**
Allen, Claude **68**
Allen, Debbie **13, 42**
Allen, Dick **85**
Allen, Ethel D. **13**
Allen, Eugene **79**
Allen, Geri **92**
Allen, Larry **109**
Allen, Lucy **85**
Allen, Macon Bolling **104**
Allen, Marcus **20**
Allen, Ray **82**
Allen, Robert L. **38**
Allen, Samuel W. **38**
Allen, Tina **22, 75**
Allen, Will **74**
Allen-Buillard, Melba **55**
Allison, Luther **111**
Alonso, Laz **87**
Als, Hilton **105**
Alston, Charles **33**
Altidore, Jozy **109**
Amaker, Norman **63**
Amaker, Tommy **62**
Amaki, Amalia **76**
Amerie **52**
Ames, Wilmer **27**
Ammons, Albert **112**
Ammons, Gene **112**
Ammons, James H. **81**
Amos, Emma **63**
Amos, John **8, 62**
Amos, Wally **9**
Amy, Curtis **114**
Anderson, Anthony **51, 77**
Anderson, Carl **48**
Anderson, Charles Edward **37**
Anderson, Eddie "Rochester" **30**
Anderson, Elmer **25**
Anderson, Ezzrett **95**
Anderson, Fred **87**
Anderson, Jamal **22**

Anderson, Lauren **72**
Anderson, Maceo **111**
Anderson, Marcia **115**
Anderson, Marian **2, 33**
Anderson, Michael P. **40**
Anderson, Mike **63**
Anderson, Norman B. **45**
Anderson, Reuben V. **81**
Anderson, William G(ilchrist) **57**
Andrews, Benny **22, 59**
Andrews, Bert **13**
Andrews, Inez **108**
Andrews, Raymond **4**
Andrews, Tina **74**
Angelou, Maya **1, 15**
Ansa, Tina McElroy **14**
Anthony, Carmelo **46, 94**
Anthony, Wendell **25**
apl.de.ap **84**
Aplin-Brownlee, Vivian **96**
Appiah, Kwame Anthony **67, 101**
Archer, Dennis **7, 36**
Archer, Lee, Jr. **79**
Archibald, Tiny **90**
Archie-Hudson, Marguerite **44**
Ardoin, Alphonse **65**
Arenas, Gilbert **84**
Arkadie, Kevin **17**
Armstrong, Govind **81**
Armstrong, Henry **104**
Armstrong, Louis **2**
Armstrong, Robb **15**
Armstrong, Vanessa Bell **24**
Arnez J **53**
Arnold, Billy Boy **112**
Arnold, Tichina **63**
Arnwine, Barbara **28**
Arrington, Richard **24, 100**
Arroyo, Martina **30**
Artest, Ron **52**
Asante, Molefi Kete **3**
A$AP Rocky **109**
Ashanti **37, 96**
Ashe, Arthur **1, 18**
Ashford, Calvin, Jr. **74**
Ashford, Emmett **22**
Ashford, Evelyn **63**
Ashford, Nickolas **21, 97**
Ashley & JaQuavis **107**
Ashley-Ward, Amelia **23**
Ashong, Derrick **86**
Asim, Jabari **71**
Asomugha, Nnamdi **100**
Atkins, Cholly **40**

Atkins, Erica **34**
Atkins, Juan **50**
Atkins, Russell **45**
Atkins, Tina **34**
Attaway, William **102**
Aubert, Alvin **41**
Aubespin, Mervin **95**
Augusta, Alexander T. **111**
Auguste, Donna **29**
Austin, Bobby W. **95**
Austin, Gloria **63**
Austin, Jim **63**
Austin, Junius C. **44**
Austin, Lloyd **101**
Austin, Lovie **40**
Austin, Patti **24**
Austin, Wanda M. **94**
Autrey, Wesley **68**
Avant, Clarence **19, 86**
Avant, Nicole A. **90**
Avery, Byllye Y. **66**
Ayers, Roy **16**
Ayler, Albert **104**
Babatunde, Obba **35**
Babyface **10, 31, 82**
Bacon-Bercey, June **38**
Badu, Erykah **22, 114**
Bahati, Wambui **60**
Bailey, Buster **38**
Bailey, Chauncey **68**
Bailey, Clyde **45**
Bailey, DeFord **33**
Bailey, Pearl **14**
Bailey, Philip **63**
Bailey, Radcliffe **19**
Bailey, Xenobia **11**
Baines, Harold **32**
Baiocchi, Regina Harris **41**
Baisden, Michael **25, 66**
Baker, Anita **21, 48**
Baker, Augusta **38**
Baker, Delbert W. **110**
Baker, Dusty **8, 43, 72, 110**
Baker, Ella **5**
Baker, Gwendolyn Calvert **9**
Baker, Houston A., Jr. **6**
Baker, Josephine **3**
Baker, LaVern **26**
Baker, Matt **76**
Baker, Maxine B. **28**
Baker, Mickey **95**
Baker, Thurbert **22**
Baker, Vernon Joseph **65, 87**
Bakewell, Danny **99**

Baldwin, Cynthia 74, 107
Baldwin, James 1
Ballance, Frank W. 41
Ballard, Allen Butler, Jr. 40
Ballard, Florence 112
Ballard, Hank 41
Ballard, John 95
Baltimore, Richard Lewis, III 71
Bambaataa, Afrika 34
Bambara, Toni Cade 10
Bandele, Asha 36
Banks, Azealia 107
Banks, Ernie 33
Banks, Jeffrey 17
Banks, Lloyd 113
Banks, Michelle 59
Banks, Paula A. 68
Banks, Tyra 11, 50
Banks, William 11
Banneker, Benjamin 93
Banner, David 55
Bannister, Edward Mitchell 88
Baquet, Dean 63
Baraka, Amiri 1, 38
Baraka, Sho 109
Barbee, Lloyd Augustus 71
Barber, Ronde 41
Barber, Tiki 57, 107
Barboza, Anthony 10
Barclay, Paris 37, 94
Barden, Donald H. 9, 20, 89
Barker, Danny 32
Barkley, Charles 5, 66
Barksdale, Don 103
Barlow, Roosevelt 49
Barnes, Ernie 16, 78
Barnes, Katreese 97
Barnes, Melody 75
Barnes, Roosevelt "Booba" 33
Barnes, Steven 54
Barnett, Amy Du Bois 46
Barnett, Etta Moten 56
Barnett, Herman 112
Barnett, Marguerite 46
Barney, Lem 26
Barnhill, David 30
Barrax, Gerald William 45
Barrett, Andrew C. 12
Barrett, Jacquelyn 28
Barrino, Fantasia 53, 94
Barrow, Willie T. 85
Barry, Marion S(hepilov, Jr.) 7, 44
Barthé, Earl 78
Barthe, Richmond 15
Basie, Count 23
Baskett, James 102
Basquiat, Jean-Michel 5
Bass, Charlotta Spears 40
Bass, Fontella 104, 109
Bass, Karen 70
Bassett, Angela 6, 23, 62
Baszile, Jennifer 79
Bates, Daisy 13
Bates, Karen Grigsby 40
Bates, Peg Leg 14
Bath, Patricia E. 37
Batiste, Alvin 66
Batiste, Jonathan 108
Batiste, Lionel 105
Battle, Kathleen 70
Baugh, David 23
Baylor, Don 6
Baylor, Elgin 93

Baylor, Helen 36
Beach, Michael 26
Beal, Bernard B. 46
Beals, Jennifer 12
Beals, Melba Pattillo 15, 94
Bearden, Romare 2, 50
Beasley, Jamar 29
Beasley, Phoebe 34
Beatty, Talley 35
Beaty, Zelmo 115
Beauvais, Garcelle 29, 95
Bechet, Sidney 18
Beckford, Tyson 11, 68
Beckham, Barry 41
Beckwith, Naomi 101
Becton, Julius W., Jr. 110
Belafonte, Harry 4, 65
Belgrave, Cynthia 75
Belgrave, Marcus 77
Bell, Carey 114
Bell, Carl C. 111
Bell, Darrin 77
Bell, Derrick 6, 98
Bell, James "Cool Papa" 36
Bell, James A. 50
Bell, James Madison 40
Bell, LeRoy 98
Bell, Michael 40
Bell, Robert Mack 22
Bell, Thom 112
Bell, W. Kamau 107
Bellamy, Bill 12
Bellamy, Terry 58
Belle, Albert 10
Belle, Regina 1, 51
Belton, Sharon Sayles 9, 16
Benberry, Cuesta 65
Benét, Eric 28, 77
Benham, Robert 78
Ben-Israel, Ben Ami 11
Benjamin, Andre 45
Benjamin, Regina 20, 75
Benjamin, Steve 98
Benjamin, Tritobia Hayes 53
Bennett, Estelle 77
Bennett, George Harold "Hal" 45
Bennett, Gwendolyn B. 59
Bennett, Lerone, Jr. 5, 84
Bennett, Richard 97
Benson, Angela 34
Benson, Obie 96
Bentley, Lamont 53
Berrien, Jacqueline A. 93
Berry, Edwin C. 81
Berry, Halle 4, 19, 57, 91
Berry, Bertice 8, 55
Berry, Chuck 29
Berry, Fred "Rerun" 48
Berry, Mary Frances 7
Berry, Moses 84
Berry, Theodore 31
Berrysmith, Don Reginald 49
Bethune, Mary McLeod 4
Betsch, MaVynee 28
Bettis, Jerome 64
Betts, Keter 85
Betts, R. Dwayne 86
Bevel, James L. 75
Beverly, Frankie 25
Bey, Yasiin 30, 96
Beyoncé 39, 70, 105
Bibb, Eric 49
Bibb, Henry and Mary 54

Bickerstaff, Bernie 21
Big Daddy Kane 79
Big Sean 96
Biggers, John 20, 33
Biggers, Sanford 62
Bilal 101
Billops, Camille 82
Billy Ward and the Dominoes 105
bin Wahad, Dhoruba 85
Bing, Dave 3, 59, 78
Bingham, Howard 96
Birch, Adolpho A., Jr. 85
Birch, Glynn R. 61
Birdman 110
Birdsong, Cindy 113
Bishop, Sanford D., Jr. 24, 111
Bishop, Stephen 95
Bivins, Michael 72
Black, Albert 51
Black, Barry C. 47
Black, Joe 75
Black, Keith Lanier 18, 84
Black Thought 63
Blackburn, Robert 28
Blackman, Toni 86
Blackmon, Brenda 58
Blackshear, Leonard 52
Blackwell, David 79
Blackwell, Kenneth, Sr. 61
Blackwell, Otis 98
Blackwell, Robert D., Sr. 52
Blackwell, Unita 17
Blacque, Taurean 58
Blade, Brian 88
Blair, Jayson 50
Blair, Paul 36
Blake, Asha 26
Blake, Charles E. 82
Blake, Eubie 29
Blake, James 43
Blakely, Edward J. 88
Blakey, Art 37
Blanchard, Terence 43
Blanco, Mykki 106
Bland, Bobby 36, 113
Bland, Edward 111
Bland, Eleanor Taylor 39
Blanks, Billy 22
Blanks, Deborah K. 69
Blanton, Dain 29
Blanton, Jimmy 108
Blassingame, John Wesley 40
Blaylock, Ronald 86
Blayton, Jesse B., Sr. 55
Bleu, Corbin 65
Blige, Mary J. 20, 34, 60, 97
Blind Boys of Alabama, The 99
Blitz the Ambassador 115
Blockson, Charles L. 42
Bloomer, George 86
Blow, Charles M. 73
Blow, Kurtis 31
Bluford, Guy 2, 35
Bluitt, Juliann S. 14
B.o.B. 91
Bobb, Robert C. 83
Bobo, Lawrence 60
Bogle, Donald 34
Bogues, Tyrone "Muggsy" 56
Bolden, Buddy 39
Bolden, Charles Frank, Jr. 7, 78
Bolden, Frank E. 44
Bolden, Tonya 32

Bolin, Jane 22, 59
Bolton, Terrell D. 25
Bolton-Holifield, Ruthie 28
Bond, Beverly 53
Bond, J. Max, Jr. 76
Bond, Julian 2, 35, 106
Bonds, Barry 6, 34, 63, 99
Bonds, Bobby 43
Bonds, Margaret 39
Bonet, Lisa 58
Bonner, Leroy 113
Bonney, Tabi 98
Bontemps, Arna 8
Booker, Cory Anthony 68
Booker, Simeon 23
Boozer, Bob 103
Borders, James 9
Borders, William Holmes 94
Boseman, Chadwick 111
Bosh, Chris 85
Bosley, Freeman, Jr. 7
Bostic, Joe 95
Boston, Kelvin E. 25
Boston, Lloyd 24
Boulware, Harold R. 109
Bow Wow 35
Bowe, Riddick 6, 107
Bowen, John W. E., Sr. 89
Bowen, Ruth 83
Bowman, Bertie 71
Bowser, Yvette Lee 17
Boyd, Edward 70
Boyd, Gerald M. 32, 59
Boyd, Gwendolyn 49
Boyd, John W., Jr. 20, 72
Boyd, Melba Joyce 86
Boyd, T. B., III 6
Boykin, Keith 14
Boykin, Otis 92
Boykin, Phillip 102
Boyz II Men 82
Bozella, Dewey 97
Bradford, Mark 89
Bradley, Adam 101
Bradley, David Henry, Jr. 39
Bradley, Ed 2, 59
Bradley, J. Robert 65
Bradley, Jennette B. 40
Bradley, Thomas 2, 20
Bradshaw, Tiny 102
Brady, St. Elmo 107
Brady, Wayne 32, 71
Brae, C. Michael 61
Braithwaite, William Stanley 52
Bramlett, Joseph 91
Branch, William Blackwell 39
Brand, Elton 31
Brandon, Barbara 3
Brandon, Terrell 16
Brandy 14, 34, 72
Branham, George, III 50
Branson, Herman 87
Brashear, Carl 29
Brashear, Donald 39
Braugher, Andre 13, 58, 91
Braun, Carol Moseley 4, 42
Brawley, Benjamin 44
Braxton, Brad 77
Braxton, Toni 15, 61, 91
Brazier, Arthur M. 115
Brazile, Donna 25, 70
Brewer, Rosalind 100
Bridges, Ruby 77

Bridges, Sheila 36
Bridges, Todd 37
Bridgewater, Dee Dee 32, 92
Bridgforth, Glinda 36
Briggs, Curtis 84
Brimm, Charles E. 105
Brimmer, Andrew 2, 48, 106
Briscoe, Connie 15
Briscoe, Marlin 37
Britt, Donna 28
Broadbent, Hydeia 36
Brock, Lou 18
Brock, Roslyn McCallister 86
Bromery, Randolph Wilson 85
Broner, Adrien 109
Bronner, Nathaniel H., Sr. 32
Brooke, Edward W. 8, 88
Brookins, Hamel Hartford 102
Brooks, Aaron 33
Brooks, Avery 9, 98
Brooks, Derrick 43
Brooks, Golden 62
Brooks, Gwendolyn 1, 28
Brooks, Hadda 40
Brooks, Mehcad 62
Brooks, Tyrone 59
Broonzy, Big Bill 82
Brower, William 49
Brown, Aja 115
Brown, Alvin 96
Brown, Angela M. 54
Brown, Anne 76
Brown, Anthony G. 72
Brown, Antron 85
Brown, Bobby 58
Brown, Byrd 49
Brown, Byron W. 72
Brown, Cecil M. 46
Brown, Charles 23
Brown, Charlotte Hawkins 106
Brown, Chris 74, 109
Brown, Chuck 78, 102
Brown, Clarence Gatemouth 59
Brown, Claude 38
Brown, Clifford 86
Brown, Cora 33
Brown, Corrine 24, 90
Brown, Cupcake 63
Brown, Donald 19
Brown, Eddie C. 35
Brown, Elaine 8
Brown, Ernest 80
Brown, Erroll M. 23
Brown, Foxy 25
Brown, Frederick J. 102
Brown, George Leslie 62
Brown, Hallie Quinn 100
Brown, Homer S. 47
Brown, James 15, 60
Brown, James 22
Brown, Jamie Foster 91
Brown, Janice Rogers 43
Brown, Jesse 6, 41
Brown, Jesse Leroy 31
Brown, Jim 11, 95
Brown, Joe 29
Brown, Joyce F. 25
Brown, Kwame R. 91
Brown, Lee P. 1, 24, 109
Brown, Les 5
Brown, Lloyd Louis 42
Brown, Marie Dutton 12
Brown, Mike 77, 107

Brown, Nappy 73
Brown, Oliver Leon 94
Brown, Oscar, Jr. 53
Brown, Patrick "Sleepy" 50
Brown, Raymond 102
Brown, Robert 65
Brown, Ron 5
Brown, Ronald K. 91
Brown, Ruth 90
Brown, Sterling Allen 10, 64
Brown, Tony 3
Brown, Uzee 42
Brown, Vivian 27
Brown, Warren 61
Brown, Wesley 23
Brown, Wesley A. 102
Brown, Willa 40
Brown, Willard 36
Brown, William Wells 99
Brown, Willie 7, 85
Brown, Zora Kramer 12
Browne, Roscoe Lee 66
Brownlee, Lawrence 88
Broyard, Anatole 68
Broyard, Bliss 68
Bruce, Blanche Kelso 33
Bruce, Bruce 56
Bruce, Isaac 26
Brunson, Dorothy 1, 87
Bryan, Ashley 41, 104
Bryant, Cullen 81
Bryant, John 26
Bryant, John R. 45
Bryant, Kobe 15, 31, 71, 110
Bryant, Paul 115
Bryant, Ray 95
Bryant, Wayne R. 6
Bryant, William Benson 61
Buchanan, Ray 32
Buckley, Gail Lumet 39
Buckley, Victoria 24
Buckner, Milt 110
Budden, Joe 108
Buery, Richard, Jr. 97
Bullard, Eugene 12
Bullins, Ed 25
Bullock, Steve 22
Bully-Cummings, Ella 48
Bumbry, Grace 5
Bunch, Lonnie G., III 91
Bunche, Ralph J. 5
Bunkley, Anita Richmond 39
Buress, Hannibal 101
Burgess, John 46
Burgess, Marjorie L. 55
Burke, Clarence, Jr. 112
Burke, Selma 16
Burke, Solomon 31, 86
Burke, Yvonne Brathwaite 42
Burks, Juanita P. 95
Burks, Mary Fair 40
Burleigh, Henry Thacker 56
Burley, Dan 96
Burnett, Charles 16, 68
Burnim, Mickey L. 48
Burns, Anthony 102
Burns, Eddie 44
Burns, Ursula 60
Burnside, R. L. 56
Burrell, Tom 21, 51
Burris, Chuck 21
Burris, Roland W. 25, 75
Burroughs, Margaret Taylor 9

Burroughs, Nannie Helen 96
Burrows, Stephen 31
Burrus, William Henry "Bill" 45
Burt-Murray, Angela 59
Burton, Bill 96
Burton, LeVar 8
Burwell, Bryan 83
Busby, Jheryl 3, 74
Bush, Gordon 82
Bush, Reggie 59, 88
Butler, George, Jr. 70
Butler, Jerry 26
Butler, Leroy, III 17
Butler, Louis 70
Butler, Octavia 8, 43, 58
Butler, Paul D. 17
Butler, Selena Sloan 98
Butts, Calvin O., III 9, 90
Butts, Cassandra 78
Bynoe, Peter C. B. 40
Bynum, Juanita 31, 71
Byrd, Donald 10
Byrd, Donald 109
Byrd, Eugene 64
Byrd, Marlon 112
Byrd, Michelle 19
Byrd, Robert 11
Cabell, Enos 102
Cadillacs 107
Cadoria, Sherian Grace 14
Caesar, Shirley 19
Cage, Byron 53
Cain, Herman 15, 92
Calabrese, Karyn 89
Caldwell, Benjamin 46
Caldwell, Earl 60
Caldwell, Jim 81
Caldwell, Kirbyjon 55
Calhoun, Lillian Scott 87
Callender, Clive O. 3
Callier, Terry 106
Calloway, Blanche 100
Calloway, Cab 14
Cameron, James 80
Camp, Kimberly 19
Campanella, Roy 25
Campbell, Bebe Moore 6, 24, 59
Campbell, Bill 9, 76
Campbell, Donald J. 66
Campbell, E. Simms 13
Campbell, Earl 104
Campbell, Mary Schmidt 43
Campbell, Milt 113
Campbell-Martin, Tisha 8, 42
Cam'ron 104
Canada, Geoffrey 23
Canady, Alexa 28
Cannon, Katie 10
Cannon, Nick 47, 73
Cannon, Reuben 50
Cara, Irene 77
Carney, William H. 104
Carr, Johnnie 69
Carr, Keela 74
Cardozo, Francis L. 33
Carew, Rod 20
Carey, Mariah 32, 53, 69
Cargill, Victoria A. 43
Carlos, John 97
Carolina Chocolate Drops 111
Carr, Kurt 56
Carr, Leroy 49
Carroll, Diahann 9

Carroll, L. Natalie 44
Carroll, Rocky 74
Carruthers, George R. 40
Carson, André 69
Carson, Benjamin 1, 35, 76
Carson, Johnnie 85
Carson, Julia 23, 69
Carson, Lisa Nicole 21
Carter, Anson 24
Carter, Benny 46
Carter, Betty 19
Carter, Butch 27
Carter, Cris 21, 109
Carter, Edward A., Jr. 104
Carter, Herbert E. 108
Carter, Jill P. 110
Carter, Joe 30
Carter, Joye Maureen 41
Carter, Kenneth 53
Carter, Majora 77
Carter, Mandy 11
Carter, Nell 39
Carter, Pamela Lynn 67
Carter, Regina 23
Carter, Robert L. 51, 100
Carter, Ron 104
Carter, Rubin 26
Carter, Stephen L. 4
Carter, Troy 98
Carter, Vince 26
Carter, Warrick L. 27
Cartey, Wilfred 47
Cartiér, Xam Wilson 41
Carver, George Washington 4
Cary, Lorene 3
Cary, Mary Ann Shadd 30
Cash, Rosalind 28
Cash, Swin 59
Cashin, Sheryll 63
CasSelle, Malcolm 11
Castor, Jimmy 100
Catchings, Tamika 43
Catlett, Elizabeth 2
Catto, Octavius V. 83
Cayton, Horace 26
Cedric the Entertainer 29, 60, 115
Celestin, Josaphat 101
Cenac, Wyatt 94
Chadiha, Jeffri 57
Chamberlain, Wilt 18, 47
Chambers, Julius 3
Chamillionaire 82
Chancler, Ndugu 115
Chandler, Gene 105
Chandler, Tyson 114
Chaney, Don 98
Chaney, John 67
Chanticleer, Raven 91
Chapman, Nathan A., Jr. 21
Chapman, Susan E. 94
Chapman, Tracy 26
Chappell, Emma 18
Chappell, Roy M. 95
Chappelle, Dave 50, 115
Charles, Ezzard 95
Charles, Ray 16, 48
Charleston, Oscar 39
Chase, Debra Martin 49, 96
Chase, John Saunders, Jr. 99
Chase, Leah 57
Chase-Riboud, Barbara 20, 46
Chatard, Peter 44
Chavis, Benjamin 6

Cheadle, Don **19, 52**
Checker, Chubby **28**
Cheeks, Maurice **47, 106**
Chenault, John **40**
Chenault, Kenneth **4, 36, 108**
Cherry, Deron **40**
Chesnutt, Charles **29**
Chestnut, J. L., Jr. **73**
Chestnut, Morris **31**
Chew, Robert F. **109**
Chideya, Farai **14, 61**
Chief Keef **112**
Childers, Lulu Vere **95**
Childress, Alice **15**
Childress, Alvin **114**
Chiles, Nick **98**
Chineworth, Mary Alice **79**
Chinn, May Edward **26**
Chisholm, Daquan **93**
Chisholm, Samuel **32**
Chisholm, Shirley **2, 50**
Christian, Barbara T. **44**
Christian, Jodie **103**
Christian, Spencer **15**
Christian-Green, Donna M. **17**
Christie, Angella **36**
Christie, Ron **83**
Chuck D **9**
Churchwell, Robert, Sr. **76**
Ciara **56, 115**
Ciara, Barbara **69**
Clack, Zoanne **73**
Claiborne, Loretta **34**
Clark, Carl **101**
Clark, Celeste **15**
Clark, Joe **1**
Clark, Kenneth B. **5, 52**
Clark, Mamie Phipps **79**
Clark, Mattie Moss **61**
Clark, Patrick **14**
Clark, Septima **7**
Clark, Sharón **105**
Clark, Wahida **107**
Clark, Yvonne Young **95**
Clark-Cole, Dorinda **66**
Clarke, Anna Mac **95**
Clarke, Cheryl **32**
Clarke, Hope **14**
Clarke, John Henrik **20**
Clarke, Kenny **27**
Clarke, Stanley **115**
Clarke, Yvette **92**
Clark-Sheard, Karen **22, 114**
Clash, Kevin **14, 93**
Clay, Bryan **57, 74**
Clay, Otis **112**
Clay, William Lacy **8**
Clay, William Lacy, Jr. **95**
Clayton, Constance **1**
Clayton, Eva M. **20**
Clayton, Gerald **111**
Clayton, Mayme Agnew **62**
Clayton, Merry **112**
Clayton, Xernona **3, 45**
Claytor, Helen **14, 52**
Cleage, Pearl **17, 64**
Cleaver, Eldridge **5**
Cleaver, Emanuel **4, 45, 68, 107**
Cleaver, Kathleen **29**
Clemente, Rosa **74**
Clement-Holmes, Linda **94**
Clements, George **2**
Clemmons, Reginal G. **41**

Clemons, Clarence **41**
Clemons, Michael "Pinball" **64**
Clendenon, Donn **26, 56**
Cleveland, James **19**
Cliff, Michelle **42**
Clifton, Lucille **14, 64, 91**
Clifton, Nathaniel "Sweetwater" **47**
Clinton, George **9, 93**
Clovers, The **104**
Clyburn, James E. **21, 71**
Clyburn, Mignon **78**
C-Murder **99**
Coachman, Alice **18**
Coasters, The **102**
Coates, Ta-Nehisi **76**
Cobb, Arnett **114**
Cobb, Jewel Plummer **42**
Cobb, W. Montague **39**
Cobb, William Jelani **59**
Cobbs, Bill **101**
Cobbs, Price M. **9**
Cobbs, Tasha **114**
Cochran, Johnnie **11, 39, 52**
Cockrel, Kenneth V., Jr. **79**
Cockrel, Kenneth Vern, Sr. **79**
CoCo Brother **93**
Cody, Radmilla **99**
Cohen, Anthony **15**
Cohen, Cathy J. **88**
Colbert, Tom **115**
Colbert, Virgis William **17**
Cole, J. **97**
Cole, Johnnetta B. **5, 43**
Cole, Keyshia **63, 107**
Cole, Lorraine **48**
Cole, Maria **104**
Cole, Nat "King" **17**
Cole, Natalie **17, 60, 84**
Cole, Rebecca **38**
Coleman, Bessie **9**
Coleman, Donald **24, 62**
Coleman, Gary **35, 86**
Coleman, George **106**
Coleman, James E., Jr. **79**
Coleman, Ken **57**
Coleman, Leonard S., Jr. **12**
Coleman, Mary **46**
Coleman, Michael B. **28, 79**
Coleman, Ornette **39, 69**
Coleman, Ronald S. **110**
Coleman, Wanda **48**
Coleman, William F., III **61**
Coleman, William T. **76**
Colemon, Johnnie **11**
Coles, Alice **80**
Colescott, Robert **69**
Collins, Albert **12**
Collins, Barbara-Rose **7, 87**
Collins, Bootsy **31**
Collins, Cardiss **10, 80**
Collins, Janet **33, 64**
Collins, Jason **111**
Collins, Lyn **53**
Collins, Marva **3, 71**
Collins, Patricia Hill **67**
Collins, Paul **61**
Colston, Hal **72**
Colter, Cyrus J. **36**
Coltrane, Alice **70**
Coltrane, John **19**
Coltrane, Ravi **71**
Combs, Sean **17, 43, 92**
Comer, James P. **6**

Common **31, 63, 98**
Compton-Rock, Malaak **86**
Cone, James H. **3, 82**
Coney, PonJola **48**
Connerly, Ward **14**
Conrad, Barbara Smith **90**
Conrad, Cecilia A. **94**
Contee, Cheryl **88**
Contours, The **109**
Conyers, John, Jr. **4, 45, 111**
Conyers, Monica **85**
Conyers, Nathan G. **24**
Coogler, Ryan **114**
Cook, Charles "Doc" **44**
Cook, (Will) Mercer **40**
Cook, Samuel DuBois **14**
Cook, Suzan D. Johnson **22**
Cook, Toni **23**
Cook, Will Marion **40**
Cooke, Marcia **60**
Cooke, Marvel **31**
Cook-Parrish, Mary Virginia **95**
Coolio **103**
Cooper, Andrew W. **36**
Cooper, Andy "Lefty" **63**
Cooper, Anna Julia **20**
Cooper, Barry **33**
Cooper, Charles "Chuck" **47**
Cooper, Chuck **75**
Cooper, Edward S. **6**
Cooper, Evern **40**
Cooper, Helene **74**
Cooper, J. California **12, 85**
Cooper, Lisa **73**
Cooper, Margaret J. **46**
Cooper, Michael **31**
Cooper, Tarzan **96**
Cooper Cafritz, Peggy **43**
Cooper-Dyke, Cynthia **17, 89**
Copeland, Johnny **110**
Copeland, Michael **47**
Copeland, Shemekia **110**
Coppola, Imani Francesca **82**
Corbi, Lana **42**
Corley, Tony **62**
Cornelius, Don **4, 100**
Cornish, Sam **50**
Cornwell, Edward E., III **70**
Correia, De'Jaun **93**
Cortez, Jayne **43, 109**
Corthron, Kia **43**
Cortor, Eldzier **42**
Cosby, Bill **7, 26, 59**
Cosby, Camille **14, 80**
Cose, Ellis **5, 50**
Cosey, Pete **103**
Cotter, Joseph Seamon, Sr. **40**
Cottrell, Comer **11**
Council, LaVerne **94**
Counter, S. Allen **74**
Cousin, Ertharin **105**
Cousins, DeMarcus **108**
Cowans, Adger W. **20**
Cowboy Troy **54**
Cox, Bryan **83**
Cox, Donald Lee **93**
Cox, Elbert Frank **111**
Cox, Ida **42**
Cox, Joseph Mason Andrew **51**
Cox, Renée **67**
Cox, William E. **68**
Craig, Carl **31, 71**
Craig-Jones, Ellen Walker **44**

Crawford, Carl **90**
Crawford, Hank **77**
Crawford, Randy **19**
Cray, Robert **30**
Creagh, Milton **27**
Crennel, Romeo **54, 107**
Crenshaw, Kimberlé Williams **88**
Crew, Rudy **16, 113**
Crew, Spencer R. **55**
Crichlow, Ernest **75**
Crisp, Coco **109**
Crite, Allan Rohan **29**
Croal, N'Gai **76**
Crocker, Frankie **29**
Crockett, George W., Jr. **10, 64**
Cromartie, Antonio **115**
Croom, Sylvester **50**
Cross, Dolores E. **23**
Crosthwait, David **93**
Crothers, Scatman **19**
Crouch, Andraé **27, 115**
Crouch, Hubert **95**
Crouch, Stanley **11, 87**
Crowder, Henry **16**
Crowdy, William Saunders **109**
Crudup, Arthur **115**
Crum, George **101**
Crump, Steven **96**
Crumpler, Rebecca Lee **89**
Cruse, Harold **54**
Crutchfield, James N. **55**
Cruz, Victor **107**
Cuffe, Paul **98**
Cullen, Countee **8**
Cullers, Vincent T. **49**
Culp, Curley **110**
Culpepper, Daunte **32, 85**
Cummings, Elijah E. **24, 102**
Cuney, William Waring **44**
Cunningham, Evelyn **23, 85**
Cunningham, Randall **23**
Curren$y **114**
Currie, Betty **21**
Currie, Ulysses **73**
Curry, George E. **23**
Curry, Mark **17**
Curry, Michael **85**
Curry, Stephen **110**
Curson, Ted **108**
Curtis, Christopher Paul **26, 113**
Curtis-Hall, Vondie **17**
Da Don, Polow **86**
Dabiri, John **93**
DaCosta, YaYa **98**
Daemyon, Jerald **64**
Dailey, Ulysses Grant **87**
Dale, Clamma **103**
Daly, Marie Maynard **37**
Dameron, Tadd **103**
Dandridge, Dorothy **3**
Dandridge, Ray **36**
Dandridge, Raymond Garfield **45**
D'Angelo **27**
Daniels, Lee **36, 76**
Daniels, Mel **106**
Daniels-Carter, Valerie **23**
Danner, Margaret Esse **49**
Danquah, Meri Nana Ama **93**
Dantley, Adrian **72**
Dara, Olu **35**
Darden, Calvin **38**
Darden, Christopher **13**
Dash, Damon **31, 113**

Dash, Darien 29
Dash, Julie 4
Dash, Leon 47
Datcher, Michael 60
Davenport, Cow Cow 115
David, Keith 27
Davidson, Jaye 5
Davidson, Tommy 21
Davis, Allison 12
Davis, Altovise 76
Davis, Angela 5, 114
Davis, Angela J. 88
Davis, Anthony 11
Davis, Arthur Paul 41
Davis, Artur 41
Davis, Belva 61
Davis, Ben 115
Davis, Benjamin O., Jr. 2, 43
Davis, Benjamin O., Sr. 4
Davis, Bing 84
Davis, Carl 105
Davis, Charles T. 48
Davis, Chuck 33
Davis, Danny K. 24, 79
Davis, Doris A. 100
Davis, Ed 24
Davis, Eisa 68
Davis, Ernie 48
Davis, Erroll B., Jr. 57
Davis, Frank Marshall 47
Davis, Gary 41
Davis, George 36
Davis, Gordon J. 76
Davis, Guy 36
Davis, James E. 50
Davis, Mia Amber 94
Davis, Mike 41
Davis, Miles 4
Davis, Milt 74
Davis, Nolan 45
Davis, Ossie 5, 50
Davis, Piper 19
Davis, Ruth 37
Davis, Shani 58, 84
Davis, Terrell 20
Davis, Thulani 61
Davis, Tyrone 54
Davis, Viola 34, 76, 100
Davis, Wade, Jr. 103
Davis, Wild Bill 114
Dawes, Dominique 11
Dawkins, Jimmy 111
Dawkins, Wayne 20
Dawn, Marpessa 75
Dawson, Andre 85
Dawson, Matel "Mat," Jr. 39
Dawson, Michael C. 63
Dawson, Rosario 72
Dawson, William Levi 39
Day, Leon 39
Days, Drew S., III 10
De' Alexander, Quinton 57
de Lavallade, Carmen 78
de Passe, Suzanne 25
De Priest, Oscar Stanton 80
De Shields, André 72
De Veaux, Alexis 44
Dean, Fred 98
Dean, Mark E. 35
Deas, Gerald 85
DeBaptiste, George 32
DeBarge, El 89
DeBerry, Lois M. 115

DeCarava, Roy 42, 81
Deconge-Watson, Lovenia 55
Dee, Merri 55
Dee, Ruby 8, 50, 68
Deezer D 53
DeFrantz, Anita 37
Deggans, Eric 71
DeJongh, John, Jr. 85
DeLaine, Joseph A. 110
Delaney, Beauford 19
Delaney, Joe 76
Delaney, Joseph 30
Delany, Bessie 12
Delany, Martin R. 27
Delany, Sadie 12
Delany, Samuel R., Jr. 9
Delco, Wilhemina 33
DeLille, Henriette 30
Dells, The 109
Dellums, Ronald 2, 81
DeLoach, Nora 30
Delpit, Lisa 101
Delsarte, Louis 34
Demby, William 51
Dennard, Brazeal 37
Dennis, Gary C. 91
Dent, Richard 97
Dent, Thomas C. 50
DePreist, James 37, 109
DePrince, Michaela 104
Derülo, Jason 93
DeVard, Jerri 61
DeVaughn, Raheem 91
Devers, Gail 7, 87
Devine, Loretta 24
Dewitty, Thelma 114
Dial, Thornton 114
Diamond, Lydia R. 101
Dickens, Helen Octavia 14, 64
Dickenson, Vic 38
Dickerson, Debra J. 60
Dickerson, Eric 27, 108
Dickerson, Ernest R. 6, 17
Dickey, Eric Jerome 21, 56
Diddley, Bo 39, 72
Diesel, Vin 29
Diggs, Charles C. 21
Diggs, Taye 25, 63
Diggs-Taylor, Anna 20
Dillard, Godfrey J. 45
Dillon, Leo 103
Dinkins, David 4
Divine, Father 7
Dixie Cups, The 109
Dixon, Bill 87
Dixon, Dean 68
Dixon, Ivan 69
Dixon, Julian C. 24
Dixon, Margaret 14
Dixon, Sharon Pratt 1
Dixon, Sheila 68
Dixon, Willie 4
DJ Clue? 111
DJ Jazzy Jeff 32
DJ Lance Rock 94
DJ Screw 110
DMX 28, 64
Dobbs, John Wesley 89
Dobbs, Mattiwilda 34
Dobson, Tamara 111
Doby, Lawrence Eugene, Sr. 16, 41
Dodson, Howard, Jr. 7, 52
Dodson, Owen Vincent 38

Dogan, Matthew Winifred 91
Dokes, Michael 105
Doley, Harold, Jr. 26
Dollar, Creflo 106
Domingo, Colman 94
Domino, Fats 20
Donald, Arnold Wayne 36
Donaldson, Jeff 46
Donegan, Dorothy 19
Dorham, Kenny 113
Dorn, Michael 112
Dorrell, Karl 52
Dorsey, Lee 65
Dorsey, Thomas Andrew 15
Dorsey, Thomas J. 90
Dortch, Thomas W., Jr. 45
Dougherty, Mary Pearl 47
Douglas, Aaron 7
Douglas, Bob 96
Douglas, Derek 88
Douglas, Donya 97
Douglas, Emory 89
Douglass, Frederick 87
Dourdan, Gary 37
Dove, Rita 6, 78, 101
Dove, Ulysses 5
Downing, George T. 91
Downing, Will 19
Dramatics, The 106
Draper, Sharon Mills 16, 43
Dre, Dr. 10, 14, 30
Drew, Alvin, Jr. 67
Drew, Charles Richard 7
Drexler, Clyde 4, 61
Driskell, David C. 7
Driver, David E. 11
Driver, Donald 99
Drummond, William J. 40
Du Bois, David Graham 45
Du Bois, W. E. B. 3
du Cille, Michel 74
DuBois, Joshua 88
DuBois, Shirley Graham 21
Ducksworth, Marilyn 12
Dudley, Edward R. 58
Due, Patricia Stephens 100
Due, Tananarive 30
Duerson, Dave 93
Duggins, George 64
Duke, Bill 3, 96
Duke, George 21, 113
Dukes, Hazel Nell 56
Dumars, Joe 16, 65
Dumas, Henry 41
Dumpson, James R. 108
Dunbar, Paul Laurence 8
Dunbar-Nelson, Alice Ruth Moore 44
Duncan, Michael Clarke 26, 104
Duncan, Tim 20, 91
Duncan, Todd 76
Dungey, Merrin 62
Dungy, Camille 86
Dungy, Tony 17, 42, 59
Dunham, Katherine 4, 59
Dunlap, Ericka 55
Dunn, Jerry 27
Dunn, Warrick 90
Dunner, Leslie B. 45
Dunnigan, Alice Allison 41
Dunston, Georgia Mae 48
Duplechan, Larry 55
DuPree, Johnny 96

Dupri, Jermaine 13, 46
Durant, Kevin 76, 107
Durham, Bobby 73
Durham, James 90
Duthiers, Vladimir 109
Dutton, Charles S. 4, 22
DuVernay, Ava 98
Dworkin, Aaron P. 52
Dwight, Edward 65
Dye, Jermaine 58
Dyett, Walter 113
Dyson, Michael Eric 11, 40
Eagleson, William Lewis 90
Early, Gerald 15
Easley, Annie J. 61
Easton, Hosea 91
Ebanks, Michelle 60
Eckstine, Billy 28
Edelin, Ramona Hoage 19
Edelman, Marian Wright 5, 42
Edison, Harry 114
Edley, Christopher 2, 48
Edley, Christopher F., Jr. 48
Edmonds, Terry 17
Edmonds, Tracey 16, 64
Edmunds, Gladys 48
Edwards, Donna 77
Edwards, Esther Gordy 43
Edwards, Harry 2
Edwards, Herman 51
Edwards, Lena Frances 76
Edwards, Melvin 22
Edwards, Teresa 14, 95
Edwards, Willarda V. 59
Edwards, Willis 104
El Wilson, Barbara 35
Elder, Larry 25
Elder, Lee 6
Elder, Lonne, III 38
Elders, Joycelyn 6
Eldridge, Roy 37
Elie, Lolis Eric 97
Elise, Kimberly 32, 101
Ellerbe, Brian 22
Ellington, Duke 5
Ellington, E. David 11
Ellington, Mercedes 34
Elliott, Missy 31, 90
Elliott, Sean 26
Ellis, Aunjanue 108
Ellis, Charles H., III 79
Ellis, Clarence A. 38
Ellis, Dock 78
Ellis, Jimmy 44
Ellis, Larry R. 110
Ellis, Nelsan 105
Ellis, Trey 97
Ellis-Lamkins, Phaedra 88
Ellison, Keith 59
Ellison, Ralph 7
Elmore, Ronn 21
Emanuel, James A. 46
Emeagwali, Dale 31
En Vogue 100
Ephriam, Mablean 29
Epperson, Sharon 54
Epps, Archie C., III 45
Epps, Mike 60
Epps, Omar 23, 59
Ericsson-Jackson, Aprille 28
Ervin, Anthony 66
Ervin, Booker 106

Ervin, Clark Kent 82
Erving, Julius 18, 47
Escobar, Damien 56
Escobar, Tourie 56
Esposito, Giancarlo 9
Espy, Mike 6
Estes, Rufus 29
Estes, Simon 28
Estes, Sleepy John 33
Eubanks, Kevin 15, 108
Eugene-Richard, Margie 63
Europe, James Reese 10
Evans, Darryl 22
Evans, Etu 55
Evans, Faith 22
Evans, Harry 25
Evans, Mari 26
Evans, Melvin H. 88
Evans, Warren C. 76
Eve 29
Everett, Carl 103
Everett, Francine 23
Everett, Percival 93
Evers, Medgar 3
Evers, Myrlie 8
Ewing, Patrick 17, 73
Fabio, Sarah Webster 48
Fabolous 93
Fabre, Shelton 71
Fagan, Garth 18, 98
Fair, Ronald L. 47
Faison, Donald 50
Faison, Frankie 55
Faison, George 16
Falana, Lola 42
Falconer, Etta Zuber 59
Fales-Hill, Susan 88
Fargas, Antonio 50
Farley, Christopher John 54
Farley, James Conway 99
Farmer, Art 38
Farmer, Forest J. 1
Farmer, James 2, 64
Farmer-Paellmann, Deadria 43
Farr, Mel 24
Farrakhan, Louis 2, 15
Farrell, Herman D., Jr. 81
Farris, Isaac Newton, Jr. 63
Fattah, Chaka 11, 70, 112
Faulk, Marshall 35, 96
Fauntroy, Walter E. 11
Fauset, Crystal Dreda Bird 100
Fauset, Jessie 7
Favors, Steve 23
Fax, Elton 48
Feelings, Muriel 44
Feelings, Tom 11, 47
Felix, Allyson 48, 98
Felix, Larry R. 64
Felix Da Housecat 110
Feemster, Herbert 72
Fennoy, Ilene 72
Fenty, Adrian 60, 88
Ferbos, Lionel 95
Ferguson, Roger W., Jr. 25, 112
Ferguson, Ronald F. 75
Ferguson, Vernice D. 108
Ferrell, Rachelle 29
Fetchit, Stepin 32
Fiasco, Lupe 64
Fielder, Cecil 2, 112
Fielder, Prince Semien 68
Fields, C. Virginia 25

Fields, Cleo 13
Fields, Evelyn J. 27
Fields, Felicia P. 60
Fields, Julia 45
Fields, Kim 36
50 Cent 46, 83
Files, Lolita 35
Fils-Aimé, Reggie 74
Fine, Sam 60
Finley, Ron 110
Finner-Williams, Paris Michele 62
Fishbone 101
Fishburne, Laurence 4, 22, 70
Fisher, Ada Lois Sipuel 76
Fisher, Ada M. 76
Fisher, Antwone 40
Fisher, Derek 97
Fisher, Gail 85
Fisher, Miles Mark 91
Fisk Jubilee Singers 112
Fitzgerald, Ella 1, 18
Five Keys, The 104
Flack, Roberta 19
Flake, Floyd H. 18, 110
Flamingos, The 108
Flanagan, Tommy 69
Flavor Flav 67
Fleming, Erik R. 75
Fleming, Raymond 48
Fletcher, Arthur A. 63
Fletcher, Benjamin 90
Fletcher, Bill, Jr. 41
Fletcher, Buddy 16, 108
Fletcher, Geoffrey 85
Flo Rida 78
Flood, Curt 10, 93
Flowers, Sylester 50
Flowers, Vonetta 35
Floyd, Elson S. 41
Forbes, Calvin 46
Forbes, James A., Jr. 71
Ford, Barney 90
Ford, Cheryl 45
Ford, Clyde W. 40
Ford, Harold E(ugene) 42
Ford, Harold E(ugene), Jr. 16, 70
Ford, Jack 39
Ford, Johnny 70
Ford, Nick Aaron 44
Ford, T-Model 91, 113
Ford, Wallace 58
Forman, James 7, 51
Forman, James, Jr. 89
Forrest, Leon 44
Forrest, Vernon 40, 79
Forté, John 74
Forte, Linda Diane 54
Fortune, James 92
Foster, Andrew 79
Foster, Arian 114
Foster, Ezola 28
Foster, Frank 97
Foster, George "Pops" 40
Foster, Henry W., Jr. 26
Foster, Jylla Moore 45
Foster, Marie 48
Foster, William P. 88
Fowler, Reggie 51
Fox, Donal 114
Fox, John R. 105
Fox, Vivica A. 15, 53
Foxx, Anthony 81
Foxx, Jamie 15, 48

Foxx, Redd 2
Foye, K'wan 97
Francis, Norman (C.) 60
Francis, Thais 93
Francois, Terry A. 106
Franklin, Aretha 11, 44, 115
Franklin, C. L. 68
Franklin, Hardy R. 9, 87
Franklin, J. E. 44
Franklin, John Hope 5, 77
Franklin, Kirk 15, 49, 97
Franklin, Shirley 34, 80
Franti, Michael 93
Fraser, Sarah Loguen 100
Frazer, Jendayi 68
Frazer, Victor O. 98
Frazier, E. Franklin 10
Frazier, Joe 19, 98
Frazier, Kenneth 97
Frazier, Kevin 58
Frazier, Oscar 58
Frazier, Ryan 89
Frazier, Walt 91
Frazier-Lyde, Jacqui 31
Freelon, Nnenna 32
Freeman, Aaron 52
Freeman, Al, Jr. 11, 105
Freeman, Charles 19
Freeman, Harold P. 23
Freeman, Leonard 27
Freeman, Marianna 23
Freeman, Morgan 2, 20, 62, 100
Freeman, Paul 39
Freeman, Von 104
Freeman, Yvette 27
French, Albert 18
French, D. M. 94
Fresh, Doug E. 93
Friday, Jeff 24
Fryer, Roland G. 56
Fudge, Ann (Marie) 11, 55
Fudge, Marcia L. 76
Fulani, Lenora 11
Fuller, A. Oveta 43
Fuller, Arthur 27
Fuller, Blind Boy 86
Fuller, Charles 8
Fuller, Curtis 115
Fuller, Howard L. 37
Fuller, Hoyt 44
Fuller, Meta Vaux Warrick 27
Fuller, S. B. 13
Fuller, Solomon Carter, Jr. 15
Fuller, Thomas O. 90
Fuller, Vivian 33
Funderburg, I. Owen 38
Funnye, Capers C., Jr. 73
Fuqua, Antoine 35
Fuqua, Harvey 90
Futch, Eddie 33
Future 109
Gaines, Brenda 41
Gaines, Clarence E., Sr. 55
Gaines, Ernest J. 7
Gaines, Grady 38
Gaines, Lloyd 79
Gaines, Matthew 95
Gaines, Patrice 106
Gaiter, Dorothy J. 80
Gaither, Alonzo Smith (Jake) 14
Gaither, Israel L. 65
Gamble, Kenny 85
Gamble, Oscar 113

Gans, Joe 91
Gant, Richard 105
Gantt, Harvey 1
Gap Band, The 100
Gardere, Jeffrey 76
Gardner, Chris 65
Gardner, Edward G. 45
Garland, Red 115
Garner, Erroll 76
Garner, Tyron 99
Garnet, Henry Highland 100
Garnett, Kevin 14, 70
Garrett, James F. 78
Garrett, Joyce Finley 59
Garrison, Zina 2
Garvin, Gerry 78
Gary, Willie E. 12
Gaskins, Eric 64
Gaskins, Rudy 74
Gaspard, Patrick 84
Gaston, Arthur George 3, 38, 59
Gaston, Cito 71
Gaston, Marilyn Hughes 60
Gates, Henry Louis, Jr. 3, 38, 67
Gates, Sylvester James, Jr. 15
Gates, William 97
Gay, Tyson 114
Gaye, Marvin 2
Gaye, Nona 56
Gayle, Addison, Jr. 41
Gayle, Helene D. 3, 46
Gaynor, Gloria 36
Gentry, Alvin 23
George, Eddie 80
George, Nelson 12, 101
George, Zelma Watson 42
Gervin, George 80
Geto Boys 115
Ghostface Killah 90
Gibbons, Gary 107
Gibbs, Marla 86
Gibbs, Mifflin W. 99
Gibson, Althea 8, 43
Gibson, Bob 33
Gibson, Donald Bernard 40
Gibson, John Trusty 87
Gibson, Johnnie Mae 23
Gibson, Josh 22
Gibson, Kenneth Allen 6
Gibson, Ted 66
Gibson, Truman K., Jr. 60
Gibson, Tyrese 27, 62
Gibson, William F. 6
Giddings, Paula 11
Gidron, Richard D. 68
Gilbert, Christopher 50
Gilbert, John Wesley 91
Giles, Roscoe C. 93
Gill, Gerald 69
Gill, Johnny 51
Gill, Turner 83
Gilles, Ralph 61
Gillespie, Dizzy 1
Gilliam, Frank 23
Gilliam, Joe 31
Gilliam, Sam 16
Gilliard, Steve 69
Gilmore, Artis 101
Gilmore, Marshall 46
Gilpin, Charles Sidney 81
Ginuwine 35
Giovanni, Nikki 9, 39, 85
Gist, Carole 1

Givens, Adele 62
Givens, Robin 4, 25, 58
Givhan, Robin Deneen 72
Glanville, Douglas Metunwa 82
Glasper, Robert 101
Glass, Ron 111
Gloster, Hugh Morris, Sr. 90
Glover, Cedric B. 103
Glover, Corey 34
Glover, Danny 1, 24, 103
Glover, Donald 85
Glover, Keith 79
Glover, Nathaniel, Jr. 12
Glover, Savion 14
Goapele 55
Goines, Donald 19
Goings, Russell 59
Goldberg, Whoopi 4, 33, 69
Golden, Marita 19, 99
Golden, Thelma 10, 55
Golden Gate Quartet 104
Goldsberry, Ronald 18
Golson, Benny 37
Golston, Allan C. 55
Gomes, Peter J. 15, 93
Gomez, Jewelle 30
Gomez-Preston, Cheryl 9
Gomillion, Charles 90
Goode, Mal 13
Goode, W. Wilson 4
Gooden, Dwight 20
Gooden, Linda 94
Gooding, Cuba, Jr. 16, 62
Goodlett, Carlton B. 91
Goodman, Al 87
Goodman, Kim C. 94
Goodnight, Paul 32
Gorden, W. C. 71
Gordon, Bruce S. 41, 53, 82
Gordon, Carl 87
Gordon, Dexter 25
Gordon, Ed 10, 53
Gordone, Charles 15
Gordon-Reed, Annette 74
Gordy, Berry, Jr. 1
Goss, Carol A. 55
Goss, Tom 23
Gossett, Louis, Jr. 7
Gotti, Irv 39
Gourdin, Edward O. 93
Gourdine, Meredith 33
Gourdine, Simon 11
Grace, George H. 48
Graham, Katerina 99
Graham, Lawrence Otis 12
Graham, Lorenz 48
Graham, Stedman 13
Graham, Trevor 84
Granderson, Curtis 66
Granderson, LZ 103
Granger, Lester B. 75
Grant, Augustus O. 71
Grant, Bernie 57
Grant, Frank 100
Grant, Gwendolyn Goldsby 28
Granville, Evelyn Boyd 36
Gravely, Samuel L., Jr. 5, 49
Graves, Butch 77
Graves, Denyce Antoinette 19, 57
Graves, Earl G. 1, 35
Gray, Darius 69
Gray, Dobie 99
Gray, F. Gary 14, 49

Gray, Farrah 59
Gray, Fred 37
Gray, Ida 41
Gray, Macy 29
Gray, Vincent C. 88
Gray, William H., III 3
Gray, Willie 46
Gray, Yeshimbra "Shimmy" 55
Greaves, R. B. 106
Greaves, William 38
Greely, M. Gasby 27
Green, A. C. 32
Green, Al 13, 47, 74
Green, Cee Lo 70, 103
Green, Darrell 39, 74
Green, Dennis 5, 45
Green, Grant 56
Green, Isaac H. 79
Green, Jonathan 54
Green, Nancy 112
Greene, Frank S., Jr. 101
Greene, Jimmy 74
Greene, Joe 10
Greene, Maurice 27, 77
Greene, Petey 65
Greene, Richard Thaddeus, Sr. 67
Greenfield, Eloise 9
Greenhouse, Bunnatine "Bunny" 57
Greenlee, Sam 48
Greenwood, L. C. 115
Greenwood, Monique 38
Greer, Hal 92
Gregory, Ann 63
Gregory, Dick 1, 54
Gregory, Frederick 8, 51
Gregory, Wilton 37
Grier, Bobby 95
Grier, David Alan 28
Grier, Eliza Ann 90
Grier, Mike 43
Grier, Pam 9, 31, 86
Grier, Roosevelt 13
Griffey, Dick 89
Griffey, Ken, Jr. 12, 73
Griffin, Anthony 71
Griffin, Bessie Blout 43
Griffin, Blake 98
Griffin, Johnny 71
Griffin, LaShell 51
Griffin, Robert, III 107
Griffith, Emile 113
Griffith, Mark Winston 8
Griffith, Yolanda 25
Griffith-Joyner, Florence 28
Grillo, Evelio 95
Grimké, Archibald H. 9
Grist, Reri 84
Groff, Peter 96
Grooms, Henry R(andall) 50
Guillaume, Robert 3, 48
Guinier, Lani 7, 30
Gumbel, Bryant 14, 80
Gumbel, Greg 8
Gunn, Moses 10
Gurira, Danai 73
Guru 84
Guy, George "Buddy" 31
Guy, Jasmine 2
Guy, Rosa 5
Guyot, Lawrence 108
Guy-Sheftall, Beverly 13, 92
Guyton, Tyree 9, 94
Gwynn, Tony 18, 83

Haddon, Dietrick 55
Hageman, Hans 36
Hageman, Ivan 36
Hagler, Marvelous Marvin 102
Hailey, JoJo 22
Hailey, K-Ci 22
Hairston, Jester 88
Hairston, Sam 88
Hale, Clara 16
Hale, Lorraine 8
Haley, Alex 4
Haley, George Williford Boyce 21
Hall, Aaron 57
Hall, Alvin D. 86
Hall, Arsenio 58
Hall, Arthur 39
Hall, Elliott S. 24
Hall, Juanita 62
Hall, Kevan 61
Hall, Lloyd A. 8
Hall, Tamron 96
Halliburton, Warren J. 49
Ham, Cynthia Parker 58
Hamblin, Ken 10
Hamburg, Beatrix 84
Hamburg, Margaret 78
Hamer, Fannie Lou 6
Hamilton, Anthony 61
Hamilton, Leonard 100
Hamilton, Lisa Gay 71
Hamilton, Samuel C. 47
Hamilton, Vicki 95
Hamilton, Virginia 10
Hamlin, Larry Leon 49, 62
Hammond, Fred 23
Hammonds, Evelynn 69
Hammons, David 69
Hampton, Fred 18
Hampton, Henry 6
Hampton, Lionel 17, 41
Hancock, Herbie 20, 67
Handy, W. C. 8
Haney, Lee 77
Hannah, Marc 10
Hansberry, Lorraine 6
Hansberry, Tony, II 93
Hansberry, William Leo 11
Hansen, Austin 88
Hardaway, Anfernee 13, 111
Hardaway, Tim 35
Harden, Monique 97
Hardin Armstrong, Lil 39
Harding, Vincent 67
Hardison, Bethann 12
Hardison, Kadeem 22
Hare, Nathan 44
Harewood, Dorian 104
Harkless, Necia Desiree 19
Harmon, Clarence 26
Harold, Erika 54
Harold Melvin & the Blue Notes 105
Harper, Ben 34, 62
Harper, Frances Ellen Watkins 11
Harper, Hill 32, 65, 97
Harper, Michael S. 34
Harper, Rachel M. 92
Harrell, Andre 9, 30
Harrington, Oliver W. 9
Harris, Alice 7
Harris, Barbara 12
Harris, Barry 68
Harris, Bernard A. 90

Harris, Bill 72
Harris, Carla A. 67
Harris, Corey 39, 73
Harris, Damon 110
Harris, E. Lynn 12, 33
Harris, Eddy L. 18
Harris, Franco 97
Harris, Gary L. 87
Harris, James 79
Harris, Jay T. 19
Harris, Jessica B. 91
Harris, Kamala D. 64
Harris, Leslie 6
Harris, Lyle Ashton 83
Harris, Major 110
Harris, Marcelite Jordon 16
Harris, Mary Styles 31
Harris, Maya Lakshmi 88
Harris, Monica 18
Harris, Patricia Roberts 2
Harris, Richard E. 61
Harris, Robin 7
Harris, Sylvia 70
Harris, Wesley L. 92
Harris, Wood 114
Harris, Wynonie 102
Harris-Lacewell, Melissa 81
Harrison, Alvin 28
Harrison, Calvin 28
Harrison, Charles 72
Harris-Stewart, Lusia 90
Harry, Jackée 111
Harsh, Vivian Gordon 14
Hart, Alvin Youngblood 61
Hart, Kevin 103
Hart, Thomas A., Sr. 113
Hartman, Johnny 109
Harvard, Beverly 11
Harvey, Steve 18, 58
Harvey, William R. 42
Haskins, Clem 23
Haskins, James 36, 54
Hassell, Leroy Rountree, Sr. 41
Hastie, William H. 8
Hastings, Alcee L. 16
Hatcher, Andrew T. 90
Hatcher, Richard G. 55
Hatchett, Glenda 32
Hathaway, Donny 18
Hathaway, Isaac Scott 33
Hathaway, Lalah 57, 88
Havens, Richie 111
Hawkins, Augustus F. 68
Hawkins, Coleman 9
Hawkins, Connie 91
Hawkins, Edwin 113
Hawkins, Erskine 14
Hawkins, La-Van 17, 54
Hawkins, Screamin' Jay 30
Hawkins, Steven 14
Hawkins, Tramaine 16
Hawkins, Walter 87
Hayden, Carla D. 47
Hayden, Lewis 105
Hayden, Palmer 13
Hayden, Robert 12
Hayes, Bob 77
Hayes, Cecil N. 46
Hayes, Dennis 54
Hayes, Elvin 93
Hayes, Isaac 20, 58, 73
Hayes, James C. 10
Hayes, Roland 4

Hayes, Teddy 40
Haygood, Wil 83
Haynes, Elizabeth Ross 102
Haynes, George Edmund 8
Haynes, Marques 22
Haynes, Roy 87
Haynes, Trudy 44
Haynie, Sharon 94
Haysbert, Dennis 42, 106
Haysbert, Raymond V., Sr. 87
Haywood, Gar Anthony 43
Haywood, Jimmy 58
Haywood, Margaret A. 24
Haywood, Spencer 99
Hazel, Darryl B. 50
Hazzard, Walt 98
Healy, James Augustine 30
Healy, Michael 90
Heard, Gar 25
Heard, Nathan C. 45
Hearns, Thomas 29
Heath, Percy 100
Heavy D 58, 98
Hector, Jamie 98
Hedgeman, Anna Arnold 22
Height, Dorothy I. 2, 23, 78
Hemingway, Anthony 107
Hemphill, Essex 10
Hemphill, Jessie Mae 33, 59
Hemsley, Sherman 19, 104
Henderson, Cornelius Langston 26
Henderson, David 53
Henderson, Fletcher 32
Henderson, George Washington 101
Henderson, Gordon 5
Henderson, Henry Fairfax, Jr. 89
Henderson, Jeff 72
Henderson, Rickey 28, 78
Henderson, Stephen E. 45
Henderson, Thelton E. 68
Henderson, Wade J. 14
Henderson, Zelma 71
Hendrix, Jimi 10
Hendryx, Nona 56
Hendy, Francis 47
Henries, A. Doris Banks 44
Henry, Aaron 19
Henry, Clarence "Frogman" 46
Henry, Dwight 104
Henry, Joshua 94
Henry, Troy 85
Henson, Darrin 33
Henson, Josiah 90
Henson, Matthew 2
Henson, Taraji P. 58, 77
Herbert, Bob 63, 96
Hercules, Frank 44
Herenton, Willie W. 24, 81
Herman, Alexis M. 15
Hernandez, Aileen Clarke 13
Herndon, Alonzo Franklin 89
Herndon, Angelo 90
Hernton, Calvin C. 51
Hickman, Fred 11
Higginbotham, A. Leon, Jr. 13, 25
Higginbotham, Jay C. 37
Higginsen, Vy 65
Hightower, Dennis F. 13
Hill, Andrew 66
Hill, Anita 5, 65
Hill, Bonnie Guiton 20
Hill, Calvin 19

Hill, Donna 32
Hill, Dulé 29
Hill, Grant 13, 94
Hill, Hugh Morgan 83
Hill, Janet 19
Hill, Jemele 109
Hill, Jesse, Jr. 13
Hill, Lauryn 20, 53, 111
Hill, Leslie Pinckney 44
Hill, Marc Lamont 80
Hill, Michael 95
Hill, Oliver W. 24, 63
Hill, Peter 92
Hill, Wyllstyne D. 94
Hillard, Terry 25
Hillary, Barbara 65
Hilliard, Asa Grant, III 66
Hilliard, David 7, 105
Hilliard, Earl F. 24
Hilliard, Wendy 53
Hilson, Keri 84
Himes, Chester 8
Hinderas, Natalie 5
Hine, Darlene Clark 24
Hines, Earl "Fatha" 39
Hines, Garrett 35
Hines, Gregory 1, 42
Hinton, Milt 30
Hinton, William Augustus 8
Hoagland, Everett H. 45
Hobson, Julius W. 44
Hobson, Mellody 40
Hodge, Derrick 114
Hogan, Beverly Wade 50
Holder, Eric, Jr. 9, 76, 104
Holder, Laurence 34
Holdsclaw, Chamique 24, 110
Holiday, Billie 1
Holiday, Jrue 115
Holland, Endesha Ida Mae 3, 57
Holland, Kimberly N. 62
Holland, Robert, Jr. 11
Holland-Dozier-Holland 36
Holloway, Brenda 65
Holloway, Loleatta 115
Hollowell, Donald L. 57
Holmes, Amy 69
Holmes, Clint 57
Holmes, Hamilton E. 82
Holmes, Larry 20, 68
Holmes, Santonio 87
Holmes, Shannon 70
Holmes, T. J. 98
Holsey, Lucius Henry 92
Holstein, Casper 89
Holt, Lester 66
Holt, Nora 38
Holt Baker, Arlene 73
Holton, Hugh, Jr. 39
Holyfield, Evander 6
Honeywood, Varnette P. 54, 88
Honoré, Russel L. 64
Hood, James Walker 91
Hooker, John Lee 30
hooks, bell 5, 90
Hooks, Benjamin L. 2, 85
Hooks, Robert 76
Hope, John 8
Hope, Lugenia Burns 89
Hopkins, Bernard 35, 69, 105
Hopkins, Donald R. 89
Hopkins, Lightnin' 83
Horn, Shirley 32, 56

Horne, Frank 44
Horne, Lena 5, 86
Horsford, Steven 88
Horton, Andre 33
Horton, Big Walter 115
Horton, Gladys 92
Horton, James Oliver 58
Horton, Suki 33
Horton, Willie 104
Hoskins, Harold K. 103
Houghton, Israel 92
House, Son 8
Houston, Charles Hamilton 4
Houston, Cissy 20, 83
Houston, Whitney 7, 28, 83, 100
Howard, Ayanna 65
Howard, Desmond 16, 58
Howard, Dwight 113
Howard, Juwan 15
Howard, M. William, Jr. 26
Howard, Michelle 28
Howard, Perry Wilbon, Jr. 112
Howard, Ryan 65, 113
Howard, Sherri 36
Howard, Terrence 59, 94
Howell, Ayinde 91
Howlin' Wolf 9
Howroyd, Janice Bryant 42
Hoyte, Lenon 50
Hrabowski, Freeman A., III 22
Hubbard, Arnette Rhinehart 38
Hubbard, Freddie 75
Hudlin, Reginald 9, 86
Hudlin, Warrington 9
Hudson, Cheryl 15
Hudson, Ernie 72
Hudson, Jennifer 63, 83
Hudson, Wade 15
Huff, Leon 86
Huggins, Edie 71
Huggins, Larry 21
Huggins, Nathan Irvin 52
Hughes, Albert 7
Hughes, Allen 7
Hughes, Cathy 27
Hughes, Dora 88
Hughes, Ebony 57
Hughes, Langston 4
Hughley, D. L. 23, 76
Hull, Akasha Gloria 45
Humphrey, Bobbi 20
Humphries, Frederick 20
Hunt, Darnell 92
Hunt, Richard 6
Hunter, Alberta 42
Hunter, Billy 22, 109
Hunter, Clementine 45
Hunter, Ivory Joe 106
Hunter, Lindsey 110
Hunter, Torii 43, 109
Hunter-Gault, Charlayne 6, 31
Hurston, Zora Neale 3
Hurt, Byron 61
Hurt, Mississippi John 84
Hurtt, Harold 46
Hutch, Willie 62
Hutcherson, Bobby 115
Hutcherson, Hilda Yvonne 54
Hutchinson, Earl Ofari 24
Hutson, Jean Blackwell 16
Hyde, Cowan F. "Bubba" 47
Hyman, Earle 25, 79
Hyman, Phyllis 19

Ibrahim, Fuad 109
Ice Cube 8, 30, 60
Iceberg Slim 11
Ice-T 6, 31, 96
Iman, Chanel 66
Imani Winds 113
Ifill, Gwen 28
Imes, Elmer Samuel 39
India.Arie 34
Ingram, James 84
Ingram, Rex 5
Ink Spots, The 102
Innis, Roy 5
Irvin, Michael 64
Irvin, Monford Merrill 31
Irvin, Vernon 65
Irving, Barrington, Jr. 112
Irving, Kyrie 102
Irving, Larry, Jr. 12
Irvis, K. Leroy 67
Isaacs, Cheryl Boone 113
Isaacs, John 76
Isley, Marvin 87
Isley, Ronald 25, 56
Iverson, Allen 24, 46
Iverson, Johnathan Lee 22, 100
Ivey, Phil 72, 106
J Dilla 102
Ja Rule 35, 91
Jackson, Alexine Clement 22
Jackson, Alphonso R. 48
Jackson, Brenda 87
Jackson, Deborah 94
Jackson, Earl 31
Jackson, Edison O. 67
Jackson, Frank G. 76
Jackson, Fred James 25
Jackson, George 14
Jackson, George 19
Jackson, Hal 41, 104
Jackson, Isaiah 3
Jackson, Jamea 64
Jackson, James A. 90
Jackson, Janet 6, 30, 68
Jackson, Jermaine 79
Jackson, Jesse 1, 27, 72
Jackson, Jesse, Jr. 14, 45, 81, 108
Jackson, Joe 78
Jackson, John 36
Jackson, Judith D. 57
Jackson, LaToya 95
Jackson, Lisa 77
Jackson, Mae 57
Jackson, Mahalia 5
Jackson, Mannie 14
Jackson, Mary 73
Jackson, Maynard 2, 41
Jackson, Michael 19, 53, 76
Jackson, Millie 25
Jackson, Milt 26
Jackson, Phillip 115
Jackson, Rampage 83
Jackson, Randy 40
Jackson, Reggie 15
Jackson, Rickey 88
Jackson, Samuel L. 8, 19, 63, 102
Jackson, Sandi 108
Jackson, Sheneska 18
Jackson, Shirley Ann 12
Jackson, Tito 81
Jackson, Tom 70
Jackson, Vera 40
Jackson 5 103

Jackson Lee, Sheila 20
Jacob, John E. 2
Jacobs, Harriet 104
Jacobs, Regina 38
Jacquet, Illinois 49
Jaheim 58
Jakes, Thomas "T. D." 17, 43
Jamal, Ahmad 69
Jamerson, James 59
James, Charles H., III 62
James, Daniel, Jr. 16
James, Donna A. 51
James, Elmore 114
James, Etta 13, 52, 100
James, G. Larry 74
James, Juanita 13
James, LeBron 46, 78, 105
James, Nikki M. 94
James, Rick 19
James, Sharpe 23, 69
James, Skip 38
James, Sly 107
James Bracken and Vivian Bracken 107
Jamison, Judith 7, 67, 96
Jarreau, Al 21, 65, 105
Jarrett, Valerie 73
Jarrett, Vernon D. 42
Jarvis, Charlene Drew 21
Jarvis, Erich 67
Jarvis, Kristen 85
Jasper, John J. 91
Jasper, Kenji 39
Jay-Z 27, 69, 103
Jealous, Benjamin Todd 70, 113
Jefferson, Blind Lemon 81
Jefferson, Denise 87
Jefferson, Margo 108
Jefferson, Mildred Fay 89
Jefferson, William J. 25, 72
Jeffries, Leonard 8
Jemison, Mae C. 1, 35
Jemison, Major L. 48
Jenifer, Franklyn G. 2
Jenkins, Beverly 14
Jenkins, Ella 15
Jenkins, Kris 98
Jenkins, Ray 77
Jennings, Lyfe 56, 69
Jerkins, Rodney 31
Jeter, Claude 75
Jeter, Derek 27, 93
Jimmy Jam 13
Joe, Yolanda 21
John, Daymond 23, 114
Johns, Vernon 38
Johnson, Angela 52
Johnson, Anthony M. 92
Johnson, Avery 62
Johnson, Beverly 2, 102
Johnson, Buddy 36
Johnson, Bumpy 102
Johnson, Calvin 108
Johnson, Chad 108
Johnson, Charles 1, 82
Johnson, Charles S. 12
Johnson, Chris 92
Johnson, Clark 96
Johnson, Clifford "Connie" 52
Johnson, Conrad O. 97
Johnson, Dennis 89
Johnson, Eddie Bernice 8, 90
Johnson, Edward Austin 107

Johnson, Eunice W. 83
Johnson, Fenton 91
Johnson, George E. 29
Johnson, Georgia Douglas 41
Johnson, Gus 92
Johnson, Hall 90
Johnson, Hank, Jr. 80
Johnson, Harry E. 57
Johnson, Harvey, Jr. 24, 82
Johnson, J. J. 37
Johnson, Jack 8
Johnson, James Weldon 5
Johnson, Je'Caryous 63
Johnson, Jeh C. 76
Johnson, Jeh Vincent 44
Johnson, Joe 94
Johnson, John H. 3, 54
Johnson, John Henry 96
Johnson, Johnnie 56
Johnson, Judy 105
Johnson, Katherine (Coleman Goble) 61
Johnson, Kevin 70
Johnson, Keyshawn 91
Johnson, Larry 28
Johnson, Le'Andria 108
Johnson, Leroy R. 89
Johnson, Levi 48
Johnson, Lonnie 85
Johnson, Lonnie G. 32, 93
Johnson, Magic 3, 39, 101
Johnson, Mamie "Peanut" 40
Johnson, Mat 31, 105
Johnson, Michael 13
Johnson, Mordecai Wyatt 79
Johnson, Norma H. 17, 97
Johnson, R. M. 36
Johnson, Rafer 33
Johnson, Robert 2
Johnson, Robert L. 3, 39
Johnson, Robert T. 17
Johnson, Rodney Van 28
Johnson, Sandra K. 94
Johnson, Sheila Crump 48
Johnson, Shoshana 47
Johnson, Syl 97
Johnson, Syleena 98
Johnson, Tommy 106
Johnson, Virginia 9
Johnson, William 91
Johnson, William Henry 3
Johnson-George, Tamara 79
Johnson-Powell, Gloria 107
Joiner, Charlie 102
Jolley, Willie 28
Jones, Absalom 52
Jones, Adam 103
Jones, Adam 114
Jones, Alex 64
Jones, Andruw 98
Jones, Bill T. 1, 46, 80
Jones, Bobby 20, 94
Jones, Booker T. 84
Jones, Carl 7
Jones, Caroline 29
Jones, Clara Stanton 51
Jones, Clarence B. 114
Jones, Cobi N'Gai 18
Jones, Cullen 73
Jones, Deacon 92, 112
Jones, Donell 29
Jones, Doris W. 62
Jones, E. Edward, Sr. 45

Jones, Ed "Too Tall" 46
Jones, Edith Mae Irby 65
Jones, Edward P. 43, 67
Jones, Elaine R. 7, 45
Jones, Elvin 14, 68
Jones, Emil, Jr. 74
Jones, Etta 35
Jones, Eugene Kinckle 79
Jones, Frederick McKinley 68
Jones, Gayl 37
Jones, Genevieve 101
Jones, Hank 57, 86
Jones, Ingrid Saunders 18
Jones, James Earl 3, 49, 79
Jones, John 89
Jones, Jonah 39
Jones, K. C. 83
Jones, Lois Mailou 13
Jones, Lou 64
Jones, Marion 21, 66
Jones, Merlakia 34
Jones, Orlando 30
Jones, Papa Jo 99
Jones, Paul R. 76
Jones, Quincy 8, 30
Jones, Randy 35
Jones, Rashida 101
Jones, Robbie 113
Jones, Robert Elijah 90
Jones, Robert G. 81
Jones, Sam 85
Jones, Sarah 39
Jones, Sharon 86
Jones, Tayari 96
Jones, Thad 68
Jones, Theodore T., Jr. 108
Jones, Thomas W. 41
Jones, Van 70
Jones, Wayne 53
Jones, William A., Jr. 61
Jones-Drew, Maurice 113
Joplin, Scott 6
Jordan, Barbara 4, 78
Jordan, Deloris 108
Jordan, Eddie 82
Jordan, Eddie 83
Jordan, June 7, 35
Jordan, Louis 104
Jordan, Michael 6, 21
Jordan, Michael B. 97
Jordan, Montell 23
Jordan, Vernon E. 3, 35
Joseph, Jamal 101
Joseph, Kathie-Ann 56
Josey, E. J. 10
Joyce, Dru 81
Joyner, Marjorie Stewart 26
Joyner, Matilda Sissieretta 15
Joyner, Tom 19, 90
Joyner-Kersee, Jackie 5
Julian, Hubert 90
Julian, Percy Lavon 6
July, William 27
Just, Ernest Everett 3
Justice, David 18
Juvenile 96
Kaigler, Denise 63
Kaiser, Cecil 42
Kandi 83
Kani, Karl 10
Karenga, Maulana 10, 71
Karim, Benjamin 61
Kaufman, Bob 105

Kaufman, Monica 66
Kay, Connie 114
Kay, Ulysses 37
Kearney, Beverly 109
Kearney, Janis 54
Kearse, Amalya Lyle 12
Keckley, Elizabeth 90
Kee, John P. 43
Keene, John 73
Keflezighi, Meb 49
Keith, Damon J. 16, 74
Keith, Floyd A. 61
Kelis 58
Kelley, Cliff 75
Kelley, Elijah 65
Kelley, Malcolm David 59
Kellogg, Clark 64
Kelly, Jim 113
Kelly, Patrick 3
Kelly, R. 18, 44, 71
Kelly, Robin 114
Kem 47
Kemp, Herb 94
Kendrick, Erika 57
Kendricks, Eddie 22
Kennedy, Adrienne 11
Kennedy, Cortez 104
Kennedy, Florynce 12, 33
Kennedy, Randall 40
Kennedy-Overton, Jayne Harris 46
Kenney, John A., Jr. 48
Kenoly, Ron 45
Kenyatta, Robin 54
Kerry, Leon G. 46
Key & Peele 107
Keyes, Alan 11, 105
Keys, Alicia 32, 68
Khalifa, Wiz 96
Khan, Chaka 12, 50
Khanga, Yelena 6
Kid Cudi 83
Kidd, Jason 86
Kidd, Mae Street 39
Killens, John O. 54
Killings, Debra 57
Killingsworth, Cleve, Jr. 54
Kilpatrick, Carolyn Cheeks 16
Kilpatrick, Kwame 34, 71
Kimbro, Dennis 10
Kimbro, Henry A. 25
Kimbro, Warren 76
Kincaid, Bernard 28
Kincaid, Jamaica 4, 109
King, Alonzo 38
King, B. B. 7
King, Barbara 22
King, Bernice 4, 81
King, Colbert I. 69
King, Coretta Scott 3, 57
King, Dexter 10
King, Don 14
King, Freddie 92
King, Gayle 19, 99
King, Martin Luther, III 20
King, Martin Luther, Jr. 1
King, Martin Luther, Sr. 89
King, Preston 28
King, Reatha Clark 65
King, Regina 22, 45
King, Robert Arthur 58
King, Robert Hillary 84
King, Rodney 103
King, Teresa 80

King, Woodie, Jr. 27
King, Yolanda 6
King Curtis 92
Kingston, Sean 94
Kirby, George 14
Kirk, Clara 95
Kirk, Ron 11, 75, 111
Kirkland, Eddie 99
Kitt, Eartha 16, 75
Kitt, Sandra 23
Kittles, Rick 51
Kitwana, Bakari 86
Klugh, Earl 59
Knight, Etheridge 37
Knight, Gladys 16, 66
Knight, Marie 80
Knight, Suge 11, 30, 102
Knowles, Mathew 96
Knowles, Tina 61
Knowling, Robert E., Jr. 38
Knox, Simmie 49
Knuckles, Frankie 42
Komunyakaa, Yusef 9
Kong, B. Waine 50
Kool Moe Dee 37
Koontz, Elizabeth Duncan 101
Kotto, Yaphet 7
Kountz, Samuel L. 10
Kravitz, Lenny 10, 34
Krigger, Kevin 111
KRS-One 34
K-Swift 73
Kunjufu, Jawanza 3, 50
Kweli, Talib 93
La Roca, Pete 107
La Salle, Eriq 12
LaBelle, Patti 13, 30
LaChanze 93
Lacks, Henrietta 101
Lacy, Marc 111
Lacy, Sam 30, 46
Ladd, Ernie 64
Ladner, Joyce A. 42
Lafontant, Jewel Stradford 3, 51
Lamar, Jake 96
Lamar, Kendrick 105
Lampkin, Daisy 19
Lampley, Oni Faida 43, 71
Lancaster, Byard 105
Lance, Major 111
Lane, Charles 3
Lane, Dick 92
Lane, Lunsford 93
Lane, Vincent 5
Lane, William Henry 90
Langford, Larry P. 74
Langhart Cohen, Janet 19, 60
Langston, John Mercer 101
Lanier, Bob 47
Lanier, Willie 33
Lankford, Ray 23
Larkin, Barry 24
Larrieux, Amel 63
Lars, Byron 32
Larsen, Nella 10
Laryea, Thomas Davies, III 67
LaSalle, Denise 111
Lashley, Bobby 63
Lassiter, Roy 24
Lateef, Yusef 91
Lathan, Sanaa 27
Latimer, Lewis H. 4
Lattany, Kristin Hunter 88

Lattimore, Kenny 35
LaVette, Bettye 85
Lavizzo-Mourey, Risa 48
Lawless, Theodore K. 8
Lawrence, Donald 99
Lawrence, Jacob 4, 28
Lawrence, Margaret Morgan 100
Lawrence, Martin 6, 27
Lawrence, Robert H., Jr. 16
Lawrence-Lightfoot, Sara 10
Laws, Hubert 90
Lawson, James M., Jr. 90
Lawson, Jennifer 1, 50
Laymon, Kiese 113
Layton, William 87
Leadbelly 82
Leakes, NeNe 107
Leary, Kathryn D. 10
Leavell, Dorothy R. 17
Lecrae 108
Ledisi 73
Lee, Annie Frances 22
Lee, Barbara 25, 102
Lee, Bertram M., Sr. 46
Lee, Canada 8
Lee, Consuela 84
Lee, Debra L. 62
Lee, Eric P. 79
Lee, Jarena 100
Lee, Joe A. 45
Lee, Joie 1
Lee, Leslie 85
Lee, Malcolm D. 75
Lee, Raphael C. 87
Lee, Robert 112
Lee, Spike 5, 19, 86
Lee-Smith, Hughie 5, 22
Leevy, Carrol M. 42
Leffall, Lasalle, Jr. 3, 64
LeFlore, Lyah Beth 96
Legend, John 67
Leggs, Kingsley 62
Leland, Mickey 2
Lemmons, Kasi 20
Lemon, Alton T. 112
Lemon, Don 94
Lennox, Betty 31
LeNoire, Rosetta 37
Lenox, Adriane 59
Leon, Kenny 10, 98
Leonard, Buck 67
Leonard, Sugar Ray 15
Leslie, Lisa 16, 73
Lester, Bill 42, 85
Lester, Julius 9, 115
Lesure, James 64
LeTang, Henry 66
Letson, Al 39
Levert, Eddie 70
Levert, Gerald 22, 59
Lewis, Ananda 28
Lewis, Aylwin B. 51, 88
Lewis, Butch 71, 99
Lewis, Byron E. 13
Lewis, Carl 4, 97
Lewis, David Levering 9
Lewis, Delano 7
Lewis, Edmonia 10
Lewis, Edward T. 21
Lewis, Emmanuel 36
Lewis, George 104
Lewis, Henry 38
Lewis, Jamal 115

Lewis, John 2, 46, 83
Lewis, Marvin 51, 87
Lewis, Norman 39
Lewis, Oliver 56
Lewis, Ramsey 35, 70
Lewis, Ray 33, 109
Lewis, Reginald F. 6
Lewis, Samella 25
Lewis, Shirley A. R. 14
Lewis, Terry 13
Lewis, Thomas 19
Lewis, William Henry 89
Lewis, William M., Jr. 40
Lewis-Hall, Freda 105
Lewis-Thornton, Rae 32
Ligging, Alfred, III 43
Lighty, Chris 105
Ligon, Glenn 82
Lil' Kim 28
Lil Wayne 66, 84
Liles, Kevin 42, 99
Lincoln, Abbey 3, 88
Lincoln, C. Eric 38
Lindsay, Peta 100
Lindsey, Tommie 51
Lipscomb, Mance 49
LisaRaye 27
Lister, Marquita 65
Liston, Sonny 33
Little, Benilde 21
Little, Booker 105
Little, Floyd 86
Little, Larry 90
Little, Robert L. 2
Little Anthony & the Imperials 107
Little Milton 36, 54
Little Richard 15
Little Walter 36
Littlepage, Craig 35
LL Cool J 16, 49, 94
Llewellyn, J. Bruce 13, 85
Lloyd 99
Lloyd, Earl 26
Lloyd, John Henry "Pop" 30
Lloyd, Reginald 64
Locke, Alain 10
Locke, Attica 85
Locke, Eddie 44
Lofton, James 42
Lofton, Kenny 12
Logan, Onnie Lee 14
Logan, Rayford W. 40
Loguen, J. W. 91
Lomax, Louis E. 90
Lomax, Michael L. 58
Long, Eddie L. 29, 89
Long, Huey 79
Long, Loretta 58
Long, Nia 17, 95
Long, Richard Alexander 65
Lopes, Davey 92
Lopes, Lisa "Left Eye" 36
Lorde, Audre 6
Lott, Ronnie 9
Loueke, Lionel 88
Louis, Errol T. 8
Louis, Joe 5
Louis, Willie 113
Loury, Glenn 36
Love, Darlene 23, 92
Love, Ed 58
Love, Laura 50
Love, Loni 113

Love, Mia 96
Love, Nat 9
Love, Reggie 77
Lovell, Whitfield 74
Lover, Ed 10
Loving, Alvin, Jr. 35, 53
Loving, Mildred 69
Lowe, Herbert 57
Lowe, Sidney 64
Lowery, Evelyn Gibson 115
Lowery, Joseph 2
Lowery, Myron 80
Lowry, A. Leon 60
Lucas, Bill 97
Lucas, John 7
Lucie, Lawrence 80
Lucien, Jon 66
Luckett, Letoya 61
Lucy, William 50
Lucy Foster, Autherine 35
Ludacris 37, 60
Luke, Derek 61
Lumbly, Carl 47
Lumet, Jenny 80
Luna, Donyale 88
Luper, Clara 94
Luter, Fred, Jr. 103
Lyles, Lester Lawrence 31
Lymon, Frankie 22
Lynch, Loretta E. 103
Lynch, Shola 61
Lynch, William, Jr. 115
Lynne, Gloria 115
Lyons, Henry 12
Lyons, James E., Sr. 102
Lyttle, Hulda Margaret 14
Mabley, Moms 15
Mabrey, Vicki 26
Mabry, Marcus 70
Mac, Bernie 29, 61, 72
Mac Daddy 111
Mack, Iris 105
Mack, Tony 104
Mackey, Biz 82
Mackey, Nathaniel 75
Mackie, Anthony 102
Madame Sul-Te-Wan 95
Madhubuti, Haki 7, 85
Madison, Joseph E. 17
Madison, Paula 37, 99
Madison, Romell 45
Madlib 88
Magic Slim 110
Mahal, Taj 39
Mahorn, Rick 60
Maitreya, Sananda 85
Majette, Denise 41
Major, Clarence 9
Majors, Jeff 41
Malco, Romany 71
Mallett, Conrad, Jr. 16
Mallory, Mark 62
Malone, Annie 13
Malone, Karl 18, 51, 90
Malone, Maurice 32
Malone, Moses 79
Malone Jones, Vivian 59
Malveaux, Floyd 54
Malveaux, Julianne 32, 70
Malveaux, Suzanne 88
Mane, Gucci 91
Manigault, Earl "The Goat" 15
Manley, Audrey Forbes 16

Mann, Tamela 92
Manning, Frankie 78
Manuel, Jerry 94
Marable, Manning 10, 102
March, William Carrington 56
Marcille, Eva 97
Marian Anderson String Quartet 111
Mariner, Jonathan 41
Marino, Eugene Antonio 30
Mario 71
Markham, Pigmeat 106
Marrow, Queen Esther 24
Marsalis, Branford 34, 103
Marsalis, Delfeayo 41
Marsalis, Ellis 90
Marsalis, Wynton 16, 90
Marsh, Henry, III 32
Marshall, Bella 22
Marshall, Kerry James 59
Marshall, Paule 7, 77
Marshall, Thurgood 1, 44
Marshall, William 107
Martin, Curtis 104
Martin, Darnell 43, 78
Martin, Duane 108
Martin, Helen 31
Martin, Jesse L. 31
Martin, Louis E. 16
Martin, Michel 97
Martin, Roberta 58
Martin, Roland S. 49, 84
Martin, Ruby Grant 49
Martin, Sara 38
Martin, Trayvon 105
Mase 24
Masekela, Sal 106
Mason, Biddy 89
Mason, Charles Harrison 107
Mason, Felicia 31
Mason, Herman, Jr. 83
Mason, Judi Ann 112
Mason, Ronald 27
Massaquoi, Hans J. 30
Massenburg, Kedar 23, 110
Massey, Brandon 40
Massey, Walter E. 5, 45
Massie, Samuel Proctor, Jr. 29
Master P 21, 115
Matejka, Adrian 87
Mathabane, Mark 5, 99
Mathis, Greg 26
Mathis, Johnny 20
Matson, Ollie 93
Matthews, Ameena 105
Matthews, Benjamin 93
Matthews, Mark 59
Matthews Shatteen, Westina 51
Matzeliger, Jan 93
Maupin, John E., Jr. 92
Maxey, Randall 46
Maxis, Theresa 62
Maxwell 20, 81
May, Derrick 41
Mayberry-Stewart, Melodie 94
Maye, Lee 111
Mayfield, Curtis 2, 43
Mayhew, Martin R. 76
Mayhew, Richard 39
Maynard, Nancy Hicks 73
Maynard, Robert C. 7
Maynor, Dorothy 19
Mayo, Whitman 32
Mays, Benjamin E. 7

Mays, Leslie A. 41
Mays, William G. 34
Mays, Willie 3
Mayweather, Floyd 57, 104
MC Breed 75
M.C. Hammer 20, 80
MC Lyte 34, 108
McAdoo, Bob 75
McAnulty, William E., Jr. 66
McBay, Henry C. 91
McBride, Bryant 18
McBride, Chi 73
McBride, James 35, 87
McCabe, Jewell Jackson 10
McCall, H. Carl 27
McCall, Nathan 8
McCann, Renetta 44
McCarthy, Sandy 64
McCarty, Osceola 16
McCauley, Gina 76
McClellan, George Marion 91
McClendon, Forrest 94
McClendon, Lisa 61
McClinton, Marion Isaac 77
McClurkin, Donnie 25
McCoo, Marilyn 53
McCovey, Willie 103
McCoy, Elijah 8
McCracklin, Jimmy 108
McCrary, Darius 111
McCrary Anthony, Crystal 70
McCray, Nikki 18
McCullough, DeAndre 106
McCullough, Geraldine 58, 79
McDaniel, Hattie 5
McDaniel, Randall Cornell 81
McDaniels, Ralph 79
McDonald, Audra 20, 62
McDonald, Erroll 1
McDonald, Gabrielle Kirk 20
McDougall, Gay J. 11, 43
McDuffie, Dwayne 62
McEwen, Mark 5
McFadden, Bernice L. 39
McFarlan, Tyron 60
McFarland, Roland 49
McFerrin, Bobby 68
McFerrin, Robert, Sr. 94
McGee, Charles 10
McGee, James D. 74
McGee, James Madison 46
McGee, Vonetta 95
McGhee, Heather C. 106
McGhee, Sharon K. 113
McGill, Anthony 76
McGlowan, Angela 64, 86
McGrady, Tracy 80
McGriff, Fred 24
McGriff, Jimmy 72
McGruder, Aaron 28, 56
McGruder, Robert 22, 35
McGuire, Raymond J. 57
McHenry, Donald F. 83
McJunkin, George 93
McKay, Claude 6
McKay, Nellie Yvonne 17, 57
McKee, Lonette 12
McKenzie, Vashti M. 29
McKinney, Cynthia 11, 52, 74
McKinney, Nina Mae 40
McKinney-Whetstone, Diane 27
McKinnon, Isaiah 9
McKissack, Leatrice 80

McKissick, Floyd B. 3
McKnight, Brian 18, 34
McLean, Jackie 78
McLendon, John B., Jr. 89
McLeod, Gus 27
McMillan, Rosalynn A. 36
McMillan, Terry 4, 17, 53
McMillan, Tracy 93
McMurray, Georgia L. 36
McNabb, Donovan 29
McNair, Ronald 3, 58
McNair, Steve 22, 47, 79
McNeil, Lori 1
McPhail, Sharon 2
McPherson, David 32
McPherson, James Alan 70
McQueen, Butterfly 6, 54
McRae, Carmen 77
McRae, Hal 84
McShann, Jay 110
McTell, Blind Willie 89
McWhorter, John 35
McWorter, Free Frank 91
Meadows, Tim 30
Meek, Carrie 6, 36
Meek, Kendrick 41, 89
Meeks, Gregory 25
Meeks, James T. 92
Mehretu, Julie 85
Mell, Patricia 49
Melton, Frank 81
Melton, Harold D. 79
Meminger, Dean 114
Memphis Minnie 33
Memphis Slim 105
Menard, John Willis 90
Mengestu, Dinaw 66, 114
Mercado-Valdes, Frank 43
Meredith, James H. 11
Merkerson, S. Epatha 47, 83
Merriweather, Big Maceo 109
Metcalfe, Ralph 26
Method Man 81
Mfume, Kweisi 6, 41
Michaux, Solomon Lightfoot 91
Micheaux, Oscar 7
Michele, Michael 31
Mickelbury, Penny 28
Mickens, Ronald Elbert 105
Middleton, Reggie 105
Midnight Star 110
Mighty Clouds of Joy 110
Miguel 98
Miles, Buddy 69
Miles, William 112
Millender-McDonald, Juanita 21, 61
Miller, Bebe 3
Miller, Cheryl 10, 74
Miller, Clyde 113
Miller, Dorie 29
Miller, Larry G. 72
Miller, Marcus 84
Miller, Omar Benson 93
Miller, Patina 94
Miller, Pepper 96
Miller, Reggie 33
Miller, Warren F., Jr. 53
Miller, Wentworth 75
Miller-Travis, Vernice 64
Millinder, Lucky 101
Millines Dziko, Trish 28
Millner, Denene 76
Mills, Florence 22

Mills, Joseph C. 51
Mills, Sam 33
Mills, Stephanie 36
Mills, Steve 47
Mills Brothers, The 99
Milner, Ron 39
Milton, DeLisha 31
Minaj, Nicki 86
Ming, Mel 106
Mingo, Frank 32
Mingus, Charles 15
Minkins, Shadrach 104
Minoso, Minnie 89
Minor, DeWayne 32
Mitchell, Arthur 2, 47
Mitchell, Arthur Wergs 91
Mitchell, Brian Stokes 21
Mitchell, Clarence M., Jr. 88
Mitchell, Corinne 8
Mitchell, Dwike 111
Mitchell, Elvis 67
Mitchell, Kel 66
Mitchell, Leona 42
Mitchell, Loften 31
Mitchell, Nicole 66
Mitchell, Parren J. 42, 66
Mitchell, Russ 21, 73
Mitchell, Sam 82
Mitchell, Shireen 89
Mitchell, Stephanie 36
Mitchell, Willie 114
Mo', Keb' 36
Mohammed, Nazr 64
Mohammed, W. Deen 27
Mokae, Zakes 80
Monáe, Janelle 86
Monica 21
Mo'Nique 35, 84
Monk, Art 38, 73
Monk, Thelonious 1
Monroe, Bryan 71
Monroe, Earl 89
Monroe, Mary 35
Montgomery, Isaiah T. 91
Montgomery, Robbie 101
Montgomery, Tim 41
Montgomery, Wes 88
Moody, James 83
Moody-Adams, Michele 76
Moon, Warren 8, 66
Mooney, Paul 37
Moonglows, The 108
Moore, Barbara C. 49
Moore, Chante 26
Moore, Davey 105
Moore, Dorothy Rudd 46
Moore, Gwendolynne S. 55
Moore, Harry T. 29
Moore, Jessica Care 30
Moore, Johnny B. 38
Moore, Juanita 83
Moore, LeRoi 72
Moore, Maya 94
Moore, Melba 21
Moore, Minyon 45
Moore, Shemar 21, 112
Moore, Undine Smith 28
Moore, Wes 86
Moorer, Michael 19
Moose, Charles 40
Moran, Jason 89
Morgan, Garrett 1
Morgan, Gertrude 63

Morgan, Irene 65
Morgan, Joe 9, 96
Morgan, Lee 102
Morgan, Rose 11
Morgan, Tracy 61, 102
Morial, Ernest "Dutch" 26
Morial, Marc H. 20, 51
Morón, Alonzo G. 91
Morris, Garrett 31
Morris, Greg 28
Morris, Mercury 114
Morris, Raheem 77
Morrison, Sam 50
Morrison, Toni 2, 15, 86
Morrison, Vanessa 84
Morrow, E. Frederic 100
Morton, Azie Taylor 48
Morton, Ferdinand Q. 90
Morton, Frederick A., Jr. 93
Morton, Jelly Roll 29
Morton, Joe 18
Moses, Edwin 8
Moses, Gilbert 12
Moses, Robert Parris 11
Mosley, Shane 32
Mosley, Walter 5, 25, 68
Moss, Carlton 17
Moss, J. 64
Moss, Otis, Jr. 72
Moss, Otis, III 72
Moss, Preacher 63
Moss, Randy 23, 90
Mossell, Gertrude Bustill 40
Mossell, Nathan Francis 91
Moten, Etta 18
Motley, Archibald, Jr. 30
Motley, Constance Baker 10, 55
Motley, Marion 26
Moton, Robert Russa 83
Mourning, Alonzo 17, 44
Moutoussamy-Ashe, Jeanne 7
Mowry, Jess 7
Mowry, Tamera 79
Mowry, Tia 78
Moyo, Karega Kofi 36
Moyo, Yvette Jackson 36
Muhammad, Ava 31
Muhammad, Elijah 4
Muhammad, Jabir Herbert 72
Muhammad, Khallid Abdul 10, 31
Mullen, Harryette 34
Mullen, Nicole C. 45
Muncie, Chuck 112
Murphy, Charles 95
Murphy, Eddie 4, 20, 61
Murphy, John H. 42
Murphy, Laura M. 43
Murray, Albert L. 33
Murray, Cecil 12, 47
Murray, Eddie 12
Murray, Lenda 10
Murray, Pauli 38
Murray, Tai 47
Murrell, Sylvia Marilyn 49
Muse, Clarence Edouard 21
Musiq 37, 84
Mya 35
Myers, Lou 110
Myers, Walter Dean 8, 70
Myles, Kim 69
Nabrit, Samuel Milton 47
Nagin, Ray 42, 57, 88
Nail, John E. 92

Nance, Cynthia 71
Nanula, Richard D. 20
Napoleon, Benny N. 23
Nas 33, 111
Nash, Diane 72
Nash, Joe 55
Nash, Johnny 40
Nash, Niecy 66, 115
Nash, Shannon King 84
Nate Dogg 92
Naughton, Naturi 97
Navarro, Fats 104
Naylor, Gloria 10, 42
Ndegeocello, Meshell 15, 83
Neal, Elise 29
Neal, Larry 38
Neal, Mark Anthony 74
Neal, Raful 44
Neals, Otto 73
Nelly 32, 90
Nelson, Jill 6, 54
Nelson, Kadir 115
Nelson, Oliver 113
Nelson, Sophia A. 93
Nelson, Stanley 92
Nelson Meigs, Andrea 48
Neville, Aaron 21
Neville, Arthel 53
New Edition 101
Newcombe, Don 24
Newkirk, Pamela 69
Newman, David 76
Newman, Lester C. 51
Newsome, Ozzie 26
Newton, Cam 96
Newton, Huey 2
Ne-Yo 65
Ngaujah, Sahr 86
Nicholas, Denise 82
Nicholas, Fayard 20, 57
Nicholas, Harold 20
Nichols, Nichelle 11
Nissel, Angela 42
Nix, Robert N. C., Jr. 51
Nixon, Edgar Daniel 100
Nixon, Otis 111
N'Namdi, George R. 17
Noble, Gil 76
Noble, Ronald 46
Noble Drew Ali 100
Norman, Christina 47
Norman, Jessye 5
Norman, Maidie 20
Norman, Pat 10
Norris, Michele 83
Northup, Solomon 115
Norton, Eleanor Holmes 7, 93
Norton, Ken 101, 115
Norton, Meredith 72
Notorious B.I.G. 20
Nottage, Lynn 66
Nugent, Richard Bruce 39
Nunez, Elizabeth 62, 112
Nunn, Annetta 43
Nutter, Michael 69, 112
Obadele, Imari 84
Obama, Barack 49, 74, 91
Obama, Michelle 61, 90
O'Brien, Soledad 88
Ocean, Frank 100
Odetta 37, 74
Odom, Lamar 81
Ogden, Jonathan 110

Oglesby, Zena 12
Ogletree, Charles, Jr. 12, 47
O'Grady, Lorraine 73
Ojikutu, Bayo 66
Ojikutu, Bisola 65
Ol' Dirty Bastard 52
Olden, Georg(e) 44
O'Leary, Hazel 6
Oliver, Garrett 95
Oliver, Jerry 37
Oliver, Joe "King" 42
Oliver, John J., Jr. 48
Oliver, Kimberly 60
Oliver, Pam 54
Oliver, Paul 115
Omarion 107
Omarosa 69, 110
112 114
O'Neal, Frederick 99
O'Neal, Patrice 99
O'Neal, Rodney 88
O'Neal, Ron 46
O'Neal, Shaquille 8, 30, 95
O'Neal, Stanley 38, 67
O'Neil, Buck 19, 59
Onyewu, Oguchi 60
Orange, James 74
Orioles, The 100
Orlandersmith, Dael 42
Orman, Roscoe 55
Ormes, Jackie 73
Osbey, Brenda Marie 102
Osborne, Jeffrey 26
Osborne, Na'taki 54
Otis, Clarence, Jr. 55
Otis, Clyde 67
Ouattara, Morou 74
Owens, Helen 48
Owens, Jack 38
Owens, Jesse 2
Owens, Major 6
Owens, Terrell 53, 106
Pace, Betty 59
Pace, Orlando 21
Packer, Daniel 56
Packer, Will 71
Packer, Z. Z. 64
Page, Alan 7
Page, Clarence 4
Page, Greg 78
Page, Inman 82
Paige, Rod 29
Paige, Satchel 7
Painter, Nell Irvin 24, 88
Palmer, Keke 68
Palmer, Rissi 65
Palmer, Violet 59
Parham, Marjorie B. 71
Parish, Robert 43
Parker, Barrington D. 92
Parker, Candace 74
Parker, Charlie 20
Parker, Jim 64
Parker, Kellis E. 30
Parker, Maceo 72
Parker, Nicole Ari 52
Parker, Pat 19
Parker, Ray, Jr. 85
Parker, Star 70
Parker, Vernon 97
Parks, Bernard C. 17
Parks, Gordon 1, 35, 58
Parks, Henry Green, Jr. 89

Parks, Rosa 1, 35, 56
Parks, Suzan-Lori 34, 85
Parlan, Horace 108
Parr, Russ 51
Parsons, James 14
Parsons, Richard Dean 11, 33
Paterson, Basil A. 69
Paterson, David A. 59
Patrick, Deval 12, 61
Patterson, Floyd 19, 58
Patterson, Frederick Douglass 12
Patterson, Gilbert Earl 41
Patterson, J. O., Jr. 80
Patterson, Louise 25
Patterson, Mary Jane 54
Patton, Antwan 45
Patton, Charley 107
Patton, Paula 62
Paul, Chris 84, 100
Payne, Allen 13
Payne, Donald M. 2, 57, 112
Payne, Ethel L. 28
Payne, Freda 58
Payne, Les 89
Payne, Ulice, Jr. 42
Payne, William D. 60
Payton, Benjamin F. 23
Payton, Gary 99
Payton, John 48
Payton, Philip A., Jr. 88
Payton, Walter 11, 25
Pearson, Felicia 99
Peck, Carolyn 23
Peebles, Ann 114
Peete, Calvin 11
Peete, Holly Robinson 20
Peete, Rodney 60
Pena, Paul 58
Pendergrass, Teddy 22, 83
Penguins, The 107
Peoples, Dottie 22
Perez, Anna 1
Perkins, Eddie 103
Perkins, Edward 5
Perkins, James, Jr. 55
Perkins, Marion 38
Perkins, Pinetop 70
Perkins, Tony 24
Perren, Freddie 60
Perrineau, Harold, Jr. 51
Perrot, Kim 23
Perry, Herman 89
Perry, James 83
Perry, Joe 95
Perry, Laval 64
Perry, Lowell 30
Perry, Matthew J., Jr. 96
Perry, Steve 98
Perry, Tyler 40, 54, 103
Perry, Warren 56
Person, Waverly 9, 51
Peters, Brock 96
Peters, Clarke 103
Peters, Margaret 43
Peters, Matilda 43
Petersen, Frank E. 31
Peterson, Adrian 109
Peterson, James 38
Peterson, James 81
Peterson, Jesse Lee 81
Peterson, Karen Carter 90
Peterson, Marvin "Hannibal" 27
Petioni, Muriel 99

Petry, Ann **19**
Pettiford, Oscar **106**
Phifer, Mekhi **25, 103**
Phillips, Carl **111**
Phillips, Charles E., Jr. **57, 109**
Phillips, Esther **107**
Phillips, Helen L. **63**
Phillips, Joseph C. **73**
Phillips, Teresa L. **42**
Phipps, Wintley **59**
Pickens, James, Jr. **59**
Pickett, Bill **11**
Pickett, Cecil **39**
Pierce, Elijah **84**
Pierce, Harold **75**
Pierce, Paul **71**
Pierce, Wendell **90**
Pierre, Percy Anthony **46**
Pincham, R. Eugene, Sr. **69**
Pinchback, P. B. S. **9**
Pinckney, Bill **42**
Pinckney, Sandra **56**
Pindell, Howardena **55**
Pinder, Jefferson **77**
Pinderhughes, John **47**
Pinkett, Randal **61**
Pinkett Smith, Jada **10, 41, 95**
Pinkney, Fayette **80**
Pinkney, Jerry **15**
Pinkston, W. Randall **24**
Pinn, Vivian Winona **49**
Piper, Adrian **71**
Pippen, Scottie **15, 89**
Pippin, Horace **9**
Pitts, Byron **71**
Pitts, Derrick **77**
Pitts, Leonard, Jr. **54, 85**
Pitts, Robb **84**
Pitts, Skip **103**
Platters, The **99**
Player, Willa B. **43**
Pleasant, Mary Ellen **9**
Pleasure P **84**
Plessy, Homer Adolph **31**
Plinton, James O., Jr. **98**
P.M. Dawn **54**
Poindexter, Hildrus A. **87**
Poitier, Sidney **11, 36**
Poitier, Sydney Tamiia **65**
Polite, Carlene Hatcher **82**
Pollard, Fritz **53**
Pollard, William L. **91**
Pope.L, William **72**
Porter, Billy **112**
Porter, James A. **11**
Porter, Terry **75**
Potter, Myrtle **40**
Pough, Terrell **58**
Pounder, CCH **72**
Poussaint, Alvin F. **5, 67**
Poussaint, Renee **78**
Powell, Adam Clayton, Jr. **3**
Powell, Benny **87**
Powell, Bud **24**
Powell, Colin **1, 28, 75**
Powell, Debra A. **23**
Powell, Keith **101**
Powell, Kevin **31, 74**
Powell, Maxine **8, 115**
Powell, Michael **32**
Powell, Mike **7**
Powell, Renee **34**
Powell, William J. **82**

Power, Will **83**
Pratt, Awadagin **31**
Pratt, Geronimo **18, 95**
Pratt, Kyla **57**
Preer, Evelyn **82**
Premice, Josephine **41**
Pressley, Condace L. **41**
Preston, Billy **39, 59**
Price, David **101**
Price, Florence **37**
Price, Frederick K. C. **21**
Price, Glenda **22**
Price, Hugh B. **9, 54**
Price, Kelly **23**
Price, Leontyne **1**
Price, Lisa **97**
Price, Richard **51**
Pride, Charley **26**
Primas, Randy **106**
Primus, Pearl **6**
Prince **18, 65**
Prince, Richard E. **71**
Prince, Ron **64**
Prince, Tayshaun **68**
Prince-Bythewood, Gina **31, 77**
Pritchard, Robert Starling **21**
Procope, Ernesta **23**
Procope, John Levy **56**
Professor Longhair **109**
Proof **101**
Prophet, Nancy Elizabeth **42**
Prothrow-Stith, Deborah **10**
Pruitt, Wendell O. **106**
Pryce, Trevor **89**
Pryor, Rain **65**
Pryor, Richard **3, 24, 56**
Puckett, Kirby **4, 58**
Pugh, Charles **81**
Purdie, Bernard **77**
Purnell, Silas **59**
Puryear, Martin **42, 101**
Putney, Martha S. **75**
Quander, Nellie **102**
Quarles, Benjamin Arthur **18**
Quarles, Norma **25**
Quarterman, Lloyd Albert **4**
Queen Latifah **1, 16, 58**
?uestlove **74**
Quigless, Helen G. **49**
Quince, Peggy A. **69**
Quivers, Robin **61**
Rabb, Maurice F., Jr. **58**
Radcliffe, Ted **74**
Ragin, Derek Lee **84**
Rahman, Aishah **37**
Raines, Franklin **14, 107**
Raines, Tim **107**
Rainey, Ma **33**
Ralph, Sheryl Lee **18, 108**
Ramsey, Charles H. **21, 69**
Rand, A. Barry **6**
Randall, Alice **38**
Randall, Dudley **8, 55**
Randall, Vernellia R. **95**
Randle, John **87**
Randle, Theresa **16**
Randolph, A. Philip **3**
Randolph, Linda A. **52**
Randolph, Willie **53**
Rangel, Charles B. **3, 52, 85**
Ransome, James E. **88**
Raoul, Kwame **55**
Rapier, James T. **82**

Rashad, Ahmad **18**
Rashad, Phylicia **21**
Raspberry, William **2**
Ravens, The **103**
Raven-Symoné **44, 113**
Rawlings-Blake, Stephanie **93**
Rawlinson, Johnnie B. **79**
Rawls, Lou **17, 57**
Ray, Carline **113**
Ray, Charlotte E. **60**
Ray, Gene Anthony **47**
Ray J **86**
Razaf, Andy **19**
Reagins, Tony **94**
Reagon, Bernice Johnson **7**
Reagon, Toshi **76**
Reason, J. Paul **19**
Reaves, Donald J. **102**
Record, Eugene **60**
Redd, Dana **93**
Reddick, Lance **52**
Reddick, Lawrence Dunbar **20**
Redding, Ann Holmes **77**
Redding, J. Saunders **26**
Redding, Louis L. **26**
Redding, Otis **16**
Redman **81**
Redman, Joshua **30**
Redmond, Eugene **23**
Redwood, John Henry **78**
Reece, Marcel **114**
Reed, A. C. **36**
Reed, Ishmael **8**
Reed, Jimmy **38**
Reed, Joe L. **110**
Reed, Kasim **82**
Reed, Natina **106**
Reed, Willis, Jr. **86**
Reed Hall, Alaina **83**
Reedy, Jessica **101**
Reems, Ernestine Cleveland **27**
Rees, Dee **100**
Reese, Della **6, 20, 96**
Reese, Jerry **103**
Reese, Milous J., Jr. **51**
Reese, Pokey **28**
Reese, Tracy **54**
Reeves, Bass **100**
Reeves, Dianne **32**
Reeves, Gregory **49**
Reeves, Martha **85**
Reeves, Rachel J. **23**
Reeves, Triette Lipsey **27**
Reid, Antonio "L.A." **28**
Reid, Ira De A. **100**
Reid, Irvin D. **20**
Reid, Senghor **55**
Reid, Tim **56**
Reid, Vernon **34**
Revels, Hiram Rhoades **98**
Reverend Ike **79**
Reynolds, Harold **77**
Reynolds, Star Jones **10, 27, 61**
Rhames, Ving **14, 50**
Rhimes, Shonda Lynn **67**
Rhoden, Dwight **40**
Rhoden, William C. **67**
Rhodes, Jewell Parker **84**
Rhodes, Ray **14**
Rhone, Sylvia **2**
Rhymefest **97**
Rhymes, Busta **31**
Rhyne, Melvin **109**

Ribbs, Willy T. **2**
Ribeau, Sidney **70**
Ribeiro, Alfonso **17**
Rice, Condoleezza **3, 28, 72**
Rice, Constance LaMay **60**
Rice, Emmett J. **94**
Rice, Jerry **5, 55, 89**
Rice, Jim **75**
Rice, Linda Johnson **9, 41**
Rice, Louise Allen **54**
Rice, Norm **8**
Rice, Ray **112**
Rice, Susan **74, 103**
Richard, Dawn **92**
Richard, J. R. **87**
Richards, Beah **30**
Richards, Hilda **49**
Richards-Ross, Sanya **66, 98**
Richardson, Desmond **39**
Richardson, Donna **39**
Richardson, Julieanna **81**
Richardson, LaTanya **71**
Richardson, Laura **81**
Richardson, Nolan **9**
Richardson, Rupert **67**
Richardson, Salli **68**
Richie, Leroy C. **18**
Richie, Lionel **27, 65, 114**
Richmond, Cedric **93**
Richmond, Mitch **19**
Rideau, Iris **46**
Ridley, John **69**
Riggins, Karriem **102**
Riggs, Marlon **5, 44**
Riles, Wilson C. **79**
Riley, Amber **97**
Riley, Boots **89**
Riley, Helen Caldwell Day **13**
Riley, Rochelle **50**
Rillieux, Norbert **92**
Ringgold, Faith **4, 81**
Riperton, Minnie **32**
Rivers, Doc **25, 81**
Rivers, Eugene F., III **81**
Rivers, Sam **95**
Roach, Max **21, 63**
Roaf, Andrée Layton **106**
Roaf, Willie **106**
Roberts, Darryl **70**
Roberts, Deborah **35**
Roberts, Kimberly Rivers **72**
Roberts, Lillian **83**
Roberts, Marcus **19, 113**
Roberts, Mike **57**
Roberts, Robin **16, 54, 113**
Roberts, Roy S. **14**
Robertson, Gil L., IV **85**
Robertson, Oscar **26**
Robeson, Eslanda Goode **13**
Robeson, Paul **2**
Robey, Don **115**
Robinson, Aminah **50**
Robinson, Bill "Bojangles" **11**
Robinson, Bishop L. **66**
Robinson, Cleo Parker **38**
Robinson, Craig **103**
Robinson, Craig **107**
Robinson, Dave **110**
Robinson, David **24, 90**
Robinson, Eddie G. **10**
Robinson, Eugene **77**
Robinson, Fatima **34**
Robinson, Fenton **38**

Robinson, Flynn 112
Robinson, Frank 9, 87
Robinson, Ida B. 106
Robinson, Jackie 6
Robinson, Joann Gibson 100
Robinson, LaVaughn 69
Robinson, Malcolm S. 44
Robinson, Matt 69
Robinson, Max 3
Robinson, Patrick 19, 71
Robinson, Rachel 16
Robinson, Randall 7, 46
Robinson, Reginald R. 53
Robinson, Sharon 22
Robinson, Shaun 36
Robinson, Smokey 3, 49
Robinson, Spottswood W., III 22
Robinson, Sugar Ray 18
Robinson, Sylvia 79
Robinson, Will 51, 69
Robinson-Berry, Joan 94
Roble, Abdi 71
Roby, Kimberla Lawson 86
Roche, Joyce M. 17
Rochon, Lela 16
Rochon, Stephen W. 78
Rock, Chris 3, 22, 66
Rock, John S. 113
Rock, The 29, 66
Rock, Tony 108
Rodgers, Johnathan 6, 51
Rodgers, Rod 36
Rodman, Dennis 12, 44, 96
Rodriguez, Cheryl 64
Rodriguez, Jimmy 47
Rogers, Alan G. 72
Rogers, Bobby 110
Rogers, Desirée 88
Rogers, Jimmy 38
Rogers, Joe 27
Rogers, Joel Augustus 30
Rogers, John W., Jr. 5, 52
Rogers, Rodney Ray 106
Roker, Al 12, 49
Roker, Roxie 68
Rolle, Esther 13, 21
Rolle, Janet 97
Rolle, Myron 98
Rollins, Charlemae Hill 27
Rollins, Howard E., Jr. 16
Rollins, Jimmy 70
Rollins, Sonny 37, 94
Romanthony 115
Romeo 98
Rondo, Rajon 111
Roots, The 101
Rose, Anika Noni 70
Rose, Derrick 82
Rose, Jalen 108
Ross, Charles 27
Ross, Diana 8, 27
Ross, Don 27
Ross, Isaiah "Doc" 40
Ross, Rick 79, 104
Ross, Tracee Ellis 35
Ross-Lee, Barbara 67
Roundfield, Danny 109
Roundtree, Dovey 80
Roundtree, Richard 27
Rouse, Cecilia 93
Rowan, Carl T. 1, 30
Rowe-Adams, Jackie 109
Rowell, Victoria 13, 68

Rowland, Kelly 100
Roxanne Shante 33
Roy, Brandon 98
Roy, Kenny 51
Rubin, Chanda 37
Rucker, Darius 34, 74, 108
Rudolph, Maya 46, 106
Rudolph, Wilma 4
Ruffin, Josephine St. Pierre 75
Ruffins, Kermit 85
Ruley, Ellis 38
Run 31, 73, 75
RuPaul 17, 91
Rush, Bobby 26, 76
Rush, Bobby 78
Rush, Otis 38
Rushen, Patrice 12
Rushing, Jimmy 37
Russell, Bill 8
Russell, Brenda 52
Russell, Herman Jerome 17
Russell, Nipsey 66
Russell-McCloud, Patricia A. 17
Russwurm, John Brown 100
Rust, Art, Jr. 83
Rustin, Bayard 4
RZA 80
Saar, Alison 16
Saar, Betye 80
Sabathia, CC 74
St. Jacques, Raymond 8
Saint James, Synthia 12
St. John, Kristoff 25
St. Julien, Marlon 29
St. Patrick, Mathew 48
Saldana, Zoe 72
Sallee, Charles 38
Salter, Nikkole 73
Salters, Lisa 71
Sam and Dave 102
Samara, Noah 15
Sample, Joe 51
Sampson, Charles 13
Sanchez, Sonia 17, 51
Sanders, Angelia 86
Sanders, Barry 1, 53
Sanders, Bob 72
Sanders, Deion 4, 31, 96
Sanders, Joseph R., Jr. 11
Sanders, Malika 48
Sanders, Pharoah 64
Sanders, Satch 77
Sands, Diana 87
Sanford, Isabel 53
Sanneh, Kelefa 96
Santamaria, Mongo 81
Santiago-Hudson, Ruben 85
Santigold 96
Sapp, Marvin 74
Sapp, Warren 38, 109
Sapphire 14, 95
Sasser, Sean 113
Satcher, David 7, 57, 111
Savage, Augusta 12
Sawyer, Eugene 81
Sayers, Gale 28
Sayles Belton, Sharon 9, 16
Sbraga, Kevin 88
Scantlebury-White, Velma 64
Schiavocampo, Mara 97
Schmoke, Kurt 1, 48
Schuyler, George Samuel 40
Schuyler, Philippa 50

Scott, C(ornelius) A(dolphus) 29
Scott, David 41
Scott, Dread 106
Scott, George 55
Scott, George 113
Scott, Harold Russell, Jr. 61
Scott, Hazel 66
Scott, Jill 29, 83
Scott, John T. 65
Scott, "Little" Jimmy 48
Scott, Milton 51
Scott, Robert C. 23
Scott, Stuart 34
Scott, Tim 87
Scott, Wendell Oliver, Sr. 19
Scott-Heron, Gil 94
Scott-Young, Mona 101
Scurry, Briana 27
Seals, Son 56
Sears, Leah Ward 5, 79
Sears, Stephanie 53
Sebree, Charles 40
Secada, Jon 97
Seele, Pernessa 46
Seele, John 18
Senna, Danzy 93
Sermon, Erick 81
Serrano, Andres 3
Sewell, Terri 93
Seymour, Richard 101
Seymour, Teddy 110
Seymour, William J. 106
Shabazz, Attallah 6
Shabazz, Betty 7, 26
Shabazz, Ilyasah 36
Shadd, Abraham D. 81
Shakur, Afeni 67
Shakur, Assata 6
Shakur, Tupac 14
Shakur, Yusef 85
Shange, Ntozake 8, 89
Shanice 112
Shank, Suzanne F. 77
Shannon, Randy 82
Sharpe, Shannon 97
Sharper, Darren 32
Sharpton, Al 21, 97
Shavers, Cheryl 31
Shaw, Bernard 2, 28
Shaw, Marlena 105
Shaw, William J. 30
Sheard, Kierra 61, 114
Sheffield, Gary 16, 108
Shell, Art 1, 66
Shelton, Paula Young 86
Shepherd, Sherri 55
Shepp, Archie 101
Sherrod, Clayton 17
Sherrod, Shirley 87
Shider, Garry 87
Shinhoster, Earl 32
Shipp, E. R. 15
Shipp, Matthew 107
Shippen, John 43
Shirelles, The 111
Shirley, Donald 111
Shirley, George 33
Shockley, Ann Allen 84
Shores, Arthur D. 99
Short, Bobby 52
Short, Columbus 79
Shorter, Wayne 75
Showers, Reggie 30

Shropshire, Thomas B. 49
Shuttlesworth, Fred 47, 98
Sidibe, Gabourey 84
Sidner, Sara 105
Sifford, Charlie 4, 49
Sigur, Wanda 44
Silas, Paul 24
Silver, Horace 26
Siméus, Dumas M. 25, 110
Simkins, Modjeska Monteith 112
Simmons, Bob 29
Simmons, E. Denise 79
Simmons, Gary 58
Simmons, Henry 55
Simmons, Jamal 72
Simmons, Kimora Lee 51, 83
Simmons, Russell 1, 30
Simmons, Ruth J. 13, 38
Simms, Margaret 94
Simon, Joe 109
Simon, Lateefah 95
Simone, Nina 15, 41
Simpson, Carole 6, 30
Simpson, Lorna 4, 36
Simpson, Merton D. 110
Simpson, O. J. 15, 100
Simpson, Valerie 21, 97
Simpson-Hoffman, N'kenge 52
Sims, Danny 106
Sims, Howard "Sandman" 48
Sims, Lowery Stokes 27
Sims, Naomi 29, 79
Sinbad 1, 16
Singletary, Mike 4, 76
Singleton, John 2, 30
Sinkford, Jeanne C. 13
Sir Mix-A-Lot 82
Sisqo 30
Sissle, Noble 29
Sister Souljah 11, 100
Sizemore, Barbara A. 26, 110
Sizemore, Grady 96
Skinner, Kiron K. 65
Sklarek, Norma Merrick 25, 101
Slater, Rodney E. 15
Slaughter, John Brooks 53
Sledge, Percy 39
Sleet, Gregory M. 109
Sleet, Moneta, Jr. 5
Slice, Kimbo 73
Slick Rick 93
Slim Thug 86
Slocumb, Jonathan 52
Slyde, Jimmy 70
Smalls, Robert 82
Smaltz, Audrey 12
Smiley, Rickey 59
Smiley, Tavis 20, 68
Smith, Amanda Berry 109
Smith, Anna Deavere 6, 44
Smith, B(arbara) 11
Smith, Barbara 28
Smith, Bessie 3
Smith, Bruce 80
Smith, Bruce W. 53
Smith, Bubba 96
Smith, Cecilia 102
Smith, Cladys "Jabbo" 32
Smith, Clarence 113
Smith, Clarence O. 21
Smith, Damu 54
Smith, Danyel 40
Smith, DeMaurice 92

Smith, Dr. Lonnie 49
Smith, Emmitt 7, 87
Smith, Greg 28
Smith, Hilton 29
Smith, Ian 62
Smith, Jaden 82
Smith, Jane E. 24
Smith, Jessie Carney 35
Smith, John L. 22
Smith, Joshua 10
Smith, Kemba 70
Smith, Kenny 114
Smith, LaQuan 113
Smith, Lee 101
Smith, Lonnie Liston 49
Smith, Lovie 66, 107
Smith, Malcolm A. 75
Smith, Mamie 32
Smith, Marie F. 70
Smith, Marvin 46
Smith, Mary Carter 26
Smith, Ming 100
Smith, Morgan 46
Smith, Myrna 92
Smith, Nate 49
Smith, Neil 109
Smith, Ozzie 77
Smith, Princella 86
Smith, Randy 81
Smith, Reggie 113
Smith, Rick 72
Smith, Roger Guenveur 12
Smith, Stephen A. 69
Smith, Stuff 37
Smith, Tasha 73
Smith, Tommie 102
Smith, Trixie 34
Smith, Tubby 18, 83
Smith, Vincent D. 48
Smith, Will 8, 18, 53
Smith, Willi 8
Smith, Willie 107
Smith, Willow 92
Smyre, Calvin 90
Smythe Haith, Mabel 61
Sneed, Paula A. 18
Snipes, Wesley 3, 24, 67
Snoop Dogg 35, 84
Snow, Samuel 71
Snowden, Frank M., Jr. 67
Snowden, Gail 108
Sohn, Sonja 100
Solange 97
Solomon, Jimmie Lee 38
Somi 85
Sommore 61
Songz, Trey 88
Southern, Eileen 56
Southgate, Martha 58
Sowell, Thomas 2, 99
Spaniels, The 105
Spann, Otis 107
Sparks, Jordin 66
Spaulding, Charles Clinton 9
Spearman, Leonard H. O., Sr. 81
Spears, Warren 52
Spector, Ronnie 77
Speech 82
Spencer, Anne 27
Spencer, Michael G. 87
Spencer, Octavia 100
Spencer, Vaino H. 99
Spigner, Archie 81

Spikes, Dolores 18
Spiller, Bill 64
Sprewell, Latrell 23
Spriggs, William 67
Springer, Ashton, Jr. 115
Stackhouse, Jerry 30
Staley, Dawn 57
Stallings, George A., Jr. 6
Stallworth, John 102
Stampley, Micah 54
Stanford, John 20
Stanford, Olivia Lee Dilworth 49
Stanton, Alysa 78
Stanton, Robert 20
Staples, Brent 8
Staples, Cleotha 113
Staples, Mavis 50, 88
Staples, "Pops" 32
Stargell, Willie 29
Staton, Candi 27
Staton, Dakota 62
Staupers, Mabel K. 7
Stearnes, Norman "Turkey" 31
Steave-Dickerson, Kia 57
Steele, Claude 13, 97
Steele, Lawrence 28
Steele, Michael 38, 73, 91
Steele, Sage 115
Steele, Shelby 13, 82
Steinberg, Martha Jean "The
    Queen" 28
Stephens, Charlotte Andrews 14
Stephens, Sloane 105
Stew 69
Steward, David L. 36
Steward, Emanuel 18, 106
Stewart, Alison 13
Stewart, Billy 112
Stewart, Ella 39
Stewart, James, Jr. 60, 98
Stewart, Kordell 21, 111
Stewart, Maria W. Miller 19
Stewart, Nzingha 89
Stewart, Paul Wilbur 12
Stewart, Tonea Harris 78
Stewart, Tricky 98
Stickney, Phyllis Yvonne 108
Sticky Fingaz 86
Still, William Grant 37
Stingley, Darryl 69
Stinson, Denise L. 59
Stith, Charles R. 73
Stith, Tom 93
Stokes, Carl 10, 73
Stokes, Louis 3
Stone, Angie 31
Stone, Chuck 9
Stone, Jesse 98
Stone, Sly 85
Stone, Toni 15
Stoney, Michael 50
Stoudemire, Amar'e 59, 106
Stout, Juanita Kidd 24
Stout, Renee 63
Stoute, Steve 38
Stowers, Freddie 107
Stradford, J. B. 101
Strahan, Michael 35, 81
Strautmanis, Michael 87
Strawberry, Darryl 22
Strayhorn, Billy 31
Street, John F. 24
Street, Richard 110

Streeter, Sarah 45
Streeter, Sevyn 115
Stringer, C. Vivian 13, 66
Stringer, Korey 35
Stringer, Vickie 58
Strode, Woody 111
Strong, Barrett 89
Studdard, Ruben 46
Sudarkasa, Niara 4
Sudduth, Jimmy Lee 65
Sugarhill Gang, The 79
Suggs, Terrell 108
Sullivan, Jazmine 81
Sullivan, Leon H. 3, 30
Sullivan, Louis 8
Sullivan, Maxine 37
Sumlin, Hubert 101
Summer, Donna 25, 102
Sumner, Francis Cecil 112
Sun Ra 60
Sundiata, Sekou 66
Sutphen, Mona 77
Suttles, Mule 108
Sutton, Percy E. 42, 82
Swan Silvertones, The 110
Swann, Bettye 109
Swann, Lynn 28
Sweat, Keith 19
Sweatshirt, Earl 114
Sweatt, Heman Marion 114
Sweet, Ossian 68
Sweet Honey in the Rock 106
Swizz Beatz 108
Swoopes, Sheryl 12, 56
Swygert, H. Patrick 22
Sykes, Roosevelt 20
Sykes, Wanda 48, 81
Syler, Rene 53
Tademy, Lalita 36
Tail Dragger 112
Tait, Michael 57
Take 6 112
Talbert, David E. 34, 93
Talbert, Mary B. 77
Talley, André Leon 56, 106
Tamar-kali 63
Tamia 24, 55
Tampa Red 63
Tancil, Gladys Quander 59
Tanksley, Ann 37
Tanner, Henry Ossawa 1
Tanner, Jack E. 100
Taste of Honey, A 115
Tate, Buddy 108
Tate, Eleanora E. 20, 55
Tate, Grady 106
Tate, John 107
Tate, Larenz 15
Tatum, Art 28
Tatum, Beverly Daniel 42, 84
Tatum, Elinor R. 78
Tatum, Jack 87
Tatum, Reece 104
Tatum, Wilbert 76
Taulbert, Clifton Lemoure 19
Tavares 115
Taylor, Billy 23, 92
Taylor, Bo 72
Taylor, Cecil 70
Taylor, Charles 20
Taylor, Ephren W., II 61
Taylor, Gardner C. 76

Taylor, Helen (Lavon Hollingshed)
    30
Taylor, Jason 70
Taylor, Jermain 60
Taylor, Koko 40, 80
Taylor, Kristin Clark 8
Taylor, Lawrence 25
Taylor, Lonzie Odie 96
Taylor, Marshall Walter "Major" 62
Taylor, Meshach 4
Taylor, Mildred D. 26
Taylor, Natalie 47
Taylor, Recy 92
Taylor, Regina 9, 46, 97
Taylor, Robert Robinson 80
Taylor, Robert Rochon 104
Taylor, Ron 35
Taylor, Susan C. 62
Taylor, Susan L. 10, 86
Taylor, Susie King 13
T-Boz 108
Tchicai, John 102
Teague, Bob 111
Teasley, Lisa 92
Teer, Barbara Ann 81
Temple, Ed 109
Temple, Lewis 102
Terrell, Dorothy A. 24
Terrell, Mary Church 9
Terrell, Tammi 32
Terrell-Kearney, Kim 83
Terrence J 108
Terry, Clark 39
Terry, Sonny 88
Tharpe, Rosetta 65
The-Dream 74
Thigpen, Ed 110
Thigpen, Lynne 17, 41
Thomas, Alma 14
Thomas, Arthur Ray 52
Thomas, Carla 96
Thomas, Clarence 2, 39, 65
Thomas, Claudia Lynn 64
Thomas, Debi 26
Thomas, Derrick 25
Thomas, Emmitt 71
Thomas, Frank 12, 51
Thomas, Franklin A. 5, 49
Thomas, Irma 29
Thomas, Isiah 7, 26, 65
Thomas, Jefferson 88
Thomas, Michael 69
Thomas, Mickalene 61
Thomas, Rozonda 34, 78
Thomas, Rufus 20, 96
Thomas, Sean Patrick 35
Thomas, Thurman 75
Thomas, Trisha R. 65
Thomas, Vivien 9
Thomas-Graham, Pamela 29
Thomas-Greenfield, Linda 99
Thompson, Bennie G. 26
Thompson, Cynthia Bramlett 50
Thompson, Don 56, 108
Thompson, John Douglas 81
Thompson, John W. 26
Thompson, Kenan 52
Thompson, Larry D. 39
Thompson, Tazewell 13
Thompson, Tina 25, 75
Thompson, William C., Jr. 35, 114
Thoms, Tracie 61
Thornton, Big Mama 33

Thornton, Yvonne S. 69
Thrash, Dox 35
Threadgill, Henry 97
Thrower, Willie 35
Thurman, Howard 3
Thurman, Wallace 16
Thurmond, Nate 88
Thurston, Baratunde 79, 101
Thurston, Stephen J. 49
Tiant, Luis 102
Till, Emmett 7
Tillard, Conrad 47
Tillis, Frederick 40
Tillman, Deborah 98
Tillman, Dorothy 76
Tillman, George, Jr. 20
Timbaland 32
Tingling, Milton A. 110
Tinsley, Boyd 50
Tirico, Mike 68
Tisdale, Wayman 50
Tobias, Channing H. 79
Tobin, Patricia 75
Todman, Terence A. 55
Tolbert, James L. 112
Tolbert, Terence 74
Toler, Burl 80
Tolliver, Mose 60
Tolliver, William 9
Tolson, Melvin 37
Tolton, Augustine 62
Tomlinson, LaDainian 65, 112
Tonex 54
Toney, James 89
Tooks, Lance 62
Toomer, Jean 6
Toote, Gloria E. A. 64
Torres, Gina 52
Torry, Guy 31
Touré, Askia (Muhammad Abu Bakr
    el) 47
Touré, Faya Ora Rose 56
Toussaint, Allen 60
Towns, Edolphus 19, 75
Townsend, Robert 4, 23
T-Pain 73, 111
Trammps, The 108
Travis, Tracey T. 94
Tresvant, Ralph 57
Trethewey, Natasha 103
Tribbett, Tye 81
Tribble, Israel, Jr. 8
Trina 114
Trombone Shorty 97
Trotter, Donne E. 28
Trotter, Lloyd G. 56
Trotter, Monroe 9
Troupe, Quincy 83
Trouppe, Quincy Thomas, Sr. 84
True, Rachel 82
Trueheart, William E. 49
Tubbs Jones, Stephanie 24, 72
Tubman, Harriet 9
Tucker, C. Delores 12, 56
Tucker, Chris 13, 23, 62
Tucker, Cynthia 15, 61
Tucker, Rosina 14
Tuckson, Reed V. 71
Tunie, Tamara 63
Tunnell, Emlen 54
Turman, Glynn 100
Turnbull, Charles Wesley 62
Turnbull, Walter 13, 60

Turner, Big Joe 92
Turner, Henry McNeal 5
Turner, Ike 68
Turner, Tina 6, 27
2 Chainz 105
Tyler, Aisha N. 36
Tyler, the Creator 100
Tyner, McCoy 92
Tyree, Omar Rashad 21
Tyson, Andre 40
Tyson, Asha 39
Tyson, Cicely 7, 51, 112
Tyson, Mike 28, 44, 93
Tyson, Neil deGrasse 15, 65
Uggams, Leslie 23, 114
Ulmer, James 79
Underwood, Blair 7, 27, 76
Union, Gabrielle 31, 92
Unseld, Wes 23
Upshaw, Gene 18, 47, 72
Usher 23, 56, 95
Usry, James L. 23
Ussery, Terdema, II 29
Utendahl, John 23
Valentino, Bobby 62
Van Lierop, Robert 53
Van Peebles, Mario 2, 51
Van Peebles, Melvin 7, 95
Vance, Courtney B. 15, 60
Vance, Jim 110
VanDerZee, James 6
Vandross, Luther 13, 48, 59
Vanzant, Iyanla 17, 47, 108
Vaughan, Sarah 13
Vaughn, Countess 53
Vaughn, Gladys Gary 47
Vaughn, Mo 16
Vaughn, Viola 70
Vaughns, Cleopatra 46
Vega, Marta Moreno 61
Velez-Rodriguez, Argelia 56
Verdelle, A. J. 26
Vereen, Ben 4
Verrett, Shirley 66, 91
Vesey, Denmark 100
Via, Dennis 108
Vick, Michael 39, 65, 94
Villarosa, Clara 85
Vincent, Marjorie Judith 2
Vincent, Troy 91
Vinson, Eddie 112
Von Lipsey, Roderick K. 11
Waddles, Charleszetta "Mother" 10,
    49
Wade, Dwyane 61, 103
Wade-Gayles, Gloria Jean 41
Wagner, Albert 78
Wagner, Annice 22
Wainwright, Joscelyn 46
Waka Flocka Flame 110
Walcott, Dennis M. 112
Walcott, Jersey Joe 102
Waldon, Alton R., Jr. 98
Waldron, Mal 109
Wale 92
Walker, Albertina 10, 58, 89
Walker, A'lelia 14
Walker, Alice I, 43
Walker, Arthur, II 87
Walker, Bernita Ruth 53
Walker, Cedric "Ricky" 19
Walker, Chet 106
Walker, Cora T. 68

Walker, Dianne 57
Walker, George 37
Walker, Herschel 1, 69
Walker, Hezekiah 34
Walker, John T. 50
Walker, Joseph Edison 111
Walker, Kara 16, 80
Walker, LeRoy T. 106
Walker, Lucius, Jr. 88
Walker, Madame C. J. 7
Walker, Maggie Lena 17
Walker, Margaret 29
Walker, Ray 109
Walker, Rebecca 50
Walker, T. J. 7
Walker, T-Bone 111
Walker, Teshima 114
Walker, Tristan 98
Walker, Wyatt Tee 80
Wall, Orindatus S. B. 92
Wallace, Ben 54
Wallace, Joaquin 49
Wallace, Michele Faith 13
Wallace, Perry E. 47
Wallace, Phyllis A. 9
Wallace, Rasheed 56
Wallace, Sippie 1
Wallace, William 75
Waller, Fats 29
Wallis, Quvenzhané 109
Walters, Ronald 83
Walton, Cedar 114
Ward, Andre 62
Ward, Benjamin 68
Ward, Douglas Turner 42
Ward, Hines 84
Ward, Lloyd 21, 46
Ward, Willa 105
Ward, William E. 107
Ware, Andre 37
Ware, Carl H. 30
Ware, David S. 106
Ware, DeMarcus 92
Warfield, Marsha 2
Warfield, William 94
Waring, Laura Wheeler 99
Warner, Malcolm-Jamal 22, 36, 110
Warren, Michael 27
Warwick, Dionne 18, 111
Washington, Alonzo 29
Washington, Booker T. 4
Washington, Denzel 1, 16, 93
Washington, Dinah 22
Washington, Ebonya 79
Washington, Elsie B. 78
Washington, Fredi 10
Washington, Gene 63
Washington, Grover, Jr. 17, 44
Washington, Harold 6
Washington, Harriet A. 69
Washington, Hayma 86
Washington, Isaiah 62
Washington, James, Jr. 38
Washington, James Melvin 50
Washington, Kenny 50
Washington, Kenny 107
Washington, Kerry 46, 107
Washington, Laura S. 18
Washington, MaliVai 8
Washington, Mary T. 57
Washington, Ora Mae 115
Washington, Patrice Clarke 12
Washington, Pauletta Pearson 86

Washington, Regynald G. 44
Washington, Val 12
Washington, Walter 45
Wasow, Omar 15
Waters, Benny 26
Waters, Ethel 7
Waters, Maxine 3, 67, 103
Waters, Muddy 34
Watkins, Craig 97
Watkins, Donald 35
Watkins, Joe 86
Watkins, Levi, Jr. 9
Watkins, Perry 12
Watkins, Shirley R. 17
Watkins, Ted 104
Watkins, Walter C. 24
Watley, Jody 54
Watson, Bob 25
Watson, Carlos 50
Watson, Diane 41
Watson, Johnny "Guitar" 18
Watt, Garland W. 113
Watt, Mel 26, 105
Wattleton, Faye 9
Watts, André 42, 101
Watts, J. C., Jr. 14, 38
Watts, Reggie 52, 102
Watts, Rolonda 9
Wayans, Damien 78
Wayans, Damon 8, 41
Wayans, Keenen Ivory 18
Wayans, Kim 80
Wayans, Marlon 29, 82
Wayans, Shawn 29
Weathers, Carl 10
Weaver, Afaa Michael 37
Weaver, Mike 109
Weaver, Robert C. 8, 46
Webb, Chick 105
Webb, Veronica 10, 95
Webb, Wellington 3, 81
Webb-Christburg, Sheyann 110
Webber, Chris 15, 30, 59
Webster, Katie 29
Wedgeworth, Robert W. 42
Weeks, Thomas, III 70
Weems, Carrie Mae 63
Weems, Renita J. 44
Wein, Joyce 62
Welburn, Edward T. 50
Welch, Elisabeth 52
Welcome, Verda Freeman 112
Wells, Henrietta Bell 69
Wells, James Lesesne 10
Wells, Junior 102
Wells, Mary 28
Wells, Vernon 91
Wells, Willie 105
Wells-Barnett, Ida B. 8
Welsing, Frances Cress 5
Wesley, Dorothy Porter 19
Wesley, Richard 73
Wesley, Rutina 97
Wesley, Valerie Wilson 18
West, Allen 89
West, Cornel 5, 33, 80
West, Dorothy 12, 54
West, James E. 87
West, Kanye 52, 93
West, Togo D., Jr. 16
Westbrook, Kelvin 50
Westbrook, Peter 20
Westbrooks, Bobby 51

Whack, Rita Coburn 36
Whalum, Kirk 37, 64
Wharton, A. C., Jr. 110
Wharton, Clifton R., Jr. 7
Wharton, Clifton Reginald, Sr. 36
Wheat, Alan 14
Wheaton, James 103
Whitaker, Forest 2, 49, 67
Whitaker, Mark 21, 47
Whitaker, Pernell 10, 89
White, Armond 80
White, Augustus, III 100
White, Barry 13, 41
White, Bill 1, 48
White, Charles 39
White, Dondi 34
White, Frank 95
White, Jesse 22, 75
White, Jessica 83
White, Jo Jo 112
White, John H. 27
White, Josh 86
White, Josh, Jr. 52
White, Linda M. 45
White, Lois Jean 20
White, Maurice 29
White, Michael Jai 71
White, Michael R. 5
White, Reggie 6, 50
White, Sylvain 96
White, Terri 82
White, Walter F. 4
White, Willye 67
White-Hammond, Gloria 61
Whitehead, Colson 77
Whitfield, Fred 23
Whitfield, LeRoy 84
Whitfield, Lynn 18
Whitfield, Mal 60
Whitfield, Norman 73
Whitfield, Van 34
Whitlock, Jason 78
Whitmore, George 106
Whitney, Davey L. 110
Whitney, Marva 109
Wideman, John Edgar 5, 87
Widener, Warren 99
Wilbekin, Emil 63
Wilbon, Michael 68
Wilder, L. Douglas 3, 48
Wiley, Kehinde 62
Wiley, Ralph 8, 78
Wilkens, J. Ernest, Jr. 43
Wilkens, Lenny 11, 88
Wilkerson, Isabel 71
Wilkins, David 77
Wilkins, Dominique 74
Wilkins, Ray 47
Wilkins, Roger 2, 84
Wilkins, Roy 4
Wilkins, Thomas Alphonso 71
will.i.am 64
Williams, Ann Claire 82
Williams, Anthony 21
Williams, Armstrong 29
Williams, Bert 18
Williams, Billy 86
Williams, Billy Dee 8, 105
Williams, Clarence 33
Williams, Clarence 70
Williams, Clarence, III 26
Williams, Claude 80
Williams, Cootie 114

Williams, Daniel Hale 2
Williams, David Rudyard 50
Williams, David W. 110
Williams, Deniece 36
Williams, Deron 92
Williams, Doug 22, 112
Williams, Dudley 60
Williams, Eddie N. 44
Williams, Evelyn 10
Williams, Fannie Barrier 27
Williams, Frederick (B.) 63
Williams, George Washington 18
Williams, Gregory 11
Williams, Hosea Lorenzo 15, 31
Williams, J. Mayo 83
Williams, Jody 113
Williams, Joe 5, 25
Williams, John A. 27
Williams, Juan 35, 80
Williams, Ken 68
Williams, Lauryn 58
Williams, Lindsey 75
Williams, Maggie 7, 71
Williams, Malinda 57
Williams, Marco 53
Williams, Mary Lou 15
Williams, Michael Kenneth 97
Williams, Michael L. 86
Williams, Michelle 73
Williams, Montel 4, 57
Williams, Nat D. 91
Williams, Natalie 31
Williams, O. S. 13
Williams, Patricia 11, 54
Williams, Paul 112
Williams, Paul R. 9
Williams, Pharrell 47, 82
Williams, Preston Warren, II 64
Williams, Rhonda Y. 86
Williams, Ricky 85
Williams, Robert F. 11
Williams, Ronald A. 57
Williams, Russell, II 70
Williams, Samm-Art 21
Williams, Saul 31
Williams, Serena 20, 41, 73
Williams, Sherley Anne 25
Williams, Stanley "Tookie" 29, 57
Williams, Stevie 71
Williams, Ted 91
Williams, Terrie M. 35
Williams, Tony 67
Williams, Vanessa A. 32, 66
Williams, Vanessa L. 4, 17
Williams, Venus 17, 34, 62
Williams, Walter E. 4
Williams, Wendy 62
Williams, William T. 11
Williams, Willie L. 4
Williamson, Fred 67
Williamson, Mykelti 22
Williamson, Sonny Boy 84
Willie, Louis, Jr. 68
Willingham, Tyrone 43
Willis, Bill 68
Willis, Deborah 85
Willis, Dontrelle 55
Willis, Patrick 99
Williston, David Augustus 99
Wills, Harry 80
Wills, Maury 73
Wilson, Abram 104
Wilson, August 7, 33, 55

Wilson, Brian Courtney 94
Wilson, Cassandra 16
Wilson, Chandra 57
Wilson, Charlie 31, 77
Wilson, Debra 38
Wilson, Demond 102
Wilson, Donald E. 88
Wilson, Dorien 55
Wilson, Ellis 39
Wilson, Flip 21
Wilson, Frank 106
Wilson, Frederica 92
Wilson, Gerald 49
Wilson, Jackie 60
Wilson, Jimmy 45
Wilson, John 109
Wilson, Lionel 99
Wilson, Margaret Bush 79
Wilson, Mary 28
Wilson, Nancy 10, 98
Wilson, Natalie 38
Wilson, Phill 9, 104
Wilson, Stephanie 72
Wilson, Sunnie 7, 55
Wilson, Tracey Scott 777
Wilson, William Julius 20
Winans, Angie 36
Winans, BeBe 14
Winans, CeCe 14, 43
Winans, David 77
Winans, Debbie 36
Winans, Marvin L. 17
Winans, Ronald 54
Winans, Vickie 24
Winfield, Dave 5, 91
Winfield, Paul 2, 45
Winfrey, Oprah 2, 15, 61, 106
Winkfield, Jimmy 42
Winslow, Kellen 83
Wisdom, Kimberlydawn 57
Withers, Bill 61
Withers, Ernest C. 68, 88
Withers-Mendes, Elisabeth 64
Witherspoon, Jimmy 113
Witherspoon, John 38
Witt, Edwin T. 26
Wolfe, Ann 82
Wolfe, George C. 6, 43
Womack, Bobby 60, 92
Wonder, Stevie 11, 53
Wood, Willie 111
Woodard, Alfre 9, 108
Woodard, Lynette 67
Woodruff, Hale 9
Woodruff, John 68
Woods, Abraham, Jr. 74
Woods, Belita 103
Woods, Cheyenne 103
Woods, Georgie 57
Woods, Granville T. 5
Woods, Jacqueline 52
Woods, Mattiebelle 63
Woods, Renn 110
Woods, Scott 55
Woods, Sylvia 34, 104
Woods, Teri 69
Woods, Tiger 14, 31, 81
Woodson, Ali Ollie 89
Woodson, Carter G. 2
Woodson, Mike 78
Woodson, Robert L. 10
Woodson, Rod 79
Woolard, Jamal 102

Worrill, Conrad 12
Worthy, James 49
Worthy, Kym 84
Wray, Noble 114
Wright, Antoinette 60
Wright, Beverly 97
Wright, Bruce McMarion 3, 52
Wright, Chalky 103
Wright, Charles H. 35
Wright, Deborah C. 25
Wright, Jeffrey 54, 111
Wright, Jeremiah A., Jr. 45, 69, 103
Wright, Lewin 43
Wright, Louis Tompkins 4
Wright, Nathan, Jr. 56
Wright, O. V. 114
Wright, Rayfield 70
Wright, Richard 5
Wright, Richard Robert, Sr. 100
Wright, Sarah E. 95
Wright, Timothy 74
Wyatt, Addie L. 56
Wynn, Albert R. 25, 77
X, Malcolm 1
X, Marvin 45
Xuma, Madie Hall 59
Xzibit 78
Yancy, Dorothy Cowser 42
Yarbrough, Camille 40
Yarbrough, Cedric 51
Yates, Jack 114
Yayo, Tony 113
Yearwood, Lennox, Jr. 112
Yerby, Frank 96
Yette, Samuel F. 63
Ying Yang Twins 112
Yoba, Malik 11
York, Dwight D. 71
York, Vincent 40
Young, Al 82
Young, Andrew 3, 48, 110
Young, Charles 77
Young, Coleman 1, 20
Young, Darren 114
Young, Donald, Jr. 57
Young, Jean Childs 14
Young, Jimmy 54
Young, John 111
Young, Lee 72
Young, Lee Thompson 114
Young, Lester 37
Young, Perry H. 100
Young, Roger Arliner 29
Young, Whitney M., Jr. 4
Young Jeezy 63
Youngblood, Johnny Ray 8
Youngblood, Shay 32
Zane 71
Zollar, Alfred 40
Zollar, Jawole Willa Jo 28
Zook, Kristal Brent 62
Z-Ro 109

Angolan
Bonga, Kuenda 13
dos Santos, Isabel 114
dos Santos, José Eduardo 43, 114
Lopes, Leila 99
Neto, António Agostinho 43
Roberto, Holden 65

Savimbi, Jonas **2, 34**

Antiguan
Kincaid, Jamaica **4, 109**
McGuire, George Alexander **80**
Spencer, Winston Baldwin **68**
Williams, Denise **40**

Aruban
Williams, David Rudyard **50**

Australian
Freeman, Cathy **29**
Irving, Kyrie **102**
Mundine, Anthony **56**
Rose, Lionel **56**

Austrian
Kodjoe, Boris **34, 89**

Bahamian
Christie, Perry Gladstone **53**
Ferguson, Amos **81**
Ingraham, Hubert A. **19**
Pindling, Lynden **81**
Spence, Joseph **49**

Barbadian
Adams, Grantley **82**
Arthur, Owen **33**
Brathwaite, Kamau **36**
Clarke, Austin C. **32**
Foster, Cecil **32**
Fresh, Doug E. **93**
Grandmaster Flash **33, 60**
Kamau, Kwadwo Agymah **28**
Lamming, George **35**
Rihanna **65, 102**

Belizean
Barrow, Dean **69**
Jones, Marion **21, 66**
Palacio, Andy **96**
Shyne **101**

Beninese
Gantin, Bernardin **70**
Hounsou, Djimon **19, 45**
Joachim, Paulin **34**
Kerekou, Ahmed (Mathieu) **1**
Kidjo, Angelique **50**
Loueke, Lionel **88**
Soglo, Nicéphore **15**
Yayi, Boni T. **84**

Bermudian
Cameron, Earl **44**
Gordon, Pamela **17**
Smith, Jennifer **21**

Bissau-Guinean
Cabral, Amílcar **104**
Sanhá Malam Bacai **84, 101**
Vieira, João Bernardo **14, 84**

Botswanan
Dow, Unity **104**
Khama, Ian **95**
Masire, Quett **5**
Mogae, Festus Gontebanye **19, 79**

Brazilian
Brown, Carlinhos **81**
Caymmi, Dorival **72**
da Silva, Benedita **5**
dos Santos, Manuel Francisco **65**

Gil, Gilberto **53**
Jorge, Seu **73**
Leônidas **96**
Machado de Assis **74**
Mello, Breno **73**
Moura, Paulo **87**
Nascimento, Abdias do **93**
Nascimento, Milton **2, 64**
Pelé **7**
Pitta, Celso **17**
Querino, Manuel Raimundo **84**
Ronaldinho **69**
Silva, Anderson **96**
Silva, Marina **80**

British
Abbott, Diane **9**
Adjaye, David **38, 78**
Adoboli, Kweku **106**
Akinnuoye-Agbaje, Adewale **56**
Akomfrah, John **37**
Amos, Valerie **41**
Anderson, Ho Che **54**
Anthony, Trey **63**
Appiah, Kwame Anthony **67, 101**
Armah, Esther **87**
Armatrading, Joan **32**
Bailey Rae, Corinne **83**
Barnes, John **53**
Bassey, Shirley **25**
Berry, James **41**
Blackwood, Maureen **37**
Boateng, Ozwald **35, 113**
Boateng, Paul Yaw **56**
Breeze, Jean "Binta" **37**
Brown, Melanie **73**
Campbell, Naomi **1, 31**
Carby, Hazel **27**
Charles, John **108**
Christie, Linford **8**
Cole, Ashley **106**
Coleridge-Taylor, Samuel **75**
Crooks, Garth **53**
Cruz, Taio **104**
D'Aguiar, Fred **50**
Danjah, Terror **91**
David, Craig **31, 53**
Davidson, Jaye **5**
DeGale, James **74**
Edwards, Trevor **54**
Ejiofor, Chiwetel **67**
Elba, Idris **49, 89**
Emmanuel, Alphonsia **38**
Equiano, Olaudah **78**
Estelle **75**
Evans, Diana **72**
Farah, Mo **104**
Fenton, Kevin **87**
Ferdinand, Rio **82**
Forna, Aminatta **95**
Garrett, Sean **57**
Gladwell, Malcolm **62**
Griffin, Angela **80**
Hall, Stuart **78**
Hamilton, Lewis **66**
Harewood, David **52**
Harris, Naomie **55**
Haye, David **82**
Henriques, Julian **37**
Henry, Lenny **9, 52**
Holmes, Kelly **47**
Ibrahim, Mo **67, 115**
Ince, Paul **83**

Jamelia **51**
James, David **84**
Jean-Baptiste, Marianne **17, 46**
Johnson, Ken **106**
Jordan, Ronny **26**
Julien, Isaac **3**
Kay, Jackie **37**
Kinch, Soweto **108**
King, Oona **27**
Kwei-Armah, Kwame **84**
Lester, Adrian **46**
Lewis, Denise **33**
Lewis, Lennox **27**
Lewis, Leona **75**
Lindo, Delroy **18, 45**
Markham, E. A. **37**
Mbatha-Raw, Gugu **89**
McGrath, Pat **72**
McKinney Hammond, Michelle **51**
McQueen, Steve **84**
Miller, Wentworth **75**
Ming, Mel **106**
Morris, William "Bill" **51**
Muamba, Fabrice **104**
Mvula, Laura **110**
Newton, Thandie **26, 114**
Okonedo, Sophie **67**
Oyelowo, David **82**
Pitt, David Thomas **10**
Rascal, Dizzee **82**
Regis, Cyrille **51**
Sade **15, 92**
Sandé, Emeli **113**
Scantlebury, Janna **47**
Seacole, Mary **54**
Seal **14, 75**
Sesay, Isha **107**
Siji **56**
Slash **75**
Slick Rick **93**
Smith, Anjela Lauren **44**
Smith, Richard **51**
Smith, Zadie **51**
Stoutt, H. Lavity **83**
Stuart, Moira **82**
Taylor, John (David Beckett) **16**
Thomason, Marsha **47**
Tinie Tempah **115**
Tricky **98**
Walker, Eamonn **37**
Williams, Roy **89**

Burkinabé
Compaore, Blaise **87**
Sankara, Thomas **17**
Somé, Malidoma Patrice **10**

Burundian
Bigirimana, Gael **115**
Ndadaye, Melchior **7**
Nkurunziza, Pierre **78**
Ntaryamira, Cyprien **8**

Cameroonian
Ahidjo, Ahmadou **81**
Bebey, Francis **45**
Beti, Mongo **36**
Biya, Chantal **89**
Biya, Paul **28, 114**
Eto'o, Samuel **73**
Kotto, Yaphet **7**
Milla, Roger **2**
Njawe, Pius **87**
Oyono, Ferdinand **38**

Song, Alex **105**

Canadian
Alexander, Lincoln **106**
Auguste, Arnold A. **47**
Augustine, Jean **53**
Bannister, Edward Mitchell **88**
Bell, Ralph S. **5**
Best, Carrie **80**
Boyd, Suzanne **52**
Brand, Dionne **32**
Brathwaite, Fred **35**
Brown, Rosemary **62**
Brown, Sean **52**
Carnegie, Herbert **25**
Chanté, Keshia **50**
Chong, Rae Dawn **62**
Clarke, Austin **32**
Clarke, George **32**
Cools, Anne **64**
Cooper, Afua **53**
Cox, Deborah **28**
Croal, N'Gai **76**
Curling, Alvin **34**
Dixon, George **52**
Doig, Jason **45**
Drake **86**
Edugyan, Esi **98**
Elliot, Lorris **37**
Fiona, Melanie **84**
Foster, Cecil **32**
Fox, Rick **27**
Fuhr, Grant **1, 49**
Grand-Pierre, Jean-Luc **46**
Hammond, Lenn **34**
Harris, Claire **34**
Henry, Joshua **94**
Iginla, Jarome **35**
Isaac, Julius **34**
James, Vanessa **84**
Jean, Michaëlle; **70**
Jenkins, Fergie **46**
Johnson, Ben **1**
Johnson, Clark **96**
Kane, Evander **97**
K'naan **76**
Laraque, Georges **48**
Lewis, Daurene **72**
Mayers, Jamal **39**
McKegney, Tony **3**
Mollel, Tololwa **38**
Neale, Haydain **52**
O'Ree, Willie **5**
Peterson, Oscar **52**
Philip, Marlene Nourbese **32**
Reuben, Gloria **15**
Richards, Lloyd **2**
Rodrigues, Percy **68**
Sadlier, Rosemary **62**
Salvador, Bryce **51**
Scarlett, Millicent **49**
Senior, Olive **37**
Sparks, Corinne Etta **53**
Vanity **67**
Verna, Gelsy **70**
Weekes, Kevin **67**
Williams, Denise **40**

Cape Verdean
Antunes, Lúcio **109**
Évora, Cesária **12, 99**
Grace, Sweet Daddy **104**

Pereira, Aristides **30, 97**

Caymanian
Ebanks, Selita **67**

Central African
Bozizé, François **96**

Chadian
Déby, Idriss **30**
Habré, Hissène **6, 104**

Colombian
Pomare, Eleo **72**

Congolese (Democratic Republic of the Congo)
Kabila, Joseph **30**
Kabila, Laurent **20**
Kintaudi, Leon **62**
Kolosoy, Wendo **73**
Lubanga, Thomas **104**
Mobutu Sese Seko **1, 56**
Muamba, Fabrice **104**
Mudimbe, V. Y. **61**
Mutombo, Dikembe **7, 107**
Nkunda, Laurent **75**
Ntaganda, Bosco **111**

Congolese (Republic of the Congo)
Lumumba, Patrice **33**
Sassou-Nguesso, Denis **103**

Costa Rican
McDonald, Erroll **1**

Cuban
Dihigo, Martín **103**
Ferrer, Ibrahim **41**
Güines, Tata **69**
Hernández, Orlando **96**
León, Tania **13**
Maceo, Antonio **82**
Minoso, Minnie **89**
Portuondo, Omara **53**
Puig, Yasiel **113**
Quirot, Ana **13**
Rodríguez, Arsenio **87**
Santamaria, Mongo **81**
Savón, Félix **105**
Secada, Jon **97**
Stevenson, Teófilo **103**
Tiant, Luis **102**
Valdés, Chucho **89**
Velez-Rodriguez, Argelia **56**

Curaçaoan
Jones, Andruw **98**

Danish
Tchicai, John **102**

Dominican (from Dominica)
Charles, Mary Eugenia **10, 55**
Charles, Pierre **52**
Skerrit, Roosevelt **72**

Dominican (from Dominican Republic)
Cano, Robinson **97**
Horford, Al **107**
Martinez, Pedro **81**
Ortiz, David **52, 82**
Perez, Pascual **108**
Sosa, Sammy **21, 44**

Virgil, Ozzie **48**

Dutch
Ali, Ayaan Hirsi **58, 92**
Davids, Edgar **106**
Liberia-Peters, Maria Philomena **12**

Ecuadoran
Benítez, Christian **113**

Equatorial Guinean
Moussambani, Eric **105**
Obiang, Teodoro **103**

Eritrean
Afewerki, Isaias **98**
Keflezighi, Meb **49**

Ethiopian
Aberra, Amsale **67**
Abune Paulos **105**
Afro, Teddy **78**
Astatke, Mulatu **81**
Bekele, Kenenisa **75**
Birra, Ali **113**
Desalegn, Hailemariam **105**
Dibaba, Tirunesh **73, 109**
Gabre-Medhin, Tsegaye **64**
Gebrselassie, Haile **70**
Gerima, Haile **38, 80**
Haile Selassie **7**
Ibrahim, Fuad **109**
Kebede, Liya **59**
Mengistu, Haile Mariam **65**
Samuelsson, Marcus **53**
Zenawi, Meles **3, 99**

Filipino
apl.de.ap **84**

French
Baker, Josephine **3**
Baldwin, James **1**
Baugé, Grégory **86**
Bebey, Francis **45**
Bonaly, Surya **7**
Boulogne, Joseph, Chevalier de Saint-Georges **94**
Chase-Riboud, Barbara **20, 46**
Dieudonné **67**
Evra, Patrice **102**
Fanon, Frantz **44**
Henry, Thierry **66**
James, Vanessa **84**
Kanouté, Fred **68**
Noah, Yannick **4, 60**
Parker, Tony **75**
Song, Alex **105**
Sy, Omar **109**
Tanner, Henry Ossawa **1**
Thiam, Tidjane **104**
White, Sylvain **96**

Gabonese
Bongo, Ali Ben **80**
Bongo, Omar **1, 79**

Gambian
Bensouda, Fatou **103**
Jammeh, Yahya **23, 104**
Peters, Lenrie **43**
Sanneh, Kelefa **96**

German
Massaquoi, Hans J. **30**

Ghanaian
Adoboli, Kweku **106**
Adu, Freddy **67**
Aidoo, Ama Ata **38**
Ali, Mohammed Naseehu **60**
Annan, Kofi Atta **15, 48**
Appiah, Kwame Anthony **67, 101**
Armah, Ayi Kwei **49**
Atta Mills, John **75**
Awoonor, Kofi **37, 115**
Awuah, Patrick **111**
Balotelli, Mario **104**
Bartels, Peggielene **80**
Blitz the Ambassador **115**
Danquah, Meri Nana Ama **93**
Dawuni, Rocky **94**
DuBois, Shirley Graham **21**
Gyan, Asamoah **87**
Jawara, Dawda Kairaba **11**
Kufuor, John Agyekum **54, 82**
Lee, Robert **112**
Mahama, John Dramani **103**
Mensah, John **87**
Mensah, Thomas **48**
Nkrumah, Kwame **3**
Rawlings, Jerry **9**
Rawlings, Nana Konadu Agyeman **13**
Yeboah, Emmanuel Ofosu **53**

Grenadian
Bishop, Maurice **39**
Gairy, Eric Matthew **83**
Isaac, Julius **34**
Mitchell, Keith **82**

Guinean
Camara, Moussa Dadis **76**
Condé, Alpha **95**
Conté, Lansana **7, 76**
Diallo, Amadou **27**
Diawara, Djeli Moussa **111**
Niane, Katoucha **70**
Touré, Sekou **6**

Guyanese
Amos, Valerie **41**
Beaton, Norman **14**
Burnham, Forbes **66**
Carter, Martin **49**
Dabydeen, David **48**
D'Aguiar, Fred **50**
Damas, Léon-Gontran **46**
Dathorne, O. R. **52**
Griffith, Patrick A. **64**
Jagan, Cheddi **16**
Lefel, Edith **41**
van Sertima, Ivan **25**

Haitian
Aristide, Jean-Bertrand **6, 45**
Auguste, Rose-Anne **13**
Beauvais, Garcelle **29, 95**
Beauvoir, Max **74**
Beken **111**
Celestin, Josaphat **101**
Charlemagne, Manno **11**
Christophe, Henri **9**
Danticat, Edwidge **15, 68**
Delice, Ronald **48**
Delice, Rony **48**
Hector, Jamie **98**
Jean, Wyclef **20, 86**
Jean-Juste, Gérard **78**

Jean-Louis, Jimmy **76**
Jeune, Vitolio **98**
Laferriere, Dany **33**
Laraque, Paul **67**
Laroche, Joseph Philippe Lemercier **85**
Magloire, Paul Eugène **68**
Manigat, Mirlande **90**
Martelly, Michel **90**
Pascal-Trouillot, Ertha **3**
Peck, Raoul **32**
Pierre, Andre **17**
Pierre-Louis, Michèle **75**
Préval, René **87**
Siméus, Dumas M. **25, 110**
Verna, Gelsy **70**
Villard-Appolon, Malya **106**

Hungarian
Watts, André **42, 101**

Irish
Adebari, Rotimi **83**
Mumba, Samantha **29**

Italian
Balotelli, Mario **104**
Esposito, Giancarlo **9**
Kyenge, Cécile **113**

Ivorian
Bedie, Henri Konan **21**
Blondy, Alpha **30**
Dadié, Bernard **34**
De Bankolé, Isaach **78**
Drogba, Didier **78**
Gbagbo, Laurent **43, 90**
Guéï, Robert **66**
Houphouët-Boigny, Félix **4, 64**
Ouattara **43**
Ouattara, Alassane **90**
Ouattara, Morou **74**
Thiam, Tidjane **104**
Touré, Yaya **99**

Jamaican
Ashley, Maurice **15, 47**
Banton, Buju **93**
Barnes, John **53**
Barnes, Lloyd **77**
Barrett, Lindsay **43**
Beenie Man **32**
Belafonte, Harry **4, 65**
Bennett, Louise **69**
Bennett, Richard **97**
Berry, James **41**
Big Youth **107**
Bolt, Usain **73, 104**
Brown, Dennis **99**
Burning Spear **79**
Campbell-Brown, Veronica **102**
Channer, Colin **36**
Cliff, Jimmy **28, 92**
Cliff, Michelle **42**
Coke, Christopher **108**
Cooper, Afua **53**
Cox, Renée **67**
Curling, Alvin **34**
Dekker, Desmond **104**
Dodd, Coxsone **99**
Dunbar, Sly **34**
Ellis, Alton **74**
Ellis, Hortense **97**
Ewing, Patrick **17, 73**

Fagan, Garth **18, 98**
Fenton, Kevin **87**
Figueroa, John J. **40**
Ford, Vincent **75**
Fraser-Pryce, Shelly-Ann **113**
Garvey, Marcus **1**
Golding, Bruce **78**
Goodison, Lorna **71**
Graham, Trevor **84**
Griffiths, Marcia **29**
Hamilton, Tanya **93**
Hammond, Lenn **34**
Hearne, John Edgar Caulwell **45**
Heavy D **58, 98**
Hibbert, Toots **103**
Holness, Andrew **99**
Irving, Barrington, Jr. **112**
Isaacs, Gregory **89**
James, Marlon **85**
Johnson, Ben **1**
Johnson, Linton Kwesi **37**
Joseph, Kathie-Ann **56**
Kingston, Sean **94**
Kong, B. Waine **50**
Manley, Edna **26**
Manley, Ruth **34**
Marks, Audrey **99**
Marley, Bob **5**
Marley, Rita **32, 70**
Marley, Stephen **100**
Marley, Ziggy **41**
McGregor, Stephen **99**
McKay, Claude **6**
McKenzie, Jaunel **73**
Minott, Sugar **86**
Moody, Ronald **30**
Morrison, Keith **13**
Mowatt, Judy **38**
Palmer, Everard **37**
Patterson, Orlando **4**
Patterson, P. J. **6, 20**
Perry, Lee **19, 103**
Perry, Ruth **19**
Ranglin, Ernest **78**
Reece, E. Albert **63**
Rhoden, Wayne **70**
Rhone, Trevor **80**
Rogers, Joel Augustus **30**
Russwurm, John Brown **100**
Senior, Olive **37**
Shaggy **31**
Shakespeare, Robbie **34**
Sharpe, Samuel **103**
Shearer, Hugh **107**
Simpson Miller, Portia **62, 100**
Sinclair, Madge **78**
Steely **80**
Taylor, Karin **34**
Tosh, Peter **9**
White, Willard **53**
Yabby You **83**

Kenyan
Cheruiyot, Robert **69**
Juma, Calestous **57**
Kariuki, J. M. **67**
Kenyatta, Jomo **5**
Kenyatta, Uhuru **110**
Kibaki, Mwai **60**
Kipsang, Wilson **115**
Kobia, Samuel **43**
Loroupe, Tegla **59**
Maathai, Wangari **43, 97**

Mazrui, Ali A. **12**
Mboya, Tom **107**
Moi, Daniel Arap **1, 35**
Mutu, Wangechi **44**
Mwangi, Meja **40**
Ngilu, Charity **58**
Ngugi wa Thiong'o **29, 61, 101**
Odinga, Raila **67, 110**
Otunga, Maurice Michael **55**
Rudisha, David **112**
Tergat, Paul **59**
Wambugu, Florence **42**
Wanjiru, Sammy **94**

Korean
Ward, Hines **84**

Lesothoian
Mofolo, Thomas **37**
Mosisili, Pakalitha **96**

Liberian
Conneh, Sekou Damate, Jr. **51**
Cooper, Lisa **73**
Doe, Samuel K. **100**
Fuller, Solomon Carter, Jr. **15**
Gbowee, Leymah **76**
Keith, Rachel Boone **63**
Perry, Ruth **15**
Sawyer, Amos **2**
Sirleaf, Ellen Johnson **71**
Taylor, Charles **20**
Tolbert, William R. **100**
Tubman, William **99**
Weah, George **58**

Malawian
Banda, Hastings Kamuzu **6, 54**
Banda, Joyce **101**
Kayira, Legson **40**
Malawi Mouse Boys **114**
Muluzi, Bakili **14, 76**

Malian
Amadou & Mariam **113**
Diawara, Fatoumata **114**
Keïta, Ibrahim Boubacar **113**
Keita, Salif **83**
Sangare, Oumou **18, 99**
Souleymane, Mahamane **78**
Touré, Amadou Toumani **18**
Traore, Dioncounda **103**

Martinican
Césaire, Aimé **48, 69**
Palcy, Euzhan **94**

Mozambican
Chissano, Joaquim **7, 55, 67**
Couto, Mia **45**
Diogo, Luisa Dias **63**
Guebuza, Armando **81**
Machel, Graça **16, 102**
Machel, Samora Moises **8**
Mutola, Maria **12**

Namibian
Mbuende, Kaire **12**
Nujoma, Samuel **10**
Pohamba, Hifikepunye **95**

Nigerian
Abacha, Sani **11, 70**
Abani, Chris **77**
Abiola, Moshood **70**

Abiola-Costello, Hafsat **108**
Abubakar, Abdulsalami **66**
Achebe, Chinua **6, 99, 111**
Ade, King Sunny **41**
Adichie, Chimamanda Ngozi **64**
Ake, Claude **30**
Akinola, Peter Jasper **65**
Akpan, Uwem **70**
Akunyili, Dora Nkem **58**
Amadi, Elechi **40**
Amata, Jeta **111**
Arinze, Francis **19**
Azikiwe, Nnamdi **13**
Babangida, Ibrahim **4**
Babatunde, Rotimi **104**
Bandele, Biyi **68**
Clark-Bekedermo, J. P. **44**
Darego, Agbani **52**
D'banj **107**
Ekwensi, Cyprian **37**
Emeagwali, Philip **30**
Emecheta, Buchi **30**
Fela **1, 42**
Jonathan, Goodluck **83**
Kuti, Femi **47, 110**
Lawal, Kase L. **45**
Obasanjo, Olusegun **5, 22**
Obasanjo, Stella **32, 56**
Ogunlesi, Adebayo O. **37**
Ojukwu, Odumegwu **99**
Okara, Gabriel **37**
Okigbo, Christopher **102**
Okocha, Jay Jay **99**
Okonjo-Iweala, Ngozi **101**
Okosuns, Sonny **71**
Olagundoye, Toks **113**
Olajuwon, Hakeem **2, 72**
Olatunji, Babatunde **36**
Olojede, Dele **59**
Olopade, Olufunmilayo Falusi **58**
Onwueme, Tess Osonye **23**
Onwurah, Ngozi **38**
Osotimehin, Babatunde **107**
Prince Twins Seven-Seven **95**
Rotimi, Ola **1**
Sade **15, 92**
Saro-Wiwa, Kenule **39**
Siji **56**
Sowande, Fela **39**
Soyinka, Wole **4, 93**
Tutuola, Amos **30**
Ujiri, Masai **107**
Ukpabio, Helen **86**
Wiwa, Ken **67**
Yar'Adua, Umaru **69, 89**

Nigerien
Bombino **112**
Issoufou, Mahamadou **102**
Tandja, Mamadou **33, 78**

Norwegian
Brown, Anne **76**

Panamanian
Bailey, Preston **64**
Williams, Juan **35, 80**

Peruvian
Baca, Susana **80**

Polish
Bridgetower, George **78**

Portuguese
Souza, Carmen **111**

Puerto Rican
Cepeda, Orlando **98**
Schomburg, Arthur Alfonso **9**

Russian
Khanga, Yelena **6**

Rwandan
Bizimungu, Pasteur **19**
Habyarimana, Juvenal **8**
Ilibagiza, Immaculée **66**
Kabera, Eric **104**
Kagame, Paul **54**
Mushikiwabo, Louise **88**
Rusesabagina, Paul **60**

St. Kitts and Nevis
Douglas, Bob **96**
Douglas, Denzil Llewellyn **53**

Saint Lucian
Compton, John **65**

Saudi
Amoudi, Mohammed al- **88**
Kalbani, Adil **77**

Senegalese
Acogny, Germaine **55**
Akon **68**
Ba, Mariama **30**
Boye, Madior **30**
Diop, Birago **53**
Diop, Cheikh Anta **4**
Diouf, Abdou **3**
Evra, Patrice **102**
Maal, Baaba **66**
Mbaye, Mariétou **31**
Mboup, Souleymane **10**
Ndiaye, Iba **74**
N'Dour, Youssou **1, 53, 79**
Sall, Macky **101**
Sané, Pierre Gabriel **21**
Sembène, Ousmane **13, 62**
Senghor, Augustin Diamancoune **66**
Senghor, Léopold Sédar **12, 66**
Sy, Oumou **65**
Wade, Abdoulaye **66**

Sierra Leonean
Beah, Ishmael **69**
Cheney-Coker, Syl **43**
DePrince, Michaela **104**
Jones, Monty **66**
Kabbah, Ahmad Tejan **23**
Koroma, Ernest Bai **84**
Sankoh, Foday **74**
Sesay, Isha **107**
Yumkella, Kandeh **105**

Somali
Ahmed, Sharif **80**
Ali, Ayaan Hirsi **58, 92**
Ali Mahdi Mohamed **5**
Dirie, Waris **56**
Farah, Mo **104**
Farah, Nuruddin **27**
Iman **4, 33, 87**
K'naan **76**
Mohamud, Hassan Sheikh **105**
Omar, Samia Yusuf **107**

Roble, Abdi 71

South African
Abrahams, Peter 39
Adams, Paul 50
Biko, Steven 4
Brutus, Dennis 38
Buthelezi, Mangosuthu Gatsha 9
Butler, Jonathan 28
Chaka Chaka, Yvonne 112
Chweneyagae, Presley 63
Dandala, Mvume 77
Dlamini-Zuma, Nkosazana 34, 105
Dube, Lucky 77
Grae, Jean 51
Hani, Chris 6
Head, Bessie 28
Jansen, Jonathan 102
Jim, Songezo 111
Ka Dinizulu, Mcwayizeni 29
Kente, Gibson 52
Khumalo, Leleti 51
Kuzwayo, Ellen 68
Ladysmith Black Mambazo 103
LaGuma, Alex 30
Lebo M 109
Luthuli, Albert 13
Mabuza, Lindiwe 18
Mabuza-Suttle, Felicia 43
Madikizela-Mandela, Winnie 2, 35, 112
Mahlasela, Vusi 65
Makeba, Miriam 2, 50, 74
Malema, Julius 98
Mandela, Nelson 1, 14, 77
Maponya, Maishe 101
Maponya, Richard 101
Masekela, Barbara 18
Masekela, Hugh 1, 106
Mathabane, Mark 5, 99
Matshikiza, Pumeza 115
Mbeki, Govan A. 80
Mbeki, Thabo 14, 73
Mhlaba, Raymond 55

Mokae, Zakes 80
Motlanthe, Kgalema 74
Mphalele, Es'kia (Ezekiel) 40
Naki, Hamilton 63
Ngubane, Ben 33
Nkoli, Simon 60
Nkosi, Lewis 46
Ntshona, Winston 52
Nyanda, Siphiwe 21
Nzo, Alfred 15
Petersen, Neal 96
Plaatje, Sol T. 80
Ramaphosa, Cyril 3
Ramphele, Mamphela 29
Rapelang Rabana 112
Sisulu, Albertina 57, 95
Sisulu, Sheila Violet Makate 24
Sisulu, Walter 47
Sono, Jomo 86
Thugwane, Josia 21
Tutu, Desmond (Mpilo) 6, 44
Tutu, Nontombi Naomi 57
Zuma, Jacob 33, 75

South Sudanese
Kiir, Salva Mayardit 85, 103
Wek, Alek 18, 63, 105

Spanish
Eto'o, Samuel 73

Sudanese
Bashir, Halima 73
Bashir, Omar al- 77
Bol, Manute 1
Cham, Adongo Agada Akway 77
Garang, John 105
Hussein, Lubna 80
Nour, Nawal M. 56
Salih, Al-Tayyib 37

Swazi
Mswati III 56

Swedish
Hendricks, Barbara 3, 67
Valdés, Bebo 75

Tanzanian
Kikwete, Jakaya Mrisho 73
Mkapa, Benjamin W. 16, 77
Mollel, Tololwa 38
Mongella, Gertrude 11
Mwinyi, Ali Hassan 1, 77
Nyerere, Julius 5
Ongala, Remmy 9, 91
Rugambwa, Laurean 20

Togolese
Eyadéma, Gnassingbé 7, 52
Gnassingbé, Faure 67
Soglo, Nicéphore 15

Trinidadian
Anthony, Michael 29
Auguste, Arnold A. 47
Brand, Dionne 32
Carmichael, Stokely 5, 26
Cartey, Wilfred 47
Dymally, Mervyn 42
Francis, Thais 93
Guy, Rosa 5
Harris, Claire 34
Hendy, Francis 47
Hercules, Frank 44
Hill, Errol 40
Holder, Geoffrey 78
Julian, Hubert 90
London, Theophilus 95
Lord Kitchener 110
Lushington, Augustus Nathaniel 56
Nakhid, David 25
Nunez, Elizabeth 62, 112
Petioni, Muriel 99
Primus, Pearl 6
Rudder, David 79
Shorty, Ras, I 47
Toussaint, Lorraine 32
Williams, Eric Eustace 65

Tunisian
Memmi, Albert 37

Ugandan
Amin, Idi 42
Arac de Nyeko, Monica 66
Atim, Julian 66
Atyam, Angelina 55
Kato, David 103
Kisekka, Samson 112
Kony, Joseph 101
Museveni, Yoweri 4
Mutebi, Ronald 25
Obote, Milton 63
Okaalet, Peter 58
Sentamu, John 58

West Indian
Césaire, Aimé 48, 69
Coombs, Orde M. 44
Innis, Roy 5
Knight, Gwendolyn 63
Pitt, David Thomas 10
Rojas, Don 33
Staupers, Mabel K. 7
Taylor, Susan L. 10, 86
Walcott, Derek 5, 94

Zambian
Chiluba, Frederick 56, 80
Chitalu, Godfrey 108
Kaunda, Kenneth 2
Moyo, Dambisa 76
Mwanawasa, Levy 72
Sata, Michael 102
Zulu, Princess Kasune 54

Zimbabwean
Chideya, Farai 14
Marechera, Dambudzo 39
Moyo, Lovemore 76
Mtukudzi, Oliver 109
Mugabe, Robert 10, 71
Mukoko, Jestina 75
Muzorewa, Abel 85
Nkomo, Joshua 4, 65
Tsvangirai, Morgan 26, 72
Vera, Yvonne 32

Cumulative Occupation Index

Volume numbers appear in **bold**

Art and design

Abele, Julian **55**
Aberra, Amsale **67**
Adjaye, David **38, 78**
Allen, Tina **22, 75**
Alston, Charles **33**
Amaki, Amalia **76**
Amos, Emma **63**
Anderson, Ho Che **54**
Andrews, Benny **22, 59**
Andrews, Bert **13**
Armstrong, Robb **15**
Ashford, Calvin, Jr. **74**
Bailey, Preston **64**
Bailey, Radcliffe **19**
Bailey, Xenobia **11**
Baker, Matt **76**
Bannister, Edward Mitchell **88**
Barboza, Anthony **10**
Barnes, Ernie **16, 78**
Barthé, Earl **78**
Barthe, Richmond **15**
Basquiat, Jean-Michel **5**
Bearden, Romare **2, 50**
Beasley, Phoebe **34**
Beckwith, Naomi **101**
Bell, Darrin **77**
Benberry, Cuesta **65**
Benjamin, Tritobia Hayes **53**
Biggers, John **20, 33**
Biggers, Sanford **62**
Billops, Camille **82**
Bingham, Howard **96**
Blackburn, Robert **28**
Bond, J. Max, Jr. **76**
Bradford, Mark **89**
Brandon, Barbara **3**
Brown, Donald **19**
Brown, Frederick J. **102**
Brown, Robert **65**
Bryan, Ashley **41, 104**
Burke, Selma **16**
Burroughs, Margaret Taylor **9**
Camp, Kimberly **19**
Campbell, E. Simms **13**
Campbell, Mary Schmidt **43**
Catlett, Elizabeth **2**
Chanticleer, Raven **91**
Chase, John Saunders, Jr. **99**
Chase-Riboud, Barbara **20, 46**
Colescott, Robert **69**
Collins, Paul **61**
Cortor, Eldzier **42**

Cowans, Adger W. **20**
Cox, Renée **67**
Crichlow, Ernest **75**
Crite, Allan Rohan **29**
Davis, Bing **84**
De Veaux, Alexis **44**
DeCarava, Roy **42, 81**
Delaney, Beauford **19**
Delaney, Joseph **30**
Delsarte, Louis **34**
Dial, Thornton **114**
Dillon, Leo **103**
Donaldson, Jeff **46**
Douglas, Aaron **7**
Douglas, Emory **89**
Driskell, David C. **7**
du Cille, Michel **74**
Dwight, Edward **65**
Edwards, Melvin **22**
El Wilson, Barbara **35**
Ewing, Patrick **17, 73**
Farley, James Conway **99**
Fax, Elton **48**
Feelings, Tom **11, 47**
Ferguson, Amos **81**
Fine, Sam **60**
Freeman, Leonard **27**
Fuller, Meta Vaux Warrick **27**
Gantt, Harvey **1**
Garvin, Gerry **78**
Gilles, Ralph **61**
Gilliam, Sam **16**
Golden, Thelma **10, 55**
Goodnight, Paul **32**
Green, Jonathan **54**
Guyton, Tyree **9, 94**
Hammons, David **69**
Hansen, Austin **88**
Harkless, Necia Desiree **19**
Harrington, Oliver W. **9**
Harris, Lyle Ashton **83**
Harrison, Charles **72**
Hathaway, Isaac Scott **33**
Hayden, Palmer **13**
Hayes, Cecil N. **46**
Holder, Geoffrey **78**
Honeywood, Varnette P. **54, 88**
Hope, John **8**
Hudson, Cheryl **15**
Hudson, Wade **15**
Hunt, Richard **6**
Hunter, Clementine **45**
Hutson, Jean Blackwell **16**
Jackson, Earl **31**

Jackson, Mary **73**
Jackson, Vera **40**
Johnson, Jeh Vincent **44**
Johnson, William Henry **3**
Jones, Lois Mailou **13**
Jones, Paul R. **76**
King, Robert Arthur **58**
Kitt, Sandra **23**
Knight, Gwendolyn **63**
Knox, Simmie **49**
Lawrence, Jacob **4, 28**
Lee, Annie Frances **22**
Lee-Smith, Hughie **5, 22**
Lewis, Edmonia **10**
Lewis, Norman **39**
Lewis, Samella **25**
Ligon, Glenn **82**
Lovell, Whitfield **74**
Loving, Alvin, Jr. **35, 53**
Manley, Edna **26**
Marshall, Kerry James **59**
Mayhew, Richard **39**
McCullough, Geraldine **58, 79**
McDuffie, Dwayne **62**
McGee, Charles **10**
McGruder, Aaron **28, 56**
McQueen, Steve **84**
Mehretu, Julie **85**
Mitchell, Corinne **8**
Moody, Ronald **30**
Morrison, Keith **13**
Motley, Archibald, Jr. **30**
Moutoussamy-Ashe, Jeanne **7**
Mutu, Wangechi **44**
Myles, Kim **69**
Nascimento, Abdias do **93**
Nelson, Kadir **115**
Ndiaye, Iba **74**
Neals, Otto **73**
N'Namdi, George R. **17**
Nugent, Richard Bruce **39**
O'Grady, Lorraine **73**
Olden, Georg(e) **44**
Ormes, Jackie **73**
Ouattara **43**
Perkins, Marion **38**
Pierce, Elijah **84**
Pierre, Andre **17**
Pindell, Howardena **55**
Pinder, Jefferson **77**
Pinderhughes, John **47**
Pinkney, Jerry **15**
Piper, Adrian **71**
Pippin, Horace **9**

Pope.L, William **72**
Porter, James A. **11**
Prince Twins Seven-Seven **95**
Prophet, Nancy Elizabeth **42**
Puryear, Martin **42, 101**
Querino, Manuel Raimundo **84**
Ransome, James E. **88**
Reid, Senghor **55**
Ringgold, Faith **4, 81**
Roble, Abdi **71**
Ruley, Ellis **38**
Saar, Alison **16**
Saar, Betye **80**
Saint James, Synthia **12**
Sallee, Charles **38**
Sanders, Joseph R., Jr. **11**
Savage, Augusta **12**
Scott, Dread **106**
Scott, John T. **65**
Sebree, Charles **40**
Serrano, Andres **3**
Shabazz, Attallah **6**
Shonibare, Yinka **58**
Simmons, Gary **58**
Simpson, Lorna **4, 36**
Simpson, Merton D. **110**
Sims, Lowery Stokes **27**
Sklarek, Norma Merrick **25, 101**
Sleet, Moneta, Jr. **5**
Smith, Bruce W. **53**
Smith, Marvin **46**
Smith, Ming **100**
Smith, Morgan **46**
Smith, Vincent D. **48**
Steave-Dickerson, Kia **57**
Stout, Renee **63**
Sudduth, Jimmy Lee **65**
Tanksley, Ann **37**
Tanner, Henry Ossawa **1**
Taylor, Lonzie Odie **96**
Taylor, Robert Robinson **80**
Thomas, Alma **14**
Thrash, Dox **35**
Tolliver, Mose **60**
Tolliver, William **9**
Tooks, Lance **62**
VanDerZee, James **6**
Verna, Gelsy **70**
Wagner, Albert **78**
Wainwright, Joscelyn **46**
Walker, A'lelia **14**
Walker, Kara **16, 80**
Waring, Laura Wheeler **99**
Washington, Alonzo **29**

189

Washington, James, Jr. 38
Weems, Carrie Mae 63
Wells, James Lesesne 10
White, Charles 39
White, Dondi 34
White, John H. 27
Wiley, Kehinde 62
Williams, Clarence 70
Williams, O. S. 13
Williams, Paul R. 9
Williams, William T. 11
Willis, Deborah 85
Williston, David Augustus 99
Wilson, Ellis 39
Wilson, John 109
Withers, Ernest C. 68, 88
Woodruff, Hale 9

Business

Abbott, Robert Sengstacke 27
Abiola, Moshood 70
Adams, Eula L. 39
Adams, Jenoyne 60
Adkins, Rod 41
Adoboli, Kweku 106
Akil, Mara Brock 60, 82
Al-Amin, Jamil Abdullah 6
Alexander, Archie Alphonso 14
Allen-Buillard, Melba 55
Ames, Wilmer 27
Amos, Wally 9
Amoudi, Mohammed al- 88
Archer, Lee, Jr. 79
Armstrong, Govind 81
Auguste, Donna 29
Austin, Gloria 63
Austin, Jim 63
Austin, Wanda M. 94
Avant, Clarence 19, 86
Avant, Nicole A. 90
Baker, Ella 5
Baker, Gwendolyn Calvert 9
Baker, Maxine 28
Bakewell, Danny 99
Banks, Jeffrey 17
Banks, Paula A. 68
Banks, William 11
Barden, Donald H. 9, 20, 89
Barrett, Andrew C. 12
Beal, Bernard B. 46
Beamon, Bob 30
Beasley, Phoebe 34
Bell, James A. 50
Bennett, Richard 97
Bing, Dave 3, 59, 78
Blackshear, Leonard 52
Blackwell, Robert D., Sr. 52
Blaylock, Ronald 86
Blayton, Jesse B., Sr. 55
Bolden, Frank E. 44
Borders, James 9
Boston, Kelvin E. 25
Boston, Lloyd 24
Bowen, Ruth 83
Boyd, Edward 70
Boyd, Gwendolyn 49
Boyd, John W., Jr. 20, 72
Boyd, T. B., III 6
Bradley, Jennette B. 40
Brae, C. Michael 61
Brewer, Rosalind 100
Bridges, Sheila 36
Bridgforth, Glinda 36

Briggs, Curtis 84
Brimmer, Andrew 2, 48, 106
Bronner, Nathaniel H., Sr. 32
Brown, Eddie C. 35
Brown, Jamie Foster 91
Brown, Les 5
Brown, Marie Dutton 12
Brunson, Dorothy 1, 87
Bryant, John 26
Burgess, Marjorie L. 55
Burks, Juanita P. 95
Burns, Ursula 60
Burrell, Tom 21, 51
Burroughs, Margaret Taylor 9
Burrus, William Henry 45
Burt-Murray, Angela 59
Butler, George, Jr. 70
Cain, Herman 15, 92
Calabrese, Karyn 89
Caldwell, Earl 60
Cameron, James 80
Carter, Pamela Lynn 67
CasSelle, Malcolm 11
Chamberlain, Wilt 18, 47
Chapman, Nathan A., Jr. 21
Chapman, Susan E. 94
Chappell, Emma 18
Chase, Leah 57
Chenault, Kenneth 4, 36, 108
Cherry, Deron 40
Chisholm, Samuel J. 32
Clark, Celeste 15
Clark, Patrick 14
Clay, William Lacy 8
Clayton, Xernona 3, 45
Clement-Holmes, Linda 94
Clyburn, Mignon 78
Cobbs, Price M. 9
Coke, Christopher 108
Colbert, Virgis William 17
Coleman, Donald 24, 62
Coleman, Ken 57
Compton-Rock, Malaak 86
Conyers, Nathan G. 24
Cooper, Barry 33
Cooper, Evern 40
Corbi, Lana 42
Cornelius, Don 4, 100
Cosby, Camille 14, 80
Cottrell, Comer 11
Council, LaVerne 94
Cox, William E. 68
Creagh, Milton 27
Crum, George 101
Cuffe, Paul 98
Cullers, Vincent T. 49
Daniels-Carter, Valerie 23
Darden, Calvin 38
Dash, Darien 29
Davis, Belva 61
Davis, Ed 24
Davis, Erroll B., Jr. 57
Dawson, Matel, Jr. 39
de Passe, Suzanne 25
Dean, Mark 35
Dee, Merri 55
Delany, Bessie 12
Delany, Martin R. 27
Delany, Sadie 12
DeVard, Jerri 61
Diallo, Amadou 27
Doley, Harold, Jr. 26
Donald, Arnold Wayne 36

Dorsey, Thomas J. 90
dos Santos, Isabel 114
Downing, George T. 91
Dre, Dr. 10, 14, 30
Driver, David E. 11
Ducksworth, Marilyn 12
Duerson, Dave 93
Easley, Annie J. 61
Ebanks, Michelle 60
Edelin, Ramona Hoage 19
Edmonds, Tracey 16, 64
Edmunds, Gladys 48
Edwards, Trevor 54
El Wilson, Barbara 35
Elder, Lee 6
Ellington, E. David 11
Evans, Darryl 22
Evers, Myrlie 8
Farmer, Forest J. 1
Farr, Mel 24
Farrakhan, Louis 15
Fauntroy, Walter E. 11
Ferguson, Roger W., Jr. 25, 112
Ferdinand, Rio 82
50 Cent 46, 83
Fils-Aimé, Reggie 74
Fletcher, Buddy 16, 108
Flowers, Sylester 50
Ford, Barney 90
Ford, Harold E(ugene), Jr. 16, 70
Forte, Linda Diane 54
Foster, Jylla Moore 45
Fowler, Reggie 51
Franklin, Hardy R. 9
Frazier, Kenneth 97
Friday, Jeff 24
Fryer, Roland G. 56
Fudge, Ann 11, 55
Fuller, S. B. 13
Funderburg, I. Owen 38
Gaines, Brenda 41
Gardner, Chris 65
Gardner, Edward G. 45
Garrett, James F. 78
Gaskins, Rudy 74
Gaston, Arthur George 3, 38, 59
Gibbs, Mifflin W. 99
Gibson, John Trusty 87
Gibson, Kenneth Allen 6
Gibson, Ted 66
Gidron, Richard D. 68
Gilles, Ralph 61
Goings, Russell 59
Goldsberry, Ronald 18
Golston, Allan C. 55
Gooden, Linda 94
Goodman, Kim C. 94
Gordon, Bruce S. 41, 53, 82
Gordon, Pamela 17
Gordy, Berry, Jr. 1
Goss, Carol A. 55
Goss, Tom 23
Grace, George H. 48
Graham, Stedman 13
Graves, Butch 77
Graves, Earl G. 1, 35
Gray, Farrah 59
Greely, M. Gasby 27
Green, Isaac H. 79
Green, Nancy 112
Greene, Richard Thaddeus, Sr. 67
Greenwood, Monique 38
Griffith, Mark Winston 8

Grooms, Henry R(andall) 50
Hale, Lorraine 8
Hall, Alvin D. 86
Ham, Cynthia Parker 58
Hamer, Fannie Lou 6
Hamilton, Samuel C. 47
Handy, W. C. 8
Hannah, Marc 10
Hardison, Bethann 12
Harrell, Andre 9, 30
Harris, Alice 7
Harris, Carla A. 67
Harris, E. Lynn 12, 33
Harris, Monica 18
Harris, Richard E. 61
Hart, Thomas A., Sr. 113
Harvey, Steve 18, 58
Harvey, William R. 42
Hawkins, La-Van 17, 54
Hayden, Carla D. 47
Haysbert, Raymond V., Sr. 87
Hazel, Darryl B. 50
Henderson, Gordon 5
Henderson, Henry Fairfax, Jr. 89
Henry, Dwight 104
Henry, Lenny 9, 52
Henry, Troy 85
Herndon, Alonzo Franklin 89
Hightower, Dennis F. 13
Hill, Bonnie Guiton 20
Hill, Calvin 19
Hill, Janet 19
Hill, Jesse, Jr. 13
Hill, Peter 92
Hobson, Mellody 40
Holland, Kimberly N. 62
Holland, Robert, Jr. 11
Holmes, Larry 20, 68
Holstein, Casper 89
Howell, Ayinde 91
Howroyd, Janice Bryant 42
Hudlin, Warrington 9
Hudson, Cheryl 15
Hudson, Wade 15
Huggins, Larry 21
Hughes, Cathy 27
Ibrahim, Mo 67, 115
Ice Cube 8, 30, 60
Irvin, Vernon 65
Jackson, George 19
Jackson, Hal 41, 104
Jackson, Joe 78
Jackson, Mannie 14
Jackson, Michael 19, 53, 76
Jakes, Thomas "T. D." 17, 43
James, Charles H., III 62
James, Donna A. 51
James, Juanita 13
Jenkins, Ray 77
John, Daymond 23, 114
Johnson, Bumpy 102
Johnson, Eunice W. 83
Johnson, George E. 29
Johnson, John H. 3, 54
Johnson, Kevin 70
Johnson, Robert L. 3, 39
Johnson, Sheila Crump 48
Johnson, William 91
Jolley, Willie 28
Jones, Carl 7
Jones, Caroline 29
Jones, Ingrid Saunders 18
Jones, John 89

Jones, Thomas W. 41
Jones, Wayne 53
Jordan, Michael 6, 21
Jordan, Montell 23
Joyner, Marjorie Stewart 26
Julian, Percy Lavon 6
Kaigler, Denise 63
Keith, Floyd A. 61
Kelly, Patrick 3
Kemp, Herb 94
Kendrick, Erika 57
Kidd, Mae Street 39
Killingsworth, Cleve, Jr. 54
Kimbro, Dennis 10
King, Dexter 10
King, Don 14
Knowles, Tina 61
Knowling, Robert E., Jr. 38
Lane, Vincent 5
Langhart Cohen, Janet 19, 60
Lanier, Willie 33
Laryea, Thomas Davies, III 67
Lawal, Kase L. 45
Lawless, Theodore K. 8
Lawson, Jennifer 1, 50
Leary, Kathryn D. 10
Leavell, Dorothy R. 17
Lee, Annie Frances 22
Lee, Bertram M., Sr. 46
Lee, Debra L. 62
Leonard, Sugar Ray 15
Lewis, Aylwin B. 51, 88
Lewis, Byron E. 13
Lewis, Delano 7
Lewis, Edward T. 21
Lewis, Reginald F. 6
Lewis, William M., Jr. 40
Ligging, Alfred, III 43
Llewellyn, J. Bruce 13, 85
Long, Eddie L. 29, 89
Louis, Errol T. 8
Lucas, John 7
Lucy, William 50
Mack, Iris 105
Malone, Annie 13
Maponya, Richard 101
March, William Carrington 56
Marks, Audrey 99
Marshall, Bella 22
Matthews Shatteen, Westina 51
Matzeliger, Jan 93
Mayberry-Stewart, Melodie 94
Maynard, Robert C. 7
Mays, Leslie A. 41
Mays, William G. 34
McCabe, Jewell Jackson 10
McCann, Renetta 44
McCoy, Elijah 8
McDonald, Erroll 1
McGee, James Madison 46
McGuire, Raymond J. 57
McKissack, Leatrice 80
McLeod, Gus 27
McPherson, David 32
McWorter, Free Frank 91
Middleton, Reggie 105
Miller, Larry G. 72
Miller, Pepper 96
Millines Dziko, Trish 28
Mills, Steve 47
Mingo, Frank 32
Mitchell, Shireen 89
Monk, Art 38, 73

Monroe, Bryan 71
Montgomery, Isaiah T. 91
Montgomery, Robbie 101
Moore, Wes 86
Morgan, Garrett 1
Morgan, Rose 11
Morris, William 51
Moyo, Karega Kofi 36
Moyo, Yvette Jackson 36
Muhammad, Jabir Herbert 72
Nagin, Ray 42, 57, 88
Nail, John E. 92
Nanula, Richard D. 20
Nash, Diane 72
Nelson Meigs, Andrea 48
Nichols, Nichelle 11
Norman, Christina 47
Ogunlesi, Adebayo O. 37
Oliver, Garrett 95
Olojede, Dele 59
O'Neal, Rodney 88
O'Neal, Stanley 38, 67
Otis, Clarence, Jr. 55
Ouattara, Morou 74
Packer, Daniel 56
Parham, Marjorie B. 71
Parks, Henry Green, Jr. 89
Parsons, Richard Dean 11, 33
Payton, Philip A., Jr. 88
Peck, Carolyn 23
Perez, Anna 1
Perkins, James, Jr. 55
Perry, Laval 64
Perry, Lowell 30
Phillips, Charles E., Jr. 57, 109
Pierce, Harold 75
Pinckney, Bill 42
Pinkett, Randal 61
Pleasant, Mary Ellen 9
Plinton, James O., Jr. 98
Potter, Myrtle 40
Price, Frederick K. C. 21
Price, Hugh B. 9, 54
Price, Lisa 97
Procope, Ernesta 23
Procope, John Levy 56
Queen Latifah 1, 16, 58
Quivers, Robin 61
Raines, Franklin 14, 107
Rand, A. Barry 6
Reeves, Rachel J. 23
Reid, Antonio "L.A." 28
Rhone, Sylvia 2
Rice, Linda Johnson 9, 41
Rice, Norm 8
Richardson, Donna 39
Richie, Leroy C. 18
Rideau, Iris 46
Roberts, Mike 57
Roberts, Roy S. 14
Robertson, Oscar 26
Robeson, Eslanda Goode 13
Robinson, Jackie 6
Robinson, Rachel 16
Robinson, Randall 7, 46
Roche, Joyce M. 17
Rodgers, Johnathan 6, 51
Rodriguez, Jimmy 47
Rogers, Desirée 88
Rogers, John W., Jr. 5, 52
Rojas, Don 33
Rolle, Janet 97
Ross, Charles 27

Ross, Diana 8, 27
Russell, Bill 8
Russell, Herman Jerome 17
Russell-McCloud, Patricia 17
Saint James, Synthia 12
Samara, Noah 15
Samuelsson, Marcus 53
Sanders, Angelia 86
Sanders, Dori 8
Sbraga, Kevin 88
Scott, C. A. 29
Scott, Milton 51
Scott, Tim 87
Sengstacke, John 18
Shakur, Afeni 67
Shank, Suzanne F. 77
Shropshire, Thomas B. 49
Siméus, Dumas M. 25, 110
Simmons, Kimora Lee 51, 83
Simmons, Russell 1, 30
Sims, Naomi 29, 79
Smith, B(arbara) 11
Smith, Clarence O. 21
Smith, Jane E. 24
Smith, Joshua 10
Smith, Willi 8
Sneed, Paula A. 18
Snowden, Gail 108
Spaulding, Charles Clinton 9
Staley, Dawn 57
Stanford, Olivia Lee Dilworth 49
Steinberg, Martha Jean "The
    Queen" 28
Steward, David L. 36
Stewart, Ella 39
Stewart, Paul Wilbur 12
Stinson, Denise L. 59
Stradford, J. B. 101
Stringer, Vickie 58
Sullivan, Leon H. 3, 30
Sutton, Percy E. 42, 82
Taylor, Ephren W., II 61
Taylor, Karin 34
Taylor, Kristin Clark 8
Taylor, Natalie 47
Taylor, Robert Rochon 104
Taylor, Susan L. 10, 86
Temple, Lewis 102
Terrell, Dorothy A. 24
Thiam, Tidjane 104
Thomas, Franklin A. 5, 49
Thomas, Jefferson 88
Thomas-Graham, Pamela 29
Thompson, Cynthia Bramlett 50
Thompson, Don 56, 108
Thompson, John W. 26
Tobin, Patricia 75
Travis, Tracey T. 94
Tribble, Israel, Jr. 8
Trotter, Lloyd G. 56
Trotter, Monroe 9
Tuckson, Reed V. 71
Tyson, Asha 39
Ussery, Terdema, II 29
Utendahl, John 23
VanDerZee, James 6
Vaughn, Gladys Gary 47
Vaughns, Cleopatra 46
Villarosa, Clara 85
Walker, A'lelia 14
Walker, Cedric 19
Walker, Joseph Edison 111
Walker, Madame C. J. 7

Walker, Maggie Lena 17
Walker, Ray 109
Walker, T. J. 7
Walker, Tristan 98
Ward, Lloyd 21, 46
Ware, Carl H. 30
Washington, Alonzo 29
Washington, Mary T. 57
Washington, Regynald G. 44
Washington, Val 12
Wasow, Omar 15
Watkins, Donald 35
Watkins, Walter C., Jr. 24
Wein, Joyce 62
Welburn, Edward T. 50
Wells-Barnett, Ida B. 8
Westbrook, Kelvin 50
Wharton, Clifton R., Jr. 7
White, Linda M. 45
White, Walter F. 4
Wilkins, Ray 47
Williams, Armstrong 29
Williams, Lindsey 75
Williams, O. S. 13
Williams, Paul R. 9
Williams, Ronald A. 57
Williams, Terrie 35
Williams, Walter E. 4
Williams, Wendy 62
Willie, Louis, Jr. 68
Wilson, Sunnie 7, 55
Woods, Jacqueline 52
Woods, Sylvia 34, 104
Woodson, Robert L. 10
Wright, Antoinette 60
Wright, Charles H. 35
Wright, Deborah C. 25
Wright, Rayfield 70
Wright, Richard Robert, Sr. 100
Yoba, Malik 11
Young, Perry H. 100
Zollar, Alfred 40

Dance
Acogny, Germaine 55
Adams, Jenoyne 60
Ailey, Alvin 8
Allen, Debbie 13, 42
Anderson, Lauren 72
Anderson, Maceo 111
Atkins, Cholly 40
Babatunde, Obba 35
Baker, Josephine 3
Bates, Peg Leg 14
Beatty, Talley 35
Brown, Ernest 80
Brown, Ronald K. 91
Byrd, Donald 10
Chanticleer, Raven 91
Clarke, Hope 14
Collins, Janet 33, 64
Davis, Chuck 33
de Lavallade, Carmen 78
DePrince, Michaela 104
Dove, Ulysses 5
Dunham, Katherine 4, 59
Ellington, Mercedes 34
Fagan, Garth 18, 98
Falana, Lola 42
Glover, Savion 14
Hall, Arthur 39
Henson, Darrin 33
Hines, Gregory 1, 42

Jamison, Judith **7, 67, 96**
Jefferson, Denise **87**
Jeune, Vitolio **98**
Johnson, Ken **106**
Johnson, Virginia **9**
Jones, Bill T. **1, 46, 80**
Jones, Doris W. **62**
King, Alonzo **38**
Lane, William Henry **90**
LeTang, Henry **66**
Manning, Frankie **78**
Miller, Bebe **3**
Mills, Florence **22**
Mitchell, Arthur **2, 47**
Moten, Etta **18**
Muse, Clarence Edouard **21**
Nash, Joe **55**
Nicholas, Fayard **20, 57**
Nicholas, Harold **20**
Nichols, Nichelle **11**
Polite, Carlene Hatcher **82**
Pomare, Eleo **72**
Premice, Josephine **41**
Primus, Pearl **6**
Ray, Gene Anthony **47**
Rhoden, Dwight **40**
Ribeiro, Alfonso **17**
Richardson, Desmond **39**
Robinson, Bill "Bojangles" **11**
Robinson, Cleo Parker **38**
Robinson, Fatima **34**
Robinson, LaVaughn **69**
Rodgers, Rod **36**
Sims, Howard "Sandman" **48**
Slyde, Jimmy **70**
Spears, Warren **52**
Tyson, Andre **40**
Vereen, Ben **4**
Walker, Dianne **57**
Washington, Fredi **10**
Williams, Dudley **60**
Zollar, Jawole Willa Jo **28**

Education

Abani, Chris **77**
Abercrumbie, P. Eric **95**
Ackerman, Arlene **108**
Adams, Leslie **39**
Adams-Ender, Clara **40**
Adkins, Rutherford H. **21**
Aidoo, Ama Ata **38**
Ake, Claude **30**
Albert, Octavia V. R. **100**
Alexander, Margaret Walker **22**
Alexander, Michelle **98**
Allen, Robert L. **38**
Allen, Samuel W. **38**
Allen-Buillard, Melba **55**
Alston, Charles **33**
Amadi, Elechi **40**
Ammons, James H. **81**
Anderson, Charles Edward **37**
Appiah, Kwame Anthony **67, 101**
Archer, Dennis **7**
Archie-Hudson, Marguerite **44**
Aristide, Jean-Bertrand **6, 45**
Asante, Molefi Kete **3**
Aubert, Alvin **41**
Austin, Bobby W. **95**
Awuah, Patrick **111**
Bacon-Bercey, June **38**
Bahati, Wambui **60**
Baiocchi, Regina Harris **41**

Baker, Augusta **38**
Baker, Delbert W. **110**
Baker, Gwendolyn Calvert **9**
Baker, Houston A., Jr. **6**
Baldwin, Cynthia **74, 107**
Ballard, Allen Butler, Jr. **40**
Bambara, Toni Cade **10**
Baraka, Amiri **1, 38**
Barbee, Lloyd Augustus **71**
Barboza, Anthony **10**
Barnett, Marguerite **46**
Barthé, Earl **78**
Bath, Patricia E. **37**
Batiste, Alvin **66**
Beals, Melba Pattillo **15, 94**
Beckham, Barry **41**
Belgrave, Marcus **77**
Bell, Derrick **6, 98**
Benberry, Cuesta **65**
Benjamin, Tritobia Hayes **53**
Berry, Bertice **8, 55**
Berry, Mary Frances **7**
Bethune, Mary McLeod **4**
Biggers, John **20, 33**
Black, Albert **51**
Blackwell, David **79**
Blakely, Edward J. **88**
Blassingame, John Wesley **40**
Blockson, Charles L. **42**
Bluitt, Juliann S. **14**
Bobo, Lawrence **60**
Bogle, Donald **34**
Bolden, Tonya **32**
Bosley, Freeman, Jr. **7**
Boyd, Melba Joyce **86**
Boyd, T. B., III **6**
Bradley, Adam **101**
Bradley, David Henry, Jr. **39**
Branch, William Blackwell **39**
Brathwaite, Kamau **36**
Braun, Carol Moseley **4, 42**
Briscoe, Marlin **37**
Bromery, Randolph Wilson **85**
Brown, Claude **38**
Brown, Hallie Quinn **100**
Brown, Joyce F. **25**
Brown, Sterling Allen **10, 64**
Brown, Uzee **42**
Brown, Wesley **23**
Brown, Willa **40**
Bruce, Blanche Kelso **33**
Brutus, Dennis **38**
Bunch, Lonnie G., III **91**
Burke, Selma **16**
Burke, Yvonne Brathwaite **42**
Burks, Mary Fair **40**
Burnim, Mickey L. **48**
Burroughs, Margaret Taylor **9**
Burroughs, Nannie Helen **96**
Butler, Paul D. **17**
Butler, Selena Sloan **98**
Butts, Calvin O., III **9, 90**
Callender, Clive O. **3**
Campbell, Bebe Moore **6, 24, 59**
Campbell, Mary Schmidt **43**
Cannon, Katie **10**
Carby, Hazel **10**
Cardozo, Francis L. **33**
Carnegie, Herbert **25**
Carruthers, George R. **40**
Carter, Herbert E. **108**
Carter, Joye Maureen **41**
Carter, Kenneth **53**

Carter, Warrick L. **27**
Cartey, Wilfred **47**
Carver, George Washington **4**
Cary, Lorene **3**
Cary, Mary Ann Shadd **30**
Catlett, Elizabeth **2**
Cayton, Horace **26**
Chaney, John **67**
Cheney-Coker, Syl **43**
Childers, Lulu Vere **95**
Clark, Joe **1**
Clark, Kenneth B. **5, 52**
Clark, Septima **7**
Clark, Yvonne Young **95**
Clarke, Cheryl **32**
Clarke, George **32**
Clarke, John Henrik **20**
Clayton, Constance **1**
Cleaver, Kathleen Neal **29**
Clements, George **2**
Clemmons, Reginal G. **41**
Cobb, Jewel Plummer **42**
Cobb, W. Montague **39**
Cobb, William Jelani **59**
Cobbs, Price M. **9**
Cohen, Anthony **15**
Cohen, Cathy J. **88**
Cole, Johnnetta B. **5, 43**
Coleman, William F., III **61**
Colescott, Robert **69**
Collins, Janet **33, 64**
Collins, Marva **3, 71**
Collins, Patricia Hill **67**
Comer, James P. **6**
Coney, PonJola **48**
Conrad, Cecilia A. **94**
Cook, Mercer **40**
Cook, Samuel DuBois **14**
Cook, Toni **23**
Cooper, Afua **53**
Cooper, Anna Julia **20**
Cooper, Edward S. **6**
Cooper Cafritz, Peggy **43**
Copeland, Michael **47**
Cotter, Joseph Seamon, Sr. **40**
Cottrell, Comer **11**
Counter, S. Allen **74**
Cox, Elbert Frank **111**
Cox, Joseph Mason Andrew **51**
Cox, William E. **68**
Creagh, Milton **27**
Crenshaw, Kimberlé Williams **88**
Crew, Rudy **16, 113**
Crew, Spencer R. **55**
Cross, Dolores E. **23**
Crouch, Hubert **95**
Cruse, Harold **54**
Cullen, Countee **8**
Daly, Marie Maynard **37**
Dathorne, O. R. **52**
Davis, Allison **12**
Davis, Angela J. **88**
Davis, Arthur P. **41**
Davis, Charles T. **48**
Davis, Erroll B., Jr. **57**
Davis, George **36**
Davis, Milt **74**
Dawson, William Levi **39**
Days, Drew S., III **10**
Deconge-Watson, Lovenia **55**
Delany, Sadie **12**
Delany, Samuel R., Jr. **9**
Delco, Wilhemina R. **33**

Delpit, Lisa **101**
Delsarte, Louis **34**
Dennard, Brazeal **37**
Dewitty, Thelma **114**
Dickens, Helen Octavia **14, 64**
Diop, Cheikh Anta **4**
Dixon, Margaret **14**
Dodson, Howard, Jr. **7, 52**
Dodson, Owen Vincent **38**
Dogan, Matthew Winifred **91**
Donaldson, Jeff **46**
Douglas, Aaron **7**
Dove, Ulysses **5**
Draper, Sharon Mills **16, 43**
Driskell, David C. **7**
Drummond, William J. **40**
Du Bois, David Graham **45**
Dumas, Henry **41**
Dunbar-Nelson, Alice Ruth Moore **44**
Dunnigan, Alice Allison **41**
Dunston, Georgia Mae **48**
Dymally, Mervyn **42**
Dyson, Michael Eric **11, 40**
Early, Gerald **15**
Edelin, Ramona Hoage **19**
Edelman, Marian Wright **5, 42**
Edley, Christopher **2, 48**
Edley, Christopher F., Jr. **48**
Edwards, Harry **2**
Elders, Joycelyn **6**
Elliot, Lorris **37**
Ellis, Clarence A. **38**
Ellison, Ralph **7**
Epps, Archie C., III **45**
Evans, Mari **26**
Everett, Percival **93**
Falconer, Etta Zuber **59**
Fauset, Jessie **7**
Favors, Steve **23**
Feelings, Muriel **44**
Ferguson, Ronald F. **75**
Figueroa, John J. **40**
Fleming, Raymond **48**
Fletcher, Bill, Jr. **41**
Floyd, Elson S. **41**
Ford, Jack **39**
Forman, James, Jr. **89**
Foster, Ezola **28**
Foster, Henry W., Jr. **26**
Foster, William P. **88**
Francis, Norman (C.) **60**
Franklin, Hardy R. **9, 87**
Franklin, John Hope **5, 77**
Franklin, Robert M. **13**
Frazier, E. Franklin **10**
Fryer, Roland G. **56**
Fuller, A. Oveta **43**
Fuller, Arthur **27**
Fuller, Howard L. **37**
Fuller, Solomon Carter, Jr. **15**
Futrell, Mary Hatwood **33**
Gaines, Ernest J. **7**
Gates, Henry Louis, Jr. **3, 38, 67**
Gates, Sylvester James, Jr. **15**
Gayle, Addison, Jr. **41**
George, Zelma Watson **42**
Gerima, Haile **38, 80**
Gibson, Donald Bernard **40**
Giddings, Paula **11**
Gilbert, John Wesley **91**
Gill, Gerald **69**
Gloster, Hugh Morris, Sr. **90**

Gomes, Peter J. **15, 93**
Gomez, Jewelle **30**
Gomillion, Charles **90**
Goodison, Lorna **71**
Granville, Evelyn Boyd **36**
Greenfield, Eloise **9**
Groff, Peter **96**
Guinier, Lani **7, 30**
Guy-Sheftall, Beverly **13, 92**
Hageman, Hans and Ivan **36**
Hale, Lorraine **8**
Hall, Stuart **78**
Halliburton, Warren J. **49**
Hamburg, Beatrix **84**
Hammonds, Evelynn **69**
Handy, W. C. **8**
Hansberry, William Leo **11**
Harding, Vincent **67**
Harkless, Necia Desiree **19**
Harper, Michael S. **34**
Harris, Alice **7**
Harris, Barry **68**
Harris, Bill **72**
Harris, Gary L. **87**
Harris, Jay T. **19**
Harris, Jessica B. **91**
Harris, Patricia Roberts **2**
Harris-Lacewell, Melissa **81**
Harsh, Vivian Gordon **14**
Harvey, William R. **42**
Haskins, James **36, 54**
Hathaway, Isaac Scott **33**
Hayden, Carla D. **47**
Hayden, Robert **12**
Haynes, George Edmund **8**
Henderson, George Washington **101**
Henderson, Stephen E. **45**
Henries, A. Doris Banks **44**
Herenton, Willie W. **24, 81**
Hill, Andrew **66**
Hill, Anita **5, 65**
Hill, Bonnie Guiton **20**
Hill, Errol **40**
Hill, Leslie Pinckney **44**
Hill, Marc Lamont **80**
Hilliard, Asa Grant, III **66**
Hine, Darlene Clark **24**
Hinton, William Augustus **8**
Hoagland, Everett H. **45**
Hogan, Beverly Wade **50**
Holland, Endesha Ida Mae **3, 57**
Holt, Nora **38**
Hope, John **8**
Horton, James Oliver **58**
Houston, Charles Hamilton **4**
Hoyte, Lenon **50**
Hrabowski, Freeman A., III **22**
Huggins, Nathan Irvin **52**
Hughes, Ebony **57**
Hull, Akasha Gloria **45**
Humphries, Frederick **20**
Hunt, Darnell **92**
Hunt, Richard **6**
Hutcherson, Hilda Yvonne **54**
Hutson, Jean Blackwell **16**
Imes, Elmer Samuel **39**
Jackson, Edison O. **67**
Jackson, Fred James **25**
Jackson, Vera **40**
Jansen, Jonathan **102**
Jarrett, Vernon D. **42**
Jarvis, Charlene Drew **21**

Jarvis, Erich **67**
Jefferson, Denise **87**
Jefferson, Margo **108**
Jeffries, Leonard **8**
Jenifer, Franklyn G. **2**
Jenkins, Ella **15**
Johns, Vernon **38**
Johnson, Anthony M. **92**
Johnson, Conrad O. **97**
Johnson, Hazel **22**
Johnson, James Weldon **5**
Johnson, Katherine **61**
Johnson, Mordecai Wyatt **79**
Jones, Clara Stanton **51**
Jones, Edward P. **43, 67**
Jones, Gayl **37**
Jones, Ingrid Saunders **18**
Jones, Lois Mailou **13**
Joplin, Scott **6**
Jordan, June **7, 35**
Joseph, Jamal **101**
Josey, E. J. **10**
Just, Ernest Everett **3**
Karenga, Maulana **10, 71**
Kay, Ulysses **37**
Keith, Damon J. **16, 74**
Kennedy, Florynce **12, 33**
Kennedy, Randall **40**
Kilpatrick, Carolyn Cheeks **16**
Kimbro, Dennis **10**
King, Preston **28**
King, Reatha Clark **65**
Kittles, Rick **51**
Komunyakaa, Yusef **9**
Koontz, Elizabeth Duncan **101**
Kunjufu, Jawanza **3, 50**
Ladner, Joyce A. **42**
Lawrence, Jacob **4, 28**
Lawrence-Lightfoot, Sara **10**
Lee, Annie Frances **22**
Lee, Joe A. **45**
Leevy, Carrol M. **42**
Leffall, Lasalle **3, 64**
Lewis, David Levering **9**
Lewis, Norman **39**
Lewis, Samella **25**
Lewis, Shirley A. R. **14**
Lewis, Thomas **19**
Liberia-Peters, Maria Philomena **12**
Lincoln, C. Eric **38**
Lindsey, Tommie **51**
Locke, Alain **10**
Logan, Rayford W. **40**
Lomax, Michael L. **58**
Long, Loretta **58**
Long, Richard Alexander **65**
Lorde, Audre **6**
Loury, Glenn **36**
Loving, Alvin, Jr. **35, 53**
Lowry, A. Leon **60**
Lucy Foster, Autherine **35**
Luper, Clara **94**
Lyons, James E., Sr. **102**
Lyttle, Hulda Margaret **14**
Mackey, Nathaniel **75**
Major, Clarence **9**
Malveaux, Floyd **54**
Manley, Audrey Forbes **16**
Marable, Manning **10, 102**
Markham, E. A. **37**
Marsalis, Ellis **90**
Marshall, Paule **7, 77**
Masekela, Barbara **18**

Mason, Herman, Jr. **83**
Mason, Ronald **27**
Massey, Walter E. **5, 45**
Massie, Samuel P., Jr. **29**
Matejka, Adrian **87**
Maupin, John E., Jr. **92**
Mayhew, Richard **39**
Maynard, Robert C. **7**
Maynor, Dorothy **19**
Mayo, Whitman **32**
Mays, Benjamin E. **7**
McBay, Henry C. **91**
McCarty, Osceola **16**
McCullough, Geraldine **58, 79**
McDaniel, Randall Cornell **81**
McKay, Nellie Yvonne **17, 57**
McLendon, John B., Jr. **89**
McMillan, Terry **4, 17, 53**
McMurray, Georgia L. **36**
McPherson, James Alan **70**
McWhorter, John **35**
Mell, Patricia **49**
Memmi, Albert **37**
Meredith, James H. **11**
Millender-McDonald, Juanita **21, 61**
Mitchell, Corinne **8**
Mitchell, Nicole **66**
Mitchell, Sharon **36**
Mofolo, Thomas Mokopu **37**
Mollel, Tololwa **38**
Mongella, Gertrude **11**
Moody-Adams, Michele **76**
Mooney, Paul **37**
Moore, Barbara C. **49**
Moore, Harry T. **29**
Moore, Melba **21**
Morón, Alonzo G. **91**
Morrison, Keith **13**
Morrison, Sam **50**
Morrison, Toni **2, 15, 86**
Moses, Robert Parris **11**
Moton, Robert Russa **83**
Mphalele, Es'kia (Ezekiel) **40**
Mudimbe, V. Y. **61**
Mullen, Harryette **34**
Murray, Pauli **38**
Nabrit, Samuel Milton **47**
Nance, Cynthia **71**
Naylor, Gloria **10, 42**
Neal, Larry **38**
Neal, Mark Anthony **74**
Newkirk, Pamela **69**
Newman, Lester C. **51**
N'Namdi, George R. **17**
Norman, Maidie **20**
Nour, Nawal M. **56**
Obadele, Imari **84**
Ogletree, Charles, Jr. **12, 47**
Ojikutu, Bisola **65**
Oliver, Kimberly **60**
Onwueme, Tess Osonye **23**
Onwurah, Ngozi **38**
Owens, Helen **48**
Page, Alan **7**
Page, Inman **82**
Paige, Rod **29**
Painter, Nell Irvin **24, 88**
Palmer, Everard **37**
Parker, Kellis E. **30**
Patterson, Frederick Douglass **12**
Patterson, Mary Jane **54**
Patterson, Orlando **4**
Payton, Benjamin F. **23**

Perry, Steve **98**
Perry, Warren **56**
Peters, Margaret **43**
Peters, Matilda **43**
Peterson, James **81**
Pickett, Cecil **39**
Pinckney, Bill **42**
Pindell, Howardena **55**
Piper, Adrian **71**
Player, Willa B. **43**
Pollard, William L. **91**
Porter, James A. **11**
Poussaint, Alvin F. **5, 67**
Powell, Benny **87**
Price, Florence **37**
Price, Glenda **22**
Price, Richard **51**
Primus, Pearl **6**
Prophet, Nancy Elizabeth **42**
Purnell, Silas **59**
Putney, Martha S. **75**
Quarles, Benjamin Arthur **18**
Querino, Manuel Raimundo **84**
Quigless, Helen G. **49**
Rahman, Aishah **37**
Ramphele, Mamphela **29**
Randall, Vernellia R. **95**
Reagon, Bernice Johnson **7**
Reaves, Donald J. **102**
Reddick, Lawrence Dunbar **20**
Redding, J. Saunders **26**
Redmond, Eugene **23**
Reid, Ira De A. **100**
Reid, Irvin D. **20**
Rhodes, Jewell Parker **84**
Ribeau, Sidney **70**
Rice, Condoleezza **3, 28, 72**
Rice, Louise Allen **54**
Richards, Hilda **49**
Riles, Wilson C. **79**
Robinson, Joann Gibson **100**
Robinson, Sharon **22**
Robinson, Spottswood W., III **22**
Rodriguez, Cheryl **64**
Rogers, Joel Augustus **30**
Rollins, Charlemae Hill **27**
Ross-Lee, Barbara **67**
Rouse, Cecilia **93**
Russell-McCloud, Patricia **17**
Russwurm, John Brown **100**
Salih, Al-Tayyib **37**
Sallee, Charles Louis, Jr. **38**
Schomburg, Arthur Alfonso **9**
Sears, Stephanie **53**
Senior, Olive **37**
Shabazz, Betty **7, 26**
Shange, Ntozake **8, 89**
Shelton, Paula Young **86**
Shipp, E. R. **15**
Shirley, George **33**
Shockley, Ann Allen **84**
Simkins, Modjeska Monteith **112**
Simmons, Ruth J. **13, 38**
Sinkford, Jeanne C. **13**
Sisulu, Sheila Violet Makate **24**
Sizemore, Barbara A. **26, 110**
Smith, Anna Deavere **6**
Smith, Barbara **28**
Smith, Jessie Carney **35**
Smith, John L. **22**
Smith, Mary Carter **26**
Smith, Tubby **18, 83**
Snowden, Frank M., Jr. **67**

Southern, Eileen 56
Sowande, Fela 39
Spearman, Leonard H. O., Sr. 81
Spears, Warren 52
Spikes, Dolores 18
Spriggs, William 67
Stanford, John 20
Steele, Claude 13, 97
Steele, Shelby 13, 82
Stephens, Charlotte Andrews 14
Stewart, Maria W. Miller 19
Stewart, Tonea Harris 78
Stone, Chuck 9
Sudarkasa, Niara 4
Sullivan, Louis 8
Swygert, H. Patrick 22
Talbert, Mary B. 77
Tancil, Gladys Quander 59
Tanksley, Ann 37
Tatum, Beverly Daniel 42, 84
Taylor, Helen (Lavon Hollingshed) 30
Taylor, Susie King 13
Terrell, Mary Church 9
Thomas, Alma 14
Thomas, Michael 69
Thurman, Howard 3
Tillis, Frederick 40
Tillman, Deborah 98
Tobias, Channing H. 79
Toler, Burl 80
Tolson, Melvin 37
Tribble, Israel, Jr. 8
Trueheart, William E. 49
Tucker, Rosina 14
Turnbull, Charles Wesley 62
Turnbull, Walter 13, 60
Tutu, Desmond 6
Tutu, Nontombi Naomi 57
Tutuola, Amos 30
Tyson, Andre 40
Tyson, Asha 39
Tyson, Neil deGrasse 15, 65
Usry, James L. 23
van Sertima, Ivan 25
Vaughn, Viola 70
Vega, Marta Moreno 61
Velez-Rodriguez, Argelia 56
Verna, Gelsy 70
Wade-Gayles, Gloria Jean 41
Walcott, Dennis M. 112
Walcott, Derek 5, 94
Walker, George 37
Wallace, Michele Faith 13
Wallace, Perry E. 47
Wallace, Phyllis A. 9
Walters, Ronald 83
Washington, Booker T. 4
Watkins, Shirley R. 17
Wattleton, Faye 9
Weaver, Afaa Michael 37
Wedgeworth, Robert W. 42
Wells, Henrietta Bell 69
Wells, James Lesesne 10
Wells-Barnett, Ida B. 8
Welsing, Frances Cress 5
Wesley, Dorothy Porter 19
Wesley, Richard 73
West, Cornel 5, 33, 80
Wharton, Clifton R., Jr. 7
White, Charles 39
White, Lois Jean 20
Wilkens, J. Ernest, Jr. 43

Wilkins, Roger 2, 84
Williams, David Rudyard 50
Williams, Fannie Barrier 27
Williams, Gregory 11
Williams, Patricia 11, 54
Williams, Rhonda Y. 86
Williams, Sherley Anne 25
Williams, Walter E. 4
Wilson, Donald E. 88
Wilson, William Julius 22
Woodruff, Hale 9
Woodson, Carter G. 2
Worrill, Conrad 12
Wright, Antoinette 60
Wright, Richard Robert, Sr. 100
Xuma, Madie Hall 59
Yancy, Dorothy Cowser 42
Young, Jean Childs 14
Zook, Kristal Brent 62

Fashion
Aberra, Amsale 67
Bailey, Xenobia 11
Banks, Jeffrey 17
Banks, Tyra 11, 50
Barboza, Anthony 10
Beals, Jennifer 12
Beauvais, Garcelle 29, 95
Beckford, Tyson 11, 68
Boateng, Ozwald 35, 113
Bond, Beverly 53
Bonney, Tabi 98
Boyd, Suzanne 52
Bridges, Sheila 36
Brown, Joyce F. 25
Burrows, Stephen 31
Campbell, Naomi 1, 31
Chanticleer, Raven 91
DaCosta, YaYa 98
Darego, Agbani 52
Davidson, Jaye 5
Davis, Mia Amber 94
De' Alexander, Quinton 57
Delice, Ronald 48
Delice, Rony 48
Dirie, Waris 56
Dobson, Tamara 111
Ebanks, Selita 67
Evans, Etu 55
Finley, Ron 110
Gaskins, Eric 64
Gibson, Ted 66
Givhan, Robin Deneen 72
Hall, Kevan 61
Harold, Erika 54
Henderson, Gordon 5
Hendy, Francis 47
Iman 4, 33, 87
Iman, Chanel 66
John, Daymond 23, 114
Johnson, Beverly 2, 102
Johnson, Eunice W. 83
Jones, Carl 7
Jones, Genevieve 101
Kani, Karl 10
Kebede, Liya 59
Keckley, Elizabeth 90
Kelly, Patrick 3
Kodjoe, Boris 34, 89
Lars, Byron 32
Lopes, Leila 99
Luna, Donyale 88
Malone, Maurice 32

Marcille, Eva 97
McGrath, Pat 72
McKenzie, Jaunel 73
Michele, Michael 31
Niane, Katoucha 70
Onwurah, Ngozi 38
Powell, Maxine 8, 115
Reese, Tracy 54
Rhymes, Busta 31
Robinson, Patrick 19, 71
Rochon, Lela 16
Rowell, Victoria 13, 68
Simmons, Kimora Lee 51, 83
Sims, Naomi 29, 79
Smaltz, Audrey 12
Smith, B(arbara) 11
Smith, LaQuan 113
Smith, Willi 8
Smythe Haith, Mabel 61
Steele, Lawrence 28
Stoney, Michael 50
Sy, Oumou 65
Talley, André Leon 56, 106
Taylor, Karin 34
Walker, T. J. 7
Webb, Veronica 10, 95
Wek, Alek 18, 63, 105
White, Jessica 83
Williams, Serena 20, 41, 73

Film
Aaliyah 30
Aaron, Quinton 82
Adebimpe, Tunde 75
Akinnuoye-Agbaje, Adewale 56
Akomfrah, John 37
Ali, Tatyana 73
Allain, Stephanie 49
Allen, Debbie 13, 42
Alonso, Laz 87
Amata, Jeta 111
Amos, John 8, 62
Anderson, Anthony 51, 77
Anderson, Eddie "Rochester" 30
Andrews, Tina 74
Armah, Esther 87
Babatunde, Obba 35
Babyface 10, 31, 82
Baker, Josephine 3
Banks, Michelle 59
Banks, Tyra 11, 50
Barclay, Paris 37, 94
Barnett, Etta Moten 56
Baskett, James 102
Bassett, Angela 6, 23, 62
Beach, Michael 26
Beals, Jennifer 12
Beckford, Tyson 11, 68
Belafonte, Harry 4, 65
Bellamy, Bill 12
Bennett, Louise 69
Bentley, Lamont 53
Berry, Fred "Rerun" 48
Berry, Halle 4, 19, 57, 91
Bey, Yasiin 30, 96
Billops, Camille 82
Bivins, Michael 72
Blackwood, Maureen 37
Bleu, Corbin 65
Bogle, Donald 34
Boseman, Chadwick 111
Brady, Wayne 32, 71
Brandy 14, 34, 72

Breeze, Jean "Binta" 37
Brooks, Golden 62
Brooks, Hadda 40
Brown, Jim 11, 95
Brown, Tony 3
Browne, Roscoe Lee 66
Burnett, Charles 16, 68
Byrd, Michelle 19
Byrd, Robert 11
Calloway, Cab 14
Campbell, Naomi 1, 31
Campbell-Martin, Tisha 8, 42
Cannon, Nick 47, 73
Cannon, Reuben 50
Cara, Irene 77
Carroll, Diahann 9
Carroll, Rocky 74
Carson, Lisa Nicole 21
Cash, Rosalind 28
Cedric the Entertainer 29, 60, 115
Chase, Debra Martin 49, 96
Cheadle, Don 19, 52
Chestnut, Morris 31
Chong, Rae Dawn 62
Chweneyagae, Presley 63
Cobbs, Bill 101
Common 31, 63, 98
Coogler, Ryan 114
Crump, Steven 96
Curtis-Hall, Vondie 17
DaCosta, YaYa 98
Dandridge, Dorothy 3
Daniels, Lee 36, 76
Dash, Julie 4
David, Keith 27
Davidson, Jaye 5
Davidson, Tommy 21
Davis, Eisa 68
Davis, Guy 36
Davis, Ossie 5, 50
Davis, Sammy, Jr. 18
Davis, Viola 34, 76, 100
Dawn, Marpessa 75
Dawson, Rosario 72
De Bankolé, Isaach 78
de Passe, Suzanne 25
De Shields, André 72
Dee, Ruby 8, 50, 68
Devine, Loretta 24
Dickerson, Ernest 6, 17
Diesel, Vin 29
Dieudonné 67
Diggs, Taye 25, 63
Dixon, Ivan 69
DMX 28, 64
Dobson, Tamara 111
Domingo, Colman 94
Driskell, David C. 7
Duke, Bill 3, 96
Duncan, Michael Clarke 26, 104
Dutton, Charles S. 4, 22
DuVernay, Ava 98
Earthquake 55
Ejiofor, Chiwetel 67
Elba, Idris 49, 89
Elder, Lonne, III 38
Elie, Lolis Eric 97
Elise, Kimberly 32, 101
Ellis, Aunjanue 108
Ellis, Nelsan 105
Ellis, Trey 97
Emmanuel, Alphonsia 38
Epps, Omar 23, 59

Esposito, Giancarlo 9
Evans, Darryl 22
Everett, Francine 23
Faison, Donald 50
Faison, Frankie 55
Fetchit, Stepin 32
Fishburne, Laurence 4, 22, 70
Fisher, Antwone 40
Fisher, Gail 85
Fletcher, Geoffrey 85
Fox, Rick 27
Fox, Vivica A. 15, 53
Foxx, Jamie 15, 48
Franklin, Carl 11
Freeman, Al, Jr. 11, 105
Freeman, Morgan 2, 20, 62, 100
Freeman, Yvette 27
Friday, Jeff 24
Fuller, Charles 8
Fuqua, Antoine 35
Gant, Richard 105
Gaye, Nona 56
Gerima, Haile 38, 80
Gibbs, Marla 86
Gibson, Tyrese 27, 62
Givens, Adele 62
Glover, Danny 1, 24, 103
Glover, Donald 85
Glover, Savion 14
Goldberg, Whoopi 4, 33, 69
Gooding, Cuba, Jr. 16, 62
Gordon, Dexter 25
Gossett, Louis, Jr. 7
Gray, F. Gary 14, 49
Greaves, William 38
Grier, David Alan 28
Grier, Pam 9, 31, 86
Gunn, Moses 10
Gurira, Danai 73
Hairston, Jester 88
Hall, Juanita 62
Hamilton, Lisa Gay 71
Hamilton, Tanya 93
Hampton, Henry 6
Harewood, David 52
Harewood, Dorian 104
Harper, Hill 32, 65, 97
Harris, Leslie 6
Harris, Naomie 55
Harris, Robin 7
Hart, Kevin 103
Hayes, Teddy 40
Hector, Jamie 98
Henriques, Julian 37
Henry, Dwight 104
Henry, Lenny 9, 52
Henson, Darrin 33
Henson, Taraji P. 58, 77
Hines, Gregory 1, 42
Hooks, Robert 76
Horne, Lena 5, 86
Hounsou, Djimon 19, 45
Howard, Sherri 36
Howard, Terrence 59, 94
Howell, Ayinde 91
Hudlin, Reginald 9, 86
Hudlin, Warrington 9
Hudson, Ernie 72
Hudson, Jennifer 63, 83
Hughes, Albert 7
Hughes, Allen 7
Hurt, Byron 61
Ice Cube 8, 30, 60

Ice-T 6, 31, 96
Ingram, Rex 5
Isaacs, Cheryl Boone 113
Jackson, George 19
Jackson, Janet 6, 30, 68
Jackson, Rampage 83
Jackson, Samuel L. 8, 19, 63, 102
Jean, Michaëlle; 70
Jean-Baptiste, Marianne 17, 46
Jean-Louis, Jimmy 76
Johnson, Clark 96
Jones, James Earl 3, 49, 79
Jones, Orlando 30
Jones, Quincy 8, 30
Jones, Rashida 101
Jones, Robbie 113
Jordan, Michael B. 97
Jorge, Seu 73
Julian, Hubert 90
Julien, Isaac 3
Kabera, Eric 104
Kelley, Elijah 65
Kelly, Jim 113
Keys, Alicia 32, 68
Khumalo, Leleti 51
King, Regina 22, 45
King, Woodie, Jr. 27
Kirby, George 14
Kitt, Eartha 16, 75
Kodjoe, Boris 34, 89
Kool Moe Dee 37
Kotto, Yaphet 7
Kunjufu, Jawanza 3, 50
Lane, Charles 3
Lathan, Sanaa 27
Lawrence, Martin 6, 27, 60
Lebo M 109
Lee, Joie 1
Lee, Malcolm D. 75
Lee, Spike 5, 19, 86
Lemmons, Kasi 20
LeNoire, Rosetta 37
Lester, Adrian 46
Lewis, Samella 25
Lil' Kim 28
Lincoln, Abbey 3, 88
Lindo, Delroy 18, 45
LisaRaye 27
LL Cool J 16, 49, 94
Long, Nia 17, 95
Love, Loni 113
Lover, Ed 10
Luke, Derek 61
Lumet, Jenny 80
Luna, Donyale 88
Lynch, Shola 61
Mac, Bernie 29, 61, 72
Mackie, Anthony 102
Madame Sul-Te-Wan 95
Malco, Romany 71
Mann, Tamela 92
Marcille, Eva 97
Marshall, William 107
Martin, Darnell 43, 78
Martin, Duane 108
Martin, Helen 31
Mason, Judi Ann 112
Mbatha-Raw, Gugu 89
McBride, Chi 73
McDaniel, Hattie 5
McGee, Vonetta 95
McKee, Lonette 12
McKinney, Nina Mae 40

McQueen, Butterfly 6, 54
McQueen, Steve 84
Meadows, Tim 30
Mello, Breno 73
Micheaux, Oscar 7
Miles, William 112
Miller, Omar Benson 93
Miller, Wentworth 75
Mitchell, Kel 66
Mokae, Zakes 80
Mo'Nique 35, 84
Mooney, Paul 37
Moore, Chante 26
Moore, Juanita 83
Moore, Melba 21
Morris, Garrett 31
Morrison, Vanessa 84
Morton, Joe 18
Moses, Gilbert 12
Moss, Carlton 17
Murphy, Charles 95
Murphy, Eddie 4, 20, 61
Muse, Clarence Edouard 21
Nash, Johnny 40
Naughton, Naturi 97
Neal, Elise 29
Nelson, Stanley 92
Newton, Thandie 26, 114
Nicholas, Fayard 20, 57
Nicholas, Harold 20
Nichols, Nichelle 11
Norman, Maidie 20
Okonedo, Sophie 67
O'Neal, Ron 46
O'Neal, Shaquille 8, 30, 95
Onwurah, Ngozi 38
Oyelowo, David 82
Packer, Will 71
Palcy, Euzhan 94
Palmer, Keke 68
Parker, Nicole Ari 52
Parks, Gordon 1, 35, 58
Patton, Paula 62
Payne, Allen 13
Peck, Raoul 32
Perrineau, Harold, Jr. 51
Perry, Tyler 40, 54, 103
Peters, Brock 96
Peters, Clarke 103
Pierce, Wendell 90
Pinkett Smith, Jada 10, 41, 95
Poitier, Sidney 11, 36
Poitier, Sydney Tamiia 65
Pounder, CCH 72
Pratt, Kyla 57
Preer, Evelyn 82
Prince-Bythewood, Gina 31, 77
Pryor, Richard 3, 24, 56
Queen Latifah 1, 16, 58
Ralph, Sheryl Lee 18, 108
Randle, Theresa 16
Reddick, Lance 52
Reed, Natina 106
Rees, Dee 100
Reuben, Gloria 15
Rhames, Ving 14, 50
Rhimes, Shonda Lynn 67
Rhymes, Busta 31
Richards, Beah 30
Richardson, LaTanya 71
Richardson, Salli 68
Ridley, John 69
Riggs, Marlon 5, 44

Riley, Amber 97
Roberts, Darryl 70
Roberts, Kimberly Rivers 72
Robinson, Craig 103
Robinson, Matt 69
Robinson, Shaun 36
Rochon, Lela 16
Rock, Chris 3, 22, 66
Rock, The 29, 66
Rodrigues, Percy 68
Rolle, Esther 13, 21
Rollins, Howard E., Jr. 16
Rose, Anika Noni 70
Ross, Diana 8, 27
Roundtree, Richard 27
Rowell, Victoria 13, 68
Rudolph, Maya 46, 106
St. Jacques, Raymond 8
St. John, Kristoff 25
Saldana, Zoe 72
Salter, Nikkole 73
Sands, Diana 87
Schultz, Michael A. 6
Scott, Hazel 66
Scott, Jill 29, 83
Sembène, Ousmane 13, 62
Shakur, Tupac 14
Shepherd, Sherri 55
Short, Columbus 79
Sidibe, Gabourey 84
Sinbad 1, 16
Sinclair, Madge 78
Singleton, John 2, 30
Sisqo 30
Smith, Anjela Lauren 44
Smith, Anna Deavere 6, 44
Smith, Bubba 96
Smith, Jaden 82
Smith, Roger Guenveur 12
Smith, Tasha 73
Smith, Will 8, 18, 53
Smith, Willow 92
Snipes, Wesley 3, 24, 67
Solange 97
Souleymane, Mahamane 78
Spencer, Octavia 100
Strode, Woody 111
Sullivan, Maxine 37
Sy, Omar 109
Sykes, Wanda 48, 81
Tate, Larenz 15
Taylor, Meshach 4
Taylor, Regina 9, 46, 97
Terrence J 108
Thigpen, Lynne 17, 41
Thomas, Sean Patrick 35
Thompson, Kenan 52
Thurman, Wallace 16
Tillman, George, Jr. 20
Torres, Gina 52
Torry, Guy 31
Toussaint, Lorraine 32
Townsend, Robert 4, 23
True, Rachel 82
Tucker, Chris 13, 23, 62
Tunie, Tamara 63
Turman, Glynn 100
Turner, Tina 6, 27
Tyler, Aisha N. 36
Tyson, Cicely 7, 51, 112
Underwood, Blair 7, 27, 76
Union, Gabrielle 31, 92
Usher 23, 56, 95

Van Lierop, Robert 53
Van Peebles, Mario 2, 51
Van Peebles, Melvin 7, 95
Vance, Courtney B. 15, 60
Vanity 67
Vereen, Ben 4
Walker, Eamonn 37
Wallace, William 75
Wallis, Quvenzhané 109
Ward, Douglas Turner 42
Washington, Denzel 1, 16, 93
Washington, Fredi 10
Washington, Kerry 46, 107
Waters, Ethel 7
Wayans, Damien 78
Wayans, Damon 8, 41
Wayans, Keenen Ivory 18
Wayans, Kim 80
Wayans, Marlon 29, 82
Wayans, Shawn 29
Weathers, Carl 10
Wesley, Richard 73
Wesley, Rutina 97
Wheaton, James 103
Whitaker, Forest 2, 49, 67
White, Armond 80
White, Michael Jai 71
White, Sylvain 96
Whitfield, Lynn 18
Williams, Billy Dee 8, 105
Williams, Clarence, III 26
Williams, Marco 53
Williams, Michael Kenneth 97
Williams, Russell, II 70
Williams, Samm-Art 21
Williams, Saul 31
Williams, Vanessa A. 32, 66
Williams, Vanessa L. 4, 17
Williamson, Fred 67
Williamson, Mykelti 22
Wilson, Debra 38
Wilson, Dorien 55
Winfield, Paul 2, 45
Witherspoon, John 38
Woodard, Alfre 9, 108
Woolard, Jamal 102
Wright, Jeffrey 54, 111
Yarbrough, Cedric 51
Yoba, Malik 11

**Government and politics--
international**
Abacha, Sani 11, 70
Abbott, Diane 9
Abiola, Moshood 70
Abubakar, Abdulsalami 66
Adebari, Rotimi 83
Afewerki, Isaias 98
Ahidjo, Ahmadou 81
Ahmadiya, Dora Nkem58
Alexander, Lincoln 106
Ali Mahdi Mohamed 5
Amadi, Elechi 40
Amin, Idi 42
Amos, Valerie 41
Annan, Kofi Atta 15, 48
Aristide, Jean-Bertrand 6, 45
Arthur, Owen 33
Atta Mills, John 75
Augustine, Jean 53
Avant, Nicole A. 90
Azikiwe, Nnamdi 13
Babangida, Ibrahim 4

Baker, Gwendolyn Calvert 9
Banda, Hastings Kamuzu 6, 54
Banda, Joyce 101
Barnes, Melody 75
Barrow, Dean 69
Bartels, Peggielene 80
Bashir, Omar al- 77
Bedie, Henri Konan 21
Berry, Mary Frances 7
Biko, Steven 4
Bishop, Maurice 39
Biya, Chantal 89
Biya, Paul 28, 114
Bizimungu, Pasteur 19
Boateng, Paul Yaw 56
Bongo, Ali Ben 80
Bongo, Omar 1, 79
Boye, Madior 30
Bozizé, François 96
Brown, Rosemary 62
Bunche, Ralph J. 5
Burnham, Forbes 66
Buthelezi, Mangosuthu Gatsha 9
Cabral, Amílcar 104
Camara, Moussa Dadis 76
Césaire, Aimé 48, 69
Cham, Adongo Agada Akway 77
Charlemagne, Manno 11
Charles, Mary Eugenia 10, 55
Charles, Pierre 52
Chiluba, Frederick 56, 80
Chissano, Joaquim 7, 55, 67
Christie, Perry Gladstone 53
Christophe, Henri 9
Compaore, Blaise 87
Compton, John 65
Condé, Alpha 95
Conneh, Sekou Damate, Jr. 51
Conté, Lansana 7, 76
Cools, Anne 64
Cousin, Ertharin 115
Curling, Alvin 34
da Silva, Benedita 5
Dadié, Bernard 34
Dandala, Mvume 77
Davis, Ruth 37
Déby, Idriss 30
Desalegn, Hailemariam 105
Diogo, Luisa Dias 63
Diop, Cheikh Anta 4
Diouf, Abdou 3
Dlamini-Zuma, Nkosazana 34, 105
Doe, Samuel K. 100
dos Santos, José Eduardo 43, 114
Douglas, Denzil Llewellyn 53
Ekwensi, Cyprian 37
Eyadéma, Gnassingbé 7, 52
Fela 1, 42
Gairy, Eric Matthew 83
Garang, John 105
Gbagbo, Laurent 43, 90
Gnassingbé, Faure 67
Golding, Bruce 78
Gordon, Pamela 17
Grant, Bernie 57
Guebuza, Armando 81
Habré, Hissène 6, 104
Habyarimana, Juvenal 8
Haile Selassie 7
Haley, George Williford Boyce 21
Hani, Chris 6
Holness, Andrew 99
Houphouët-Boigny, Félix 4, 64

Hussein, Lubna 80
Ifill, Gwen 28
Ingraham, Hubert A. 19
Isaac, Julius 34
Issoufou, Mahamadou 102
Jagan, Cheddi 16
Jammeh, Yahya 23, 104
Jawara, Dawda Kairaba 11
Jean, Michaëlle; 70
Jean, Wyclef 20, 86
Jonathan, Goodluck 83
Ka Dinizulu, Mcwayizeni 29
Kabbah, Ahmad Tejan 23
Kabila, Joseph 30
Kabila, Laurent 20
Kabunda, Kenneth 2
Kagame, Paul 54
Kariuki, J. M. 67
Keïta, Ibrahim Boubacar 113
Kenyatta, Jomo 5
Kenyatta, Uhuru 110
Kerekou, Ahmed (Mathieu) 1
Khama, Ian 95
Kibaki, Mwai 60
Kiir, Salva Mayardit 85, 103
Kikwete, Jakaya Mrisho 73
King, Oona 27
Kisekka, Samson 112
Kony, Joseph 101
Koroma, Ernest Bai 84
Kufuor, John Agyekum 54, 82
Kyenge, Cécile 113
Laraque, Paul 67
Lewis, Daurene 72
Liberia-Peters, Maria Philomena 12
Lubanga, Thomas 104
Lumumba, Patrice 33
Luthuli, Albert 13
Maathai, Wangari 43, 97
Mabuza, Lindiwe 18
Machel, Graça 16, 102
Machel, Samora Moises 8
Magloire, Paul Eugène 68
Mahama, John Dramani 103
Malema, Julius 98
Mandela, Nelson 1, 14, 77
Mandela, Winnie 2, 35, 112
Manigat, Mirlande 90
Marks, Audrey 99
Martelly, Michel 90
Masekela, Barbara 18
Masire, Quett 5
Mbeki, Govan A. 80
Mbeki, Thabo 14, 73
Mboya, Tom 107
Mbuende, Kaire 12
Mengistu, Haile Mariam 65
Mhlaba, Raymond 55
Mitchell, Keith 82
Mkapa, Benjamin W. 16, 77
Mobutu Sese Seko 1, 56
Mogae, Festus Gontebanye 19, 79
Mohamud, Hassan Sheikh 105
Moi, Daniel Arap 1, 35
Mongella, Gertrude 11
Mosisili, Pakalitha 96
Motlanthe, Kgalema 74
Moyo, Dambisa 76
Moyo, Lovemore 76
Mswati III 56
Mugabe, Robert 10, 71
Mukoko, Jestina 75
Muluzi, Bakili 14, 76

Museveni, Yoweri 4
Mushikiwabo, Louise 88
Mutebi, Ronald 25
Muzorewa, Abel 85
Mwanawasa, Levy 72
Mwinyi, Ali Hassan 1, 77
Nascimento, Abdias do 93
Ndadaye, Melchior 3
Nelson, Sophia A. 93
Neto, António Agostinho 43
Ngilu, Charity 58
Ngubane, Ben 33
Nkoli, Simon 60
Nkomo, Joshua 4, 65
Nkrumah, Kwame 3
Nkurunziza, Pierre 78
Ntaryamira, Cyprien 8
Nujoma, Samuel 10
Nyanda, Siphiwe 21
Nyerere, Julius 5
Nzo, Alfred 15
Obasanjo, Olusegun 5, 22
Obasanjo, Stella 32, 56
Obiang, Teodoro 103
Obote, Milton 63
Odinga, Raila 67, 110
Okara, Gabriel 37
Okonjo-Iweala, Ngozi 101
Ouattara, Alassane 90
Oyono, Ferdinand 38
Pascal-Trouillot, Ertha 3
Patterson, P. J. 6, 20
Pereira, Aristides 30, 97
Perkins, Edward 5
Perry, Ruth 15
Pierre-Louis, Michèle 75
Pindling, Lynden 81
Pitt, David Thomas 10
Pitta, Celso 17
Pohamba, Hifikepunye 95
Préval, René 87
Ramaphosa, Cyril 3
Rawlings, Jerry 9
Rawlings, Nana Konadu Agyeman 13
Roberto, Holden 65
Robinson, Randall 7, 46
Russwurm, John Brown 100
Sall, Macky 101
Sampson, Edith S. 4
Sanhá Malam Bacai 84, 101
Sankara, Thomas 17
Sankoh, Foday 74
Sassou-Nguesso, Denis 103
Sata, Michael 102
Savimbi, Jonas 2, 34
Sawyer, Amos 2
Senghor, Augustin Diamacoune 66
Senghor, Léopold Sédar 12, 66
Shearer, Hugh 107
Silva, Marina 80
Simpson Miller, Portia 62, 100
Sirleaf, Ellen Johnson 71
Sisulu, Walter 47
Skerrit, Roosevelt 72
Skinner, Kiron K. 65
Smith, Jennifer 21
Soglo, Nicephore 15
Spencer, Winston Baldwin 68
Tandja, Mamadou 33, 78
Taylor, Charles 20
Taylor, John (David Beckett) 16
Thiam, Tidjane 104

Todman, Terence A. 55
Tolbert, William R. 100
Touré, Amadou Toumani 18
Touré, Sekou 6
Traore, Dioncounda 103
Tsvangirai, Morgan 26, 72
Tubman, William 99
Tutu, Desmond (Mpilo) 6, 44
Van Lierop, Robert 53
Vieira, João Bernardo 14, 84
Wade, Abdoulaye 66
Weah, George 58
Wharton, Clifton R., Jr. 7
Wharton, Clifton Reginald, Sr. 36
Williams, Eric Eustace 65
Wiwa, Ken 67
Yar'Adua, Umaru 69, 89
Yayi, Boni T. 84
Yumkella, Kandeh 105
Zenawi, Meles 3, 99
Zuma, Jacob G. 33, 75

Government and politics--U.S.

Adams, Floyd, Jr. 12
Adams, Grantley 82
Ahmed, Sharif 80
Alexander, Archie Alphonso 14
Alexander, Clifford 26
Allen, Claude 68
Allen, Ethel D. 13
Allen, Eugene 79
Archer, Dennis 7, 36
Arrington, Richard 24, 100
Avant, Clarence 19, 86
Baker, Thurbert 22
Ballance, Frank W. 41
Baltimore, Richard Lewis, III 71
Barbee, Lloyd Augustus 71
Barrett, Andrew C. 12
Barrett, Jacqueline 28
Barry, Marion S. 7, 44
Bass, Karen 70
Becton, Julius W., Jr. 110
Bell, Michael 40
Bellamy, Terry 58
Belton, Sharon Sayles 9, 16
Benjamin, Steve 98
Berrien, Jacqueline A. 93
Berry, Edwin C. 81
Berry, Mary Frances 7
Berry, Theodore M. 31
Bethune, Mary McLeod 4
Bing, Dave 3, 59, 78
Bishop, Sanford D., Jr. 24, 111
Blackwell, Kenneth, Sr. 61
Blackwell, Unita 17
Bobb, Robert C. 83
Bond, Julian 2, 35, 106
Booker, Cory Anthony 68
Bosley, Freeman, Jr. 7
Bowman, Bertie 71
Boykin, Keith 14
Bradley, Jennette B. 40
Bradley, Thomas 2
Braun, Carol Moseley 4, 42
Brazile, Donna 25, 70
Brimmer, Andrew 2, 48, 106
Brooke, Edward W. 8, 88
Brookins, Hamel Hartford 102
Brooks, Tyrone 59
Brown, Aja 115
Brown, Alvin 96
Brown, Anthony G. 72

Brown, Byrd 49
Brown, Byron W. 72
Brown, Cora 33
Brown, Corrine 24, 90
Brown, Elaine 8
Brown, George Leslie 62
Brown, Jesse 6, 41
Brown, Kwame R. 91
Brown, Les 5
Brown, Ron 5
Brown, Willie 7, 85
Bruce, Blanche K. 33
Bryant, Wayne R. 6
Buckley, Victoria (Vicki) 24
Bunche, Ralph J. 5
Burke, Yvonne Brathwaite 42
Burris, Chuck 21
Burris, Roland W. 25, 75
Burton, Bill 96
Bush, Gordon 82
Butler, Jerry 26
Butts, Cassandra 78
Caesar, Shirley 19
Campbell, Bill 9, 76
Cardozo, Francis L. 33
Carson, André 69
Carson, Johnnie 85
Carson, Julia 23, 69
Carter, Jill P. 110
Carter, Pamela Lynn 67
Celestin, Josaphat 101
Chavis, Benjamin 6
Chisholm, Shirley 2, 50
Christian-Green, Donna M. 17
Christie, Ron 83
Clarke, Yvette 92
Clay, William Lacy 8
Clay, William Lacy, Jr. 95
Clayton, Eva M. 20
Cleaver, Eldridge 5
Cleaver, Emanuel 4, 45, 68, 107
Clemente, Rosa 74
Clyburn, James E. 21, 71
Clyburn, Mignon 78
Cockrel, Kenneth V., Jr. 79
Cockrel, Kenneth Vern, Sr. 79
Coleman, Mary 46
Coleman, Michael B. 28, 79
Coleman, William T. 76
Collins, Barbara-Rose 7, 87
Collins, Cardiss 10, 80
Colter, Cyrus J. 36
Connerly, Ward 14
Conyers, John, Jr. 4, 45, 111
Conyers, Monica 85
Cook, Mercer 40
Cose, Ellis 5, 50
Craig-Jones, Ellen Walker 44
Crockett, George W., Jr. 10, 64
Cummings, Elijah E. 24, 102
Cunningham, Evelyn 23, 85
Currie, Betty 21
Currie, Ulysses 73
Davis, Artur 41
Davis, Benjamin O., Jr. 2, 43
Davis, Benjamin O., Sr. 4
Davis, Danny K. 24, 79
Davis, Doris A. 100
Davis, Gordon J. 76
Davis, James E. 50
Days, Drew S., III 10
De Priest, Oscar Stanton 80
DeBerry, Lois M. 115

DeJongh, John, Jr. 85
Delany, Martin R. 27
Delco, Wilhemina R. 33
Dellums, Ronald 2, 81
Diggs, Charles R. 21
Dinkins, David 4
Dixon, Julian C. 24
Dixon, Sharon Pratt 1
Dixon, Sheila 68
Dougherty, Mary Pearl 47
Douglas, Derek 88
Du Bois, W. E. B. 3
Dudley, Edward R. 58
Dukes, Hazel Nell 56
Dunbar-Nelson, Alice Ruth Moore 44
DuPree, Johnny 96
Dymally, Mervyn 42
Easley, Annie J. 61
Edmonds, Terry 17
Edwards, Donna 77
Edwards, Willis 104
Ellison, Keith 59
Ervin, Clark Kent 82
Espy, Mike 6
Evans, Melvin H. 88
Farmer, James 2, 64
Farrakhan, Louis 2
Farrell, Herman D., Jr. 81
Fattah, Chaka 11, 70, 112
Fauntroy, Walter E. 11
Fauset, Crystal Dreda Bird 100
Felix, Larry R. 64
Fenty, Adrian 60, 88
Fields, C. Virginia 25
Fields, Cleo 13
Fisher, Ada M. 76
Flake, Floyd H. 18, 110
Fleming, Erik R. 75
Fletcher, Arthur A. 63
Flipper, Henry O. 3
Ford, Harold E(ugene) 42
Ford, Harold E(ugene), Jr. 16, 70
Ford, Jack 39
Ford, Johnny 70
Fortune, T. Thomas 6
Foster, Ezola 28
Foxx, Anthony 81
Francois, Terry A. 106
Franklin, Shirley 34, 80
Franks, Gary 2
Frazer, Jendayi 68
Frazer, Victor O. 98
Frazier, Ryan 89
Fudge, Marcia L. 76
Fulani, Lenora 11
Fuller, Thomas O. 90
Gaines, Matthew 95
Gantt, Harvey 1
Garrett, Joyce Finley 59
Garvey, Marcus 1
Gaspard, Patrick 84
Gibbs, Mifflin W. 99
Gibson, Johnnie Mae 23
Gibson, Kenneth Allen 6
Gibson, William F. 6
Glover, Cedric B. 103
Goode, W. Wilson 4
Gravely, Samuel L., Jr. 5, 49
Gray, Vincent C. 88
Gray, William H., III 3
Grillo, Evelio 95
Grimké, Archibald H. 9

Groff, Peter 96
Guinier, Lani 7, 30
Haley, George Williford Boyce 21
Hamer, Fannie Lou 6
Harmon, Clarence 26
Harris, Alice 7
Harris, Patricia Roberts 2
Harvard, Beverly 11
Hastie, William H. 8
Hastings, Alcee L. 16
Hatcher, Andrew T. 90
Hatcher, Richard G. 55
Hawkins, Augustus F. 68
Hayes, James C. 10
Henderson, Thelton E. 68
Henry, Aaron 19
Herenton, Willie W. 24, 81
Herman, Alexis M. 15
Hernandez, Aileen Clarke 13
Hill, Bonnie Guiton 20
Hilliard, Earl F. 24
Hobson, Julius W. 44
Holder, Eric H., Jr. 9, 76, 104
Holmes, Amy 69
Holt Baker, Arlene 73
Horsford, Steven 88
Howard, Perry Wilbon, Jr. 112
Hughes, Dora 88
Ifill, Gwen 28
Irving, Larry, Jr. 12
Irvis, K. Leroy 67
Jackson, Alphonso R. 48
Jackson, Frank G. 76
Jackson, George 14
Jackson, Jesse 1, 27, 72
Jackson, Jesse, Jr. 14, 45, 81, 108
Jackson, Lisa 77
Jackson, Mae 57
Jackson, Maynard 2, 41
Jackson, Sandi 108
Jackson, Shirley Ann 12
Jackson Lee, Sheila 20
Jacob, John E. 2
James, Sharpe 23, 69
James, Sly 107
Jarrett, Valerie 73
Jarvis, Charlene Drew 21
Jarvis, Kristen 85
Jefferson, William J. 25, 72
Johnson, Eddie Bernice 8, 90
Johnson, Edward Austin 107
Johnson, Hank, Jr. 80
Johnson, Harvey, Jr. 24, 82
Johnson, James Weldon 5
Johnson, Jeh C. 76
Johnson, Katherine (Coleman Goble) 61
Johnson, Kevin 70
Johnson, Leroy R. 89
Johnson, Norma H. 17, 97
Johnson, Robert T. 17
Jones, Elaine R. 7, 45
Jones, Emil, Jr. 74
Jones, John 89
Jordan, Barbara 4, 78
Jordan, Vernon 3, 35
Kelley, Cliff 75
Kelly, Robin 114
Kennard, William Earl 18
Keyes, Alan 11, 105
Kidd, Mae Street 39
Kilpatrick, Carolyn Cheeks 16
Kilpatrick, Kwame 34, 71

Kincaid, Bernard 28
King, Martin Luther, III 20
Kirk, Ron 11, 75, 111
Lafontant, Jewel Stradford 3, 51
Langford, Larry P. 74
Langston, John Mercer 101
Layton, William 87
Lee, Barbara 25, 102
Leland, Mickey 2
Lewis, Delano 7
Lewis, John 2, 46, 83
Lewis, William Henry 89
Lindsay, Peta 100
Love, Mia 96
Love, Reggie 77
Lowery, Myron 80
Lynch, William, Jr. 115
Mack, Tony 104
Majette, Denise 41
Mallett, Conrad, Jr. 16
Mallory, Mark 62
Marsh, Henry, III 32
Marshall, Bella 22
Marshall, Thurgood 1, 44
Martin, Louis E. 16
Martin, Ruby Grant 49
McCall, H. Carl 27
McGee, James D. 74
McGee, James Madison 46
McGlowan, Angela 64, 86
McHenry, Donald F. 83
McKinney, Cynthia 11, 52, 74
McKissick, Floyd B. 3
Meek, Carrie 6, 36
Meek, Kendrick 41, 89
Meeks, Gregory 25
Meeks, James T. 92
Melton, Frank 81
Menard, John Willis 90
Meredith, James H. 11
Metcalfe, Ralph 26
Mfume, Kweisi 6, 41
Millender-McDonald, Juanita 21, 61
Mitchell, Arthur Wergs 91
Mitchell, Parren J. 42, 66
Moore, Gwendolynne S. 55
Moore, Minyon 45
Morial, Ernest "Dutch" 26
Morial, Marc H. 20, 51
Morrow, E. Frederic 100
Morton, Azie Taylor 48
Morton, Ferdinand Q. 90
Moses, Robert Parris 11
Murrell, Sylvia Marilyn 49
Nagin, Ray 42, 57, 88
Nix, Robert N. C., Jr. 51
Norton, Eleanor Holmes 7, 93
Nutter, Michael 69, 112
Obama, Barack 49, 74, 91
Obama, Michelle 61, 90
O'Leary, Hazel 6
Owens, Major 6
Page, Alan 7
Paige, Rod 29
Parker, Vernon 97
Paterson, Basil A. 69
Paterson, David A. 59
Patrick, Deval 12, 61
Patterson, J. O., Jr. 80
Patterson, Louise 25
Payne, Donald M. 2, 57, 112
Payne, William D. 60
Perez, Anna 1

Perkins, Edward 5
Perkins, James, Jr. 55
Perry, James 83
Perry, Lowell 30
Peterson, Karen Carter 90
Pinchback, P. B. S. 9
Pitts, Robb 84
Powell, Adam Clayton, Jr. 3
Powell, Colin 1, 28, 75
Powell, Debra A. 23
Powell, Michael 32
Primas, Randy 106
Pugh, Charles 81
Randolph, A. Philip 3
Rangel, Charles B. 3, 52, 85
Raoul, Kwame 55
Rapier, James T. 82
Rawlings-Blake, Stephanie 93
Redd, Dana 93
Reed, Joe L. 110
Reed, Kasim 82
Reeves, Gregory 49
Reeves, Martha 85
Reeves, Triette Lipsey 27
Revels, Hiram Rhoades 98
Rice, Condoleezza 3, 28, 72
Rice, Emmett J. 94
Rice, Norm 8
Rice, Susan 74, 103
Richardson, Laura 81
Richardson, Rupert 67
Richmond, Cedric 93
Riles, Wilson C. 79
Roberts, Lillian 83
Robinson, Bishop L. 66
Robinson, Randall 7, 46
Rochon, Stephen W. 78
Rogers, Desirée 88
Rogers, Joe 27
Ross, Don 27
Rouse, Cecilia 93
Rush, Bobby 26, 76
Rustin, Bayard 4
Sampson, Edith S. 4
Sanders, Malika 48
Sawyer, Eugene 81
Sayles Belton, Sharon 9
Schmoke, Kurt 1, 48
Scott, David 41
Scott, Robert C. 23
Scott, Tim 87
Sewell, Terri 93
Shakur, Assata 6
Shavers, Cheryl 31
Shelton, Paula Young 86
Sherrod, Shirley 87
Simmons, E. Denise 79
Simmons, Jamal 72
Simpson, Carole 6, 30
Sisulu, Sheila Violet Makate 24
Slater, Rodney E. 15
Smith, Malcolm A. 75
Smith, Nate 49
Smith, Princella 86
Smyre, Calvin 90
Smythe Haith, Mabel 61
Spearman, Leonard H. O., Sr. 81
Spencer, Vaino H. 99
Spigner, Archie 81
Stanton, Robert 20
Staupers, Mabel K. 7
Steele, Michael 38, 73, 91
Stewart, Nzingha 89

Stokes, Carl 10, 73
Stokes, Louis 3
Stone, Chuck 9
Stoutt, H. Lavity 83
Strautmanis, Michael 87
Street, John F. 24
Sullivan, Louis 8
Sutphen, Mona 77
Sutton, Percy E. 42, 82
Taylor, Robert Rochon 104
Terry, Clark 39
Thomas, Clarence 2, 39, 65
Thomas-Greenfield, Linda 99
Thompson, Bennie G. 26
Thompson, Larry D. 39
Thompson, William C., Jr. 35, 114
Tillman, Dorothy 76
Todman, Terence A. 55
Tolbert, Terence 74
Toote, Gloria E. A. 64
Towns, Edolphus 19, 75
Tribble, Israel, Jr. 8
Trotter, Donne E. 28
Tubbs Jones, Stephanie 24, 72
Tucker, C. Delores 12, 56
Turnbull, Charles Wesley 62
Turner, Henry McNeal 5
Usry, James L. 23
Vaughn, Gladys Gary 47
Von Lipsey, Roderick K. 11
Waldon, Alton R., Jr. 98
Wallace, Phyllis A. 9
Washington, Harold 6
Washington, Val 12
Washington, Walter 45
Waters, Maxine 3, 67, 103
Watkins, Craig 97
Watkins, Joe 86
Watkins, Shirley R. 17
Watson, Diane 41
Watt, Mel 26, 105
Watts, J. C., Jr. 14, 38
Weaver, Robert C. 8, 46
Webb, Wellington 3, 81
Welcome, Verda Freeman 112
West, Allen 89
Wharton, A. C., Jr. 110
Wharton, Clifton R., Jr. 7
Wharton, Clifton Reginald, Sr. 36
Wheat, Alan 14
White, Jesse 22, 75
White, Michael R. 5
Widener, Warren 99
Wilder, L. Douglas 3, 48
Williams, Anthony 21
Williams, Eddie N. 44
Williams, George Washington 18
Williams, Hosea Lorenzo 15, 31
Williams, Maggie 7, 71
Williams, Michael L. 86
Wilson, Frederica 92
Wilson, Lionel 99
Wilson, Margaret Bush 79
Woods, Abraham, Jr. 74
Wynn, Albert 25, 77
Young, Andrew 3, 48, 110

Law
Alexander, Clifford 26
Alexander, Joyce London 18
Alexander, Michelle 98
Alexander, Sadie Tanner Mossell
   22

Ali, Russlynn H. 92
Allen, Macon Bolling 104
Allen, Samuel W. 38
Amaker, Norman 63
Anderson, Reuben V. 81
Archer, Dennis 7, 36
Arnwine, Barbara 28
Bailey, Clyde 45
Baldwin, Cynthia 74, 107
Banks, William 11
Barbee, Lloyd Augustus 71
Barrett, Andrew C. 12
Barrett, Jacqueline 28
Baugh, David 23
Benham, Robert 78
Benjamin, Steve 98
Bensouda, Fatou 103
Berrien, Jacqueline A. 93
Berry, Theodore M. 31
Birch, Adolpho A., Jr. 85
Bolin, Jane 22, 59
Bolton, Terrell D. 25
Booker, Cory Anthony 68
Bosley, Freeman, Jr. 7
Boulware, Harold R. 109
Boykin, Keith 14
Bradley, Thomas 2
Brooke, Edward W. 8, 88
Brown, Byrd 49
Brown, Cora 33
Brown, Cupcake 63
Brown, Homer S. 47
Brown, Janice Rogers 43
Brown, Joe 29
Brown, Lee P. 1, 24, 109
Brown, Ron 5
Bryant, Wayne R. 6
Bryant, William Benson 61
Buery, Richard, Jr. 97
Bully-Cummings, Ella 48
Burris, Roland W. 25, 75
Butler, Louis 70
Butler, Paul D. 17
Bynoe, Peter C. B. 40
Campbell, Bill 9, 76
Carter, Pamela Lynn 67
Carter, Robert L. 51, 100
Carter, Stephen L. 4
Cashin, Sheryll 63
Chambers, Julius 3
Chestnut, J. L., Jr. 73
Cleaver, Kathleen Neal 29
Clendenon, Donn 26, 56
Cochran, Johnnie 11, 39, 52
Colbert, Tom 115
Coleman, James E., Jr. 79
Coleman, William T. 76
Colter, Cyrus J. 36
Crenshaw, Kimberlé Williams 88
Darden, Christopher 13
Davis, Angela J. 88
Davis, Artur 41
Davis, Gordon J. 76
Days, Drew S., III 10
DeFrantz, Anita 37
Dillard, Godfrey J. 45
Dow, Unity 104
Edley, Christopher 2, 48
Edley, Christopher F., Jr. 48
Ellington, E. David 11
Ephriam, Mablean 29
Ervin, Clark Kent 82
Espy, Mike 6

Evans, Warren C. 76
Farmer-Paellmann, Deadria 43
Feemster, Herbert 72
Fenty, Adrian 60, 88
Fields, Cleo 13
Finner-Williams, Paris Michele 62
Fisher, Ada Lois Sipuel 76
Ford, Wallace 58
Forman, James, Jr. 89
Foxx, Anthony 81
Frazer, Victor O. 98
Freeman, Charles 19
Gaines, Lloyd 79
Gary, Willie E. 12
Gibson, Johnnie Mae 23
Glover, Nathaniel, Jr. 12
Gomez-Preston, Cheryl 9
Gordon-Reed, Annette 74
Gourdin, Edward O. 93
Graham, Lawrence Otis 12
Gray, Fred 37
Gray, Willie 46
Greenhouse, Bunnatine 57
Grimké, Archibald H. 9
Guinier, Lani 7, 30
Haley, George Williford Boyce 21
Hall, Elliott S. 24
Harden, Monique 97
Harris, Kamala D. 64
Harris, Maya Lakshmi 88
Harris, Patricia Roberts 2
Harvard, Beverly 11
Hassell, Leroy Rountree, Sr. 41
Hastie, William H. 8
Hatcher, Richard G. 55
Hatchett, Glenda 32
Hawkins, Augustus F. 68
Hawkins, Steven 14
Hayes, Dennis 54
Haywood, Margaret A. 24
Henderson, Thelton E. 68
Higginbotham, A. Leon, Jr. 13, 25
Hill, Anita 5, 65
Hillard, Terry 25
Hills, Oliver W. 24
Holder, Eric H., Jr. 9, 76, 104
Hollowell, Donald L. 57
Holton, Hugh, Jr. 39
Hooks, Benjamin L. 2, 85
Houston, Charles Hamilton 4
Howard, Perry Wilbon, Jr. 112
Hubbard, Arnette Rhinehart 38
Hurtt, Harold 46
Isaac, Julius 34
Jackson, Maynard 2, 41
Jackson Lee, Sheila 20
Johnson, Edward Austin 107
Johnson, Harry E. 57
Johnson, James Weldon 5
Johnson, Jeh C. 76
Johnson, Leroy R. 89
Johnson, Norma H. 17, 97
Jones, Clarence B. 114
Jones, Elaine R. 7, 45
Jones, Theodore T., Jr. 108
Jones, Van 70
Jordan, Eddie 82
Jordan, Vernon E. 3, 35
Kearse, Amalya Lyle 12
Keith, Damon J. 16, 74
Kennard, William Earl 18
Kennedy, Florynce 12, 33
Kennedy, Randall 40

Kibaki, Mwai 60
La Roca, Pete 107
Lafontant, Jewel Stradford 3, 51
Lewis, Delano 7
Lewis, William Henry 89
Lloyd, Reginald 64
Lynch, Loretta E. 103
Majette, Denise 41
Mallett, Conrad, Jr. 16
Mandela, Nelson 1, 14, 77
Marsh, Henry, III 32
Marshall, Thurgood 1, 44
Mathis, Greg 26
McAnulty, William E., Jr. 66
McCrary Anthony, Crystal 70
McDonald, Gabrielle Kirk 20
McDougall, Gay J. 11, 43
McGhee, Heather C. 106
McKinnon, Isaiah 9
McPhail, Sharon 2
Meeks, Gregory 25
Melton, Harold D. 79
Mitchell, Arthur Wergs 91
Mitchell, Clarence M., Jr. 88
Moose, Charles 40
Morial, Ernest "Dutch" 26
Morton, Ferdinand Q. 90
Morton, Frederick A., Jr. 93
Motley, Constance Baker 10, 55
Muhammad, Ava 31
Murray, Pauli 38
Nance, Cynthia 71
Napoleon, Benny N. 23
Nash, Shannon King 84
Nelson, Sophia A. 93
Nix, Robert N. C., Jr. 51
Noble, Ronald 46
Nunn, Annetta 43
Obama, Michelle 61, 90
Ogletree, Charles, Jr. 12, 47
Ogunlesi, Adebayo O. 37
Oliver, Jerry 37
Page, Alan 7
Parker, Barrington D. 92
Parker, Kellis E. 30
Parks, Bernard C. 17
Parsons, James 14
Parsons, Richard Dean 11, 33
Pascal-Trouillot, Ertha 3
Paterson, Basil A. 69
Patrick, Deval 12
Payne, Ulice, Jr. 42
Payton, John 48
Perry, Lowell 30
Perry, Matthew J., Jr. 96
Philip, Marlene Nourbese 32
Pincham, R. Eugene, Sr. 69
Powell, Michael 32
Quince, Peggy A. 69
Ramsey, Charles H. 21, 69
Raoul, Kwame 55
Rawlinson, Johnnie B. 79
Ray, Charlotte E. 60
Redding, Louis L. 26
Reed, Kasim 82
Reeves, Bass 100
Reynolds, Star Jones 10, 27, 61
Rice, Constance LaMay 60
Richie, Leroy C. 18
Roaf, Andrée Layton 106
Robinson, Bishop L. 66
Robinson, Malcolm S. 44
Robinson, Randall 7, 46

Rock, John S. 113
Roundtree, Dovey 80
Russell-McCloud, Patricia 17
Sampson, Edith S. 4
Schmoke, Kurt 1, 48
Sears, Leah Ward 5, 79
Shores, Arthur D. 99
Sleet, Gregory M. 109
Smith, DeMaurice 92
Solomon, Jimmie Lee 38
Sparks, Corinne Etta 53
Stokes, Louis 3
Stout, Juanita Kidd 24
Strautmanis, Michael 87
Sutton, Percy E. 42, 82
Tanner, Jack E. 100
Taylor, John (David Beckett) 16
Thomas, Arthur Ray 52
Thomas, Clarence 2, 39, 65
Thomas, Franklin A. 5, 49
Thompson, Larry D. 39
Tingling, Milton A. 110
Tolbert, James L. 112
Touré, Faya Ora Rose 56
Tubbs Jones, Stephanie 24, 72
Van Lierop, Robert 53
Wagner, Annice 22
Wainwright, Joscelyn 46
Waldon, Alton R., Jr. 98
Walker, Cora T. 68
Wallace, Perry E. 47
Ward, Benjamin 68
Washington, Harold 6
Watkins, Craig 97
Watkins, Donald 35
Watt, Garland W. 113
Watt, Melvin 26
Wharton, Clifton Reginald, Sr. 36
Widener, Warren 99
Wilder, L. Douglas 3, 48
Wilkins, David 77
Williams, Ann Claire 82
Williams, David W. 110
Williams, Evelyn 10
Williams, Gregory 11
Williams, Patricia 11, 54
Williams, Willie L. 4
Wilson, Jimmy 45
Worthy, Kym 84
Wray, Noble 114
Wright, Bruce McMarion 3, 52
Wynn, Albert 25, 77

Military
Abacha, Sani 11, 70
Adams Early, Charity 13, 34
Adams-Ender, Clara 40
Alexander, Margaret Walker 22
Amin, Idi 42
Anderson, Marcia 115
Archer, Lee, Jr. 79
Austin, Lloyd 101
Babangida, Ibrahim 4
Baker, Vernon Joseph 65, 87
Bashir, Omar al- 77
Becton, Julius W., Jr. 110
Bennett, Richard 97
Black, Barry C. 47
Bolden, Charles Frank, Jr. 7, 78
Brashear, Carl 29
Brown, Anthony G. 72
Brown, Erroll M. 23
Brown, Jesse 6, 41

Brown, Jesse Leroy 31
Brown, Wesley A. 102
Brown, Willa 40
Bullard, Eugene 12
Cadoria, Sherian Grace 14
Carney, William H. 104
Carter, Edward A., Jr. 104
Chappell, Roy M. 95
Chissano, Joaquim 7, 55, 67
Christophe, Henri 9
Clark, Carl 101
Clarke, Anna Mac 95
Clemmons, Reginal G. 41
Coleman, Ronald S. 110
Compaore, Blaise 87
Conté, Lansana 7, 76
Cooke, Marcia 60
Davis, Benjamin O., Jr. 2, 43
Davis, Benjamin O., Sr. 4
Drew, Alvin, Jr. 67
Duggins, George 64
Ellis, Larry R. 110
Europe, James Reese 10
Eyadéma, Gnassingbé 7, 52
Fields, Evelyn J. 27
Flipper, Henry O. 3
Fox, John R. 105
Gravely, Samuel L., Jr. 5, 49
Gregory, Frederick 8, 51
Guéï, Robert 66
Habré, Hissène 6, 104
Habyarimana, Juvenal 8
Harris, Marcelite Jordan 16
Healy, Michael 90
Honoré, Russel L. 64
Hoskins, Harold K. 103
Howard, Michelle 28
Jackson, Fred James 25
James, Daniel, Jr. 16
Johnson, Hazel 22
Johnson, Shoshana 47
Julian, Hubert 90
Kagame, Paul 54
Kerekou, Ahmed (Mathieu) 1
Khama, Ian 95
King, Teresa 80
Kony, Joseph 101
Laraque, Paul 67
Lawrence, Robert H., Jr. 16
Lubanga, Thomas 104
Lyles, Lester 31
Maceo, Antonio 82
Magloire, Paul Eugène 68
Matthews, Mark 59
Miller, Dorie 29
Nkunda, Laurent 75
Ntaganda, Bosco 111
Nyanda, Siphiwe 21
Obasanjo, Olusegun 5, 22
Ojukwu, Odumegwu 99
Perry, Herman 89
Petersen, Frank E. 31
Plinton, James O., Jr. 98
Powell, Colin 1, 28, 75
Pruitt, Wendell O. 106
Rawlings, Jerry 9
Reason, J. Paul 19
Rochon, Stephen W. 78
Rogers, Alan G. 72
Scantlebury, Janna 47
Smalls, Robert 82
Snow, Samuel 71
Stanford, John 20

Staupers, Mabel K. 7
Stokes, Louis 3
Stowers, Freddie 107
Touré, Amadou Toumani 18
Via, Dennis 108
Von Lipsey, Roderick K. 11
Ward, William E. 107
Watkins, Perry 12
West, Togo, D., Jr. 16
Wilson, Jimmy 45
Wright, Lewin 43
Young, Charles 77

Music
Aaliyah 30
Abdullah, Kazem 97
Ace, Johnny 36
Acklin, Barbara Jean 107
Adams, Johnny 39
Adams, Leslie 39
Adams, Oleta 18
Adams, Yolanda 17, 67
Adderley, Julian "Cannonball" 30
Adderley, Nat 29
Ade, King Sunny 41
Adebimpe, Tunde 75
Afro, Teddy 78
Akinmusire, Ambrose 103
Akon 68
Albright, Gerald 23
Alert, Kool DJ 33
Ali, Rashied 79
Allen, Betty 83
Allen, Geri 92
Allison, Luther 111
Amadou & Mariam 113
Amerie 52
Ammons, Albert 112
Ammons, Gene 112
Amy, Curtis 114
Anderson, Carl 48
Anderson, Fred 87
Anderson, Marian 2, 33
Andrews, Inez 108
apl.de.ap 84
Ardoin, Alphonse 65
Armatrading, Joan 32
Armstrong, Louis 2
Armstrong, Vanessa Bell 24
Arnold, Billy Boy 112
Arroyo, Marina 30
A$AP Rocky 109
Ashanti 37, 96
Ashford, Nickolas 21, 97
Ashong, Derrick 86
Astatke, Mulatu 81
Atkins, Juan 50
Attaway, William 102
Austin, Lovie 40
Austin, Patti 24
Avant, Clarence 19, 86
Avant, Nicole A. 90
Ayers, Roy 16
Ayler, Albert 104
Babyface 10, 31, 82
Baca, Susana 80
Badu, Erykah 22, 114
Bailey, Buster 38
Bailey, DeFord 33
Bailey, Pearl 14
Bailey, Philip 63
Bailey Rae, Corinne 83
Baiocchi, Regina Harris 41

Baker, Anita 21, 48
Baker, Josephine 3
Baker, LaVern 26
Baker, Mickey 95
Ballard, Florence 112
Ballard, Hank 41
Bambaataa, Afrika 34
Banks, Azealia 107
Banks, Lloyd 113
Banner, David 55
Banton, Buju 93
Baraka, Sho 109
Barker, Danny 32
Barnes, Katreese 97
Barnes, Lloyd 77
Barnes, Roosevelt "Booba" 33
Barrino, Fantasia 53, 94
Basie, Count 23
Bass, Fontella 104, 109
Bassey, Shirley 25
Batiste, Alvin 66
Batiste, Jonathan 108
Batiste, Lionel 105
Battle, Kathleen 70
Baylor, Helen 36
Bebey, Francis 45
Bechet, Sidney 18
Beenie Man 32
Beken 111
Belafonte, Harry 4, 65
Belgrave, Marcus 77
Bell, Carey 114
Bell, LeRoy 98
Bell, Thom 112
Belle, Regina 1, 51
Benét, Eric 28, 77
Benjamin, Andre 45
Bennett, Estelle 77
Benson, Obie 96
Bentley, Lamont 53
Berry, Chuck 29
Betts, Keter 85
Beverly, Frankie 25
Bey, Yasiin 30, 96
Beyoncé 39, 70, 105
Bibb, Eric 49
Big Daddy Kane 79
Big Sean 96
Big Youth 107
Bilal 101
Billy Ward and the Dominoes 105
Birdman 110
Birdsong, Cindy 113
Birra, Ali 113
Bivins, Michael 72
Black Thought 63
Blackman, Toni 86
Blackwell, Otis 98
Blade, Brian 88
Blake, Eubie 29
Blakey, Art 37
Blanchard, Terence 43
Blanco, Mykki 106
Bland, Bobby 36, 113
Bland, Edward 111
Blanton, Jimmy 108
Bleu, Corbin 65
Blige, Mary J. 20, 34, 60, 97
Blind Boys of Alabama, The 99
Blitz the Ambassador 115
Blondy, Alpha 30
Blow, Kurtis 31
B.o.B. 91

Bolden, Buddy 39
Bombino 112
Bond, Beverly 53
Bonds, Margaret 39
Bonga, Kuenda 13
Bonner, Leroy 113
Bonney, Tabi 98
Boulogne, Joseph, Chevalier de Saint-Georges 94
Bow Wow 35
Boykin, Phillip 102
Boyz II Men 82
Bradley, J. Robert 65
Bradshaw, Tiny 102
Brae, C. Michael 61
Brandy 14, 34, 72
Braxton, Toni 15, 61, 91
Bridgetower, George 78
Bridgewater, Dee Dee 32, 92
Brooks, Hadda 40
Broonzy, Big Bill 82
Brown, Angela M. 54
Brown, Anne 76
Brown, Bobby 58
Brown, Carlinhos 81
Brown, Charles 23
Brown, Chris 74, 109
Brown, Chuck 78, 102
Brown, Clarence Gatemouth 59
Brown, Clifford 86
Brown, Dennis 99
Brown, Foxy 25
Brown, James 15, 60
Brown, Melanie 73
Brown, Nappy 73
Brown, Oscar, Jr. 53
Brown, Patrick "Sleepy" 50
Brown, Ruth 90
Brown, Uzee 42
Brownlee, Lawrence 88
Bryant, Paul 115
Bryant, Ray 95
Buckner, Milt 110
Budden, Joe 108
Bumbry, Grace 5
Burke, Clarence, Jr. 112
Burke, Solomon 31, 86
Burleigh, Henry Thacker 56
Burley, Dan 96
Burning Spear 79
Burns, Eddie 44
Burnside, R. L. 56
Busby, Jheryl 3, 74
Butler, George, Jr. 70
Butler, Jerry 26
Butler, Jonathan 28
Byrd, Donald 109
Cadillacs 107
Caesar, Shirley 19
Cage, Byron 53
Callier, Terry 106
Calloway, Blanche 100
Calloway, Cab 1
Campbell-Martin, Tisha 8, 42
Cam'ron 104
Cannon, Nick 47, 73
Carey, Mariah 32, 53, 69
Carolina Chocolate Drops 111
Carr, Kurt 56
Carr, Leroy 49
Carter, Benny 46
Carter, Betty 19
Carter, Nell 39

Carter, Regina 23
Carter, Ron 104
Carter, Troy 98
Carter, Warrick L. 27
Cartiér, Xam Wilson 41
Castor, Jimmy 100
Caymmi, Dorival 72
Chaka Chaka, Yvonne 112
Chamillionaire 82
Chancler, Ndugu 115
Chandler, Gene 105
Chanté, Keshia 50
Chapman, Tracy 26
Charlemagne, Manno 11
Charles, Ray 16, 48
Cheatham, Doc 17
Checker, Chubby 28
Chenault, John 40
Chief Keef 112
Childers, Lulu Vere 95
Chi-Lites 106
Christian, Jodie 103
Christie, Angella 36
Chuck D 9
Ciara 56, 115
Clark, Mattie Moss 61
Clark, Sharón 105
Clark-Cole, Dorinda 66
Clarke, Kenny 27
Clarke, Stanley 115
Clark-Sheard, Karen 22, 114
Clay, Otis 112
Clayton, Gerald 111
Clayton, Merry 112
Clemons, Clarence 41
Cleveland, James 19
Cliff, Jimmy 28, 92
Clinton, George 9, 93
Clovers, The 104
C-Murder 99
Coasters, The 102
Cobb, Arnett 114
Cobbs, Tasha 114
Cody, Radmilla 99
Cole, J. 97
Cole, Keyshia 63, 107
Cole, Maria 104
Cole, Nat "King" 17
Cole, Natalie 17, 60, 84
Coleman, George 106
Coleman, Ornette 39, 69
Coleridge-Taylor, Samuel 75
Collins, Albert 12
Collins, Bootsy 31
Collins, Lyn 53
Coltrane, Alice 70
Coltrane, John 19
Coltrane, Ravi 71
Combs, Sean 17, 43, 92
Common 31, 63, 98
Conrad, Barbara Smith 90
Contours, The 109
Cook, Charles "Doc" 44
Cook, Will Marion 40
Cooke, Sam 17
Coolio 103
Copeland, Johnny 110
Copeland, Shemekia 110
Coppola, Imani Francesca 82
Cosey, Pete 103
Count Basie 23
Cowboy Troy 54
Cox, Deborah 28

Cox, Ida 42
Craig, Carl 31, 71
Crawford, Hank 77
Crawford, Randy 19
Cray, Robert 30
Creagh, Milton 27
Crocker, Frankie 29
Crothers, Scatman 19
Crouch, Andraé 27, 115
Crowder, Henry 16
Crudup, Arthur 115
Cruz, Taio 104
Curren$y 114
Curson, Ted 108
Da Don, Polow 86
Daemyon, Jerald 64
Dale, Clamma 103
Dameron, Tadd 103
D'Angelo 27
Danjah, Terror 91
Dara, Olu 35
Dash, Damon 31, 113
Dash, Darien 29
Davenport, Cow Cow 115
David, Craig 31, 53
Davis, Anthony 11
Davis, Carl 105
Davis, Gary 41
Davis, Guy 36
Davis, Miles 4
Davis, Sammy, Jr. 18
Davis, Tyrone 54
Davis, Wild Bill 114
Dawkins, Jimmy 111
Dawson, William Levi 39
Dawuni, Rocky 94
D'banj 107
de Passe, Suzanne 25
DeBarge, El 89
Deezer D 53
Dekker, Desmond 104
Dells, The 109
Dennard, Brazeal 37
DePreist, James 37, 109
Derülo, Jason 93
DeVaughn, Raheem 91
Diawara, Djeli Moussa 111
Diawara, Fatoumata 114
Dickenson, Vic 38
Diddley, Bo 39, 72
Dixie Cups, The 109
Dixon, Bill 87
Dixon, Dean 68
Dixon, Willie 4
DJ Clue? 111
DJ Jazzy Jeff 32
DJ Lance Rock 94
DJ Screw 110
DMX 28, 64
Dobbs, Mattiwilda 34
Dodd, Coxsone 99
Domino, Fats 20
Donegan, Dorothy 19
Dorham, Kenny 113
Dorsey, Lee 65
Dorsey, Thomas 15
Downing, Will 19
Drake 86
Dramatics, The 106
Dre, Dr. 10, 14, 30
Dube, Lucky 77
Duke, George 21, 113
Dumas, Henry 41

Duncan, Todd 76
Dunner, Leslie B. 45
Duplechan, Larry 55
Dupri, Jermaine 13, 46
Durham, Bobby 73
Dworkin, Aaron P. 52
Dyett, Walter 113
Earth, Wind & Fire 98
Earthquake 55
Eckstine, Billy 28
Edison, Harry 114
Edmonds, Tracey 16, 64
Edwards, Esther Gordy 43
Eldridge, Roy 37
Ellington, Duke 5
Elliott, Missy 31, 90
Ellis, Alton 74
Ellis, Hortense 97
En Vogue 100
Ervin, Booker 106
Escobar, Damien 56
Escobar, Tourie 56
Estelle 75
Estes, Simon 28
Estes, Sleepy John 33
Eubanks, Kevin 15, 108
Europe, James Reese 10
Evans, Faith 22
Eve 29
Évora, Cesária 12, 99
Fabolous 93
Falana, Lola 42
Farmer, Art 38
Fat Boys 92
Feemster, Herbert 72
Fela 1, 42
Felix Da Housecat 110
Ferbos, Lionel 95
Ferrell, Rachelle 29
Ferrer, Ibrahim 41
Fiasco, Lupe 64
50 Cent 46, 83
Fiona, Melanie 84
Fishbone 101
Fisk Jubilee Singers 112
Fitzgerald, Ella 8, 18
Five Keys, The 104
Flack, Roberta 19
Flamingos, The 108
Flanagan, Tommy 69
Flavor Flav 67
Flo Rida 78
Ford, T-Model 91, 113
Ford, Vincent 75
Forté, John 74
Fortune, James 92
Foster, Frank 97
Foster, George "Pops" 40
Foster, William P. 88
Fox, Donal 114
Franklin, Aretha 11, 44, 115
Franklin, Kirk 15, 49, 97
Franti, Michael 93
Freelon, Nnenna 32
Freeman, Paul 39
Freeman, Von 104
Freeman, Yvette 27
Fresh, Doug E. 93
Fuller, Blind Boy 86
Fuller, Curtis 115
Fuqua, Antoine 35
Fuqua, Harvey 90
Future 109

Gaines, Grady 38
Gamble, Kenny 85
Gap Band, The 100
Garland, Red 115
Garner, Erroll 76
Garrett, Sean 57
Gaye, Marvin 2
Gaye, Nona 56
Gaynor, Gloria 36
George, Zelma Watson 42
Geto Boys 115
Ghostface Killah 90
Gibson, Althea 8, 43
Gibson, Tyrese 27, 62
Gil, Gilberto 53
Gill, Johnny 51
Ginuwine 35
Glasper, Robert 101
Glover, Corey 34
Goapele 55
Golden Gate Quartet 104
Golson, Benny 37
Goodman, Al 87
Gordon, Dexter 25
Gordy, Berry, Jr. 1
Gotti, Irv 39
Grae, Jean 51
Graham, Katerina 99
Grandmaster Flash 33, 60
Graves, Denyce Antoinette 19, 57
Gray, Dobie 99
Gray, F. Gary 14, 49
Gray, Macy 29
Greaves, R. B. 106
Greaves, William 38
Greely, M. Gasby 27
Green, Al 13, 47, 74
Green, Cee Lo 70, 103
Green, Grant 56
Greene, Jimmy 74
Griffey, Dick 89
Griffin, Johnny 71
Griffin, LaShell 51
Griffiths, Marcia 29
Grist, Reri 84
Güines, Tata 69
Guru 84
Guy, Buddy 31
Haddon, Dietrick 55
Hailey, JoJo 22
Hailey, K-Ci 22
Hairston, Jester 88
Hall, Aaron 57
Hall, Juanita 62
Hamilton, Anthony 61
Hammond, Fred 23
Hammond, Lenn 34
Hampton, Lionel 17, 41
Hancock, Herbie 20, 67
Handy, W. C. 8
Hardin Armstrong, Lil 39
Harold Melvin & the Blue Notes 105
Harper, Ben 34, 62
Harrell, Andre 9, 30
Harris, Barry 68
Harris, Corey 39, 73
Harris, Damon 110
Harris, Major 110
Harris, Wynonie 102
Hart, Alvin Youngblood 61
Hartman, Johnny 109

Hathaway, Donny 18
Hathaway, Lalah 57, 88
Havens, Richie 111
Hawkins, Coleman 9
Hawkins, Edwin 113
Hawkins, Erskine 14
Hawkins, Screamin' Jay 30
Hawkins, Tramaine 16
Hawkins, Walter 87
Hayes, Isaac 20, 58, 73
Hayes, Roland 4
Hayes, Teddy 40
Haynes, Roy 87
Heath, Percy 100
Heavy D 58, 98
Hemphill, Jessie Mae 33, 59
Henderson, Fletcher 32
Hendricks, Barbara 3, 67
Hendrix, Jimi 10
Hendryx, Nona 56
Henry, Clarence "Frogman" 46
Hibbert, Toots 103
Higginbotham, J. C. 37
Higginsen, Vy 65
Hill, Andrew 66
Hill, Lauryn 20, 53, 111
Hilson, Keri 84
Hinderas, Natalie 5
Hines, Earl "Fatha" 39
Hinton, Milt 30
Hodge, Derrick 114
Holiday, Billie 1
Holland-Dozier-Holland 36
Holloway, Brenda 65
Holloway, Loleatta 115
Holmes, Clint 57
Holt, Nora 38
Hooker, John Lee 30
Hopkins, Lightnin' 83
Horn, Shirley 32, 56
Horne, Lena 5, 86
Horton, Big Walter 115
Horton, Gladys 92
Houghton, Israel 92
House, Son 8
Houston, Cissy 20, 83
Houston, Whitney 7, 28, 83, 100
Howell, Ayinde 91
Howlin' Wolf 9
Hubbard, Freddie 75
Hudson, Jennifer 63, 83
Huff, Leon 86
Humphrey, Bobbi 20
Hunter, Alberta 42
Hunter, Ivory Joe 106
Hurt, Mississippi John 84
Hutch, Willie 62
Hutcherson, Bobby 115
Hyman, Phyllis 19
Ice Cube 8, 30, 60
Ice-T 6, 31, 96
Imani Winds 113
India.Arie 34
Ingram, James 84
Ink Spots, The 102
Isaacs, Gregory 89
Isley, Marvin 87
Isley, Ronald 25, 56
J Dilla 102
Ja Rule 35, 91
Jackson, Fred James 25
Jackson, George 19
Jackson, Hal 41, 104

Jackson, Isaiah 3
Jackson, Janet 6, 30, 68
Jackson, Jermaine 79
Jackson, John 36
Jackson, LaToya 95
Jackson, Mahalia 5
Jackson, Michael 19, 53, 76
Jackson, Millie 25
Jackson, Milt 26
Jackson, Randy 40
Jackson, Tito 81
Jackson 5 103
Jacquet, Illinois 49
Jaheim 58
Jamal, Ahmad 69
Jamelia 51
Jamerson, James 59
James, Elmore 114
James, Etta 13, 52, 100
James, Rick 17
James, Skip 38
James Bracken and Vivian Bracken
  107
Jarreau, Al 21, 65, 105
Jay-Z 27, 69, 103
Jean, Wyclef 20, 86
Jefferson, Blind Lemon 81
Jenkins, Ella 15
Jennings, Lyfe 56, 69
Jerkins, Rodney 31
Jeter, Claude 75
Jimmy Jam 13
Johnson, Buddy 36
Johnson, Conrad O. 97
Johnson, Hall 90
Johnson, J. J. 37
Johnson, James Weldon 5
Johnson, Johnnie 56
Johnson, Ken 106
Johnson, Le'Andria 108
Johnson, Lonnie 85
Johnson, Robert 2
Johnson, Syl 97
Johnson, Syleena 98
Johnson, Tommy 106
Johnson-George, Tamara 79
Jones, Bobby 20, 94
Jones, Booker T. 84
Jones, Donell 29
Jones, Elvin 14, 68
Jones, Etta 35
Jones, Hank 57, 86
Jones, Jonah 39
Jones, Papa Jo 99
Jones, Quincy 8, 30
Jones, Robert G. 81
Jones, Sharon 86
Jones, Thad 68
Joplin, Scott 6
Jordan, Louis 104
Jordan, Montell 23
Jordan, Ronny 26
Jorge, Seu 73
Joyner, Matilda Sissieretta 15
Juvenile 96
Kandi 83
Kay, Connie 114
Kay, Ulysses 37
Kee, John P. 43
Keita, Salif 83
Kelis 58
Kelley, Elijah 65
Kelly, R. 18, 44, 71

Kem 47
Kendricks, Eddie 22
Kenoly, Ron 45
Kenyatta, Robin 54
Keys, Alicia 32, 68
Khalifa, Wiz 96
Khan, Chaka 12, 50
Kid Cudi 83
Kidjo, Angelique 50
Killings, Debra 57
Kinch, Soweto 108
King, B. B. 7
King, Freddie 92
King Curtis 92
Kingston, Sean 94
Kirkland, Eddie 99
Kitt, Eartha 16, 75
Klugh, Earl 59
K'naan 76
Knight, Gladys 16, 66
Knight, Marie 80
Knight, Suge 11, 30, 102
Knowles, Mathew 96
Knowles, Tina 61
Knuckles, Frankie 42
Kolosoy, Wendo 73
Kool Moe Dee 37
Kravitz, Lenny 10, 34
KRS-One 34
K-Swift 73
Kuti, Femi 47, 110
Kweli, Talib 93
La Roca, Pete 107
LaBelle, Patti 13, 30
Ladysmith Black Mambazo 103
Lamar, Kendrick 105
Lancaster, Byard 105
Lance, Major 111
Larrieux, Amel 63
LaSalle, Denise 111
Lateef, Yusef 91
Lattimore, Kenny 35
LaVette, Bettye 85
Lawrence, Donald 99
Laws, Hubert 90
Leadbelly 82
Lebo M 109
Lecrae 108
Ledisi 73
Lee, Consuela 84
Lefel, Edith 41
Legend, John 67
León, Tania 13
Levert, Eddie 70
Levert, Gerald 22, 59
Lewis, Ananda 28
Lewis, Butch 71, 99
Lewis, George 104
Lewis, Henry 38
Lewis, Leona 75
Lewis, Ramsey 35, 70
Lewis, Terry 13
Lighty, Chris 105
Lil' Kim 28
Lil Wayne 66, 84
Liles, Kevin 42, 99
Lincoln, Abbey 3, 88
Lipscomb, Mance 49
Lister, Marquita 65
Little, Booker 105
Little Anthony & the Imperials 107
Little Milton 36, 54
Little Richard 15

Little Walter 36
LL Cool J 16, 49, 94
Lloyd 99
Locke, Eddie 44
London, Theophilus 95
Long, Huey 79
Lopes, Lisa "Left Eye" 36
Lord Kitchener 110
Loueke, Lionel 88
Love, Darlene 23, 92
Love, Ed 58
Love, Laura 50
Lover, Ed 10
Lucie, Lawrence 80
Lucien, Jon 66
Luckett, Letoya 61
Ludacris 37, 60
Lymon, Frankie 22
Lynne, Gloria 115
Maal, Baaba 66
Mac Daddy 111
Madlib 88
Magic Slim 110
Mahal, Taj 39
Mahlasela, Vusi 65
Maitreya, Sananda 85
Majors, Jeff 41
Makeba, Miriam 2, 50, 74
Malawi Mouse Boys 114
Mane, Gucci 91
Mann, Tamela 92
Marian Anderson String Quartet 111
Mario 71
Marley, Bob 5
Marley, Rita 32, 70
Marley, Stephen 100
Marley, Ziggy 41
Marrow, Queen Esther 24
Marsalis, Branford 34, 103
Marsalis, Delfeayo 41
Marsalis, Ellis 90
Marsalis, Wynton 16, 90
Martelly, Michel 90
Martin, Roberta 58
Martin, Sara 38
Mary Mary 34, 92
Mase 24
Masekela, Hugh 1, 106
Massenburg, Kedar 23, 110
Master P 21, 115
Mathis, Johnny 20
Matshikiza, Pumeza 115
Matthews, Benjamin 93
Maxwell 20, 81
May, Derrick 41
Maye, Lee 111
Mayfield, Curtis 2, 43
Maynor, Dorothy 19
MC Breed 75
M.C. Hammer 20, 80
MC Lyte 34, 108
McClendon, Lisa 61
McClurkin, Donnie 25
McCoo, Marilyn 53
McCracklin, Jimmy 108
McDaniel, Hattie 5
McFerrin, Bobby 68
McFerrin, Robert, Sr. 94
McGill, Anthony 76
McGregor, Stephen 99
McGriff, Jimmy 72
McKee, Lonette 12
McKinney, Nina Mae 40

McKnight, Brian 18, 34
McLean, Jackie 78
McPherson, David 32
McRae, Carmen 77
McShann, Jay 110
McTell, Blind Willie 89
Memphis Minnie 33
Memphis Slim 105
Merriweather, Big Maceo 109
Method Man 81
Midnight Star 110
Mighty Clouds of Joy 110
Miguel 98
Miles, Buddy 69
Miller, Marcus 84
Millinder, Lucky 101
Mills, Stephanie 36
Mills Brothers, The 99
Minaj, Nicki 86
Mingus, Charles 15
Minott, Sugar 86
Mitchell, Dwike 111
Mitchell, Leona 42
Mitchell, Nicole 66
Mitchell, Willie 114
Mo', Keb' 36
Monáe, Janelle 86
Monica 21
Monk, Thelonious 1
Montgomery, Robbie 101
Montgomery, Wes 88
Moody, James 83
Moonglows, The 108
Moore, Chante 26
Moore, Dorothy Rudd 46
Moore, Johnny B. 38
Moore, LeRoi 72
Moore, Melba 21
Moore, Undine Smith 28
Moran, Jason 89
Morgan, Lee 102
Morton, Jelly Roll 29
Moses, Gilbert 12
Moss, J 64
Moten, Etta 18
Moura, Paulo 87
Mowatt, Judy 38
Mtukudzi, Oliver 109
Mullen, Nicole C. 45
Mumba, Samantha 29
Murphy, Eddie 4, 20, 61
Murray, Tai 47
Muse, Clarence Edouard 21
Musiq 37, 84
Mvula, Laura 110
Mya 35
Nas 33, 111
Nascimento, Milton 2, 64
Nash, Johnny 40
Nate Dogg 92
Naughton, Naturi 97
Navarro, Fats 104
Ndegeocello, Meshell 15, 83
N'Dour, Youssou 1, 53, 79
Neal, Raful 44
Neale, Haydain 52
Nelly 32, 90
Nelson, Oliver 113
Neville, Aaron 21
New Edition 101
Newman, David 76
Ne-Yo 65
Nicholas, Fayard 20, 57

Nicholas, Harold 20
Noah, Yannick 4, 60
Norman, Jessye 5
Notorious B.I.G. 20
Ocean, Frank 100
Odetta 37, 74
O'Jays, The 98
Okosuns, Sonny 71
Ol' Dirty Bastard 52
Olatunji, Babatunde 36
Oliver, Joe "King" 42
Omarion 107
112 114
O'Neal, Shaquille 8, 30, 95
Ongala, Remmy 9, 91
Orioles, The 100
Osborne, Jeffrey 26
Otis, Clyde 67
OutKast 35
Owens, Jack 38
Palacio, Andy 96
Palmer, Keke 68
Palmer, Rissi 65
Parker, Charlie 20
Parker, Maceo 72
Parker, Ray, Jr. 85
Parks, Gordon 1, 35, 58
Parlan, Horace 108
Patton, Antwan 45
Patton, Charley 107
Payne, Freda 58
Peebles, Ann 114
Pena, Paul 58
Pendergrass, Teddy 22, 83
Penguins, The 107
Peoples, Dottie 22
Perkins, Pinetop 70
Perren, Freddie 60
Perry, Lee 19, 103
Perry, Ruth 19
Peterson, James 38
Peterson, Marvin "Hannibal" 27
Peterson, Oscar 52
Pettiford, Oscar 106
Phillips, Esther 107
Phillips, Helen L. 63
Phipps, Wintley 59
Pinkney, Fayette 80
Pitts, Skip 103
Platters, The 99
Pleasure P 84
P.M. Dawn 54
Portuondo, Omara 53
Powell, Benny 87
Powell, Bud 24
Pratt, Awadagin 31
Premice, Josephine 41
Preston, Billy 39, 59
Price, Florence 37
Price, Kelly 23
Price, Leontyne 1
Pride, Charley 26
Prince 18, 65
Pritchard, Robert Starling 21
Professor Longhair 109
Proof 101
Pryce, Trevor 89
Pryor, Rain 65
Public Enemy 98
Purdie, Bernard 77
Queen Latifah 1, 16, 58
?uestlove 74
Ragin, Derek Lee 84

Rainey, Ma 33
Randall, Alice 38
Ranglin, Ernest 78
Rascal, Dizzee 82
Ravens, The 103
Ray, Carline 113
Ray J 86
Razaf, Andy 19
Reagon, Bernice Johnson 7
Reagon, Toshi 76
Record, Eugene 60
Redman 81
Redman, Joshua 30
Reed, A. C. 36
Reed, Jimmy 38
Reed, Natina 106
Reedy, Jessica 101
Reese, Della 6, 20, 96
Reeves, Dianne 32
Reeves, Martha 85
Reid, Antonio "L.A." 28
Reid, Vernon 34
Rhoden, Wayne 70
Rhone, Sylvia 2
Rhymefest 97
Rhymes, Busta 31
Rhyne, Melvin 109
Richard, Dawn 92
Richie, Lionel 27, 65, 114
Riggins, Karriem 102
Rihanna 65, 102
Riley, Boots 89
Riperton, Minnie 32
Rivers, Sam 95
Roach, Max 21, 63
Roberts, Kimberly Rivers 72
Roberts, Marcus 19, 113
Robeson, Paul 2
Robinson, Fenton 38
Robinson, Reginald R. 53
Robinson, Smokey 3, 49
Robinson, Sylvia 79
Rodríguez, Arsenio 87
Rogers, Bobby 110
Rogers, Jimmy 38
Rollins, Sonny 37, 94
Romanthony 115
Romeo 98
Roots, The 101
Ross, Diana 8, 27
Ross, Isaiah "Doc" 40
Ross, Rick 79, 104
Rowland, Kelly 100
Roxanne Shante 33
Rucker, Darius 34, 74, 108
Rudder, David 79
Ruffins, Kermit 85
Run 31, 73
Run-DMC 31, 75
RuPaul 17, 91
Rush, Bobby 78
Rush, Otis 38
Rushen, Patrice 12
Rushing, Jimmy 37
Russell, Brenda 52
RZA 80
Sade 15, 92
Sam and Dave 102
Sample, Joe 51
Sandé, Emeli 113
Sanders, Angelia 86
Sanders, Pharoah 64

Sangare, Oumou 18, 99
Santamaria, Mongo 81
Santigold 96
Sapp, Marvin 74
Scarlett, Millicent 49
Schuyler, Philippa 50
Scott, George 55
Scott, Hazel 66
Scott, Jill 29, 83
Scott, "Little" Jimmy 48
Scott-Heron, Gil 94
Scott-Young, Mona 101
Seal 14, 75
Seals, Son 56
Secada, Jon 97
Sermon, Erick 81
Shaggy 31
Shakur, Afeni 67
Shakur, Tupac 14
Shanice 112
Shaw, Marlena 105
Sheard, Kierra 61, 114
Shepp, Archie 101
Shider, Garry 87
Shipp, Matthew 107
Shirelles, The 111
Shirley, Donald 111
Shirley, George 33
Short, Bobby 52
Shorter, Wayne 75
Shorty, Ras, I 47
Shyne 101
Siji 56
Silver, Horace 26
Simmons, Russell 1, 30
Simon, Joe 109
Simone, Nina 15, 41
Simpson, Valerie 21, 97
Simpson-Hoffman, N'kenge 52
Sims, Danny 106
Sir Mix-A-Lot 82
Sisqo 30
Sissle, Noble 29
Sister Souljah 11, 100
Slash 75
Sledge, Percy 39
Slick Rick 93
Slim Thug 86
Sly & Robbie 34
Smith, Bessie 3
Smith, Cecilia 102
Smith, Cladys "Jabbo" 32
Smith, Clarence 113
Smith, Dr. Lonnie 49
Smith, Lonnie Liston 49
Smith, Mamie 32
Smith, Myrna 92
Smith, Stuff 37
Smith, Trixie 34
Smith, Will 8, 18, 53
Smith, Willie 107
Smith, Willow 92
Snoop Dogg 35, 84
Solange 97
Somi 85
Songz, Trey 88
Southern, Eileen 56
Souza, Carmen 111
Sowande, Fela 39
Spaniels, The 105
Spann, Otis 107
Sparks, Jordin 66
Spector, Ronnie 77

Speech 82
Spence, Joseph 49
Stampley, Micah 54
Stanford, Olivia Lee Dilworth 49
Staples, Cleotha 113
Staples, Mavis 50, 88
Staples, "Pops" 32
Staton, Candi 27
Staton, Dakota 62
Steely 80
Steinberg, Martha Jean "The Queen" 28
Stew 69
Stewart, Billy 112
Stewart, Tricky 98
Sticky Fingaz 86
Still, William Grant 37
Stone, Angie 31
Stone, Jesse 98
Stone, Sly 85
Stoute, Steve 38
Strayhorn, Billy 31
Street, Richard 110
Streeter, Sarah 45
Streeter, Sevyn 115
Strong, Barrett 89
Studdard, Ruben 46
Sugarhill Gang, The 79
Sullivan, Jazmine 81
Sullivan, Maxine 37
Sumlin, Hubert 101
Summer, Donna 25, 102
Sun Ra 60
Sundiata, Sekou 66
Supremes, The 33
Swan Silvertones, The 110
Swann, Bettye 109
Sweat, Keith 19
Sweatshirt, Earl 114
Sweet Honey in the Rock 106
Swizz Beatz 108
Sykes, Roosevelt 20
Tail Dragger 112
Tait, Michael 57
Take 6 112
Tamar-kali 63
Tamia 24, 55
Tampa Red 63
Taste of Honey, A 115
Tate, Buddy 108
Tate, Grady 106
Tatum, Art 28
Tavares 115
Taylor, Billy 23, 92
Taylor, Cecil 70
Taylor, Koko 40, 80
T-Boz 108
Tchicai, John 102
Tempations, The 33
Terrell, Tammi 32
Terry, Clark 39
Terry, Sonny 88
Tharpe, Rosetta 65
The-Dream 74
Thigpen, Ed 110
Thomas, Carla 96
Thomas, Irma 29
Thomas, Rozonda 34, 78
Thomas, Rufus 20, 96
Thornton, Big Mama 33
Threadgill, Henry 97
Three Mo' Tenors 35
Thurston, Stephen J. 49

Tillis, Frederick 40
Timbaland 32
Tinie Tempah 115
Tinsley, Boyd 50
Tisdale, Wayman 50
TLC 34
Tonex 54
Tosh, Peter 9
Toussaint, Allen 60
T-Pain 73, 111
Trammps, The 108
Tresvant, Ralph 57
Tribbett, Tye 81
Tricky 98
Trina 114
Trombone Shorty 97
Turnbull, Walter 13, 60
Turner, Big Joe 92
Turner, Ike 68
Turner, Tina 6, 27
2 Chainz 105
Tyler, the Creator 100
Tyner, McCoy 92
Uggams, Leslie 23, 114
Ulmer, James 79
Usher 23, 56, 95
Valdés, Bebo 75
Valdés, Chucho 89
Valentino, Bobby 62
Vandross, Luther 13, 48, 59
Vanity 67
Vaughan, Sarah 13
Vereen, Ben 4
Verrett, Shirley 66, 91
Vinson, Eddie 112
Waka Flocka Flame 110
Waldron, Mal 109
Wale 92
Walker, Albertina 10, 58, 89
Walker, Cedric 19
Walker, George 37
Walker, Hezekiah 34
Walker, T-Bone 111
Wallace, Sippie 1
Waller, Fats 29
Walton, Cedar 114
Ward, Willa 105
Ware, David S. 106
Warfield, William 94
Warwick, Dionne 18, 111
Washington, Dinah 22
Washington, Grover, Jr. 17, 44
Washington, Kenny 107
Waters, Benny 26
Waters, Ethel 7
Waters, Muddy 34
Watley, Jody 54
Watson, Johnny "Guitar" 18
Watts, André 42, 101
Watts, Reggie 52, 102
Webb, Chick 105
Webster, Katie 29
Wein, Joyce 62
Welch, Elisabeth 52
Wells, Junior 102
Wells, Mary 28
West, Kanye 52, 93
Whalum, Kirk 37, 64
White, Barry 13, 41
White, Josh 86
White, Josh, Jr. 52
White, Maurice 29
White, Willard 53

Whitfield, Norman 73
Whitney, Marva 109
Wilkins, Thomas Alphonso 71
will.i.am 64
Williams, Bert 18
Williams, Clarence 33
Williams, Claude 80
Williams, Cootie 114
Williams, Deniece 36
Williams, Denise 40
Williams, J. Mayo 83
Williams, Jody 113
Williams, Joe 5, 25
Williams, Mary Lou 15
Williams, Michelle 73
Williams, Nat D. 91
Williams, Paul 112
Williams, Pharrell 47, 82
Williams, Saul 31
Williams, Tony 67
Williams, Vanessa L. 4, 17
Williamson, Sonny Boy 84
Wilson, Abram 104
Wilson, Brian Courtney 94
Wilson, Cassandra 16
Wilson, Charlie 31, 77
Wilson, Frank 106
Wilson, Gerald 49
Wilson, Jackie 60
Wilson, Mary 28
Wilson, Nancy 10, 98
Wilson, Natalie 38
Winans, Angie 36
Winans, BeBe 14
Winans, CeCe 14, 43
Winans, David 77
Winans, Debbie 36
Winans, Marvin L. 17
Winans, Ronald 54
Winans, Vickie 24
Withers, Bill 61
Withers-Mendes, Elisabeth 64
Witherspoon, Jimmy 113
Womack, Bobby 60, 92
Wonder, Stevie 11, 53
Woods, Belita 103
Woods, Georgie 57
Woods, Scott 55
Woodson, Ali Ollie 89
Woolard, Jamal 102
Wright, O. V. 114
Wright, Timothy 74
Xzibit 78
Yabby You 83
Yarbrough, Camille 40
Yayo, Tony 113
Ying Yang Twins 112
Yoba, Malik 11
York, Vincent 40
Young, Lee 72
Young, Lester 37
Young Jeezy 63
Z-Ro 109

Religion

Abernathy, Ralph David 1
Abune Paulos 105
Adams, Yolanda 17, 67
Agyeman, Jaramogi Abebe 10, 63
Akinola, Peter Jasper 65
Akpan, Uwem 70
Al-Amin, Jamil Abdullah 6
Anthony, Wendell 25

Arinze, Francis 19
Aristide, Jean-Bertrand 6, 45
Armstrong, Vanessa Bell 24
Austin, Junius C. 44
Baker, Delbert W. 110
Banks, William 11
Barrow, Willie T. 85
Baylor, Helen 36
Beauvoir, Max 74
Bell, Ralph S. 5
Ben-Israel, Ben Ami 11
Berry, Moses 84
Black, Barry C. 47
Blake, Charles E. 82
Blanks, Deborah K. 69
Bloomer, George 86
Borders, William Holmes 94
Bowen, John W. E., Sr. 89
Boyd, T. B., III 6
Braxton, Brad 77
Brazier, Arthur M. 115
Brookins, Hamel Hartford 102
Bryant, John R. 45
Burgess, John 46
Butts, Calvin O., III 9, 90
Bynum, Juanita 31, 71
Caesar, Shirley 19
Cage, Byron 53
Caldwell, Kirbyjon 55
Cannon, Katie 10
Cardozo, Francis L. 33
Carr, Kurt 56
Chavis, Benjamin 6
Chineworth, Mary Alice 79
Cleaver, Emanuel 4, 45, 68, 107
Clements, George 2
Cleveland, James 19
Colemon, Johnnie 11
Collins, Janet 33, 64
Coltrane, Alice 70
Cone, James H. 3, 82
Cook, Suzan D. Johnson 22
Crouch, Andraé 27, 115
Crowdy, William Saunders 109
Dandala, Mvume 77
DeLille, Henriette 30
Divine, Father 7
Dollar, Creflo 106
DuBois, Joshua 88
Dyson, Michael Eric 11, 40
Easton, Hosea 91
Ellis, Charles H., III 79
Elmore, Ronn 21
Fabre, Shelton 71
Farrakhan, Louis 2, 15
Fauntroy, Walter E. 11
Fisher, Miles Mark 91
Flake, Floyd H. 18, 110
Forbes, James A., Jr. 71
Franklin, C. L. 68
Franklin, Robert M. 13
Fuller, Thomas O. 90
Funnye, Capers C., Jr. 73
Gaither, Israel L. 65
Gantin, Bernardin 70
Gilmore, Marshall 46
Gomes, Peter J. 15, 93
Grace, Sweet Daddy 104
Gray, Darius 69
Gray, William H., III 3
Green, Al 13, 47, 74
Gregory, Wilton 37
Grier, Roosevelt 13

Haddon, Dietrick 55
Haile Selassie 7
Harding, Vincent 67
Harris, Barbara 12
Hawkins, Tramaine 16
Hawkins, Walter 87
Hayes, James C. 10
Healy, James Augustine 30
Holsey, Lucius Henry 92
Hood, James Walker 91
Hooks, Benjamin L. 2, 85
Howard, M. William, Jr. 26
Jackson, Jesse 1, 27, 72
Jakes, Thomas "T. D." 17, 43
Jasper, John J. 91
Jean-Juste, Gérard 78
Jemison, Major L. 48
Johns, Vernon 38
Jones, Absalom 52
Jones, Alex 64
Jones, E. Edward, Sr. 45
Jones, Robert Elijah 90
Jones, William A., Jr. 61
Kalbani, Adil 77
Karim, Benjamin 61
Kelly, Leontine 33
King, Barbara 22
King, Bernice 4, 81
King, Martin Luther, Jr. 1
King, Martin Luther, Sr. 89
Kobia, Samuel 43
Lawson, James M., Jr. 90
Lee, Eric P. 79
Lee, Jarena 100
Lewis-Thornton, Rae 32
Lincoln, C. Eric 38
Little Richard 15
Loguen, J. W. 91
Long, Eddie L. 29, 89
Lowery, Joseph 2
Lowry, A. Leon 60
Luter, Fred, Jr. 103
Lyons, Henry 12
Majors, Jeff 41
Marino, Eugene Antonio 30
Mason, Charles Harrison 107
Maxis, Theresa 62
Mays, Benjamin E. 7
McClellan, George Marion 91
McClurkin, Donnie 25
McGuire, George Alexander 80
McKenzie, Vashti M. 29
Meeks, James T. 92
Michaux, Solomon Lightfoot 91
Miller, Clyde 113
Morgan, Gertrude 63
Moss, J 64
Moss, Otis, Jr. 72
Moss, Otis III 72
Muhammad, Ava 31
Muhammad, Elijah 4
Muhammad, Jabir Herbert 72
Muhammad, Khallid Abdul 10, 31
Muhammed, W. Deen 27
Murray, Cecil 12, 47
Muzorewa, Abel 85
Noble Drew Ali 100
Okaalet, Peter 58
Otunga, Maurice Michael 55
Patterson, Gilbert Earl 41
Patterson, J. O., Jr. 80
Peterson, Jesse Lee 81
Phipps, Wintley 59

Pierre, Andre 17
Powell, Adam Clayton, Jr. 3
Price, Frederick K. C. 21
Redding, Ann Holmes 77
Reems, Ernestine Cleveland 27
Reese, Della 6, 20, 96
Reverend Ike 79
Riley, Helen Caldwell Day 13
Rivers, Eugene F., III 81
Robinson, Ida B. 106
Rogers, Alan G. 72
Roundtree, Dovey 80
Rugambwa, Laurean 20
Sapp, Marvin 74
Scott, George 55
Senghor, Augustin Diamancoune 66
Sentamu, John 58
Seymour, William J. 106
Shabazz, Betty 7, 26
Sharpe, Samuel 103
Sharpton, Al 21, 97
Shaw, William J. 30
Shuttlesworth, Fred 47, 98
Slocumb, Jonathan 52
Smith, Amanda Berry 109
Somé, Malidoma Patrice 10
Stallings, George A., Jr. 6
Stampley, Micah 54
Stanton, Alysa 78
Steinberg, Martha Jean "The
    Queen" 28
Stith, Charles R. 73
Sullivan, Leon H. 3, 30
Taylor, Gardner C. 76
Taylor, Lonzie Odie 96
Thurman, Howard 3
Tillard, Conrad 47
Tolton, Augustine 62
Tonex 54
Tribbett, Tye 81
Turner, Henry McNeal 5
Tutu, Desmond (Mpilo) 6, 44
Ukpabio, Helen 86
Vanity 67
Vanzant, Iyanla 17, 47, 108
Waddles, Charleszetta "Mother" 10,
    49
Walker, Hezekiah 34
Walker, John T. 50
Walker, Lucius, Jr. 88
Walker, Wyatt Tee 80
Washington, James Melvin 50
Waters, Ethel 7
Watkins, Joe 86
Weeks, Thomas, III 70
Weems, Renita J. 44
White, Reggie 6, 50
White-Hammond, Gloria 61
Williams, Frederick (B.) 63
Williams, Hosea Lorenzo 15, 31
Williams, Preston Warren, II 64
Wilson, Frank 106
Wilson, Natalie 38
Winans, BeBe 14
Winans, CeCe 14, 43
Winans, Marvin L. 17
Winans, Ronald 54
Woods, Abraham, Jr. 74
Wright, Jeremiah A., Jr. 45, 69, 103
Wright, Nathan, Jr. 56
Wright, Timothy 74
Wyatt, Addie L. 56
X, Malcolm 1

Yates, Jack 114
Yearwood, Lennox, Jr. 112
York, Dwight D. 71
Youngblood, Johnny Ray 8

Science and technology

Adams-Campbell, Lucille L. 60
Adkins, Rod 41
Adkins, Rutherford H. 21
Alcorn, George Edward, Jr. 59
Alexander, Archie Alphonso 14
Alexander, Joseph L. 95
Allen, Ethel D. 13
Allen, Will 74
Anderson, Charles Edward 37
Anderson, Michael P. 40
Anderson, Norman B. 45
Anderson, William G(ilchrist) 57
Atim, Julian 66
Augusta, Alexander T. 111
Auguste, Donna 29
Auguste, Rose-Anne 13
Austin, Wanda M. 94
Bacon-Bercey, June 38
Banda, Hastings Kamuzu 6, 54
Banneker, Benjamin 93
Barnett, Herman 112
Bashir, Halima 73
Bath, Patricia E. 37
Bell, Carl C. 111
Benjamin, Regina 20, 75
Benson, Angela 34
Bishop, Stephen 95
Black, Keith Lanier 18, 84
Blackwell, David 79
Bluford, Guy 2, 35
Bluitt, Juliann S. 14
Bolden, Charles Frank, Jr. 7, 78
Boykin, Otis 92
Brady, St. Elmo 107
Branson, Herman 87
Brimm, Charles E. 105
Brown, Vivian 27
Brown, Willa 40
Bullard, Eugene 12
Callender, Clive O. 3
Campbell, Donald J. 66
Canady, Alexa 28
Cargill, Victoria A. 43
Carroll, L. Natalie 44
Carruthers, George R. 40
Carson, Benjamin 1, 35, 76
Carter, Joye Maureen 41
Carter, Majora 77
Carver, George Washington 4
CasSelle, Malcolm 11
Chatard, Peter 44
Chinn, May Edward 26
Christian, Spencer 15
Clack, Zoanne 73
Clark, Mamie Phipps 79
Clark, Yvonne Young 95
Cobb, W. Montague 39
Cobbs, Price M. 9
Cole, Rebecca 38
Coleman, Bessie 9
Coleman, Ken 57
Comer, James P. 6
Coney, PonJola 48
Cooper, Edward S. 6
Cooper, Lisa 73
Cornwell, Edward E., III 70
Counter, S. Allen 74

Crosthwait, David 93
Crouch, Hubert 95
Crumpler, Rebecca Lee 89
Dabiri, John 93
Dailey, Ulysses Grant 87
Daly, Marie Maynard 37
Davis, Allison 12
Dean, Mark 35
Deas, Gerald 85
Deconge-Watson, Lovenia 55
Delany, Bessie 12
Delany, Martin R. 27
Dennis, Gary C. 91
Dickens, Helen Octavia 14, 64
Diop, Cheikh Anta 4
Douglas, Donya 97
Drew, Alvin, Jr. 67
Drew, Charles Richard 7
Dunham, Katherine 4, 59
Dunston, Georgia Mae 48
Durham, James 90
Edwards, Lena Frances 76
Edwards, Willarda V. 59
Elders, Joycelyn 6
Ellington, E. David 11
Ellis, Clarence A. 38
Emeagwali, Dale 31
Emeagwali, Philip 30
Ericsson-Jackson, Aprille 28
Fennoy, Ilene 72
Fenton, Kevin 87
Ferguson, Vernice D. 108
Fields, Evelyn J. 27
Fisher, Ada M. 76
Fisher, Rudolph 17
Flipper, Henry O. 3
Flowers, Sylester 50
Foster, Henry W., Jr. 26
Fraser, Sarah Loguen 100
Freeman, Harold P. 23
French, D. M. 94
Fulani, Lenora 11
Fuller, A. Oveta 43
Fuller, Arthur 27
Fuller, Solomon Carter, Jr. 15
Gardere, Jeffrey 76
Gaston, Marilyn Hughes 60
Gates, Sylvester James, Jr. 15
Gayle, Helene D. 3, 46
Gibbons, Gary 107
Gibson, Kenneth Allen 6
Gibson, William F. 6
Giles, Roscoe C. 93
Gilliard, Steve 69
Goodlett, Carlton B. 91
Gourdine, Meredith 33
Grant, Augustus O. 71
Granville, Evelyn Boyd 36
Gray, Ida 41
Greene, Frank S., Jr. 101
Gregory, Frederick 8, 51
Grier, Eliza Ann 90
Griffin, Anthony 71
Griffin, Bessie Blout 43
Griffith, Patrick A. 64
Hall, Lloyd A. 8
Hamburg, Margaret 78
Hamilton, Vicki 95
Hammonds, Evelynn 69
Hannah, Marc 10
Hansberry, Tony, II 93
Harris, Bernard A. 90
Harris, Gary L. 87

Harris, Mary Styles 31
Harris, Wesley L. 92
Haynie, Sharon 94
Haywood, Jimmy 58
Henderson, Cornelius Langston 26
Henderson, Henry Fairfax, Jr. 89
Henson, Matthew 2
Hill, Wyllstyne D. 94
Hillary, Barbara 65
Hinton, William Augustus 8
Holmes, Hamilton E. 82
Hopkins, Donald R. 89
Hughes, Dora 88
Howard, Ayanna 65
Hutcherson, Hilda Yvonne 54
Imes, Elmer Samuel 39
Irving, Barrington, Jr. 112
Irving, Larry, Jr. 12
Jackson, Deborah 94
Jackson, Lisa 77
Jackson, Shirley Ann 12
Jarvis, Erich 67
Jawara, Dawda Kairaba 11
Jefferson, Mildred Fay 89
Jemison, Mae C. 1, 35
Jenifer, Franklyn G. 2
Johnson, Anthony M. 92
Johnson, Lonnie G. 32, 93
Johnson, Sandra K. 94
Johnson-Powell, Gloria 107
Jones, Edith Mae Irby 65
Jones, Frederick McKinley 68
Jones, Monty 66
Jones, Randy 35
Jones, Wayne 53
Joseph, Kathie-Ann 56
Julian, Hubert 90
Julian, Percy Lavon 6
Juma, Calestous 57
Just, Ernest Everett 3
Keith, Rachel Boone 63
Kenney, John A., Jr. 48
King, Reatha Clark 65
Kintaudi, Leon 62
Kittles, Rick 51
Knowling, Robert E., Jr. 38
Kong, B. Waine 50
Kountz, Samuel L. 10
Kyenge, Cécile 113
Lacks, Henrietta 101
Laroche, Joseph Philippe Lemercier
    85
Laryea, Thomas Davies, III 67
Latimer, Lewis H. 4
Lavizzo-Mourey, Risa 48
Lawless, Theodore K. 8
Lawrence, Margaret Morgan 100
Lawrence, Robert H., Jr. 16
Lee, Raphael C. 87
Lee, Robert 112
Leevy, Carrol M. 42
Leffall, Lasalle 3, 64
Lewis, Daurene 72
Lewis, Delano 7
Lewis-Hall, Freda 105
Logan, Onnie Lee 14
Lushington, Augustus Nathaniel 56
Lyttle, Hulda Margaret 14
Madison, Romell 45
Malveaux, Floyd 54
Manley, Audrey Forbes 16
Massey, Walter E. 5, 45
Massie, Samuel P., Jr. 29

Maupin, John E., Jr. 92
Maxey, Randall 46
Mays, William G. 34
Mboup, Souleymane 10
McBay, Henry C. 91
McCoy, Elijah 8
McJunkin, George 93
McNair, Ronald 3, 58
Mensah, Thomas 48
Mickens, Ronald Elbert 105
Miller, Warren F., Jr. 53
Millines Dziko, Trish 28
Mills, Joseph C. 51
Morgan, Garrett 1
Mossell, Nathan Francis 91
Murray, Pauli 38
Nabrit, Samuel Milton 47
Naki, Hamilton 63
Neto, António Agostinho 43
Nour, Nawal M. 56
Ojikutu, Bisola 65
Olopade, Olufunmilayo Falusi 58
Osborne, Na'taki 54
Pace, Betty 59
Perry, Warren 56
Person, Waverly 9, 51
Peters, Lenrie 43
Petioni, Muriel 99
Pickett, Cecil 39
Pierre, Percy Anthony 46
Pinn, Vivian Winona 49
Pitt, David Thomas 10
Pitts, Derrick 77
Poindexter, Hildrus A. 87
Poussaint, Alvin F. 5, 67
Price, Richard 51
Prothrow-Stith, Deborah 10
Quarterman, Lloyd Albert 4
Rabb, Maurice F., Jr. 58
Randolph, Linda A. 52
Rapelang Rabana 112
Reece, E. Albert 63
Reese, Milous J., Jr. 51
Riley, Helen Caldwell Day 13
Rillieux, Norbert 92
Robeson, Eslanda Goode 13
Robinson, Rachel 16
Robinson-Berry, Joan 94
Roker, Al 12, 49
Ross-Lee, Barbara 67
Samara, Noah 15
Satcher, David 7, 57, 111
Schiavocampo, Mara 97
Seacole, Mary 54
Shabazz, Betty 7, 26
Shavers, Cheryl 31
Sigur, Wanda 44
Sinkford, Jeanne C. 13
Slaughter, John Brooks 53
Smith, Ian 62
Smith, Richard 51
Spencer, Michael G. 87
Staples, Brent 8
Staupers, Mabel K. 7
Stewart, Ella 39
Sullivan, Louis 8
Sumner, Francis Cecil 112
Sweet, Ossian 68
Taylor, Susan C. 62
Terrell, Dorothy A. 24
Thomas, Vivien 9
Thornton, Yvonne S. 69
Tuckson, Reed V. 71

Tyson, Neil deGrasse 15, 65
Walker, Arthur, II 87
Walker, Joseph Edison 111
Walker, Tristan 98
Wambugu, Florence 42
Washington, Patrice Clarke 12
Watkins, Levi, Jr. 9
Wein, Joyce 62
Welsing, Frances Cress 5
West, James E. 87
Westbrooks, Bobby 51
White, Augustus, III 100
White-Hammond, Gloria 61
Wilkens, J. Ernest, Jr. 43
Williams, Daniel Hale 2
Williams, David Rudyard 50
Williams, O. S. 13
Wilson, Donald E. 88
Wilson, Stephanie 72
Wisdom, Kimberlydawn 57
Witt, Edwin T. 26
Woods, Granville T. 5
Wright, Louis Tompkins 4
Young, Roger Arliner 29

Social issues

Abbott, Diane 9
Abbott, Robert Sengstacke 27
Abernathy, Ralph David 1
Abiola-Costello, Hafsat 108
Abu-Jamal, Mumia 15
Adams, Sheila J. 25
Agyeman, Jaramogi Abebe 10, 63
Ake, Claude 30
Al-Amin, Jamil Abdullah 6
Alexander, Clifford 26
Alexander, Sadie Tanner Mossell 22
Allen, Lucy 85
Allen, Will 74
Ali, Muhammad 2, 16, 52
Allen, Ethel D. 13
Amaker, Norman 63
Andrews, Benny 22, 59
Angelou, Maya 1, 15
Annan, Kofi Atta 15, 48
Anthony, Wendell 25
Appiah, Kwame Anthony 67, 101
Arac de Nyeko, Monica 66
Archer, Dennis 7
Aristide, Jean-Bertrand 6, 45
Arnwine, Barbara 28
Asante, Molefi Kete 3
Ashe, Arthur 1, 18
Atyam, Angelina 55
Auguste, Rose-Anne 13
Austin, Bobby W. 95
Autrey, Wesley 68
Avery, Byllye Y. 66
Azikiwe, Nnamdi 13
Ba, Mariama 30
Baisden, Michael 25, 66
Baker, Ella 5
Baker, Gwendolyn Calvert 9
Baker, Houston A., Jr. 6
Baker, Josephine 3
Baker, Thurbert 22
Baldwin, James 1
Ballard, John 95
Banks, Paula A. 68
Barbee, Lloyd Augustus 71
Barlow, Roosevelt 49
Barnett, Etta Moten 56

Barrow, Willie T. 85
Bass, Charlotta Spears 40
Bates, Daisy 13
Bell, Derrick 6, 98
Bell, Ralph S. 5
Berry, Bertice 8, 55
Berry, Edwin C. 81
Berry, Mary Frances 7
Berrysmith, Don Reginald 49
Bethune, Mary McLeod 4
Betsch, MaVynee 28
Betts, R. Dwayne 86
Bevel, James L. 75
Bibb, Henry and Mary 54
Biko, Steven 4
bin Wahad, Dhoruba 85
Birch, Glynn R. 61
Black, Albert 51
Blackwell, Unita 17
Blakely, Edward J. 88
Bobo, Lawrence 60
Bolin, Jane 22, 59
Bond, Julian 2, 35, 106
Bonga, Kuenda 13
Booker, Cory Anthony 68
Bosley, Freeman, Jr. 7
Boyd, Gwendolyn 49
Boyd, John W., Jr. 20, 72
Boyd, T. B., III 6
Boykin, Keith 14
Bozella, Dewey 97
Bradley, David Henry, Jr. 39
Braun, Carol Moseley 4, 42
Brazier, Arthur M. 115
Bridges, Ruby 77
Broadbent, Hydeia 36
Brock, Roslyn McCallister 86
Brown, Byrd 49
Brown, Charlotte Hawkins 106
Brown, Cora 33
Brown, Eddie C. 35
Brown, Elaine 8
Brown, Homer S. 47
Brown, Jesse 6, 41
Brown, Jim 11, 95
Brown, Les 5
Brown, Lloyd Louis 10 42
Brown, Oliver Leon 94
Brown, Oscar, Jr. 53
Brown, Tony 3
Brown, Willa 40
Brown, Zora Kramer 12
Brutus, Dennis 38
Bryant, Wayne R. 6
Buery, Richard, Jr. 97
Bullock, Steve 22
Bunch, Lonnie G., III 91
Bunche, Ralph J. 5
Burks, Mary Fair 40
Burns, Anthony 102
Burroughs, Margaret Taylor 9
Burroughs, Nannie Helen 96
Butler, Paul D. 17
Butler, Selena Sloan 98
Butts, Calvin O., III 9, 90
Cameron, James 80
Campbell, Bebe Moore 6, 24, 59
Canada, Geoffrey 23
Carby, Hazel 27
Carlos, John 97
Carmichael, Stokely 5, 26
Carr, Johnnie 69
Carr, Keela 74

Carter, Majora 77
Carter, Mandy 11
Carter, Rubin 26
Carter, Stephen L. 4
Cary, Lorene 3
Cary, Mary Ann Shadd 30
Catto, Octavius V. 83
Cayton, Horace 26
Chavis, Benjamin 6
Chestnut, J. L., Jr. 73
Chideya, Farai 14, 61
Childress, Alice 15
Chisholm, Daquan 93
Chissano, Joaquim 7, 55, 67
Christophe, Henri 9
Clark, Joe 1
Clark, Kenneth B. 5, 52
Clark, Septima 7
Clay, William Lacy 8
Clayton, Mayme Agnew 62
Claytor, Helen 14, 52
Cleaver, Eldridge 5
Cleaver, Kathleen Neal 29
Clements, George 2
Cobbs, Price M. 9
Cole, Johnnetta B. 5, 43
Cole, Lorraine 48
Coles, Alice 80
Collins, Patricia Hill 67
Colston, Hal 72
Comer, James P. 6
Compton-Rock, Malaak 86
Connerly, Ward 14
Cook, Toni 23
Cooke, Marvel 31
Cook-Parrish, Mary Virginia 95
Cooper, Anna Julia 20
Cooper, Edward S. 6
Cooper, Margaret J. 46
Correia, De'Jaun 93
Cosby, Bill 7, 26, 59
Cosby, Camille 14, 80
Cose, Ellis 5, 50
Cox, Donald Lee 93
Creagh, Milton 27
Crew, Spencer R. 55
Cruse, Harold 54
Cuffe, Paul 98
da Silva, Benedita 5
Davis, Angela 5, 114
Davis, Artur 41
Davis, Danny K. 24
Dawson, Matel, Jr. 39
Dawson, Michael C. 63
DeBaptiste, George 32
DeLaine, Joseph A. 110
Delany, Martin R. 27
Dellums, Ronald 2, 81
Dent, Thomas C. 50
Diallo, Amadou 27
Dickerson, Ernest 6
Dieudonné 67
Diop, Cheikh Anta 4
Dirie, Waris 56
Divine, Father 7
Dixon, Margaret 14
Dobbs, John Wesley 89
Dodson, Howard, Jr. 7, 52
Dortch, Thomas W., Jr. 45
Douglas, Derek 88
Douglass, Frederick 87
Drew, Charles Richard 7
Du Bois, W. E. B. 3

DuBois, Shirley Graham 21
Due, Patricia Stephens 100
Duggins, George 64
Dukes, Hazel Nell 56
Dumas, Henry 41
Dumpson, James R. 108
Dunham, Katherine 4, 59
Eagleson, William Lewis 90
Early, Gerald 15
Easton, Hosea 91
Edelin, Ramona Hoage 19
Edelman, Marian Wright 5, 42
Edley, Christopher 2, 48
Edwards, Harry 2
Edwards, Lena Frances 76
Elder, Larry 25
Ellis-Lamkins, Phaedra 88
Ellison, Ralph 7
Esposito, Giancarlo 9
Espy, Mike 6
Eugene-Richard, Margie 63
Europe, James Reese 10
Evers, Medgar 3
Evers, Myrlie 8
Farmer, James 2, 64
Farrakhan, Louis 15
Farris, Isaac Newton, Jr. 63
Fauntroy, Walter E. 11
Fauset, Jessie 7
Fela 1, 42
Fields, C. Virginia 25
Finley, Ron 110
Finner-Williams, Paris Michele 62
Fletcher, Benjamin 90
Fletcher, Bill, Jr. 41
Forbes, James A., Jr. 71
Forman, James 7, 51
Fortune, T. Thomas 6
Foster, Marie 48
Franklin, Hardy R. 9
Franklin, John Hope 5, 77
Franklin, Robert M. 13
Frazier, E. Franklin 10
French, D. M. 94
Fulani, Lenora 11
Fuller, Arthur 27
Fuller, Charles 8
Gaines, Ernest J. 7
Gamble, Kenny 85
Gardner, Chris 65
Garner, Tyron 99
Garnet, Henry Highland 100
Garvey, Marcus 1
Gates, Henry Louis, Jr. 3, 38, 67
Gayle, Helene D. 3
Gbowee, Leymah 76
George, Nelson 12, 101
George, Zelma Watson 42
Gibson, Kenneth Allen 6
Gibson, William F. 6
Gilbert, Christopher 50
Gist, Carole 1
Golston, Allan C. 55
Gomez, Jewelle 30
Gomez-Preston, Cheryl 9
Gomillion, Charles 90
Goss, Carol A. 55
Gossett, Louis, Jr. 7
Graham, Lawrence Otis 12
Granger, Lester B. 75
Gray, Fred 37
Greene, Petey 65
Gregory, Dick 1, 54

Gregory, Wilton 37
Grier, Roosevelt 13
Griffith, Mark Winston 8
Grimké, Archibald H. 9
Guy, Rosa 5
Guyot, Lawrence 108
Hale, Lorraine 8
Haley, Alex 4
Hall, Elliott S. 24
Hall, Stuart 78
Hamblin, Ken 10
Hamer, Fannie Lou 6
Hampton, Fred 18
Hampton, Henry 6
Hani, Chris 6
Hansberry, William Leo 11
Harden, Monique 97
Harding, Vincent 67
Harper, Frances Ellen Watkins 11
Harrington, Oliver W. 9
Harris, Alice 7
Harris, Leslie 6
Harris, Marcelite Jordan 16
Harris, Patricia Roberts 2
Hawkins, Augustus F. 68
Hawkins, Steven 14
Hayden, Lewis 105
Hayes, Dennis 54
Haynes, Elizabeth Ross 102
Haynes, George Edmund 8
Hedgeman, Anna Arnold 22
Height, Dorothy I. 2, 23, 78
Henderson, Thelton E. 68
Henderson, Wade J. 14
Henderson, Zelma 71
Henry, Aaron Edd 19
Henry, Lenny 9, 52
Henson, Josiah 90
Hernandez, Aileen Clarke 13
Herndon, Angelo 90
Hernton, Calvin C. 51
Hill, Anita 5, 65
Hill, Jesse, Jr. 13
Hill, Oliver W. 24, 63
Hilliard, Asa Grant, III 66
Hilliard, David 7, 105
Holland, Endesha Ida Mae 3, 57
Holt Baker, Arlene 73
Hood, James Walker 91
hooks, bell 5, 90
Hooks, Benjamin L. 2, 85
Hope, Lugenia Burns 89
Houston, Charles Hamilton 4
Howard, M. William, Jr. 26
Hoyte, Lenon 50
Hubbard, Arnette Rhinehart 38
Huggins, Nathan Irvin 52
Hughes, Albert 7
Hughes, Allen 7
Hughes, Langston 4
Hunt, Darnell 92
Hunter-Gault, Charlayne 6, 31
Hutchinson, Earl Ofari 24
Hutson, Jean Blackwell 16
Ingram, Rex 5
Innis, Roy 5
Irvis, K. Leroy 67
Jackson, Edison O. 67
Jackson, Fred James 25
Jackson, George 14
Jackson, Jesse 1, 27, 72
Jackson, Judith D. 57
Jackson, Phillip 115

Jacob, John E. 2
Jagan, Cheddi 16
James, Daniel, Jr. 16
Jansen, Jonathan 102
Jealous, Benjamin Todd 70, 113
Jean, Wyclef 20, 86
Jeffries, Leonard 8
Jenkins, Ray 77
Johnson, Charles S. 12
Johnson, James Weldon 5
Johnson, Kevin 70
Jolley, Willie 28
Jones, Clarence B. 114
Jones, Cullen 73
Jones, Elaine R. 7, 45
Jones, Eugene Kinckle 79
Jones, John 89
Jones, Van 70
Jones, William A., Jr. 61
Jordan, June 7, 35
Jordan, Vernon E. 3, 35
Joseph, Kathie-Ann 56
Josey, E. J. 10
Joyner, Marjorie Stewart 26
Joyner, Tom 19, 90
Julian, Percy Lavon 6
Karim, Benjamin 61
Kato, David 103
Kaunda, Kenneth 2
Keita, Salif 83
Kelley, Cliff 75
Kennedy, Florynce 12, 33
Khanga, Yelena 6
Kidd, Mae Street 39
Kimbro, Warren 76
King, Bernice 4, 81
King, Coretta Scott 3, 57
King, Dexter 10
King, Martin Luther, III 20
King, Martin Luther, Jr. 1
King, Martin Luther, Sr. 89
King, Preston 28
King, Robert Hillary 84
King, Rodney 103
King, Yolanda 6
Kirk, Clara 95
Kitwana, Bakari 86
Koontz, Elizabeth Duncan 101
Kuzwayo, Ellen 68
Ladner, Joyce A. 42
LaGuma, Alex 30
Lampkin, Daisy 19
Lane, Charles 3
Lane, Vincent 5
Langston, John Mercer 101
Laraque, Paul 67
Lawson, James M., Jr. 90
Lee, Canada 8
Lee, Eric P. 79
Leland, Mickey 2
Lemon, Alton T. 112
Lewis, Ananda 28
Lewis, Delano 7
Lewis, Thomas 19
Lewis-Thornton, Rae 32
Little, Robert L. 2
Logan, Rayford W. 40
Loguen, J. W. 91
Louis, Errol T. 8
Louis, Willie 113
Loving, Mildred 69
Lowery, Evelyn Gibson 115
Lowery, Joseph 2

Lowry, A. Leon 60
Lucas, John 7
Lucy, William 50
Lucy Foster, Autherine 35
Luper, Clara 94
Maathai, Wangari 43, 97
Mabuza-Suttle, Felicia 43
Madison, Joseph E. 17
Makeba, Miriam 2, 50, 74
Malone Jones, Vivian 59
Malveaux, Julianne 32, 70
Mandela, Nelson 1, 14, 77
Mandela, Winnie 2, 35, 112
Manley, Audrey Forbes 16
Maponya, Maishe 101
Marable, Manning 10, 102
Marshall, Paule 7, 77
Marshall, Thurgood 1, 44
Martin, Louis E. 16
Martin, Trayvon 105
Masekela, Barbara 18
Mason, Biddy 89
Mason, Ronald 27
Matthews, Ameena 105
Maynard, Robert C. 7
Mays, Benjamin E. 7
Mbeki, Thabo 14, 73
McCabe, Jewell Jackson 10
McCarty, Osceola 16
McDougall, Gay J. 11, 43
McKay, Claude 6
McKenzie, Vashti M. 29
McKinney Hammond, Michelle 51
McKissick, Floyd B. 3
McMurray, Georgia L. 36
McQueen, Butterfly 6, 54
McWhorter, John 35
McWorter, Free Frank 91
Meredith, James H. 11
Mfume, Kweisi 6, 41
Mhlaba, Raymond 55
Micheaux, Oscar 7
Millender-McDonald, Juanita 21, 61
Miller, Clyde 113
Miller-Travis, Vernice 64
Millines Dziko, Trish 28
Minkins, Shadrach 104
Mitchell, Clarence M., Jr. 88
Mkapa, Benjamin W. 16, 77
Mongella, Gertrude 11
Moore, Gwendolynne S. 55
Moore, Harry T. 29
Morgan, Irene 65
Morial, Ernest "Dutch" 26
Moses, Robert Parris 11
Moss, Otis, Jr. 72
Mossell, Gertrude Bustill 40
Motley, Constance Baker 10, 55
Moton, Robert Russa 83
Moutoussamy-Ashe, Jeanne 7
Mowry, Jess 7
Muhammad, Elijah 4
Muhammad, Khallid Abdul 10, 31
Mukoko, Jestina 75
Murphy, Laura M. 43
Murray, Pauli 38
Nash, Diane 72
Ndadaye, Melchior 7
Nelson, Jill 6, 54
Newton, Huey 2
Niane, Katoucha 70
Nixon, Edgar Daniel 100
Nkoli, Simon 60

Nkrumah, Kwame 3
Noble, Gil 76
Norman, Pat 10
Nour, Nawal M. 56
Nzo, Alfred 15
Obasanjo, Olusegun 5
Oglesby, Zena 12
Ojikutu, Bisola 65
O'Neal, Frederick 99
Orange, James 74
Ormes, Jackie 73
Osborne, Na'taki 54
Osotimehin, Babatunde 107
Owens, Major 6
Page, Alan 7
Page, Clarence 4
Parker, Kellis E. 30
Parker, Pat 19
Parks, Rosa 1, 35, 56
Parr, Russ 51
Patterson, Frederick Douglass 12
Patterson, Louise 25
Patterson, Orlando 4
Patterson, P. J. 6, 20
Perkins, Edward 5
Perry, James 83
Perry, Matthew J., Jr. 96
Peterson, Jesse Lee 81
Pitt, David Thomas 10
Pleasant, Mary Ellen 9
Plessy, Homer Adolph 31
Pough, Terrell 58
Poussaint, Alvin F. 5, 67
Powell, Adam Clayton, Jr. 3
Powell, Kevin 31, 74
Pratt, Geronimo 18, 95
Pressley, Condace L. 41
Price, Hugh B. 9, 54
Primus, Pearl 6
Pritchard, Robert Starling 21
Prothrow-Stith, Deborah 10
Quander, Nellie 102
Quarles, Benjamin Arthur 18
Quigless, Helen G. 49
Ramaphosa, Cyril 3
Ramphele, Mamphela 29
Ramsey, Charles H. 21, 69
Rand, A. Barry 6
Randolph, A. Philip 3
Randolph, Linda A. 52
Rawlings, Nana Konadu Agyeman 13
Reagon, Bernice Johnson 7
Reed, Ishmael 8
Reid, Ira De A. 100
Rice, Louise Allen 54
Rice, Norm 8
Richards, Hilda 49
Richardson, Julieanna 81
Richardson, Rupert 67
Riggs, Marlon 5
Riley, Boots 89
Riley, Helen Caldwell Day 13
Rivers, Eugene F., III 81
Roberts, Lillian 83
Robeson, Eslanda Goode 13
Robeson, Paul 2
Robinson, Jackie 6
Robinson, Rachel 16
Robinson, Randall 7, 46
Robinson, Sharon 22
Robinson, Spottswood W., III 22
Roble, Abdi 71

Rock, John S. 113
Rodriguez, Cheryl 64
Rolle, Myron 98
Rowan, Carl T. 1, 30
Rowe-Adams, Jackie 109
Rowell, Victoria 13, 68
Ruffin, Josephine St. Pierre 75
Rusesabagina, Paul 60
Russwurm, John Brown 100
Rustin, Bayard 4
Sampson, Edith S. 4
Sanders, Malika 48
Sané, Pierre Gabriel 21
Sapphire 14, 95
Saro-Wiwa, Kenule 39
Sasser, Sean 113
Savimbi, Jonas 2, 34
Sawyer, Amos 2
Sayles Belton, Sharon 9, 16
Scantlebury-White, Velma 64
Seacole, Mary 54
Seale, Bobby 3
Sears, Stephanie 53
Seele, Pernessa 46
Senghor, Léopold Sédar 12
Shabazz, Attallah 6
Shabazz, Betty 7, 26
Shadd, Abraham D. 81
Shakur, Afeni 67
Shakur, Assata 6
Shakur, Yusef 85
Sharpe, Samuel 103
Sharpton, Al 21, 97
Sherrod, Shirley 87
Shinhoster, Earl 32
Shuttlesworth, Fred 47, 98
Sifford, Charlie 4, 49
Simkins, Modjeska Monteith 112
Simms, Margaret 94
Simon, Lateefah 95
Sisulu, Albertina 57, 95
Sisulu, Sheila Violet Makate 24
Sleet, Moneta, Jr. 5
Smith, Anna Deavere 6
Smith, Barbara 28
Smith, Damu 54
Smith, Greg 28
Smith, Kemba 70
Smith, Marie F. 70
Smith, Nate 49
Smith, Tommie 102
Snowden, Frank M., Jr. 67
Sohn, Sonja 100
Spriggs, William 67
Stallings, George A., Jr. 6
Staupers, Mabel K. 7
Steele, Claude 13, 97
Steele, Shelby 13, 82
Stewart, Alison 13
Stewart, Ella 39
Stewart, Maria W. Miller 19
Stone, Chuck 9
Sullivan, Leon H. 3, 30
Sweatt, Heman Marion 114
Sweet, Ossian 68
Talbert, Mary B. 77
Tate, Eleanora E. 20, 55
Tatum, Wilbert 76
Taulbert, Clifton Lemoure 19
Taylor, Bo 72
Taylor, Mildred D. 26
Taylor, Recy 92
Taylor, Robert Rochon 104

Terrell, Mary Church 9
Thomas, Arthur Ray 52
Thomas, Franklin A. 5, 49
Thomas, Jefferson 88
Thompson, Bennie G. 26
Thompson, Cynthia Bramlett 50
Thurman, Howard 3
Thurman, Wallace 16
Till, Emmett 7
Tobias, Channing H. 79
Toomer, Jean 6
Tosh, Peter 9
Touré, Askia (Muhammad Abu Bakr el) 47
Touré, Faya Ora Rose 56
Tribble, Israel, Jr. 8
Trotter, Donne E. 28
Trotter, Monroe 9
Tsvangirai, Morgan 26, 72
Tubman, Harriet 9
Tucker, C. Delores 12, 56
Tucker, Cynthia 15, 61
Tucker, Rosina 14
Tutu, Desmond 6
Tyree, Omar Rashad 21
Vaughn, Viola 70
Vega, Marta Moreno 61
Velez-Rodriguez, Argelia 56
Vesey, Denmark 100
Villard-Appolon, Malya 106
Vincent, Marjorie Judith 2
Waddles, Charleszetta "Mother" 10, 49
Walcott, Derek 5, 94
Walker, A'lelia 14
Walker, Alice 1, 43
Walker, Bernita Ruth 53
Walker, Lucius, Jr. 88
Wall, Orindatus S. B. 92
Wallace, Joaquin 49
Wallace, Michele Faith 13
Wallace, Phyllis A. 9
Wallace, William 75
Washington, Booker T. 4
Washington, Ebonya 79
Washington, Fredi 10
Washington, Harold 6
Washington, Pauletta Pearson 86
Watkins, Ted 104
Wattleton, Faye 9
Webb-Christburg, Sheyann 110
Wells, Henrietta Bell 69
Wells, James Lesesne 10
Wells-Barnett, Ida B. 8
Welsing, Frances Cress 5
West, Cornel 5, 33, 80
White, Michael R. 5
White, Reggie 6, 50
White, Walter F. 4
White, Willye 67
White-Hammond, Gloria 61
Whitmore, George 106
Wilkins, Roy 4
Williams, Armstrong 29
Williams, Evelyn 10
Williams, Fannie Barrier 27
Williams, George Washington 18
Williams, Hosea Lorenzo 15, 31
Williams, Maggie 7, 71
Williams, Montel 4, 57
Williams, Patricia 11, 54
Williams, Robert F. 11
Williams, Stanley "Tookie" 29, 57

Williams, Walter E. 4
Williams, Willie L. 4
Wilson, August 7, 33, 55
Wilson, Margaret Bush 79
Wilson, Phill 9, 104
Wilson, Sunnie 7, 55
Wilson, William Julius 22
Withers, Ernest C. 68, 88
Wiwa, Ken 67
Wolfe, George C. 6, 43
Woodson, Robert L. 10
Worrill, Conrad 12
Wright, Beverly 97
Wright, Charles H. 35
Wright, Louis Tompkins 4
Wright, Nathan, Jr. 56
Wright, Richard 5
Wyatt, Addie L. 56
X, Malcolm 1
Xuma, Madie Hall 59
Yancy, Dorothy Cowser 42
Yarbrough, Camille 40
Yearwood, Lennox, Jr. 112
Yeboah, Emmanuel Ofosu 53
Yoba, Malik 11
Young, Jean Childs 14
Young, Whitney M., Jr. 4
Youngblood, Johnny Ray 8
Yumkella, Kandeh 105
Zulu, Princess Kasune 54

Sports
Aaron, Hank 5
Abdul-Jabbar, Kareem 8
Abdur-Rahim, Shareef 28
Adams, Paul 50
Adu, Freddy 67
Alexander, Shaun 58
Ali, Laila 27, 63
Ali, Muhammad 2, 16, 52
Allen, Dick 85
Allen, Larry 109
Allen, Marcus 20
Allen, Ray 82
Altidore, Jozy 109
Amaker, Tommy 62
Amos, John B. 62
Anderson, Elmer 25
Anderson, Ezzrett 95
Anderson, Jamal 22
Anderson, Mike 63
Anderson, Viv 58
Anthony, Carmelo 46, 94
Antunes, Lúcio 109
Archibald, Tiny 90
Arenas, Gilbert 84
Armstrong, Henry 104
Artest, Ron 52
Ashe, Arthur 1, 18
Ashford, Emmett 22
Ashford, Evelyn 63
Ashley, Maurice 15, 47
Asomugha, Nnamdi 100
Baines, Harold 32
Baker, Dusty 8, 43, 72, 110
Balotelli, Mario 104
Banks, Ernie 33
Barber, Ronde 41
Barber, Tiki 57, 107
Barkley, Charles 5, 66
Barksdale, Don 103
Barnes, Ernie 16, 78
Barnes, John 53

Barnes, Steven 54
Barney, Lem 26
Barnhill, David 30
Baugé, Grégory 86
Baylor, Don 6
Baylor, Elgin 93
Beamon, Bob 30
Beasley, Jamar 29
Beaty, Zelmo 115
Bekele, Kenenisa 75
Bell, James "Cool Papa" 36
Belle, Albert 10
Benítez, Christian 113
Bettis, Jerome 64
Bickerstaff, Bernie 21
Bing, Dave 3, 59, 78
Bigirimana, Gael 115
Bivins, Michael 72
Black, Joe 75
Blair, Paul 36
Blake, James 43
Blanks, Billy 22
Blanton, Dain 29
Bogues, Tyrone "Muggsy" 56
Bol, Manute 1
Bolt, Usain 73, 104
Bolton-Holifield, Ruthie 28
Bonaly, Surya 7
Bonds, Barry 6, 34, 63, 99
Bonds, Bobby 43
Bonheur, Yannick 84
Boozer, Bob 103
Bosh, Chris 85
Bostic, Joe 95
Bowe, Riddick 6, 107
Bozella, Dewey 97
Bramlett, Joseph 91
Brand, Elton 31
Brandon, Terrell 16
Branham, George, III 50
Brashear, Donald 39
Brathwaite, Fred 35
Briscoe, Marlin 37
Brock, Lou 18
Broner, Adrien 109
Brooks, Aaron 33
Brooks, Derrick 43
Brown, Antron 85
Brown, James 22
Brown, Jim 11, 95
Brown, Mike 77, 107
Brown, Raymond 102
Brown, Sean 52
Brown, Willard 36
Bruce, Isaac 26
Bryant, Cullen 81
Bryant, Kobe 15, 31, 71, 110
Buchanan, Ray 32
Bush, Reggie 59, 88
Butler, Leroy, III 17
Bynoe, Peter C. B. 40
Byrd, Marlon 112
Cabell, Enos 102
Caldwell, Jim 81
Campanella, Roy 25
Campbell, Earl 104
Campbell, Milt 113
Campbell-Brown, Veronica 102
Cano, Robinson 97
Carew, Rod 20
Carlos, John 97
Carnegie, Herbert 25
Carter, Anson 24

Carter, Butch 27
Carter, Cris 21, 109
Carter, Joe 30
Carter, Kenneth 53
Carter, Rubin 26
Carter, Vince 26
Cash, Swin 59
Catchings, Tamika 43
Cepeda, Orlando 98
Chamberlain, Wilt 18, 47
Chandler, Tyson 114
Chaney, Don 98
Chaney, John 67
Charles, Ezzard 95
Charles, John 108
Charleston, Oscar 39
Cheeks, Maurice 47, 106
Cherry, Deron 40
Cheruiyot, Robert 69
Chitalu, Godfrey 108
Christie, Linford 8
Claiborne, Loretta 34
Clay, Bryan 57, 74
Clemons, Michael "Pinball" 64
Clendenon, Donn 26, 56
Clifton, Nathaniel "Sweetwater" 47
Coachman, Alice 18
Cole, Ashley 106
Coleman, Leonard S., Jr. 12
Collins, Jason 111
Cooper, Andy "Lefty" 63
Cooper, Charles "Chuck" 47
Cooper, Michael 31
Cooper, Tarzan 96
Cooper-Dyke, Cynthia 17, 89
Copeland, Michael 47
Corley, Tony 62
Cottrell, Comer 11
Cousins, DeMarcus 108
Cox, Bryan 83
Crawford, Carl 90
Crennel, Romeo 54, 107
Crisp, Coco 109
Cromartie, Antonio 115
Crooks, Garth 53
Croom, Sylvester 50
Cruz, Victor 107
Culp, Curley 110
Culpepper, Daunte 32, 85
Cunningham, Randall 23
Curry, Michael 85
Curry, Stephen 110
Dandridge, Ray 36
Daniels, Mel 106
Dantley, Adrian 72
Davids, Edgar 106
Davis, Ben 115
Davis, Ernie 48
Davis, Mike 41
Davis, Milt 74
Davis, Piper 19
Davis, Shani 58, 84
Davis, Terrell 20
Davis, Wade, Jr. 103
Dawes, Dominique 11
Dawson, Andre 85
Day, Leon 39
Dean, Fred 98
DeFrantz, Anita 37
DeGale, James 74
Delaney, Joe 76
Dent, Richard 97
Devers, Gail 7, 87

Dibaba, Tirunesh 73, 109
Dickerson, Eric 27, 108
Dihigo, Martín 103
Dixon, George 52
Doby, Lawrence Eugene, Sr. 16, 41
Doig, Jason 45
Dokes, Michael 105
Dorrell, Karl 52
dos Santos, Manuel Francisco 65
Douglas, Bob 96
Drew, Charles Richard 7
Drexler, Clyde 4, 61
Driver, Donald 99
Drogba, Didier 78
Duerson, Dave 93
Dumars, Joe 16, 65
Duncan, Tim 20, 91
Dungy, Tony 17, 42, 59
Dunn, Jerry 27
Dunn, Warrick 90
Durant, Kevin 76, 107
Dye, Jermaine 58
Edwards, Harry 2
Edwards, Herman 51
Edwards, Teresa 14, 95
Elder, Lee 6
Ellerbe, Brian 22
Elliott, Sean 26
Ellis, Dock 78
Ellis, Jimmy 44
Ervin, Anthony 66
Erving, Julius 18, 47
Eto'o, Samuel 73
Everett, Carl 103
Evra, Patrice 102
Ewing, Patrick 17, 73
Farah, Mo 104
Farr, Mel 24
Faulk, Marshall 35, 96
Felix, Allyson 48, 98
Ferdinand, Rio 82
Fielder, Cecil 2, 112
Fielder, Prince 68
Fisher, Derek 97
Flood, Curt 10, 93
Flowers, Vonetta 35
Ford, Cheryl 45
Foreman, George 1, 15
Forrest, Vernon 40, 79
Foster, Andrew 79
Foster, Arian 114
Fowler, Reggie 51
Fox, Rick 27
Fraser-Pryce, Shelly-Ann 113
Frazier, Joe 19, 98
Frazier, Walt 91
Frazier-Lyde, Jacqui 31
Freeman, Cathy 29
Freeman, Marianna 23
Fuhr, Grant 1, 49
Fuller, Vivian 33
Futch, Eddie 33
Gaines, Clarence E., Sr. 55
Gaither, Alonzo Smith (Jake) 14
Gamble, Oscar 113
Gans, Joe 91
Garnett, Kevin 14, 70
Garrison, Zina 2
Gaston, Cito 71
Gates, William 97
Gay, Tyson 114
Gebrselassie, Haile 70
Gentry, Alvin 23

George, Eddie 80
Gervin, George 80
Gibson, Althea 8, 43
Gibson, Bob 33
Gibson, Josh 22
Gibson, Truman K., Jr. 60
Gill, Turner 83
Gilliam, Frank 23
Gilliam, Joe 31
Gilmore, Artis 101
Glanville, Douglas Metunwa 82
Gooden, Dwight 20
Gorden, W. C. 71
Goss, Tom 23
Gourdine, Meredith 33
Gourdine, Simon 11
Graham, Trevor 84
Granderson, Curtis 66
Grand-Pierre, Jean-Luc 46
Grant, Frank 100
Gray, Yeshimbra "Shimmy" 55
Green, A. C. 32
Green, Darrell 39, 74
Green, Dennis 5, 45
Greene, Joe 10
Greene, Maurice 27, 77
Greenwood, L. C. 115
Greer, Hal 92
Gregg, Eric 16
Gregory, Ann 63
Grier, Bobby 95
Grier, Mike 43
Grier, Roosevelt 1
Griffey, Ken, Jr. 12, 73
Griffin, Blake 98
Griffin, Robert, III 107
Griffith, Emile 113
Griffith, Yolanda 25
Griffith-Joyner, Florence 28
Gumbel, Greg 8
Gwynn, Tony 18, 83
Gyan, Asamoah 87
Hagler, Marvelous Marvin 102
Hairston, Sam 88
Hamilton, Leonard 100
Hamilton, Lewis 66
Haney, Lee 77
Hardaway, Anfernee 13, 111
Hardaway, Tim 35
Harris, Franco 97
Harris, James 79
Harris, Sylvia 70
Harrison, Alvin 28
Harrison, Calvin 28
Harris-Stewart, Lusia 90
Hart, Thomas A., Sr. 113
Haskins, Clem 23
Hawkins, Connie 91
Haye, David 82
Hayes, Bob 77
Hayes, Elvin 93
Haywood, Spencer 99
Hazzard, Walt 98
Heard, Gar 25
Hearns, Thomas 29
Henderson, Rickey 28, 78
Henry, Thierry 66
Hernández, Orlando 96
Hickman, Fred 11
Hill, Calvin 19
Hill, Grant 13, 94
Hill, Michael 95
Hillary, Barbara 65

Hilliard, Wendy 53
Hines, Garrett 35
Holdsclaw, Chamique 24, 110
Holiday, Jrue 115
Holland, Kimberly N. 62
Holmes, Kelly 47
Holmes, Larry 20, 68
Holmes, Santonio 87
Holyfield, Evander 6
Hopkins, Bernard 35, 69, 105
Horford, Al 107
Horton, Andre 33
Horton, Suki 33
Horton, Willie 104
Howard, Desmond 16, 58
Howard, Dwight 113
Howard, Juwan 15
Howard, Ryan 65, 113
Howard, Sherri 36
Hunter, Billy 22, 109
Hunter, Lindsey 110
Hunter, Torii 43, 109
Hyde, Cowan F. "Bubba" 47
Ibrahim, Fuad 109
Iginla, Jarome 35
Ince, Paul 83
Irvin, Michael 64
Irvin, Monte 31
Irving, Kyrie 102
Isaacs, John 76
Iverson, Allen 24, 46
Ivey, Phil 72, 106
Jackson, Jamea 64
Jackson, Mannie 14
Jackson, Rampage 83
Jackson, Reggie 15
Jackson, Rickey 88
Jackson, Tom 70
Jacobs, Regina 38
James, David 84
James, G. Larry 74
James, LeBron 46, 78, 105
James, Vanessa 84
Jenkins, Fergie 46
Jenkins, Kris 98
Jeter, Derek 27, 93
Jim, Songezo 111
Johnson, Avery 62
Johnson, Ben 1
Johnson, Calvin 108
Johnson, Chad 108
Johnson, Chris 92
Johnson, Clifford "Connie" 52
Johnson, Dennis 89
Johnson, Gus 92
Johnson, Jack 8
Johnson, Joe 94
Johnson, John Henry 96
Johnson, Judy 105
Johnson, Kevin 70
Johnson, Keyshawn 91
Johnson, Larry 28
Johnson, Levi 48
Johnson, Magic 3, 39, 101
Johnson, Mamie "Peanut" 40
Johnson, Michael 13
Johnson, Rafer 33
Johnson, Rodney Van 28
Joiner, Charlie 102
Jones, Adam 103
Jones, Adam 114
Jones, Andruw 98
Jones, Cobi N'Gai 18

Jones, Cullen 73
Jones, Deacon 92, 112
Jones, Ed "Too Tall" 46
Jones, K. C. 83
Jones, Lou 64
Jones, Marion 21, 66
Jones, Merlakia 34
Jones, Randy 35
Jones, Robbie 113
Jones, Roy, Jr. 22
Jones, Sam 85
Jones-Drew, Maurice 113
Jordan, Eddie 83
Jordan, Michael 6, 21
Joyce, Dru 81
Joyner-Kersee, Jackie 5
Justice, David 18
Kaiser, Cecil 42
Kane, Evander 97
Kanouté, Fred 68
Kearney, Beverly 109
Keflezighi, Meb 49
Keith, Floyd A. 61
Kellogg, Clark 64
Kelly, Jim 113
Kennedy, Cortez 104
Kennedy-Overton, Jayne Harris 46
Kerry, Leon G. 46
Kidd, Jason 86
Kimbro, Henry A. 25
King, Don 14
Kipsang, Wilson 115
Krigger, Kevin 111
Lacy, Sam 30, 46
Ladd, Ernie 64
Lane, Dick 92
Lanier, Bob 47
Lanier, Willie 33
Lankford, Ray 23
Laraque, Georges 48
Larkin, Barry 24
Lashley, Bobby 63
Lassiter, Roy 24
Lee, Canada 8
Lennox, Betty 31
Leonard, Buck 67
Leonard, Sugar Ray 15
Leônidas 96
Leslie, Lisa 16, 73
Lester, Bill 42, 85
Lewis, Butch 71, 99
Lewis, Carl 4, 97
Lewis, Denise 33
Lewis, Jamal 115
Lewis, Lennox 27
Lewis, Marvin 51, 87
Lewis, Oliver 56
Lewis, Ray 33, 109
Liston, Sonny 33
Little, Floyd 86
Little, Larry 90
Littlepage, Craig 35
Lloyd, Earl 26
Lloyd, John Henry "Pop" 30
Lofton, James 42
Lofton, Kenny 12
Lopes, Davey 92
Loroupe, Tegla 59
Lott, Ronnie 9
Louis, Joe 5
Love, Nat 9
Love, Reggie 77
Lowe, Sidney 64

Lucas, Bill 97
Lucas, John 7
Mackey, Biz 82
Madison, Paula 37, 99
Mahorn, Rick 60
Malone, Karl 18, 51, 90
Malone, Moses 79
Manigault, Earl "The Goat" 15
Manuel, Jerry 94
Mariner, Jonathan 41
Martin, Curtis 104
Martinez, Pedro 81
Masekela, Sal 106
Matson, Ollie 93
Maye, Lee 111
Mayers, Jamal 39
Mayhew, Martin R. 76
Mays, Willie 3
Mayweather, Floyd 57, 104
McAdoo, Bob 75
McBride, Bryant 18
McCarthy, Sandy 64
McCovey, Willie 103
McCray, Nikki 18
McDaniel, Randall Cornell 81
McGrady, Tracy 80
McGriff, Fred 24
McKegney, Tony 3
McLendon, John B., Jr. 89
McNabb, Donovan 29
McNair, Steve 22, 47, 79
McNeil, Lori 1
McRae, Hal 84
Mello, Breno 73
Meminger, Dean 114
Mensah, John 87
Metcalfe, Ralph 26
Milla, Roger 2
Miller, Cheryl 10, 74
Miller, Larry G. 72
Miller, Reggie 33
Mills, Sam 33
Milton, DeLisha 31
Minor, DeWayne 32
Minoso, Minnie 89
Mitchell, Sam 82
Mohammed, Nazr 64
Monk, Art 38, 73
Monroe, Earl 89
Montgomery, Tim 41
Moon, Warren 8, 66
Moore, Davey 105
Moore, Maya 94
Moorer, Michael 19
Morgan, Joe 9, 96
Morris, Mercury 114
Morris, Raheem 77
Moses, Edwin 8
Mosley, Shane 32
Moss, Randy 23, 90
Motley, Marion 26
Mourning, Alonzo 17, 44
Moussambani, Eric 105
Muamba, Fabrice 104
Muhammad, Jabir Herbert 72
Muncie, Chuck 112
Mundine, Anthony 56
Murray, Eddie 12
Murray, Lenda 10
Mutola, Maria 12
Mutombo, Dikembe 7, 107
Nakhid, David 25
Newcombe, Don 24

Newsome, Ozzie 26
Newton, Cam 96
Nixon, Otis 111
Noah, Yannick 4, 60
Norton, Ken 101, 115
Odom, Lamar 81
Ogden, Jonathan 110
Okocha, Jay Jay 99
Olajuwon, Hakeem 2, 72
Oliver, Pam 54
Oliver, Paul 115
Omar, Samia Yusuf 107
O'Neal, Shaquille 8, 30, 95
O'Neil, Buck 19, 59
Onyewu, Oguchi 60
O'Ree, Willie 5
Ortiz, David 52, 82
Owens, Jesse 2
Owens, Terrell 53, 106
Pace, Orlando 21
Page, Alan 7
Page, Greg 78
Paige, Satchel 7
Palmer, Violet 59
Parish, Robert 43
Parker, Candace 74
Parker, Jim 64
Parker, Tony 75
Patterson, Floyd 19, 58
Paul, Chris 84, 100
Payton, Gary 99
Payton, Walter 11, 25
Peck, Carolyn 23
Peete, Calvin 11
Peete, Rodney 60
Pelé 7
Perez, Pascual 108
Perkins, Eddie 103
Perrot, Kim 23
Perry, Joe 95
Perry, Lowell 30
Peters, Margaret 43
Peters, Matilda 43
Petersen, Neal 96
Peterson, Adrian 109
Phillips, Teresa L. 42
Pickett, Bill 11
Pierce, Paul 71
Pippen, Scottie 15, 89
Pollard, Fritz 53
Porter, Terry 75
Powell, Mike 7
Powell, Renee 34
Powell, William J. 82
Price, David 101
Pride, Charley 26
Prince, Ron 64
Prince, Tayshaun 68
Pryce, Trevor 89
Puckett, Kirby 4, 58
Puig, Yasiel 113
Quirot, Ana 13
Radcliffe, Ted 74
Raines, Tim 107
Randle, John 87
Randolph, Willie 53
Rashad, Ahmad 18
Ready, Stephanie 33
Reagins, Tony 94
Reece, Marcel 114
Reed, Willis, Jr. 86
Reese, Jerry 103
Reese, Pokey 28

Regis, Cyrille 51
Reynolds, Harold 77
Rhoden, William C. 67
Rhodes, Ray 14
Ribbs, Willy T. 2
Rice, Jerry 5, 55, 89
Rice, Jim 75
Rice, Ray 112
Richard, J. R. 87
Richards-Ross, Sanya 66, 98
Richardson, Donna 39
Richardson, Nolan 9
Richmond, Mitch 19
Rivers, Doc 25, 81
Roaf, Willie 106
Robertson, Oscar 26
Robinson, Craig 107
Robinson, Dave 110
Robinson, David 24, 90
Robinson, Eddie G. 10, 61
Robinson, Flynn 112
Robinson, Frank 9, 87
Robinson, Jackie 6
Robinson, Sugar Ray 18
Robinson, Will 51, 69
Rodman, Dennis 12, 44, 96
Rogers, Rodney Ray 106
Rolle, Myron 98
Rollins, Jimmy 70
Ronaldinho 69
Rondo, Rajon 111
Rose, Derrick 82
Rose, Jalen 108
Rose, Lionel 56
Roundfield, Danny 109
Roy, Brandon 98
Rubin, Chanda 37
Rudisha, David 112
Rudolph, Wilma 4
Russell, Bill 8
Sabathia, CC 74
St. Julien, Marlon 29
Salvador, Bryce 51
Sampson, Charles 13
Sanders, Barry 1, 53
Sanders, Bob 72
Sanders, Deion 4, 31, 96
Sanders, Satch 77
Sapp, Warren 38, 109
Savón, Félix 105
Sayers, Gale 28
Scott, George 113
Scott, Stuart 34
Scott, Wendell Oliver, Sr. 19
Scurry, Briana 27
Seymour, Richard 101
Seymour, Teddy 110
Shannon, Randy 82
Sharpe, Shannon 97
Sharper, Darren 32
Sheffield, Gary 16, 108
Shell, Art 1, 66
Shippen, John 43
Showers, Reggie 30
Sifford, Charlie 4, 49
Silas, Paul 24
Silva, Anderson 96
Simmons, Bob 29
Simpson, O. J. 15, 100
Singletary, Mike 4, 76
Sizemore, Grady 96
Slice, Kimbo 73
Smith, Bruce 80

Smith, Bubba 96
Smith, Emmitt 7, 87
Smith, Hilton 29
Smith, Kenny 114
Smith, Lee 101
Smith, Lovie 66, 107
Smith, Neil 109
Smith, Ozzie 77
Smith, Randy 81
Smith, Reggie 113
Smith, Rick 72
Smith, Stephen A. 69
Smith, Tommie 102
Smith, Tubby 18, 83
Solomon, Jimmie Lee 38
Song, Alex 105
Sono, Jomo 86
Sosa, Sammy 21, 44
Spiller, Bill 64
Sprewell, Latrell 23
Stackhouse, Jerry 30
Staley, Dawn 57
Stallworth, John 102
Stargell, Willie 29
Stearns, Norman "Turkey" 31
Steele, Sage 115
Stephens, Sloane 105
Stevenson, Teófilo 103
Steward, Emanuel 18, 106
Stewart, James, Jr. 60, 98
Stewart, Kordell 21, 111
Stingley, Darryl 69
Stith, Tom 93
Stone, Toni 15
Stoudemire, Amar'e 59, 106
Strahan, Michael 35, 81
Strawberry, Darryl 22
Stringer, C. Vivian 13, 66
Stringer, Korey 35
Strode, Woody 111
Suggs, Terrell 108
Suttles, Mule 108
Swann, Lynn 28
Swoopes, Sheryl 12, 56
Tate, John 107
Tatum, Jack 87
Tatum, Reece 104
Taylor, Jason 70
Taylor, Jermain 60
Taylor, Lawrence 25
Taylor, Marshall Walter "Major" 62
Temple, Ed 109
Tergat, Paul 59
Terrell-Kearney, Kim 83
Thomas, Debi 26
Thomas, Derrick 25
Thomas, Emmitt 71
Thomas, Frank 12, 51
Thomas, Isiah 7, 26, 65
Thomas, Thurman 75
Thompson, Tina 25, 75
Thrower, Willie 35
Thugwane, Josia 21
Thurmond, Nate 88
Tiant, Luis 102
Tirico, Mike 68
Tisdale, Wayman 50
Toler, Burl 80
Tomlinson, LaDainian 65, 112
Toney, James 89
Touré, Yaya 99
Trouppe, Quincy Thomas, Sr. 84
Tunnell, Emlen 54

Turman, Glynn 100
Tyson, Mike 28, 44, 93
Ujiri, Masai 107
Unseld, Wes 23
Upshaw, Gene 18, 47, 72
Ussery, Terdema, II 29
Vanessa James and Yannick Bon-
    heur 84
Vick, Michael 39, 65, 94
Vincent, Troy 91
Virgil, Ozzie 48
Wade, Dwyane 61, 103
Walcott, Jersey Joe 102
Walker, Chet 106
Walker, Herschel 1, 69
Walker, LeRoy T. 106
Wallace, Ben 54
Wallace, Perry E. 47
Wallace, Rasheed 56
Wanjiru, Sammy 94
Ward, Andre 62
Ward, Hines 84
Ware, Andre 37
Ware, DeMarcus 92
Washington, Gene 63
Washington, Kenny 50
Washington, MaliVai 8
Washington, Ora Mae 115
Watson, Bob 25
Watts, J. C., Jr. 14, 38
Weah, George 58
Weathers, Carl 10
Weaver, Mike 109
Webber, Chris 15, 30, 59
Weekes, Kevin 67
Wells, Vernon 91
Wells, Willie 105
Westbrook, Peter 20
Whitaker, Pernell 10, 89
White, Bill 1, 48
White, Frank 95
White, Jesse 22, 75
White, Jo Jo 112
White, Reggie 6, 50
White, Willye 67
Whitfield, Fred 23
Whitfield, Mal 60
Whitney, Davey L. 110
Wilbon, Michael 68
Wilkens, Lenny 11, 88
Wilkins, Dominique 74
Williams, Billy 86
Williams, Deron 92
Williams, Doug 22, 112
Williams, J. Mayo 83
Williams, Ken 68
Williams, Lauryn 58
Williams, Natalie 31
Williams, Ricky 85
Williams, Serena 20, 41, 73
Williams, Stevie 71
Williams, Venus 17, 34, 62
Williamson, Fred 67
Willingham, Tyrone 43
Willis, Bill 68
Willis, Dontrelle 55
Willis, Patrick 99
Wills, Harry 80
Wills, Maury 73
Winfield, Dave 5, 91
Winkfield, Jimmy 42
Winslow, Kellen 83
Wolfe, Ann 82

Wood, Willie 111
Woodard, Lynette 67
Woodruff, John 68
Woods, Cheyenne 103
Woods, Tiger 14, 31, 81
Woodson, Mike 78
Woodson, Rod 79
Worthy, James 49
Wright, Chalky 103
Wright, Rayfield 70
Yeboah, Emmanuel Ofosu 53
Young, Darren 114
Young, Donald, Jr. 57
Young, Jimmy 54
Young, John 111

Television

Akil, Mara Brock 60, 82
Akinnuoye-Agbaje, Adewale 56
Alexander, Khandi 43
Ali, Tatyana 73
Allen, Byron 3, 24, 97
Allen, Debbie 13, 42
Allen, Marcus 20
Alonso, Laz 87
Amos, John 8, 62
Anderson, Anthony 51, 77
Anderson, Eddie "Rochester" 30
Andrews, Tina 74
Arkadie, Kevin 17
Arnez J 53
Arnold, Tichina 63
Babatunde, Obba 35
Banks, Michelle 59
Banks, William 11
Barclay, Paris 37, 94
Bassett, Angela 6, 23, 62
Beach, Michael 26
Beaton, Norman 14
Beauvais, Garcelle 29, 95
Bell, LeRoy 98
Bell, W. Kamau 107
Bellamy, Bill 12
Bennett, Louise 69
Bentley, Lamont 53
Berry, Bertice 8, 55
Berry, Fred "Rerun" 48
Bey, Yasiin 30, 96
Blackmon, Brenda 58
Blackwood, Maureen 37
Blacque, Taurean 58
Blake, Asha 26
Bleu, Corbin 65
Bonet, Lisa 58
Boseman, Chadwick 111
Boston, Kelvin E. 25
Bowser, Yvette Lee 17
Bradley, Ed 2, 59
Brady, Wayne 32, 71
Brandy 14, 34, 72
Braugher, Andre 13, 58, 91
Bridges, Todd 37
Brooks, Avery 9, 98
Brooks, Golden 62
Brooks, Hadda 40
Brooks, Mehcad 62
Brown, James 22
Brown, Joe 29
Brown, Les 5
Brown, Tony 3
Brown, Vivian 27
Brown, Warren 61
Browne, Roscoe Lee 66

Bruce, Bruce 56
Buress, Hannibal 101
Burnett, Charles 16, 68
Burton, LeVar 8
Byrd, Eugene 64
Byrd, Robert 11
Caldwell, Benjamin 46
Cameron, Earl 44
Campbell, Naomi 1, 31
Campbell-Martin, Tisha 8, 42
Cannon, Nick 47, 73
Cannon, Reuben 50
Cara, Irene 77
Carroll, Rocky 74
Carroll, Diahann 9
Carson, Lisa Nicole 21
Carter, Nell 39
Cash, Rosalind 28
Cedric the Entertainer 29, 60, 115
Cenac, Wyatt 94
Chappelle, Dave 50, 115
Chase, Debra Martin 49, 96
Cheadle, Don 19, 52
Chestnut, Morris 31
Chew, Robert F. 109
Chideya, Farai 14, 61
Childress, Alvin 114
Christian, Spencer 15
Ciara, Barbara 69
Clack, Zoanne 73
Clash, Kevin 14, 93
Clayton, Xernona 3, 45
Cobbs, Bill 101
CoCo Brother 93
Cole, Keyshia 63, 107
Cole, Nat "King" 17
Coleman, Gary 35, 86
Common 31, 63, 98
Coolio 103
Corbi, Lana 42
Cornelius, Don 4, 100
Cosby, Bill 7, 26, 59
Crothers, Scatman 19
Crump, Steven 96
Curry, Mark 17
Curtis-Hall, Vondie 17
DaCosta, YaYa 98
Davidson, Tommy 21
Davis, Eisa 68
Davis, Mia Amber 94
Davis, Ossie 5, 50
Davis, Viola 34, 76, 100
de Passe, Suzanne 25
De Shields, André 72
Dee, Ruby 8, 50, 68
Deezer D 53
Devine, Loretta 24
Dickerson, Ernest 6
Diggs, Taye 25, 63
Dixon, Ivan 69
DJ Lance Rock 94
Dorn, Michael 112
Dourdan, Gary 37
Drake 86
Dre, Dr. 10
Duke, Bill 3, 96
Dungey, Merrin 62
Duthiers, Vladimir 109
Dutton, Charles S. 4, 22
Earthquake 55
Ejiofor, Chiwetel 67
Elba, Idris 49, 89
Elder, Larry 25

Elie, Lolis Eric 97
Elise, Kimberly 32, 101
Ellis, Aunjanue 108
Ellis, Trey 97
Emmanuel, Alphonsia 38
Ephriam, Mablean 29
Epperson, Sharon 54
Erving, Julius 18, 47
Esposito, Giancarlo 9
Eubanks, Kevin 15, 108
Evans, Harry 25
Faison, Donald 50
Faison, Frankie 55
Falana, Lola 42
Fales-Hill, Susan 88
Fargas, Antonio 50
Fields, Kim 36
Fishburne, Laurence 4, 22, 70
Fisher, Gail 85
Fox, Rick 27
Foxx, Jamie 15, 48
Foxx, Redd 2
Frazier, Kevin 58
Freeman, Aaron 52
Freeman, Morgan 2, 20, 62, 100
Freeman, Yvette 27
Gaines, Ernest J. 7
Gant, Richard 105
Gardere, Jeffrey 76
Garvin, Gerry 78
Gibbs, Marla 86
Gibson, Tyrese 27, 62
Givens, Adele 62
Givens, Robin 4, 25, 58
Glass, Ron 111
Glover, Danny 1, 24, 103
Glover, Donald 85
Glover, Savion 14
Goldberg, Whoopi 4, 33, 69
Goode, Mal 13
Gooding, Cuba, Jr. 16, 62
Gordon, Carl 87
Gordon, Ed 10, 53
Gossett, Louis, Jr. 7
Graham, Katerina 99
Gray, Darius 69
Greely, M. Gasby 27
Greene, Petey 65
Grier, David Alan 28
Grier, Pam 9, 31, 86
Griffin, Angela 80
Guillaume, Robert 3, 48
Gumbel, Bryant 14, 80
Gumbel, Greg 8
Gunn, Moses 10
Gurira, Danai 73
Guy, Jasmine 2
Hairston, Jester 88
Haley, Alex 4
Hall, Arsenio 58
Hall, Tamron 96
Hamilton, Lisa Gay 71
Hampton, Henry 6
Hardison, Kadeem 22
Harewood, David 52
Harewood, Dorian 104
Harper, Hill 32, 65, 97
Harrell, Andre 9, 30
Harris, Naomie 55
Harris, Robin 7
Harris, Wood 114
Harry, Jackée 111
Hart, Kevin 103

Harvey, Steve 18, 58
Hatchett, Glenda 32
Hayes, Isaac 20, 58, 73
Haynes, Trudy 44
Haysbert, Dennis 42, 106
Hector, Jamie 98
Hemingway, Anthony 107
Hemsley, Sherman 19, 104
Henderson, Jeff 72
Henriques, Julian 37
Henry, Lenny 4, 52
Henson, Darrin 33
Henson, Taraji P. 58, 77
Hickman, Fred 11
Hill, Dulé 29
Hill, Marc Lamont 80
Hinderas, Natalie 5
Hines, Gregory 1, 42
Holmes, Amy 69
Holmes, T. J. 28
Holt, Lester 66
Hooks, Robert 76
Hounsou, Djimon 19, 45
Howard, Sherri 36
Howard, Terrence 59, 94
Hudson, Ernie 72
Huggins, Edie 71
Hughley, D. L. 23, 76
Hunter-Gault, Charlayne 6, 31
Hyman, Earle 25, 79
Ice-T 6, 31, 96
Ifill, Gwen 28
Ingram, Rex 5
Jackson, George 19
Jackson, Janet 6, 30, 68
Jackson, Randy 40
Jackson, Tom 70
Jarrett, Vernon D. 42
Jenkins, Kris 98
Joe, Yolanda 21
Johnson, Clark 96
Johnson, Linton Kwesi 37
Johnson, Robert L. 3, 39
Johnson, Rodney Van 28
Jones, James Earl 3, 49, 79
Jones, Orlando 30
Jones, Quincy 8, 30
Jones, Rashida 101
Jones, Robbie 113
Jordan, Michael B. 97
Kandi 83
Kaufman, Monica 66
Kelley, Malcolm David 59
Kennedy-Overton, Jayne Harris 46
Key & Peele 107
Keys, Alicia 32, 68
Kid Cudi 83
King, Gayle 19, 99
King, Regina 22, 45
King, Woodie, Jr. 27
Kirby, George 14
Kitt, Eartha 16, 75
Knight, Gladys 16, 66
Kodjoe, Boris 34, 89
Kotto, Yaphet 7
Kwei-Armah, Kwame 84
La Salle, Eriq 12
LaBelle, Patti 13, 30
Langhart Cohen, Janet 19, 60
Lathan, Sanaa 27
Lawrence, Martin 6, 27, 60
Lawson, Jennifer 1, 50
Leakes, NeNe 107

Lee, Leslie 85
LeFlore, Lyah Beth 96
Lemmons, Kasi 20
Lemon, Don 94
Lesure, James 64
Lewis, Ananda 28
Lewis, Byron E. 13
Lewis, Emmanuel 36
Lil' Kim 28
Lindo, Delroy 18, 45
LisaRaye 27
LL Cool J 16, 49, 94
Lofton, James 42
Long, Loretta 58
Long, Nia 17, 95
Love, Loni 113
Lover, Ed 10
Luke, Derek 61
Lumbly, Carl 47
Mabrey, Vicki 26
Mabuza-Suttle, Felicia 43
Mac, Bernie 29, 61, 72
Madison, Paula 37, 99
Malco, Romany 71
Malveaux, Suzanne 88
Mann, Tamela 92
Marcille, Eva 97
Marshall, William 107
Markham, Pigmeat 106
Martin, Duane 108
Martin, Helen 31
Martin, Jesse L. 31
Martin, Michel 97
Masekela, Sal 106
Mason, Judi Ann 112
Mathis, Greg 26
Mayo, Whitman 32
Mbatha-Raw, Gugu 89
McBride, Chi 73
McCrary, Darius 111
McCrary Anthony, Crystal 70
McCullough, DeAndre 106
McDaniel, Hattie 5
McDaniels, Ralph 79
McEwen, Mark 5
McFarland, Roland 49
McGee, Vonetta 95
McGlowan, Angela 64, 86
McKee, Lonette 12
McKenzie, Vashti M. 29
McKinney, Nina Mae 40
McQueen, Butterfly 6, 54
Meadows, Tim 30
Mello, Breno 73
Melton, Frank 81
Mercado-Valdes, Frank 43
Merkerson, S. Epatha 47, 83
Michele, Michael 31
Mickelbury, Penny 28
Miles, William 112
Miller, Omar Benson 93
Miller, Wentworth 75
Ming, Mel 106
Mitchell, Brian Stokes 21
Mitchell, Kel 66
Mitchell, Russ 21, 73
Mokae, Zakes 80
Mo'Nique 35, 84
Montgomery, Robbie 101
Mooney, Paul 37
Moore, Chante 26
Moore, Melba 21
Moore, Shemar 21, 112

Morgan, Tracy **61, 102**
Morris, Garrett **31**
Morris, Greg **28**
Morton, Frederick A., Jr. **93**
Morton, Joe **18**
Moses, Gilbert **12**
Moss, Carlton **17**
Mowry, Tamera **79**
Mowry, Tia **78**
Murphy, Charles **95**
Murphy, Eddie **4, 20, 61**
Muse, Clarence Edouard **21**
Myers, Lou **110**
Myles, Kim **69**
Nash, Johnny **40**
Nash, Niecy **66, 115**
Naughton, Naturi **97**
Neal, Elise **29**
Nicholas, Denise **82**
Nichols, Nichelle **11**
Nissel, Angela **42**
Neville, Arthel **53**
Noble, Gil **76**
Norman, Christina **47**
Norman, Maidie **20**
O'Brien, Soledad **88**
Okonedo, Sophie **67**
Olagundoye, Toks **113**
Oliver, Pam **54**
Omarosa **69, 110**
O'Neal, Patrice **99**
Onwurah, Ngozi **38**
Orman, Roscoe **55**
Palcy, Euzhan **94**
Palmer, Keke **68**
Parker, Nicole Ari **52**
Parr, Russ **51**
Payne, Allen **13**
Pearson, Felicia **99**
Peete, Holly Robinson **20**
Peete, Rodney **60**
Perkins, Tony **24**
Perrineau, Harold, Jr. **51**
Perry, Lowell **30**
Perry, Tyler **40, 54, 103**
Peters, Brock **96**
Peters, Clarke **103**
Phifer, Mekhi **25, 103**
Phillips, Joseph C. **73**
Pickens, James, Jr. **59**
Pierce, Wendell **90**
Pinckney, Sandra **56**
Pinkett Smith, Jada **10, 41, 95**
Pinkston, W. Randall **24**
Pitts, Byron **71**
Poitier, Sydney Tamiia **65**
Pounder, CCH **72**
Poussaint, Renee **78**
Powell, Keith **101**
Price, Frederick K. C. **21**
Price, Hugh B. **9, 54**
Prince-Bythewood, Gina **31, 77**
Pugh, Charles **81**
Quarles, Norma **25**
Queen Latifah **1, 16, 58**
Quivers, Robin **61**
Ralph, Sheryl Lee **18, 108**
Randle, Theresa **16**
Rashad, Ahmad **18**
Rashad, Phylicia **21**
Raven-Symoné **44, 113**
Ray, Gene Anthony **47**
Ray J **86**

Reddick, Lance **52**
Reed Hall, Alaina **83**
Reese, Della **6, 20, 96**
Reid, Tim **56**
Reuben, Gloria **15**
Reynolds, Star Jones **10, 27, 61**
Rhimes, Shonda Lynn **67**
Ribeiro, Alfonso **17**
Richards, Beah **30**
Richardson, Donna **39**
Richardson, LaTanya **71**
Richardson, Salli **68**
Ridley, John **69**
Riley, Amber **97**
Roberts, Deborah **35**
Roberts, Robin **16, 54, 113**
Robinson, Craig **103**
Robinson, Matt **69**
Robinson, Max **3**
Robinson, Shaun **36**
Rochon, Lela **16**
Rock, Chris **3, 22, 66**
Rock, Tony **108**
Rodgers, Johnathan **6, 51**
Rodrigues, Percy **68**
Roker, Al **12, 49**
Roker, Roxie **68**
Rolle, Esther **13, 21**
Rollins, Howard E., Jr. **16**
Romeo **98**
Roots, The **101**
Rose, Jalen **108**
Ross, Tracee Ellis **35**
Roundtree, Richard **27**
Rowan, Carl T. **1, 30**
Rowell, Victoria **13, 68**
Rowland, Kelly **100**
Rudolph, Maya **46, 106**
Run **31, 73**
RuPaul **17, 91**
Russell, Bill **8**
Russell, Nipsey **66**
Rust, Art, Jr. **83**
St. Jacques, Raymond **8**
St. John, Kristoff **25**
St. Patrick, Mathew **48**
Saldana, Zoe **72**
Salters, Lisa **71**
Sands, Diana **87**
Sanford, Isabel **53**
Santiago-Hudson, Ruben **85**
Sasser, Sean **113**
Schiavocampo, Mara **97**
Schultz, Michael A. **6**
Scott, Hazel **66**
Scott, Jill **29, 83**
Scott, Stuart **34**
Scott-Young, Mona **101**
Shaw, Bernard **2, 28**
Sesay, Isha **107**
Shepherd, Sherri **55**
Sidner, Sara **105**
Simmons, Henry **55**
Simmons, Jamal **72**
Simmons, Kimora Lee **51, 83**
Simpson, Carole **6, 30**
Simpson, O. J. **15, 100**
Sinbad **1, 16**
Sinclair, Madge **78**
Smiley, Tavis **20, 68**
Smith, Anjela Lauren **44**
Smith, B(arbara) **11**
Smith, Ian **62**

Smith, Roger Guenveur **12**
Smith, Tasha **73**
Smith, Will **8, 18, 53**
Sohn, Sonja **100**
Spencer, Octavia **100**
Stewart, Alison **13**
Stewart, Nzingha **89**
Stickney, Phyllis Yvonne **108**
Stokes, Carl **10, 73**
Stone, Chuck **9**
Strahan, Michael **35, 81**
Stuart, Moira **82**
Sykes, Wanda **48, 81**
Syler, Rene **53**
Swann, Lynn **28**
Tate, Larenz **15**
Taylor, Jason **70**
Taylor, Karin **34**
Taylor, Meshach **4**
Taylor, Regina **9, 46, 97**
Teague, Bob **111**
Terrence J **108**
Thigpen, Lynne **17, 41**
Thomas-Graham, Pamela **29**
Thomason, Marsha **47**
Thompson, Kenan **52**
Thoms, Tracie **61**
Thurston, Baratunde **79, 101**
Tillman, Deborah **98**
Tirico, Mike **68**
Torres, Gina **52**
Torry, Guy **31**
Toussaint, Lorraine **32**
Townsend, Robert **4, 23**
True, Rachel **82**
Tucker, Chris **13, 23, 62**
Tunie, Tamara **63**
Turman, Glynn **100**
Tyler, Aisha N. **36**
Tyson, Cicely **7, 51, 112**
Uggams, Leslie **23, 114**
Underwood, Blair **7, 27, 76**
Union, Gabrielle **31, 92**
Usher **23, 56, 95**
Van Peebles, Mario **2, 51**
Vance, Jim **110**
Vaughn, Countess **53**
Vereen, Ben **4**
Walker, Chet **106**
Walker, Eamonn **37**
Ware, Andre **37**
Warfield, Marsha **2**
Warner, Malcolm-Jamal **22, 36, 110**
Warren, Michael **27**
Washington, Denzel **1, 16, 93**
Washington, Hayma **86**
Washington, Isaiah **62**
Washington, Kerry **46, 107**
Watson, Carlos **50**
Watts, Rolonda **9**
Wayans, Damien **78**
Wayans, Damon **8, 41**
Wayans, Kim **80**
Wayans, Keenen Ivory **18**
Wayans, Marlon **29, 82**
Wayans, Shawn **29**
Weathers, Carl **10**
Wesley, Richard **73**
Wesley, Rutina **97**
Whack, Rita Coburn **36**
Wheaton, James **103**
Whitfield, Lynn **1, 18**
Wilbon, Michael **68**

Williams, Armstrong **29**
Williams, Clarence, III **26**
Williams, Juan **35, 80**
Williams, Malinda **57**
Williams, Michael Kenneth **97**
Williams, Montel **4, 57**
Williams, Russell, II **70**
Williams, Samm-Art **21**
Williams, Vanessa A. **32, 66**
Williams, Vanessa L. **4, 17**
Williams, Wendy **62**
Williamson, Mykelti **22**
Wills, Maury **73**
Wilson, Chandra **57**
Wilson, Debra **38**
Wilson, Demond **102**
Wilson, Dorien **55**
Wilson, Flip **21**
Winfield, Paul **2, 45**
Winfrey, Oprah **2, 15, 61, 106**
Witherspoon, John **38**
Woodard, Alfre **9, 108**
Wright, Jeffrey **54, 111**
Yarbrough, Cedric **51**
Yoba, Malik **11**
Young, Lee Thompson **114**

Theater
Adams, Osceola Macarthy **31**
Ailey, Alvin **8**
Aldridge, Ira **99**
Alexander, Khandi **43**
Allen, Debbie **13, 42**
Anderson, Carl **48**
Andrews, Bert **13**
Angelou, Maya **1, 15**
Anthony, Trey **63**
Arkadie, Kevin **17**
Armstrong, Vanessa Bell **24**
Arnez J **53**
Babatunde, Obba **35**
Babatunde, Rotimi **104**
Bandele, Biyi **68**
Baraka, Amiri **1, 38**
Barclay, Paris **37, 94**
Barnett, Etta Moten **56**
Barrett, Lindsay **43**
Baskett, James **102**
Beach, Michael **26**
Beaton, Norman **14**
Belafonte, Harry **4, 65**
Belgrave, Cynthia **75**
Bennett, Louise **69**
Blanco, Mykki **106**
Borders, James **9**
Boseman, Chadwick **111**
Boykin, Phillip **102**
Branch, William Blackwell **39**
Braugher, Andre **13, 58, 91**
Brooks, Avery **9, 98**
Brown, Oscar, Jr. **53**
Brown, Ruth **90**
Browne, Roscoe Lee **66**
Bruce, Bruce **56**
Caldwell, Benjamin **46**
Calloway, Cab **14**
Cameron, Earl **44**
Campbell, Naomi **1**
Cara, Irene **77**
Carroll, Rocky **74**
Carroll, Vinnette **29**
Carter, Nell **39**
Cash, Rosalind **28**

Cheadle, Don 19, 52
Chenault, John 40
Childress, Alice 15
Clarke, Hope 14
Cleage, Pearl 17, 64
Cook, Will Marion 40
Cooper, Chuck 75
Corthron, Kia 43
Curtis-Hall, Vondie 17
Dadié, Bernard 34
David, Keith 27
Davis, Altovise 76
Davis, Eisa 68
Davis, Ossie 5, 50
Davis, Sammy, Jr. 18
Davis, Viola 34, 76, 100
Dawn, Marpessa 75
De Shields, André 72
Dee, Ruby 8, 50, 68
Devine, Loretta 24
Diamond, Lydia R. 101
Dieudonné 67
Diggs, Taye 25, 63
Dixon, Ivan 69
Dodson, Owen Vincent 38
Domingo, Colman 94
Dunham, Katherine 4, 59
Dutton, Charles S. 4, 22
Ejiofor, Chiwetel 67
Elba, Idris 49, 89
Elder, Lonne, III 38
Ellis, Nelsan 105
Emmanuel, Alphonsia 38
Epps, Mike 60
Esposito, Giancarlo 9
Europe, James Reese 10
Faison, Frankie 55
Falana, Lola 42
Fargas, Antonio 50
Fields, Felicia P. 60
Fishburne, Laurence 4, 22, 70
Francis, Thais 93
Franklin, J. E. 44
Freeman, Aaron 52
Freeman, Al, Jr. 11, 105
Freeman, Yvette 27
Fuller, Charles 8
Gibson, John Trusty 87
Gilpin, Charles Sidney 81
Givens, Adele 62
Glover, Danny 1, 24, 103
Glover, Keith 79
Glover, Savion 14
Goldberg, Whoopi 4, 33, 69
Gordone, Charles 15
Gossett, Louis, Jr. 7
Graves, Denyce Antoinette 19, 57
Greaves, William 38
Guillaume, Robert 3, 48
Gunn, Moses 10
Gurira, Danai 73
Hall, Juanita 62
Hamilton, Lisa Gay 71
Hamlin, Larry Leon 49, 62
Hansberry, Lorraine 6
Harewood, David 52
Harris, Bill 72
Harris, Robin 7
Hayes, Teddy 40
Henry, Joshua 94
Higginsen, Vy 65
Hill, Errol 40
Hill, Hugh Morgan 83

Hines, Gregory 1, 42
Holder, Geoffrey 78
Holder, Laurence 34
Holland, Endesha Ida Mae 3, 57
Hooks, Robert 76
Hyman, Earle 25, 79
Hyman, Phyllis 19
Ingram, Rex 5
Iverson, Johnathan Lee 22, 100
Jackson, Millie 25
James, Nikki M. 94
Jamison, Judith 7, 67, 96
Jean-Baptiste, Marianne 17, 46
Johnson, Je'Caryous 63
Jones, James Earl 3, 49, 79
Jones, Sarah 39
Joyner, Matilda Sissieretta 15
Kente, Gibson 52
Khumalo, Leleti 51
King, Woodie, Jr. 27
Kitt, Eartha 16, 75
Kotto, Yaphet 7
Kwei-Armah, Kwame 84
La Salle, Eriq 12
LaChanze 93
Lacy, Marc 111
Lampley, Oni Faida 43, 71
Lathan, Sanaa 27
Lee, Canada 8
Lee, Leslie 85
Leggs, Kingsley 62
Lemmons, Kasi 20
LeNoire, Rosetta 37
Lenox, Adriane 59
Leon, Kenny 10, 98
Lester, Adrian 46
Letson, Al 39
Lindo, Delroy 18, 45
Lister, Marquita 65
Mackie, Anthony 102
Mann, Tamela 92
Maponya, Maishe 101
Marrow, Queen Esther 24
Martin, Helen 31
Martin, Jesse L. 31
Mason, Judi Ann 112
Mbatha-Raw, Gugu 89
McClendon, Forrest 94
McClinton, Marion Isaac 77
McDaniel, Hattie 5
McDonald, Audra 20, 62
McFarlan, Tyron 60
McKee, Lonette 12
McQueen, Butterfly 6, 54
Merkerson, S. Epatha 47, 83
Mickelbury, Penny 28
Miller, Patina 94
Mills, Florence 22
Milner, Ron 39
Mitchell, Brian Stokes 21
Mokae, Zakes 80
Mollel, Tololwa 38
Moore, Melba 21
Moses, Gilbert 12
Moss, Carlton 17
Moss, Preacher 63
Moten, Etta 18
Muse, Clarence Edouard 21
Nascimento, Abdias do 93
Ngaujah, Sahr 86
Nicholas, Fayard 20, 57
Nicholas, Harold 20
Norman, Maidie 20

Nottage, Lynn 66
Ntshona, Winston 52
Okonedo, Sophie 67
O'Neal, Frederick 99
Orlandersmith, Dael 42
Oyelowo, David 82
Payne, Allen 13
Perrineau, Harold, Jr. 51
Perry, Tyler 40, 54, 103
Peters, Brock 96
Peters, Clarke 103
Pierce, Wendell 90
Porter, Billy 112
Pounder, CCH 72
Powell, Keith 101
Power, Will 83
Preer, Evelyn 82
Premice, Josephine 41
Primus, Pearl 6
Pryor, Rain 65
Randle, Theresa 16
Rashad, Phylicia 21
Redwood, John Henry 78
Richards, Beah 30
Richards, Lloyd 2
Richardson, Desmond 39
Richardson, LaTanya 71
Robeson, Paul 2
Rolle, Esther 13, 21
Rollins, Howard E., Jr. 16
Rose, Anika Noni 70
Rotimi, Ola 1
St. Jacques, Raymond 8
Salter, Nikkole 73
Sands, Diana 87
Sanford, Isabel 53
Santiago-Hudson, Ruben 85
Schultz, Michael A. 6
Scott, Harold Russell, Jr. 61
Shabazz, Attallah 6
Slocumb, Jonathan 52
Smiley, Rickey 59
Smith, Anjela Lauren 44
Smith, Anna Deavere 6, 44
Smith, Roger Guenveur 12
Snipes, Wesley 3, 24, 67
Sommore 61
Soyinka, Wole 4, 93
Springer, Ashton, Jr. 115
Stew 69
Stewart, Tonea Harris 78
Sundiata, Sekou 66
Talbert, David E. 34, 93
Taylor, Meshach 4
Taylor, Regina 9, 46, 97
Taylor, Ron 35
Teer, Barbara Ann 81
Thigpen, Lynne 17, 41
Thompson, John Douglas 81
Thompson, Tazewell 13
Thurman, Wallace 16
Torres, Gina 52
Toussaint, Lorraine 32
Townsend, Robert 4, 23
Turman, Glynn 100
Uggams, Leslie 23, 114
Underwood, Blair 7, 27, 76
Vance, Courtney B. 15, 60
Vereen, Ben 4
Walcott, Derek 5, 94
Walker, Eamonn 37
Ward, Douglas Turner 42
Warfield, William 94

Washington, Fredi 10
Waters, Ethel 7
Wesley, Rutina 97
Wheaton, James 103
Whitaker, Forest 2, 49, 67
White, Terri 82
White, Willard 53
Whitfield, Lynn 18
Williams, Bert 18
Williams, Clarence, III 26
Williams, Michelle 73
Williams, Samm-Art 21
Williamson, Mykelti 22
Wilson, August 7, 33, 55
Wilson, Dorien 55
Wilson, Tracey Scott 777
Winfield, Paul 2, 45
Withers-Mendes, Elisabeth 64
Wolfe, George C. 6, 43
Woods, Renn 110
Wright, Jeffrey 54, 111
Yarbrough, Cedric 51

Writing
Abani, Chris 77
Abrahams, Peter 39
Abu-Jamal, Mumia 15
Achebe, Chinua 6, 99, 111
Adams, Jenoyne 60
Adams-Ender, Clara 40
Adichie, Chimamanda Ngozi 64
Aidoo, Ama Ata 38
Ake, Claude 30
Akpan, Uwem 70
Al-Amin, Jamil Abdullah 6
Alexander, Elizabeth 75
Alexander, Kwame 98
Alexander, Margaret Walker 22
Ali, Ayaan Hirsi 58, 92
Ali, Hana Yasmeen 52
Ali, Mohammed Naseehu 60
Allen, Robert L. 38
Allen, Samuel W. 38
Als, Hilton 105
Amadi, Elechi 40
Ames, Wilmer 27
Anderson, Ho Che 54
Andrews, Raymond 4
Andrews, Tina 74
Angelou, Maya 1, 15
Ansa, Tina McElroy 14
Anthony, Michael 29
Aplin-Brownlee, Vivian 96
Arac de Nyeko, Monica 66
Aristide, Jean-Bertrand 6, 45
Arkadie, Kevin 17
Armah, Ayi Kwei 49
Armah, Esther 87
Asante, Molefi Kete 3
Ashley & JaQuavis 107
Ashley-Ward, Amelia 23
Asim, Jabari 71
Atkins, Cholly 40
Atkins, Russell 45
Attaway, William 102
Aubert, Alvin 41
Aubespin, Mervin 95
Auguste, Arnold A. 47
Awoonor, Kofi 37, 115
Azikiwe, Nnamdi 13
Ba, Mariama 30
Babatunde, Rotimi 104
Bahati, Wambui 60

Bailey, Chauncey 68
Baiocchi, Regina Harris 41
Baisden, Michael 25, 66
Baker, Augusta 38
Baker, Houston A., Jr. 6
Baldwin, James 1
Ballard, Allen Butler, Jr. 40
Bambara, Toni Cade 10
Bandele, Asha 36
Bandele, Biyi 68
Baquet, Dean 63
Baraka, Amiri 1, 38
Barnes, Steven 54
Barnett, Amy Du Bois 46
Barrax, Gerald William 45
Barrett, Lindsay 43
Bashir, Halima 73
Bass, Charlotta Spears 40
Baszile, Jennifer 79
Bates, Karen Grigsby 40
Beah, Ishmael 69
Beals, Melba Pattillo 15, 94
Bebey, Francis 45
Beckham, Barry 41
Bell, James Madison 40
Benberry, Cuesta 65
Bennett, George Harold 45
Bennett, Gwendolyn B. 59
Bennett, Lerone, Jr. 5, 84
Bennett, Louise 69
Benson, Angela 34
Berry, James 41
Berry, Mary Frances 7
Best, Carrie 80
Beti, Mongo 36
Betts, R. Dwayne 86
Bishop, Maurice 39
Blackman, Toni 86
Blair, Jayson 50
Bland, Eleanor Taylor 39
Blassingame, John Wesley 40
Blockson, Charles L. 42
Blow, Charles M. 73
Bluitt, Juliann S. 14
Bolden, Tonya 32
Bontemps, Arna 8
Booker, Simeon 23
Borders, James 9
Bostic, Joe 95
Boston, Lloyd 24
Boyd, Gerald M. 32, 59
Boyd, Melba Joyce 86
Boyd, Suzanne 52
Bradley, Adam 101
Bradley, David Henry, Jr. 39
Braithwaite, William Stanley 52
Branch, William Blackwell 39
Brand, Dionne 32
Brathwaite, Kamau 36
Brawley, Benjamin 44
Breeze, Jean "Binta" 37
Briscoe, Connie 15
Britt, Donna 28
Brooks, Gwendolyn 1, 28
Brower, William 49
Brown, Cecil M. 46
Brown, Claude 38
Brown, Elaine 8
Brown, Les 5
Brown, Lloyd Louis 10, 42
Brown, Marie Dutton 12
Brown, Sterling Allen 10, 64
Brown, Tony 3

Brown, Wesley 23
Brown, William Wells 99
Broyard, Anatole 68
Broyard, Bliss 68
Brutus, Dennis 38
Bryan, Ashley 41, 104
Buckley, Gail Lumet 39
Bullins, Ed 25
Bunche, Ralph J. 5
Bunkley, Anita Richmond 39
Burgess, Marjorie L. 55
Burley, Dan 96
Burroughs, Margaret Taylor 9
Burwell, Bryan 83
Butler, Octavia 8, 43, 58
Bynum, Juanita 31, 71
Caldwell, Earl 60
Calhoun, Lillian Scott 87
Campbell, Bebe Moore 6, 24, 59
Carby, Hazel 27
Carmichael, Stokely 5, 26
Carroll, Vinnette 29
Carter, Joye Maureen 41
Carter, Martin 49
Carter, Stephen L. 4
Cartey, Wilfred 47
Cartiér, Xam Wilson 41
Cary, Lorene 3
Cary, Mary Ann Shadd 30
Cayton, Horace 26
Cenac, Wyatt 94
Césaire, Aimé 48, 69
Chadiha, Jeffri 57
Channer, Colin 36
Chase-Riboud, Barbara 20, 46
Chenault, John 40
Cheney-Coker, Syl 43
Chesnutt, Charles 29
Chideya, Farai 14, 61
Childress, Alice 15
Chiles, Nick 98
Christian, Barbara T. 44
Churchwell, Robert, Sr. 76
Clack, Zoanne 73
Clark, Kenneth B. 5, 52
Clark, Septima 7
Clark, Wahida 107
Clark-Bekedermo, J. P. 44
Clarke, Austin C. 32
Clarke, Cheryl 32
Clarke, George 32
Cleage, Pearl 17, 64
Cleaver, Eldridge 5
Cliff, Michelle 42
Clifton, Lucille 14, 64, 91
Coates, Ta-Nehisi 76
Cobb, William Jelani 59
Cobbs, Price M. 9
Cohen, Anthony 15
Cole, Johnnetta B. 5, 43
Coleman, Wanda 48
Collins, Patricia Hill 67
Colter, Cyrus J. 36
Comer, James P. 6
Contee, Cheryl 88
Cook, Suzan D. Johnson 22
Cooke, Marvel 31
Cook-Parrish, Mary Virginia 95
Coombs, Orde M. 44
Cooper, Afua 53
Cooper, Andrew W. 36
Cooper, Anna Julia 20
Cooper, Helene 74

Cooper, J. California 12, 85
Cornish, Sam 50
Cortez, Jayne 43, 109
Cosby, Bill 7, 26, 59
Cose, Ellis 5, 50
Cotter, Joseph Seamon, Sr. 40
Couto, Mia 45
Cox, Joseph Mason Andrew 51
Creagh, Milton 27
Croal, N'Gai 76
Crouch, Stanley 11, 87
Cruse, Harold 54
Crutchfield, James N. 55
Cullen, Countee 8
Cuney, William Waring 44
Cunningham, Evelyn 23, 85
Curry, George E. 23
Curtis, Christopher Paul 26, 113
Dabydeen, David 48
Dadié, Bernard 34
D'Aguiar, Fred 50
Damas, Léon-Gontran 46
Dandridge, Raymond Garfield 45
Danner, Margaret Esse 49
Danquah, Meri Nana Ama 93
Danticat, Edwidge 15, 68
Dash, Leon 47
Datcher, Michael 60
Dathorne, O. R. 52
Davis, Allison 12
Davis, Charles T. 48
Davis, Eisa 68
Davis, Frank Marshall 47
Davis, George 36
Davis, Nolan 45
Davis, Thulani 61
Dawkins, Wayne 20
de Passe, Suzanne 25
De Veaux, Alexis 44
Deggans, Eric 71
Delany, Martin R. 27
Delany, Samuel R., Jr. 9
DeLoach, Nora 30
Demby, William 51
Dent, Thomas C. 50
Dickerson, Debra J. 60
Dickey, Eric Jerome 21, 56
Diop, Birago 53
Diop, Cheikh Anta 4
Dodson, Howard, Jr. 7, 52
Dodson, Owen Vincent 38
Douglass, Frederick 87
Dove, Rita 6, 78, 101
Draper, Sharon Mills 16, 43
Driskell, David C. 7
Driver, David E. 11
Drummond, William J. 40
Du Bois, David Graham 45
Du Bois, W. E. B. 3
DuBois, Shirley Graham 21
Due, Tananarive 30
Dumas, Henry 41
Dunbar, Paul Laurence 8
Dunbar-Nelson, Alice Ruth Moore 44
Dungy, Camille 86
Dunham, Katherine 4, 59
Dunnigan, Alice Allison 41
Duplechan, Larry 55
Dyson, Michael Eric 11, 40
Eagleson, William Lewis 90
Edmonds, Terry 17
Edugyan, Esi 98

Ekwensi, Cyprian 37
Elder, Lonne, III 38
Elie, Lolis Eric 97
Elliot, Lorris 37
Ellis, Trey 97
Ellison, Ralph 7
Elmore, Ronn 21
Emanuel, James A. 46
Emecheta, Buchi 30
Equiano, Olaudah 78
Estes, Rufus 29
Evans, Diana 72
Evans, Mari 26
Everett, Percival 93
Fabio, Sarah Webster 48
Fair, Ronald L. 47
Fales-Hill, Susan 88
Fanon, Frantz 44
Farah, Nuruddin 27
Farley, Christopher John 54
Farrakhan, Louis 15
Fauset, Jessie 7
Feelings, Muriel 44
Feelings, Tom 11, 47
Fields, Julia 45
Figueroa, John J. 40
Files, Lolita 35
Finner-Williams, Paris Michele 62
Fisher, Antwone 40
Fisher, Rudolph 17
Fleming, Raymond 48
Fletcher, Bill, Jr. 41
Fletcher, Geoffrey 85
Forbes, Calvin 46
Ford, Clyde W. 40
Ford, Nick Aaron 44
Ford, Wallace 58
Forman, James 7, 51
Forna, Aminatta 95
Forrest, Leon 44
Fortune, T. Thomas 6
Foster, Cecil 32
Foster, Jylla Moore 45
Foye, K'wan 97
Franklin, John Hope 5, 77
Franklin, Robert M. 13
Frazier, E. Franklin 10
Frazier, Oscar 58
French, Albert 18
Fuller, Charles 8
Fuller, Hoyt 44
Gabre-Medhin, Tsegaye 64
Gaines, Ernest J. 7
Gaines, Patrice 106
Gaiter, Dorothy J. 80
Gardner, Chris 65
Gaston, Marilyn Hughes 60
Gates, Henry Louis, Jr. 3, 38, 67
Gayle, Addison, Jr. 41
George, Nelson 12, 101
Gibson, Donald Bernard 40
Giddings, Paula 11
Gilbert, Christopher 50
Gilliard, Steve 69
Giovanni, Nikki 9, 39, 85
Givhan, Robin Deneen 72
Gladwell, Malcolm 62
Gloster, Hugh Morris, Sr. 90
Glover, Donald 85
Goines, Donald 19
Golden, Marita 19, 99
Gomez, Jewelle 30
Goodison, Lorna 71

Goodlett, Carlton B. 91
Gordon-Reed, Annette 74
Graham, Lawrence Otis 12
Graham, Lorenz 48
Granderson, LZ 103
Grant, Gwendolyn Goldsby 28
Gray, Darius 69
Greaves, William 38
Greenfield, Eloise 9
Greenlee, Sam 48
Greenwood, Monique 38
Griffith, Mark Winston 8
Grimké, Archibald H. 9
Guy, Rosa 5
Guy-Sheftall, Beverly 13, 92
Haley, Alex 4
Halliburton, Warren J. 49
Hamblin, Ken 10
Hamilton, Virginia 10
Hansberry, Lorraine 6
Harding, Vincent 67
Hare, Nathan 44
Harkless, Necia Desiree 19
Harper, Frances Ellen Watkins 11
Harper, Hill 32, 65, 97
Harper, Michael S. 34
Harper, Rachel M. 92
Harrington, Oliver W. 9
Harris, Bill 72
Harris, Claire 34
Harris, Eddy L. 18
Harris, Jay 19
Harris, Jessica B. 91
Harris, Leslie 6
Harris, Monica 18
Harrison, Alvin 28
Harrison, Calvin 28
Haskins, James 36, 54
Hayden, Robert 12
Hayes, Teddy 40
Haygood, Wil 83
Haywood, Gar Anthony 43
Head, Bessie 28
Heard, Nathan C. 45
Hearne, John Edgar Caulwell 45
Hemphill, Essex 10
Henderson, David 53
Henderson, Stephen E. 45
Henries, A. Doris Banks 44
Henriques, Julian 37
Henry, Lenny 9, 52
Henson, Josiah 90
Henson, Matthew 2
Herbert, Bob 63, 96
Hercules, Frank 44
Herndon, Angelo 90
Hernton, Calvin C. 51
Hill, Donna 32
Hill, Errol 40
Hill, Jemele 109
Hill, Leslie Pinckney 44
Hilliard, David 7, 105
Hoagland, Everett H. 45
Hobson, Julius W. 44
Holland, Endesha Ida Mae 3, 57
Holmes, Shannon 70
Holt, Nora 38
Holton, Hugh, Jr. 39
hooks, bell 5, 90
Horne, Frank 44
Hrabowski, Freeman A., III 22
Hudlin, Reginald 9, 86
Hudson, Cheryl 15

Hudson, Wade 15
Hughes, Langston 4
Hull, Akasha Gloria 45
Hunter-Gault, Charlayne 6, 31
Hurston, Zora Neale 3
Iceberg Slim 11
Ifill, Gwen 28
Ilibagiza, Immaculée 66
Jackson, Brenda 87
Jackson, Fred James 25
Jackson, George 14
Jackson, James A. 90
Jackson, Sheneska 18
Jacobs, Harriet 104
James, Marlon 85
Jarrett, Vernon D. 42
Jasper, Kenji 39
Jefferson, Margo 108
Jenkins, Beverly 14
Joachim, Paulin 34
Joe, Yolanda 21
Johnson, Angela 52
Johnson, Charles 1, 82
Johnson, Charles S. 12
Johnson, Fenton 91
Johnson, Georgia Douglas 41
Johnson, James Weldon 5
Johnson, John H. 3, 54
Johnson, Linton Kwesi 37
Johnson, Mat 31, 105
Johnson, R. M. 36
Johnson, Sandra K. 94
Johnson, William 91
Jolley, Willie 28
Jones, Edward P. 43, 67
Jones, Gayl 37
Jones, Orlando 30
Jones, Sarah 39
Jones, Tayari 96
Jordan, Deloris 108
Jordan, June 7, 35
Joseph, Jamal 101
Josey, E. J. 10
July, William 27
Just, Ernest Everett 3
Kamau, Kwadwo Agymah 28
Karenga, Maulana 10, 71
Kariuki, J. M. 67
Kaufman, Bob 105
Kay, Jackie 37
Kayira, Legson 40
Kearney, Janis 54
Keckley, Elizabeth 90
Keene, John 73
Kendrick, Erika 57
Kennedy, Adrienne 11
Kennedy, Florynce 12, 33
Kennedy, Randall 40
Khanga, Yelena 6
Killens, John O. 54
Kimbro, Dennis 10
Kincaid, Jamaica 4, 109
King, Colbert I. 69
King, Coretta Scott 3, 57
King, Preston 28
King, Woodie, Jr. 27
Kitt, Sandra 23
Kitwana, Bakari 86
Knight, Etheridge 37
Kobia, Samuel 43
Komunyakaa, Yusef 9
Kunjufu, Jawanza 3, 50
Lacy, Marc 111

Lacy, Sam 30, 46
Ladner, Joyce A. 42
Laferriere, Dany 33
LaGuma, Alex 30
Lamar, Jake 96
Lamming, George 35
Lampley, Oni Faida 43, 71
Lane, Lunsford 93
Larsen, Nella 10
Lateef, Yusef 91
Lattany, Kristin Hunter 88
Lawrence, Martin 6, 27, 60
Lawrence-Lightfoot, Sara 10
Laymon, Kiese 113
Lee, Jarena 100
LeFlore, Lyah Beth 96
Lemmons, Kasi 20
Lemon, Don 94
Lester, Julius 9, 115
Letson, Al 39
Lewis, David Levering 9
Lewis, Samella 25
Lincoln, C. Eric 38
Little, Benilde 21
Locke, Alain 10
Locke, Attica 85
Lomax, Louis E. 90
Lorde, Audre 6
Louis, Errol T. 8
Loury, Glenn 36
Lowe, Herbert 57
Mabry, Marcus 70
Mabuza-Suttle, Felicia 43
Machado de Assis 74
Mackey, Nathaniel 75
Madhubuti, Haki 7, 85
Major, Clarence 9
Makeba, Miriam 2, 50, 74
Malveaux, Julianne 32, 70
Manley, Ruth 34
Marechera, Dambudzo 39
Markham, E. A. 37
Marshall, Paule 7, 77
Martin, Michel 97
Martin, Roland S. 49, 84
Mason, Felicia 31
Mason, Herman, Jr. 83
Massaquoi, Hans J. 30
Matejka, Adrian 87
Mathabane, Mark 5, 99
Maynard, Nancy Hicks 73
Maynard, Robert C. 7
Mays, Benjamin E. 7
Mbaye, Mariétou 31
McBride, James 35, 87
McCall, Nathan 8
McCauley, Gina 76
McClellan, George Marion 91
McCrary Anthony, Crystal 70
McDuffie, Dwayne 62
McFadden, Bernice L. 39
McGhee, Sharon K. 113
McGruder, Robert 22, 35
McKay, Claude 6
McKinney Hammond, Michelle 51
McKinney-Whetstone, Diane 27
McMillan, Rosalynn A. 36
McMillan, Terry 4, 17, 53
McMillan, Tracy 93
McPherson, James Alan 70
Memmi, Albert 37
Menard, John Willis 90
Mengestu, Dinaw 66, 114

Meredith, James H. 11
Mfume, Kweisi 6, 41
Micheaux, Oscar 7
Mickelbury, Penny 28
Miller, Pepper 96
Millner, Denene 76
Milner, Ron 39
Mitchell, Elvis 67
Mitchell, Loften 31
Mitchell, Russ 21, 73
Mitchell, Sharon 36
Mofolo, Thomas Mokopu 37
Mollel, Tololwa 38
Monroe, Bryan 71
Monroe, Mary 35
Moore, Jessica Care 30
Moore, Wes 86
Morrison, Toni 2, 15, 86
Mosley, Walter 5, 25, 68
Moss, Carlton 17
Mossell, Gertrude Bustill 40
Moutoussamy-Ashe, Jeanne 7
Mowry, Jess 7
Mphalele, Es'kia (Ezekiel) 40
Mudimbe, V. Y. 61
Mugo, Micere Githae 32
Mullen, Harryette 34
Murphy, John H. 42
Murray, Albert L. 33
Murray, Pauli 38
Mwangi, Meja 40
Myers, Walter Dean 8, 70
Nash, Shannon King 84
Naylor, Gloria 10, 42
Neal, Larry 38
Neal, Mark Anthony 74
Nelson, Jill 6, 54
Nelson, Kadir 115
Neto, António Agostinho 43
Newkirk, Pamela 69
Newton, Huey 2
Ngugi wa Thiong'o 29, 61, 101
Nissel, Angela 42
Njawe, Pius 87
Nkosi, Lewis 46
Norris, Michele 83
Northup, Solomon 115
Norton, Meredith 72
Nugent, Richard Bruce 39
Nunez, Elizabeth 62, 112
Ojikutu, Bayo 66
Okara, Gabriel 37
Okigbo, Christopher 102
Oliver, John J., Jr. 48
Onwueme, Tess Osonye 23
Orlandersmith, Dael 42
Osbey, Brenda Marie 102
Oyono, Ferdinand 38
Packer, Z. Z. 64
Page, Clarence 4
Painter, Nell Irvin 24, 88
Palmer, Everard 37
Parker, Pat 19
Parker, Star 70
Parks, Suzan-Lori 34, 85
Patterson, Orlando 4
Payne, Ethel L. 28
Payne, Les 89
Pearson, Felicia 99
Peters, Lenrie 43
Petersen, Neal 96
Petry, Ann 19
Philip, Marlene Nourbese 32

Phillips, Carl 111
Phillips, Joseph C. 73
Piper, Adrian 71
Pitts, Leonard, Jr. 54, 85
Plaatje, Sol T. 80
Polite, Carlene Hatcher 82
Poussaint, Alvin F. 5, 67
Poussaint, Renee 78
Powell, Adam Clayton, Jr. 3
Powell, Kevin 31, 74
Power, Will 83
Pressley, Condace L. 41
Prince, Richard E. 71
Pryce, Trevor 89
Quarles, Benjamin Arthur 18
Rahman, Aishah 37
Randall, Alice 38
Randall, Dudley 8, 55
Rapier, James T. 82
Raspberry, William 2
Reddick, Lawrence Dunbar 20
Redding, J. Saunders 26
Redmond, Eugene 23
Reed, Ishmael 8
Reid, Ira De A. 100
Rhimes, Shonda Lynn 67
Rhoden, William C. 67
Rhodes, Jewell Parker 84
Rhone, Trevor 80
Richards, Beah 30
Ridley, John 69
Riggs, Marlon 5
Riley, Rochelle 50
Ringgold, Faith 4, 81
Robertson, Gil L., IV 85
Robeson, Eslanda Goode 13
Robinson, Aminah 50
Robinson, Eugene 77
Robinson, Matt 69
Roby, Kimberla Lawson 86
Rogers, Joel Augustus 30
Rollins, Charlamae Hill 27
Rotimi, Ola 1
Rowan, Carl T. 1, 30
Ruffin, Josephine St. Pierre 75
Run 31, 73
Russwurm, John Brown 100
Rust, Art, Jr. 83
Sadlier, Rosemary 62
Saint James, Synthia 12
St. John, Kristoff 25
Salih, Al-Tayyib 37

Sanchez, Sonia 17, 51
Sanders, Dori 8
Sanneh, Kelefa 96
Sapphire 14, 95
Saro-Wiwa, Kenule 39
Shelton, Paula Young 86
Schomburg, Arthur Alfonso 9
Schuyler, George Samuel 40
Scott-Heron, Gil 94
Seale, Bobby 3
Sembène, Ousmane 13, 62
Senghor, Léopold Sédar 12, 66
Sengstacke, John 18
Senior, Olive 37
Senna, Danzy 93
Shabazz, Attallah 6
Shabazz, Ilyasah 36
Shakur, Assata 6
Shakur, Yusef 85
Shange, Ntozake 8, 89
Shaw, Bernard 2, 28
Shipp, E. R. 15
Shockley, Ann Allen 84
Simone, Nina 15, 41
Simpson, Carole 6, 30
Singletary, Mike 4, 76
Singleton, John 2, 30
Sister Souljah 11, 100
Skinner, Kiron K. 65
Smiley, Tavis 20, 68
Smith, Anna Deavere 6
Smith, B(arbara) 11
Smith, Barbara 28
Smith, Bruce W. 53
Smith, Danyel 40
Smith, Jessie Carney 35
Smith, Mary Carter 26
Smith, Stephen A. 69
Smith, Zadie 51
Snowden, Frank M., Jr. 67
Somé, Malidoma Patrice 10
Southgate, Martha 58
Sowell, Thomas 2, 99
Soyinka, Wole 4, 93
Spencer, Anne 27
Spriggs, William 67
Staples, Brent 8
Stewart, Alison 13
Stone, Chuck 9
Stringer, Vickie 58
Sundiata, Sekou 66
Tademy, Lalita 36

Talbert, David E. 34, 93
Tate, Eleanora E. 20, 55
Tatum, Beverly Daniel 42, 84
Tatum, Elinor R. 78
Tatum, Wilbert 76
Taulbert, Clifton Lemoure 19
Taylor, Kristin Clark 8
Taylor, Mildred D. 26
Taylor, Susan C. 62
Taylor, Susan L. 10, 86
Teasley, Lisa 92
Thomas, Michael 69
Thomas, Trisha R. 65
Thomas-Graham, Pamela 29
Thornton, Yvonne S. 69
Thurman, Howard 3
Thurston, Baratunde 79, 101
Tillis, Frederick 40
Tolson, Melvin 37
Toomer, Jean 6
Touré, Askia (Muhammad Abu Bakr
  el) 47
Townsend, Robert 4
Trethewey, Natasha 103
Trotter, Monroe 9
Troupe, Quincy 83
Tucker, Cynthia 15, 61
Turner, Henry McNeal 5
Tutuola, Amos 30
Tyree, Omar Rashad 21
Tyson, Asha 39
van Sertima, Ivan 25
Vanzant, Iyanla 17, 47, 108
Vega, Marta Moreno 61
Vera, Yvonne 32
Verdelle, A. J. 26
Wade-Gayles, Gloria Jean 41
Walcott, Derek 5, 94
Walker, Alice 1, 43
Walker, Margaret 29
Walker, Rebecca 50
Walker, Teshima 114
Wallace, Michele Faith 13
Wallace, Phyllis A. 9
Walters, Ronald 83
Ward, Douglas Turner 42
Washington, Booker T. 4
Washington, Elsie B. 78
Washington, Harriet A. 69
Washington, James, Jr. 38
Washington, Laura S. 18
Weaver, Afaa Michael 37

Weems, Renita J. 44
Wells-Barnett, Ida B. 8
Wesley, Dorothy Porter 19
Wesley, Richard 73
Wesley, Valerie Wilson 18
West, Cornel 5, 33, 80
West, Dorothy 12, 54
Whack, Rita Coburn 36
Wharton, Clifton R., Jr. 7
Whitaker, Mark 21, 47
White, Armond 80
White, Walter F. 4
Whitehead, Colson 77
Whitfield, LeRoy 84
Whitfield, Van 34
Whitlock, Jason 78
Wideman, John Edgar 5, 87
Wilbekin, Emil 63
Wiley, Ralph 8, 78
Wilkerson, Isabel 71
Wilkins, Roger 2, 84
Wilkins, Roy 4
Williams, Armstrong 29
Williams, George Washington 18
Williams, John A. 27
Williams, Juan 35, 80
Williams, Patricia 11, 54
Williams, Robert F. 11
Williams, Roy 89
Williams, Saul 31
Williams, Sherley Anne 25
Williams, Wendy 62
Wilson, August 7, 33, 55
Wilson, Mary 28
Wilson, William Julius 22
Winans, Marvin L. 17
Wiwa, Ken 67
Wolfe, George C. 6, 43
Woods, Mattiebelle 63
Woods, Scott 55
Woods, Teri 69
Woodson, Carter G. 2
Worrill, Conrad 12
Wright, Bruce McMarion 3, 52
Wright, Richard 5
Wright, Sarah E. 95
X, Marvin 45
Yarbrough, Camille 40
Yerby, Frank 96
Yette, Samuel F. 63
Young, Al 82
Young, Whitney M., Jr. 4
Youngblood, Shay 32
Zane 71
Zook, Kristal Brent 62

Cumulative Subject Index

Volume numbers appear in **bold**

A cappella
Cooke, Sam **17**
Fisk Jubilee Singers **112**
Ladysmith Black Mambazo **103**
Reagon, Bernice Johnson **7**
Swan Silvertones, The **110**
Sweet Honey in the Rock **106**
Take 6 **112**

AA
See Alcoholics Anonymous

AAAS
See American Association for the Advancement of Science

AARP
Dixon, Margaret **14**
Smith, Marie F. **70**

ABC
See American Broadcasting Company

Abstract expressionism
Alston, Charles **33**
Bearden, Romare **2, 50**
Delaney, Beauford **19**
Lewis, Norman **39**
Simpson, Merton D. **110**
Thomas, Alma **14**
Woodruff, Hale **9**

Academy awards
Berry, Halle **4, 19, 57, 91**
Cara, Irene **77**
Fletcher, Geoffrey **85**
Foxx, Jamie **15, 48**
Freeman, Morgan **2, 20, 62, 100**
Goldberg, Whoopi **4, 33, 69**
Gooding, Cuba, Jr. **16, 62**
Gossett, Louis, Jr. **7**
Hancock, Herbie **20, 67**
Hayes, Isaac **20, 58, 73**
Hudson, Jennifer **63, 83**
McDaniel, Hattie **5**
Mo'Nique **35, 84**
Poitier, Sidney **11, 36**
Prince **18, 65**
Richie, Lionel **27, 65, 114**
Spencer, Octavia **100**
Washington, Denzel **1, 16, 93**
Whitaker, Forest **2, 49, 67**
Williams, Russell, II **70**

Wonder, Stevie **11, 53**

ACLU
See American Civil Liberties Union

Acquired immune deficiency syndrome (AIDS)
Ashe, Arthur **1, 18**
Atim, Julian **66**
Broadbent, Hydeia **36**
Cargill, Victoria A. **43**
Fenton, Kevin **87**
Gayle, Helene D. **3, 46**
Hale, Lorraine **8**
Lewis-Thornton, Rae **32**
Mboup, Souleymane **10**
Moutoussamy-Ashe, Jeanne **7**
Norman, Pat **10**
Ojikutu, Bisola **65**
Okaalet, Peter **58**
Pickett, Cecil **39**
Sasser, Sean **113**
Seele, Pernessa **46**
Whitfield, LeRoy **84**
Wilson, Phill **9, 104**
Zulu, Princess Kasune **54**

Acting
Aaliyah **30**
Aaron, Quinton **82**
Adams, Osceola Macarthy **31**
Adebimpe, Tunde **75**
Akinnuoye-Agbaje, Adewale **56**
Aldridge, Ira **99**
Alexander, Khandi **43**
Ali, Tatyana **73**
Allen, Debbie **13, 42**
Alonso, Laz **87**
Amos, John **8, 62**
Anderson, Anthony **51, 77**
Anderson, Carl **48**
Anderson, Eddie "Rochester" **30**
Andrews, Tina **74**
Angelou, Maya **1, 15**
Armstrong, Vanessa Bell **24**
Ashanti **37, 96**
Babatunde, Obba **35**
Bahati, Wambui **60**
Bailey, Pearl **14**
Baker, Josephine **3**
Banks, Michelle **59**
Barnett, Etta Moten **56**
Baskett, James **102**
Bassett, Angela **6, 23, 62**
Beach, Michael **26**

Beals, Jennifer **12**
Beaton, Norman **14**
Beauvais, Garcelle **29, 95**
Belgrave, Cynthia **75**
Bennett, Louise **69**
Bentley, Lamont **53**
Berry, Fred "Rerun" **48**
Berry, Halle **4, 19, 57, 91**
Bey, Yasiin **30, 96**
Bivins, Michael **72**
Blacque, Taurean **58**
Blanks, Billy **22**
Bonet, Lisa **58**
Borders, James **9**
Boseman, Chadwick **111**
Bow Wow **35**
Boykin, Phillip **102**
Brady, Wayne **32, 71**
Branch, William Blackwell **39**
Braugher, Andre **13, 58, 91**
Bridges, Todd **37**
Brooks, Avery **9, 98**
Brooks, Golden **62**
Brooks, Mehcad **62**
Brown, Jim **11, 95**
Browne, Roscoe Lee **66**
Byrd, Eugene **64**
Caesar, Shirley **19**
Calloway, Cab **14**
Cameron, Earl **44**
Campbell, Naomi **1, 31**
Campbell-Martin, Tisha **8, 42**
Cannon, Nick **47, 73**
Cara, Irene **77**
Carroll, Diahann **9**
Carroll, Rocky **74**
Carson, Lisa Nicole **21**
Carey, Mariah **32, 53, 69**
Cash, Rosalind **28**
Cedric the Entertainer **29, 60, 115**
Cheadle, Don **19, 52**
Chestnut, Morris **31**
Chew, Robert F. **109**
Childress, Alice **15**
Childress, Alvin **114**
Chong, Rae Dawn **62**
Chweneyagae, Presley **63**
Clarke, Hope **14**
Cobbs, Bill **101**
Coleman, Gary **35, 86**
Combs, Sean **17, 43, 92**
Common **31, 63, 98**
Cooper, Chuck **75**
Cosby, Bill **7, 26, 59**

Crothers, Scatman **19**
Curry, Mark **17**
Curtis-Hall, Vondie **17**
DaCosta, YaYa **98**
Dandridge, Dorothy **3**
David, Keith **27**
Davidson, Jaye **5**
Davis, Altovise **76**
Davis, Eisa **68**
Davis, Guy **36**
Davis, Ossie **5, 50**
Davis, Sammy, Jr. **18**
Davis, Viola **34, 76, 100**
Dawn, Marpessa **75**
Dawson, Rosario **72**
De Bankolé, Isaach **78**
De Shields, André **72**
Dee, Ruby **8, 50, 68**
Devine, Loretta **24**
Diesel, Vin **29**
Diggs, Taye **25, 63**
Dixon, Ivan **69**
DMX **28, 64**
Dobson, Tamara **111**
Domingo, Colman **94**
Dorn, Michael **112**
Dourdan, Gary **37**
Duke, Bill **3, 96**
Duncan, Michael Clarke **26, 104**
Dungey, Merrin **62**
Dutton, Charles S. **4, 22**
Ejiofor, Chiwetel **67**
Elba, Idris **49, 89**
Elise, Kimberly **32, 101**
Ellis, Aunjanue **108**
Ellis, Nelsan **105**
Emmanuel, Alphonsia **38**
Epps, Mike **60**
Epps, Omar **23, 59**
Esposito, Giancarlo **9**
Everett, Francine **23**
Faison, Donald **50**
Faison, Frankie **55**
Fargas, Antonio **50**
Fetchit, Stepin **32**
Fields, Felicia P. **60**
Fields, Kim **36**
Fishburne, Laurence **4, 22, 70**
Fisher, Gail **85**
Fox, Rick **27**
Fox, Vivica A. **15, 53**
Foxx, Jamie **15, 48**
Foxx, Redd **2**
Francis, Thais **93**

Freeman, Al, Jr. 11, 105
Freeman, Morgan 2, 20, 62, 100
Freeman, Yvette 27
Gant, Richard 105
Gaye, Nona 56
Gibbs, Marla 86
Gibson, Tyrese 27, 62
Gilpin, Charles Sidney 81
Ginuwine 35
Givens, Adele 62
Givens, Robin 4, 25, 58
Glass, Ron 111
Glover, Danny 1, 24, 103
Glover, Donald 85
Goldberg, Whoopi 4, 33, 69
Gooding, Cuba, Jr. 16, 62
Gordon, Dexter 25
Gossett, Louis, Jr. 7
Graham, Katerina 99
Greaves, William 38
Grier, David Alan 28
Grier, Pam 9, 31, 86
Griffin, Angela 80
Guillaume, Robert 3, 48
Gunn, Moses 10
Gurira, Danai 73
Guy, Jasmine 2
Hairston, Jester 88
Hamilton, Lisa Gay 71
Hamlin, Larry Leon 49, 62
Hammond, Fred 23
Hardison, Kadeem 22
Harewood, David 52
Harewood, Dorian 104
Harper, Hill 32, 65, 97
Harris, Naomie 55
Harris, Robin 7
Harris, Wood 114
Harry, Jackée 111
Harvey, Steve 18, 58
Hawkins, Screamin' Jay 30
Hayes, Isaac 20, 58, 73
Haysbert, Dennis 42, 106
Hector, Jamie 98
Hemsley, Sherman 19, 104
Henry, Dwight 104
Henry, Joshua 94
Henry, Lenny 9, 52
Henson, Taraji P. 58, 77
Hill, Dulé 29
Hines, Gregory 1, 42
Holder, Geoffrey 78
Hooks, Robert 76
Horne, Lena 5, 86
Hounsou, Djimon 19, 45
Houston, Whitney 7, 28, 83, 100
Howard, Sherri 36
Howard, Terrence 59, 94
Howell, Ayinde 91
Hudson, Ernie 72
Hudson, Jennifer 63, 83
Hughley, D. L. 23, 76
Hyman, Earle 25, 79
Ice Cube 8, 30, 60
Ice-T 6, 31, 96
Ingram, Rex 5
Jackson, Millie 25
Jackson, Samuel L. 8, 19, 63, 102
James, Nikki M. 94
Jean-Baptiste, Marianne 17, 46
Jean-Louis, Jimmy 76
Johnson, Clark 96
Johnson, Rodney Van 28

Jones, James Earl 3, 49, 79
Jones, Orlando 30
Jones, Rashida 101
Jones, Robbie 113
Jordan, Michael B. 97
Jorge, Seu 73
Kelley, Elijah 65
Kelley, Malcolm David 59
Kelly, Jim 113
Kennedy-Overton, Jayne Harris 46
Khumalo, Leleti 51
Kid Cudi 83
King, Regina 22, 45
King, Woodie, Jr. 27
Kirby, George 14
Kitt, Eartha 16, 75
Knight, Gladys 16, 66
Kodjoe, Boris 34, 89
Kotto, Yaphet 7
La Salle, Eriq 12
LaBelle, Patti 13, 30
LaChanze 93
Lampley, Oni Faida 43, 71
Lane, Charles 3
Lassiter, Roy 24
Lathan, Sanaa 27
Lawrence, Martin 6, 27, 60
Leakes, NeNe 107
Lee, Canada 8
Lee, Joie 1
Leggs, Kingsley 62
Lemmons, Kasi 20
LeNoire, Rosetta 37
Lenox, Adriane 59
Lester, Adrian 46
Lesure, James 64
Lewis, Emmanuel 36
Lincoln, Abbey 3, 88
Lindo, Delroy 18, 45
LisaRaye 27
LL Cool J 16, 49, 94
Long, Nia 17, 95
Luke, Derek 61
Lumbly, Carl 47
Mabley, Jackie "Moms" 15
Mac, Bernie 29, 61, 72
Mackie, Anthony 102
Madame Sul-Te-Wan 95
Malco, Romany 71
Mann, Tamela 92
Maponya, Maishe 101
Marcille, Eva 97
Mario 71
Marrow, Queen Esther 24
Marshall, William 107
Martin, Duane 108
Martin, Helen 31
Martin, Jesse L. 31
Mayo, Whitman 32
Mbatha-Raw, Gugu 89
M.C. Hammer 20, 80
McBride, Chi 73
McClendon, Forrest 94
McClinton, Marion Isaac 77
McCrary, Darius 111
McCullough, DeAndre 106
McDaniel, Hattie 5
McDonald, Audra 20, 62
McGee, Vonetta 95
McKee, Lonette 12
McKinney, Nina Mae 40
McQueen, Butterfly 6, 54
Meadows, Tim 30

Mello, Breno 73
Merkerson, S. Epatha 47, 83
Michele, Michael 31
Miller, Omar Benson 93
Miller, Patina 94
Miller, Wentworth 75
Mitchell, Brian Stokes 21
Mitchell, Kel 66
Mokae, Zakes 80
Mo'Nique 35, 84
Moore, Chante 26
Moore, Juanita 83
Moore, Shemar 21, 112
Morgan, Tracy 61, 102
Morris, Garrett 31
Morris, Greg 28
Morton, Joe 18
Moten, Etta 18
Mowry, Tamera 79
Mowry, Tia 78
Murphy, Charles 95
Murphy, Eddie 4, 20, 61
Muse, Clarence Edouard 21
Myers, Lou 110
Nash, Johnny 40
Nash, Niecy 66, 115
Naughton, Naturi 97
Neal, Elise 29
Newton, Thandie 26, 114
Ngaujah, Sahr 86
Nicholas, Denise 82
Nicholas, Fayard 20, 57
Nicholas, Harold 20
Nichols, Nichelle 11
Norman, Maidie 20
Notorious B.I.G. 20
Ntshona, Winston 52
Okonedo, Sophie 67
Olagundoye, Toks 113
O'Neal, Frederick 99
O'Neal, Ron 46
O'Neal, Shaquille 8, 30, 95
Orlandersmith, Dael 42
Orman, Roscoe 55
Oyelowo, David 82
Parker, Nicole Ari 52
Patton, Paula 62
Payne, Allen 13
Payne, Freda 58
Pearson, Felicia 99
Peete, Holly Robinson 20
Perrineau, Harold, Jr. 51
Peters, Brock 96
Peters, Clarke 103
Phifer, Mekhi 25, 103
Phillips, Joseph C. 73
Pickens, James, Jr. 59
Pierce, Wendell 90
Pinkett Smith, Jada 10, 41, 95
Poitier, Sidney 11, 36
Poitier, Sydney Tamiia 65
Porter, Billy 112
Pounder, CCH 72
Pratt, Kyla 57
Preer, Evelyn 82
Premice, Josephine 41
Pryor, Rain 65
Pryor, Richard 3, 24, 56
Queen Latifah 1, 16, 58
Ralph, Sheryl Lee 18, 108
Randle, Theresa 16
Rashad, Phylicia 21
Raven-Symoné 44, 113

Ray, Gene Anthony 47
Reddick, Lance 52
Reed, Natina 106
Reed Hall, Alaina 83
Reese, Della 6, 20, 96
Reid, Tim 56
Reuben, Gloria 15
Rhames, Ving 14, 50
Rhymes, Busta 31
Ribeiro, Alfonso 17
Richards, Beah 30
Richards, Lloyd 2
Richardson, LaTanya 71
Richardson, Salli 68
Riley, Amber 97
Robeson, Paul 2
Robinson, Craig 103
Robinson, Shaun 36
Rock, Chris 3, 22, 66
Rock, The 29 66
Rodgers, Rod 36
Rodrigues, Percy 68
Roker, Roxie 68
Rolle, Esther 13, 21
Rollins, Howard E., Jr. 17
Romeo 98
Rose, Anika Noni 70
Ross, Diana 8, 27
Ross, Tracee Ellis 35
Roundtree, Richard 27
Rowell, Victoria 13, 68
Rowland, Kelly 100
Rudolph, Maya 46, 106
St. Jacques, Raymond 8
St. John, Kristoff 25
St. Patrick, Mathew 48
Saldana, Zoe 72
Salter, Nikkole 73
Sands, Diana 87
Sanford, Isabel 53
Santiago-Hudson, Ruben 85
Scott, Hazel 66
Scott, Jill 29, 83
Shakur, Tupac 14
Short, Columbus 79
Sidibe, Gabourey 84
Simmons, Henry 55
Sinbad 1, 16
Sinclair, Madge 78
Sisqo 30
Smith, Anjela Lauren 44
Smith, Anna Deavere 6, 44
Smith, B(arbara) 11
Smith, Bubba 96
Smith, Jaden 82
Smith, Roger Guenveur 12
Smith, Tasha 73
Smith, Will 8, 18, 53
Smith, Willow 92
Snipes, Wesley 3, 24, 67
Snoop Dogg 35, 84
Sohn, Sonja 100
Solange 97
Sommore 61
Spencer, Octavia 100
Stewart, Tonea Harris 78
Sticky Fingaz 86
Strode, Woody 111
Sy, Omar 109
Sykes, Wanda 48, 81
Tamia 97
Tate, Larenz 15
Taylor, Meshach 4

Taylor, Regina 9, 46, 97
Taylor, Ron 35
Terrence J 108
Thigpen, Lynne 17, 41
Thomas, Sean Patrick 35
Thomason, Marsha 47
Thompson, John Douglas 81
Thompson, Kenan 52
Thompson, Tazewell 13
Thoms, Tracie 61
Torres, Gina 52
Torry, Guy 31
Toussaint, Lorraine 32
Townsend, Robert 4, 23
True, Rachel 82
Tucker, Chris 13, 23, 62
Tunie, Tamara 63
Turman, Glynn 100
Turner, Tina 6, 27
Tyler, Aisha N. 36
Tyson, Cicely 7, 51, 112
Uggams, Leslie 23, 114
Underwood, Blair 7, 27, 76
Union, Gabrielle 31, 92
Usher 23, 56, 95
Van Peebles, Mario 2, 51
Van Peebles, Melvin 7, 95
Vance, Courtney B. 15, 60
Vanity 67
Vereen, Ben 4
Walker, Eamonn 37
Wallis, Quvenzhané 109
Ward, Douglas Turner 42
Warfield, Marsha 2
Warfield, William 94
Warner, Malcolm-Jamal 22, 36, 110
Warren, Michael 27
Washington, Denzel 1, 16, 93
Washington, Fredi 10
Washington, Isaiah 62
Washington, Kerry 46, 107
Waters, Ethel 7
Wayans, Damon 8, 41
Wayans, Keenen Ivory 18
Wayans, Kim 80
Wayans, Marlon 29, 82
Wayans, Shawn 29
Weathers, Carl 10
Wesley, Rutina 97
Wheaton, James 103
Whitaker, Forest 2, 49, 67
White, Michael Jai 71
White, Terri 82
Whitfield, Lynn 18
Williams, Bert 18
Williams, Billy Dee 8, 105
Williams, Clarence, III 26
Williams, Joe 5, 25
Williams, Malinda 57
Williams, Michael Kenneth 97
Williams, Samm-Art 21
Williams, Saul 31
Williams, Vanessa A. 32, 66
Williams, Vanessa L. 4, 17
Williamson, Fred 67
Williamson, Mykelti 22
Wilson, Chandra 57
Wilson, Debra 38
Wilson, Demond 102
Wilson, Dorien 55
Wilson, Flip 21
Winfield, Paul 2, 45
Winfrey, Oprah 2, 15, 61, 106

Withers-Mendes, Elisabeth 64
Witherspoon, John 38
Woodard, Alfre 9, 108
Woods, Renn 110
Woodson, Ali Ollie 89
Wright, Jeffrey 54, 111
Yarbrough, Cedric 51
Yoba, Malik 11
Young, Lee Thompson 114

Adoption and foster care
Clements, George 2
Hale, Clara 16
Hale, Lorraine 8
Oglesby, Zena 12
Rowell, Victoria 13, 68

Advertising
Barboza, Anthony 10
Boyd, Edward 70
Burrell, Tom 21, 51
Campbell, E. Simms 13
Chisholm, Samuel J. 32
Coleman, Donald 24, 62
Cullers, Vincent T. 49
Gaskins, Rudy 74
Green, Nancy 112
Jones, Caroline R. 29
Jordan, Montell 23
Kemp, Herb 94
Lewis, Byron E. 13
McKinney Hammond, Michelle 51
Mingo, Frank 32
Olden, Georg(e) 44
Pinderhughes, John 47
Roche, Joyce M. 17

Affirmative action
Arnwine, Barbara 28
Coleman, William T. 76
Edley, Christopher F., Jr. 48
Higginbotham, A. Leon, Jr. 13, 25
Maynard, Robert C. 7
Thompson, Bennie G. 26

AFL-CIO
See American Federation of Labor
   and Congress of Industrial Organizations

African American art
Jones, Paul R. 76

African American folklore
Bailey, Xenobia 11
Brown, Sterling Allen 10, 64
Dial, Thornton 114
Driskell, David C. 7
Ellison, Ralph 7
Gaines, Ernest J. 7
Hamilton, Virginia 10
Hurston, Zora Neale 3
Lester, Julius 9, 115
Tillman, George, Jr. 20
Williams, Bert 18
Yarbrough, Camille 40

African American history
Benberry, Cuesta 65
Bennett, Lerone, Jr. 5, 84
Berry, Mary Frances 7
Blackshear, Leonard 52
Blockson, Charles L. 42
Burroughs, Margaret Taylor 9
Camp, Kimberly 19

Chase-Riboud, Barbara 20, 46
Clarke, John Henrik 20
Clayton, Mayme Agnew 62
Cobb, William Jelani 59
Coombs, Orde M. 44
Cooper, Anna Julia 20
Dodson, Howard, Jr. 7, 52
Douglas, Aaron 7
DuBois, Shirley Graham 21
Dyson, Michael Eric 11, 40
Feelings, Tom 11, 47
Franklin, John Hope 5, 77
Gaines, Ernest J. 7
George, Nelson 12, 101
Gill, Gerald 69
Gordon-Reed, Annette 74
Haley, Alex 4
Halliburton, Warren J. 49
Harkless, Necia Desiree 19
Harris, Richard E. 61
Hine, Darlene Clark 24
Jones, Edward P. 43, 67
Lewis, David Levering 9
Marable, Manning 10, 102
Mason, Herman, Jr. 83
Painter, Nell Irvin 24, 88
Pritchard, Robert Starling 21
Putney, Martha S. 75
Quarles, Benjamin Arthur 18
Richardson, Julieanna 81
Schomburg, Arthur Alfonso 9
Shadd, Abraham D. 81
Southern, Eileen 56
Tancil, Gladys Quander 59
Woodson, Carter G. 2
Yarbrough, Camille 40

African American literature
Andrews, Raymond 4
Angelou, Maya 1, 15
Baisden, Michael 25, 66
Baker, Houston A., Jr. 6
Baldwin, James 1
Bambara, Toni Cade 1
Baraka, Amiri 1, 38
Bennett, George Harold "Hal" 45
Bontemps, Arna 8
Briscoe, Connie 15
Brooks, Gwendolyn 1, 28
Brown, Claude 38
Brown, Wesley 23
Brown, William Wells 99
Burroughs, Margaret Taylor 9
Campbell, Bebe Moore 6, 24, 59
Cary, Lorene 3
Childress, Alice 15
Cleage, Pearl 17, 64
Cullen, Countee 8
Davis, Arthur P. 41
Davis, Nolan 45
Dickey, Eric Jerome 21, 56
Du Bois, W. E. B. 3
Dunbar, Paul Laurence 8
Ellison, Ralph 7
Evans, Mari 26
Fair, Ronald L. 47
Fauset, Jessie 7
Feelings, Tom 11, 47
Fisher, Rudolph 17
Ford, Nick Aaron 44
Fuller, Charles 8
Gaines, Ernest J. 7
Gates, Henry Louis, Jr. 3, 38, 67

Gayle, Addison, Jr. 41
Gibson, Donald Bernard 40
Giddings, Paula 11
Giovanni, Nikki 9, 39, 85
Goines, Donald 19
Golden, Marita 19, 99
Guy, Rosa 5
Haley, Alex 4
Hansberry, Lorraine 6
Harper, Frances Ellen Watkins 11
Heard, Nathan C. 45
Himes, Chester 8
Holland, Endesha Ida Mae 3, 57
Holmes, Shannon 70
Hughes, Langston 4
Hull, Akasha Gloria 45
Hurston, Zora Neale 3
Iceberg Slim 11
Joe, Yolanda 21
Johnson, Charles 1, 82
Johnson, James Weldon 5
Jones, Gayl 37
Jordan, June 7, 35
July, William 27
Kitt, Sandra 23
Larsen, Nella 10
Little, Benilde 21
Lorde, Audre 6
Madhubuti, Haki 7, 85
Major, Clarence 9
Marshall, Paule 7, 77
McKay, Claude 6
McKay, Nellie Yvonne 17, 57
McKinney-Whetstone, Diane 27
McMillan, Terry 4, 17, 53
McPherson, James Alan 70
Morrison, Toni 2, 15, 86
Mowry, Jess 7
Naylor, Gloria 10, 42
Petry, Ann 19
Pinkney, Jerry 15
Rahman, Aishah 37
Randall, Dudley 8, 55
Redding, J. Saunders 26
Redmond, Eugene 23
Reed, Ishmael 8
Ringgold, Faith 4, 81
Sanchez, Sonia 17, 51
Schomburg, Arthur Alfonso 9
Schuyler, George Samuel 40
Shange, Ntozake 8, 89
Smith, Mary Carter 26
Taylor, Mildred D. 26
Thomas, Trisha R. 65
Thurman, Wallace 16
Toomer, Jean 6
Tyree, Omar Rashad 21
Verdelle, A. J. 26
Villarosa, Clara 85
Walker, Alice 1, 43
Wesley, Valerie Wilson 18
Wideman, John Edgar 5, 87
Williams, John A. 27
Williams, Sherley Anne 25
Wilson, August 7, 33, 55
Wolfe, George C. 6, 43
Wright, Richard 5
Wright, Sarah E. 95
Yarbrough, Camille 40

African American studies
Alexander, Elizabeth 75
Baszile, Jennifer 79

Brawley, Benjamin 44
Carby, Hazel 27
Christian, Barbara T. 44
De Veaux, Alexis 44
Ford, Nick Aaron 44
Hare, Nathan 44
Harris-Lacewell, Melissa 81
Henderson, Stephen E. 45
Huggins, Nathan Irvin 52
Long, Richard Alexander 65
Neal, Mark Anthony 74
Peterson, James 81
West, Cornel 5, 33, 80

African art
Simpson, Merton D. 110

African Canadian literature
Elliott, Lorris 37
Foster, Cecil 32
Senior, Olive 37

African dance
Acogny, Germaine 55
Adams, Jenoyne 60
Ailey, Alvin 8
Davis, Chuck 33
Primus, Pearl 6

African history
Chase-Riboud, Barbara 20, 46
Clarke, John Henrik 20
Counter, S. Allen 74
Diop, Cheikh Anta 4
Dodson, Howard, Jr. 7, 52
DuBois, Shirley Graham 21
Feelings, Muriel 44
Halliburton, Warren J. 49
Hansberry, William Leo 11
Harkless, Necia Desiree 19
Henries, A. Doris Banks 44
Hilliard, Asa Grant, III 66
Jawara, Dawda Kairaba 11
Marshall, Paule 7, 77
van Sertima, Ivan 25

African literature
Abrahams, Peter 39
Achebe, Chinua 6, 99, 111
Aidoo, Ama Ata 38
Akpan, Uwem 70
Amadi, Elechi 40
Arac de Nyeko, Monica 66
Armah, Ayi Kwei 49
Awoonor, Kofi 37, 115
Babatunde, Rotimi 104
Bandele, Biyi 68
Barrett, Lindsay 43
Beti, Mongo 36
Brutus, Dennis 38
Cartey, Wilfred 47
Cheney-Coker, Syl 43
Couto, Mia 45
Dadié, Bernard 34
Dathorne, O. R. 52
Ekwensi, Cyprian 37
Farah, Nuruddin 27
Gabre-Medhin, Tsegaye 64
Head, Bessie 28
Kayira, Legson 40
Memmi, Albert 37
Mofolo, Thomas 37
Mphalele, Es'kia 40
Mwangi, Meja 40

Ngugi wa Thiong'o 29, 61, 101
Okigbo, Christopher 102
Onwueme, Tess Osonye 23
Oyono, Ferdinand 38
Peters, Lenrie 43
Rotimi, Ola 1
Salih, Al-Tayyib 37
Saro-Wiwa, Kenule 39
Soyinka, Wole 4, 93

African Methodist Episcopal Church (AME)
Blanks, Deborah K. 69
Brookins, Hamel Hartford 102
Bryant, John R. 45
Flake, Floyd H. 18, 110
Lee, Jarena 100
Loguen, J. W. 91
McKenzie, Vashti M. 29
Mudimbe, V. Y. 61
Murray, Cecil 12, 47
Roundtree, Dovey 80
Turner, Henry McNeal 5
Youngblood, Johnny Ray 8

African music
Ade, King Sunny 41
Afro, Teddy 78
Amadou & Mariam 113
Ashong, Derrick 86
Birra, Ali 113
Bombino 112
Chaka Chaka, Yvonne 112
Diawara, Djeli Moussa 111
Diawara, Fatoumata 114
Fela 1, 42
Keita, Salif 83
Kidjo, Angelique 50
Kolosoy, Wendo 73
Kuti, Femi 47, 110
Maal, Baaba 66
Mahlasela, Vusi 65
Makeba, Miriam 2, 50, 74
Malawi Mouse Boys 114
Nascimento, Milton 2 64
Sangare, Oumou 18, 99
Somi 85

African National Congress (ANC)
Dlamini-Zuma, Nkosazana 34, 105
Hani, Chris 6
Ka Dinizulu, Mcwayizeni 29
Kaunda, Kenneth 2
Kuzwayo, Ellen 68
Luthuli, Albert 13
Madikizela-Mandela, Winnie 2, 35, 112
Malema, Julius 98
Mandela, Nelson 1, 14, 77
Masekela, Barbara 18
Mbeki, Govan A. 80
Mbeki, Thabo 14, 73
Mhlaba, Raymond 55
Motlanthe, Kgalema 74
Nkomo, Joshua 4, 65
Nyanda, Siphiwe 21
Nzo, Alfred 15
Ramaphosa, Cyril 3
Sisulu, Albertina 57, 95
Sisulu, Walter 47
Tutu, Desmond Mpilo 6, 44
Weems, Renita J. 44
Xuma, Madie Hall 59

Zuma, Jacob 33, 75

African Union
Diouf, Abdou 3
Dlamini-Zuma, Nkosazana 34, 105
Haile Selassie 7
Kaunda, Kenneth 2
Kenyatta, Jomo 5
Nkrumah, Kwame 3
Nujoma, Samuel 10
Nyerere, Julius 5
Sassou-Nguesso, Denis 103
Touré, Sekou 6

Afro-Brazilian music
Brown, Carlinhos 81
Caymmi, Dorival 72
Gil, Gilberto 53
Jorge, Seu 73
Moura, Paulo 87

Afrocentricity
Asante, Molefi Kete 3
Biggers, John 20, 33
Diop, Cheikh Anta 4
Hansberry, William Leo 11
Sanchez, Sonia 17, 51
Turner, Henry McNeal 5

Afro-Cuban music
Lefel, Edith 41
Rodríguez, Arsenio 87
Santamaria, Mongo 81
Secada, Jon 97

Afro-Peruvian music
Baca, Susana 80

Agriculture
Allen, Will 74
Boyd, John W., Jr. 20, 72
Carver, George Washington 4
Finley, Ron 110
Hall, Lloyd A. 8
Jones, Monty 66
Masire, Quett 5
Sanders, Dori 8
Wambugu, Florence 42

AHA
See American Heart Association

AIDS
See Acquired immune deficiency syndrome

Akron Beacon Journal
Crutchfield, James N. 55

ALA
See American Library Association

Alabama state government
Davis, Artur 41
Ford, Johnny 70
Gray, Fred 37
Rapier, James T. 82

Alcoholics Anonymous (AA)
Lucas, John 7

All Afrikan People's Revolutionary Party
Carmichael, Stokely 5, 26
Moses, Robert Parris 11

Alpha & Omega Ministry
White, Reggie 6, 50

Alpha Kappa Alpha Sorority
Quander, Nellie 102
White, Linda M. 45

Alternative music
Santigold 96

Alvin Ailey American Dance Theater
Ailey, Alvin 8
Clarke, Hope 14
Dove, Ulysses 5
Faison, George 16
Jamison, Judith 7, 67, 96
Jefferson, Denise 87
Primus, Pearl 6
Rhoden, Dwight 40
Richardson, Desmond 39
Spears, Warren 52
Tyson, Andre 40
Williams, Dudley 60

Ambassadors
Avant, Nicole A. 90
Awoonor, Kofi 37, 115
Braun, Carol Moseley 4, 42
Carson, Johnnie 85
Cook, Mercer 40
Davis, Ruth 37
Dudley, Edward R. 58
Dymally, Mervyn 42
Frazer, Jendayi 68
Mbuende, Kaire 12
Perkins, Edward 5
Smythe Haith, Mabel 61
Spearman, Leonard H. O., Sr. 81
Stith, Charles R. 73
Todman, Terence A. 55
Watson, Diane 41
Wharton, Clifton Reginald, Sr. 36
Whitfield, Mal 60

AME
See African Methodist Episcopal Church

American Association for the Advancement of Science (AAAS)
Cobb, W. Montague 39
Massey, Walter E. 5, 45
Pickett, Cecil 39

American Ballet Theatre
Dove, Ulysses 5
Richardson, Desmond 39

American Bar Association
Archer, Dennis 7, 36
Pincham, R. Eugene, Sr. 69
Thompson, Larry D. 39
Walker, Cora T. 68

American Book Award
Baraka, Amiri 1, 38
Bates, Daisy 13
Bradley, David Henry, Jr. 39
Clark, Septima 7
Ellis, Trey 97
Gates, Henry Louis, Jr. 3, 38, 67
Lorde, Audre 6
Loury, Glenn 36

Marshall, Paule **7, 77**
Sanchez, Sonia **17, 51**
Troupe, Quincy **83**
Walker, Alice **1, 43**

American Broadcasting Company (ABC)
Christian, Spencer **15**
Goode, Mal **13**
Martin, Michel **97**
Mickebury, Penny **28**
Reynolds, Star Jones **10, 27, 61**
Roberts, Robin **16, 54, 113**
Robinson, Max **3**
Simpson, Carole **6, 30**

American Cancer Society
Ashe, Arthur **1, 18**
Leffall, Lasalle **3, 64**
Riperton, Minnie **32**
Thomas, Arthur Ray **52**

American Choral Directors Association
Adams, Leslie **39**

American Civil Liberties Union (ACLU)
Baugh, David **23**
Harris, Maya Lakshmi **88**
Murphy, Laura M. **43**
Murray, Pauli **38**
Pincham, R. Eugene, Sr. **69**

American Civil War
Augusta, Alexander T. **111**
Carney, William H. **104**

American Economic Association
Loury Glenn **36**

American Enterprise Institute
Woodson, Robert L. **10**

American Express Company
Adams, Eula L. **39**
Chapman, Susan E. **94**
Chenault, Kenneth **4, 36, 108**
Goodman, Kim C. **94**

American Federation of Labor and Congress of Industrial Organizations (AFL-CIO)
Fletcher, Bill, Jr. **41**
Holt Baker, Arlene **73**
O'Neal, Frederick **99**
Randolph, A. Philip **3**

American Guild of Organists
Adams, Leslie **39**

American Heart Association (AHA)
Cooper, Edward S. **6**
Grant, Augustus O. **71**
Richardson, Donna **39**

American Idol
Barrino, Fantasia **53, 94**
Hudson, Jennifer **63, 83**
Jackson, Randy **40**

American Library Association (ALA)
Franklin, Hardy R. **9, 87**
Hayden, Carla D. **47**

Jones, Clara Stanton **51**
Josey, E. J. **10**
McFadden, Bernice L. **39**
Rollins, Charlamae Hill **27**
Wedgeworth, Robert W. **42**

American Negro Theater
Martin, Helen **31**
O'Neal, Frederick **99**

American Nuclear Society
Wilkens, J. Ernest, Jr. **43**

American Nurses Association (ANA)
Kennedy, Adrienne **11**
Staupers, Mabel K. **7**

American Psychological Association (APA)
Anderson, Norman B. **45**

American Red Cross
Bullock, Steve **22**
Drew, Charles Richard **7**

American Society of Magazine Editors
Curry, George E. **23**

American Tennis Association
Gibson, Althea **8, 43**
Peters, Margaret and Matilda **43**

American Writers Association
Schuyler, George Samuel **40**

Amsterdam News
Bostic, Joe **95**
Burley, Dan **96**
Cooper, Andrew W. **36**
Holt, Nora **38**
Tatum, Elinor R. **78**
Tatum, Wilbert **76**

ANA
See American Nurses Association

ANC
See African National Congress

Anglican Church
Akinola, Peter Jasper **65**
Tutu, Desmond Mpilo **6, 44**

Angolan government
dos Santos, José Eduardo **43, 114**
Neto, António Agostinho **43**

Anheuser-Busch distribution
Cherry, Deron **40**

Anthropology
Asante, Molefi Kete **3**
Cole, Johnnetta B. **5, 43**
Davis, Allison **12**
Diop, Cheikh Anta **4**
Dunham, Katherine **4, 59**
Hansberry, William Leo **11**
Primus, Pearl **6**
Robeson, Eslanda Goode **13**
Rodriguez, Cheryl **64**

Antoinette Perry awards
See Tony awards

APA
See American Psychological Association

Apartheid
Abrahams, Peter **39**
Ashe, Arthur **18**
Biko, Steven **4**
Brutus, Dennis **38**
Butler, Jonathan **28**
Howard, M. William, Jr. **26**
Jansen, Jonathan **102**
Ka Dinizulu, Mcwayizeni **29**
Kuzwayo, Ellen **68**
LaGuma, Alex **30**
Luthuli, Albert **13**
Madikizela-Mandela, Winnie **2, 35, 112**
Mahlasela, Vusi **65**
Makeba, Miriam **2, 50, 74**
Mandela, Nelson **1, 14, 77**
Maponya, Maishe **101**
Masekela, Hugh **1, 106**
Mbeki, Thabo **14, 73**
McDougall, Gay J. **11, 43**
Mhlaba, Raymond **55**
Mphalele, Es'kia **40**
Nkoli, Simon **60**
Ntshona, Winston **52**
Nyanda, Siphiwe **21**
Nzo, Alfred **15**
Plaatje, Sol T. **80**
Ramaphosa, Cyril **3**
Ramphele, Mamphela **29**
Robinson, Randall **7, 46**
Sisulu, Albertina **57, 95**
Sisulu, Walter **47**
Sullivan, Leon H. **13, 30**
Tutu, Desmond Mpilo **6, 44**

Apollo
Williams, O. S. **13**

Apollo Theater
Sims, Howard **48**
Sutton, Percy E. **42, 82**

Archaeology
Gilbert, John Wesley **91**
McJunkin, George **93**
Perry, Warren **56**

Architecture
Abele, Julian **55**
Adjaye, David **38, 78**
Bond, J. Max, Jr. **76**
Chase, John Saunders, Jr. **99**
Gantt, Harvey **1**
Johnson, Jeh Vincent **44**
King, Robert Arthur **58**
McKissack, Leatrice **80**
Sklarek, Norma Merrick **25, 101**
Taylor, Robert Robinson **80**
Williams, Paul R. **9**

Argonne National Laboratory
Massey, Walter E. **5, 45**
Quarterman, Lloyd Albert **4**

Ariel Capital Management
Hobson, Mellody **40**
Rogers, John W., Jr. **5, 52**

Arista Records
Lattimore, Kenny **35**
Reid, Antonio "L.A." **28**

Arkansas government
Elders, Joycelyn **6**

Arkansas Supreme Court
Roaf, Andrée Layton **106**

Art history
Amaki, Amalia **76**
Benjamin, Tritobia Hayes **53**
Campbell, Mary Schmidt **43**

Astronauts
Anderson, Michael P. **40**
Bluford, Guy **2, 35**
Bolden, Charles Frank, Jr. **7, 78**
Gregory, Frederick **8, 51**
Harris, Bernard A. **90**
Jemison, Mae C. **1, 35**
Lawrence, Robert H., Jr. **16**
McNair, Ronald **3, 58**
Wilson, Stephanie **72**

Astronomy
Banneker, Benjamin **93**
Pitts, Derrick **77**

Astrophysics
Alcorn, George Edward, Jr. **59**
Carruthers, George R. **40**
Walker, Arthur, II **87**

Atlanta Baptist College
See Morehouse College

Atlanta Board of Education
Mays, Benjamin E. **7**

Atlanta Braves baseball team
Aaron, Hank **5**
Jones, Andruw **98**
Justice, David **18**
Lucas, Bill **97**
McGriff, Fred **24**

Atlanta city government
Campbell, Bill **9, 76**
Franklin, Shirley **34, 80**
Jackson, Maynard **2, 41**
Pitts, Robb **84**
Reed, Kasim **82**
Williams, Hosea Lorenzo **15, 31**
Young, Andrew **3, 48, 110**

Atlanta Police Department
Harvard, Beverly **11**

Authors Guild
Schuyler, George Samuel **40**

Authors League of America
Abrahams, Peter **39**
Cotter, Joseph Seamon, Sr. **40**

Automobile dealership
Farr, Mel **24**
Gidron, Richard D. **68**
Parker, Jim **64**

Aviation
Brown, Jesse Leroy **31**
Brown, Willa **40**
Bullard, Eugene **12**
Coleman, Bessie **9**

Irving, Barrington, Jr. 112
Julian, Hubert 90
McLeod, Gus 27
Petersen, Frank E. 31
Plinton, James O., Jr. 98
Roy, Kenny 51
Turner, Henry McNeal 5
Young, Perry H. 100

Bahamian government
Christie, Perry Gladstone 53
Pindling, Lynden 81

Ballet
Ailey, Alvin 8
Allen, Debbie 13, 42
Anderson, Lauren 72
Collins, Janet 33, 64
DePrince, Michaela 104
Dove, Ulysses 5
Faison, George 16
Jamison, Judith 7, 67, 96
Johnson, Virginia 9
Jones, Doris W. 62
Mitchell, Arthur 2, 47
Nichols, Nichelle 11
Parks, Gordon 1, 35, 58
Rhoden, Dwight 40
Richardson, Desmond 39
Rowell, Victoria 13, 68
Tyson, Andre 40

Baltimore city government
Dixon, Sheila 68
Rawlings-Blake, Stephanie 93
Robinson, Bishop L. 66
Schmoke, Kurt 1, 48

Baltimore Orioles baseball team
Baylor, Don 6
Blair, Paul 36
Carter, Joe 30
Jackson, Reggie 15
Robinson, Frank 9, 87

Banking
Blaylock, Ronald 86
Boyd, T. B., III 6
Bradley, Jennette B. 40
Bridgforth, Glinda 36
Bryant, John 26
Chapman, Nathan A., Jr. 21
Chappell, Emma 18
Forte, Linda Diane 54
Funderburg, I. Owen 38
Greene, Richard Thaddeus, Sr. 67
Griffith, Mark Winston 8
Harris, Carla A. 67
Lawless, Theodore K. 8
Louis, Errol T. 8
March, William Carrington 56
McGuire, Raymond J. 57
Morgan, Rose 11
Parsons, Richard Dean 11
Snowden, Gail 108
Taylor, Robert Rochon 104
Utendahl, John 23
Walker, Maggie Lena 17
Watkins, Donald 35
Watkins, Walter C. 24
Willie, Louis, Jr. 68
Wright, Deborah C. 25

Wright, Richard Robert, Sr. 100

Baptist
Austin, Junius C. 44
Borders, William Holmes 94
Bradley, J. Robert 65
Braxton, Brad 77
Butts, Calvin O., III 9, 90
Davis, Gary 41
Forbes, James A., Jr. 71
Franklin, C. L. 68
Fuller, Thomas O. 90
Gomes, Peter J. 15, 93
Hooks, Benjamin L. 2, 85
Jasper, John J. 91
Jemison, Major L. 48
Jones, E. Edward, Sr. 45
King, Martin Luther, Sr. 89
Long, Eddie L. 29, 89
Luter, Fred, Jr. 103
Meeks, James T. 92
Moss, Otis, Jr. 72
Rogers, Alan G. 72
Sharpe, Samuel 103
Sharpton, Al 21, 97
Shuttlesworth, Fred 47, 98
Taylor, Gardner C. 76
Taylor, Lonzie Odie 96
Thurston, Stephen J. 49
Walker, Lucius, Jr. 88
Walker, Wyatt Tee 80
Yates, Jack 114

Barbadian government
Adams, Grantley 82
Arthur, Owen 33

Baseball
Aaron, Hank 5
Allen, Dick 85
Anderson, Elmer 25
Ashford, Emmett 22
Baines, Harold 32
Baker, Dusty 8, 43, 72, 110
Banks, Ernie 33
Barnhill, David 30
Baylor, Don 6
Bell, James "Cool Papa" 36
Belle, Albert 10
Black, Joe 75
Blair, Paul 36
Bonds, Barry 6, 34, 63, 99
Bonds, Bobby 43
Brock, Lou 18
Brown, Raymond 102
Brown, Willard 36
Byrd, Marlon 112
Cabell, Enos 102
Campanella, Roy 25
Cano, Robinson 97
Carew, Rod 20
Carter, Joe 30
Cepeda, Orlando 98
Charleston, Oscar 39
Clendenon, Donn 26, 56
Coleman, Leonard S., Jr. 12
Cooper, Andy "Lefty" 63
Cottrell, Comer 11
Crawford, Carl 90
Crisp, Coco 109
Dandridge, Ray 36
Davis, Piper 19
Dawson, Andre 85
Day, Leon 39

Dihigo, Martín 103
Doby, Lawrence Eugene, Sr. 16
Dye, Jermaine 58
Ellis, Dock 78
Everett, Carl 103
Fielder, Cecil 2, 112
Fielder, Prince 68
Flood, Curt 10, 93
Foster, Andrew 79
Gamble, Oscar 113
Gaston, Cito 71
Gibson, Bob 33
Gibson, Josh 22
Glanville, Douglas Metunwa 82
Gooden, Dwight 20
Granderson, Curtis 66
Grant, Frank 100
Gregg, Eric 16
Griffey, Ken, Jr. 12, 73
Gwynn, Tony 18, 83
Hairston, Sam 88
Henderson, Rickey 28, 78
Hernández, Orlando 96
Horton, Willie 104
Howard, Ryan 65, 113
Hunter, Torii 43, 109
Hyde, Cowan F. "Bubba" 47
Irvin, Monte 31
Jackson, Reggie 15
Jenkins, Fergie 46
Jeter, Derek 27, 93
Johnson, Clifford "Connie" 52
Johnson, Judy 105
Johnson, Mamie "Peanut" 40
Jones, Adam 114
Jones, Andruw 98
Justice, David 18
Kaiser, Cecil 42
Kimbro, Henry A. 25
Lacy, Sam 30, 46
Lankford, Ray 23
Larkin, Barry 24
Lloyd, John Henry "Pop" 30
Lofton, Kenny 12
Lopes, Davey 92
Lucas, Bill 97
Mackey, Biz 82
Manuel, Jerry 94
Mariner, Jonathan 41
Martinez, Pedro 81
Maye, Lee 111
Mays, Willie 3
McCovey, Willie 103
McGriff, Fred 24
McRae, Hal 84
Minoso, Minnie 89
Morgan, Joe 9, 96
Murray, Eddie 12
Newcombe, Don 24
Nixon, Otis 111
O'Neil, Buck 19, 59
Ortiz, David 52, 82
Paige, Satchel 7
Perez, Pascual 108
Price, David 101
Pride, Charley 26
Puckett, Kirby 4, 58
Puig, Yasiel 113
Radcliffe, Ted 74
Raines, Tim 107
Randolph, Willie 53
Reagins, Tony 94
Reese, Pokey 28

Reynolds, Harold 77
Rice, Jim 75
Richard, J. R. 87
Robinson, Frank 9, 87
Robinson, Jackie 6
Robinson, Sharon 22
Rollins, Jimmy 70
Sabathia, CC 74
Sanders, Deion 4, 31, 96
Scott, George 113
Sheffield, Gary 16, 108
Sizemore, Grady 96
Smith, Hilton 29
Smith, Lee 101
Smith, Ozzie 77
Smith, Reggie 113
Sosa, Sammy 21, 44
Stargell, Willie 29
Stearnes, Norman "Turkey" 31
Stone, Toni 15
Strawberry, Darryl 22
Suttles, Mule 108
Thomas, Frank 12, 51
Tiant, Luis 102
Trouppe, Quincy Thomas, Sr. 84
Vaughn, Mo 16
Virgil, Ozzie 48
Watson, Bob 25
Wells, Vernon 91
Wells, Willie 105
White, Bill 1, 48
White, Frank 95
Whitney, Davey L. 110
Williams, Billy 86
Williams, Ken 68
Willis, Dontrelle 55
Wills, Maury 73
Winfield, Dave 5, 91

Baseball Hall of Fame
Banks, Ernie 33
Bell, James "Cool Papa" 36
Brown, Raymond 102
Brown, Willard 36
Campanella, Roy 25
Cepeda, Orlando 98
Charleston, Oscar 39
Dandridge, Ray 36
Dawson, Andre 85
Day, Leon 39
Dihigo, Martín 103
Doby, Lawrence Eugene, Sr. 16, 41
Foster, Andrew 79
Gibson, Josh 22
Gwynn, Tony 18, 83
Henderson, Rickey 28, 78
Irvin, Monte 31
Johnson, Judy 105
Leonard, Buck 67
Lloyd, John Henry "Pop" 30
Mackey, Biz 82
McCovey, Willie 103
Morgan, Joe 9, 96
Paige, Satchel 7
Rice, Jim 75
Robinson, Frank 9, 87
Robinson, Jackie 6
Smith, Hilton 29
Smith, Ozzie 77
Stearnes, Norman "Turkey" 31
Wells, Willie 105
Williams, Billy 86

Winfield, Dave **5, 91**

Basket making
Jackson, Mary **73**

Basketball
Abdul-Jabbar, Kareem **8**
Abdur-Rahim, Shareef **28**
Allen, Ray **82**
Amaker, Tommy **62**
Anderson, Mike **63**
Anthony, Carmelo **46, 94**
Archibald, Tiny **90**
Arenas, Gilbert **84**
Artest, Ron **52**
Barkley, Charles **5, 66**
Barksdale, Don **103**
Baylor, Elgin **93**
Beaty, Zelmo **115**
Bing, Dave **3, 59, 78**
Bogues, Tyrone "Muggsy" **56**
Bol, Manute **1**
Bolton-Holifield, Ruthie **28**
Bosh, Chris **85**
Brand, Elton **31**
Brandon, Terrell **16**
Brown, Mike **77, 107**
Bryant, Kobe **15, 31, 71, 110**
Bynoe, Peter C. B. **40**
Carter, Butch **27**
Carter, Kenneth **53**
Carter, Vince **26**
Catchings, Tamika **43**
Chamberlain, Wilt **18, 47**
Chandler, Tyson **114**
Chaney, Don **98**
Chaney, John **67**
Cheeks, Maurice **47, 106**
Clifton, Nathaniel "Sweetwater" **47**
Collins, Jason **111**
Cooper, Charles "Chuck" **47**
Cooper, Michael **31**
Cooper, Tarzan **96**
Cooper-Dyke, Cynthia **17, 89**
Cousins, DeMarcus **108**
Curry, Michael **85**
Curry, Stephen **110**
Daniels, Mel **106**
Dantley, Adrian **72**
Davis, Mike **41**
Douglas, Bob **96**
Drexler, Clyde **4, 61**
Dumars, Joe **16, 65**
Duncan, Tim **20, 91**
Dunn, Jerry **27**
Durant, Kevin **76, 107**
Edwards, Teresa **14, 95**
Ellerbe, Brian **22**
Elliott, Sean **26**
Erving, Julius **18, 47**
Ewing, Patrick **17, 73**
Fisher, Derek **97**
Fox, Rick **27**
Frazier, Walt **91**
Freeman, Marianna **23**
Gaines, Clarence E., Sr. **55**
Garnett, Kevin **14, 70**
Gates, William **97**
Gentry, Alvin **23**
Gilmore, Artis **101**
Gourdine, Simon **11**
Gray, Yeshimbra "Shimmy" **55**
Green, A. C. **32**

Greer, Hal **92**
Griffin, Blake **98**
Griffith, Yolanda **25**
Hamilton, Leonard **100**
Hardaway, Anfernee **13, 111**
Hardaway, Tim **35**
Harris-Stewart, Lusia **90**
Haskins, Clem **23**
Hawkins, Connie **91**
Hayes, Elvin **93**
Haynes, Marques **22**
Haywood, Spencer **99**
Hazzard, Walt **98**
Heard, Gar **25**
Hill, Grant **13, 94**
Holdsclaw, Chamique **24, 110**
Holiday, Jrue **115**
Horford, Al **107**
Howard, Dwight **113**
Howard, Juwan **15**
Hunter, Billy **22, 109**
Hunter, Lindsey **110**
Irving, Kyrie **102**
Isaacs, John **76**
Iverson, Allen **24, 46**
James, LeBron **46, 78, 105**
Johnson, Avery **62**
Johnson, Dennis **89**
Johnson, Gus **92**
Johnson, Joe **94**
Johnson, Kevin **70**
Johnson, Larry **28**
Johnson, Magic **3, 39, 101**
Jones, K. C. **83**
Jones, Merlakia **34**
Jones, Robbie **113**
Jones, Roy, Jr. **22**
Jones, Sam **85**
Jordan, Eddie **83**
Jordan, Michael **6, 21**
Joyce, Dru **81**
Justice, David **18**
Kellogg, Clark **64**
Kidd, Jason **86**
Lanier, Bob **47**
Lennox, Betty **31**
Leslie, Lisa **16, 73**
Lloyd, Earl **26**
Lowe, Sidney **64**
Lucas, John **7**
Mahorn, Rick **60**
Malone, Karl **18, 51, 90**
Malone, Moses **79**
Manigault, Earl "The Goat" **15**
McAdoo, Bob **75**
McGrady, Tracy **80**
McLendon, John B., Jr. **89**
Meminger, Dean **114**
Miller, Cheryl **10, 74**
Milton, DeLisha **31**
Mitchell, Sam **82**
Mohammed, Nazr **64**
Monroe, Earl **89**
Mourning, Alonzo **17, 44**
Mutombo, Dikembe **7, 107**
Odom, Lamar **81**
Olajuwon, Hakeem **2, 72**
O'Neal, Shaquille **8, 30, 95**
Palmer, Violet **59**
Parish, Robert **43**
Parker, Candace **74**
Parker, Tony **75**
Paul, Chris **84, 100**

Payton, Gary **99**
Peck, Carolyn **23**
Phillips, Teresa L. **42**
Pierce, Paul **71**
Pippen, Scottie **15, 89**
Porter, Terry **75**
Prince, Tayshaun **68**
Reed, Willis, Jr. **86**
Richardson, Nolan **9**
Richmond, Mitch **19**
Rivers, Doc **25, 81**
Robertson, Oscar **26**
Robinson, Craig **107**
Robinson, David **24, 90**
Robinson, Flynn **112**
Robinson, Will **51, 69**
Rodman, Dennis **12, 44, 96**
Rogers, Rodney Ray **106**
Rondo, Rajon **111**
Rose, Derrick **82**
Rose, Jalen **108**
Roundfield, Danny **109**
Roy, Brandon **98**
Russell, Bill **8**
Sanders, Satch **77**
Silas, Paul **24**
Smith, Kenny **114**
Smith, Randy **81**
Smith, Stephen A. **69**
Smith, Tubby **18, 83**
Sprewell, Latrell **23**
Stackhouse, Jerry **30**
Staley, Dawn **57**
Stith, Tom **93**
Stoudemire, Amar'e **59, 106**
Stringer, C. Vivian **13, 66**
Swoopes, Sheryl **12, 56**
Ujiri, Masai **107**
Ussery, Terdema, II **29**
Tatum, Reece **104**
Thomas, Isiah **7, 26, 65**
Thompson, Tina **25, 75**
Thurmond, Nate **88**
Tisdale, Wayman **50**
Unseld, Wes **23**
Wade, Dwyane **61, 103**
Walker, Chet **106**
Wallace, Ben **54**
Wallace, Perry E. **47**
Wallace, Rasheed **56**
Washington, Ora Mae **115**
Webber, Chris **15, 30, 59**
White, Jo Jo **112**
Whitney, Davey L. **110**
Wilkens, Lenny **11, 88**
Williams, Deron **92**
Williams, Natalie **31**
Woodard, Lynette **67**
Woodson, Mike **78**
Worthy, James **49**

Basketball Hall of Fame
Abdul-Jabbar, Kareem **8**
Archibald, Tiny **90**
Barkley, Charles **5, 66**
Barksdale, Don **103**
Baylor, Elgin **93**
Bing, Dave **3, 59, 78**
Boozer, Bob **103**
Chamberlain, Wilt **18, 47**
Chaney, John **67**
Cooper, Tarzan **96**
Cooper-Dyke, Cynthia **17, 89**

Daniels, Mel **106**
Dantley, Adrian **72**
Douglas, Bob **96**
Drexler, Clyde **4, 61**
Dumars, Joe **16, 65**
Edwards, Teresa **14, 95**
Ewing, Patrick **17, 73**
Frazier, Walt **91**
Gaines, Clarence E., Sr. **55**
Gates, William **97**
Gervin, George **80**
Gilmore, Artis **101**
Greer, Hal **92**
Harris-Stewart, Lusia **90**
Hawkins, Connie **91**
Hayes, Elvin **93**
Haynes, Marques **22**
Johnson, Dennis **89**
Johnson, Gus **92**
Johnson, Magic **3, 39, 101**
Jones, K. C. **83**
Jones, Sam **85**
Lanier, Bob **47**
Lloyd, Earl **26**
Malone, Karl **18, 51, 90**
Malone, Moses **79**
McAdoo, Bob **75**
McLendon, John B., Jr. **89**
Miller, Cheryl **10, 74**
Monroe, Earl **89**
Olajuwon, Hakeem **2, 72**
Parish, Robert **43**
Pippen, Scottie **15, 89**
Reed, Willis, Jr. **86**
Robertson, Oscar **26**
Robinson, David **24, 90**
Rodman, Dennis **12, 44, 96**
Russell, Bill **8**
Sanders, Satch **77**
Thomas, Isiah **7, 26, 65**
Thurmond, Nate **88**
Unseld, Wes **23**
Walker, Chet **106**
Wilkens, Lenny **11, 88**
Wilkins, Dominique **74**
Woodard, Lynette **67**
Worthy, James **49**

Bass
Blanton, Jimmy **108**
Carter, Ron **104**
Clarke, Stanley **115**
Foster, George "Pops" **40**
Isley, Marvin **87**
Jamerson, James **59**
Pettiford, Oscar **106**

BBC
See British Broadcasting Company

Beatrice International
See TLC Beatrice International Holdings, Inc.

Beauty salons and products
Cottrell, Comer **11**
Fine, Sam **60**
Fuller, S. B. **13**
Gardner, Edward G. **45**
Gibson, Ted **66**
Johnson, George E. **29**
Johnson, William **91**
Joyner, Marjorie Stewart **26**
Malone, Annie **13**

Price, Lisa **97**
Roche, Joyce M. **17**
Stanford, Olivia Lee Dilworth **49**
Walker, Madame C. J. **7**

Bebop
Carter, Betty **19**
Clarke, Kenny **27**
Coltrane, John **19**
Dameron, Tadd **103**
Davis, Miles **4**
Eckstine, Billy **28**
Fitzgerald, Ella **8, 18**
Freeman, Von **104**
Gillespie, Dizzy **1**
Gordon, Dexter **25**
Hancock, Herbie **20, 67**
Harris, Barry **68**
Hawkins, Coleman **9**
Jackson, Milt **26**
Navarro, Fats **104**
Parker, Charlie **20**
Powell, Bud **24**
Roach, Max **21, 63**
Vaughan, Sarah **13**

Ben & Jerry's Homemade Ice Cream, Inc.
Holland, Robert, Jr. **11**

Bennett College
Cole, Johnnetta B. **5, 43**
Player, Willa B. **43**

Benin government
Kerekou, Ahmed **1**
Soglo, Nicéphore **15**
Yayi, Boni T. **84**

Bermuda government
Gordon, Pamela **17**

BET
See Black Entertainment Television

Bethune-Cookman College
Bethune, Mary McLeod **4**

Big Easy Award
Adams, Johnny **39**

Bill and Melinda Gates Foundation
Golston, Allan C. **55**

Bing Group, The
Bing, Dave **3, 59, 78**
Lloyd, Earl **26**

Biology
Cobb, Jewel Plummer **42**
Crouch, Hubert **95**
Emeagwali, Dale **31**
Jarvis, Erich **67**
Malveaux, Floyd **54**
Pickett, Cecil **39**

Biotechnology
Dabiri, John **93**
Haynie, Sharon **94**
Juma, Calestous **57**
Wambugu, Florence **42**

Birmingham (AL) city government
Arrington, Richard **24, 100**
Kincaid, Bernard **28**

Langford, Larry P. **74**
Nunn, Annetta **43**

Birmingham (AL) Police Department
Nunn, Annetta **43**
Woods, Abraham, Jr. **74**

Bishop College
Cottrell, Comer **11**

Black Alliance for Educational Options
Fuller, Howard L. **37**

Black American West Museum
Stewart, Paul Wilbur **12**

Black arts movement
Barrett, Lindsay **43**
Caldwell, Benjamin **46**
Cornish, Sam **50**
Cortez, Jayne **43, 109**
Cruse, Harold **54**
Dent, Thomas C. **50**
Donaldson, Jeff **46**
Dumas, Henry **41**
Gayle, Addison, Jr. **41**
Giovanni, Nikki **9, 39, 85**
Henderson, David **53**
Hoagland, Everett H. **45**
Neal, Larry **38**
Pomare, Eleo **72**
Smith, Vincent D. **48**
Touré, Askia (Muhammad Abu Bakr el) **47**
X, Marvin **45**

Black Cabinet
Hastie, William H. **8**

Black Coaches Association (BCA)
Freeman, Marianna **23**
Keith, Floyd A. **61**

Black Consciousness movement
Biko, Steven **4**
Fanon, Frantz **44**
Fuller, Hoyt **44**
Muhammad, Elijah **4**
Ramphele, Mamphela **29**

***Black Enterprise* magazine**
Graves, Butch **77**
Graves, Earl G. **1, 35**
Wallace, Phyllis A. **9**

Black Entertainment Television (BET)
Ames, Wilmer **27**
Gordon, Ed **10, 53**
Greely, M. Gasby **27**
Holmes, T. J. **98**
Johnson, Robert L. **3, 39**
Johnson, Sheila Crump **48**
Jones, Bobby **20, 94**
Lee, Debra L. **62**
McCrary Anthony, Crystal **70**
Rolle, Janet **97**
Smiley, Tavis **20, 68**

Black Filmmakers Hall of Fame
Barnett, Etta Moten **18, 56**
Blake, Eubie **29**

Browne, Roscoe Lee **66**
Carroll, Diahann **9**
Carter, Benny **46**
Cash, Rosalind **28**
Crothers, Scatman **19**
Davis, Sammy, Jr. **18**
de Passe, Suzanne **25**
Dee, Ruby **8, 50, 68**
Dixon, Ivan **69**
Dunham, Katherine **4, 59**
Fetchit, Stepin **32**
Glover, Danny **1, 24, 103**
Greaves, William **38**
Johnson, Hall **90**
Lincoln, Abbey **3, 88**
Madame Sul-Te-Wan **95**
McDaniel, Hattie **5**
McKinney, Nina Mae **40**
McQueen, Butterfly **6, 54**
Micheaux, Oscar **7**
Miles, William **112**
Muse, Clarence Edouard **21**
Nicholas, Fayard **20, 57, 61**
Nicholas, Harold **20**
Norman, Maidie **20**
Parks, Gordon **1, 35, 58**
Peters, Brock **96**
Poitier, Sidney **11, 36**
Robeson, Paul **2**
Schultz, Michael A. **6**
Tyson, Cicely **7, 51, 112**
Van Peebles, Melvin **7, 95**
Washington, Fredi **10**
Williams, Billy Dee **8, 105**
Wilson, August **7, 33, 55**

Black History Month
Woodson, Carter G. **2**

Black nationalism
Baraka, Amiri **1, 38**
Caldwell, Benjamin **46**
Carmichael, Stokely **5, 26**
Cuffe, Paul **98**
Donaldson, Jeff **46**
Farrakhan, Louis **2**
Forman, James **7, 51**
Garvey, Marcus **1**
Heard, Nathan C. **45**
Innis, Roy **5**
Muhammad, Elijah **4**
Obadele, Imari **84**
Turner, Henry McNeal **5**
X, Malcolm **1**
York, Dwight D. **71**

Black Panther Party (BPP)
Abu-Jamal, Mumia **15**
Al-Amin, Jamil Abdullah **6**
bin Wahad, Dhoruba **85**
Brown, Elaine **8**
Carmichael, Stokely **5**
Cleaver, Eldridge **5**
Cleaver, Kathleen Neal **29**
Coates, Ta-Nehisi **76**
Cox, Donald Lee **93**
Davis, Angela **5, 114**
Douglas, Emory **89**
Forman, James **7, 51**
Hampton, Fred **18**
Hilliard, David **7, 105**
Jackson, George Lester **14**
Joseph, Jamal **101**
Kimbro, Warren **76**

Neal, Larry **38**
Newton, Huey **2**
Pratt, Geronimo **18, 95**
Rush, Bobby **26, 76**
Seale, Bobby **3**
Shakur, Afeni **67**
Shakur, Assata **6**

Black Power movement
Al-Amin, Jamil Abdullah **6**
Brown, Elaine **8**
Carmichael, Stokely **5, 26**
Dodson, Howard, Jr. **7, 52**
Donaldson, Jeff **46**
Dumas, Henry **41**
Hare, Nathan **44**
McKissick, Floyd B. **3**
Stone, Chuck **9**

Black Think Tank
Hare, Nathan **44**

Blackvoices.com
Cooper, Barry **33**

***Black World* magazine**
See *Negro Digest* magazine

Blogging
Contee, Cheryl **88**

Blues
Ace, Johnny **36**
Allison, Luther **111**
Amy, Curtis **114**
Arnold, Billy Boy **112**
Austin, Lovie **40**
Barnes, Roosevelt "Booba" **33**
Bell, Carey **114**
Bibb, Eric **49**
Bland, Bobby **36, 113**
Bombino **112**
Broonzy, Big Bill **82**
Brown, Charles **23**
Brown, Nappy **73**
Burns, Eddie **44**
Burnside, R. L. **56**
Carr, Leroy **49**
Clark, Sharón **105**
Clarke, Kenny **27**
Collins, Albert **12**
Copeland, Johnny **110**
Copeland, Shemekia **110**
Cox, Ida **42**
Cray, Robert **30**
Crudup, Arthur **115**
Davis, Gary **41**
Davis, Guy **36**
Davis, Tyrone **54**
Dawkins, Jimmy **111**
Dixon, Willie **4**
Dorsey, Thomas **15**
Estes, Sleepy John **33**
Évora, Cesária **12, 99**
Ford, T-Model **91, 113**
Freeman, Yvette **27**
Fuller, Blind Boy **86**
Gaines, Grady **38**
Guy, Buddy **31**
Handy, W. C. **8**
Harris, Corey **39, 73**
Harris, Wynonie **102**
Hemphill, Jessie Mae **33, 59**
Holiday, Billie **1**
Hooker, John Lee **30**

Hopkins, Lightnin' 83
House, Son 8
Howlin' Wolf 9
Hunter, Alberta 42
Hurt, Mississippi John 84
Jackson, John 36
James, Elmore 114
James, Skip 38
Jefferson, Blind Lemon 81
Johnson, Buddy 36
Johnson, Lonnie 85
Johnson, Syl 97
Johnson, Tommy 106
King, B. B. 7
King, Freddie 92
Kirkland, Eddie 99
LaVette, Bettye 85
Leadbelly 82
Lipscomb, Mance 49
Little Milton 36
Little Walter 36
Magic Slim 110
Mahal, Taj 39
Martin, Sara 38
McCracklin, Jimmy 108
McGriff, Jimmy 72
McShann, Jay 110
McTell, Blind Willie 89
Memphis Slim 105
Merriweather, Big Maceo 109
Mo', Keb' 36
Moore, Johnny B. 38
Muse, Clarence Edouard 21
Neal, Raful 44
Odetta 37, 74
Owens, Jack 38
Parker, Charlie 20
Patton, Charley 107
Peebles, Ann 114
Pena, Paul 58
Perkins, Pinetop 70
Peterson, James 38
Professor Longhair 109
Rawls, Lou 17, 57
Reed, A. C. 36
Reed, Jimmy 38
Robinson, Fenton 38
Rogers, Jimmy 38
Ross, Isaiah "Doc" 40
Rush, Bobby 78
Rush, Otis 38
Seals, Son 56
Smith, Bessie 3
Smith, Clarence 113
Smith, Mamie 32
Smith, Trixie 34
Spann, Otis 107
Streeter, Sarah 45
Sumlin, Hubert 101
Sykes, Roosevelt 20
Tail Dragger 112
Tampa Red 63
Taylor, Koko 40, 80
Terry, Sonny 88
Turner, Big Joe 92
Turner, Ike 68
Walker, T-Bone 111
Wallace, Sippie 1
Washington, Dinah 22
Waters, Ethel 7
Waters, Muddy 34
Watson, Johnny "Guitar" 18
Webster, Katie 29

Wells, Junior 102
White, Josh, Jr. 52
Williams, Jody 113
Williams, Joe 5, 25
Williamson, Sonny Boy 84
Witherspoon, Jimmy 113

Blues Hall of Fame
Allison, Luther 111
Bland, Bobby 36, 113
Broonzy, Big Bill 82
Crudup, Arthur 115
Hopkins, Lightnin' 83
Hunter, Alberta 42
Hurt, Mississippi John 84
Little Milton 36
Williamson, Sonny Boy 84

Bobsledding
Flowers, Vonetta 35
Hines, Garrett 35
Jones, Randy 35
Moses, Edwin 8

Bodybuilding
Haney, Lee 77
Murray, Lenda 10

Boeing Company, The
Bell, James A. 50
Grooms, Henry R(andall) 50
Mills, Joseph C. 51
Robinson-Berry, Joan 94

Boogie-woogie music
Brooks, Hadda 40
Smith, Clarence 113

The Boondocks
McGruder, Aaron 28, 56

Boston Celtics basketball team
Allen, Ray 82
Chaney, Don 98
Cooper, Charles "Chuck" 47
Fox, Rick 27
Garnett, Kevin 14, 70
Parish, Robert 43
Pierce, Paul 71
Rivers, Doc 25, 81
Russell, Bill 8
Sanders, Satch 77
Silas, Paul 24
White, Jo Jo 112

Boston Red Sox baseball team
Baylor, Don 6
Ortiz, David 52, 82
Rice, Jim 75
Tiant, Luis 102
Vaughn, Mo 16

Botswanan government
Khama, Ian 95
Masire, Quett 5
Mogae, Festus Gontebanye 19, 79

Bowling
Branham, George, III 50
Terrell-Kearney, Kim 83

Boxing
Ali, Laila 27, 63
Ali, Muhammad 2, 16, 52

Armstrong, H, 107enry 104
Bowe, Riddick 6, 107
Bozella, Dewey 97
Broner, Adrien 109
Carter, Rubin 26
Charles, Ezzard 95
DeGale, James 74
Dixon, George 52
Dokes, Michael 105
Ellis, Jimmy 44
Foreman, George 1, 15
Forrest, Vernon 40, 79
Frazier, Joe 19, 98
Frazier-Lyde, Jacqui 31
Futch, Eddie 33
Gans, Joe 91
Gibson, Truman K., Jr. 60
Griffith, Emile 113
Hagler, Marvelous Marvin 102
Haye, David 82
Hearns, Thomas 29
Holmes, Larry 20, 68
Holyfield, Evander 6
Hopkins, Bernard 35, 69, 105
Johnson, Jack 8
Jones, Roy, Jr. 22
King, Don 14
Lee, Canada 8
Leonard, Sugar Ray 15
Lewis, Butch 71, 99
Lewis, Lennox 27
Louis, Joe 5
Mayweather, Floyd 57, 104
Moore, Davey 105
Moorer, Michael 19
Mosley, Shane 32
Muhammad, Jabir Herbert 72
Mundine, Anthony 56
Norton, Ken 101, 115
Page, Greg 78
Patterson, Floyd 19, 58
Perkins, Eddie 103
Robinson, Sugar Ray 18
Rose, Lionel 56
Savón, Félix 105
Stevenson, Teófilo 103
Steward, Emanuel 18, 106
Tate, John 107
Taylor, Jermain 60
Toney, James 89
Tyson, Mike 28, 44, 93
Walcott, Jersey Joe 102
Ward, Andre 62
Weaver, Mike 109
Whitaker, Pernell 10, 89
Wills, Harry 80
Wolfe, Ann 82
Wright, Chalky 103
Young, Jimmy 54

Boys and Girls Clubs
Brooks, Derrick 43
Gaines, Brenda 41

Boys Choir of Harlem
Turnbull, Walter 13, 60

BPP
See Black Panther Party

Brazilian government
da Silva, Benedita 5
Nascimento, Abdias do 93

Silva, Marina 80

Breast cancer awareness
Brown, Zora Kramer 12
Norton, Meredith 72
Riperton, Minnie 32

British Broadcasting Company (BBC)
Armah, Esther 87
Figueroa, John J. 40
Stuart, Moira 82

British Film Institute
Akomfrah, John 37

British government
Abbott, Diane 9
Amos, Valerie 41
Boateng, Paul Yaw 56
Grant, Bernie 57
King, Oona 27
Pitt, David Thomas 10

British Virgin Islands government
Stoutt, H. Lavity 83

Broadcasting
Allen, Byron 3, 24, 97
Ashley, Maurice 15, 47
Bettis, Jerome 64
Blackmon, Brenda 58
Bostic, Joe 95
Bradley, Ed 2, 59
Branch, William Blackwell 39
Brown, Les 5
Brown, Tony 3
Brown, Vivian 27
Brunson, Dorothy 1, 87
Clayton, Xernona 3, 45
Cornelius, Don 4, 100
Crump, Steven 96
Dee, Merri 55
Elder, Larry 25
Evans, Harry 25
Figueroa, John J. 40
Freeman, Aaron 52
Goode, Mal 13
Gumbel, Bryant 14, 80
Gumbel, Greg 8
Hall, Tamron 96
Hamblin, Ken 10
Hickman, Fred 11
Holt, Lester 66
Hunter-Gault, Charlayne 6, 31
Jackson, Hal 41, 104
Johnson, Rafer 33
Johnson, Robert L. 3, 39
Joyner, Tom 19, 90
Kellogg, Clark 64
Kennedy-Overton, Jayne Harris 46
King, Gayle 19, 99
Langhart Cohen, Janet 19, 60
Lawson, Jennifer 1, 50
Lemon, Don 94
Lewis, Delano 7
Lomax, Louis E. 90
Mabrey, Vicki 26
Madison, Joseph E. 17
McEwen, Mark 5
McFarland, Roland 49
Melton, Frank 81
Mickelbury, Penny 28
Miller, Cheryl 10, 74

Ming, Mel **106**
Mitchell, Russ **21, 73**
Morgan, Joe **9, 96**
Morton, Frederick A., Jr. **93**
Neville, Arthel **53**
Peete, Rodney **60**
Pinckney, Sandra **56**
Pinkston, W. Randall **24**
Quarles, Norma **25**
Reynolds, Star Jones **10, 27, 61**
Roberts, Deborah **35**
Roberts, Robin **16, 54, 113**
Rodgers, Johnathan **6, 51**
Rose, Jalen **108**
Russell, Bill **8**
Sanders, Deion **4, 31, 96**
Shaw, Bernard **2, 28**
Simmons, Jamal **72**
Simpson, Carole **6, 30**
Smiley, Tavis **20, 68**
Steele, Sage **115**
Stewart, Alison **13**
Swann, Lynn **28**
Syler, Rene **53**
Tirico, Mike **68**
Watts, Rolonda **9**
White, Bill **1, 48**
Williams, Armstrong **29**
Williams, Juan **35, 80**
Williams, Montel **4, 57**
Winfrey, Oprah **2, 15, 61, 106**

Broadside Press
Hoagland, Everett H. **45**
Randall, Dudley **8, 55**

Brookings Institute
Ladner, Joyce A. **42**

Brooklyn Dodgers baseball team
Black, Joe **75**
Campanella, Roy **25**
Newcombe, Don **24**
Robinson, Jackie **6**

Brotherhood of Sleeping Car Porters
Randolph, A. Philip **3**
Tucker, Rosina **14**

Brown University
Beckham, Barry **41**
Simmons, Ruth **13, 38**

Brown v. Board of Education of Topeka
Boulware, Harold R. **109**
Brown, Oliver Leon **94**
Carter, Robert L. **51, 100**
Clark, Kenneth B. **5, 52**
Franklin, John Hope **5, 77**
Henderson, Zelma **71**
Hill, Oliver W. **24, 63**
Houston, Charles Hamilton **4**
Malone Jones, Vivian **59**
Marshall, Thurgood **1, 44**
Motley, Constance Baker **10, 55**
Redding, Louis L. **26**
Robinson, Spottswood W., III **22**
Simkins, Modjeska Monteith **112**

Buffalo Bills football team
Simpson, O. J. **15, 100**
Smith, Bruce **80**

Thomas, Thurman **75**

Bull-riding
Sampson, Charles **13**

Burundian government
Ndadaye, Melchior **7**
Nkurunziza, Pierre **78**
Ntaryamira, Cyprien **8**

Busing (anti-busing legislation)
Bosley, Freeman, Jr. **7**

Cabinet
See U.S. Cabinet

Cable News Network (CNN)
Chideya, Farai **14, 61**
Hickman, Fred **11**
Malveaux, Suzanne **88**
O'Brien, Soledad **88**
Quarles, Norma **25**
Rolle, Janet **97**
Shaw, Bernard **2, 28**
Sidner, Sara **105**
Watson, Carlos **50**

Caldecott medal
Dillon, Leo **103**
Pinkney, Jerry **15**

California Angels baseball team
See Los Angeles Angels baseball team

California state government
Bass, Karen **70**
Brown, Janice Rogers **43**
Brown, Willie **7, 85**
Dixon, Julian C. **24**
Dymally, Mervyn **42**
Hawkins, Augustus F. **68**
Lee, Barbara **25, 102**
Millender-McDonald, Juanita **21, 61**
Richardson, Laura **81**
Riles, Wilson C. **79**
Waters, Maxine **3, 67, 103**
Watson, Diane **41**

California State University
Cobb, Jewel Plummer **42**
Karenga, Maulana **10, 71**

California Supreme Court
Brown, Janice Rogers **43**

Calypso
Belafonte, Harry **4, 65**
Lord Kitchener **110**
Premice, Josephine **41**
Rhoden, Wayne **70**
Rudder, David **79**

Cameroonian government
Ahidjo, Ahmadou **81**
Biya, Paul **28, 114**
Oyono, Ferdinand **38**

Canadian Football League (CFL)
Anderson, Ezzrett **95**
Clemons, Michael "Pinball" **64**
Gilliam, Frank **23**
Moon, Warren **8, 66**
Thrower, Willie **35**

Weathers, Carl **10**

Canadian government
Alexander, Lincoln **106**
Augustine, Jean **53**
Brown, Rosemary **62**
Cools, Anne **64**
Jean, Michaëlle; **70**
Lewis, Daurene **72**
Sparks, Corinne Etta **53**

Cancer research
Adams-Campbell, Lucille L. **60**
Chinn, May Edward **26**
Clark, Celeste **15**
Daly, Marie Maynard **37**
Dunston, Georgia Mae **48**
Freeman, Harold P. **23**
Leffall, Lasalle **3, 64**
Olopade, Olufunmilayo Falusi **58**

Capital punishment
Correia, De'Jaun **93**
Hawkins, Steven **14**

Caribbean dance
Ailey, Alvin **8**
Dunham, Katherine **4, 59**
Fagan, Garth **18, 98**
Nichols, Nichelle **11**
Primus, Pearl **6**

Caribbean literature/West Indian literature
Beken **111**
Breeze, Jean "Binta" **37**
Carter, Martin **49**
Cartey, Wilfred **47**
Channer, Colin **36**
Coombs, Orde M. **44**
Dabydeen, David **48**
Guy, Rosa **5**
Hearne, John Edgar Caulwell **45**
Markham, E. A. **37**
Marshall, Paule **7, 77**
McKay, Claude **6**
Nunez, Elizabeth **62, 112**
Walcott, Derek **5, 94**

Caribbean music
Ellis, Alton **74**
Ellis, Hortense **97**
Lefel, Edith **41**
Ranglin, Ernest **78**

Casting
Cannon, Reuben **50**

Cartoonists
Armstrong, Robb **15**
Bell, Darrin **77**
Brandon, Barbara **3**
Brown, Robert **65**
Campbell, E. Simms **13**
Fax, Elton **48**
Harrington, Oliver W. **9**
McDuffie, Dwayne **62**
McGruder, Aaron **28, 56**
Ormes, Jackie **73**
Smith, Bruce W. **53**

Catering
See Restaurants/Catering/Cooking

Catholicism
See Roman Catholic Church

CBC
See Congressional Black Caucus

CBS
See Columbia Broadcasting System

CDC
See Centers for Disease Control and Prevention

CDF
See Children's Defense Fund

Celebrities for a Drug-Free America
Vereen, Ben **4**

Censorship
Butts, Calvin O., III **9, 90**

Centers for Disease Control and Prevention (CDC)
Fenton, Kevin **87**
Gayle, Helene D. **3**
Satcher, David **7, 57, 111**
Wisdom, Kimberlydawn **57**

Central African Republic government
Bozizé, François **96**

Central Intercollegiate Athletic Association (CIAA)
Kerry, Leon G. **46**
Yancy, Dorothy Cowser **42**

Certified public accountant
Jones, Thomas W. **41**
Washington, Mary T. **57**

CFL
See Canadian Football League

Chadian government
Déby, Idriss **30**
Habré, Hissène **6, 104**

Chama Cha Mapinduzi (Tanzania; Revolutionary Party)
Kikwete, Jakaya Mrisho **73**
Mkapa, Benjamin W. **16, 77**
Mongella, Gertrude **11**
Mwinyi, Ali Hassan **1, 77**
Nyerere, Julius **5**

Chemistry
Brady, St. Elmo **107**
Daly, Marie Maynard **37**
Donald, Arnold Wayne **36**
Hall, Lloyd A. **8**
Haynie, Sharon **94**
Humphries, Frederick **20**
Julian, Percy Lavon **6**
King, Reatha Clark **65**
Massie, Samuel Proctor, Jr. **29**
Mays, William G. **34**
McBay, Henry C. **91**
Mensah, Thomas **48**
Quarterman, Lloyd Albert **4**

Chess
Ashley, Maurice **15, 47**

Chicago Bears football team
Dent, Richard **97**
Page, Alan **7**

Payton, Walter **11, 25**
Sayers, Gale **28**
Singletary, Mike **4, 76**
Thrower, Willie **35**

Chicago Black Arts Movement
Cortor, Eldzier **42**
Sebree, Charles **40**

Chicago Bulls basketball team
Brand, Elton **31**
Jordan, Michael **6, 21**

Chicago city government
Berry, Edwin C. **81**
De Priest, Oscar Stanton **80**
Jackson, Sandi **108**
Jones, Emil, Jr. **74**
Jones, John **89**
Kelley, Cliff **75**
Lane, Vincent **5**
Metcalfe, Ralph **26**
Sawyer, Eugene **81**
Taylor, Robert Rochon **104**
Tillman, Dorothy **76**
Washington, Harold **6**

Chicago Cubs baseball team
Banks, Ernie **33**
Bonds, Bobby **43**
Carter, Joe **30**
Sosa, Sammy **21, 44**
Williams, Billy **86**

Chicago Defender
Abbott, Robert Sengstacke **27**
Burley, Dan **96**
Holt, Nora **38**
Martin, Roland S. **49, 84**
Ormes, Jackie **73**
Payne, Ethel L. **28**

Chicago Eight
Seale, Bobby **3**

Chicago Negro Chamber of Commerce
Fuller, S. B. **13**

Chicago Police Department
Hillard, Terry **25**
Holton, Hugh, Jr. **39**

Chicago Reporter
Calhoun, Lillian Scott **87**
Washington, Laura S. **18**

Chicago Tribune
Page, Clarence **4**

Chicago White Sox baseball team
Baines, Harold **32**
Bonds, Bobby **43**
Doby, Lawrence Eugene, Sr. **16, 41**
Johnson, Clifford "Connie" **52**
Thomas, Frank **12, 51**
Williams, Ken **68**

Child care
Tillman, Deborah **98**

Children's Defense Fund (CDF)
Edelman, Marian Wright **5, 42**
Williams, Maggie **7, 71**

Children's literature
Asim, Jabari **71**
Berry, James **41**
Bryan, Ashley **41, 104**
Curtis, Christopher Paul **26, 113**
De Veaux, Alexis **44**
Feelings, Muriel **44**
Graham, Lorenz **48**
Greenfield, Eloise **9**
Haskins, James **36, 54**
Johnson, Angela **52**
Jordan, Deloris **108**
Lester, Julius **9, 115**
Mollel, Tololwa **38**
Myers, Walter Dean **8, 20**
Nelson, Kadir **115**
Okara, Gabriel **37**
Palmer, Everard **37**
Shelton, Paula Young **86**
Yarbrough, Camille **40**

Chi-Lites
Record, Eugene **60**

Chiropractics
Ford, Clyde W. **40**
Reese, Milous J., Jr. **51**
Westbrooks, Bobby **51**

Choreography
Acogny, Germaine **55**
Ailey, Alvin **8**
Alexander, Khandi **43**
Allen, Debbie **13, 42**
Atkins, Cholly **40**
Babatunde, Obba **35**
Beatty, Talley **35**
Brown, Ronald K. **91**
Byrd, Donald **10**
Collins, Janet **33, 64**
Davis, Chuck **33**
de Lavallade, Carmen **78**
de Passe, Suzanne **25**
De Shields, André **72**
Dove, Ulysses **5**
Dunham, Katherine **4, 59**
Ellington, Mercedes **34**
Fagan, Garth **18, 98**
Faison, George **16**
Glover, Savion **14**
Hall, Arthur **39**
Henson, Darrin **33**
Jamison, Judith **7, 67, 96**
Jeune, Vitolio **98**
Johnson, Virginia **9**
Jones, Bill T. **1, 46, 80**
King, Alonzo **38**
LeTang, Henry **66**
Manning, Frankie **78**
Miller, Bebe **3**
Mitchell, Arthur **2, 47**
Nicholas, Fayard **20, 57**
Nicholas, Harold **20**
Pomare, Eleo **72**
Primus, Pearl **6**
Rhoden, Dwight **40**
Richardson, Desmond **39**
Robinson, Cleo Parker **38**
Robinson, Fatima **34**
Rodgers, Rod **36**
Spears, Warren **52**
Tyson, Andre **40**

Zollar, Jawole **28**

Chrysler Corporation
Colbert, Virgis William **17**
Farmer, Forest **1**
Gilles, Ralph **61**
Richie, Leroy C. **18**

Church of God in Christ
Blake, Charles E. **82**
Franklin, Robert M. **13**
Hayes, James C. **10**
Patterson, Gilbert Earl **41**
Yearwood, Lennox, Jr. **112**

CIAA
See Central Intercollegiate Athletic Association

Cincinnati city government
Berry, Theodore M. **31**
Mallory, Mark **62**

Cincinnati Reds baseball team
Blair, Paul **36**
Larkin, Barry **24**
Morgan, Joe **9, 96**
Reese, Pokey **28**
Robinson, Frank **9, 87**

Cinematography
Dickerson, Ernest **6, 17**

Circus
Iverson, Johnathan Lee **22, 100**
McFarlan, Tyron **60**
Walker, Cedric "Ricky" **19**

Citigroup
Gaines, Brenda **41**
Jones, Thomas W. **41**
McGuire, Raymond J. **57**

City government--U.S.
Bell, Michael **40**
Bellamy, Terry **58**
Benjamin, Steve **98**
Bobb, Robert C. **83**
Bradley, Jennette B. **40**
Brown, Aja **115**
Brown, Alvin **96**
Brown, Willie **7, 85**
Burris, Chuck **21**
Bush, Gordon **82**
Caesar, Shirley **19**
Celestin, Josaphat **101**
Clayton, Constance **1**
Cleaver, Emanuel **4, 45, 68, 107**
Coleman, Michael **28, 79**
Craig-Jones, Ellen Walker **44**
Davis, Doris A. **100**
Dellums, Ronald **2, 81**
DuPree, Johnny **96**
Ford, Jack **39**
Ford, Johnny **70**
Foxx, Anthony **81**
Francois, Terry A. **106**
Gibbs, Mifflin W. **99**
Glover, Cedric B. **103**
Hatcher, Richard G. **55**
Hayes, James C. **10**
Herenton, Willie W. **24, 81**
James, Sly **107**
Johnson, Harvey, Jr. **24, 82**
Love, Mia **96**
Lowery, Myron **80**

Mack, Tony **104**
Mallett, Conrad, Jr. **16**
Marsh, Henry **32**
McPhail, Sharon **2**
Melton, Frank **81**
Morial, Ernest "Dutch" **26**
Morial, Marc H. **20, 51**
Murrell, Sylvia Marilyn **49**
Parker, Vernon **97**
Patterson, J. O., Jr. **80**
Perkins, James, Jr. **55**
Powell, Adam Clayton, Jr. **3**
Powell, Debra A. **23**
Primas, Randy **106**
Redd, Dana **93**
Usry, James L. **23**
Wharton, A. C., Jr. **110**
Widener, Warren **99**
Wilson, Lionel **99**

Civil rights
Abbott, Diane **9**
Abernathy, Ralph **1**
Agyeman, Jaramogi Abebe **10, 63**
Al-Amin, Jamil Abdullah **6**
Alexander, Clifford **26**
Alexander, Michelle **98**
Amaker, Norman **63**
Angelou, Maya **1, 15**
Anthony, Wendell **25**
Aristide, Jean-Bertrand **6, 45**
Arnwine, Barbara **28**
Baker, Ella **5**
Baker, Josephine **3**
Ballance, Frank W. **41**
Ballard, John **95**
Barbee, Lloyd Augustus **71**
Barrow, Willie T. **85**
Bashir, Halima **73**
Bass, Charlotta Spears **40**
Bates, Daisy **13**
Baugh, David **23**
Beals, Melba Pattillo **15, 94**
Bell, James Madison **40**
Berry, Theodore M. **31**
Bevel, James L. **75**
Biko, Steven **4**
Bond, Julian **2, 35, 106**
Booker, Simeon **23**
Borders, William Holmes **94**
Boyd, John W., Jr. **20, 72**
Bradle, David Henry, Jr. **39**
Bridges, Ruby **77**
Brock, Roslyn McCallister **86**
Brooks, Tyrone **59**
Brown, Byrd **49**
Brown, Charlotte Hawkins **106**
Brown, Elaine **8**
Brown, Homer S. **47**
Brown, Tony **3**
Brown, Wesley **23**
Brown, Willa **40**
Burks, Mary Fair **40**
Caldwell, Earl **60**
Cameron, James **80**
Carmichael, Stokely **5, 26**
Carr, Johnnie **69**
Carter, Mandy **11**
Carter, Rubin **26**
Cary, Mary Ann Shadd **30**
Catto, Octavius V. **83**
Cayton, Horace **26**
Chambers, Julius **3**

Chavis, Benjamin **6**
Chestnut, J. L., Jr. **73**
Clark, Septima **7**
Clay, William Lacy **8**
Cleaver, Eldridge **5**
Cleaver, Kathleen Neal **29**
Clyburn, James E. **21, 71**
Cobb, W. Montague **39**
Cobbs, Price M. **9**
Coleman, James E., Jr. **79**
Cooper, Anna Julia **20**
Cunningham, Evelyn **23, 85**
Davis, Angela **5, 114**
Davis, Artur **41**
Davis, James E. **50**
Dent, Thomas C. **50**
Diallo, Amadou **27**
Diggs, Charles C. **21**
Divine, Father **7**
Dobbs, John Wesley **89**
Dodson, Howard, Jr. **7, 52**
Douglass, Frederick **87**
Du Bois, W. E. B. **3**
Dudley, Edward R. **58**
Due, Patricia Stephens **100**
Dukes, Hazel Nell **56**
Dumas, Henry **41**
Eagleson, William Lewis **90**
Edwards, Willis **104**
Ellison, Ralph **7**
Evers, Medgar **3**
Evers, Myrlie **8**
Farmer, James **2, 64**
Farmer-Paellmann, Deadria **43**
Fisher, Ada Lois Sipuel **76**
Forman, James **7, 51**
Fortune, T. Thomas **6**
Foster, Marie **48**
Franklin, C. L. **68**
French, D. M. **94**
Gaines, Ernest J. **7**
Gaines, Lloyd **79**
Gibson, William F. **6**
Gomillion, Charles **90**
Granger, Lester B. **75**
Gray, Fred **37**
Gregory, Dick **1, 54**
Grillo, Evelio **95**
Grimké, Archibald H. **9**
Guinier, Lani **7, 30**
Guyot, Lawrence **108**
Haley, George Williford Boyce **21**
Hall, Elliott S. **24**
Hamer, Fannie Lou **6**
Hampton, Fred **18**
Hampton, Henry **6**
Harding, Vincent **67**
Harper, Frances Ellen Watkins **11**
Harris, Patricia Roberts **2**
Hastie, William H. **8**
Hatcher, Richard G. **55**
Hawkins, Augustus F. **68**
Hawkins, Steven **14**
Hayes, Dennis **54**
Hedgeman, Anna Arnold **22**
Height, Dorothy I. **2, 23, 78**
Henderson, Thelton E. **68**
Henry, Aaron **19**
Higginbotham, A. Leon, Jr. **13, 25**
Hill, Jesse, Jr. **13**
Hill, Oliver W. **24, 63**
Hilliard, David **7, 105**
Hobson, Julius W. **44**

Holland, Endesha Ida Mae **3, 57**
Hollowell, Donald L. **57**
Hooks, Benjamin L. **2, 85**
Hope, Lugenia Burns **89**
Houston, Charles Hamilton **4**
Howard, M. William, Jr. **26**
Irvis, K. Leroy **67**
Jackson, Alexine Clement **22**
Jackson, Jesse **1, 27, 72**
James, Daniel, Jr. **16**
Jarrett, Vernon D. **42**
Jenkins, Ray **77**
Johns, Vernon **38**
Johnson, Georgia Douglas **41**
Johnson, James Weldon **5**
Johnson, Norma H. **17, 97**
Jones, Clarence B. **114**
Jones, Elaine R. **7, 45**
Jones, John **89**
Jones, William A., Jr. **61**
Jordan, Barbara **4, 78**
Jordan, June **7, 35**
Jordan, Vernon E. **3, 35**
Julian, Percy Lavon **6**
Karim, Benjamin **61**
Kennedy, Florynce **12, 33**
Kenyatta, Jomo **5**
Kidd, Mae Street **39**
King, Bernice **4, 81**
King, Coretta Scott **3, 57**
King, Martin Luther, III **20**
King, Martin Luther, Jr. **1**
King, Martin Luther, Sr. **89**
King, Preston **28**
King, Robert Hillary **84**
King, Rodney **103**
King, Yolanda **6**
Ladner, Joyce A. **42**
Lampkin, Daisy **19**
Lawson, James M., Jr. **90**
Lewis, William Henry **89**
Logan, Rayford W. **40**
Louis, Willie **113**
Loving, Mildred **69**
Lowery, Evelyn Gibson **115**
Lowery, Joseph **2**
Lowry, A. Leon **60**
Lucy Foster, Autherine **35**
Luper, Clara **94**
Madikizela-Mandela, Winnie **2, 35, 112**
Makeba, Miriam **2, 50, 74**
Malone Jones, Vivian **59**
Mandela, Nelson **1, 14, 77**
Martin, Louis E. **16**
Martin, Ruby Grant **49**
Mays, Benjamin E. **7**
Mbeki, Thabo **14, 73**
McDonald, Gabrielle Kirk **20**
McDougall, Gay J. **11, 43**
McKissick, Floyd B. **3**
Meredith, James H. **11**
Metcalfe, Ralph **26**
Miller, Clyde **113**
Mitchell, Clarence M., Jr. **88**
Morgan, Irene **65**
Moore, Barbara C. **49**
Moore, Harry T. **29**
Morial, Ernest "Dutch" **26**
Moses, Robert Parris **11**
Moss, Otis, Jr. **72**
Motley, Constance Baker **10, 55**
Mowry, Jess **7**

Murphy, Laura M. **43**
Murray, Pauli **38**
Nash, Diane **72**
Ndadaye, Melchior **7**
Nelson, Jill **6, 54**
Newton, Huey **2**
Nixon, Edgar Daniel **100**
Nkoli, Simon **60**
Nkomo, Joshua **4, 65**
Noble, Gil **76**
Nunn, Annetta **43**
Nzo, Alfred **15**
Orange, James **74**
Parker, Kellis E. **30**
Parks, Rosa **1, 35, 56**
Patrick, Deval **12, 61**
Patterson, Louise **25**
Patterson, Orlando **4**
Perry, Matthew J., Jr. **96**
Pincham, R. Eugene, Sr. **69**
Pinchback, P. B. S. **9**
Player, Willa B. **43**
Pleasant, Mary Ellen **9**
Plessy, Homer Adolph **31**
Poitier, Sidney **11, 36**
Powell, Adam Clayton, Jr. **3**
Price, Hugh B. **9, 54**
Ramaphosa, Cyril **3**
Randolph, A. Philip **3**
Redding, Louis L. **26**
Rivers, Eugene F., III **81**
Robeson, Paul **2**
Robinson, Jackie **6**
Robinson, Joann Gibson **100**
Robinson, Rachel **16**
Robinson, Randall **7, 46**
Robinson, Sharon **22**
Robinson, Spottswood W., III **22**
Roundtree, Dovey **80**
Rush, Bobby **26, 76**
Rustin, Bayard **4**
Sadlier, Rosemary **62**
Sanders, Malika **48**
Sané, Pierre Gabriel **21**
Saro-Wiwa, Kenule **39**
Seale, Bobby **3**
Shabazz, Attallah **6**
Shabazz, Betty **7, 26**
Shakur, Assata **6**
Sharpton, Al **21, 97**
Shelton, Paula Young **86**
Shinhoster, Earl **32**
Shores, Arthur D. **99**
Shuttlesworth, Fred **47, 98**
Simkins, Modjeska Monteith **112**
Simon, Lateefah **95**
Simone, Nina **15, 41**
Sisulu, Albertina **57, 95**
Sisulu, Sheila Violet Makate **24**
Sleet, Moneta, Jr. **5**
Smith, Barbara **28**
Staupers, Mabel K. **7**
Sullivan, Leon H. **3, 30**
Sutton, Percy E. **42, 82**
Sweet, Ossian **68**
Taylor, Recy **92**
Taylor, Robert Rochon **104**
Thompson, Bennie G. **26**
Thurman, Howard **3**
Till, Emmett **7**
Tillman, Dorothy **76**
Tolson, Melvin B. **37**
Touré, Faya Ora Rose **56**

Trotter, Monroe **9**
Tsvangirai, Morgan **26, 72**
Turner, Henry McNeal **5**
Walker, Rebecca **50**
Washington, Booker T. **4**
Washington, Fredi **10**
Weaver, Robert C. **8, 46**
Webb-Christburg, Sheyann **110**
Wells, James Lesesne **10**
Wells-Barnett, Ida B. **8**
White, Walter F. **4**
Whitmore, George **106**
Wilkins, Roy **4**
Williams, Evelyn **10**
Williams, Fannie Barrier **27**
Williams, Hosea Lorenzo **15, 31**
Williams, Robert F. **11**
Williams, Walter E. **4**
Wilson, William Julius **22**
Woods, Abraham, Jr. **74**
Woodson, Robert L. **10**
Wright, Nathan, Jr. **56**
X, Malcolm **1**
Yoba, Malik **11**
Young, Jean Childs **14**
Young, Whitney M., Jr. **4**

Clarinet
Bechet, Sidney **18**
McGill, Anthony **76**

Classical music
Abdullah, Kazem **97**
Adams, Leslie **39**
Baiocchi, Regina Harris **41**
Bonds, Margaret **39**
Brown, Uzee **42**
Burleigh, Henry Thacker **56**
Coleridge-Taylor, Samuel **75**
Cook, Will Marion **40**
Dawson, William Levi **39**
DePreist, James **37, 109**
Dixon, Dean **68**
Dunner, Leslie B. **45**
Fox, Donal **114**
Freeman, Paul **39**
Imani Winds **113**
Kay, Ulysses **37**
Lewis, Henry **38**
Marian Anderson String Quartet **111**
McFerrin, Bobby **68**
McGill, Anthony **76**
Moore, Dorothy Rudd **46**
Murray, Tai **47**
Pratt, Awadagin **31**
Price, Florence **37**
Schuyler, Philippa **50**
Sowande, Fela **39**
Still, William Grant **37**
Tillis, Frederick **40**
Walker, George **37**
Wilkins, Thomas Alphonso **71**
Williams, Denise **40**

Classical singers
Anderson, Marian **2, 33**
Battle, Kathleen **70**
Bumbry, Grace **5**
Burleigh, Henry Thacker **56**
Hayes, Roland **4**
Hendricks, Barbara **3, 67**
Lister, Marquita **65**
Norman, Jessye **5**
Price, Leontyne **1**

Three Mo' Tenors **35**
Williams, Denise **40**

Cleo Parker Robinson Dance Ensemble
Robinson, Cleo Parker **38**

Clergy
Abune Paulos **105**
Agyeman, Jaramogi Abebe **10, 63**
Anthony, Wendell **25**
Baker, Delbert W. **110**
Bell, Ralph S. **5**
Ben-Israel, Ben Ami **11**
Berry, Moses **84**
Black, Barry C. **47**
Bloomer, George **86**
Bowen, John W. E., Sr. **89**
Burgess, John **46**
Bynum, Juanita **31, 71**
Caesar, Shirley **19**
Caldwell, Kirbyjon **55**
Cleveland, James **19**
Cook, Suzan D. Johnson **22**
Crowdy, William Saunders **109**
Dollar, Creflo **106**
Dyson, Michael Eric **11, 40**
Easton, Hosea **91**
Ellis, Charles H., III **79**
Falana, Lola **42**
Gilmore, Marshall **46**
Grace, Sweet Daddy **104**
Gregory, Wilton **37**
Henson, Josiah **90**
Holsey, Lucius Henry **92**
Hood, James Walker **91**
Howard, M. William, Jr. **26**
Jakes, Thomas "T. D." **17, 43**
James, Skip **38**
Jemison, Major L. **48**
Johns, Vernon **38**
Jones, Absalom **52**
Jones, Alex **64**
Jones, Robert Elijah **90**
Jones, William A., Jr. **61**
Karim, Benjamin **61**
Kee, John P. **43**
Kelly, Leontine **33**
King, Barbara **22**
King, Bernice **4, 81**
Kobia, Samuel **43**
Lee, Eric P. **79**
Lincoln, C. Eric **38**
Maxis, Theresa **62**
McClurkin, Donnie **25**
McGuire, George Alexander **80**
McKenzie, Vashti M. **29**
Michaux, Solomon Lightfoot **91**
Morgan, Gertrude **63**
Noble Drew Ali **100**
Okaalet, Peter **58**
Otunga, Maurice Michael **55**
Peterson, Jesse Lee **81**
Phipps, Wintley **59**
Reems, Ernestine Cleveland **27**
Reese, Della **6, 20, 96**
Reverend Ike **79**
Robinson, Ida B. **106**
Sentamu, John **58**
Smith, Amanda Berry **109**
Taylor, Gardner C. **76**
Thurman, Howard **3**
Thurston, Stephen J. **49**

Tillard, Conrad **47**
Tolton, Augustine **62**
Ukpabio, Helen **86**
Walker, John T. **50**
Washington, James Melvin **50**
Watkins, Joe **86**
Weeks, Thomas, III **70**
Weems, Renita J. **44**
White-Hammond, Gloria **61**
Williams, David Rudyard **50**
Williams, Frederick (B.) **63**
Williams, Preston Warren, II **64**
Winans, Marvin L. **17**
Wright, Nathan, Jr. **56**

Cleveland Browns football team
Brown, Jim **11, 95**
Hill, Calvin **19**
Motley, Marion **26**
Newsome, Ozzie **26**
Willis, Bill **68**

Cleveland city government
Jackson, Frank G. **76**
Stokes, Carl **10, 73**
White, Michael R. **5**

Cleveland Foundation
Adams, Leslie **39**

Cleveland Indians baseball team
Belle, Albert **10**
Bonds, Bobby **43**
Carter, Joe **30**
Doby, Lawrence Eugene, Sr. **16, 41**
Justice, David **18**
Lofton, Kenny **12**
Murray, Eddie **12**
Paige, Satchel **7**
Robinson, Frank **9, 87**
Sabathia, CC **74**
Sizemore, Grady **96**

CLIO Awards
Lewis, Emmanuel **36**

Clothing design
Aberra, Amsale **67**
Bailey, Xenobia **11**
Bonney, Tabi **98**
Burrows, Stephen **31**
Gaskins, Eric **64**
Henderson, Gordon **5**
Jones, Carl **7**
Kani, Karl **10**
Kelly, Patrick **3**
Lars, Byron **32**
Malone, Maurice **32**
Pinkett Smith, Jada **10, 41, 95**
Robinson, Patrick **19, 71**
Smith, Willi **8**
Walker, T. J. **7**
Williams, Serena **20, 41, 73**

CNBC
Epperson, Sharon **54**
Thomas-Graham, Pamela **29**

CNN
See Cable News Network

Coaching
Amaker, Tommy **62**
Anderson, Mike **63**

Ashley, Maurice **15, 47**
Baker, Dusty **8, 43, 72, 110**
Baylor, Don **6**
Bickerstaff, Bernie **21**
Bonds, Bobby **43**
Brown, Mike **77, 107**
Caldwell, Jim **81**
Campanella, Roy **25**
Carew, Rod **20**
Carter, Butch **27**
Carter, Kenneth **53**
Chaney, Don **98**
Chaney, John **67**
Cheeks, Maurice **47, 106**
Cooper, Michael **31**
Cox, Bryan **83**
Crennel, Romeo **54, 107**
Curry, Michael **85**
Davis, Mike **41**
Dorrell, Karl **52**
Dungy, Tony **17, 42, 59**
Dunn, Jerry **27**
Edwards, Herman **51**
Ellerbe, Brian **22**
Freeman, Marianna **23**
Gaines, Clarence E., Sr. **55**
Gaither, Alonzo Smith (Jake) **14**
Gaston, Cito **71**
Gates, William **97**
Gentry, Alvin **23**
Gibson, Althea **8, 43**
Gibson, Bob **33**
Gill, Turner **83**
Gorden, W. C. **71**
Graham, Trevor **84**
Gray, Yeshimbra "Shimmy" **55**
Green, Dennis **5, 45**
Greene, Joe **10**
Hamilton, Leonard **100**
Hart, Thomas A., Sr. **113**
Haskins, Clem **23**
Hazzard, Walt **98**
Heard, Gar **25**
Johnson, Avery **62**
Jordan, Eddie **83**
Joyce, Dru **81**
Kearney, Beverly **109**
Keith, Floyd A. **61**
Lewis, Marvin **51, 87**
Lofton, James **42**
Manuel, Jerry **94**
Miller, Cheryl **10, 74**
Mitchell, Sam **82**
Morris, Raheem **77**
O'Neil, Buck **19, 59**
Parish, Robert **43**
Phillips, Teresa L. **42**
Rhodes, Ray **14**
Richardson, Nolan **9**
Rivers, Doc **25, 81**
Robinson, Craig **107**
Robinson, Eddie G. **10, 61**
Robinson, Frank **9, 87**
Robinson, Will **51, 69**
Russell, Bill **8**
Sanders, Satch **77**
Shannon, Randy **82**
Shell, Art **1, 66**
Silas, Paul **24**
Simmons, Bob **29**
Singletary, Mike **4, 76**
Smith, Lovie **66, 107**
Smith, Tubby **18, 83**

Stringer, C. Vivian **13, 66**
Thomas, Emmitt **71**
Tunnell, Emlen **54**
White, Frank **95**
White, Jesse **22, 75**
Whitney, Davey L. **110**
Williams, Doug **22, 112**
Willingham, Tyrone **43**
Wills, Maury **73**

Coca-Cola Company
Llewellyn, J. Bruce **13, 85**
Ware, Carl T. **30**

Coca-Cola Foundation
Jones, Ingrid Saunders **18**

Collage
Andrews, Benny **22, 59**
Bearden, Romare **2, 50**
Bradford, Mark **89**
Driskell, David C. **7**
Pindell, Howardena **55**
Pinder, Jefferson **77**
Robinson, Aminah **50**
Saar, Betye **80**
Thomas, Mickalene **61**
Verna, Gelsy **70**

College and university administration
Abercrumbie, P. Eric **95**
Ammons, James H. **81**
Archie-Hudson, Marguerite **44**
Austin, Bobby W. **95**
Awuah, Patrick **111**
Baker, Delbert W. **110**
Ballard, Allen Butler, Jr. **40**
Barnett, Marguerite **46**
Becton, Julius W., Jr. **110**
Bromery, Randolph Wilson **85**
Burnim, Mickey L. **48**
Christian, Barbara T. **44**
Cole, Johnnetta B. **5, 43**
Cook, Samuel DuBois **14**
Crew, Rudy **16, 113**
Cross, Dolores E. **23**
Davis, Erroll B., Jr. **57**
Dogan, Matthew Winifred **91**
Favors, Steve **23**
Floyd, Elson S. **41**
Ford, Nick Aaron **44**
Francis, Norman (C.) **60**
Gilbert, John Wesley **91**
Harvey, William R. **42**
Hill, Leslie Pinckney **44**
Hogan, Beverly Wade **50**
Horne, Frank **44**
Jackson, Edison O. **67**
King, Reatha Clark **65**
Lee, Joe A. **45**
Lewis, Shirley A. R. **14**
Lomax, Michael L. **58**
Lyons, James E., Sr. **102**
Mason, Ronald **27**
Massey, Walter E. **5, 45**
Maupin, John E., Jr. **92**
Mell, Patricia **49**
Moody-Adams, Michele **76**
Morón, Alonzo G. **91**
Nance, Cynthia **71**
Newman, Lester C. **51**
Page, Inman **82**
Pollard, William L. **91**

Reaves, Donald J. 102
Ribeau, Sidney 70
Sizemore, Barbara A. 26, 110
Trueheart, William E. 49

Colorado Rockies baseball team
Baylor, Don 6

Colorado state government
Brown, George Leslie 62
Buckley, Victoria (Vikki) 24
Groff, Peter 96
Rogers, Joe 27

Columbia Broadcasting System (CBS)
Bradley, Ed 2, 59
Kellogg, Clark 64
Mabrey, Vicki 26
McEwen, Mark 5
Mitchell, Russ 21, 73
Olden, Georg(e) 44
Pinkston, W. Randall 24
Pitts, Byron 71
Rodgers, Johnathan 6, 51
Ware, Andre 37

Columbia Records
Jackson, Randy 40
Knowles, Tina 61
Olatunji, Babatunde 36
Williams, Deniece 36

Columbia University
Huggins, Nathan Irvin 52
Joseph, Jamal 101
Marable, Manning 10, 102
Moody-Adams, Michele 76
Steele, Claude 13, 97

Comedy
Allen, Byron 3, 24, 97
Amos, John 8, 62
Anderson, Anthony 51, 77
Anderson, Eddie "Rochester" 30
Anthony, Trey 63
Arnez J 53
Beaton, Norman 14
Bell, W. Kamau 107
Bellamy, Bill 12
Berry, Bertice 8, 55
Brady, Wayne 32, 71
Bruce, Bruce 56
Buress, Hannibal 101
Cannon, Nick 47, 73
Cedric the Entertainer 29, 60, 115
Cenac, Wyatt 94
Chappelle, Dave 50, 115
Cosby, Bill 7, 26, 59
Curry, Mark 17
Davidson, Tommy 21
Davis, Sammy, Jr. 18
Dieudonné 67
Earthquake 55
Epps, Mike 60
Foxx, Jamie 15, 48
Foxx, Redd 2
Freeman, Aaron 52
Givens, Adele 62
Glover, Donald 85
Goldberg, Whoopi 4, 33, 69
Harris, Robin 7
Hart, Kevin 103
Harvey, Steve 18, 58

Henry, Lenny 9, 52
Hughley, D. L. 23, 76
Key & Peele 107
Kirby, George 14
Lawrence, Martin 6, 27, 60
Love, Loni 113
Mabley, Jackie "Moms" 15
Mac, Bernie 29, 61, 72
Markham, Pigmeat 106
Mayo, Whitman 32
McEwen, Mark 5
Meadows, Tim 30
Mooney, Paul 37
Morgan, Tracy 61, 102
Morris, Garrett 31
Moss, Preacher 63
Murphy, Charles 95
Murphy, Eddie 4, 20, 61
Nash, Niecy 66, 115
O'Neal, Patrice 99
Powell, Keith 101
Pryor, Richard 3, 24, 56
Robinson, Craig 103
Rock, Chris 3, 22, 66
Rock, Tony 108
Russell, Nipsey 66
Schultz, Michael A. 6
Slocumb, Jonathan 52
Smiley, Rickey 59
Sommore 61
Stickney, Phyllis Yvonne 108
Sykes, Wanda 48, 81
Thompson, Kenan 52
Thurston, Baratunde 79, 101
Torry, Guy 31
Townsend, Robert 4, 23
Tucker, Chris 13, 23, 62
Tyler, Aisha N. 36
Watts, Reggie 52, 102
Wayans, Damon 8, 41
Wayans, Keenen Ivory 18
Wayans, Kim 80
Wayans, Marlon 29, 82
Wayans, Shawn 29
Wilson, Debra 38
Wilson, Flip 21
Witherspoon, John 38
Yarbrough, Cedric 51

Comerica Bank
Forte, Linda Diane 54

Commercial art
Freeman, Leonard 27

Communist Party
Brown, Lloyd Louis 42
Davis, Angela 5, 114
Herndon, Angelo 90
Patterson, Louise 25
Wright, Richard 5

Community activism
Brazier, Arthur M. 115
Buery, Richard, Jr. 97
Harden, Monique 97
Kimbro, Warren 76
Matthews, Ameena 105
Rowe-Adams, Jackie 109
Shakur, Yusef 85
Simon, Lateefah 95
Watkins, Ted 104

Yearwood, Lennox, Jr. 112

Computer graphics
Coleman, Ken 57
Hannah, Marc 10

Computer science
Adkins, Rod 41
Auguste, Donna 29
Dean, Mark 35
Easley, Annie J. 61
Ellis, Clarence 38
Emeagwali, Philip 30
Irvin, Vernon 65
Laryea, Thomas Davies, III 67
Mensah, Thomas 48
Millines Dziko, Trish 28
Zollar, Alfred 40

Conceptual art
Allen, Tina 22, 75
Bailey, Xenobia 11
Blanco, Mykki 106
Cortez, Jayne 43, 109
Harris, Lyle Ashton 83
London, Theophilus 95
O'Grady, Lorraine 73
Piper, Adrian 71
Pope.L, William 72
Robinson, Aminah 50
Scott, Dread 106
Shonibare, Yinka 58
Simpson, Lorna 4, 36

Conductors
Abdullah, Kazem 97
Calloway, Blanche 100
Calloway, Cab 14
Cook, Will Marion 40
Dawson, William Levi 39
DePreist, James 37, 109
Dixon, Dean 68
Dunner, Leslie B. 45
Foster, William P. 88
Freeman, Paul 39
Hairston, Jester 88
Jackson, Isaiah 3
León, Tania 13
Lewis, Henry 38

Congolese government (Democratic Republic of the Congo)
Kabila, Joseph 30
Kabila, Laurent 20
Mobutu Sese Seko 1, 56

Congolese government (Republic of the Congo)
Lumumba, Patrice 33
Sassou-Nguesso, Denis 103

Congress of Racial Equality (CORE)
Farmer, James 2, 64
Hobson, Julius W. 44
Innis, Roy 5
Jackson, Jesse 1, 27, 72
McKissick, Floyd B. 3
Rustin, Bayard 4

Congressional Black Caucus (CBC)
Christian-Green, Donna M. 17
Clay, William Lacy 8

Clay, William Lacy, Jr. 95
Clyburn, James E. 21, 71
Collins, Cardiss 10, 80
Cummings, Elijah E. 24, 102
Dellums, Ronald 2, 81
Diggs, Charles C. 21
Fauntroy, Walter E. 11
Gray, William H., III 3
Hastings, Alcee L. 16
Hawkins, Augustus F. 68
Johnson, Eddie Bernice 8, 90
Leland, Mickey 2
Mfume, Kweisi 6, 41
Mitchell, Parren J. 42, 66
Owens, Major 6
Payton, John 48
Rangel, Charles B. 3, 52, 85
Scott, Robert C. 23
Stokes, Louis 3
Thompson, Bennie G. 26
Towns, Edolphus 19, 75

Construction industry
Bennett, Richard 97
Russell, Herman Jerome 17

Contemporary Christian music
Baraka, Sho 109
Griffin, LaShell 51
Lecrae 108
Tait, Michael 57

Continental Basketball Association (CBA)
Davis, Mike 41
Thomas, Isiah 7, 26, 65
Ussery, Terdema, II 29

Cooking
See Restaurants/Catering/Cooking

CORE
See Congress of Racial Equality

Coretta Scott King Awards
Bryan, Ashley 41, 104
Clifton, Lucille 14, 64, 91
Curtis, Christopher Paul 26, 113
Dillon, Leo 103
Draper, Sharon Mills 16, 43
Fax, Elton 48
Greenfield, Eloise 9
Hamilton, Virginia 10
Haskins, James 36, 54
Johnson, Angela 52
Lester, Julius 9, 115
Morrison, Toni 2, 15, 86
Nelson, Kadir 115
Rollins, Charlemae Hill 27
Taylor, Mildred D. 26

Coronet
Oliver, Joe "King" 42

Corporate executive
Adams, Eula L. 39
Brewer, Rosalind 100
Coleman, Ken 57
Cottrell, Comer 11
Dortch, Thomas W., Jr. 45
Frazier, Kenneth 97
Hannah, Marc 10
Hill, Wyllstyne D. 94
Jackson, Mannie 14

James, Donna A. **51**
Johnson, George E. **29**
Knowling, Robert **38**
Lewis, William M., Jr. **40**
Lewis-Hall, Freda **105**
Mays, Leslie A. **41**
Ogunlesi, Adebayo **37**
Phillips, Charles E., Jr. **57, 109**
Rand, A. Barry **6**
Scott, Milton **51**
Siméus, Dumas M. **25, 110**
Smith, Joshua **10**
Thompson, Cynthia Bramlett **50**
Walker, Joseph Edison **111**
Westbrook, Kelvin **50**

Corporation for Public Broadcasting (CPB)
Brown, Tony **3**

Cosmetology
Cottrell, Comer **11**
Fuller, S. B. **13**
McGrath, Pat **72**
Morgan, Rose **11**
Powell, Maxine **8, 115**
Roche, Joyce M. **17**
Walker, A'lelia **14**
Walker, Madame C. J. **7**

Council on Legal Education Opportunities (CLEO)
Henderson, Wade J. **14**
Henry, Aaron **19**

Count Basie Orchestra
Count Basie **23**
Dickenson, Vic **38**
Eldridge, Roy **37**
Foster, Frank **97**
Jacquet, Illinois **49**
Johnson, J. J. **37**
Jones, Papa Jo **99**
Jones, Thad **68**
Powell, Benny **87**
Rushing, Jimmy **37**
Terry, Clark **39**
Williams, Joe **5, 25**
Young, Lester **37**

Country music
Bailey, DeFord **33**
Carolina Chocolate Drops **111**
Cowboy Troy **54**
Gray, Dobie **99**
Palmer, Rissi **65**
Pride, Charley **26**
Randall, Alice **38**
Rucker, Darius **34, 74, 108**

Cowboys
Love, Nat **9**
Pickett, Bill **11**

CPB
See Corporation for Public Broadcasting

Craftwork
Hill, Peter **92**

Creative Artists Agency
Nelson Meigs, Andrea **48**

Creole music
Ardoin, Alphonse **65**

Cricket
Adams, Paul **50**

Critical race theory
Crenshaw, Kimberlé Williams **88**
Williams, Patricia **11, 54**

Crusader
Williams, Robert F. **11**

Cuban League
Charleston, Oscar **39**
Day, Leon **39**

Cuban military
Maceo, Antonio **82**

Cuban music
Ferrer, Ibrahim **41**
Portuondo, Omara **53**
Valdés, Bebo **75**
Valdés, Chucho **89**

Cubism
Bearden, Romare **2, 50**
Green, Jonathan **54**

Culinary arts
Allen, Eugene **79**
Brown, Warren **61**
Calabrese, Karyn **89**
Chase, Leah **57**
Clark, Patrick **14**
Estes, Rufus **29**
Evans, Darryl **22**
Garvin, Gerry **78**
Henderson, Jeff **72**
Ouattara, Morou **74**
Samuelsson, Marcus **53**
Sasser, Sean **113**

Cultural pluralism
Locke, Alain **10**
Vega, Marta Moreno **61**

Curator/exhibition designer
Amaki, Amalia **76**
Beckwith, Naomi **101**
Camp, Kimberly **19**
Campbell, Mary Schmidt **43**
Golden, Thelma **10, 55**
Hoyte, Lenon **50**
Hutson, Jean Blackwell **16**
Pindell, Howardena **55**
Sanders, Joseph R., Jr. **11**
Sims, Lowery Stokes **27**
Stewart, Paul Wilbur **12**

Cy Young Award
Gibson, Bob **33**
Gooden, Dwight **20**
Jenkins, Fergie **46**
Martinez, Pedro **81**
Newcombe, Don **24**
Sabathia, CC **74**

Cycling
Baugé, Grégory **86**
Jim, Songezo **111**
Taylor, Marshall Walter "Major" **62**
Yeboah, Emmanuel Ofosu **53**

Dallas city government
Kirk, Ron **11, 75, 111**

Dallas Cowboys football team
Allen, Larry **109**
Hayes, Bob **77**

Hill, Calvin **19**
Irvin, Michael **64**
Jones, Ed "Too Tall" **46**
Smith, Emmitt **7, 87**
Wright, Rayfield **70**

Dallas Police Department
Bolton, Terrell D. **25**

Dance Theatre of Harlem
DePrince, Michaela **104**
Johnson, Virginia **9**
King, Alonzo **38**
Mitchell, Arthur **2, 47**
Nicholas, Fayard **20, 57**
Nicholas, Harold **20**
Peters, Brock **96**

DAV
See Disabled American Veterans

Daytona Institute
See Bethune-Cookman College

D.C. sniper
Moose, Charles **40**

Def Jam Records
Jay-Z **27, 69, 103**
Liles, Kevin **42, 99**
LL Cool J **16, 49, 94**
Simmons, Russell **1, 30**

Defense Communications Agency
Gravely, Samuel L., Jr. **5, 49**

Delta Sigma Theta Sorority
Rice, Louise Allen **54**

Dentistry
Bluitt, Juliann S. **14**
Delany, Bessie **12**
Gray, Ida **41**
Lee, Robert **112**
Madison, Romell **45**
Maupin, John E., Jr. **92**
Rock, John S. **113**
Sinkford, Jeanne C. **13**

Denver Broncos football team
Barnes, Ernie **16, 78**
Briscoe, Marlin **37**
Davis, Terrell **20**
Jackson, Tom **70**
Little, Floyd **86**
Sharpe, Shannon **97**

Denver city government
Webb, Wellington **3, 81**

Denver Nuggets basketball team
Bickerstaff, Bernie **21**
Bynoe, Peter C. B. **40**
Hardaway, Tim **35**
Lee, Bertram M., Sr. **46**

Depression/The Great Depression
Hampton, Henry **6**

Dermatology
Taylor, Susan C. **62**

Destiny's Child
Beyoncé **39, 70, 105**
Luckett, Letoya **61**

Rowland, Kelly **100**
Williams, Michelle **73**

Detective fiction
See Mystery/detective fiction

Detroit city government
Archer, Dennis **7, 36**
Bing, Dave **3, 59, 78**
Cockrel, Kenneth V., Jr. **79**
Cockrel, Kenneth Vern, Sr. **79**
Collins, Barbara-Rose **7, 87**
Conyers, Monica **85**
Crockett, George W., Jr. **10, 64**
Evans, Warren C. **76**
Garrett, Joyce Finley **59**
Kilpatrick, Kwame **34, 71**
Marshall, Bella **22**
Pugh, Charles **81**
Reeves, Martha **85**
Young, Coleman **1, 20**

Detroit Lions football team
Barney, Lem **26**
Farr, Mel **24**
Johnson, Levi **48**
Mayhew, Martin R. **76**
Sanders, Barry **1, 53**
Ware, Andre **37**

Detroit Pistons basketball team
Bing, Dave **3, 59, 78**
Dumars, Joe **16, 65**
Gentry, Alvin **23**
Hill, Grant **13, 94**
Hunter, Lindsey **110**
Lanier, Bob **47**
Lloyd, Earl **26**
Lowe, Sidney **64**
Mahorn, Rick **60**
Mohammed, Nazr **64**
Prince, Tayshaun **68**
Robinson, Will **51, 69**
Rodman, Dennis **12, 44, 96**
Stackhouse, Jerry **30**
Thomas, Isiah **7, 26, 65**
Wallace, Ben **54**
Webber, Chris **15, 30, 59**

Detroit Police Department
Bully-Cummings, Ella **48**
Gomez-Preston, Cheryl **9**
McKinnon, Isaiah **9**
Napoleon, Benny N. **23**

Detroit Tigers baseball team
Fielder, Cecil **2, 112**
Horton, Willie **104**
Virgil, Ozzie **48**

Diabetes
Fennoy, Ilene **72**
Wisdom, Kimberlydawn **57**

Diamond mining
Masire, Quett **5**

Dictators
Abacha, Sani **11, 70**
Afewerki, Isaias **98**
Ahidjo, Ahmadou **81**
Amin, Idi **42**
Bashir, Omar al- **77**
Biya, Paul **28, 114**

Compaore, Blaise 87
Conté, Lansana 7, 76
Eyadéma, Gnassingbé 7, 52
Gbagbo, Laurent 43, 90
Habré, Hissène 6, 104
Kabila, Laurent 20
Mengistu, Haile Mariam 65
Moi, Daniel Arap 1, 35
Mswati III 56
Mugabe, Robert 10, 71
Obiang, Teodoro 103
Sassou-Nguesso, Denis 103
Traore, Dioncounda 103
Touré, Sekou 6
Zenawi, Meles 3, 99

Diner's Club
Gaines, Brenda 41

Diplomatic Corps
See U.S. Department of State

Disabled American Veterans (DAV)
Brown, Jesse 6, 41

Disco
Gaynor, Gloria 36
Holloway, Loleatta 115
Payne, Freda 58
Perren, Freddie 60
Shaw, Marlena 105
Staton, Candi 27
Summer, Donna 25, 102
Tavares 115
Trammps, The 108

Distance running
Cheruiyot, Robert 69
Kipsang, Wilson 115
Loroupe, Tegla 59
Tergat, Paul 59
Wanjiru, Sammy 94

Diving
Brashear, Carl 29

DJ
Alert, Kool DJ Red 32
Atkins, Juan 50
Bond, Beverly 53
DJ Clue? 111
DJ Jazzy Jeff 32
DJ Lance Rock 94
DJ Screw 110
Felix Da Housecat 110
Grandmaster Flash 33, 60
Knuckles, Frankie 42
Love, Ed 58

Documentary film
Billops, Camille 82
Blackwood, Maureen 37
Branch, William Blackwell 39
Byrd, Robert 11
Crump, Steven 96
Dash, Julie 4
DuVernay, Ava 98
Elie, Lolis Eric 97
Gray, Darius 69
Greaves, William 38
Hampton, Henry 6
Henry, Lenny 9, 52
Hudlin, Reginald 9, 86
Hudlin, Warrington 9

Hurt, Byron 61
Jean, Michaëlle; 70
Julien, Isaac 3
Kabera, Eric 104
Lynch, Shola 61
Miles, William 112
Nelson, Stanley 92
Peck, Raoul 32
Rees, Dee 100
Riggs, Marlon 5, 44
Roberts, Kimberly Rivers 72
Whack, Rita Coburn 36
Williams, Marco 53

Dollmaking
El Wilson, Barbara 35

Dominica government
Charles, Mary Eugenia 10, 55
Charles, Pierre 52
Skerrit, Roosevelt 72

Dove Award
Baylor, Helen 36
Winans, CeCe 14, 43

Drama Desk Awards
Carter, Nell 39
Taylor, Ron 35
Wesley, Richard 73

Dreamland Orchestra
Cook, Charles "Doc" 44

Drug abuse prevention
Clements, George 2
Creagh, Milton 27
Hale, Lorraine 8
Harris, Alice 7
Lucas, John 7

Drug synthesis
Julian, Percy Lavon 6
Pickett, Cecil 39

Drums
Ali, Rashied 79
Batiste, Lionel 105
Blade, Brian 88
Blakey, Art 37
Brown, Carlinhos 81
Chancler, Ndugu 115
Durham, Bobby 73
Güines, Tata 69
Haynes, Roy 87
Jones, Elvin 14, 68
Kay, Connie 114
La Roca, Pete 107
Locke, Eddie 44
Miles, Buddy 69
Purdie, Bernard 77
Rodríguez, Arsenio 87
Tate, Grady 106
Thigpen, Ed 110
Washington, Kenny 107
Webb, Chick 105
Williams, Tony 67
Young, Lee 72

Dunham Dance Company
Dunham, Katherine 4, 59

DuSable Museum of African American History
Burroughs, Margaret Taylor 9
Wright, Antoinette 60

E Street Band
Clemons, Clarence 41

East Harlem School at Exodus House
Hageman, Hans 36
Hageman, Ivan 36

Ebonics
Cook, Toni 23

Ebony magazine
Bennett, Lerone, Jr. 5, 84
Branch, William Blackwell 39
Cullers, Vincent T. 49
Fuller, Hoyt 44
Johnson, Eunice W. 83
Johnson, John H. 3, 54
Massaquoi, Hans J. 30
Rice, Linda Johnson 9, 41
Sleet, Moneta, Jr. 5

Ebony Museum of African American History
See DuSable Museum of African American History

Economics
Ake, Claude 30
Arthur, Owen 33
Boyd, T. B., III 6
Brimmer, Andrew 2, 48, 106
Brown, Tony 3
Conrad, Cecilia A. 94
Fryer, Roland G. 56
Gibson, William F. 6
Hampton, Henry 6
Juma, Calestous 57
Malveaux, Julianne 32, 70
Masire, Quett 5
Moyo, Dambisa 76
Okonjo-Iweala, Ngozi 101
Pitta, Celso 17
Raines, Franklin 14, 107
Robinson, Randall 7, 46
Simms, Margaret 94
Sowell, Thomas 2, 99
Spriggs, William 67
Sullivan, Leon H. 3, 30
Wallace, Phyllis A. 9
Washington, Ebonya 79
Wharton, Clifton R., Jr. 7
White, Michael R. 5
Williams, Walter E. 4
Woodson, Robert L. 10

Editing
Abani, Chris 77
Aubert, Alvin 41
Bass, Charlotta Spears 40
Brown, Lloyd Louis 42
Curry, George E. 23
Delany, Martin R. 27
Dumas, Henry 41
Murphy, John H. 42
Schuyler, George Samuel 40

Edmonton Oilers hockey team
Fuhr, Grant 1, 49
Grier, Mike 43
Laraque, Georges 48

EEC
See European Economic Community

EEOC
See Equal Employment Opportunity Commission

Elder Foundation
Elder, Lee 6

Electronic music
Atkins, Juan 50
Craig, Carl 31, 71
Felix Da Housecat 110
May, Derrick 41
Romanthony 115

Emerge (Savoy) magazine
Ames, Wilmer 27
Curry, George E. 23

Emmy awards
Allen, Debbie 13, 42
Amos, John 8, 62
Ashe, Arthur 1, 18
Barclay, Paris 37, 94
Barnes, Katreese 97
Belafonte, Harry 4, 65
Bradley, Ed 2, 59
Branch, William Blackwell 39
Brown, James 22
Brown, Les 5
Browne, Roscoe Lee 66
Carter, Nell 39
Clayton, Xernona 3, 45
Cosby, Bill 7, 26, 59
Curtis-Hall, Vondie 17
De Shields, André 72
Dee, Ruby 8, 50, 68
Fisher, Gail 85
Foxx, Redd 2
Freeman, Al, Jr. 11, 105
Goldberg, Whoopi 4, 33, 69
Gossett, Louis, Jr. 7
Guillaume, Robert 3, 48
Gumbel, Greg 8
Hunter-Gault, Charlayne 6, 31
Jones, James Earl 3, 49, 79
Kitt, Eartha 16, 75
La Salle, Eriq 12
Mabrey, Vicki 26
Martin, Michel 97
McQueen, Butterfly 6, 54
Moore, Shemar 21, 112
Parks, Gordon 1, 35, 58
Pinkston, W. Randall 24
Quarles, Norma 25
Richards, Beah 30
Robinson, Max 3
Rock, Chris 3, 22, 66
Rolle, Esther 13, 21
St. John, Kristoff 25
Schiavocampo, Mara 97
Taylor, Billy 23, 92
Thigpen, Lynne 17, 41
Tyson, Cicely 7, 51, 112
Uggams, Leslie 23, 114
Washington, Hayma 86
Wayans, Damon 8, 41
Whack, Rita Coburn 36
Whitfield, Lynn 18
Williams, Montel 4, 57
Williams, Russell, II 70
Williams, Sherley Anne 25
Winfrey, Oprah 2, 15, 61, 106

Woodard, Alfre **9, 108**

Endocrinology
Elders, Joycelyn **6**
Fennoy, Ilene **72**

Energy
Cose, Ellis **5, 50**
Lawal, Kase L. **45**
O'Leary, Hazel **6**
Yumkella, Kandeh **105**

Engineering
Alexander, Archie Alphonso **14**
Anderson, Charles Edward **37**
Auguste, Donna **29**
Austin, Wanda M. **94**
Benson, Angela **34**
Boyd, Gwendolyn **49**
Boykin, Otis **92**
Burns, Ursula **60**
Clark, Yvonne Young **95**
Crosthwait, David **93**
Dabiri, John **93**
Douglas, Donya **97**
Emeagwali, Philip **30**
Ericsson-Jackson, Aprille **28**
Gibson, Kenneth Allen **6**
Gourdine, Meredith **33**
Greene, Frank S., Jr. **101**
Grooms, Henry R(andall) **50**
Harris, Gary L. **87**
Harris, Wesley L. **92**
Henderson, Cornelius Langston **26**
Henderson, Henry Fairfax, Jr. **89**
Howard, Ayanna **65**
Johnson, Anthony M. **92**
Johnson, Sandra K. **94**
Jones, Wayne **53**
Laroche, Joseph Philippe Lemercier **85**
Laryea, Thomas Davies, III **67**
McCoy, Elijah **8**
Miller, Warren F., Jr. **53**
Mills, Joseph C. **51**
O'Neal, Rodney **88**
Pierre, Percy Anthony **46**
Price, Richard **51**
Rillieux, Norbert **92**
Robinson-Berry, Joan **94**
Sigur, Wanda **44**
Slaughter, John Brooks **53**
Spencer, Michael G. **87**
Trotter, Lloyd G. **56**
West, James E. **87**
Wilkens, J. Ernest, Jr. **43**
Williams, O. S. **13**

Entertainment promotion
Bowen, Ruth **83**
Carter, Troy **98**
Isaacs, Cheryl Boone **113**
Lewis, Butch **71, 99**

Entrepreneur
Bakewell, Danny **99**
Barden, Donald H. **9, 20, 89**
Burks, Juanita P. **95**
Dash, Damon **31, 113**
Dash, Darien **29**
Downing, George T. **91**
Fletcher, Buddy **16, 108**
Fudge, Ann (Marie) **11, 55**
Gardner, Edward G. **45**

Gaston, Arthur George **3, 38, 59**
Gordy, Berry, Jr. **1**
Graves, Earl G. **1, 35**
Henderson, Henry Fairfax, Jr. **89**
Herndon, Alonzo Franklin **89**
John, Daymond **23, 114**
Johnson, John H. **3, 54**
Jones, Carl **7**
Lewis, Reginald F. **6**
Maponya, Richard **101**
McCann, Renetta **44**
Middleton, Reggie **105**
Otis, Clarence, Jr. **55**
Parks, Henry Green, Jr. **89**
Payton, Philip A., Jr. **88**
Perry, Tyler **40, 54, 103**
Rapelang Rabana **112**
Roberts, Mike **57**
Spaulding, Charles Clinton **9**
Steward, David L. **36**
Walker, Madame C. J. **7**
Walker, Maggie Lena **17**
Walker, T. J. **7**
Winfrey, Oprah **2, 15, 61, 106**
Woods, Granville T. **5**

Environmental issues
Betsch, MaVynee **28**
Carter, Majora **77**
Ellis-Lamkins, Phaedra **88**
Eugene-Richard, Margie **63**
Harden, Monique **97**
Hill, Bonnie Guiton **20**
Jackson, Lisa **77**
Jones, Van **70**
Maathai, Wangari **43, 97**
Miller-Travis, Vernice **64**
Osborne, Na'taki **54**
Saro-Wiwa, Kenule **39**
Wright, Beverly **97**

Epidemiology
Fenton, Kevin **87**
Gayle, Helene D. **3**
Poindexter, Hildrus A. **87**

Episcopalian
Burgess, John **46**
Harris, Barbara **12**
Jones, Absalom **52**
Redding, Ann Holmes **77**
Walker, John T. **50**
Williams, Frederick (B.) **63**

Equal Employment Opportunity Commission (EEOC)
Alexander, Clifford **26**
Berrien, Jacqueline A. **93**
Hill, Anita **5, 65**
Lewis, Delano **7**
Norton, Eleanor Holmes **7, 93**
Thomas, Clarence **2, 39, 65**
Wallace, Phyllis A. **9**

Equatorial Guinean government
Obiang, Teodoro **103**

Eritrean government
Afewerki, Isaias **98**

ESPN
Jackson, Tom **70**
Lewis, Ray **33, 109**
Masekela, Sal **106**

Roberts, Robin **16, 54, 113**
Salters, Lisa **71**
Scott, Stuart **34**
Smith, Stephen A. **69**
Tirico, Mike **68**
Wilbon, Michael **68**

***Essence* magazine**
Bandele, Asha **36**
Burt-Murray, Angela **59**
De Veaux, Alexis **44**
Ebanks, Michelle **60**
Grant, Gwendolyn Goldsby **28**
Greenwood, Monique **38**
Lewis, Edward T. **21**
Parks, Gordon **1, 35, 58**
Smith, Clarence O. **21**
Taylor, Susan L. **10, 86**
Wesley, Valerie Wilson **18**

Essence Award
Broadbent, Hydeia **36**
McMurray, Georgia L. **36**

Ethiopian government
Desalegn, Hailemariam **105**
Haile Selassie **7**
Mengistu, Haile Mariam **65**
Zenawi, Meles **3, 99**

Etiquette
Bates, Karen Grigsby **40**

European Economic Community (EEC)
Diouf, Abdou **3**

Event planning
Bailey, Preston **64**
Williams, Lindsey **75**

Executive Leadership Council
Jackson, Mannie **14**

Exiled heads of state
Amin, Idi **42**
Aristide, Jean-Bertrand **6, 45**
Mengistu, Haile Mariam **65**
Mobutu Sese Seko **1, 56**

Exploration
Bishop, Stephen **95**
Henson, Matthew **2**

Famine relief
See World hunger

Fannie Mae
Jackson, Maynard **2, 41**
Raines, Franklin **14, 107**

Fashion
Aberra, Amsale **67**
Biya, Chantal **89**
Boateng, Ozwald **35, 113**
Boyd, Suzanne **52**
Chanticleer, Raven **91**
DaCosta, YaYa **98**
Delice, Ronald **48**
Delice, Rony **48**
Evans, Etu **55**
Fine, Sam **60**
Finley, Ron **110**
Gaskins, Eric **64**
Givhan, Robin Deneen **72**
Hall, Kevan **61**

Hendy, Francis **47**
Jones, Genevieve **101**
Keckley, Elizabeth **90**
Knowles, Tina **61**
Lars, Byron **32**
Luna, Donyale **88**
Malone, Maurice **32**
McGrath, Pat **72**
Reese, Tracy **54**
Simmons, Kimora Lee **51, 83**
Smaltz, Audrey **12**
Smith, LaQuan **113**
Steele, Lawrence **28**
Stoney, Michael **50**
Sy, Oumou **65**
Talley, André Leon **56, 106**
White, Jessica **83**

Fashion Institute of Technology (FIT)
Brown, Joyce F. **25**

FCC
See Federal Communications Commission

Federal Bureau of Investigation (FBI)
Gibson, Johnnie Mae **23**
Harvard, Beverly **11**

Federal Communications Commission (FCC)
Barrett, Andrew C. **12**
Clyburn, Mignon **78**
Hughes, Cathy **27**
Kennard, William Earl **18**
Powell, Michael **32**
Russell-McCloud, Patricia A. **17**

Federal Court of Canada
Isaac, Julius **34**

Federal Emergency Management Agency
Becton, Julius W., Jr. **110**

Federal Reserve Bank
Brimmer, Andrew **2, 48, 106**
Ferguson, Roger W., Jr. **25, 112**
Layton, William **87**
Rice, Emmett J. **94**

Feed the Hungry program
Williams, Hosea Lorenzo **15, 31**

Fencing
Boulogne, Joseph, Chevalier de Saint-Georges **94**
Westbrook, Peter **20**

Fiction
Adams, Jenoyne **60**
Adichie, Chimamanda Ngozi **64**
Alexander, Margaret Walker **22**
Ali, Mohammed Naseehu **60**
Amadi, Elechi **40**
Anthony, Michael **29**
Ansa, Tina McElroy **14**
Armah, Ayi Kwei **49**
Ashley & JaQuavis **107**
Attaway, William **102**
Ba, Mariama **30**
Baiocchi, Regina Harris **41**
Baisden, Michael **25, 66**
Bandele, Biyi **68**

Beckham, Barry **41**
Benson, Angela **34**
Berry, James **41**
Bolden, Tonya **32**
Bradley, David Henry, Jr. **39**
Brand, Dionne **32**
Briscoe, Connie **15**
Brown, Cecil M. **46**
Brown, Lloyd Louis **42**
Bunkley, Anita Richmond **39**
Butler, Octavia **8, 43, 58**
Campbell, Bebe Moore **6, 24, 59**
Cartiér, Xam Wilson **41**
Chase-Riboud, Barbara **20, 46**
Cheney-Coker, Syl **43**
Chesnutt, Charles **29**
Clark, Wahida **107**
Clarke, Austin **32**
Cleage, Pearl **17, 64**
Cliff, Michelle **42**
Colter, Cyrus J. **36**
Cooper, J. California **12, 85**
Creagh, Milton **27**
Danticat, Edwidge **15, 68**
Dathorne, O. R. **52**
Demby, William **51**
Diop, Birago **53**
Draper, Sharon Mills **16, 43**
Due, Tananarive **30**
Dumas, Henry **41**
Dunbar-Nelson, Alice Ruth Moore **44**
Duplechan, Larry **55**
Edugyan, Esi **98**
Ellis, Trey **97**
Emecheta, Buchi **30**
Evans, Diana **72**
Everett, Percival **93**
Fair, Ronald L. **47**
Fales-Hill, Susan **88**
Farah, Nuruddin **27**
Farley, Christopher John **54**
Files, Lolita **35**
Ford, Nick Aaron **44**
Ford, Wallace **58**
Forna, Aminatta **95**
Forrest, Leon **44**
Foye, K'wan **97**
Gomez, Jewelle **30**
Gray, Darius **69**
Greenlee, Sam **48**
Harper, Rachel M. **92**
Harris, E. Lynn **12, 33**
Haywood, Gar Anthony **43**
Hercules, Frank **44**
Hill, Donna **32**
Holton, Hugh, Jr. **39**
Horne, Frank **44**
Jackson, Sheneska **18**
Jakes, Thomas "T. D." **17, 43**
James, Marlon **85**
Jasper, Kenji **39**
Jenkins, Beverly **14**
Johnson, Georgia Douglas **41**
Jones, Edward P. **43, 67**
Jones, Gayl **37**
Jones, Tayari **96**
Kamau, Kwadwo Agymah **28**
Kay, Jackie **37**
Kayira, Legson **40**
Keene, John **73**
Kendrick, Erika **57**
Killens, John O. **54**

Kincaid, Jamaica **4, 109**
Laferriere, Dany **33**
LaGuma, Alex **30**
Lamar, Jake **96**
Lamming, George **35**
Lattany, Kristin Hunter **88**
Laymon, Kiese **113**
LeFlore, Lyah Beth **96**
Locke, Attica **85**
Machado de Assis **74**
Marechera, Dambudzo **39**
Markham, E. A. **37**
Mason, Felicia **31**
Mathabane, Mark **5, 99**
Mbaye, Mariétou **31**
McCrary Anthony, Crystal **70**
McFadden, Bernice L. **39**
McKinney-Whetstone, Diane **27**
McMillan, Rosalynn A. **36**
McMillan, Terry **4, 17, 53**
Memmi, Albert **37**
Mengestu, Dinaw **66, 114**
Mitchell, Sharon **36**
Monroe, Mary **35**
Mosley, Walter **5, 25, 68**
Mossell, Gertrude Bustill **40**
Mphalele, Es'kia **40**
Mwangi, Meja **40**
Naylor, Gloria **10, 42**
Nkosi, Lewis **46**
Nugent, Richard Bruce **39**
Okara, Gabriel **37**
Ojikutu, Bayo **66**
Packer, Z. Z. **64**
Peters, Lenrie **43**
Philip, Marlene Nourbese **32**
Polite, Carlene Hatcher **82**
Randall, Alice **38**
Ridley, John **69**
Roby, Kimberla Lawson **86**
Sapphire **14, 95**
Schuyler, George Samuel **40**
Senior, Olive **37**
Senna, Danzy **93**
Smith, Danyel **40**
Smith, Zadie **51**
Southgate, Martha **58**
Tate, Eleanora E. **20, 55**
Taylor, Mildred D. **26**
Teasley, Lisa **92**
Thomas, Michael **69**
Thomas-Graham, Pamela **29**
Tutuola, Amos **30**
Vera, Yvonne **32**
Verdelle, A. J. **26**
Walker, Margaret **29**
Weaver, Afaa Michael **37**
Whitehead, Colson **77**
Whitfield, Van **34**
Williams, Sherley Anne **25**
Williams, Stanley "Tookie" **29, 57**
Woods, Teri **69**
Yarbrough, Camille **40**
Yerby, Frank **96**
Young, Al **82**
Youngblood, Shay **32**
Zane **71**

Figure skating
Bonaly, Surya **7**
Bonheur, Yannick **84**
James, Vanessa **84**
Thomas, Debi **26**

Vanessa James and Yannick Bonheur **84**

Film criticism
Mitchell, Elvis **67**

Film direction/video direction
Akomfrah, John **37**
Allain, Stephanie **49**
Barclay, Paris **37, 94**
Blackwood, Maureen **37**
Bonney, Tabi **98**
Burnett, Charles **16, 68**
Byrd, Robert **11**
Coogler, Ryan **114**
Daniels, Lee **36, 76**
Dash, Julie **4**
Dickerson, Ernest **6, 17**
Duke, Bill **3, 96**
DuVernay, Ava **98**
Franklin, Carl **11**
Fuqua, Antoine **35**
Gerima, Haile **38, 80**
Gray, Darius **69**
Gray, F. Gary **14, 49**
Greaves, William **38**
Hamilton, Tanya **93**
Harris, Leslie **6**
Hayes, Teddy **40**
Henriques, Julian **37**
Hudlin, Reginald **9, 86**
Hudlin, Warrington **9**
Hughes, Albert **7**
Hughes, Allen **7**
Hurt, Byron **61**
Jackson, George **19**
Johnson, Clark **96**
Julien, Isaac **3**
Lane, Charles **3**
Lee, Malcolm D. **75**
Lee, Spike **5, 19, 86**
Lemmons, Kasi **20**
Lewis, Samella **25**
Martin, Darnell **43, 78**
McQueen, Steve **84**
Micheaux, Oscar **7**
Morton, Joe **18**
Moses, Gilbert **12**
Moss, Carlton **17**
Mwangi, Meja **40**
Onwurah, Ngozi **38**
Palcy, Euzhan **94**
Peck, Raoul **32**
Perry, Tyler **40, 54, 103**
Prince-Bythewood, Gina **31, 77**
Rees, Dee **100**
Riggs, Marlon **5, 44**
Roberts, Darryl **70**
St. Jacques, Raymond **8**
Schultz, Michael A. **6**
Sembène, Ousmane **13, 62**
Singleton, John **2, 30**
Smith, Roger Guenveur **12**
Souleymane, Mahamane **78**
Tillman, George, Jr. **20**
Townsend, Robert **4, 23**
Tyler, Aisha N. **36**
Underwood, Blair **7, 27, 76**
Van Peebles, Mario **2, 51**
Van Peebles, Melvin **7, 95**
Wallace, William **75**
Ward, Douglas Turner **42**
Wayans, Damon **8, 41**

Wayans, Keenen Ivory **18**
White, Sylvain **96**
Whitaker, Forest **2, 49, 67**

Film production
Allain, Stephanie **49**
Amata, Jeta **111**
Chase, Debra Martin **49, 96**
Daniels, Lee **36, 76**
Gerima, Haile **38, 80**
Greaves, William **38**
Isaacs, Cheryl Boone **113**
Julian, Hubert **90**
Morrison, Vanessa **84**
Onwurah, Ngozi **38**
Packer, Will **71**
Patton, Paula **62**
Robinson, Matt **69**
Stewart, Nzingha **89**
Tyler, Aisha N. **36**
Van Lierop, Robert **53**
Walker, Chet **106**
Ward, Douglas Turner **42**
Wayans, Damien **78**
Whitaker, Forest **2, 49, 67**
Williams, Marco **53**
Williams, Russell, II **70**
Williamson, Fred **67**

Film scores
Blanchard, Terence **43**
Crouch, Andraé **27, 115**
Hancock, Herbie **20, 67**
Jones, Quincy **8, 30**
Lebo M **109**
Prince **18, 65**
RZA **80**

Finance
Adams, Eula L. **39**
Adoboli, Kweku **106**
Banks, Jeffrey **17**
Bell, James A. **50**
Boston, Kelvin E. **25**
Brown, Eddie C. **35**
Bryant, John **26**
Chapman, Nathan A., Jr. **21**
Chapman, Susan E. **94**
Doley, Harold, Jr. **26**
Epperson, Sharon **54**
Ferguson, Roger W., Jr. **25, 112**
Fletcher, Buddy **16, 108**
Funderburg, I. Owen **38**
Gaines, Brenda **41**
Griffith, Mark Winston **8**
Hall, Alvin D. **86**
Harris, Carla A. **67**
Hobson, Mellody **40**
Jones, Thomas W. **41**
Lawless, Theodore K. **8**
Lewis, William M., Jr. **40**
Louis, Errol T. **8**
Mack, Iris **105**
Marshall, Bella **22**
Moyo, Dambisa **76**
Nash, Shannon King **84**
O'Neal, Stanley **38, 67**
Rogers, John W., Jr. **5, 52**
Ross, Charles **27**
Shank, Suzanne F. **77**
Taylor, Ephren W., II **61**

Travis, Tracey T. **94**

Firefighters
Barlow, Roosevelt **49**
Bell, Michael **40**

Fisk University
Imes, Elmer Samuel **39**
Johnson, Charles S. **12**
Phillips, Teresa L. **42**
Smith, John L. **22**

Fitness
Richardson, Donna **39**
Smith, Ian **62**

Florida A & M University
Ammons, James H. **81**
Foster, William P. **88**
Gaither, Alonzo Smith (Jake) **14**
Humphries, Frederick **20**

Florida Marlins baseball team
Hill, Michael **95**
Mariner, Jonathan **41**

Florida state government
Brown, Corrine **24, 90**
Meek, Carrie **6, 36**
Meek, Kendrick **41, 89**
Menard, John Willis **90**
Tribble, Israel, Jr. **8**
Wilson, Frederica **92**

Florida Supreme Court
Quince, Peggy A. **69**

Flute
Laws, Hubert **90**

Folk music
Bailey, DeFord **33**
Beken **111**
Broonzy, Big Bill **82**
Callier, Terry **106**
Carolina Chocolate Drops **111**
Chapman, Tracy **26**
Charlemagne, Manno **11**
Cody, Radmilla **99**
Cuney, William Waring **44**
Davis, Gary **41**
Dawson, William Levi **39**
Handy, W. C. **8**
Harper, Ben **34, 62**
Havens, Richie **111**
House, Son **8**
Jenkins, Ella **15**
Love, Laura **50**
Odetta **37, 74**
Reagon, Toshi **76**
Southern, Eileen **56**
Spence, Joseph **49**
White, Josh **86**
Williams, Denise **40**

Food products
Amos, Wally **9**
Briggs, Curtis **84**
Oliver, Garrett **95**
Parks, Henry Green, Jr. **89**
Siméus, Dumas M. **25, 110**

Football
Buchanan, Ray **32**
Clemons, Michael "Pinball" **64**
Davis, Ernie **48**

Dorrell, Karl **52**
Dungy, Tony **17, 42, 59**
Gaither, Alonzo Smith (Jake) **14**
Gill, Turner **83**
Gorden, W. C. **71**
Grier, Bobby **95**
Grier, Roosevelt **13**
Jones, Ed "Too Tall" **46**
Keith, Floyd A. **61**
Lanier, Willie **33**
Lewis, Marvin **51, 87**
Lewis, William Henry **89**
McNabb, Donovan **29**
Perry, Lowell **30**
Pollard, Fritz **53**
Prince, Ron **64**
Robinson, Eddie G. **10, 61**
Shannon, Randy **82**
Simmons, Bob **29**
Smith, Lovie **66, 107**
Watts, J. C., Jr. **14, 38**
Weathers, Carl **10**
Williams, Doug **22, 112**
Willingham, Tyrone **43**
Willis, Bill **68**
Woodson, Rod **79**

Football Hall of Fame, professional
Allen, Larry **109**
Allen, Marcus **20**
Barney, Lem **26**
Briscoe, Marlin **37**
Brown, Jim **11, 95**
Campbell, Earl **104**
Carter, Cris **21, 109**
Culp, Curley **110**
Dean, Fred **98**
Dent, Richard **97**
Dickerson, Eric **27, 108**
Faulk, Marshall **35, 96**
Green, Darrell **39, 74**
Greene, Joe **10**
Harris, Franco **97**
Hayes, Bob **77**
Irvin, Michael **64**
Jackson, Rickey **88**
Johnson, John Henry **96**
Joiner, Charlie **102**
Jones, Deacon **92, 112**
Kennedy, Cortez **104**
Lane, Dick **92**
Lanier, Willie **33**
Little, Floyd **86**
Little, Larry **90**
Lofton, James **42**
Lott, Ronnie **9**
Martin, Curtis **104**
Matson, Ollie **93**
McDaniel, Randall Cornell **81**
Monk, Art **38, 73**
Moon, Warren **8, 66**
Motley, Marion **26**
Newsome, Ozzie **26**
Ogden, Jonathan **110**
Page, Alan (Cedric) **7**
Parker, Jim **64**
Payton, Walter (Jerry) **11, 25**
Perry, Joe **95**
Pollard, Fritz **53**
Randle, John **87**
Rice, Jerry **5, 55, 89**
Roaf, Willie **106**

Robinson, Dave **110**
Sanders, Barry **1, 53**
Sanders, Deion **4, 31, 96**
Sapp, Warren **38, 109**
Sayers, Gale **28**
Sharpe, Shannon **97**
Shell, Art **1, 66**
Simpson, O. J. **15, 100**
Singletary, Mike **4, 76**
Smith, Bruce **80**
Smith, Emmitt **7, 87**
Stallworth, John **102**
Swann, Lynn **28**
Taylor, Lawrence **25**
Thomas, Derrick **25**
Thomas, Emmitt **71**
Thomas, Thurman **75**
Tunnell, Emlen **54**
Upshaw, Gene **18, 47, 72**
White, Reggie **6, 50**
Willis, Bill **68**
Winslow, Kellen **83**
Wood, Willie **111**
Woodson, Rod **79**
Wright, Rayfield **70**

Ford Foundation
Franklin, Robert M. **13**
Thomas, Franklin A. **5, 49**

Ford Motor Company
Cherry, Deron **40**
Dawson, Matel, Jr. **39**
Goldsberry, Ronald **18**
Hazel, Darryl B. **50**
McMillan, Rosalynn A. **36**

Foreign investment
Amoudi, Mohammed al- **88**
dos Santos, Isabel **114**

Forensic science
Griffin, Bessie Blout **43**

Foster care
Hale, Clara **16**
Hale, Lorraine **8**

Fox Broadcasting Company
Corbi, Lana **42**
McFarland, Roland **49**
Oliver, Pam **54**
Strahan, Michael **35, 81**

Freddie Mac
Baker, Maxine **28**

French West Africa
Camara, Moussa Dadis **76**
Diouf, Abdou **3**
Ndiaye, Iba **74**

Funeral homes
March, William Carrington **56**

Funk music
Ayers, Roy **16**
Bonner, Leroy **113**
Brown, James **15, 60**
Castor, Jimmy **100**
Clinton, George **9, 93**
Collins, Bootsy **31**
Collins, Lyn **53**
Gap Band, The **100**
Johnson, Conrad O. **97**
Love, Laura **50**

Midnight Star **110**
Monáe, Janelle **86**
Parker, Maceo **72**
Parker, Ray, Jr. **85**
Purdie, Bernard **77**
Shider, Garry **87**
Stone, Sly **85**
Watson, Johnny "Guitar" **18**
Woods, Belita **103**

Fusion
Davis, Miles **4**
Jones, Quincy **8, 30**
Williams, Tony **67**

Gabonese government
Bongo, Ali Ben **80**
Bongo, Omar **1, 79**

Gambian government
Jammeh, Yahya **23, 104**
Jawara, Dawda Kairaba **11**

Gambling
Ivey, Phil **72, 106**

Gangs
Coke, Christopher **108**
Matthews, Ameena **105**
Shakur, Yusef **85**
Taylor, Bo **72**
Williams, Stanley "Tookie" **29, 57**

Garifuna music
Palacio, Andy **96**

Gay and lesbian issues
Boykin, Keith **14**
Carter, Mandy **11**
Clarke, Cheryl **32**
Collins, Jason **111**
Davis, Wade, Jr. **103**
De Veaux, Alexis **44**
Garner, Tyron **99**
Hemphill, Essex **10**
Julien, Isaac **3**
Kato, David **103**
Norman, Pat **10**
Riggs, Marlon **5, 44**
Wilson, Phill **9, 104**

Genealogy
Allen, Lucy **85**
Blockson, Charles L. **42**
Haley, Alex **4**

***General Hospital* TV series**
Cash, Rosalind **28**

General Motors Corporation
O'Neal, Stanley **38, 67**
Roberts, Roy S. **14**
Welburn, Edward T. **50**

Genetics
Dunston, Georgia Mae **48**
Harris, Mary Styles **31**
Kittles, Rick **51**
Olopade, Olufunmilayo Falusi **58**

Geometric symbolism
Douglas, Aaron **7**

Geophysics
Person, Waverly **9, 51**

George Foster Peabody Broadcasting Award
Bradley, Ed 2, 59
Hunter-Gault, Charlayne 6, 31
Mac, Bernie 29, 61, 72
Shaw, Bernard 2

Georgia state government
Baker, Thurbert 22
Bishop, Sanford D., Jr. 24, 111
Bond, Julian 2, 35, 106
Brooks, Tyrone 59
Johnson, Hank, Jr. 80
Johnson, Leroy R. 89
Majette, Denise 41
McKinney, Cynthia 11, 52, 74
Reed, Kasim 82
Scott, David 41
Smyre, Calvin 90
Williams, Hosea Lorenzo 15, 31

Georgia Supreme Court
Benham, Robert 78
Melton, Harold D. 79
Sears, Leah Ward 5, 79

Ghanaian government
Atta Mills, John 75
Bartels, Peggielene 80
Kufuor, John Agyekum 54, 82
Lee, Robert 112
Mahama, John Dramani 103
Nkrumah, Kwame 3
Rawlings, Jerry 9

Girl Scouts of the USA
Thompson, Cynthia Bramlett 50

Goddard Space Flight Center
Douglas, Donya 97
Ericsson-Jackson, Aprille 28

Golden Globe awards
Allen, Debbie 13, 42
Bassett, Angela 6, 23, 62
Cara, Irene 77
Carroll, Diahann 9
Fisher, Gail 85
Freeman, Morgan 2, 20, 62, 100
Ross, Diana 8, 27
Spencer, Octavia 100
Taylor, Regina 9, 46, 97

Golden Pen award
McFadden, Bernice L. 39

Golf
Bramlett, Joseph 91
Davis, Ben 115
Elder, Lee 6
Gibson, Althea 8, 43
Gregory, Ann 63
Jackson, Fred James 25
Peete, Calvin 11
Powell, William J. 82
Richmond, Mitch 19
Shippen, John 43
Sifford, Charlie 4, 49
Spiller, Bill 64
Woods, Cheyenne 103
Woods, Tiger 14, 31, 81

Gospel music
Adams, Oleta 18
Adams, Yolanda 17, 67

Andrews, Inez 108
Armstrong, Vanessa Bell 24
Bass, Fontella 104, 109
Baylor Helen 36
Blind Boys of Alabama, The 99
Bonds, Margaret 39
Bradley, J. Robert 65
Caesar, Shirley 19
Cage, Byron 53
Clark, Mattie Moss 61
Clark-Cole, Dorinda 66
Clark-Sheard, Karen 22, 114
Clayton, Merry 112
Cleveland, James 19
Christie, Angella 36
Cobbs, Tasha 114
Cooke, Sam 17
Crouch, Andraé 27, 115
Davis, Gary 41
Dorsey, Thomas 15
Fortune, James 92
Franklin, Aretha 11, 44, 115
Franklin, Kirk 15, 49, 97
Gaynor, Gloria 36
Golden Gate Quartet 104
Green, Al 13, 47, 74
Haddon, Dietrick 55
Hammond, Fred 23
Hawkins, Edwin 113
Hawkins, Tramaine 16
Hawkins, Walter 87
Higginsen, Vy 65
Holloway, Loleatta 115
Houghton, Israel 92
Houston, Cissy 20, 83
Jackson, Mahalia 5
Jeter, Claude 75
Johnson, Le'Andria 108
Jones, Bobby 20, 94
Kee, John P. 43
Kenoly, Ron 45
Killings, Debra 57
Knight, Gladys 16, 66
Knight, Marie 80
Lassiter, Roy 24
Lawrence, Donald 99
Little Richard 15
Majors, Jeff 41
Mann, Tamela 92
Marrow, Queen Esther 24
Martin, Roberta 58
Mary Mary 34, 92
Mayfield, Curtis 2, 43
McClendon, Lisa 61
McClurkin, Donnie 25
Mighty Clouds of Joy 110
Mills, Stephanie 36
Monica 21
Moss, J 64
Mullen, Nicole C. 45
Peoples, Dottie 22
Phipps, Wintley 59
Preston, Billy 39, 59
Reagon, Bernice Johnson 7
Reedy, Jessica 101
Reese, Della 6, 20, 96
Sapp, Marvin 74
Scott, George 55
Sheard, Kierra 61, 114
Stampley, Micah 54
Staples, Cleotha 113
Staples, Mavis 50, 88
Staples, "Pops" 32

Staton, Candi 27
Steinberg, Martha Jean "The Queen" 28
Swan Silvertones, The 110
Sweet Honey in the Rock 106
Take 6 112
Tharpe, Rosetta 65
Tonex 54
Tribbett, Tye 81
Walker, Albertina 10, 58, 89
Walker, Hezekiah 34
Ward, Willa 105
Washington, Dinah 22
Whalum, Kirk 37, 64
Williams, Deniece 36
Williams, Michelle 73
Wilson, Brian Courtney 94
Wilson, Natalie 38
Winans, Angie 36
Winans, BeBe 14
Winans, CeCe 14, 43
Winans, David 77
Winans, Debbie 36
Winans, Marvin L. 17
Winans, Ronald 54
Winans, Vickie 24
Wright, O. V. 114
Wright, Timothy 74

Graffiti art
Scott, Dread 106
White, Dondi 34

Grammy Awards
Adams, Oleta 18
Adderley, Nat 29
Babyface 10, 31, 82
Badu, Erykah 22, 114
Battle, Kathleen 70
Belafonte, Harry 4, 65
Beyoncé 39, 70, 105
Blade, Brian 88
Blige, Mary J. 20, 34, 60, 97
Blind Boys of Alabama, The 99
Brandy 14, 34, 72
Caesar, Shirley 19
Cara, Irene 77
Carolina Chocolate Drops 111
Carter, Ron 104
Chapman, Tracy 26
Cleveland, James 19
Cole, Natalie 17, 60, 84
Combs, Sean 17, 43, 92
Coolio 103
Cosby, Bill 7, 26, 59
Cray, Robert 30
Crouch, Andraé 27, 115
Davis, Miles 4
Dee, Ruby 8, 50, 68
Duke, George 21, 113
Earth, Wind & Fire 98
Ellington, Duke 5
Estelle 75
Évora, Cesária 12, 99
Ferrer, Ibrahim 41
Fitzgerald, Ella 8
Forté, John 74
Franklin, Aretha 11, 44, 115
Gamble, Kenny 85
Gaye, Marvin 2
Gaynor, Gloria 36
Gibson, Tyrese 27, 62
Glover, Corey 34

Goldberg, Whoopi 4, 33, 69
Gray, Macy 29
Green, Cee Lo 70, 103
Guy, Buddy 31
Harris, Damon 110
Hathaway, Donny 18
Hawkins, Tramaine 16
Hawkins, Walter 87
Hayes, Isaac 20, 58, 73
Hill, Lauryn 20, 53, 111
Holland-Dozier-Holland 36
Hooker, John Lee 30
Houston, Cissy 20, 83
Houston, Whitney 7, 28, 83, 100
Hubbard, Freddie 75
Isley, Ronald 25, 56
Jackson, Janet 6, 30, 68
Jackson, Michael 19, 53, 76
James, Etta 13, 52, 100
Jarreau, Al 21, 65, 105
Jay-Z 27, 69, 103
Jean, Wyclef 20, 86
Jimmy Jam 13
Johnson, Le'Andria 108
Jones, Bobby 20, 94
Jones, Quincy 8, 30
Kee, John P. 43
Kelly, R. 18, 44, 71
Keys, Alicia 32, 68
Knight, Gladys 16, 66
Knuckles, Frankie 42
LaBelle, Patti 13, 30
Lecrae 108
Lawrence, Donald 99
Lebo M 109
Legend, John 67
Lewis, Terry 13
Lopes, Lisa 36
Mahal, Taj 39
Maitreya, Sananda 85
Makeba, Miriam 2, 50, 74
Marley, Ziggy 41
Marsalis, Branford 34, 103
M.C. Hammer 20, 80
Method Man 81
Mighty Clouds of Joy 110
Mills, Stephanie 36
Mo', Keb' 36
Moore, LeRoi 72
Murphy, Eddie 4, 20, 61
Norman, Jessye 5
Obama, Barack 49, 74, 91
Olatunji, Babatunde 36
Perkins, Pinetop 70
Poitier, Sidney 11, 36
Price, Leontyne 1
Pride, Charley 26
Prince 18, 65
Queen Latifah 1, 16, 58
?uestlove 74
Redding, Otis 16
Reid, Vernon 34
Rhymefest 97
Richie, Lionel 27, 65, 114
Rihanna 65, 102
Robinson, Smokey 3, 49
Rollins, Sonny 37, 94
Roots, The 101
Ross, Isaiah "Doc" 40
Rucker, Darius 34, 74, 108
Sade 15, 92
Scott, Jill 29, 83
Seal 14, 75

Shaggy 31
Shorter, Wayne 75
Simon, Joe 109
Slash 75
Smith, Will 8, 18
Stewart, Tricky 98
Street, Richard 110
Summer, Donna 25, 102
Swizz Beatz 108
Temptations, The 33
Trammps, The 108
Turner, Tina 6, 27
Walker, Hezekiah 34
Warwick, Dionne 18, 111
West, Kanye 52, 93
White, Barry 13, 41
White, Maurice 29
Whitfield, Norman 73
Williams, Deniece 36
Williams, Joe 5, 25
Williams, Michelle 73
Williams, Paul 112
Wilson, Nancy 10, 98
Winans, CeCe 14, 43
Winans, Marvin L. 17
Wonder, Stevie 11, 53

Grand Ole Opry
Bailey, DeFord 33

Graphic novels
Anderson, Ho Che 54
Johnson, Mat 31, 105
Jones, Rashida 101
McDuffie, Dwayne 62
Tooks, Lance 62

Green Bay Packers football team
Brooks, Aaron 33
Butler, Leroy, III 17
Driver, Donald 99
Howard, Desmond 16, 58
Sharper, Darren 32
White, Reggie 6, 50
Wood, Willie 111

Green Party
Clemente, Rosa 74
McKinney, Cynthia 11, 52, 74

Grenadian government
Bishop, Maurice 39
Gairy, Eric Matthew 83
Mitchell, Keith 82

Guardian
Trotter, Monroe 9

Guggenheim fellowship
Miles, William 112
Pope.L, William 72
Rollins, Sonny 37, 94
Taylor, Cecil 70
Wilson, Ellis 39

Guinea government
Camara, Moussa Dadis 76
Condé, Alpha 95
Conté, Lansana 7, 76
Touré, Sekou 6

Guinea-Bissau government
Cabral, Amílcar 104
Sanhá Malam Bacai 84, 101

Vieira, João 14, 84

Guitar
Ade, King Sunny 41
Baker, Mickey 95
Barker, Danny 32
Barnes, Roosevelt "Booba" 33
Bibb, Eric 49
Brown, Clarence Gatemouth 59
Butler, Jonathan 28
Burns, Eddie 44
Burnside, R. L. 56
Caymmi, Dorival 72
Collins, Bootsy 31
Copeland, Johnny 110
Cosey, Pete 103
Cray, Robert 30
Davis, Gary 41
Dawkins, Jimmy 111
Diddley, Bo 39, 72
Estes, Sleepy John 33
Fuller, Blind Boy 86
Green, Grant 56
Guy, Buddy 31
Harris, Corey 39, 73
Hemphill, Jessie Mae 33, 59
Hendrix, Jimi 10
House, Son 8
Hooker, John Lee 30
Hopkins, Lightnin' 83
Howlin' Wolf 9
James, Elmore 114
Johnson, Robert 2
Johnson, Syl 97
Johnson, Tommy 106
Jordan, Ronny 26
Killings, Debra 57
King, B. B. 7
King, Freddie 92
Klugh, Earl 59
Kolosoy, Wendo 73
Kravitz, Lenny 10, 34
Leadbelly 82
Lipscomb, Mance 49
Long, Huey 79
Loueke, Lionel 88
Magic Slim 110
Marley, Bob 5
Mayfield, Curtis 2, 43
McTell, Blind Willie 89
Montgomery, Wes 88
Ndegeocello, Meshell 15, 83
Ongala, Remmy 9, 91
Parker, Ray, Jr. 85
Patton, Charley 107
Pena, Paul 58
Pitts, Skip 103
Ranglin, Ernest 78
Rodríguez, Arsenio 87
Rush, Bobby 78
Seals, Son 56
Shider, Garry 87
Slash 75
Spence, Joseph 49
Sumlin, Hubert 101
Ulmer, James 79
Walker, T-Bone 111
Watson, Johnny "Guitar" 18
White, Josh 86
Williams, Jody 113

Guyanese government
Burnham, Forbes 66
Jagan, Cheddi 16

Gymnastics
Dawes, Dominique 11
Hilliard, Wendy 53
White, Jesse 22, 75

Hair care
See Beauty salons and products

Haitian government
Aristide, Jean-Bertrand 6, 45
Manigat, Mirlande 90
Martelly, Michel 90
Pascal-Trouillot, Ertha 3
Pierre-Louis, Michèle 75
Préval, René 87

Hale House
Hale, Clara 16
Hale, Lorraine 8

Harlem Globetrotters
Chamberlain, Wilt 18, 47
Gates, William 97
Haynes, Marques 22
Jackson, Mannie 14
Tatum, Reece 104
Woodard, Lynette 67

Harlem Renaissance
Alexander, Margaret Walker 22
Bennett, Gwendolyn B. 59
Christian, Barbara T. 44
Crichlow, Ernest 75
Cullen, Countee 8
Cuney, William Waring 44
Dandridge, Raymond Garfield 45
Davis, Arthur P. 41
Delaney, Beauford 19
Ellington, Duke 5
Fauset, Jessie 7
Fisher, Rudolph 17
Frazier, E. Franklin 10
Horne, Frank 44
Hughes, Langston 4
Hurston, Zora Neale 3
Imes, Elmer Samuel 39
Johnson, Georgia Douglas 41
Johnson, James Weldon 5
Johnson, William Henry 3
Larsen, Nella 10
Locke, Alain 10
McKay, Claude 6
Mills, Florence 22
Morton, Ferdinand Q. 90
Nail, John E. 92
Nugent, Richard Bruce 39
Patterson, Louise 25
Payton, Philip A., Jr. 88
Petry, Ann 19
Thurman, Wallace 16
Toomer, Jean 6
VanDerZee, James 6
Waring, Laura Wheeler 99
West, Dorothy 12, 54
Wilson, Ellis 39

Harlem Writers Guild
Guy, Rosa 5
Killens, John O. 54

Wesley, Valerie Wilson 18

Harmonica
Arnold, Billy Boy 112
Bailey, DeFord 33
Barnes, Roosevelt "Booba" 33
Bell, Carey 114
Burns, Eddie 44
Horton, Big Walter 115
Howlin' Wolf 9
Neal, Raful 44
Ross, Isaiah "Doc" 40
Terry, Sonny 88

Harp
Coltrane, Alice 70
Majors, Jeff 41

Harvard Law School
Bell, Derrick 6, 98
Dickerson, Debra J. 60
Ogletree, Charles, Jr. 12, 47
Wilkins, David 77

Harvard University
Amaker, Tommy 62
Epps, Archie C., III 45
Ferguson, Ronald F. 75
Gomes, Peter J. 15, 93
Hammonds, Evelynn 69
Huggins, Nathan Irvin 52
Loury, Glenn 36
Poindexter, Hildrus A. 87

Head Start
Edelman, Marian Wright 5, 42
Taylor, Helen 30

Health care reform
Adams-Campbell, Lucille L. 60
Berrysmith, Don Reginald 49
Brown, Jesse 6, 41
Carroll, L. Natalie 44
Cole, Lorraine 48
Cooper, Edward S. 6
Dirie, Waris 56
Gibson, Kenneth A. 6
Hughes, Dora 88
Hughes, Ebony 57
Kintaudi, Leon 62
Lavizzo-Mourey, Risa 48
Potter, Myrtle 40
Randall, Vernellia R. 95
Richardson, Rupert 67
Tuckson, Reed V. 71
Vaughn, Viola 70
Williams, Daniel Hale 2
Williams, David Rudyard 50

Heart disease
Cooper, Edward S. 6
Grant, Augustus O. 71
Watkins, Levi, Jr. 9

Heisman Trophy
Allen, Marcus 20
Bush, Reggie 59, 88
Campbell, Earl 104
Davis, Ernie 48
George, Eddie 80
Griffin, Robert, III 107
Howard, Desmond 16, 58
Newton, Cam 96
Sanders, Barry 1, 53
Simpson, O. J. 15, 100

Walker, Herschel **1, 69**
Ware, Andre **37**
Williams, Ricky **85**

Heroism
Autrey, Wesley **68**
Delaney, Joe **76**

HEW
See U.S. Department of Health,
　Education, and Welfare

HHS
See U.S. Department of Health and
　Human Services

Hip-hop music
Akon **68**
apl.de.ap **84**
Ashanti **37, 96**
Banks, Azealia **107**
Baraka, Sho **109**
Benjamin, Andre **45**
Blackman, Toni **86**
Blige, Mary J. **20, 34, 60, 97**
Blitz the Ambassador **115**
B.o.B. **91**
Bradley, Adam **101**
Budden, Joe **108**
Cole, J. **97**
Combs, Sean **17, 43, 92**
D'banj **107**
DJ Clue? **111**
Elliott, Missy **31, 90**
Estelle **75**
Fabolous **93**
Fat Boys **92**
Fiasco, Lupe **64**
Forté, John **74**
Franti, Michael **93**
Fresh, Doug E. **93**
Garrett, Sean **57**
Ghostface Killah **90**
Glasper, Robert **101**
Guru **84**
Hill, Lauryn **20, 53, 111**
Hodge, Derrick **114**
Jean, Wyclef **20, 86**
Jennings, Lyfe **56, 69**
Kid Cudi **83**
Kitwana, Bakari **86**
K-Swift **73**
Kweli, Talib **93**
Lighty, Chris **105**
Lil Wayne **66, 84**
Madlib **88**
Mane, Gucci **91**
Method Man **81**
Miguel **98**
Minaj, Nicki **86**
Nelly **32, 90**
Nate Dogg **92**
Patton, Antwan **45**
Peterson, James **81**
Public Enemy **98**
?uestlove **74**
Rascal, Dizzee **82**
Redman **81**
Riggins, Karriem **102**
Roots, The **101**
Run **31, 73**
Scott-Young, Mona **101**
Sermon, Erick **81**
Slick Rick **93**

Smith, Danyel **40**
Swizz Beatz **108**
Tricky **98**
2 Chainz **105**
Wale **92**
West, Kanye **52, 93**
will.i.am **64**
Williams, Pharrell **47, 82**

Hip-hop theater
Power, Will **83**

Historians
Blassingame, John Wesley **40**
Bogle, Donald **34**
Cooper, Afua **53**
Crew, Spencer R. **55**
Cruse, Harold **54**
Fisher, Miles Mark **91**
Franklin, John Hope **5, 77**
Gates, Henry Louis, Jr. **3, 38, 67**
Giddings, Paula **11**
Hammonds, Evelynn **69**
Harris, Jessica B. **91**
Horton, James Oliver **58**
Huggins, Nathan Irvin **52**
Logan, Rayford W. **40**
Nash, Joe **55**
Moore, Wes **86**
Patterson, Orlando **4**
Querino, Manuel Raimundo **84**
Reddick, Lawrence Dunbar **20**
Rogers, Joel Augustus **30**
Sadlier, Rosemary **62**
Skinner, Kiron K. **65**
Snowden, Frank M., Jr. **67**
Washington, James Melvin **50**
Williams, George Washington **18**
Williams, Rhonda Y. **86**

Hockey
Carnegie, Herbert **25**
Doig, Jason **45**
Grand-Pierre, Jean-Luc **46**

Horse racing
Harris, Sylvia **70**
Krigger, Kevin **111**
Minor, DeWayne **32**
St. Julien, Marlon **29**
Winkfield, Jimmy **42**

House of Representatives
See U.S. House of Representatives

Houston Astros baseball team
Richard, J. R. **87**
Watson, Bob **25**

Houston Oilers football team
McNair, Steve **22, 47, 79**
Moon, Warren **8, 66**

**Houston Rockets basketball
team**
Lucas, John **7**
Olajuwon, Hakeem **2, 72**
Smith, Kenny **114**

Howard University
Adams-Campbell, Lucille L. **60**
Benjamin, Tritobia Hayes **53**
Branson, Herman **87**
Cardozo, Francis L. **33**
Childers, Lulu Vere **95**

Cobb, W. Montague **39**
Davis, Arthur P. **41**
Dodson, Owen **38**
Gerima, Haile **38, 80**
Harris, Gary L. **87**
Jenifer, Franklyn G. **2**
Johnson, Mordecai Wyatt **79**
Ladner, Joyce A. **42**
Langston, John Mercer **101**
Locke, Alain **10**
Logan, Rayford W. **40**
Malveaux, Floyd **54**
Neal, Larry **38**
Payton, Benjamin F. **23**
Porter, James A. **11**
Reid, Irvin D. **20**
Ribeau, Sidney **70**
Robinson, Spottswood W., III **22**
Snowden, Frank M., Jr. **67**
Sowande, Fela **39**
Spriggs, William **67**
Swygert, H. Patrick **22**
Wells, James Lesesne **10**
Wesley, Dorothy Porter **19**
White, Charles **39**
Young, Roger Arliner **29**

HUD
See U.S. Department of Housing
　and Urban Development

Hugo awards
Butler, Octavia **8, 43, 58**
Delany, Samuel R., Jr. **9**

Human resources
Howroyd, Janice Bryant **42**

Human rights
Abiola-Costello, Hafsat **108**
Atyam, Angelina **55**
Carter, Mandy **11**
Dow, Unity **104**
Harden, Monique **97**
Kato, David **103**
Maathai, Wangari **43, 97**
McDougall, Gay J. **11, 43**
Mukoko, Jestina **75**

Hunter College
DeCarava, Roy **42, 81**
Mayhew, Richard **39**
Thomas, Michael **69**

IBM
Adkins, Rod **41**
Blackwell, Robert D., Sr. **52**
Dean, Mark **35**
Foster, Jylla Moore **45**
Thompson, John W. **26**
Zollar, Alfred **40**

Ice skating
See Figure skating

Illinois state government
Braun, Carol Moseley **4, 42**
Burris, Roland W. **25, 75**
Colter, Cyrus J. **36**
Jones, Emil, Jr. **74**
Kelly, Robin **114**
Meeks, James T. **92**
Obama, Barack **49, 74, 91**
Raoul, Kwame **55**
Trotter, Donne E. **28**

Washington, Harold **6**
White, Jesse **22, 75**

Illustrations
Anderson, Ho Che **54**
Baker, Matt **76**
Biggers, John **20, 33**
Bryan, Ashley **41, 104**
Campbell, E. Simms **13**
Crichlow, Ernest **75**
Dillon, Leo **103**
Fax, Elton **48**
Honeywood, Varnette P. **54, 88**
Hudson, Cheryl **15**
Kitt, Sandra **23**
Nelson, Kadir **115**
Pinkney, Jerry **15**
Ransome, James E. **88**
Saint James, Synthia **12**
Simmons, Gary **58**

IMF
See International Monetary Fund

Indiana state government
Carson, Julia **23, 69**
Carter, Pamela Lynn **67**

**Indianapolis Colts football
team**
Caldwell, Jim **81**
Dungy, Tony **17, 42, 59**
Sanders, Bob **72**

Indianapolis 500
Ribbs, Willy T. **2**

Industrial design
Harrison, Charles **72**

Information technology
Blackwell, Robert D., Sr. **52**
Coleman, Ken **57**
Council, LaVerne **94**
Gooden, Linda **94**
Hamilton, Vicki **95**
Hill, Wyllstyne D. **94**
Mayberry-Stewart, Melodie **94**
Pinkett, Randal **61**
Smith, Joshua **10**
Steward, David L. **36**
Walker, Tristan **98**
Woods, Jacqueline **52**
Zollar, Alfred **40**

Insurance
Gaston, Arthur George **3, 38, 59**
Herndon, Alonzo Franklin **89**
Hill, Jesse, Jr. **13**
Holstein, Casper **89**
James, Donna A. **51**
Kidd, Mae Street **39**
Killingsworth, Cleve, Jr. **54**
Procope, Ernesta **23**
Procope, John Levy **56**
Scott, Tim **87**
Spaulding, Charles Clinton **9**
Thiam, Tidjane **104**
Vaughns, Cleopatra **46**
Williams, Ronald A. **57**
Willie, Louis, Jr. **68**

Interior design
Ashford, Calvin, Jr. **74**
Bridges, Sheila **36**

De' Alexander, Quinton 57
Ham, Cynthia Parker 58
Hayes, Cecil N. 46
King, Robert Arthur 58
Myles, Kim 69
Steave-Dickerson, Kia 57
Taylor, Karin 34

International Monetary Fund (IMF)
Babangida, Ibrahim 4
Chissano, Joaquim 7, 55, 67
Diouf, Abdou 3
Patterson, P. J. 6, 20

Internet
CasSelle, Malcolm 11
Cooper, Barry 33
Ellington, E. David 11
Gilliard, Steve 69
Knowling, Robert 38
Mitchell, Shireen 89
Thomas-Graham, Pamela 29
Thompson, John W. 26
Walker, Tristan 98

Interpol
Noble, Ronald 46

Interscope Geffen A & M Records
Stoute, Steve 38

Inventions
Chisholm, Daquan 93
Johnson, Lonnie G. 32, 93
Jones, Frederick McKinley 68
Julian, Percy Lavon 6
Latimer, Lewis H. 4
Matzeliger, Jan 93
McCoy, Elijah 8
Morgan, Garrett 1
Temple, Lewis 102
West, James E. 87
Woods, Granville T. 5

Investment banking
Jones, Clarence B. 114
McGuire, Raymond J. 57

Investment management
Beal, Bernard B. 46
Bryant, John 26
Ford, Wallace 58
Gardner, Chris 65
Goings, Russell 59
Green, Isaac H. 79
Harris, Carla A. 67
Middleton, Reggie 105
Procope, Ernesta 23
Rogers, John W., Jr. 5, 52
Utendahl, John 23

Islam
Ali, Ayaan Hirsi 58, 92
Kalbani, Adil 77
Muhammed, W. Deen 27
Noble Drew Ali 100
Redding, Ann Holmes 77

Italian government
Kyenge, Cécile 113

Ivory Coast government
Bedie, Henri Konan 21
Gbagbo, Laurent 43, 90

Guéï, Robert 66
Houphouët-Boigny, Félix 4, 64
Ouattara, Alassane 90
Thiam, Tidjane 104

Jackson State University
Mason, Ronald 27

Jamaican government
Golding, Bruce 78
Holness, Andrew 99
Marks, Audrey 99
Patterson, P. J. 6, 20
Shearer, Hugh 107
Simpson Miller, Portia 62, 100

Jazz
Adderley, Julian "Cannonball" 30
Adderley, Nat 29
Akinmusire, Ambrose 103
Albright, Gerald 23
Ali, Rashied 79
Allen, Geri 92
Ammons, Albert 112
Ammons, Gene 112
Amy, Curtis 114
Anderson, Carl 48
Anderson, Fred 87
Armstrong, Louis 2
Astatke, Mulatu 81
Austin, Lovie 40
Austin, Patti 24
Ayers, Roy 16
Ayler, Albert 104
Bailey, Buster 38
Bailey, Philip 63
Barker, Danny 32
Batiste, Alvin 66
Batiste, Jonathan 108
Batiste, Lionel 105
Bechet, Sidney 18
Belgrave, Marcus 77
Belle, Regina 1, 51
Betts, Keter 85
Blade, Brian 88
Blakey, Art 37
Blanchard, Terence 43
Bland, Edward 111
Blanton, Jimmy 108
Bolden, Buddy 39
Bridgewater, Dee Dee 32, 92
Brown, Clifford 86
Bryant, Ray 95
Buckner, Milt 110
Burley, Dan 96
Butler, Jonathan 28
Byrd, Donald 109
Callier, Terry 106
Calloway, Blanche 100
Calloway, Cab 14
Carter, Benny 46
Carter, Regina 23
Carter, Ron 104
Carter, Warrick L. 27
Cartiér, Xam Wilson 41
Charles, Ray 16, 48
Cheatham, Doc 17
Christian, Jodie 103
Clark, Sharón 105
Clarke, Kenny 27
Clayton, Gerald 111
Cobb, Arnett 114
Cole, Maria 104
Cole, Nat "King" 17

Cole, Natalie 17, 60, 84
Coleman, George 106
Coleman, Ornette 39, 69
Coltrane, Alice 70
Coltrane, John 19
Coltrane, Ravi 71
Cook, Charles "Doc" 44
Cosey, Pete 103
Count Basie 23
Crawford, Hank 77
Crawford, Randy 19
Crothers, Scatman 19
Crouch, Stanley 11, 87
Crowder, Henry 16
Curson, Ted 108
Daemyon, Jerald 64
Dara, Olu 35
Davis, Anthony 11
Davis, Frank Marshall 47
Davis, Miles 4
Davis, Wild Bill 114
Dickenson, Vic 38
Dixon, Bill 87
Donegan, Dorothy 19
Dorham, Kenny 113
Downing, Will 19
Duke, George 21, 113
Dumas, Henry 41
Durham, Bobby 73
Dyett, Walter 113
Eckstine, Billy 28
Edison, Harry 114
Eldridge, Roy 37
Ellington, Duke 5
Ellison, Ralph 7
Ervin, Booker 106
Eubanks, Kevin 15, 108
Farmer, Art 38
Ferbos, Lionel 95
Ferbos, Lionel 95
Ferrell, Rachelle 29
Fitzgerald, Ella 8, 18
Flanagan, Tommy 69
Foster, Frank 97
Foster, George "Pops" 40
Fox, Donal 114
Freelon, Nnenna 32
Freeman, Von 104
Freeman, Yvette 27
Fuller, Arthur 27
Garner, Erroll 76
Gillespie, Dizzy 1
Glasper, Robert 101
Golson, Benny 37
Gordon, Dexter 25
Green, Grant 56
Greene, Jimmy 74
Griffin, Johnny 71
Güines, Tata 69
Hampton, Lionel 17, 41
Hancock, Herbie 20, 67
Hardin Armstrong, Lil 39
Harris, Barry 68
Hartman, Johnny 109
Hawkins, Coleman 9
Haynes, Roy 87
Heath, Percy 100
Henderson, Fletcher 32
Higginbotham, J. C. 37
Hill, Andrew 66
Hinton, Milt 30
Hodge, Derrick 114

Holiday, Billie 1
Horn, Shirley 32, 56
Hubbard, Freddie 75
Hyman, Phyllis 19
Jackson, Milt 26
Jacquet, Illinois 49
Jamal, Ahmad 69
James, Etta 13, 52, 100
Jarreau, Al 21, 65, 105
Johnson, Buddy 36
Johnson, J. J. 37
Johnson, Ken 106
Johnson, Lonnie 85
Jones, Elvin 14, 68
Jones, Etta 35
Jones, Hank 57, 86
Jones, Jonah 39
Jones, Papa Jo 99
Jones, Quincy 8, 30
Jones, Thad 68
Jordan, Louis 104
Jordan, Ronny 26
Kay, Connie 114
Kenyatta, Robin 54
Klugh, Earl 59
La Roca, Pete 107
Lancaster, Byard 105
Lateef, Yusef 91
Laws, Hubert 90
Ledisi 73
Lee, Consuela 84
Lewis, George 104
Lewis, Ramsey 35, 70
Lincoln, Abbey 3, 88
Little, Booker 105
Locke, Eddie 44
Long, Huey 79
Loueke, Lionel 88
Lucie, Lawrence 80
Lucien, Jon 66
Lynne, Gloria 115
Marsalis, Branford 34, 103
Marsalis, Delfeayo 41
Marsalis, Ellis 90
Marsalis, Wynton 16, 90
McBride, James 35, 87
McGriff, Jimmy 72
McLean, Jackie 78
McRae, Carmen 77
Miller, Marcus 84
Millinder, Lucky 101
Mills, Florence 22
Mingus, Charles 15
Mitchell, Dwike 111
Mitchell, Nicole 66
Monk, Thelonious 1
Montgomery, Wes 88
Moody, James 83
Moore, Melba 21
Moran, Jason 89
Morgan, Lee 102
Morton, Jelly Roll 29
Muse, Clarence Edouard 21
Nascimento, Milton 2, 64
Navarro, Fats 104
Nelson, Oliver 113
Newman, David 76
Oliver, Joe "King" 42
Parker, Charlie 20
Parker, Maceo 72
Parlan, Horace 108
Payne, Freda 58
Peterson, Marvin "Hannibal" 27

Peterson, Oscar 52
Pettiford, Oscar 106
Powell, Benny 87
Powell, Bud 24
Purdie, Bernard 77
Ray, Carline 113
Redman, Joshua 30
Reeves, Dianne 32
Rhyne, Melvin 109
Riggins, Karriem 102
Rivers, Sam 95
Roach, Max 21, 63
Roberts, Marcus 19, 113
Rollins, Sonny 37, 94
Ruffins, Kermit 85
Rushing, Jimmy 37
Sample, Joe 51
Santamaria, Mongo 81
Scarlett, Millicent 49
Scott, Hazel 66
Scott, "Little" Jimmy 48
Shaw, Marlena 105
Shepp, Archie 101
Shipp, Matthew 107
Shirley, Donald 111
Shorter, Wayne 75
Silver, Horace 26
Simpson-Hoffman, N'kenge 52
Sissle, Noble 29
Smith, Bessie 3
Smith, Cecilia 102
Smith, Cladys "Jabbo" 32
Smith, Dr. Lonnie 49
Smith, Lonnie Liston 49
Smith, Stuff 37
Smith, Willie 107
Somi 85
Souza, Carmen 111
Staton, Dakota 62
Strayhorn, Billy 31
Sullivan, Maxine 37
Sun Ra 60
Swann, Lynn 28
Take 6 112
Tampa Red 63
Tate, Buddy 108
Tate, Grady 106
Taylor, Billy 23, 92
Taylor, Cecil 70
Tchicai, John 102
Terry, Clark 39
Thigpen, Ed 110
Threadgill, Henry 97
Tisdale, Wayman 50
Trombone Shorty 97
Tyner, McCoy 92
Ulmer, James 79
Valdés, Bebo 75
Valdés, Chucho 89
Vaughan, Sarah 13
Vinson, Eddie 112
Waldron, Mal 109
Waller, Fats 29
Walton, Cedar 114
Ware, David S. 106
Washington, Dinah 22
Washington, Grover, Jr. 17, 44
Washington, Kenny 107
Waters, Benny 26
Watson, Johnny "Guitar" 18
Watts, Reggie 52, 102
Webb, Chick 105
Webster, Katie 29

Wein, Joyce 62
Whalum, Kirk 37, 64
White, Maurice 29
Williams, Claude 80
Williams, Cootie 114
Williams, Joe 5, 25
Williams, Mary Lou 15
Williams, Tony 67
Wilson, Abram 104
Wilson, Cassandra 16
Wilson, Gerald 49
Wilson, Nancy 10, 98
York, Vincent 40
Young, Lee 72
Young, Lester 37

Jet magazine
Johnson, John H. 3, 54
Massaquoi, Hans J. 30
Sleet, Moneta, Jr. 5

Jockeys
Harris, Sylvia 70
Lewis, Oliver 56
Winkfield, Jimmy 42

Johnson C. Smith University
Yancy, Dorothy Cowser 42

Johnson Products
Johnson, George E. 29

Johnson Publishing Company, Inc.
Booker, Simeon 23
Johnson, Eunice W. 83
Johnson, John H. 3, 54
Monroe, Bryan 71
Rice, Linda Johnson 9, 41
Rogers, Desirée 88
Sleet, Moneta, Jr. 5

Joint Center for Political and Economic Studies
Williams, Eddie N. 44

Joint Chiefs of Staff
See U.S. Joint Chiefs of Staff

Journalism
Abbott, Robert Sengstacke 27
Abrahams, Peter 39
Abu-Jamal, Mumia 15
Als, Hilton 105
Ansa, Tina McElroy 14
Aplin-Brownlee, Vivian 96
Ashley-Ward, Amelia 23
Asim, Jabari 71
Aubespin, Mervin 95
Auguste, Arnold A. 47
Azikiwe, Nnamdi 13
Bailey, Chauncey 68
Baquet, Dean 63
Barnett, Amy Du Bois 46
Barrett, Lindsay 43
Bass, Charlotta Spears 40
Bates, Karen Grigsby 40
Bennett, Gwendolyn B. 59
Bennett, Lerone, Jr. 5, 84
Best, Carrie 80
Blair, Jayson 50
Blake, Asha 26
Blow, Charles M. 73
Bolden, Frank E. 44
Booker, Simeon 23

Borders, James 9
Boyd, Gerald M. 32, 59
Boyd, Suzanne 52
Bradley, Ed 2, 59
Britt, Donna 28
Brower, William 49
Brown, George Leslie 62
Brown, Lloyd Louis 42
Brown, Tony 3
Buckley, Gail Lumet 39
Burt-Murray, Angela 59
Burwell, Bryan 83
Caldwell, Earl 60
Campbell, Bebe Moore 6, 24, 59
Cary, Mary Ann Shadd 30
Cayton, Horace 26
Chadiha, Jeffri 57
Chideya, Farai 14, 61
Chiles, Nick 98
Churchwell, Robert, Sr. 76
Ciara, Barbara 69
Cooke, Marvel 31
Cook-Parrish, Mary Virginia 95
Cooper, Andrew W. 36
Cooper, Barry 33
Cooper, Helene 74
Cose, Ellis 5, 50
Croal, N'Gai 76
Crouch, Stanley 11, 87
Crump, Steven 96
Crutchfield, James N. 55
Cullen, Countee 8
Cunningham, Evelyn 23, 85
Dash, Leon 47
Datcher, Michael 60
Davis, Belva 61
Davis, Frank Marshall 47
Davis, Thulani 61
Dawkins, Wayne 20
Deggans, Eric 71
Douglass, Frederick 87
Drummond, William J. 40
Due, Tananarive 30
Dunnigan, Alice Allison 41
Duthiers, Vladimir 109
Eagleson, William Lewis 90
Edmonds, Terry 17
Elie, Lolis Eric 97
Epperson, Sharon 54
Farley, Christopher John 54
Forman, James 7, 51
Fortune, T. Thomas 6
Fuller, Hoyt 44
Gaiter, Dorothy J. 80
Giddings, Paula 11
Gilliard, Steve 69
Givhan, Robin Deneen 72
Goode, Mal 13
Gordon, Ed 10, 53
Granderson, LZ 103
Grimké, Archibald H. 9
Gumbel, Bryant 14, 80
Gumbel, Greg 8
Hall, Tamron 96
Hare, Nathan 44
Harrington, Oliver W. 9
Harris, Claire 34
Harris, Jay 19
Harris, Richard E. 61
Hatcher, Andrew T. 90
Haygood, Wil 83
Haynes, Trudy 44
Henriques, Julian 37

Herbert, Bob 63, 96
Hickman, Fred 11
Hill, Jemele 109
Holmes, T. J. 98
Holt, Lester 66
Huggins, Edie 71
Hunter-Gault, Charlayne 6, 31
Ifill, Gwen 28
Jackson, James A. 90
Jarrett, Vernon D. 42
Jasper, Kenji 39
Jealous, Benjamin Todd 70, 113
Joachim, Paulin 34
Johnson, Georgia Douglas 41
Kaufman, Monica 66
Kearney, Janis 54
Khanga, Yelena 6
Killens, John O. 54
King, Colbert I. 69
King, Gayle 19, 99
Kitwana, Bakari 86
Knight, Etheridge 37
LaGuma, Alex 30
Lacy, Sam 30, 46
Lamar, Jake 96
Lampkin, Daisy 19
Leavell, Dorothy R. 17
Lemon, Don 94
Lewis, Edward T. 21
Lomax, Louis E. 90
Lowe, Herbert 57
Mabrey, Vicki 26
Mabry, Marcus 70
Mabuza-Suttle, Felicia 43
Malveaux, Suzanne 88
Martin, Louis E. 16
Martin, Michel 97
Mason, Felicia 31
Maynard, Nancy Hicks 73
Maynard, Robert C. 7
Mbeki, Govan A. 80
McBride, James 35, 87
McCall, Nathan 8
McGruder, Robert 22, 35
McKay, Claude 6
Mickelbury, Penny 28
Mitchell, Elvis 67
Mitchell, Russ 21, 73
Mkapa, Benjamin W. 16, 77
Monroe, Bryan 71
Mossell, Gertrude Bustill 40
Mukoko, Jestina 75
Murphy, John H. 42
Murray, Pauli 38
Nelson, Jill 6, 54
Neville, Arthel 53
Newkirk, Pamela 69
Njawe, Pius 87
Nkosi, Lewis 46
Noble, Gil 76
Norris, Michele 83
O'Brien, Soledad 88
Oliver, Pam 54
Olojede, Dele 59
Page, Clarence 4
Palmer, Everard 37
Parham, Marjorie B. 71
Parker, Star 70
Parks, Gordon 1, 35, 58
Payne, Ethel L. 28
Payne, Les 89
Perez, Anna 1
Perkins, Tony 24

Phillips, Joseph C. **73**
Pinkston, W. Randall **24**
Pitts, Byron **71**
Pitts, Leonard, Jr. **54, 85**
Plaatje, Sol T. **80**
Poussaint, Renee **78**
Pressley, Condace L. **41**
Price, Hugh B. **9, 54**
Prince, Richard E. **71**
Pugh, Charles **81**
Quarles, Norma **25**
Rapier, James T. **82**
Raspberry, William **2**
Reed, Ishmael **8**
Reeves, Rachel J. **23**
Rhoden, William C. **67**
Riley, Rochelle **50**
Robertson, Gil L., IV **85**
Robinson, Eugene **77**
Robinson, Max **3**
Rodgers, Johnathan **6, 51**
Ross, Don **27**
Rowan, Carl T. **1, 30**
Russwurm, John Brown **100**
Rust, Art, Jr. **83**
Salih, Al-Tayyib **37**
Salters, Lisa **71**
Sanders, Pharoah **64**
Sanneh, Kelefa **96**
Schiavocampo, Mara **97**
Schuyler, George Samuel **40**
Schuyler, Philippa **50**
Senior, Olive **37**
Sesay, Isha **107**
Shaw, Bernard **2, 28**
Shipp, E. R. **15**
Sidner, Sara **105**
Simpson, Carole **6, 30**
Smith, Clarence O. **21**
Smith, Danyel **40**
Smith, Stephen A. **69**
Sowell, Thomas **2, 99**
Staples, Brent **8**
Stewart, Alison **13**
Stokes, Carl **10, 73**
Stone, Chuck **9**
Syler, Rene **53**
Tate, Eleanora E. **20, 55**
Tatum, Elinor R. **78**
Tatum, Wilbert **76**
Taylor, Kristin Clark **8**
Teague, Bob **111**
Thurman, Wallace **16**
Tolson, Melvin B. **37**
Trotter, Monroe **9**
Tucker, Cynthia **15, 61**
Walker, Teshima **114**
Wallace, Michele Faith **13**
Washington, Elsie B. **78**
Washington, Harriet A. **69**
Watson, Carlos **50**
Watts, Rolonda **9**
Wells-Barnett, Ida B. **8**
Wesley, Valerie Wilson **18**
Whitaker, Mark **21, 47**
White, Armond **80**
Whitfield, LeRoy **84**
Whitlock, Jason **78**
Wilbekin, Emil **63**
Wilbon, Michael **68**
Wiley, Ralph **8, 78**
Wilkerson, Isabel **71**
Wilkins, Roger **2, 84**

Williams, Armstrong **29**
Williams, Clarence **70**
Williams, Juan **35, 80**
Wiwa, Ken **67**
Woods, Mattiebelle **63**
Yette, Samuel F. **63**
Zook, Kristal Brent **62**

Judaism
Funnye, Capers C., Jr. **73**
Stanton, Alysa **78**

Judiciary
Allen, Macon Bolling **104**
Gibbs, Mifflin W. **99**
Hatchett, Glenda **32**
Hubbard, Arnette **38**
Sampson, Edith S. **4**
Spencer, Vaino H. **99**
Watt, Garland W. **113**

Kansas City Chiefs football team
Allen, Marcus **20**
Cherry, Deron **40**
Delaney, Joe **76**
Dungy, Tony **17, 42, 59**
Smith, Neil **109**
Thomas, Derrick **25**
Thomas, Emmitt **71**

Kansas City Royals baseball team
White, Frank **95**

Kansas State University
Prince, Ron **64**

Kappa Alpha Psi
Hamilton, Samuel C. **47**

Kentucky Derby
Krigger, Kevin **111**
Winkfield, Jimmy **42**

Kentucky Negro Educational Association
Cotter, Joseph Seamon, Sr. **40**

Kentucky state government
Kidd, Mae Street **39**

Kenyan government
Kariuki, J. M. **67**
Kenyatta, Jomo **5**
Kenyatta, Uhuru **110**
Kibaki, Mwai **60**
Maathai, Wangari **43, 97**
Mboya, Tom **107**
Moi, Daniel Arap **1, 35**
Ngilu, Charity **58**
Odinga, Raila **67, 110**

King Center
See Martin Luther King Jr. Center for Nonviolent Social Change

King Oliver's Creole Band
Armstrong, Louis **2**
Hardin Armstrong, Lil **39**
Oliver, Joe "King" **42**

King's Troop of the Royal Horse Artillery
Scantlebury, Janna **47**

Kraft General Foods
Fudge, Ann (Marie) **11, 55**
Sneed, Paula A. **18**

Kwanzaa
Karenga, Maulana **10, 71**

Labour Party
Amos, Valerie **41**

Ladies Professional Golfers Association (LPGA)
Gibson, Althea **8, 43**
Powell, Renee **34**
Woods, Cheyenne **103**

LaFace Records
Babyface **10, 31, 82**
Benjamin, Andre **45**
OutKast **35**
Patton, Antwan **45**
Reid, Antonio "L.A." **28**

Landscape architecture
Williston, David Augustus **99**

LAPD
See Los Angeles Police Department

Latin American folk music
Nascimento, Milton **2, 64**

Latin baseball leagues
Kaiser, Cecil **42**

Law education
Alexander, Michelle **98**
Bell, Derrick **6, 98**
Carter, Stephen L. **4**
Forman, James, Jr. **89**
Guinier, Lani **7, 30**
Johnson, Edward Austin **107**
Langston, John Mercer **101**
Williams, Patricia **11, 54**

Law enforcement
Alexander, Joyce London **18**
Barrett, Jacquelyn **28**
Bolton, Terrell D. **25**
Bradley, Thomas **2, 20**
Brown, Lee P. **1, 24, 109**
Bully-Cummings, Ella **48**
Evans, Warren C. **76**
Feemster, Herbert **72**
Freeman, Charles **19**
Gibson, Johnnie Mae **23**
Glover, Nathaniel, Jr. **12**
Gomez-Preston, Cheryl **9**
Harvard, Beverly **11**
Hillard, Terry **25**
Holton, Hugh, Jr. **39**
Hurtt, Harold **46**
Johnson, Norma H. **17, 97**
Johnson, Robert T. **17**
Jordan, Eddie **82**
McKinnon, Isaiah **9**
Moose, Charles **40**
Napoleon, Benny N. **23**
Noble, Ronald **46**
Oliver, Jerry **37**
Parks, Bernard C. **17**
Ramsey, Charles H. **21, 69**
Reeves, Bass **100**
Robinson, Bishop L. **66**
Schmoke, Kurt **1, 48**

Smith, Richard **51**
Thomas, Franklin A. **5, 49**
Wainwright, Joscelyn **46**
Ward, Benjamin **68**
Watkins, Craig **97**
Williams, Willie L. **4**
Wilson, Jimmy **45**
Wray, Noble **114**

LDF
See NAACP Legal Defense and Educational Fund

League of Nations
Haile Selassie **7**

Legal Defense Fund
See NAACP Legal Defense and Educational Fund

Lesotho government
Mosisili, Pakalitha **96**

Lexicography
Major, Clarence **9**

Liberian government
Doe, Samuel K. **100**
Henries, A. Doris Banks **44**
Russwurm, John Brown **100**
Sawyer, Amos **2**
Sirleaf, Ellen Johnson **71**
Tolbert, William R. **100**
Tubman, William **99**
Weah, George **58**

Library science
Bontemps, Arna **8**
Franklin, Hardy R. **9, 87**
Harsh, Vivian Gordon **14**
Hutson, Jean Blackwell **16**
Jones, Clara Stanton **51**
Josey, E. J. **10**
Kitt, Sandra **23**
Larsen, Nella **10**
Morrison, Sam **50**
Owens, Major **6**
Rollins, Charlemae Hill **27**
Shockley, Ann Allen **84**
Smith, Jessie Carney **35**
Spencer, Anne **27**
Wedgeworth, Robert W. **42**
Wesley, Dorothy Porter **19**

Librettos
Chenault, John **40**

Lincoln University (MO)
Page, Inman **82**
Randall, Dudley **8, 55**

Lincoln University (PA)
Cuney, William Waring **44**
Sudarkasa, Niara **4**

Literacy Volunteers of America
Amos, Wally **9**

Literary criticism
Braithwaite, William Stanley **52**
Brown, Sterling Allen **10, 64**
Broyard, Anatole **68**
Cartey, Wilfred **47**
Christian, Barbara T. **44**
Cook, Mercer **40**
De Veaux, Alexis **44**

Emanuel, James A. 46
Fleming, Raymond 48
Ford, Nick Aaron 44
Joachim, Paulin 34
Mackey, Nathaniel 75
Mugo, Micere Githae 32
Ngugi wa Thiong'o 29, 61, 101
Redding, J. Saunders 26
Reed, Ishmael 8
Smith, Barbara 28
Wesley, Valerie Wilson 18
West, Cornel 5, 33, 80

Litigation
Allen, Lucy 85
Baldwin, Cynthia 74, 107
Cochran, Johnnie 11, 39, 52
Gary, Willie E. 12
Payne, Ulice, Jr. 42
Rock, John S. 113
Sweatt, Heman Marion 114
Tolbert, James L. 112
Watt, Garland W. 113
Worthy, Kym 84

"Little Rock Nine"
Bates, Daisy 13
Beals, Melba Pattillo 15, 94
Thomas, Jefferson 88

Lobbying
Boyd, John W., Jr. 20, 72
Brown, Elaine 8
Brown, Jesse 6, 41
Brown, Ron 5
Christie, Ron 83
Hart, Thomas A., Sr. 113
Lee, Canada 8
Mallett, Conrad, Jr. 16
Reeves, Gregory 49
Robinson, Randall 7, 46
Wynn, Albert R. 25, 77

Los Angeles Angels baseball team
Baylor, Don 6
Bonds, Bobby 43
Reagins, Tony 94

Los Angeles city government
Bradley, Thomas 2, 20
Brookins, Hamel Hartford 102
Edwards, Willis 104
Evers, Myrlie 8

Los Angeles Clippers basketball team
Baylor, Elgin 93
Brand, Elton 31
Griffin, Blake 98

Los Angeles Dodgers baseball team
Newcombe, Don 24
Strawberry, Darryl 22
Wills, Maury 73

Los Angeles Lakers basketball team
Abdul-Jabbar, Kareem 8
Baylor, Elgin 93
Chamberlain, Wilt 18, 47
Fisher, Derek 97
Fox, Rick 27
Green, A. C. 32

Hazzard, Walt 98
Johnson, Magic 3, 39, 101
Odom, Lamar 81
O'Neal, Shaquille 8, 30, 95
Worthy, James 49

Los Angeles Philharmonic
Lewis, Henry 38

Los Angeles Police Department (LAPD)
Parks, Bernard C. 17
Smith, Richard 51
Williams, Willie L. 4

Los Angeles Times newspaper
Baquet, Dean 63
Drummond, William J. 40

Lost-Found Nation of Islam
Ali, Muhammad 2, 16, 52
Ellison, Keith 59
Farrakhan, Louis 2, 15
Heard, Nathan C. 45
Karim, Benjamin 61
Muhammad, Ava 31
Muhammad, Elijah 4
Muhammad, Jabir Herbert 72
Muhammad, Khallid Abdul 10, 31
Muhammed, W. Deen 27
Sutton, Percy E. 42, 82
Tillard, Conrad 47
X, Malcolm 1
X, Marvin 45

Louisiana state government
Fields, Cleo 13
Francis, Norman (C.) 60
Glover, Cedric B. 103
Jefferson, William J. 25, 72
Morial, Ernest "Dutch" 26
Peterson, Karen Carter 90
Pinchback, P. B. S. 9
Richardson, Rupert 67
Richmond, Cedric 93

LPGA
See Ladies Professional Golfers Association

Lunar surface ultraviolet camera
See Ultraviolet camera/spectrograph

Lynching (anti-lynching legislation)
Moore, Harry T. 29
Till, Emmett 7

MacArthur Foundation Fellowship
Allen, Will 74
Benjamin, Regina 20, 75
Butler, Octavia 8, 43, 58
Carter, Majora 77
Carter, Regina 23
Cooper, Lisa 73
Dabiri, John 93
Gordon-Reed, Annette 74
Hammons, David 69
Harris, Corey 39, 73
Jackson, Mary 73
Johnson, Angela 52
Johnson, Charles 1, 82
Jones, Edward P. 43, 67

Lee, Raphael C. 87
Lindsey, Tommie 51
Lovell, Whitfield 74
Mehretu, Julie 85
Moran, Jason 89
Nelson, Stanley 92
Olopade, Olufunmilayo Falusi 58
Parks, Suzan-Lori 34, 85
Robinson, Aminah 50
Taylor, Cecil 70
Walcott, Derek 5, 94
Whitehead, Colson 77
Williams, Patricia 11, 54

MacNeil/Lehrer NewsHour
Hunter-Gault, Charlayne 6, 31

Mad TV
Jones, Orlando 30
Wilson, Debra 38

Madame C. J. Walker Manufacturing Company
Joyner, Marjorie Stewart 26
Walker, A'lelia 14
Walker, Madame C. J. 7

Major League Baseball administration
Hill, Michael 95
Lucas, Bill 97
Mariner, Jonathan 41
Solomon, Jimmie Lee 38
Young, John 111

Malawian government
Banda, Hastings Kamuzu 6, 54
Banda, Joyce 101
Muluzi, Bakili 14, 76

Malian government
Keïta, Ibrahim Boubacar 113
Touré, Amadou Toumani 18
Traore, Dioncounda 103

Manhattan Project
Quarterman, Lloyd Albert 4
Wilkens, J. Ernest, Jr. 43

March on Washington/Freedom March
Baker, Josephine 3
Belafonte, Harry 4, 65
Bunche, Ralph J. 5
Davis, Ossie 5, 50
Fauntroy, Walter E. 11
Forman, James 7, 51
Franklin, John Hope 5, 77
Hedgeman, Anna Arnold 22
Jackson, Mahalia 5
Jones, Clarence B. 114
King, Coretta Scott 3, 57
King, Martin Luther, Jr. 1
Lewis, John 2, 46, 83
Meredith, James H. 11
Randolph, A. Philip 3
Rustin, Bayard 4
Sleet, Moneta, Jr. 5
Wilkins, Roy 4
Woods, Abraham, Jr. 74
Young, Whitney M., Jr. 4

Marketing
DeVard, Jerri 61
Edwards, Trevor 54

Fils-Aimé, Reggie 74
Gaskins, Rudy 74
Jackson, James A. 90
Kaigler, Denise 63
Kendrick, Erika 57
Leary, Kathryn D. 10
Miller, Pepper 96
Moyo, Karega Kofi 36
Moyo, Yvette Jackson 36
Rolle, Janet 97

Martial arts
Barnes, Steven 54
Copeland, Michael 47
Kelly, Jim 113
Slice, Kimbo 73

Martin Luther King Jr. Center for Nonviolent Social Change
Dodson, Howard, Jr. 7, 52
Farris, Isaac Newton, Jr. 63
King, Bernice 4, 81
King, Coretta Scott 3, 57
King, Dexter 10
King, Martin Luther, Jr. 1
King, Yolanda 6

Martin Luther King Jr. National Memorial Project
Johnson, Harry E. 57

Marxism
Baraka, Amiri 1, 38
Bishop, Maurice 39
Jagan, Cheddi 16
Machel, Samora Moises 8
Nkrumah, Kwame 3
Sankara, Thomas 17

Maryland state government
Brown, Anthony G. 72
Carter, Jill P. 110
Currie, Ulysses 73
Lyons, James E., Sr. 102
Steele, Michael 38, 73, 91
Welcome, Verda Freeman 112

Massachusetts state government
Brooke, Edward W. 8, 88
Gourdin, Edward O. 93
Hayden, Lewis 105
Lewis, William Henry 89
Patrick, Deval 12, 61

Masters Golf Tournament
Elder, Lee 6
Woods, Tiger 14, 31, 81

Mathematics
Alcorn, George Edward, Jr. 59
Banneker, Benjamin 93
Blackwell, David 79
Cox, Elbert Frank 111
Deconge-Watson, Lovenia 55
Emeagwali, Philip 30
Falconer, Etta Zuber 59
Gates, Sylvester James, Jr. 15
Granville, Evelyn Boyd 36
Johnson, Katherine (Coleman Goble) 61
Price, Richard 51

Wilkens, J. Ernest, Jr. **43**

Maxwell House Coffee Company
Fudge, Ann (Marie) **11, 55**

McDonald's Corporation
Thompson, Don **56, 108**

McGill University (Canada)
Elliott, Lorris **37**

MCP
See Malawi Congress Party

Medical examiners
Carter, Joye Maureen **41**

Medicine
Adams-Campbell, Lucille L. **60**
Anderson, William G(ilchrist) **57**
Atim, Julian **66**
Augusta, Alexander T. **111**
Banda, Hastings Kamuzu **6, 54**
Barnett, Herman **112**
Bashir, Halima **73**
Benjamin, Regina **20, 75**
Black, Keith Lanier **18, 84**
Brimm, Charles E. **105**
Callender, Clive O. **3**
Carroll, L. Natalie **44**
Carter, Joye Maureen **41**
Chatard, Peter **44**
Chinn, May Edward **26**
Christian-Green, Donna M. **17**
Cobb, W. Montague **39**
Cole, Rebecca **38**
Comer, James P. **6**
Coney, PonJola **48**
Cooper, Edward S. **6**
Cooper, Lisa **73**
Cornwell, Edward E., III **70**
Counter, S. Allen **74**
Crumpler, Rebecca Lee **89**
Dailey, Ulysses Grant **87**
Deas, Gerald **85**
Dickens, Helen Octavia **14, 64**
Drew, Charles Richard **7**
Durham, James **90**
Edwards, Lena Frances **76**
Edwards, Willarda V. **59**
Elders, Joycelyn **6**
Fennoy, Ilene **72**
Fisher, Ada M. **76**
Fisher, Rudolph **17**
Flowers, Sylester **50**
Foster, Henry W., Jr. **26**
Fraser, Sarah Loguen **100**
Freeman, Harold P. **23**
French, D. M. **94**
Fuller, Solomon Carter, Jr. **15**
Gayle, Helene D. **3**
Gibbons, Gary **107**
Gibson, William F. **6**
Giles, Roscoe C. **93**
Goodlett, Carlton B. **91**
Grant, Augustus O. **71**
Grier, Eliza Ann **90**
Griffin, Anthony **71**
Griffith, Patrick A. **64**
Hamburg, Margaret **78**
Hansberry, Tony, II **93**
Harris, Bernard A. **90**
Hinton, William Augustus **8**
Holmes, Hamilton E. **82**

Hopkins, Donald R. **89**
Hutcherson, Hilda Yvonne **54**
Jefferson, Mildred Fay **89**
Jemison, Mae C. **1, 35**
Johnson, R. M. **36**
Jones, Edith Mae Irby **65**
Joseph, Kathie-Ann **56**
Keith, Rachel Boone **63**
Kenney, John A., Jr. **48**
Kintaudi, Leon **62**
Kong, B. Waine **50**
Kountz, Samuel L. **10**
Kyenge, Cécile **113**
Lacks, Henrietta **101**
Lavizzo-Mourey, Risa **48**
Lawless, Theodore K. **8**
Lee, Raphael C. **87**
Leevy, Carrol M. **42**
Leffall, Lasalle **3, 64**
Logan, Onnie Lee **14**
Malveaux, Floyd **54**
Maxey, Randall **46**
Mossell, Nathan Francis **91**
Naki, Hamilton **63**
Nour, Nawal M. **56**
Okaalet, Peter **58**
Olopade, Olufunmilayo Falusi **58**
Pace, Betty **59**
Petioni, Muriel **99**
Pinn, Vivian Winona **49**
Pitt, David Thomas **10**
Poussaint, Alvin F. **5, 67**
Rabb, Maurice F., Jr. **58**
Randolph, Linda A. **52**
Reece, E. Albert **63**
Ross-Lee, Barbara **67**
Scantlebury-White, Velma **64**
Smith, Ian **62**
Stewart, Ella **39**
Sullivan, Louis **8**
Sweet, Ossian **68**
Taylor, Susan C. **62**
Thomas, Claudia Lynn **64**
Thomas, Vivien **9**
Thornton, Yvonne S. **69**
Tuckson, Reed V. **71**
Walker, Joseph Edison **111**
Washington, Harriet A. **69**
Watkins, Levi, Jr. **9**
Welsing, Frances Cress **5**
White, Augustus, III **100**
White-Hammond, Gloria **61**
Williams, Daniel Hale **2**
Wilson, Donald E. **88**
Witt, Edwin T. **26**
Wright, Charles H. **35**
Wright, Louis Tompkins **4**

Meharry Medical College
Coney, PonJola **48**
Foster, Henry W., Jr. **26**
Griffith, Patrick A. **64**
Lyttle, Hulda Margaret **14**

Men's movement
Somé, Malidoma Patrice **10**

Merrill Lynch & Co., Inc.
Ford, Harold E(ugene), Jr. **16, 70**
Matthews Shatteen, Westina **51**
O'Neal, Stanley **38, 67**

Meteorology
Anderson, Charles Edward **37**
Bacon-Bercey, June **38**

Mexican baseball league
Bell, James "Cool Papa" **36**
Dandridge, Ray **36**

Miami Dolphins football team
Cox, Bryan **83**
Greene, Joe **10**
Little, Larry **90**
Morris, Mercury **114**
Williams, Ricky **85**

Michigan state government
Brown, Cora **33**
Collins, Barbara-Rose **7, 87**
Kilpatrick, Carolyn Cheeks **16**
Kilpatrick, Kwame **34, 71**
Reeves, Triette Lipsey **27**
Wisdom, Kimberlydawn **57**

Michigan Supreme Court
Archer, Dennis **7, 36**
Mallett, Conrad, Jr. **16**

Michigan State University
Wharton, Clifton R., Jr. **7**

Midwifery
Logan, Onnie Lee **14**
Mason, Biddy **89**
Robinson, Sharon **22**

Military police
Cadoria, Sherian Grace **14**

Militia
Kony, Joseph **101**
Lubanga, Thomas **104**
Nkunda, Laurent **75**
Ojukwu, Odumegwu **99**

Miller Brewing Company
Colbert, Virgis William **17**
Shropshire, Thomas B. **49**

Millinery
Bailey, Xenobia **11**

Million Man March
Farrakhan, Louis **2, 15**
Hawkins, La-Van **17, 54**
Worrill, Conrad **12**

Milwaukee Brewers baseball team
Aaron, Hank **5**
Baylor, Don **6**

Milwaukee Bucks basketball team
Abdul-Jabbar, Kareem **8**
Robertson, Oscar **26**

Minneapolis city government
Belton, Sharon Sayles **9, 16**

Minnesota Supreme Court
Page, Alan **7**

Minnesota Timberwolves basketball team
Garnett, Kevin **14, 70**

Minnesota Twins baseball team
Baylor, Don **6**
Carew, Rod **20**

Puckett, Kirby **4, 58**

Minnesota Vikings football team
Carter, Cris **21, 109**
Culpepper, Daunte **32, 85**
Cunningham, Randall **23**
Dungy, Tony **17, 42, 59**
Fowler, Reggie **51**
Gilliam, Frank **23**
Green, Dennis **5, 45**
McDaniel, Randall Cornell **81**
Moon, Warren **8, 66**
Moss, Randy **23, 90**
Page, Alan **7**
Peterson, Adrian **109**
Randle, John **87**
Rashad, Ahmad **18**
Stringer, Korey **35**

Minority Business Enterprise Legal Defense and Education Fund
Mitchell, Parren J. **42, 66**

Minstrel shows
Lane, William Henry **90**
McDaniel, Hattie **5**

Miss America
Dunlap, Ericka **55**
Harold, Erika **54**
Vincent, Marjorie Judith **2**
Williams, Vanessa L. **4, 17**

Miss Universe
Lopes, Leila **99**

Miss USA
Gist, Carole **1**

Miss World
Darego, Agbani **52**

Mississippi state government
Anderson, Reuben V. **81**
Fleming, Erik R. **75**

Missouri state government
Wilson, Margaret Bush **79**

Mixed martial arts
Jackson, Rampage **83**
Silva, Anderson **96**

Modeling
Allen-Buillard, Melba **55**
Banks, Tyra **11, 50**
Beauvais, Garcelle **29, 95**
Beckford, Tyson **11, 68**
Berry, Halle **4, 19, 57, 91**
Campbell, Naomi **1, 31**
Darego, Agbani **52**
Davis, Mia Amber **94**
Dirie, Waris **56**
Dobson, Tamara **111**
Ebanks, Selita **67**
Gibson, Tyrese **27, 62**
Hardison, Bethann **12**
Hounsou, Djimon **19, 45**
Iman **4, 33, 87**
Iman, Chanel **66**
Johnson, Beverly **2, 102**
Kebede, Liya **59**
Kodjoe, Boris **34, 89**
Langhart Cohen, Janet **19, 60**

Leslie, Lisa **16, 73**
LisaRaye **27**
Lopes, Leila **99**
Marcille, Eva **97**
McKenzie, Jaunel **73**
Michele, Michael **31**
Niane, Katoucha **70**
Onwurah, Ngozi **38**
Rochon, Lela **16**
RuPaul **17, 91**
Simmons, Kimora Lee **51, 83**
Sims, Naomi **29, 79**
Smith, B(arbara) **11**
Tamia **24, 55**
Taylor, Karin **34**
Watley, Jody **54**
Webb, Veronica **10, 95**
Wek, Alek **18, 63, 105**

Modern dance
Ailey, Alvin **8**
Allen, Debbie **13, 42**
Brown, Ronald K. **91**
Byrd, Donald **10**
Collins, Janet **33, 64**
Davis, Chuck **33**
Diggs, Taye **25, 63**
Dove, Ulysses **5**
Fagan, Garth **18, 98**
Faison, George **16**
Henson, Darrin **33**
Jeune, Vitolio **98**
Jones, Bill T. **1, 46, 80**
King, Alonzo **38**
Kitt, Eartha **16, 75**
Miller, Bebe **3**
Pomare, Eleo **72**
Primus, Pearl **6**
Spears, Warren **52**
Vereen, Ben **4**
Williams, Dudley **60**

Montgomery bus boycott
Abernathy, Ralph David **1**
Baker, Ella **5**
Burks, Mary Fair **40**
Carr, Johnnie **69**
Jackson, Mahalia **5**
Killens, John O. **54**
King, Martin Luther, Jr. **1**
Nixon, Edgar Daniel **100**
Parks, Rosa **1, 35, 56**
Robinson, Joann Gibson **100**
Rustin, Bayard **4**

**Montgomery County (MD) Po-
lice Department**
Moose, Charles **40**

Montreal Expos baseball team
Dawson, Andre **85**
Doby, Lawrence Eugene, Sr. **16, 41**

Morehouse College
Brown, Uzee **42**
Gloster, Hugh Morris, Sr. **90**
Hope, John **8**
Mays, Benjamin E. **7**
Satcher, David **7, 57, 111**

Motivational speaking
Bahati, Wambui **60**
Baisden, Michael **66**
Bozella, Dewey **97**
Brown, Les **5**

Bunkley, Anita Richmond **39**
Creagh, Milton **27**
Gardner, Chris **65**
Grant, Gwendolyn Goldsby **28**
Gray, Farrah **59**
Jolley, Willie **28**
July, William **27**
Kimbro, Dennis **10**
Russell-McCloud, Patricia **17**
Shabazz, Ilyasah **36**
Tyson, Asha **39**

Motorcycle racing
Brown, Antron **85**
Showers, Reggie **30**
Stewart, James, Jr. **60, 98**

Motown Records
Atkins, Cholly **40**
Avant, Clarence **19, 86**
Ballard, Florence **112**
Birdsong, Cindy **113**
Bizimungu, Pasteur **19**
Busby, Jheryl **3, 74**
de Passe, Suzanne **25**
Edwards, Esther Gordy **43**
Gaye, Marvin **2**
Gordy, Berry, Jr. **1**
Harrell, Andre **9, 30**
Holland-Dozier-Holland **36**
Holloway, Brenda **65**
Hutch, Willie **62**
Jackson, George **19**
Jamerson, James **59**
Jones, Robert G. **81**
Kendricks, Eddie **22**
Knight, Gladys **16, 66**
Massenburg, Kedar **23, 110**
Powell, Maxine **8, 115**
Richie, Lionel **27, 65, 114**
Robinson, Smokey **3, 49**
Ross, Diana **8, 27**
Sanders, Angelia **86**
Supremes, The **33**
Terrell, Tammi **32**
Wells, Mary **28**
Whitfield, Norman **73**
Wilson, Frank **106**
Wilson, Mary **28**
Wonder, Stevie **11, 53**

Mount Holyoke College
Tatum, Beverly Daniel **42, 84**

**Movement for Democratic
Change (MDC)**
Moyo, Lovemore **76**
Tsvangirai, Morgan **26, 72**

Mozambican government
Chissano, Joaquim **7, 55, 67**
Diogo, Luisa Dias **63**
Guebuza, Armando **81**
Machel, Graça **16, 102**
Machel, Samora Moises **8**

Multimedia art
Amaki, Amalia **76**
Bailey, Xenobia **11**
Lovell, Whitfield **74**
Pinder, Jefferson **77**
Robinson, Aminah **50**

Simpson, Lorna **4, 36**

Muppets, The
Clash, Kevin **14, 93**

Murals
Alston, Charles **33**
Biggers, John **20, 33**
Douglas, Aaron **7**
Lee-Smith, Hughie **5**
Walker, Kara **16, 80**

Museum of Modern Art
Pindell, Howardena **55**
Smith, Ming **100**

Music Critics Circle
Holt, Nora **38**

Music publishing
Avant, Nicole A. **90**
Edmonds, Tracey **16, 64**
Griffey, Dick **89**
Handy, W. C. **8**
Holland-Dozier-Holland **36**
Humphrey, Bobbi **20**
Jackson, George **19**
James, Rick **17**
Mayfield, Curtis **2, 43**
Otis, Clyde **67**
Pryce, Trevor **89**
Redding, Otis **16**
Riley, Boots **89**
Shakur, Afeni **67**
Shorty, Ras, I **47**
Strong, Barrett **89**

Music Television (MTV)
Bellamy, Bill **12**
Chideya, Farai **14, 61**
Morton, Frederick A., Jr. **93**
Norman, Christina **47**
Powell, Kevin **31, 74**
Run **31, 73**

Musical composition
Armatrading, Joan **32**
Ashford, Nickolas **21, 97**
Ashford and Simpson **21, 97**
Attaway, William **102**
Baiocchi, Regina Harris **41**
Ballard, Hank **41**
Bebey, Francis **45**
Bell, LeRoy **98**
Benson, Obie **96**
Bland, Edward **111**
Blige, Mary J. **20, 34, 60, 97**
Bonds, Margaret **39**
Bonga, Kuenda **13**
Boulogne, Joseph, Chevalier de
   Saint-Georges **94**
Bridgetower, George **78**
Brown, Dennis **99**
Brown, Patrick "Sleepy" **50**
Brown, Uzee **42**
Burke, Solomon **31, 86**
Burleigh, Henry Thacker **56**
Caesar, Shirley **19**
Carter, Ron **104**
Carter, Warrick L. **27**
Castor, Jimmy **100**
Chapman, Tracy **26**
Charlemagne, Manno **11**
Charles, Ray **16, 48**
Cleveland, James **19**

Cole, J. **97**
Cole, Natalie **17, 60, 84**
Coleman, Ornette **39, 69**
Collins, Bootsy **31**
Cook, Will Marion **40**
Davis, Anthony **11**
Davis, Miles **4**
Davis, Sammy, Jr. **18**
Dawson, William Levi **39**
Diddley, Bo **39, 72**
Domino, Fats **20**
Ellington, Duke **5**
Europe, James Reese **10**
Evans, Faith **22**
Freeman, Paul **39**
Fuller, Arthur **27**
Gamble, Kenny **85**
Garrett, Sean **57**
Gaynor, Gloria **36**
Gillespie, Dizzy **1**
Golson, Benny **37**
Greaves, R. B. **106**
Green, Al **13, 47, 74**
Hailey, JoJo **22**
Hailey, K-Ci **22**
Handy, W. C. **8**
Harris, Corey **39, 73**
Hathaway, Donny **18**
Hayes, Isaac **20, 58, 73**
Hayes, Teddy **40**
Hibbert, Toots **103**
Holland-Dozier-Holland **36**
Holmes, Clint **57**
Holt, Nora **38**
Humphrey, Bobbi **20**
Hutch, Willie **62**
Isley, Ronald **25, 56**
Jackson, Fred James **25**
Jackson, Michael **19, 53, 76**
Jackson, Randy **40**
James, Rick **17**
Jerkins, Rodney **31**
Johnson, Buddy **36**
Johnson, Georgia Douglas **41**
Jones, Jonah **39**
Jones, Quincy **8, 30**
Jones, Thad **68**
Joplin, Scott **6**
Jordan, Montell **23**
Jordan, Ronny **26**
Kay, Ulysses **37**
Kee, John P. **43**
Kelly, R. **18, 44, 71**
Keys, Alicia **32, 68**
Kidjo, Angelique **50**
Killings, Debra **57**
King, B. B. **7**
Lebo M **109**
León, Tania **13**
Lewis, George **104**
Little Milton **36, 54**
Little Walter **36**
Mahlasela, Vusi **65**
Majors, Jeff **41**
Martin, Roberta **58**
Maxwell **20, 81**
Mayfield, Curtis **2, 43**
M.C. Hammer **20, 80**
McClurkin, Donnie **25**
McFerrin, Bobby **68**
Mills, Stephanie **36**
Mitchell, Brian Stokes **21**
Monica **21**

Moore, Chante 26
Moore, Dorothy Rudd 46
Moore, Undine Smith 28
Muse, Clarence Edouard 21
Nash, Johnny 40
Ndegeocello, Meshell 15, 83
Nelson, Oliver 113
Osborne, Jeffrey 26
Otis, Clyde 67
Parker, Ray, Jr. 85
Pratt, Awadagin 31
Price, Florence 37
Prince 18, 65
Pritchard, Robert Starling 21
Redding, Otis 16
Reed, A. C. 36
Reid, Antonio "L.A." 28
Roach, Max 21, 63
Robinson, Reginald R. 53
Run-DMC 31, 75
Russell, Brenda 52
Santigold 96
Scott-Heron, Gil 94
Seal 14, 75
Shirley, Donald 111
Shorty, Ras, I 47
Silver, Horace 26
Simone, Nina 15, 41
Simpson, Valerie 21, 97
Solange 97
Somi 85
Sowande, Fela 39
Stewart, Tricky 98
Still, William Grant 37
Strayhorn, Billy 31
Sundiata, Sekou 66
Sweat, Keith 19
Threadgill, Henry 97
Tillis, Frederick 40
Trombone Shorty 97
Usher 23, 56, 95
Van Peebles, Melvin 7, 95
Walker, George 37
Washington, Grover, Jr. 17, 44
Williams, Deniece 36
Williams, Tony 67
Wilson, Abram 104
Wilson, Frank 106
Winans, Angie 36
Winans, Debbie 36
Withers, Bill 61

Musical direction
Barnes, Katreese 97
Bonds, Margaret 39
Johnson, Ken 106
Rushen, Patrice 12

Musicology
George, Zelma Watson 42

Mystery/detective fiction
Bates, Karen Grigsby 40
Bland, Eleanor Taylor 39
Creagh, Milton 27
DeLoach, Nora 30
Hayes, Teddy 40
Haywood, Gar Anthony 43
Himes, Chester 8
Holton, Hugh, Jr. 39
Mickelbury, Penny 28
Mosley, Walter 5, 25, 68
Thomas-Graham, Pamela 29

Wesley, Valerie Wilson 18

Mystic Seaport Museum
Pinckney, Bill 42

NAACP
See National Association for the
Advancement of Colored People

NAACP Image Awards
Alexander, Michelle 98
Brandy 14, 34, 72
Fields, Kim 36
Freeman, Morgan 2, 20, 62, 100
Glover, Danny 1, 24, 103
Lawrence, Martin 6, 27, 60
Mac, Bernie 29, 61, 72
McRae, Carmen 77
Moore, Shemar 21, 112
Nelson, Kadir 115
Okonedo, Sophie 67
Prince-Bythewood, Gina 31, 77
Rhimes, Shonda Lynn 67
Spencer, Octavia 100
Taylor, Regina 9, 46, 97
Warner, Malcolm-Jamal 22, 36, 110
Washington, Kerry 46, 107
Wesley, Richard 73

**NAACP Legal Defense and
Educational Fund (LDF)**
Berrien, Jacqueline A. 93
Chambers, Julius 3
Coleman, James E., Jr. 79
Coleman, William T. 76
Days, Drew S., III 10
Edelman, Marian Wright 5, 42
Fisher, Ada Lois Sipuel 76
Guinier, Lani 7, 30
Jones, Elaine R. 7, 45
Julian, Percy Lavon 6
Marshall, Thurgood 1, 44
Motley, Constance Baker 10, 55
Rice, Constance LaMay 60
Smith, Kemba 70
Smythe Haith, Mabel 61

NABJ
See National Association of Black
Journalists

NACW
See National Association of Colored Women

Namibian government
Mbuende, Kaire 12
Nujoma, Samuel 10
Pohamba, Hifikepunye 95

NASA
See National Aeronautics and
Space Administration

NASCAR
See National Association for Stock
Car Auto Racing

Nation of Islam
See Lost-Found Nation of Islam

**National Aeronautics and
Space Administration (NASA)**
Anderson, Michael P. 40
Bluford, Guy 2, 35
Bolden, Charles Frank, Jr. 7, 78
Campbell, Donald J. 66

Carruthers, George R. 40
Douglas, Donya 97
Drew, Alvin, Jr. 67
Easley, Annie J. 61
Ericsson-Jackson, Aprille 28
Gregory, Frederick 8, 51
Harris, Bernard A. 90
Jemison, Mae C. 1, 35
Johnson, Katherine (Coleman
Goble) 61
Johnson, Lonnie G. 32, 93
McNair, Ronald 3, 58
Mills, Joseph C. 51
Nichols, Nichelle 11
Sigur, Wanda 44
Wilson, Stephanie 72

**National Association for the
Advancement of Colored
People (NAACP)**
Anderson, Reuben V. 81
Anderson, William G(ilchrist) 57
Anthony, Wendell 25
Austin, Junius C. 44
Ballance, Frank W. 41
Brock, Roslyn McCallister 86
Brown, Homer S. 47
Chambers, Julius 3
Chavis, Benjamin 6
Cobb, W. Montague 39
Du Bois, W. E. B. 3
DuBois, Shirley Graham 21
Dukes, Hazel Nell 56
Farmer, James 2, 64
Fuller, S. B. 13
Grimké, Archibald H. 9
Hampton, Fred 18
Harrington, Oliver W. 9
Hayes, Dennis 54
Henderson, Wade 14
Hollowell, Donald L. 57
Hooks, Benjamin L. 2, 85
Houston, Charles Hamilton 4
Jealous, Benjamin Todd 70, 113
Kidd, Mae Street 39
Lampkin, Daisy 19
Madison, Joseph E. 17
Marshall, Thurgood 1, 44
McKissick, Floyd B. 3
McPhail, Sharon 2
Meredith, James H. 11
Mfume, Kweisi 6, 41
Mitchell, Clarence M., Jr. 88
Moore, Harry T. 29
Morgan, Irene 65
Moses, Robert Parris 11
Motley, Constance Baker 10, 55
Moyo, Yvette Jackson 36
Owens, Major 6
Payton, John 48
Richardson, Rupert 67
Rustin, Bayard 4
Simkins, Modjeska Monteith 112
Sutton, Percy E. 42, 82
Talbert, Mary B. 77
Terrell, Mary Church 9
Tobias, Channing H. 79
Tucker, C. Delores 12, 56
Van Lierop, Robert 53
White, Walter F. 4
Wilkins, Roy 4
Williams, Hosea Lorenzo 15, 31
Wilson, Margaret Bush 79

Wright, Louis Tompkins 4

**National Association of Black
Journalists (NABJ)**
Curry, George E. 23
Dawkins, Wayne 20
Harris, Jay T. 19
Jarrett, Vernon D. 42
Lowe, Herbert 57
Payne, Les 89
Pressley, Condace L. 41
Rice, Linda Johnson 9, 41
Shipp, E. R. 15
Stone, Chuck 9
Washington, Laura S. 18

**National Association of
Broadcasters Hall of Fame**
Jackson, Hal 41, 104

**National Association of Col-
ored Women (NACW)**
Bethune, Mary McLeod 4
Butler, Selena Sloan 98
Cook-Parrish, Mary Virginia 95
Cooper, Margaret J. 46
Harper, Frances Ellen Watkins 11
Lampkin, Daisy 19
Ruffin, Josephine St. Pierre 75
Stewart, Ella 39
Talbert, Mary B. 77
Terrell, Mary Church 9

**National Association of Social
Workers**
Jackson, Judith D. 57
McMurray, Georgia L. 36

**National Association for Stock
Car Auto Racing (NASCAR)**
Lester, Bill 42, 85

**National Baptist Convention
USA**
Bradley, J. Robert 65
Jones, E. Edward, Sr. 45
Lyons, Henry 12
Shaw, William J. 30
Thurston, Stephen J. 49

National Bar Association
Alexander, Joyce London 18
Alexander, Sadie Tanner Mossell
22
Archer, Dennis 7, 36
Bailey, Clyde 45
Hubbard, Arnette 38
McPhail, Sharon 2
Pincham, R. Eugene, Sr. 69
Quince, Peggy A. 69
Ray, Charlotte E. 60
Robinson, Malcolm S. 44
Thompson, Larry D. 39
Walker, Cora T. 68

**National Basketball Players
Association**
Erving, Julius 18, 47
Ewing, Patrick 17, 73
Fisher, Derek 97
Gourdine, Simon 11
Hunter, Billy 22, 109

**National Black Farmers Asso-
ciation (NBFA)**
Boyd, John W., Jr. 20, 72

National Black Fine Art Show
Wainwright, Joscelyn 46

National Book Award
Ellison, Ralph 7
Haley, Alex 4
Johnson, Charles 1, 82
Mackey, Nathaniel 75
Patterson, Orlando 4

National Broadcasting Company (NBC)
Gumbel, Bryant 14, 80
Hinderas, Natalie 5
Holt, Lester 66
Ifill, Gwen 28
Johnson, Rodney Van 28
Madison, Paula 37, 99
Reynolds, Star Jones 10, 27, 61
Roker, Al 12, 49
Schiavocampo, Mara 97
Simpson, Carole 6, 30
Thomas-Graham, Pamela 29
Williams, Montel 4, 57

National Brotherhood of Skiers (NBS)
Horton, Andre 33
Horton, Suki 33

National Coalition of 100 Black Women (NCBW)
Mays, Leslie A. 41
McCabe, Jewell Jackson 10

National Council of Churches
Howard, M. William, Jr. 26

National Council of Negro Women (NCNW)
Bethune, Mary McLeod 4
Blackwell, Unita 17
Cole, Johnnetta B. 5, 43
Height, Dorothy I. 2, 23, 78
Lampkin, Daisy 19
Smith, Jane E. 24
Staupers, Mabel K. 7

National Council on the Arts
Robinson, Cleo Parker 38

National Cowboys of Color Museum and Hall of Fame
Austin, Gloria 63
Austin, Jim 63
Pickett, Bill 11
Pride, Charley 26
Sampson, Charles 13

National Dental Association
Madison, Romell 45

National Education Association (NEA)
Futrell, Mary Hatwood 33
Koontz, Elizabeth Duncan 101

National Endowment for the Arts (NEA)
Barthé, Earl 78
Bradley, David Henry, Jr. 39
Brown, Chuck 78, 102
Hall, Arthur 39
Hemphill, Essex 10
Pope.L, William 72
Serrano, Andres 3

Williams, John A. 27
Williams, William T. 11

National Football League (NFL)
Alexander, Shaun 58
Allen, Larry 109
Allen, Marcus 20
Anderson, Jamal 22
Asomugha, Nnamdi 100
Barber, Ronde 41
Barber, Tiki 57, 107
Barney, Lem 26
Bettis, Jerome 64
Briscoe, Marlin 37
Brooks, Aaron 33
Brooks, Derrick 43
Brown, Jim 11, 95
Bruce, Isaac 26
Bryant, Cullen 81
Bush, Reggie 59, 88
Butler, Leroy, III 17
Caldwell, Jim 81
Campbell, Earl 104
Carter, Cris 21, 109
Cherry, Deron 40
Cox, Bryan 83
Crennel, Romeo 54, 107
Cromartie, Antonio 115
Croom, Sylvester 50
Cruz, Victor 107
Culp, Curley 110
Culpepper, Daunte 32, 85
Cunningham, Randall 23
Davis, Milt 74
Davis, Terrell 20
Davis, Wade, Jr. 103
Dean, Fred 98
Delaney, Joe 76
Dent, Richard 97
Dickerson, Eric 27, 108
Driver, Donald 99
Duerson, Dave 93
Dunn, Warrick 90
Edwards, Herman 51
Farr, Mel 24
Faulk, Marshall 35, 96
Foster, Arian 114
Fowler, Reggie 51
George, Eddie 80
Gilliam, Frank 23
Gilliam, Joe 31
Green, Darrell 39, 74
Green, Dennis 5, 45
Greene, Joe 10
Greenwood, L. C. 115
Griffin, Robert, III 107
Harris, Franco 97
Harris, James 79
Hill, Calvin 19
Holmes, Santonio 87
Howard, Desmond 16, 58
Irvin, Michael 64
Jackson, Rickey 88
Jackson, Tom 70
Jenkins, Kris 98
Johnson, Calvin 108
Johnson, Chad 108
Johnson, Chris 92
Johnson, John Henry 96
Johnson, Keyshawn 91
Johnson, Levi 48
Joiner, Charlie 102

Jones, Adam 103
Jones, Deacon 92, 112
Jones-Drew, Maurice 113
Kennedy, Cortez 104
Ladd, Ernie 64
Lane, Dick 92
Lewis, Jamal 115
Lewis, Ray 33, 109
Little, Floyd 86
Little, Larry 90
Lofton, James 42
Lott, Ronnie 9
Martin, Curtis 104
Matson, Ollie 93
Mayhew, Martin R. 76
McDaniel, Randall Cornell 81
McNair, Steve 22, 47, 79
Monk, Art 38, 73
Moon, Warren 8, 66
Morris, Mercury 114
Moss, Randy 23, 90
Motley, Marion 26
Muncie, Chuck 112
Newsome, Ozzie 26
Newton, Cam 96
Ogden, Jonathan 110
Oliver, Pam 54
Oliver, Paul 115
Owens, Terrell 53, 106
Pace, Orlando 21
Page, Alan 7
Parker, Jim 64
Payton, Walter 11, 25
Peete, Rodney 60
Perry, Joe 95
Peterson, Adrian 109
Pryce, Trevor 89
Randle, John 87
Rashad, Ahmad 18
Reece, Marcel 114
Reese, Jerry 103
Rhodes, Ray 14
Rice, Jerry 5, 55, 89
Rice, Ray 112
Roaf, Willie 106
Robinson, Dave 110
Rolle, Myron 98
Sanders, Barry 1, 53
Sanders, Bob 72
Sanders, Deion 4, 31, 96
Sapp, Warren 38, 109
Sayers, Gale 28
Seymour, Richard 101
Sharpe, Shannon 97
Sharper, Darren 32
Shell, Art 1, 66
Simpson, O. J. 15, 100
Singletary, Mike 4, 76
Smith, Bubba 96
Smith, Bruce 80
Smith, DeMaurice 92
Smith, Emmitt 7, 87
Smith, Neil 109
Smith, Rick 72
Stallworth, John 102
Stewart, Kordell 21, 111
Stingley, Darryl 69
Strahan, Michael 35, 81
Stringer, Korey 35
Strode, Woody 111
Suggs, Terrell 108
Swann, Lynn 28
Tatum, Jack 87

Taylor, Jason 70
Taylor, Lawrence 25
Thomas, Derrick 25
Thomas, Emmitt 71
Thomas, Thurman 75
Thrower, Willie 35
Toler, Burl 80
Tomlinson, LaDainian 65, 112
Tunnell, Emlen 54
Upshaw, Gene 18, 47, 72
Vick, Michael 39, 65, 94
Vincent, Troy 91
Walker, Herschel 1, 69
Ward, Hines 84
Ware, Andre 37
Ware, DeMarcus 92
Washington, Kenny 50
White, Reggie 6, 50
Williams, Doug 22, 112
Williams, J. Mayo 83
Williams, Ricky 85
Williamson, Fred 67
Willis, Patrick 99
Winslow, Kellen 83
Wood, Willie 111
Wright, Rayfield 70

National Hockey League (NHL)
Brashear, Donald 39
Brathwaite, Fred 35
Brown, Sean 52
Doig, Jason 45
Fuhr, Grant 1, 49
Grand-Pierre, Jean-Luc 46
Grier, Mike 43
Iginla, Jarome 35
Kane, Evander 97
Laraque, Georges 48
Mayers, Jamal 39
McBride, Bryant 18
McCarthy, Sandy 64
McKegney, Tony 3
O'Ree, Willie 5
Salvador, Bryce 51
Weekes, Kevin 67

National Institutes of Health (NIH)
Anderson, Norman B. 45
Cargill, Victoria A. 43
Dunston, Georgia Mae 48
Gibbons, Gary 107
Pinn, Vivian Winona 49

National Inventors Hall of Fame
Carruthers, George R. 40

National Medical Association
Cole, Lorraine 48
Giles, Roscoe C. 93
Maxey, Randall 46
Ojikutu, Bisola 65

National Newspaper Publishers Association
Cooper, Andrew W. 36
Jealous, Benjamin Todd 70, 113
Oliver, John J., Jr. 48

National Oceanic and Atmospheric Administration
Bacon-Bercey, June 38
Fields, Evelyn J. 27

National Organization for Women (NOW)
Hernandez, Aileen Clarke 13
Kennedy, Florynce 12, 33
Murray, Pauli 38

National Parent Teacher Association
Butler, Selena Sloan 98

National Public Radio (NPR)
Abu-Jamal, Mumia 15
Bates, Karen Grigsby 40
Drummond, William J. 40
Early, Gerald 15
Lewis, Delano 7
Martin, Michel 97
Mitchell, Elvis 67
Norris, Michele 83
Smiley, Tavis 20, 68
Walker, Teshima 114
Williams, Juan 35, 80
Zook, Kristal Brent 62

National Rifle Association (NRA)
Williams, Robert F. 11

National Science Foundation (NSF)
Jackson, Deborah 94
Massey, Walter E. 5, 45

National Security Council
Frazer, Jendayi 68
Powell, Colin 1, 28, 75
Rice, Condoleezza 3, 28, 72
Rice, Susan 74, 103
Sutphen, Mona 77

National Union for the Total Independence of Angola (UNITA)
Roberto, Holden 65
Savimbi, Jonas 2, 34

National Urban League
Barrow, Willie T. 85
Berry, Edwin C. 81
Brown, Ron 5
Gordon, Bruce S. 41, 53, 82
Granger, Lester B. 75
Greely, M. Gasby 27
Haynes, George Edmund 8
Jacob, John E. 2
Jones, Eugene Kinckle 79
Jordan, Vernon E. 3, 35
Price, Hugh B. 9, 54
Spriggs, William 67
Young, Whitney M., Jr. 4

National Wildlife Federation
Osborne, Na'taki 54

National Women's Hall of Fame
Cary, Mary Ann Shadd 30
Kelly, Leontine 33
Talbert, Mary B. 77

NBC
See National Broadcasting Company

NCBW
See National Coalition of 100 Black Women

NCNW
See National Council of Negro Women

NEA
See National Education Association; National Endowment for the Arts

Nebula awards
Butler, Octavia 8, 43, 58
Delany, Samuel R., Jr. 9

Négritude
Césaire, Aimé 48, 69
Damas, Léon-Gontran 46
Ndiaye, Iba 74

Negro Ensemble Company
Cash, Rosalind 28
Gordon, Carl 87
Hooks, Robert 76
Rolle, Esther 13, 21
Schultz, Michael A. 6
Ward, Douglas Turner 42

Negro Leagues
Banks, Ernie 33
Barnhill, David 30
Bell, James "Cool Papa" 36
Black, Joe 75
Brown, Raymond 102
Brown, Willard 36
Campanella, Roy 25
Charleston, Oscar 39
Dandridge, Ray 36
Davis, Piper 19
Day, Leon 39
Dihigo, Martín 103
Foster, Andrew 79
Gibson, Josh 22
Grant, Frank 100
Hairston, Sam 88
Hyde, Cowan F. "Bubba" 47
Irvin, Monte 31
Johnson, Clifford "Connie" 52
Johnson, Judy 105
Johnson, Mamie "Peanut" 40
Kaiser, Cecil 42
Kimbro, Henry A. 25
Leonard, Buck 67
Lloyd, John Henry "Pop" 30
Mackey, Biz 82
Morton, Ferdinand Q. 90
O'Neil, Buck 19, 59
Paige, Charley 26
Pride, Charley 26
Radcliffe, Ted 74
Smith, Hilton 29
Stearnes, Norman "Turkey" 31
Stone, Toni 15
Suttles, Mule 108
Wells, Willie 105
Whitney, Davey L. 110

Netherlands Antilles government
Liberia-Peters, Maria Philomena 12

Neurosurgery
Black, Keith Lanier 18, 84
Canady, Alexa 28

Carson, Benjamin 1, 35, 76
Dennis, Gary C. 91

Neustadt International Prize for Literature
Brathwaite, Kamau 36

Nevada state government
Horsford, Steven 88

New Jersey state government
Bryant, Wayne R. 6
Payne, William D. 60

New Negro movement
See Harlem Renaissance

New Orleans city government
Henry, Troy 85
Mason, Ronald 27
Nagin, Ray 42, 57, 88
Perry, James 83

New Orleans Saints football team
Brooks, Aaron 33
Mills, Sam 33

New York City government
Campbell, Mary Schmidt 43
Davis, Gordon J. 76
Dinkins, David 4
Farrell, Herman D., Jr. 81
Fields, C. Virginia 25
Ford, Wallace 58
Hageman, Hans 36
Paterson, Basil A. 69
Spigner, Archie 81
Sutton, Percy E. 42
Thompson, William, Jr. 35, 114
Tolbert, Terence 74
Walcott, Dennis M. 112

New York Daily News
Cose, Ellis 5, 50

New York Drama Critics Circle Award
Hansberry, Lorraine 6

New York Giants football team
Barber, Tiki 57, 107
Reese, Jerry 103
Strahan, Michael 35, 81
Taylor, Lawrence 25

New York Jets football team
Jenkins, Kris 98
Martin, Curtis 104

New York Knicks basketball team
Ewing, Patrick 17, 73
Johnson, Larry 28
Meminger, Dean 114
Reed, Willis, Jr. 86
Stith, Tom 93

New York Mets baseball team
Clendenon, Donn 26, 56
Manuel, Jerry 94

New York Public Library
Baker, Augusta 38
Dodson, Howard, Jr. 7, 52

New York Shakespeare Festival
Browne, Roscoe Lee 66
Gunn, Moses 10
Wolfe, George C. 6, 43

New York state government
Brown, Byron W. 72
Farrell, Herman D., Jr. 81
Johnson, Edward Austin 107
McCall, H. Carl 27
Meeks, Gregory 25
Motley, Constance Baker 10, 55
Owens, Major 6
Paterson, Basil A. 69
Paterson, David A. 59
Smith, Malcolm A. 75
Waldon, Alton R., Jr. 98

New York State Supreme Court
Dudley, Edward R. 58
Jones, Theodore T., Jr. 108
Tingling, Milton A. 110
Wright, Bruce McMarion 3, 52

New York Stock Exchange
Doley, Harold, Jr. 26

New York Times
Blair, Jayson 50
Blow, Charles M. 73
Boyd, Gerald M. 32, 59
Broyard, Anatole 68
Caldwell, Earl 60
Cooper, Helene 74
Herbert, Bob 63, 96
Hunter-Gault, Charlayne 6, 31
Ifill, Gwen 28
Mabry, Marcus 70
Price, Hugh B. 9, 54
Rhoden, William C. 67
Wilkins, Roger 2, 84

New York University
Campbell, Mary Schmidt 43
Newkirk, Pamela 69

New York Yankees baseball team
Baylor, Don 6
Bonds, Bobby 43
Cano, Robinson 97
Jackson, Reggie 15
Jeter, Derek 27, 93
Sabathia, CC 74
Strawberry, Darryl 22
Watson, Bob 25
Winfield, Dave 5, 91

Newark (NJ) city government
Booker, Cory Anthony 68
Gibson, Kenneth Allen 6
James, Sharpe 23, 69

Newbery medal
Curtis, Christopher Paul 26, 113

Newsday
Olojede, Dele 59

Newsweek
Mabry, Marcus 70

NFL
See National Football League

NHL
See National Hockey League

Niagara movement
Du Bois, W. E. B. 3
Hope, John 8
Talbert, Mary B. 77
Trotter, Monroe 9

Nickelodeon
DJ Lance Rock 94
Thompson, Kenan 52

Nigerian government
Abiola, Moshood 70
Abubakar, Abdulsalami 66
Akunyili, Dora Nkem 58
Jonathan, Goodluck 83
Obasanjo, Olusegun 5
Okonjo-Iweala, Ngozi 101
Yar'Adua, Umaru 69, 89

Nigerian military
Abacha, Sani 11, 70
Abiola, Moshood 70
Babangida, Ibrahim 4
Obasanjo, Olusegun 5, 22
Ojukwu, Odumegwu 99

Nigerien government
Issoufou, Mahamadou 102
Tandja, Mamadou 33, 78

NIH
See National Institutes of Health

Nike, Inc.
Edwards, Trevor 54
Miller, Larry G. 72

Nobel Peace Prize
Annan, Kofi Atta 15, 48
Bunche, Ralph J. 5
King, Martin Luther, Jr. 1
Luthuli, Albert 13
Maathai, Wangari 43, 97
Obama, Barack 49, 74, 91
Tutu, Desmond Mpilo 6, 44

Nobel Prize in Literature
Morrison, Toni 2, 15, 86
Soyinka, Wole 4, 93
Walcott, Derek 5, 94

Noma Award for Publishing in African
Ba, Mariama 30

Nonfiction
Abrahams, Peter 39
Adams-Ender, Clara 40
Ali, Hana Yasmeen 52
Allen, Debbie 13, 42
Allen, Robert L. 38
Andrews, Tina 74
Atkins, Cholly 40
Baisden, Michael 66
Bashir, Halima 73
Beah, Ishmael 69
Blassingame, John Wesley 40
Blockson, Charles L. 42
Bogle, Donald 34
Brown, Cecil M. 46
Brown, Lloyd Louis 42
Broyard, Bliss 68
Buckley, Gail Lumet 39

Carby, Hazel 27
Carter, Stephen L. 4
Cashin, Sheryll 63
Chiles, Nick 98
Cobb, William Jelani 59
Cole, Johnnetta B. 5, 43
Cook, Mercer 40
Cox, Joseph Mason Andrew 51
Cruse, Harold 54
Danquah, Meri Nana Ama 93
Datcher, Michael 60
Davis, Angela J. 88
Davis, Arthur P. 41
Davis, George 36
Davis, Thulani 61
Dickerson, Debra J. 60
Dunnigan, Alice Allison 41
Elliott, Lorris 37
Fax, Elton 48
Fine, Sam 60
Finner-Williams, Paris Michele 62
Fisher, Antwone 40
Forna, Aminatta 95
Foster, Cecil 32
Gayle, Addison, Jr. 41
Gladwell, Malcolm 62
Golden, Marita 19, 99
Greenwood, Monique 38
Harrison, Alvin 28
Harrison, Calvin 28
Henderson, David 53
Henries, A. Doris Banks 44
Henriques, Julian 37
Hercules, Frank 44
Hernton, Calvin C. 51
Hill, Errol 40
Horne, Frank 44
Ilibagiza, Immaculée 66
Jefferson, Margo 108
Johnson, Sandra K. 94
Johnson, William 91
Jolley, Willie 28
Jordan, Vernon E. 7, 35
Kayira, Legson 40
Kearney, Janis 54
Kennedy, Randall 40
Kincaid, Jamaica 4, 109
Knight, Etheridge 37
Ladner, Joyce A. 42
Lampley, Oni Faida 43, 71
Lane, Lunsford 93
Laymon, Kiese 113
Lee, Jarena 100
Lincoln, C. Eric 38
Mabuza-Suttle, Felicia 43
Malveaux, Julianne 32, 70
Manley, Ruth 34
Mathabane, Mark 5, 99
Matthews Shatteen, Westina 51
McKenzie, Vashti M. 29
McKinney Hammond, Michelle 51
McWhorter, John 35
Miller, Pepper 96
Mossell, Gertrude Bustill 40
Murray, Pauli 38
Naylor, Gloria 10, 42
Neal, Mark Anthony 74
Newkirk, Pamela 69
Nissel, Angela 42
Norton, Meredith 72
Parks, Rosa 1, 35, 56
Pearson, Felicia 99
Petersen, Neal 96

Pitts, Leonard, Jr. 54, 85
Reid, Ira De A. 100
Run 31, 73
Rusesabagina, Paul 60
Sadler, Rosemary 62
Shakur, Yusef 85
Smith, Jessie Carney 35
Steele, Shelby 13, 82
Thornton, Yvonne S. 69
Wade-Gayles, Gloria Jean 41
Walker, Rebecca 50
Wambugu, Florence 42
Wilkens, J. Ernest, Jr. 43
Williams, Terrie 35
Williams, Wendy 62
Wiwa, Ken 67
Wright, Nathan, Jr. 56
Zook, Kristal Brent 62

North Carolina state government
Ballance, Frank W. 41
Fuller, Thomas O. 90
Watt, Mel 26, 105

North Carolina State University
Lowe, Sidney 64

North Pole
Counter, S. Allen 74
Delany, Martin R. 27
Henson, Matthew 2
Hillary, Barbara 65
McLeod, Gus 27

NOW
See National Organization for Women

NPR
See National Public Radio

NRA
See National Rifle Association

NSF
See National Science Foundation

Nuclear energy
O'Leary, Hazel 6
Packer, Daniel 56
Quarterman, Lloyd Albert 4

Nuclear Regulatory Commission
Jackson, Shirley Ann 12

Nursing
Adams-Ender, Clara 40
Auguste, Rose-Anne 13
Ferguson, Vernice D. 108
Hillary, Barbara 65
Hughes, Ebony 57
Hunter, Alberta 42
Johnson, Hazel 22
Johnson, Mamie "Peanut" 40
Larsen, Nella 10
Lewis, Daurene 72
Lyttle, Hulda Margaret 14
Richards, Hilda 49
Riley, Helen Caldwell Day 13
Robinson, Rachel 16
Robinson, Sharon 22
Seacole, Mary 54
Shabazz, Betty 7, 26

Staupers, Mabel K. 7
Taylor, Susie King 13

Nutrition
Clark, Celeste 15
Gregory, Dick 1, 54
Smith, Ian 62
Watkins, Shirley R. 17

Oakland Athletics baseball team
Baylor, Don 6
Henderson, Rickey 28, 78
Jackson, Reggie 15

Oakland Tribune
Bailey, Chauncey 68
Maynard, Nancy Hicks 73
Maynard, Robert C. 7

OAU
See African Union

Obie awards
Browne, Roscoe Lee 66
Carter, Nell 39
De Shields, André 72
Freeman, Morgan 2, 20, 62, 100
Freeman, Yvette 27
Orlandersmith, Dael 42
Sands, Diana 87
Thigpen, Lynne 17, 41

Office of Civil Rights
See U.S. Department of Education

Ohio state government
Brown, Les 5
Ford, Jack 39
Stokes, Carl 10, 73
White, Michael R. 5
Williams, George Washington 18

Oklahoma Hall of Fame
Mitchell, Leona 42

Oklahoma state government
Ross, Don 27

Oklahoma Supreme Court
Colbert, Tom 115

Olympics
Ali, Muhammad 2, 16, 52
Barksdale, Don 103
Beamon, Bob 30
Bekele, Kenenisa 75
Bolt, Usain 73, 104
Bonaly, Surya 7
Bonheur, Yannick 84
Boozer, Bob 103
Bowe, Riddick 6, 107
Campbell, Milt 113
Campbell-Brown, Veronica 102
Carlos, John 97
Christie, Linford 8
Clay, Bryan 57, 74
Coachman, Alice 18
Davis, Shani 58, 84
Dawes, Dominique 11
DeFrantz, Anita 37
DeGale, James 74
Devers, Gail 7, 87
Dibaba, Tirunesh 73, 109
Edwards, Teresa 14, 95
Ervin, Anthony 66

Eto'o, Samuel **73**
Farah, Mo **104**
Felix, Allyson **48, 98**
Flowers, Vonetta **35**
Fraser-Pryce, Shelly-Ann **113**
Frazier, Joe **19, 98**
Freeman, Cathy **29**
Garrison, Zina **2**
Gay, Tyson **114**
Gebrselassie, Haile **70**
Gourdin, Edward O. **93**
Gourdine, Meredith **33**
Greene, Maurice **27, 77**
Griffith, Yolanda **25**
Griffith-Joyner, Florence **28**
Harrison, Alvin **28**
Harrison, Calvin **28**
Harris-Stewart, Lusia **90**
Hayes, Bob **77**
Hazzard, Walt **98**
Hernández, Orlando **96**
Hines, Garrett **35**
Holmes, Kelly **47**
Holyfield, Evander **6**
Howard, Sherri **36**
Iginla, Jarome **35**
James, G. Larry **74**
James, Vanessa **84**
Johnson, Ben **1**
Johnson, Michael **13**
Johnson, Rafer **33**
Jones, Cullen **73**
Jones, Lou **64**
Jones, Randy **35**
Joyner-Kersee, Jackie **5**
Keflezighi, Meb **49**
Kidd, Jason **86**
Kipsang, Wilson **115**
Lewis, Carl **4, 97**
Malone, Karl **18, 51, 90**
Matson, Ollie **93**
Metcalfe, Ralph **26**
Miller, Cheryl **10, 74**
Montgomery, Tim **41**
Moses, Edwin **8**
Moussambani, Eric **105**
Mutola, Maria **12**
Omar, Samia Yusuf **107**
Owens, Jesse **2**
Powell, Mike **7**
Quirot, Ana **13**
Richards-Ross, Sanya **66, 98**
Rudolph, Wilma **4**
Savón, Félix **105**
Scurry, Briana **27**
Smith, Tommie **102**
Stevenson, Teófilo **103**
Temple, Ed **109**
Thomas, Debi **26**
Thugwane, Josia **21**
Vanessa James and Yannick Bonheur **84**
Wade, Dwyane **61, 103**
Walker, LeRoy T. **106**
Wanjiru, Sammy **94**
Ward, Andre **62**
Ward, Lloyd **21, 46**
Westbrook, Peter **20**
Whitaker, Pernell **10, 89**
White, Willye **67**
Whitfield, Mal **60**
Williams, Lauryn **58**

Woodruff, John **68**

***On a Roll* Radio**
Smith, Greg **28**

Oncology
Leffall, Lasalle **3, 64**

100 Black Men of America
Dortch, Thomas W., Jr. **45**
Llewellyn, J. Bruce **13, 85**

Ontario Legislature
Curling, Alvin **34**

Opera
Adams, Leslie **39**
Allen, Betty **83**
Anderson, Marian **2, 33**
Arroyo, Martina **30**
Battle, Kathleen **70**
Brown, Angela M. **54**
Brown, Anne **76**
Brown, Uzee **42**
Brownlee, Lawrence **88**
Bumbry, Grace **5**
Collins, Janet **33, 64**
Conrad, Barbara Smith **90**
Dale, Clamma **103**
Davis, Anthony **11**
Dobbs, Mattiwilda **34**
Duncan, Todd **76**
Estes, Simon **28**
Freeman, Paul **39**
Graves, Denyce Antoinette **19, 57**
Greely, M. Gasby **27**
Grist, Reri **84**
Hendricks, Barbara **3, 67**
Joplin, Scott **6**
Joyner, Matilda Sissieretta **15**
Lister, Marquita **65**
Matshikiza, Pumeza **115**
Matthews, Benjamin **93**
Maynor, Dorothy **19**
McDonald, Audra **20, 62**
McFerrin, Robert, Sr. **94**
Mitchell, Leona **42**
Norman, Jessye **5**
Phillips, Helen L. **63**
Price, Leontyne **1**
Ragin, Derek Lee **84**
Simpson-Hoffman, N'kenge **52**
Still, William Grant **37**
Three Mo' Tenors **35**
Verrett, Shirley **66, 91**
Warfield, William **94**
White, Willard **53**

Ophthalmology
Bath, Patricia E. **37**

Oracle Corporation
Phillips, Charles E., Jr. **57, 109**
Woods, Jacqueline **52**

Organ
Bryant, Paul **115**
Buckner, Milt **110**
Davis, Wild Bill **114**
McGriff, Jimmy **72**
Rhyne, Melvin **109**

Organization executive
Edelin, Ramona Hoage **19**
Gayle, Helene D. **3, 46**

Jackson, Phillip **115**
McGhee, Heather C. **106**

Organization of African Unity
See African Union

Organization Us
Karenga, Maulana **10, 71**

Organized crime
Coke, Christopher **108**
Holstein, Casper **89**
Johnson, Bumpy **102**

Osteopathy
Allen, Ethel D. **13**
Anderson, William G(ilchrist) **57**
Ross-Lee, Barbara **67**

Painting
Alston, Charles **33**
Amos, Emma **63**
Andrews, Benny **22, 59**
Bailey, Radcliffe **19**
Bannister, Edward Mitchell **88**
Barnes, Ernie **16, 78**
Barthe, Richmond **15**
Basquiat, Jean-Michel **5**
Bearden, Romare **2, 50**
Beasley, Phoebe **34**
Biggers, John **20, 33**
Bradford, Mark **89**
Brown, Frederick J. **102**
Campbell, E. Simms **13**
Colescott, Robert **69**
Collins, Paul **61**
Cortor, Eldzier **42**
Cowans, Adger W. **20**
Crichlow, Ernest **75**
Crite, Allan Rohan **29**
Davis, Bing **84**
Delaney, Beauford **19**
Delaney, Joseph **30**
Delsarte, Louis **34**
Douglas, Aaron **7**
Driskell, David C. **7**
Ferguson, Amos **81**
Freeman, Leonard **27**
Gilliam, Sam **16**
Goodnight, Paul **32**
Green, Jonathan **54**
Guyton, Tyree **9, 94**
Harkless, Necia Desiree **19**
Hayden, Palmer **13**
Holder, Geoffrey **78**
Honeywood, Varnette P. **54, 88**
Hunter, Clementine **45**
Jackson, Earl **31**
Johnson, William Henry **3**
Jones, Lois Mailou **13**
Knight, Gwendolyn **63**
Knox, Simmie **49**
Lawrence, Jacob **4, 28**
Lee, Annie Frances **22**
Lee-Smith, Hughie **5, 22**
Lewis, Norman **39**
Lewis, Samella **25**
Ligon, Glenn **82**
Loving, Alvin, Jr. **35, 53**
Major, Clarence **9**
Marshall, Kerry James **59**
Mayhew, Richard **39**
McGee, Charles **10**
Mehretu, Julie **85**

Mitchell, Corinne **8**
Motley, Archibald, Jr. **30**
Mutu, Wangechi **44**
Nascimento, Abdias do **93**
Ndiaye, Iba **74**
Neals, Otto **73**
Nugent, Richard Bruce **39**
Ouattara **43**
Pierre, Andre **17**
Pindell, Howardena **55**
Pippin, Horace **9**
Porter, James A. **11**
Prince Twins Seven-Seven **95**
Ransome, James E. **88**
Reid, Senghor **55**
Ringgold, Faith **4, 81**
Ruley, Ellis **38**
Sallee, Charles **38**
Sebree, Charles **40**
Simpson, Merton D. **110**
Smith, Vincent D. **48**
Sudduth, Jimmy Lee **65**
Tanksley, Ann **37**
Tanner, Henry Ossawa **1**
Thomas, Alma **14**
Thomas, Mickalene **61**
Tolliver, Mose **60**
Tolliver, William **9**
Verna, Gelsy **70**
Wagner, Albert **78**
Waring, Laura Wheeler **99**
Washington, James, Jr. **38**
Wells, James Lesesne **10**
White, Charles **39**
Wiley, Kehinde **62**
Williams, William T. **11**
Wilson, Ellis **39**
Wilson, John **109**
Woodruff, Hale **9**

Pan-Africanism
Carmichael, Stokely **5, 26**
Clarke, John Henrik **20**
Cuffe, Paul **98**
Du Bois, David Graham **45**
Garvey, Marcus **1**
Haile Selassie **7**
Kenyatta, Jomo **5**
Lee, Robert **112**
Logan, Rayford W. **40**
Madhubuti, Haki **7, 85**
Marshall, Paule **7, 77**
Nkrumah, Kwame **3**
Nyerere, Julius **5**
Touré, Sekou **6**
Turner, Henry McNeal **5**

PBS
See Public Broadcasting Service

Peace Corps
See U.S. Peace Corps

Pediatrics
Carson, Benjamin **1, 35, 76**
Elders, Joycelyn **6**
Fennoy, Ilene **72**
Lawrence, Margaret Morgan **100**
Witt, Edwin T. **26**

PEN/Faulkner award
Bradley, David Henry, Jr. **39**
Mayhew, Richard **39**

Wideman, John Edgar 5, 87

Pennsylvania state government
Allen, Ethel D. 13
Brown, Homer S. 47
Fattah, Chaka 11, 70, 112
Fauset, Crystal Dreda Bird 100
Irvis, K. Leroy 67
Nix, Robert N. C., Jr. 51

Pennsylvania Supreme Court
Baldwin, Cynthia 74, 107

Pentecostal church
Brazier, Arthur M. 115
DuBois, Joshua 88
Mason, Charles Harrison 107
Patterson, Gilbert Earl 41
Patterson, J. O., Jr. 80
Rivers, Eugene F., III 81
Sapp, Marvin 74
Seymour, William J. 106
Wright, Timothy 74

People United to Serve Humanity (PUSH)
Barrow, Willie T. 85
Jackson, Jesse 1, 27, 72
Jackson, Jesse, Jr. 14, 45, 81, 108

PepsiCo Inc.
Banks, Paula A. 68
Boyd, Edward 70

Perkins Prize
Jones, Thomas W. 41

PGA
See Professional Golfers' Association

Pharmaceuticals
Flowers, Sylester 50
Frazier, Kenneth 97
Lewis-Hall, Freda 105
Potter, Myrtle 40

Pharmacist
Akunyili, Dora Nkem 58
Flowers, Sylester 50
Pickett, Cecil 39
Stewart, Ella 39

Phi Beta Sigma Fraternity
Thomas, Arthur Ray 52

Philadelphia city government
Allen, Ethel D. 13
Goode, W. Wilson 4
Nutter, Michael 69, 112
Street, John F. 24

Philadelphia Eagles football team
Cunningham, Randall 23
McNabb, Donovan 29
Rhodes, Ray 14
White, Reggie 6, 50

Philadelphia Flyers hockey team
Brashear, Donald 39
Charleston, Oscar 39

Philadelphia Phillies baseball team
Howard, Ryan 65, 113
Rollins, Jimmy 70

Philadelphia 76ers basketball team
Barkley, Charles 5, 66
Bol, Manute 1
Chamberlain, Wilt 18, 47
Erving, Julius 18, 47
Iverson, Allen 24, 46
Stackhouse, Jerry 30

Philanthropy
Banks, Paula A. 68
Brown, Eddie C. 35
Cole, Maria 104
Cooper, Evern 40
Cosby, Bill 7, 26, 59
Cosby, Camille 14, 80
Dawson, Matel, Jr. 39
Edley, Christopher 2, 48
Gardner, Chris 65
Gray, Willie 46
Ibrahim, Mo 67, 115
Johnson, Kevin 70
Johnson, Sheila Crump 48
Jones, Paul R. 76
Lavizzo-Mourey, Risa 48
Malone, Annie 13
McCarty, Osceola 16
Millines Dziko, Trish 28
Pleasant, Mary Ellen 9
Reeves, Rachel J. 23
Rolle, Myron 98
Thomas, Franklin A. 5, 49
Waddles, Charleszetta "Mother" 10, 49
Walker, Madame C. J. 7
Washington, Pauletta Pearson 86
Wein, Joyce 62
White, Reggie 6, 50
Williams, Fannie Barrier 27
Wonder, Stevie 11, 53

Philosophy
Appiah, Kwame Anthony 67, 101
Hall, Stuart 78
Piper, Adrian 71
Toomer, Jean 6
West, Cornel 5, 33, 80

Photography
Andrews, Bert 13
Barboza, Anthony 10
Bingham, Howard 96
Cowans, Adger W. 20
Cox, Renée 67
DeCarava, Roy 42, 81
Farley, James Conway 99
Hansen, Austin 88
Harris, Lyle Ashton 83
Hinton, Milt 30
Moutoussamy-Ashe, Jeanne 7
Parks, Gordon 1, 35, 58
Pinderhughes, John 47
Robeson, Eslanda Goode 13
Roble, Abdi 71
Serrano, Andres 3
Simpson, Lorna 4, 36
Sleet, Moneta, Jr. 5
Smith, Marvin 46
Smith, Ming 100

Smith, Morgan 46
Tanner, Henry Ossawa 1
Thomas, Mickalene 61
Taylor, Lonzie Odie 96
VanDerZee, James 6
Weems, Carrie Mae 63
White, John H. 27
Williams, Clarence 70
Willis, Deborah 85

Photojournalism
Ashley-Ward, Amelia 23
du Cille, Michel 74
Jackson, Vera 40
Moutoussamy-Ashe, Jeanne 7
Parks, Gordon 1, 35, 58
Sleet, Moneta, Jr. 5
Van Lierop, Robert 53
Wallace, William 75
White, John H. 27
Williams, Clarence 70
Withers, Ernest C. 68, 88
Yette, Samuel F. 63

Physical therapy
Elders, Joycelyn 6
Griffin, Bessie Blout 43

Physics
Adkins, Rutherford H. 21
Branson, Herman 87
Gates, Sylvester James, Jr. 15
Gourdine, Meredith 33
Imes, Elmer Samuel 39
Jackson, Deborah 94
Jackson, Shirley Ann 12
Johnson, Anthony M. 92
Massey, Walter E. 5, 45
Mickens, Ronald Elbert 105
Tyson, Neil deGrasse 15, 65

Piano
Adams, Leslie 39
Allen, Geri 92
Ammons, Albert 112
Austin, Lovie 40
Batiste, Jonathan 108
Bonds, Margaret 39
Brooks, Hadda 40
Bryant, Ray 95
Buckner, Milt 110
Cartiér, Xam Wilson 41
Christian, Jodie 103
Clayton, Gerald 111
Cole, Nat "King" 17
Coltrane, Alice 70
Cook, Charles "Doc" 44
Count Basie 23
Dameron, Tadd 103
Davenport, Cow Cow 115
Davis, Wild Bill 114
Domino, Fats 20
Donegan, Dorothy 19
Duke, George 21, 113
Ellington, Duke 5
Flanagan, Tommy 69
Fox, Donal 114
Garland, Red 115
Garner, Erroll 76
Hancock, Herbie 20, 67
Hardin Armstrong, Lil 39
Harris, Barry 68
Hayes, Isaac 20, 58, 73
Hinderas, Natalie 5

Hines, Earl "Fatha" 39
Horn, Shirley 32, 56
Jamal, Ahmad 69
Johnson, Johnnie 56
Jones, Hank 57, 86
Joplin, Scott 6
Keys, Alicia 32, 68
Lee, Consuela 84
Marsalis, Ellis 90
McRae, Carmen 77
McShann, Jay 110
Merriweather, Big Maceo 109
Mitchell, Dwike 111
Monk, Thelonious 1
Moran, Jason 89
Parlan, Horace 108
Perkins, Pinetop 70
Peterson, Oscar 52
Powell, Bud 24
Pratt, Awadagin 31
Preston, Billy 39, 59
Price, Florence 37
Pritchard, Robert Starling 21
Professor Longhair 109
Roberts, Marcus 19, 113
Robinson, Reginald R. 53
Sample, Joe 51
Schuyler, Philippa 50
Scott, Hazel 66
Shipp, Matthew 107
Shirley, Donald 111
Silver, Horace 26
Simone, Nina 15, 41
Smith, Willie 107
Sun Ra 60
Swann, Lynn 28
Southern, Eileen 56
Spann, Otis 107
Sykes, Roosevelt 20
Taylor, Billy 23, 92
Taylor, Cecil 70
Turner, Ike 68
Tyner, McCoy 92
Valdés, Bebo 75
Valdés, Chucho 89
Vaughan, Sarah 13
Waldron, Mal 109
Walker, George 37
Waller, Fats 29
Walton, Cedar 114
Watts, André 42, 101
Webster, Katie 29
Williams, Mary Lou 15

Pittsburgh Pirates baseball team
Bonds, Barry 6, 34, 63, 99
Clendenon, Donn 26, 56
Ellis, Dock 78
Stargell, Willie 29

Pittsburgh Steelers football team
Dungy, Tony 17, 42, 59
Gilliam, Joe 31
Greene, Joe 10
Greenwood, L. C. 115
Harris, Franco 97
Perry, Lowell 30
Stallworth, John 102
Stewart, Kordell 21, 111
Swann, Lynn 28
Ward, Hines 84

Woodson, Rod 79

Planned Parenthood Federation of America Inc.
Wattleton, Faye 9

Playboy
Brown, Robert 65
Taylor, Karin 34

Playwright
Anthony, Trey 63
Arkadie, Kevin 17
Armah, Esther 87
Babatunde, Rotimi 104
Baldwin, James 1
Bandele, Biyi 68
Barrett, Lindsay 43
Beckham, Barry 41
Branch, William Blackwell 39
Brown, Cecil M. 46
Brown, Oscar, Jr. 53
Bullins, Ed 25
Caldwell, Benjamin 46
Carroll, Vinnette 29
Césaire, Aimé 48, 69
Chenault, John 40
Childress, Alice 15
Clark-Bekedermo, J. P. 44
Clarke, George 32
Cleage, Pearl 17, 64
Corthron, Kia 43
Cotter, Joseph Seamon, Sr. 40
Cox, Joseph Mason Andrew 51
Dadié, Bernard 34
Davis, Eisa 68
De Veaux, Alexis 44
Dent, Thomas C. 50
Diamond, Lydia R. 101
Dodson, Owen 38
Domingo, Colman 94
Elder, Larry, III 38
Evans, Mari 26
Farah, Nuruddin 27
Franklin, J. E. 44
Glover, Keith 79
Gordone, Charles 15
Gurira, Danai 73
Hansberry, Lorraine 6
Harris, Bill 72
Hayes, Teddy 40
Hill, Errol 40
Hill, Leslie Pinckney 44
Holder, Laurence 34
Hughes, Langston 4
Johnson, Georgia Douglas 41
Johnson, Je'Caryous 63
Jones, Sarah 39
Kennedy, Adrienne 11
Kente, Gibson 52
King, Woodie, Jr. 27
Kwei-Armah, Kwame 84
Lampley, Oni Faida 43, 71
Lee, Leslie 85
Long, Richard Alexander 65
Maponya, Maishe 101
Marechera, Dambudzo 39
Mason, Judi Ann 112
McClinton, Marion Isaac 77
McGhee, Sharon K. 113
Milner, Ron 39
Mitchell, Loften 31
Moss, Carlton 17
Mugo, Micere Githae 32

Ngugi wa Thiong'o 29, 61, 101
Nottage, Lynn 66
Onwueme, Tess Osonye 23
Orlandersmith, Dael 42
Parks, Suzan-Lori 34, 85
Perry, Tyler 40, 54, 103
Rahman, Aishah 37
Redwood, John Henry 78
Rhone, Trevor 80
Salter, Nikkole 73
Sanchez, Sonia 17, 51
Santiago-Hudson, Ruben 85
Schuyler, George Samuel 40
Sebree, Charles 40
Smith, Anna Deavere 6, 44
Talbert, David E. 34, 93
Taylor, Regina 9, 46, 97
Teer, Barbara Ann 81
Thurman, Wallace 17
Tolson, Melvin B. 37
Walcott, Derek 5, 94
Ward, Douglas Turner 42
Wesley, Richard 73
Williams, Roy 89
Williams, Samm-Art 21
Wilson, August 7, 33, 55
Wilson, Tracey Scott 777
Wolfe, George C. 6, 43
Youngblood, Shay 32

Poet laureate (U.S.)
Dove, Rita 6, 78, 101
Trethewey, Natasha 103

Poetry
Abani, Chris 77
Adams, Jenoyne 60
Alexander, Elizabeth 75
Alexander, Kwame 98
Alexander, Margaret Walker 22
Allen, Samuel L. 38
Angelou, Maya 1, 15
Atkins, Russell 45
Aubert, Alvin 41
Baiocchi, Regina Harris 41
Bandele, Asha 36
Barrax, Gerald William 45
Barrett, Lindsay 43
Bell, James Madison 40
Bennett, Gwendolyn B. 59
Bennett, Louise 69
Berry, James 41
Blanco, Mykki 106
Bontemps, Arna 8
Boyd, Melba Joyce 86
Braithwaite, William Stanley 52
Brand, Dionne 32
Brathwaite, Kamau 36
Breeze, Jean "Binta" 37
Brooks, Gwendolyn 1, 28
Brown, Cecil M. 46
Brutus, Dennis 38
Burgess, Marjorie L. 55
Carter, Martin 49
Cartey, Wilfred 47
Césaire, Aimé 48, 69
Chenault, John 40
Cheney-Coker, Syl 43
Clark-Bekedermo, J. P. 44
Clarke, Cheryl 32
Clarke, George 32
Cleage, Pearl 17, 64
Cliff, Michelle 42

Clifton, Lucille 14, 64, 91
Coleman, Wanda 48
Cooper, Afua 53
Cornish, Sam 50
Cortez, Jayne 43, 109
Cotter, Joseph Seamon, Sr. 40
Cox, Joseph Mason Andrew 51
Cuney, William Waring 44
Dabydeen, David 48
Dadié, Bernard 34
D'Aguiar, Fred 50
Damas, Léon-Gontran 46
Dandridge, Raymond Garfield 45
Danner, Margaret Esse 49
Datcher, Michael 60
Davis, Charles T. 48
Davis, Frank Marshall 47
De Veaux, Alexis 44
Dent, Thomas C. 50
Dodson, Owen 38
Dove, Rita 6, 78, 101
Draper, Sharon Mills 16, 43
Dumas, Henry 41
Dunbar, Paul Laurence 8
Dunbar-Nelson, Alice Ruth Moore 44
Dungy, Camille 86
Emanuel, James A. 46
Evans, Mari 26
Fabio, Sarah Webster 48
Fair, Ronald L. 47
Figueroa, John J. 40
Fisher, Antwone 40
Fleming, Raymond 48
Forbes, Calvin 46
Ford, Nick Aaron 44
Frazier, Oscar 58
Gabre-Medhin, Tsegaye 64
Gilbert, Christopher 50
Goings, Russell 59
Goodison, Lorna 71
Harkless, Necia Desiree 19
Harper, Frances Ellen Watkins 11
Harper, Michael S. 34
Harris, Bill 72
Harris, Claire 34
Hayden, Robert 12
Henderson, David 53
Hernton, Calvin C. 51
Hill, Leslie Pinckney 44
Hoagland, Everett H. 45
Horne, Frank 44
Hughes, Langston 7
Jackson, Fred James 25
Joachim, Paulin 34
Johnson, Fenton 91
Johnson, Georgia Douglas 41
Johnson, Linton Kwesi 37
Jones, Sarah 39
Kaufman, Bob 105
Kay, Jackie 37
Keene, John 73
Knight, Etheridge 37
Lacy, Marc 111
Laraque, Paul 67
Letson, Al 39
Lorde, Audre 6
Mackey, Nathaniel 75
Manley, Ruth 34
Marechera, Dambudzo 39
Matejka, Adrian 87
McClellan, George Marion 91
Moore, Jessica Care 30

Mugo, Micere Githae 32
Mullen, Harryette 34
Naylor, Gloria 10, 42
Neto, António Agostinho 43
Nugent, Richard Bruce 39
Okara, Gabriel 37
Okigbo, Christopher 102
Osbey, Brenda Marie 102
Parker, Pat 19
Peters, Lenrie 43
Philip, Marlene Nourbese 32
Phillips, Carl 111
Powell, Kevin 31, 74
Quigless, Helen G. 49
Randall, Dudley 8, 55
Redmond, Eugene 23
Richards, Beah 30
Sanchez, Sonia 17, 51
Sapphire 14, 95
Scott-Heron, Gil 94
Senghor, Léopold Sédar 12
Senior, Olive 37
Smith, Mary Carter 26
Spencer, Anne 27
Sundiata, Sekou 66
Tolson, Melvin B. 37
Touré, Askia (Muhammad Abu Bakr el) 47
Trethewey, Natasha 103
Troupe, Quincy 83
van Sertima, Ivan 25
Walker, Margaret 29
Washington, James, Jr. 38
Weaver, Afaa Michael 37
Williams, Saul 31
Williams, Sherley Anne 25
Woods, Scott 55
Young, Al 82

Poetry Slam, Inc.
Woods, Scott 55

Political science
Ake, Claude 30
Cohen, Cathy J. 88
Dawson, Michael C. 63
Harris-Lacewell, Melissa 81
Skinner, Kiron K. 65
Walters, Ronald 83
Watson, Carlos 50

Politics
Adebari, Rotimi 83
Alexander, Archie Alphonso 14
Ali, Ayaan Hirsi 58, 92
Allen, Claude 68
Austin, Junius C. 44
Avant, Clarence 19, 86
Barnes, Melody 75
Barrow, Dean 69
Blackwell, Unita 17
Boye, Madior 30
Brazile, Donna 25, 70
Brown, Oscar, Jr. 53
Burris, Roland W. 25, 75
Burton, Bill 96
Buthelezi, Mangosuthu Gatsha 9
Butler, Jerry 26
Cain, Herman 15, 92
Césaire, Aimé 48, 69
Chideya, Farai 14, 61
Coleman, Mary 46
Compton, John 65
Conneh, Sekou Damate, Jr. 51

Connerly, Ward 14
Davis, James E. 50
Edmonds, Terry 17
Fields, Julia 45
Foster, Ezola 28
Frazier, Ryan 89
Greenlee, Sam 48
Hatcher, Andrew T. 90
Henry, Aaron 19
Holmes, Amy 69
Ingraham, Hubert A. 19
Jackson, Mae 57
Jarrett, Valerie 73
Kelley, Cliff 75
Keyes, Alan 11, 105
Lindsay, Peta 100
Lynch, William, Jr. 115
Magloire, Paul Eugène 68
McGlowan, Angela 64, 86
Moore, Minyon 45
Morton, Ferdinand Q. 90
Nelson, Sophia A. 93
Obasanjo, Stella 32
Pereira, Aristides 30, 97
Perry, Ruth 15
Pitta, Celso 17
Reed, Joe L. 110
Sankoh, Foday 74
Simmons, E. Denise 79
Simmons, Jamal 72
Sisulu, Sheila Violet Makate 24
Smith, Jennifer 21
Smith, Princella 86
Spencer, Winston Baldwin 68
Watkins, Joe 86
Williams, Eddie N. 44
Williams, Eric Eustace 65
Williams, Maggie 7, 71

Pop music
Ashford, Nickolas 21, 97
Ashford and Simpson 21, 97
Babyface 10, 31, 82
Bailey, Pearl 14
Bailey Rae, Corinne 83
Bassey, Shirley 25
Benson, Obie 96
Birdsong, Cindy 113
Bleu, Corbin 65
Brown, Bobby 58
Brown, Melanie 73
Butler, Jonathan 28
Cannon, Nick 47, 73
Carey, Mariah 32, 53, 69
Chanté, Keshia 50
Checker, Chubby 28
Clayton, Merry 112
Coasters, The 102
Cole, Nat "King" 17
Coppola, Imani Francesca 82
Cox, Deborah 28
Cruz, Taio 104
David, Craig 31, 53
Derülo, Jason 93
Dixie Cups, The 109
Ferrell, Rachelle 29
Graham, Katerina 99
Gray, Macy 29
Hailey, JoJo 22
Hailey, K-Ci 22
Harris, Damon 110
Harris, Major 110
Hawkins, Screamin' Jay 30

Hayes, Isaac 20, 58, 73
Holmes, Clint 57
Horton, Gladys 92
Houston, Whitney 7, 28, 83, 100
Hudson, Jennifer 63, 83
Humphrey, Bobbi 20
Ink Spots, The 102
Isley, Ronald 25, 56
Jackson, Janet 6, 30, 68
Jackson, Jermaine 79
Jackson, LaToya 95
Jackson, Michael 19, 53, 76
Jackson 5 103
James, Rick 17
Jones, Booker T. 84
Jones, Quincy 8, 30
Jordan, Montell 23
Kelis 58
Kendricks, Eddie 22
Keys, Alicia 32, 68
Khan, Chaka 12, 50
Kingston, Sean 94
Knowles, Mathew 96
LaBelle, Patti 13, 30
Lewis, Leona 75
Luckett, Letoya 61
Martelly, Michel 90
Mathis, Johnny 20
McFerrin, Bobby 68
Mills Brothers, The 99
Monica 21
Moore, Chante 26
Mtukudzi, Oliver 109
Mumba, Samantha 29
Mvula, Laura 110
Mya 35
Naughton, Naturi 97
Neville, Aaron 21
New Edition 101
Ne-Yo 65
Noah, Yannick 4, 60
Osborne, Jeffrey 26
Otis, Clyde 67
Palmer, Keke 68
P.M. Dawn 54
Preston, Billy 39, 59
Prince 18, 65
Raven-Symoné 44, 113
Reid, Antonio "L.A." 28
Reid, Vernon 34
Richie, Lionel 27, 65, 114
Rihanna 65, 102
Robinson, Smokey 3, 49
Rogers, Bobby 110
Rowland, Kelly 100
Rucker, Darius 34, 74, 108
Sandé, Emeli 113
Seal 14, 75
Secada, Jon 97
Shirelles, The 111
Short, Bobby 52
Simpson, Valerie 21, 97
Sisqo 30
Smith, Myrna 92
Smith, Willow 92
Solange 97
Staton, Candi 27
Street, Richard 110
Streeter, Sevyn 115
Summer, Donna 25, 102
Supremes, The 33
Sweat, Keith 19
Temptations, The 33

The-Dream 74
Thomas, Irma 29
Turner, Tina 6, 27
Usher 23, 56, 95
Vanity 67
Warwick, Dionne 18, 111
Washington, Dinah 22
Washington, Grover, Jr. 17, 44
Washington, Val 12
Welch, Elisabeth 52
White, Barry 13, 41
White, Josh, Jr. 52
will.i.am 64
Williams, Paul 112
Wilson, Jackie 60
Wilson, Mary 28
Withers-Mendes, Elisabeth 64
Wonder, Stevie 11, 53

Portland (OR) Police Department
Moose, Charles 40

Portland Trail Blazers basketball team
Drexler, Clyde 4, 61
Miller, Larry G. 72
Porter, Terry 75
Roy, Brandon 98

Pratt Institute
Mayhew, Richard 39

Presbyterianism
Cannon, Katie 10

Pride Economic Enterprises
Barry, Marion S. 7, 44

Princeton University
Appiah, Kwame Anthony 67, 101
Blanks, Deborah K. 69
Harris-Lacewell, Melissa 81
Rouse, Cecilia 93
Simmons, Ruth 13, 38

Printmaking
Blackburn, Robert 28
Crichlow, Ernest 75
Neals, Otto 73
Tanksley, Ann 37
Thrash, Dox 35
Wells, James Lesesne 10
Wilson, John 109

Prison ministry
Bell, Ralph S. 5

Prison reform
Betts, R. Dwayne 86

Procter & Gamble
Clement-Holmes, Linda 94

Professional Golfers' Association (PGA)
Bramlett, Joseph 91
Elder, Lee 6
Powell, Renee 34
Sifford, Charlie 4, 49
Woods, Tiger 14, 31, 81

Professional Women's Club of Chicago
Gray, Ida 41

Proposition 209
Connerly, Ward 14

Prosecution
Bensouda, Fatou 103
Darden, Christopher 13
Worthy, Kym 84

Provincial Freeman
Cary, Mary Ann Shadd 30

Psychiatry
Bell, Carl C. 111
Cobbs, Price M. 9
Comer, James P. 6
Fanon, Frantz 44
Fuller, Solomon Carter, Jr. 15
Hamburg, Beatrix 84
Johnson-Powell, Gloria 107
Lawrence, Margaret Morgan 100
Poussaint, Alvin F. 5, 67
Welsing, Frances Cress 5

Psychology
Anderson, Norman B. 45
Archie-Hudson, Marguerite 44
Brown, Joyce F. 25
Clark, Kenneth B. 5, 52
Clark, Mamie Phipps 79
Edwards, Harry 2
Finner-Williams, Paris Michele 62
Fulani, Lenora 11
Gardere, Jeffrey 76
Gilbert, Christopher 50
Hale, Lorraine 8
Hare, Nathan 44
Hilliard, Asa Grant, III 66
Staples, Brent 8
Steele, Claude 13, 97
Sumner, Francis Cecil 112
Tatum, Beverly Daniel 42, 84

Psychotheraphy
Berrysmith, Don Reginald 49
Ford, Clyde W. 40

Public Broadcasting Service (PBS)
Brown, Les 5
Brown, Tony 3
Creagh, Milton 27
Hampton, Henry 6
Hunter-Gault, Charlayne 6, 31
Ifill, Gwen 28
Lawson, Jennifer 1, 50
Long, Loretta 58
Lynch, Shola 61
Roker, Al 12, 49

Public housing
Lane, Vincent 5
Perry, James 83
Reems, Ernestine Cleveland 27

Public policy
Douglas, Derek 88

Public relations
Barrett, Andrew C. 12
Calhoun, Lillian Scott 87
Compton-Rock, Malaak 86
Edmonds, Terry 17
Graham, Stedman 13
Jones, Robert G. 81
McCabe, Jewell Jackson 10

Perez, Anna **1**
Pritchard, Robert Starling **21**
Rowan, Carl T. **1, 30**
Taylor, Kristin Clark **8**
Tobin, Patricia **75**

Public schools
Ackerman, Arlene **108**
Baker, Gwendolyn Calvert **9**
Clayton, Constance **1**
Coleman, William F., III **61**
Collins, Marva **3, 71**
Crew, Rudy **16, 113**
Dewitty, Thelma **114**
Lemon, Alton T. **112**

Public speaking
Bell, James Madison **40**
Brown, Hallie Quinn **100**
Douglass, Frederick **87**
Kennedy, Randall **40**

Publishing
Abbott, Robert Sengstacke **27**
Alexander, Kwame **98**
Ames, Wilmer **27**
Ashley-Ward, Amelia **23**
Aubert, Alvin **41**
Auguste, Arnold A. **47**
Baisden, Michael **25, 66**
Bakewell, Danny **99**
Boston, Lloyd **24**
Boyd, T. B., III **6**
Brown, Jamie Foster **91**
Brown, Marie Dutton **12**
Cary, Mary Ann Shadd **30**
Coombs, Orde M. **44**
Cox, William E. **68**
Dawkins, Wayne **20**
Driver, David E. **11**
Ducksworth, Marilyn **12**
Dumas, Henry **41**
Fuller, Hoyt **44**
Giddings, Paula **11**
Goodlett, Carlton B. **91**
Harris, Jay **19**
Harris, Monica **18**
Hill, Bonnie Guiton **20**
Hudson, Cheryl **15**
Hudson, Wade **15**
James, Juanita **13**
Jones, Quincy **8, 30**
Kunjufu, Jawanza **3, 50**
Lawson, Jennifer **1, 50**
Leavell, Dorothy R. **17**
Lewis, Edward T. **21**
Lorde, Audre **6**
Madhubuti, Haki **7, 85**
Maynard, Nancy Hicks **73**
Maynard, Robert C. **7**
McDonald, Erroll **1**
Moore, Jessica Care **30**
Morgan, Garrett **1**
Murphy, John H. **42**
Parks, Gordon **1, 35, 58**
Perez, Anna **1**
Randall, Dudley **8, 55**
Scott, C. A. **29**
Sengstacke, John **18**
Smith, Clarence O. **21**
Stinson, Denise L. **59**
Stringer, Vickie **58**
Tyree, Omar Rashad **21**
Vanzant, Iyanla **17, 47, 108**

Walker, Alice **1, 43**
Washington, Alonzo **29**
Washington, Laura S. **18**
Wells-Barnett, Ida B. **8**
Williams, Armstrong **29**
Woods, Teri **69**

Pulitzer Prize
Brooks, Gwendolyn **1, 28**
Dove, Rita **6, 78, 101**
Fuller, Charles **8**
Givhan, Robin Deneen **72**
Gordone, Charles **15**
Haley, Alex **4**
Jefferson, Margo **108**
Komunyakaa, Yusef **9**
Lewis, David Levering **9**
Marable, Manning **10, 102**
McPherson, James Alan **70**
Morrison, Toni **2, 15, 86**
Newkirk, Pamela **69**
Page, Clarence **4**
Parks, Suzan-Lori **34, 85**
Payne, Les **89**
Pitts, Leonard, Jr. **54, 85**
Robinson, Eugene **77**
Shipp, E. R. **15**
Sleet, Moneta, Jr. **5**
Walker, Alice **1, 43**
Walker, George **37**
White, John H. **27**
Wilkins, Roger **2, 84**
Wilson, August **7, 33, 55**

Puppetry
Clash, Kevin **14, 93**

PUSH
See People United to Serve Humanity

Quiltmaking
Benberry, Cuesta **65**
Ringgold, Faith **4, 81**

Qwest Records
Jones, Quincy **8, 30**

Race car driving
Brown, Antron **85**
Hamilton, Lewis **66**
Lester, Bill **42, 85**
Ribbs, Willy T. **2**
Scott, Wendell Oliver, Sr. **19**

Race relations
Abbott, Diane **9**
Alexander, Clifford **26**
Anthony, Wendell **25**
Asante, Molefi Kete **3**
Baldwin, James **1**
Bethune, Mary McLeod **4**
Bobo, Lawrence **60**
Booker, Simeon **23**
Bosley, Freeman, Jr. **7**
Boyd, T. B., III **6**
Bradley, David Henry, Jr. **39**
Branch, William Blackwell **39**
Brown, Elaine **8**
Butler, Paul D. **17**
Cary, Lorene **3**
Cashin, Sheryll **63**
Cayton, Horace **26**
Chavis, Benjamin **6**
Clark, Kenneth B. **5, 52**

Clark, Septima **7**
Cobbs, Price M. **9**
Cochran, Johnnie **11, 39, 52**
Cole, Johnnetta B. **5, 43**
Comer, James P. **6**
Cone, James H. **3, 82**
Cook, Suzan D. Johnson **22**
Cook, Toni **23**
Cosby, Bill **7, 26, 59**
Davis, Angela **5, 114**
Davis, Benjamin O., Jr. **2, 43**
Davis, Benjamin O., Sr. **4**
Delany, Martin R. **27**
Diallo, Amadou **27**
Dickerson, Debra J. **60**
Divine, Father **7**
DuBois, Shirley Graham **21**
Dunbar-Nelson, Alice Ruth Moore **44**
Dyson, Michael Eric **11, 40**
Edelman, Marian Wright **5, 42**
Elder, Lee **6**
Ellison, Ralph **7**
Farmer, James **2, 64**
Farmer-Paellmann, Deadria **43**
Farrakhan, Louis **2**
Fauset, Jessie **7**
Franklin, John Hope **5, 77**
Fuller, Charles **8**
Gibson, William F. **6**
Goode, W. Wilson **4**
Graham, Lawrence Otis **12**
Gregory, Dick **1, 54**
Grimké, Archibald H. **9**
Hall, Elliott S. **24**
Hampton, Henry **6**
Harris, Alice **7**
Hastie, William H. **8**
Haynes, George Edmund **8**
Henry, Aaron **19**
Henry, Lenny **9, 52**
Hill, Oliver W. **24, 63**
Hope, John **8**
Howard, M. William, Jr. **26**
Hunt, Darnell **92**
Ingram, Rex **5**
Jeffries, Leonard **8**
Jones, Elaine R. **7, 45**
Khanga, Yelena **6**
King, Bernice **4, 81**
King, Coretta Scott **3, 57**
King, Martin Luther, Jr. **1**
King, Yolanda **6**
Lane, Charles **3**
Lee-Smith, Hughie **5, 22**
Lorde, Audre **6**
Mabuza-Suttle, Felicia **43**
Mandela, Nelson **1, 14, 77**
Martin, Louis E. **16**
Martin, Trayvon **105**
Maynard, Robert C. **7**
McDougall, Gay J. **11, 43**
McKay, Claude **6**
Meredith, James H. **11**
Micheaux, Oscar **7**
Moore, Harry T. **29**
Mosley, Walter **5, 25, 68**
Muhammad, Khallid Abdul **10, 31**
Page, Clarence **4**
Pitt, David Thomas **10**
Poussaint, Alvin F. **5, 67**
Price, Frederick K. C. **21**
Price, Hugh B. **9, 54**

Reid, Ira De A. **100**
Robeson, Paul **2**
Robinson, Spottswood W., III **22**
Shabazz, Attallah **6**
Sifford, Charlie **4, 49**
Simpson, Carole **6, 30**
Sister Souljah **11, 100**
Sisulu, Sheila Violet Makate **24**
Smith, Anna Deavere **6, 44**
Sowell, Thomas **2, 99**
Spaulding, Charles Clinton **9**
Staples, Brent **8**
Steele, Shelby **13, 82**
Stradford, J. B. **101**
Taulbert, Clifton Lemoure **19**
Till, Emmett **7**
Tutu, Desmond Mpilo **6, 44**
Tutu, Nontombi Naomi **57**
Tyree, Omar Rashad **21**
Walcott, Derek **5, 94**
Walker, Maggie **17**
Washington, Booker T. **4**
Washington, Harold **6**
Wells-Barnett, Ida B. **8**
Welsing, Frances Cress **5**
Wiley, Ralph **8, 78**
Wilkins, Roy **4**
Williams, Gregory **11**
Williams, Hosea Lorenzo **15, 31**
Williams, Walter E. **4**
Wilson, Sunnie **7, 55**
Wright, Richard **5**
Young, Whitney M., Jr. **4**

Radio
Abrahams, Peter **39**
Abu-Jamal, Mumia **15**
Alert, Kool DJ Red **33**
Anderson, Eddie "Rochester" **30**
Ashong, Derrick **86**
Banks, William **11**
Baskett, James **102**
Bates, Karen Grigsby **40**
Beasley, Phoebe **34**
Blayton, Jesse B., Sr. **55**
Booker, Simeon **23**
Branch, William Blackwell **39**
CoCo Brother **93**
Crocker, Frankie **29**
Dre, Dr. **10, 14, 30**
Elder, Larry **25**
Fuller, Charles **8**
Gibson, Truman K., Jr. **60**
Goode, Mal **13**
Greene, Petey **65**
Gumbel, Greg **8**
Hamblin, Ken **10**
Haynes, Trudy **44**
Holt, Nora **38**
Hughes, Cathy **27**
Jackson, Hal **41, 104**
Jarrett, Vernon D. **42**
Joe, Yolanda **21**
Joyner, Tom **19, 90**
Kelley, Cliff **75**
Lewis, Delano **7**
Lewis, Ramsey **35, 70**
Ligging, Alfred, III **43**
Love, Ed **58**
Lover, Ed **10**
Ludacris **37, 60**
Luper, Clara **94**
Madison, Joseph E. **17**

Majors, Jeff **41**
McGhee, Sharon K. **113**
Michaux, Solomon Lightfoot **91**
Mickelbury, Penny **28**
Moss, Carlton **17**
Parr, Russ **51**
Pressley, Condace L. **41**
Pugh, Charles **81**
Quivers, Robin **61**
Samara, Noah **15**
Smiley, Rickey **59**
Smiley, Tavis **20, 68**
Smith, Greg **28**
Steinberg, Martha Jean "The
    Queen" **28**
Stuart, Moira **82**
Thomas, Rufus **20, 96**
Tirico, Mike **68**
Whack, Rita Coburn **36**
Williams, Armstrong **29**
Williams, Nat D. **91**
Williams, Ted **91**
Williams, Wendy **62**
Woods, Georgie **57**
Yarbrough, Camille **40**

Radio Hall of Fame
Jackson, Hal **41, 104**
Joyner, Tom **19, 90**
Williams, Wendy **62**

Ragtime
Blake, Eubie **29**
Europe, James Reese **10**
Joplin, Scott **6**
Robinson, Reginald R. **53**
Sissle, Noble **29**

Rap music
Alert, Kool DJ Red **33**
A$AP Rocky **109**
Bambaataa, Afrika **34**
Banks, Lloyd **113**
Banner, David **55**
Benjamin, Andre **45**
Bey, Yasiin **30, 96**
Big Daddy Kane **79**
Big Sean **96**
Birdman **110**
Black Thought **63**
Blackman, Toni **86**
Blow, Kurtis **31**
B.o.B. **91**
Bonney, Tabi **98**
Bow Wow **35**
Bradley, Adam **101**
Brown, Foxy **25**
Cam'ron **104**
Chamillionaire **82**
Chief Keef **112**
Chuck D. **9**
C-Murder **99**
Combs, Sean **17, 43, 92**
Common **31, 63, 98**
Coolio **103**
Curren$y **114**
Da Don, Polow **86**
Deezer D **53**
DJ Jazzy Jeff **32**
DJ Screw **110**
DMX **28, 64**
Drake **86**
Dre, Dr. **10, 14, 30**
Dupri, Jermaine **13, 46**

Dyson, Michael Eric **11, 40**
Elliott, Missy **31, 90**
Eve **29**
Fabolous **93**
Fat Boys **92**
50 Cent **46, 83**
Flavor Flav **67**
Flo Rida **78**
Future **109**
Geto Boys **115**
Ghostface Killah **90**
Gotti, Irv **39**
Grae, Jean **51**
Grandmaster Flash **33, 60**
Gray, F. Gary **14, 49**
Harrell, Andre **9, 30**
Heavy D **58, 98**
Ice Cube **8, 30, 60**
Ice-T **6, 31, 96**
J Dilla **102**
Ja Rule **35, 91**
Jay-Z **27, 69, 103**
Jones, Quincy **8, 30**
Juvenile **96**
Khalifa, Wiz **96**
Kid Cudi **83**
K'naan **76**
Knight, Suge **11, 30, 102**
KRS-One **34**
Kweli, Talib **93**
Lamar, Kendrick **105**
Lighty, Chris **105**
Lil' Kim **28**
Lil Wayne **66, 84**
LL Cool J **16, 49, 94**
London, Theophilus **95**
Lopes, Lisa **36**
Lover, Ed **10**
Ludacris **37, 60**
Mac Daddy **111**
Madlib **88**
Mane, Gucci **91**
Mase **24**
Master P **21, 115**
MC Breed **75**
M.C. Hammer **20, 80**
MC Lyte **34, 108**
McDaniels, Ralph **79**
Method Man **81**
Nas **33, 111**
Nate Dogg **92**
Nelly **32, 90**
Notorious B.I.G. **20**
Ol' Dirty Bastard **52**
O'Neal, Shaquille **8, 30, 95**
OutKast **35**
Peterson, James **81**
Proof **101**
Public Enemy **98**
Queen Latifah **1, 16, 58**
?uestlove **74**
Ray J **86**
Redman **81**
Rhymefest **97**
Rhymes, Busta **31**
Riley, Boots **89**
Roberts, Kimberly Rivers **72**
Romeo **98**
Ross, Rick **79, 104**
Run-DMC **31, 75**
RZA **80**
Sermon, Erick **81**
Shakur, Afeni **67**

Shakur, Tupac **14**
Shyne **101**
Simmons, Russell **1, 30**
Sir Mix-A-Lot **82**
Sister Souljah **11, 100**
Slick Rick **93**
Slim Thug **86**
Smith, Will **8, 18, 53**
Snoop Dogg **35, 84**
Speech **82**
Sticky Fingaz **86**
Sugarhill Gang, The **79**
Sweatshirt, Earl **114**
Timbaland **32**
Tinie Tempah **115**
T-Pain **73, 111**
Trina **114**
2 Chainz **105**
Tyler, the Creator **100**
Waka Flocka Flame **110**
Wale **92**
Woolard, Jamal **102**
Xzibit **78**
Yarbrough, Camille **40**
Yayo, Tony **113**
Ying Yang Twins **112**
Young Jeezy **63**
Z-Ro **109**

Rastafarianism
Burning Spear **79**
Dube, Lucky **77**
Haile Selassie **7**
Marley, Bob **5**
Marley, Rita **32, 70**
Tosh, Peter **9**

Reader's Choice Award
Holton, Hugh, Jr. **39**

Reading Is Fundamental
Trueheart, William E. **49**

Real estate development
Amoudi, Mohammed al- **88**
Bakewell, Danny **99**
Burks, Juanita P. **95**
Chapman, Susan E. **94**
Lane, Vincent **5**
Maponya, Richard **101**
Marshall, Bella **22**
Nail, John E. **92**
Payton, Philip A., Jr. **88**
Russell, Herman Jerome **17**
Toote, Gloria E. A. **64**

Record producer
Albright, Gerald **23**
Ayers, Roy **16**
Babyface **10, 31, 82**
Bambaataa, Afrika **34**
Barnes, Lloyd **77**
Bivins, Michael **72**
Butler, George, Jr. **70**
Carter, Troy **98**
Cole, J. **97**
Coleman, Ornette **39, 69**
Da Don, Polow **86**
Danjah, Terror **91**
Davis, Carl **105**
de Passe, Suzanne **25**
DJ Jazzy Jeff **32**
Dodd, Coxsone **99**
Dre, Dr. **10, 14, 30**

Duke, George **21, 113**
Dupri, Jermaine **13, 46**
Elliott, Missy **31, 90**
Felix Da Housecat **110**
Fuqua, Harvey **90**
Gotti, Irv **39**
Hailey, JoJo **22**
Hailey, K-Ci **22**
Hammond, Fred **23**
Hawkins, Walter **87**
Huff, Leon **86**
Ice Cube **8, 30, 60**
Ja Rule **35, 91**
Jackson, George **19**
Jackson, Joe **78**
Jackson, Michael **19, 53, 76**
Jackson, Randy **40**
Jean, Wyclef **20, 86**
Jerkins, Rodney **31**
Jimmy Jam **13**
Jones, Quincy **8, 30**
Kelly, R. **18, 44, 71**
Knowles, Mathew **96**
Lewis, Terry **13**
Marley, Rita **32, 70**
Marley, Stephen **100**
Mayfield, Curtis **2, 43**
McGregor, Stephen **99**
Minott, Sugar **86**
Mitchell, Willie **114**
Osborne, Jeffrey **26**
Prince **18, 65**
Queen Latifah **1, 16, 58**
Reid, Antonio "L.A." **28**
Robinson, Sylvia **79**
Sermon, Erick **81**
Sims, Danny **106**
Stewart, Tricky **98**
Sweat, Keith **19**
Timbaland **32**
Turner, Ike **68**
Tyler, the Creator **100**
Vandross, Luther **13, 48, 59**
White, Barry **13, 41**
Whitfield, Norman **73**
Williams, J. Mayo **83**
Williams, Pharrell **47, 82**
Yabby You **83**
Young, Lee **72**

Recording executive
Birdman **110**
Brae, C. Michael **61**
Busby, Jheryl **3, 74**
Butler, George, Jr. **70**
Dash, Damon **31, 113**
de Passe, Suzanne **25**
Dupri, Jermaine **13, 46**
Gordy, Berry, Jr. **1**
Gotti, Irv **39**
Harrell, Andre **9, 30**
Jackson, George **19**
Jackson, Randy **40**
James Bracken and Vivian Bracken
    107
Jimmy Jam **13**
Jones, Quincy **8, 30**
Knight, Suge **11, 30, 102**
Lewis, Terry **13**
Liles, Kevin **42, 99**
Massenburg, Kedar **23, 110**
Master P **21, 115**
Mayfield, Curtis **2, 43**

McPherson, David 32
Reid, Antonio "L.A." 28
Rhone, Sylvia 2
Robey, Don 115
Sanders, Angelia 86
Simmons, Russell 1, 30
Williams, J. Mayo 83

Reggae
Afro, Teddy 78
Banton, Buju 93
Barnes, Lloyd 77
Beenie Man 32
Big Youth 107
Blondy, Alpha 30
Brown, Dennis 99
Burning Spear 79
Cliff, Jimmy 28, 92
Dawuni, Rocky 94
Dekker, Desmond 104
Dodd, Coxsone 99
Dube, Lucky 77
Ellis, Alton 74
Ellis, Hortense 97
Ford, Vincent 75
Griffiths, Marcia 29
Hammond, Lenn 34
Hibbert, Toots 103
Isaacs, Gregory 89
Johnson, Linton Kwesi 37
Marley, Bob 5
Marley, Rita 32, 70
Marley, Stephen 100
Marley, Ziggy 41
McGregor, Stephen 99
Minott, Sugar 86
Mowatt, Judy 38
Perry, Lee 19, 103
Perry, Ruth 19
Rhoden, Wayne 70
Shaggy 31
Sly & Robbie 34
Steely 80
Tosh, Peter 9
Yabby You 83

Republican Party
Allen, Ethel D. 13
Fisher, Ada M. 76
Howard, Perry Wilbon, Jr. 112
Scott, Tim 87
Steele, Michael 38, 73, 91
Toote, Gloria E. A. 64

Restaurants/Catering/Cooking
Armstrong, Govind 81
Cain, Herman 15, 92
Calabrese, Karyn 89
Crum, George 101
Daniels-Carter, Valerie 23
Dorsey, Thomas J. 90
Downing, George T. 91
Ford, Barney 90
Garvin, Gerry 78
Hawkins, La-Van 17, 54
Henry, Dwight 104
Howell, Ayinde 91
James, Charles H., III 62
Lewis, Aylwin B. 51, 88
Montgomery, Robbie 101
Otis, Clarence, Jr. 55
Ouattara, Morou 74
Pierce, Harold 75
Rodriguez, Jimmy 47

Samuelsson, Marcus 53
Sbraga, Kevin 88
Smith, B(arbara) 11
Washington, Regynald G. 44
Williams, Lindsey 75
Woods, Sylvia 34, 104

Rhode Island School of Design
Bannister, Edward Mitchell 88
Prophet, Nancy Elizabeth 42

Rhodes scholar
Booker, Cory Anthony 68
Braxton, Brad 77
Kennedy, Randall 40
Locke, Alain 10
Pinkett, Randal 61
Rice, Susan 74, 103
Rolle, Myron 98
Wideman, John Edgar 5, 87

Rhythm and blues/soul music
Aaliyah 30
Ace, Johnny 36
Acklin, Barbara Jean 107
Adams, Johnny 39
Adams, Oleta 18
Akon 68
Amerie 52
Ashanti 37, 96
Ashford, Nickolas 21, 97
Ashford and Simpson 21, 97
Austin, Patti 24
Ayers, Roy 16
Babyface 10, 31, 82
Badu, Erykah 22, 114
Bailey, Philip 63
Baker, Anita 21, 48
Baker, LaVern 26
Baker, Mickey 95
Ballard, Florence 112
Ballard, Hank 41
Barrino, Fantasia 53, 94
Bass, Fontella 104, 109
Baylor, Helen 36
Belgrave, Marcus 77
Bell, LeRoy 98
Bell, Thom 112
Belle, Regina 1, 51
Benét, Eric 28, 77
Berry, Chuck 29
Beverly, Frankie 25
Beyoncé 39, 70, 105
Bilal 101
Billy Ward and the Dominoes 105
Bivins, Michael 72
Blige, Mary J. 20, 34, 60, 97
Boyz II Men 82
Bradshaw, Tiny 102
Brandy 14, 34, 72
Braxton, Toni 15, 61, 91
Brooks, Hadda 40
Brown, Bobby 58
Brown, Charles 23
Brown, Chris 74, 109
Brown, Chuck 78, 102
Brown, Clarence Gatemouth 59
Brown, James 15, 60
Brown, Nappy 73
Brown, Oscar, Jr. 53
Brown, Ruth 90
Burke, Clarence, Jr. 112
Burke, Solomon 31, 86

Busby, Jheryl 3, 74
Butler, Jerry 26
Cadillacs 107
Carey, Mariah 32, 53, 69
Castor, Jimmy 100
Chandler, Gene 105
Charles, Ray 16, 48
Chi-Lites 106
Ciara 56, 115
Clay, Otis 112
Clinton, George 9, 93
Clovers, The 104
Cole, Keyshia 63, 107
Cole, Natalie 17, 60, 84
Contours, The 109
Cooke, Sam 17
Cox, Deborah 28
Crawford, Hank 77
D'Angelo 27
David, Craig 31, 53
Davis, Tyrone 54
DeBarge, El 89
Dells, The 109
Derülo, Jason 93
DeVaughn, Raheem 91
Diddley, Bo 39, 72
Domino, Fats 20
Dorsey, Lee 65
Downing, Will 19
Dramatics, The 106
Dre, Dr. 14, 30
Dupri, Jermaine 13, 46
Earth, Wind & Fire 98
En Vogue 100
Escobar, Damien 56
Escobar, Tourie 56
Evans, Faith 22
Feemster, Herbert 72
Fiona, Melanie 84
Five Keys, The 104
Flamingos, The 108
Franklin, Aretha 11, 44, 115
Fuqua, Harvey 90
Gamble, Kenny 85
Gap Band, The 100
Garrett, Sean 57
Gaye, Marvin 2
Gaynor, Gloria 36
Gibson, Tyrese 27, 62
Gill, Johnny 51
Ginuwine 35
Goapele 55
Goodman, Al 87
Gotti, Irv 39
Gray, Dobie 99
Gray, Macy 29
Greaves, R. B. 106
Green, Al 13, 47, 74
Green, Cee Lo 70, 103
Hailey, JoJo 22
Hailey, K-Ci 22
Hall, Aaron 57
Hamilton, Anthony 61
Harold Melvin & the Blue Notes 105
Harris, Corey 39, 73
Harris, Damon 110
Harris, Major 110
Hart, Alvin Youngblood 61
Hathaway, Donny 18
Hathaway, Lalah 57, 88
Hayes, Isaac 20, 58, 73
Hendryx, Nona 56

Henry, Clarence "Frogman" 46
Hill, Lauryn 20, 53, 111
Hilson, Keri 84
Holloway, Brenda 65
Houston, Cissy 20, 83
Houston, Whitney 7, 28, 83, 100
Huff, Leon 86
Hunter, Ivory Joe 106
Hyman, Phyllis 19
India.Arie 34
Ingram, James 84
Isley, Marvin 87
Isley, Ronald 25, 56
Jackson, Janet 6, 30, 68
Jackson, Michael 19, 53, 76
Jackson, Millie 25
Jackson, Tito 81
Jaheim 58
Jamelia 51
James, Etta 13, 52, 100
James, Rick 17
Jennings, Lyfe 56, 69
Johnson, Robert 2
Johnson, Syl 97
Johnson, Syleena 98
Johnson-George, Tamara 79
Jones, Booker T. 84
Jones, Donell 29
Jones, Quincy 8, 30
Jones, Sharon 86
Jordan, Louis 104
Jordan, Montell 23
Kandi 83
Kay, Connie 114
Kelly, R. 18, 44, 71
Kem 47
Kendricks, Eddie 22
Keys, Alicia 32, 68
King Curtis 92
Knight, Gladys 16, 66
Knight, Marie 80
LaBelle, Patti 13, 30
Lance, Major 111
Larrieux, Amel 63
LaSalle, Denise 111
Lattimore, Kenny 35
LaVette, Bettye 85
Ledisi 73
Legend, John 67
Levert, Eddie 70
Levert, Gerald 22, 59
Little Anthony & the Imperials 107
Little Richard 15
Lloyd 99
Lopes, Lisa 36
Love, Darlene 23, 92
Luckett, Letoya 61
Maitreya, Sananda 85
Mario 71
Maxwell 20, 81
Maye, Lee 111
Mayfield, Curtis 2, 43
McCoo, Marilyn 53
McKnight, Brian 18, 34
Midnight Star 110
Miguel 98
Miles, Buddy 69
Millinder, Lucky 101
Mitchell, Willie 114
Monáe, Janelle 86
Monica 21
Montgomery, Robbie 101
Moonglows, The 108

Moore, Chante **26**
Moore, Melba **21**
Musiq **37, 84**
Mvula, Laura **110**
Mya **35**
Nash, Johnny **40**
Ndegeocello, Meshell **15, 83**
Neale, Haydain **52**
Neville, Aaron **21**
New Edition **101**
Ne-Yo **65**
Notorious B.I.G. **20**
Ocean, Frank **100**
O'Jays, The **98**
Omarion **107**
112 **114**
Orioles, The **100**
Otis, Clyde **67**
Parker, Maceo **72**
Parker, Ray, Jr. **85**
Peebles, Ann **114**
Pendergrass, Teddy **22, 83**
Penguins, The **107**
Phillips, Esther **107**
Pinkney, Fayette **80**
Pitts, Skip **103**
Platters, The **99**
Pleasure P **84**
Preston, Billy **39, 59**
Price, Kelly **23**
Prince **18, 65**
Ravens, The **103**
Reagon, Toshi **76**
Record, Eugene **60**
Redding, Otis **16**
Reed, A. C. **36**
Reed, Natina **106**
Reeves, Martha **85**
Richard, Dawn **92**
Riperton, Minnie **32**
Robinson, Smokey **3, 49**
Rogers, Bobby **110**
Ross, Diana **8, 27**
Russell, Brenda **52**
Sade **15, 92**
Sam and Dave **102**
Sample, Joe **51**
Scott, Jill **29, 83**
Scott, "Little" Jimmy **48**
Scott-Heron, Gil **94**
Shanice **112**
Shaw, Marlena **105**
Siji **56**
Simon, Joe **109**
Simpson, Valerie **21, 97**
Sisqo **30**
Sledge, Percy **39**
Songz, Trey **88**
Spaniels, The **105**
Sparks, Jordin **66**
Staton, Candi **27**
Steinberg, Martha Jean "The
   Queen" **28**
Stewart, Billy **112**
Stone, Angie **31**
Stone, Jesse **98**
Street, Richard **110**
Streeter, Sevyn **115**
Strong, Barrett **89**
Studdard, Ruben **46**
Sullivan, Jazmine **81**
Supremes, The **33**
Swann, Bettye **109**

Sweat, Keith **19**
Tamia **24, 55**
Taste of Honey, A **115**
Tavares **115**
T-Boz **108**
Temptations, The **33**
Terrell, Tammi **32**
The-Dream **74**
Thomas, Carla **96**
Thomas, Irma **29**
Thomas, Rozonda **34, 78**
Thomas, Rufus **20, 96**
TLC **34**
Tresvant, Ralph **57**
Turner, Ike **68**
Turner, Tina **6, 27**
Ulmer, James **79**
Usher **23, 56, 95**
Valentino, Bobby **62**
Vandross, Luther **13, 48, 59**
Warwick, Dionne **18, 111**
Watley, Jody **54**
Wells, Mary **28**
West, Kanye **52, 93**
White, Barry **13, 41**
Whitney, Marva **109**
Williams, Michelle **73**
Williams, Paul **112**
Wilson, Cassandra **16**
Wilson, Charlie **31, 77**
Wilson, Mary **28**
Wilson, Nancy **10, 98**
Withers, Bill **61**
Witherspoon, Jimmy **113**
Womack, Bobby **60, 92**
Wonder, Stevie **11, 53**
Woods, Belita **103**
Woodson, Ali Ollie **89**
Wright, O. V. **114**

**Robert C. Maynard Institute
for Journalism Education**
Harris, Jay T. **19**
Maynard, Nancy Hicks **73**
Maynard, Robert C. **7**

Rock and Roll Hall of Fame
Ballard, Florence **112**
Ballard, Hank **41**
Bennett, Estelle **77**
Berry, Chuck **29**
Bland, Bobby **36, 113**
Brown, Charles **23**
Burke, Solomon **31, 86**
Clinton, George **9, 93**
Cole, Nat "King" **17**
Davis, Miles **4**
Diddley, Bo **39, 72**
Franklin, Aretha **11, 44, 115**
Gamble, Kenny **85**
Grandmaster Flash **33, 60**
Green, Al **13, 47, 74**
Guy, Buddy **31**
Harris, Damon **110**
Hayes, Isaac **20, 58, 73**
Holiday, Billie **1**
Holland-Dozier-Holland **36**
Hooker, John Lee **30**
Isley, Marvin **87**
Isley, Ronald **25, 56**
Jackson, Mahalia **5**
Jackson, Michael **19, 53, 76**
Jackson, Tito **81**

Jackson 5 **103**
Jamerson, James **59**
James, Etta **13, 52, 100**
Johnson, Johnnie **56**
Jones, Booker T. **84**
Jones, Quincy **8, 30**
Knight, Gladys **16, 66**
Love, Darlene **23, 92**
Mayfield, Curtis **2, 43**
Morton, Jelly Roll **29**
Orioles, The **100**
Prince **18, 65**
Public Enemy **98**
Reeves, Martha **85**
Ross, Diana **8, 27**
Run-DMC **31, 75**
Sam and Dave **102**
Shider, Garry **87**
Sledge, Percy **39**
Spector, Ronnie **77**
Steinberg, Martha Jean "The
   Queen" **28**
Stone, Jesse **98**
Stone, Sly **85**
Summer, Donna **25, 102**
Supremes, The **33**
Toussaint, Allen **60**
Turner, Big Joe **92**
Turner, Ike **68**
Turner, Tina **6, 27**
Walker, T-Bone **111**
Wilson, Jackie **60**
Wilson, Mary **28**
Wonder, Stevie **11, 53**

Rock music
Adebimpe, Tunde **75**
Ballard, Hank **41**
Bennett, Estelle **77**
Berry, Chuck **29**
Blackwell, Otis **98**
Clemons, Clarence **41**
Diddley, Bo **39, 72**
Domino, Fats **20**
Edwards, Esther Gordy **43**
Fishbone **101**
Glover, Corey **34**
Hendrix, Jimi **10**
Johnson, Johnnie **56**
King Curtis **92**
Kravitz, Lenny **10, 34**
Little Richard **15**
Lymon, Frankie **22**
Mayfield, Curtis **2, 43**
Miles, Buddy **69**
Moore, LeRoi **72**
Preston, Billy **39, 59**
Prince **18, 65**
Reagon, Toshi **76**
Reid, Vernon **34**
Run-DMC **31, 75**
Slash **75**
Spector, Ronnie **77**
Stew **69**
Stone, Jesse **98**
Stone, Sly **85**
Tait, Michael **57**
Tamar-kali **63**
Tinsley, Boyd **50**
Toussaint, Allen **60**
Turner, Ike **68**
Turner, Big Joe **92**
Turner, Tina **6, 27**

will.i.am **64**
Wilson, Jackie **60**

Rockefeller Foundation
Price, Hugh B. **9, 54**

Rockets
Williams, O. S. **13**

Rodeo
Nash, Johnny **40**
Pickett, Bill **11**
Sampson, Charles **13**
Turman, Glynn **100**
Whitfield, Fred **23**

Roman Catholic Church
Akpan, Uwem **70**
Arinze, Francis **19**
Aristide, Jean-Bertrand **6, 45**
Chineworth, Mary Alice **79**
Clements, George **2**
DeLille, Henriette **30**
Fabre, Shelton **71**
Gantin, Bernardin **70**
Gregory, Wilton D. **37**
Guy, Rosa **5**
Healy, James Augustine **30**
Jean-Juste, Gérard **78**
Jones, Alex **64**
Marino, Eugene Antonio **30**
Otunga, Maurice Michael **55**
Rugambwa, Laurean **20**
Senghor, Augustin Diamacoune **66**
Stallings, George A., Jr. **6**

Romance fiction
Bunkley, Anita Richmond **39**
Hill, Donna **32**
Jackson, Brenda **87**
Washington, Elsie B. **78**

Royalty
Christophe, Henri **9**
Ka Dinizulu, Mcwayizeni **29**
Mswati III **56**
Mutebi, Ronald **25**

Rugby
Mundine, Anthony **56**

Rutgers University
Gibson, Donald Bernard **40**

Rwandan government
Habyarimana, Juvenal **8**
Kagame, Paul **54**
Mushikiwabo, Louise **88**

**Sacramento Kings basketball
team**
Russell, Bill **8**
Webber, Chris **15, 30, 59**

Sailing
Petersen, Neal **96**
Pinckney, Bill **42**
Seymour, Teddy **110**

**St. Kitts and Nevis govern-
ment**
Douglas, Denzil Llewellyn **53**

St. Louis Blues hockey team
Brathwaite, Fred **35**
Mayers, Jamal **39**

St. Louis Cardinals baseball team
Baylor, Don 6
Bonds, Bobby 43
Brock, Lou 18
Flood, Curt 10, 93
Gibson, Bob 33
Lankford, Ray 23
Smith, Ozzie 77

St. Louis city government
Bosley, Freeman, Jr. 7
Harmon, Clarence 26

Salvation Army
Gaither, Israel L. 65

San Antonio Spurs basketball team
Duncan, Tim 20, 91
Elliott, Sean 26
Gervin, George 80
Mohammed, Nazr 64
Parker, Tony 75
Robinson, David 24, 90

San Diego Chargers football team
Barnes, Ernie 16, 78
Joiner, Charlie 102
Oliver, Paul 115
Tomlinson, LaDainian 65, 112
Winslow, Kellen 83

San Diego Padres baseball team
Carter, Joe 30
Gwynn, Tony 18, 83
McGriff, Fred 24
Smith, Ozzie 77
Winfield, Dave 5, 91

San Francisco 49ers football team
Green, Dennis 5, 45
Hayes, Bob 77
Lott, Ronnie 9
Perry, Joe 95
Rice, Jerry 5, 55, 89
Singletary, Mike 4, 76
Washington, Gene 63
Willis, Patrick 99

San Francisco Giants baseball team
Bonds, Barry 6, 34, 63, 99
Bonds, Bobby 43
Carter, Joe 30
Mays, Willie 3
McCovey, Willie 103
Strawberry, Darryl 22

Saturday Night Live
Barnes, Katreese 97
Meadows, Tim 30
Morgan, Tracy 61, 102
Morris, Garrett 31
Murphy, Eddie 4, 20, 61
Rock, Chris 3, 22, 66
Rudolph, Maya 46, 106
Thompson, Kenan 52

Saxophone
Adderley, Julian "Cannonball" 30
Albright, Gerald 23

Ammons, Gene 112
Amy, Curtis 114
Anderson, Fred 87
Ayler, Albert 104
Bechet, Sidney 18
Clemons, Clarence 41
Cobb, Arnett 114
Coleman, George 106
Coltrane, John 19
Coltrane, Ravi 71
Crawford, Hank 77
Ervin, Booker 106
Foster, Frank 97
Freeman, Von 104
Golson, Benny 37
Gordon, Dexter 25
Greene, Jimmy 74
Griffin, Johnny 71
Hawkins, Coleman 9
Jacquet, Illinois 49
Kay, Ulyssess 37
Kenyatta, Robin 54
Kinch, Soweto 108
King Curtis 92
McLean, Jackie 78
Moody, James 83
Moore, LeRoi 72
Moura, Paulo 87
Nelson, Oliver 113
Newman, David 76
Parker, Charlie 20
Parker, Maceo 72
Redman, Joshua 30
Rivers, Sam 95
Rollins, Sonny 37, 94
Sanders, Pharoah 64
Shepp, Archie 101
Shider, Garry 87
Shorter, Wayne 75
Tate, Buddy 108
Tchicai, John 102
Vinson, Eddie 112
Ware, David S. 106
Washington, Grover, Jr. 17, 44
Waters, Benny 26
Whalum, Kirk 37, 64
York, Vincent 40
Young, Lester 37

Schomburg Center for Research in Black Culture
Andrews, Bert 13
Dodson, Howard, Jr. 7, 52
Hutson, Jean Blackwell 16
Morrison, Sam 50
Reddick, Lawrence Dunbar 20
Schomburg, Arthur Alfonso 9

School desegregation
Boulware, Harold R. 109
Bridges, Ruby 77
Brown, Oliver Leon 94
Chestnut, J. L., Jr. 73
DeLaine, Joseph A. 110
Fortune, T. Thomas 6
Hobson, Julius W. 44
Holmes, Hamilton E. 82
Sweatt, Heman Marion 114

Science fiction
Barnes, Steven 54
Butler, Octavia 8, 43, 58

Delany, Samuel R., Jr. 9

SCLC
See Southern Christian Leadership Conference

Scotland Yard
Griffin, Bessie Blout 43

Screenplay writing
Akil, Mara Brock 60, 82
Brown, Cecil M. 46
Clack, Zoanne 73
Davis, Thulani 61
Elder, Lonne, III 38
Ellis, Trey 97
Fisher, Antwone 40
Fletcher, Geoffrey 85
Greaves, William 38
Jones, Orlando 30
Lancaster, Byard 105
Lumet, Jenny 80
Mason, Judi Ann 112
McMillan, Tracy 93
Nissel, Angela 42
Prince-Bythewood, Gina 31, 77
Pryce, Trevor 89
Rhimes, Shonda Lynn 67
Rhone, Trevor 80
Ridley, John 69
Robinson, Matt 69
Singleton, John 2, 30
Talbert, David E. 34, 93
Van Peebles, Melvin 7, 95
Wesley, Richard 73

Sculpture
Allen, Tina 22, 75
Amos, Emma 63
Bailey, Radcliffe 19
Barthe, Richmond 15
Biggers, John 20, 33
Biggers, Sanford 62
Billops, Camille 82
Brown, Donald 19
Burke, Selma 16
Catlett, Elizabeth 2
Chanticleer, Raven 91
Chase-Riboud, Barbara 20, 46
Cortor, Eldzier 42
Dwight, Edward 65
Edwards, Melvin 22
Fuller, Meta Vaux Warrick 27
Guyton, Tyree 9, 94
Hammons, David 69
Hathaway, Isaac Scott 33
Hunt, Richard 6
Lewis, Edmonia 10
Lewis, Samella 25
Manley, Edna 26
Marshall, Kerry James 59
McCullough, Geraldine 58, 79
McGee, Charles 10
Moody, Ronald 30
Neals, Otto 73
Perkins, Marion 38
Pierce, Elijah 84
Prophet, Nancy Elizabeth 42
Puryear, Martin 42, 101
Saar, Alison 16
Saar, Betye 80
Savage, Augusta 12
Scott, John T. 65
Shabazz, Attallah 6

Simmons, Gary 58
Stout, Renee 63
Washington, James, Jr. 38
Wilson, John 109

Seattle city government
Rice, Norm 8

Seattle Mariners baseball team
Griffey, Ken, Jr. 12, 73
Reynolds, Harold 77

Seattle Supersonics basketball team
Bickerstaff, Bernie 21
Payton, Gary 99
Silas, Paul 24

Security and defense services
Garrett, James F. 78

Senegalese government
Diouf, Abdou 3
Sall, Macky 101
Senghor, Léopold Sédar 66
Wade, Abdoulaye 66

Sesame Street
Byrd, Eugene 64
Clash, Kevin 14, 93
Glover, Savion 14
Long, Loretta 58
Orman, Roscoe 55
Reed Hall, Alaina 83
Robinson, Matt 69

Sexual harassment
Gomez-Preston, Cheryl 9
Hill, Anita 5, 65
McCauley, Gina 76
Thomas, Clarence 2, 39, 65
Auguste, Arnold A. 47

Ship captain
Cuffe, Paul 98

Sickle cell anemia
Edwards, Willarda V. 59
Pace, Betty 59

Sierra Leone government
Kabbah, Ahmad Tejan 23
Koroma, Ernest Bai 84

Skateboarding
Williams, Stevie 71

Skiing
Horton, Andre 33
Horton, Suki 33

Skillman Foundation
Goss, Carol A. 55

Slavery
Albert, Octavia V. R. 100
Asante, Molefi Kete 3
Bibb, Henry and Mary 54
Blackshear, Leonard 52
Blassingame, John Wesley 40
Brown, William Wells 99
Burns, Anthony 102
Chase-Riboud, Barbara 20, 46
Cooper, Anna Julia 20
Douglas, Aaron 7
Du Bois, W. E. B. 3

Dunbar, Paul Laurence **8**
Durham, James **90**
Easton, Hosea **91**
Equiano, Olaudah **78**
Farmer-Paellmann, Deadria **43**
Gaines, Ernest J. **7**
Garnet, Henry Highland **100**
Gordon-Reed, Annette **74**
Haley, Alex **4**
Harper, Frances Ellen Watkins **11**
Hayden, Lewis **105**
Henson, Josiah **90**
Huggins, Nathan Irvin **52**
Jacobs, Harriet **104**
Johnson, Charles **1, 82**
Jones, Edward P. **43, 67**
Keckley, Elizabeth **90**
Lane, Lunsford **93**
Langston, John Mercer **101**
Mason, Biddy **89**
McWorter, Free Frank **91**
Minkins, Shadrach **104**
Montgomery, Isaiah T. **91**
Muhammad, Elijah **4**
Northup, Solomon **115**
Patterson, Orlando **4**
Pleasant, Mary Ellen **9**
Reeves, Bass **100**
Russwurm, John Brown **100**
Sharpe, Samuel **103**
Stephens, Charlotte Andrews **14**
Stewart, Maria W. Miller **19**
Tancil, Gladys Quander **59**
Taylor, Susie King **13**
Tubman, Harriet **9**
Vesey, Denmark **100**
Wall, Orindatus S. B. **92**
Yates, Jack **114**

Smithsonian Institution
Bunch, Lonnie G., III **91**

Smith College
Mayhew, Richard **39**
Simmons, Ruth **13, 38**

SNCC
See Student Nonviolent Coordinating Committee

Soccer
Adu, Freddy **67**
Altidore, Jozy **109**
Anderson, Viv **58**
Antunes, Lúcio **109**
Balotelli, Mario **104**
Barnes, John **53**
Beasley, Jamar **29**
Benítez, Christian **113**
Bigirimana, Gael **115**
Charles, John **108**
Chitalu, Godfrey **108**
Cole, Ashley **106**
Crooks, Garth **53**
Davids, Edgar **106**
dos Santos, Manuel Francisco **65**
Drogba, Didier **78**
Eto'o, Samuel **73**
Evra, Patrice **102**
Ferdinand, Rio **82**
Gyan, Asamoah **87**
Henry, Thierry **66**
Ibrahim, Fuad **109**
Ince, Paul **83**

James, David **84**
Jones, Cobi N'Gai **18**
Kanouté, Fred **68**
Leônidas **96**
Mello, Breno **73**
Mensah, John **87**
Milla, Roger **2**
Muamba, Fabrice **104**
Nakhid, David **25**
Okocha, Jay Jay **99**
Onyewu, Oguchi **60**
Pelé **7**
Regis, Cyrille **51**
Ronaldinho **69**
Scurry, Briana **27**
Song, Alex **105**
Sono, Jomo **86**
Touré, Yaya **99**
Weah, George **58**

Social science/social criticism
Austin, Bobby W. **95**
Berry, Mary Frances **7**
Black, Albert **51**
Bobo, Lawrence **60**
Cayton, Horace **26**
Clark, Kenneth B. **5, 52**
Cobbs, Price M. **9**
Collins, Patricia Hill **67**
Edwards, Harry **2**
Frazier, E. Franklin **10**
George, Zelma Watson **42**
Hall, Stuart **78**
Hare, Nathan **44**
Harris, Eddy L. **18**
Haynes, George Edmund **8**
hooks, bell **5, 90**
Hunt, Darnell **92**
Ladner, Joyce A. **42**
Lawrence-Lightfoot, Sara **10**
Marable, Manning **10, 102**
Reid, Ira De A. **100**
Williams, David Rudyard **50**
Woodson, Robert L. **10**

Social work
Auguste, Rose-Anne **13**
Berry, Bertice **8, 55**
Berrysmith, Don Reginald **49**
Brown, Cora **33**
Canada, Geoffrey **23**
Coles, Alice **80**
Colston, Hal **72**
Compton-Rock, Malaak **86**
Dumpson, James R. **108**
Dunham, Katherine **4, 59**
Fields, C. Virginia **25**
Finner-Williams, Paris Michele **62**
Gbowee, Leymah **76**
Granger, Lester B. **75**
Grillo, Evelio **95**
Hale, Clara **16**
Hale, Lorraine **8**
Harris, Alice **7**
Haynes, George Edmund **8**
Jackson, Judith D. **57**
Jackson, Mae **57**
King, Barbara **22**
Kirk, Clara **95**
Lewis, Thomas **19**
Little, Robert L. **2**
Quander, Nellie **102**
Robinson, Rachel **16**

Sears, Stephanie **53**
Smith, Damu **54**
Vaughn, Viola **70**
Waddles, Charleszetta "Mother" **10, 49**
Walker, Bernita Ruth **53**
Wallace, Joaquin **49**
Wells, Henrietta Bell **69**
White-Hammond, Gloria **61**
Thrower, Willie **35**
Young, Whitney M., Jr. **4**

Soledad Brothers
Jackson, George Lester **14**

Somalian government
Ahmed, Sharif **80**
Mohamud, Hassan Sheikh **105**

Soul food
Williams, Lindsey **75**
Woods, Sylvia **34, 104**

Soul Train
Baylor, Helen **36**
Cornelius, Don **4, 100**
D'Angelo **27**
Winans, CeCe **14, 43**

South African Communist Party
Hani, Chris **6**
Mhlaba, Raymond **55**

South African government
Dandala, Mvume **77**
Dlamini-Zuma, Nkosazana **34, 105**
Mhlaba, Raymond **55**
Motlanthe, Kgalema **74**
Sisulu, Walter **47**
Zuma, Jacob **33, 75**

South Carolina state government
Cardozo, Francis L. **33**
Scott, Tim **87**

South Sudan government
Kiir, Salva Mayardit **85, 103**

Southeastern University
Jarvis, Charlene Drew **21**

Southern Christian Leadership Conference (SCLC)
Abernathy, Ralph **1**
Barrow, Willie T. **85**
Brooks, Tyrone **59**
Chavis, Benjamin **6**
Hooks, Benjamin L. **2, 85**
Jackson, Jesse **1, 27, 72**
Jones, William A., Jr. **61**
King, Bernice **4, 81**
King, Martin Luther, Jr. **1**
King, Martin Luther, III **20**
Lawson, James M., Jr. **90**
Lee, Eric P. **79**
Lowery, Joseph **2**
Moses, Robert Parris **11**
Moss, Otis, Jr. **72**
Nash, Diane **72**
Orange, James **74**
Rustin, Bayard **4**
Shuttlesworth, Fred **47, 98**
Walker, Wyatt Tee **80**

Williams, Hosea Lorenzo **15, 31**

Southern Syncopated Orchestra
Cook, Will Marion **40**

Space shuttle
Gregory, Frederick **8, 51**
Jemison, Mae C. **1, 35**
McNair, Ronald **3, 58**
Wilson, Stephanie **72**

Special Olympics
Clairborne, Loretta **34**

Speedskating
Davis, Shani **58, 84**

Spelman College
Cobb, William Jelani **59**
Cole, Johnnetta B. **5, 43**
Falconer, Etta Zuber **59**
Price, Glenda **22**
Simmons, Ruth **13, 38**
Tatum, Beverly Daniel **42, 84**
Wade-Gayles, Gloria Jean **41**

Sphinx Organization
Dworkin, Aaron P. **52**

Spingarn medal
Aaron, Hank **5**
Ailey, Alvin **8**
Anderson, Marian **2, 33**
Angelou, Maya **1, 15**
Bates, Daisy **13**
Belafonte, Harry **4, 65**
Bethune, Mary McLeod **4**
Bond, Julian **2, 35, 106**
Bradley, Thomas **2, 20**
Braithwaite, William Stanley **52**
Brooke, Edward W. **8, 88**
Bunche, Ralph J. **5**
Burleigh, Henry Thacker **56**
Carson, Benjamin **1, 35, 76**
Carter, Robert L. **51, 100**
Carver, George Washington **4**
Chesnutt, Charles **29**
Clark, Kenneth B. **5, 52**
Conyers, John, Jr. **4, 45, 111**
Cosby, Bill **7, 26, 59**
Davis, Sammy, Jr. **18**
Dee, Ruby **8, 50, 68**
Drew, Charles Richard **7**
Du Bois, W. E. B. **3**
Ellington, Duke **5**
Evers, Medgar **3**
Evers, Myrlie **8**
Franklin, John Hope **5, 77**
Gilpin, Charles Sidney **81**
Graves, Earl G. **1, 35**
Grimké, Archibald H. **9**
Haley, Alex **4**
Hastie, William H. **8**
Hayes, Roland **4**
Height, Dorothy I. **2, 23, 78**
Higginbotham, A. Leon, Jr. **13, 25**
Hill, Oliver W. **24, 63**
Hinton, William Augustus **8**
Hooks, Benjamin L. **2, 85**
Hope, John **8**
Horne, Lena **5, 86**
Houston, Charles Hamilton **4**
Hughes, Langston **4**
Jackson, Jesse **1, 27, 72**

Johnson, James Weldon 5
Johnson, John H. 3, 54
Johnson, Mordecai Wyatt 79
Jordan, Barbara 4, 78
Jordan, Vernon E. 3, 35
Julian, Percy Lavon 6
Just, Ernest Everett 3
Keith, Damon J. 16, 74
King, Martin Luther, Jr. 1
Lawless, Theodore K. 8
Lawrence, Jacob 4
Lewis, John 2, 46, 83
Logan, Rayford 40
Marshall, Thurgood 1, 44
Mays, Benjamin E. 7
Mitchell, Clarence M., Jr. 88
Moore, Harry T. 29
Motley, Constance Baker 10, 55
Moton, Robert Russa 83
Parks, Gordon 1, 35, 58
Parks, Rosa 1, 35, 56
Patterson, Frederick Douglass 12
Powell, Colin 1, 28, 75
Price, Leontyne 1
Randolph, A. Philip 3
Riles, Wilson C. 79
Robeson, Paul 2
Robinson, Jackie 6
Rowan, Carl T. 1, 30
Staupers, Mabel K. 7
Sullivan, Leon H. 3, 30
Sutton, Percy E. 42, 82
Talbert, Mary B. 77
Tobias, Channing H. 79
Tyson, Cicely 7, 51, 112
Weaver, Robert C. 8, 46
White, Walter F. 4
Wilder, L. Douglas 3, 48
Wilkins, Roy 4
Williams, Paul R. 9
Winfrey, Oprah 2, 15, 61, 106
Woodson, Carter G. 2
Wright, Louis Tompkins 4
Wright, Richard 5
Young, Andrew 3, 48, 110
Young, Charles 77
Young, Coleman 1, 20

Spirituals
Anderson, Marian 2, 33
Carr, Kurt 56
Fisher, Miles Mark 91
Hairston, Jester 88
Hayes, Roland 4
Jackson, Mahalia 5
Johnson, Hall 90
Joyner, Matilda Sissieretta 15
Norman, Jessye 5
Reese, Della 6, 20, 96
Williams, Denise 40

Sports administration
Fuller, Vivian 33
Goss, Tom 23
Kerry, Leon G. 46
Lee, Bertram M., Sr. 46
Littlepage, Craig 35
Mills, Steve 47
Payne, Ulice, Jr. 42
Phillips, Teresa L. 42
Randolph, Willie 53
Ujiri, Masai 107

Ussery, Terdema, II 29

Sports agent
Holland, Kimberly N. 62

Stanford University
Bobo, Lawrence 60
Rice, Condoleezza 3, 28, 72
Steele, Claude 13, 97
Walker, Arthur, II 87
Washington, Gene 63

State University of New York
Baraka, Amiri 1, 38
Butts, Calvin O., III 9, 90
Clemente, Rosa 74
Wharton, Clifton R., Jr. 7

Stellar Awards
Baylor, Helen 36
Hawkins, Walter 87
Lawrence, Donald 99
Sapp, Marvin 74
Tribbett, Tye 81
Walker, Hezekiah 34

Storytelling
Baker, Augusta 38
Bennett, Louise 69
Hill, Hugh Morgan 83

Student Nonviolent Coordinating Committee (SNCC)
Al-Amin, Jamil Abdullah 6
Anderson, William G(ilchrist) 57
Barry, Marion S. 7, 44
Blackwell, Unita 17
Carmichael, Stokely 5, 26
Clark, Septima 7
Forman, James 7, 51
Hamer, Fannie Lou 6
Holland, Endesha Ida Mae 3, 57
Moses, Robert Parris 11
Nash, Diane 72
Poussaint, Alvin F. 5, 67
Touré, Askia (Muhammad Abu Bakr el) 47

Sudan government
Bashir, Omar al- 77
Cham, Adongo Agada Akway 77
Garang, John 105

Sun Microsystems
Tademy, Lalita 36

Sundance Film Festival
Coogler, Ryan 114
DuVernay, Ava 98
Harris, Leslie 6
Nelson, Stanley 92

Supreme Court
See U.S. Supreme Court

Surfing
Corley, Tony 62

Surrealism
Ellison, Ralph 7
Lee-Smith, Hughie 5, 22

Swaziland government
Mswati III 56

Swimming
Ervin, Anthony 66
Jones, Cullen 73

Moussambani, Eric 105

Talk Soup
Tyler, Aisha N. 36

Talladega College
Archie-Hudson, Marguerite 44

Tampa Bay Buccaneers football team
Barber, Ronde 41
Brooks, Derrick 43
Dungy, Tony 17, 42, 59
McDaniel, Randall Cornell 81
Morris, Raheem 77
Sapp, Warren 38, 109

Tanganyikan African National Union (TANU)
Kikwete, Jakaya Mrisho 73
Nyerere, Julius 5

TANU
See Tanganyikan African National Union

Tanzanian African National Union (TANU)
See Tanganyikan African National Union

Tap dancing
Anderson, Maceo 111
Atkins, Cholly 40
Bates, Peg Leg 14
Brown, Ernest 80
Glover, Savion 14
Hines, Gregory 1, 42
Lane, William Henry 90
Robinson, LaVaughn 69
Sims, Howard "Sandman" 48
Slyde, Jimmy 70
Walker, Dianne 57

Teacher of the Year Award
Draper, Sharon Mills 16, 43
Oliver, Kimberly 60

Teachers Insurance and Annuity Association and the College Retirement Equities Fund (TIAA-CREF)
Wharton, Clifton R., Jr. 7

Teaching
Abani, Chris 77
Adams-Ender, Clara 40
Alexander, Margaret Walker 22
Amadi, Elechi 40
Archie-Hudson, Marguerite 44
Aubert, Alvin 41
Baiocchi, Regina Harris 41
Ballard, Allen Butler, Jr. 40
Beals, Melba Pattillo 15, 94
Belgrave, Marcus 77
Bibb, Henry and Mary 54
Blassingame, John Wesley 40
Branch, William Blackwell 39
Brawley, Benjamin 44
Brown, Charlotte Hawkins 106
Burroughs, Nannie Helen 96
Campbell, Mary Schmidt 43
Cardozo, Francis L. 33
Carter, Joye Maureen 41
Chenault, John 40
Cheney-Coker, Syl 43

Clarke, John Henrik 20
Clemmons, Reginal G. 41
Cobb, Jewel Plummer 42
Cobb, W. Montague 39
Cole, Johnnetta B. 5, 43
Colescott, Robert 69
Collins, Patricia Hill 67
Cook, Mercer 40
Cooper Cafritz, Peggy 43
Cortor, Eldzier 42
Cotter, Joseph Seamon, Sr. 40
Crouch, Hubert 95
Dailey, Ulysses Grant 87
Davis, Arthur P. 41
Davis, Gary 41
Davis, George 36
Davis, Milt 74
De Veaux, Alexis 44
Delpit, Lisa 101
Dennard, Brazeal 37
Draper, Sharon Mills 16, 43
Drummond, William J. 40
Dumas, Henry 41
Dunnigan, Alice Allison 41
Dyett, Walter 113
Dymally, Mervyn 42
Early, Gerald 15
Everett, Percival 93
Falconer, Etta Zuber 59
Feelings, Muriel 44
Ferguson, Ronald F. 75
Figueroa, John J. 40
Ford, Nick Aaron 44
Forrest, Leon 44
Fuller, A. Oveta 43
Fuller, Arthur 27
Fuller, Howard L. 37
Gates, Sylvester James, Jr. 15
Gayle, Addison, Jr. 41
Gill, Gerald 69
Granville, Evelyn Boyd 36
Hall, Arthur 39
Hamburg, Beatrix 84
Hammonds, Evelynn 69
Harding, Vincent 67
Hare, Nathan 44
Harris, Barry 68
Haskins, James 36, 54
Henries, A. Doris Banks 44
Hill, Errol 40
Hill, Leslie Pinckney 44
Horne, Frank 44
Humphries, Frederick 20
Imes, Elmer Samuel 39
Jackson, Fred James 25
Jansen, Jonathan 102
Jarrett, Vernon D. 42
Jarvis, Erich 67
Kennedy, Randall 40
Ladner, Joyce A. 42
Leevy, Carrol M. 42
Lewis, Norman 39
Lindsey, Tommie 51
Luper, Clara 94
Logan, Rayford W. 40
McCullough, Geraldine 58, 79
Mickens, Ronald Elbert 105
Mitchell, Parren J. 42, 66
Moore, Harry T. 29
Mphalele, Es'kia 40
Naylor, Gloria 10, 42
Norman, Maidie 20
Oliver, Kimberly 60

Owens, Helen **48**
Palmer, Everard **37**
Patterson, Mary Jane **54**
Perry, Steve **98**
Peters, Margaret and Matilda **43**
Player, Willa B. **43**
Prophet, Nancy Elizabeth **42**
Putney, Martha S. **75**
Querino, Manuel Raimundo **84**
Ray, Charlotte E. **60**
Redmond, Eugene **23**
Reid, Senghor **55**
Rhodes, Jewell Parker **84**
Ross-Lee, Barbara **67**
Shockley, Ann Allen **84**
Simpson-Hoffman, N'kenge **52**
Smith, Anna Deavere **6, 44**
Smith, John L. **22**
Toler, Burl **80**
Tutu, Nontombi Naomi **57**
Wambugu, Florence **42**
Watson, Diane **41**
Wells, Henrietta Bell **69**
Wesley, Richard **73**
Wilkens, J. Ernest, Jr. **43**
Yancy, Dorothy Cowser **42**
Yarbrough, Camille **40**
York, Vincent **40**

Teatro Experimental do Negro
Nascimento, Abdias do **93**

Telecommunications
Clyburn, Mignon **78**
Gordon, Bruce S. **41, 53, 82**
Ibrahim, Mo **67, 115**
Irvin, Vernon **65**
Rapelang Rabana **112**
Wilkins, Ray **47**

Television
Akil, Mara Brock **60, 82**
Allen, Byron **3, 24, 97**
Arkadie, Kevin **17**
Arnold, Tichina **63**
Banks, Tyra **11, 50**
Blake, Asha **26**
Bowser, Yvette Lee **17**
Brady, Wayne **32, 71**
Brown, Bobby **58**
Brown, James **22**
Brown, Joe **29**
Brown, Vivian **27**
Burnett, Charles **16, 68**
Carter, Nell **39**
Chase, Debra Martin **49, 96**
Clack, Zoanne **73**
CoCo Brother **93**
Corbi, Lana **42**
Creagh, Milton **27**
de Passe, Suzanne **25**
Deezer D **53**
Earthquake **55**
Elder, Larry **25**
Ephriam, Mablean **29**
Evans, Harry **25**
Falana, Lola **42**
Fales-Hill, Susan **88**
Frazier, Kevin **58**
Gardere, Jeffrey **76**
George, Nelson **12, 101**
Gray, Willie **46**
Greely, M. Gasby **27**
Greene, Petey **65**

Hall, Arsenio **58**
Hatchett, Glenda **32**
Haynes, Trudy **44**
Henriques, Julian **37**
Hill, Marc Lamont **80**
Jackson, George **19**
Jackson, Randy **40**
Jackson, Tom **70**
Jarrett, Vernon D. **42**
Joe, Yolanda **21**
Kandi **83**
LeFlore, Lyah Beth **96**
Long, Loretta **58**
Lomax, Louis E. **90**
Mabuza-Suttle, Felicia **43**
Mathis, Greg **26**
McCrary Anthony, Crystal **70**
McFarland, Roland **49**
McGlowan, Angela **64, 86**
McKenzie, Vashti M. **29**
Mercado-Valdes, Frank **43**
Mitchell, Russ **21, 73**
Moss, Carlton **16**
Neville, Arthel **53**
Nissel, Angela **42**
Norman, Christina **47**
Omarosa **69, 110**
Palmer, Keke **68**
Perry, Tyler **40, 54, 103**
Pitts, Byron **71**
Poussaint, Renee **78**
Price, Frederick K. C. **21**
Prince-Bythewood, Gina **31, 77**
Quarles, Norma **25**
Reynolds, Star Jones **10, 27, 61**
Rhimes, Shonda Lynn **67**
Ridley, John **69**
Roberts, Deborah **35**
Roker, Al **12, 49**
Russell, Nipsey **66**
Salters, Lisa **71**
Shepherd, Sherri **55**
Simmons, Kimora Lee **51, 83**
Smiley, Tavis **20, 68**
Stewart, Nzingha **89**
Stuart, Moira **82**
Taylor, Jason **70**
Taylor, Karin **34**
Tillman, Deborah **98**
Vance, Jim **110**
Vaughn, Countess **53**
Wainwright, Joscelyn **46**
Washington, Hayma **86**
Watson, Carlos **50**
Wayans, Damien **78**
Wayans, Damon **8, 41**
Wayans, Marlon **29, 82**
Wayans, Shawn **29**
Williams, Armstrong **29**
Williams, Wendy **62**

Television direction
Barclay, Paris **37, 94**
Duke, Bill **3, 96**
Hemingway, Anthony **107**
Johnson, Clark **96**
Warner, Malcolm-Jamal **22, 36, 110**
Whack, Rita Coburn **36**

Tennessee state government
DeBerry, Lois M. **115**
Ford, Harold E. **42**

Tennessee State University
Clark, Yvonne Young **95**
Phillips, Teresa L. **42**

Tennessee Supreme Court
Birch, Adolpho A., Jr. **85**

Tennessee Titans football team
George, Eddie **80**
McNair, Steve **22, 47, 79**
Rolle, Myron **98**

Tennis
Ashe, Arthur **1, 18**
Blake, James **43**
Garrison, Zina **2**
Gibson, Althea **8, 43**
Jackson, Jamea **64**
McNeil, Lori **1**
Noah, Yannick **4, 60**
Peters, Margaret and Matilda **43**
Rubin, Chanda **37**
Stephens, Sloane **105**
Washington, MaliVai **8**
Washington, Ora Mae **115**
Williams, Samm-Art **21**
Williams, Serena **20, 41, 73**
Williams, Venus **17, 34, 62**
Young, Donald, Jr. **57**

Texas Rangers baseball team
Bonds, Bobby **43**
Cottrell, Comer **11**

Texas state government
Delco, Wilhemina **33**
Gaines, Matthew **95**
Johnson, Eddie Bernice **8, 90**
Jordan, Barbara **4, 78**

Theater administration/ownership
Austin, Lovie **40**
Banks, Michelle **59**
Borders, James **9**
Cox, Ida **42**
Gibson, John Trusty **87**
Hamlin, Larry Leon **49, 62**
Leggs, Kingsley **62**
LeNoire, Rosetta **37**
Leon, Kenny **10, 98**
Marsalis, Delfeayo **41**
Spears, Warren **52**

Theatrical direction/production
Belgrave, Cynthia **75**
Glover, Keith **79**
Hall, Juanita **62**
Hayes, Teddy **40**
Leon, Kenny **10, 98**
McClinton, Marion Isaac **77**
Milner, Ron **39**
Perry, Tyler **40, 54, 103**
Scott, Harold Russell, Jr. **61**
Springer, Ashton, Jr. **115**
Taylor, Regina **9, 46, 97**
Teer, Barbara Ann **81**
Thompson, Tazewell **13**
Wolfe, George C. **6, 43**

Theology
Cone, James H. **3, 82**
Franklin, Robert M. **13**

Harding, Vincent **67**
Henderson, George Washington **101**

TIAA-CREF
See Teachers Insurance and Annuity Association and the College Retirement Equities Fund

Time Warner Inc.
Ames, Wilmer **27**
Parsons, Richard Dean **11, 33**

TLC Beatrice International Holdings, Inc.
Lewis, Reginald F. **6**

Togolese government
Eyadéma, Gnassingbé **7, 52**
Gnassingbé, Faure **67**

The Tonight Show
Eubanks, Kevin **15, 108**

Tony Awards
Allen, Debbie **13, 42**
Bailey, Pearl **14**
Belafonte, Harry **4, 65**
Carroll, Diahann **9**
Carter, Nell **39**
Clarke, Hope **14**
Cooper, Chuck **75**
Davis, Viola **34, 76, 100**
Faison, George **16**
Falana, Lola **42**
Fishburne, Laurence **4, 22, 70**
Glover, Savion **14**
Goldberg, Whoopi **4, 33, 69**
Hall, Juanita **62**
Hines, Gregory **1, 42**
Horne, Lena **5, 86**
Hyman, Phyllis **19**
James, Nikki M. **94**
Jones, Bill T. **1, 46, 80**
Jones, James Earl **3, 49, 79**
Jones, Sarah **39**
LaChanze **93**
Lenox, Adriane **59**
McDonald, Audra **20, 62**
Mitchell, Brian Stokes **21**
Mokae, Zakes **80**
Moore, Melba **21**
Porter, Billy **112**
Premice, Josephine **41**
Rashad, Phylicia **21**
Richards, Lloyd **2**
Rose, Anika Noni **70**
Santiago-Hudson, Ruben **85**
Thigpen, Lynne **17, 41**
Tyson, Cicely **7, 51, 112**
Uggams, Leslie **23, 114**
Vereen, Ben **4**
Washington, Denzel **1, 16, 93**
Wilson, August **7, 33, 55**
Wolfe, George C. **6, 43**
Wright, Jeffrey **54, 111**

Toronto Blue Jays baseball team
Carter, Joe **30**
Gaston, Cito **71**
McGriff, Fred **24**

Toronto Raptors basketball team
Carter, Butch 27
Carter, Vince 26
Olajuwon, Hakeem 2, 72
Thomas, Isiah 7, 26, 65

Tourism
Edmunds, Gladys 48

Track and field
Ashford, Evelyn 63
Beamon, Bob 30
Bekele, Kenenisa 75
Bolt, Usain 73, 104
Campbell, Milt 113
Campbell-Brown, Veronica 102
Carlos, John 97
Christie, Linford 8
Clay, Bryan 57, 74
Devers, Gail 7, 87
Dibaba, Tirunesh 73, 109
Farah, Mo 104
Felix, Allyson 48, 98
Fraser-Pryce, Shelly-Ann 113
Freeman, Cathy 29
Gay, Tyson 114
Gebrselassie, Haile 70
Graham, Trevor 84
Greene, Maurice 27, 77
Griffith-Joyner, Florence 28
Harrison, Alvin 28
Harrison, Calvin 28
Hayes, Bob 77
Holmes, Kelly 47
Jacobs, Regina 38
James, G. Larry 74
Johnson, Michael 13
Johnson, Rodney Van 28
Jones, Lou 64
Jones, Marion 21, 66
Joyner-Kersee, Jackie 5
Kearney, Beverly 109
Keflezighi, Meb 49
Lewis, Carl 4, 97
Matson, Ollie 93
Metcalfe, Ralph 26
Montgomery, Tim 41
Moses, Edwin 8
Mutola, Maria 12
Omar, Samia Yusuf 107
Owens, Jesse 2
Pollard, Fritz 53
Powell, Mike 7
Quirot, Ana 13
Richards-Ross, Sanya 66, 98
Rudisha, David 112
Rudolph, Wilma 4
Smith, Tommie 102
Temple, Ed 109
Thugwane, Josia 21
Walker, LeRoy T. 106
White, Willye 67
Whitfield, Mal 60
Williams, Lauryn 58
Woodruff, John 68

Transplant surgery
Alexander, Joseph L. 95
Callender, Clive O. 3
Kountz, Samuel L. 10

Transport and General Workers' Union
Morris, William "Bill" 51

Trombone
Fuller, Curtis 115
Lewis, George 104
Marsalis, Delfeayo 41
Powell, Benny 87
Trombone Shorty 97

Trumpet
Adderley, Nat 29
Akinmusire, Ambrose 103
Armstrong, Louis 2
Belgrave, Marcus 77
Blanchard, Terence 43
Brown, Clifford 86
Byrd, Donald 109
Curson, Ted 108
Dara, Olu 35
Davis, Miles 4
Dixon, Bill 87
Dorham, Kenny 113
Edison, Harry 114
Eldridge, Roy 37
Ellison, Ralph 7
Farmer, Art 38
Ferbos, Lionel 95
Gillespie, Dizzy 1
Hubbard, Freddie 75
Jones, Jonah 39
Jones, Thad 68
Little, Booker 105
Marsalis, Wynton 16, 90
Masekela, Hugh 1, 106
Morgan, Lee 102
Navarro, Fats 104
Smith, Cladys "Jabbo" 32
Terry, Clark 39
Williams, Cootie 114
Wilson, Abram 104
Wilson, Gerald 49

Tuskegee Airmen
Archer, Lee, Jr. 79
Bromery, Randolph Wilson 85
Brown, Willa 40
Carter, Herbert E. 108
Chappell, Roy M. 95
Davis, Benjamin O., Jr. 2, 43
Haysbert, Raymond V., Sr. 87
Hoskins, Harold K. 103
James, Daniel, Jr. 16
Plinton, James O., Jr. 98
Pruitt, Wendell O. 106
Young, Perry H. 100

Tuskegee University
Carver, George Washington 4
Dawson, William Levi 39
Gomillion, Charles 90
Moton, Robert Russa 83
Patterson, Frederick Douglass 12
Payton, Benjamin F. 23
Taylor, Robert Robinson 80
Williston, David Augustus 99

UCC
See United Church of Christ

Ugandan government
Amin, Idi 42
Kisekka, Samson 112

Museveni, Yoweri 4
Obote, Milton 63

UN
See United Nations

UNCF
See United Negro College Fund

Underground Railroad
Blockson, Charles L. 42
Cohen, Anthony 15
Crew, Spencer R. 55
DeBaptiste, George 32
Shadd, Abraham D. 81

UNIA
See Universal Negro Improvement Association

Unions
Brown, Lloyd Louis 42
Burrus, William Henry "Bill" 45
Clay, William Lacy 8
Ellis-Lamkins, Phaedra 88
Europe, James Reese 10
Farmer, James 2, 64
Fletcher, Benjamin 90
Fletcher, Bill, Jr. 41
Holt Baker, Arlene 73
Lucy, William 50
McGee, James Madison 46
Morris, William "Bill" 51
Ramaphosa, Cyril 3
Randolph, A. Philip 3
Roberts, Lillian 83
Smith, Nate 49
Tucker, Rosina 14
Wyatt, Addie L. 56

UNIP
See United National Independence Party

UNITA
See National Union for the Total Independence of Angola

United Church of Christ (UCC)
Chavis, Benjamin 6
Forbes, James A., Jr. 71
Miller, Clyde 113
Moss, Otis, III 72
Wright, Jeremiah A., Jr. 45, 69, 103

United Democratic Front (UDF; Malawi)
Muluzi, Bakili 14, 76

United Methodist Church
Caldwell, Kirbyjon 55
Cleaver, Emanuel 4, 45, 68, 107
Lawson, James M., Jr. 90
Lewis, Shirley A. R. 14
Muzorewa, Abel 85
Stith, Charles R. 73

United Nations (UN)
Annan, Kofi Atta 15, 48
Bunche, Ralph J. 5
Cousin, Ertharin 115
Diouf, Abdou 3
Frazier, E. Franklin 10
Juma, Calestous 57
Lafontant, Jewel Stradford 3, 51
McDonald, Gabrielle Kirk 20

McHenry, Donald F. 83
Mongella, Gertrude 11
Osotimehin, Babatunde 107
Perkins, Edward 5
Rice, Susan 74, 103
Smythe Haith, Mabel 61
Young, Andrew 3, 48, 110
Yumkella, Kandeh 105

United Negro College Fund (UNCF)
Boyd, T. B., III 6
Bunkley, Anita Richmond 39
Creagh, Milton 27
Dawson, Matel, Jr. 39
Edley, Christopher 2, 48
Lomax, Michael L. 58
Patterson, Frederick Douglass 12

United Parcel Service
Cooper, Evern 40
Darden, Calvin 38
Washington, Patrice Clarke 12

United Somali Congress
Ali Mahdi Mohamed 5

United States Football League (USFL)
White, Reggie 6, 50
Williams, Doug 22, 112

Universal Negro Improvement Association (UNIA)
Austin, Junius C. 44
Garvey, Marcus 1
McGuire, George Alexander 80

University administration
See College and university administration

University of Alabama
Davis, Mike 41
Lucy Foster, Autherine 35

University of California–Berkeley
Blackwell, David 79
Drummond, William J. 40
Edley, Christopher F., Jr. 48

University of Chicago Hospitals
Lee, Raphael C. 87

University of Michigan
Amaker, Tommy 62
Dillard, Godfrey J. 45
Fuller, A. Oveta 43
Goss, Tom 23
Gray, Ida 41
Imes, Elmer Samuel 39
Hill, Errol 40

***Upscale* magazine**
Bronner, Nathaniel H., Sr. 32

Urban League (regional)
Adams, Sheila J. 25
Clayton, Xernona 3, 45
Jacob, John E. 2
Layton, William 87
Walcott, Dennis M. 112

Young, Whitney M., Jr. **4**

Urban planning/renewal
Allen, Will **74**
Blakely, Edward J. **88**
Bosley, Freeman, Jr. **7**
Brown, Aja **115**
Carter, Majora **77**
Harris, Alice **7**
Lane, Vincent **5**

U.S. Air Force
Anderson, Michael P. **40**
Davis, Benjamin O., Jr. **2, 43**
Drew, Alvin, Jr. **67**
Dwight, Edward **65**
Gregory, Frederick **8, 51**
Harris, Marcelite Jordan **16**
James, Daniel, Jr. **16**
Johnson, Lonnie G. **32, 93**
Jones, Wayne **53**
Lyles, Lester **31**

U.S. Army
Adams-Ender, Clara **40**
Anderson, Marcia **115**
Augusta, Alexander T.**111**
Austin, Lloyd **101**
Baker, Vernon Joseph **65, 87**
Becton, Julius W., Jr. **110**
Brown, Anthony G. **72**
Cadoria, Sherian Grace **14**
Carter, Edward A., Jr. **104**
Clarke, Anna Mac **95**
Clemmons, Reginal G. **41**
Davis, Benjamin O., Sr. **4**
Delany, Martin R. **27**
Ellis, Larry R. **110**
Flipper, Henry O. **3**
Fox, John R. **105**
Greenhouse, Bunnatine "Bunny" **57**
Honoré, Russel L. **64**
Jackson, Fred James **25**
Johnson, Hazel **22**
Johnson, Shoshana **47**
King, Teresa **80**
Matthews, Mark **59**
Perry, Herman **89**
Poindexter, Hildrus A. **87**
Powell, Colin **1, 28, 75**
Rogers, Alan G. **72**
Snow, Samuel **71**
Stanford, John **20**
Stowers, Freddie **107**
Via, Dennis **108**
Ward, William E. **107**
Watkins, Perry **12**
West, Allen **89**
West, Togo D., Jr. **16**
Young, Charles **77**

U.S. Army Air Corps
Anderson, Charles Edward **37**

U.S. Atomic Energy Commission
Nabrit, Samuel Milton **47**

U.S. Attorney's Office
Jordan, Eddie **82**
Lafontant, Jewel Stradford **3, 51**
Lynch, Loretta E. **103**

U.S. Bureau of Engraving and Printing
Felix, Larry R. **64**

U.S. Cabinet
Brown, Ron **5**
Elders, Joycelyn **6**
Espy, Mike **6**
Harris, Patricia Roberts **2**
Herman, Alexis M. **15**
Kirk, Ron **11, 75, 111**
O'Leary, Hazel **6**
Powell, Colin **1, 28, 75**
Rice, Condoleezza **3, 28, 72**
Slater, Rodney E. **15**
Sullivan, Louis **8**
Weaver, Robert C. **8, 46**

U.S. Coast Guard
Brown, Erroll M. **23**
Healy, Michael **90**
Rochon, Stephen W. **78**

U.S. Commission on Civil Rights
Berry, Mary Frances **7**
Edley, Christopher **2, 48**
Fletcher, Arthur A. **63**

U.S. Conference of Catholic Bishops
Gregory, Wilton D. **37**

U.S. Court of Appeals
Hastie, William H. **8**
Higginbotham, A. Leon, Jr. **13, 25**
Kearse, Amalya Lyle **12**
Keith, Damon J. **16, 74**
Rawlinson, Johnnie B. **79**
Williams, Ann Claire **82**

U.S. Department of Agriculture (USDA)
Espy, Mike **6**
Layton, William **87**
Sherrod, Shirley **87**
Vaughn, Gladys Gary **47**
Watkins, Shirley R. **17**
Williams, Hosea Lorenzo **15, 31**

U.S. Department of Commerce
Brown, Ron **5**
Irving, Larry, Jr. **12**
Morrow, E. Frederic **100**
Shavers, Cheryl **31**

U.S. Department of Defense
Greenhouse, Bunnatine "Bunny" **57**
Johnson, Jeh C. **76**
Tribble, Israel, Jr. **8**

U.S. Department of Education
Ali, Russlynn H. **92**
Groff, Peter **96**
Hill, Anita **5, 65**
Hill, Bonnie Guiton **20**
Paige, Rod **29**
Purnell, Silas **59**
Thomas, Clarence **2, 39, 65**
Tribble, Israel, Jr. **8**
Velez-Rodriguez, Argelia **56**

U.S. Department of Energy
O'Leary, Hazel **6**

U.S. Department of Health and Human Services (HHS)
See also U.S. Department of Health, Education, and Welfare
Gaston, Marilyn Hughes **60**
Hamburg, Margaret **78**
Hughes, Dora **88**

U.S. Department of Health, Education, and Welfare (HEW)
Harris, Patricia Roberts **2**
Randolph, Linda A. **52**
Spearman, Leonard H. O., Sr. **81**
Sullivan, Louis **8**

U.S. Department of Housing and Urban Development (HUD)
Blackwell, J. Kenneth, Sr. **61**
Gaines, Brenda **41**
Harris, Patricia Roberts **2**
Jackson, Alphonso R. **48**
Weaver, Robert C. **8, 46**

U.S. Department of Justice
Campbell, Bill **9, 76**
Days, Drew S., III **10**
Guinier, Lani **7, 30**
Harris, Maya Lakshmi **88**
Holder, Eric, Jr. **9, 76, 104**
Lafontant, Jewel Stradford **3, 51**
Lewis, Delano **7**
Patrick, Deval **12, 61**
Payton, John **48**
Thompson, Larry D. **39**
Williams, Michael L. **86**

U.S. Department of Labor
Crockett, George W., Jr. **10, 64**
Fletcher, Arthur A. **63**
Herman, Alexis M. **15**

U.S. Department of State
Baltimore, Richard Lewis, III **71**
Bethune, Mary McLeod **4**
Bunche, Ralph J. **5**
Davis, Ruth **37**
Dougherty, Mary Pearl **47**
Frazer, Jendayi **68**
Ervin, Clark Kent **82**
Garrett, Joyce Finley **59**
Grimké, Archibald H. **9**
Haley, George Williford Boyce **21**
Harris, Patricia Roberts **2**
Lafontant, Jewel Stradford **3, 51**
McGee, James D. **74**
Powell, Colin **1, 28, 75**
Rice, Condoleezza **3, 28, 72**
Rice, Susan **74, 103**
Stokes, Carl **10, 73**
Sutphen, Mona **77**
Thomas-Greenfield, Linda **99**
Van Lierop, Robert **53**
Wharton, Clifton R., Jr. **7**
Wharton, Clifton Reginald, Sr. **36**

U.S. Department of the Treasury
Morton, Azie Taylor **48**

U.S. Department of Transportation
Coleman, William T. **76**
Davis, Benjamin O., Jr. **2, 43**

U.S. Department of Veterans Affairs
Brown, Jesse **6, 41**

U.S. Diplomatic Corps
See U.S. Department of State

U.S. District Attorney
Harris, Kamala D. **64**
Lloyd, Reginald **64**

U.S. District Court judge
Bryant, William Benson **61**
Carter, Robert L. **51, 100**
Cooke, Marcia **60**
Diggs-Taylor, Anna **20**
Henderson, Thelton E. **68**
Johnson, Norma H. **17, 97**
Keith, Damon J. **16, 74**
Parker, Barrington D. **92**
Parsons, James **14**
Perry, Matthew J., Jr. **96**
Sleet, Gregory M. **109**
Tanner, Jack E. **100**
Williams, Ann Claire **82**
Williams, David W. **110**

U.S. Dream Academy
Phipps, Wintley **59**

U.S. Environmental Protection Agency
Jackson, Lisa **77**

U.S. Foreign Service
See U.S. Department of State

U.S. Geological Survey
Bromery, Randolph Wilson **85**
Person, Waverly **9, 51**

U.S. House of Representatives
Archie-Hudson, Marguerite **44**
Ballance, Frank W. **41**
Bishop, Sanford D., Jr. **24, 111**
Brown, Corrine **24, 90**
Burke, Yvonne Brathwaite **42**
Carson, André **69**
Carson, Julia **23, 69**
Chisholm, Shirley **2, 50**
Clarke, Yvette **92**
Clay, William Lacy **8**
Clay, William Lacy, Jr. **95**
Clayton, Eva M. **20**
Cleaver, Emanuel **4, 45, 68, 107**
Clyburn, James E. **21, 71**
Collins, Barbara-Rose **7, 87**
Collins, Cardiss **10, 80**
Conyers, John, Jr. **4, 45, 111**
Crockett, George W., Jr. **10, 64**
Cummings, Elijah E. **24, 102**
Davis, Artur **41**
Davis, Danny K. **24, 79**
De Priest, Oscar Stanton **80**
Dellums, Ronald **2, 81**
Diggs, Charles C. **21**
Dixon, Julian C. **24**
Dymally, Mervyn **42**
Edwards, Donna **77**
Ellison, Keith **59**
Espy, Mike **6**
Fattah, Chaka **11, 70, 112**
Fauntroy, Walter E. **11**
Fields, Cleo **13**

Flake, Floyd H. **18, 110**
Ford, Harold E(ugene) **42**
Ford, Harold E(ugene), Jr. **16, 70**
Franks, Gary **2**
Frazer, Victor O. **98**
Fudge, Marcia L. **76**
Gray, William H., III **3**
Hastings, Alcee L. **16**
Hawkins, Augustus F. **68**
Hilliard, Earl F. **24**
Jackson, Jesse, Jr. **14, 45, 81, 108**
Jackson Lee, Sheila **20**
Jefferson, William J. **25, 72**
Johnson, Eddie Bernice **8, 90**
Johnson, Hank, Jr. **80**
Jordan, Barbara **4, 78**
Kelly, Robin **114**
Kilpatrick, Carolyn Cheeks **16**
Langston, John Mercer **101**
Lee, Barbara **25, 102**
Leland, Mickey **2**
Lewis, John **2, 46, 83**
Majette, Denise **41**
McKinney, Cynthia **11, 52, 74**
Meek, Carrie **6, 36**
Meek, Kendrick **41, 89**
Meeks, Gregory **25**
Menard, John Willis **90**
Metcalfe, Ralph **26**
Mfume, Kweisi **6, 41**
Millender-McDonald, Juanita **21, 61**
Mitchell, Arthur Wergs **91**
Mitchell, Parren J. **42, 66**
Moore, Gwendolynne S. **55**
Norton, Eleanor Holmes **7, 93**
Owens, Major **6**
Payne, Donald M. **2, 57, 112**
Pinchback, P. B. S. **9**
Powell, Adam Clayton, Jr. **3**
Rangel, Charles B. **3, 52, 85**
Rapier, James T. **82**
Richardson, Laura **81**
Richmond, Cedric **93**
Rush, Bobby **26, 76**
Scott, David **41**
Scott, Robert C. **23**
Sewell, Terri **93**
Smalls, Robert **82**
Stokes, Louis **3**
Thompson, Bennie G. **26**
Towns, Edolphus **19, 75**
Tubbs Jones, Stephanie **24, 72**
Waldon, Alton R., Jr. **98**
Washington, Harold **6**
Waters, Maxine **3, 67, 103**
Watson, Diane **41**
Watt, Mel **26, 105**
Watts, J. C., Jr. **14, 38**
West, Allen **89**
Wheat, Alan **14**
Wilson, Frederica **92**
Wynn, Albert R. **25, 77**
Young, Andrew **3, 48, 110**

U.S. Information Agency
Allen, Samuel **38**

U.S. Marines
Bennett, Richard **97**
Bolden, Charles Frank, Jr. **7, 78**
Brown, Jesse **6, 41**
Coleman, Ronald S. **110**
Petersen, Franke E. **31**

Von Lipsey, Roderick K. **11**

U.S. Navy
Black, Barry C. **47**
Brashear, Carl **29**
Brown, Jesse Leroy **31**
Brown, Wesley A. **102**
Clark, Carl **101**
Doby, Lawrence Eugene, Sr. **16, 41**
Fields, Evelyn J. **27**
Gravely, Samuel L., Jr. **5, 49**
Howard, Michelle **28**
Miller, Dorie **29**
Pinckney, Bill **42**
Pruitt, Wendell O. **106**
Reason, J. Paul **19**
Wright, Lewin **43**

U.S. Peace Corps
Days, Drew S., III **10**
Johnson, Rafer **33**
Lewis, Delano **7**

U.S. presidency
Obama, Barack **49, 74, 91**

U.S. Register of the Treasury
Bruce, Blanche Kelso **33**

U.S. Senate
Black, Barry C. **47**
Bowman, Bertie **71**
Braun, Carol Moseley **4, 42**
Brooke, Edward W. **8, 88**
Bruce, Blanche Kelso **33**
Burris, Roland W. **25, 75**
Obama, Barack **49, 74, 91**
Pinchback, P. B. S. **9**
Revels, Hiram Rhoades **98**

U.S. State Department
See U.S. Department of State

U.S. Supreme Court
Marshall, Thurgood **1, 44**
Thomas, Clarence **2, 39, 65**

U.S. surgeon general
Benjamin, Regina **20, 75**
Elders, Joycelyn **6**
Satcher, David **7, 57, 111**

U.S. Virgin Islands government
Christian-Green, Donna M. **17**
DeJongh, John, Jr. **85**
Evans, Melvin H. **88**
Frazer, Victor O. **98**
Hastie, William H. **8**
Turnbull, Charles Wesley **62**

USDA
See U.S. Department of Agriculture

USFL
See United States Football League

Vancouver Grizzlies basketball team
Abdur-Rahim, Shareef **28**

Vaudeville
Anderson, Eddie "Rochester" **30**
Austin, Lovie **40**
Bates, Peg Leg **14**
Cox, Ida **42**
Davis, Sammy, Jr. **18**

Gilpin, Charles Sidney **81**
Johnson, Jack **8**
Martin, Sara **38**
McDaniel, Hattie **5**
Mills, Florence **22**
Robinson, Bill "Bojangles" **11**
Waters, Ethel **7**

Veterans's issues
Carr, Keela **74**

Veterinary science
Jawara, Dawda Kairaba **11**
Lushington, Augustus Nathaniel **56**
Thomas, Vivien **9**

Vibe
Jones, Quincy **8, 30**
Smith, Danyel **40**
Wilbekin, Emil **63**

Vibraphone
Hampton, Lionel **17, 41**
Hutcherson, Bobby **115**
Smith, Cecilia **102**

Victim's Bill of Rights
Dee, Merri **55**

Video gaming
Croal, N'Gai **76**
Fils-Aimé, Reggie **74**

Vietnam Veterans of America
Duggins, George **64**

Village Voice
Cooper, Andrew W. **36**
Crouch, Stanley **11**

Violin
Boulogne, Joseph, Chevalier de Saint-Georges **94**
Bridgetower, George **78**
Daemyon, Jerald **64**
Dworkin, Aaron P. **52**
Escobar, Damien **56**
Escobar, Tourie **56**
Murray, Tai **47**
Smith, Stuff **37**
Tinsley, Boyd **50**
Williams, Claude **80**

Virginia state government
Marsh, Henry **32**
Martin, Ruby Grant **49**
Wilder, L. Douglas **3, 48**

Virginia Supreme Court
Hassell, Leroy Rountree, Sr. **41**

Virology
Fuller, A. Oveta **43**

Vogue magazine
Talley, André Leon **56, 106**

Volleyball
Blanton, Dain **29**

Voodoo
Beauvoir, Max **74**
Dunham, Katherine **4, 59**
Guy, Rosa **5**
Hurston, Zora Neale **3**

Pierre, Andre **17**

Voting rights
Cary, Mary Ann Shadd **30**
Chestnut, J. L., Jr. **73**
Clark, Septima **7**
Forman, James **7, 51**
Hamer, Fannie Lou **6**
Harper, Frances Ellen Watkins **11**
Hill, Jesse, Jr. **13**
Lampkin, Daisy **19**
Mandela, Nelson **1, 14, 77**
Moore, Harry T. **29**
Moses, Robert Parris **11**
Terrell, Mary Church **9**
Touré, Faya Ora Rose **56**
Trotter, Monroe **9**
Tubman, Harriet **9**
Wells-Barnett, Ida B. **8**
Williams, Hosea Lorenzo **15, 31**

WAAC (Women's Auxiliary Army Corps)
See Women's Army Corps

WAC
See Women's Army Corps

War criminals
Lubanga, Thomas **104**
Ntaganda, Bosco **111**
Sankoh, Foday **74**

Washington, D.C., city government
Barry, Marion S. **7, 44**
Brown, Kwame R. **91**
Cooper Cafritz, Peggy **43**
Dixon, Sharon Pratt **1**
Fenty, Adrian **60, 88**
Gray, Vincent C. **88**
Hobson, Julius W. **44**
Jarvis, Charlene Drew **21**
Neal, Larry **38**
Norton, Eleanor Holmes **7, 93**
Washington, Walter **45**
Williams, Anthony **21**

Washington Post
Aplin-Brownlee, Vivian **96**
Britt, Donna **28**
Gaines, Patrice **106**
Givhan, Robin Deneen **72**
Haygood, Wil **83**
Ifill, Gwen **28**
King, Colbert I. **69**
Maynard, Robert C. **7**
McCall, Nathan **8**
Nelson, Jill **6, 54**
Raspberry, William **2**

Washington Redskins football team
Green, Darrell **39, 74**
Monk, Art **38, 73**

Washington Week in Review
TV series
Ifill, Gwen **28**

Washington Wizards basketball team
Bickerstaff, Bernie **21**
Heard, Gar **25**
Howard, Juwan **15**

Unseld, Wes **23**
Webber, Chris **15, 30, 59**

Weather
Brown, Vivian **27**
Christian, Spencer **15**
McEwen, Mark **5**
Roker, Al **12, 49**

Welfare reform
Bryant, Wayne R. **6**
Carson, Julia **23, 69**
Parker, Star **70**
Wallace, Joaquin **49**
Williams, Walter E. **4**

West Indian folk songs
Rhoden, Wayne **70**

West Indian literature
See Caribbean literature/West Indian literature

West Point
Davis, Benjamin O., Jr. **2, 43**
Flipper, Henry O. **3**
Young, Charles **77**

White House
Allen, Eugene **79**
Burton, Bill **96**
Butts, Cassandra **78**
Christie, Ron **83**
Currie, Betty **21**
Gaspard, Patrick **84**
Hatcher, Andrew T. **90**
Jarvis, Kristen **85**
Keckley, Elizabeth **90**
Love, Reggie **77**
Obama, Michelle **61, 90**
Rochon, Stephen W. **78**
Rogers, Desirée **88**
Rouse, Cecilia **93**
Strautmanis, Michael **87**

Wine/winemaking
Allen-Buillard, Melba **55**
Rideau, Iris **46**
Walker, Ray **109**

Wisconsin Supreme Court
Butler, Louis **70**

Women Helping Offenders
Holland, Endesha Ida Mae **3, 57**

Women's Army Corps (WAC)
Adams Earley, Charity **13, 34**
Cadoria, Sherian Grace **14**
Clarke, Anna Mac **95**

Women's Auxiliary Army Corps
See Women's Army Corps

Women's issues
Abiola-Costello, Hafsat **108**
Allen, Ethel D. **13**
Angelou, Maya **1, 15**
Avery, Byllye Y. **66**
Ba, Mariama **30**
Bashir, Halima **73**
Brown, Elaine **8**
Burroughs, Nannie Helen **96**
Campbell, Bebe Moore **6, 24, 59**
Cannon, Katie **10**
Carby, Hazel **27**

Cary, Mary Ann Shadd **30**
Charles, Mary Eugenia **10, 55**
Chinn, May Edward **26**
Christian, Barbara T. **44**
Christian-Green, Donna M. **17**
Clark, Septima **7**
Cook-Parrish, Mary Virginia **95**
Cooper, Anna Julia **20**
De Veaux, Alexis **44**
Edwards, Lena Frances **76**
Elders, Joycelyn **6**
Evans, Diana **72**
Fauset, Jessie **7**
Giddings, Paula **11**
Gomez, Jewelle **30**
Grimké, Archibald H. **9**
Guy-Sheftall, Beverly **13, 92**
Hale, Clara **16**
Hale, Lorraine **8**
Hamer, Fannie Lou **6**
Harper, Frances Ellen Watkins **11**
Harris, Leslie **6**
Harris, Patricia Roberts **2**
Haynes, Elizabeth Ross **102**
Height, Dorothy I. **2, 23, 78**
Hernandez, Aileen Clarke **13**
Hill, Anita **5, 65**
Hine, Darlene Clark **24**
Holland, Endesha Ida Mae **3, 57**
hooks, bell **5, 90**
Hughes, Ebony **57**
Hull, Akasha Gloria **45**
Hussein, Lubna **80**
Jackson, Alexine Clement **22**
Joe, Yolanda **21**
Jordan, June **7, 35**
Koontz, Elizabeth Duncan **101**
Lampkin, Daisy **19**
Larsen, Nella **10**
Lorde, Audre **6**
Marshall, Paule **7, 77**
Mbaye, Mariétou **31**
McCabe, Jewell Jackson **10**
McCauley, Gina **76**
McKenzie, Vashti M. **29**
McMillan, Terry **4, 17, 53**
Millender-McDonald, Juanita **21, 61**
Millner, Denene **76**
Mongella, Gertrude **11**
Mossell, Gertrude Bustill **40**
Naylor, Gloria **10, 42**
Nelson, Jill **6, 54**
Niane, Katoucha **70**
Nichols, Nichelle **11**
Ormes, Jackie **73**
Parker, Pat **19**
Rawlings, Nana Konadu Agyeman **13**
Ruffin, Josephine St. Pierre **75**
Shange, Ntozake **8, 89**
Sherrod, Shirley **87**
Simpson, Carole **6, 30**
Smith, Barbara **28**
Smith, Jane E. **24**
Talbert, Mary B. **77**
Terrell, Mary Church **9**
Tubman, Harriet **9**
Vanzant, Iyanla **17, 47, 108**
Villard-Appolon, Malya **106**
Walker, Alice **1, 43**
Walker, Rebecca **50**
Wallace, Michele Faith **13**
Williams, Fannie Barrier **27**

Xuma, Madie Hall **59**

Women's Leadership Forum
Shabazz, Ilyasah **36**

Women's National Basketball Association
Bolton-Holifield, Ruthie **28**
Cash, Swin **59**
Catchings, Tamika **43**
Cooper, Cynthia **17**
Edwards, Teresa **14, 95**
Ford, Cheryl **45**
Griffith, Yolanda **25**
Holdsclaw, Chamique **24, 110**
Jones, Merlakia **34**
Lennox, Betty **31**
Leslie, Lisa **16, 73**
Madison, Paula **37, 99**
McCray, Nikki **18**
Miller, Cheryl **10, 74**
Milton, DeLisha **31**
Moore, Maya **94**
Palmer, Violet **59**
Parker, Candace **74**
Peck, Carolyn **23**
Perrot, Kim **23**
Staley, Dawn **57**
Swoopes, Sheryl **12, 56**
Thompson, Tina **25, 75**
Williams, Natalie **31**
Woodard, Lynette **67**

Workplace equity
Clark, Septima **7**
Hill, Anita **5, 65**
Nelson, Jill **6, 54**
Simpson, Carole **6, 30**

Works Progress (Projects) Administration (WPA)
Alexander, Margaret Walker **22**
Blackburn, Robert **28**
DeCarava, Roy **42, 81**
Douglas, Aaron **7**
Dunham, Katherine **4, 59**
Fauset, Crystal Dreda Bird **100**
Hall, Juanita **62**
Lawrence, Jacob **4, 28**
Lee-Smith, Hughie **5, 22**
Murray, Pauli **38**
Sallee, Charles **38**
Sebree, Charles **40**
Winkfield, Jimmy **42**
Wright, Richard **5**

World Bank
Okonjo-Iweala, Ngozi **101**
Soglo, Nicéphore **15**

World beat
Fela **1, 42**
Maal, Baaba **66**
N'Dour, Youssou **1, 53, 79**
Okosuns, Sonny **71**
Ongala, Remmy **9, 91**

World Cup
dos Santos, Manuel Francisco **65**
Gyan, Asamoah **87**
Mensah, John **87**
Milla, Roger **2**
Pelé **7**

Scurry, Briana **27**

World hunger
Iman **4, 33, 87**
Leland, Mickey **2**
Masire, Quett **5**

World Wrestling Entertainment (WWE) Hall of Fame
Ladd, Ernie **64**

WPA
See Works Progress (Projects) Administration

Wrestling
Ladd, Ernie **64**
Lashley, Bobby **63**
Rock, The **29, 66**
Young, Darren **114**

Xerox Corp.
Burns, Ursula **60**
Rand, A. Barry **6**

Yale Repertory Theater
Dutton, Charles S. **4, 22**
Richards, Lloyd **2**

Yale University
Blassingame, John Wesley **40**
Carby, Hazel **27**
Davis, Charles T. **48**
Hill, Errol **40**
Neal, Larry **38**

YMCA
See Young Men's Christian Association

Yoruban folklore
Soyinka, Wole **4, 93**

Young adult literature
Anderson, Ho Che **54**
Bolden, Tonya **32**
Ekwensi, Cyprian **37**
Johnson, Angela **52**
Millner, Denene **76**
Myers, Walter Dean **8, 20**

Young Men's Christian Association (YMCA)
Goode, Mal **13**
Hope, John **8**
Tobias, Channing H. **79**

Young Women's Christian Association (YWCA)
Clark, Septima **7**
Claytor, Helen **14, 52**
Height, Dorothy I. **2, 23, 78**
Jackson, Alexine Clement **22**
Jenkins, Ella **15**
Stewart, Ella **39**
Xuma, Madie Hall **59**

YWCA
See Young Women's Christian Association

Zairian government
Mobutu Sese Seko **1, 56**

Zambian government
Chiluba, Frederick **56, 80**
Mwanawasa, Levy **72**
Sata, Michael **102**

Cumulative Name Index

Volume numbers appear in **bold**

Aaliyah 1979–2001 **30**

Aaron, Hank 1934— **5**

Aaron, Henry Louis *See Aaron, Hank*

Aaron, Quinton 1984— **82**

Abacha, Sani 1943–1998 **11, 70**

Abani, Chris 1966— **77**

Abbott, Diane 1953— **9**

Abbott, Robert Sengstacke 1868–1940 **27**

Abdul-Jabbar, Kareem 1947— **8**

Abdullah, Imaam Isa *See York, Dwight D.*

Abdullah, Kazem 1979(?)— **97**

Abdulmajid, Iman Mohamed *See Iman*

Abdul-Rahman, Mahdi *See Hazzard, Walt*

Abdur-Rahim, Shareef 1976— **28**

Abele, Julian 1881–1950 **55**

Abercrumbie, P. Eric 1948— **95**

Abernathy, Ralph David 1926–1990 **1**

Aberra, Amsale 1954— **67**

Abiola, Moshood 1937–1998 **70**

Abiola-Costello, Hafsat 1974— **108**

Abrahams, Peter 1919— **39**

Abu-Jamal, Mumia 1954— **15**

Abubakar, Abdulsalami 1942— **66**

Abune Paulos 1935–2012 **105**

Ace, Johnny 1929–1954 **36**

Achebe, Albert Chinualumogu *See Achebe, Chinua*

Achebe, Chinua 1930–2013 **6, 99, 111**

Ackerman, Arlene 1947–2013 **108**

Acklin, Barbara Jean 1943–1998 **107**

Acogny, Germaine 1944— **55**

Adam, Mariam *See Imani Winds*

Adams, Eula L. 1950— **39**

Adams, Floyd, Jr. 1945— **12**

Adams, Grantley 1898–1971 **82**

Adams, H. Leslie *See Adams, Leslie*

Adams, Jenoyne (?)— **60**

Adams, Johnny 1932–1998 **39**

Adams, Leslie 1932— **39**

Adams, Oleta 19(?)(?)— **18**

Adams, Osceola Macarthy 1890–1983 **31**

Adams, Paul 1977— **50**

Adams, Sheila J. 1943— **25**

Adams, Yolanda 1961— **17, 67**

Adams-Campbell, Lucille L. 1953— **60**

Adams Earley, Charity (Edna) 1918— **13, 34**

Adams-Ender, Clara 1939— **40**

Adderley, Julian "Cannonball" 1928–1975 **30**

Adderley, Nat 1931–2000 **29**

Adderley, Nathaniel *See Adderley, Nat*

Ade, Sunny King 1946— **41**

Adebari, Rotimi 1963(?)— **83**

Adebimpe, Tunde 1975— **75**

Adeniyi, Sunday *See Ade, Sunny King*

Adichie, Chimamanda Ngozi 1977— **64**

Adjaye, David 1966— **38, 78**

Adkins, Rod 1958— **41**

Adkins, Rutherford H. 1924–1998 **21**

Adoboli, Kweku 1980— **106**

Adu, Freddy 1989— **67**

Adu, Fredua Koranteng *See Adu, Freddy*

Adu, Helen Folasade *See Sade*

Afewerki, Isaias 1946— **98**

Afro, Teddy 1976— **78**

Agyeman, Jaramogi Abebe 1911–2000 **10, 63**

Agyeman Rawlings, Nana Konadu 1948— **13**

Ahidjo, Ahmadou 1924–1989 **81**

Ahmed, Sharif 1964— **80**

Aidoo, Ama Ata 1942— **38**

Aiken, Loretta Mary *See Mabley, Jackie "Moms"*

Ailey, Alvin 1931–1989 **8**

Ainsworth, Leonard Victor *See Gray, Dobie*

Ake, Claude 1939–1996 **30**

Akil, Mara Brock 1970— **60, 82**

Akinmusire, Ambrose 1982— **103**

Akinnuoye-Agbaje, Adewale 1967— **56**

Akinola, Peter Jasper 1944— **65**

Akintimehin, Olubowale Victor *See Wale*

Akomfrah, John 1957— **37**

Akon 1973(?)— **68**

Akpan, Uwem 1971— **70**

Akunyili, Dora Nkem 1954— **58**

Al-Amin, Jamil Abdullah 1943— **6**

Albert, Octavia V. R. 1853–1890(?) **100**

Albright, Gerald 1947— **23**

Alcindor, Ferdinand Lewis *See Abdul-Jabbar, Kareem*

Alcorn, George Edward, Jr. 1940— **59**

Aldridge, Ira 1807–1867 **99**

Alert, Kool DJ Red 19(?)(?)— **33**

Alexander, Archie Alphonso 1888–1958 **14**

Alexander, Clifford 1933— **26**

Alexander, Elizabeth 1962— **75**

Alexander, John Marshall *See Ace, Johnny*

Alexander, Joseph L. 1930–2002 **95**

Alexander, Joyce London 1949— **18**

Alexander, Khandi 1957— **43**

Alexander, Kwame 1969(?)— **98**

Alexander, Lincoln 1922–2012 **106**

Alexander, Margaret Walker 1915–1998 **22**

Alexander, Michelle 1967— **98**

Alexander, Sadie Tanner Mossell 1898–1989 **22**

Alexander, Shaun 1977— **58**

Ali, Ayaan Hirsi 1969— **58, 92**

Ali, Hana Yasmeen 1976— **52**

Ali, Laila 1977— **27, 63**

Ali, Mohammed Naseehu 1971— **60**

Ali, Muhammad 1942— **2, 16, 52**

Ali, Rashied 1935–2009 **79**

Ali, Russlynn H. 1971(?)— **92**

Ali, Tatyana 1979— **73**

Ali Mahdi Mohamed 1940— **5**

Allain, Stephanie 1959— **49**

Allen, Betty 1927–2009 **83**

Allen, Byron 1961— **3, 24, 97**

Allen, Claude 1960— **68**

Allen, Debbie 1950— **13, 42**

Allen, Dick 1942— **85**

Allen, Ethel D. 1929–1981 **13**

Allen, Eugene 1919— **79**

Allen, Fulton *See Fuller, Blind Boy*

Allen, Geri 1957— **92**

Allen, Larry 1971— **109**

Allen, Lucy 1932— **85**

Allen, Macon Bolling 1816–1894 **104**

Allen, Marcus 1960— **20**

Allen, Ora Denise *See LaSalle, Denise*

Allen, Ray 1975— **82**

Allen, Richard 1760–1831 **14**

Allen, Robert L. 1942— **38**

Allen, Samuel W. 1917— **38**

Allen, Tina 1949–2008 **22, 75**

Allen, Will 1949— **74**

Allen-Buillard, Melba 1960— **55**

Allison, Luther 1939–1997 **111**

Allison, Verne *See Dells, The*

Almoctar, Goumour *See Bombino*

Alonso, Laz 1974— **87**

Als, Hilton 1961— **105**

Alston, Charles Henry 1907–1977 **33**

Altidore, Josmer *See Altidore, Jozy*

Altidore, Jozy 1989— **109**

Amadi, Elechi 1934— **40**

Amadou & Mariam **113**

Amaker, Harold Tommy, Jr. *See Amaker, Tommy*

Amaker, Norman 1935–2000 **63**

Amaker, Tommy 1965— **62**

Amaki, Amalia 1949— **76**

Amata, Jeta 1975— **111**

Amerie 1980— **52**

Ames, Wilmer 1950–1993 **27**

Amin, Idi 1925–2003 **42**

Ammons, Albert 1907–1949 **112**

Ammons, Gene 1925–1974 **112**

Ammons, James H. 1952(?)— **81**

Amos, Emma 1938— **63**

Amos, John 1941— **8, 62**

Amos, Valerie 1954— **41**

Amos, Wally 1937— **9**

Amy, Curtis 1927–2002 **114**

Amoudi, Mohammed al- 1946— **88**

Anderson, Anthony 1970— **51, 77**

Anderson, Carl 1945–2004 **48**

Anderson, Charles Edward 1919–1994 **37**

Anderson, Eddie "Rochester" 1905–1977 **30**

Anderson, Elmer 1941— **25**

Anderson, Ezzrett 1920— **95**

Anderson, Fred 1929–2010 **87**

Anderson, Ho Che 1969— **54**

Anderson, Jamal 1972— **22**

Anderson, Kisean *See Kingston, Sean*

Anderson, Lauren 1965— **72**

Anderson, Maceo 1910–2001 **111**

Anderson, Marcia 1958(?)— **115**

Anderson, Marian 1902— **2, 33**

Anderson, Michael P. 1959–2003 **40**

Anderson, Mike 1959— **63**

Anderson, Norman B. 1955— **45**

Anderson, Reuben V. 1942— **81**

Anderson, Sean Michael Leonard *See Big Sean*

Anderson, Sugarfoot *See Anderson, Ezzrett*

Anderson, Viv 1956— **58**

Anderson, William G(ilchrist) 1927— **57**

Andre 3000 *See Benjamin, Andre*

Andrews, Benny 1930–2006 **22, 59**

Andrews, Bert 1929–1993 **13**

Andrews, Inez 1929–2012 **108**

Andrews, Mark *See Sisqo*

Andrews, Raymond 1934–1991 **4**

Andrews, Tina 1951— **74**

Andrews, Troy *See Trombone Shorty*

Angelou, Maya 1928— **1, 15**

Anna Marie *See Lincoln, Abbey*

Annan, Kofi Atta 1938— **15, 48**

Ansa, Tina McElroy 1949— **14**

Anthony, Carmelo 1984— **46, 94**

Anthony, Crystal *See McCrary Anthony, Crystal*

Anthony, Michael 1930(?)— **29**

Anthony, Trey 1974— **63**

Anthony, Wendell 1950— **25**

Antunes, Lúcio 1966— **109**

apl.de.ap 1974— **84**

Aplin-Brownlee, Vivian 1946–2007 **96**

Appiah, Kwame Anthony 1954— **67, 101**

Arac de Nyeko, Monica 1979— **66**

Arach, Monica *See Arac de Nyeko, Monica*

Archer, Dennis (Wayne) 1942— **7, 36**

Archer, Lee, Jr. 1919— **79**

Archer, Michael D'Angelo *See D'Angelo*

Archer, Osceola *See Adams, Osceola Macarthy*

Archibald, Nathaniel *See Archibald, Tiny*

Archibald, Tiny 1948— **90**

Archie-Hudson, Marguerite 1937— **44**

Ardoin, Alphonse 1915–2007 **65**

Arenas, Gilbert 1982— **84**

Arinze, Francis 1932— **19**

Aristide, Jean-Bertrand 1953— **6, 45**

Arkadie, Kevin 1957— **17**

Armah, Ayi Kwei 1939— **49**

Armah, Esther 1963— **87**

Armatrading, Joan 1950— **32**

Armstrong, Govind 1968— **81**

Armstrong, Henry 1912–1988 **104**

Armstrong, Louis 1900–1971 **2**

Armstrong, Robb 1962— **15**

Armstrong, Vanessa Bell 1953— **24**

Arnez J, 1966(?)— **53**

Arnold, Billy Boy 1935— **112**

Arnold, Monica *See Monica*

Arnold, Tichina 1971— **63**

Arnold, William *See Arnold, Billy Boy*

Arnwine, Barbara 1951(?)— **28**

Arrington, Richard 1934— **24, 100**

Arroyo, Martina 1936— **30**

Artest, Ron 1979— **52**

Arthur, Owen 1949— **33**

Asante, Molefi Kete 1942— **3**

A$AP Rocky 1988— **109**

Ashanti 1980— **37, 96**

Ashe, Arthur Robert, Jr. 1943–1993 **1, 18**

Ashford, Calvin, Jr. 1935(?)–2008 **74**

Ashford, Emmett 1914–1980 **22**

Ashford, Evelyn 1957— **63**

Ashford, Nickolas 1941–2011 **21, 97**

Ashford and Simpson **21, 97**

Ashley, Maurice 1966— **15, 47**

Ashley & JaQuavis **107**

Ashley-Ward, Amelia 1957— **23**

Ashong, Derrick 1975— **86**

Asim, Jabari 1962— **71**

Asomugha, Nnamdi 1981— **100**

Astatke, Mulatu 1942(?)— **81**

Atim, Julian 1980(?)— **66**

Atkins, Cholly 1930–2003 **40**

Atkins, David *See Sinbad*

Atkins, Erica 1972— *See Mary Mary*

Atkins, Jeffrey *See Ja Rule*

Atkins, Juan 1962— **50**

Atkins, Russell 1926— **45**

Atkins, Tina 1974— *See Mary Mary*

Atta Mills, John 1944— **75**

Attaway, William 1911–1986 **102**

Atyam, Angelina 1946— **55**

Aubert, Alvin 1930— **41**

Aubespin, Mervin 1937— **95**

Augusta, Alexander T. 1825–1890 **111**

Auguste, Arnold A. 1946— **47**

Auguste, Donna 1958— **29**

Auguste, (Marie Carmele) Rose-Anne 1963— **13**

Augustine, Jean 1937— **53**

Austin, Bobby W. 1944— **95**

Austin, Gloria 1956— **63**

Austin, Jim 1951— **63**

Austin, Junius C. 1887–1968 **44**

Austin, Lloyd 1953— **101**

Austin, Lovie 1887–1972 **40**

Austin, Patti 1948— **24**

Austin, Wanda M. 1953(?)— **94**

Autrey, Wesley 1956— **68**

Avant, Clarence 1931— **19, 86**

Avant, Nicole A. 1968— **90**

Avery, Byllye Y. 1937— **66**

Awoonor, Kofi 1935–2013 **37, 115**

Awoonor-Williams, George *See Awoonor, Kofi*

Awoyinka, Adesiji *See Siji*

Awuah, Patrick 1965— **111**

Ayers, Roy 1940— **16**

Ayler, Albert 1936–1970 **104**

Azikiwe, Nnamdi 1904–1996 **13**

Ba, Mariama 1929–1981 **30**

Babangida, Ibrahim (Badamasi) 1941— **4**

Babatunde, Obba 19(?)(?)— **35**

Babatunde, Rotimi 19(?)(?)— **104**

Babyface 1959— **10, 31, 82**

Baca, Susana 1954— **80**

Bacon-Bercey, June 1942— **38**

Badu, Erykah 1971— **22, 114**

Bagayoko, Amadou *See Amadou & Mariam*

Bahati, Wambui 1950(?)— **60**

Bailey, Buddy *See Clovers, The*

Bailey, Buster 1902–1967 **38**

Bailey, Chauncey 1949–2007 **68**

Bailey, Clyde 1946— **45**

Bailey, DeFord 1899–1982 **33**

Bailey, Jimmy *See Cadillacs*

Bailey, Pearl Mae 1918–1990 **14**

Bailey, Philip 1951— **63**

Bailey, Preston 1948(?)— **64**

Bailey, Radcliffe 1968— **19**

Bailey, William C. *See Bailey, Buster*

Bailey, Xenobia 1955(?)— **11**

Bailey Rae, Corinne 1979— **83**

Baines, Harold 1959— **32**

Baiocchi, Regina Harris 1956— **41**

Baisden, Michael 1963— **25, 66**

Baker, Anita 1957— **21, 48**

Baker, Arlene Holt *See Holt Baker, Arlene*

Baker, Augusta 1911–1998 **38**

Baker, Constance *See Motley, Constance Baker*

Baker, Delbert W. 1953— **110**

Baker, Dusty 1949— **8, 43, 72, 110**

Baker, Ella 1903–1986 **5**

Baker, George *See Divine, Father*

Baker, Gwendolyn Calvert 1931— **9**

Baker, Houston A(lfred), Jr. 1943— **6**

Baker, Johnnie B., Jr. *See Baker, Dusty*

Baker, Josephine 1906–1975 **3**

Baker, LaVern 1929–1997 **26**

Baker, Matt 1921–1959 **76**

Baker, Maxine 1952— **28**

Baker, Mickey 1925— **95**

Baker, Thurbert 1952— **22**

Baker, Vernon Joseph 1919–2010 **65, 87**

Bakewell, Danny 1946— **99**

Balance, Frank W. 1942— **41**

Baldwin, Cynthia 1945— **74, 107**

Baldwin, James 1924–1987 **1**

Ballard, Allen Butler, Jr. 1930— **40**

Ballard, Florence 1943–1976 **112**

See also Supremes, The

Ballard, Hank 1927–2003 **41**

Ballard, John 1830–1905 **95**

Balotelli, Mario 1990— **104**

Baltimore, Richard Lewis, III 1946— **71**

Bambaataa, Afrika 1958— **34**

Bambara, Toni Cade 1939— **10**

Banda, Hastings Kamuzu 1898(?)–1997 **6, 54**

Banda, Joyce 1950— **101**

Bandele, Asha 1970(?)— **36**

Bandele, Biyi 1967— **68**

Bandele-Thomas, Biyi *See Bandele, Biyi*

Banks, A. Doris *See Henries, A. Doris Banks*

Banks, Azealia 1991— **107**

Banks, Ernie 1931— **33**

Banks, Jeffrey 1953— **17**

Banks, Lloyd 1982— **113**

Banks, Michelle 1968(?)— **59**

Banks, Paula A. 1950— **68**

Banks, Ron *See Dramatics, The*

Banks, Tyra 1973— **11, 50**

Banks, William (Venoid) 1903–1985 **11**

Banneker, Benjamin 1731–1806 **93**

Banner, David 1975(?)— **55**

Bannister, Edward Mitchell 1828–1901 **88**

Banton, Buju 1973— **93**

Baquet, Dean 1956— **63**

Baraka, Amiri 1934— **1, 38**

Baraka, Sho 19(?)(?)— **109**

Barbee, Lloyd Augustus 1925–2002 **71**

Barber, Atiim Kiambu Hakeem-Ah *See Barber, Tiki*

Barber, Ronde 1975— **41**

Barber, Tiki 1975— **57, 107**

Barboza, Anthony 1944— **10**

Barclay, Paris 1956— **37, 94**

Barden, Donald H. 1943— **9, 20, 89**

Barker, Danny 1909–1994 **32**

Barkley, Charles 1963— **5, 66**

Barksdale, Chuck *See Dells, The*

Barksdale, Don 1923–1993 **103**

Barlow, Roosevelt 1917–2003 **49**

Barnes, Ernie 1938–2009 **16, 78**

Barnes, John 1963— **53**

Barnes, Katreese 196(?)— **97**

Barnes, Lloyd 1944— **77**

Barnes, Melody 1964— **75**

Barnes, Prentiss *See Moonglows, The*

Barnes, Roosevelt "Booba" 1936–1996 **33**

Barnes, Steven 1952— **54**

Barnett, Amy Du Bois 1969— **46**

Barnett, Etta Moten 1901–2004 **18, 56**

Barnett, Herman 1926–1973 **112**

Barnett, Marguerite 1942–1992 **46**

Barney, Lem 1945— **26**

Barnhill, David 1914–1983 **30**

Barnwell, Ysaye *See Sweet Honey in the Rock*

Barrax, Gerald William 1933— **45**

Barrett, Andrew C. 1942(?)— **12**

Barrett, Jacqueline 1950— **28**

Barrett, Lindsay 1941— **43**

Barrett, Mario Dewar *See Mario*

Barrino, Fantasia 1984— **53, 94**

Barrow, Dean 1951— **69**

Barrow, Jamal *See Shyne*

Barrow, Joseph Louis *See Louis, Joe*

Barrow, Willie T. 1924— **85**

Barry, Marion S(hepilov, Jr.) 1936— **7, 44**

Bartels, Peggielene 1953(?)— **80**

Barthé, Earl 19(?)(?)— **78**

Barthe, Richmond 1901–1989 **15**

Barwuah, Mario *See Balotelli, Mario*

Bashir, Halima 1979— **73**

Bashir, Omar al- 1944— **77**

Basie, William James *See Count Basie*

Baskett, James 1904–1948 **102**

Basquiat, Jean-Michel 1960–1988 **5**

Bass, Charlotta Amanda Spears 1874–1969 **40**

Bass, Fontella 1940–2012 **104, 109**

Bass, Karen 1953— **70**

Bassett, Angela 1958— **6, 23, 62**

Bassey, Shirley 1937— **25**

Baszile, Jennifer 1969(?)— **79**

Bates, Clayton *See Bates, Peg Leg*

Bates, Daisy (Lee Gatson) 1914(?)— **13**
Bates, Elias *See Diddley, Bo*
Bates, Karen Grigsby 19(?)(?)— **40**
Bates, Peg Leg 1907— **14**
Bath, Patricia E. 1942— **37**
Batiste, Alvin 1932–2007 **66**
Batiste, Jonathan 1986— **108**
Batiste, Lionel 1932(?)–2012 **105**
Battle, Kathleen 1948— **70**
Baugé, Grégory 1985— **86**
Baugh, David 1947— **23**
Baylor, Don(ald Edward) 1949— **6**
Baylor, Elgin 1934— **93**
Baylor, Helen 1953— **36**
Bazawule, Samuel *See Blitz the Ambassador*
Beach, Michael 1963— **26**
Beah, Ishmael 1980— **69**
Beal, Bernard B. 1954(?)— **46**
Beals, Jennifer 1963— **12**
Beals, Melba Pattillo 1941— **15, 94**
Beamon, Bob 1946— **30**
Bearden, Romare 1912–1988 **2, 50**
Beasley, Jamar 1979— **29**
Beasley, Myrlie *See Evers, Myrlie*
Beasley, Phoebe 1943— **34**
Beaton, Norman Lugard 1934–1994 **14**
Beatty, Talley 1923(?)–1995 **35**
Beaty, Zelmo 1939–2013 **115**
Beauvais, Garcelle 1966— **29, 95**
Beauvoir, Max 1936(?)— **74**
Bebey, Francis 1929–2001 **45**
Bechet, Sidney 1897–1959 **18**
Beck, Robert *See Iceberg Slim*
Beckford, Tyson 1970— **11, 68**
Beckham, Barry 1944— **41**
Beckwith, Naomi 1976— **101**
Becton, Julius W., Jr. 1926— **110**
Bedie, Henri Konan 1934— **21**
Beenie Man 1973— **32**
Bekele, Kenenisa 1982— **75**
Beken 1956(?)— **111**
Belafonte, Harold George, Jr. *See Belafonte, Harry*
Belafonte, Harry 1927— **4, 65**
Belgrave, Cynthia 1920–1997 **75**
Belgrave, Marcus 1936— **77**
Bell, Carey 1936–2007 **114**
Bell, Carl C. 1947— **111**
Bell, Cool Papa *See Bell, James "Cool Papa"*
Bell, Darrin 1975— **77**
Bell, Derrick 1930–2011 **6, 98**
Bell, James "Cool Papa" 1901–1991 **36**
Bell, James A. 1948— **50**
Bell, James Madison 1826–1902 **40**
Bell, LeRoy 1951— **98**
Bell, Michael 1955— **40**
Bell, Ralph S. 1934— **5**
Bell, Ricky *See New Edition*
Bell, Robert Mack 1943— **22**
Bell, Thom 1943— **112**
Bell, Thomas Randolph *See Bell, Thom*
Bell, W. Kamau 19(?)(?)— **107**
Bell, Walter Kamau *See Bell, W. Kamau*
Bellamy, Bill 1967— **12**
Bellamy, Terry 1972— **58**
Belle, Albert (Jojuan) 1966— **10**

Belle, Regina 1963— **1, 51**
Belton, Sharon Sayles 1951— **9, 16**
Benberry, Cuesta 1923–2007 **65**
Benét, Eric 1966— **28, 77**
Benham, Robert 1946— **78**
Ben-Israel, Ben Ami 1940(?)— **11**
Benítez, Christian 1986–2013 **113**
Benjamin, Andre (3000) 1975— **45** *See also OutKast*
Benjamin, Regina 1956— **20, 75**
Benjamin, Steve 1969— **98**
Benjamin, Tritobia Hayes 1944— **53**
Bennett, Estelle 1941–2009 **77**
Bennett, George Harold "Hal" 1930— **45**
Bennett, Gwendolyn B. 1902–1981 **59**
Bennett, Lerone, Jr. 1928— **5, 84**
Bennett, Louise 1919–2006 **69**
Bennett, Richard 1980(?)— **97**
Benson, Angela 19(?)(?)— **34**
Benson, Obie 1936–2005 **96**
Benson, Renaldo *See Benson, Obie*
Bensouda, Fatou 1961— **103**
Bentley, Lamont 1973–2005 **53**
Bernard, Marvin *See Yayo, Tony*
Berrien, Jacqueline A. 1961— **93**
Berry, Bertice 1960— **8, 55**
Berry, Bill *See Berry, Edwin C.*
Berry, Charles Edward Anderson *See Berry, Chuck*
Berry, Chuck 1926— **29**
Berry, Edwin C. 1910–1987 **81**
Berry, Fred "Rerun" 1951–2003 **48**
Berry, Halle 1966— **4, 19, 57, 91**
Berry, James 1925— **41**
Berry, Mary Frances 1938— **7**
Berry, Moses 1950(?)— **84**
Berry, Theodore M. 1905–2000 **31**
Berrysmith, Don Reginald 1936— **49**
Best, Carrie 1903–2001 **80**
Betha, Mason Durrell 1977(?)— **24**
Bethune, Mary (Jane) McLeod 1875–1955 **4**
Beti, Mongo 1932–2001 **36**
Betsch, MaVynee 1935— **28**
Bettis, Jerome 1972— **64**
Betts, Keter 1928–2005 **85**
Betts, R. Dwayne 1979(?)— **86**
Bevel, James L. 1936–2008 **75**
Beverly, Frankie 1946— **25**
Bey, Yasiin 1973— **30, 96**
Beyoncé 1981— **39, 70, 105**
Bibb, Eric 1951— **49**
Bibb, Henry 1815–1854 **54**
Bibb, Mary 1820–1877 **54**
Bickerstaff, Bernard Tyrone 1944— **21**
Big Bank Hank *See Sugarhill Gang, The*
Big Boi *See Patton, Antwan*
Big Daddy Kane 1968— **79**
Big Sean 1977— **96**
Big Youth 1949— **107**
Biggers, John 1924–2001 **20, 33**
Biggers, Sanford 1970— **62**
Bigirimana, Gael 1993— **115**
Biko, Stephen *See Biko, Steven (Bantu)*

Biko, Steven (Bantu) 1946–1977 **4**
Bilal 1979— **101**
Billingslea, Joe *See Contours, The*
Billong, Alexandre Dimitri Song *See Song, Alex*
Billops, Camille 1933— **82**
Billy Ward and the Dominoes **105**
bin Wahad, Dhoruba 1943— **85**
Bing, Dave 1943— **3, 59, 78**
Bingham, Howard 1939— **96**
Birch, Adolpho A., Jr. 1932— **85**
Birch, Glynn R. 195(?)— **61**
Birdman 1969— **110**
Birdsong, Cindy 1939— **113**
Birra, Ali 1948— **113**
Bishop, Eric *See Foxx, Jamie*
Bishop, Maurice 1944–1983 **39**
Bishop, Sanford D., Jr. 1947— **24, 111**
Bishop, Stephen 1820–1857 **95**
Bivins, Michael 1968— **72** *See also New Edition*
Biya, Chantal 1970— **89**
Biya, Paul 1933— **28, 114**
Biyidi-Awala, Alexandre *See Beti, Mongo*
Bizimungu, Pasteur 1951— **19**
Black, Albert 1940— **51**
Black, Barry C. 1948— **47**
Black, Joe 1924–2002 **75**
Black, Keith Lanier 1957— **18, 84**
Black Kold Madina *See Roberts, Kimberly Rivers*
Black Thought 1972— **63**
Blackburn, Robert 1920— **28**
Blackman, Toni 1968— **86**
Blackmon, Brenda 1952— **58**
Blackmore, Amos Wells *See Wells, Junior*
Blackshear, Leonard 1943— **52**
Blackwell, David 1919— **79**
Blackwell, Kenneth, Sr. 1948— **61**
Blackwell, Otis 1932–2002 **98**
Blackwell, Robert D., Sr. 1937— **52**
Blackwell, Unita 1933— **17**
Blackwood, Maureen 1960— **37**
Blacque, Taurean 1941— **58**
Blade, Brian 1970— **88**
Blair, Jayson 1976— **50**
Blair, Maxine *See Powell, Maxine*
Blair, Paul 1944— **36**
Blake, Asha 1961(?)— **26**
Blake, Charles E. 1940— **82**
Blake, Eubie 1883–1983 **29**
Blake, James 1979— **43**
Blake, James Hubert *See Blake, Eubie*
Blakely, Edward J. 1938— **88**
Blakey, Art(hur) 1919–1990 **37**
Blanchard, Terence 1962— **43**
Blanco, Mykki 1986(?)— **106**
Bland, Bobby 1930–2013 **36, 113**
Bland, Bobby "Blue" *See Bland, Bobby*
Bland, Edward 1926–2013 **111**
Bland, Eleanor Taylor 1944–2010 **39**
Blanks, Billy 1955(?)— **22**
Blanks, Deborah K. 1958— **69**
Blanton, Dain 1971— **29**
Blanton, Jimmy 1918–1942 **108**
Blassingame, John Wesley 1940–2000 **40**

Blaylock, Ronald 1960(?)— **86**
Blayton, Jesse B., Sr. 1897–1977 **55**
Bleu, Corbin 1989— **65**
Blige, Mary J. 1971— **20, 34, 60, 97**
Blind Boys of Alabama, The **99**
Blitz the Ambassador 1982— **115**
Blockson, Charles L. 1933— **42**
Blondy, Alpha 1953— **30**
Bloomer, George 1963— **86**
Blow, Charles M. 1968(?)— **73**
Blow, Kurtis 1959— **31**
Bluford, Guion Stewart, Jr. *See Bluford, Guy*
Bluford, Guy 1942— **2, 35**
Bluitt, Juliann Stephanie 1938— **14**
Boateng, Ozwald 1968(?)— **35, 113**
Boateng, Paul Yaw 1951— **56**
B.o.B. 1988— **91**
Bobb, Robert C. 1945— **83**
Bobo, Lawrence 1958— **60**
Bogle, Donald 19(?)(?)— **34**
Bogues, Tyrone "Muggsy" 1965— **56**
Bol, Manute 1963— **1**
Bolden, Buddy 1877–1931 **39**
Bolden, Charles Frank, Jr. 1946— **7, 78**
Bolden, Charles Joseph *See Bolden, Buddy*
Bolden, Frank E. 1913–2003 **44**
Bolden, Tonya 1959— **32**
Bolin, Jane 1908–2007 **22, 59**
Bolling, Allen Macon *See Allen, Macon Bolling*
Bolt, Usain 1986— **73, 104**
Bolton, Terrell D. 1959(?)— **25**
Bolton-Holifield, Ruthie 1967— **28**
Bombino 1980— **112**
Bonaly, Surya 1973— **7**
Bond, Beverly 1970— **53**
Bond, J. Max, Jr. 1935— **76**
Bond, Julian 1940— **2, 35, 106**
Bonds, Barry 1964— **6, 34, 63, 99**
Bonds, Bobby 1946— **43**
Bonds, Margaret 1913–1972 **39**
Bonet, Lisa 1967— **58**
Boney, Lisa Michelle *See Bonet, Lisa*
Bonga, Kuenda 1942— **13**
Bongo, Albert-Bernard *See Bongo, Omar*
Bongo, Ali Ben 1959— **80**
Bongo, Omar 1935–2009 **1, 79**
Bonheur, Yannick 1982— **84**
Bonner, Leroy 1943–2013 **113**
Bonney, Tabi 1978(?)— **98**
Bontemps, Arna(ud Wendell) 1902–1973 **8**
Booker, Cory Anthony 1969— **68**
Booker, Simeon 1918— **23**
Boozer, Bob 1937–2012 **103**
Borders, James (Buchanan, IV) 1949— **9**
Borders, William Holmes 1905–1993 **94**
Boseman, Chadwick 1982— **111**
Bosh, Chris 1984— **85**
Bosley, Freeman (Robertson), Jr. 1954— **7**
Bossard, Henry K. *See Swan Silvertones, The*
Bostic, Joe 1909–1988 **95**

Boston, Kelvin E. 1955(?)— **25**
Boston, Lloyd 1970(?)— **24**
Boulogne, Joseph, Chevalier de Saint-Georges 1745(?)–1799 **94**
Boulware, Harold R. 1913–1983 **109**
Bow Wow 1987— **35**
Bowe, Riddick 1967— **6, 107**
Bowen, John W. E., Sr. 1855–1933 **89**
Bowen, Ruth 1924–2009 **83**
Bowman, Bertie 1931— **71**
Bowman, Herbert *See Bowman, Bertie*
Bowser, Yvette Lee 1965(?)— **17**
Boyd, Edward 1914–2007 **70**
Boyd, Gerald M. 1950–2006 **32, 59**
Boyd, Gwendolyn 1955— **49**
Boyd, John W., Jr. 1965— **20, 72**
Boyd, Melba Joyce 1950— **86**
Boyd, Steven *See Dramatics, The*
Boyd, Suzanne 1963— **52**
Boyd, T(heophilus) B(artholomew), III 1947— **6**
Boye, Madior 1940— **30**
Boykin, Keith 1965— **14**
Boykin, Otis 1920–1982 **92**
Boykin, Phillip 1968— **102**
Boyz II Men **82**
Bozella, Dewey 1959— **97**
Bozizé, François 1946— **96**
Bracken, James 1909–1972 **107**
Bracken, Vivian 1921–1989 **107**
Bradford, Mark 1961— **89**
Bradley, Adam 1974— **101**
Bradley, Alton *See Golden Gate Quartet*
Bradley, David Henry, Jr. 1950— **39**
Bradley, Ed 1941–2006 **2, 59**
Bradley, J. Robert 1919–2007 **65**
Bradley, Jennette B. 1952— **40**
Bradley, Thomas 1917— **2, 20**
Bradshaw, Myron C. *See Bradshaw, Tiny*
Bradshaw, Tiny 1907–1958 **102**
Brady, St. Elmo 1884–1966 **107**
Brady, Wayne 1972— **32, 71**
Brae, C. Michael 1963(?)— **61**
Braithwaite, William Stanley 1878–1962 **52**
Bramlett, Joseph 1988— **91**
Branch, William Blackwell 1927— **39**
Brand, Dionne 1953— **32**
Brand, Elton 1979— **31**
Brandon, Barbara 1960(?)— **3**
Brandon, Thomas Terrell 1970— **16**
Brandy 1979— **14, 34, 72**
Branham, George, III 1962— **50**
Branson, Herman 1914–1995 **87**
Brashear, Carl Maxie 1931— **29**
Brashear, Donald 1972— **39**
Brathwaite, Fred 1972— **35**
Brathwaite, Kamau 1930— **36**
Brathwaite, Lawson Edward *See Kamau Brathwaite*
Braugher, Andre 1962— **13, 58, 91**
Braun, Carol Moseley 1947— **4, 42**
Brawley, Benjamin 1882–1939 **44**
Braxton, Brad 1969(?)— **77**
Braxton, Gene *See Herndon, Angelo*
Braxton, Toni 1967— **15, 61, 91**

Brazier, Arthur M. 1921–2010 **115**
Brazile, Donna 1959— **25, 70**
Breaux, Christopher *See Ocean, Frank*
Breed, Eric T. *See MC Breed*
Breed, MC *See MC Breed*
Breedlove, Sarah *See Walker, Madame C. J.*
Breeze, Jean "Binta" 1956— **37**
Brembly, Paul *See Golden Gate Quartet*
Brewer, Rosalind 1962— **100**
Bridges, Christopher *See Ludacris*
Bridges, Ruby 1954— **77**
Bridges, Sheila 1964— **36**
Bridges, Todd 1965— **37**
Bridgetower, George 1780(?)–1860 **78**
Bridgewater, Dee Dee 1950— **32, 92**
Bridgforth, Glinda 1952— **36**
Briggs, Curtis 1952(?)— **84**
Brimm, Charles E. 1924–2010 **105**
Brimmer, Andrew 1926–2012 **2, 48, 106**
Briscoe, Connie 1952— **15**
Briscoe, Marlin 1946(?)— **37**
Britt, Donna 1954(?)— **28**
Broadbent, Hydeia 1984— **36**
Brock, Lou 1939— **18**
Brock, Michael *See Dramatics, The*
Brock, Roslyn McCallister 1965— **86**
Brodie, Roosevelt *See Harold Melvin & the Blue Notes*
Bromery, Randolph Wilson 1926— **85**
Broner, Adrien 1989— **109**
Bronner, Nathaniel H., Sr. 1914–1993 **32**
Brooke, Edward W. 1919— **8, 88**
Brookins, Hamel Hartford 1925–2012 **102**
Brooks, Aaron 1976— **33**
Brooks, Avery 1948— **9, 98**
Brooks, Derrick 1973— **43**
Brooks, Golden 1970— **62**
Brooks, Gwendolyn 1917–2000 **1, 28**
Brooks, Hadda 1916–2002 **40**
Brooks, Mehcad 1980— **62**
Brooks, Orville *See Golden Gate Quartet*
Brooks, Robert Calvin *See Bland, Bobby*
Brooks, Tyrone 1945— **59**
Broonzy, Big Bill 1893–1958 **82**
Brother Blue *See Hill, Hugh Morgan*
Brower, William 1916–2004 **49**
Brown, Aja 1982— **115**
Brown, Alvin 1963— **96**
Brown, Andre *See Dre, Dr.*
Brown, Angela M. 1964(?)— **54**
Brown, Anne 1912–2009 **76**
Brown, Anthony G. 1961— **72**
Brown, Antron 1976— **85**
Brown, Beverly *See Dixie Cups, The*
Brown, Bill *See Billy Ward and the Dominoes*
Brown, Bobby 1969— **58** *See also New Edition*
Brown, Buck *See Brown, Robert*

Brown, Byrd 1930–2001 **49**
Brown, Byron W. 1958— **72**
Brown, Carlinhos 1962— **81**
Brown, Cecil M. 1943— **46**
Brown, Charles 1922–1999 **23**
Brown, Charlotte Hawkins 1883–1961 **106**
Brown, Chris 1989— **74, 109**
Brown, Chuck 1936–2012 **78, 102**
Brown, Clarence Gatemouth 1924–2005 **59**
Brown, Claude 1937–2002 **38**
Brown, Clifford 1930–1956 **86**
Brown, Cora 1914–1972 **33**
Brown, Corrine 1946— **24, 90**
Brown, Cupcake 1964— **63**
Brown, Dennis 1957–1999 **99**
Brown, Donald 1963— **19**
Brown, Eddie C. 1940— **35**
Brown, Elaine 1943— **8**
Brown, Ernest 1916–2009 **80**
Brown, Erroll M. 1950(?)— **23**
Brown, Foxy 1979— **25**
Brown, Frederick J. 1945–2012 **102**
Brown, George Leslie 1926–2006 **62**
Brown, H. Rap *See Al-Amin, Jamil Abdullah*
Brown, Hallie Quinn 1850(?)–1949 **100**
Brown, Harley *See Dramatics, The*
Brown, Homer S. 1896–1977 **47**
Brown, Hubert Gerold *See Al-Amin, Jamil Abdullah*
Brown, James 1933–2006 **15, 60**
Brown, James 1951— **22**
Brown, James Mack *See Dramatics, The*
Brown, James Nathaniel *See Brown, Jim*
Brown, James Willie, Jr. *See Komunyakaa, Yusef*
Brown, Jamie Foster 19(?)(?)— **91**
Brown, Janice Rogers 1949— **43**
Brown, Jesse 1944–2003 **6, 41**
Brown, Jesse Leroy 1926–1950 **31**
Brown, Jim 1936— **11, 95**
Brown, Joe 19(?)(?)— **29**
Brown, Joyce F. 1946— **25**
Brown, Kwame R. 1970— **91**
Brown, Lawrence Darrow *See Gray, Dobie*
Brown, Lee P. 1937— **1, 24, 109**
Brown, Les(lie Calvin) 1945— **5**
Brown, Lloyd Louis 1913–2003 **42**
Brown, Melanie 1975— **73**
Brown, Mike 1970— **77, 107**
Brown, Nappy 1929–2008 **73**
Brown, Oliver Leon 1918–1961 **94**
Brown, Oscar, Jr. 1926–2005 **53**
Brown, Patrick "Sleepy" 1970— **50**
Brown, Raymond 1908–1965 **102**
Brown, Robert 1936–2007 **65**
Brown, Ron(ald Harmon) 1941–1996 **5**
Brown, Ronald K. 1966— **91**
Brown, Rosemary 1930–2003 **62**
Brown, Ruth 1928–2006 **90**
Brown, Sean 1976— **52**
Brown, Sterling Allen 1901–1989 **10, 64**
Brown, Tony 1933— **3**
Brown, Uzee 1950— **42**
Brown, Vivian 1964— **27**

Brown, Warren 1971(?)— **61**
Brown, Wesley 1945— **23**
Brown, Wesley A. 1927–2012 **102**
Brown, Willa Beatrice 1906–1992 **40**
Brown, Willard 1911(?)–1996 **36**
Brown, William Anthony *See Brown, Tony*
Brown, William Wells 1814(?)–1884 **99**
Brown, Willie 1934— **7, 85**
Brown, Zora Kramer 1949— **12**
Brown Bomber, The *See Louis, Joe*
Browne, Roscoe Lee 1925–2007 **66**
Brownlee, Lawrence 1972(?)— **88**
Broyard, Anatole 1920–1990 **68**
Broyard, Bliss 1966— **68**
Bruce, Blanche Kelso 1849–1898 **33**
Bruce, Bruce 19(?)(?)— **56**
Bruce, Isaac 1972— **26**
Brunson, Dorothy 1938— **1, 87**
Brutus, Dennis 1924— **38**
Bryan, Ashley 1923— **41, 104**
Bryant, Cullen 1951–2009 **81**
Bryant, John 1966— **26**
Bryant, John R. 1943— **45**
Bryant, Kobe 1978— **15, 31, 71, 110**
Bryant, Paul 1933–2010 **115**
Bryant, Ray 1931–2011 **95**
Bryant, Wayne R(ichard) 1947— **6**
Bryant, William Benson 1911–2005 **61**
Bryant, William Cullen *See Bryant, Cullen*
Buchanan, Manley Augustus *See Big Youth*
Buchanan, Ray 1971— **32**
Buckley, Gail Lumet 1937— **39**
Buckley, Victoria (Vikki) 1947–1999 **24**
Buckner, Milt 1915–1977 **110**
Budden, Joe 1980— **108**
Budden, Joseph Anthony, II *See Budden, Joe*
Buery, Richard, Jr. 1972— **97**
Buff Love *See Fat Boys*
Bullard, Eugene Jacques 1894–1961 **12**
Bullins, Ed 1935— **25**
Bullock, Anna Mae *See Turner, Tina*
Bullock, Steve 1936— **22**
Bully-Cummings, Ella 1957(?)— **48**
Bumbry, Grace (Ann) 1937— **5**
Bunch, Lonnie G., III 1952— **91**
Bunche, Ralph J(ohnson) 1904–1971 **5**
Bunkley, Anita Richmond 19(?)(?)— **39**
Buress, Hannibal 1983— **101**
Burgess, John 1909–2003 **46**
Burgess, Marjorie L. 1929— **55**
Burgess, Marlina *See Shaw, Marlena*
Burke, Clarence, Jr. 1949–2013 **112**
Burke, Selma Hortense 1900–1995 **16**
Burke, Solomon 1940— **31, 86**
Burke, Yvonne Brathwaite 1932— **42**

Burks, Juanita P. 1920— **95**

Burks, Mary Fair 1920–1991 **40**

Burleigh, Henry Thacker 1866–1949 **56**

Burley, Dan 1907–1962 **96**

Burley, Mary Lou See Williams, Mary Lou

Burnett, Charles 1944— **16, 68**

Burnett, Chester Arthur See Howlin' Wolf

Burnett, Dorothy 1905–1995 **19**

Burnham, Forbes 1923–1985 **66**

Burnim, Mickey L. 1949— **48**

Burning Spear 194(?)— **79**

Burns, Anthony 1834–1862 **102**

Burns, Eddie 1928— **44**

Burns, Jesse Louis See Jackson, Jesse

Burns, Ursula 1958— **60**

Burnside, R. L. 1926–2005 **56**

Burrell, Orville Richard See Shaggy

Burrell, Stanley Kirk See M.C. Hammer

Burrell, Tom 1939— **21, 51**

Burris, Chuck 1951— **21**

Burris, Roland W. 1937— **25, 75**

Burroughs, Margaret Taylor 1917— **9**

Burroughs, Nannie Helen 1879(?)–1961 **96**

Burrows, Stephen 1943— **31**

Burrus, William Henry "Bill" 1936— **45**

Burruss, Kandi See Kandi

Burt-Murray, Angela 1970— **59**

Burton, Bill 1977— **96**

Burton, LeVar 1957— **8**

Burwell, Bryan 1955— **83**

Busby, Jheryl 1949–2008 **3, 74**

Bush, Gordon 1942— **82**

Bush, Reggie 1985— **59, 88**

Bushwick Bill See Geto Boys

Buthelezi, Mangosuthu Gatsha 1928— **9**

Butler, George, Jr. 1931–2008 **70**

Butler, Jerry 1939— **26**

Butler, Jonathan 1961— **28**

Butler, Leroy, III 1968— **17**

Butler, Louis 1952— **70**

Butler, Octavia 1947–2006 **8, 43, 58**

Butler, Paul D. 1961— **17**

Butler, Selena Sloan 1872(?)–1964 **98**

Butts, Calvin O., III 1949— **9, 90**

Butts, Cassandra 1965— **78**

Bwino, Ndiwa See Malawi Mouse Boys

Bynoe, Peter C. B. 1951— **40**

Bynum, Juanita 1959— **31, 71**

Byrd, Donald 1932–2013 **109**

Byrd, Donald 1949— **10**

Byrd, Eugene 1975— **64**

Byrd, Henry Roeland See Professor Longhair

Byrd, Marlon 1977— **112**

Byrd, Michelle 1965— **19**

Byrd, Robert (Oliver Daniel, III) 1952— **11**

Byron, JoAnne Deborah See Shakur, Assata

Cabell, Enos 1949— **102**

Cabral, Amílcar 1924–1973 **104**

Cade, Toni See Bambara, Toni Cade

Cadillacs **107**

Cadoria, Sherian Grace 1940— **14**

Caesar, Shirley 1938— **19**

Cage, Byron 1965(?)— **53**

Cain, Herman 1945— **15, 92**

Calabrese, Karyn 1947— **89**

Caldwell, Benjamin 1937— **46**

Caldwell, Earl 1941(?)— **60**

Caldwell, Jim 1955— **81**

Caldwell, Kirbyjon 1953(?)— **55**

Calhoun, Cora See Austin, Lovie

Calhoun, Lillian Scott 1923–2006 **87**

Callaway, Thomas DeCarlo See Green, Cee Lo

Callender, Clive O(rville) 1936— **3**

Callier, Terry 1945–2012 **106**

Calloway, Blanche 1902–1978 **100**

Calloway, Cab 1907–1994 **14**

Calloway, Reggie See Midnight Star

Calloway, Vincent See Midnight Star

Camara, Moussa Dadis 1964— **76**

Cameron, Earl 1917— **44**

Cameron, James 1914–2006 **80**

Camp, Georgia Blanche Douglas See Johnson, Georgia Douglas

Camp, Kimberly 1956— **19**

Campanella, Roy 1921–1993 **25**

Campbell, Bebe Moore 1950–2006 **6, 24, 59**

Campbell, Bill 1954— **9, 76**

Campbell, Charleszetta Lena See Waddles, Charleszetta (Mother)

Campbell, Donald J. 1935— **66**

Campbell, E(lmer) Simms 1906–1971 **13**

Campbell, Earl 1955— **104**

Campbell, Mary Schmidt 1947— **43**

Campbell, Milt 1933–2012 **113**

Campbell, Milton See Little Milton

Campbell, Naomi 1970— **1, 31**

Campbell, Tisha See Campbell-Martin, Tisha

Campbell-Brown, Veronica 1982— **102**

Campbell-Martin, Tisha 1969— **8, 42**

Cam'ron 1976— **104**

Canada, Geoffrey 1954— **23**

Canady, Alexa 1950— **28**

Canegata, Leonard Lionel Cornelius See Lee, Canada

Cannon, Katie 1950— **10**

Cannon, Nick 1980— **47, 73**

Cannon, Reuben 1946— **50**

Cano, Robinson 1982— **97**

Canó Mercedes, Robinson José See Cano, Robinson

Cara, Irene 1959— **77**

Carby, Hazel 1948— **27**

Cardozo, Francis L. 1837–1903 **33**

Carew, Rod 1945— **20**

Carey, Jake See Flamingos, The

Carey, Mariah 1970— **32, 53, 69**

Carey, Zeke See Flamingos, The

Cargill, Victoria A. 19(?)(?)— **43**

Carlos, John 1945— **97**

Carmichael, Stokely 1941–1998 **5, 26**

Carnegie, Herbert 1919— **25**

Carney, William H. 1840–1908 **104**

Carolina Chocolate Drops **111**

Carr, Johnnie 1911–2008 **69**

Carr, Keela 1973— **74**

Carr, Kurt 196(?)— **56**

Carr, Leroy 1905–1935 **49**

Carroll, Diahann 1935— **9**

Carroll, Earl See Cadillacs

Carroll, L. Natalie 1950— **44**

Carroll, Rocky 1963— **74**

Carroll, Vinnette 1922— **29**

Carruthers, George R. 1939— **40**

Carson, André 1974— **69**

Carson, Benjamin 1951— **1, 35, 76**

Carson, Johnnie 1943— **85**

Carson, Josephine See Baker, Josephine

Carson, Julia 1938–2007 **23, 69**

Carson, Lisa Nicole 1969— **21**

Carter, Anson 1974— **24**

Carter, Ben See Ben-Israel, Ben Ami

Carter, Benny 1907–2003 **46**

Carter, Betty 1930— **19**

Carter, Butch 1958— **27**

Carter, Cris 1965— **21, 109**

Carter, Dwayne Michael, Jr. See Lil Wayne

Carter, Edward A., Jr. 1916–1963 **104**

Carter, Herbert E. 1919–2012 **108**

Carter, Jill P. 1964— **110**

Carter, Joe 1960— **30**

Carter, Johnny See Dells, The; Flamingos, The

Carter, Joye Maureen 1957— **41**

Carter, Kenneth 1959(?)— **53**

Carter, Majora 1966— **77**

Carter, Mandy 1946— **11**

Carter, Martin 1927–1997 **49**

Carter, Nell 1948–2003 **39**

Carter, Pamela Lynn 1949— **67**

Carter, Regina 1966(?)— **23**

Carter, Rob See Dramatics, The

Carter, Robert L. 1917–2012 **51, 100**

Carter, Ron 1937— **104**

Carter, Rubin 1937— **26**

Carter, Shawn Corey See Jay-Z

Carter, Stephen L(isle) 1954— **4**

Carter, Troy 1973(?)— **98**

Carter, Vince 1977— **26**

Carter, Warrick L. 1942— **27**

Cartey, Wilfred 1931–1992 **47**

Cartiér, Xam Wilson 1949— **41**

Carver, George Washington 1861(?)–1943 **4**

Cary, Lorene 1956— **3**

Cary, Mary Ann Shadd 1823–1893 **30**

Casel, Nitanju Bolade See Sweet Honey in the Rock

Cash, Nayvadius See Future

Cash, Rosalind 1938–1995 **28**

Cash, Swin 1979— **59**

Cashin, Sheryll 1962— **63**

CasSelle, Malcolm 1970— **11**

Castor, Jimmy 1940–2012 **100**

Catchings, Tamika 1979— **43**

Catlett, Elizabeth 1919— **2**

Catto, Octavius V. 1839–1871 **83**

Caymmi, Dorival 1914–2008 **72**

Cayton, Horace 1903–1970 **26**

Cedric the Entertainer 1964— **29, 60, 115**

Cee Lo See Green, Cee Lo

Celestin, Joe See Celestin, Josaphat

Celestin, Josaphat 1956— **101**

Cenac, Wyatt 1976— **94**

Cepeda, Orlando 1937— **98**

Césaire, Aimé 1913–2008 **48, 69**

Chadiha, Jeffri 1970— **57**

Chaka Chaka, Yvonne 1965— **112**

Cham, Adongo Agada Akway 1954(?)— **77**

Chamberlain, Wilt 1936–1999 **18, 47**

Chambers, James See Cliff, Jimmy

Chambers, Julius (LeVonne) 1936— **3**

Chamillionaire 1979— **82**

Champion, Betty Jean See Swann, Bettye

Chandler, Gene 1937— **105**

Chandler, Tyson 1982— **114**

Chaney, Don 1946— **98**

Chaney, John 1932— **67**

Channer, Colin 1963— **36**

Chanté, Keshia 1988— **50**

Chanticleer, Raven 1928–2002 **91**

Chapman, Nathan A., Jr. 1957— **21**

Chapman, Susan E. 1968— **94**

Chapman, Tracy 1964— **26**

Chappell, Emma C. 1941— **18**

Chappell, Roy M. 1921–2002 **95**

Chappelle, Dave 1973— **50, 115**

Charlemagne, Emmanuel See Charlemagne, Manno

Charlemagne, Manno 1948— **11**

Charles, Ezzard 1921–1975 **95**

Charles, John 1944–2002 **108**

Charles, Mary Eugenia 1919–2005 **10, 55**

Charles, Pierre 1954–2004 **52**

Charles, Ray 1930–2004 **16, 48**

Charleston, Oscar 1896–1954 **39**

Chase, Debra Martin 1956— **49, 96**

Chase, John Saunders, Jr. 1925— **99**

Chase, Leah 1923— **57**

Chase-Riboud, Barbara 1939— **20, 46**

Chatard, Peter 1936— **44**

Chatman, John Len See Memphis Slim

Chavis, Benjamin (Franklin, Jr.) 1948— **6**

Chea, Alvin See Take 6

Cheadle, Don 1964— **19, 52**

Cheatham, Doc 1905–1997 **17**

Checker, Chubby 1941— **28**

Cheeks, Maurice 1956— **47, 106**

Chenault, John 1952— **40**

Chenault, Kenneth 1951— **4, 36, 108**

Cheney-Coker, Syl 1945— **43**

Cheruiyot, Robert 1978— **69**

Cherry, Deron 1959— **40**

Cherry, Nicole See Marian Anderson String Quartet

Chesimard, JoAnne (Deborah) See Shakur, Assata

Chesnutt, Charles 1858–1932 **29**

Chestnut, J. L., Jr. 1930–2008 **73**

Chestnut, Morris 1969— **31**

Chew, Robert F. 1960–2013 **109**

Chideya, Farai 1969— **14, 61**

Chief Black Thunderbird Eagle *See York, Dwight D.*

Chief Keef 1995— **112**

Childers, Lulu Vere 1870–1946 **95**

Childress, Alice 1920–1994 **15**

Childress, Alvin 1907–1986 **114**

Chiles, Nick 1965— **98**

Chi-Lites **106**

Chiluba, Frederick 1943— **56, 80**

Chineworth, Mary Alice 1917— **79**

Chinn, May Edward 1896–1980 **26**

Chisholm, Daquan 1993— **93**

Chisholm, Samuel J. 1942— **32**

Chisholm, Shirley 1924–2005 **2, 50**

Chissano, Joaquim 1939— **7, 55, 67**

Chitalu, Godfrey 1947–1993 **108**

Chong, Rae Dawn 1961— **62**

Christian, Barbara T. 1946–2000 **44**

Christian, Jodie 1932-2012 **103**

Christian, Spencer 1947— **15**

Christian-Green, Donna M. 1945— **17**

Christie, Angella **36**

Christie, Linford 1960— **8**

Christie, Perry Gladstone 1944— **53**

Christie, Ron 1969(?)— **83**

Christophe, Henri 1767–1820 **9**

Chuck D 1960— **9** *See also Public Enemy*

Church, Bruce *See Bruce, Bruce*

Churchwell, Robert, Sr. 1917–2009 **76**

Chweneyagae, Presley 1984— **63**

Ciara 1985— **56, 115**

Ciara, Barbara 195(?)— **69**

Cissé, Souleymane *See Souleymane, Mahamane*

Clack, Zoanne 1968(?)— **73**

Claiborne, Loretta 1953— **34**

Chancler, Leon *See Chancler, Ndugu*

Chancler, Ndugu 1952— **115**

Clark, Carl 1916— **101**

Clark, Celeste (Clesteen) Abraham 1953— **15**

Clark, Joe 1939— **1**

Clark, John Pepper *See Clark-Bekederemo, J. P.*

Clark, Kenneth B. 1914–2005 **5, 52**

Clark, Kristin *See Taylor, Kristin Clark*

Clark, Mamie Phipps 1917–1983 **79**

Clark, Mattie Moss 1925–1994 **61**

Clark, Patrick 1955— **14**

Clark, Septima (Poinsette) 1898–1987 **7**

Clark, Sharón 1961— **105**

Clark, Wahida 19(?)(?)— **107**

Clark, Yvonne Young 1929— **95**

Clark-Bekederemo, J. P. 1935— **44**

Clark-Cole, Dorinda 1957— **66**

Clarke, Anna Mac 1919–1944 **95**

Clarke, Austin C. 1934— **32**

Clarke, Cheryl 1947— **32**

Clarke, George Elliott 1960— **32**

Clarke, Hope 1943(?)— **14**

Clarke, John Henrik 1915–1998 **20**

Clarke, Kenny 1914–1985 **27**

Clarke, Patrice Francise *See Washington, Patrice Clarke*

Clarke, Peter *See Peters, Clarke*

Clarke, Stanley 1951— **115**

Clarke, Yvette 1964— **92**

Clark-Sheard, Karen 1960— **22, 114**

Clash, Kevin 1960— **14, 93**

Clay, Bryan 1980— **57, 74**

Clay, Cassius Marcellus, Jr. *See Ali, Muhammad*

Clay, Otis 1942— **112**

Clay, William Lacy 1931— **8**

Clay, William Lacy, Jr. 1956— **95**

Clayton, Constance 1937— **1**

Clayton, Eva M. 1934— **20**

Clayton, Gerald 1984— **111**

Clayton, Mayme Agnew 1923–2006 **62**

Clayton, Merry 1948— **112**

Clayton, Xernona 1930— **3, 45**

Claytor, Helen 1907–2005 **14, 52**

Cleage, Albert B., Jr. *See Agyeman, Jaramogi Abebe*

Cleage, Pearl 1948— **17, 64**

Cleaver, Eldridge 1935— **5**

Cleaver, Emanuel, II 1944— **4, 45, 68, 107**

Cleaver, Kathleen Neal 1945— **29**

Clemente, Rosa 1972— **74**

Clement-Holmes, Linda 1962— **94**

Clements, George (Harold) 1932— **2**

Clemmons, Reginal G. 19(?)(?)— **41**

Clemons, Clarence 1942— **41**

Clemons, Michael "Pinball" 1965— **64**

Clendenon, Donn 1935–2005 **26, 56**

Cleveland, James 1932(?)–1991 **19**

Cliff, Jimmy 1948— **28, 92**

Cliff, Michelle 1946— **42**

Clifton, Lucille 1936–2010 **14, 64, 91**

Clifton, Nathaniel "Sweetwater" 1922(?)–1990 **47**

Clinkscale, Aja Lena *See Brown, Aja*

Clinton, George 1941— **9, 93**

Clovers, The **104**

Clyburn, James E. 1940— **21, 71**

Clyburn, Mignon 1962— **78**

C-Murder 1971— **99**

Coachman, Alice 1923— **18**

Coasters, The **102**

Coates, Ta-Nehisi 1975— **76**

Cobb, Arnett 1918–1989 **114**

Cobb, Jewel Plummer 1924— **42**

Cobb, Monty *See Cobb, W. Montague*

Cobb, W. Montague 1904–1990 **39**

Cobb, William Jelani 1969— **59**

Cobbs, Bill 1934— **101**

Cobbs, Natasha *See Cobbs, Tasha*

Cobbs, Price M(ashaw) 1928— **9**

Cobbs, Tasha 1981— **114**

Cochran, Johnnie 1937–2005 **11, 39, 52**

Cockrel, Kenneth V., Jr. 1965— **79**

Cockrel, Kenneth Vern, Sr. 1938–1989 **79**

CoCo Brother 19(?)(?)— **93**

Cody, Radmilla 1975— **99**

Coggins, Danny *See Moonglows, The*

Cohen, Anthony 1963— **15**

Cohen, Cathy J. 1962— **88**

Coke, Christopher 1969— **108**

Colbert, Thomas *See Colbert, Tom*

Colbert, Tom 1949— **115**

Colbert, Virgis William 1939— **17**

Cole, Ashley 1980— **106**

Cole, J. 1985— **97**

Cole, Johnnetta B(etsch) 1936— **5, 43**

Cole, Keyshia 1981— **63, 107**

Cole, Lorraine 195(?)— **48**

Cole, Maria 1922–2012 **104**

Cole, Nat "King" 1919–1965 **17**

Cole, Natalie 1950— **17, 60, 84**

Cole, Rebecca 1846–1922 **38**

Coleman, Ashley Antoinette Snell *See Ashley & JaQuavis*

Coleman, Bessie 1892–1926 **9**

Coleman, Donald 1952— **24, 62**

Coleman, Gary 1968–2010 **35, 86**

Coleman, George 1935— **106**

Coleman, James E., Jr. 1948(?)— **79**

Coleman, JaQuavis Javon *See Ashley & JaQuavis*

Coleman, Ken 1942— **57**

Coleman, Leonard S., Jr. 1949— **12**

Coleman, Mary 1946— **46**

Coleman, Michael B. 1954— **28, 79**

Coleman, Ornette 1930— **39, 69**

Coleman, Ronald S. 1948— **110**

Coleman, Troy *See Cowboy Troy*

Coleman, Valerie *See Imani Winds*

Coleman, Wanda 1946— **48**

Coleman, William F., III 1955(?)— **61**

Coleman, William T. 1920— **76**

Colemon, Johnnie 1921(?)— **11**

Coleridge-Taylor, Samuel 1875–1912 **75**

Coles, Alice 1951(?)— **80**

Coles, Dennis *See Ghostface Killah*

Colescott, Robert 1925— **69**

Collins, Albert 1932–1993 **12**

Collins, Barbara-Rose 1939— **7, 87**

Collins, Bootsy 1951— **31**

Collins, Cardiss 1931— **10, 80**

Collins, Clarence *See Little Anthony & the Imperials*

Collins, Janet 1917–2003 **33, 64**

Collins, Jason 1978— **111**

Collins, Lyn 1948–2005 **53**

Collins, Marva 1936— **3, 71**

Collins, Patricia Hill 1948— **67**

Collins, Paul 1936— **61**

Collins, William *See Collins, Bootsy*

Colston, Hal 1953(?)— **72**

Colter, Cyrus J. 1910–2002 **36**

Coltrane, Alice 1937–2007 **70**

Coltrane, John William 1926–1967 **19**

Coltrane, Ravi 1965— **71**

Combs, Sean 1969— **17, 43, 92**

Comer, James P(ierpont) 1934— **6**

Common 1972— **31, 63, 98**

Compaore, Blaise 1951— **87**

Compton, John 1925–2007 **65**

Compton-Rock, Malaak 1969— **86**

Condé, Alpha 1938— **95**

Condrey, Cory *See CoCo Brother*

Cone, James H. 1938— **3, 82**

Coney, PonJola 1951— **48**

Conley, Nellie *See Madame Sul-Te-Wan*

Conneh, Sekou Damate, Jr. 1960— **51**

Connerly, Ward 1939— **14**

Connor, William *See Swan Silvertones, The*

Conrad, Barbara Smith 1940(?)— **90**

Conrad, Cecilia A. 1955— **94**

Conté, Lansana 1934(?)–2008 **7, 76**

Contee, Cheryl 1971— **88**

Contours, The **109**

Conyers, John, Jr. 1929— **4, 45, 111**

Conyers, Monica 1964— **85**

Conyers, Nathan G. 1932— **24**

Coogler, Ryan 1986— **114**

Cook, Charles "Doc" 1891–1958 **44**

Cook, (Will) Mercer 1903–1987 **40**

Cook, Sam 1931–1964 **17**

Cook, Samuel DuBois 1928— **14**

Cook, Suzan D. Johnson 1957— **22**

Cook, Toni 1944— **23**

Cook, Victor Trent *See Three Mo' Tenors*

Cook, Wesley *See Abu-Jamal, Mumia*

Cook, Will Marion 1869–1944 **40**

Cooke, Charles L. *See Cook, Charles "Doc"*

Cooke, Marcia 1954— **60**

Cooke, Marvel 1901(?)–2000 **31**

Cook-Parrish, Mary Virginia 1862(?)–1945 **95**

Cooks, Patricia 1944–1989 **19**

Coolio 1963— **103**

Cools, Anne 1943— **64**

Coombs, Orde M. 1939–1984 **44**

Cooper, Afua 1957— **53**

Cooper, Andrew Lewis *See Cooper, Andy "Lefty"*

Cooper, Andrew W. 1928–2002 **36**

Cooper, Andy "Lefty" 1898–1941 **63**

Cooper, Anna Julia 1858–1964 **20**

Cooper, Barry 1956— **33**

Cooper, Charles "Chuck" 1926–1984 **47**

Cooper, Charles Theodore *See Cooper, Tarzan*

Cooper, Chuck 1954— **75**

Cooper, Cynthia *See Cooper-Dyke, Cynthia*

Cooper, Edward S(awyer) 1926— **6**

Cooper, Evern 19(?)(?)— **40**

Cooper, Helene 1966— **74**

Cooper, J. California 1932(?)— **12, 85**

Cooper, Jeffrey *See Midnight Star*

Cooper, Lisa 1963— **73**

Cooper, Marcus *See Pleasure P*

Cooper, Margaret J. 194(?)— **46**

Cooper, Michael 1956— **31**

Cooper, Tarzan 1907–1980 **96**

Cooper Cafritz, Peggy 1947— **43**

Cooper-Dyke, Cynthia 1963— **17, 89**

Copeland, Johnny 1937–1997 **110**

Copeland, Michael 1954— **47**

Copeland, Shemekia 1979— **110**

Coppola, Imani Francesca 1978— **82**

Corbi, Lana 1955— **42**

Corley, Tony 1949— **62**

Cornelius, Don 1936–2012 **4, 100**

Cornish, Sam 1935— **50**

Cornwell, Edward E., III 1956— **70**

Correia, Antoné De'Jaun *See Correia, De'Jaun*

Correia, De'Jaun 1994— **93**

Cortez, Jayne 1934–2012 **43, 109**

Corthron, Kia 1961— **43**

Cortor, Eldzier 1916— **42**

Cosby, Bill 1937— **7, 26, 59**

Cosby, Camille 1945— **14, 80**

Cosby, William Henry, Jr. *See Cosby, Bill*

Cose, Ellis 1951— **5, 50**

Cosey, Pete 1943–2012 **103**

Cosey, Peter Palus *See Cosey, Pete*

Cotter, Joseph Seamon, Sr. 1861–1949 **40**

Cottrell, Comer 1931— **11**

Council, LaVerne 1961(?)— **94**

Count Basie 1904–1984 **23**

Counter, S. Allen 1944— **74**

Courtney, Opal, Jr. *See Spaniels, The*

Cousin, Ertharin 1957— **115**

Cousins, DeMarcus 1990— **108**

Couto, Mia 1955— **45**

Coverley, Louise Bennett *See Bennett, Louise*

Cowans, Adger W. 1936— **20**

Cowboy Troy, 1970— **54**

Cox, Bryan 1968— **83**

Cox, Deborah 1974(?)— **28**

Cox, Donald Lee 1936–2011 **93**

Cox, Elbert Frank 1895–1969 **111**

Cox, Ida 1896–1967 **42**

Cox, Joseph Mason Andrew 1930— **51**

Cox, Renée 1960— **67**

Cox, William E. 1942— **68**

Cozart, Keith *See Chief Keef*

Craig, Carl 1969— **31, 71**

Craig-Jones, Ellen Walker 1906–2000 **44**

Crawford, Carl 1981— **90**

Crawford, Hank 1934–2009 **77**

Crawford, Randy 1952— **19**

Crawford, Veronica *See Crawford, Randy*

Cray, Robert 1953— **30**

Creagh, Milton 1957— **27**

Cream, Arnold Raymond *See Walcott, Jersey Joe*

Crennel, Romeo 1947— **54, 107**

Crenshaw, Kimberlé Williams 1959— **88**

Crenshaw, Robert *See Swan Silvertones, The*

Crew, Rudolph F. *See Crew, Rudy*

Crew, Rudy 1950— **16, 113**

Crew, Spencer R. 1949— **55**

Crichlow, Ernest 1914–2005 **75**

Crisp, Coco 1979— **109**

Crisp, Covelli Loyce *See Crisp, Coco*

Crite, Allan Rohan 1910–2007 **29**

Croal, N'Gai 1972— **76**

Crocker, Frankie 1937–2000 **29**

Crockett, George W., Jr. 1909–1997 **10, 64**

Cromartie, Antonio 1984— **115**

Crooks, Garth 1958— **53**

Croom, Sylvester 1954— **50**

Cross, Dolores E. 1938— **23**

Crosthwait, David 1892–1976 **93**

Crothers, Benjamin Sherman *See Crothers, Scatman*

Crothers, Scatman 1910–1986 **19**

Crouch, Andraé 1942— **27, 115**

Crouch, Hubert 1906–1980 **95**

Crouch, Stanley 1945— **11, 87**

Crowder, Henry 1895–1954(?) **16**

Crowdy, William Saunders 1847–1908 **109**

Crudup, Arthur 1905–1974 **115**

Crudup, Big Boy *See Crudup, Arthur*

Crum, George 1822–1914 **101**

Crump, Lavell *See Banner, David*

Crump, Steven 1957— **96**

Crumpler, Rebecca Lee 1831–1895 **89**

Cruse, Harold 1916–2005 **54**

Crutchfield, James N. 1947— **55**

Cruz, Taio 1983— **104**

Cruz, Victor 1986— **107**

Cuffe, Paul 1759–1817 **98**

Cullen, Countee 1903–1946 **8**

Cullers, Vincent T. 1924(?)–2003 **49**

Culp, Curley 1946— **110**

Culp, Napoleon Brown Goodson *See Brown, Nappy*

Culpepper, Daunte 1977— **32, 85**

Cummings, Elijah E. 1951— **24, 102**

Cuney, William Waring 1906–1976 **44**

Cunningham, Evelyn 1916–2010 **23, 85**

Cunningham, Randall 1963— **23**

Curling, Alvin 1939— **34**

Curren$y 1981— **114**

Currie, Betty 1939(?)— **21**

Currie, Ulysses 1937— **73**

Curry, George E. 1947— **23**

Curry, Mark 1964— **17**

Curry, Michael 1968— **85**

Curry, Stephen 1988— **110**

Curson, Ted 1935–2012 **108**

Curtis, Christopher Paul 1953— **26, 113**

Curtis-Hall, Vondie 1956— **17**

Da Don, Polow 1978— **86**

da Silva, Benedita 1942— **5**

da Silva, Jorge Mário *See Jorge, Seu*

da Silva, Leônidas *See Leônidas*

Dabiri, John 1980(?)— **93**

Dabydeen, David 1956— **48**

DaCosta, YaYa 1982— **98**

Dacres, Desmond Adolphus *See Dekker, Desmond*

Dadié, Bernard 1916— **34**

Daemyon, Jerald 1970(?)— **64**

D'Aguiar, Fred 1960— **50**

Dailey, Ulysses Grant 1885–1961 **87**

Dale, Clamma 1948— **103**

Daly, Marie Maynard 1921— **37**

Damas, Léon-Gontran 1912–1978 **46**

Dameron, Tadd 1917–1965 **103**

Dance, Kelvin *See Kitwana, Bakari*

Dandala, Mvume 1951— **77**

Dandridge, Dorothy 1922–1965 **3**

Dandridge, Ray 1913–1994 **36**

Dandridge, Raymond Garfield 1882–1930 **45**

D'Angelo 1974— **27**

Daniels, Gertrude *See Haynes, Trudy*

Daniels, Jerry *See Ink Spots, The*

Daniels, Lee 1959— **36, 76**

Daniels, Mel 1944— **106**

Daniels-Carter, Valerie 19(?)(?)— **23**

Danjah, Terror 1977— **91**

Danner, Margaret Esse 1915–1986 **49**

Danquah, Meri Nana Ama 1967— **93**

Danticat, Edwidge 1969— **15, 68**

Dantley, Adrian 1956— **72**

Dara, Olu 1941— **335**

D'Arby, Terence Trent *See Maitreya, Sananda*

Darden, Calvin 1950— **38**

Darden, Christopher 1957— **13**

Darego, Agbani 1982— **52**

Dash, Damon 1971— **31, 113**

Dash, Darien 1972(?)— **29**

Dash, Julie 1952— **4**

Dash, Leon 1944— **47**

Datcher, Michael 1967— **60**

Dathorne, O. R. 1934— **52**

Davenport, Arthur *See Fattah, Chaka*

Davenport, Charles Edward *See Davenport, Cow Cow*

Davenport, Cow Cow 1894–1955 **115**

David, Craig 1981— **31, 53**

David, Keith 1954— **27**

Davids, Edgar 1973— **106**

Davidson, Jaye 1967(?)— **5**

Davidson, Tommy 1963(?)— **21**

Davis, Allison 1902–1983 **12**

Davis, Altovise 1943–2009 **76**

Davis, Angela 1944— **5, 114**

Davis, Angela J. 1956— **88**

Davis, Anthony 1951— **11**

Davis, Anthony Moses *See Beenie Man*

Davis, Arthur P. 1904–1996 **41**

Davis, Artur 1967— **41**

Davis, Belva 1932— **61**

Davis, Ben 1912–2013 **115**

Davis, Benjamin O(liver), Jr. 1912–2002 **2, 43**

Davis, Benjamin O(liver), Sr. 1877–1970 **4**

Davis, Bing 1937— **84**

Davis, Carl 1934–2012 **105**

Davis, Charles T. 1918–1981 **48**

Davis, Chuck 1937— **33**

Davis, Danny K. 1941— **24, 79**

Davis, Doris A. 1936(?)— **100**

Davis, Douglas E. *See Fresh, Doug E.*

Davis, Ed 1911–1999 **24**

Davis, Eisa 1971— **68**

Davis, Erellon Benjamin *See Davis, Ben*

Davis, Ernie 1939–1963 **48**

Davis, Erroll B., Jr. 1944— **57**

Davis, Frank Marshall 1905–1987 **47**

Davis, Gary 1896–1972 **41**

Davis, George 1939— **36**

Davis, Gordon J. 1941— **76**

Davis, Guy 1952— **36**

Davis, Jamelia Niela *See Jamelia*

Davis, James E. 1962–2003 **50**

Davis, Lorenzo "Piper" 1917–1997 **19**

Davis, Mia Amber 1974–2011 **94**

Davis, Mike 1960— **41**

Davis, Miles (Dewey, III) 1926–1991 **4**

Davis, Milt 1929–2008 **74**

Davis, Nolan 1942— **45**

Davis, Ossie 1917–2005 **5, 50**

Davis, Rob *See Dramatics, The*

Davis, Robert Earl, Jr. *See DJ Screw*

Davis, Ruth 1943— **37**

Davis, Sammy, Jr. 1925–1990 **18**

Davis, Shani 1982— **58, 84**

Davis, Terrell 1972— **20**

Davis, Thulani 1948— **61**

Davis, Tyrone 1938–2005 **54**

Davis, Viola 1965— **34, 76, 100**

Davis, Wade, Jr. 1977— **103**

Davis, Wild Bill 1918–1995 **114**

Davis, William Strethen *See Davis, Wild Bill*

Dawes, Dominique (Margaux) 1976— **11**

Dawkins, James Henry *See Dawkins, Jimmy*

Dawkins, Jimmy 1936–2013 **111**

Dawkins, Wayne 1955— **20**

Dawn, Marpessa 1934–2008 **75**

Dawson, Andre 1954— **85**

Dawson, Matel "Mat," Jr. 1921–2002 **39**

Dawson, Michael C. 1951— **63**

Dawson, Rosario 1979— **72**

Dawson, William Levi 1899–1900 **39**

Dawuni, Rocky 1969— **94**

Day, Leon 1916–1995 **39**

Days, Drew S(aunders, III) 1941— **10**

D'banj 1980— **107**

De' Alexander, Quinton 19??— **57**

de Assís Moreira, Ronaldo *See Ronaldinho*

De Bankolé, Isaach 1957— **78**

de Carvalho, Barcelo *See Bonga, Kuenda*

de Lavallade, Carmen 1931— **78**

de Passe, Suzanne 1948(?)— **25**

De Priest, Oscar Stanton 1871–1951 **80**

De Shields, André 1946— **72**

De Veaux, Alexis 1948— **44**

"Deadwood Dick" *See Love, Nat*

Dean, Fred 1952— **98**

Dean, Kasseem David *See Swizz Beatz*

Dean, Mark E. 1957— **35**

Deas, Gerald 1931— **85**

Deauphin, Jean-Prosper *See Beken*

DeBaptiste, George 1814(?)–1875 **32**

DeBarge, El 1961— **89**

DeBerry, Lois M. 1945–2013 **115**

Déby, Idriss 1952— **30**

DeCarava, Roy 1919–2009 **42, 81**

Deconge-Watson, Lovenia 1933— **55**

Dee, Merri 1936— **55**

Dee, Ruby 1924— **8, 50, 68**

Deezer D 1965— **53**

DeFrantz, Anita 1952— **37**

DeGale, James 1986— **74**

Deggans, Eric 1965— **71**

DeJongh, John, Jr. 1957— **85**

Dekker, Desmond 1941–2006 **104**

DeLaine, Joseph A. 1898–1974 **110**

Delaney, Beauford 1901–1979 **19**

Delaney, Joe 1958–1983 **76**

Delaney, Joseph 1904–1991 **30**

Delany, Annie Elizabeth 1891–1995 **12**

Delany, Martin R. 1812–1885 **27**

Delany, Samuel R(ay), Jr. 1942— **9**

Delany, Sarah (Sadie) 1889— **12**

Delco, Wilhemina R. 1929— **33**

Delice, Ronald 1966— **48**

Delice, Rony 1966— **48**

DeLille, Henriette 1813–1862 **30**

Dells, The **109**

Dellums, Ronald 1935— **2, 81**

DeLoach, Nora 1940–2001 **30**

Delpit, Lisa 1952— **101**

Delsarte, Louis 1944— **34**

Demby, William 1922— **51**

Demps, Larry *See Dramatics, The*

Dennard, Brazeal 1929— **37**

Dennis, Gary C. 1950— **91**

Dent, Cedric *See Take 6*

Dent, Richard 1960— **97**

Dent, Thomas C. 1932–1998 **50**

Dent, Tom *See Dent, Thomas C.*

Dentley, Khristian *See Take 6*

DePreist, James 1936–2013 **37, 109**

DePrince, Michaela 1995— **104**

Derham, James *See Durham, James*

Derülo, Jason 1989— **93**

Desalegn, Hailemariam 1965— **105**

Desrouleaux, Jason *See Derülo, Jason*

DeVard, Jerri 1957(?)— **61**

DeVaughn, Raheem 1975— **91**

Devers, Gail 1966— **7, 87**

Devine, Loretta 1953— **24**

Devine, Major J. *See Divine, Father*

DeVoe, Ronnie *See New Edition*

DeWese, Mohandas *See Kool Moe Dee*

Dewitty, Thelma 1912–1977 **114**

Di Genius *See McGregor, Stephen*

Dial, Thornton 1928— **114**

Diallo, Amadou 1976–1999 **27**

Diamond, Lydia R. 1969— **101**

Diawara, Djeli Moussa 1962— **111**

Diawara, Fatoumata 1982— **114**

Dibaba, Tirunesh 1985— **73, 109**

Dickens, Helen Octavia 1909–2001 **14, 64**

Dickenson, Vic 1906–1984 **38**

Dickerson, Debra J. 1959— **60**

Dickerson, Eric 1960— **27, 108**

Dickerson, Ernest 1952(?)— **6, 17**

Dickerson, Isaac *See Fisk Jubilee Singers*

Dickey, Eric Jerome 1961— **21, 56**

Diddley, Bo 1928–2008 **39, 72**

Diesel, Vin 1967(?)— **29**

Dieudonné 1966— **67**

Diggs, Charles C. 1922–1998 **21**

Diggs, Robert Fitzgerald *See RZA*

Diggs, Scott *See Diggs, Taye*

Diggs, Taye 1972— **25, 63**

Diggs-Taylor, Anna 1932— **20**

Dihigo, Martín 1905(?)–1971 **103**

Dilla, J *See J Dilla*

Dillard, Godfrey J. 1948— **45**

Dillard, Tramar *See Flo Rida*

Dillon, Leo 1933–2012 **103**

Dinkins, David 1927— **4**

Diogo, Luisa Dias 1958— **63**

Diop, Birago 1906–1989 **53**

Diop, Cheikh Anta 1923–1986 **4**

Diouf, Abdou 1935— **3**

Dirie, Waris 1965(?)— **56**

Divine, Father 1877(?)–1965 **7**

Dixie Cups, The **109**

Dixon, Bill 1925–2010 **87**

Dixon, Dean 1915–1976 **68**

Dixon, George 1870–1909 **52**

Dixon, Ivan 1931–2008 **69**

Dixon, Julian C. 1934— **24**

Dixon, Margaret 192(?)— **14**

Dixon, Rodrick *See Three Mo' Tenors*

Dixon, Sharon Pratt 1944— **1**

Dixon, Sheila 1953— **68**

Dixon, Willie (James) 1915–1992 **4**

DJ Clue? 1975— **111**

DJ Jazzy Jeff 1965— **32**

DJ Lance Rock 1965— **94**

DJ Ready Red *See Geto Boys*

DJ Red Alert *See Alert, Kool DJ Red*

DJ Screw 1971–2000 **110**

Dlamini-Zuma, Nkosazana 1949— **34, 105**

DMC *See Run-DMC*

DMX 1970— **28, 64**

do Nascimento, Edson Arantes *See Pelé*

Dobbs, John Wesley 1882–1961 **89**

Dobbs, Mattiwilda 1925— **34**

Dobson, Tamara 1947–2006 **111**

Doby, Larry *See Doby, Lawrence Eugene, Sr.*

Doby, Lawrence Eugene, Sr. 1924–2003 **16, 41**

Dodd, Clement Seymour *See Dodd, Coxsone*

Dodd, Coxsone 1932–2004 **99**

Dodson, Howard, Jr. 1939— **7, 52**

Dodson, Owen 1914–1983 **38**

Doe, Samuel K. 1951–1990 **100**

Dogan, Matthew Winifred 1863–1947 **91**

Doig, Jason 1977— **45**

Dokes, Michael 1958— **105**

Doley, Harold, Jr. 1947— **26**

Dollar, Creflo 1962— **106**

Domingo, Colman 1969— **94**

Domini, Rey *See Lorde, Audre (Geraldine)*

Domino, Fats 1928— **20**

Donald, Arnold Wayne 1954— **36**

Donaldson, Jeff 1932–2004 **46**

Donegan, Dorothy 1922–1998 **19**

Donovan, Kevin *See Bambaataa, Afrika*

Dorham, Kenny 1924–1972 **113**

Dorham, McKinley Howard *See Dorham, Kenny*

Dorhan, Carlita *See Taste of Honey, A*

Dorn, Michael 1952— **112**

Dorrell, Karl 1963— **52**

Dorsey, Lee 1926–1986 **65**

Dorsey, Thomas Andrew 1899–1993 **15**

Dorsey, Thomas J. 1812(?)–1875 **90**

Dortch, Thomas W., Jr. 1950— **45**

dos Santos, Isabel 1973— **114**

dos Santos, José Eduardo 1942— **43, 114**

dos Santos, Manuel Francisco 1933 **65**

Dougherty, Mary Pearl 1915–2003 **47**

Douglas, Aaron 1899–1979 **7**

Douglas, Ashanti Shequoiya *See Ashanti*

Douglas, Bob 1882–1979 **96**

Douglas, Denzil Llewellyn 1953— **53**

Douglas, Derek 1971— **88**

Douglas, Donya 1970(?)— **97**

Douglas, Emory 1943— **89**

Douglas, Lizzie *See Memphis Minnie*

Douglass, Frederick 1817(?)–1895 **87**

Doumbia, Mariam *See Amadou & Mariam*

Dourdan, Gary 1966— **37**

Dove, Rita 1952— **6, 78, 101**

Dove, Ulysses 1947— **5**

Dow, Unity 1959— **104**

Downing, George T. 1819–1903 **91**

Downing, Will 19(?)(?)— **19**

Dozier, Lamont *See Holland-Dozier-Holland*

Dr. J *See Erving, Julius*

Drake 1986— **86**

Drake, Lavern *See Cadillacs*

Dramatics, The **106**

Draper, Sharon Mills 1952— **16, 43**

Drayton, William Jonathan, Jr. *See Flavor Flav*

Dre, Dr. 1965(?)— **10, 14, 30**

Dream, The *See The-Dream*

Drew, Alvin, Jr. 1962— **67**

Drew, Charles Richard 1904–1950 **7**

Drew, Maurice *See Jones-Drew, Maurice*

Drew, Timothy *See Noble Drew Ali*

Drew Ali *See Noble Drew Ali*

Drexler, Clyde 1962— **4, 61**

Driskell, David C(lyde) 1931— **7**

Driver, David E. 1955— **11**

Driver, Donald 1975— **99**

D-Roc *See Ying Yang Twins*

Drogba, Didier 1978— **78**

Drummond, William J. 1944— **40**

Du Bois, David Graham 1925— **45**

Du Bois, W(illiam) E(dward) B(urghardt) 1868–1963 **3**

du Cille, Michel 1955(?)— **74**

Dube, Lucky 1964–2007 **77**

DuBois, Joshua 1982— **88**

DuBois, Shirley Graham 1907–1977 **21**

Duchemin, Alamaine *See Maxis, Theresa*

Duchemin, Marie *See Maxis, Theresa*

Duchemin, Theresa Maxis *See Maxis, Theresa*

Ducksworth, Marilyn 1957— **12**

Duckworth, Kendrick Lamar *See Lamar, Kendrick*

Dudley, Edward R. 1911–2005 **58**

Dudus *See Coke, Christopher*

Due, Patricia Stephens 1939–2012 **100**

Due, Tananarive 1966— **30**

Duerson, Dave 1960–2011 **93**

Duggins, George 1943–2005 **64**

Duke, Bill 1943— **3, 96**

Duke, George 1946–2013 **21, 113**

Dukes, Hazel Nell 1932— **56**

Dumars, Joe 1963— **16, 65**

Dumas, Henry 1934–1968 **41**

Dumpson, James R. 1909–2012 **108**

Dunbar, Alice *See Dunbar-Nelson, Alice Ruth Moore*

Dunbar, Paul Laurence 1872–1906 **8**

Dunbar, Sly 1952— *See Sly & Robbie*

Dunbar-Nelson, Alice Ruth Moore 1875–1935 **44**

Duncan, Cleveland *See Penguins, The*

Duncan, Michael Clarke 1957–2012 **26, 104**

Duncan, Tim 1976— **20, 91**

Duncan, Todd 1903–1998 **76**

Dungey, Merrin 1971— **62**

Dungy, Camille 1972— **86**

Dungy, Tony 1955— **17, 42, 59**

Dunham, Katherine 1910–2006 **4, 59**

Dunlap, Ericka 1982(?)— **55**

Dunn, Jerry 1953— **27**

Dunn, Warrick 1975— **90**

Dunner, Leslie B. 1956— **45**

Dunnigan, Alice Allison 1906–1983 **41**

Dunston, Georgia Mae 1944— **48**

Duplechan, Larry 1956— **55**

DuPree, Johnny 1953— **96**

Dupri, Jermaine 1972— **13, 46**

Durant, Kevin 1988— **76, 107**

Durham, Bobby 1937–2008 **73**

Durham, James 1762–1834(?) **90**

Durham, Robert Joseph *See Durham, Bobby*

Duthiers, Vladimir 1969— **109**

Dutton, Charles S. 1951— **4, 22**

Dutton, Marie Elizabeth 1940— **12**

DuVernay, Ava 1972— **98**

Dwight, Edward 1933— **65**

Dworkin, Aaron P. 1970— **52**

Dye, Jermaine 1974— **58**

Dyett, Walter 1901–1969 **113**

Dymally, Mervyn 1926— **42**

Dyson, Michael Eric 1958— **11, 40**

Eagleson, William Lewis 1835–1899 **90**

Early, Deloreese Patricia *See Reese, Della*

Early, Gerald (Lyn) 1952— **15**

Earth, Wind & Fire **98**

Earthquake, 1963— **55**

Easley, Annie J. 1933— **61**
Easton, Hosea 1798–1837 **91**
Ebanks, Michelle 1962— **60**
Ebanks, Selita 1983— **67**
Eckstein, William Clarence See Eckstine, Billy
Eckstine, Billy 1914–1993 **28**
Edelin, Ramona Hoage 1945— **19**
Edelman, Marian Wright 1939— **5, 42**
Edgerton, Khia Danielle See K-Swift
Edison, Harry 1915(?)–1999 **114**
Edison, Harry "Sweets" See Edison, Harry
Edley, Christopher 1928–2003 **2, 48**
Edley, Christopher F., Jr. 1953— **48**
Edmonds, Kenneth See Babyface
Edmonds, Terry 1950(?)— **17**
Edmonds, Tracey 1967— **16, 64**
Edmunds, Gladys 1951(?)— **48**
Edugyan, Esi 1978— **98**
Edwards, Dennis See Contours, The
Edwards, Donna 1958— **77**
Edwards, Eli See McKay, Claude
Edwards, Esther Gordy 1920(?)— **43**
Edwards, Harry 1942— **2**
Edwards, Herman 1954— **51**
Edwards, Lena Frances 1900–1986 **76**
Edwards, Melvin 1937— **22**
Edwards, Teresa 1964— **14, 95**
Edwards, Trevor 1962— **54**
Edwards, Willarda V. 1951— **59**
Edwards, Willis 1946–2012 **104**
Eikerenkoetter, Frederick J., II See Reverend Ike
Ejiofor, Chiwetal 1977(?)— **67**
Ekwensi, Cyprian 1921— **37**
El Wilson, Barbara 1959— **35**
Elam, Keith See Guru
Elba, Idris 1972— **49, 89**
Elder, Larry 1952— **25**
Elder, (Robert) Lee 1934— **6**
Elder, Lonne, III 1931–1996 **38**
Elders, Joycelyn (Minnie) 1933— **6**
Eldridge, Roy 1911–1989 **37**
El-Hajj Malik El-Shabazz See X, Malcolm
Elie, Lolis Eric 1985— **97**
Elise, Kimberly 1967— **32, 101**
Ellerbe, Brian 1963— **22**
Ellington, Duke 1899–1974 **5**
Ellington, E. David 1960— **11**
Ellington, Edward Kennedy See Ellington, Duke
Ellington, Mercedes 1939— **34**
Ellington, Robert See Dramatics, The
Elliott, Lorris 1931–1999 **37**
Elliott, Missy 1971— **31, 90**
Elliott, Sean 1968— **26**
Ellis, Alton 1938–2008 **74**
Ellis, Aunjanue 1969— **108**
Ellis, Charles H., III 1958(?)— **79**
Ellis, Clarence A. 1943— **38**
Ellis, Dock 1945–2008 **78**
Ellis, Hortense 1941–2000 **97**
Ellis, Jimmy 1940— **44**
Ellis, Jimmy, II See Trammps, The

Ellis, Larry R. 1946— **110**
Ellis, Monica See Imani Winds
Ellis, Nelsan 1981— **105**
Ellis, Trey 1962— **97**
Ellis-Lamkins, Phaedra 1976— **88**
Ellison, Keith 1963— **59**
Ellison, Ralph (Waldo) 1914–1994 **7**
Elmore, Ronn 1957— **21**
El-Shabazz, El-Hajj Malik See X, Malcolm
Emanuel, James A. 1921— **46**
Emeagwali, Dale 1954— **31**
Emeagwali, Philip 1954— **30**
Emecheta, Buchi 1944— **30**
Emmanuel, Alphonsia 1956— **38**
En Vogue **100**
English, Alvin See Contours, The
Ensley, Carol Denise See Nash, Niecy
Ephriam, Mablean 1949(?)— **29**
Epperson, Sharon 1969(?)— **54**
Epps, Archie C., III 1937–2003 **45**
Epps, Mike 1970— **60**
Epps, Omar 1973— **23, 59**
Epps, Tauheed See 2 Chainz
Equiano, Olaudah 1745(?)–1797 **78**
Ericsson-Jackson, Aprille 19(?)(?)— **28**
Ervin, Anthony 1981— **66**
Ervin, Booker 1930–1970 **106**
Ervin, Clark Kent 1959— **82**
Erving, Julius 1950— **18, 47**
Escobar, Damien 1987— **56**
Escobar, Tourie 1985— **56**
Esposito, Giancarlo (Giusseppi Alessandro) 1958— **9**
Espy, Alphonso Michael See Espy, Mike
Espy, Mike 1953— **6**
Estelle 1980— **75**
Esters, Monica Ann See Conyers, Monica
Estes, Rufus 1857–19(?)(?) **29**
Estes, Simon 1938— **28**
Estes, Sleepy John 1899–1977 **33**
Eto'o, Samuel 1981— **73**
Eubanks, Kevin 1957— **15, 108**
Eugene-Richard, Margie 1941— **63**
Europe, (William) James Reese 1880–1919 **10**
Evans, Darryl 1961— **22**
Evans, Diana 1972(?)— **72**
Evans, Ernest See Checker, Chubby
Evans, Etu 1969— **55**
Evans, Faith 1973(?)— **22**
Evans, Greene See Fisk Jubilee Singers
Evans, Harry 1956(?)— **25**
Evans, Mari 1923— **26**
Evans, Melvin H. 1917–1984 **88**
Evans, Warren C. 1948— **76**
Eve 1979— **29**
Everett, Carl 1971— **103**
Everett, Francine 1917–1999 **23**
Everett, Percival 1956— **93**
Everett, Ronald McKinley See Karenga, Maulana
Evers, Medgar (Riley) 1925–1963 **3**
Evers, Myrlie 1933— **8**
Évora, Cesária 1941–2011 **12, 99**
Evra, Patrice 1981— **102**

Ewing, Patrick 1962— **17, 73**
Eyadéma, Gnassingbé 1937–2005 **7, 52**
Fabio, Sarah Webster 1928–1979 **48**
Fabolous 1977— **93**
Fabre, Shelton 1963— **71**
Fagan, Garth 1940— **18, 98**
Fair, Leroy See Contours, The
Fair, Ronald L. 1932— **47**
Faison, Donald 1974— **50**
Faison, Frankie 1949— **55**
Faison, George William 1946— **16**
Falana, Lola 1942— **42**
Falconer, Etta Zuber 1933–2002 **59**
Fales-Hill, Susan 1962— **88**
Fanon, Frantz 1925–1961 **44**
Fantasia See Barrino, Fantasia
Farah, Mo 1983— **104**
Farah, Nuruddin 1945— **27**
Fargas, Antonio 1946(?)— **50**
Farley, Christopher John 1966— **54**
Farley, James Conway 1854–1910(?) **99**
Farmer, Art(hur Stewart) 1928–1999 **38**
Farmer, Forest J(ackson) 1941— **1**
Farmer, James 1920–1999 **2, 64**
Farmer-Paellmann, Deadria 1966— **43**
Farr, Mel 1944— **24**
Farrakhan, Louis 1933— **2, 15**
Farrell, Herman D., Jr. 1932— **81**
Farris, Isaac Newton, Jr. 1962— **63**
Fat Boys **92**
Father Goose See Rhoden, Wayne
Fattah, Chaka 1956— **11, 70, 112**
Faulk, Marshall 1973— **35, 96**
Fauntroy, Walter E(dward) 1933— **11**
Fauset, Crystal Dreda Bird 1893–1965 **100**
Fauset, Jessie (Redmon) 1882–1961 **7**
Favors, Steve 1948— **23**
Fax, Elton 1909–1993 **48**
Feaster, Robert Franklin See Sundiata, Sekou
Feelings, Muriel 1938— **44**
Feelings, Tom 1933–2003 **11, 47**
Feemster, Herbert 1942— **72**
Fela 1938–1997 **1, 42**
Felix, Allyson 1985— **48, 98**
Felix, Larry R. (?)— **64**
Felix Da Housecat 1971— **110**
Fennoy, Ilene 1947— **72**
Fenton, Kevin 1966(?)— **87**
Fenty, Adrian 1970— **60, 88**
Fenty, Robyn Rihanna See Rihanna
Ferbos, Lionel 1911— **95**
Ferdinand, Rio 1978— **82**
Ferguson, Amos 1920–2009 **81**
Ferguson, Kevin See Slice, Kimbo
Ferguson, Roger W., Jr. 1951— **25, 112**
Ferguson, Ronald F. 1950(?)— **75**
Ferguson, Vernice D. 1928–2012 **108**
Ferrell, Rachelle 1961— **29**
Ferrer, Ibrahim 1927— **41**
Fetchit, Stepin 1892–1985 **32**
Fiasco, Lupe 1982— **64**
Fielder, Cecil 1963— **2, 112**

Fielder, Prince 1984— **68**
Fields, C. Virginia 1946— **25**
Fields, Cleo 1962— **13**
Fields, Evelyn J. 1949— **27**
Fields, Felicia P. (?)— **60**
Fields, Julia 1938— **45**
Fields, Kim 1969— **36**
50 Cent 1976— **46, 83**
Figueroa, John J. 1920–1999 **40**
Files, Lolita 1964(?)— **35**
Fils-Aimé, Reggie 1961— **74**
Fine, Sam 1969— **60**
Finley, Ron 1978(?)— **110**
Finner-Williams, Paris Michele 1951— **62**
Fiona, Melanie 1983— **84**
Fishbone **101**
Fishburne, Larry See Fishburne, Laurence
Fishburne, Laurence 1961— **4, 22, 70**
Fisher, Ada Lois Sipuel 1924–1995 **76**
Fisher, Ada M. 1947— **76**
Fisher, Antwone Quenton 1959— **40**
Fisher, Derek 1974— **97**
Fisher, Gail 1935–2000 **85**
Fisher, George See Peters, Brock
Fisher, Miles Mark 1899–1970 **91**
Fisher, Rudolph John Chauncey 1897–1934 **17**
Fisher, Thelma See Dewitty, Thelma
Fisk Jubilee Singers **112**
Fitzgerald, Ella 1918–1996 **8, 18**
Five Blind Boys of Alabama, The See Blind Boys of Alabama, The
Five Keys, The **104**
Flack, Roberta 1940— **19**
Flake, Floyd H. 1945— **18, 110**
Flamingos, The **108**
Flanagan, Tommy 1930–2001 **69**
Flash, Grandmaster See Grandmaster Flash
Flavor Flav 1959— **67** See also Public Enemy
Fleming, Erik R. 1965— **75**
Fleming, Raymond 1945— **48**
Flemons, Dom See Carolina Chocolate Drops
Flemons, Wade See Earth, Wind & Fire
Fletcher, Alphonse, Jr. See Fletcher, Buddy
Fletcher, Arthur A. 1924–2005 **63**
Fletcher, Benjamin 1890–1949 **90**
Fletcher, Bill, Jr. 1954— **41**
Fletcher, Buddy 1965— **16, 108**
Fletcher, Geoffrey 1970— **85**
Flipper, Henry O(ssian) 1856–1940 **3**
Flo Rida 1979— **78**
Flood, Curt 1938–1997 **10, 93**
Florence, Kenneth Howard See Norton, Ken
Flowers, Sylester 1935— **50**
Flowers, Vonetta 1973— **35**
Floyd, Elson S. 1956— **41**
Folks, Byron See Allen, Byron
Forbes, Audrey Manley 1934— **16**
Forbes, Calvin 1945— **46**
Forbes, James A., Jr. 1935— **71**
Ford, Barney 1822–1902 **90**

Ford, Cheryl 1981— **45**

Ford, Clyde W. 1951— **40**

Ford, Harold E(ugene) 1945— **42**

Ford, Harold E(ugene), Jr. 1970—
16, 70

Ford, Jack 1947— **39**

Ford, James Lewis Carter See
Ford, T-Model

Ford, Johnny 1942— **70**

Ford, Nick Aaron 1904–1982 **44**

Ford, T-Model 1920(?)–2013 **91,
113**

Ford, Vincent 1940(?)–2008 **75**

Ford, Wallace 1950— **58**

Ford, Willie See Dramatics, The

Foreman, George 1948— **1, 15**

Forman, James 1928–2005 **7, 51**

Forman, James, Jr. 1967— **89**

Forna, Aminatta 1964— **95**

Forrest, Leon 1937–1997 **44**

Forrest, Vernon 1971–2009 **40, 79**

Forté, John 1975— **74**

Forte, Linda Diane 1952— **54**

Fortune, James 1977(?)— **92**

Fortune, T(imothy) Thomas
1856–1928 **6**

Foster, Andrew 1879–1930 **79**

Foster, Arian 1986— **114**

Foster, Cecil (A.) 1954— **32**

Foster, Ezola 1938— **28**

Foster, Frank 1928–2011 **97**

Foster, George "Pops" 1892–1969
40

Foster, Henry W., Jr. 1933— **26**

Foster, Jylla Moore 1954— **45**

Foster, Marie 1917–2003 **48**

Foster, Rube See Foster, Andrew

Foster, William P. 1919–2010 **88**

Four Tops, The See Benson, Obie

Fowler, Reggie 1959— **51**

Fowles, Gloria See Gaynor, Gloria

Fox, Donal 1952— **114**

Fox, John R. 1917–1944 **105**

Fox, Rick 1969— **27**

Fox, Ulrich Alexander See Fox,
Rick

Fox, Vivica A. **15, 53**

Foxx, Anthony 1971— **81**

Foxx, Jamie 1967— **15, 48**

Foxx, Redd 1922–1991 **2**

Foye, K'wan 19(?)(?)— **97**

Francis, Norman (C.) 1931— **60**

Francis, Thais 1980— **93**

Francois, Terry A. 1940–1989 **106**

Franklin, Aretha 1942— **11, 44, 115**

Franklin, C. L. 1915–1984 **68**

Franklin, Carl 1949— **11**

Franklin, Elmo See Mighty Clouds
of Joy

Franklin, Hardy R. 1929–2004 **9, 87**

Franklin, J. E. 1937— **44**

Franklin, John Hope 1915–2009 **5,
77**

Franklin, Kirk 1970— **15, 49, 97**

Franklin, Robert M(ichael) 1954—
13

Franklin, Shante Anthony See Cur-
ren$y

Franklin, Shirley 1945— **34, 80**

Franks, Gary 1954(?)— **2**

Franti, Michael 1966— **93**

Fraser, Sarah Loguen 1850–1933
100

Fraser, Shelly-Ann See Fraser-
Pryce, Shelly-Ann

Fraser-Pryce, Shelly-Ann 1986—
113

Frazer, Jendayi 196(?)— **68**

Frazer, Victor O. 1943— **98**

Frazier, Edward Franklin
1894–1962 **10**

Frazier, Joe 1944–2011 **19, 98**

Frazier, Kenneth 1954— **97**

Frazier, Kevin 1964— **58**

Frazier, Oscar 1956–2005 **58**

Frazier, Ryan 1977— **89**

Frazier, Walt 1945— **91**

Frazier-Lyde, Jacqui 1961— **31**

Fredericks, Henry Saint Claire See
Mahal, Taj

Freelon, Nnenna 1954— **32**

Freeman, Aaron 1956— **52**

Freeman, Al, Jr. 1934–2012 **11, 105**

Freeman, Albert Cornelius, Jr. See
Freeman, Al, Jr.

Freeman, Cathy 1973— **29**

Freeman, Charles Eldridge 1933—
19

Freeman, Harold P. 1933— **23**

Freeman, Leonard 1950— **27**

Freeman, Marianna 1957— **23**

Freeman, Morgan 1937— **2, 20,
62, 100**

Freeman, Paul 1936— **39**

Freeman, Von 1923–2012 **104**

Freeman, Yvette **27**

French, Albert 1943— **18**

French, D. M. 1924–2011 **94**

Fresh, Doug E. 1966— **93**

Fresh Prince, The See Smith, Will

Friday, Jeff 1964(?)— **24**

Fryer, Roland G. 1977— **56**

Fudge, Ann (Marie) 1951— **11, 55**

Fudge, Marcia L. 1952— **76**

Fuhr, Grant 1962— **1, 49**

Fulani, Lenora (Branch) 1950— **11**

Fuller, A. Oveta 1955— **43**

Fuller, Arthur 1972— **27**

Fuller, Blind Boy 1907(?)–1941 **86**

Fuller, Charles (Henry) 1939— **8**

Fuller, Curtis 1934— **115**

Fuller, Howard L. 1941— **37**

Fuller, Hoyt 1923–1981 **44**

Fuller, Meta Vaux Warrick
1877–1968 **27**

Fuller, S. B. 1895–1988 **13**

Fuller, Solomon Carter, Jr.
1872–1953 **15**

Fuller, Thomas O. 1867–1942 **90**

Fuller, Vivian 1954— **33**

Funches, Johnny See Dells, The

Funderburg, I. Owen 1924–2002 **38**

Funnye, Capers C., Jr. 1952(?)—
73

Fuqua, Antoine 1966— **35**

Fuqua, Charlie See Ink Spots, The

Fuqua, Harvey 1927–2010 **90** See
also Moonglows, The

Futch, Eddie 1911–2001 **33**

Future 1983— **109**

Gabre-Medhin, Tsegaye 1936–2006
64

Gabriel, Athelgra Neville See Dixie
Cups, The

Gaines, Brenda 19(?)(?)— **41**

Gaines, Clarence E., Sr.
1923–2005 **55**

Gaines, Ernest J(ames) 1933— **7**

Gaines, Grady 1934— **38**

Gaines, LaDonna Andrea See
Summer, Donna

Gaines, Lloyd 1911–19(?)(?) **79**

Gaines, Matthew 1840–1900 **95**

Gaines, Patrice 1950— **106**

Gairy, Eric Matthew 1922–1997 **83**

Gaiter, Dorothy J. 1950(?)— **80**

Gaither, Israel L. 1944— **65**

Gaither, Jake 1903–1994 **14**

Gamble, Kenny 1943— **85**

Gamble, Oscar 1949— **113**

Gans, Joe 1874–1910 **91**

Gant, Kenneth See Midnight Star

Gant, Richard 1944— **105**

Gantin, Bernardin 1922–2008 **70**

Gantt, Harvey (Bernard) 1943— **1**

Gap Band, The **100**

Garang, John 1945–2005 **105**

Gardere, Jeffrey 1956— **76**

Gardner, Carl See Coasters, The

Gardner, Chris 1954— **65**

Gardner, Edward G. 1925— **45**

Garland, Red 1923–1984 **115**

Garland, William M. See Garland,
Red

Garner, Erroll 1921–1977 **76**

Garner, Tyron 1967–2006 **99**

Garnet, Henry Highland 1815–1882
100

Garnett, Kevin (Maurice) 1976—
14, 70

Garrett, James F. 1942— **78**

Garrett, Joyce Finley 1931–1997 **59**

Garrett, Sean 1979— **57**

Garrincha See dos Santos, Manuel
Francisco

Garrison, Zina 1963— **2**

Gartin, Lydia See Diamond, Lydia
R.

Garvey, Marcus 1887–1940 **1**

Garvin, Gerry 1967(?)— **78**

Gary, Willie Edward 1947— **12**

Gaskins, Eric 1958— **64**

Gaskins, Rudy 1960(?)— **74**

Gaspard, Patrick 1967— **84**

Gaston, Arthur George 1892–1996
3, 38, 59

Gaston, Cito 1944— **71**

Gaston, Clarence Edwin See Gaston, Cito

Gaston, Marilyn Hughes 1939— **60**

Gates, Henry Louis, Jr. 1950— **3,
38, 67**

Gates, Pop See Gates, William

Gates, Rosalind See Brewer, Rosalind

Gates, Sylvester James, Jr. 1950—
15

Gates, William 1917–1999 **97**

Gay, Council See Contours, The

Gay, Marvin Pentz, Jr. See Gaye,
Marvin

Gay, Tyson 1982— **114**

Gaye, Marvin 1939–1984 **2**

Gaye, Nona 1974— **56**

Gayle, Addison, Jr. 1932–1991 **41**

Gayle, Helene D. 1955— **3, 46**

Gaynor, Gloria 1947— **36**

Gbagbo, Laurent 1945— **43, 90**

Gbowee, Leymah 1971(?)— **76**

Gebrselassie, Haile 1973— **70**

Gentry, Alvin 1954— **23**

Gentry, Melvin See Midnight Star

George, Eddie 1973— **80**

George, Nelson 1957— **12, 101**

George, Zelma Watson 1903–1994
42

Gerima, Haile 1946— **38, 80**

Gervin, George 1952— **80**

Geto Boys **115**

Ghostface Killah 1970— **90**

Gibbons, Gary 1956— **107**

Gibbs, Marla 1931— **86**

Gibbs, Mifflin W. 1823–1915 **99**

Gibson, Althea 1927–2003 **8, 43**

Gibson, Bob 1935— **33**

Gibson, Donald Bernard 1933— **40**

Gibson, John Trusty 1878–1937 **87**

Gibson, Johnnie Mae 1949— **23**

Gibson, Josh 1911–1947 **22**

Gibson, Kenneth Allen 1932— **6**

Gibson, Ted 1965— **66**

Gibson, Truman K., Jr. 1912–2005
60

Gibson, Tyrese 1978— **27, 62**

Gibson, William F(rank) 1933— **6**

Giddens, Rhiannon See Carolina
Chocolate Drops

Giddings, Paula (Jane) 1947— **11**

Gidron, Richard D. 1939–2007 **68**

Gil, Gilberto 1942— **53**

Gilbert, Christopher 1949— **50**

Gilbert, John Wesley 1864–1923 **91**

Giles, Cameron See Cam'ron

Giles, Roscoe C. 1890–1970 **93**

Gill, Gerald 1948–2007 **69**

Gill, Johnny 1966— **51** See also
New Edition

Gill, Turner 1962— **83**

Gilles, Ralph 1970— **61**

Gillespie, Dizzy 1917–1993 **1**

Gillespie, John Birks See Gillespie,
Dizzy

Gilliam, Frank 1934(?)— **23**

Gilliam, Joe, Jr. 1950–2000 **31**

Gilliam, Sam 1933— **16**

Gilliard, Steve 1964–2007 **69**

Gillis, Jesse, Jr. See Harold Melvin
& the Blue Notes

Gilmore, Artis 1949— **101**

Gilmore, Marshall 1931— **46**

Gilpin, Charles Sidney 1878–1930
81

Ginuwine 1975(?)— **35**

Ginyard, Caleb J. C. See Golden
Gate Quartet

Giovanni, Nikki 1943— **9, 39, 85**

Gist, Carole 1970(?)— **1**

Givens, Adele 19(?)(?)— **62**

Givens, Cliff See Billy Ward and the
Dominoes; Golden Gate Quartet

Givens, Robin 1964— **4, 25, 58**

Givhan, Robin Deneen 1964— **72**

Gladwell, Malcolm 1963— **62**

Glanville, Douglas Metunwa 1970—
82

Glasper, Robert 1978— **101**

Glass, Ron 1945— **111**

Gloster, Hugh Morris, Sr.
1911–2002 **90**

Glover, Cedric B. 1965— **103**

Glover, Corey 1964— **34**

Glover, Danny 1948— **1, 24, 103**

Glover, Donald 1983— **85**

Glover, Keith 1966— **79**
Glover, Nathaniel, Jr. 1943— **12**
Glover, Savion 1974— **14**
Gnassingbé, Faure 1966— **67**
Goapele 1977— **55**
"The Goat" *See Manigault, Earl "The Goat"*
Godbolt, James Titus *See Slyde, Jimmy*
Goines, Donald 1937(?)–1974 **19**
Goings, Russell 1932(?)— **59**
Goldberg, Whoopi 1955— **4, 33, 69**
Golden, Marita 1950— **19, 99**
Golden, Thelma 1965— **10, 55**
Golden Gate Quartet **104**
Golding, Bruce 1947— **78**
Goldsberry, Ronald 1942— **18**
Golson, Benny 1929— **37**
Golston, Allan C. 1967(?)— **55**
Gomes, Peter J. 1942–2011 **15, 93**
Gomez, Jewelle 1948— **30**
Gomez-Preston, Cheryl 1954— **9**
Gomillion, Charles 1900–1995 **90**
Goode, Mal(vin Russell) 1908–1995 **13**
Goode, W(oodrow) Wilson 1938— **4**
Gooden, Dwight 1964— **20**
Gooden, Linda 1953(?)— **94**
Gooden, Lolita *See Roxanne Shante*
Gooding, Cuba, Jr. 1968— **16, 62**
Goodison, Lorna 1947— **71**
Goodlett, Carlton B. 1914–1997 **91**
Goodman, Al 1943–2010 **87**
Goodman, Kim C. 1966— **94**
Goodnight, Paul 1946— **32**
Gorden, W. C. 1930— **71**
Gorden, William C. *See Gorden, W. C.*
Gordon, Billy *See Contours, The*
Gordon, Bruce S. 1946— **41, 53, 82**
Gordon, Carl 1932–2010 **87**
Gordon, Dexter 1923–1990 **25**
Gordon, Ed 1960— **10, 53**
Gordon, Pamela 1955— **17**
Gordone, Charles 1925–1995 **15**
Gordon-Reed, Annette 1958— **74**
Gordy, Berry, Jr. 1929— **1**
Goreed, Joseph *See Williams, Joe*
Goss, Carol A. 1947— **55**
Goss, Tom 1946— **23**
Gossett, Louis, Jr. 1936— **7**
Gotti, Irv 1971— **39**
Gourdin, Edward O. 1897–1966 **93**
Gourdine, Anthony *See Little Anthony & the Imperials*
Gourdine, Meredith 1929–1998 **33**
Gourdine, Simon (Peter) 1940— **11**
Graca, Marcelino Manuel da *See Grace, Sweet Daddy*
Grace, Charles Manuel *See Grace, Sweet Daddy*
Grace, George H. 1948— **48**
Grace, Sweet Daddy 1881–1960 **104**
Grae, Jean 1976— **51**
Graham, Aubrey Drake *See Drake*
Graham, Katerina 1989— **99**
Graham, Lawrence Otis 1962— **12**
Graham, Lorenz 1902–1989 **48**
Graham, Stedman 1951(?)— **13**

Graham, Trevor 1962(?)— **84**
Grandberry, Omari Ishmael *See Omarion*
Granderson, Curtis 1981— **66**
Granderson, LZ 1972— **103**
Grandmaster Flash 1958— **33, 60**
Grand-Pierre, Jean-Luc 1977— **46**
Granger, Lester B. 1896–1976 **75**
Grant, Augustus O. 1946(?)— **71**
Grant, Bernie 1944–2000 **57**
Grant, Frank 1865–1937 **100**
Grant, Gwendolyn Goldsby 19(?)(?)— **28**
Granville, Evelyn Boyd 1924— **36**
Gravely, Samuel L., Jr. 1922–2004 **5, 49**
Graves, Alexander *See Moonglows, The*
Graves, Butch 1962— **77**
Graves, Denyce Antoinette 1964— **19, 57**
Graves, Earl G(ilbert) 1935— **1, 35**
Graves, Earl Gilbert, Jr. *See Graves, Butch*
Gray, Darius 1945— **69**
Gray, Dobie 1940(?)–2011 **99**
Gray, F. Gary 1969— **14, 49**
Gray, Farrah 1984— **59**
Gray, Fred Sr. 1930— **37**
Gray, Frizzell *See Mfume, Kweisi*
Gray (Nelson Rollins), Ida 1867–1953 **41**
Gray, Macy 1970— **29**
Gray, Terius *See Juvenile*
Gray, Vincent C. 1942— **88**
Gray, William H., III 1941— **3**
Gray, Willie 1947— **46**
Gray, Yeshimbra "Shimmy" 1972— **55**
Greaves, R. B. 1943–2012 **106**
Greaves, William 1926— **38**
Greely, M. Gasby 1946— **27**
Greely, Margaret Gasby *See Greely, M. Gasby*
Green, A. C. 1963— **32**
Green, Al 1946— **13, 47, 74**
Green, Cee Lo 1974— **70, 103**
Green, Darrell 1960— **39, 74**
Green, Dennis 1949— **5, 45**
Green, Grant 1935–1979 **56**
Green, Isaac H. 1959— **79**
Green, Jerry *See Contours, The*
Green, Jonathan 1955— **54**
Green, Nancy 1834–1923 **112**
Greene, Frank S., Jr. 1938–2009 **101**
Greene, Jimmy 1975— **74**
Greene, Joe 1946— **10**
Greene, Maurice 1974— **27, 77**
Greene, Petey 1931–1984 **65**
Greene, Ralph Waldo *See Greene, Petey*
Greene, Richard Thaddeus, Sr. 1913–2006 **67**
Greene, Talib Kweli *See Kweli, Talib*
Greenfield, Eloise 1929— **9**
Greenfield, Ronnie Spector *See Spector, Ronnie*
Greenhouse, Bunnatine "Bunny" 1944— **57**
Greenlee, Sam 1930— **48**
Greenwood, L. C. 1946–2013 **115**
Greenwood, Monique 1959— **38**

Greer, Hal 1936— **92**
Gregg, Eric 1951— **16**
Gregory, Ann 1912–1990 **63**
Gregory, Dick 1932— **1, 54**
Gregory, Frederick 1941— **8, 51**
Gregory, Gerald *See Spaniels, The*
Gregory, Wilton 1947— **37**
Grier, Bobby 1933— **95**
Grier, David Alan 1955— **28**
Grier, Eliza Ann 1863(?)–1902 **90**
Grier, Mike 1975— **43**
Grier, Pam 1949— **9, 31, 86**
Grier, Roosevelt (Rosey) 1932— **13**
Griffey, Dick 1938–2010 **89**
Griffey, Ken, Jr. 1969— **12, 73**
Griffin, Angela 1976— **80**
Griffin, Anthony 1960— **71**
Griffin, Bessie Blout 1914— **43**
Griffin, Blake 1989— **98**
Griffin, John Arnold, III *See Griffin, Johnny*
Griffin, Johnny 1928–2008 **71**
Griffin, LaShell 1967— **51**
Griffin, Robert, III 1990— **107**
Griffith, Emile 1938–2013 **113**
Griffith, Mark Winston 1963— **8**
Griffith, Patrick A. 1944— **64**
Griffith, Yolanda 1970— **25**
Griffith-Joyner, Florence 1959–1998 **28**
Griffiths, Marcia 1948(?)— **29**
Grillo, Evelio 1919–2008 **95**
Grimké, Archibald H(enry) 1849–1930 **9**
Grist, Reri 1932— **84**
Groff, Peter 1963— **96**
Grooms, Henry R(andall) 1944— **50**
Guarionex *See Schomburg, Arthur Alfonso*
Guebuza, Armando 1943— **81**
Guéï, Robert 1941–2002 **66**
Guillaume, Robert 1927— **3, 48**
Güines, Tata 1930–2008 **69**
Guinier, (Carol) Lani 1950— **7, 30**
Gumbel, Bryant 1948— **14, 80**
Gumbel, Greg 1946— **8**
Gunn, Moses 1929–1993 **10**
Gurira, Danai 1978(?)— **73**
Guru 1961–2010 **84**
Guy, Billy *See Coasters, The*
Guy, (George) Buddy 1936— **31**
Guy, Jasmine 1964(?)— **2**
Guy, Rosa 1925(?)— **5**
Guyot, Lawrence 1939–2012 **108**
Guy-Sheftall, Beverly 1946— **13, 92**
Guyton, Tyree 1955— **9, 94**
Gwynn, Tony 1960— **18, 83**
Gyan, Asamoah 1985— **87**
Habré, Hissène 1942— **6, 104**
Habyarimana, Juvenal 1937–1994 **8**
Haddon, Dietrick 1973(?)— **55**
Hageman, Hans 19(?)(?)— **36**
Hageman, Ivan 19(?)(?)— **36**
Hagler, Marvelous Marvin 1954— **102**
Haile Selassie 1892–1975 **7**
Hailey, JoJo 1971— **22**
Hailey, K-Ci 1969— **22**
Hairston, Jester 1901–2000 **88**
Hairston, Sam 1920–1997 **88**

Haju, Gerard *See Malawi Mouse Boys*
Hale, Clara 1902–1992 **16**
Hale, Lorraine 1926(?)— **8**
Hale, Nathaniel Dawayne *See Nate Dogg*
Haley, Alex (Palmer) 1921–1992 **4**
Haley, George Williford Boyce 1925— **21**
Hall, Aaron 1963— **57**
Hall, Alvin D. 1952— **86**
Hall, Arsenio 1955— **58**
Hall, Arthur 1943–2000 **39**
Hall, Elliott S. 1938(?)— **24**
Hall, Juanita 1901–1968 **62**
Hall, Kevan 19(?)(?)— **61**
Hall, Lloyd A(ugustus) 1894–1971 **8**
Hall, Syren *See Fiona, Melanie*
Hall, Stuart 1932— **78**
Hall, Tamron 1970— **96**
Halliburton, Warren J. 1924— **49**
Hallim, Melanie Fiona *See Fiona, Melanie*
Ham, Cynthia Parker 1970(?)— **58**
Hamblin, Ken 1940— **10**
Hamburg, Beatrix 1923— **84**
Hamburg, Margaret 1955— **78**
Hamer, Fannie Lou (Townsend) 1917–1977 **6**
Hamilton, Anthony 1971— **61**
Hamilton, Leonard 1948— **100**
Hamilton, Lewis 1985— **66**
Hamilton, Lisa Gay 1964— **71**
Hamilton, Samuel C. 19(?)(?)— **47**
Hamilton, Tanya 1968— **93**
Hamilton, Vicki 1964(?)— **95**
Hamilton, Virginia 1936— **10**
Hamlin, Larry Leon 1948–2007 **49, 62**
Hammer, M. C. *See M.C. Hammer*
Hammond, Fred 1960— **23**
Hammond, Lenn 1970(?)— **34**
Hammonds, Evelynn 1953— **69**
Hammons, David 1943— **69**
Hampton, Fred 1948–1969 **18**
Hampton, Henry (Eugene, Jr.) 1940— **6**
Hampton, Lionel 1908(?)–2002 **17, 41**
Hancock, Herbie 1940— **20, 67**
Handy, W(illiam) C(hristopher) 1873–1937 **8**
Haney, Lee 1959— **77**
Hani, Chris 1942–1993 **6**
Hani, Martin Thembisile *See Hani, Chris*
Hannah, Marc (Regis) 1956— **10**
Hansberry, Lorraine (Vivian) 1930–1965 **6**
Hansberry, Tony, II 1994— **93**
Hansberry, William Leo 1894–1965 **11**
Hansen, Austin 1910–1996 **88**
Happy Land Jubilee Singers *See Blind Boys of Alabama, The*
Hardaway, Anfernee 1971— **13, 111**
Hardaway, Penny *See Hardaway, Anfernee*
Hardaway, Tim 1966— **35**
Harden, Monique 1968— **97**
Hardin Armstrong, Lil 1898–1971 **39**

Hardin, Lillian Beatrice *See Hardin Armstrong, Lil*

Harding, Vincent 1931— **67**

Hardison, Bethann 19(?)(?)— **12**

Hardison, Kadeem 1966— **22**

Hardy, Antonio *See Big Daddy Kane*

Hardy, Nell *See Carter, Nell*

Hare, Nathan 1934— **44**

Harewood, David 1965— **52**

Harewood, Dorian 1950— **104**

Harkless, Necia Desiree 1920— **19**

Harmon, Clarence 1940(?)— **26**

Harold, Erika 1980(?)— **54**

Harold Melvin & the Blue Notes **105**

Harper, Ben 1969— **34, 62**

Harper, Frances E(llen) W(atkins) 1825–1911 **11**

Harper, Frank *See Harper, Hill*

Harper, Hill 1966— **32, 65, 97**

Harper, Michael S. 1938— **34**

Harper, Rachel M. 1972— **92**

Harrell, Andre (O'Neal) 1962(?)— **9, 30**

Harrington, Carey Bell *See Bell, Carey*

Harrington, Oliver W(endell) 1912— **9**

Harris, Addie *See Shirelles, The*

Harris, Alice 1934— **7**

Harris, Barbara 1930— **12**

Harris, Barry 1929— **68**

Harris, Bernard A. 1956— **90**

Harris, Bill *See Clovers, The*

Harris, Bill 1941— **72**

Harris, Carla A. 1962— **67**

Harris, Ciara Princess *See Ciara*

Harris, Claire 1937— **34**

Harris, Corey 1969— **39, 73**

Harris, Damon 1950–2013 **110**

Harris, E. Lynn 1957— **12, 33**

Harris, Eddy L. 1956— **18**

Harris, Franco 1950— **97**

Harris, Gary L. 1953— **87**

Harris, James 1947— **79**

Harris, James, III *See Jimmy Jam*

Harris, Jay **19**

Harris, Jessica B. 1948— **91**

Harris, Kamala D. 1964— **64**

Harris, Leslie 1961— **6**

Harris, Lyle Ashton 1965— **83**

Harris, Major 1947–2012 **110**

Harris, Marcelite Jordon 1943— **16**

Harris, Mary Styles 1949— **31**

Harris, Maya Lakshmi 1966— **88**

Harris, Monica 1968— **18**

Harris, Naomie 1976— **55**

Harris, Otis Robert, Jr. *See Harris, Damon*

Harris, Patricia Roberts 1924–1985 **2**

Harris, Richard E. 1912(?)— **61**

Harris, Rhonda *See Vanzant, Iyanla*

Harris, Robin 1953–1990 **7**

Harris, Shack *See Harris, James*

Harris, Sherwin David *See Harris, Wood*

Harris, "Sweet" Alice *See Harris, Alice*

Harris, Sylvia 1967(?)— **70**

Harris, Wesley L. 1941— **92**

Harris, William Anthony *See Harris, Bill*

Harris, Wood 1969— **114**

Harris, Wynonie 1915(?)–1969 **102**

Harris-Lacewell, Melissa 1973— **81**

Harrison, Alvin 1974— **28**

Harrison, Calvin 1974— **28**

Harrison, Charles 1931— **72**

Harrison, Mya *See Mya*

Harris-Stewart, Lusia 1955— **90**

Harry, Jackée 1956— **111**

Harsh, Vivian Gordon 1890–1960 **14**

Hart, Alvin Youngblood 1963— **61**

Hart, Gregory Edward *See Hart, Alvin Youngblood*

Hart, Kevin 1980— **103**

Hart, Thomas A., Sr. 1919–2013 **113**

Hartman, Johnny 1923–1983 **109**

Harvard, Beverly (Joyce Bailey) 1950— **11**

Harvey, Steve 1956— **18, 58**

Harvey, William R. 1941— **42**

Haskins, Clem 1943— **23**

Haskins, James 1941–2005 **36, 54**

Hassell, Leroy Rountree, Sr. 1955— **41**

Hastie, William H(enry) 1904–1976 **8**

Hastings, Alcee Lamar 1936— **16**

Hatcher, Andrew T. 1923–1990 **90**

Hatcher, Richard G. 1933— **55**

Hatchett, Glenda 1951(?)— **32**

Hathaway, Donny 1945–1979 **18**

Hathaway, Isaac Scott 1874–1967 **33**

Hathaway, Lalah 1968— **57, 88**

Haughton, Aaliyah *See Aaliyah*

Havens, Richard Pierce *See Havens, Richie*

Havens, Richie 1941–2013 **111**

Hawkins, Adrienne Lita *See Kennedy, Adrienne*

Hawkins, Augustus F. 1907–2007 **68**

Hawkins, Barbara Ann *See Dixie Cups, The*

Hawkins, Coleman 1904–1969 **9**

Hawkins, Connie 1942— **91**

Hawkins, Edwin 1943— **113**

Hawkins, Erskine Ramsey 1914–1993 **14**

Hawkins, Jamesetta *See James, Etta*

Hawkins, La-Van 1960— **17, 54**

Hawkins, Rosa Lee *See Dixie Cups, The*

Hawkins, "Screamin'" Jay 1929–2000 **30**

Hawkins, Steven Wayne 1962— **14**

Hawkins, Tramaine Aunzola 1951— **16**

Hawkins, Walter 1949–2010 **87**

Hayden, Carla D. 1952— **47**

Hayden, Lewis 1811–1889 **105**

Hayden, Palmer 1890–1973 **13**

Hayden, Robert Earl 1913–1980 **12**

Haye, David 1980— **82**

Hayes, Bob 1942–2002 **77**

Hayes, Cecil N. 1945— **46**

Hayes, Dennis 1951— **54**

Hayes, Elvin 1945— **93**

Hayes, Isaac 1942–2008 **20, 58, 73**

Hayes, James C. 1946— **10**

Hayes, Robert Lee *See Hayes, Bob*

Hayes, Roland 1887–1977 **4**

Hayes, Teddy 1951— **40**

Haygood, Wil 1954— **83**

Haynes, Cornell, Jr. *See Nelly*

Haynes, Elizabeth Ross 1883–1953 **102**

Haynes, George Edmund 1880–1960 **8**

Haynes, Marques 1926— **22**

Haynes, Roy 1925— **87**

Haynes, Trudy 1926— **44**

Haynie, Sharon 1955— **94**

Haysbert, Dennis 1954— **42, 106**

Haysbert, Raymond V., Sr. 1920–2010 **87**

Haywood, Gar Anthony 1954— **43**

Haywood, Jimmy 1993(?)— **58**

Haywood, Margaret A. 1912— **24**

Haywood, Spencer 1949— **99**

Hazel, Darryl B. 1949— **50**

Hazzard, Walt 1942–2011 **98**

Head, Bessie 1937–1986 **28**

Healy, James Augustine 1830–1900 **30**

Healy, Michael 1839–1904 **90**

Heard, Gar 1948— **25**

Heard, Nathan C. 1936–2004 **45**

Hearne, John Edgar Caulwell 1926–1994 **45**

Hearns, Thomas 1958— **29**

Heath, Percy 1923–2005 **100**

Heavy D 1967–2011 **58, 98**

Hector, Jamie 1975— **98**

Hedgeman, Anna Arnold 1899–1990 **22**

Hedgeman, Peyton Cole *See Hayden, Palmer*

Height, Dorothy I. 1912— **2, 23, 78**

Hemingway, Anthony 1977— **107**

Hemphill, Essex 1957— **10**

Hemphill, Jessie Mae 1923–2006 **33, 59**

Hemsley, Sherman 1938–2012 **19, 104**

Henderson, Cornelius Langston 1888(?)–1976 **26**

Henderson, David 1942— **53**

Henderson, Fletcher 1897–1952 **32**

Henderson, George Washington 1850–1936 **101**

Henderson, Gordon 1957— **5**

Henderson, Henry Fairfax, Jr. 1928— **89**

Henderson, Jeff 1964— **72**

Henderson, Natalie Leota *See Hinderas, Natalie*

Henderson, Rickey 1958— **28, 78**

Henderson, Stephen E. 1925–1997 **45**

Henderson, Thelton E. 1933— **68**

Henderson, Wade 1944(?)— **14**

Henderson, Zelma 1920–2008 **71**

Hendricks, Barbara 1948— **3, 67**

Hendrix, James Marshall *See Hendrix, Jimi*

Hendrix, Jimi 1942–1970 **10**

Hendrix, Johnny Allen *See Hendrix, Jimi*

Hendryx, Nona 1944— **56**

Hendy, Francis 195(?)— **47**

Henries, A. Doris Banks 1913–1981 **44**

Henriques, Julian 1955(?)— **37**

Henry, Aaron Edd 1922–1997 **19**

Henry, Clarence "Frogman" 1937— **46**

Henry, Dwight 1963— **104**

Henry, Joshua 1994— **94**

Henry, Lenny 1958— **9, 52**

Henry, Marianne *See Marian Anderson String Quartet*

Henry, Richard Bullock *See Obadele, Imari*

Henry, Thierry 1977— **66**

Henry, Troy 1960(?)— **85**

Henson, Darrin 1970(?)— **33**

Henson, Josiah 1789–1883 **90**

Henson, Matthew (Alexander) 1866–1955 **2**

Henson, Taraji P. 1970— **58, 77**

Herbert, Bob 1945— **63, 96**

Hercules, Frank 1911–1996 **44**

Herenton, Willie W. 1940— **24, 81**

Herman, Alexis Margaret 1947— **15**

Hernandez, Aileen Clarke 1926— **13**

Hernández, Orlando 1965— **96**

Herndon, Alonzo Franklin 1858–1927 **89**

Herndon, Angelo 1913–1997 **90**

Hernton, Calvin C. 1932–2001 **51**

Hibbert, Frederick Nathaniel *See Hibbert, Toots*

Hibbert, Toots 1946— **103**

Hickman, Fred(erick Douglass) 1951— **11**

Hicks, Ulysses *See Five Keys, The*

Hicks Maynard, Nancy *See Maynard, Nancy Hicks*

Higginbotham, A(loysius) Leon, Jr. 1928–1998 **13, 25**

Higginbotham, Jack *See Higginbotham, Jay C.*

Higginbotham, Jay C. 1906–1973 **37**

Higginsen, Vy 1945(?)— **65**

Hightower, Dennis F(owler) 1941— **13**

Hill, Andrew 1931–2007 **66**

Hill, Anita 1956— **5, 65**

Hill, Beatrice *See Moore, Melba*

Hill, Bonnie Guiton 1941— **20**

Hill, Calvin 1947— **19**

Hill, Donna 1955— **32**

Hill, Dulé 1975(?)— **29**

Hill, Errol 1921— **40**

Hill, Grant 1972— **13, 94**

Hill, Hugh Morgan 1921–2009 **83**

Hill, Janet 1947— **19**

Hill, Jemele 1975— **109**

Hill, Jesse, Jr. 1927— **13**

Hill, Lauryn 1975— **20, 53, 111**

Hill, Leslie Pinckney 1880–1960 **44**

Hill, Marc Lamont 1978— **80**

Hill, Michael 1971— **95**

Hill, Oliver W. 1907–2007 **24, 63**

Hill, Peter 1767–1829 **92**

Hill, Tamia *See Tamia*

Hill, Wyllstyne D. 1949(?)— **94**

Hillard, Terry 1954— **25**

Hillary, Barbara 1923(?)— **65**

Hilliard, Asa Grant, III 1933–2007 **66**

Hilliard, David 1942— **7, 105**

Hilliard, Earl F. 1942— **24**

Hilliard, Wendy 196(?)— **53**

Hilson, Keri 1982— **84**
Himes, Chester 1909–1984 **8**
Hinderas, Natalie 1927–1987 **5**
Hine, Darlene Clark 1947— **24**
Hines, Earl "Fatha" 1905–1983 **39**
Hines, Garrett 1969— **35**
Hines, Gregory (Oliver) 1946–2003 **1, 42**
Hinton, Milt 1910–2000 **30**
Hinton, William Augustus 1883–1959 **8**
Hoagland, Everett H. 1942— **45**
Hoagland, Jaheim See Jaheim
Hobson, Julius W. 1919–1977 **44**
Hobson, Mellody 1969— **40**
Hodge, Derrick 1979— **114**
Hogan, Beverly Wade 1951— **50**
Hoggs, Billy See Contours, The
Holder, Eric, Jr. 1951— **9, 76, 104**
Holder, Geoffrey 1930— **78**
Holder, Laurence 1939— **34**
Holdsclaw, Chamique 1977— **24, 110**
Holiday, Billie 1915–1959 **1**
Holiday, Jrue 1990— **115**
Holland, Brian See Holland-Dozier-Holland
Holland, Eddie See Holland-Dozier-Holland
Holland, Endesha Ida Mae 1944–2006 **3, 57**
Holland, Kimberly N. 19(?)(?)— **62**
Holland, Robert, Jr. 1940— **11**
Holland-Dozier-Holland **36**
Holloway, Brenda 1946— **65**
Holloway, Loleatta 1946–2011 **115**
Hollowell, Donald L. 1917–2004 **57**
Holmes, Amy 1973— **69**
Holmes, Benjamin See Fisk Jubilee Singers
Holmes, Clint 1946— **57**
Holmes, De'Angelo See Ying Yang Twins
Holmes, Hamilton E. 1941–1995 **82**
Holmes, Kelly 1970— **47**
Holmes, Larry 1949— **20, 68**
Holmes, Loutelious Ann, Jr. See Holmes, T. J.
Holmes, Santonio 1984— **87**
Holmes, Shannon 1973(?)— **70**
Holmes, T. J. 1977— **98**
Holness, Andrew 1972— **99**
Holsey, Lucius Henry 1842–1920 **92**
Holstein, Casper 1876–1944 **89**
Holt, Lester 1959— **66**
Holt, Morris See Magic Slim
Holt, Nora 1885(?)–1974 **38**
Holt Baker, Arlene 1951— **73**
Holte, Patricia Louise See LaBelle, Patti
Holton, DeShaun Dupree See Proof
Holton, Hugh, Jr. 1947–2001 **39**
Holyfield, Evander 1962— **6**
Honeywood, Varnette P. 1950–2010 **54, 88**
Honoré, Russel L. 1947— **64**
Hood, James Walker 1831–1918 **91**
Hooker, John Lee 1917–2000 **30**
hooks, bell 1952— **5, 90**
Hooks, Benjamin L. 1925–2010 **2, 85**
Hooks, Robert 1937— **76**

Hope, John 1868–1936 **8**
Hope, Lugenia Burns 1871–1947 **89**
Hopgood, Hadda See Brooks, Hadda
Hopkins, Bernard 1965— **35, 69, 105**
Hopkins, Donald R. 1941— **89**
Hopkins, Lightnin' 1912–1982 **83**
Hopkins, Sam See Hopkins, Lightnin'
Horford, Al 1988— **107**
Horford Reynoso, Alfred Joel See Horford, Al
Horn, Shirley 1934–2005 **32, 56**
Horne, Frank 1899–1974 **44**
Horne, Lena 1917–2010 **5, 86**
Horsford, Steven 1973— **88**
Horton, Andre 1979— **33**
Horton, Big Walter 1918(?)–1981 **115**
Horton, Gladys 1945–2011 **92**
Horton, James Oliver 1943— **58**
Horton, (Andreana) Suki 1982— **33**
Horton, Walter See Horton, Big Walter
Horton, Willie 1942— **104**
Hoskins, Harold K. 1927–2012 **103**
Houghton, Israel 1971— **92**
Hounsou, Djimon 1964— **19, 45**
Houphouët, Dia See Houphouët-Boigny, Félix
Houphouët-Boigny, Félix 1905–1993 **4, 64**
House, Eddie James, Jr. See House, Son
House, Eugene See House, Son
House, Son 1902–1988 **8**
Houston, Charles Hamilton 1895–1950 **4**
Houston, Cissy 1933— **20, 83**
Houston, Whitney 1963–2012 **7, 28, 83, 100**
Howard, Ayanna 1972— **65**
Howard, Corinne See Mitchell, Corinne
Howard, Desmond 1970— **16, 58**
Howard, Dwight 1985— **113**
Howard, Juwan Antonio 1973— **15**
Howard, M. William, Jr. 1946— **26**
Howard, Michelle 1960— **28**
Howard, Perry Wilbon, Jr. 1877–1961 **112**
Howard, Ryan 1979— **65, 113**
Howard, Sherri 1962— **36**
Howard, Terrence 1969— **59, 94**
Howard, William See Dramatics, The
Howell, Ayinde 1978— **91**
Howlin' Wolf 1910–1976 **9**
Howroyd, Janice Bryant 1953— **42**
Hoyte, Lenon 1905–1999 **50**
Hrabowski, Freeman A., III 1950— **22**
Hubbard, Arnette 19(?)(?)— **38**
Hubbard, Freddie 1948–2008 **75**
Hubbard, Frederick DeWayne See Hubbard, Freddie
Huddleston, William Emanuel See Lateef, Yusef
Hudlin, Reginald 1961— **9, 86**
Hudlin, Warrington, Jr. 1953(?)— **9**
Hudson, Cheryl 19(?)(?)— **15**
Hudson, Ernie 1945— **72**

Hudson, James See Spaniels, The
Hudson, Jennifer 1981— **63, 83**
Hudson, Saul See Slash
Hudson, Wade 1946— **15**
Huff, Leon 1942— **86**
Huggins, Edie 1935–2008 **71**
Huggins, Larry 1950— **21**
Huggins, Nathan Irvin 1927–1989 **52**
Hughes, Albert 1972— **7**
Hughes, Allen 1972— **7**
Hughes, Cathy 1947(?)— **27**
Hughes, Dora 1970(?)— **88**
Hughes, Ebony 1948— **57**
Hughes, (James Mercer) Langston 1902–1967 **4**
Hughes, Leon See Coasters, The
Hughley, D. L. 1963— **23, 76**
Hughley, Darryl Lynn See Hughley, D. L.
Hull, Akasha Gloria 1944— **45**
Humphrey, Bobbi 1950— **20**
Humphries, Frederick 1935— **20**
Hunt, Darnell 1962— **92**
Hunt, Richard (Howard) 1935— **6**
Hunter, Alberta 1895–1984 **42**
Hunter, Billy 1942— **22, 109**
Hunter, Charlayne See Hunter-Gault, Charlayne
Hunter, Clementine 1887–1988 **45**
Hunter, George William See Hunter, Billy
Hunter, Ivory Joe 1914–1974 **106**
Hunter, Lindsey 1970— **110**
Hunter, Torii 1975— **43, 109**
Hunter-Gault, Charlayne 1942— **6, 31**
Hurston, Zora Neale 1891–1960 **3**
Hurt, Byron 1970— **61**
Hurt, Mississippi John 1892(?)–1966 **84**
Hurtt, Harold 1947(?)— **46**
Hussein, Lubna 1970(?)— **80**
Hutch, Willie 1944–2005 **62**
Hutcherson, Bobby 1941— **115**
Hutcherson, Hilda Yvonne 1955— **54**
Hutchinson, Earl Ofari 1945— **24**
Hutson, Jean Blackwell 1914— **16**
Hyde, Cowan F. "Bubba" 1908–2003 **47**
Hyman, Earle 1926— **25, 79**
Hyman, Phyllis 1949(?)–1995 **19**
Ibrahim, Fuad 1991— **109**
Ibrahim, Ibee See Ibrahim, Fuad
Ibrahim, Mo 1946— **67, 115**
Ice Cube 1969— **8, 30, 60**
Iceberg Slim 1918–1992 **11**
Ice-T 1958— **6, 31, 96**
Ifill, Gwen 1955— **28**
Iginla, Jarome 1977— **35**
Ilibagiza, Immaculée 1972(?)— **66**
Iman 1955— **4, 33, 87**
Iman, Chanel 1989— **66**
Imani Winds **113**
Imes, Elmer Samuel 1883–1941 **39**
Ince, Paul 1967— **83**
India.Arie 1975— **34**
Ingraham, Hubert A. 1947— **19**
Ingram, James 1952— **84**
Ingram, Raphael See Five Keys, The
Ingram, Rex 1895–1969 **5**

Ingram, Ripley See Five Keys, The
Ink Spots, The **102**
Innis, Roy (Emile Alfredo) 1934— **5**
Irvin, Michael 1966— **64**
Irvin, (Monford Merrill) Monte 1919— **31**
Irvin, Vernon 1961— **65**
Irving, Barrington, Jr. 1983— **112**
Irving, Clarence (Larry) 1955— **12**
Irving, Kyrie 1992— **102**
Irvis, K. Leroy 1917(?)–2006 **67**
Isaac, Julius 1928— **34**
Isaacs, Cheryl Boone 1949— **113**
Isaacs, Gregory 1951–2010 **89**
Isaacs, John 1915–2009 **76**
Isles, Bill See O'Jays, The
Isley, Marvin 1953–2010 **87**
Isley, Ronald 1941— **25, 56**
Issoufou, Mahamadou 1952— **102**
Iverson, Allen 1975— **24, 46**
Iverson, Johnathan Lee 1976— **22, 100**
Ivey, Artis, Jr. See Coolio
Ivey, Phil 1976— **72, 106**
J Dilla 1974–2006 **102**
Ja Rule 1976— **35, 91**
Jackée See Harry, Jackée
Jackson, Alexine Clement 1936— **22**
Jackson, Alphonso R. 1946— **48**
Jackson, Brenda 1953— **87**
Jackson, Deborah 1952— **94**
Jackson, Earl 1948— **31**
Jackson, Edison O. 1943(?)— **67**
Jackson, Eric, Jr. See Ying Yang Twins
Jackson, Frank G. 1946— **76**
Jackson, Fred James 1950— **25**
Jackson, George 1960(?)— **19**
Jackson, George Lester 1941–1971 **14**
Jackson, Hal 1915–2012 **41, 104**
Jackson, Henry Melody, Jr. See Armstrong, Henry
Jackson, Isaiah (Allen) 1945— **3**
Jackson, Jackie See Jackson 5
Jackson, Jamea 1986— **64**
Jackson, James A. 1878–1960 **90**
Jackson, James Curtis, III See 50 Cent
Jackson, Janet 1966— **6, 30, 68**
Jackson, Jennie See Fisk Jubilee Singers
Jackson, Jermaine 1954— **79** See also Jackson 5
Jackson, Jesse 1941— **1, 27, 72**
Jackson, Jesse, Jr. 1965— **14, 45, 81, 108**
Jackson, Joe 1929— **78**
Jackson, John 1924–2002 **36**
Jackson, John David See Fabolous
Jackson, Judith D. 1950— **57**
Jackson, LaToya 1956— **95**
Jackson, Lisa 1962— **77**
Jackson, Mae 1941–2005 **57**
Jackson, Mahalia 1911–1972 **5**
Jackson, Marlon See Jackson 5
Jackson, Mannie 1939— **14**
Jackson, Mary 1945— **73**
Jackson, Maynard 1938–2003 **2, 41**
Jackson, Michael 1958–2009 **19, 53, 76** See also Jackson 5
Jackson, Millie 1944— **25**

Jackson, Milt 1923–1999 **26**

Jackson, O'Shea *See Ice Cube*

Jackson, Otis, Jr. *See Madlib*

Jackson, Phillip 1950— **115**

Jackson, Quinton *See Jackson, Rampage*

Jackson, Rampage 1978— **83**

Jackson, Randy 1956— **40**

Jackson, Reginald Martinez 1946— **15**

Jackson, Rickey 1958— **88**

Jackson, Samuel L. 1948— **8, 19, 63, 102**

Jackson, Sandi 1963— **108**

Jackson, Sheneska 1970(?)— **18**

Jackson, Shirley Ann 1946— **12**

Jackson, Tito 1953— **81** *See also Jackson 5*

Jackson, Tom 1951— **70**

Jackson, Vera 1912— **40**

Jackson, Vivian *See Yabby You*

Jackson, Willie *See Spaniels, The*

Jackson, Zelda Mavin *See Ormes, Jackie*

Jackson 5 **103**

Jackson Lee, Sheila 1950— **20**

Jaco, Wasalu Muhammad *See Fiasco, Lupe*

Jacob, John E(dward) 1934— **2**

Jacobs, Harriet 1813–1897 **104**

Jacobs, Marion Walter *See Little Walter*

Jacobs, Regina 1963— **38**

Jacquet, Illinois 1922(?)–2004 **49**

Jagan, Cheddi 1918–1997 **16**

Jaheim 1978— **58**

Jakes, Thomas "T.D." 1957— **17, 43**

Jam, Jimmy *See Jimmy Jam*

Jam Master Jay *See Run-DMC*

Jamal, Ahmad 1930— **69**

Jamelia 1981— **51**

Jamerson, James 1936–1983 **59**

James, Charles H., III 1959(?)— **62**

James, Daniel "Chappie," Jr. 1920–1978 **16**

James, David 1970— **84**

James, Donna A. 1957— **51**

James, Elmo *See James, Elmore*

James, Elmore 1918–1963 **114**

James, Etta 1938–2012 **13, 52, 100**

James, G. Larry 1947–2008 **74**

James, Juanita (Therese) 1952— **13**

James, LeBron 1984— **46, 78, 105**

James, Marlon 1970— **85**

James, Nikki M. 1981— **94**

James, Sharpe 1936— **23, 69**

James, Skip 1902–1969 **38**

James, Sly 1951— **107**

James, Sylvester, Jr. *See James, Sly*

James, Vanessa 1987— **84**

James Bracken and Vivian Bracken **107**

Jamison, Judith 1943— **7, 67, 96**

Jammeh, Yahya 1965— **23, 104**

Jansen, Jonathan 1956— **102**

Jarreau, Al 1940— **21, 65, 105**

Jarreau, Alwyn Lopez *See Jarreau, Al*

Jarrett, Valerie 1956— **73**

Jarrett, Vernon D. 1921— **42**

Jarvis, Charlene Drew 1941— **21**

Jarvis, Erich 1965— **67**

Jarvis, Kristen 1981(?)— **85**

Jasper, John J. 1812–1901 **91**

Jasper, Kenji 1976(?)— **39**

Jawara, Dawda Kairaba 1924— **11**

Jawara, Jali Musa *See Diawara, Djeli Moussa*

Jay-Z 1969— **27, 69, 103**

Jealous, Benjamin Todd 1973— **70, 113**

Jean, Michaëlle 1957— **70**

Jean, Wyclef 1970— **20, 86**

Jean-Baptiste, Marianne 1967— **17, 46**

Jean-Juste, Gérard 1946–2009 **78**

Jean-Louis, Jimmy 1968— **76**

Jeffers, Eve Jihan *See Eve*

Jefferson, Blind Lemon 1893(?)–1929 **81**

Jefferson, Denise 1944–2010 **87**

Jefferson, Margo 1947— **108**

Jefferson, Mildred Fay 1927–2010 **89**

Jefferson, William J. 1947— **25, 72**

Jeffries, Leonard 1937— **8**

Jemison, Mae C. 1957— **1, 35**

Jemison, Major L. 1955(?)— **48**

Jenifer, Franklyn G(reen) 1939— **2**

Jenkins, Beverly 1951— **14**

Jenkins, Ella (Louise) 1924— **15**

Jenkins, Fergie 1943— **46**

Jenkins, Hubby *See Carolina Chocolate Drops*

Jenkins, Jay *See Young Jeezy*

Jenkins, Kris 1979— **98**

Jenkins, Ray 1920–2009 **77**

Jenkins, Terrence *See Terrence J*

Jennings, Chester *See Jennings, Lyfe*

Jennings, Lyfe 1973— **56, 69**

Jerkins, Rodney 1978(?)— **31**

Jesu, Kunjoya Mwa *See Malawi Mouse Boys*

Jeter, Claude 1914–2009 **75** *See also Swan Silvertones*

Jeter, Derek 1974— **27, 93**

Jeune, Vitolio 1982— **98**

Jim, Songezo 1990— **111**

Jimmy Jam 1959— **13**

Joachim, Paulin 1931— **34**

Joe, Yolanda 19(?)(?)— **21**

John, Daymond 1969— **23, 114**

Johns, Vernon 1892–1965 **38**

Johnson, Angela 1961— **52**

Johnson, Anthony M. 1954— **92**

Johnson, Arnez *See Arnez J*

Johnson, Avery 1965— **62**

Johnson, Ben 1961— **1**

Johnson, Beverly 1952— **2, 102**

Johnson, Buddy 1915–1977 **36**

Johnson, Bumpy 1905(?)–1968 **102**

Johnson, Calvin 1985— **108**

Johnson, Camará DaCosta *See DaCosta, YaYa*

Johnson, Carol Diann *See Carroll, Diahann*

Johnson, Caryn E. *See Goldberg, Whoopi*

Johnson, Chad 1978— **108**

Johnson, Charles 1948— **1, 82**

Johnson, Charles Arthur *See St. Jacques, Raymond*

Johnson, Charles Spurgeon 1893–1956 **12**

Johnson, Chris 1985— **92**

Johnson, Clarence *See Chi-Lites*

Johnson, Clark 1954— **96**

Johnson, Clifford "Connie" 1922–2004 **52**

Johnson, Conrad O. 1915–2008 **97**

Johnson, Dennis 1954–2007 **89**

Johnson, Donald Ray *See Taste of Honey, A*

Johnson, Dwayne *See Rock, The*

Johnson, Earvin *See Johnson, Magic*

Johnson, Eddie Bernice 1935— **8, 90**

Johnson, Edward Austin 1860–1944 **107**

Johnson, Ellsworth Raymond *See Johnson, Bumpy*

Johnson, Eunice W. 1916–2010 **83**

Johnson, Fenton 1888–1958 **91**

Johnson, George E. 1927— **29**

Johnson, Georgia Douglas 1880–1966 **41**

Johnson, Gus 1938–1987 **92**

Johnson, Hall 1888–1970 **90**

Johnson, Hank, Jr. 1954— **80**

Johnson, Harry E. 1954— **57**

Johnson, Harvey, Jr. 1947(?)— **24, 82**

Johnson, Hazel 1927— **22**

Johnson, Hubert *See Contours, The*

Johnson, J. J. 1924–2001 **37**

Johnson, Jack 1878–1946 **8**

Johnson, James Louis *See Johnson, J. J.*

Johnson, James Weldon 1871–1938 **5**

Johnson, James William *See Johnson, James Weldon*

Johnson, Janice Marie *See Taste of Honey, A*

Johnson, Je'Caryous 1977— **63**

Johnson, Jeh C. 1957— **76**

Johnson, Jeh Vincent 1931— **44**

Johnson, Joan Marie *See Dixie Cups, The*

Johnson, Joe *See Golden Gate Quartet*

Johnson, Joe 1981— **94**

Johnson, John Arthur *See Johnson, Jack*

Johnson, John H. 1918–2005 **3, 54**

Johnson, John Henry 1929–2011 **96**

Johnson, Johnnie 1924–2005 **56**

Johnson, Judy 1899–1989 **105**

Johnson, Katherine (Coleman Goble) 1918— **61**

Johnson, Ken 1914–1941 **106**

Johnson, Kevin 1966— **70**

Johnson, Keyshawn 1972— **91**

Johnson, Larry 1969— **28**

Johnson, Le'Andria 1983— **108**

Johnson, Leroy R. 1928— **89**

Johnson, Levi 1950— **48**

Johnson, Linton Kwesi 1952— **37**

Johnson, Lonnie 1899(?)–1970 **85**

Johnson, Lonnie G. 1949— **32, 93**

Johnson, Louis *See Swan Silvertones, The*

Johnson, Magic 1959— **3, 39, 101**

Johnson, Mamie "Peanut" 1932— **40**

Johnson, Marguerite *See Angelou, Maya*

Johnson, Mat 1970— **31, 105**

Johnson, Michael (Duane) 1967— **13**

Johnson, Michelle *See Ndegeocello, Meshell*

Johnson, Mordecai Wyatt 1890–1976 **79**

Johnson, Norma H. 1932–2011 **17, 97**

Johnson, R. M. 1968— **36**

Johnson, Rafer 1934— **33**

Johnson, Robert 1911–1938 **2**

Johnson, Robert L. 1946(?)— **3, 39**

Johnson, Robert T. 1948— **17**

Johnson, Rodney Van 19(?)(?)— **28**

Johnson, Sandra K. 1960(?)— **94**

Johnson, Sheila Crump 1949(?)— **48**

Johnson, Shoshana 1973— **47**

Johnson, Syl 1938— **97**

Johnson, Syleena 1977— **98**

Johnson, Taalib *See Musiq*

Johnson, Tommy 1896–1956 **106**

Johnson, Virginia (Alma Fairfax) 1950— **9**

Johnson, William 1809–1851 **91**

Johnson, William Henry 1901–1970 **3**

Johnson, William Julius *See Johnson, Judy*

Johnson, Willie *See Golden Gate Quartet*

Johnson, Woodrow Wilson *See Johnson, Buddy*

Johnson, Wycliffe *See Steely*

Johnson-Brown, Hazel W. *See Johnson, Hazel*

Johnson-George, Tamara 1971— **79**

Johnson-Powell, Gloria 1937— **107**

Joiner, Alvin Nathaniel *See Xzibit*

Joiner, Charlie 1947— **102**

Jolley, Willie 1956— **28**

Jonathan, Goodluck 1957— **83**

Jones, Absalom 1746–1818 **52**

Jones, Adam 1983— **103**

Jones, Adam 1985— **114**

Jones, Alex 1941— **64**

Jones, Andruw 1977— **98**

Jones, Anthony *See Jones, Van*

Jones, Bill T. 1952— **1, 46, 80**

Jones, Bob *See Jones, Robert G.*

Jones, Bobby 1938— **20, 94**

Jones, Booker T. 1944— **84**

Jones, Carl 1955(?)— **7**

Jones, Caroline R. 1942— **29**

Jones, Clara Stanton 1913–2012 **51**

Jones, Clarence B. 1931— **114**

Jones, Cobi N'Gai 1970— **18**

Jones, Creadel *See Chi-Lites*

Jones, Cullen 1984— **73**

Jones, Daron *See 112*

Jones, David D. *See Jones, Deacon*

Jones, Deacon 1938–2013 **92, 112**

Jones, Donell 1973— **29**

Jones, Doris W. 1914(?)–2006 **62**

Jones, E. Edward, Sr. 1931— **45**

Jones, Ed "Too Tall" 1951— **46**
Jones, Edith Mae Irby 1927— **65**
Jones, Edward P. 1950— **43, 67**
Jones, Elaine R. 1944— **7, 45**
Jones, Elvin 1927–2004 **14, 68**
Jones, Emil, Jr. 1935— **74**
Jones, Etta 1928–2001 **35**
Jones, Eugene Kinckle 1885–1954 **79**
Jones, Frederick McKinley 1893–1961 **68**
Jones, Frederick Russell See Jamal, Ahmad
Jones, Gayl 1949— **37**
Jones, Genevieve 1975(?)— **101**
Jones, Hank 1918–2010 **57, 86**
Jones, Ingrid Saunders 1945— **18**
Jones, James Earl 1931— **3, 49, 79**
Jones, James Yancy See Tail Dragger
Jones, Jo See Jones, Papa Jo
Jones, John 1816–1879 **89**
Jones, Jonah 1909–2000 **39**
Jones, Jonathan David Samuel See Jones, Papa Jo
Jones, K. C. 1932— **83**
Jones, Kelis See Kelis
Jones, Kimberly Denise See Lil' Kim
Jones, Kirk See Sticky Fingaz
Jones, Le Roi See Baraka, Amiri
Jones, Lillie Mae See Carter, Betty
Jones, Lois Mailou 1905— **13**
Jones, Lou 1932–2006 **64**
Jones, Marion 1975— **21, 66**
Jones, Merlakia 1973— **34**
Jones, Monty 1951(?)— **66**
Jones, Nasir bin Olu Dara See Nas
Jones, Ollie See Ravens, The
Jones, Orlando 1968— **30**
Jones, Orville See Ink Spots, The
Jones, Papa Jo 1911–1985 **99**
Jones, Paul R. 1928— **76**
Jones, Quincy (Delight) 1933— **8, 30**
Jones, Randy 1969— **35**
Jones, Rashida 1976— **101**
Jones, Robert Elijah 1872–1960 **90**
Jones, Robert Elliott See Jones, Jonah
Jones, Robert G. 1936–2008 **81**
Jones, Robbie 1977— **113**
Jones, Roy Jr. 1969— **22**
Jones, Russell See Ol' Dirty Bastard
Jones, Ruth Lee See Washington, Dinah
Jones, Sam 1933— **85**
Jones, Sarah 1974— **39**
Jones, Sharon 1955(?)— **86**
Jones, Sissieretta See Joyner, Matilda Sissieretta
Jones, Star See Reynolds, Star Jones
Jones, Tayari 1970— **96**
Jones, Thad 1923–1986 **68**
Jones, Theodore T., Jr. 1944–2012 **108**
Jones, Thomas W. 1949— **41**
Jones, Van 1968— **70**
Jones, Wayne 1952— **53**

Jones, William A., Jr. 1934–2006 **61**
Jones-Drew, Maurice 1985— **113**
Joplin, Scott 1868–1917 **6**
Jordan, Barbara 1936–1996 **4, 78**
Jordan, Deloris 1941— **108**
Jordan, Eddie 1952— **82**
Jordan, Eddie 1955— **83**
Jordan, Eric Benét See Benét, Eric
Jordan, June 1936— **7, 35**
Jordan, Louis 1908–1975 **104**
Jordan, Michael 1963— **6, 21**
Jordan, Michael B. 1987— **97**
Jordan, Montell 1968(?)— **23**
Jordan, Ronny 1962— **26**
Jordan, Vernon E(ulion, Jr.) 1935— **3, 35**
Jorge, Seu 1970— **73**
Joseph, Edward See Joseph, Jamal
Joseph, Jamal 1953— **101**
Joseph, Kathie-Ann 1970(?)— **56**
Josey, E. J. 1924— **10**
Joyce, Dru 1955— **81**
Joyner, Jacqueline See Joyner-Kersee, Jackie
Joyner, Marjorie Stewart 1896–1994 **26**
Joyner, Matilda Sissieretta 1869(?)–1933 **15**
Joyner, Tom 1949(?)— **19, 90**
Joyner-Kersee, Jackie 1962— **5**
Julian, Hubert 1897–1983 **90**
Julian, Percy Lavon 1899–1975 **6**
Julien, Isaac 1960— **3**
July, William, II 19(?)(?)— **27**
Juma, Calestous 1953— **57**
Junior, Marvin See Dells, The
Just, Ernest Everett 1883–1941 **3**
Justice, David Christopher 1966— **18**
Juvenile 1975— **96**
Ka Dinizulu, Israel See Ka Dinizulu, Mcwayizeni
Ka Dinizulu, Mcwayizeni 1932–1999 **29**
Kabbah, Ahmad Tejan 1932— **23**
Kabera, Eric 1970— **104**
Kabila, Joseph 1968(?)— **30**
Kabila, Laurent 1939— **20**
Kachinwe, Zondiwe See Malawi Mouse Boys
Kagame, Paul 1957— **54**
Kahlil, Aisha See Sweet Honey in the Rock
Kaigler, Denise 1962— **63**
Kaine See Ying Yang Twins
Kaiser, Cecil 1916–2011 **42**
Kalbani, Adil 1959(?)— **77**
Kamau, Johnstone See Kenyatta, Jomo
Kamau, Kwadwo Agymah 1960(?)— **28**
Kandi 1976— **83**
Kane, Evander 1991— **97**
Kani, Karl 1968(?)— **10**
Kanouté, Fred 1977— **68**
Karenga, Maulana 1941— **10, 71**
Karim, Benjamin 1932–2005 **61**
Kariuki, J. M. 1929–1975 **67**
Kassahun, Tewodros See Afro, Teddy
Kato, David 1964–2011 **103**
Katoucha See Niane, Katoucha

Kaufman, Bob 1925–1986 **105**
Kaufman, Monica 1948(?)— **66**
Kaufman, Robert Garnell See Kaufman, Bob
Kaunda, Kenneth (David) 1924— **2**
Kay, Connie 1927–1994 **114**
Kay, Jackie 1961— **37**
Kay, Ulysses 1917–1995 **37**
Kayira, Legson 1942— **40**
Kearney, Beverly 1958— **109**
Kearney, Janis 1953— **54**
Kearse, Amalya Lyle 1937— **12**
Kebede, Liya 1978— **59**
Keckley, Elizabeth 1818–1907 **90**
Kee, John P. 1962— **43**
Keene, John 1965— **73**
Keflezighi, Meb 1975— **49**
Keïta, Ibrahim Boubacar 1945— **113**
Keita, Salif 1949— **83**
Keith, Damon J. 1922— **16, 74**
Keith, Floyd A. 1948— **61**
Keith, Michael See **112**
Keith, Rachel Boone 1924–2007 **63**
Kelis 1979— **58**
Kelley, Cliff 1941— **75**
Kelley, Elijah 1986— **65**
Kelley, Malcolm David 1992— **59**
Kellogg, Clark 1961— **64**
Kelly, Chris See Mac Daddy
Kelly, Jim 1946–2013 **113**
Kelly, Leontine 1920— **33**
Kelly, Patrick 1954(?)–1990 **3**
Kelly, R. 1967— **18, 44, 71**
Kelly, Robert Sylvester See Kelly, R.
Kelly, Robin 1956— **114**
Kelly, Sharon Pratt See Dixon, Sharon Pratt
Kelly, Winzell See Dramatics, The
Kem 196(?)— **47**
Kemp, Herb 1941–2011 **94**
Kendrick, Erika 1975— **57**
Kendricks, Eddie 1939–1992 **22**
Kennard, William Earl 1957— **18**
Kennedy, Adrienne 1931— **11**
Kennedy, Cortez 1968— **104**
Kennedy, Florynce Rae 1916–2000 **12, 33**
Kennedy, Lelia McWilliams Robinson 1885–1931 **14**
Kennedy, Randall 1954— **40**
Kennedy-Overton, Jayne Harris 1951— **46**
Kenner-Jackson, Doris See Shirelles, The
Kenney, John A., Jr. 1914–2003 **48**
Kenoly, Ron 1944— **45**
Kente, Gibson 1932–2004 **52**
Kenyatta, Jomo 1891(?)–1978 **5**
Kenyatta, Robin 1942–2004 **54**
Kenyatta, Uhuru 1961— **110**
Kerekou, Ahmed (Mathieu) 1933— **1**
Kerry, Leon G. 1949(?)— **46**
Key, Keegan-Michael See Key & Peele
Key & Peele **107**
Keyes, Alan 1950— **11, 105**
Keys, Alicia 1981— **32, 68**
Kgositsile, Thebe Neruda See Sweatshirt, Earl
Khalifa, Wiz 1987— **96**

Khama, Ian 1953— **95**
Khan, Chaka 1953— **12, 50**
Khanga, Yelena 1962— **6**
Khumalo, Leleti 1970— **51**
Kibaki, Mwai 1931— **60**
Kibble, Joey See Take 6
Kibble, Mark See Take 6
Kid Cudi 1984— **83**
Kidd, Jason 1973— **86**
Kidd, Mae Street 1904–1995 **39**
Kidjo, Angelique 1960— **50**
Kiir, Salva Mayardit 1951— **85, 103**
Kikwete, Jakaya Mrisho 1950— **73**
Killens, John O. 1967–1987 **54**
Killings, Debra 196(?)— **57**
Killingsworth, Cleve, Jr. 1952— **54**
Kilpatrick, Carolyn Cheeks 1945— **16**
Kilpatrick, Kwame 1970— **34, 71**
Kimble, Perry See Taste of Honey, A
Kimbro, Dennis (Paul) 1950— **10**
Kimbro, Henry A. 1912–1999 **25**
Kimbro, Warren 1934–2009 **76**
Kincaid, Bernard 1945— **28**
Kincaid, Jamaica 1949— **4, 109**
Kinch, Soweto 1978— **108**
King, Alonzo 19(?)(?)— **38**
King, B. B. 1925— **7**
King, Barbara 19(?)(?)— **22**
King, Bernice 1963— **4, 81**
King, Colbert I. 1939— **69**
King, Coretta Scott 1927–2006 **3, 57**
King, Dexter (Scott) 1961— **10**
King, Don 1931— **14**
King, Freddie 1934–1976 **92**
King, Gayle 1954— **19, 99**
King, Martin Luther, III 1957— **20**
King, Martin Luther, Jr. 1929–1968 **1**
King, Martin Luther, Sr. 1899–1984 **89**
King, Oona 1967— **27**
King, Preston 1936— **28**
King, Reatha Clark 1938— **65**
King, Regina 1971— **22, 45**
King, Riley B. See King, B. B.
King, Robert Arthur 1945— **58**
King, Robert Hillary 1942— **84**
King, Rodney 1965–2012 **103**
King, Teresa 1961— **80**
King, Woodie Jr. 1937— **27**
King, Yolanda (Denise) 1955— **6**
King Curtis 1934–1971 **92**
Kingston, Sean 1990— **94**
Kintaudi, Leon 1949(?)— **62**
Kintaudi, Ngoma Miezi See Kintaudi, Leon
Kiprotich, Wilson Kipsang See Kipsang, Wilson
Kipsang, Wilson 1982— **115**
Kirby, George 1924–1995 **14**
Kirk, Clara 1941— **95**
Kirk, Ron 1954— **11, 75, 111**
Kirkland, Eddie 1923–2011 **99**
Kirnan, Conrad Henry See Kay, Connie
Kisekka, Samson 1912–1999 **112**
Kisule, David Kato See Kato, David
Kitt, Eartha 1927–2008 **16, 75**
Kitt, Sandra 1947— **23**
Kittles, Rick 1976(?)— **51**

Kitwana, Bakari 19(?)(?)— 86
Klugh, Earl 1953— 59
K'naan 1978— 76
Knight, Etheridge 1931–1991 37
Knight, Gladys 1944— 16, 66
Knight, Gwendolyn 1913–2005 63
Knight, Marie 1925(?)–2009 80
Knight, Marion Hugh, Jr. See
Knight, Suge
Knight, Suge 1965— 11, 30, 102
Knowles, Beyoncé See Beyoncé
Knowles, Mathew 1952— 96
Knowles, Solange See Solange
Knowles, Tina 1954(?)— 61
Knowling, Robert Jr. 1955(?)— 38
Knox, Simmie 1935— 49
Knuckles, Frankie 1955— 42 See
also Roots, The
Kobia, Samuel 1947— 43
Kodjoe, Boris 1973— 34, 89
Kolosoy, Wendo 1925–2008 73
Komunyakaa, Yusef 1941— 9
Kone, Seydou See Blondy, Alpha
Kong, B. Waine 1943— 50
Kony, Joseph 1961(?)— 101
Kool DJ Red Alert See Alert, Kool
DJ Red
Kool Moe Dee 1963— 37
Kool Rock Ski See Fat Boys
Koontz, Elizabeth Duncan
1919–1989 101
Koroma, Ernest Bai 1953— 84
Kotto, Yaphet (Fredrick) 1944— 7
Kountz, Samuel L(ee) 1930–1981
10
Kravitz, Lenny 1964— 10, 34
Kravitz, Leonard See Kravitz,
Lenny
Krigger, Kevin 1983— 111
KRS-One 1965— 34
Krute, Fred See Alert, Kool DJ Red
K-Swift 1978–2008 73
Kufuor, John Agyekum 1938— 54,
82
Kunjufu, Jawanza 1953— 3, 50
Kuti, Fela Anikulapo See Fela
Kuti, Femi 1962— 47, 110
Kuzwayo, Ellen 1914–2006 68
Kwei-Armah, Kwame 1967— 84
Kweli, Talib 1975— 93
Kyenge, Cécile 1964— 113
Kyles, Cedric Antonio See Cedric
the Entertainer
La Menthe, Ferdinand Joseph See
Morton, Jelly Roll
La Roca, Pete 1938–2012 107
La Salle, Eriq 1962— 12
LaBelle, Patti 1944— 13, 30
LaChanze 1961— 93
Lacks, Henrietta 1921–1951 101
Lacy, Marc 1969— 111
Lacy, Sam 1903–2003 30, 46
Lacy, Walter Marcellus See Lacy,
Marc
Ladd, Ernie 1938–2007 64
Ladner, Joyce A. 1943— 42
Ladysmith Black Mambazo 103
Laferriere, Dany 1953— 33
Lafontant, Jewel Stradford
1922–1997 3, 51
Lafontant-MANkarious, Jewel
Stradford See Lafontant, Jewel
Stradford

LaGuma, Alex 1925–1985 30
Lamar, Jake 1961— 96
Lamar, Kendrick 1987— 105
Lamming, George 1927— 35
Lamont, William Joseph See Billy
Ward and the Dominoes
Lampkin, Daisy 1883(?)–1965 19
Lampley, Oni Faida 1959–2008 43,
71
Lampley, Vera See Lampley, Oni
Faida
Lancaster, Byard 1942–2012 105
Lance, Major 1939–1994 111
Lane, Charles 1953— 3
Lane, Dick 1927–2002 92
Lane, Lunsford 1803–18(?)(?) 93
Lane, Vincent 1942— 5
Lane, William Henry
1825(?)–1852(?) 90
Langford, Larry P. 1948— 74
Langford, William See Golden Gate
Quartet
Langhart Cohen, Janet 1941— 19,
60
Langston, John Mercer 1829–1897
101
Lanier, Bob 1948— 47
Lanier, Willie 1945— 33
Lankford, Raymond Lewis 1967—
23
Laraque, Georges 1976— 48
Laraque, Paul 1920–2007 67
Larkin, Barry 1964— 24
Laroche, Joseph Philippe Lemercier
1889–1912 85
Larrieux, Amel 1973(?)— 63
Lars, Byron 1965— 32
Larsen, Nella 1891–1964 10
Laryea, Thomas Davies, III 1979—
67
LaSalle, Denise 1939— 111
Lashley, Bobby 1976— 63
Lashley, Franklin Roberto See
Lashley, Bobby
Lassiter, Roy 1969— 24
Lateef, Yusef 1920— 91
Lathan, Sanaa 1971— 27
Latimer, Lewis H(oward)
1848–1928 4
Lattany, Kristin Hunter 1931–2008
88
Lattimore, Kenny 1970(?)— 35
LaVette, Bettye 1946— 85
Lavizzo-Mourey, Risa 1954— 48
Lawal, Kase L. 19(?)(?)— 45
Lawless, Theodore K(enneth)
1892–1971 8
Lawrence, Diedra See Marian
Anderson String Quartet
Lawrence, Donald 1958— 99
Lawrence, Jacob (Armstead)
1917–2000 4, 28
Lawrence, Margaret Morgan
1914— 100
Lawrence, Martin 1965— 6, 27, 60
Lawrence, Robert Henry, Jr.
1935–1967 16
Lawrence-Lightfoot, Sara 1944—
10
Laws, Hubert 1939— 90
Lawson, James M., Jr. 1928— 90
Lawson, Jennifer 1946— 1, 50
Laymon, Kiese 197(?)— 113
Layton, William 1915–2007 87

Leadbelly 1885–1949 82
Leakes, NeNe 1967— 107
Leary, Kathryn D. 1952— 10
Leavell, Dorothy R. 1944— 17
Lebo M 1964— 109
Lecrae 1979— 108
Ledbetter, Hudson William See
Leadbelly
Ledisi 197(?)— 73
Lee, Annie Frances 1935— 22
Lee, Barbara 1946— 25, 102
Lee, Bertram M., Sr. 1939–2003 46
Lee, Beverly See Shirelles, The
Lee, Canada 1907–1952 8
Lee, Consuela 1926–2009 84
Lee, Debra L. 1954— 62
Lee, Don Luther See Madhubuti,
Haki R.
Lee, Eric P. 1958— 79
Lee, Gabby See Lincoln, Abbey
Lee, Jarena 1783–1855(?) 100
Lee, Joe A. 1946(?)— 45
Lee, Joie 1962(?)— 1
Lee, Leslie 1935— 85
Lee, Malcolm D. 1970— 75
Lee, Raphael C. 1949— 87
Lee, Robert 1920–2010 112
Lee, Shelton Jackson See Lee,
Spike
Lee, Spike 1957— 5, 19, 86
Lee-Smith, Hughie 1915— 5, 22
Leevy, Carrol M. 1920— 42
Lefel, Edith 1963–2003 41
Leffall, Lasalle, Jr. 1930— 3, 64
LeFlore, Lyah Beth 1970— 96
Legend, John 1978— 67
Legendary Orioles, The See Ori-
oles, The
Leggs, Kingsley 196(?)— 62
Leland, George Thomas See Le-
land, Mickey
Leland, Mickey 1944–1989 2
Lemmons, Kasi 1961— 20
Lemon, Alton T. 1928–2013 112
Lemon, Don 1966— 94
Lennox, Betty 1976— 31
LeNoire, Rosetta 1911–2002 37
Lenox, Adriane 1956— 59
Leon, Kenny 1956— 10, 98
León, Tania 1943— 13
Leonard, Buck 1907— 67
Leonard, Sugar Ray 1956— 15
Leonard, Walter Fenner See Leor-
nard, Buck
Leônidas 1913–2004 96
Leslie, Lisa 1972— 16, 73
Lester, Adrian 1968— 46
Lester, Bill 1961— 42, 85
Lester, Bobby See Moonglows, The
Lester, Julius 1939— 9, 115
Lester, Robert See Chi-Lites
Lesure, James 1975— 64
LeTang, Henry 1915–2007 66
Letson, Al 1972— 39
Levert, Eddie 1942— 70 See also
O'Jays, The
Levert, Gerald 1966–2006 22, 59
Levi, Moses See Shyne
Lewis, Amisho Baraka See Baraka,
Sho
Lewis, Aylwin B. 1954— 51, 88
Lewis, Butch 1946–2011 71, 99
Lewis, Byron E(ugene) 1931— 13

Lewis, Carl 1961— 4, 97
Lewis, Daurene 194(?)— 72
Lewis, David Levering 1936— 9
Lewis, Delano (Eugene) 1938— 7
Lewis, Denise 1972— 33
Lewis, Earl See Flamingos, The
Lewis, (Mary) Edmonia
1845(?)–1911(?) 10
Lewis, Edward T. 1940— 21
Lewis, Emmanuel 1971— 36
Lewis, Frederick Carlton See
Lewis, Carl
Lewis, George 1952— 104
Lewis, Henry 1932–1996 38
Lewis, Jamal 1979— 115
Lewis, John 1940— 2, 46, 83
Lewis, Lennox 1965— 27
Lewis, Leona 1985— 75
Lewis, Marvin 1958— 51, 87
Lewis, Norman 1909–1979 39
Lewis, Oliver 1856–1924 56
Lewis, Ramsey 1935— 35, 70
Lewis, Ray 1975— 33, 109
Lewis, Reginald F. 1942–1993 6
Lewis, Ronald See Lewis, Butch
Lewis, Samella 1924— 25
Lewis, Shirley Ann Redd 1937— 14
Lewis, Terry 1956— 13
Lewis, Thomas 1939— 19
Lewis, William Henry 1868–1949
89
Lewis, William M., Jr. 1956— 40
Lewis-Hall, Freda 1955(?)— 105
Lewis-Thornton, Rae 1962— 32
Ligging, Alfred, III 1965— 43
Lighty, Chris 1968–2012 105
Lighty, Darrell Steven See Lighty,
Chris
Ligon, Glenn 1960— 82
Ligon, Joe See Mighty Clouds of
Joy
Lil' Bow Wow See Bow Wow
Lil' Kim 1975— 28
Lil' Romeo See Romeo
Lil Wayne 1982— 66, 84
Lilakoi Moon See Bonet, Lisa
Liles, Kevin 1968— 42, 99
Lincoln, Abbey 1930–2010 3, 88
Lincoln, C(harles) Eric 1924–2000
38
Lindo, Allen Pineda See apl.de.ap
Lindo, Delroy 1952— 18, 45
Lindsay, Peta 1984— 100
Lindsey, Tommie 1951— 51
Lipscomb, Belinda See Midnight
Star
Lipscomb, Mance 1895–1976 49
LisaRaye 1967— 27
Lister, Marquita 1965(?) 65
Liston, (Charles) Sonny
1928(?)–1970 33
Little, Benilde 1958— 21
Little, Booker 1938–1961 105
Little, Floyd 1942— 86
Little, Larry 1945— 90
Little, Malcolm See X, Malcolm
Little, Robert L(angdon) 1938— 2
Little Anthony See Little Anthony &
the Imperials
Little Anthony & the Imperials 107
Little Milton 1934–2005 36, 54
Little Richard 1932— 15
Little Walter 1930–1968 36

Little Warrior See Barrow, Willie T.
Littlepage, Craig 1951— 35
LL Cool J 1968— 16, 49, 94
Llewellyn, J. Bruce 1927–2010 13, 85
Lloyd 1986— 99
Lloyd, Christopher See Banks, Lloyd
Lloyd, Earl 1928(?)— 26
Lloyd, John Henry "Pop" 1884–1965 30
Lloyd, Reginald 1967— 64
Locke, Alain 1886–1954 10
Locke, Attica 1974— 85
Locke, Eddie 1930— 44
Lofton, James 1956— 42
Lofton, Kenneth 1967— 12
Lofton, Ramona See Sapphire
Logan, Onnie Lee 1910(?)–1995 14
Logan, Rayford W. 1897–1982 40
Loguen, J. W. 1813–1872 91
Lomax, Louis E. 1922–1970 90
Lomax, Michael L. 1947— 58
London, Theophilus 1987— 95
Long, Eddie L. 1953— 29, 89
Long, Huey 1904–2009 79
Long, Loretta 1940— 58
Long, Nia 1970— 17, 95
Long, Richard Alexander 1927— 65
Loper, Ramon See Five Keys, The
Lopes, Davey 1945— 92
Lopes, Leila 1986— 99
Lopes, Lisa 1971–2002 36 See also TLC
Lord, Tracy See Little Anthony & the Imperials
Lord Kitchener 1922–2000 110
Lord Pitt of Hampstead See Pitt, David Thomas
Lorde, Audre (Geraldine) 1934–1992 6
Lorenzo, Irving See Gotti, Irv
Loroupe, Tegla 1973— 59
Lott, Ronnie 1959— 9
Loueke, Lionel 1973(?)— 88
Louis, Errol T. 1962— 8
Louis, Joe 1914–1981 5
Louis, Willie 1937–2013 113
Loury, Glenn 1948— 36
Love, Darlene 1941— 23, 92
Love, Ed 1932(?)— 58
Love, Laura 1960— 50
Love, Loni 1971— 113
Love, Mia 1975— 96
Love, Nat 1854–1921 9
Love, Reggie 1982— 77
Lovelace, Bobby See Midnight Star
Lovell, Whitfield 1959— 74
Lover, Ed 10
Loving, Alvin, Jr., 1935–2005 35, 53
Loving, Mildred 1939–2008 69
Lowe, Herbert 1962— 57
Lowe, Sidney 1960— 64
Lowery, Evelyn Gibson 1925–2013 115
Lowery, Joseph E. 1924— 2
Lowery, Myron 1946(?)— 80
Lowry, A. Leon 1913–2005 60
Lubanga, Thomas 1960— 104
Lucas, Bill 1936–1979 97
Lucas, Harold See Clovers, The
Lucas, John 1953— 7

Lucas, William DeVaughn See Lucas, Bill
Lucie, Lawrence 1907–2009 80
Lucien, Jon 1942–2007 66
Luckett, Letoya 1981— 61
Lucy, William 1933— 50
Lucy Foster, Autherine 1929— 35
Ludacris, 1978— 37, 60
Lufeyo, Jameson See Malawi Mouse Boys
Luke, Derek 1974— 61
Lumbly, Carl 1952— 47
Lumet, Jenny 1967— 80
Lumpkin, Elgin Baylor See Ginuwine
Lumumba, Patrice 1925–1961 33
Luna, Donyale 1946–1979 88
Luper, Clara 1923–2011 94
Lushington, Augustus Nathaniel 1869–1939 56
Luter, Fred, Jr. 1956— 103
Luthuli, Albert (John Mvumbi) 1898(?)–1967 13
Lyfe See Jennings, Lyfe
Lyle, Marcenia See Stone, Toni
Lyles, Lester Lawrence 1946— 31
Lymon, Frankie 1942–1968 22
Lynch, Bill See Lynch, William, Jr
Lynch, Loretta E. 1959— 103
Lynch, Shola 1969— 61
Lynch, William, Jr. 1941–2013 115
Lynn, Lonnie Rashid, Jr. See Common
Lynne, Gloria 1929(?)–2013 115
Lyons, Henry 1942(?)— 12
Lyons, James E., Sr. 1944(?)— 102
Lyttle, Hulda Margaret 1889–1983 14
Maal, Baaba 1953— 66
Maathai, Wangari 1940–2011 43, 97
Mabior, John Garang de See Garang, John
Mabley, Jackie "Moms" 1897(?)–1975 15
Mabrey, Vicki 1957(?)— 26
Mabry, Marcus 1967— 70
Mabuza, Lindiwe 1938— 18
Mabuza-Suttle, Felicia 1950— 43
Mac, Bernie 1957–2008 29, 61, 72
Mac Daddy 1978–2013 111
Maceo, Antonio 1845–1896 82
Machado de Assis 1839–1908 74
Machaka, Yvonne See Chaka Chaka, Yvonne
Machel, Graça 1945— 16, 102
Machel, Samora Moises 1933–1986 8
Mack, Iris 1955(?)— 105
Mack, Tony 1966— 104
Mackey, Biz 1897–1965 82
Mackey, Nathaniel 1947— 75
Mackie, Anthony 1979— 102
Madame Sul-Te-Wan 1873–1959 95
Madhubuti, Haki R. 1942— 7, 85
Madikizela-Mandela, Winnie 1934— 2, 35, 112
Madison, Joseph E. 1949— 17
Madison, Paula 1952— 37, 99
Madison, Romell 1952— 45
Madlib 1973— 88
Magan, Ayaan Hirsi See Ali, Ayaan Hirsi

Magic Slim 1937–2013 110
Magloire, Paul Eugène 1907–2001 68
Mahal, Taj 1942— 39
Mahama, John Dramani 1958— 103
Mahlasela, Vusi 1965— 65
Mahorn, Rick 1958— 60
Maillard, Carol See Sweet Honey in the Rock
Mainor, Dorothy Leigh 1910(?)–1996 19
Maitreya, Sananda 1962— 85
Majette, Denise 1955— 41
Major, Clarence 1936— 9
Majors, Jeff 1960(?)— 41
Makeba, Miriam 1932–2008 2, 50, 74
Malawi Mouse Boys 114
Malco, Romany 1968— 71
Malcolm X See X, Malcolm
Malema, Julius 1981— 98
Mallett, Conrad, Jr. 1953— 16
Mallory, Mark 1962— 62
Malone, Annie (Minerva Turnbo Pope) 1869–1957 13
Malone, Karl 1963— 18, 51, 90
Malone, Maurice 1965— 32
Malone, Moses 1955— 79
Malone Jones, Vivian 1942–2005 59
Malonga, Eric Moussambani See Moussambani, Eric
Malphurs, Juaquin James See Waka Flocka Flame
Malveaux, Floyd 1940— 54
Malveaux, Julianne 1953— 32, 70
Malveaux, Suzanne 1966— 88
Mandela, Nelson 1918— 1, 14, 77
Mandela, Winnie See Madikizela-Mandela, Winnie
Mane, Gucci 1980— 91
Manigat, Mirlande 1940— 90
Manigault, Earl "The Goat" 1943— 15
Manigault, Omarosa See Omarosa
Manigault-Stallworth, Omarosa See Omarosa
Manley, Audrey Forbes 1934— 16
Manley, Edna 1900–1987 26
Manley, Ruth 1947— 34
Mann, Tamela 1966— 92
Manning, Frankie 1914–2009 78
Manning, Marva Ann See Whitney, Marva
Manson, John See Swan Silvertones, The
Manuel, Jerry 1953— 94
Maponya, Maishe 1951— 101
Maponya, Richard 1926— 101
Marable, Manning 1950–2011 10, 102
March, William Carrington 1923–2002 56
Marchand, Inga See Foxy Brown
Marcille, Eva 1984— 97
Marechera, Charles William See Marechera, Dambudzo
Marechera, Dambudzo 1952–1987 39
Marechera, Tambudzai See Marechera, Dambudzo
Marian Anderson String Quartet 111
Mariner, Jonathan 1954(?)— 41

Marino, Eugene Antonio 1934–2000 30
Mario 1986— 71
Markham, Dewey See Markham, Pigmeat
Markham, E(dward) A(rchibald) 1939— 37
Markham, Pigmeat 1904–1981 106
Marks, Audrey 19(?)(?)— 99
Marle, Milton See Billy Ward and the Dominoes
Marley, Bob 1945–1981 5
Marley, David See Marley, Ziggy
Marley, Rita 1947— 32, 70
Marley, Robert Nesta See Marley, Bob
Marley, Stephen 1972— 100
Marley, Ziggy 1968— 41
Marrow, Queen Esther 1943(?)— 24
Marrow, Tracy See Ice-T
Marsalis, Branford 1960— 34, 103
Marsalis, Delfeayo 1965— 41
Marsalis, Ellis 1934— 90
Marsalis, Wynton 1961— 16, 90
Marsh, Henry L., III 1934(?)— 32
Marshall, Bella 1950— 22
Marshall, Gloria See Sudarkasa, Niara
Marshall, Kerry James 1955— 59
Marshall, Paule 1929— 7, 77
Marshall, Thurgood 1908–1993 1, 44
Marshall, Valenza Pauline Burke See Marshall, Paule
Marshall, William 1924–2003 107
Martelly, Michel 1961— 90
Martha Jean "The Queen" See Steinberg, Martha Jean
Martin, Curtis 1973— 104
Martin, Darnell 1964— 43, 78
Martin, Duane 1965— 108
Martin, Helen 1909–2000 31
Martin, Jesse L. 19(?)(?)— 31
Martin, Johnny See Mighty Clouds of Joy
Martin, Louis Emanuel 1912–1997 16
Martin, Michel 19(?)(?)— 97
Martin, Roberta 1907–1969 58
Martin, Roland S. 1968— 49, 84
Martin, Ruby Grant 1933–2003 49
Martin, Sara 1884–1955 38
Martin, Trayvon 1995–2012 105
Martinez, Pedro 1971— 81
Marvin X See X, Marvin
Mary Mary 34, 92
Mase 1977(?)— 24
Masekela, Barbara 1941— 18
Masekela, Hugh 1939— 1, 106
Masekela, Sal 1971— 106
Masire, Quett (Ketumile Joni) 1925— 5
Mason, Biddy 1818–1891 89
Mason, Charles Harrison 1866–1961 107
Mason, Felicia 1963(?)— 31
Mason, Herman, Jr. 1962— 83
Mason, Judi Ann 1955–2009 112
Mason, Ronald 1949— 27
Massaquoi, Hans J. 1926— 30
Massenburg, Kedar 1963(?)— 23, 110
Massey, Bobby See O'Jays, The

Massey, Brandon 1973— **40**

Massey, Walter E(ugene) 1938— **5, 45**

Massie, Samuel Proctor, Jr. 1919— **29**

Master Gee See Sugarhill Gang, The

Master P 1970— **21, 115**

Matejka, Adrian 1971(?)— **87**

Mathabane, Johannes See Mathabane, Mark

Mathabane, Mark 1960— **5, 99**

Mathis, Greg 1960— **26**

Mathis, Johnny 1935— **20**

Matshikiza, Pumeza 1979(?)— **115**

Matson, Ollie 1930–2011 **93**

Matta, Adam See Carolina Chocolate Drops

Matthews, Ameena 19(?)(?)— **105**

Matthews, Benjamin 1932–2006 **93**

Matthews, Denise See Vanity

Matthews, Mark 1894–2005 **59**

Matthews Shatteen, Westina 1948— **51**

Matzeliger, Jan 1852–1889 **93**

Mauldin, Jermaine Dupri See Dupri, Jermaine

Maupin, John E., Jr. 1946— **92**

Maxey, Randall 1941— **46**

Maxis, Theresa 1810–1892 **62**

Maxwell 1973— **20, 81**

May, Derrick 1963— **41**

Mayberry-Stewart, Melodie 1948— **94**

Maye, Arthur Lee See Maye, Lee

Maye, Lee 1934–2002 **111**

Mayers, Jamal 1974— **39**

Mayers, Rakim See A$AP Rocky

Mayes, Lenny See Dramatics, The

Mayfield, Curtis 1942–1999 **2, 43**

Mayhew, Martin R. 1965— **76**

Mayhew, Richard 1924— **39**

Maynard, Nancy Hicks 1946–2008 **73**

Maynard, Robert C(lyve) 1937–1993 **7**

Maynor, Dorothy 1910–1996 **19**

Mayo, Whitman 1930–2001 **32**

Mays, Benjamin E(lijah) 1894–1984 **7**

Mays, Leslie A. 19(?)(?)— **41**

Mays, William G. 1946— **34**

Mays, William Howard, Jr. See Mays, Willie

Mays, Willie 1931— **3**

Mayweather, Floyd 1977— **57, 104**

Mazrui, Ali Al'Amin 1933— **12**

M'bala M'bala, Dieudonné See Dieudonné

Mbatha-Raw, Gugu 1983— **89**

Mbaye, Mariétou 1948— **31**

Mbeki, Govan A. 1910–2001 **80**

Mbeki, Thabo 1942— **14, 73**

Mboup, Souleymane 1951— **10**

Mboya, Thomas Joseph Odhiambo See Mboya, Tom

Mboya, Tom 1930–1969 **107**

Mbuende, Kaire Munionganda 1953— **12**

MC Breed 1971–2008 **75**

M.C. Hammer 1963— **20, 80**

MC Lyte 1971— **34, 108**

McAdoo, Bob 1951— **75**

McAnulty, William E., Jr. 1947–2007 **66**

McBay, Henry C. 1914–1995 **91**

McBride, Bryant Scott 1965— **18**

McBride, Chi 1961— **73**

McBride, James 1957— **35, 87**

McCabe, Jewell Jackson 1945— **10**

McCall, H. Carl 1938(?)— **27**

McCall, Nathan 1955— **8**

McCalla, Leyla See Carolina Chocolate Drops

McCann, Renetta 1957(?)— **44**

McCarthy, Sandy 1972— **64**

McCarty, Osceola 1908— **16**

McCary, Michael S. See Boyz II Men

McCauley, Gina 1976(?)— **76**

McClellan, George Marion 1860–1934 **91**

McClendon, Forrest 1965— **94**

McClendon, Lisa 1975(?)— **61**

McClinton, Marion Isaac 1954— **77**

McClurkin, Donnie 1961— **25**

McCoo, Marilyn 1943— **53**

McCovey, Willie 1938— **103**

McCowin, Michael See Mighty Clouds of Joy

McCoy, Elijah 1844–1929 **8**

McCracklin, Jimmy 1921–2012 **108**

McCrary, Crystal See McCrary Anthony, Crystal

McCrary, Darius 1976— **111**

McCrary Anthony, Crystal 1969— **70**

McCray, Nikki 1972— **18**

McCullough, Bernard Jeffrey See Mac, Bernie

McCullough, DeAndre 1977–2012 **106**

McCullough, Geraldine 1917–2008 **58, 79**

McDaniel, Hattie 1895–1952 **5**

McDaniel, Prudence See Marian Anderson String Quartet

McDaniel, Randall Cornell 1964— **81**

McDaniels, Darryl See DMC

McDaniels, Ralph 19(?)(?)— **79**

McDonald, Audra 1970— **20, 62**

McDonald, Erroll 1954(?)— **1**

McDonald, Gabrielle Kirk 1942— **20**

McDougall, Gay J. 1947— **11, 43**

McDuffie, Dwayne 1962— **62**

McElroy, Sollie See Flamingos, The

McEwen, Mark 1954— **5**

McFadden, Bernice L. 1966— **39**

McFarlan, Tyron 1971(?)— **60**

McFarland, Roland 1940— **49**

McFerrin, Bobby 1950— **68**

McFerrin, Robert, Jr. See McFerrin, Bobby

McFerrin, Robert, Sr. 1921–2006 **94**

McGee, Charles 1924— **10**

McGee, James D. 1949— **74**

McGee, James Madison 1940— **46**

McGee, Vonetta 1945–2010 **95**

McGhee, Heather C. 1981— **106**

McGhee, Sharon K. 1957–2012 **113**

McGill, Anthony 1979— **76**

McGill, Lucius See Dells, The

McGill, Mickey See Dells, The

McGlowan, Angela 1970— **64, 86**

McGrady, Tracy 1979— **80**

McGrath, Pat 1970— **72**

McGregor, Stephen 1990— **99**

McGriff, Fred 1963— **24**

McGriff, James Harrell See McGriff, Jimmy

McGriff, Jimmy 1936–2008 **72**

McGruder, Aaron 1974— **28, 56**

McGruder, Robert 1942— **22, 35**

McGuire, George Alexander 1866–1934 **80**

McGuire, Raymond J. 1957(?)(—) **57**

McHenry, Donald F. 1936— **83**

McIntosh, Winston Hubert See Tosh, Peter

McIntyre, Natalie See Gary, Macy

McJunkin, George 1851–1922 **93**

McKay, Claude 1889–1948 **6**

McKay, Festus Claudius See McKay, Claude

McKay, Nellie Yvonne 19(?)(?)–2006 **17, 57**

McKee, Lonette 1952— **12**

McKegney, Tony 1958— **3**

McKenzie, Jaunel 1986— **73**

McKenzie, Vashti M. 1947— **29**

McKinney, Cynthia 1955— **11, 52, 74**

McKinney, Nina Mae 1912–1967 **40**

McKinney Hammond, Michelle 1957— **51**

McKinney-Whetstone, Diane 1954(?)— **27**

McKinnon, Ike See McKinnon, Isaiah

McKinnon, Isaiah 1943— **9**

McKissack, Leatrice 1930— **80**

McKissick, Floyd B(ixler) 1922–1981 **3**

McKnight, Brian 1969— **18, 34**

McKnight, Claude V., III See Take 6

McLean, Jackie 1931–2006 **78**

McLendon, John B., Jr. 1915–1999 **89**

McLeod, Gus 1955(?)— **27**

McMillan, Rosalynn A. 1953— **36**

McMillan, Terry 1951— **4, 17, 53**

McMillan, Tracy 1964— **93**

McMurray, Georgia L. 1934–1992 **36**

McNabb, Donovan 1976— **29**

McNair, Ronald 1950–1986 **3, 58**

McNair, Steve 1973–2009 **22, 47, 79**

McNeil, David See Billy Ward and the Dominoes

McNeil, Lori 1964(?)— **1**

McPhail, Sharon 1948— **2**

McPhatter, Clyde See Billy Ward and the Dominoes

McPherson, David 1968— **32**

McPherson, James Alan 1943— **70**

McQuater, Matthew See Clovers, The

McQueen, Butterfly 1911–1995 **6, 54**

McQueen, Steve 1969— **84**

McRae, Carmen 1920–1994 **77**

McRae, Hal 1945— **84**

McShann, Jay 1916–2006 **110**

McTell, Blind Willie 1901–1959 **89**

McVey, Joseph Wayne See Z-Ro

McWhorter, John 1965— **35**

McWorter, Free Frank 1777–1854 **91**

Meadows, Tim 1961— **30**

Meek, Carrie (Pittman) 1926— **6, 36**

Meek, Kendrick 1966— **41, 89**

Meeks, Gregory 1953— **25**

Meeks, James T. 1956— **92**

Mehretu, Julie 1970— **85**

Meles Zenawi See Zenawi, Meles

Mell, Patricia 1953— **49**

Mello, Breno 1931–2008 **73**

Melton, Frank 1949–2009 **81**

Melton, Harold D. 1966— **79**

Melvin, Harold See Harold Melvin & the Blue Notes

Meminger, Dean 1948–2013 **114**

Memmi, Albert 1920— **37**

Memphis Minnie 1897–1973 **33**

Memphis Slim 1915–1988 **105**

Menard, John Willis 1838–1893 **90**

Mengestu, Dinaw 1978— **66, 114**

Mengistu, Haile Mariam 1937— **65**

Mensah, John 1982— **87**

Mensah, Thomas 1950— **48**

Mercado-Valdes, Frank 1962— **43**

Meredith, James H(oward) 1933— **11**

Merkerson, S. Epatha 1952— **47, 83**

Merriweather, Big Maceo 1905–1953 **109**

Merriweather, Major See Merriweather, Big Maceo

Mescudi, Scott Ramon Seguro See Kid Cudi

Messenger, The See Divine, Father

Metcalfe, Ralph 1910–1978 **26**

Method Man 1971— **81**

Meyer, June See Jordan, June

Mfume, Kweisi 1948— **6, 41**

Mhinga, Yvonne See Chaka Chaka, Yvonne

Mhlaba, Raymond 1920–2005 **55**

Michaux, Solomon Lightfoot 1884–1968 **91**

Micheaux, Oscar (Devereaux) 1884–1951 **7**

Michele, Michael 1966— **31**

Mickelbury, Penny 1948— **28**

Mickens, Ronald Elbert 1943— **105**

Mickle, Dale See Dixie Cups, The

Middleton, Reggie 1967— **105**

Midnight Star **110**

Mighty Clouds of Joy **110**

Miguel 1986(?)— **98**

Miles, Buddy 1947–2008 **69**

Miles, George Allen, Jr. See Miles, Buddy

Miles, William 1931–2013 **112**

Milla, Roger 1952— **2**

Millender-McDonald, Juanita 1938–2007 **21, 61**

Miller, Bebe 1950— **3**

Miller, Cheryl 1964— **10, 74**

Miller, Clyde 1927–2011 **113**

Miller, Corey See C-Murder

Miller, Dorie 1919–1943 **29**

Miller, Doris See Miller, Dorie

Miller, Larry G. 1950(?)— **72**

Miller, Marcus 1959— **84**

Miller, Maria 1803–1879 **19**

Miller, Omar Benson 1978— **93**
Miller, Patina 1984— **94**
Miller, Pepper 1953— **96**
Miller, Percy *See Master P*
Miller, Percy Romeo, Jr. *See Romeo*
Miller, Portia Simpson *See Simpson Miller, Portia*
Miller, Reggie 1965— **33**
Miller, Rice *See Williamson, Sonny Boy*
Miller, Romeo *See Romeo*
Miller, Warren F., Jr. 1943— **53**
Miller, Wentworth 1972— **75**
Miller-Travis, Vernice 1959— **64**
Millinder, Lucius Venable *See Millinder, Lucky*
Millinder, Lucky 1900–1966 **101**
Millines Dziko, Trish 1957— **28**
Millner, Denene 1969(?)— **76**
Mills, Dylan Kwabena *See Rascal, Dizzee*
Mills, Florence 1896–1927 **22**
Mills, Joseph C. 1946— **51**
Mills, Sam 1959— **33**
Mills, Stephanie 1957— **36**
Mills, Steve 1960(?)— **47**
Mills Brothers, The **99**
Milner, Ron 1938— **39**
Milton, DeLisha 1974— **31**
Minaj, Nicki 1984— **86**
Ming, Mel 1944— **106**
Mingo, Frank L. 1939–1989 **32**
Mingus, Charles Jr. 1922–1979 **15**
Minkins, Shadrach 1814(?)–1875 **104**
Minor, DeWayne 1956— **32**
Minoso, Minnie 1925— **89**
Minott, Sugar 1956–2010 **86**
Mitchell, Arthur 1934— **2, 47**
Mitchell, Arthur Wergs 1883–1968 **91**
Mitchell, Brian Stokes 1957— **21**
Mitchell, Clarence M., Jr. 1911–1984 **88**
Mitchell, Corinne 1914–1993 **8**
Mitchell, Dwike 1930–2013 **111**
Mitchell, Elvis 1958— **67**
Mitchell, Ivory, Jr. *See Mitchell, Dwike*
Mitchell, Keith 1946— **82**
Mitchell, Kel 1978— **66**
Mitchell, Leona 1949— **42**
Mitchell, Loften 1919–2001 **31**
Mitchell, Nicole 1967(?)— **66**
Mitchell, Parren J. 1922–2007 **42, 66**
Mitchell, Russ 1960— **21, 73**
Mitchell, Sam 1963— **82**
Mitchell, Sharon 1962— **36**
Mitchell, Shireen 1970— **89**
Mitchell, Willie 1928–2010 **114**
Mizell, Jason *See Run-DMC*
Mkapa, Benjamin W. 1938— **16, 77**
Mo', Keb' 1952— **36**
Mobutu Sese Seko 1930–1997 **1, 56**
Moctar, Omara *See Bombino*
Mofolo, Thomas (Mokopu) 1876–1948 **37**
Mogae, Festus Gontebanye 1939— **19, 79**
Mohamed, Ali Mahdi *See Ali Mahdi Mohamed*

Mohammed, Nazr 1977— **64**
Mohammed, W. Deen 1933— **27**
Mohammed, Warith Deen *See Mohammed, W. Deen*
Mohamud, Hassan Sheikh 1955— **105**
Mohlabane, Goapele *See Goapele*
Moi, Daniel Arap 1924— **1, 35**
Mokae, Zakes 1934–2009 **80**
Mollel, Tololwa 1952— **38**
Monáe, Janelle 1985— **86**
Mongella, Gertrude 1945— **11**
Monica 1980— **21**
Mo'Nique 1967— **35, 84**
Monk, Art 1957— **38, 73**
Monk, Thelonious 1917–1982 **1**
Monroe, Bryan 1965— **71**
Monroe, Earl 1944— **89**
Monroe, Mary 19(?)(?)— **35**
Monteith, Mary Modjeska *See Simkins, Modjeska Monteith*
Montgomery, Isaiah T. 1847–1924 **91**
Montgomery, Robbie 1940— **101**
Montgomery, Tim 1975— **41**
Montgomery, Wes 1923–1968 **88**
Moody, James 1925— **83**
Moody, Ronald 1900–1984 **30**
Moody-Adams, Michele 1956— **76**
Moon, Warren 1956— **8, 66**
Mooney, Paul 19(?)(?)— **37**
Moonglows, The **108**
Moore, Alice Ruth *See Dunbar-Nelson, Alice Ruth Moore*
Moore, Anthony *See Romanthony*
Moore, Barbara C. 1949— **49**
Moore, Bobby *See Rashad, Ahmad*
Moore, Chante 1970(?)— **26**
Moore, Davey 1933–1963 **105**
Moore, David Schultz *See Moore, Davey*
Moore, Dorothy Rudd 1940— **46**
Moore, Gwendolynne S. 1951— **55**
Moore, Harry T. 1905–1951 **29**
Moore, Jessica Care 1971— **30**
Moore, Johnny B. 1950— **38**
Moore, Juanita 1922— **83**
Moore, Kevin *See Mo', Keb'*
Moore, Lecrae *See Lecrae*
Moore, LeRoi 1961–2008 **72**
Moore, Maya 1989— **94**
Moore, Melba 1945— **21**
Moore, Minyon 19(?)(?)— **45**
Moore, Richard *See bin Wahad, Dhoruba*
Moore, Sam *See Sam and Dave*
Moore, Shemar 1970— **21, 112**
Moore, Undine Smith 1904–1989 **28**
Moore, Wes 1978— **86**
Moorer, Lana *See MC Lyte*
Moorer, Michael 1967— **19**
Moose, Charles 1953— **40**
Morake, Lebohang *See Lebo M*
Morales, Mark 1960— *See Fat Boys*
Moran, Jason 1975— **89**
Morgan, Garrett (Augustus) 1877–1963 **1**
Morgan, Gertrude 1900–1986 **63**
Morgan, Irene 1917–2007 **65**
Morgan, Joe 1943— **9, 96**
Morgan, Lee 1938–1972 **102**

Morgan, Rose (Meta) 1912(?)— **11**
Morgan, Tracy 1968— **61, 102**
Morgan Lawrence, Margaret *See Lawrence, Margaret Morgan*
Morganfield, McKinley *See Muddy Waters*
Morial, Ernest "Dutch" 1929–1989 **26**
Morial, Marc H. 1958— **20, 51**
Morón, Alonzo G. 1909–1971 **91**
Morris, Eugene Edward *See Morris, Mercury*
Morris, Garrett 1937— **31**
Morris, Greg 1934–1996 **28**
Morris, Mercury 1947— **114**
Morris, Nathan *See Boyz II Men*
Morris, Raheem 1976— **77**
Morris, Wanya *See Boyz II Men*
Morris, William "Bill" 1938— **51**
Morris, Stevland Judkins *See Wonder, Stevie*
Morrison, Keith 1942— **13**
Morrison, Mary Thelma *See Washington, Mary T.*
Morrison, Sam 1936— **50**
Morrison, Toni 1931— **2, 15, 86**
Morrison, Vanessa 1969(?)— **84**
Morrow, E. Frederic 1909–1994 **100**
Morton, Azie Taylor 1936–2003 **48**
Morton, Ferdinand Q. 1881–1949 **90**
Morton, Frederick A., Jr. 1967(?)— **93**
Morton, Jelly Roll 1885(?)–1941 **29**
Morton, Joe 1947— **18**
Mos Def *See Bey, Yasiin*
Moseley-Braun, Carol *See Braun, Carol Moseley*
Moses, Edwin 1955— **8**
Moses, Gilbert, III 1942–1995 **12**
Moses, Robert Parris 1935— **11**
Mosisili, Pakalitha 1945— **96**
Mosley, "Sugar" Shane 1971— **32**
Mosley, Tim *See Timbaland*
Mosley, Walter 1952— **5, 25, 68**
Moss, Bryant *See Moss, Preacher*
Moss, Carlton 1909–1997 **17**
Moss, J. (?)— **64**
Moss, Otis, Jr. 1935— **72**
Moss, Otis, III 1971(?)— **72**
Moss, Preacher 1967— **63**
Moss, Randy 1977— **23, 90**
Moss, Shad Gregory *See Lil' Bow Wow*
Mossell, Gertrude Bustill 1855–1948 **40**
Mossell, Nathan Francis 1856–1946 **91**
Moten, Etta *See Barnett, Etta Moten*
Motlanthe, Kgalema 1949— **74**
Motley, Archibald, Jr. 1891–1981 **30**
Motley, Constance Baker 1921–2005 **10, 55**
Motley, Marion 1920–1999 **26**
Moton, Robert Russa 1867–1940 **83**
Moura, Paulo 1932–2010 **87**
Mourning, Alonzo 1970— **17, 44**
Moussambani, Eric 1978— **105**
Moutoussamy-Ashe, Jeanne 1951— **7**
Mowatt, Judy 1952(?)— **38**

Mowry, Jess 1960— **7**
Mowry, Tamera 1978— **79**
Mowry, Tia 1978— **78**
Moyo, Dambisa 1970(?)— **76**
Moyo, Karega Kofi 19(?)(?)— **36**
Moyo, Lovemore 1965— **76**
Moyo, Yvette Jackson 1953— **36**
Mphalele, Es'kia (Ezekiel) 1919— **40**
Mswati III 1968— **56**
Mtukudzi, Oliver 1952— **109**
Muamba, Fabrice 1988— **104**
Mudimbe, V. Y. 1941— **61**
Mugabe, Robert 1924— **10, 71**
Mugo, Madeleine *See Mugo, Micere Githae*
Mugo, Micere Githae 1942— **32**
Muhajir, El *See X, Marvin*
Muhammad, Ava 1951— **31**
Muhammad, Elijah 1897–1975 **4**
Muhammad, Jabir Herbert 1929–2008 **72**
Muhammad, Khallid Abdul 1951(?)— **10, 31**
Mukoko, Jestina 1957(?)— **75**
Mullen, Harryette 1953— **34**
Mullen, Nicole C. 1967— **45**
Muluzi, Bakili 1943— **14, 76**
Mumba, Samantha 1983— **29**
Mumford, Eugene *See Billy Ward and the Dominoes; Golden Gate Quartet*
Muncie, Chuck 1953–2013 **112**
Muncie, Harry Vance *See Muncie, Chuck*
Mundine, Anthony 1975— **56**
Munsey, Harry Vance *See Muncie, Chuck*
Murphy, Charles 1959— **95**
Murphy, Charlie *See Murphy, Charles*
Murphy, Eddie 1961— **4, 20, 61**
Murphy, Edward Regan *See Murphy, Eddie*
Murphy, John H. 1916— **42**
Murphy, Laura M. 1955— **43**
Murphy McKenzie, Vashti *See McKenzie, Vashti M.*
Murray, Albert L. 1916— **33**
Murray, Cecil 1929— **12, 47**
Murray, Eddie 1956— **12**
Murray, Lenda 1962— **10**
Murray, Pauli 1910–1985 **38**
Murray, Tai 1982— **47**
Murrell, Sylvia Marilyn 1947— **49**
Musa, Ali, Mohammed *See Birra, Ali*
Muse, Clarence Edouard 1889–1979 **21**
Museveni, Yoweri (Kaguta) 1944(?)— **4**
Mushikiwabo, Louise 1961— **88**
Musiq 1977— **37, 84**
Mutebi, Ronald 1956— **25**
Mutola, Maria de Lurdes 1972— **12**
Mutombo, Dikembe 1966— **7, 107**
Mutu, Wangechi 19(?)(?)— **44**
Muzorewa, Abel 1925–2010 **85**
Mvula, Laura 1987— **110**
Mwanawasa, Levy 1948–2008 **72**
Mwangi, Meja 1948— **40**
Mwinyi, Ali Hassan 1925— **1, 77**
Mya 1979— **35**
Myers, Dwight *See Heavy D*

Myers, Lewis Eddy See Myers, Lou

Myers, Lou 1935(?)–2013 110

Myers, Walter Dean 1937— 8, 70

Myers, Walter Milton See Myers, Walter Dean

Myles, John H. See Swan Silver-tones, The

Myles, Kim 1974— 69

Myrie, Mark Anthony See Banton, Buju

Nabrit, Samuel Milton 1905–2003 47

Nagin, Ray 1956— 42, 57, 88

Nail, John E. 1883–1947 92

Najm, Faheem Rasheed See T-Pain

Nakhid, David 1964— 25

Naki, Hamilton 1926–2005 63

Nance, Cynthia 1958— 71

Nanula, Richard D. 1960— 20

Napoleon, Benny N. 1956(?)— 23

Nas 1973— 33, 111

Nascimento, Abdias do 1914–2011 93

Nascimento, Milton 1942— 2, 64

Nash, Diane 1938— 72

Nash, Joe 1919–2005 55

Nash, Johnny 1940— 40

Nash, Niecy 1970— 66, 115

Nash, Shannon King 1971— 84

Nash, Terius Youngdell See The-Dream

Nate Dogg 1969–2011 92

Naughton, Naturi 1984— 97

Navarro, Fats 1923–1950 104

Navarro, Theodore, Jr. See Navarro, Fats

Naylor, Gloria 1950— 10, 42

Nazario, Zoe Yadira Zaldaña See Saldana, Zoe

Ndadaye, Melchior 1953–1993 7

Ndegeocello, Meshell 1968— 15, 83

Ndiaye, Iba 1928–2008 74

N'Dour, Youssou 1959— 1, 53, 79

Ndungane, Winston Njongonkulu 1941— 16

Neal, Elise 1970— 29

Neal, Larry 1937–1981 38

Neal, Mark Anthony 1965(?)— 74

Neal, Raful 1936— 44

Neale, Haydain 1970— 52

Neals, Otto 1930— 73

Nelly 1974— 32, 90

Nelson, Jill 1952— 6, 54

Nelson, Kadir 1974— 115

Nelson, Oliver 1932–1975 113

Nelson, Prince Rogers See Prince

Nelson, Sophia A. 1967— 93

Nelson, Stanley 1951— 92

Nelson Meigs, Andrea 1968— 48

Neto, António Agostinho 1922— 43

Nettles, Marva Deloise See Collins, Marva

Neverson, Tremaine Aldon See Songz, Trey

Neville, Aaron 1941— 21

Neville, Arthel 1962— 53

New Edition 101

Newcombe, Don 1926— 24

Newkirk, Pamela 1957— 69

Newman, David 1933–2009 76

Newman, Lester C. 1952— 51

Newsome, Ozzie 1956— 26

Newton, Cam 1989— 96

Newton, Huey (Percy) 1942–1989 2

Newton, Thandie 1972— 26, 114

Newton, Thandiwe See Newton, Thandie

Ne-Yo 1982— 65

Ngaujah, Sahr 1976— 86

Ngengi, Kamau wa See Kenyatta, Jomo

Ngilu, Charity 1952— 58

Ngubane, (Baldwin Sipho) Ben 1941— 33

Nguema Mbasogo, Teodoro Obiang See Obiang, Teodoro

Ngugi, James T. See Ngugi wa Thiong'o

Ngugi wa Thiong'o 1938— 29, 61, 101

Niane, Katoucha 1960–2008 70

Nicholas, Denise 1944— 82

Nicholas, Fayard 1914–2006 20, 57, 61

Nicholas, Harold 1921— 20

Nichols, Grace See Nichols, Nichelle

Nichols, James Thomas See Bell, James "Cool Papa"

Nichols, Nichelle 1933(?)— 11

Nissel, Angela 1974— 42

Nix, Robert N. C., Jr. 1928–2003 51

Nixon, Edgar Daniel 1899–1987 100

Nixon, Otis 1959— 111

Njawe, Pius 1957–2010 87

Njongonkulu, Winston Ndungane 1941— 16

Nkoli, Simon 1957–1998 60

Nkomo, Joshua 1917–1999 4, 65

Nkosi, Lewis 1936— 46

Nkrumah, Kwame 1909–1972 3

Nkunda, Laurent 1967— 75

Nkurunziza, Pierre 1963— 78

N'Namdi, George R. 1946— 17

Noah, Yannick 1960— 4, 60

Noble, Gil 1932— 76

Noble, Reginald See Redman

Noble, Ronald 1957— 46

Noble Drew Ali 1886–1929 100

Norman, Christina 1960(?)— 47

Norman, Jessye 1945— 5

Norman, Maidie 1912–1998 20

Norman, Pat 1939— 10

Norris, Michele 1961— 83

Northup, Solomon 1808–1863(?) 115

Norton, Eleanor Holmes 1937— 7, 93

Norton, Ken 1943–2013 101, 115

Norton, Meredith 1970(?)— 72

Norwood, Brandy See Brandy

Norwood, William Raymond, Jr. See Ray J

Notorious B.I.G. 1972–1997 20

Nottage, Cynthia DeLores See Tucker, C. DeLores

Nottage, Lynn 1964— 66

Nour, Nawal M. 1965(?)— 56

Ntaganda, Bosco 1972— 111

Ntaryamira, Cyprien 1955–1994 8

Ntshona, Winston 1941— 52

Nugent, Richard Bruce 1906–1987 39

Nujoma, Samuel 1929— 10

Nunez, Elizabeth 1944— 62, 112

Nunez-Harrell, Elizabeth See Nunez, Elizabeth

Nunn, Annetta 1959— 43

Nunn, Bobby See Coasters, The

Nutter, Michael 1957— 69, 112

Nuttin' but Stringz See Escobar, Tourie, and Escobar, Damien

Nyanda, Siphiwe 1950— 21

Nyerere, Julius (Kambarage) 1922— 5

Nzo, Alfred (Baphethuxolo) 1925— 15

Obadele, Imari 1930–2010 84

Obama, Barack 1961— 49, 74, 91

Obama, Michelle 1964— 61, 90

Obasanjo, Olusegun 1937— 5, 22

Obasanjo, Stella 1945–2005 32, 56

Obiang, Teodoro 1942— 103

Obote, Milton 1925–2005 63

O'Brien, Soledad 1966— 88

Ocean, Frank 1987— 100

Ochocinco, Chad See Johnson, Chad

ODB See Ol' Dirty Bastard

Odetta 1930— 37, 74

Odinga, Raila 1945— 67, 110

Odom, Lamar 1979— 81

Odumegwu-Ojukwu, Chukwuemeka See Ojukwu, Odumegwu

Ogden, Jonathan 1974— 110

Oglesby, Zena 1947— 12

Ogletree, Charles, Jr. 1952— 12, 47

O'Grady, Lorraine 1934— 73

Ogunlesi, Adebayo O. 19(?)(?)— 37

O'Jays, The 98

Ojikutu, Bayo 1971— 66

Ojikutu, Bisola 1974— 65

Ojukwu, Emeka See Ojukwu, Odumegwu

Ojukwu, Odumegwu 1933–2011 99

Okaalet, Peter 1953— 58

Okara, Gabriel 1921— 37

Okigbo, Christopher 1932–1967 102

Okogwu, Patrick Chukwuemeka See Tinie Tempah

Okonedo, Sophie 1969— 67

Okonjo-Iweala, Ngozi 1954— 101

Okonma, Tyler See Tyler, the Creator

Okosuns, Sonny 1947–2008 71

Okocha, Augustine Azuka See Okocha, Jay Jay

Okocha, Jay Jay 1973— 99

Ol' Dirty Bastard 1968–2004 52

Olagundoye, Olatokunbo Susan Olasobunmi Abeke See Olagundoye, Toks

Olagundoye, Toks 1975— 113

Olajuwon, Akeem See Olajuwon, Hakeem

Olajuwon, Hakeem 1963— 2, 72

Olatunji, Babatunde 1927— 36

Olden, Georg(e) 1920–1975 44

O'Leary, Hazel (Rollins) 1937— 6

Oliver, Bilal Sayeed See Bilal

Oliver, Garrett 1962— 95

Oliver, Jerry 1947— 37

Oliver, Joe "King" 1885–1938 42

Oliver, John J., Jr. 1945— 48

Oliver, Kimberly 1976— 60

Oliver, Pam 1961— 54

Oliver, Paul 1984–2013 115

Olojede, Dele 1961— 59

Olopade, Olufunmilayo Falusi 1957(?)— 58

Omar, Samia Yusuf 1991–2012 107

Omarion 1984— 107

Omarosa 1974— 69, 110 112 114

O'Neal, Frederick 1905–1992 99

O'Neal, Patrice 1969–2011 99

O'Neal, Rodney 1954— 88

O'Neal, Ron 1937–2004 46

O'Neal, Shaquille 1972— 8, 30, 95

O'Neal, Stanley 1951— 38, 67

O'Neil, Buck 1911–2006 19, 59

O'Neil, John Jordan See O'Neil, Buck

Ongala, Ramadhani Mtoro See Ongala, Remmy

Ongala, Remmy 1947–2010 9, 91

Onile-Ere, Adetayo Ayowale See Cruz, Taio

Onwueme, Tess Osonye 1955— 23

Onwurah, Ngozi 1966(?)— 38

Onyewu, Oguchi 1982— 60

Orange, James 1942–2008 74

O'Ree, William Eldon See O'Ree, Willie

O'Ree, Willie 1935— 5

Orioles, The 100

Orlandersmith, Dael 1959— 42

Orman, Roscoe 1944— 55

Ormes, Jackie 1911–1985 73

Ortiz, David 1975— 52, 82

Osbey, Brenda Marie 1957— 102

Osborne, Jeffrey 1948— 26

Osborne, Na'taki 1974— 54

Osotimehin, Babatunde 1949— 107

Otis, Clarence, Jr. 1956— 55

Otis, Clyde 1924— 67

Otunga, Maurice Michael 1923–2003 55

Ouattara 1957— 43

Ouattara, Alassane 1942— 90

Ouattara, Morou 1966— 74

Ousley, Curtis See King Curtis

Ousmane, Sembène See Sembène, Ousmane

OutKast 35

Owens, Dana See Queen Latifah

Owens, Helen 1937— 48

Owens, Henry See Golden Gate Quartet

Owens, J. C. See Owens, Jesse

Owens, Jack 1904–1997 38

Owens, James Cleveland See Owens, Jesse

Owens, Jesse 1913–1980 2

Owens, Major (Robert) 1936— 6

Owens, Paul See Swan Silver-tones, The

Owens, Terrell 1973— 53, 106

Oyebanjo, Dapo Daniel See D'banj

Oyelowo, David 1976— 82

Oyewale, Taiwo Bamidele Olaniyi See Prince Twins Seven-Seven

Oyono, Ferdinand 1929— 38

P. Diddy See Combs, Sean

Pace, Betty 1954— 59

Pace, Orlando 1975— 21

Packer, Daniel 1947— **56**
Packer, Will 1974(?)— **71**
Packer, Z. Z. 1973— **64**
Page, Alan (Cedric) 1945— **7**
Page, Clarence 1947— **4**
Page, Greg 1958–2009 **78**
Page, Inman 1853–1935 **82**
Paige, Leroy Robert See Paige, Satchel
Paige, Rod 1933— **29**
Paige, Satchel 1906–1982 **7**
Painter, Nell Irvin 1942— **24, 88**
Palacio, Andy 1960–2008 **96**
Palcy, Euzhan 1958— **94**
Palmer, Everard 1930— **37**
Palmer, Keke 1993— **68**
Palmer, Rissi 1981— **65**
Palmer, Violet 1964— **59**
Papa Wendo See Kolosoy, Wendo
Parham, Marjorie B. 1918— **71**
Parish, Robert 1953— **43**
Parker, Barrington D. 1915–1993 **92**
Parker, Candace 1986— **74**
Parker, Charlie 1920–1955 **20**
Parker, Jim 1934–2005 **64**
Parker, Kellis E. 1942–2000 **30**
Parker, (Lawrence) Kris(hna) See KRS-One
Parker, LarStella Irby See Parker, Star
Parker, Maceo 1943— **72**
Parker, Nicole Ari 1970— **52**
Parker, Q See 112
Parker, Quinnes See 112
Parker, Ray, Jr. 1954— **85**
Parker, Star 1956— **70**
Parker, Tony 1982— **75**
Parker, Vernon 1959— **97**
Parks, Bernard C. 1943— **17**
Parks, Gordon 1912–2006 **1, 35, 58**
Parks, Henry Green, Jr. 1916–1989 **89**
Parks, Rosa 1913–2005 **1, 35, 56**
Parks, Suzan-Lori 1963— **34, 85**
Parlan, Horace 1931— **108**
Parr, Russ 196(?)— **51**
Parsons, James Benton 1911–1993 **14**
Parsons, Richard Dean 1948— **11, 33**
Pascal-Trouillot, Ertha 1943— **3**
Paterson, Basil A. 1926— **69**
Paterson, David A. 1954— **59**
Patillo, Melba Joy 1941— **15**
Patrick, Deval 1956— **12, 61**
Patterson, Floyd 1935–2006 **19, 58**
Patterson, Frederick Douglass 1901–1988 **12**
Patterson, Gilbert Earl 1939— **41**
Patterson, J. O., Jr. 1935— **80**
Patterson, Louise 1901–1999 **25**
Patterson, Mary Jane 1840–1894 **54**
Patterson, Orlando 1940— **4**
Patterson, P(ercival) J(ames) 1936(?)— **6, 20**
Patterson, Robert, Jr. See Ali, Rashied
Patton, Antwan 1975— **45** See also OutKast
Patton, Charley 1891(?)–1934 **107**
Patton, Paula 1975— **62**

Paul, Chris 1985— **84, 100**
Payne, Allen 1962(?)— **13**
Payne, Donald M. 1934–2012 **2, 57, 112**
Payne, Ethel L. 1911–1991 **28**
Payne, Freda 1942— **58**
Payne, Hazel See Taste of Honey, A
Payne, Les 1941— **89**
Payne, Ulice, Jr. 1955— **42**
Payne, William D. 1932— **60**
Payton, Benjamin F. 1932— **23**
Payton, Gary 1968— **99**
Payton, John 1946— **48**
Payton, Philip A., Jr. 1876–1917 **88**
Payton, Walter 1954–1999 **11, 25**
Peake, Tadley Ewing See Dameron, Tadd
Peaker, Franklin See Harold Melvin & the Blue Notes
Pearman, Raven-Symoné Christina See Raven-Symoné
Pearson, Felicia 1980— **99**
Peck, Carolyn 1966(?)— **23**
Peck, Raoul 1953— **32**
Peebles, Ann 1947— **114**
Peebles, Annie Murray See Peebles, Ann
Peele, Jordan See Key & Peele
Peete, Calvin 1943— **11**
Peete, Holly Robinson 1965— **20**
Peete, Rodney 1966— **60**
Pelé 1940— **7**
Pena, Paul 1950–2005 **58**
Pendergrass, Teddy 1950–2010 **22, 83**
Penguins, The **107**
Penniman, Richard Wayne See Little Richard
Peoples, Dottie 19(?)(?)— **22**
Pereira, Aristides 1923–2011 **30, 97**
Perez, Anna 1951— **1**
Perez, Pascual 1957–2012 **108**
Perkins, Anthony 1959(?)— **24**
Perkins, Eddie 1937–2012 **103**
Perkins, Edward (Joseph) 1928— **5**
Perkins, James, Jr. 1953(?)— **55**
Perkins, Joe Willie See Perkins, Pinetop
Perkins, Marion 1908–1961 **38**
Perkins, Pinetop 1913— **70**
Perren, Freddie 1943–2004 **60**
Perrineau, Harold, Jr. 1968— **51**
Perrot, Kim 1967–1999 **23**
Perry, Emmitt, Jr. See Perry, Tyler
Perry, Herman 1922–1945 **89**
Perry, James 1975— **83**
Perry, Joe 1927–2011 **95**
Perry, Laval 195(?)— **64**
Perry, Lee 1936— **19, 103**
Perry, Lincoln See Fetchit, Stepin
Perry, Lowell 1931–2001 **30**
Perry, Matthew J., Jr. 1921–2011 **96**
Perry, Rainford Hugh See Perry, Lee
Perry, Ruth 1936— **19**
Perry, Ruth Sando 1939— **15**
Perry, Scratch See Perry, Lee
Perry, Steve 1970— **98**
Perry, Tyler 1969— **40, 54, 103**
Perry, Warren 1942(?)— **56**
Person, Waverly 1927— **9, 51**

Peters, Brock 1927–2005 **96**
Peters, Clarke 1952— **103**
Peters, Lenrie 1932— **43**
Peters, Margaret 1915— **43**
Peters, Maria Philomena 1941— **12**
Peters, Matilda 1917— **43**
Petersen, Frank E. 1932— **31**
Petersen, Neal 1967— **96**
Peterson, Adrian 1985— **109**
Peterson, Hannibal See Peterson, Marvin
Peterson, James 19(?)(?)— **81**
Peterson, James 1937— **38**
Peterson, Jesse Lee 1949— **81**
Peterson, Karen Carter 1969— **90**
Peterson, Marvin 1948— **27**
Peterson, Oscar 1925— **52**
Petioni, Muriel 1914 –2011 **99**
Petry, Ann 1909–1997 **19**
Pettiford, Oscar 1922–1960 **106**
Phifer, Mekhi 1974— **25, 103**
Philip, M. Nourbese See Philip, Marlene Nourbese
Philip, Marlene Nourbese 1947— **32**
Phillips, Arthur See Dramatics, The
Phillips, Bobby See Cadillacs
Phillips, Carl 1959— **111**
Phillips, Charles E., Jr. 1959— **57, 109**
Phillips, Esther 1935–1984 **107**
Phillips, Helen L. 1919–2005 **63**
Phillips, Joseph C. 1962— **73**
Phillips, Teresa L. 1958— **42**
Phipps, Wintley 1955— **59**
Pickens, James, Jr. 1954— **59**
Pickett, Bill 1870–1932 **11**
Pickett, Cecil 1945— **39**
Pierce, Elijah 1892–1984 **84**
Pierce, Harold 1917-1988 **75**
Pierce, Maryland See Five Keys, The
Pierce, Paul 1977— **71**
Pierce, Wendell 1962— **90**
Pierre, Andre 1915— **17**
Pierre, Percy Anthony 1939— **46**
Pierre-Louis, Michèle 1947— **75**
Pigford, Eva See Marcille, Eva
Pimentel, Miguel Jontel See Miguel
Pincham, R. Eugene, Sr. 1925–2008 **69**
Pinchback, P(inckney) B(enton) S(tewart) 1837–1921 **9**
Pinckney, Bill 1935— **42**
Pinckney, Sandra 194(?)— **56**
Pindell, Howardena 1943— **55**
Pinder, Jefferson 1970— **77**
Pinderhughes, John 1946— **47**
Pindling, Lynden 1930–2000 **81**
Pinkett, Jada See Pinkett Smith, Jada
Pinkett, Randal 1971— **61**
Pinkett Smith, Jada 1971— **10, 41, 95**
Pinkney, Fayette 1948–2009 **80**
Pinkney, Jerry 1939— **15**
Pinkston, W. Randall 1950— **24**
Pinn, Vivian Winona 1941— **49**
Piper, Adrian 1948— **71**
Pippen, Scottie 1965— **15, 89**
Pippin, Horace 1888–1946 **9**
Pitt, David Thomas 1913–1994 **10**

Pitta (do Nascimento), Celso (Roberto) 19(?)(?)— **17**
Pitts, Byron 1960— **71**
Pitts, Charles See Pitts, Skip
Pitts, Derrick 1956(?)— **77**
Pitts, Leonard, Jr. 1957— **54, 85**
Pitts, Robb 1941— **84**
Pitts, Robert Lee See Pitts, Robb
Pitts, Skip 1947–2012 **103**
Plaatje, Sol T. 1876–1932 **80**
Platters, The **99**
Player, Willa B. 1909–2003 **43**
Pleasant, Loretta See Lacks, Henrietta
Pleasant, Mary Ellen 1814–1904 **9**
Pleasure P 1984— **84**
Plessy, Homer Adolph 1862–1925 **31**
Plinton, James O., Jr. 1914–1996 **98**
P.M. Dawn, **54**
Pohamba, Hifikepunye 1935— **95**
Poindexter, Hildrus A. 1901–1987 **87**
Poitier, Sidney 1927— **11, 36**
Poitier, Sydney Tamiia 1973— **65**
Polite, Carlene Hatcher 1932–2009 **82**
Polite, Lloyd, Jr. See Lloyd
Pollard, Fritz 1894–1986 **53**
Pollard, William L. 1945(?)— **91**
Pomare, Eleo 1937–2008 **72**
Poole, Elijah See Muhammad, Elijah
Pope.L, William 1955— **72**
Porter, Billy 1969— **112**
Porter, Countee Leroy See Cullin, Countee
Porter, Dorothy See Wesley, Dorothy Porter
Porter, James A(mos) 1905–1970 **11**
Porter, Maggie See Fisk Jubilee Singers
Porter, Terry 1963— **75**
Portuondo, Omara 1930— **53**
Potter, Myrtle 1958— **40**
Potts, Sylvester See Contours, The
Pough, Terrell 1987(?)–2005 **58**
Pounder, Carol Christine Hilaria See Pounder, CCH
Pounder, CCH 1952— **72**
Poussaint, Alvin F. 1934— **5, 67**
Poussaint, Renee 1944— **78**
Powell, Adam Clayton, Jr. 1908–1972 **3**
Powell, Benny 1930–2010 **87**
Powell, Bud 1924–1966 **24**
Powell, Colin 1937— **1, 28, 75**
Powell, Debra A. 1964— **23**
Powell, Keith 1979(?)— **101**
Powell, Kevin 1966— **31, 74**
Powell, Maxine 1915–2013 **8, 115**
Powell, Michael Anthony See Powell, Mike
Powell, Michael K. 1963— **32**
Powell, Mike 1963— **7**
Powell, Renee 1946— **34**
Powell, William See O'Jays, The
Powell, William J. 1916–2009 **82**
Power, Will 1970— **83**
Prater, Dave See Sam and Dave
Pratt, Awadagin 1966— **31**

Pratt, Elmer See Pratt, Geronimo
Pratt, Geronimo 1947–2011 **18, 95**
Pratt, Kyla 1986— **57**
Pratt Dixon, Sharon See Dixon, Sharon Pratt
Preer, Evelyn 1896–1932 **82**
Premice, Josephine 1926–2001 **41**
Pressley, Condace L. 1964— **41**
Preston, Billy 1946–2006 **39, 59**
Preston, William Everett See Preston, Billy
Préval, René 1943— **87**
Price, David 1985— **101**
Price, Florence 1887–1953 **37**
Price, Frederick K. C. 1932— **21**
Price, Glenda 1939— **22**
Price, Hugh B. 1941— **9, 54**
Price, Kelly 1973(?)— **23**
Price, Leontyne 1927— **1**
Price, Lisa 1962— **97**
Price, Richard 1930(?)— **51**
Pride, Charley 1938(?)— **26**
Primas, Randy 1949–2012 **106**
Primus, Pearl 1919— **6**
Prince 1958— **18, 65**
Prince, Richard E. 1947— **71**
Prince, Ron 1969— **64**
Prince, Tayshaun 1980— **68**
Prince Johnny C See Geto Boys
Prince Markie Dee See Fat Boys
Prince Twins Seven-Seven 1944–2011 **95**
Prince-Bythewood, Gina 1969— **31, 77**
Pritchard, Robert Starling 1927— **21**
Procope, Ernesta 19(?)(?)— **23**
Procope, John Levy 1925–2005 **56**
Professor Griff See Public Enemy
Professor Longhair 1918–1980 **109**
Proof 1973–2006 **101**
Prophet, Nancy Elizabeth 1890–1960 **42**
Prothrow, Deborah Boutin See Prothrow-Stith, Deborah
Prothrow-Stith, Deborah 1954— **10**
Pruitt, Wendell O. 1920–1945 **106**
Pryce, Trevor 1975— **89**
Pryor, Rain 1969— **65**
Pryor, Richard 1940–2005 **3, 24, 56**
Public Enemy **98**
Puckett, Kirby 1960–2006 **4, 58**
Puff Daddy See Combs, Sean
Pugh, Charles 1971— **81**
Puig, Yasiel 1990— **113**
Purdie, Bernard 1939— **77**
Purnell, Silas 1923–2003 **59**
Puryear, Martin 1941— **42, 101**
Putney, Martha S. 1916–2008 **75**
Puzey, Leonard See Ravens, The
Quander, Nellie 1880–1961 **102**
Quarles, Benjamin Arthur 1904–1996 **18**
Quarles, Norma 1936— **25**
Quarterman, Lloyd Albert 1918–1982 **4**
Quattlebaum, Michael David, Jr. See Blanco, Mykki
Queen Latifah 1970— **1, 16, 58**
Querino, Manuel Raimundo 1851–1923 **84**
?uestlove 1971— **74** See Roots, The

Quigless, Helen G. 1944–2004 **49**
Quince, Peggy A. 1948— **69**
Quirot, Ana (Fidelia) 1963— **13**
Quivers, Robin 1952— **61**
Rabb, Maurice F., Jr. 1932–2005 **58**
Rabia, Aliyah See Staton, Dakota
Radcliffe, Ted 1902–2005 **74**
Radcliffe, Theodore Roosevelt See Radcliffe, Ted
Ragin, Derek Lee 1958— **84**
Rahman, Aishah 1936— **37**
Raines, Franklin 1949— **14, 107**
Raines, Rock See Raines, Tim
Raines, Tim 1959— **107**
Rainey, Ma 1886–1939 **33**
Ralph, Sheryl Lee 1956— **18, 108**
Ramaphosa, (Matamela) Cyril 1952— **3**
Rambough, Lori Ann See Sommore
Ramphele, Mamphela 1947— **29**
Ramsey, Charles H. 1948— **21, 69**
Rand, A(ddison) Barry 1944— **6**
Randall, Alice 1959— **38**
Randall, Dudley 1914–2000 **8, 55**
Randall, Vernellia R. 1948— **95**
Randle, John 1967— **87**
Randle, Theresa 1967— **16**
Randolph, A(sa) Philip 1889–1979 **3**
Randolph, Linda A. 1941— **52**
Randolph, Willie 1954— **53**
Rangel, Charles B. 1930— **3, 52, 85**
Ranglin, Ernest 1932— **78**
Rankin Don See Rhoden, Wayne
Ransome, James E. 1961— **88**
Raoul, Kwame 1964— **55**
Rapelang Rabana 198(?)— **112**
Rapier, James T. 1837–1883 **82**
Ras Tafari See Haile Selassie
Rascal, Dizzee 1985— **82**
Rashad, Ahmad 1949— **18**
Rashad, Phylicia 1948— **21**
Raspberry, William 1935— **2**
Raven See Raven-Symoné
Ravens, The **103**
Raven-Symoné 1985— **44, 113**
Rawlings, Jerry (John) 1947— **9**
Rawlings-Blake, Stephanie 1970— **93**
Rawlinson, Johnnie B. 1952— **79**
Rawls, Lou 1936–2006 **17, 57**
Ray, Carline 1925–2013 **113**
Ray, Charlotte E. 1850–1911 **60**
Ray, Gene Anthony 1962–2003 **47**
Ray J 1981— **86**
Raymond, Usher See Usher
Razaf, Andy 1895–1973 **19**
Razafkeriefo, Andreamentania Paul See Razaf, Andy
Ready, Stephanie 1975— **33**
Reagins, Tony 1967— **94**
Reagon, Bernice Johnson 1942— **7**
Reagon, Toshi 1964— **76**
Reason, Joseph Paul 1943— **19**
Reaves, Donald J. 1946— **102**
Record, Eugene 1940–2005 **60**
See also Chi-Lites
Redd, Dana 1968— **93**
Reddick, Lance 19(?)(?)— **52**
Reddick, Lawrence Dunbar 1910–1995 **20**
Redding, Ann Holmes 1951— **77**

Redding, J. Saunders 1906–1988 **26**
Redding, Louis L. 1901–1998 **26**
Redding, Otis, Jr. 1941— **16**
Redman 1970— **81**
Redman, Joshua 1969— **30**
Redmond, Eugene 1937— **23**
Redwood, John Henry 1942–2003 **78**
Reece, E. Albert 1950— **63**
Reece, Marcel 1985— **114**
Reed, A. C. 1926— **36**
Reed, Alaina See Reed Hall, Alaina
Reed, Ishmael 1938— **8**
Reed, Jimmy 1925–1976 **38**
Reed, Joe L. 1939(?)— **110**
Reed, Kasim 1969— **82**
Reed, Larry See Dramatics, The
Reed, Natina 1979–2012 **106**
Reed, Willie See Louis, Willie
Reed, Willis, Jr. 1942— **86**
Reed Amini, Alaina See Reed Hall, Alaina
Reed Hall, Alaina 1946–2009 **83**
Reedy, Jessica 1988— **101**
Reems, Ernestine Cleveland 1932— **27**
Rees, Dee 197(?)— **100**
Reese, Calvin See Reese, Pokey
Reese, Della 1931— **6, 20, 96**
Reese, Jerry 1963— **103**
Reese, Milous J., Jr. 1904— **51**
Reese, Pokey 1973— **28**
Reese, Tracy 1964— **54**
Reeves, Bass 1838–1910 **100**
Reeves, Dianne 1956— **32**
Reeves, Gregory 1952— **49**
Reeves, Martha 1941— **85**
Reeves, Rachel J. 1950(?)— **23**
Reeves, Shirley Alston See Shirelles, The
Reeves, Triette Lipsey 1963— **27**
Regis, Cyrille 1958— **51**
Reid, Antonio "L.A." 1958(?)— **28**
Reid, Ira De A. 1901–1968 **100**
Reid, Irvin D. 1941— **20**
Reid, L.A. See Reid, Antonio "L.A."
Reid, Senghor 1976— **55**
Reid, Tim 1944— **56**
Reid, Vernon 1958— **34**
Reivers, Corbin Bleu See Corbin Bleu
Reuben, Gloria 19(?)(?)— **15**
Rev Run See Run; Run-DMC
Revels, Hiram Rhoades 1827–1901 **98**
Reverend Ike 1935–2009 **79**
Reynolds, Harold 1960— **77**
Reynolds, L. J. See Dramatics, The
Reynolds, Star Jones 1962(?)— **10, 27, 61**
Rhames, Ving 1959— **14, 50**
Rhimes, Shonda Lynn 1970— **67**
Rhoden, Dwight 1962— **40**
Rhoden, Wayne 1966— **70**
Rhoden, William C. 1950(?)— **67**
Rhodes, Jewell Parker 1954— **84**
Rhodes, Ray 1950— **14**
Rhone, Sylvia 1952— **2**
Rhone, Trevor 1940–2009 **80**
Rhymefest 1977— **97**
Rhymes, Busta 1972— **31**
Rhyne, Melvin 1936–2013 **109**

Ribbs, William Theodore, Jr. See Ribbs, Willy T.
Ribbs, Willy T. 1956— **2**
Ribeau, Sidney 1947(?)— **70**
Ribeiro, Alfonso 1971— **17**
Rice, Condoleezza 1954— **3, 28, 72**
Rice, Constance LaMay 1956— **60**
Rice, Emmett J. 1920–2011 **94**
Rice, Jerry 1962— **5, 55, 89**
Rice, Jim 1953— **75**
Rice, Linda Johnson 1958— **9, 41**
Rice, Louise Allen 1941— **54**
Rice, Norm(an Blann) 1943— **8**
Rice, Ray 1987— **112**
Rice, Susan 1964— **74, 103**
Richard, Dawn 1983— **92**
Richard, J. R. 1950— **87**
Richards, Beah 1926–2000 **30**
Richards, Hilda 1936— **49**
Richards, Lloyd 1923(?)— **2**
Richards, Sanya See Richards-Ross, Sanya
Richards-Ross, Sanya 1985— **66, 98**
Richardson, Desmond 1969— **39**
Richardson, Donna 1962— **39**
Richardson, Elaine Potter See Kincaid, Jamaica
Richardson, Julieanna 1954— **81**
Richardson, LaTanya 1949— **71**
Richardson, Laura 1962— **81**
Richardson, Nolan 1941— **9**
Richardson, Pat See Norman, Pat
Richardson, Rupert 1930–2008 **67**
Richardson, Salli 1967— **68**
Richie, Leroy C. 1941— **18**
Richie, Lionel 1949— **27, 65, 114**
Richmond, Cedric 1973— **93**
Richmond, Mitchell James 1965— **19**
Ricks, Jimmy See Ravens, The
Riddick, Clyde See Golden Gate Quartet
Rideau, Iris 1940(?)— **46**
Ridenhour, Carlton See Chuck D.
Ridley, John 1965— **69**
Riggins, Karriem 1975— **102**
Riggs, Marlon 1957–1994 **5, 44**
Rihanna 1988— **65, 102**
Riles, Wilson C. 1917–1999 **79**
Riley, Amber 1986— **97**
Riley, Boots 1971— **89**
Riley, Helen Caldwell Day 1926— **13**
Riley, Rochelle 1959(?)— **50**
Rillieux, Norbert 1806–1894 **92**
Ringgold, Faith 1930— **4, 81**
Riperton, Minnie 1947–1979 **32**
Rivers, Doc 1961— **25, 81**
Rivers, Eugene F., III 1950— **81**
Rivers, Glenn See Rivers, Doc
Rivers, Kim See Roberts, Kimberly Rivers
Rivers, Sam 1923— **95**
Roach, Max 1924–2007 **21, 63**
Roaf, Andrée Layton 1941–2009 **106**
Roaf, William Layton See Roaf, Willie
Roaf, Willie 1970— **106**
Roberto, Holden 1923–2007 **65**

Roberts, Aldwyn See Lord Kitchener

Roberts, Darryl 1962(?)— 70

Roberts, Deborah 1960— 35

Roberts, Ian See Kwei-Armah, Kwame

Roberts, James See Lover, Ed

Roberts, Kimberly Rivers 1981(?)— 72

Roberts, Kristina LaFerne See Zane

Roberts, Lillian 1928— 83

Roberts, Marcus 1963— 19, 113

Roberts, Marthaniel See Roberts, Marcus

Roberts, Mike 1948— 57

Roberts, Robin 1960— 16, 54, 113

Roberts, Roy S. 1939(?)— 14

Roberts, William Leonard, II See Ross, Rick

Robertson, Gil L., IV 1964— 85

Robertson, Lance See DJ Lance Rock

Robertson, Oscar 1938— 26

Robeson, Eslanda Goode 1896–1965 13

Robeson, Paul (Leroy Bustill) 1898–1976 2

Robey, Don 1903–1975 115

Robinson, Aminah 1940— 50

Robinson, Bill "Bojangles" 1878–1949 11

Robinson, Bishop L. 1927— 66

Robinson, Cleo Parker 1948(?)— 38

Robinson, Craig 1962— 107

Robinson, Craig 1971— 103

Robinson, Darren 1967–1995 See Fat Boys

Robinson, Dave 1941— 110

Robinson, David 1965— 24, 90

Robinson, Eddie G. 1919–2007 10, 61

Robinson, Eugene 1955— 77

Robinson, Fatima 19(?)(?)— 34

Robinson, Fenton 1935–1997 38

Robinson, Flynn 1941–2013 112

Robinson, Frank 1935— 9, 87

Robinson, Ida B. 1891–1946 106

Robinson, Jack Roosevelt See Robinson, Jackie

Robinson, Jackie 1919–1972 6

Robinson, Joann Gibson 1912–1992 100

Robinson, Justin See Carolina Chocolate Drops

Robinson, LaVaughn 1927–2008 69

Robinson, Louise See Sweet Honey in the Rock

Robinson, Luther See Robinson, Bill "Bojangles"

Robinson, Malcolm S. 1948— 44

Robinson, Matt 1937–2002 69

Robinson, Matthew, Jr. See Robinson, Matt

Robinson, Max 1939–1988 3

Robinson, Patrick 1966— 19, 71

Robinson, Rachel 1922— 16

Robinson, Randall 1941— 7, 46

Robinson, Reginald R. 1972— 53

Robinson, Sharon 1950— 22

Robinson, Shaun 19(?)(?)— 36

Robinson, Smokey 1940— 3, 49

Robinson, Spottswood W., III 1916–1998 22

Robinson, Sugar Ray 1921— 18

Robinson, Sylvia 1936— 79

Robinson, Will 1911–2008 51, 69

Robinson, William, Jr. See Robinson, Smokey

Robinson-Berry, Joan 19(?)(?)— 94

Roble, Abdi 1964— 71

Roby, Kimberla Lawson 1965— 86

Roche, Joyce M. 1947— 17

Rochester See Anderson, Eddie "Rochester"

Rochon, Lela 1965(?)— 16

Rochon, Stephen W. 1950(?)— 78

Rock, Chris 1967(?)— 3, 22, 66

Rock, John S. 1825–1866 113

Rock, John Sweat See Rock, John S.

Rock, John Swett See Rock, John S.

Rock, The 1972— 29, 66

Rock, Tony 1974— 108

Rodgers, Johnathan 1946— 6, 51

Rodgers, Rod 1937–2002 36

Rodman, Dennis 1961— 12, 44, 96

Rodney, Winston See Burning Spear

Rodrigues, Percy 1918–2007 68

Rodríguez, Arsenio 1911–1970 87

Rodriguez, Cheryl 1952— 64

Rodriguez, Jimmy 1963(?)— 47

Rogers, Alan G. 1967–2008 72

Rogers, Bobby 1940–2013 110

Rogers, Desirée 1959— 88

Rogers, Jimmy 1924–1997 38

Rogers, Joe 1964— 27

Rogers, Joel Augustus 1883(?)–1996 30

Rogers, John W., Jr. 1958— 5, 52

Rogers, Kelis See Kelis

Rogers, Nat See Little Anthony & the Imperials

Rogers, Rodney Ray 1971— 106

Rojas, Don 1949— 33

Roker, Al 1954— 12, 49

Roker, Roxie 1929–1995 68

Rolle, Esther 1920–1998 13, 21

Rolle, Janet 1961— 97

Rolle, Myron 1986— 98

Rollins, Billy See Contours, The

Rollins, Charlemae Hill 1897–1979 27

Rollins, Howard E., Jr. 1950–1996 16

Rollins, Ida Gray Nelson See Gray (Nelson Rollins), Ida

Rollins, James Calvin, III See Rollins, Jimmy

Rollins, Jimmy 1978— 70

Rollins, Sonny 1930— 37, 94

Rollins, Theodore Walter See Rollins, Sonny

Romanthony 1967–2013 115

Romeo 1989— 98

Ronaldinho 1980— 69

Rondo, Rajon 1986— 111

Rooakhptah, Amunnubi See York, Dwight D.

Roots, The 101

Rose, Anika Noni 1972— 70

Rose, Derrick 1988— 82

Rose, Jalen 1973— 108

Rose, Lionel 1948— 56

Ross, Araminta See Tubman, Harriet

Ross, Charles 1957— 27

Ross, Diana 1944— 8, 27

Ross, Don 1941— 27

Ross, Isaiah "Doc" 1925–1993 40

Ross, Rick 1976— 79, 104

Ross, Tracee Ellis 1972— 35

Rosser, Frederick Douglas, III See Young, Darren

Ross-Lee, Barbara 1942— 67

Rotimi, (Emmanuel Gladstone) Ola-(wale) 1938— 1

Roundfield, Danny 1953–2012 109

Roundtree, Dovey 1914— 80

Roundtree, Richard 1942— 27

Rouse, Cecilia 1963— 93

Rowan, Carl T(homas) 1925— 1, 30

Rowe-Adams, Jackie 194(?)— 109

Rowell, Victoria 1960— 13, 68

Rowland, Kelly 1981— 100

Roxanne Shante 1969— 33

Roy, Brandon 1984— 98

Roy, Kenny 1990(?)— 51

Rubin, Chanda 1976— 37

Rucker, Darius 1966— 34, 74, 108

Rudder, David 1953— 79

Rudisha, David 1988— 112

Rudolph, Maya 1972— 46, 106

Rudolph, Wilma (Glodean) 1940— 4

Ruffin, Joseph Lee See Shakur, Yusef

Ruffin, Josephine St. Pierre 1842–1924 75

Ruffins, Kermit 1964— 85

Rugambwa, Laurean 1912–1997 20

Ruley, Ellis 1882–1959 38

Run 1964— 31, 73, 75

Run-DMC 31, 75

RuPaul 1960— 17, 91

Rusesabagina, Paul 1954— 60

Rush, Bobby 1940— 78

Rush, Bobby 1946— 26, 76

Rush, Otis 1934— 38

Rushen, Patrice 1954— 12

Rushing, Jimmy 1903–1972 37

Russell, Bill 1934— 8

Russell, Brenda 1944(?)— 52

Russell, Herman Jerome 1931(?)— 17

Russell, Nipsey 1924–2005 66

Russell, William Felton See Russell, Bill

Russell-McCloud, Patricia 1946— 17

Russwurm, John Brown 1799–1851 100

Rust, Art, Jr. 1927–2010 83

Rustin, Bayard 1910–1987 4

Rutling, Thomas See Fisk Jubilee Singers

RZA 1969— 80

Saar, Alison 1956— 16

Saar, Betye 1926— 80

Sabathia, Carsten Charles, Jr. See Sabathia, CC

Sabathia, CC 1980— 74

Sade 1959— 15, 92

Sadler, Joseph See Grandmaster Flash

Sadlier, Rosemary 19(?)(?)— 62

St. Jacques, Raymond 1930–1990 8

Saint James, Synthia 1949— 12

St. John, Kristoff 1966— 25

St. Julien, Marlon 1972— 29

St. Patrick, Mathew 1969— 48

Saint-Georges, Chevalier de See Boulogne, Joseph, Chevalier de Saint-Georges

Saint-Georges, Joseph Boulogne See Boulogne, Joseph, Chevalier de Saint-Georges

Saldana, Zoe 1978— 72

Salih, Al-Tayyib 1929— 37

Sall, Macky 1961— 101

Sallee, Charles 1911— 38

Salley, Sam See Harold Melvin & the Blue Notes

Salter, Nikkole 1979(?)— 73

Salters, Alisia See Salters, Lisa

Salters, Lisa 1966(?)— 71

Salvador, Bryce 1976— 51

Sam and Dave 102

Samara, Noah 1956— 15

SAMO See Basquiat, Jean-Michel

Sample, Joe 1939— 51

Sampson, Charles 1957— 13

Sampson, Edith S(purlock) 1901–1979 4

Samuel, Sealhenry Olumide See Seal

Samuelsson, Marcus 1970— 53

Sanchez, Sonia 1934— 17, 51

Sandé, Emeli 1987— 113

Sanders, Angelia 1961(?)— 86

Sanders, Barry 1968— 1, 53

Sanders, Bob 1981— 72

Sanders, Deion 1967— 4, 31, 96

Sanders, Demond See Sanders, Bob

Sanders, Dori(nda) 1935— 8

Sanders, Joseph R(ichard, Jr.) 1954— 11

Sanders, Malika 1973— 48

Sanders, Pharoah 1940— 64

Sanders, Rose M. See Touré, Faya Ora Rose

Sanders, Satch 1938— 77

Sanders, Thomas Ernest See Sanders, Satch

Sands, Diana 1934–1973 87

Sané, Pierre Gabriel 1948–1998 21

Sanford, Isabel 1917–2004 53

Sanford, John Elroy See Foxx, Redd

Sangare, Oumou 1968— 18, 99

Sanhá Malam Bacai 1947–2012 84, 101

Sankara, Thomas 1949–1987 17

Sankoh, Foday 1937–2003 74

Sanneh, Kelefa 1975— 96

Santamaria, Mongo 1917–2003 81

Santiago-Hudson, Ruben 1956— 85

Santigold 1976— 96

Santogold See Santigold

Santos de Freitas, Antonio Carlos See Brown, Carlinhos

Sapp, Marvin 1966(?)— 74

Sapp, Rhonda LaChanze See LaChanze

Sapp, Warren 1972— 38, 109

Sapphire 1950— 14, 95

Saro-Wiwa, Kenule 1941–1995 39

Sasser, Sean 1968–2013 113

Sassou-Nguesso, Denis 1943— 103

Sata, Michael 1937— 102

Satcher, David 1941— 7, 57, 111

Satchmo See Armstrong, (Daniel) Louis

Saunders, Mahalia See Ellis, Hortense

Savage, Augusta Christine 1892(?)–1962 12

Savimbi, Jonas (Malheiro) 1934–2002 2, 34

Savón, Félix 1967— 105

Sawyer, Amos 1945— 2

Sawyer, Eugene 1934–2008 81

Saxton, Shirley Childress See Sweet Honey in the Rock

Sayers, Gale 1943— 28

Sayles Belton, Sharon See Belton, Sharon Sayles

Sbraga, Kevin 1979(?)— 88

Scandrick, Marvin See 112

Scandrick, Slim See 112

Scantlebury, Janna 1984(?)— 47

Scantlebury-White, Velma 1955— 64

Scarface See Geto Boys

Scarlett, Millicent 1971— 49

Schiavocampo, Mara 1979— 97

Schmoke, Kurt 1949— 1, 48

Schomburg, Arthur Alfonso 1874–1938 9

Schomburg, Arturo Alfonso See Schomburg, Arthur Alfonso

Schultz, Michael A. 1938— 6

Schuyler, George Samuel 1895–1977 40

Schuyler, Philippa 1931–1967 50

Scott, C. A. 1908–2000 29

Scott, Coretta See King, Coretta Scott

Scott, Cornelius Adolphus See Scott, C. A.

Scott, David 1946— 41

Scott, Dread 1965— 106

Scott, George 1929–2005 55 See also Blind Boys of Alabama, The

Scott, George 1944–2013 113

Scott, Harold Russell, Jr. 1935–2006 61

Scott, Hazel 1920–1981 66

Scott, Jeff See Imani Winds

Scott, Jill 1972— 29, 83

Scott, John T. 1940–2007 65

Scott, "Little" Jimmy 1925— 48

Scott, Milton 1956— 51

Scott, Robert C. 1947— 23

Scott, Stuart 1965— 34

Scott, Tim 1965— 87

Scott, Wendell Oliver, Sr. 1921–1990 19

Scott-Heron, Gil 1949–2011 94

Scott-Young, Mona 1967(?)— 101

Scruggs, Mary Elfrieda See Williams, Mary Lou

Scurry, Briana 1971— 27

Seacole, Mary 1805–1881 54

Seal 14, 75

Seale, Bobby 1936— 3

Seale, Robert George See Seale, Bobby

Seals, Frank See Seals, Son

Seals, Son 1942–2004 56

Sears, Leah Ward 1955— 5, 79

Sears, Stephanie 1964— 53

Sears-Collins, Leah J(eanette) See Sears, Leah Ward

Sebree, Charles 1914–1985 40

Secada, Jon 1962— 97

Secada, Juan Francisco See Secada, Jon

Seele, Pernessa 1954— 46

Selassie, Haile See Haile Selassie

Sembène, Ousmane 1923–2007 13, 62

Senghor, Augustin Diamacoune 1928–2007 66

Senghor, Léopold Sédar 1906–2001 12, 66

Sengstacke, John Herman Henry 1912–1997 18

Senior, Olive 1941— 37

Senna, Danzy 1970— 93

Sentamu, John 1949— 58

Sermon, Erick 1968— 81

Serrano, Andres 1951(?)— 3

Sesay, Isha 1976— 107

Seven-Seven, Prince Twins See Prince Twins Seven-Seven

Sewell, Terri 1965— 93

Seymour, Richard 1979— 101

Seymour, Teddy 1941(?)— 110

Seymour, William J. 1879–1922 106

Shabazz, Attallah 1958— 6

Shabazz, Betty 1936–1997 7, 26

Shabazz, Ilyasah 1962— 36

Shadd, Abraham D. 1801–1882 81

Shaggy 1968— 31

Shakespeare, Robbie 1953— See Sly & Robbie

Shakur, Afeni 1947— 67

Shakur, Assata 1947— 6

Shakur, Meshell Suihailia Bashir See Ndegeocello, Meshell

Shakur, Tupac Amaru 1971–1996 14

Shakur, Yusef 1973— 85

Shange, Ntozake 1948— 8, 89

Shanice 1973— 112

Shank, Suzanne F. 1962(?)— 77

Shannon, Randy 1966— 82

Sharpe, Samuel 1801(?)–1832 103

Sharpe, Shannon 1968— 97

Sharper, Darren 1975— 32

Sharpton, Al 1954— 21, 97

Shavers, Cheryl 19(?)(?)— 31

Shaw, Bernard 1940— 2, 28

Shaw, Ernesto D., Jr. See DJ Clue?

Shaw, Marlena 1942— 105

Shaw, William J. 1934— 30

Sheard, Kierra 1987— 61, 114

Sheard, Kiki See Sheard, Kierra

Shearer, Hugh 1923–2004 107

Sheffey, Asa Bundy See Hayden, Robert Earl

Sheffield, Gary 1968— 16, 108

Shell, Art 1946— 1, 66

Shelton, Billy See Clovers, The

Shelton, Paula Young 1961— 86

Shepherd, Sherri 1970— 55

Shepp, Archie 1937— 101

Sheppard, Ella See Fisk Jubilee Singers

Sherrod, Clayton 1944— 17

Sherrod, Shirley 1948— 87

Shider, Garry 1953–2010 87

Shinhoster, Earl 1950(?)–2000 32

Shipp, E. R. 1955— 15

Shipp, Matthew 1960— 107

Shippen, John 1879–1968 43

Shirelles, The 111

Shirley, Donald 1927–2013 111

Shirley, George I. 1934— 33

Shocklee, Hank See Public Enemy

Shockley, Ann Allen 1927— 84

Shonibare, Yinka 1962— 58

Shores, Arthur D. 1904–1996 99

Short, Bobby 1924–2005 52

Short, Columbus 1982— 79

Shorter, Wayne 1933— 75

Shorty, Ras, I 1941–2000 47

Showers, Reggie 1964— 30

Shropshire, Thomas B. 1925–2003 49

Shuttlesworth, Fred 1922–2011 47, 98

Shyne 1978— 101

Sidibe, Gabourey 1983— 84

Sidner, Sara 1972— 105

Sifford, Charlie 1922— 4, 49

Sigur, Wanda 1958— 44

Siji 1971(?)— 56

Silas, Paul 1943— 24

Silva, Anderson 1975— 96

Silva, Marina 1958— 80

Silver, Horace 1928— 26

Siméus, Dumas M. 1939— 25, 110

Simkins, Modjeska Monteith 1899–1992 112

Simmons, Bill See Midnight Star

Simmons, Bob 1948— 29

Simmons, E. Denise 19(?)(?)— 79

Simmons, Gary 1964— 58

Simmons, Henry 1970— 55

Simmons, Jamal 1971— 72

Simmons, Joseph See Run; Run-DMC

Simmons, Kimora Lee 1975— 51, 83

Simmons, Russell 1957(?)— 1, 30

Simmons, Ruth J. 1945— 13, 38

Simms, Margaret 1946— 94

Simon, Joe 1943— 109

Simon, Lateefah 1977— 95

Simone, Nina 1933–2003 15, 41

Simpson, Carole 1940— 6, 30

Simpson, Lorna 1960— 4, 36

Simpson, Merton D. 1928–2013 110

Simpson, O. J. 1947— 15, 100

Simpson, Valerie 1946— 21, 97

Simpson-Hoffman, N'kenge 1975(?)— 52

Simpson Miller, Portia 1945— 62, 100

Sims, Danny 1936–2012 106

Sims, Howard "Sandman" 1917–2003 48

Sims, Lowery Stokes 1949— 27

Sims, Naomi 1948–2009 29, 79

Sims, Peter See La Roca, Pete

Sinbad 1957(?)— 1, 16

Sinclair, Floyd See Mayweather, Floyd

Sinclair, Madge 1938–1995 78

Singletary, Mike 1958— 4, 76

Singleton, John 1968— 2, 30

Sinkford, Jeanne C. 1933— 13

Sir Mix-A-Lot 1963— 82

Sirleaf, Ellen Johnson 1938— 71

Sisqo 1976— 30

Sissle, Noble 1889–1975 29

Sister Souljah 1964— 11, 100

Sisulu, Albertina 1918–2011 57, 95

Sisulu, Sheila Violet Makate 1948(?)— 24

Sisulu, Walter 1912–2003 47

Sizemore, Barbara A. 1927–2004 26, 110

Sizemore, Grady 1982— 96

Skerrit, Roosevelt 1972— 72

Skinner, Kiron K. 1962(?) 65

Sklarek, Norma Merrick 1926–2012 25, 101

Slash 1975— 75

Slater, Rodney Earl 1955— 15

Slaughter, John Brooks 1934— 53

Sledge, Percy 1940— 39

Sleet, Gregory M. 1951— 109

Sleet, Moneta (J.), Jr. 1926— 5

Slice, Kimbo 1974— 73

Slick Rick 1965— 93

Slim See 112

Slim Jukebox, The See Geto Boys

Slim Thug 1980— 86

Slocumb, Jonathan 19(?)(?)— 52

Sly & Robbie 34

Slyde, Jimmy 1927–2008 70

Smalls, Robert 1839–1915 82

Smaltz, Audrey 1937(?)— 12

Smiley, Rickey 1968— 59

Smiley, Tavis 1964— 20, 68

Smith, Amanda Berry 1837–1915 109

Smith, Anjela Lauren 1973— 44

Smith, Anna Deavere 1950— 6, 44

Smith, Arthur Lee, See Asante, Molefi Kete

Smith, B. See Smith, B(arbara)

Smith, B(arbara) 1949(?)— 11

Smith, Barbara 1946— 28

Smith, Bessie 1894–1937 3

Smith, Bruce 1984— 80

Smith, Bruce W. 19(?)(?)— 53

Smith, Bubba 1945–2011 96

Smith, Carl Reginald See Smith, Reggie

Smith, Cecilia 1960(?)— 102

Smith, Charles Aaron See Smith, Bubba

Smith, Che See Rhymefest

Smith, Cladys "Jabbo" 1908–1991 32

Smith, Clarence 1904–1929 113

Smith, Clarence O. 1933— 21

Smith, Clifford See Method Man

Smith, Damu 1951— 54

Smith, Dante Terrell See Bey, Yasiin

Smith, Danyel 1966(?)— 40

Smith, DeMaurice 1964— 92

Smith, Dickie See Five Keys, The

Smith, Dr. Lonnie 1942— 49

Smith, Emmitt 1969— 7, 87

Smith, Greg 1964— 28

Smith, Hezekiah Leroy Gordon See Smith, Stuff

Smith, Hilton 1912–1983 29

Smith, Ian 1970(?)— 62

Smith, Jabbo See Smith, Cladys "Jabbo"

Smith, Jaden 1998— **82**
Smith, James Todd *See LL Cool J*
Smith, Jane E. 1946— **24**
Smith, Jennifer 1947— **21**
Smith, Jessie Carney 1930— **35**
Smith, John L. 1938— **22**
Smith, Joshua (Isaac) 1941— **10**
Smith, Kemba 1971— **70**
Smith, Kenneth *See Smith, Kenny*
Smith, Kenny 1965— **114**
Smith, LaQuan 1988— **113**
Smith, Lee 1957— **101**
Smith, Lenithia Bonita *See Leakes, NeNe*
Smith, Lonnie Liston 1940— **49**
Smith, Lovie 1958— **66, 107**
Smith, Malcolm A. 1956— **75**
Smith, Mamie 1883–1946 **32**
Smith, Marie F. 1939— **70**
Smith, Marvin 1910–2003 **46**
Smith, Mary Carter 1919— **26**
Smith, Ming 19(?)(?)— **100**
Smith, Morgan 1910–1993 **46**
Smith, Myrna 1941–2010 **92**
Smith, Nate 1929— **49**
Smith, Neil 1966— **109**
Smith, Orlando *See Smith, Tubby*
Smith, Ozzie 1954— **77**
Smith, Pinetop *See Smith, Clarence*
Smith, Princella 1983— **86**
Smith, Randy 1948–2009 **81**
Smith, Reggie 1945— **113**
Smith, Richard 1957— **51**
Smith, Rick 1969— **72**
Smith, Roger Guenveur 1960— **12**
Smith, Shaffer Chimere *See Ne-Yo*
Smith, Stephen A. 1967— **69**
Smith, Stuff 1909–1967 **37**
Smith, Tasha 1971— **73**
Smith, Tommie 1944— **102**
Smith, Trevor, Jr. *See Rhymes, Busta*
Smith, Trixie 1895–1943 **34**
Smith, Tubby 1951— **18, 83**
Smith, Vincent D. 1929–2003 **48**
Smith, Walker, Jr. *See Robinson, Sugar Ray*
Smith, Will 1968— **8, 18, 53**
Smith, Willi (Donnell) 1948–1987 **8**
Smith, Willie 1897(?)–1973 **107**
Smith, Willow 2000— **92**
Smith, Zadie 1975— **51**
Smyre, Calvin 1947— **90**
Smythe Haith, Mabel 1918–2006 **61**
Sneed, Paula A. 1947— **18**
Snipes, Wesley 1962— **3, 24, 67**
Snoop Dogg 1971— **35, 84**
Snow, Samuel 1923–2008 **71**
Snowden, Frank M., Jr. 1911–2007 **67**
Snowden, Gail 1945— **108**
Soglo, Nicéphore 1935— **15**
Sohn, Sonja 1964— **100**
Solange 1986— **97**
Solomon, Jimmie Lee 1947(?)— **38**
Somé, Malidoma Patrice 1956— **10**
Somi 1979— **85**
Sommore, 1966— **61**
Song, Alex 1987— **105**
Songz, Trey 1984— **88**
Sono, Jomo 1955— **86**

Sosa, Sammy 1968— **21, 44**
Soto Alejo, Federico Arístides *See Güines, Tata*
Soulchild, Musiq *See Musiq*
Souleymane, Mahamane 1940— **78**
Southern, Eileen 1920–2002 **56**
Southgate, Martha 1960(?)— **58**
Souza, Carmen 1981— **111**
Sowande, Fela 1905–1987 **39**
Sowande, Olufela Obafunmilayo *See Sowande, Fela*
Sowell, Thomas 1930— **2, 99**
Soyinka, Wole 1934— **4, 93**
Spaniels, The **105**
Spann, Otis 1930(?)–1970 **107**
Sparks, Corinne Etta 1953— **53**
Sparks, Jordin 1989— **66**
Spaulding, Charles Clinton 1874–1952 **9**
Spearman, Leonard H. O., Sr. 1929–2008 **81**
Spears, Warren 1954–2005 **52**
Speck, George *See Crum, George*
Spector, Ronnie 1943— **77**
Speech 1968— **82**
Spellman-Diaz, Toyin *See Imani Winds*
Spence, Joseph 1910–1984 **49**
Spencer, Anne 1882–1975 **27**
Spencer, Michael G. 1952— **87**
Spencer, Octavia 1972— **100**
Spencer, Vaino H. 1920— **99**
Spencer, Winston Baldwin 1948— **68**
Spigner, Archie 1928— **81**
Spikes, Dolores Margaret Richard 1936— **18**
Spiller, Bill 1913–1988 **64**
Sprewell, Latrell 1970— **23**
Spriggs, William 195(?)— **67**
Springer, Ashton, Jr. 1930–2013 **115**
Stackhouse, Jerry 1974— **30**
Staley, Dawn 1970— **57**
Stallings, Felix, Jr. *See Felix Da Housecat*
Stallings, George A(ugustus), Jr. 1948— **6**
Stallworth, John 1952— **102**
Stampley, Micah 1971— **54**
Stanford, John 1938— **20**
Stanford, Olivia Lee Dilworth 1914–2004 **49**
Stanton, Alysa 1963— **78**
Stanton, Robert 1940— **20**
Staples, Brent 1951— **8**
Staples, Cleotha 1934–2013 **113**
Staples, Mavis 1939(?)— **50, 88**
Staples, "Pops" 1915–2000 **32**
Staples, Roebuck *See Staples, "Pops"*
Staples, Ron *See Mighty Clouds of Joy*
Stargell, Willie 1940(?)–2001 **29**
Staton, Candi 1940(?)— **27**
Staton, Dakota 1930(?)–2007 **62**
Staupers, Mabel K(eaton) 1890–1989 **7**
Stearnes, Norman "Turkey" 1901–1979 **31**
Steave-Dickerson, Kia 1970— **57**
Steele, Claude 1946— **13, 97**
Steele, Lawrence 1963— **28**
Steele, Michael 1958— **38, 73, 91**

Steele, Sage 1972— **115**
Steele, Shelby 1946— **13, 82**
Steely 1962–2009 **80**
Steinberg, Martha Jean 1930(?)–2000 **28**
Stephens, Charlotte Andrews 1854–1951 **14**
Stephens, John *See Legend, John*
Stephens, Myrtle *See Potter, Myrtle*
Stephens, Sloane 1993— **105**
Stevens, Yvette *See Khan, Chaka*
Stevenson, Teófilo 1952–2012 **103**
Stew 1961— **69**
Steward, David L. 19(?)(?)— **36**
Steward, Emanuel 1944–2012 **18, 106**
Stewart, Alison 1966(?)— **13**
Stewart, Billy 1937–1970 **112**
Stewart, Bubba *See Stewart, James, Jr.*
Stewart, Christopher Alan *See Stewart, Tricky*
Stewart, Ella 1893–1987 **39**
Stewart, James, Jr. 1985— **60, 98**
Stewart, Kordell 1972— **21, 111**
Stewart, Mark *See Stew*
Stewart, Nzingha 1974— **89**
Stewart, Paul Wilbur 1925— **12**
Stewart, Sylvester *See Stone, Sly*
Stewart, Tonea Harris 1947— **78**
Stewart, Tricky 1974— **98**
Stickney, Phyllis Yvonne 19(?)(?)— **108**
Sticky Fingaz 1970— **86**
Still, William Grant 1895–1978 **37**
Stingley, Darryl 1951–2007 **69**
Stinson, Denise L. 1954— **59**
Stith, Charles R. 1949— **73**
Stith, Tom 1939–2010 **93**
Stockman, Shawn *See Boyz II Men*
Stokes, Carl 1927–1996 **10, 73**
Stokes, Louis 1925— **3**
Stone, Angie 1965(?)— **31**
Stone, Charles Sumner, Jr. *See Stone, Chuck*
Stone, Chuck 1924— **9**
Stone, Jesse 1901–1999 **98**
Stone, Sly 1943— **85**
Stone, Toni 1921–1996 **15**
Stoney, Michael 1969— **50**
Stott, Dorothy M. *See Stout, Renee*
Stott, Dot *See Stout, Renee*
Stoudemire, Amar'e 1982— **59, 106**
Stout, Juanita Kidd 1919–1998 **24**
Stout, Renee 1958— **63**
Stoute, Steve 1971(?)— **38**
Stoutt, H. Lavity 1929–1995 **83**
Stowers, Freddie 1896–1918 **107**
Stradford, J. B. 1861–1935 **101**
Strahan, Michael 1971— **35, 81**
Strain, Sammy *See Little Anthony & the Imperials*
Strautmanis, Michael 1969— **87**
Strawberry, Darryl 1962— **22**
Strayhorn, Billy 1915–1967 **31**
Street, John F. 1943(?)— **24**
Street, Richard 1942–2013 **110**
Streeter, Amber Denise *See Streeter, Sevyn*
Streeter, Sarah 1953— **45**
Streeter, Sevyn 1986— **115**
Stringer, C. Vivian 1948— **13, 66**
Stringer, Korey 1974–2001 **35**

Stringer, Vickie 196(?)— **58**
Strode, Woodrow Wilson Woolwine *See Strode, Woody*
Strode, Woody 1914–1994 **111**
Stroman, Nathaniel *See Earthquake*
Strong, Barrett 1941— **89**
Stuart, Moira 1949— **82**
Stubbs, Joe *See Contours, The*
Studdard, Ruben 1978— **46**
Sudarkasa, Niara 1938— **4**
Sudduth, Jimmy Lee 1910–2007 **65**
Sugarhill Gang, The **79**
Suggs, Terrell 1982— **108**
Sullivan, Jazmine 1987— **81**
Sullivan, Leon H(oward) 1922— **3, 30**
Sullivan, Louis (Wade) 1933— **8**
Sullivan, Maxine 1911–1987 **37**
Sul-Te-Wan, Madame *See Madame Sul-Te-Wan*
Sumlin, Hubert 1931–2011 **101**
Summer, Donna 1948–2012 **25, 102**
Sumner, Francis Cecil 1926–1973 **112**
Sun Ra, 1914–1993 **60**
Sundiata, Sekou 1948–2007 **66**
Supremes, The **33**
Sutphen, Mona 1967— **77**
Suttles, George *See Suttles, Mule*
Suttles, Mule 1900–1966 **108**
Suttles, Warren *See Ravens, The*
Sutton, Percy E. 1920–2009 **42, 82**
Swan Silvertones, The **110**
Swann, Bettye 1944— **109**
Swann, Lynn 1952— **28**
Swaray, Fanta Estelle *See Estelle*
Sweat, Keith 1961(?)— **19**
Sweatshirt, Earl 1994— **114**
Sweatt, Heman Marion 1912–1982 **114**
Sweet, Ossian 1895–1960 **68**
Sweet Honey in the Rock **106**
Swizz Beatz 1978— **108**
Swoopes, Sheryl 1971— **12, 56**
Swygert, H. Patrick 1943— **22**
Sy, Omar 1978— **109**
Sy, Oumou 1952— **65**
Sykes, Roosevelt 1906–1984 **20**
Sykes, Wanda 1964— **48, 81**
Syler, Rene 1963— **53**
Tademy, Lalita 1948— **36**
Tafari Makonnen *See Haile Selassie*
Tail Dragger 1940— **112**
Tait, Michael 1966— **57**
Take 6 **112**
Talbert, David E. 1966(?)— **34, 93**
Talbert, Mary B. 1866–1923 **77**
Talley, André Leon 1949— **56, 106**
Tamar-kali 1973(?)— **63**
Tamia 1975— **24, 55**
Tampa Red 1904(?)–1980 **63**
Tancil, Gladys Quander 1921–2002 **59**
Tandja, Mamadou 1938— **33, 78**
Tanksley, Ann (Graves) 1934— **37**
Tanner, Henry Ossawa 1859–1937 **1**
Tanner, Jack E. 1919–2006 **100**
Taste of Honey, A **115**
Tate, Bruce *See Penguins, The*

Tate, Buddy 1913–2001 **108**

Tate, Eleanora E. 1948— **20, 55**

Tate, George Holmes *See Tate, Buddy*

Tate, Grady 1932— **106**

Tate, John 1955–1998 **107**

Tate, Larenz 1975— **15**

Tate, Minnie *See Fisk Jubilee Singers*

Tatum, Art 1909–1956 **28**

Tatum, Beverly Daniel 1954— **42, 84**

Tatum, Elinor R. 197(?)— **78**

Tatum, Jack 1948— **87**

Tatum, Reece 1921–1967 **104**

Tatum, Wilbert 1933–2009 **76**

Taulbert, Clifton Lemoure 1945— **19**

Tavares **115**

Tavares, Butch *See Tavares*

Tavares, Chubby *See Tavares*

Tavares, Pooch *See Tavares*

Tavares, Ralph *See Tavares*

Tavares, Tiny *See Tavares*

Taylor, Bennie *See Dramatics, The*

Taylor, Billy 1921–2010 **23, 92**

Taylor, Bo 1966–2008 **72**

Taylor, Cecil 1929— **70**

Taylor, Charles 1948— **20**

Taylor, Darren *See Taylor, Bo*

Taylor, Ephren W., II 1982— **61**

Taylor, Gardner C. 1918— **76**

Taylor, Helen (Lavon Hollingshed) 1942–2000 **30**

Taylor, Jason 1974— **70**

Taylor, Jermain 1978— **60**

Taylor, John (David Beckett) 1952— **16**

Taylor, Karin 1971— **34**

Taylor, Katrina Laverne *See Trina*

Taylor, Koko 1928–2009 **40, 80**

Taylor, Kristin Clark 1959— **8**

Taylor, Lawrence 1959— **25**

Taylor, Lonzie Odie 1899–1977 **96**

Taylor, Marshall Walter "Major" 1878–1932 **62**

Taylor, Meshach 1947(?)— **4**

Taylor, Mildred D. 1943— **26**

Taylor, Natalie 1959— **47**

Taylor, Recy 1919— **92**

Taylor, Regina 1960— **9, 46, 97**

Taylor, Robert Robinson 1868–1942 **80**

Taylor, Robert Rochon 1899–1957 **104**

Taylor, Ron 1952–2002 **35**

Taylor, Susan C. 1957— **62**

Taylor, Susan L. 1946— **10, 86**

Taylor, Susie King 1848–1912 **13**

T-Boz 1970— **108** *See also TLC*

Tchicai, John 1936— **102**

Teague, Bob 1929–2013 **111**

Teasley, Lisa 1962— **92**

Teer, Barbara Ann 1937–2008 **81**

Temple, Ed 1927— **109**

Temple, Lewis 1800–1854 **102**

Temptations, The **33**

Tergat, Paul 1969— **59**

Terminator X *See Public Enemy*

Terrell, Dorothy A. 1945— **24**

Terrell, Mary (Elizabeth) Church 1863–1954 **9**

Terrell, Tammi 1945–1970 **32**

Terrell-Kearney, Kim 1965— **83**

Terrence J 1982— **108**

Terrill, Saunders *See Terry, Sonny*

Terry, Clark 1920— **39**

Terry, Sonny 1911–1986 **88**

Tharpe, Rosetta 1915–1973 **65**

Thaws, Adrian Nicholas Matthews *See Tricky*

The Artist *See Prince*

The-Dream 1982— **74**

Thiam, Aliaune Akon *See Akon*

Thiam, Tidjane 1962— **104**

Thigpen, Ed 1930–2010 **110**

Thigpen, Lynne 1948–2003 **17, 41**

Thomas, Alma Woodsey 1891–1978 **14**

Thomas, Arthur Ray 1951— **52**

Thomas, Carla 1942— **96**

Thomas, Clarence 1948— **2, 39, 65**

Thomas, Claudia Lynn 1950— **64**

Thomas, David *See Take 6*

Thomas, Debi 1967— **26**

Thomas, Derrick 1967–2000 **25**

Thomas, Emmitt 1943— **71**

Thomas, Frank 1968— **12, 51**

Thomas, Franklin A. 1934— **5, 49**

Thomas, Irma 1941— **29**

Thomas, Isiah 1961— **7, 26, 65**

Thomas, Jefferson 1942–2010 **88**

Thomas, Michael 1967— **69**

Thomas, Mickalene 1971— **61**

Thomas, Rozonda 1971— **78** *See also TLC*

Thomas, Rufus 1917–2001 **20, 96**

Thomas, Sean Patrick 1970— **35**

Thomas, Stayve Jerome *See Slim Thug*

Thomas, Thurman 1966— **75**

Thomas, Todd *See Speech*

Thomas, Trisha R. 1964— **65**

Thomas, Vivien (T.) 1910–1985 **9**

Thomas-Graham, Pamela 1963(?)— **29**

Thomas-Greenfield, Linda 1952— **99**

Thomason, Marsha 1976— **47**

Thomaz, Cameron Jibril *See Khalifa, Wiz*

Thompson, Ahmir *See ?uestlove*

Thompson, Bennie G. 1948— **26**

Thompson, Cynthia Bramlett 1949— **50**

Thompson, Dearon *See Deezer D*

Thompson, Don 1963— **56, 108**

Thompson, John Douglas 1964— **81**

Thompson, John W. 1949— **26**

Thompson, Kenan 1978— **52**

Thompson, Larry D. 1945— **39**

Thompson, Marshall *See Chi-Lites*

Thompson, Sylvester *See Johnson, Syl*

Thompson, Tazewell (Alfred, Jr.) 1954— **13**

Thompson, Tina 1975— **25, 75**

Thompson, William C., Jr. 1953— **35, 114**

Thoms, Tracie 1975— **61**

Thornton, Big Mama 1926–1984 **33**

Thornton, Yvonne S. 1947— **69**

Thrash, Dox 1893–1965 **35**

Threadgill, Henry 1944— **97**

Three Mo' Tenors **35**

Thrower, Willie 1930–2002 **35**

Thugwane, Josia 1971— **21**

Thurman, Howard 1900–1981 **3**

Thurman, Wallace Henry 1902–1934 **16**

Thurmond, Nate 1941— **88**

Thurston, Baratunde 1977— **79, 101**

Thurston, Stephen J. 1952— **49**

Tiant, Luis 1940— **102**

Till, Emmett (Louis) 1941–1955 **7**

Tillard, Conrad 1964— **47**

Tillis, Frederick 1930— **40**

Tillman, Deborah 1962(?)— **98**

Tillman, Dorothy 1947— **76**

Tillman, George, Jr. 1968— **20**

Timbaland 1971— **32**

Tingling, Milton A. 1953— **110**

Tinie Tempah 1988— **115**

Tinsley, Boyd 1964— **50**

Tirico, Michael *See Tirico, Mike*

Tirico, Mike 1966— **68**

Tisby, Dexter *See Penguins, The*

Tisdale, Wayman 1964— **50**

TLC **34**

Tobias, Channing H. 1882–1961 **79**

Tobin, Patricia 1943–2008 **75**

Todd, Franck *See Golden Gate Quartet*

Todman, Terence A. 1926— **55**

Tolbert, James L. 1926–2013 **112**

Tolbert, Terence 1964— **74**

Tolbert, William R. 1913–1980 **100**

Toler, Burl 1928–2009 **80**

Tolliver, Mose 1915(?)–2006 **60**

Tolliver, William (Mack) 1951— **9**

Tolson, Melvin B(eaunorus) 1898–1966 **37**

Tolton, Augustine 1854–1897 **62**

Tomlinson, LaDainian 1979— **65, 112**

Tonex, 1978(?)— **54**

Toney, James 1968— **89**

Tooks, Lance 1962— **62**

Toomer, Jean 1894–1967 **6**

Toomer, Nathan Pinchback *See Toomer, Jean*

Toote, Gloria E. A. 1931— **64**

Toots and the Maytals *See Hibbert, Toots*

Torres, Gina 1969— **52**

Torry, Guy 19(?)(?)— **31**

Tosh, Peter 1944–1987 **9**

Touré, Amadou Toumani 1948(?)— **18**

Touré, Askia (Muhammad Abu Bakr el) 1938— **47**

Touré, Faya Ora Rose 1945— **56**

Touré, Sekou 1922–1984 **6**

Touré, Yaya 1983— **99**

Toussaint, Allen 1938— **60**

Toussaint, Lorraine 1960— **32**

Townes, Jeffrey Allan *See DJ Jazzy Jeff*

Towns, Edolphus 1934— **19, 75**

Townsend, Robert 1957— **4, 23**

T-Pain 1985— **73, 111**

Trammell, Kimberly N. *See Holland, Kimberly N.*

Trammps, The **108**

Traore, Dioncounda 1942— **103**

Travis, Tracey T. 1962— **94**

Tresvant, Ralph 1968— **57** *See also New Edition*

Trethewey, Natasha 1966— **103**

Tribbett, Tye 1977— **81**

Tribble, Israel, Jr. 1940— **8**

Tricky 1967— **98**

Trina 1974— **114**

Trombone Shorty 1986— **97**

Trotter, Donne E. 1950— **28**

Trotter, Lloyd G. 1945(?)— **56**

Trotter, (William) Monroe 1872–1934 **9**

Trotter, Tariq Luqmaan *See Black Thought; Roots, The*

Trouillot, Ertha Pascal *See Pascal-Trouillot, Ertha*

Troupe, Quincy 1943— **83**

Trouppe, Quincy Thomas, Sr. 1912–1993 **84**

True, Rachel 1966— **82**

Trueheart, William E. 1942— **49**

Tsvangirai, Morgan 1952— **26, 72**

Tubbs Jones, Stephanie 1949–2008 **24, 72**

Tubman, Harriet 1820(?)–1913 **9**

Tubman, William 1895–1971 **99**

Tucker, C. Delores 1927–2005 **12, 56**

Tucker, Chris 1972— **13, 23, 62**

Tucker, Cynthia 1955— **1561**

Tucker, Rosina Budd Harvey Corrothers 1881–1987 **14**

Tuckson, Reed V. 1951(?)— **71**

Tuku *See Mtukudzi, Oliver*

Tunie, Tamara 1959— **63**

Tunnell, Emlen 1925–1975 **54**

Ture, Kwame *See Carmichael, Stokely*

Turman, Glynn 1947— **100**

Turnbull, Charles Wesley 1935— **62**

Turnbull, Walter 1944— **13, 60**

Turner, Big Joe 1911–1985 **92**

Turner, Henry McNeal 1834–1915 **5**

Turner, Ike 1931–2007 **68**

Turner, Izear *See Turner, Ike*

Turner, Tina 1939— **6, 27**

Tutu, Desmond (Mpilo) 1931— **6, 44**

Tutu, Nontombi Naomi 1960— **57**

Tutuola, Amos 1920–1997 **30**

2 Chainz 1976— **105**

Tyler, Aisha N. 1970— **36**

Tyler, the Creator 1991— **100**

Tyner, McCoy 1938— **92**

Tyree, Omar Rashad 1969— **21**

Tyrese *See Gibson, Tyrese*

Tyson, Andre 1960— **40**

Tyson, Asha 1970— **39**

Tyson, Cicely 1924(?)— **7, 51, 112**

Tyson, Mike 1966— **28, 44, 93**

Tyson, Neil deGrasse 1958— **15, 65**

Uggams, Leslie 1943— **23, 114**

Ujiri, Masai 1970— **107**

Ukpabio, Helen 1969— **86**

Ulmer, James 1942— **79**

Underwood, Blair 1964— **7, 27, 76**

Union, Gabrielle 1972— **31, 92**

Unseld, Wes 1946— **23**

Upshaw, Gene 1945–2008 **18, 47, 72**

Usher 1977— **23, 56, 95**

Usry, James L. 1922— **23**

Ussery, Terdema Lamar, II 1958— 29

Utendahl, John 1956— 23

Valdés, Bebo 1918— 75

Valdés, Chucho 1941— 89

Valdés, Dionisio Ramón Emilio See Valdés, Bebo

Valentine, Johnny See Mighty Clouds of Joy

Valentino, Bobby 1980— 62

Van Lierop, Robert 1939— 53

Van Loan, James See Billy Ward and the Dominoes

Van Peebles, Mario 1957— 2, 51

Van Peebles, Melvin 1932— 7, 95

van Sertima, Ivan 1935— 25

Vance, Courtney B. 1960— 15, 60

Vance, Jim 1942— 110

VanDerZee, James (Augustus Joseph) 1886–1983 6

Vandross, Luther 1951–2005 13, 48, 59

Vanessa James and Yannick Bonheur 84

Vanity 1959— 67

Vann, Harold Moore See Muhammad, Khallid Abdul

Vanzant, Iyanla 1953— 17, 47, 108

Vaughan, Sarah (Lois) 1924–1990 13

Vaughn, Countess 1978— 53

Vaughn, Gladys Gary 1942(?)— 47

Vaughn, Mo 1967— 16

Vaughn, Viola 1947— 70

Vaughns, Cleopatra 1940— 46

Vega, Marta Moreno 1942(?)— 61

Velez-Rodriguez, Argelia 1936— 56

Vera, Yvonne 1964— 32

Verdelle, A. J. 1960— 26

Vereen, Ben(jamin Augustus) 1946— 4

Verna, Gelsy 1961–2008 70

Verrett, Shirley 1931–2010 66, 91

Vesey, Denmark 1767(?)–1822 100

Via, Dennis 1958(?)— 108

Vibra-Naires, The See Orioles, The

Vick, Michael 1980— 39, 65, 94

Vieira, João Bernardo 1939–2009 14, 84

Villard-Appolon, Malya 1959(?)— 106

Villarosa, Clara 1930(?)— 85

Vincent, Marjorie Judith 1965(?)— 2

Vincent, Mark See Diesel, Vin

Vincent, Troy 1971— 91

Vinson, Cleanhead See Vinson, Eddie

Vinson, Eddie 1917–1988 112

Virgil, Ozzie 1933— 48

Vogue, En See En Vogue

Von Lipsey, Roderick 1959— 11

wa Ngengi, Kamau See Kenyatta, Jomo

Waddles, Charleszetta 1912–2001 10, 49

Waddles, Mother See Waddles, Charleszetta

Wade, Abdoulaye 1926— 66

Wade, Dwyane 1982— 61, 103

Wade, Harold See Trammps, The

Wade, Stanley See Trammps, The

Wade-Gayles, Gloria Jean 1937(?)— 41

Wagner, Albert 1924–2006 78

Wagner, Annice 1937— 22

Wainwright, Joscelyn 1941— 46

Waka Flocka Flame 1986— 110

Walcott, Dennis M. 1951— 112

Walcott, Derek 1930— 5, 94

Walcott, Jersey Joe 1914–1994 102

Waldon, Alton R., Jr. 1936— 98

Waldron, Mal 1925–2002 109

Wale 1984— 92

Walker, Aaron Thibeaux See Walker, T-Bone

Walker, Albertina 1929–2010 10, 58, 89

Walker, Alice 1944— 1, 43

Walker, Arthur, II 1936–2001 87

Walker, Bernita Ruth 1946— 53

Walker, Cedric "Ricky" 1953— 19

Walker, Chet 1940— 106

Walker, Cora T. 1922–2006 68

Walker, Dianne 1951— 57

Walker, Eamonn 1961(?)— 37

Walker, Eliza See Fisk Jubilee Singers

Walker, George 1922— 37

Walker, Greg See Taste of Honey, A

Walker, Herschel 1962— 1, 69

Walker, Hezekiah 1962— 34

Walker, John T. 1925–1989 50

Walker, Joseph Edison 1880–1958 111

Walker, Kara 1969— 16, 80

Walker, Kurt See Blow, Kurtis

Walker, LeRoy T. 1918–2012 106

Walker, Lucius, Jr. 1930–2010 88

Walker, Madame C. J. 1867–1919 7

Walker, Maggie Lena 1867(?)–1934 17

Walker, Margaret 1915–1998 29

Walker, Nellie Marian See Larsen, Nella

Walker, Ray 1981— 109

Walker, Rebecca 1969— 50

Walker, T. J. 1961(?)— 7

Walker, T-Bone 1910–1975 111

Walker, Teshima 1968–2013 114

Walker, Thomas See Walker, T. J.

Walker, Tristan 1984— 98

Walker, Wyatt Tee 1929— 80

Wall, Orindatus S. B. 1825–1891 92

Wallace, Ben 1974— 54

Wallace, Joaquin 1965— 49

Wallace, Michele Faith 1952— 13

Wallace, Perry E. 1948— 47

Wallace, Phyllis A(nn) 1920(?)–1993 9

Wallace, Rasheed 1974— 56

Wallace, Richard See Mighty Clouds of Joy

Wallace, Ruby Ann See Dee, Ruby

Wallace, Sippie 1898–1986 1

Wallace, William 1939–2008 75

Waller, Fats 1904–1943 29

Waller, Thomas Wright See Waller, Fats

Wallis, Quvenzhané 2003— 109

Walters, Richard See Slick Rick

Walters, Ronald 1938— 83

Walton, Alex See Moonglows, The

Walton, Cedar 1934–2013 114

Walton, Cora See Taylor, Koko

Wambugu, Florence 1953— 42

Wamutombo, Dikembe Mutombo Mpolondo Mukamba Jean Jacque See Mutombo, Dikembe

Wanjiru, Sammy 1986–2011 94

Ward, Andre 1984— 62

Ward, Benjamin 1926–2002 68

Ward, Billy See Billy Ward and the Dominoes

Ward, Douglas Turner 1930— 42

Ward, Hines 1976— 84

Ward, Lloyd 1949— 21, 46

Ward, Willa 1920–2012 105

Ward, William E. 1949— 107

Ware, Andre 1968— 37

Ware, Carl H. 1943— 30

Ware, David S. 1949–2012 106

Ware, DeMarcus 1982— 92

Warfield, Marsha 1955— 2

Warfield, William 1920–2002 94

Waring, Laura Wheeler 1887–1948 99

Warner, Malcolm-Jamal 1970— 22, 36, 110

Warren, Ernest See Spaniels, The

Warren, Mervyn See Take 6

Warren, Michael 1946— 27

Warrick, Marie Dionne See Warwick, Dionne

Warsame, Keinan Abdi See K'naan

Warwick, Dionne 1940— 18, 111

Washington, Alonzo 1967— 29

Washington, Booker T(aliaferro) 1856–1915 4

Washington, Denzel 1954— 1, 16, 93

Washington, Dinah 1924–1963 22

Washington, Ebonya 1973(?)— 79

Washington, Elsie B. 1942–2009 78

Washington, Fred(er)i(cka Carolyn) 1903–1994 10

Washington, Gene 1947— 63

Washington, Grover, Jr. 1943–1999 17, 44

Washington, Harold 1922–1987 6

Washington, Harriet A. 1951— 69

Washington, Hayma 19(?)(?)— 86

Washington, Isaiah 1963— 62

Washington, James, Jr. 1909(?)–2000 38

Washington, James Melvin 1948–1997 50

Washington, Kenny 1918–1971 50

Washington, Kenny 1958— 107

Washington, Kerry 1977— 46, 107

Washington, Laura S. 1956(?)— 18

Washington, MaliVai 1969— 8

Washington, Mary T. 1906–2005 57

Washington, Ora Mae 1899(?)–1971 115

Washington, Patrice Clarke 1961— 12

Washington, Pauletta Pearson 1950— 86

Washington, Regynald G. 1954(?)— 44

Washington, Tamia Reneé See Tamia

Washington, Valores James 1903–1995 12

Washington, Walter 1915–2003 45

Wasow, Omar 1970— 15

Waters, Benny 1902–1998 26

Waters, Ethel 1895–1977 7

Waters, Maxine 1938— 3, 67, 103

Waters, Muddy 1915–1983 34

Watkins, Craig 1967— 97

Watkins, Donald 1948— 35

Watkins, Frances Ellen See Harper, Frances Ellen Watkins

Watkins, Gloria Jean See hooks, bell

Watkins, Joe 1953— 86

Watkins, Levi, Jr. 1945— 9

Watkins, Perry James Henry 1948–1996 12

Watkins, Shirley R. 1938— 17

Watkins, Ted 1923(?)–1993 104

Watkins, Tionne See T-Boz; TLC

Watkins, Walter C. 1946— 24

Watley, Jody 1959— 54

Watson, Bo See Midnight Star

Watson, Bob 1946— 25

Watson, Carlos 1970— 50

Watson, Diane 1933— 41

Watson, Ivory See Ink Spots, The

Watson, Johnny "Guitar" 1935–1996 18

Watt, Garland W. 1932–2013 113

Watt, Mel 1945— 26, 105

Wattleton, (Alyce) Faye 1943— 9

Watts, Andr&ecute; 1946— 42, 101

Watts, J(ulius) C(aesar), Jr. 1957— 14, 38

Watts, Reggie 1972— 52, 102

Watts, Rolonda 1959— 9

Wayans, Damien 198(?)— 78

Wayans, Damon 1961— 8, 41

Wayans, Keenen Ivory 1958— 18

Wayans, Kim 1961— 80

Wayans, Marlon 1972— 29, 82

Wayans, Shawn 1971— 29

Waymon, Eunice Kathleen See Simone, Nina

Weah, George 1966— 58

Weathers, Carl 1948— 10

Weaver, Afaa Michael 1951— 37

Weaver, Michael S. See Weaver, Afaa Michael

Weaver, Mike 1951— 109

Weaver, Robert C. 1907–1997 8, 46

Webb, Chick 1909–1939 105

Webb, Sheyann See Webb-Christburg, Sheyann

Webb, Veronica 1965— 10, 95

Webb, Wellington 1941— 3, 81

Webb, William Henry See Webb, Chick

Webb-Christburg, Sheyann 1956— 110

Webber, Chris 1973— 15, 30, 59

Webster, Katie 1936–1999 29

Wedgeworth, Robert W. 1937— 42

Weekes, Kevin 1975— 67

Weeks, Thomas, III 1967— 70

Weems, Carrie Mae 1953— 63

Weems, Renita J. 1954— 44

Wein, Joyce 1928–2005 62

Wek, Alek 1977— 18, 63, 105

Welburn, Edward T. 1950— 50

Welch, Elisabeth 1908–2003 52

Welcome, Verda Freeman 1907–1990 112

Welles, Rosalind See Washington, Elsie B.

Wells, Henrietta Bell 1912–2008 **69**

Wells, James Lesesne 1902–1993 **10**

Wells, Junior 1934–1998 **102**

Wells, Mary 1943–1992 **28**

Wells, Vernon 1978— **91**

Wells, Willie 1906–1989 **105**

Wells-Barnett, Ida B(ell) 1862–1931 **8**

Welsing, Frances (Luella) Cress 1935– **5**

Wendo See Kolosoy, Wendo

Wesley, Dorothy Porter 1905–1995 **19**

Wesley, Richard 1945— **73**

Wesley, Rutina 1979— **97**

Wesley, Valerie Wilson 194(?)— **18**

West, Allen 1961— **89**

West, Bernie See Five Keys, The

West, Cornel 1953— **5, 33, 80**

West, Dorothy 1907–1998 **12, 54**

West, James E. 1931— **87**

West, Kanye 1977— **52, 93**

West, Rudy See Five Keys, The

West, Togo Dennis, Jr. 1942— **16**

Westbrook, Kelvin 1955— **50**

Westbrook, Peter 1952— **20**

Westbrooks, Bobby 1930(?)–1995 **51**

Whack, Rita Coburn 1958— **36**

Whalum, Kirk 1958— **37, 64**

Wharton, A. C., Jr. 1944— **110**

Wharton, Clifton R(eginald), Jr. 1926— **7**

Wharton, Clifton Reginald, Sr. 1899–1990 **36**

Wheat, Alan Dupree 1951— **14**

Wheaton, James 1924–2002 **103**

Whitaker, Forest 1961– **2, 49, 67**

Whitaker, Mark 1957— **21, 47**

Whitaker, Pernell 1964— **10, 89**

Whitaker, "Sweet Pea" See Whitaker, Pernell

White, Armond 1954(?)— **80**

White, Augustus, III 1936— **100**

White, Barry 1944–2003 **13, 41**

White, Bill 1933(?)– **1, 48**

White, Charlie See Billy Ward and the Dominoes

White, Charles 1918–1979 **39**

White, (Donald) Dondi 1961–1998 **34**

White, Frank 1950— **95**

White, Jesse 1934— **22, 75**

White, Jessica 1984— **83**

White, Jo Jo 1946— **112**

White, John H. 1945— **27**

White, Joseph Henry See White, Jo Jo

White, Josh 1914(?)–1969 **86**

White, Josh, Jr. 1940— **52**

White, Linda M. 1942— **45**

White, Lois Jean 1938— **20**

White, Maurice 1941— **29** See also Earth, Wind & Fire

White, Michael Jai 1967— **71**

White, Michael R(eed) 1951— **5**

White, Reggie 1961–2004 **6, 50**

White, Reginald Howard See White, Reggie

White, Santi See Santigold

White, Sylvain 1971— **96**

White, Terri 1948— **82**

White, Walter F(rancis) 1893–1955 **4**

White, Willard 1946— **53**

White, William DeKova See White, Bill

White, Willye 1939— **67**

White-Hammond, Gloria 1951(?)— **61**

Whitehead, Colson 1969— **77**

Whitehead, Don See Earth, Wind & Fire

Whitfield, Fred 1967— **23**

Whitfield, LeRoy 1969–2005 **84**

Whitfield, Lynn 1954— **18**

Whitfield, Mal 1924— **60**

Whitfield, Norman 1940–2008 **73**

Whitfield, Van 1960(?)— **34**

Whitlock, Jason 1967— **78**

Whitmore, George 1944–2012 **106**

Whitney, Davey L. 1930— **110**

Whitney, Marva 1944–2012 **109**

Whittaker, Hudson See Tampa Red

Wideman, John Edgar 1941– **5, 87**

Widener, Warren 1938— **99**

Wilbekin, Emil 1968— **63**

Wilbon, Michael 1958— **68**

Wilburn, Nayvadius See Future

Wilder, L. Douglas 1931– **3, 48**

Wiley, Kehinde 1977— **62**

Wiley, Ralph 1952–2004 **8, 78**

Wilkens, J. Ernest, Jr. 1923– **43**

Wilkens, Lenny 1937– **11, 88**

Wilkens, Leonard Randolph See Wilkens, Lenny

Wilkerson, Isabel 1961— **71**

Wilkerson, Robert King See King, Robert Hillary

Wilkins, David 1956— **77**

Wilkins, Dominique 1960— **74**

Wilkins, Elbert See Dramatics, The

Wilkins, Ray 1951— **47**

Wilkins, Roger 1932— **2, 84**

Wilkins, Roy 1901–1981 **4**

Wilkins, Thomas Alphonso 1956— **71**

will.i.am 1975— **64**

Williams, Alice Faye See Shakur, Afeni

Williams, Ann Claire 1949— **82**

Williams, Anthony 1951— **21**

Williams, Anthony Charles See Tonex

Williams, Armstrong 1959— **29**

Williams, Bernard See Harold Melvin & the Blue Notes

Williams, Bert 1874–1922 **18**

Williams, Billy 1938— **86**

Williams, Billy Dee 1937— **8, 105**

Williams, Bryan See Birdman

Williams, Calvin See Golden Gate Quartet

Williams, Carl See Kani, Karl

Williams, Charles Melvin See Williams, Cootie

Williams, Clarence 1893(?)–1965 **33**

Williams, Clarence 1967— **70**

Williams, Clarence, III 1939— **26**

Williams, Claude 1908–2004 **80**

Williams, Cootie 1908(?)–1985 **114**

Williams, Curtis See Penguins, The

Williams, Daniel Hale (III) 1856–1931 **2**

Williams, David Rudyard 1954— **50**

Williams, David W. 1910–2000 **110**

Williams, Deniece 1951— **36**

Williams, Denise 1958— **40**

Williams, Deron 1984— **92**

Williams, Doug 1955— **22, 112**

Williams, Dudley 1938— **60**

Williams, Eddie N. 1932— **44**

Williams, Eric Eustace 1911–1981 **65**

Williams, Evelyn 1922(?)— **10**

Williams, Fannie Barrier 1855–1944 **27**

Williams, Frederick (B.) 1939–2006 **63**

Williams, George Washington 1849–1891 **18**

Williams, Gertrude See Morgan, Gertrude

Williams, Gregory (Howard) 1943— **11**

Williams, Hosea Lorenzo 1926— **15, 31**

Williams, J. Mayo 1894–1980 **83**

Williams, Jody 1935— **113**

Williams, Joe 1918–1999 **5, 25**

Williams, John A. 1925— **27**

Williams, Joseph Leon See Williams, Jody

Williams, Juan 1954— **35, 80**

Williams, Ken 1964— **68**

Williams, Lauryn 1983— **58**

Williams, Lindsey 1966— **75**

Williams, Maggie 1954— **7, 71**

Williams, Malinda 1975— **57**

Williams, Marco 1956— **53**

Williams, Margaret Ann See Williams, Maggie

Williams, Mary Lou 1910–1981 **15**

Williams, Michael Kenneth 1966— **97**

Williams, Michael L. 1953— **86**

Williams, Michelle 1980— **73**

Williams, Montel 1956— **4, 57**

Williams, Nat D. 1907–1983 **91**

Williams, Natalie 1970— **31**

Williams, O(swald) S. 1921— **13**

Williams, Patricia 1951— **11, 54**

Williams, Paul 1939–1971 **112** See also Temptations, The

Williams, Paul R(evere) 1894–1980 **9**

Williams, Paulette Linda See Shange, Ntozake

Williams, Pharrell 1973— **47, 82**

Williams, Preston Warren, II 1939(?)— **64**

Williams, Rhonda Y. 1967(?)— **86**

Williams, Ricky 1977— **85**

Williams, Robert F(ranklin) 1925— **11**

Williams, Robert Peter See Guillaume, Robert

Williams, Ronald A. 1949— **57**

Williams, Roy 1968— **89**

Williams, Russell, II 1952— **70**

Williams, Samuel Arthur 1946— **21**

Williams, Saul 1972— **31**

Williams, Serena 1981— **20, 41, 73**

Williams, Sherley Anne 1944–1999 **25**

Williams, Stanley "Tookie" 1953–2005 **29, 57**

Williams, Stevie 1979— **71**

Williams, Ted 1957— **91**

Williams, Terrie M. 1954— **35**

Williams, Tony 1945–1997 **67**

Williams, Vanessa A. 1963— **32, 66**

Williams, Vanessa L. 1963— **4, 17**

Williams, Venus 1980— **17, 34, 62**

Williams, Walter See O'Jays, The

Williams, Walter E(dward) 1936— **4**

Williams, Wendy 1964— **62**

Williams, Wilbert See Mighty Clouds of Joy

Williams, William December See Williams, Billy Dee

Williams, William T(homas) 1942— **11**

Williams, Willie L(awrence) 1943— **4**

Williamson, Fred 1938— **67**

Williamson, Lisa See Sister Souljah

Williamson, Mykelti 1957— **22**

Williamson, Sonny Boy 1899(?)–1965 **84**

Willie, Louis, Jr. 1923–2007 **68**

Willie D See Geto Boys

Willingham, Tyrone 1953— **43**

Willis, Bill 1921–2007 **68**

Willis, Cheryl See Hudson, Cheryl

Willis, Deborah 1948— **85**

Willis, Dontrelle 1982— **55**

Willis, Patrick 1985— **99**

Willis, William Karnet See Willis, Bill

Williston, David Augustus 1868–1962 **99**

Wills, Harry 1889(?)–1958 **80**

Wills, Maury 1932— **73**

Wilson, Abram 1973–2012 **104**

Wilson, August 1945–2005 **7, 33, 55**

Wilson, Brian Courtney 19(?)(?)— **94**

Wilson, Cassandra 1955— **16**

Wilson, Chandra 1969— **57**

Wilson, Charlie 1953— **31, 77** See also Gap Band, The

Wilson, Debra 1970(?)— **38**

Wilson, Demond 1946— **102**

Wilson, Donald E. 1936(?)— **88**

Wilson, Dorien 1962(?)— **55**

Wilson, Ellis 1899–1977 **39**

Wilson, Frank 1940–2012 **106**

Wilson, Frederica 1942— **92**

Wilson, Flip 1933–1998 **21**

Wilson, Gerald 1918— **49**

Wilson, Gloria Mai See Lynne, Gloria

Wilson, Grady Demond See Wilson, Demond

Wilson, Jackie 1934–1984 **60** See also Billy Ward and the Dominoes

Wilson, Jimmy 1946— **45**

Wilson, John 1922— **109**

Wilson, Lionel 1915–1998 **99**

Wilson, Margaret Bush 1919–2009 **79**

Wilson, Mary 1944 **28**

Wilson, Nancy 1937— **10, 98**

Wilson, Natalie 1972(?)— **38**

Wilson, Orlandus See Golden Gate Quartet

Wilson, Paul See Flamingos, The

Wilson, Phill 1956— **9, 104**
Wilson, Robert *See Gap Band, The*
Wilson, Ronnie *See Gap Band, The*
Wilson, Shanice Lorraine *See Shanice*
Wilson, Stephanie 1966— **72**
Wilson, Sunnie 1908–1999 **7, 55**
Wilson, Tracey Scott 1967(?)— **77**
Wilson, William Julius 1935— **22**
Wilson, William Nathaniel *See Wilson, Sunnie*
Wimbley, Damon 1966— *See Fat Boys*
Winans, Angie 1968— **36**
Winans, Benjamin 1962— **14**
Winans, CeCe 1964— **14, 43**
Winans, David 1934–2009 **77**
Winans, Debbie 1972— **36**
Winans, Marvin L. 1958— **17**
Winans, Ronald 1956–2005 **54**
Winans, Vickie 1953(?)— **24**
Winfield, Dave 1951— **5, 91**
Winfield, David Mark *See Winfield, Dave*
Winfield, Paul (Edward) 1941–2004 **2, 45**
Winfrey, Oprah 1954— **2, 15, 61, 106**
Winkfield, Jimmy 1882–1974 **42**
Winley, Harold *See Clovers, The*
Winslow, Kellen 1957— **83**
Wisdom, Kimberlydawn 1956— **57**
Withers, Bill 1938— **61**
Withers, Ernest C. 1922–2007 **68, 88**
Withers-Mendes, Elisabeth 1973(?)— **64**
Witherspoon, Jimmy 1920(?)–1997 **113**
Witherspoon, John 1942— **38**
Witt, Edwin T. 1920— **26**
Wiwa, Ken 1968— **67**
Wiz Khalifa *See Khalifa, Wiz*
Wofford, Chloe Anthony *See Morrison, Toni*
Wolde Yohannes, Gebre Medhin *See Abune Paulos*
Wolfe, Ann 1971— **82**

Wolfe, George C. 1954— **6, 43**
Womack, Bobby 1944— **60, 92**
Womack, Solomon *See Swan Silvertones, The*
Wonder, Stevie 1950— **11, 53**
Wonder Mike *See Sugarhill Gang, The*
Wood, William Vernell *See Wood, Willie*
Wood, Willie 1936— **111**
Woodard, Alfre 1953— **9, 108**
Woodard, Lynette 1959— **67**
Woodbridge, Hudson *See Tampa Red*
Woodruff, Hale (Aspacio) 1900–1980 **9**
Woodruff, John 1915–2007 **68**
Woods, Abraham, Jr. 1928–2008 **74**
Woods, Belita 1948–2012 **103**
Woods, Cheyenne 1990— **103**
Woods, Eldrick *See Woods, Tiger*
Woods, Georgie 1927–2005 **57**
Woods, Granville T. 1856–1910 **5**
Woods, Jacqueline 1962— **52**
Woods, Mattiebelle 1902–2005 **63**
Woods, Renn 1958— **110**
Woods, Scott 1971— **55**
Woods, Sylvia 1926–2012 **34, 104**
Woods, Teri 1968— **69**
Woods, Thomas *See Clovers, The*
Woods, Tiger 1975— **14, 31, 81**
Woodson, Ali Ollie 1951–2010 **89**
Woodson, Carter G(odwin) 1875–1950 **2**
Woodson, Mike 1958— **78**
Woodson, Robert L. 1937— **10**
Woodson, Rod 1965— **79**
Woolard, Jamal 1975— **102**
Wooldridge, Anna Marie *See Lincoln, Abbey*
Worrill, Conrad 1941— **12**
Worthy, James 1961— **49**
Worthy, Kym 1956— **84**
Wray, Noble 1960— **114**
Wright, Albert *See Wright, Chalky*
Wright, Antoinette 195(?)— **60**
Wright, Beverly 1947— **97**

Wright, Bruce McMarion 1918–2005 **3, 52**
Wright, Chalky 1912–1957 **103**
Wright, Charles H. 1918–2002 **35**
Wright, Clyde *See Golden Gate Quartet*
Wright, Deborah C. 1958— **25**
Wright, Erica *See Badu, Erykah*
Wright, Ernest, Jr. *See Little Anthony & the Imperials*
Wright, Jeffrey 1965— **54, 111**
Wright, Jeremiah A., Jr. 1941— **45, 69, 103**
Wright, Lewin 1962— **43**
Wright, Louis Tompkins 1891–1952 **4**
Wright, Nathan, Jr. 1923–2005 **56**
Wright, O. V. 1939–1980 **114**
Wright, Overton Vertis *See Wright, O. V.*
Wright, Rayfield 1945— **70**
Wright, Richard 1908–1960 **5**
Wright, Richard Robert, Sr. 1855–1947 **100**
Wright, Sarah E. 1928–2009 **95**
Wright, Timothy 1947— **74**
Wyatt, Addie L. 1924— **56**
Wylie, Mary T. Washington *See Washington, Mary T.*
Wynn, Albert R. 1951— **25, 77**
X, Malcolm 1925–1965 **1**
X, Marvin 1944— **45**
Xuma, Madie Hall 1894–1982 **59**
Xzibit 1974— **78**
Yabby You 1946–2010 **83**
Yancey, James DeWitt *See J Dilla*
Yancy, Dorothy Cowser 1944— **42**
Yar'Adua, Umaru 1951–2010 **69, 89**
Yarbrough, Camille 1938— **40**
Yarbrough, Cedric 1971— **51**
Yasiin *See Bey, Yasiin*
Yates, Jack 1828–1897 **114**
Yates, John Henry *See Yates, Jack*
Yayi, Boni T. 1952— **84**
Yayo, Tony 1978— **113**
Yearwood, Lennox, Jr. 1969— **112**
Yeboah, Emmanuel Ofosu 1977— **53**

Yerby, Frank 1916–1991 **96**
Yette, Samuel F. 1929— **63**
Ying Yang Twins **112**
Yoba, (Abdul-)Malik (Kashie) 1967— **11**
York, Dwight D. 1945— **71**
York, Malachi Z. *See York, Dwight D.*
York, Vincent 1952— **40**
Young, Al 1939— **82**
Young, Andre Ramelle *See Dre, Dr.*
Young, Andrew 1932— **3, 48, 110**
Young, Charles 1864–1922 **77**
Young, Coleman 1918–1997 **1, 20**
Young, Darren 1979— **114**
Young, Dewey *See Swan Silvertones, The*
Young, Donald, Jr. 1989— **57**
Young, Earl *See Trammps, The*
Young, Jean Childs 1933–1994 **14**
Young, Jimmy 1948–2005 **54**
Young, John 1949— **111**
Young, Ledisi Anibade *See Ledisi*
Young, Lee 1914–2008 **72**
Young, Lee Thompson 1984–2013 **114**
Young, Leonidas Raymond *See Young, Lee*
Young, Perry H. 1919–1998 **100**
Young, Roger Arliner 1899–1964 **29**
Young, Thomas *See Three Mo' Tenors*
Young, Whitney M(oore), Jr. 1921–1971 **4**
Young Jeezy 1977— **63**
Youngblood, Johnny Ray 1948— **8**
Youngblood, Shay 1959— **32**
Yumkella, Kandeh 1959— **105**
Zane 1967(?)— **71**
Zenawi, Meles 1955— **3, 99**
Zollar, Alfred 1955(?)— **40**
Zollar, Jawole Willa Jo 1950— **28**
Zook, Kristal Brent 1966(?)— **62**
Z-Ro 1977— **109**
Zulu, Princess Kasune 1977— **54**
Zuma, Jacob 1942— **33, 75**
Zuma, Nkosazana Dlamini *See Dlamini-Zuma, Nkosazana*

$165.00